Literature

Literature

Fiction

Poetry

Drama

Joseph K. Davis
University of Southern Mississippi

Panthea R. Broughton
Louisiana State University

Michael Wood
Columbia University

Scott, Foresman and Company
Glenview, Illinois
Dallas, Tex.
Oakland, N.J.
Palo Alto, Cal.
Abingdon, England

Library of Congress Cataloging in Publication Data

Main entry under title:
Literature: fiction, poetry & drama.

   Includes index.
   1. Literature—Collections. I. Davis, Joseph K.
II. Broughton, Panthea Reid. III. Wood, Michael.
PN6014.L584   808.8   76–43372
ISBN 0–673–15009–7
1 2 3 4 5 6-RRC-82 81 80 79 78 77 76

Acknowledgments

Conrad Aiken. "Sound of Breaking" from *Collected Poems* by Conrad Aiken. Copyright © 1953, 1970 by Conrad Aiken. Reprinted by permission of Oxford University Press, Inc.

A. R. Ammons. "Cascadilla Falls" reprinted from *Uplands, New Poems* by A. R. Ammons. By permission of W. W. Norton & Company, Inc. Copyright © 1970 by A. R. Ammons. "Hippie Hop" reprinted from *Collected Poems: 1951–1971* by A. R. Ammons. By permission of W. W. Norton & Company, Inc. Copyright © 1972 by A. R. Ammons.

Sherwood Anderson. "Death in the Woods" from *American Mercury*, September 1926. Copyright 1926 by The American Mercury Inc. Renewed 1953 by Eleanor Copenhaver Anderson. Reprinted by permission of Harold Ober Associates Incorporated.

John Ashbery. "These Lacustrine Cities" from *Rivers and Mountains* by John Ashbery. Copyright © 1962, 1963, 1964, 1966 by John Ashbery. Reprinted by permission of Holt, Rinehart and Winston, Publishers.

W. H. Auden. "In Memory of W. B. Yeats," "Musée des Beaux Arts," and "The Unknown Citizen," copyright 1940 and renewed 1968 by W. H. Auden. Reprinted from *Collected Shorter Poems 1927–1957*. "It's No Use Raising a Shout" from *Poems* by W. H. Auden. Copyright 1934 and renewed 1962 by W. H. Auden. All poems reprinted by permission of Random House, Inc. and Faber and Faber Ltd.

Imamu Amiri Baraka (LeRoi Jones). "A Poem for Speculative Hipsters" from *The Dead Lecturer*, published by Grove Press. Copyright © 1964 by LeRoi Jones (Imamu Amiri Baraka). Reprinted by permission of The Sterling Lord Agency, Inc.

Donald Barthelme. "The Balloon" reprinted with the permission of Farrar, Straus & Giroux, Inc. From *Unspeakable Practices, Unnatural Acts* by Donald Barthelme. Copyright © 1966, 1968 by Donald Barthelme.

Matsuo Bashō. "The Way of Haiku" from *Haiku*, Vol. 1, translated by R. H. Blyth. Reprinted by permission of The Hokuseido Press. "The Unknown Flower" and "Coolness" from *An Introduction to Haiku* by Harold G. Henderson. Copyright © 1958 by Harold G. Henderson. Reprinted by permission of Doubleday & Company, Inc.

E. C. Bentley. "John Stuart Mill" from *Clerihews Complete* by E. C. Bentley. Reprinted by permission of the Estate of E. C. Bentley.

John Berryman. Three "Dream Songs" (Nos. 14, 266, and 382) reprinted with the permission of Farrar, Straus & Giroux, Inc. from *The Dream Songs* by John Berryman. Copyright © 1959, 1962, 1963, 1964, 1965, 1966, 1967, 1968, 1969 by John Berryman.

Robert Bly. "In a Train" and "Surprised by Evening" reprinted from *Silence in the Snowy Fields*, Wesleyan University Press, 1962, copyright © 1962 by Robert Bly, reprinted with his permission. "When the Dumb Speak" (p. 62) from *The Light Around the Body* by Robert Bly. Copyright © 1967 by Robert Bly. By permission of Harper & Row, Publishers.

Heinrich Böll. "Christmas Every Day" translated by Denver Lindley. Reprinted by permission of Joan Davis. Copyright © 1957 by Heinrich Böll.

Arna Bontemps. "Southern Mansion" from *Personals* published by Paul Breman. Copyright © 1963 by Arna Bontemps. Reprinted by permission of Harold Ober Associates Incorporated.

Jorge Luis Borges. "Dreamtigers" from *Dreamtigers* by Jorge Luis Borges, translated by Mildred Boyer and Harold Morland. Copyright © 1964 by Jorge Luis Borges. All rights reserved. Reprinted by permission of the University of Texas Press. "The Secret Miracle" translated by Harriet de Onís, from *Labyrinths and Other Writings*. Copyright © 1962 by New Directions Publishing Corporation. Reprinted by permission of New Directions Publishing Corporation.

Kay Boyle. "Astronomer's Wife" from *The White Horses of Vienna and Other Stories*. Copyright 1936, © 1964 by Kay Boyle. Reprinted by permission of A. Watkins, Inc.

Ray Bradbury. "August 2002: Night Meeting" from *The Martian Chronicles* by Ray Bradbury. Copyright 1946, 1948, 1949, 1950, 1958 by Ray Bradbury. Reprinted by permission of Harold Matson Company, Inc.

Richard Brautigan. "Homage to the San Francisco YMCA" from *Revenge of the Lawn* by Richard Brautigan. Copyright © 1963, 1964, 1965, 1966, 1967, 1969, 1970, 1971 by Richard Brautigan. Reprinted by permission of Simon and Schuster.

Gwendolyn Brooks. "Old Mary" and "We Real Cool" (© 1959 by Gwendolyn Brooks Blakely); "Of De Witt Williams on His Way to Lincoln Cemetery" (© 1945 by Gwendolyn Brooks Blakely) from *The World of Gwendolyn*
(continued on page 1141)

Preface

One of our primary aims in *Literature* is to help students become more aware of the connection between their own lives and the study of literature. More important, the text also tries to increase their sensitivity to the craftsmanship involved in the creation of effective literary works. In attempting to fulfill these aims, we have provided a collection of stories, poems, and plays that are appealing and teachable, along with discussions of the elements of literature that are comprehensive and flexible. In approaching literature through an examination of its various components, we have focused on the relationships between the part and the functioning whole, between craft and content, and between literature and life.

Believing that literature is best studied, understood, and appreciated when it is best represented, we have included selections that combine literary excellence with illustrative aptness and student appeal. Some are well-known classics; others are less familiar and more contemporary. Those within each of the chapters serve to exemplify the particular literary element under discussion. Moreover, a group of works "for further study," included at the end of each of the three major sections, provides instructors and students with the opportunity to select additional pieces for reading and discussion.

The conviction that good literature ought to be made accessible and examined with some idea of its craft and content is reflected in the editorial apparatus. Pertinent study questions follow many of the selections. Explanatory footnotes help students with such troublesome matters as unfamiliar allusions, foreign phrases, and particularly difficult passages in individual works. Subsections, identified as "Notes," examine special literary techniques and forms. A special section, "Writing Themes about Literature," should be useful to students in developing papers which deal with literary topics. A comprehensive Glossary of Literary and Critical Terms provides accessible definitions of all the terms discussed within the text.

The organization of *Literature* into three separate sections—fiction, poetry, and drama—follows the sequence in which these genres are usually taught. Each section is self-contained and thus may be taken up individually or in conjunction with one or both of the other sections. As parallel units, the fiction and the poetry sections each begin with a chapter which introduces the genre and end with a chapter which looks at its subject "in wider perspective." The ten chapters in between consider essential components of fiction and poetry. Instructors may wish to assign the first six basic chapters in the fiction and the poetry and later to sample, or perhaps to omit, the remaining six chapters. The drama section departs from this scheme in order to trace the historical evolution of the drama from classical tragedy to modern symbolism and expressionism. At the same time, this section examines important developments in stagecraft.

We wish to express our gratitude and professional admiration to Stan Stoga, our editor at Scott, Foresman, whose dedicated and intelligent contribution to the text has enriched it immeasurably. Sharing in our thanks is Richard Welna, Executive Editor at Scott, Foresman, who conceived the idea for the book and who has consistently encouraged us throughout its development. Many colleagues in the profession have given invaluable advice and timely assistance in the creation of *Literature*. Among them are Milly S. Barranger, Tulane University; John Fiero, University of Southwestern Louisiana; John I. Fischer, Louisiana State University; Quentin Gehle, Virginia Polytechnic Institute; William Harmon, University of North Carolina at Chapel Hill; Ralph E. Hitt, Jane Hinton, and Sara Woodward, Mississippi State University for Women; Janet H. Hobbs, North Carolina State University; M. X. Lesser, Northeastern University; Charles W. Moorman and Frank O'Hare, University of Southern Mississippi; Mary Northcut, Richland College; Jeffrey R. Prince, Northwestern University; David L. Rankin, Winthrop College; Theresa Santangelo, Fullerton College; Robert Spechard, European Division of the University of Maryland; Ted R. Spivey, Georgia State University; Norman F. Weaver, New York State University College at Buffalo; and Richard A. Wilan, Northern Virginia Community College.

Joseph K. Davis
Panthea R. Broughton
Michael Wood

Contents

Fiction

Stories for Further Study 379

Poetry

Chapter 1   The Experience of Poetry 455

Chapter 2   Language   475

Chapter 3   Imagery   492

Chapter 4 Metaphor and Simile 509

Chapter 5 Symbol and Allegory 525

Chapter 6   Irony and Paradox   547

Chapter 7   Tone   **564**

Chapter 8   Sound   **579**

Chapter 9   Rhythm and Meter   **599**

Chapter 10   Form and Pattern   **621**

Poems for Further Study 682

Drama

I
Fiction

Chapter 1
Story

Our language is a convenient and practical tool. We use it to perform all kinds of everyday tasks: telling a lost motorist how to get to Main Street; describing to a dentist how an aching tooth feels; persuading a prospective employer of our talents and skills; comparing the merits and deficiencies of the candidates for state governor. It is difficult to get through even the most routine tasks without using language. And although we may avoid conversation with a clerk or a cashier when we are in a hurry, language is so essential to human existence that most of us find it distressing to go through a single day without talking to somebody about something, however trivial or routine a matter it might be.

It is even more distressing to be unable to share with someone our experiences and feelings and ideas. We need to put into words what has happened to us or what we have heard has happened to someone else. And so we tell stories. The incidents, jokes, anecdotes, and brief tales that we tell may be crude or sophisticated, spontaneous or contrived, factual or exaggerated. Yet they are alike in being expressions of our human need to share a story. The French writer and philosopher Jean Paul Sartre found that need a fundamental human characteristic. He wrote that "a man is always a teller of tales, he lives surrounded by his stories and the stories of others, he sees everything that happens to him through them; and he tries to live his own life as if he were telling a story."

Because we are all, as Sartre said, natural tellers of tales and because we tell best what we know best, we sift through our experiences to find those incidents that can be dramatized and sometimes elaborated to make good stories. These we retell. Most of us instinctively know which incidents are worth retelling. We usually do not describe, even to our most loyal friends, what we had for breakfast. If, however, the stove explodes in the kitchen, someone is injured, our dining room fills with smoke, then eating is forgotten. We now have had an experience at breakfast which we will tell and perhaps retell again and again. Such an experience is news. It works a compulsion upon us because whenever an event breaks a pattern or reverses our expectations it is notable, memorable, and important. In other words, it is particular. As such it may also be humorous, sad, touching, lively, terrifying, glamorous, or exciting; but because it is out of the ordinary, we feel compelled to relate it to other people.

We may, on the other hand, occasionally remember an incident precisely because it breaks no patterns. Instead of reversing our expectations, it confirms them. Such an incident may prove how shrewd our friend Jim is, how dull a particular town is, how difficult chemistry is, even how routine breakfast was. We try to shape such materials into manageable tales in the hope that someone will understand and reply, "Sure, that's how it is." Sometimes our simplest tales not only confirm our attitudes about a particular person or situation, but they also seem broadly applicable to human experience. They are, in other words, universal. We retell certain select incidents, then, either because they appear unique or because they reveal something universal in the human condition.

Fiction writers tell stories for exactly the same reasons. They are fascinated by the particularity or the universality of their raw materials and are compelled to shape them into stories. And though *particular* and *universal* sound like contradictory terms, the best stories are always both at once. They are particular because they startle and delight by presenting in a fresh way things we have not seen or noticed and events we have never experienced in quite the same way. Yet at the same time they are universal because they are true to experiences and understandings that extend beyond peculiar or limited places, times, and incidents.

The following short story by Saki, for instance, is a bizarre tale about a boy whose pet ferret kills his guardian. This is the type of gory incident that makes newspaper headlines and that often provides raw material for sadistic gossip. But Saki's story offers more than sensational news or gossip. Though it shocks us with the extraordinary, it consoles us with the ordinary. That is, it confirms and reinforces our ordinary, basic assumptions about loneliness, repression, and resentment at the same time that it startles us with a very peculiar incident. Let us see how Saki manages to yoke the unusual and the universal together in such a very short story.

Saki [H. H. Munro] (1870–1916)
Sredni Vashtar

Conradin was ten years old, and the doctor had pronounced his profes-sional opinion that the boy would not live another five years. The doctor was silky and effete, and counted for little, but his opinion was endorsed by Mrs. De Ropp, who counted for nearly everything. Mrs. De Ropp was Conradin's cousin and guardian, and in his eyes she represented those three-fifths of the world that are necessary and disagreeable and real; the other two-fifths, in per-petual antagonism to the foregoing, were summed up in himself and his imagi-nation. One of these days Conradin supposed he would succumb to the mas-tering pressure of wearisome necessary things—such as illnesses and coddling restrictions and drawn-out dullness. Without his imagination, which was ram-pant under the spur of loneliness, he would have succumbed long ago.

Mrs. De Ropp would never, in her honestest moments, have confessed to herself that she disliked Conradin, though she might have been dimly aware that thwarting him "for his good" was a duty which she did not find particu-larly irksome. Conradin hated her with a desperate sincerity which he was perfectly able to mask. Such few pleasures as he could contrive for himself gained an added relish from the likelihood that they would be displeasing to his guardian, and from the realm of his imagination she was locked out—an un-clean thing, which should find no entrance.

In the dull, cheerless garden, overlooked by so many windows that were ready to open with a message not to do this or that, or a reminder that medi-cines were due, he found little attraction. The few fruit-trees that it contained were set jealously apart from his plucking, as though they were rare specimens of their kind blooming in an arid waste; it would probably have been difficult to find a market-gardener who would have offered ten shillings for their entire yearly produce. In a forgotten corner, however, almost hidden behind a dismal shrubbery, was a disused tool-shed of respectable proportions, and within its walls Conradin found a haven, something that took on the varying aspects of a playroom and a cathedral. He had peopled it with a legion of familiar phantoms, evoked partly from fragments of history and partly from his own brain, but it also boasted two inmates of flesh and blood. In one corner lived a ragged-plumaged Houdan hen, on which the boy lavished an affection that had scarcely another outlet. Further back in the gloom stood a large hutch, divided into two compartments, one of which was fronted with close iron bars. This was the abode of a large polecat-ferret, which a friendly butcher-boy had once smuggled, cage and all, into its present quarters, in exchange for a long-secreted hoard of small silver. Conradin was dreadfully afraid of the lithe, sharp-fanged beast, but it was his most treasured possession. Its very presence in the tool-shed was a secret and fearful joy, to be kept scrupulously from the knowledge of the Woman, as he privately dubbed his cousin. And one day, out of Heaven knows what material, he spun the beast a wonderful name, and from that moment it grew into a god and a religion. The Woman indulged in religion once a week at a church near by, and took Conradin with her, but to him the church service was an alien rite in the House of Rimmon. Every Thursday, in the dim and musty silence of the tool-shed, he worshipped with mystic and elaborate ceremonial before the wooden hutch where dwelt Sredni Vashtar, the great ferret. Red flowers in their season and scarlet berries in the winter-time were offered at his shrine, for he was a god who laid some special stress on the fierce impatient side of things, as opposed to the Woman's religion, which, as far as Conradin could observe, went to great lengths in the contrary direction. And on great festivals powdered nutmeg was strewn in front of his hutch, an important feature of the offering being that the nutmeg had to be stolen. These festivals were of irregular occurrence, and were chiefly appointed to celebrate some passing event. On one occasion, when Mrs. De Ropp suffered from acute toothache for three days, Conradin kept up the festival during the entire three days, and almost succeeded in persuading himself that Sredni Vashtar was personally responsible for the toothache. If the malady had lasted for another day the supply of nutmeg would have given out.

The Houdan hen was never drawn into the cult of Sredni Vashtar. Conradin had long ago settled that she was an Anabaptist. He did not pretend to have the remotest knowledge as to what an Anabaptist was, but he privately hoped that it was dashing and not very respectable. Mrs. De Ropp was the ground plan on which he based and detested all respectability.

After a while Conradin's absorption in the tool-shed began to attract the notice of his guardian. "It is not good for him to be pottering down there in all weathers," she promptly decided, and at breakfast one morning she announced that the Houdan hen had been sold and taken away overnight. With her short-sighted eyes she peered at Conradin, waiting for an outbreak of rage and sorrow, which she was ready to rebuke with a flow of excellent precepts and reasoning. But Conradin said nothing: there was nothing to be said. Something perhaps in his white set face gave her a momentary qualm, for at tea that afternoon there was toast on the table, a delicacy which she usually banned on the ground that it was bad for him; also because the making of it "gave trouble," a deadly offence in the middle-class feminine eye.

"I thought you liked toast," she exclaimed, with an injured air, observing that he did not touch it.

"Sometimes," said Conradin.

In the shed that evening there was an innovation in the worship of the hutch-god. Conradin had been wont to chant his praises, tonight he asked a boon.

"Do one thing for me, Sredni Vashtar."

The thing was not specified. As Sredni Vashtar was a god he must be supposed to know. And choking back a sob as he looked at that other empty corner, Conradin went back to the world he so hated.

And every night, in the welcome darkness of his bedroom, and every evening in the dusk of the tool-shed, Conradin's bitter litany went up: "Do one thing for me, Sredni Vashtar."

Mrs. De Ropp noticed that the visits to the shed did not cease, and one day she made a further journey of inspection.

"What are you keeping in that locked hutch?" she asked. "I believe it's guinea-pigs. I'll have them all cleared away."

Conradin shut his lips tight, but the Woman ransacked his bedroom till she found the carefully hidden key, and forthwith marched down to the shed to complete her discovery. It was a cold afternoon, and Conradin had been bidden to keep to the house. From the furthest window of the dining-room the door of the shed could just be seen beyond the corner of the shrubbery, and there Conradin stationed himself. He saw the Woman enter, and then he imagined her opening the door of the sacred hutch and peering down with her short-sighted eyes into the thick straw bed where his god lay hidden. Perhaps she would prod at the straw in her clumsy impatience. And Conradin fervently breathed his prayer for the last time. But he knew as he prayed that he did not believe. He knew that the Woman would come out presently with that pursed smile he loathed so well on her face, and that in an hour or two the gardener would carry away his wonderful god, a god no longer, but a simple brown ferret in a hutch. And he knew that the Woman would triumph always as she triumphed now, and that he would grow ever more sickly under her pestering and domineering and superior wisdom, till one day nothing would matter much more with him, and the doctor would be proved right. And in the sting and misery of his defeat, he began to chant loudly and defiantly the hymn of his threatened idol:

Sredni Vashtar went forth,
His thoughts were red thoughts and his teeth were white.
His enemies called for peace, but he brought them death.
Sredni Vashtar the Beautiful.

And then of a sudden he stopped his chanting and drew closer to the window-pane. The door of the shed still stood ajar as it had been left, and the minutes were slipping by. They were long minutes, but they slipped by nevertheless. He watched the starlings running and flying in little parties across the lawn; he counted them over and over again, with one eye always on that swinging door. A sour-faced maid came in to lay the table for tea, and still Conradin stood and waited and watched. Hope had crept by inches into his heart, and now a look of triumph began to blaze in his eyes that had only known the wistful patience of defeat. Under his breath, with a furtive exultation, he began once again the pæan of victory and devastation. And presently his eyes were rewarded: out through that doorway came a long, low, yellow-and-brown beast, with eyes a-blink at the waning daylight, and dark wet stains around the fur of jaws and throat. Conradin dropped on his knees. The great polecat-ferret made its way down to a small brook at the foot of the garden, drank for a moment, then crossed a little plank bridge and was lost to sight in the bushes. Such was the passing of Sredni Vashtar.

"Tea is ready," said the sour-faced maid; "where is the mistress?"

"She went down to the shed some time ago," said Conradin.

And while the maid went to summon her mistress to tea, Conradin fished a toasting-fork out of the sideboard drawer and proceeded to toast himself a piece of bread. And during the toasting of it and the buttering of it with much butter and the slow enjoyment of eating it, Conradin listened to the noises and silences which fell in quick spasms beyond the dining-room door. The loud foolish screaming of the maid, the answering chorus of wondering ejaculations from the kitchen region, the scuttering footsteps and hurried embassies for outside help, and then, after a lull, the scared sobbings and the shuffling tread of those who bore a heavy burden into the house.

"Whoever will break it to the poor child? I couldn't for the life of me!" exclaimed a shrill voice. And while they debated the matter among themselves, Conradin made himself another piece of toast.

In this story the seemingly idle pastimes of a sickly, shy ten-year-old boy slowly take on sinister aspects as the events in the toolshed become laced with horror. The apparently trivial though somewhat sad story of Conradin's bleak existence becomes a tale of hatred, loneliness, pagan religious rites, and finally violence and death. Here is news—the ordinary transformed into the extraordinary. The story told is hardly a simple, everyday one. Yet Saki makes even these weird events seem believable. We may say, in fact, that in his treatment of these events Saki creates **verisimilitude**—the appearance or likeness of what is true and actual. At the same time he also makes us aware of the tale's particularity and universal significance.

In achieving this effect, Saki provides a few carefully selected details. He tells us only that Conradin is an orphan, that he is ten years old, that he may not live another five years, and that he is now in the care of his cousin, Mrs. De Ropp. Perhaps another, less skillful storyteller would have explained Mrs. De Ropp's financial situation, told what happened to her husband and Conradin's parents, and described the house. Saki reports none of these matters. He omits them because they are not essential to our understanding of Conradin's mental and emotional state. The details that are included, however, are all vital and essential. The garden is dull and cheerless; the overlooking windows are a source of intrusion, not joy. Even the shrubbery is dismal. All such details, even apparently insignificant ones, are weighted to convey more than mere surface observations. Part of Saki's artistry is simply selection—knowing what to include, what to exclude.

In such a firmly controlled story, the artist tries to prune every word that does not contribute to the desired effect. Writing in 1842, Edgar Allan Poe said that in short fiction "every word *tells,* and there is not a word that does not tell." In the carefully crafted short story every word suggests something significant, and so we should read short fiction almost as closely as we would a poem. In "Sredni Vashtar," for instance, we should notice that the word *succumbed* is used twice in the first paragraph. First, it clearly refers to the dull routine of "wearisome necessary things" that threaten Conradin, but its second use is less explicit. Does Saki mean that without his imagination the boy would have succumbed to respectability or to death? Or perhaps Saki means both—perhaps they are one and the same.

This question is never explicitly resolved. Rather Saki goes on in the second paragraph to define the conflict between Conradin and his guardian so explicitly that Mrs. De Ropp herself seems almost responsible for the boy's limited prospects. Saki's careful selection of details in the third paragraph vividly reveals Conradin's bleak existence and his need to defend himself against his guardian's authority by dismissing it and creating his own private world. Her religion is conventional and respectable, but Conradin's is exotic, since with his imagination, he creates a cathedral, fashions a religion, and even produces a god.

Saki manages in the first three paragraphs not only to make us understand how a ten-year-old boy might use red flowers, scarlet berries, and powdered nutmeg to worship a polecat-ferret, but he also tempts us to approve. He prepares us for Mrs. De Ropp's gruesome death, which we feel is somehow fitting, and which we are startled to find ourselves condoning. Normally, if we had read or heard that a woman had been bitten to death by a polecat-ferret, we would have been appalled. If we had discovered that her foster son had worshipped the ferret and prayed to it to kill her, we would label him "deviant" or seriously "delinquent." Yet Saki realigns our sympathies so that we are shocked less by Conradin than by Mrs. De Ropp and perhaps by our own reactions.

Saki accomplishes this response through a number of techniques— by narrating the tale from Conradin's perspective; by avoiding a description of the horrid death itself; and by carefully selecting details so that everything mentioned contributes to the tale's single effect. That effect is intensified because Saki has associated Conradin's strange behavior with the forces of life, that of the woman with death. Even in their particularity, the unusual incidents of the tale suggest larger, universal issues. And the impact of the story depends upon how well the small and the large implications of the narrative underscore each other, upon how well Saki has yoked the particular and the universal together and shaped them into a unified piece of fiction.

The story Saki tells is the sort that we would retell whenever such a strange event happened. If anyone we know or even had heard of told us or one of our friends what happened to Conradin and Mrs. De Ropp, we would probably repeat it, saying "You know that girl Sarah? Well, she lives about six blocks from where that woman was killed and she heard . . . ." We would repeat the story because such shocking incidents carry their own force and drama and convey a thrill whenever they are retold.

If Sammy in the following story by John Updike, however, told us what happened to him one Thursday afternoon, most of us would not recount the incident. We might convey only a simple bit of information: "You know Sammy who works in the A & P? Well, he quit his job—had an argument with his boss." Few of us would sense the drama in this incident and even fewer of us would be able to convey it. Yet a writer like Updike sees and conveys the particular and the universal significance in this apparently commonplace incident in a familiar A & P on an ordinary Thursday afternoon. Recognizing that accomplishment is the basis of understanding how a well-crafted story works.

John Updike   (b. 1932)
A & P

In walks these three girls in nothing but bathing suits. I'm in the third checkout slot, with my back to the door, so I don't see them until they're over by the bread. The one that caught my eye first was the one in the plaid green two-piece. She was a chunky kid, with a good tan and a sweet broad soft-looking can with those two crescents of white just under it, where the sun never seems to hit, at the top of the backs of her legs. I stood there with my hand on a box of HiHo crackers trying to remember if I rang it up or not. I ring it up again and the customer starts giving me hell. She's one of these cash-register-watchers, a witch about fifty with rouge on her cheekbones and no eyebrows, and I know it made her day to trip me up. She'd been watching cash registers for fifty years and probably never seen a mistake before.

By the time I got her feathers smoothed and her goodies into a bag—she gives me a little snort in passing, if she'd been born at the right time they would have burned her over in Salem—by the time I get her on her way the girls had circled around the bread and were coming back, without a pushcart, back my way along the counters, in the aisle between the checkouts and the Special bins. They didn't even have shoes on. There was this chunky one, with the two-piece—it was bright green and the seams on the bra were still sharp and her belly was still pretty pale so I guessed she just got it (the suit)—there was this one, with one of those chubby berry-faces, the lips all bunched together under her nose, this one, and a tall one, with black hair that hadn't quite frizzed right, and one of these sunburns right across under the eyes, and a chin that was too long—you know, the kind of girl other girls think is very "striking" and "attractive" but never quite makes it, as they very well know, which is why they like her so much—and then the third one, that wasn't quite so tall. She was the queen. She kind of led them, the other two peeking around and making their shoulders round. She didn't look around, not this queen, she just walked straight on slowly, on these long white prima-donna legs. She came down a little hard on her heels, as if she didn't walk in bare feet that much, putting down her heels and then letting the weight move along to her toes as if she was testing the floor with every step, putting a little deliberate extra action into it. You never know for sure how girls' minds work (do you really think it's a mind in there or just a little buzz like a bee in a glass jar?) but you got the idea she had talked the other two into coming in here with her, and now she was showing them how to do it, walk slow and hold yourself straight.

She had on a kind of dirty-pink—beige maybe, I don't know—bathing suit with a little nubble all over it and, what got me, the straps were down. They were off her shoulders looped loose around the cool tops of her arms, and I guess as a result the suit had slipped a little on her, so all around the top of the cloth there was this shining rim. If it hadn't been there you wouldn't have known there could have been anything whiter than those shoulders. With the straps pushed off, there was nothing between the top of the suit and the top of her head except just *her,* this clean bare plane of the top of her chest down from the shoulder bones like a dented sheet of metal tilted in the light. I mean, it was more than pretty.

She had a sort of oaky hair that the sun and salt had bleached, done up in a bun that was unravelling, and a kind of prim face. Walking into the A & P with your straps down, I suppose it's the only kind of face you *can* have. She held her head so high her neck, coming up out of those white shoulders, looked kind of stretched, but I didn't mind. The longer her neck was, the more of her there was.

She must have felt in the corner of her eye me and over my shoulder Stokesie in the second slot watching, but she didn't tip. Not this queen. She kept her eyes moving across the racks, and stopped, and turned so slow it made my stomach rub the inside of my apron, and buzzed to the other two, who kind of huddled against her for relief, and then they all three of them went up the cat-and-dog-food - breakfast - cereal - macaroni - rice - raisins - seasonings - spreads - spaghetti - soft-drinks - crackers - and - cookies aisle. From the third slot I look straight up this aisle to the meat counter, and I watched them all the way. The fat one with the tan sort of fumbled with the cookies, but on second thought she put the package back. The sheep pushing their carts down the aisle—the girls were walking against the usual traffic (not that we have one-way signs or anything)—were pretty hilarious. You could see them, when Queenie's white shoulders dawned on them, kind of jerk, or hop, or hiccup, but their eyes snapped back to their own baskets and on they pushed. I bet you could set off dynamite in an A & P and the people would by and large keep reaching and checking oatmeal off their lists and muttering "Let me see, there was a third thing, began with A, asparagus, no, ah, yes, applesauce!" or whatever it is they do mutter. But there was no doubt, this jiggled them. A few house-slaves in pin curlers even looked around after pushing their carts past to make sure what they had seen was correct.

You know, it's one thing to have a girl in a bathing suit down on the beach, where what with the glare nobody can look at each other much anyway, and another thing in the cool of the A & P, under the fluorescent lights, against all those stacked packages, with her feet paddling along naked over our checkerboard green-and-cream rubber-tile floor.

"Oh Daddy," Stokesie said beside me. "I feel so faint."

"Darling," I said. "Hold me tight." Stokesie's married, with two babies chalked up on his fuselage already, but as far as I can tell that's the only difference. He's twenty-two, and I was nineteen this April.

"Is it done?" he asks, the responsible married man finding his voice. I forgot to say he thinks he's going to be manager some sunny day, maybe in 1990 when it's called the Great Alexandrov and Petrooshki Tea Company or something.

What he meant was, our town is five miles from a beach, with a big summer colony out on the Point, but we're right in the middle of town, and the women generally put on a shirt or shorts or something before they get out of the car into the street. And anyway these are usually women with six children and varicose veins mapping their legs and nobody, including them, could care less. As I say, we're right in the middle of town, and if you stand at our front doors you can see two banks and the Congregational church and the newspaper store and three real-estate offices and about twenty-seven old freeloaders tearing up Central Street because the sewer broke again. It's not as if we're on the Cape; we're north of Boston and there's people in this town haven't seen the ocean for twenty years.

The girls had reached the meat counter and were asking McMahon something. He pointed, they pointed, and they shuffled out of sight behind a pyramid of Diet Delight peaches. All that was left for us to see was old McMahon patting his mouth and looking after them sizing up their joints. Poor kids, I began to feel sorry for them, they couldn't help it.

Now here comes the sad part of the story, at least my family says it's sad, but I don't think it's so sad myself. The store's pretty empty, it being Thursday afternoon, so there was nothing much to do except lean on the register and wait for the girls to show up again. The whole store was like a pinball machine and I didn't know which tunnel they'd come out of. After a while they come around out of the far aisle, around the light bulbs, records at discount of the Caribbean Six or Tony Martin Sings or some such gunk you wonder they waste the wax on, six-packs of candy bars, and plastic toys done up in cellophane that fall apart when a kid looks at them anyway. Around they come, Queenie still leading the way, and holding a little gray jar in her hand. Slots Three through Seven are unmanned and I could see her wondering between Stokes and me, but Stokesie with his usual luck draws an old party in baggy gray pants who stumbles up with four giant cans of pineapple juice (what do these bums *do* with all that pineapple juice? I've often asked myself) so the girls come to me. Queenie puts down the jar and I take it into my fingers icy cold. Kingfish Fancy Herring Snacks in Pure Sour Cream: 49¢. Now her hands are empty, not a ring or a bracelet, bare as God made them, and I wonder where the money's coming from. Still with that prim look she lifts a folded dollar bill out of the hollow at the center of her nubbled pink top. The jar went heavy in my hand. Really, I thought that was so cute.

Then everybody's luck begins to run out. Lengel comes in from haggling with a truck full of cabbages on the lot and is about to scuttle into that door marked MANAGER behind which he hides all day when the girls touch his eye. Lengel's pretty dreary, teaches Sunday school and the rest, but he doesn't miss that much. He comes over and says, "Girls, this isn't the beach."

Queenie blushes, though maybe it's just a brush of sunburn I was noticing for the first time, now that she was so close. "My mother asked me to pick up a jar of herring snacks." Her voice kind of startled me, the way voices do when you see the people first, coming out so flat and dumb yet kind of tony, too, the way it ticked over "pick up" and "snacks." All of a sudden I slid right down her voice into her living room. Her father and the other men were standing around in ice-cream coats and bow ties and the women were in sandals picking up herring snacks on toothpicks off a big glass plate and they were all holding drinks the color of water with olives and sprigs of mint in them. When my parents have somebody over they get lemonade and if it's a real racy affair Schlitz in tall glasses with "They'll Do It Every Time" cartoons stencilled on.

"That's all right," Lengel said. "But this isn't the beach." His repeating this struck me as funny, as if it had just occurred to him, and he had been thinking all these years the A & P was a great big dune and he was the head lifeguard. He didn't like my smiling—as I say he doesn't miss much—but he concentrates on giving the girls that sad Sunday-school-superintendent stare.

Queenie's blush is no sunburn now, and the plump one in plaid, that I liked better from the back—a really sweet can—pipes up, "We weren't doing any shopping. We just came in for the one thing."

"That makes no difference," Lengel tells her, and I could see from the way his eyes went that he hadn't noticed she was wearing a two-piece before. "We want you decently dressed when you come in here."

"We *are* decent," Queenie says suddenly, her lower lip pushing, getting sore now that she remembers her place, a place from which the crowd that runs the A & P must look pretty crummy. Fancy Herring Snacks flashed in her very blue eyes.

"Girls, I don't want to argue with you. After this come in here with your shoulders covered. It's our policy." He turns his back. That's policy for you. Policy is what the kingpins want. What the others want is juvenile delinquency.

All this while, the customers had been showing up with their carts but, you know, sheep, seeing a scene, they had all bunched up on Stokesie, who shook open a paper bag as gently as peeling a peach, not wanting to miss a word. I could feel in the silence everybody getting nervous, most of all Lengel, who asks me, "Sammy, have you rung up their purchase?"

I thought and said "No" but it wasn't about that I was thinking. I go through the punches, 4, 9, GROC, TOT—it's more complicated than you think, and after you do it often enough, it begins to make a little song, that you hear words to, in my case "Hello (*bing*) there, you (*gung*) hap-py pee-pul (*splat*)!"—the *splat* being the drawer flying out. I uncrease the bill, tenderly as you may imagine, it just having come from between the two smoothest scoops of vanilla I had ever known were there, and pass a half and a penny into her narrow pink palm, and nestle the herrings in a bag and twist its neck and hand it over, all the time thinking.

The girls, and who'd blame them, are in a hurry to get out, so I say "I quit" to Lengel quick enough for them to hear, hoping they'll stop and watch me, their unsuspected hero. They keep right on going, into the electric eye; the door flies open and they flicker across the lot to their car, Queenie and Plaid and Big Tall Goony-Goony (not that as raw material she was so bad), leaving me with Lengel and a kink in his eyebrow.

"Did you say something, Sammy?"

"I said I quit."

"I thought you did."

"You didn't have to embarrass them."

"It was they who were embarrassing us."

I started to say something that came out "Fiddle-de-do." It's a saying of my grandmother's, and I know she would have been pleased.

"I don't think you know what you're saying," Lengel said.

"I know you don't," I said. "But I do." I pull the bow at the back of my apron and start shrugging it off my shoulders. A couple of customers that had been heading for my slot begin to knock against each other, like scared pigs in a chute.

Lengel sighs and begins to look very patient and old and gray. He's been a friend of my parents for years. "Sammy, you don't want to do this to your Mom and Dad," he tells me. It's true, I don't. But it seems to me that once you begin a gesture it's fatal not to go through with it. I fold the apron, "Sammy" stitched in red on the pocket, and put it on the counter, and drop the bow tie on top of it. The bow tie is theirs, if you've ever wondered. "You'll feel this for the rest of your life," Lengel says, and I know that's true, too, but remembering how he made that pretty girl blush makes me so scrunchy inside I punch the No Sale tab and the machine whirs "pee-pul" and the drawer splats out. One advantage to this scene taking place in summer, I can follow this up with a clean exit, there's no fumbling around getting your coat and galoshes, I just saunter into the electric eye in my white shirt that my mother ironed the night before, and the door heaves itself open, and outside the sunshine is skating around on the asphalt.

I look around for my girls, but they're gone, of course. There wasn't anybody but some young married screaming with her children about some candy they didn't get by the door of a powder-blue Falcon station wagon. Looking back in the big windows, over the bags of peat moss and aluminum lawn furniture stacked on the pavement, I could see Lengel in my place in the slot, checking the sheep through. His face was dark gray and his back stiff, as if he's just had an injection of iron, and my stomach kind of fell as I felt how hard the world was going to be to me hereafter.

When we finish reading "A & P" we too feel, "Yes, the world *is* hard—that's how it is." We come to that recognition because the story is so authentic we cannot question it and because Sammy's feelings are so much like our own. Reading "Sredni Vashtar," we have the sense that the author's voice is shaping the tale for us. Reading "A & P," we have the illusion that there is no author at all. It really does not sound as if John Updike sat down at a desk and wrote and polished a piece of short fiction, but rather as if an actual boy named Sammy casually spoke to us in his own voice—which somehow got transcribed into written words.

Sammy's voice sounds authentic for a number of reasons. He does not explain who or where he is but merely begins talking as if to himself or to someone he knows. He initially describes the girls as if he had been asked a question about the merchandise: "they're over by the bread." He repeats trivial opinions and cute sayings that he apparently does not believe, remarking, for instance, that girls have no minds at the same time that he is becoming fascinated with their casual attitude. He does not know what the color beige is or that martinis are not served with mint sprigs. He can be inarticulate: "I mean, it was more than pretty"; and "Really, I thought that was so cute"; and "you know." Yet he can also speak in a racily poetic fashion, saying that Stokesie has "two babies chalked up on his fuselage already" or describing Queenie taking the dollar bill from the top of her bathing suit "between the two smoothest scoops of vanilla I had ever known were there." Most of the time though Sammy speaks stumblingly and haltingly. Sometimes he repeats himself and sometimes he forgets what he means to say, but in his very hesitancy Sammy talks in a conversational manner familiar to most of us.

The chatty quality of the narrative may seem so artless that we might conclude that "A & P" is not as carefully crafted as "Sredni Vashtar." Certainly it is hard to believe that in "A & P" every word "tells" as it does in "Sredni Vashtar." Nevertheless, in Updike's story vague, repetitious, and apparently irrelevant words tell too; for they let us know a great deal about Sammy. Although we get the impression that "A & P" is a casual, loose, and rambling narrative, if we look carefully we will see that it too is a tight, coherent story in which all details contribute to a unified effect.

Consider the A & P and its patrons. There is nothing extraordinary about the store. Aisles and rows and registers and check-outs and bins and counters seem to be slots and tunnels in a pinball machine. The products are alike in their ordinariness—HiHo crackers and bread and light bulbs and cookies and Diet Delight Peaches. These products are uniformly ordinary and, like the plastic toys that "fall apart when a kid looks at them anyway," they lack quality and substance. Everything Sammy says about the shoppers implies that, like the stacked packages sold at the store, they too are ordinary. They wear pin curls and have varicose veins and carry shopping lists; they watch cash registers and push their carts with the traffic. Sammy calls them sheep. And the store's manager, Lengel, with his dreary sense of regularity and policy, typifies them.

It is against a backdrop of such conformers that Queenie, with her "long white prima-donna legs," stands out as a nonconformist. She carries herself proudly, leads her two friends around, and has her bathing-suit straps pushed down over her shoulders, an indication of her indifference to group values and conventional opinions. Her purchase of Kingfish Fancy Herring Snacks in Pure Sour Cream further sets her apart from the crowd and establishes what seems to Sammy a discriminating sense of quality.

Updike has set up two contrasting ways of living: conformity and independence, mediocrity and the quest for quality. And he has made every detail in the story contribute to our sense of the difference between the two. As in "Sredni Vashtar," there is in this story a conflict between two opposing forces. But in "Sredni Vashtar," no matter how much the polecat-ferret fulfills Conradin's wishes, it acts as an outside agent so that the death of Mrs. De Ropp seems beyond Conradin's control.

In "A & P," however, the two opposing forces are not engaged in a life-and-death struggle. Their conflict is not so dramatic, but it is nonetheless real. And the issue is Sammy's decision to choose one side or another. At first he is committed to the A & P and all that it represents; he regards the girls as intruders and stares at them as sex objects. Then seeing old McMahon behind the meat counter "patting his mouth and looking after them sizing up their joints," be begins to feel sorry for them. Despite Sammy's sense of how different his own background is from Queenie's, he sides with her against the forces of conformity. Quitting his job and turning in the bow tie and the apron with "Sammy" stitched in red across it is a perfect expression of his disaffection with middle-class values. Yet this act only temporarily resolves the conflict. For Sammy lives in a world in which nonconformity is punished severely. It is a world which is going to be hard on him.

Before reading this story, all of us probably knew that the world frequently ignores heroes and punishes nonconformists; such an understanding is more or less universal. Yet in reading "A & P" we discover something of what that truth may actually mean to Sammy, with whom we identify, and to ourselves. Because we intimately share in Sammy's yearnings and frustrations, we therefore *know*, as we did not quite know before we began reading, how it is for the nonconformist. Updike has made a familiar truth fresh and real to us.

"Sredni Vashtar" brings us to think about something we are unlikely to have known before. "A & P" brings us to think with fresh conviction about something we are likely to have known before. Yet both stories are similar in yoking a particular situation with a universal understanding. Reading these two very different stories together also reveals that good fiction does not have to follow any definite pattern but that, regardless of the kind of story, it must be unified to achieve a definite effect. In order to do this the author must use the elements of fiction to best advantage. And we need to study these elements in order to appreciate and judge the author's achievement and enhance our reading pleasure.

Before we look more closely at the craft of fiction, however, we need to expand an idea suggested at the beginning of this chapter: that judging fiction is not fundamentally different from judging the stories and anecdotes our friends tell. On one hand, some people cannot make an interesting narrative out of the most bizarre or exciting experience. A few individuals, on the other hand, can take humdrum experiences like buying a pair of shoes, planting a garden, or working in a supermarket and transform them into exciting and compelling narratives. The good storyteller, like the serious fiction writer, makes his stories vivid, dramatic, and unified because he has an imaginative facility for ordering and controlling language. Well-crafted fiction is different in degree, not kind, from even the best of stories told in casual conversation. We react to our storytelling friends according to how well they tell their tales, and we judge fiction according to how well the author manages the elements of the craft. An explanation of the ways in which these elements function in fiction helps develop in us a better sense of how effective storytellers reveal the particular and the universal qualities in their tales.

Chapter 2
Plot

Writers of fiction invent plots in much the same way all of us try to devise a model or work out a plan for our lives. In each case an ordered framework is imposed on experience in order to contain, control, and shape it. "A & P" is a controlled fragment of experience from which Updike seems to have deleted all the tedious and irrelevant experiences Sammy might have had. Updike writes only about those events that suggest a basic conflict between conformity and independence. He works by what novelist Elizabeth Bowen calls the "whittling-away of alternatives" to create a plot and thus impose order and unity on his material. In reading "A & P" we understand Sammy's conflict as we probably would not if we were working in a supermarket. Because well-crafted fiction presents such a focused and controlled segment of life, reading it offers us another way of bringing order and meaning to our experiences.

Plot is not merely the sum total of events or their sequence. Rather it is the selecting, ordering, and arranging of incidents to suggest their importance and their relationships, their actual dependence on one another. To say that some girls in bathing suits walked into an A & P and that a clerk quit is to say only what happened. To review a story's plot, however, is to say something about the connections between the events it relates.

In the traditional plot these connections are causal. When Aristotle (384–322 B.C.) said that the plot must have a beginning, a middle, and an end, he meant that the middle must logically grow out of the beginning and that the end must be a fulfillment of the beginning and the middle. The three stages of a traditional plot follow a pattern rather like a three-part argument, with a conclusion that is a logical outgrowth of the first two statements. For instance, if you agree with the first two statements, you must agree with the third: "All draftsmen are frustrated architects. John is a draftsman. John is a frustrated architect." Similarly, the plot of "A & P" might be reviewed according to the following pattern: "The A & P excludes nonconformity. Sammy admires Queenie's nonconformity. Sammy must quit the A & P." Although not rigorously logical, such a statement of plot indicates how the story's conclusion grows out of the beginning and the middle parts. "Plot," as Elizabeth Bowen observed, "is the knowing of destination," by which she meant that its ultimate resting place must be determined by its origin and continuation or by its beginning and middle.

The traditional plot follows with variations a basic design that may be visualized as a line, which gradually rises, reaches a high point, and then moves downward. The rising line represents the gradual intensification or building-up of a problem, reaching its highest point when the problem becomes so intense that a solution must come about. The downward line represents the rapid decrease of intensity as the problem is resolved. Although this design may be varied, it usually manifests certain elements basic to most fictional plots: exposition, conflict, complication, crisis, and dénouement. Here is a diagram showing the basic plot structure and the relationship of its elements:

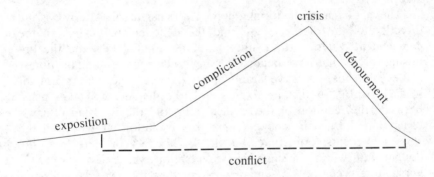

In its simplest form, **exposition** is whatever background information—time, setting, details about the characters—the author includes in order to prepare the reader for the subsequent conflict: "On a windy, gray day in the spring of 1932, Jeff Armstrong, an unemployed merchant seaman, was walking along the beach at Carmel. He had just left the shack he shared with . . . ." and so on. A more subtle and sophisticated handling of exposition occurs when the author slowly reveals bits of pertinent information as the narrative unfolds. In Stephen Crane's "A Mystery of Heroism," for example, the exposition briefly paints a vivid picture of a battle, but it is not until later on that we are given additional details about the participants.

It is less important for the exposition to supply facts than for it to contain the seed or suggestion of a **conflict,** or the opposition between forces that is intensified and then resolved during the narrative. In "A Mystery of Heroism," Crane casually mentions in his second paragraph Fred Collins' thirst. Yet this thirst soon grows into an intense conflict. Without some element of conflict, few stories or even personal anecdotes would be worth telling at all. Whether our story is about a friend's attempt to talk herself out of a traffic ticket, about the frustrating attempts to correct a computer error on a grade report, or about the difficult decision we face in choosing a career, at the heart of each lies a basic conflict. And in fiction, as in real life, conflict may take three basic forms: man against man, man against nature or his environment, or man against himself.

When the characters are caught up in their situation and the conflict intensifies, the **complication** occurs. In Guy de Maupassant's "A Fishing Excursion" circumstance prevents the two friends from enjoying themselves as they did before the military seige. Yet they challenge circumstance and involve themselves in an ever-more dangerous struggle with the forces around them. The conflict peaks at a moment of **crisis,** or the point of greatest intensity when the opposing forces interlock or reach a standstill. The crisis in Maupassant's story is the moment when the two friends must choose either personal survival or their friendship and integrity.

The crisis marks the turning point of the narrative. Afterwards the direction of the plot changes, and the dénouement begins. In the **dénouement**[1] (literally the "untying") the conflict between the opposing forces that have become entangled during the complication is settled, the loose narrative strands are tied up, and the story is brought to a close. In "A Fishing Excursion," the dénouement takes place between the mention of the leveled guns and the Prussian officer's order that the fish be cooked; here the resolution wraps up all the story's elements. Sometimes, as in "A Mystery of Heroism," the dénouement will be initiated by a reversal of expectation or by a reversed interpretation of a situation. No matter how it is accomplished, the dénouement should be embedded in the complication. In a unified piece of fiction the conflict is not settled by accident but rather by the fulfillment of the basic problem set up during the complication.

Our discussion of the five components of the standard plot structure may suggest that this design is inflexible. This is not the case, however. Plot is subject to many variations—for example, lengthening or shortening any of the elements; introducing minor crises before the major one; planting exposition at various places in the narrative or even omitting it; and shifting the order of events.

A frequent variation from the basic plot structure is the **flashback,** the presenting of scenes which took place prior to the time of the narrative. In the flashback events from the past are reenacted, while in standard exposition they are only summarized. Another familiar device for

---

1. In order to keep terminology to a minimum, we are using *dénouement* synonymously with *resolution* and *falling action.*

restructuring time is the **frame,** which presents a story from the past within a framework of present-day events. Irwin Shaw's "The Eighty-Yard Run" (Chapter 3), for instance, begins and ends with Christian Darling at the age of thirty-five on a football field. In the course of the narrative Shaw presents Christian's life between ages twenty and thirty-five in a traditional rising and falling plot design.

Probably the clearest, most consistent example of how traditional plot works can be found in detective fiction. In the **detective story** a crime, usually a murder, is solved by a detective through careful analysis and logical interpretation of clues. John Dickson Carr's "The Incautious Burglar" begins with a careful exposition that **foreshadows** or subtly hints at what is to come later in the story. The Russian writer Anton Chekhov once said that if there is a gun in the first act of a play, we can be sure it will go off in the last act. In "The Incautious Burglar" there are no guns, but there are a great many details planted in the story's first part which "go off" in its last. Here exposition contains the seed of a conflict. The initial problem is figuring out why Marcus Hunt would leave valuable paintings that are uninsured in such a vulnerable position, but the real problem—discovering who killed Hunt—soon emerges as the story unfolds.

Suspense is created by frustrating and "suspending" the reader's desire to move toward the story's outcome. In a detective story, the suspense is achieved by giving readers clues by which they can solve a crime. Yet it is sometimes difficult for the reader to put them together, since the point of most detective fiction is that the clever detective should solve the crime before the reader does. Like the reader, the people in the story devise alternate solutions, but these are usually wrong or inadequate. The crisis occurs when the plot complication becomes almost hopelessly entangled. Then the detective unravels the plot threads, solves the crime, and explains how he arrived at his conclusion, thereby bringing about the dénouement.

In "The Incautious Burglar" the dénouement, which fulfills the sinister implications of the card game that began the story, ties up all the story's loose ends. Thus the dénouement here functions as Edgar Allan Poe said it should in all stories. Poe, who established the conventions of detective fiction and whose theories about the short story have been widely influential, wrote in 1846 that

> *every plot, worth the name, must be elaborated to its dénouement before anything be attempted with the pen. It is only with the dénouement constantly in view that we can give a plot its indispensable air of consequence, or causation, by making the incidents, and especially the tone at all points, tend to the development of the intention.*

Detective fiction provides a model for the study of plot structure in short fiction because of its consistent and predictable handling of the basic elements of storytelling.

To the extent that we read fiction to learn how things will turn out, our approach may be to read for plot interest alone. We may read mystery stories to find out if the secret agent can identify the master spy before he himself is ambushed and shot; we may read adventure stories to learn if the explorers will survive among hostile natives; or we may read conventional love stories to know if a boy and a girl will stay together. Such an approach is appropriate with much popular fiction, and it is often demanded by more serious fiction as well.

In well-crafted fiction we cannot **paraphrase,** or restate in our own words, the plot by reviewing the incidents and indicating their relationships without losing much of the story's impact and meaning. Flannery O'Connor once said that a story "isn't any good unless it successfully resists paraphrase, unless it hangs on and expands in the mind." We could paraphrase the plot of "A Mystery of Heroism," for example, by saying that it "is about" a soldier who, for apparently mysterious reasons, risks his life to get a bucket of water from a well close to enemy lines, gives a drink to a fallen comrade, and returns to his lines only to have the bucket spilled by two officers. Yet this paraphrase, or even an expanded version of it, cannot come close to conveying the vividness, intensity, and impact of the story.

Reading a story for its plot should not be considered a mere matter of reading only to discover what happens. Instead, reading with the plot in mind should involve an appreciation of the craftsmanship used to put the story together. We should study plot as we might study the architectural design of a building—to see where things fit and to learn if the architect has allowed for an adequate number of elevators and windows. Similarly, we might read a story simply to see what occurs and how things turn out. But we might also study a building's design as a work of art in itself. In the same way, we study plot to appreciate how the reversal is suggested by sequences of events and their complication; how the dénouement fulfills the foreshadowing of the exposition; how the ending, whether happy or not, grows logically and inevitably out of the story's beginning and middle. Studying the architectural design of a plot, we come to appreciate the form, harmony, and beauty of the story's artistic construction.

John Dickson Carr (b. 1906)
The Incautious Burglar

Two guests, who were not staying the night at Cranleigh Court, left at shortly past eleven o'clock. Marcus Hunt saw them to the front door. Then he returned to the dining-room, where the poker-chips were now stacked into neat piles of white, red, and blue.

"Another game?" suggested Rolfe.

"No good," said Derek Henderson. His tone, as usual, was weary. "Not with just the three of us."

Their host stood by the sideboard and watched them. The long, low house, overlooking the Weald of Kent,[1] was so quiet that their voices rose with startling loudness. The dining-room, large and panelled, was softly lighted by electric wall-candles which brought out the sombre colours of the paintings. It is not often that anybody sees, in one room of an otherwise commonplace country house, two Rembrandts and a Van Dyck. There was a kind of defiance about those paintings.

To Arthur Rolfe—the art dealer—they represented enough money to make him shiver. To Derek Henderson—the art critic—they represented a problem. What they represented to Marcus Hunt was not apparent.

Hunt stood by the sideboard, his fists on his hips, smiling. He was a middle-sized, stocky man, with a full face and a high complexion. Equip him with a tuft of chin-whisker, and he would have looked like a Dutch burgher for a Dutch brush.[2] His shirt-front bulged out untidily. He watched with ironical amusement while Henderson picked up a pack of cards in long fingers, cut them into two piles, and shuffled with a sharp flick of each thumb which made the cards melt together like a conjuring trick.

Henderson yawned.

"My boy," said Hunt, "you surprise me."

"That's what I try to do," answered Henderson, still wearily. He looked up. "But why do you say so, particularly?"

Henderson was young, he was long, he was lean, he was immaculate; and he wore a beard. It was a reddish beard, which moved some people to hilarity. But he wore it with an air of complete naturalness.

"I'm surprised," said Hunt, "that you enjoy anything so bourgeois—so plebeian—as poker."

"I enjoy reading people's characters," said Henderson. "Poker's the best way to do it, you know."

Hunt's eyes narrowed. "Oh? Can you read my character, for instance?"

"With pleasure," said Henderson. Absently he dealt himself a poker-hand, face up. It contained a pair of fives, and the last card was the ace of spades. Henderson remained staring at it for a few seconds before he glanced up again.

"And I can tell you," he went on, "that *you* surprise *me*. Do you mind if

---

1. Part of a heavily-wooded region in southeastern England, near London.
2. I.e, a fit subject for a Dutch painter. In the 17th century, burghers (middle-class citizens) were popular subjects in Dutch art.

I'm frank? I had always thought of you as the Colossus of Business; the smasher; the plunger; the fellow who took the long chances. Now, you're not like that at all.''

Marcus Hunt laughed. But Henderson was undisturbed.

''You're tricky, but you're cautious. I doubt if you ever took a long chance in your life. Another surprise''—he dealt himself a new hand—''is Mr. Rolfe here. He's the man who, given the proper circumstances, would take the long chances.''

Arthur Rolfe considered this. He looked startled, but rather flattered. Though in height and build not unlike Hunt, there was nothing untidy about him. He has a square, dark face, with thin shells of eyeglasses, and a worried forehead.

''I doubt that,'' he declared, very serious about this. Then he smiled. ''A person who took long chances in my business would find himself in the soup.'' He glanced round the room. '' Anyhow, I'd be too cautious to have three pictures, with an aggregate value of thirty thousand pounds, hanging in an unprotected downstairs room with French windows giving on a terrace.'' An almost frenzied note came into his voice. ''Great Scot! Suppose a burglar——''

''Damn!'' said Henderson unexpectedly.

Even Hunt jumped.

Ever since the poker-party, an uneasy atmosphere had been growing. Hunt had picked up an apple from a silver fruit-bowl on the sideboard. He was beginning to pare it with a fruit-knife, a sharp wafer-thin blade which glittered in the light of the wall-lamps.

''You nearly made me slice my thumb off,'' he said, putting down the knife. ''What's the matter with you?''

''It's the ace of spades,'' said Henderson, still languidly. ''That's the second time it's turned up in five minutes.''

Arthur Rolfe chose to be dense. ''Well? What about it?''

''I think our young friend is being psychic,'' said Hunt, good-humoured again. ''Are you reading characters, or only telling fortunes?''

Henderson hesitated. His eyes moved to Hunt, and then to the wall over the sideboard where Rembrandt's ''Old Woman with Cap'' stared back with the immobility and skin-colouring of a red Indian. Then Henderson looked towards the French windows opening on the terrace.

''None of my affair,'' shrugged Henderson. ''It's your house and your collection and your responsibility. But this fellow Butler: what do you know about him?''

Marcus Hunt looked boisterously amused.

''Butler? He's a friend of my niece's. Harriet picked him up in London, and asked me to invite him down here. Nonsense! Butler's all right. What are you thinking, exactly?''

''Listen!'' said Rolfe, holding up his hand.

The noise they heard, from the direction of the terrace, was not repeated. It was not repeated because the person who had made it, a very bewildered and uneasy young lady, had run lightly and swiftly to the far end, where she leaned against the balustrade.

Lewis Butler hesitated before going after her. The moonlight was so clear that one could see the mortar between the tiles which paved the terrace, and trace the design of the stone urns along the balustrade. Harriet Davis wore a white gown with long and filmy skirts, which she lifted clear of the ground as she ran.

Then she beckoned to him.

She was half sitting, half leaning against the rail. Her white arms were spread out, fingers gripping the stone. Dark hair and dark eyes became even more vivid by moonlight. He could see the rapid rise and fall of her breast; he could even trace the shadow of her eyelashes.

"That was a lie, anyhow," she said.

"What was?"

"What my Uncle Marcus said. You heard him." Harriet Davis's fingers tightened still more on the balustrade. But she nodded her head vehemently, with fierce accusation. "About my knowing you. And inviting you here. I never saw you before this week-end. Either Uncle Marcus is going out of his mind, or . . . will you answer me just one question?"

"If I can."

"Very well. Are you by any chance a crook?"

She spoke with as much simplicity and directness as though she had asked him whether he might be a doctor or a lawyer. Lewis Butler was not unwise enough to laugh. She was in that mood where, to any woman, laughter is salt to a raw wound; she would probably have slapped his face.

"To be quite frank about it," he said, "I'm not. Will you tell me why you asked?"

"This house," said Harriet, looking at the moon, "used to be guarded with burglar alarms. If you as much as touched a window, the whole place started clanging like a fire-station. He had all the burglar alarms removed last week. Last week." She took her hands off the balustrade, and pressed them together hard. "The pictures used to be upstairs, in a locked room next to his bedroom. He had them moved downstairs—last week. It's almost as though my uncle *wanted* the house to be burgled."

Butler knew that he must use great care here.

"Perhaps he does." (Here she looked at Butler quickly, but did not comment.) "For instance," he went on idly, "suppose one of his famous Rembrandts turned out to be a fake? It might be a relief not to have to show it to his expert friends."

The girl shook her head.

"No." She said. "They're all genuine. You see, I thought of that too."

Now was the time to hit, and hit hard. To Lewis Butler, in his innocence, there seemed to be no particular problem. He took out his cigarette-case, and turned it over without opening it.

"Look here, Miss Davis, you're not going to like this. But I can tell you of cases in which people were rather anxious to have their property 'stolen.' If a picture is insured for more than its value, and then it is mysteriously 'stolen' one night——?"

"That might be all very well too," answered Harriet, still calmly. "Except that not one of those pictures has been insured."

The cigarette-case, which was of polished metal, slipped through Butler's fingers and fell with a clatter on the tiles. It spilled cigarettes, just as it spilled and confused his theories. As he bent over to pick it up, he could hear a church clock across the Weald strike the half-hour after eleven.

"You're sure of that?"

"I'm perfectly sure. He hasn't insured any of his pictures for as much as a penny. He says it's a waste of money."

"But——"

"Oh, I know! And I don't know why I'm talking to you like this. You're a stranger, aren't you?" She folded her arms, drawing her shoulders up as though she were cold. Uncertainty, fear, and plain nerves flicked at her eyelids. "But then Uncle Marcus is a stranger too. Do you know what I think? *I* think he's going mad."

"Hardly as bad as that, is it?"

"Yes, go on," the girl suddenly stormed at him. "*Say* it: go on and say it. That's easy enough. But you don't see him when his eyes seem to get smaller, and all that genial-country-squire look goes out of his face. He's not a fake: he hates fakes, and goes out of his way to expose them. But, if he hasn't gone clear out of his mind, what's he up to? What can he be up to?"

In something over three hours, they found out.

The burglar did not attack until half-past two in the morning. First he smoked several cigarettes in the shrubbery below the rear terrace. When he heard the church clock strike, he waited a few minutes more, and then slipped up the steps to the French windows of the dining-room.

A chilly wind stirred at the turn of the night, in the hour of suicides and bad dreams. It smoothed grass and trees with a faint rustling. When the man glanced over his shoulder, the last of the moonlight distorted his face: it showed less a face than the blob of a black cloth mask, under a greasy cap pulled down over his ears.

He went to work on the middle window, with the contents of a folding tool-kit not so large as a motorist's. He fastened two short strips of adhesive tape to the glass just beside the catch. Then his glass-cutter sliced out a small semicircle inside the tape.

It was done not without noise: it crunched like a dentist's drill in a tooth, and the man stopped to listen.

There was no answering noise. No dog barked.

With the adhesive tape holding the glass so that it did not fall and smash, he slid his gloved hand through the opening and twisted the catch. The weight of his body deadened the creaking of the window when he pushed inside.

He knew exactly what he wanted. He put the tool-kit into his pocket, and drew out an electric torch.[3] Its beam moved across to the sideboard; it touched gleaming silver, a bowl of fruit, and a wicked little knife thrust into an apple as though into someone's body; finally, it moved up the hag-face of the "Old Woman with Cap."

This was not a large picture, and the burglar lifted it down easily. He pried out glass and frame. Though he tried to roll up the canvas with great care, the brittle paint cracked across in small stars which wounded the hag's face. The

---

3. Flashlight.

burglar was so intent on this that he never noticed the presence of another person in the room.

He was an incautious burglar: he had no sixth sense which smelt murder.

Up on the second floor of the house, Lewis Butler was awakened by a muffled crash like that of metal objects falling.

He had not fallen into more than a half doze all night. He knew with certainty what must be happening, though he had no idea of why, or how, or to whom.

Butler was out of bed, and into his slippers, as soon as he heard the first faint clatter from downstairs. His dressing-gown would, as usual, twist itself up like a rolled umbrella and defy all attempts to find the arm-holes whenever he wanted to hurry. But the little flashlight was ready in the pocket.

That noise seemed to have roused nobody else. With certain possibilities in his mind, he had never in his life moved so fast once he managed to get out of his bedroom. Not using his light, he was down two flights of deep-carpeted stairs without noise. In the lower hall he could feel a draught, which meant that a window or door had been opened somewhere. He made straight for the dining-room.

But he was too late.

Once the pencil-beam of Butler's flashlight had swept round, he switched on a whole blaze of lights. The burglar was still here, right enough. But the burglar was lying very still in front of the sideboard; and, to judge by the amount of blood on his sweater and trousers, he would never move again.

"That's done it," Butler said aloud.

A silver service, including a tea-urn, had been toppled off the sideboard. Where the fruit-bowl had fallen, the dead man lay on his back among a litter of oranges, apples, and a squashed bunch of grapes. The mask still covered the burglar's face; his greasy cap was flattened still further on his ears; his gloved hands were thrown wide.

Fragments of smashed picture-glass lay round him, together with the empty frame, and the "Old Woman with Cap" had been half crumpled up under his body. From the position of the most conspicuous bloodstains, one judged that he had been stabbed through the chest with the stained fruit-knife beside him.

"*What is it?*" said a voice almost at Butler's ear.

He could not have been more startled if the fruit-knife had pricked his ribs. He had seen nobody turning on lights in the hall, nor had he heard Harriet Davis approach. She was standing just behind him, wrapped in a Japanese kimono, with her dark hair round her shoulders. But, when he explained what had happened, she would not look into the dining-room; she backed away, shaking her head violently, like an urchin ready for flight.

"You had better wake up your uncle," Butler said briskly, with a confidence he did not feel. "And the servants. I must use your telephone." Then he looked her in the eyes. "Yes, you're quite right. I think you've guessed it already. I'm a police-officer."

She nodded.

"Yes. I guessed. Who are you? And is your name really Butler?"

"I'm a sergeant of the Criminal Investigation Department. And my name really is Butler. Your uncle brought me here."

"Why?"

"I don't know. He hasn't got round to telling me."

This girl's intelligence, even when over-shadowed by fear, was direct and disconcerting. "But, if he wouldn't say why he wanted a police-officer, how did they come to send you? He'd have to tell them, wouldn't he?"

Butler ignored it. "I must see your uncle. Will you go upstairs and wake him, please?"

"I can't," said Harriet. "Uncle Marcus isn't in his room."

"Isn't——?"

"No. I knocked at the door on my way down. He's gone."

Butler took the stairs two treads at a time. Harriet had turned on all the lights on her way down, but nothing stirred in the bleak, over-decorated passages.

Marcus Hunt's bedroom was empty. His dinner-jacket had been hung up neatly on the back of a chair, shirt laid across the seat with collar and tie on top of it. Hunt's watch ticked loudly on the dressing-table. His money and keys were there too. But he had not gone to bed, for the bedspread was undisturbed.

The suspicion which came to Lewis Butler, listening to the thin insistent ticking of that watch in the drugged hour before dawn, was so fantastic that he could not credit it.

He started downstairs again, and on the way he met Arthur Rolfe blundering out of another bedroom down the hall. The art dealer's stocky body was wrapped in a flannel dressing-gown. He was not wearing his eyeglasses, which gave his face a bleary and rather caved-in expression. He planted himself in front of Butler, and refused to budge.

"Yes," said Butler. "You don't have to ask. It's a burglar."

"I knew it," said Rolfe calmly. "Did he get anything?"

"No. He was murdered."

For a moment Rolfe said nothing, but his hand crept into the breast of his dressing-gown as though he felt pain there.

"Murdered? You don't mean the *burglar* was murdered?"

"Yes."

"But why? By an accomplice, you mean? Who is the burglar?"

"That," snarled Lewis Butler, "is what I intend to find out."

In the lower hall he found Harriet Davis, who was now standing in the doorway of the dining-room and looking steadily at the body by the sideboard. Though her face hardly moved a muscle, her eyes brimmed over.

"You're going to take off the mask, aren't you?" she asked, without turning round.

Stepping with care to avoid squashed fruit and broken glass, Butler leaned over the dead man. He pushed back the peak of the greasy cap; he lifted the black cloth mask, which was clumsily held by an elastic band; and he found what he expected to find.

The burglar was Marcus Hunt—stabbed through the heart while attempting to rob his own house.

"You see, sir," Butler explained to Dr. Gideon Fell on the following afternoon, "that's the trouble. However you look at it, the case makes no sense."

Again he went over the facts.

"Why should the man burgle his own house and steal his own property?

Every one of those paintings is valuable, and not a single one is insured! Consequently, why? Was the man a simple lunatic? What did he think he was doing?''

The village of Sutton Valence, straggling like a grey-white Italian town along the very peak of the Weald, was full of hot sunshine. In the apple orchard behind the white inn of the *Tabard*, Dr. Gideon Fell sat at a garden table among wasps, with a pint tankard at his elbow. Dr. Fell's vast bulk was clad in a white linen suit. His pink face smoked in the heat, and his wary lookout for wasps gave him a regrettably wall-eyed appearance as he pondered.

He said:

''Superintendent Hadley suggested that I might—harrumph—look in here. The local police are in charge, aren't they?''

''Yes. I'm merely standing by.''

''Hadley's exact words to me were, 'It's so crazy that nobody but you will understand it.' The man's flattery becomes more nauseating every day.'' Dr. Fell scowled. ''I say. Does anything else strike you as queer about this business?''

''Well, why should a man burgle his own house?''

''No, no, no!'' growled Dr. Fell. ''Don't be obsessed with that point. Don't become hypnotized by it. For instance''—a wasp hovered near his tankard, and he distended his checks and blew it away with one vast puff like Father Neptune[4]—''for instance, the young lady seems to have raised an interesting question. If Marcus Hunt wouldn't say why he wanted a detective in the house, why did the C.I.D. consent to send you?''

Butler shrugged his shoulders.

''Because,'' he said, ''Chief Inspector Ames thought Hunt was up to funny business, and meant to stop it.''

''What sort of funny business?''

''A faked burglary to steal his own pictures for the insurance. It looked like the old, old game of appealing to the police to divert suspicion. In other words, sir, exactly what this appeared to be: until I learned (and to-day proved) that not one of those damned pictures has ever been insured for a penny.''

Butler hesitated.

''It can't have been a practical joke,'' he went on. ''Look at the elaborateness of it! Hunt put on old clothes from which all tailors' tabs and laundry marks were removed. He put on gloves and a mask. He got hold of a torch and an up-to-date kit of burglar's tools. He went out of the house by the back door; we found it open later. He smoked a few cigarettes in the shrubbery below the terrace; we found his footprints in the soft earth. He cut a pane of glass . . . but I've told you all that.''

''And then,'' mused Dr. Fell, ''somebody killed him.''

''Yes. The last and worst 'why.' Why should anybody have killed him?''

''H'm. Clues?''

''Negative.'' Butler took out his notebook. ''According to the police surgeon, he died of a direct heart-wound from a blade (presumably that fruit-knife) so thin that the wound was difficult to find. There were a number of his

---

4. In Roman mythology, the god of the sea.

finger-prints, but nobody else's. We did find one odd thing, though. A number of pieces in the silver service off the sideboard were scratched in a queer way. It looked almost as though, instead of being swept off the sideboard in a struggle, they had been piled up on top of each other like a tower; and then pushed——''

Butler paused, for Dr. Fell was shaking his big head back and forth with an expression of gargantuan distress.

"Well, well, well," he was saying; "well, well, well. And you call that negative evidence?"

"Isn't it? It doesn't explain why a man burgles his own house."

"Look here," said the doctor mildly. "I should like to ask you just one question. What is the most important point in this affair? One moment! I did not say the most interesting; I said the most important. Surely it is the fact that a man has been murdered?"

"Yes, sir. Naturally."

"I mention the fact"—the doctor was apologetic—"because it seems in danger of being overlooked. It hardly interests you. You are concerned only with Hunt's senseless masquerade. You don't mind a throat being cut; but you can't stand a leg being pulled. Why not try working at it from the other side, and asking who killed Hunt?"

Butler was silent for a long time.

"The servants are out of it," he said at length. "They sleep in another wing on the top floor; and for some reason," he hesitated, "somebody locked them in last night." His doubts, even his dreads, were beginning to take form. There was a fine blow-up over that when the house was roused. Of course, the murderer could have been an outsider."

"You know it wasn't," said Dr. Fell. "Would you mind taking me to Cranleigh Court?"

They came out on the terrace in the hottest part of the afternoon.

Dr. Fell sat down on a wicker settee, with a dispirited Harriet beside him. Derek Henderson, in flannels, perched his long figure on the balustrade. Arthur Rolfe alone wore a dark suit and seemed out of place. For the pale green and brown of the Kentish lands, which rarely acquired harsh colour, now blazed. No air stirred, no leaf moved, in that brilliant thickness of heat; and down in the garden, towards their left, the water of the swimming-pool sparkled with hot, hard light. Butler felt it like a weight on his eyelids.

Derek Henderson's beard was at once languid and yet aggressive.

"It's no good," he said. "Don't keep on asking me why Hunt should have burgled his own house. But I'll give you a tip."

"Which is?" inquired Dr. Fell.

"Whatever the reason was," returned Henderson, sticking out his neck, "it was a good reason. Hunt was much too canny and cautious ever to do anything without a good reason. I told him so last night."

Dr. Fell spoke sharply. "Cautious? Why do you say that?"

"Well, for instance. I take three cards on the draw. Hunt takes one. I bet; he sees me and raises. I cover that, and raise again. Hunt drops out. In other words, it's fairly certain he's filled his hand, but not so certain I'm holding much more than a pair. Yet Hunt drops out. So with my three sevens I bluff him out of his straight. He played a dozen hands last night just like that."

Henderson began to chuckle. Seeing the expression on Harriet's face, he checked himself and became preternaturally solemn.

"But then, of course," Henderson added, "he had a lot on his mind last night."

Nobody could fail to notice the change of tone.

"So? And what did he have on his mind?"

"Exposing somebody he had always trusted," replied Henderson coolly. "That's why I didn't like it when the ace of spades turned up so often."

"You'd better explain that," said Harriet, after a pause. "I don't know what you're hinting at, but you'd better explain that. He told you he intended to expose somebody he had always trusted?"

"No. Like myself, he hinted at it."

It was the stolid Rolfe who stormed into the conversation then. Rolfe had the air of a man determined to hold hard to reason, but finding it difficult.

"Listen to me," snapped Rolfe. "I have heard a great deal, at one time or another, about Mr. Hunt's liking for exposing people. Very well!" He slid one hand into the breast of his coat, in a characteristic gesture. "But where in the name of sanity does that leave us? He wants to expose someone. And, to do that, he puts on outlandish clothes and masquerades as a burglar. Is that sensible? I tell you, the man was mad! There's no other explanation."

"There are five other explanations," said Dr. Fell.

Derek Henderson slowly got up from his seat on the balustrade, but he sat down again at a savage gesture from Rolfe.

Nobody spoke.

"I will not, however," pursued Dr. Fell, "waste your time with four of them. We are concerned with only one explanation: the real one."

"And you know the real one?" asked Henderson sharply.

"I rather think so."

"Since when?"

"Since I had the opportunity of looking at all of you," answered Dr. Fell.

He settled back massively in the wicker settee, so that its frame creaked and cracked like a ship's bulkhead in a heavy sea. His vast chin was outthrust, and he nodded absently as though to emphasize some point that was quite clear in his own mind.

"I've already had a word with the local inspector," he went on suddenly. "He will be here in a few minutes. And, at my suggestion, he will have a request for all of you. I sincerely hope nobody will refuse."

"Request?" said Henderson. "What request?"

"It's a very hot day," said Dr. Fell, blinking towards the swimming-pool. "He's going to suggest that you all go in for a swim."

Harriet uttered a kind of despairing mutter, and turned as though appealing to Lewis Butler.

"That," continued Dr. Fell, "will be the politest way of drawing attention to the murderer. In the meantime, let me call your attention to one point in the evidence which seems to have been generally overlooked. Mr. Henderson, do you know anything about direct heart-wounds, made by a steel blade as thin as a wafer?"

"Like Hunt's wound? No. What about them?"

"There is practically no exterior bleeding," answered Dr. Fell.

"But——!" Harriet was beginning, when Butler stopped her.

"The police surgeon, in fact, called attention to that wound which was so 'difficult to find.' The victim dies almost at once; and the edges of the wound compress. But in that case," argued Dr. Fell, "how did the late Mr. Hunt come to have so much blood on his sweater, and even splashed on his trousers?"

"Well?"

"He didn't," answered Dr. Fell simply. "Mr. Hunt's blood never got on his clothes at all."

"I can't stand this," said Harriet, jumping to her feet. "I—I'm sorry, but have you gone mad yourself? Are you telling us we didn't see him lying by that sideboard, with blood on him?"

"Oh, yes. You saw that."

"Let him go on," said Henderson, who was rather white round the nostrils. "Let him rave."

"It is, I admit, a fine point," said Dr. Fell. "But it answers your question, repeated to the point of nausea, as to why the eminently sensible Mr. Hunt chose to dress up in burglar's clothes and play burglar. The answer is short and simple. He didn't."

"It must be plain to everybody," Dr. Fell went on, opening his eyes wide, "that Mr. Hunt was deliberately setting a trap for someone—the real burglar.

"He believed that a certain person might try to steal one or several of his pictures. He probably knew that this person had tried similar games before, in other country houses: that is, an inside job which was carefully planned to look like an outside job. So he made things easy for this thief, in order to trap him, with a police-officer in the house.

"The burglar, a sad fool, fell for it. This thief, a guest in the house, waited until well past two o'clock in the morning. He then put on his old clothes, mask, gloves, and the rest of it. He let himself out by the back door. He went through all the motions we have erroneously been attributing to Marcus Hunt. Then the trap snapped. Just as he was rolling up the Rembrandt, he heard a noise. He swung his light round. And he saw Marcus Hunt, in pyjamas and dressing-gown, looking at him.

"Yes, there was a fight. Hunt flew at him. The thief snatched up a fruit-knife and fought back. In that struggle, Marcus Hunt forced his opponent's hand back. The fruit-knife gashed the thief's chest, inflicting a superficial but badly bleeding gash. It sent the thief over the edge of insanity. He wrenched Marcus Hunt's wrist half off, caught up the knife, and stabbed Hunt to the heart.

"Then, in a quiet house, with a little beam of light streaming out from the torch on the sideboard, the murderer sees something that will hang him. He sees the blood from his own superficial wound seeping down his clothes.

"How is he to get rid of those clothes? He cannot destroy them, or get them away from the house. Inevitably the house will be searched, and they will be found. Without the blood-stains, they would seem ordinary clothes in his wardrobe. But with the blood-stains——

"There is only one thing he can do."

Harriet Davis was standing behind the wicker settee, shading her eyes against the glare of the sun. Her hand did not tremble when she said:

"He changed clothes with my uncle."

"That's it," growled Dr. Fell. "That's the whole sad story. The murderer dressed the body in his own clothes, making a puncture with the knife in sweater, shirt, and undervest. He then slipped on Mr. Hunt's pyjamas and dressing-gown, which at a pinch he could always claim as his own. Hunt's wound had bled hardly at all. His dressing gown, I think, had come open in the fight; so that all the thief had to trouble him was a tiny puncture in the jacket of the pyjamas.

"But, once he had done this, he had to hypnotize you all into the belief that there would have been no time for a change of clothes. He had to make it seem that the fight occurred just *then*. He had to rouse the house. So he brought down echoing thunders by pushing over a pile of silver, and slipped upstairs."

Dr. Fell paused.

"The burglar could never have been Marcus Hunt, you know," he added. "We learn that Hunt's fingerprints were all over the place. Yet the murdered man was wearing gloves."

There was a swishing of feet in the grass below the terrace, and a tread of heavy boots coming up the terrace steps. The local Inspector of police, buttoned up and steaming in his uniform, was followed by two constables.

Dr. Fell turned round a face of satisfaction.

"Ah!" he said, breathing deeply. "They've come to see about that swimming-party, I imagine. It is easy to patch up a flesh-wound with lint and cotton, or even a handkerchief. But such a wound will become infernally conspicuous in anyone who is forced to climb into bathing-trunks."

"But it couldn't have been——" cried Harriet. Her eyes moved round. Her fingers tightened on Lewis Butler's arm, an instinctive gesture which he was to remember long afterwards, when he knew her even better.

"Exactly," agreed the doctor, wheezing with pleasure. "It could not have been a long, thin, gangling fellow like Mr. Henderson. It assuredly could not have been a small and slender girl like yourself.

"There is only one person who, as we know, is just about Marcus Hunt's height and build; who could have put his own clothes on Hunt without any suspicion. That is the same person who, though he managed to staunch the wound in his chest, has been constantly running his hand inside the breast of his coat to make certain the bandage is secure. Just as Mr. Rolfe is doing now."

Arthur Rolfe sat very quiet, with his right hand still in the breast of his jacket. His face had grown smeary in the hot sunlight, but the eyes behind those thin shells of glasses remained inscrutable. He spoke only once, through dry lips, after they had cautioned him.

"I should have taken the young pup's warning," he said. "After all, he told me I would take long chances."

Questions for Study

1. How does Carr build suspense in the first two sections? Describe the methods he uses to create suspense during the robbery scene. Does he trick the reader by withholding information? How does he maintain suspense during the rest of the tale?

2. Examine the ways in which Carr presents the exposition. Does he provide all the background information early or does he gradually present it throughout the story?

Which method seems to be more subtle, inconspicuous, and natural?

3. How does Carr indicate what sort of man Marcus Hunt is? Are his schemes adequately explained?

4. Reread the story to see how many hints Carr drops that might suggest who the murderer is. Did you notice these on your first reading? Why or why not?

5. Describe the central conflict in the story. What is the crisis? Would you describe it as an intensification of the conflict? How is the dénouement suggested by the exposition and complication?

6. Set up, in the three-part form discussed on pp. 18–19, the basic plot structure of the story. Diagram the plot according to the basic design shown on p. 19. Are there any significant variations from the traditional structure?

Guy de Maupassant (1850–1893)
A Fishing Excursion

Paris was blockaded, desolate, famished. The sparrows were few, and anything that was to be had was good to eat.

On a bright morning in January, Mr. Morissot, a watchmaker by trade, but idler through circumstances, was walking along the boulevard, sad, hungry, with his hands in the pockets of his uniform trousers, when he came face to face with a brother-in-arms whom he recognized as an old-time friend.

Before the war,[1] Morissot could be seen at daybreak every Sunday, trudging along with a cane in one hand and a tin box on his back. He would take the train to Colombes and walk from there to the Isle of Marante[2] where he would fish until dark.

It was there he had met Mr. Sauvage who kept a little notion store in the Rue Notre Dame de Lorette, a jovial fellow and passionately fond of fishing like himself. A warm friendship had sprung up between these two and they would fish side by side all day, very often without saying a word. Some days, when everything looked fresh and new and the beautiful spring sun gladdened every heart, Mr. Morissot would exclaim:

"How delightful!" and Mr. Sauvage would answer:

"There is nothing to equal it."

Then again on a fall evening, when the glorious setting sun, spreading its golden mantle on the already tinted leaves, would throw strange shadows around the two friends, Sauvage would say:

"What a grand picture!"

"It beats the boulevard!" would answer Morissot. But they understood each other quite as well without speaking.

The two friends had greeted each other warmly and had resumed their walk side by side, both thinking deeply of the past and present events. They entered

---

1. The Franco-Prussian War of 1870–71. The story is set in the closing days of the war when an armistice was being negotiated.

2. This area is northwest of the center of Paris; today it lies inside the city limits.

a *café,* and when a glass of absinthe[3] had been placed before each Sauvage sighed:

"What terrible events, my friend!"

"And what weather!" said Morissot sadly; "this is the first nice day we have had this year. Do you remember our fishing excursions?"

"Do I! Alas! When shall we go again!"

After a second absinthe they emerged from the *café* feeling rather dizzy— that light-headed effect which alcohol has on an empty stomach. The balmy air had made Sauvage exuberant and he exclaimed:

"Suppose we go!"

"Where?"

"Fishing."

"Fishing! Where?"

"To our old spot, to Colombes. The French soldiers are stationed near there and I know Colonel Dumoulin will give us a pass."

"It's a go; I am with you."

An hour after, having supplied themselves with their fishing tackle, they arrived at the colonel's villa. He had smiled at their request and had given them a pass in due form.

At about eleven o'clock they reached the advance-guard, and after presenting their pass, walked through Colombes and found themselves very near their destination. Argenteuil, across the way, and the great plains toward Nanterre were all deserted. Solitary the hills of Orgemont and Sannois rose clearly above the plains; a splendid point of observation.

"See," said Sauvage pointing to the hills, "the Prussians are there."

Prussians! They had never seen one, but they knew that they were all around Paris, invisible and powerful: plundering, devastating, and slaughtering. To their superstitious terror they added a deep hatred for this unknown and victorious people.

"What if we should meet some?" said Morissot.

"We would ask them to join us," said Sauvage in true Parisian style.

Still they hesitated to advance. The silence frightened them. Finally Sauvage picked up courage.

"Come, let us go on cautiously."

They proceeded slowly, hiding behind bushes, looking anxiously on every side, listening to every sound. A bare strip of land had to be crossed before reaching the river. They started to run. At last, they reached the bank and sank into the bushes, breathless, but relieved.

Morissot thought he heard some one walking. He listened attentively, but no, he heard no sound. They were indeed alone! The little island shielded them from view. The house where the restaurant used to be seemed deserted; feeling reassured, they settled themselves for a good day's sport.

Sauvage caught the first fish, Morissot the second; and every minute they would bring one out which they would place in a net at their feet. It was indeed miraculous! They felt that supreme joy which one feels after having been deprived for months of a pleasant pastime. They had forgotten everything; even the war!

---

3. A very strong, green-colored liqueur with a bitter licorice flavor, prohibited today by law from being manufactured or sold in Europe and the United States.

Suddenly, they heard a rumbling sound and the earth shook beneath them. It was the cannon on Mont Valérien. Morissot looked up and saw a trail of smoke, which was instantly followed by another explosion. Then they followed in quick succession.

"They are at it again," said Sauvage shrugging his shoulders. Morissot, who was naturally peaceful, felt a sudden, uncontrollable anger.

"Stupid fools! What pleasure can they find in killing each other!"

"They are worse than brutes!"

"It will always be thus as long as we have governments."

"Well, such is life!"

"You mean death!" said Morissot laughing.

They continued to discuss the different political problems, while the cannon on Mont Valérien sent death and desolation among the French.

Suddenly they started. They had heard a step behind them. They turned and beheld four big men in dark uniforms, with guns pointed right at them. Their fishing-lines dropped out of their hands and floated away with the current.

In a few minutes, the Prussian soldiers had bound them, cast them into a boat, and rowed across the river to the island which our friends had thought deserted. They soon found out their mistake when they reached the house, behind which stood a score or more of soldiers. A big burly officer, seated astride a chair, smoking an immense pipe, addressed them in excellent French:

"Well, gentlemen, have you made a good haul?"

Just then, a soldier deposited at his feet the net full of fish which he had taken good care to take along with him. The officer smiled and said:

"I see you have done pretty well; but let us change the subject. You are evidently sent to spy upon me. You pretended to fish so as to put me off the scent, but I am not so simple. I have caught you and shall have you shot. I am sorry, but war is war. As you passed the advance-guard you certainly must have the password; give it to me, and I will set you free."

The two friends stood side by side, pale and slightly trembling, but they answered nothing.

"No one will ever know. You will go back home quietly and the secret will disappear with you. If you refuse, it is instant death! Choose!"

They remained motionless, silent. The Prussian officer calmly pointed to the river.

"In five minutes you will be at the bottom of this river! Surely, you have a family, friends waiting for you?"

Still they kept silent. The cannon rumbled incessantly. The officer gave orders in his own tongue, then moved his chair away from the prisoners. A squad of men advanced within twenty feet of them, ready for command.

"I give you one minute; not a second more!"

Suddenly approaching the two Frenchmen, he took Morissot aside and whispered:

"Quick, the password. Your friend will not know; he will think I have changed my mind." Morissot said nothing.

Then taking Sauvage aside he asked him the same thing, but he also was silent. The officer gave further orders and the men leveled their guns. At that moment, Morissot's eyes rested on the net full of fish lying in the grass a few feet away. The sight made him feel faint and, though he struggled against it, his eyes filled with tears. Then turning to his friend:

"Farewell! Mr. Sauvage!"

"Farewell! Mr. Morissot."

They stood for a minute, hand in hand, trembling with emotion which they were unable to control.

"Fire!" commanded the officer.

The squad of men fired as one. Sauvage fell straight on his face. Morissot, who was taller, swayed, pivoted, and fell across his friend's body, his face to the sky; while blood flowed freely from the wound in his breast. The officer gave further orders and his men disappeared. They came back presently with ropes and stones, which they tied to the feet of the two friends, and four of them carried them to the edge of the river. They swung them and threw them in as far as they could. The bodies weighted by stones sank immediately. A splash, a few ripples and the water resumed its usual calmness. The only thing to be seen was a little blood floating on the surface. The officer calmly retraced his steps toward the house muttering:

"The fish will get even now."

He perceived the net full of fish, picked it up, smiled, and called:

"Wilhelm!"

A soldier in a white apron approached. The officer handed him the fish saying:

"Fry these little things while they are still alive. They will make a delicious meal."

And having resumed his position on the chair, he puffed away at his pipe.

Questions for Study

1. The two friends, after a few drinks, are "unsteady" because of the effect of the alcohol on their empty stomachs. Find other indirect references to the famine which has overtaken Paris. How do such references further the implications of the story?

2. The story recounts what seems to be a trivial excursion against a background of significant events. What is the effect of this contrast? How does Maupassant make use of it?

3. Is Maupassant's exposition sufficient for us to understand the situation? How does he establish the depth of the friendship between the two men?

4. How does Maupassant create suspense? See if the story includes more than one crisis. If so, what happens to the suspense after each?

5. Why is Maupassant so careless about the first mention of the password?

6. How does the main crisis logically develop from an intensification of the conflict? Describe how Maupassant associates the conflict with certain universal issues. Restate the plot in three-part form.

7. Why does Maupassant not end the story with the two friends' death? Describe the conflict that remains to be settled in the resolution. What does the Prussian officer mean by saying that it is the fishes' turn now? Examine the connections the story makes between men who go fishing and the fish themselves.

8. In the often-quoted preface to his novel *Pierre and Jean,* Maupassant said about the craft of fiction: "The skill of the novelist's plan will not reside in emotional effects, in attractive writing, in a striking beginning or a moving dénouement, but in the artful building up of solid details from which the essential meaning

of the work will emerge." Does Maupassant in "A Fishing Excursion" give us "the artful building up of solid details"? Consider carefully the actual details he includes and relate them to what you feel he is trying to do in this short story.

Stephen Crane (1871–1900)
A Mystery of Heroism

The dark uniforms of the men were so coated with dust from the incessant wrestling of the two armies that the regiment almost seemed a part of the clay bank which shielded them from the shells. On the top of the hill a battery was arguing in tremendous roars with some other guns, and to the eye of the infantry, the artillerymen, the guns, the caissons, the horses, were distinctly outlined upon the blue sky. When a piece was fired, a red streak as round as a log flashed low in the heavens, like a monstrous bolt of lightning. The men of the battery wore white duck trousers, which somehow emphasized their legs; and when they ran and crowded in little groups at the bidding of the shouting officers, it was more impressive than usual to the infantry.

Fred Collins, of A Company, was saying: "Thunder! I wisht I had a drink. Ain't there any water round here?" Then somebody yelled, "There goes th' bugler!"

As the eyes of half the regiment swept in one machinelike movement there was an instant's picture of a horse in a great convulsive leap of a death wound and a rider leaning back with a crooked arm and spread fingers before his face. On the ground was the crimson terror of an exploding shell, with fibres of flame that seemed like lances. A glittering bugle swung clear of the rider's back as fell headlong the horse and the man. In the air was an odour as from a conflagration.

Sometimes they of the infantry looked down at a fair little meadow which spread at their feet. Its long, green grass was rippling gently in a breeze. Beyond it was the gray form of a house half torn to pieces by shells and by the busy axes of soldiers who had pursued firewood. The line of an old fence was now dimly marked by long weeds and by an occasional post. A shell had blown the well-house to fragments. Little lines of gray smoke ribboning upward from some embers indicated the place where had stood the barn.

From beyond a curtain of green woods there came the sound of some stupendous scuffle, as if two animals of the size of islands were fighting. At a distance there were occasional appearances of swift-moving men, horses, batteries, flags, and, with the crashing of infantry volleys were heard, often, wild and frenzied cheers. In the midst of it all Smith and Ferguson, two privates of A Company, were engaged in a heated discussion, which involved the greatest questions of the national existence.

The battery on the hill presently engaged in a frightful duel. The white legs of the gunners scampered this way and that way, and the officers redoubled their shouts. The guns, with their demeanours of stolidity and courage, were typical of something infinitely self-possessed in this clamour of death that swirled around the hill.

One of a "swing" team was suddenly smitten quivering to the ground, and his maddened brethren dragged his torn body in their struggle to escape from this turmoil and danger. A young soldier astride one of the leaders swore and fumed in his saddle, and furiously jerked at the bridle. An officer screamed out an order so violently that his voice broke and ended the sentence in a falsetto shriek.

The leading company of the infantry regiment was somewhat exposed, and the colonel ordered it moved more fully under the shelter of the hill. There was the clank of steel against steel.

A lieutenant of the battery rode down and passed them, holding his right arm carefully in his left hand. And it was as if this arm was not at all a part of him, but belonged to another man. His sober and reflective charger went slowly. The officer's face was grimy and perspiring, and his uniform was tousled as if he had been in direct grapple with an enemy. He smiled grimly when the men stared at him. He turned his horse toward the meadow.

Collins, of A Company, said: "I wisht I had a drink. I bet there's water in that there ol' well yonder!"

"Yes; but how you goin' to git it?"

For the little meadow which intervened was now suffering a terrible onslaught of shells. Its green and beautiful calm had vanished utterly. Brown earth was being flung in monstrous handfuls. And there was a massacre of the young blades of grass. They were being torn, burned, obliterated. Some curious fortune of the battle had made this gentle little meadow the object of the red hate of the shells, and each one as it exploded seemed like an imprecation in the face of a maiden.

The wounded officer who was riding across this expanse said to himself, "Why, they couldn't shoot any harder if the whole army was massed here!"

A shell struck the gray ruins of the house, and as, after the roar, the shattered wall fell in fragments, there was a noise which resembled the flapping of shutters during a wild gale of winter. Indeed, the infantry paused in the shelter of the bank appeared as men standing upon a shore contemplating a madness of the sea. The angel of calamity had under its glance the battery upon the hill. Fewer white-legged men laboured about the guns. A shell had smitten one of the pieces, and after the flare, the smoke, the dust, the wrath of this blow were gone, it was possible to see white legs stretched horizontally upon the ground. And at that interval to the rear, where it is the business of battery horses to stand with their noses to the fight awaiting the command to drag their guns out of the destruction or into it or wheresoever these incomprehensible humans demanded with whip and spur—in this line of passive and dumb spectators, whose fluttering hearts yet would not let them forget the iron laws of man's control of them—in this rank of brute-soldiers there had been relentless and hideous carnage. From the ruck of bleeding and prostrate horses, the men of the infantry could see one animal raising its stricken body with its fore legs, and turning its nose with mystic and profound eloquence toward the sky.

Some comrades joked Collins about his thirst. "Well, if yeh want a drink so bad, why don't yeh go git it!"

"Well, I will in a minnet, if yeh don't shut up!"

A lieutenant of artillery floundered his horse straight down the hill with as great concern as if it were level ground. As he galloped past the colonel of the infantry, he threw up his hand in swift salute. "We've got to get out of that," he roared angrily. He was a black-bearded officer, and his eyes, which resembled beads, sparkled like those of an insane man. His jumping horse sped along the column of infantry.

The fat major, standing carelessly with his sword held horizontally behind him and with his legs far apart, looked after the receding horseman and laughed. "He wants to get back with orders pretty quick, or there'll be no batt'ry left," he observed.

The wise young captain of the second company hazarded to the lieutenant colonel that the enemy's infantry would probably soon attack the hill, and the lieutenant colonel snubbed him.

A private in one of the rear companies looked out over the meadow, and then turned to a companion and said, "Look there, Jim!" It was the wounded officer from the battery, who some time before had started to ride across the meadow, supporting his right arm carefully with his left hand. This man had encountered a shell apparently at a time when no one perceived him, and he could now be seen lying face downward with a stirruped foot stretched across the body of his dead horse. A leg of the charger extended slantingly upward precisely as stiff as a stake. Around this motionless pair the shells still howled.

There was a quarrel in A Company. Collins was shaking his fist in the faces of some laughing comrades. "Dern yeh! I ain't afraid t' go. If yeh say much, I will go!"

"Of course, yeh will! You'll run through that there medder, won't yeh?"

Collins said, in a terrible voice, "You see now!" At this ominous threat his comrades broke into renewed jeers.

Collins gave them a dark scowl and went to find his captain. The latter was conversing with the colonel of the regiment.

"Captain," said Collins, saluting and standing at attention—in those days all trousers bagged at the knees—"captain, I want t' get permission to go git some water from that there well over yonder!"

The colonel and the captain swung about simultaneously and stared across the meadow. The captain laughed. "You must be pretty thirsty, Collins?"

"Yes, sir, I am."

"Well—ah," said the captain. After a moment, he asked, "Can't you wait?"

"No, sir."

The colonel was watching Collins's face, "Look here, my lad," he said, in a pious sort of a voice—"look here, my lad"—Collins was not a lad—"don't you think that's taking pretty big risks for a little drink of water?"

"I dunno," said Collins uncomfortably. Some of the resentment toward his companions, which perhaps had forced him into this affair, was beginning to fade. "I dunno wether 'tis."

The colonel and the captain contemplated him for a time.

"Well," said the captain finally.

"Well," said the colonel, "if you want to go, why, go."

Collins saluted. "Much obliged t' yeh."

As he moved away the colonel called after him. "Take some of the other boys' canteens with you an' hurry back now."

"Yes, sir, I will."

The colonel and the captain looked at each other then, for it had suddenly occurred that they could not for the life of them tell whether Collins wanted to go or whether he did not.

They turned to regard Collins, and as they perceived him surrounded by gesticulating comrades, the colonel said: "Well, by thunder! I guess he's going."

Collins appeared as a man dreaming. In the midst of the questions, the advice, the warnings, all the excited talk of his company mates, he maintained a curious silence.

They were very busy in preparing him for his ordeal. When they inspected him carefully it was somewhat like the examination that grooms give a horse before a race; and they were amazed, staggered by the whole affair. Their astonishment found vent in strange repetitions.

"Are yeh sure a-goin'?" they demanded again and again.

"Certainly I am," cried Collins, at last furiously.

He strode sullenly away from them. He was swinging five or six canteens by their cords. It seemed that his cap would not remain firmly on his head, and often he reached and pulled it down over his brow.

There was a general movement in the compact column. The long animal-like thing moved slightly. Its four hundred eyes were turned upon the figure of Collins.

"Well, sir, if that ain't th' derndest thing! I never thought Fred Collins had the blood in him for that kind of business."

"What's he goin' to do, anyhow?"

"He's goin' to that well there after water."

"We ain't dyin' of thirst, are we? That's foolishness."

"Well, somebody put him up to it, an' he's doin' it."

"Say, he must be a desperate cuss."

When Collins faced the meadow and walked away from the regiment, he was vaguely conscious that a chasm, the deep valley of all prides, was suddenly between him and his comrades. It was provisional, but the provision was that he return as a victor. He had blindly been led by quaint emotions, and laid himself under an obligation to walk squarely up to the face of death.

But he was not sure that he wished to make a retraction, even if he could do so without shame. As a matter of truth, he was sure of very little. He was mainly surprised.

It seemed to him supernaturally strange that he had allowed his mind to manoeuvre his body into such a situation. He understood that it might be called dramatically great.

However, he had no full appreciation of anything, excepting that he was actually conscious of being dazed. He could feel his dulled mind groping after the form and colour of this incident. He wondered why he did not feel some keen agony of fear cutting his sense like a knife. He wondered at this, because human expression had said loudly for centuries that men should feel afraid of certain things, and that all men who did not feel this fear were phenomena—heroes.

He was, then, a hero. He suffered that disappointment which we would all have if we discovered that we were ourselves capable of those deeds which we most admire in history and legend. This, then, was a hero. After all, heroes were not much.

No, it could not be true. He was not a hero. Heroes had no shames in their lives, and, as for him, he remembered borrowing fifteen dollars from a friend and promising to pay it back the next day, and then avoiding that friend for ten months. When at home his mother had aroused him for the early labour of his life on the farm, it had often been his fashion to be irritable, childish, diabolical; and his mother had died since he had come to the war.

He saw that, in this matter of the well, the canteens, the shells, he was an intruder in the land of fine deeds.

He was now about thirty paces from his comrades. The regiment had just turned its many faces toward him.

From the forest of terrific noises there suddenly emerged a little uneven line of men. They fired fiercely and rapidly at distant foliage on which appeared little puffs of white smoke. The spatter of skirmish firing was added to the thunder of the guns on the hill. The little line of men ran forward. A colour sergeant fell flat with his flag as if he had slipped on ice. There was hoarse cheering from this distant field.

Collins suddenly felt that two demon fingers were pressed into his ears. He could see nothing but flying arrows, flaming red. He lurched from the shock of this explosion, but he made a mad rush for the house, which he viewed as a man submerged to the neck in a boiling surf might view the shore. In the air, little pieces of shell howled and the earth-quake explosions drove him insane with the menace of their roar. As he ran the canteens knocked together with a rhythmical tinkling.

As he neared the house, each detail of the scene became vivid to him. He was aware of some bricks of the vanished chimney lying on the sod. There was a door which hung by one hinge.

Rifle bullets called forth by the insistent skirmishers came from the far-off bank of foliage. They mingled with the shells and the pieces of shells until the air was torn in all directions by hootings, yells, howls. The sky was full of fiends who directed all their wild rage at his head.

When he came to the well, he flung himself face downward and peered into its darkness. There were furtive silver glintings some feet from the surface. He grabbed one of the canteens and, unfastening its cap, swung it down by the cord. The water flowed slowly in with an indolent gurgle.

And now as he lay with his face turned away he was suddenly smitten with the terror. It came upon his heart like the grasp of claws. All the power faded from his muscles. For an instant he was no more than a dead man.

The canteen filled with a maddening slowness, in the manner of all bottles. Presently he recovered his strength and addressed a screaming oath to it. He leaned over until it seemed as if he intended to try to push water into it with his hands. His eyes as he gazed down into the well shone like two pieces of metal and in their expression was a great appeal and a great curse. The stupid water derided him.

There was the blaring thunder of a shell. Crimson light shone through the swift-boiling smoke and made a pink reflection on part of the wall of the well. Collins jerked out his arm and canteen with the same motion that a man would use in withdrawing his head from a furnace.

He scrambled erect and glared and hesitated. On the ground near him lay the old well bucket, with a length of rusty chain. He lowered it swiftly into the well. The bucket struck the water and then, turning lazily over, sank. When, with hand reaching tremblingly over hand, he hauled it out, it knocked often against the walls of the well and spilled some of its contents.

In running with a filled bucket, a man can adopt but one kind of gait. So through this terrible field over which screamed practical angels of death Collins ran in the manner of a farmer chased out of a dairy by a bull.

His face went staring white with anticipation—anticipation of a blow that would whirl him around and down. He would fall as he had seen other men fall, the life knocked out of them so suddenly that their knees were no more quick to touch the ground than their heads. He saw the long blue line of the regiment, but his comrades were standing looking at him from the edge of an impossible star. He was aware of some deep wheel ruts and hoofprints in the sod beneath his feet.

The artillery officer who had fallen in this meadow had been making groans in the teeth of the tempest of sound. These futile cries, wrenched from him by his agony, were heard only by shells, bullets. When wild-eyed Collins came running, this officer raised himself. His face contorted and blanched from pain, he was about to utter some great beseeching cry. But suddenly his face straightened and he called: "Say, young man, give me a drink of water, will you?"

Collins had no room amid his emotions for surprise. He was mad from the threats of destruction.

"I can't!" he screamed, and in his reply was a full description of his quaking apprehension. His cap was gone and his hair was riotous. His clothes made it appear that he had been dragged over the ground by the heels. He ran on.

The officer's head sank down and one elbow crooked. His foot in its brass-bound stirrup still stretched over the body of his horse and the other leg was under the steed.

But Collins turned. He came dashing back. His face had now turned gray and in his eyes was all terror. "Here it is! here it is!"

The officer was as a man gone in drink. His arm bent like a twig. His head drooped as if his neck were of willow. He was sinking to the ground, to lie face downward.

Collins grabbed him by the shoulder. "Here it is. Here's your drink. Turn over. Turn over, man, for God's sake!"

With Collins hauling at his shoulder, the officer twisted his body and fell with his face turned toward that region where lived the unspeakable noises of the swirling missiles. There was the faintest shadow of a smile on his lips as he looked at Collins. He gave a sigh, a little primitive breath like that from a child.

Collins tried to hold the bucket steadily, but his shaking hands caused the water to splash all over the face of the dying man. Then he jerked it away and ran on.

The regiment gave him a welcoming roar. The grimed faces were wrinkled in laughter.

His captain waved the bucket away. "Give it to the men!"

The two genial, skylarking young lieutenants were the first to gain possession of it. They played over it in their fashion.

When one tried to drink the other teasingly knocked his elbow. "Don't, Billie! You'll make me spill it," said the one. The other laughed.

Suddenly there was an oath, the thud of wood on the ground, and a swift murmur of astonishment among the ranks. The two lieutenants glared at each other. The bucket lay on the ground empty.

Questions for Study

1. Why does Crane choose to have two privates rather than two officers discuss the "greatest questions of the national existence"? Where can you find other examples of large issues made small? Of small issues made large?
2. Why does Crane describe the wounded officer so carefully? Why does he introduce so many characters who do not seem important to the plot? Why does he not make Collins an important character from the beginning?
3. Why do the officers let Collins go? Does he feel resentment? Why does he go?
4. Why does he feel that he is an "intruder in the land of fine deeds"? What does the story's title suggest about heroism? Is Collins heroic?
5. The conflict Collins experiences passes through a number of stages; the first is the conflict between his common sense and his thirst. What are the other stages? Are these stages equal or do they become increasingly serious?
6. Why does Collins go back to the wounded soldier? Would you consider that action the crisis or part of the dénouement? Why?
7. How is the dénouement prepared for in the story's exposition and complication?

Chapter 3
Character

Actions do not occur without participants and events do not signify anything without human consequences. In fiction, plots do not exist without characters. **Characters** are simply the people in the story. If animals or even objects are given human attributes in a narrative, they too function as characters; but normally when we speak of characters we mean people. And the author's task is to make these people vivid and interesting enough so that we care about them and their conflict and wish to see it resolved in some way. Thus writers of fiction must consider how best to present their characters. They can merely name them and assign them a simple function: "This is Dick. This is Jane. Dick is an ex-football player, and Jane is a doctor." Such a matter-of-fact approach to character would not sustain a reader's interest for very long. Instead the author must find a way to present situations and actions so that we care about the characters and understand who these people are and what they signify. Placing them in a situation of conflict or stress is the most effective way to accomplish both these aims.

We know that times of great stress disclose surprising things about people. A usually confident actor may discover his insecurity when faced with a demanding role; a wife may discover her strength when her husband is seriously ill; a motorcyclist may discover his courage or fear when the road twists most dangerously. According to Ernest Hemingway, an individual's courage is truly tested only in moments of extreme personal crisis. He felt that neither pity nor respect is earned until a person has risked his or her life. Thus Hemingway often writes about characters on hunting expeditions, on the battlefield, or in the bullfighting arena. Most of us would hesitate to agree with Hemingway's assumption, hoping to reveal our worth in safer ways. Nevertheless, we recognize that stress and conflict work to define our humanity in all its strengths and weaknesses.

Fiction writers create conflicts which are usually tamer than the sort Hemingway prefers but which nevertheless challenge their characters in some significant way. Characters are defined by what they are—their nature—and by what they do—their actions—in response to an opposing force. Moreover, each is defined by the other: their nature defines their actions, and their actions further define their nature.

In fiction the **protagonist,** or main character, defines himself by the interaction of what he is and what he does. Sometimes the protagonist will not respond correctly or admirably. Sometimes, in fact, he may not act at all. Even a lack of response, however, will define and further our understanding of the protagonist's nature. Whoever, or whatever, is on the other side of the conflict from the protagonist is called the **antagonist,** usually taking the form of another character. In some cases the antagonist may be an aspect of society or the environment or even some facet of the protagonist himself. Sometimes it may be a complex of many forces that work against the protagonist from outside and inside himself. If the conflict exists between people, the protagonist may seem to be the good guy or the hero, the antagonist the bad guy or the villain. Yet such labels are as inappropriate to well-crafted fiction as they are to life, since rarely in either are people and actions purely good and heroic or purely bad and villainous. In "Sredni Vashtar," for example, we could hardly call Conradin a hero, though we may be tempted to call Mrs. De Ropp a villain. Nor in "A & P" can we call Sammy a genuine hero and Lengel a villain.

Some stories are designed to frustrate our attempts to identify with heroes and participate vicariously in victory. Such fiction manages, if we are expecting a noble sheriff, to give us a villainous one; if we are expecting a shrewd detective, to give us a bungling one. These stories give us, in other words, an **anti-hero**—a character designed to undermine our expectations about heroes. In Isaac Singer's "Gimpel the Fool," Gimpel is something of an anti-hero; yet viewed in another way Gimpel seems rather heroic. Dissatisfied with the heroic mode, writers may try to present unsavory characters as protagonists, feeling that there are no rules dictating what kinds of people may be main characters in fiction. Stories can be written about people who are not even nice. If an author presents with insight and thoroughness a delinquent (as Joyce Carol Oates does in "How I Contemplated my Life from the Detroit House of Correction . . . ," Chapter 7); or a brute (as Maxim Gorki does in "Twenty-Six Men and a Girl," Chapter 6); or a failure (as Irwin Shaw does in "The Eighty-Yard Run"); or even a psychotic or criminal, such an author manages to make an unsympathetic protagonist sympathetic. Familiarity and understanding do not always breed contempt but rather occasionally destroy it. Such protagonists, if presented truthfully, can no more be totally villainous than they can be purely heroic.

This talk of protagonists and antagonists and heroes and villains may seem to imply that all conflicts in fiction are outright confrontations between characters. In most cases the protagonist is in conflict with some force larger than any one human being. And when the antagonist is another character, he is rarely just another character. In "The Eighty-Yard Run," for example, the protagonist Christian Darling is not only in conflict with his wife but with a set of values and a way of life which he cannot quite comprehend. His conflict finally is internal because of his inability to grow and relate to those around him and to the world in which he lives. In "A & P" Sammy's antagonist, represented by Lengel, is middle-class conformity. In Ralph Ellison's "Battle Royal" the protagonist is in a boxing ring with another black youth, but his real antagonist is society—its racial injustice, exploitation, and hypocrisy. In addition, he has to struggle not only against society but also against his own blindness to injustice and his timid acceptance of racial discrimination, with the result that the conflict exists both in the outside world and within himself. Similarly, in "Gimpel the Fool" Gimpel's best nature is in conflict with both pressures from outside and impulses from within, so that his nature takes shape in reaction to these pressures and impulses.

If the conflict is merely physical and thus totally external to him, the protagonist is unlikely to be changed by it. In adventure stories terrifying experiences such as high-speed car chases, rooftop fistfights, and bloody shoot-outs rarely seem to affect the main character. Usually he just kisses the beautiful girl who is inevitably waiting for him and orders a scotch-on-the-rocks. Though he has been through a great deal he has not been changed. He is a **static character,** one whose personality, attitudes, and beliefs remain fixed no matter what dramatic or bizarre situations he encounters. In serious fiction, as in life, a particular event can have a profound effect upon character. A simple matter like a girl's walking into a grocery store in a bathing suit can produce more change than any shoot-out. Yet the change should not entail a total reversal of a character's personality. Rather the **dynamic character,** whose attitudes and values are affected, usually undergoes subtle changes that only slightly affect his outward behavior but that profoundly alter his attitude toward a situation and toward life in general. Though such development is apparently slight, it is more believable. Overnight reversals of a person's character are rare in life, often unconvincing in fiction.

Some fiction does not present resolutions of conflicts between characters or forces. Instead such fiction may present a profound insight or illumination that the protagonist experiences. Thus the plot in such stories follows the crisis with a moment of awareness before the story ends. These moments of insight must carry in themselves the significance of the entire narrative. The modern Irish writer James Joyce structured the stories in *Dubliners* ("Araby" in "Stories for Further Study" is one of them) around such moments, which he called "epiph-

anies." Joyce defined an **epiphany** as a "sudden spiritual manifestation" or a revelation of something that has been ignored or hidden.
None of the three stories in this chapter includes a strictly Joycean
epiphany, but each protagonist struggles toward self-awareness. Each
develops according to what he comes to understand about himself. As
readers we participate in the protagonists' gradual movement away
from self-deception toward self-awareness. Thus we come to know
such characters from the inside. But we also know them from the outside in much the same way that we know our real-life acquaintances
—by what they do and say.

In our everyday encounters with people we develop a sort of radar
whereby we judge their state of mind and character by their actions.
We know, for example, what it means when someone avoids eye contact with us or fidgets about or gets up and paces the floor. And we
usually size up strangers according to such signals as what they do with
their hands, how they walk, whether or not they cross their legs when
they sit, how they wear their clothes, even how they keep their fingernails. In reading fiction too we know that character and actions are
manifestations of each other and that characters are not only defined
by their reactions to the conflict they face, but also by their nature.
Knowing how action illustrates character, the good fiction writer
strives for effective **characterization,** which is the way that he presents
his characters, so that each detail of the characters' manner and speech
declares in some way their identity. At the end of "The Eighty-Yard
Run" Christian is sweating profusely; in "Gimpel the Fool" Gimpel
runs when someone pretends to be a barking dog; in "Battle Royal"
the protagonist swallows blood in order to deliver his speech. Such
acts tell us better than a statement could who these people are and
what they are experiencing.

The Russian writer Anton Chekhov once warned the writer to
"avoid depicting the hero's state of mind; you ought to try to make it
clear from the hero's action." Chekhov was calling for **indirect presentation,** or characterization through action and speech, rather than for
direct presentation, or characterization through statement or explanation. Sometimes an author may need to explain certain things about his
characters through direct statement. Such direct presentation may effectively type the character or give us a concise picture of his behavior,
but too much of this kind of description would weaken the story's impact. Telling us that Jack is clumsy is not nearly as dramatic as showing
Jack spilling a bowl of soup in his lap or tripping on a flight of stairs.
"The Eighty-Yard Run" would not have been as effective a story if
Shaw had been content to tell us that the highpoint of Christian's life
was the touchdown run he made in football practice. Because we are
vividly shown the play, and especially Christian's exhilaration afterwards, the mess he makes of his later life becomes all the more ironic

and touching. While direct presentation is a valid method for summarizing character, an overreliance on it often produces a lifeless portrait rather than a study of a character in action. On the other hand, indirect presentation—"showing" rather than "telling"—is fuller and more complex and suggestive than a generalized summary could be. And so we react to this indirect method as we do to the behavior of people we know and meet. We judge the author's characterization by how fully human the characters seem to be. We consider whether their actions are consistently and plausibly motivated. We may even end up psychoanalyzing them, trying to determine, for instance, why Louise stays married to Christian in Shaw's story.

Sometimes characterization is handled rather directly through names themselves. A name that identifies a character's major trait or basic nature is termed a **characternym.** Two selections in "Stories for Further Study" illustrate this principle: the name *Faith* in Nathaniel Hawthorne's "Young Goodman Brown" and the name *Davidov* in Bernard Malamud's "Take Pity" suggest each character's role within the framework of these two narratives. To a Russian reader, the name *Ivan Ilych* in Leo Tolstoy's "The Death of Ivan Ilych" (Chapter 12) would indicate that the protagonist is a purely average man. Suggestive and symbolic names such as *Rex* (king) and *Mary* (virgin) permit the writer a subtle (and sometimes not so subtle) means of characterization.

Though a name can suggest a character's significance and a statement can declare it, effective characterization is usually a matter of presentation, not of explanation. Because of the tightness and compression of short fiction, however, only the protagonist and perhaps an auxiliary character or two can be fully developed. In well-crafted fiction, at least one major character should be what British novelist E. M. Forster called a **round character,** in other words, a multidimensional character. Forster explained that "the test of a round character is whether it is capable of surprising in a convincing way. If it never surprises, it is flat. If it does not convince, it is a flat [character] pretending to be round." A round character, Forster said, "has the incalculability of life about it." In "Sredni Vashtar" Conradin is a round character because his strange nature and bizarre behavior are presented in a believable, convincing fashion.

Flat characters, Forster wrote, "are constructed around a single idea or quality; when there is more than one factor in them, we get the beginning of the curve toward the round." When a major character is flat, or one-dimensional, no amount of melodramatic action, intricate plotting, or stylistic brilliance can bring the figure to life for us. Many writers, especially writers of popular fiction, create major characters who are so flat they are hardly characters at all: the dumb blonde, the handsome spy, the complaining mother-in-law, the crooked politician. We all know that blondes are not necessarily dumb (they may not even be true blondes!), that spies are not always handsome, that not all mothers-in-law complain, and that most politicians are not crooked. When we accept cardboard characters like these, we are either reading the story for something else—for suspense or for laughs, for example—or we are not making an effort to connect our reading to our experiences. When a writer wants to jolt us out of this comfortable attitude, he may play with our expectations and have the handsome spy turn out to be a coward or make the dumb blonde a nuclear physicist.

When acting as minor figures, flat characters perform limited, but necessary functions. They may be **stock characters,** or ready-made figures, who are brought into a story for a brief appearance. The detective story, for instance, may use as stock characters, a dim-witted police officer, a prostitute with a heart of gold, or a shifty-eyed gangster. More serious works of fiction include minor characters whose function is so limited that the writer has no need to develop them fully. The maid in "Sredni Vashtar" is such a character. She has a definite function to perform at the story's end, but we know nothing about her except that she reacts in a conventional and wrongheaded manner. Questions of her appearance, background, values, and motivation are irrelevant.

Characterization in fiction should be carefully handled so that the main characters are thoroughly defined and placed in precise focus. E. M. Forster wrote that "the hidden life that appears in external signs is hidden no longer, [when it] has entered the realm of action. And it is the function of the novelist to reveal the hidden life at its source." An author can never tell everything, not even in a very long novel, nor do all authors structure their fiction around epiphanies. Yet writers must choose and arrange their materials so that the "hidden lives" of their characters are revealed. Seeing and understanding what formerly was hidden but now is revealed, what is true but only now made evident, the reader understands what a fictional character actually is and thus what he signifies in the narrative.

Irwin Shaw (b. 1913)
The Eighty-Yard Run

The pass was high and wide and he jumped for it, feeling it slap flatly against his hands, as he shook his hips to throw off the halfback who was diving at him. The center floated by, his hands desperately brushing Darling's knee as Darling picked his feet up high and delicately ran over a blocker and an opposing linesman in a jumble on the ground near the scrimmage line. He had ten yards in the clear and picked up speed, breathing easily, feeling his thigh pads rising and falling against his legs, listening to the sound of cleats behind him, pulling away from them, watching the other backs heading him off toward the sideline, the whole picture, the men closing in on him, the blockers fighting for position, the ground he had to cross, all suddenly clear in his head, for the first time in his life not a meaningless confusion of men, sounds, speed. He smiled a little to himself as he ran, holding the ball lightly in front of him with his two hands, his knees pumping high, his hips twisting in the almost girlish run of a back in a broken field. The first halfback came at him and he fed him his leg, then swung at the last moment, took the shock of the man's shoulder without breaking stride, ran right through him, his cleats biting securely into the turf. There was only the safety man now, coming warily at him, his arms crooked, hands spread. Darling tucked the ball in, spurted at him, driving hard, hurling himself along, his legs pounding, knees high, all two hundred pounds bunched into controlled attack. He was sure he was going to get past the safety man. Without thought, his arms and legs working beautifully together, he headed right for the safety man, stiff-armed him, feeling blood spurt instantaneously from the man's nose onto his hand, seeing his face go awry, head turned, mouth pulled to one side. He pivoted away, keeping the arm locked, dropping the safety man as he ran easily toward the goal line, with the drumming of cleats diminishing behind him.

How long ago? It was autumn then, and the ground was getting hard because the nights were cold and leaves from the maples around the stadium blew across the practice fields in gusts of wind, and the girls were beginning to put polo coats over their sweaters when they came to watch practice in the afternoons. . . . Fifteen years. Darling walked slowly over the same ground in the spring twilight, in his neat shoes, a man of thirty-five dressed in a double-breasted suit, ten pounds heavier in the fifteen years, but not fat, with the years between 1925 and 1940 showing in his face.

The coach was smiling quietly to himself and the assistant coaches were looking at each other with pleasure the way they always did when one of the second stringers suddenly did something fine, bringing credit to them, making their $2,000 a year a tiny bit more secure.

Darling trotted back, smiling, breathing deeply but easily, feeling wonderful, not tired, though this was the tail end of practice and he'd run eighty yards. The sweat poured off his face and soaked his jersey and he liked the feeling, the warm moistness lubricating his skin like oil. Off in a corner of the field some players were punting and the smack of leather against the ball came pleasantly through the afternoon air. The freshmen were running signals on the next field and the quarterback's sharp voice, the pound of the eleven pairs of cleats, the "Dig, now *dig!*" of the coaches, the laughter of the players all somehow made him feel happy as he trotted back to midfield, listening to the applause and shouts of the students along the sidelines, knowing that after that run the coach would have to start him Saturday against Illinois.

Fifteen years, Darling thought, remembering the shower after the workout, the hot water steaming off his skin and the deep soapsuds and all the young voices singing with the water streaming down and towels going and managers running in and out and the sharp sweet smell of oil of wintergreen and everybody clapping him on the back as he dressed and Packard, the captain, who took being captain very seriously, coming over to him and shaking his hand and saying, "Darling, you're going to go places in the next two years."

The assistant manager fussed over him, wiping a cut on his leg with alcohol and iodine, the little sting making him realize suddenly how fresh and whole and solid his body felt. The manager slapped a piece of adhesive tape over the cut, and Darling noticed the sharp clean white of the tape against the ruddiness of the skin, fresh from the shower.

He dressed slowly, the softness of his shirt and the soft warmth of his wool socks and his flannel trousers a reward against his skin after the harsh pressure of the shoulder harness and thigh and hip pads. He drank three glasses of cold water, the liquid reaching down coldly inside of him, soothing the harsh dry places in his throat and belly left by the sweat and running and shouting of practice.

Fifteen years.

The sun had gone down and the sky was green behind the stadium and he laughed quietly to himself as he looked at the stadium, rearing above the trees, and knew that on Saturday when the 70,000 voices roared as the team came running out onto the field, part of that enormous salute would be for him. He walked slowly, listening to the gravel crunch satisfactorily under his shoes in the still twilight, feeling his clothes swing lightly against his skin, breathing the thin evening air, feeling the wind move softly in his damp hair, wonderfully cool behind his ears and at the nape of his neck.

Louise was waiting for him at the road, in her car. The top was down and he noticed all over again, as he always did when he saw her, how pretty she was, the rough blonde hair and the large, inquiring eyes and the bright mouth, smiling now.

She threw the door open. "Were you good today?" she asked.

"Pretty good," he said. He climbed in, sank luxuriously into the soft leather, stretched his legs far out. He smiled, thinking of the eighty yards. "Pretty damn good."

She looked at him seriously for a moment, then scrambled around, like a little girl, kneeling on the seat next to him, grabbed him, her hands along his ears, and kissed him as he sprawled, head back, on the seat cushion. She let go of him, but kept her head close to his, over his. Darling reached up slowly and rubbed the back of his hand against her cheek, lit softly by a street lamp a hundred feet away. They looked at each other, smiling.

Louise drove down to the lake and they sat there silently, watching the moon rise behind the hills on the other side. Finally he reached over, pulled her gently to him, kissed her. Her lips grew soft, her body sank into his, tears formed slowly in her eyes. He knew, for the first time, that he could do whatever he wanted with her.

"Tonight," he said. "I'll call for you at seven-thirty. Can you get out?"

She looked at him. She was smiling, but the tears were still full in her eyes. "All right," she said. "I'll get out. How about you? Won't the coach raise hell?"

Darling grinned. "I got the coach in the palm of my hand," he said, "Can you wait till seven-thirty?"

She grinned back at him. "No," she said.

They kissed and she started the car and they went back to town for dinner. He sang on the way home.

Christian Darling, thirty-five years old, sat on the frail spring grass, greener now than it ever would be again on the practice field, looked thoughtfully up at the stadium, a deserted ruin in the twilight. He had started on the first team that Saturday and every Saturday after that for the next two years, but it had never been as satisfactory as it should have been. He never had broken away, the longest run he'd ever made was thirty-five yards, and that in a game that was already won, and then that kid had come up from the third team, Diederich, a blank-faced German kid from Wisconsin, who ran like a bull, ripping lines to pieces Saturday after Saturday, plowing through, never getting hurt, never changing his expression, scoring more points, gaining more ground than all the rest of the team put together, making everybody's All-American, carrying the ball three times out of four, keeping everybody else out of the headlines. Darling was a good blocker and he spent his Saturday afternoons working on the big Swedes and Polacks who played tackle and end for Michigan, Illinois, Purdue, hurling into huge pile-ups, bobbing his head wildly to elude the great raw hands swinging like meat-cleavers at him as he went charging in to open up holes for Diederich coming through like a locomotive behind him. Still, it wasn't so bad. Everybody liked him and he did his job and he was pointed out on the campus and boys always felt important when they introduced their girls to him at their proms, and Louise loved him and watched him faithfully in the games, even in the mud, when your own mother wouldn't know you, and drove him around in her car keeping the top down because she was proud of him and wanted to show everybody she was Christian Darling's girl. She bought him crazy presents because her father was rich, watches, pipes, humidors, an icebox for beer for his room, curtains, wallets, a fifty-dollar dictionary.

"You'll spend every cent your old man owns," Darling protested once when she showed up at his rooms with seven different packages in her arms and tossed them onto the couch.

"Kiss me," Louise said, "and shut up."

"Do you want to break your poor old man?"

"I don't mind. I want to buy you presents."

"Why?"

"It makes me feel good. Kiss me. I don't know why. Did you know that you're an important figure?"

"Yes," Darling said gravely.

"When I was waiting for you at the library yesterday two girls saw you coming and one of them said to the other, 'That's Christian Darling. He's an important figure.'"

"You're a liar."

"I'm in love with an important figure."

"Still, why the hell did you have to give me a forty-pound dictionary?"

"I wanted to make sure," Louise said, "that you had a token of my esteem. I want to smother you in tokens of my esteem."

Fifteen years ago.

They'd married when they got out of college. There'd been other women for him, but all casual and secret, more for curiosity's sake, and vanity, women who'd thrown themselves at him and flattered him, a pretty mother at a summer camp for boys, an old girl from his home town who'd suddenly blossomed into a coquette, a friend of Louise's who had dogged him grimly for six months and had taken advantage of the two weeks that Louise went home when her mother died. Perhaps Louise had known, but she'd kept quiet, loving him completely, filling his rooms with presents, religiously watching him battling with the big Swedes and Polacks on the line of scrimmage on Saturday afternoons, making plans for marrying him and living with him in New York and going with him there to the night clubs, the theaters, the good restaurants, being proud of him in advance, tall, white-teethed, smiling, large, yet moving lightly, with an athlete's grace, dressed in evening clothes, approvingly eyed by magnificently dressed and famous women in theater lobbies, with Louise adoringly at his side.

Her father, who manufactured inks, set up a New York office for Darling to manage and presented him with three hundred accounts, and they lived on Beekman Place with a view of the river with fifteen thousand dollars a year between them, because everybody was buying everything in those days, including ink. They saw all the shows and went to all the speakeasies and spent their fifteen thousand dollars a year and in the afternoons Louise went to the art galleries and the matinees of the more serious plays that Darling didn't like to sit through and Darling slept with a girl who danced in the chorus of *Rosalie* and with the wife of a man who owned three copper mines. Darling played squash three times a week and remained as solid as a stone barn and Louise never took her eyes off him when they were in the same room together, watching him with a secret, miser's smile, with a trick of coming over to him in the middle of a crowded room and saying gravely, in a low voice, "You're the handsomest man I've ever seen in my whole life. Want a drink?"

Nineteen twenty-nine came to Darling and to his wife and father-in-law, the maker of inks, just as it came to everyone else. The father-in-law waited until 1933 and then blew his brains out and when Darling went to Chicago to see what the books of the firm looked like he found out all that was left were debts and three or four gallons of unbought ink.

"Please, Christian," Louise said, sitting in their neat Beekman Place apartment, with a view of the river and prints of paintings by Dufy and Braque and Picasso on the wall, "please, why do you want to start drinking at two o'clock in the afternoon?"

"I have nothing else to do," Darling said, putting down his glass, emptied of its fourth drink. "Please pass the whisky."

Louise filled his glass. "Come take a walk with me," she said. "We'll walk along the river."

"I don't want to walk along the river," Darling said, squinting intensely at the prints of paintings by Dufy, Braque and Picasso.

"We'll walk along Fifth Avenue."

"I don't want to walk along Fifth Avenue."

"Maybe," Louise said gently, "you'd like to come with me to some art galleries. There's an exhibition by a man named Klee. . . ."

"I don't want to go to any art galleries. I want to sit here and drink Scotch whisky," Darling said. "Who the hell hung those goddamn pictures up on the wall?"

"I did," Louise said.

"I hate them."

"I'll take them down," Louise said.

"Leave them there. It gives me something to do in the afternoon. I can hate them." Darling took a long swallow. "Is that the way people paint these days?"

"Yes, Christian. Please don't drink any more."

"Do you like painting like that?"

"Yes, dear."

"Really?"

"Really."

Darling looked carefully at the prints once more. "Little Louise Tucker. The middle-western beauty. I like pictures with horses in them. Why should you like pictures like that?"

"I just happen to have gone to a lot of galleries in the last few years . . ."

"Is that what you do in the afternoon?"

"That's what I do in the afternoon," Louise said.

"I drink in the afternoon."

Louise kissed him lightly on the top of his head as he sat there squinting at the pictures on the wall, the glass of whisky held firmly in his hand. She put on her coat and went out without saying another word. When she came back in the early evening, she had a job on a woman's fashion magazine.

They moved downtown and Louise went out to work every morning and Darling sat home and drank and Louise paid the bills as they came up. She made believe she was going to quit work as soon as Darling found a job, even though she was taking over more responsibility day by day at the magazine, interviewing authors, picking painters for the illustrations and covers, getting actresses to pose for pictures, going out for drinks with the right people, making a thousand new friends whom she loyally introduced to Darling.

"I don't like your hat," Darling said, once, when she came in in the evening and kissed him, her breath rich with martinis.

"What's the matter with my hat, Baby?" she asked, running her fingers through his hair. "Everybody says it's very smart."

"It's too damned smart," he said. "It's not for you. It's for a rich, sophisticated woman of thirty-five with admirers."

Louise laughed. "I'm practicing to be a rich sophisticated woman of thirty-five with admirers," she said. He stared soberly at her. "Now, don't look so grim, Baby. It's still the same simple little wife under the hat." She took the hat off, threw it into a corner, sat on his lap. "See? Homebody Number One."

"Your breath could run a train," Darling said, not wanting to be mean, but talking out of boredom, and sudden shock at seeing his wife curiously a stranger in a new hat, with a new expression in her eyes under the little brim, secret, confident, knowing.

Louise tucked her head under his chin so he couldn't smell her breath. "I had to take an author out for cocktails," she said. "He's a boy from the Ozark Mountains and he drinks like a fish. He's a Communist."

"What the hell is a Communist from the Ozarks doing writing for a woman's fashion magazine?"

Louise chuckled. "The magazine business is getting all mixed up these days. The publishers want to have a foot in every camp. And anyway, you can't find an author under seventy these days who isn't a Communist."

"I don't think I like you to associate with all those people, Louise," Darling said. "Drinking with them."

"He's a very nice, gentle boy," Louise said. "He reads Ernest Dowson."

"Who's Ernest Dowson?"

Louise patted his arm, stood up, fixed her hair. "He's an English poet."

Darling felt that somehow he had disappointed her. "Am I supposed to know who Ernest Dowson is?"

"No, dear. I'd better go in and take a bath."

After she had gone, Darling went over to the corner where the hat was lying and picked it up. It was nothing, a scrap of straw, a red flower, a veil, meaningless on his big hand, but on his wife's head a signal of something . . . big city, smart and knowing women drinking and dining with men other than their husbands, conversation about things a normal man wouldn't know much about, Frenchmen who painted as though they used their elbows instead of brushes, composers who wrote whole symphonies without a single melody in them, writers who knew all about politics and women who knew all about writers, the movement of the proletariat, Marx, somehow mixed up with five-dollar dinners and the best-looking women in America and fairies who made them laugh and half-sentences immediately understood and secretly hilarious and wives who called their husbands "Baby." He put the hat down, a scrap of straw and a red flower, and a little veil. He drank some whisky straight and went into the bathroom where his wife was lying deep in her bath, singing to herself and smiling from time to time like a little girl, paddling the water gently with her hands, sending up a slight spicy fragrance from the bath salts she used.

He stood over her, looking down at her. She smiled up at him, her eyes half closed, her body pink and shimmering in the warm, scented water. All over again, with all the old suddenness, he was hit deep inside him with the knowledge of how beautiful she was, how much he needed her.

"I came in here," he said, "to tell you I wish you wouldn't call me 'Baby.'"

She looked up at him from the bath, her eyes quickly full of sorrow, half-understanding what he meant. He knelt and put his arms around her, his sleeves plunged heedlessly in the water, his shirt and jacket soaking wet as he clutched her wordlessly, holding her crazily tight, crushing her breath from her, kissing her desperately, searchingly, regretfully.

He got jobs after that, selling real estate and automobiles, but somehow, although he had a desk with his name on a wooden wedge on it, and he went to the office religiously at nine each morning, he never managed to sell anything and he never made any money.

Louise was made assistant editor, and the house was always full of strange men and women who talked fast and got angry on abstract subjects like mural painting, novelists, labor unions. Negro short-story writers drank Louise's liquor, and a lot of Jews, and big solemn men with scarred faces and knotted hands who talked slowly but clearly about picket lines and battles with guns and leadpipe at mine-shaft-heads and in front of factory gates. And Louise moved among them all, confidently, knowing what they were talking about, with opinions that they listened to and argued about just as though she were a man. She knew everybody, condescended to no one, devoured books that Darling had never heard of, walked along the streets of the city, excited, at home, soaking in all the million tides of New York without fear, with constant wonder.

Her friends liked Darling and sometimes he found a man who wanted to get off in the corner and talk about the new boy who played fullback for Princeton, and the decline of the double wing-back, or even the state of the stock market, but for the most part he sat on the edge of things, solid and quiet in the high storm of words. "The dialectics of the situation . . . The theater has been given over to expert jugglers . . . Picasso? What man has a right to paint old bones and collect ten thousand dollars for them? . . . I stand firmly behind Trotsky[1] . . . Poe was the last American critic. When he died they put lilies on the grave of American criticism. I don't say this because they panned my last book, but . . ."

Once in a while he caught Louise looking soberly and consideringly at him through the cigarette smoke and the noise and he avoided her eyes and found an excuse to get up and go into the kitchen for more ice or to open another bottle.

"Come on," Cathal Flaherty was saying, standing at the door with a girl, "you've got to come down and see this. It's down on Fourteenth Street, in the old Civic Repertory, and you can only see it on Sunday nights and I guarantee you'll come out of the theater singing." Flaherty was a big young Irishman with a broken nose who was the lawyer for a longshoreman's union, and he had been hanging around the house for six months on and off, roaring and shutting everybody else up when he got in an argument. "It's a new play, *Waiting for Lefty;*[2] it's about taxi-drivers."

"Odets," the girl with Flaherty said. "It's by a guy named Odets."

"I never heard of him," Darling said.

"He's a new one," the girl said.

"It's like watching a bombardment," Flaherty said. "I saw it last Sunday night. You've got to see it."

"Come on, Baby," Louise said to Darling, excitement in her eyes already. "We've been sitting in the Sunday *Times* all day, this'll be a great change."

"I see enough taxi-drivers every day," Darling said, not because he meant that, but because he didn't like to be around Flaherty, who said things that made Louise laugh a lot and whose judgment she accepted on almost every subject. "Let's go to the movies."

"You've never seen anything like this before," Flaherty said. "He wrote this play with a baseball bat."

"Come on," Louise coaxed, "I bet it's wonderful."

"He has long hair," the girl with Flaherty said. "Odets. I met him at a party. He's an actor. He didn't say a goddam thing all night."

"I don't feel like going down to Fourteenth Street," Darling said, wishing Flaherty and his girl would get out. "It's gloomy."

"Oh, hell!" Louise said loudly. She looked coolly at Darling, as though she'd just been introduced to him and was making up her mind about him, and not very favorably. He saw her looking at him, knowing there was something new and dangerous in her face and he wanted to say something, but

---

1. Leon Trotsky (1879–1940), one of the founders of the modern communist movement. His ideas of worldwide revolution and pure communism were much in vogue in the 1930s.

2. Anticapitalistic, pro-working-class drama by Clifford Odets (1906–63) which was an immediate sensation upon its first appearance in 1935.

Flaherty was there and his damned girl, and anyway, he didn't know what to say.

"I'm going," Louise said, getting her coat. "I don't think Fourteenth Street is gloomy."

"I'm telling you," Flaherty was saying, helping her on with her coat, "it's the Battle of Gettysburg, in Brooklynese."

"Nobody could get a word out of him," Flaherty's girl was saying as they went through the door. "He just sat there all night."

The door closed. Louise hadn't said good night to him. Darling walked around the room four times, then sprawled out on the sofa, on top of the Sunday *Times*. He lay there for five minutes looking at the ceiling, thinking of Flaherty walking down the street talking in that booming voice, between the girls, holding their arms.

Louise had looked wonderful. She'd washed her hair in the afternoon and it had been very soft and light and clung close to her head as she stood there angrily putting her coat on. Louise was getting prettier every year, partly because she knew by now how pretty she was, and made the most of it.

"Nuts," Darling said, standing up. "Oh, nuts."

He put on his coat and went down to the nearest bar and had five drinks off by himself in a corner before his money ran out.

The years since then had been foggy and downhill. Louise had been nice to him, and in a way, loving and kind, they'd fought only once, when he said he was going to vote for Landon.[3] ("Oh, Christ," she'd said, "doesn't *anything* happen inside your head? Don't you read the papers? The penniless Republican!") She'd been sorry later and apologized for hurting him, but apologized as she might to a child. He'd tried hard, had gone grimly to the art galleries, the concert halls, the bookshops, trying to gain on the trail of his wife, but it was no use. He was bored, and none of what he saw or heard or dutifully read made much sense to him and finally he gave it up. He had thought, many nights as he ate dinner alone, knowing that Louise would come home late and drop silently into bed without explanation, of getting a divorce, but he knew the loneliness, the hopelessness, of not seeing her again would be too much to take. So he was good, completely devoted, ready at all times to go anyplace with her, do anything she wanted. He even got a small job, in a broker's office, and paid his own way, bought his own liquor.

Then he'd been offered the job of going from college to college as a tailor's representative. "We want a man," Mr. Rosenberg had said, "who as soon as you look at him, you say, 'There's a university man.'" Rosenberg had looked approvingly at Darling's broad shoulders and well-kept waist, at his carefully brushed hair and his honest, wrinkle-less face. "Frankly, Mr. Darling, I am willing to make you a proposition. I have inquired about you, you are favorably known on your old campus, I understand you were in the backfield with Alfred Diederich."

Darling nodded. "Whatever happened to him?"

"He is walking around in a cast for seven years now. An iron brace. He played professional football and they broke his neck for him."

---

3. Alfred Landon (b. 1887), Republican presidential candidate in 1936; he was soundly defeated by Franklin D. Roosevelt.

Darling smiled. That, at least, had turned out well.

"Our suits are an easy product to sell, Mr. Darling," Rosenberg said. "We have a handsome, custom-made garment. What has Brooks Brothers got that we haven't got? A name. No more."

"I can make fifty, sixty dollars a week," Darling said to Louise that night. "And expenses. I can save some money and then come back to New York and really get started here."

"Yes, Baby," Louise said.

"As it is," Darling said carefully, "I can make it back here once a month, and holidays and the summer. We can see each other often."

"Yes, Baby." He looked at her face, lovelier now at thirty-five than it had ever been before, but fogged over now as it had been for five years with a kind of patient, kindly, remote boredom.

"What do you say?" he asked. "Should I take it?" Deep within him he hoped fiercely, longingly, for her to say, "No, Baby, you stay right here," but she said, as he knew she'd say, "I think you'd better take it."

He nodded. He had to get up and stand with his back to her, looking out the window, because there were things plain on his face that she had never seen in the fifteen years she'd known him. "Fifty dollars is a lot of money," he said. "I never thought I'd ever see fifty dollars again." He laughed. Louise laughed, too.

Christian Darling sat on the frail green grass of the practice field. The shadow of the stadium had reached out and covered him. In the distance the lights of the university shone a little mistily in the light haze of the evening. Fifteen years. Flaherty even now was calling for his wife, buying her a drink, filling whatever bar they were in with that voice of his and that easy laugh. Darling half-closed his eyes, almost saw the boy fifteen years ago reach for the pass, slip the halfback, go skittering lightly down the field, his knees high and fast and graceful, smiling to himself because he knew he was going to get past the safety man. That was the high point, Darling thought, fifteen years ago, on an autumn afternoon, twenty years old and far from death, with the air coming easily into his lungs, and a deep feeling inside him that he could do anything, knock over anybody, outrun whatever had to be outrun. And the shower after and the three glasses of water and the cool night air on his damp head and Louise sitting hatless in the open car with a smile and the first kiss she ever really meant. The high point, an eighty-yard run in the practice, and a girl's kiss and everything after that a decline. Darling laughed. He had practiced the wrong thing, perhaps. He hadn't practiced for 1929 and New York City and a girl who would turn into a woman. Somewhere, he thought, there must have been a point where she moved up to me, was even with me for a moment, when I could have held her hand, if I'd known, held tight, gone with her. Well, he'd never known. Here he was on a playing field that was fifteen years away and his wife was in another city having dinner with another and better man, speaking with him a different, new language, a language nobody had ever taught him.

Darling stood up, smiled a little, because if he didn't smile he knew the tears would come. He looked around him. This was the spot. O'Connor's pass had come sliding out just to here . . . the high point. Darling put up his hands, felt all over again the flat slap of the ball. He shook his hips to throw off the halfback, cut back inside the center, picked his knees high as he ran gracefully over two men jumbled on the ground at the line of scrimmage, ran easily, gaining speed, for ten yards, holding the ball lightly in his two hands, swung away from the halfback diving at him, ran, swinging his hips in the almost girlish manner of a back in a broken field, tore into the safety man, his shoes drumming heavily on the turf, stiff-armed, elbow locked, pivoted, raced lightly and exultantly for the goal line.

It was only after he had sped over the goal line and slowed to a trot that he saw the boy and girl sitting together on the turf, looking at him wonderingly.

He stopped short, dropping his arms. "I . . ." he said, gasping a little, though his condition was fine and the run hadn't winded him. "I——once I played here."

The boy and the girl said nothing. Darling laughed embarrassedly, looked hard at them sitting there, close to each other, shrugged, turned and went toward his hotel, the sweat breaking out on his face and running down into his collar.

Questions for Study

1. Why does Shaw first present the eighty-yard run as if it took place in present time? How would you describe the pleasures Christian experiences during and immediately after the run?
2. How do each of the following serve to characterize Louise: buying Christian presents; hanging prints of abstract paintings on their walls; getting a job; calling Christian "Baby"; buying the hat? What other actions effectively characterize her? Are her actions effectively motivated?
3. What is the function of the minor characters in the story? Even though they are Louise's friends, why do they seem to affect Christian more than her?
4. What is the conflict in this story? Diagram the plot line, indicating the conflict and its resolution.
5. What actions effectively characterize Christian?
6. Why is the one fight between Christian and Louise about politics and not about themselves and their relationship? Why does Shaw not tell us whether or not they get divorced?

Isaac Bashevis Singer (b. 1904)
Gimpel the Fool

I

I am Gimpel the fool. I don't think myself a fool. On the contrary. But that's what folks call me. They gave me the name while I was still in school. I had seven names in all: imbecile, donkey, flax-head, dope, glump, ninny, and fool. The last name stuck. What did my foolishness consist of? I was easy to take in. They said, "Gimpel, you know the rabbi's wife has been brought to childbed?"

So I skipped school. Well, it turned out to be a lie. How was I supposed to know? She hadn't had a big belly. But I never looked at her belly. Was that really so foolish? The gang laughed and hee-hawed, stomped and danced and chanted a good-night prayer. And instead of the raisins they give when a woman's lying in, they stuffed my hand full of goat turds. I was no weakling. If I slapped someone he'd see all the way to Cracow. But I'm really not a slugger by nature. I think to myself: Let it pass. So they take advantage of me.

I was coming home from school and heard a dog barking. I'm not afraid of dogs, but of course I never want to start up with them. One of them may be mad, and if he bites there's not a Tartar in the world who can help you. So I made tracks. Then I looked around and saw the whole market-place wild with laughter. It was no dog at all but Wolf-Leib the Thief. How was I supposed to know it was he? It sounded like a howling bitch.

When the pranksters and leg-pullers found that I was easy to fool, every one of them tried his luck with me. "Gimpel, the Czar is coming to Frampol; Gimpel, the moon fell down in Turbeen; Gimpel, little Hodel Furpiece found a treasure behind the bathhouse." And I like a golem[1] believed everyone. In the first place, everything is possible, as it is written in the Wisdom of the Fathers, I've forgotten just how. Second, I had to believe when the whole town came down on me! If I ever dared to say, "Ah, you're kidding!" there was trouble. People got angry. "What do you mean! You want to call everyone a liar?" What was I to do? I believed them, and I hope at least that did them some good.

I was an orphan. My grandfather who brought me up was already bent toward the grave. So they turned me over to a baker, and what a time they gave me there! Every woman or girl who came to bake a batch of noodles had to fool me at least once. "Gimpel, there's a fair in heaven; Gimpel, the rabbi gave birth to a calf in the seventh month; Gimpel, a cow flew over the roof and laid brass eggs." A student from the yeshiva[2] came once to buy a roll, and he said, "You, Gimpel, while you stand here scraping with your baker's shovel the Messiah has come. The dead have arisen." "What do you mean?" I said. "I heard no one blowing the ram's horn!" He said, "Are you deaf?" And all began to cry, "We heard it, we heard!" Then in came Rietze the Candle-dipper and called out in her hoarse voice, "Gimpel, your father and mother have stood up from the grave. They're looking for you."

To tell the truth, I knew very well that nothing of the sort had happened, but all the same, as folks were talking, I threw on my wool vest and went out. Maybe something had happened. What did I stand to lose by looking? Well, what a cat music went up! And then I took a vow to believe nothing more. But that was no go either. They confused me so that I didn't know the big end from the small.

I went to the rabbi to get some advice. He said, "It is written, better to be a fool all your days than for one hour to be evil. You are not a fool. They are the fools. For he who causes his neighbor to feel shame loses Paradise himself." Nevertheless the rabbi's daughter took me in. As I left the rabbinical court she said, "Have you kissed the wall yet?" I said, "No; what for?" She answered, "It's the law; you've got to do it after every visit." Well, there didn't seem to

---

1. Dull-witted person; simpleton.
2. Academy for training young men in Jewish thought and traditions.

be any harm in it. And she burst out laughing. It was a fine trick. She put one over on me all right.

I wanted to go off to another town, but then everyone got busy match-making, and they were after me so they nearly tore my coat tails off. They talked at me and talked until I got water on the ear. She was no chaste maiden, but they told me she was a virgin pure. She had a limp, and they said it was deliberate, from coyness. She had a bastard, and they told me the child was her little brother. I cried, "You're wasting your time. I'll never marry that whore." But they said indignantly, "What a way to talk! Aren't you ashamed of yourself? We can take you to the rabbi and have you fined for giving her a bad name." I saw then that I wouldn't escape them so easily and I thought: They're set on making me their butt. But when you're married the husband's the master, and if that's all right with her it's agreeable to me too. Besides, you can't pass through life unscathed, nor expect to.

I went to her clay house, which was built on the sand, and the whole gang, hollering and chorusing, came after me. They acted like bear-baiters. When we came to the well they stopped all the same. They were afraid to start anything with Elka. Her mouth would open as if it were on a hinge, and she had a fierce tongue. I entered the house. Lines were strung from wall to wall and clothes were drying. Barefoot she stood by the tub, doing the wash. She was dressed in a worn hand-me-down gown of plush. She had her hair up in braids and pinned across her head. It took my breath away, almost, the reek of it all.

Evidently she knew who I was. She took a look at me and said, "Look who's here! He's come, the drip. Grab a seat."

I told her all; I denied nothing. "Tell me the truth," I said, "are you really a virgin, and is that mischievous Yechiel actually your little brother? Don't be deceitful with me, for I'm an orphan."

"I'm an orphan myself," she answered, "and whoever tries to twist you up, may the end of his nose take a twist. But don't let them think they can take advantage of me. I want a dowry of fifty guilders, and let them take up a collection besides. Otherwise they can kiss my you-know-what." She was very plainspoken. I said, "It's the bride and not the groom who gives a dowry." Then she said, "Don't bargain with me. Either a flat 'yes' or a flat 'no'—Go back where you came from."

I thought: No bread will ever be baked from *this* dough. But ours is not a poor town. They consented to everything and proceeded with the wedding. It so happened that there was a dysentery epidemic at the time. The ceremony was held at the cemetery gates, near the little corpse-washing hut. The fellows got drunk. While the marriage contract was being drawn up I heard the most pious high rabbi ask, "Is the bride a widow or a divorced woman?" And the sexton's wife answered for her, "Both a widow and divorced." It was a black moment for me. But what was I to do, run away from under the marriage canopy?

There was singing and dancing. An old granny danced opposite men, hugging a braided white *chalah*.[3] The master of revels made a "God 'a mercy" in memory of the bride's parents. The schoolboys threw burrs, as on Tishe b'Av[4]

---

3. Loaf of bread, cakelike and delicate in flavor and texture, eaten on the Sabbath and other holidays.

4. A day of fasting and deep mourning that commemorates the First (586 B.C.) and the Second (A.D. 70) destruction of the Temple in Jerusalem.

fast day. There were a lot of gifts after the sermon: a noodle board, a kneading trough, a bucket, brooms, ladles, household articles galore. Then I took a look and saw two strapping young men carrying a crib. "What do we need this for?" I asked. So they said, "Don't rack your brains about it. It's all right, it'll come in handy." I realized I was going to be rooked. Take it another way though, what did I stand to lose? I reflected: I'll see what comes of it. A whole town can't go altogether crazy.

II

At night I came where my wife lay, but she wouldn't let me in. "Say, look here, is this what they married us for?" I said. And she said, "My monthly has come." "But yesterday they took you to the ritual bath, and that's afterward, isn't it supposed to be?" "Today isn't yesterday," said she, "and yesterday's not today. You can beat it if you don't like it." In short, I waited.

Not four months later she was in childbed. The townsfolk hid their laughter with their knuckles. But what could I do? She suffered intolerable pains and clawed at the walls. "Gimpel," she cried, "I'm going. Forgive me!" The house filled with women. They were boiling pans of water. The screams rose to the welkin.[5]

The thing to do was to go to the House of Prayer to repeat Psalms, and that was what I did.

The townsfolk liked that, all right. I stood in a corner saying Psalms and prayers, and they shook their heads at me. "Pray, pray!" they told me. "Prayer never made any woman pregnant." One of the congregation put a straw to my mouth and said, "Hay for the cows." There was something to that too, by God!

She gave birth to a boy. Friday at the synagogue the sexton stood up before the Ark,[6] pounded on the reading table, and announced, "The wealthy Reb Gimpel invites the congregation to a feast in honor of the birth of a son." The whole House of Prayer rang with laughter. My face was flaming. But there was nothing I could do. After all, I *was* the one responsible for the circumcision honors and rituals.

Half the town came running. You couldn't wedge another soul in. Women brought peppered chick-peas, and there was a keg of beer from the tavern. I ate and drank as much as anyone, and they all congratulated me. Then there was a circumcision, and I named the boy after my father, may he rest in peace. When all were gone and I was left with my wife alone, she thrust her head through the bed-curtain and called me to her.

"Gimpel," said she, "why are you silent? Has your ship gone and sunk?"

"What shall I say?" I answered. "A fine thing you've done to me! If my mother had known of it she'd have died a second time."

She said, "Are you crazy, or what?"

"How can you make such a fool," I said, "of one who should be the lord and master?"

---

5. The sky.
6. The receptacle containing the written Torah, the first books of the Old Testament, central to Jewish religious doctrine.

"What's the matter with you?" she said. "What have you taken it into your head to imagine?"

I saw that I must speak bluntly and openly. "Do you think this the way to use an orphan?" I said. "You have borne a bastard."

She answered, "Drive this foolishness out of your head. The child is yours."

"How can he be mine?" I argued. "He was born seventeen weeks after the wedding."

She told me then that he was premature. I said, "Isn't he a little too premature?" She said she had had a grandmother who carried just as short a time and she resembled this grandmother of hers as one drop of water does another. She swore to it with such oaths that you would have believed a peasant at the fair if he had used them. To tell the plain truth, I didn't believe her; but when I talked it over next day with the schoolmaster he told me that the very same thing had happened to Adam and Eve. Two they went up to bed, and four they descended.

"There isn't a woman in the world who is not the granddaughter of Eve," he said.

That was how it was; they argued me dumb. But then, who really knows how such things are?

I began to forget my sorrow. I loved the child madly, and he loved me too. As soon as he saw me he'd wave his little hands and want me to pick him up, and when he was colicky I was the only one who could pacify him. I bought him a little bone teething ring and a little gilded cap. He was forever catching the evil eye[7] from someone, and then I had to run to get one of those abracadabras for him that would get him out of it. I worked like an ox. You know how expenses go up when there's an infant in the house. I don't want to lie about it; I didn't dislike Elka either, for that matter. She swore at me and cursed, and I couldn't get enough of her. What strength she had! One of her looks could rob you of the power of speech. And her orations! Pitch and sulphur, that's what they were full of, and yet somehow also full of charm. I adored her every word. She gave me bloody wounds though.

In the evening I brought her a white loaf as well as a dark one, and also poppyseed rolls I baked myself. I thieved because of her and swiped everything I could lay hands on: macaroons, raisins, almonds, cakes. I hope I may be forgiven for stealing from the Saturday pots the women left to warm in the baker's oven. I would take out scraps of meat, a chunk of pudding, a chicken leg or head, a piece of tripe, whatever I could nip quickly. She ate and became fat and handsome.

I had to sleep away from home all during the week, at the bakery. On Friday nights when I got home she always made an excuse of some sort. Either she had heartburn, or a stitch in the side or hiccups, or headaches. You know what women's excuses are. I had a bitter time of it. It was rough. To add to it, this little brother of hers, the bastard, was growing bigger. He'd put lumps on me, and when I wanted to hit back she'd open her mouth and curse so powerfully I saw a green haze floating before my eyes. Ten times a day she threat-

---

7. In Yiddish folklore, talented and beautiful children are susceptible to this form of hex, brought on by malevolent forces. It can be removed by magic formulas—"abracadabras"—either spoken or inscribed on amulets.

ened to divorce me. Another man in my place would have taken French leave and disappeared. But I'm the type that bears it and says nothing. What's one to do? Shoulders are from God, and burdens too.

One night there was a calamity in the bakery; the oven burst, and we almost had a fire. There was nothing to do but go home, so I went home. Let me, I thought, also taste the joy of sleeping in bed in mid-week. I didn't want to wake the sleeping mite and tiptoed into the house. Coming in, it seemed to me that I heard not the snoring of one but, as it were, a double snore, one a thin enough snore and the other like the snoring of a slaughtered ox. Oh, I didn't like that! I didn't like it at all. I went up to the bed, and things suddenly turned black. Next to Elka lay a man's form. Another in my place would have made an uproar, and enough noise to rouse the whole town, but the thought occurred to me that I might wake the child. A little thing like that—why frighten a little swallow, I thought. All right then, I went back to the bakery and stretched out on a sack of flour and till morning I never shut an eye. I shivered as if I had malaria. "Enough of being a donkey," I said to myself. "Gimpel isn't going to be a sucker all his life. There's a limit even to the foolishness of a fool like Gimpel."

In the morning I went to the rabbi to get advice, and it made a great commotion in the town. They sent the beadle for Elka right away. She came, carrying the child. And what do you think she did? She denied it, denied everything, bone and stone! "He's out of his head," she said. "I know nothing of dreams or divinations." They yelled at her, warned her, hammered on the table, but she stuck to her guns: it was a false accusation, she said.

The butchers and the horse-traders took her part. One of the lads from the slaughterhouse came by and said to me, "We've got our eye on you, you're a marked man." Meanwhile the child started to bear down and soiled itself. In the rabbinical court there was an Ark of the Covenant,[8] and they couldn't allow that, so they sent Elka away.

I said to the rabbi, "What shall I do?"

"You must divorce her at once," said he.

"And what if she refuses?" I asked.

He said, "You must serve the divorce. That's all you have to do."

I said, "Well, all right, Rabbi. Let me think about it."

"There's nothing to think about," said he. "You mustn't remain under the same roof with her."

"And if I want to see the child?" I asked.

"Let her go, the harlot," said he, "and her brood of bastards with her."

The verdict he gave was that I mustn't even cross her threshold—never again, as long as I should live.

During the day it didn't bother me so much. I thought: It was bound to happen, the abscess had to burst. But at night when I stretched out upon the sacks I felt it all very bitterly. A longing took me, for her and for the child. I wanted to be angry, but that's my misfortune exactly, I don't have it in me to be really angry. In the first place—this was how my thoughts went—there's bound to be a slip sometimes. You can't live without errors. Probably that lad who was with her led her on and gave her presents and what not, and women are often long on hair and short on sense, and so he got around her. And then

---

8. The chest containing scrolls on which are printed the Ten Commandments.

since she denies it so, maybe I was only seeing things? Hallucinations do happen. You see a figure or a mannikin or something, but when you come up closer it's nothing, there's not a thing there. And if that's so, I'm doing her an injustice. And when I got so far in my thoughts I started to weep. I sobbed so that I wet the flour where I lay. In the morning I went to the rabbi and told him that I had made a mistake. The rabbi wrote on with his quill, and he said that if that were so he would have to reconsider the whole case. Until he had finished I wasn't to go near my wife, but I might send her bread and money by messenger.

III

Nine months passed before all the rabbis could come to an agreement. Letters went back and forth. I hadn't realized that there could be so much erudition about a matter like this.

Meanwhile Elka gave birth to still another child, a girl this time. On the Sabbath I went to the synagogue and invoked a blessing on her. They called me up to the Torah, and I named the child for my mother-in-law—may she rest in peace. The louts and loudmouths of the town who came into the bakery gave me a going over. All Frampol refreshed its spirits because of my trouble and grief. However, I resolved that I would always believe what I was told. What's the good of *not* believing? Today it's your wife you don't believe; tomorrow it's God Himself you won't take stock in.

By an apprentice who was her neighbor I sent daily a corn or a wheat loaf, or a piece of pastry, rolls or bagels, or, when I got the chance, a slab of pudding, a slice of honeycake, or wedding strudel—whatever came my way. The apprentice was a goodhearted lad, and more than once he added something on his own. He had formerly annoyed me a lot, plucking my nose and digging me in the ribs, but when he started to be a visitor to my house he became kind and friendly. "Hey, you, Gimpel," he said to me, "you have a very decent little wife and two fine kids. You don't deserve them."

"But the things people say about her," I said.

"Well, they have long tongues," he said, "and nothing to do with them but babble. Ignore it as you ignore the cold of last winter."

One day the rabbi sent for me and said, "Are you certain, Gimpel, that you were wrong about your wife?"

I said, "I'm certain."

"Why, but look here! You yourself saw it."

"It must have been a shadow," I said.

"The shadow of what?"

"Just one of the beams, I think."

"You can go home then. You owe thanks to the Yanover rabbi. He found an obscure reference in Maimonides[9] that favored you."

I seized the rabbi's hand and kissed it.

I wanted to run home immediately. It's no small thing to be separated for so long a time from wife and child. Then I reflected: I'd better go back to work

---

9. Moses Maimonides (1135–1204), rabbi and philosopher who codified the Talmud, a collection of Jewish oral law.

now, and go home in the evening. I said nothing to anyone, although as far as my heart was concerned it was like one of the Holy Days. The women teased and twitted me as they did every day, but my thought was: Go on, with your loose talk. The truth is out, like the oil upon the water. Maimonides says it's right, and therefore it is right!

At night, when I had covered the dough to let it rise, I took my share of bread and a little sack of flour and started homeward. The moon was full and the stars were glistening, something to terrify the soul. I hurried onward, and before me darted a long shadow. It was winter, and a fresh snow had fallen. I had a mind to sing, but it was growing late and I didn't want to wake the house-holders. Then I felt like whistling, but I remembered that you don't whistle at night because it brings the demons out. So I was silent and walked as fast as I could.

Dogs in the Christian yards barked at me when I passed, but I thought: Bark your teeth out! What are you but mere dogs? Whereas I am a man, the husband of a fine wife, the father of promising children.

As I approached the house my heart started to pound as though it were the heart of a criminal. I felt no fear, but my heart went thump! thump! Well, no drawing back. I quietly lifted the latch and went in. Elka was asleep. I looked at the infant's cradle. The shutter was closed, but the moon forced its way through the cracks. I saw the newborn child's face and loved it as soon as I saw it—immediately—each tiny bone.

Then I came nearer to the bed. And what did I see but the apprentice lying there beside Elka. The moon went out all at once. It was utterly black, and I trembled. My teeth chattered. The bread fell from my hands, and my wife waked and said, "Who is that, ah?"

I muttered, "It's me."

"Gimpel?" she asked. "How come you're here? I thought it was forbidden."

"The rabbi said," I answered and shook as with a fever.

"Listen to me, Gimpel," she said, "go out to the shed and see if the goat's all right. It seems she's been sick." I have forgotten to say that we had a goat. When I heard she was unwell I went into the yard. The nannygoat was a good little creature. I had a nearly human feeling for her.

With hesitant steps I went up to the shed and opened the door. The goat stood there on her four feet. I felt her everywhere, drew her by the horns, examined her udders, and found nothing wrong. She had probably eaten too much bark. "Good night, little goat," I said. "Keep well." And the little beast answered with a "Maa" as though to thank me for the good will.

I went back. The apprentice had vanished.

"Where," I asked, "is the lad?"

"What lad?" my wife answered.

"What do you mean?" I said. "The apprentice. You were sleeping with him."

"The things I have dreamed this night and the night before," she said, "may they come true and lay you low, body and soul! An evil spirit has taken root in you and dazzles your sight." She screamed out, "You hateful creature! You moon calf! You spook! You uncouth man! Get out, or I'll scream all Frampol out of bed!"

Before I could move, her brother sprang out from behind the oven and struck me a blow on the back of the head. I thought he had broken my neck. I felt that something about me was deeply wrong, and I said, "Don't make a scandal. All that's needed now is that people should accuse me of raising spooks and *dybbuks*."[10] For that was what she had meant. "No one will touch bread of my baking."

In short, I somehow calmed her.

"Well," she said, "that's enough. Lie down, and be shattered by wheels."

Next morning I called the apprentice aside. "Listen here, brother!" I said. And so on and so forth. "What do you say?" He stared at me as though I had dropped from the roof or something.

"I swear," he said, "you'd better go to an herb doctor or some healer. I'm afraid you have a screw loose, but I'll hush it up for you." And that's how the thing stood.

To make a long story short, I lived twenty years with my wife. She bore me six children, four daughters and two sons. All kinds of things happened, but I neither saw nor heard. I believed, and that's all. The rabbi recently said to me, "Belief in itself is beneficial. It is written that a good man lives by his faith."

Suddenly my wife took sick. It began with a trifle, a little growth upon the breast. But she evidently was not destined to live long; she had no years. I spent a fortune on her. I have forgotten to say that by this time I had a bakery of my own and in Frampol was considered to be something of a rich man. Daily the healer came, and every witch doctor in the neighborhood was brought. They decided to use leeches, and after that to try cupping.[11] They even called a doctor from Lublin, but it was too late. Before she died she called me to her bed and said, "Forgive me, Gimpel."

I said, "What is there to forgive? You have been a good and faithful wife."

"Woe, Gimpel!" she said. "It was ugly how I deceived you all these years. I want to go clean to my Maker, and so I have to tell you that the children are not yours."

If I had been clouted on the head with a piece of wood it couldn't have bewildered me more.

"Whose are they?" I asked.

"I don't know," she said. "There were a lot . . . but they're not yours." And as she spoke she tossed her head to the side, her eyes turned glassy, and it was all up with Elka. On her whitened lips there remained a smile.

I imagined that, dead as she was, she was saying, "I deceived Gimpel. That was the meaning of my brief life."

IV

One night, when the period of mourning was done, as I lay dreaming on the flour sacks, there came the Spirit of Evil himself and said to me, "Gimpel, why do you sleep?"

I said, "What should I be doing? Eating *kreplach?*"[12]

---

10. An evil spirit, usually the soul of a dead person which enters a living person on whom the dead one has some claim.
11. Two techniques for bloodletting.
12. A meat- or cheese-filled dumpling.

"The whole world deceives you," he said, "and you ought to deceive the world in your turn."

"How can I deceive all the world?" I asked him.

He answered, "You might accumulate a bucket of urine every day and at night pour it into the dough. Let the sages of Frampol eat filth."

"What about the judgment in the world to come?" I said.

"There is no world to come," he said. "They've sold you a bill of goods and talked you into believing you carried a cat in your belly. What nonsense!"

"Well then," I said, "and is there a God?"

He answered, "There is no God either."

"What," I said, "*is* there, then?"

"A thick mire."

He stood before my eyes with a goatish beard and horn, long-toothed, and with a tail. Hearing such words, I wanted to snatch him by the tail, but I tumbled from the flour sacks and nearly broke a rib. Then it happened that I had to answer the call of nature, and, passing, I saw the risen dough, which seemed to say to me, "Do it." In brief, I let myself be persuaded.

At dawn the apprentice came. We kneaded the bread, scattered caraway seeds on it, and set it to bake. Then the apprentice went away, and I was left sitting in the little trench by the oven on a pile of rags. Well, Gimpel, I thought, you've revenged yourself on them for all the shame they've put on you. Outside the frost glittered, but it was warm beside the oven. The flames heated my face. I bent my head and fell into a doze.

I saw in a dream at once, Elka in her shroud. She called to me, "What have you done, Gimpel?"

I said to her, "It's all your fault," and started to cry.

"You fool!" she said. "You fool! Because I was false is everything false too? I never deceived anyone but myself. I'm paying for it all, Gimpel. They spare you nothing here."

I looked at her face. It was black; I was startled and waked, and remained sitting dumb. I sensed that everything hung in the balance. A false step now and I'd lose Eternal Life. But God gave me His help. I seized the long shovel and took out the loaves, carried them into the yard, and started to dig a hole in the frozen earth.

My apprentice came back as I was doing it. "What are you doing boss?" he said, and grew pale as a corpse.

"I know what I'm doing," I said and I buried it all before his very eyes.

Then I went home, and took my hoard from its hiding place, and divided it among the children. "I saw your mother tonight," I said. "She's turning black, poor thing."

They were so astounded they couldn't speak a word.

"Be well," I said, "and forget that such a one as Gimpel ever existed." I put on my short coat, a pair of boots, took the bag that held my prayer shawl in one hand, my stock in the other, and kissed the *mezzuzah*.[13] When people saw me in the street they were greatly surprised.

"Where are you going?" they said.

---

13. A small oblong case containing a rolled-up piece of parchment on which is printed the text of Deut. 6:4–9 and 11:13–21. It is affixed to a doorjamb to consecrate the house and to ward off evil.

I answered, "Into the world." And so I departed from Frampol.

I wandered over the land, and good people did not neglect me. After many years I became old and white; I heard a great deal, many lies and falsehoods, but the longer I lived the more I understood that there were really no lies. Whatever doesn't really happen is dreamed at night. It happens to one if it doesn't happen to another, tomorrow if not today, or a century hence if not next year. What difference can it make? Often I heard tales of which I said, "Now this is a thing that cannot happen." But before a year had elapsed I heard that it actually had come to pass somewhere.

Going from place to place, eating at strange tables, it often happens that I spin yarns—improbable things that could never have happened—about devils, magicians, windmills, and the like. The children run after me, calling, "Grandfather, tell us a story." Sometimes they ask for particular stories, and I try to please them. A fat young boy once said to me, "Grandfather, it's the same story you told us before." The little rogue, he was right.

So it is with dreams too. It is many years since I left Frampol, but as soon as I shut my eyes I am there again. And whom do you think I see? Elka. She is standing by the washtub, as at our first encounter, but her face is shining and her eyes are as radiant as the eyes of a saint, and she speaks outlandish words to me, strange things. When I wake I have forgotten it all. But while the dream lasts I am comforted. She answers all my queries, and what comes out is that all is right. I weep and implore, "Let me be with you." And she consoles me and tells me to be patient. The time is nearer than it is far. Sometimes she strokes and kisses me and weeps upon my face. When I awaken I feel her lips and taste the salt of her tears.

No doubt the world is entirely an imaginary world, but it is only once removed from the true world. At the door of the hovel where I lie, there stands the plank on which the dead are taken away. The gravedigger Jew has his spade ready. The grave waits and the worms are hungry; the shrouds are prepared— I carry them in my beggar's sack. Another *shnorrer*[14] is waiting to inherit my bed of straw. When the time comes I will go joyfully. Whatever may be there, it will be real, without complication, without ridicule, without deception. God be praised: there even Gimpel cannot be deceived.

Questions for Study

1. Why is Gimpel taken for a fool? How does Singer indicate that Gimpel may not be a fool after all?
2. Gimpel says he is incapable of feeling anger. Is this a strength or a weakness in his character? How could it be both?
3. Terrible things happen to Gimpel, yet the flavor of the story is comic. How does Singer achieve this effect? Look for phrases in the story that seem to modify what might have been bitterness on the part of Gimpel.
4. How is the character of Elka presented to us?
5. Why does Gimpel persist in believing the obvious false statements, tales, and insinuations? What does he lose by such an attitude? What does he gain?
6. Is Gimpel a static or a dynamic character? Who, or what, is his antagonist?

---

14. A professional beggar.

7. Is Gimpel's decision to leave his village consistent with his character? Explain your response, noting in particular the reasons for his telling rather bizarre things to his children.
8. Is Gimpel's final understanding about what is real and what is imaginary consistent with his earlier gullibility? What role does his religious faith play in this awareness? Is he truly a devout man or simply an unthinking believer?

Ralph Ellison (b. 1914)
Battle Royal

It goes a long way back, some twenty years. All my life I had been looking for something, and everywhere I turned someone tried to tell me what it was. I accepted their answers too, though they were often in contradiction and even self-contradictory. I was naïve. I was looking for myself and asking everyone except myself questions which I, and only I, could answer. It took me a long time and much painful boomeranging of my expectations to achieve a realization everyone else appears to have been born with: That I am nobody but myself. But first I had to discover that I am an invisible man!

And yet I am no freak of nature, nor of history. I was in the cards, other things having been equal (or unequal) eighty-five years ago. I am not ashamed of my grandparents for having been slaves. I am only ashamed of myself for having at one time been ashamed. About eighty-five years ago they were told that they were free, united with others of our country in everything pertaining to the common good, and, in everything social, separate like the fingers of the hand. And they believed it. They exulted in it. They stayed in their place, worked hard, and brought up my father to do the same. But my grandfather is the one. He was an odd old guy, my grandfather, and I am told I take after him. It was he who caused the trouble. On his deathbed he called my father to him and said, ''Son, after I'm gone I want you to keep up the fight. I never told you, but our life is a war and I have been a traitor all my born days, a spy in the enemy's country ever since I give up my gun back in the Reconstruction. Live with your head in the lion's mouth. I want you to overcome 'em with yeses, undermine 'em with grins, agree 'em to death and destruction, let 'em swoller you till they vomit or bust wide open.'' They thought the old man had gone out of his mind. He had been the meekest of men. The younger children were rushed from the room, the shades drawn and the flame of the lamp turned so low that it sputtered on the wick like the old man's breathing. ''Learn it to the younguns,'' he whispered fiercely; then he died.

But my folks were more alarmed over his last words than over his dying. It was as though he had not died at all, his words caused so much anxiety. I was warned emphatically to forget what he had said and, indeed, this is the first time it has been mentioned outside the family circle. It had a tremendous effect upon me, however. I could never be sure of what he meant. Grandfather had been a quiet old man who never made any trouble, yet on his deathbed he had called himself a traitor and a spy, and he had spoken of his meekness as a dangerous activity. It became a constant puzzle which lay unanswered in the back of my mind. And whenever things went well for me I remembered my grandfather and felt guilty and uncomfortable. It was as though I was carrying out his advice in spite of myself. And to make it worse, everyone loved me for it. I was praised by the most lily-white men of the town. I was considered an example of desirable conduct—just as my grandfather had been. And what puzzled me was that the old man had defined it as *treachery*. When I was praised for my conduct I felt a guilt that in some way I was doing something that was really against the wishes of the white folks, that if they had understood they would have desired me to act just the opposite, that I should have been sulky and mean, and that that really would have been what they wanted, even though they were fooled and thought they wanted me to act as I did. It made me afraid that some day they would look upon me as a traitor and I would be lost. Still I was more afraid to act any other way because they didn't like that at all. The old man's words were like a curse. On my graduation day I delivered an oration in which I showed that humility was the secret, indeed, the very essence of progress. (Not that I believed this—how could I, remembering my grandfather? —I only believed that it worked.) It was a great success. Everyone praised me and I was invited to give the speech at a gathering of the town's leading white citizens. It was a triumph for our whole community.

It was in the main ballroom of the leading hotel. When I got there I discovered that it was on the occasion of a smoker, and I was told that since I was to be there anyway I might as well take part in the battle royal to be fought by some of my schoolmates as part of the entertainment. The battle royal came first.

All of the town's big shots were there in their tuxedoes, wolfing down the buffet foods, drinking beer and whiskey and smoking black cigars. It was a large room with a high ceiling. Chairs were arranged in neat rows around three sides of a portable boxing ring. The fourth side was clear, revealing a gleaming space of polished floor. I had some misgivings over the battle royal, by the way. Not from a distaste for fighting, but because I didn't care too much for the other fellows who were to take part. They were tough guys who seemed to have no grandfather's curse worrying their minds. No one could mistake their toughness. And besides, I suspected that fighting a battle royal might detract from the dignity of my speech. In those pre-invisible days I visualized myself as a potential Booker T. Washington.[1] But the other fellows didn't care too much for me either, and there were nine of them. I felt superior to them in my way, and I didn't like the manner in which we were all crowded together into the servants' elevator. Nor did they like my being there. In fact, as the warmly lighted floors flashed past the elevator we had words over the fact that I, by taking part in the fight, had knocked one of their friends out of a night's work.

We were led out of the elevator through a rococo hall into an anteroom and told to get into our fighting togs. Each of us was issued a pair of boxing gloves and ushered out into the big mirrored hall, which we entered looking cautiously about us and whispering, lest we might accidentally be heard above the noise of

---

1. Black American educator and spokesman (1856–1915) who stressed the importance of industrial training as a means for blacks to achieve economic equality.

the room. It was foggy with cigar smoke. And already the whiskey was taking effect. I was shocked to see some of the most important men of the town quite tipsy. They were all there—bankers, lawyers, judges, doctors, fire chiefs, teachers, merchants. Even one of the more fashionable pastors. Something we could not see was going on up front. A clarinet was vibrating sensuously and the men were standing up and moving eagerly forward. We were a small tight group, clustered together, our bare upper bodies touching and shining with anticipatory sweat; while up front the big shots were becoming increasingly excited over something we still could not see. Suddenly I heard the school superintendent, who had told me to come, yell, "Bring up the shines, gentlemen! Bring up the little shines!"

We were rushed up to the front of the ballroom, where it smelled even more strongly of tobacco and whiskey. Then we were pushed into place. I almost wet my pants. A sea of faces, some hostile, some amused, ringed around us, and in the center, facing us, stood a magnificent blonde—stark naked. There was a dead silence. I felt a blast of cold air chill me. I tried to back away, but they were behind me and around me. Some of the boys stood with lowered heads, trembling. I felt a wave of irrational guilt and fear. My teeth chattered, my skin turned to goose flesh, my knees knocked. Yet I was strongly attracted and looked in spite of myself. Had the price of looking been blindness, I would have looked. The hair was yellow like that of a circus kewpie doll, the face heavily powdered and rouged, as though to form an abstract mask, the eyes hollow and smeared a cool blue, the color of a baboon's butt. I felt a desire to spit upon her as my eyes brushed slowly over her body. Her breasts were firm and round as the domes of East Indian temples, and I stood so close as to see the fine skin texture and beads of pearly perspiration glistening like dew around the pink and erected buds of her nipples. I wanted at one and the same time to run from the room, to sink through the floor, or go to her and cover her from my eyes and the eyes of the others with my body; to feel the soft thighs, to caress her and destroy her, to love her and murder her, to hide from her, and yet to stroke where below the small American flag tattooed upon her belly her thighs formed a capital V. I had a notion that of all in the room she saw only me with her impersonal eyes.

And then she began to dance, a slow sensuous movement; the smoke of a hundred cigars clinging to her like the thinnest of veils. She seemed like a fair bird-girl girdled in veils calling to me from the angry surface of some gray and threatening sea. I was transported. Then I became aware of the clarinet playing and the big shots yelling at us. Some threatened us if we looked and others if we did not. On my right I saw one boy faint. And now a man grabbed a silver pitcher from a table and stepped close as he dashed ice water upon him and stood him up and forced two of us to support him as his head hung and moans issued from his thick bluish lips. Another boy began to plead to go home. He was the largest of the group, wearing dark red fighting trunks much too small to conceal the erection which projected from him as though in answer to the insinuating low-registered moaning of the clarinet. He tried to hide himself with his boxing gloves.

And all the while the blonde continued dancing, smiling faintly at the big shots who watched her with fascination, and faintly smiling at our fear. I noticed a certain merchant who followed her hungrily, his lips loose and drooling. He was a large man who wore diamond studs in a shirtfront which swelled with the ample paunch underneath, and each time the blonde swayed her undulating hips he ran his hand through the thin hair of his bald head and, with his arms upheld, his posture clumsy like that of an intoxicated panda, wound his belly in a slow and obscene grind. This creature was completely hypnotized. The music had quickened. As the dancer flung herself about with a detached expression on her face, the men began reaching out to touch her. I could see their beefy fingers sink into the soft flesh. Some of the others tried to stop them and she began to move around the floor in graceful circles, as they gave chase, slipping and sliding over the polished floor. It was mad. Chairs went crashing, drinks were spilt, as they ran laughing and howling after her. They caught her just as she reached a door, raised her from the floor, and tossed her as college boys are tossed at a hazing, and above her red, fixed-smiling lips I saw the terror and disgust in her eyes, almost like my own terror and that which I saw in some of the other boys. As I watched, they tossed her twice and her soft breasts seemed to flatten against the air and her legs flung wildly as she spun. Some of the more sober ones helped her to escape. And I started off the floor, heading for the anteroom with the rest of the boys.

Some were still crying and in hysteria. But as we tried to leave we were stopped and ordered to get into the ring. There was nothing to do but what we were told. All ten of us climbed under the ropes and allowed ourselves to be blindfolded with broad bands of white cloth. One of the men seemed to feel a bit sympathetic and tried to cheer us up as we stood with our backs against the ropes. Some of us tried to grin. "See that boy over there?" one of the men said. "I want you to run across at the bell and give it to him right in the belly. If you don't get him, I'm going to get you. I don't like his looks." Each of us was told the same. The blindfolds were put on. Yet even then I had been going over my speech. In my mind each word was as bright as flame. I felt the cloth pressed into place, and frowned so that it would be loosened when I relaxed.

But now I felt a sudden fit of blind terror. I was unused to darkness. It was as though I had suddenly found myself in a dark room filled with poisonous cottonmouths. I could hear the bleary voices yelling insistently for the battle royal to begin.

"Get going in there!"

"Let me at the big nigger!"

I strained to pick up the school superintendent's voice, as though to squeeze some security out of that slightly more familiar sound.

"Let me at those black sonsabitches!" someone yelled.

"No, Jackson, no!" another voice yelled. "Here, somebody, help me hold Jack."

"I want to get at that ginger-colored nigger. Tear him limb from limb," the first voice yelled.

I stood against the ropes trembling. For in those days I was what they called ginger-colored, and he sounded as though he might crunch me between his teeth like a crisp ginger cookie.

Quite a struggle was going on. Chairs were being kicked about and I could hear voices grunting as with a terrific effort. I wanted to see, to see more desperately than ever before. But the blindfold was as tight as a thick skin-puckering scab and when I raised my gloved hands to push the layers of white aside a voice yelled, "Oh, no you don't, black bastard! Leave that alone!"

"Ring the bell before Jackson kills him a coon!" someone boomed in the sudden silence. And I heard the bell clang and the sound of feet scuffling forward.

A glove smacked against my head. I pivoted, striking out stiffly as someone went past, and felt the jar ripple along the length of my arm to my shoulder. Then it seemed as though all nine of the boys had turned upon me at once. Blows pounded me from all sides while I struck out as best I could. So many blows landed upon me that I wondered if I were not the only blindfolded fighter in the ring, or if the man called Jackson hadn't succeeded in getting me after all.

Blindfolded, I could no longer control my motions. I had no dignity. I stumbled about like a baby or a drunken man. The smoke had become thicker and with each new blow it seemed to sear and further restrict my lungs. My saliva became like hot bitter glue. A glove connected with my head, filling my mouth with warm blood. It was everywhere. I could not tell if the moisture I felt upon my body was sweat or blood. A blow landed hard against the nape of my neck. I felt myself going over, my head hitting the floor. Streaks of blue light filled the black world behind the blindfold. I lay prone, pretending that I was knocked out, but felt myself seized by hands and yanked to my feet. "Get going, black boy! Mix it up!" My arms were like lead, my head smarting from blows. I managed to feel my way to the ropes and held on, trying to catch my breath. A glove landed in my midsection and I went over again, feeling as though the smoke had become a knife jabbed into my guts. Pushed this way and that by the legs milling around me, I finally pulled erect and discovered that I could see the black, sweat-washed forms weaving in the smoky-blue atmosphere like drunken dancers weaving to the rapid drumlike thuds of blows.

Everyone fought hysterically. It was complete anarchy. Everybody fought everybody else. No group fought together for long. Two, three, four, fought one, then turned to fight each other, were themselves attacked. Blows landed below the belt and in the kidney, with the gloves open as well as closed, and with my eye partly opened now there was not so much terror. I moved carefully, avoiding blows, although not too many to attract attention, fighting from group to group. The boys groped about like blind, cautious crabs crouching to protect their mid-sections, their heads pulled in short against their shoulders, their arms stretched nervously before them, with their fists testing the smoke-filled air like the knobbed feelers of hypersensitive snails. In one corner I glimpsed a boy violently punching the air and heard him scream in pain as he smashed his hand against a ring post. For a second I saw him bent over holding his hand, then going down as a blow caught his unprotected head. I played one group against the other, slipping in and throwing a punch then stepping out of range while pushing the others into the melee to take the blows blindly aimed at me. The smoke was agonizing and there were no rounds, no bells at three minute intervals to relieve our exhaustion. The room spun around me, a swirl of lights, smoke, sweating bodies surrounded by tense white faces. I bled from both nose and mouth, the blood spattering upon my chest.

The men kept yelling, "Slug him, black boy! Knock his guts out!"

"Uppercut him! Kill him! Kill that big boy!"

Taking a fake fall, I saw a boy going down heavily beside me as though we were felled by a single blow, saw a sneaker-clad foot shoot into his groin as the two who had knocked him down stumbled upon him. I rolled out of range, feeling a twinge of nausea.

The harder we fought the more threatening the men became. And yet, I had begun to worry about my speech again. How would it go? Would they recognize my ability? What would they give me?

I was fighting automatically when suddenly I noticed that one after another of the boys was leaving the ring. I was surprised, filled with panic, as though I had been left alone with an unknown danger. Then I understood. The boys had arranged it among themselves. It was custom for the two men left in the ring to slug it out for the winner's prize. I discovered this too late. When the bell sounded two men in tuxedoes leaped into the ring and removed the blindfold. I found myself facing Tatlock, the biggest of the gang. I felt sick at my stomach. Hardly had the bell stopped ringing in my ears than it clanged again and I saw him moving swiftly toward me. Thinking of nothing else to do I hit him smash on the nose. He kept coming, bringing the rank sharp violence of stale sweat. His face was a black blank of a face, only his eyes alive—with hate of me and aglow with a feverish terror from what had happened to us all. I became anxious. I wanted to deliver my speech and he came at me as though he meant to beat it out of me. I smashed him again and again, taking his blows as they came. Then on a sudden impulse I struck him lightly and as we clinched, I whispered, "Fake like I knocked you out, you can have the prize."

"I'll break your behind," he whispered hoarsely.

"For *them?*"

"For *me*, sonofabitch."

They were yelling for us to break it up and Tatlock spun me half around with a blow, and as a joggled camera sweeps in a reeling scene, I saw the howling red faces crouching tense beneath the cloud of blue-gray smoke. For a moment the world wavered, unraveled, flowed, then my head cleared and Tatlock bounced before me. The fluttering shadow before my eyes was his jabbing left hand. Then falling foward, my head against his damp shoulder, I whispered.

"I'll make it five dollars more."

"Go to hell!"

But his muscles relaxed a trifle beneath my pressure and I breathed, "Seven?"

"Give it to your ma," he said, ripping me beneath the heart.

And while I still held him I butted him and moved away. I felt myself bombarded with punches. I fought back with hopeless desperation. I wanted to deliver my speech more than anything else in the world, because I felt only these men could judge truly my ability, and now this stupid clown was ruining my chances. I began fighting carefully now, moving in to punch him and out again with my greater speed. A lucky blow to his chin and I had him going too—until I heard a loud voice yell, "I got my money on the big boy."

Hearing this, I almost dropped my guard. I was confused: Should I try to win against the voice out there? Would not this go against my speech, and was not this a moment for humility, for nonresistance? A blow to my head as I danced about sent my right eye popping like a jack-in-the-box and settled my dilemma. The room went red as I fell. It was a dream fall, my body languid and fastidious as to where to land, until the floor became impatient and smashed up to meet me. A moment later I came to. An hypnotic voice said FIVE emphatically. And I lay there, hazily watching a dark red spot of my own blood shaping itself into a butterfly, glistening and soaking into the soiled gray world of the canvas.

When the voice drawled TEN I was lifted up and dragged to a chair. I sat dazed. My eye pained and swelled with each throb of my pounding heart and I wondered if now I would be allowed to speak. I was wringing wet, my mouth still bleeding. We were grouped along the wall now. The other boys ignored me as they congratulated Tatlock and speculated as to how much they would be paid. One boy whimpered over his smashed hand. Looking up front, I saw attendants in white jackets rolling the portable ring away and placing a small square rug in the vacant space surrounded by chairs. Perhaps, I thought, I will stand on the rug to deliver my speech.

Then the M.C. called to us, "Come on up here boys and get your money."

We ran forward to where the men laughed and talked in their chairs, waiting. Everyone seemed friendly now.

"There it is on the rug," the man said. I saw the rug covered with coins of all dimensions and a few crumpled bills. But what excited me, scattered here and there, were the gold pieces.

"Boys, it's all yours," the man said. "You get all you grab."

"That's right, Sambo," a blond man said, winking at me confidentially.

I trembled with excitement, forgetting my pain. I would get the gold and the bills, I thought. I would use both hands. I would throw my body against the boys nearest me to block them from the gold.

"Get down around the rug now," the man commanded, "and don't anyone touch it until I give the signal."

"This ought to be good," I heard.

As told, we got around the square rug on our knees. Slowly the man raised his freckled hand as we followed it upward with our eyes.

I heard, "These niggers look like they're about to pray!"

Then, "Ready," the man said. "Go!"

I lunged for a yellow coin lying on the blue design of the carpet, touching it and sending a surprised shriek to join those rising around me. I tried frantically to remove my hand but could not let go. A hot, violent force tore through my body, shaking me like a wet rat. The rug was electrified. The hair bristled up on my head as I shook myself free. My muscles jumped, my nerves jangled, writhed. But I saw that this was not stopping the other boys. Laughing in fear and embarrassment, some were holding back and scooping up the coins knocked off by the painful contortions of the others. The men roared above us as we struggled.

"Pick it up, goddamnit, pick it up!" someone called like a bass-voiced parrot. "Go on, get it!"

I crawled rapidly around the floor, picking up the coins, trying to avoid the coppers and to get greenbacks and the gold. Ignoring the shock by laughing, as I brushed the coins off quickly, I discovered that I could contain the electricity —a contradiction, but it works. Then the men began to push us onto the rug. Laughing embarrassedly, we struggled out of their hands and kept after the coins. We were all wet and slippery and hard to hold. Suddenly I saw a boy lifted into the air, glistening with sweat like a circus seal, and dropped, his wet back landing flush upon the charged rug, heard him yell and saw him literally dance upon his back, his elbows beating a frenzied tattoo upon the floor, his muscles twitching like the flesh of a horse stung by many flies. When he finally rolled off, his face was gray and no one stopped him when he ran from the floor amid booming laughter.

"Get the money," the M.C. called. "That's good hard American cash!"

And we snatched and grabbed, snatched and grabbed. I was careful not to come too close to the rug now, and when I felt the hot whiskey breath descend upon me like a cloud of foul air I reached out and grabbed the leg of a chair. It was occupied and I held on desperately.

"Leggo nigger! Leggo!"

The huge face wavered down to mine as he tried to push me free. But my body was slippery and he was too drunk. It was Mr. Colcord, who owned a chain of movie houses and "entertainment palaces." Each time he grabbed me I slipped out of his hands. It became a real struggle. I feared the rug more than I did the drunk, so I held on, surprising myself for a moment by trying to topple *him* upon the rug. It was such an enormous idea that I found myself actually carrying it out. I tried not to be obvious, yet when I grabbed his leg, trying to tumble him out of the chair, he raised up roaring with laughter, and, looking at me with soberness dead in the eye, kicked me viciously in the chest. The chair leg flew out of my hand and I felt myself going and rolled. It was as though I had rolled through a bed of hot coals. It seemed a whole century would pass before I would roll free, a century in which I was seared through the deepest levels of my body to the fearful breath within me and the breath seared and heated to the point of explosion. It'll all be over in a flash, I thought as I rolled clear. It'll all be over in a flash.

But not yet, the men on the other side were waiting, red faces swollen as though from apoplexy as they bent forward in their chairs. Seeing their fingers coming toward me I rolled away as a fumbled football rolls off the receiver's fingertips, back into the coals. That time I luckily sent the rug sliding out of place and heard the coins ringing against the floor and the boys scuffling to pick them up and the M.C. calling, "All right, boys, that's all. Go get dressed and get your money."

I was limp as a dish rag. My back felt as though it had been beaten with wires.

When we had dressed the M.C. came in and gave us each five dollars, except Tatlock, who got ten for being last in the ring. Then he told us to leave. I was not to get a chance to deliver my speech, I thought. I was going out into the dim alley in despair when I was stopped and told to go back. I returned to the ballroom, where the men were pushing back their chairs and gathering in groups to talk.

The M.C. knocked on a table for quiet. "Gentlemen," he said, "we almost forgot an important part of the program. A most serious part, gentlemen. This boy was brought here to deliver a speech which he made at his graduation yesterday . . ."

"Bravo!"

"I'm told that he is the smartest boy we've got out there in Greenwood. I'm told that he knows more big words than a pocket-sized dictionary."

Much applause and laughter.

"So now, gentlemen, I want you to give him your attention."

There was still laughter as I faced them, my mouth dry, my eye throbbing. I began slowly, but evidently my throat was tense, because they began shouting, "Louder! Louder!"

"We of the younger generation extol the wisdom of that great leader and educator,'' I shouted, ''who first spoke these flaming words of wisdom.[2] 'A ship lost at sea for many days suddenly sighted a friendly vessel. From the mast of the unfortunate vessel was seen a signal: ''Water, water; we die of thirst!'' The answer from the friendly vessel came back: ''Cast down your bucket where you are.'' The captain of the distressed vessel, at last heeding the injunction, cast down his bucket, and it came up full of fresh sparkling water from the mouth of the Amazon River.' And like him I say, and in his words, 'To those of my race who depend upon bettering their condition in a foreign land, or who underestimate the importance of cultivating friendly relations with the Southern white man, who is his next-door neighbor, I would say: ''Cast down your bucket where you are''—cast it down in making friends in every manly way of the people of all races by whom we are surrounded. . . .'''

I spoke automatically and with such fervor that I did not realize that the men were still talking and laughing until my dry mouth, filling up with blood from the cut, almost strangled me. I coughed, wanting to stop and go to one of the tall brass, sand-filled spittoons to relieve myself, but a few of the men, especially the superintendent, were listening and I was afraid. So I gulped it down, blood, saliva, and all, and continued. (What powers of endurance I had during those days! What enthusiasm! What a belief in the rightness of things!) I spoke even louder in spite of the pain. But still they talked and still they laughed, as though deaf with cotton in dirty ears. So I spoke with greater emotional emphasis. I closed my ears and swallowed blood until I was nauseated. The speech seemed a hundred times as long as before, but I could not leave out a single word. All had to be said, each memorized nuance considered, rendered. Nor was that all. Whenever I uttered a word of three or more syllables a group of voices would yell for me to repeat it. I used the phrase ''social responsibility'' and they yelled:

''What's that word you say, boy?''
''Social responsibility,'' I said.
''What?''
''Social . . .''
''Louder.''
''. . . responsibility.''
''More!''
''Respon—''
''Repeat!''
''—sibility.''

The room filled with the uproar of laughter until, no doubt, distracted by having to gulp down my blood, I made a mistake and yelled a phrase I had often seen denounced with newspaper editorials, heard debated in private.

''Social . . .''
''What?'' they yelled.
''. . . equality—''

The laughter hung smokelike in the sudden stillness. I opened my eyes, puzzled. Sounds of displeasure filled the room. The M.C. rushed forward. They

2. The quote is from a speech made by Booker T. Washington in Atlanta in 1895 in which he denounced black agitation for social betterment and encouraged blacks to achieve economic equality before seeking social equality. His views were vigorously condemned by more militant black leaders.

shouted hostile phrases at me. But I did not understand.

A small dry mustached man in the front row blared out, "Say that slowly, son!"

"What sir?"

"What you just said!"

"Social responsibility, sir," I said.

"You weren't being smart, were you, boy?" he said, not unkindly.

"No, sir!"

"You sure that about 'equality' was a mistake?"

"Oh, yes, sir," I said. "I was swallowing blood."

"Well, you had better speak more slowly so we can understand. We mean to do right by you, but you've got to know your place at all times. All right, now, go on with your speech."

I was afraid. I wanted to leave but I wanted also to speak and I was afraid they'd snatch me down.

"Thank you, sir," I said, beginning where I had left off, and having them ignore me as before.

Yet when I finished there was a thunderous applause. I was surprised to see the superintendent come forth with a package wrapped in white tissue paper, and, gesturing for quiet, address the men.

"Gentlemen, you see that I did not overpraise this boy. He makes a good speech and some day he'll lead his people in the proper paths. And I don't have to tell you that that is important in these days and times. This is a good, smart boy, and so to encourage him in the right direction, in the name of the Board of Education I wish to present him a prize in the form of this . . ."

He paused, removing the tissue paper and revealing a gleaming calfskin brief case.

". . . in the form of this first-class article from Shad Whitmore's shop."

"Boy," he said, addressing me, "take this prize and keep it well. Consider it a badge of office. Prize it. Keep developing as you are and some day it will be filled with important papers that will help shape the destiny of your people."

I was so moved that I could hardly express my thanks. A rope of bloody saliva forming a shape like an undiscovered continent drooled upon the leather and I wiped it quickly away. I felt an importance that I had never dreamed.

"Open it and see what's inside," I was told.

My fingers a-tremble, I complied, smelling the fresh leather and finding an official-looking document inside. It was a scholarship to the state college for Negroes. My eyes filled with tears and I ran awkwardly off the floor.

I was overjoyed; I did not even mind when I discovered that the gold pieces I had scrambled for were brass pocket tokens advertising a certain make of automobile.

When I reached home everyone was excited. Next day the neighbors came to congratulate me. I even felt safe from grandfather, whose deathbed curse usually spoiled my triumphs. I stood beneath his photograph with my brief case in hand and smiled triumphantly into his stolid black peasant's face. It was a face that fascinated me. The eyes seemed to follow everywhere I went.

That night I dreamed I was at a circus with him and that he refused to laugh at the clowns no matter what they did. Then later he told me to open my brief case and read what was inside and I did, finding an official envelope stamped with the state seal; and inside the envelope I found another and another, endlessly, and I thought I would fall of weariness. "Them's years," he said. "Now open that one." And I did and in it I found an engraved document containing a short message in letters of gold. "Read it," my grandfather said. "Out loud."

"To Whom It May Concern," I intoned. "Keep This Nigger-Boy Running."

I awoke with the old man's laughter ringing in my ears.

(It was a dream I was to remember and dream again for many years after. But at that time I had no insight into its meaning. First I had to attend college.)

Questions for Study

1. Why are we not told the protagonist's name?
2. To whom has his grandfather been a traitor? How does his "curse" undermine the protagonist's self-confidence? How does it distinguish him from the other "tough guys" in the battle?
3. Find as many references to being blinded or blindfolded as you can. In what different ways is the protagonist "blinded"? In what different ways does he swallow blood?
4. When he and Tatlock clinch together, what does the protagonist think Tatlock is doing "for them," the spectators? What is the protagonist doing "for them"?
5. Why does the protagonist hesitate when one man yells, "I got my money on the big boy"? Find other similar incidents of his uncertainty and explain what they reveal about his character.
6. Why is the protagonist so desperate to make his speech? Why does the superintendent want him to make it? Why do the men want him to make it? How is it appropriate that he is on the same program with the free-for-all? With the blonde dancer?
7. Why does the scholarship make the protagonist forget the brass tokens? Why does it seem to protect him from his grandfather?
8. Does the protagonist understand how he is used at the smoker? Does he experience an epiphany? If so, when? What does he seem to know, twenty years later, that he did not know at the time of the battle?

Chapter 4
Setting

The events in a story do not occur in a vacuum; they must happen in some place and at some time. In other words, fiction has setting. The term **setting** refers not only to the physical location and to the specific time or period in which the action takes place but also to the psychological and the social environment. The setting may be a vast landscape as in Ray Bradbury's Martian world of "August 2002: Night Meeting"; or it may be a confined interior such as the grocery store in Updike's "A & P." In either case, setting should help explain and clarify action and character. And it may in itself directly or indirectly convey meaning.

To assess the relative importance of setting in a particular work of fiction, we might imagine the story occurring in another time and place. If it can be updated or relocated, we may conclude that setting makes little essential contribution to the tale. The setting would then be mentioned only because events must occur somewhere. In "The Incautious Burglar," for example, setting is relatively unimportant. Even though the action takes place in a specified country mansion, it could occur in the home of any art collector anywhere without losing its effectiveness. Many stories, however, would be seriously altered or diminished by any change in setting. "Gimpel the Fool," for instance, would be altered beyond recognition if it were set anywhere other than in a Yiddish community in eastern Europe during the nineteenth century. Such a setting is more than arbitrary; it directs, shapes, and often controls the action.

Setting may function simply to establish the credibility or the believability of the story. Because Ray Bradbury's science-fiction piece is set on the planet Mars in the year 2002, the author must make the incredible seem credible. He does so largely through presenting this quite unimaginable setting in what are really a few commonplace and "earthly" terms: a roadside service station, an old-timer as attendant, an auto, a highway, a dark night. These are concrete particulars that make the almost unimaginable seem comprehensible and even familiar.

An author's purpose in creating an authentic and convincing setting is to clarify and reinforce the characters and actions in his narrative. But he may become so involved in accumulating details that he loses sight of the story. An exaggerated interest in setting is sometimes a problem in local-color fiction, or fiction that exists primarily to illustrate the particular habits, customs, and speech of a definite locale. Mark Twain's *Huckleberry Finn*, for example, contains many details of local color that portray the peculiar social customs and speech patterns common to people living along the Mississippi River in the 1850s. Yet Twain's artistry goes far beyond his vivid portrait of this region during this time to convey a theme with a much wider application.

Local-color fiction tends to accumulate details for their own sake; highly crafted fiction tends to pare down details for the story's sake. The writer of short fiction in particular has to limit and select the background details he presents. He works through selection rather than accumulation by choosing particular details of setting that carry special significance. A story may be essentially a mood piece, with all the details chosen for their psychological connotations. In such a story details of the setting which do not contribute to the effect are omitted, while everything introduced should contribute to the mood of the piece. In "A & P," for instance, Updike does not mention any special features of the store which would make it distinctive. The very ordinariness of the packaged goods and the grocery store establishes a sense of the commonplace, and this setting colors our impression of the workers and the patrons as well. In "Battle Royal" the smoke-filled, noisy, overcrowded hotel room itself becomes threatening to the narrator. Sometimes, conventional details of setting are also used less subtly to contribute to the story's "single effect." Flowers and sunshine bring out thoughts of love in romantic stories, just as abandoned houses and thunderstorms trigger fear in mystery stories.

Whether they do so in a fresh or stale manner, particular details of setting must have relevance to the narrative in order to be included. British novelist Elizabeth Bowen explains that "scene is only justified in the novel where it can be shown, or at least felt, to act upon action or character. In fact, where it has dramatic use." In Doris Lessing's "The Old Chief Mshlanga," the author tells us nothing about the young narrator's house, but she describes the African landscape in lavish, poetic detail. She does so because the young girl's actions and character are influenced by that landscape, not by the house she lives in.

Setting may explain behavior in rather obvious ways. Knowing something about the social, economic, educational, religious, and family background of people helps us understand why they act as they do. Knowing that Gimpel in "Gimpel the Fool" lives in an east European Yiddish community, that the narrator of "Battle Royal" is a young black man in the American South, and that the main character of "The Old Chief Mshlanga" is a white girl in South Africa clarifies each situation and supports the action in each story.

Setting may also be explanatory in less obvious, more subtle ways. What seems to be, for example, a surface description of a landscape may include within itself suggestions of a reality beneath or beyond the surface. In "The Old Chief Mshlanga," a description of an African mealie field begins to sound like an Anglican church: the girl pushes "through the green aisles of mealie stalks, the leaves arching like cathedrals veined with sunlight far overhead, with the packed red earth underfoot . . . ." We recognize that the child prefers to think of this land in terms of another that she cherishes in her imagination. And so we learn more about her psychology than about mealie fields. Lessing also contrasts the lush green valley where the "grass was thick and soft" and "the trees stood tall and shapely" with the white colonizers' farm where "hundreds of acres of harsh eroded soil bore trees that had been cut for the mine furnaces and had grown thin and twisted." The settlers may not literally have twisted African trees, but that description suggests the exploitation of the land. As we come to understand how the land has been violated, we sense, with a few explicit examples, how the natives too have been violated. And we find it absurd that the child's father, who has himself spoiled the landscape, wants satisfaction because one night his "big red land was trampled down by small sharp hooves" of the old chief's goats. Here we see how Lessing, with a few carefully selected details, uses setting to establish background and situation, to create a mood, and also to convey much of the story's meaning.

In the carefully crafted story, setting is neither passive nor arbitrary. In Eudora Welty's words, setting is the "gathering-spot of all that has been felt, and is about to be experienced." It is a concrete and precise focus of an entire situation. It may be a physical parallel to a psychological reality—what happens to the land in Lessing's story parallels what happens to its people. Or it may explain a situation and make it believable—what happens on Mars in Bradbury's story is both bizarre and commonplace; and thus the bizarre is made comprehensible. No matter how it is used, setting should underscore, heighten, and intensify the narrative itself.

Ray Bradbury (b. 1920)
August 2002: Night Meeting

Before going on up into the blue hills, Tomás Gomez stopped for gasoline at the lonely station.

"Kind of alone out here, aren't you, Pop?" said Tomás.

The old man wiped off the windshield of the small truck. "Not bad."

"How do you like Mars, Pop?"

"Fine. Always something new. I made up my mind when I came here last year I wouldn't expect nothing, nor ask nothing, nor be surprised at nothing. We've got to forget Earth and how things were. We've got to look at what we're in here, and how *different* it is. I get a hell of a lot of fun out of just the weather here. It's *Martian* weather. Hot as hell daytimes, cold as hell nights. I get a big kick out of the different flowers and different rain. I came to Mars to retire and I wanted to retire in a place where everything is different. An old man needs to have things different. Young people don't want to talk to him, other old people bore hell out of him. So I thought the best thing for me is a place so different that all you got to do is open your eyes and you're entertained. I got this gas station. If business picks up too much, I'll move on back to some other old highway that's not so busy, where I can earn just enough to live on and still have time to feel the *different* things here."

"You got the right idea, Pop," said Tomás, his brown hands idly on the wheel. He was feeling good. He had been working in one of the new colonies for ten days straight and now he had two days off and was on his way to a party.

"I'm not surprised at anything any more," said the old man. "I'm just looking. I'm just experiencing. If you can't take Mars for what she is, you might as well go back to Earth. Everything's crazy up here, the soil, the air, the canals, the natives (I never saw any yet, but I hear they're around), the clocks. Even my clock acts funny. Even *time* is crazy up here. Sometimes I feel I'm here all by myself, no one else on the whole damn planet. I'd take bets on it. Sometimes I feel about eight years old, my body squeezed up and everything else tall. Jesus, it's just the place for an old man. Keeps me alert and keeps me happy. You know what Mars is? It's like a thing I got for Christmas seventy years ago—don't know if you ever had one—they called them kaleidoscopes, bits of crystal and cloth and beads and pretty junk. You held it up to the sunlight and looked in through at it, and it took your breath away. All the patterns! Well, that's Mars. Enjoy it. Don't ask it to be nothing else but what it is. Jesus, you know that highway right there, built by the Martians, is over sixteen centuries old and still in good condition? That's one dollar and fifty cents, thanks and good night."

Tomás drove off down the ancient highway, laughing quietly.

It was a long road going into darkness and hills and he held to the wheel, now and again reaching into his lunch bucket and taking out a piece of candy. He had been driving steadily for an hour, with no other car on the road, no light, just the road going under, the hum, the roar, and Mars out there, so quiet. Mars was always quiet, but quieter tonight than any other. The deserts and empty seas swung by him, and the mountains against the stars.

There was a smell of Time in the air tonight. He smiled and turned the fancy in his mind. There was a thought. What did Time smell like? Like dust and clocks and people. And if you wondered what Time sounded like it sounded like water running in a dark cave and voices crying and dirt dropping down upon hollow box lids, and rain. And, going further, what did Time *look* like? Time looked like snow dropping silently into a black room or it looked like a silent film in an ancient theater, one hundred billion faces falling like those New Year balloons, down and down into nothing. That was how Time smelled and looked and sounded. And tonight—Tomás shoved a hand into the wind outside the truck—tonight you could almost *touch* Time.

He drove the truck between hills of Time. His neck prickled and he sat up, watching ahead.

He pulled into a little dead Martian town, stopped the engine, and let the silence come in around him. He sat, not breathing, looking out at the white buildings in the moonlight. Uninhabited for centuries. Perfect, faultless, in ruins, yes, but perfect, nevertheless.

He started the engine and drove another mile or more before stopping again, climbing out, carrying his lunch bucket, and walking to a little promontory where he could look back at that dusty city. He opened his thermos and poured himself a cup of coffee. A night bird flew by. He felt very good, very much at peace.

Perhaps five minutes later there was a sound. Off in the hills, where the ancient highway curved, there was a motion, a dim light, and then a murmur.

Tomás turned slowly with the coffee cup in his hand.

And out of the hills came a strange thing.

It was a machine like a jade-green insect, a praying mantis, delicately rushing through the cold air, indistinct, countless green diamonds winking over its body, and red jewels that glittered with multifaceted eyes. Its six legs fell upon the ancient highway with the sounds of a sparse rain which dwindled away, and from the back of the machine a Martian with melted gold for eyes looked down at Tomás as if he were looking into a well.

Tomás raised his hand and thought Hello! automatically but did not move his lips, for this *was* a Martian. But Tomás had swum in blue rivers on Earth, with strangers passing on the road, and eaten in strange houses with strange people, and his weapon had always been his smile. He did not carry a gun. And he did not feel the need of one now, even with the little fear that gathered about his heart at this moment.

The Martian's hands were empty too. For a moment they looked across the cool air at each other.

It was Tomás who moved first.

"Hello!" he called.

"Hello!" called the Martian in his own language.

They did not understand each other.

"Did you say hello?" they both asked.

"What did you say?" they said, each in a different tongue.

They scowled.

"Who are you?" said Tomás in English.

"What are you doing here?" In Martian; the stranger's lips moved.

"Where are you going?" they said, and looked bewildered.

"I'm Tomás Gomez."

"I'm Muhe Ca."

Neither understood, but they tapped their chests with the words and then it became clear.

And then the Martian laughed. "Wait!" Tomás felt his head touched, but no hand had touched him. "There!" said the Martian in English. "That is better!"

"You learned my language, so quick!"

"Nothing at all!"

They looked, embarrassed with a new silence, at the steaming coffee he had in one hand.

"Something different?" said the Martian, eying him and the coffee, referring to them both, perhaps.

"May I offer you a drink?" said Tomás.

"Please."

The Martian slid down from his machine.

A second cup was produced and filled, steaming. Tomás held it out.

Their hands met and—like mist—fell through each other.

"Jesus Christ!" cried Tomás, and dropped the cup.

"Name of the Gods!" said the Martian in his own tongue.

"Did you see what happened?" they both whispered.

They were very cold and terrified.

The Martian bent to touch the cup but could not touch it.

"Jesus!" said Tomás.

"Indeed." The Martian tried again and again to get hold of the cup, but could not. He stood up and thought for a moment, then took a knife from his belt. "Hey!" cried Tomás. "You misunderstand, catch!" said the Martian, and tossed it. Tomás cupped his hands. The knife fell through his flesh. It hit the ground. Tomás bent to pick it up but could not touch it, and he recoiled, shivering.

Now he looked at the Martian against the sky.

"The stars!" he said.

"The stars!" said the Martian, looking, in turn, at Tomás.

The stars were white and sharp beyond the flesh of the Martian, and they were sewn into his flesh like scintillas swallowed into the thin, phosphorescent membrane of a gelatinous sea fish. You could see stars flickering like violet eyes in the Martian's stomach and chest, and through his wrists, like jewelry.

"I can see through you!" said Tomás.

"And I through you!" said the Martian, stepping back.

Tomás felt of his own body and, feeling the warmth, was reassured. *I am real*, he thought.

The Martian touched his own nose and lips. "*I* have flesh," he said, half aloud. "*I* am alive."

Tomás stared at the stranger. "And if *I* am real, then you must be dead."

"No, you!"

"A ghost!"

"A phantom!"

They pointed at each other, with starlight burning in their limbs like daggers and icicles and fireflies, and then fell to judging their limbs again, each finding himself intact, hot, excited, stunned, awed, and the other, ah yes, that other over there, unreal, a ghostly prism flashing the accumulated light of distant worlds.

I'm drunk, thought Tomás. I won't tell anyone of this tomorrow, no, no.

They stood there on the ancient highway, neither of them moving.

"Where are you from?" asked the Martian at last.

"Earth."

"What is that?"

"There." Tomás nodded to the sky.

"When?"

"We landed over a year ago, remember?"

"No."

"And all of you were dead, all but a few. You're rare, don't you *know* that?"

"That's not true."

"Yes, dead. I saw the bodies. Black, in the rooms, in the houses, dead. Thousands of them."

"That's ridiculous. We're *alive!*"

"Mister, you're invaded, only you don't know it. You must have escaped."

"I haven't escaped; there was nothing to escape. What do you mean? I'm on my way to a festival now at the canal, near the Eniall Mountains. I was there last night. Don't you see the city there?" The Martian pointed.

Tomás looked and saw the ruins. "Why, that city's been dead thousands of years."

The Martian laughed. "Dead. I slept there yesterday!"

"And I was in it a week ago and the week before that, and I just drove through it now, and it's a heap. See the broken pillars?"

"Broken? Why, I see them perfectly. The moonlight helps. And the pillars are upright."

"There's dust in the streets," said Tomás.

"The streets are clean!"

"The canals are empty right there."

"The canals are full of lavender wine!"

"It's dead."

"It's alive!" protested the Martian, laughing more now. "Oh, you're quite wrong. See all the carnival lights? There are beautiful boats as slim as women, beautiful women as slim as boats, women the color of sand, women with fire flowers in their hands. I can see them, small, running in the streets there. That's where I'm going now, to the festival; we'll float on the waters all night long; we'll sing, we'll drink, we'll make love. Can't you *see* it?"

"Mister, that city is dead as a dried lizard. Ask any of our party. Me, I'm on my way to Green City tonight; that's the new colony we just raised over near Illinois Highway. You're mixed up. We brought in a million board feet of Oregon lumber and a couple dozen tons of good steel nails and hammered together two of the nicest little villages you ever saw. Tonight we're warming one of them. A couple rockets are coming in from Earth, bringing our wives and girl friends. There'll be barn dances and whisky——"

The Martian was now disquieted. "You say it is over *that* way?"

"There are the rockets." Tomás walked him to the edge of the hill and pointed down. "See?"

"No."

"Damn it, there they *are!* Those long silver things."

"No."

Now Tomás laughed. "You're blind!"

"I see very well. You are the one who does not see."

"But you see the new *town,* don't you?"

"I see nothing but an ocean, and water at low tide."

"Mister, that water's been evaporated for forty centuries."

"Ah, now, now, that *is* enough."

"It's true, I tell you."

The Martian grew very serious. "Tell me again. You do not see the city the way I describe it? The pillars very white, the boats very slender, the festival lights—oh, I see them *clearly!* And listen! I can hear them singing. It's no space away at all."

Tomás listened and shook his head. "No."

"And I, on the other hand," said the Martian, "cannot see what you describe. Well."

Again they were cold. An ice was in their flesh.

"Can it be . . . ?"

"What?"

"You say 'from the sky'?"

"Earth."

"Earth, a name, nothing," said the Martian. "*But* . . . as I came up the pass an hour ago . . ." He touched the back of his neck. "I felt . . ."

"Cold?"

"Yes."

"And now?"

"Cold again. Oddly. There was a thing to the light, to the hills, the road," said the Martian. "I felt the strangeness, the road, the light, and for a moment I felt as if I were the last man alive on this world. . . ."

"So did I!" said Tomás, and it was like talking to an old and dear friend, confiding, growing warm with the topic.

The Martian closed his eyes and opened them again. "This can only mean one thing. It has to do with Time. Yes. You are a figment of the Past!"

"No, you are from the Past," said the Earth Man, having had time to think of it now.

"You are so *certain.* How can you prove who is from the Past, who from the Future? What year is it?"

"Two thousand and one!"

"What does that mean to *me?*"

Tomás considered and shrugged. "Nothing."

"It is as if I told you that it is the year 4462853 s.e.c. It is nothing and more than nothing! Where is the clock to show us how the stars stand?"

"But the ruins prove it! They prove that *I* am the Future. *I* am alive, *you* are dead!"

"Everything in me denies this. My heart beats, my stomach hungers, my mouth thirsts. No, no, not dead, not alive, either of us. More alive than anything else. Caught between is more like it. Two strangers passing in the night, that is it. Two strangers passing. Ruins, you say?"

"Yes. You're afraid?"

"Who wants to see the Future, who *ever* does? A man can face the Past, but to think—the pillars *crumbled,* you say? And the sea empty, and the canals dry, and the maidens dead, and the flowers withered?" The Martian was silent, but then he looked on ahead. "But there they *are.* I *see* them. Isn't that enough for me? They wait for me now, no matter *what* you say."

And for Tomás the rockets, far away, waiting for *him,* and the town and the women from Earth. "We can never agree," he said.

"Let us agree to disagree," said the Martian. "What does it matter who is Past or Future, if we are both alive, for what follows will follow, tomorrow or in ten thousand years. How do you know that those temples are not the temples of your own civilization one hundred centuries from now, tumbled and broken? You do not know. Then don't ask. But the night is very short. There go the festival fires in the sky, and the birds."

Tomás put out his hand. The Martian did likewise in imitation.

Their hands did not touch; they melted through each other.

"Will we meet again?"

"Who knows? Perhaps some other night."

"I'd like to go with you to that festival."

"And I wish I might come to your new town, to see this ship you speak of, to see these men, to hear all that has happened."

"Good-by," said Tomás.

"Good night."

The Martian rode his green metal vehicle quietly away into the hills. The Earth Man turned his truck and drove it silently in the opposite direction.

"Good lord, what a dream that was," sighed Tomás, his hands on the wheel, thinking of the rockets, the women, the raw whisky, the Virginia reels, the party.

How strange a vision was that, thought the Martian, rushing on, thinking of the festival, the canals, the boats, the women with golden eyes, and the songs.

The night was dark. The moons had gone down. Starlight twinkled on the empty highway where now there was not a sound, no car, no person, nothing. And it remained that way all the rest of the cool dark night.

Questions for Study

1. How important are the details given in the opening conversation between Tomás Gomez and the old man at the gasoline station? How do any of them suggest later events?
2. In his first sustained speech the old station attendant gives us his views on living in a new and strange place. What precisely are these views? How do they relate to the rest of the story?
3. Tomás insists that he is the Future. Neither the Martian nor the story exactly denies this. What sort of answer does the Martian make?
4. Why cannot Tomás and the Martian touch and see the same things? What do they actually share in common? How does each relate to time and place?
5. Why does Bradbury continually emphasize time and the senses of smell, sound, sight, and touch?

6. How is the machine described? What sort of description of the Martian does Bradbury give us? Does there seem to be more of a description than there actually is? If so, why?

7. In the end both Tomás and Martian prefer to regard their meeting as merely a dream or a vision. Why do they take this view? Is this position then part of Bradbury's message? Explain your reading of the story and of what the author is trying to communicate.

8. The narrative does not end with the separation of Tomás and the Martian but with a description of the empty highway. Relate this ending to your interpretation of the story.

Doris Lessing (b. 1919)
The Old Chief Mshlanga

They were good, the years of ranging the bush over her father's farm which, like every white farm, was largely unused, broken only occasionally by small patches of cultivation. In between, nothing but trees, the long sparse grass, thorn and cactus and gully, grass and outcrop and thorn. And a jutting piece of rock which had been thrust up from the warm soil of Africa unimaginable eras of time ago, washed into hollows and whorls by sun and wind that had travelled so many thousands of miles of space and bush, would hold the weight of a small girl whose eyes were sightless for anything but a pale willowed river, a pale gleaming castle—a small girl singing: "Out flew the web and floated wide, the mirror cracked from side to side . . . ."

Pushing her way through the green aisles of the mealie[1] stalks, the leaves arching like cathedrals veined with sunlight far overhead, with the packed red earth underfoot, a fine lace of red starred witchweed would summon up a black bent figure croaking premonitions: the Northern witch, bred of cold Northern forests, would stand before her among the mealie fields, and it was the mealie fields that faded and fled, leaving her among the gnarled roots of an oak, snow falling thick and soft and white, the woodcutter's fire glowing red welcome through crowding tree trunks.

A white child, opening its eyes curiously on a sun-suffused landscape, a gaunt and violent landscape, might be supposed to accept it as her own, to take the msasa trees[2] and the thorn trees as familiars, to feel her blood running free and responsive to the swing of the seasons.

This child could not see a msasa tree, or the thorn, for what they were. Her books held tales of alien fairies, her rivers ran slow and peaceful, and she knew the shape of the leaves of an ash or an oak, the names of the little creatures that lived in English streams, when the words "the veld"[3] meant strangeness, though she could remember nothing else.

---

1. Indian corn.
2. Native African trees having small petals and leaves.
3. Unenclosed grassland in South Africa.

Because of this, for many years, it was the veld that seemed unreal; the sun was a foreign sun, and the wind spoke a strange language.

The black people on the farm were as remote as the trees and the rocks. They were an amorphous black mass, mingling and thinning and massing like tadpoles, faceless, who existed merely to serve, to say "Yes, Baas," take their money and go. They changed season by season, moving from one farm to the next, according to their outlandish needs, which one did not have to understand, coming from perhaps hundreds of miles North or East, passing on after a few months—where? Perhaps even as far away as the fabled gold mines of Johannesburg,[4] where the pay was so much better than the few shillings a month and the double handful of mealie meal twice a day which they earned in that part of Africa.

The child was taught to take them for granted: the servants in the house would come running a hundred yards to pick up a book if she dropped it. She was called "Nkosikaas"—Chieftainess, even by the black children her own age.

Later, when the farm grew too small to hold her curiosity, she carried a gun in the crook of her arm and wandered miles a day, from vlei[5] to vlei, from *kopje*[6] to *kopje*, accompanied by two dogs: the dogs and the gun were an armour against fear. Because of them she never felt fear.

If a native came into sight along the kaffir[7] paths half a mile away, the dogs would flush him up a tree as if he were a bird. If he expostulated (in his uncouth language which was by itself ridiculous) that was cheek. If one was in a good mood, it could be a matter for laughter. Otherwise one passed on, hardly glancing at the angry man in the tree.

On the rare occasions when white children met together they could amuse themselves by hailing a passing native in order to make a buffoon of him; they could set the dogs on him and watch him run; they could tease a small black child as if he were a puppy—save that they would not throw stones and sticks at a dog without a sense of guilt.

Later still, certain questions presented themselves in the child's mind; and because the answers were not easy to accept, they were silenced by an even greater arrogance of manner.

It was even impossible to think of the black people who worked about the house as friends, for if she talked to one of them, her mother would come running anxiously: "Come away; you musn't talk to natives."

It was this instilled consciousness of danger, of something unpleasant, that made it easy to laugh out loud, crudely, if a servant made a mistake in his English or if he failed to understand an order—there is a certain kind of laughter that is fear, afraid of itself.

One evening, when I was about fourteen, I was walking down the side of a mealie field that had been newly ploughed, so that the great red clods showed fresh and tumbling to the vlei beyond, like a choppy red sea; it was that hushed and listening hour, when the birds send long sad calls from tree to tree, and all

---

4. Largest city and industrial center of the Republic of South Africa.
5. Marshy depression in which water collects during the rainy season; a temporary lake.
6. Small rounded hill of the South African veld.
7. Member of a group of South African Bantu-speaking people of Ngoni stock.

the colours of earth and sky and leaf are deep and golden. I had my rifle in the curve of my arm, and the dogs were at my heels.

In front of me, perhaps a couple of hundred yards away, a group of three Africans came into sight around the side of a big antheap. I whistled the dogs close in to my skirts and let the gun swing in my hand, and advanced, waiting for them to move aside, off the path, in respect for my passing. But they came on steadily, and the dogs looked up at me for the command to chase. I was angry. It was "cheek" for a native not to stand off a path, the moment he caught sight of you.

In front walked an old man, stooping his weight on to a stick, his hair grizzled white, a dark red blanket slung over his shoulders like a cloak. Behind him came two young men, carrying bundles of pots, assegais,[8] hatchets.

The group was not a usual one. They were not natives seeking work. These had an air of dignity, of quietly following their own purpose. It was the dignity that checked my tongue. I walked quietly on, talking softly to the growling dogs, till I was ten paces away. Then the old man stopped, drawing his blanket close.

"Morning, Nkosikaas," he said, using the customary greeting for any time of the day.

"Good morning," I said. "Where are you going?" My voice was a little truculent.

The old man spoke in his own language, then one of the young men stepped forward politely and said in careful English: "My Chief travels to see his brothers beyond the river."

A Chief! I thought, understanding the pride that made the old man stand before me like an equal—more than an equal, for he showed courtesy, and I showed none.

The old man spoke again, wearing dignity like an inherited garment, still standing ten paces off, flanked by his entourage, not looking at me (that would have been rude) but directing his eyes somewhere over my head at the trees.

"You are the little Nkosikaas from the farm of Baas Jordan?"

"That's right," I said.

"Perhaps your father does not remember," said the interpreter for the old man, "but there was an affair with some goats. I remember seeing you when you were . . ." The young man held his hand at knee level and smiled.

We all smiled.

"What is your name?" I asked.

"This is Chief Mshlanga," said the young man.

"I will tell my father that I met you," I said.

The old man said: "My greetings to your father, little Nkosikaas."

"Good morning," I said politely, finding the politeness difficult, from lack of use.

"Morning, little Nkosikaas," said the old man, and stood aside to let me pass.

I went by, my gun hanging awkwardly, the dogs sniffing and growling, cheated of their favourite game of chasing natives like animals.

Not long afterwards I read in an old explorer's book the phrase: "Chief

---

8. Light spear or lance made of hardwood and tipped with iron.

Mshlanga's country." It went like this: "Our destination was Chief Mshlanga's country, to the north of the river; and it was our desire to ask his permission to prospect for gold in his territory."

The phrase "ask his permission" was so extraordinary to a white child, brought up to consider all natives as things to use, that it revived those questions, which could not be suppressed: they fermented slowly in my mind.

On another occasion one of those old prospectors who still move over Africa looking for neglected reefs, with their hammers and tents, and pans for sifting gold from crushed rock, came to the farm and, in talking of the old days, used that phrase again: "This was the Old Chief's country," he said. "It stretched from those mountains over there way back to the river, hundreds of miles of country." That was his name for our district: "The Old Chief's Country"; he did not use our name for it—a new phrase which held no implication of usurped ownership.

As I read more books about the time when this part of Africa was opened up, not much more than fifty years before, I found Old Chief Mshlanga had been a famous man, known to all the explorers and prospectors. But then he had been young; or maybe it was his father or uncle they spoke of—I never found out.

During that year I met him several times in the part of the farm that was traversed by natives moving over the country. I learned that the path up the side of the big red field where the birds sang was the recognized highway for migrants. Perhaps I even haunted it in the hope of meeting him: being greeted by him, the exchange of courtesies, seemed to answer the questions that troubled me.

Soon I carried a gun in a different spirit; I used it for shooting food and not to give me confidence. And now the dogs learned better manners. When I saw a native approaching, we offered and took greetings; and slowly that other landscape in my mind faded, and my feet struck directly on the African soil, and I saw the shapes of tree and hill clearly, and the black people moved back, as it were, out of my life: it was as if I stood aside to watch a slow intimate dance of landscape and men, a very old dance, whose steps I could not learn.

But I thought: this is my heritage, too; I was bred here; it is my country as well as the black man's country; and there is plenty of room for all of us, without elbowing each other off the pavements and roads.

It seemed it was only necessary to let free that respect I felt when I was talking with old Chief Mshlanga, to let both black and white people meet gently, with tolerance for each other's differences: it seemed quite easy.

Then, one day, something new happened. Working in our house as servants were always three natives: cook, houseboy, garden boy. They used to change as the farm natives changed: staying for a few months, then moving on to a new job, or back home to their kraals.[9] They were thought of as "good" or "bad" natives; which meant: how did they behave as servants? Were they lazy, efficient, obedient, or disrespectful? If the family felt good-humoured, the phrase was: "What can you expect from raw black savages?" If we were angry, we said: "These damned niggers, we would be much better off without them."

One day, a white policeman was on his rounds of the district, and he said

---

9. Native villages, made up of a collection of huts surrounded by a stockade.

laughingly: "Did you know you have an important man in your kitchen?"

"What!" exclaimed my mother sharply. "What do you mean?"

"A Chief's son." The policeman seemed amused. "He'll boss the tribe when the old man dies."

"He'd better not put on a Chief's son act with me," said my mother.

When the policeman left, we looked with different eyes at our cook: he was a good worker, but he drank too much at week-ends—that was how we knew him.

He was a tall youth, with very black skin, like black polished metal, his tightly-growing black hair parted white man's fashion at one side, with a metal comb from the store stuck into it; very polite, very distant, very quick to obey an order. Now that it had been pointed out, we said: "Of course, you can see. Blood always tells."

My mother became strict with him now she knew about his birth and prospects. Sometimes, when she lost her temper, she would say: "You aren't the Chief yet, you know." And he would answer her very quietly, his eyes on the ground: "Yes, Nkosikaas."

One afternoon he asked for a whole day off, instead of the customary half-day, to go home next Sunday.

"How can you go home in one day?"

"It will take me half an hour on my bicycle," he explained.

I watched the direction he took; and the next day I went off to look for this kraal; I understood he must be Chief Mshlanga's successor: there was no other kraal near enough our farm.

Beyond our boundaries on that side the country was new to me. I followed unfamiliar paths past *kopjes* that till now had been part of the jagged horizon, hazed with distance. This was Government land, which had never been cultivated by white men; at first I could not understand why it was that it appeared, in merely crossing the boundary, I had entered a completely fresh type of landscape. It was a wide green valley, where a small river sparkled, and vivid water-birds darted over the rushes. The grass was thick and soft to my calves, the trees stood tall and shapely.

I was used to our farm, whose hundreds of acres of harsh eroded soil bore trees that had been cut for the mine furnaces and had grown thin and twisted, where the cattle had dragged the grass flat, leaving innumerable criss-crossing trails that deepened each season into gullies, under the force of the rains.

This country had been left untouched, save for prospectors whose picks had struck a few sparks from the surface of the rocks as they wandered by; and for migrant natives whose passing had left, perhaps, a charred patch on the trunk of a tree where their evening fire had nestled.

It was very silent: a hot morning with pigeons cooing throatily, the midday shadows lying dense and thick with clear yellow spaces of sunlight between and in all that wide green park-like valley, not a human soul but myself.

I was listening to the quick regular tapping of a woodpecker when slowly a chill feeling seemed to grow up from the small of my back to my shoulders, in a constricting spasm like a shudder, and at the roots of my hair a tingling sensation began and ran down over the surface of my flesh, leaving me goosefleshed and cold, though I was damp with sweat. Fever? I thought; then uneasily, turned to look over my shoulder; and realized suddenly that this was fear. It was extraordinary, even humiliating. It was a new fear. For all the years I had walked by myself over this country I had never known a moment's uneasiness; in the beginning because I had been supported by a gun and the dogs, then because I had learnt an easy friendliness for the Africans I might encounter.

I had read of this feeling, how the bigness and silence of Africa, under the ancient sun, grows dense and takes shape in the mind, till even the birds seem to call menacingly, and a deadly spirit comes out of the trees and the rocks. You move warily, as if your very passing disturbs something old and evil, something dark and big and angry that might suddenly rear and strike from behind. You look at groves of entwined trees, and picture the animals that might be lurking there; you look at the river running slowly, dropping from level to level through the vlei, spreading into pools where at night the bucks come to drink, and the crocodiles rise and drag them by their soft noses into underwater caves. Fear possessed me. I found I was turning round and round, because of that shapeless menace behind me that might reach out and take me; I kept glancing at the files of *kopjes* which, seen from a different angle, seemed to change with every step so that even known landmarks, like a big mountain that had sentinelled my world since I first became conscious of it, showed an unfamiliar sunlit valley among its foothills. I did not know where I was. I was lost. Panic seized me. I found I was spinning round and round, staring anxiously at this tree and that, peering up at the sun which appeared to have moved into an eastern slant, shedding the sad yellow light of sunset. Hours must have passed! I looked at my watch and found that this state of meaningless terror had lasted perhaps ten minutes.

The point was that it was meaningless. I was not ten miles from home: I had only to take my way back along the valley to find myself at the fence; away among the foothills of the *kopjes* gleamed the roof of a neighbour's house, and a couple of hours' walking would reach it. This was the sort of fear that contracts the flesh of a dog at night and sets him howling at the full moon. It had nothing to do with what I thought or felt; and I was more disturbed by the fact that I could become its victim than of the physical sensation itself; I walked steadily on, quietened, in a divided mind, watching my own pricking nerves and apprehensive glances from side to side with a disgusted amusement. Deliberately I set myself to think of this village I was seeking, and what I should do when I entered it—if I could find it, which was doubtful, since I was walking aimlessly and it might be anywhere in the hundreds of thousands of acres of bush that stretched about me. With my mind on that village, I realized that a new sensation was added to the fear: loneliness. Now such a terror of isolation invaded me that I could hardly walk; and if it were not that I came over the crest of a small rise and saw a village below me, I should have turned and gone home. It was a cluster of thatched huts in a clearing among trees. There were neat patches of mealies and pumpkins and millet, and cattle grazed under some trees at a distance. Fowls scratched among the huts, dogs lay sleeping on the grass, and goats friezed a *kopje* that jutted up beyond a tributary of the river lying like an enclosing arm around the village.

As I came close I saw the huts were lovingly decorated with patterns of yellow and red and ochre mud on the walls; and the thatch was tied in place with plaits of straw.

This was not at all like our farm compound, a dirty and neglected place, a temporary home for migrants who had no roots in it.

And now I did not know what to do next. I called a small black boy, who was sitting on a lot playing a stringed gourd, quite naked except for the strings of blue beads round his neck, and said: "Tell the Chief I am here." The child stuck his thumb in his mouth and stared shyly back at me.

For minutes I shifted my feet on the edge of what seemed a deserted village, till at last the child scuttled off, and then some women came. They were draped in bright cloths, with brass glinting in their ears and on their arms. They also stared, silently; then turned to chatter among themselves.

I said again: "Can I see Chief Mshlanga?" I saw they caught the name; they did not understand what I wanted. I did not understand myself.

At last I walked through them and came past the huts and saw a clearing under a big shady tree, where a dozen old men sat crosslegged on the ground, talking. Chief Mshlanga was leaning back against the tree, holding a gourd in his hand, from which he had been drinking. When he saw me, not a muscle of his face moved, and I could see he was not pleased: perhaps he was afflicted with my own shyness, due to being unable to find the right forms of courtesy for the occasion. To meet me, on our own farm, was one thing; but I should not have come here. What had I expected? I could not join them socially: the thing was unheard of. Bad enough that I, a white girl, should be walking the veld alone as a white man might: and in this part of the bush where only Government officials had the right to move.

Again I stood, smiling foolishly, while behind me stood the groups of brightly-clad, chattering women, their faces alert with curiosity and interest, and in front of me sat the old men, with old lined faces, their eyes guarded, aloof. It was a village of ancients and children and women. Even the two young men who kneeled beside the Chief were not those I had seen with him previously: the young men were all away working on the white men's farms and mines, and the Chief must depend on relatives who were temporarily on holiday for his attendants.

"The small white Nkosikaas is far from home," remarked the old man at last.

"Yes," I agreed, "it is far." I wanted to say: "I have come to pay you a friendly visit, Chief Mshlanga." I could not say it. I might now be feeling an urgent helpless desire to get to know these men and women as people, to be accepted by them as a friend, but the truth was I had set out in a spirit of curiosity: I had wanted to see the village that one day our cook, the reserved and obedient young man who got drunk on Sundays, would one day rule over.

"The child of Nkosi Jordan is welcome," said Chief Mshlanga.

"Thank you," I said, and could think of nothing more to say. There was a silence, while the flies rose and began to buzz around my head; and the wind shook a little on the thick green tree that spread its branches over the old men.

"Good morning," I said at last. "I have to return now to my home."

"Morning, little Nkosikaas," said Chief Mshlanga.

I walked away from the indifferent village, over the rise past the staring amber-eyed goats, down through the tall stately trees into the great rich green valley where the river meandered and the pigeons cooed tales of plenty and the woodpecker tapped softly.

The fear had gone; the loneliness had set into stiff-necked stoicism; there was now a queer hostility in the landscape, a cold, hard, sullen indomitability that walked with me, as strong as a wall, as intangible as smoke; it seemed to say to me: you walk here as a destroyer. I went slowly homewards, with an empty heart: I had learned that if one cannot call a country to heel like a dog, neither can one dismiss the past with a smile in an easy gush of feeling, saying: I could not help it, I am also a victim.

I only saw Chief Mshlanga once again.

One night my father's big red land was trampled down by small sharp hooves, and it was discovered that the culprits were goats from Chief Mshlanga's kraal. This had happened once before, years ago.

My father confiscated all the goats. Then he sent a message to the old Chief that if he wanted them he would have to pay for the damage.

He arrived at our house at the time of sunset one evening, looking very old and bent now, walking stiffly under his regally-draped blanket, leaning on a big stick. My father sat himself down in his big chair below the steps of the house; the old man squatted carefully on the ground before him, flanked by his two young men.

The palaver was long and painful, because of the bad English of the young man who interpreted, and because my father could not speak dialect, but only kitchen kaffir.

From my father's point of view, at least two hundred pounds' worth of damage had been done to the crop. He knew he could not get the money from the old man. He felt he was entitled to keep the goats. As for the old Chief, he kept repeating angrily: "Twenty goats! My people cannot lose twenty goats! We are not rich, like the Nkosi Jordan, to lose twenty goats at once."

My father did not think of himself as rich, but rather as very poor. He spoke quickly and angrily in return, saying that the damage done meant a great deal to him, and that he was entitled to the goats.

At last it grew so heated that the cook, the Chief's son, was called from the kitchen to be interpreter, and now my father spoke fluently in English, and our cook translated rapidly so that the old man could understand how very angry my father was. The young man spoke without emotion, in a mechanical way, his eyes lowered, but showing how he felt his position by a hostile uncomfortable set of the shoulders.

It was now in the late sunset, the sky a welter of colours, the birds singing their last songs, and the cattle, lowing peacefully, moving past us towards their sheds for the night. It was the hour when Africa is most beautiful; and here was this pathetic, ugly scene, doing no one any good.

At last my father stated finally: "I'm not going to argue about it. I am keeping the goats."

The old Chief flashed back in his own language: "That means that my people will go hungry when the dry season comes."

"Go to the police, then," said my father, and looked triumphant.

There was, of course, no more to be said.

The old man sat silent, his head bent, his hands dangling helplessly over his withered knees. Then he rose, the young men helping him, and he stood facing my father. He spoke once again, very stiffly; and turned away and went home to his village.

"What did he say?" asked my father of the young man, who laughed uncomfortably and would not meet his eyes.

"What did he say?" insisted my father.

Our cook stood straight and silent, his brows knotted together. Then he spoke. "My father says: all this land, this land you call yours, is his land, and belongs to our people."

Having made this statement, he walked off into the bush after his father, and we did not see him again.

Our next cook was a migrant from Nyasaland,[10] with no expectations of greatness.

Next time the policeman came on his rounds he was told this story. He remarked: "That kraal has no right to be there; it should have been moved long ago. I don't know why no one has done anything about it. I'll have a chat with the Native Commissioner next week. I'm going over for tennis on Sunday, anyway."

Some time later we heard that Chief Mshlanga and his people had been moved two hundred miles east, to a proper Native Reserve; the Government land was going to be opened up for white settlement soon.

I went to see the village again, about a year afterwards. There was nothing there. Mounds of red mud, where the huts had been, had long swathes of rotting thatch over them, veined with the red galleries of the white ants. The pumpkin vines rioted everywhere, over the bushes, up the lower branches of trees so that the great golden balls rolled underfoot and dangled overhead; it was a festival of pumpkins. The bushes were crowding up, the new grass sprang vivid green.

The settler lucky enough to be allotted the lush warm valley (if he chose to cultivate this particular section) would find, suddenly, in the middle of a mealie field, the plants were growing fifteen feet tall, the weight of the cobs dragging at the stalks, and wonder what unsuspected vein of richness he had struck.

Questions for Study

1. The first and the second paragraphs of the story present first the African landscape and then the landscape the child cherishes in her imagination. What are the differences between the two landscapes?

2. Why does the African land on which she has always lived seem strange to the girl? How does her attitude toward it affect her attitude toward its people?

3. The girl refers several times to questions that cannot be suppressed. Why do these questions bother her? What do you suppose these questions are?

4. When she stops carrying the gun out of fear, the girl finds that the landscape in her mind fades. Why does this happen? How does it affect her relationship with the African landscape?

5. What is the difference between the land on her farm and the "completely fresh type of landscape" the girl finds across the boundary? Does that difference suggest anything more than mere differences in the make-up of the soil?

6. How does the "bigness and silence of Africa" provoke the protagonist's new fear? How does her fear seem to change the landscape?

7. How is the village different from the farm compound? Why does the girl feel

---

10. Former British protectorate in east-central Africa. It was renamed Malawi upon becoming an independent republic in 1966.

that she should not have come to the village? How does the landscape seem to change after that visit?

8. How do the child's parents look at the land and at its people? Why does the father get so upset about the goats?

9. How does the protagonist mature during the story? Find instances in which Lessing uses descriptions of the setting to convey that growth indirectly.

Chapter 5
Point of View

Plot, character, and setting are central elements in a piece of fiction. A less obvious but equally significant aspect of fiction is the author's perspective, his point of view. The term **point of view** refers to the vantage point or place from which the author reveals character, setting, and event. He can place himself a long way off, observing action with a telescopic lens, or he can move up close, examining a situation under a microscope. Finally, he himself may be one of the participants in the action. As the author begins the story we can usually sense where he stands. An author who begins "Once upon a time" sets himself at some distance from the story, while an author who begins "I can see the funnel-shaped cloud coming this way" is in the midst of the action. What we may not realize so easily is how much point of view controls content and determines meaning. To the literary theorist Percy Lubbock, point of view is the most important device of the fiction writer: ". . . the whole intricate question of method in the craft of fiction, I take to be governed by the question of the point of view—the question of the relation in which the narrator stands to the story."

Point of view is first of all a technical matter that may be signaled by pronouns which identify the teller and which indicate his perspective on the events of the story. We say that the author uses as narrative voice first-, second-, or third-person pronouns. Here is a brief outline of the three narrative voices:

Person	Pronoun	Perspective
first	*I, we*	Speaker telling his own story: "I was there."
second	*you*	Reader addressed: "You are there."
third	*he, she, it, they*	Character portrayed from the outside: "He was there."

101

Stories may be written from the second-person point of view, but this method is rarely used. An old cops-and-robbers radio show employed the second person: "You're a cop. It's a rainy Friday evening. You want to go home, but . . . ." Addressing the listener like that is awkward, and later versions of the program shifted to the first person: "It was Thursday. It was hot in Los Angeles. I was working the day-watch out of homicide. . . . My name is Friday. I'm a cop." Since the second person in fiction is hard to maintain and almost never used, it will not be considered in this discussion.

The point of view of most stories is either the first or the third person. The third person may be used in various ways to indicate the author's precise vantage point. Specifically, a third-person narrative can be *omniscient, objective,* or *limited subjective.* Each of these approaches offers special advantages that make it more appropriate for one type of narrative than for another.

The most common and conventional of the third-person perspectives is the **omniscient point of view,** in which the author is literally "all-knowing." Making no pretense of being a participant in the story, an author places himself at some distance from the tale. Not only can he tell us at will what different characters in different times and places are doing, saying, thinking, and feeling, he can also freely interpret and comment on their behavior. We are very much aware that there is a person shaping the tale and to some extent coming between us and the events of the story. This omniscient point of view might be diagramed so:

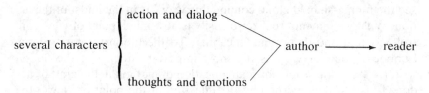

The author might say, for example, "On a rainy Friday evening, Sergeant Smith wanted to go home but he got a phone call from Naomi." The author might next record the conversation and report to us not only how Smith felt but also how Naomi on the other end of the line felt: "She was terrified." Saying that she was terrified is of course quite different from remarking that she sounded terrified. The latter is an *outside* observation, while the former is an *inside* report that only the omniscient author, looking inside the minds of his characters, can express. He can also offer inside observations about any of the other characters: "After he hung up the phone, Smith talked to Captain Hardin, who thought he was crazy to pursue the case any longer." The omniscient author also feels free to comment on the action: "Surely Sergeant Smith is too shrewd to fall for her line!" In other words, the omniscient author may offer us privileged glimpses into the inner thoughts and feelings of different characters. His narration may shift about in time and place; and he himself may intrude to explain or to offer interpretations.

The omniscient point of view is flexible and all-inclusive. It imposes no limitations on the author, but sometimes it makes the story hard to believe. Because we are sufficiently aware of the author's voice to wonder how he can know so much, the omniscient narrative may seem artificial. We can hear the stage machinery creaking as the author leaves one situation for another by saying something like, "Meanwhile in a distant city," or by asking, "And what about Naomi?" The omniscient point of view also tends to lack immediacy since action is often summarized and we are always aware of getting the tale secondhand. Moreover, modern writers have become increasingly suspicious of the claims to an all-encompassing authority that an omniscient narrative seems to make. Such an authority begins to seem improbable, perhaps even undesirable. As a consequence, many modern authors try to give the illusion that no one at all writes their stories. In *The Twentieth-Century Novel,* Joseph Warren Beach observes that in the development of the English novel from the eighteenth to the twentieth century, "the one thing that will impress you more than any other is the disappearance of the author." Authors seem determined today to make it appear as if they do not write their stories. As Beach adds, the most significant feature of modern fiction is the rule that the "story shall tell itself."

When a writer tries to give the impression that no one is telling his story, he may adopt the **objective point of view.** Here an author records only the actions and dialog of his characters in the third person and makes no attempt to reveal or interpret their inner thoughts and feelings. He does not intrude between the events and the reader:

several characters { action and dialog ⟶ reader

This approach is sometimes called the **dramatic point of view** because it gives the illusion that we are overhearing and seeing things happen, as if we were seeing them acted out on a stage. Action and dialog seem to be recorded as with a camera and a tape recorder. No voice questions, interprets, or explores any aspect of action or of behavior not directly presented. If the point of view is consistently objective, the author has shrewdly given the impression of having done nothing at all.

Ernest Hemingway, for example, has made extensive use of the objective point of view. In "The Killers," Nick Adams tries to prevent a mysterious killing, but we are never told that he feels fear, excitement, or anything at all. "The Capital of the World" (Chapter 7), however, is not strictly an objective story. Hemingway does tell us something of what the poor Spanish boy Paco loves, admires, fantasizes, and finds unbelievable. Hemingway achieves the impression of objectivity by his matter-of-fact narration of Paco's imaginary bullfight: Paco, Hemingway narrates "made the second pass, gained a little terrain on the imaginary bull and made a third pass . . . ." Hemingway uses an objective point of view for heightened effectiveness in scenes which could have been excessively emotional. When, for instance, he writes that Paco "stepped his left foot two inches too far forward and the knife did not pass, but had slipped in as easily as into a wineskin," he uses the objective point of view to make the senseless stabbing of Paco all the more horrid.

Pär Lagerkvist, another master of the objective presentation, narrates "The Children's Campaign" entirely from the outside. As an impersonal observer, he records events, snatches of dialog, and the actions of the people. Lagerkvist never explores the internal consciousness of any character. He reports reactions only as they are overtly expressed. And he never intrudes in his own voice to interpret, explain, or judge whether the destructive campaign is glorious or horrid. His narrative position is consistently objective, but his moral stance is not objective at all—it is deeply concerned and committed. Even though he reports the bloody campaign coolly, matter-of-factly—almost journalistically—his choice of details alone evokes in us a sense of the horror and absurdity of war. We are startled and perhaps even shocked by the discrepancy between the violence and the horror Lagerkvist presents and his objective manner of presentation. That shock value is effective: it is the basis of the drama and the force achieved by the objective point of view. Because it restricts itself to recording action and dialog, while excluding unexpressed thought or feeling, the objective point of view serves best in action tales. Yet in order for it not to seem blunt, dry, or even superficial, the narrative focus must be consistently controlled.

Another third-person perspective, which is a compromise between knowing everything (omniscient) and knowing nothing except external action and dialog (objective), is the **limited subjective point of view** (often called the *limited omniscient*). Here the author tells the tale from the perspective of a single character only. He uses the third person, describing the actions and dialog of the characters, but he freely tells us what the central character feels and thinks. The difference between this point of view and the omniscient is seen in the word *limited*. By his own choice the author limits his perspective to the mind of only one character, and he remains by the side of that character throughout the tale.

Anton Chekhov, for instance, writes "An Upheaval" entirely from Mashenka's point of view. Author and reader seem to be looking over Mashenka's shoulder, experiencing only what she sees and hears. We do not know what anyone else does or says when he or she is out of Mashenka's sight. Chekhov refers to Mashenka as "she," and so seems somewhat distanced from her. Yet he freely reveals what Mashenka (and no one else) is thinking: "What had happened . . . ? Was not she mixed up in something dreadful?" Chekhov does not blur the focus of his story by allowing us privileged glimpses into the minds and the hearts of any of the other characters.

The limited subjective point of view might be diagramed so:

several characters $\left\{\begin{array}{l}\text{action and dialog}\end{array}\right.$ $>$ one character's thoughts, emotions, $\longrightarrow$ reader and observations

Events happen to a character and he relates them to us. In this way we are given the illusion of simply overhearing the workings of a character's voice and mind. Neither he nor the author behind him seems to be ordering or shaping events for our benefit.

The limited subjective point of view offers both the feel of subjectivity and the appearance of objectivity. Because it is consistently restricted to one character's perspective, this point of view is more believable than the omniscient. Each of us experiences life through only one consciousness, and we can usually identify with a character who tells a story. Yet in using the third person, the author is employing a character in such a way as to make that character appear objective.

For some narratives it seems more appropriate and less artificial for a character to speak to us directly. In the **first-person point of view,** one of the characters in the story relates the tale. He may seem to be telling it orally—as if friends were sitting around swapping tales. We are aware that a character, not an outside author, is telling the story from the inside. Such a narrative voice speaks to us saying, "I did," or "I saw," or "I was there." Because the narrator speaks directly to us and because eyewitness accounts naturally seem authentic, we tend to forget that we are reading a story created by an author's imagination, not a narrative transcribed by a tape recorder.

Updike's "A & P" seems to come straight from real life, as does Sherwood Anderson's "Death in the Woods," because all first-person narratives convey the experiences, thoughts, and feelings of an actual person speaking to us. The first person offers the advantage of being persuasive and immediate, lending the story a built-in consistency and coherence. Yet one character cannot be everywhere at once. Nor can he delve into the interiors of another person's mind; nor can he plausibly know too much. The well-ordered first-person focus imposes a severe limitation upon what can be known and revealed in the story. Such a limitation would belittle and radically distort the large histori-cal, social, and political perspective of a story like Leo Tolstoy's '' The Death of Ivan Ilych'' (Chapter 12). However, it is perfectly appropriate for ''Death in the Woods,'' which is not a narrative of events but a study of a young man and his thoughts about these events.

The author must be careful in using the first-person point of view. His narrative must read as if the character were actually talking to us. Whatever the narrator observes and understands and feels and says must be consistent with and appropriate to his background and person-ality. In ''A & P'' Updike suggests certain facets of his narrator's per-sonality in the first sentence: ''In walks these three girls in nothing but bathing suits.'' Throughout the rest of the story the narrative voice re-mains in character.

Rather than allowing an ignorant character to express profound in-sights, an author usually chooses an intelligent and sensitive character as the narrative voice. Ellison's narrator in ''Battle Royal,'' for in-stance, is not very sophisticated, but he is perceptive and painfully conscious of how he and his people are being brutalized. John Cheever's narrator in ''The Angel of the Bridge'' (Chapter 7) is more sophisticated but less morally sensitive. Both of these first-person nar-rators are articulate and speak with authority and conviction. Yet even when the first-person narrator is neither apparently trustworthy nor articulate, the point of view itself can make us more receptive to what the speaker says. We may initially distrust the young and emotionally unstable narrator of ''How I Contemplated the World . . . ,'' but as she speaks to us in her own voice, our doubt vanishes and we listen to what she says.

First-person narratives work a special compulsion on their readers. The narrator speaks to us as an actual person would, and we respond as to an actual acquaintance. We must consider, however, as we do with our friends, the extent of the narrator's involvement in the tale he tells. He may be quite removed from the action itself, recording for our benefit and for his own understanding what he sees, feels, and con-cludes.

several characters { action and dialog > narrator's thoughts, emotions, → reader and observations

This diagram looks much like the one for the limited subjective point of view. In the limited subjective point of view, an author clearly identifies the center of his narrative with a character, delivering through this character everything that is given. The first-person narrator, by contrast, appears to speak for himself, not for an author. He is therefore closer to the reader in whom he confides than to the author or to other characters in the story. His perspective offers us the advantage of getting the story on two levels. Not only do we read about certain events but we also gain insight into them by seeing how a character reflects upon them. Such a story is usually less a narrative full of events than an exploration of the narrator's comprehension of those actions. Establishing as narrator a character who gains information about events and scenes he did not experience can be awkward or it can become, as in "Death in the Woods," part of the subject matter of the story itself.

A character may also tell his own story about events that happen directly to him. The stories by Updike, Ellison, and Lessing are such first-person insider narratives. (Actually, at one point in the story Lessing shifts from the third-person limited subjective to the first-person point of view.) In such tales there is little attempt at objectivity, but there is dramatic immediacy and apparent authenticity. A diagram of this first-person perspective indicates that the narrator describes and interprets the events in the story according to his perception of them:

narrator's $\left\{ \begin{array}{l} \text{thoughts, emotions, experiences; observations} \\ \text{of other characters' actions and dialog} \end{array} \right.$ $\longrightarrow$ reader

Such a character would seem authentic but could not be expected to be objective. He might tell the tale for self-serving reasons. And his viewpoint might not only be biased but also naive, insensitive, or misleading.

Wayne C. Booth in *The Rhetoric of Fiction* speaks of certain first-person narrators as *reliable* or *unreliable*. Booth insists that the principal question to be asked about the first-person point of view has to do with the trustworthiness of the narrator, who may express one set of norms, while the story itself may stand for another. In "Just Like a Tree," for instance, Ernest J. Gaines allows an unreliable narrator, James, to tell a small portion of the story even though James' understanding of other characters and their situation is limited and biased.

But why would an author intentionally use an ignorant, insensitive, or stupid character—an unreliable narrator—to tell his tale? Perhaps for the purposes of irony or satire. Such a narrator allows us to see the discrepancy between what the speaker thinks he knows and what he actually knows. It is more effective to let a character such as James reveal his own inadequacies than to have an omniscient narrator explain them to us. In this way, we have the pleasure, as we do in real life, of discovering for ourselves the discrepancies between what things appear to be and what they actually are. As readers we do not merely absorb and accept but question and reexamine. In this way we are closely involved in the narrative as it unfolds.

The most extreme attempt at reader involvement is represented in the technique of **stream-of-consciousness** writing. This method can be an extension of either the third-person limited subjective or of the first-person point of view. In either case, it does not merely reflect the character's conscious thoughts but also attempts to convey the actual flow of and interplay between the character's conscious, semiconscious, and even unconscious thoughts. Stream-of-consciousness writing is as subjective as it is possible to be. At first glance, it seems illogical because the mind's unfocused musings and irrational wanderings are never coherent, logical, or organized. Much of the responsibility for making sense of what may seem at first to be totally incoherent babblings falls upon the reader.

One of the most ambitious attempts at stream-of-consciousness writing is the end of the second section of William Faulkner's *The Sound and the Fury* (1929), which is told from the point of view of Quentin Compson. While a student at Harvard, Quentin receives word that his sister, with whom he is in love, is to be married. Here is Faulkner's attempt to recreate the disintegrating mind of a person about to commit suicide:

> *. . . you will remember that for you to go to harvard has been your mothers dream since you were born and no compson has ever disappointed a lady and i temporary it will be better for me for all of us and he every man is the arbiter of his own virtues and let no man prescribe for another mans wellbeing and i temporary and he was the saddest word of all there is nothing else in the world its not despair until time its not even time until is was*

Stream-of-consciousness writing may seem a mere exercise in cleverness or in baffling the reader. The skilled craftsman, however, uses it to try to convey a sensuous impression of the way the mind actually works, to make a poetically (if not a logically) unified narrative, and to engage the reader actively in the lives of his characters.

We know that unreliable narrators like Gaines' James or Faulkner's Quentin do not necessarily speak for the author. Thus we should resist the impulse to identify the "I," or the narrative **persona,** in a first-person story with the author. We should not forget that we are reading a work of fiction, not an autobiographical confession. Anderson's "Death in the Woods" is apparently autobiographical, and the "I" could be Anderson himself. But the persona is not Anderson. If we think of the narrator as separate from Anderson, we have the advantage of a triple perspective: ourselves watching a persona watching and/or participating in certain events which he is narrating to us.

When we read narratives, we should ask ourselves, as we do when anyone comes to us with a story to tell, "What's his angle?" or "Where does he stand?" Where a person stands affects what and how he views the events. In fiction the narrative stance or point of view determines meaning in various and subtle ways. We must know where a witness stands before we can evaluate the reliability of his testimony. We must understand someone's angle of vision before we know how to weigh what we are told. And we must understand point of view before we can appreciate the numerous, rich implications of a work of fiction.

Pär Lagerkvist (1891–1974)
The Children's Campaign

Even the children at that time received military training, were assembled in army units and exercised just as though on active service, had their own headquarters and annual manœuvres when everything was conducted as in a real state of war. The grown-ups had nothing directly to do with this training; the children actually exercised themselves and all command was entrusted to them. The only use made of adult experience was to arrange officers' training courses for specially suitable boys, who were chosen with the greatest care and who were then put in charge of the military education of their comrades in the ranks.

These schools were of high standing and there was hardly a boy throughout the land who did not dream of going to them. But the entrance tests were particularly hard; not only a perfect physique was required but also a highly developed intelligence and character. The age of admission was six to seven years and the small cadets then received an excellent training, both purely military and in all other respects, chiefly the further moulding of character. It was also greatly to one's credit in after life to have passed through one of these schools. It was really on the splendid foundation laid here that the quality, organization and efficiency of the child army rested.

Thereafter, as already mentioned, the grown-ups in no way interfered but everything was entrusted to the children themselves. No adult might meddle in the command, in organizational details or matters of promotion. Everything was managed and supervised by the children; all decisions, even the most vital, being reached by their own little general staff. No one over fourteen was allowed. The boys then passed automatically into the first age-group of the regular troops with no mean military training already behind them.

The large child army, which was the object of the whole nation's love and admiration, amounted to three army corps of four divisions: infantry, light field artillery, medical and service corps. All physically fit boys were enrolled in it and a large number of girls belonged to it as nurses, all volunteers.

Now it so happened that a smaller, quite insignificant nation behaved in a high-handed and unseemly way toward its powerful neighbour, and the insult was all the greater since this nation was by no means an equal. Indignation was great and general and, since people's feelings were running high, it was necessary to rebuke the malapert and at the same time take the chance to subjugate the country in question. In this situation the child army came forward and through its high command asked to be charged with the crushing and subduing of the foe. The news of this caused a sensation and a wave of fervour throughout the country. The proposal was given serious consideration in supreme quarters and as a result the commission was given, with some hesitation, to the children. It was in fact a task well suited to this army, and the people's obvious wishes in the matter had also to be met, if possible.

The Foreign Office therefore sent the defiant country an unacceptable ultimatum and, pending the reply, the child army was mobilized within twenty-four hours. The reply was found to be unsatisfactory and war was declared immediately.

Unparalleled enthusiasm marked the departure for the front. The intrepid little youngsters had green sprigs in the barrels of their rifles and were pelted with flowers. As is so often the case, the campaign was begun in the spring, and this time the general opinion was that there was something symbolic in it. In the capital the little commander-in-chief and chief of general staff, in the presence of huge crowds, made a passionate speech to the troops in which he expressed the gravity of the hour and his conviction of their unswerving valour and willingness to offer their lives for their country.

The speech, made in a strong voice, aroused the greatest ecstasy. The boy—who had a brilliant career behind him and had received his exalted position at the age of only twelve and a half—was acclaimed with wild rejoicing and from this moment was the avowed hero of the entire nation. There was not a dry eye, and those of the many mothers especially shone with pride and happiness. For them it was the greatest day in their lives. The troops marched past below fluttering banners, each regiment with its music corps at the head. It was an unforgettable spectacle.

There were also many touching incidents, evincing a proud patriotism, as when a little four-year-old, who had been lifted up on his mother's arm so that he could see, howled with despair and shouted, "I want to go, too. I want to go, too!" while his mother tried to hush him, explaining that he was too small. "Small am I, eh?" he exclaimed, punching her face so that her nose bled. The evening papers were full of such episodes showing the mood of the people and of the troops who were so sure of victory. The big march past was broadcast and the C.-in-C.'s speech, which had been recorded, was broadcast every evening during the days that followed, at 7:15 P.M.

Military operations had already begun, however, and reports of victory began to come in at once from the front. The children had quickly taken the offensive and on one sector of the front had inflicted a heavy defeat on the enemy, seven hundred dead and wounded and over twelve hundred prisoners, while their own losses amounted to only a hundred or so fallen. The victory was celebrated at home with indescribable rejoicing and with thanksgiving services in the churches. The newspapers were filled with accounts of individual instances of valour and pictures several columns wide of the high command, of which the leading personalities, later so well-known, began to appear now for the first time. In their joy, mothers and aunts sent so much chocolate and other sweets to the army that headquarters had to issue a strict order that all such parcels were, for the time being at any rate, forbidden, since they had made whole regiments unfit for battle and these in their turn had nearly been surrounded by the enemy.

For the child army was already far inside enemy territory and still managed to keep the initiative. The advance sector did retreat slightly in order to establish contact with its wings, but only improved its positions by so doing. A stalemate ensued in the theatre of war for some time after this.

During July, however, troops were concentrated for a big attack along the whole line and huge reserves—the child army's, in comparison with those of its opponent, were almost inexhaustible—were mustered to the front. The new offensive, which lasted for several weeks, resulted, too, in an almost decisive victory for the whole army, even though casualties were high. The children defeated the enemy all along the line, but did not manage to pursue him and thereby exploit their success to the full, because he was greatly favoured by the fact that his legs were so much longer, an advantage of which he made good use. By dint of forced marches, however, the children finally succeeded in cutting the enemy's right flank to pieces. They were now in the very heart of the country and their outposts were only a few days' march from the capital.

It was a pitched battle on a big scale and the newspapers had enormous headlines every day which depicted the dramatic course of events. At set hours the radio broadcast the gunfire and a résumé of the position. The war correspondents described in rapturous words and vivid colours the state of affairs at the front—the children's incredible feats, their indomitable courage and self-sacrifice, the whole morale of the army. It was no exaggeration. The youngsters showed the greatest bravery; they really behaved like heroes. One only had to see their discipline and contempt of death during an attack, as though they had been grown-up men at least.

It was an unforgettable sight to see them storm ahead under murderous machine-gun fire and the small medical orderlies dart nimbly forward and pick them up as they fell. Or the wounded and dying who were moved behind the front, those who had had a leg shot away or their bellies ripped open by a bayonet so that their entrails hung out—but without one sound of complaint crossing their small lips. The hand-to-hand fighting had been very fierce and a great number of children fell in this, while they were superior in the actual firing. Losses were estimated at 4000 on the enemy side and 7000 among the children, according to the secret reports. The victory had been hard won but all the more complete.

This battle became very famous and was also of far greater importance than any previously. It was now clear beyond all doubt that the children were incomparably superior in tactics, discipline and individual courage. At the same time, however, it was admitted by experts that the enemy's head-long retreat was very skilfully carried out, that his strength was evidently in defence and that he should not be underrated too much. Toward the end, also, he had unexpectedly made a stubborn resistance which had prevented any further penetration.

This observation was not without truth. In actual fact the enemy was any-thing but a warlike nation, and indeed his forces found it very difficult to hold their own. Nevertheless, they improved with practice during the fighting and became more efficient as time went on. This meant that they caused the chil-dren a good deal of trouble in each succeeding battle. They also had certain ad-vantages on their side. As their opponents were so small, for instance, it was possible after a little practice to spit several of them on the bayonet at once, and often a kick was enough to fell them to the ground.

But against this, the children were so much more numerous and also braver. They were everywhere. They swarmed over one and in between one's legs and the unwarlike people were nearly demented by all these small mon-sters who fought like fiends. Little fiends was also what they were generally called—not without reason—and this name was even adopted in the children's homeland, but there it was a mark of honour and a pet name. The enemy troops had all their work cut out merely defending themselves. At last, however, they were able to check the others' advance and even venture on one or two counter-attacks. Everything then came to a standstill for a while and there was a breathing-space.

The children were now in possession of a large part of the country. But this was not always so easy. The population did not particularly like them and proved not to be very fond of children. It was alleged that snipers fired on the boys from houses and that they were ambushed when they moved in small de-tachments. Children had even been found impaled on stakes or with their eyes gouged out, so it was said. And in many cases these stories were no doubt true. The population had quite lost their heads, were obviously goaded into a frenzy, and as they were of little use as a warlike nation and their cruelty could there-fore find no natural outlet, they tried to revenge themselves by atrocities. They felt overrun by all the foreign children as by troublesome vermin and, being at their wits' end, they simply killed whenever they had the chance. In order to put an end to these outrages the children burned one village after the other and shot hundreds of people daily, but this did not improve matters. The despicable deeds of these craven guerrillas caused them endless trouble.

At home, the accounts of all this naturally aroused the most bitter resent-ment. People's blood boiled to think that their small soldiers were treated in this way by those who had nothing to do with the war, by barbarous civilians who had no notion of established and judicial forms. Even greater indignation was caused, however, by an incident that occurred inside the occupied area some time after the big summer battle just mentioned.

A lieutenant who was out walking in the countryside came to a stream where a large, fat woman knelt washing clothes. He asked her the way to a vil-lage close by. The woman, who probably suspected him of evil intent, retorted, "What are you doing here? You ought to be at home with your mother." Whereupon the lieutenant drew his sabre to kill her, but the woman grabbed hold of him and, putting him over her knee, thwacked him black and blue with her washboard so that he was unable to sit down for several days afterward. He was so taken aback that he did nothing, armed though he was to the teeth. Luckily no one saw the incident, but there were orders that all outrages on the part of the population were to be reported to headquarters. The lieutenant therefore duly reported what had happened to him. True, it gave him little satsfaction, but as he had to obey orders he had no choice. And so it all came out.

The incident aroused a storm of rage, particularly among those at home. The infamous deed was a humiliation for the country, an insult which nothing could wipe out. It implied a deliberate violation by this militarily ignorant people of the simplest rules of warfare. Everywhere, in the press, in propaganda speeches, in ordinary conversation, the deepest contempt and disgust for the deed was expressed. The lieutenant who had so flagrantly shamed the army had his officer's epaulettes ripped off in front of the assembled troops and was declared unworthy to serve any longer in the field. He was instantly sent home to his parents, who belonged to one of the most noted families but who now had to retire into obscurity in a remote part of the country.

The woman, on the other hand, became a heroic figure among her people and the object of their rapturous admiration. During the whole of the war she and her deed were a rallying national symbol which people looked up to and which spurred them on to further effort. She subsequently became a favourite motif in the profuse literature about their desperate struggle for freedom; a vastly popular figure, brought to life again and again as time passed, now in a rugged, everyday way which appealed to the man in the street, now in heroic female form on a grandiose scale, to become gradually more and more legendary, wreathed in saga and myth. In some versions she was shot by the enemy; in others she lived to a ripe old age, loved and revered by her people.

This incident, more than anything else, helped to increase the bad feelings between the two countries and to make them wage the war with ever greater ruthlessness. In the late summer, before the autumn rains began, both armies, ignorant of each other's plans, simultaneously launched a violent offensive, which devastated both sides. On large sectors of the front the troops completely annihilated each other so that there was not a single survivor left. Any peaceful inhabitants thereabouts who were still alive and ventured out of their cellars thought that the war was over, because all were slain.

But soon new detachments came up and began fighting again. Great confusion arose in other quarters from the fact that in the heat of attack men ran past each other and had to turn around in order to go on fighting; and that some parts of the line rushed ahead while others came behind, so that the troops were both in front of and behind where they should have been and time and again attacked each other in the rear. The battle raged in this way with extreme violence and shots were fired from all directions at once.

When at last the fighting ceased and stock was taken of the situation, it appeared that no one had won. On both sides there was an equal number of fallen, 12,924, and after all attacks and retreats the position of the armies was exactly the same as at the start of the battle. It was agreed that both should claim the victory. Thereafter the rain set in and the armies went to earth in trenches and put up barbed-wire entanglements.

The children were the first to finish their trenches, since they had had more to do with that kind of thing, and settled down in them as best they could. They soon felt at home. Filthy and lousy, they lived there in the darkness as though they had never done anything else. With the adaptability of children they quickly got into the way of it. The enemy found this more difficult; he felt miserable and home-sick for the life above ground to which he was accustomed. Not so the children. When one saw them in their small grey uniforms, which were caked thick with mud, and their small gas masks, one could easily think they had been born to this existence. They crept in and out of the holes down into the earth and scampered about the passages like mice. When their burrows were attacked they were instantly up on the parapet and snapped back in blind fury. As the months passed, this hopeless, harrowing life put endurance to an increasingly severe test. But they never lost courage or the will to fight.

For the enemy the strain was often too much; the glaring pointlessness of it all made many completely apathetic. But the little ones did not react like this. Children are really more fitted for war and take more pleasure in it, while grown-ups tire of it after a while and think it is boring. The boys continued to find the whole thing exciting and they wanted to go on living as they were now. They also had a more natural herd instinct; their unity and camaraderie helped them a great deal, made it easier to hold out.

But, of course, even they suffered great hardship. Especially when winter set in with its incessant rain, a cold sleet which made everything sodden and filled the trenches with mud. It was enough to unman anyone. But it would never have entered their heads to complain. However bad things were, nothing could have made them admit it. At home everyone was very proud of them. All the cinemas showed parades behind the front and the little C.-in-C. and his generals pinning medals for bravery on their soldiers' breasts. People thought of them a great deal out there, of their little fiends, realizing that they must be having a hard time.

At Christmas, in particular, thoughts went out to them, to the lighted Christmas trees and all the sparkling childish eyes out in the trenches; in every home people sat wondering how they were faring. But the children did not think of home. They were soldiers out and out, absorbed by their duty and their new life. They attacked in several places on the morning of Christmas Eve, inflicting fairly big losses on the enemy in killed and wounded, and did not stop until it was time to open their parcels. They had the real fighting spirit which might have been a lesson even to adults.

There was nothing sentimental about them. The war had hardened and developed them, made them men. It did happen that one poor little chap burst into tears when the Christmas tree was lighted, but he was made the laughing-stock of them all. "Are you homesick for your mummy, you bastard?" they said, and kept on jeering at him all evening. He was the object of their scorn all through Christmas; he behaved suspiciously and tried to keep to himself. Once he walked a hundred yards away from the post and, because he might well have been thinking of flight, he was seized and court-martialled. He could give no reason for having absented himself, and since he had obviously intended to desert he was shot.

If those at home had been fully aware of the morale out there, they need not have worried. As it was, they wondered if the children could really hold their ground and half-regretted having entrusted them with the campaign, now that it was dragging on so long because of this nerve-racking stationary warfare. After the New Year help was even offered in secret, but it was rejected with proud indignation.

The morale of the enemy, on the other hand, was not so high. They did intend to fight to the last man, but the certainty of a complete victory was not so general as it should have been. They could not help thinking, either, how hopeless their fight really was; that in the long run they could not hold their own against these people who were armed to the very milk teeth, and this often dampened their courage.

Hardly had nature begun to come to life and seethe with the newly awakened forces of spring before the children started with incredible intensity to prepare for the decisive battle. Heavy mechanized artillery was brought up and placed in strong positions; huge troop movements went on night and day; all available fighting forces were concentrated in the very front lines. After murderous gunfire which lasted for six days, an attack was launched with great force and extreme skill. Individual bravery was, if possible, more dazzling than ever. The whole army was also a year older, and that means much at that age. But their opponents, too, were determined to do their utmost. They had assembled all their reserves, and their spirits, now that the rain had stopped and the weather was fine, were full of hope.

It was a terrible battle. The hospital trains immediately started going back from both sides packed with wounded and dying. Machine guns, tanks and gas played fearful havoc. For several days the outcome was impossible to foresee, since both armies appeared equally strong and the tide of battle constantly changed. The position gradually cleared, however. The enemy had expected the main attack in the centre, but the child army turned out to be weakest there. Use was made of this, especially because they themselves were best prepared at this very point, and this part of the children's front was soon made to waver and was forced farther and farther back by repeated attack. Advantage was also taken of an ideal evening breeze from just the right quarter to gas the children in thousands. Encouraged by their victory, the troops pursued the offensive with all their might and with equal success.

The child army's retreat, however, turned out to be a stratagem, brilliantly conceived and carried out. Its centre gave way more and more and the enemy, giving all his attention to this, forgot that at the same time he himself was wavering on both wings. In this way he ran his head into a noose. When the children considered that they had retreated far enough they halted, while the troops on the outermost wings, already far ahead, advanced swiftly until they met behind the enemy's back. The latter's entire army was thereby surrounded and in the grip of an iron hand. All the children's army had to do now was to draw the noose tighter. At last the gallant defenders had to surrender and let themselves be taken prisoner, which in fact they already were. It was the most disastrous defeat in history; not a single one escaped other than by death.

This victory became much more famous than any of the others and was eagerly studied at all military academies on account of its brilliantly executed, doubly effective encircling movement. The great general Sludelsnorp borrowed its tactics outright seventy years later at his victory over the Slivokvarks in the year 2048.

The war could not go on any longer now, because there was nothing left to fight, and the children marched to the capital with the imprisoned army between them to dictate the peace terms. These were handed over by the little commander-in-chief in the hall of mirrors in the stately old palace at a historic scene which was to be immortalized time and again in art and even now was reproduced everywhere in the weekly press. The film cameras whirred, the flashlights hissed and the radio broadcast the great moment to the world. The commander-in-chief, with austere and haughty mien and one foot slightly in front of the other, delivered the historic document with his right hand. The first and most important condition was the complete cession of the country, besides which the expenses of its capture were to be borne by the enemy, who thus had to pay the cost of the war on both sides, the last clause on account of the fact that he had been the challenging party and, according to his own admission, the cause of the war. The document was signed in dead silence, the only sound was the scratching of the fountain pen, which, according to the commentator's whisper, was solid gold and undoubtedly a future museum piece.

With this, everything was settled and the children's army returned to its own country, where it was received with indescribable rapture. Everywhere along the roads the troops were greeted with wild rejoicing; their homecoming was one long victory parade. The march into the capital and the dismissal there of the troops, which took place before vast crowds, were especially impressive. People waved and shouted in the streets as they passed, were beside themselves with enthusiasm, bands played, eyes were filled with tears of joy. Some of the loudest cheering was for the small invalids at the rear of the procession, blind and with limbs amputated, who had sacrificed themselves for their country. Many of them had already got small artificial arms and legs so that they looked just the same as before. The victory salute thundered, bayonets flashed in the sun. It was an unforgettable spectacle.

A strange, new leaf was written in the great book of history which would be read with admiration in time to come. The nation had seen many illustrious deeds performed, but never anything as proud as this. What these children had done in their devotion and fervent patriotism could never be forgotten.

Nor was it. Each spring, on the day of victory, school children marched out with flags in their hands to the cemeteries with all the small graves where the heroes rested under their small white crosses. The mounds were strewn with flowers and passionate speeches were made, reminding everyone of the glorious past, their imperishable honour and youthful, heroic spirit of self-sacrifice. The flags floated in the sun and the voices rang out clear as they sang their rousing songs, radiant childish eyes looking ahead to new deeds of glory.

Questions for Study

1. What are the characteristics of the story's objective point of view? What uses of language make it seem so objective? Why does Lagerkvist choose to narrate this story as if it were an entry in an encyclopedia or a history text?
2. Some of the terms Lagerkvist uses are staples of the journalist's vocabulary. List some of them. How do they function? Are they effective?
3. Lagerkvist speaks of "unseemly" behavior, of an "unforgettable spectacle," and of an "unforgettable sight." Do these phrases have more than one meaning? What meanings do they have?
4. Imagine that this story had been told from the following points of view: (a) a major character—perhaps the "little commander-in-chief"; (b) a minor character —perhaps the mother of one of the dead heroes; or (c) an omniscient narrator who could tell us how different characters felt and thought and who could editorialize and theorize about the campaign in his own voice. How would each of these perspectives have changed the story? By employing a consistently objective point of view, does the story gain or lose its effectiveness?

5. Several times Lagerkvist specifically reminds us of the army's youthfulness. Cite as many of these instances as you can. What is the effect of these reminders? Do they ever become painful? If so, why?

6. Why does Lagerkvist allow the children victory rather than defeat? Why continued glory rather than shame? In limiting himself to an objective vantage point, why does he express neither sympathy nor horror at the events he is reporting?

7. Is this story primarily about war or primarily about children? What sort of things does the story have to say to us about war? About children? About the attitudes of adults towards children? About adults generally?

8. What is your interpretation of this story? Note in particular the fact of its being a *children's campaign*. How is this fact worked into the meaning of the narrative?

Anton Chekhov (1860–1904)
An Upheaval

Mashenka Pavletsky, a young girl who had only just finished her studies at a boarding school, returning from a walk to the house of the Kushkins, with whom she was living as a governess, found the household in a terrible turmoil. Mihailo, the porter who opened the door to her, was excited and red as a crab.

Loud voices were heard from upstairs.

"Madame Kushkin is in a fit, most likely, or else she has quarrelled with her husband," thought Mashenka.

In the hall and in the corridor she met maidservants. One of them was crying. Then Mashenka saw, running out of her room, the master of the house himself, Nikolay Sergeitch,[1] a little man with a flabby face and a bald head, though he was not old. He was red in the face and twitching all over. He passed the governess without noticing her, and throwing up his arms, exclaimed:

"Oh, how horrible it is! How tactless! How stupid! How barbarous! Abominable!"

Mashenka went into her room, and then, for the first time in her life, it was her lot to experience in all its acuteness the feeling that is so familiar to persons in dependent positions, who eat the bread of the rich and powerful, and cannot speak their minds. There was a search going on in her room. The lady of the house, Fedosya Vassilyevna, a stout, broad-shouldered, uncouth woman with thick black eyebrows, a faintly perceptible moustache, and red hands, who was exactly like a plain, illiterate cook in face and manners, was standing, without her cap on, at the table, putting back into Mashenka's work-bag balls of wool, scraps of materials, and bits of paper. . . . Evidently the governess's arrival took her by surprise, since, on looking round and seeing the girl's pale and astonished face, she was a little taken aback, and muttered:

"*Pardon.* I . . . I upset it accidentally. . . . My sleeve caught in it. . . ."

---

1. Russians customarily refer to each other not by their surnames but by their two given names. Thus Nikolay Sergeitch is Mr. Kushkin, and Fedosya Vassilyevna is Mrs. (or Madame) Kushkin.

And saying something more, Madame Kushkin rustled her long skirts and went out. Mashenka looked round her room with wondering eyes, and, unable to understand it, not knowing what to think, shrugged her shoulders, and turned cold with dismay. What had Fedosya Vassilyevna been looking for in her work-bag? If she really had, as she said, caught her sleeve in it and upset everything, why had Nikolay Sergeitch dashed out of her room so excited and red in the face? Why was one drawer of the table pulled out a little way? The money-box, in which the governess put away ten kopeck pieces[2] and old stamps, was open. They had opened it, but did not know how to shut it, though they had scratched the lock all over. The whatnot with her books on it, the things on the table, the bed—all bore fresh traces of a search. Her linen-basket, too. The linen had been carefully folded, but it was not in the same order as Mashenka had left it when she went out. So the search had been thorough, most thorough. But what was it for? Why? What had happened? Mashenka remembered the excited porter, the general turmoil which was still going on, the weeping servant-girl; had it not all some connection with the search that had just been made in her room? Was not she mixed up in something dreadful? Mashenka turned pale, and feeling cold all over, sank on to her linen-basket.

A maidservant came into the room.

"Liza, you don't know why they have been rummaging in my room?" the governess asked her.

"Mistress has lost a brooch worth two thousand,"[3] said Liza.

"Yes, but why have they been rummaging in my room?"

"They've been searching every one, miss. They've searched all my things, too. They stripped us all naked and searched us. . . . God knows, miss, I never went near her toilet-table, let alone touching the brooch. I shall say the same at the police-station."

"But . . . why have they been rummaging here?" the governess still wondered.

"A brooch has been stolen, I tell you. The mistress has been rummaging in everything with her own hands. She even searched Mihailo, the porter, herself. It's a perfect disgrace! Nikolay Sergeitch simply looks on and cackles like a hen. But you've no need to tremble like that, miss. They found nothing here. You've nothing to be afraid of if you didn't take the brooch."

"But, Liza, it's vile . . . it's insulting," said Mashenka, breathless with indignation. "It's so mean, so low! What right had she to suspect me and to rummage in my things?"

"You are living with strangers, miss," sighed Liza. "Though you are a young lady, still you are . . . as it were . . . a servant. . . . It's not like living with your papa and mamma."

Mashenka threw herself on the bed and sobbed bitterly. Never in her life had she been subjected to such an outrage, never had she been so deeply insulted. . . . She, well-educated, refined, the daughter of a teacher, was suspected of theft; she had been searched like a street-walker! She could not imagine a greater insult. And to this feeling of resentment was added an oppressive dread of what would come next. All sorts of absurd ideas came into her

---

2. The equivalent of ten-cent coins. There were 100 kopecks to a ruble.
3. I.e., two thousand rubles.

mind. If they could suspect her of theft, then they might arrest her, strip her naked, and search her, then lead her through the street with an escort of soldiers, cast her into a cold, dark cell with mice and woodlice, exactly like the dungeon in which Princess Tarakanov[4] was imprisoned. Who would stand up for her? Her parents lived far away in the provinces; they had not the money to come to her. In the capital she was as solitary as in a desert, without friends or kindred. They could do what they liked with her.

"I will go to all the courts and all the lawyers," Mashenka thought, trembling. "I will explain to them, I will take an oath. . . . They will believe that I could not be a thief!"

Mashenka remembered that under the sheets in her basket she had some sweetmeats, which, following the habits of her schooldays, she had put in her pocket at dinner and carried off to her room. She felt hot all over, and was ashamed at the thought that her little secret was known to the lady of the house; and all this terror, shame, resentment, brought on an attack of palpitation of the heart, which set up a throbbing in her temples, in her heart, and deep down in her stomach.

"Dinner is ready," the servant summoned Mashenka.

"Shall I go, or not?"

Mashenka brushed her hair, wiped her face with a wet towel, and went into the dining-room. There they had already begun dinner. At one end of the table sat Fedosya Vassilyevna with a stupid, solemn, serious face; at the other end Nikolay Sergeitch. At the sides there were the visitors and the children. The dishes were handed by two footmen in swallowtails and white gloves. Every one knew that there was an upset in the house, that Madame Kushkin was in trouble, and every one was silent. Nothing was heard but the sound of munching and the rattle of spoons on the plates.

The lady of the house, herself, was the first to speak.

"What is the third course?" she asked the footman in a weary, injured voice.

"*Esturgeon à la russe,*"[5] answered the footman.

"I ordered that, Fenya," Nikolay Sergeitch hastened to observe. "I wanted some fish. If you don't like it, *ma chère,* don't let them serve it. I just ordered it. . . ."

Fedosya Vassilyevna did not like dishes that she had not ordered herself, and now her eyes filled with tears.

"Come, don't let us agitate ourselves," Mamikov, her household doctor, observed in a honeyed voice, just touching her arm, with a smile as honeyed. "We are nervous enough as it is. Let us forget the brooch! Health is worth more than two thousand roubles!"

"It's not the two thousand I regret," answered the lady, and a big tear rolled down her cheek. "It's the fact itself that revolts me! I cannot put up with thieves in my house. I don't regret it—I regret nothing; but to steal from me is such ingratitude! That's how they repay me for my kindness. . . ."

They all looked into their plates, but Mashenka fancied after the lady's

---

words that every one was looking at her. A lump rose in her throat; she began crying and put her handkerchief to her lips.

"*Pardon*," she muttered. "I can't help it. My head aches. I'll go away."

And she got up from the table, scraping her chair awkwardly, and went out quickly, still more overcome with confusion.

"It's beyond everything!" said Nikolay Sergeitch, frowning. "What need was there to search her room? How out of place it was!"

"I don't say she took the brooch," said Fedosya Vassilyevna, "but can you answer for her? To tell the truth, I haven't much confidence in these learned paupers."

"It really was unsuitable, Fenya. . . . Excuse me, Fenya, but you've no kind of legal right to make a search."

"I know nothing about your laws. All I know is that I've lost my brooch. And I will find the brooch!" She brought her fork down on the plate with a clatter, and her eyes flashed angrily. "And you eat your dinner, and don't interfere in what doesn't concern you!"

Nikolay Sergeitch dropped his eyes mildly and sighed. Meanwhile Mashenka, reaching her room, flung herself on her bed. She felt now neither alarm nor shame, but she felt an intense longing to go and slap the cheeks of this hard, arrogant, dull-witted, prosperous woman.

Lying on her bed she breathed into her pillow and dreamed of how nice it would be to go and buy the most expensive brooch and fling it into the face of this bullying woman. If only it were God's will that Fedosya Vassilyevna should come to ruin and wander about begging, and should taste all the horrors of poverty and dependence, and that Mashenka, whom she had insulted, might give her alms! Oh, if only she could come in for a big fortune, could buy a carriage, and could drive noisily past the windows so as to be envied by that woman!

But all these were only dreams, in reality there was only one thing left to do—to get away as quickly as possible, not to stay another hour in this place. It was true it was terrible to lose her place, to go back to her parents, who had nothing; but what could she do? Mashenka could not bear the sight of the lady of the house nor of her little room; she felt stifled and wretched here. She was so disgusted with Fedosya Vassilyevna, who was so obsessed by her illnesses and her supposed aristocratic rank, that everything in the world seemed to have become coarse and unattractive because this woman was living in it. Mashenka jumped up from the bed and began packing.

"May I come in?" asked Nikolay Sergeitch at the door; he had come up noiselessly to the door, and spoke in a soft, subdued voice. "May I?"

"Come in."

He came in and stood still near the door. His eyes looked dim and his red little nose was shiny. After dinner he used to drink beer, and the fact was perceptible in his walk, in his feeble, flabby hands.

"What's this?" he asked, pointing to the basket.

"I am packing. Forgive me, Nikolay Sergeitch, but I cannot remain in your house. I feel deeply insulted by this search!"

"I understand. . . . Only you are wrong to go. . . . Why should you? They've searched your things, but you . . . what does it matter to you? You will be none the worse for it."

Mashenka was silent and went on packing. Nikolay Sergeitch pinched his moustache, as though wondering what he should say next, and went on in an ingratiating voice:

"I understand, of course, but you must make allowances. You know my wife is nervous, headstrong; you mustn't judge her too harshly."

Mashenka did not speak.

"If you are so offended," Nikolay Sergeitch went on, "well, if you like, I'm ready to apologise. I ask your pardon."

Mashenka made no answer, but only bent lower over her box. This exhausted, irresolute man was of absolutely no significance in the household. He stood in the pitiful position of a dependent and hanger-on, even with the servants, and his apology meant nothing either.

"H'm! . . . You say nothing! That's not enough for you. In that case, I will apologise for my wife. In my wife's name. . . . She behaved tactlessly, I admit it as a gentleman. . . ."

Nikolay Sergeitch walked about the room, heaved a sigh, and went on:

"Then you want me to have it rankling here, under my heart. . . . You want my conscience to torment me. . . ."

"I know it's not your fault, Nikolay Sergeitch," said Mashenka, looking him full in the face with her big tear-stained eyes. "Why should you worry yourself?"

"Of course, no. . . . But still, don't you . . . go away. I entreat you."

Mashenka shook her head. Nikolay Sergeitch stopped at the window and drummed on the pane with his finger-tips.

"Such misunderstandings are simply torture to me," he said. "Why, do you want me to go down on my knees to you, or what? Your pride is wounded, and here you've been crying and packing up to go; but I have pride, too, and you do not spare it! Or do you want me to tell you what I would not tell as Confession? Do you? Listen; you want me to tell you what I won't tell the priest on my death-bed?"

Mashenka made no answer.

"I took my wife's brooch," Nikolay Sergeitch said quickly. "Is that enough now? Are you satisfied? Yes, I . . . took it. . . . But, of course, I count on your discretion. . . . For God's sake, not a word, not half a hint to any one!"

Mashenka, amazed and frightened, went on packing; she snatched her things, crumpled them up, and thrust them anyhow into the box and the basket. Now, after this candid avowal on the part of Nikolay Sergeitch, she could not remain another minute, and could not understand how she could have gone on living in the house before.

"And it's nothing to wonder at," Nikolay Sergeitch went on after a pause. "It's an everyday story! I need money, and she . . . won't give it to me. It was my father's money that bought this house and everything, you know! It's all mine, and the brooch belonged to my mother, and . . . it's all mine! And she took it, took possession of everything. . . . I can't go to law with her, you'll admit. . . . I beg you most earnestly, overlook it . . . stay on. *Tout comprendre, tout pardonner.*[6] Will you stay?"

---

6. A version of *tout comprendre, c'est tout pardonner*—"to understand everything is to forgive everything."

"No!" said Mashenka resolutely, beginning to tremble. "Let me alone, I entreat you!"

"Well, God bless you!" sighed Nikolay Sergeitch, sitting down on the stool near the box. "I must own I like people who still can feel resentment, contempt, and so on. I could sit here forever and look at your indignant face. . . . So you won't stay, then? I understand. . . . It's bound to be so. . . . Yes, of course. . . . It's all right for you, but for me—wo-o-o-o! . . . I can't stir a step out of this cellar. I'd go off to one of our estates, but in every one of them there are some of my wife's rascals . . . stewards, experts, damn them all! They mortgage and remortgage. . . . You mustn't catch fish, must keep off the grass, mustn't break the trees."

"Nikolay Sergeitch!" his wife's voice called from the drawing-room. "Agnia, call your master!"

"Then you won't stay?" asked Nikolay Sergeitch, getting up quickly and going towards the door. "You might as well stay, really. In the evenings I could come and have a talk with you. Eh? Stay! If you go, there won't be a human face left in the house. It's awful!"

Nikolay Sergeitch's pale, exhausted face besought her, but Mashenka shook her head, and with a wave of his hand he went out.

Half an hour later she was on her way.

Questions for Study

1. Describe the point of view of this narrative as precisely as you can.
2. At the beginning, Chekhov puts Mashenka's thoughts in quotation marks. A page or so later, though, she asks herself, "What had Fedosya Vassilyevna been looking for in her work-bag?" She asks numbers of such questions, not in quotation marks, and by the paragraph's end, Chekhov is telling us how Mashenka *feels*. Why does he make such a gradual move from apparent objectivity to subjectivity? Does this move contribute to or detract from the effectiveness of his presentation?
3. Do we know anything about what Nikolay Sergeitch thinks except through what he actually says and does? How does point of view influence our estimation of him? Would the story have changed if it had been narrated from his point of view?
4. Consider how this story would have been changed if it had been told totally objectively. How also would it have changed if it were a first-person narrative?
5. Why exactly is Mashenka so upset? What does her distress tell us about her? Are there indications in the story that Mashenka may be exceptionally naive?
6. Nikolay Sergeitch says he likes people "who still can feel resentment, contempt, and so on." What does he mean? Why is he incapable of feeling these things anymore?
7. Madame Kushkin is described as a "prosperous woman." What are the signs of prosperity in her household? What are the signs that her manners do not match her apparent social situation?
8. In "An Upheaval" there has been a crime and it is "solved" in an unexpected way. Is this story then a form of detective fiction? Specifically, how does Chekhov's presentation differ from Carr's in "The Incautious Burglar"?

Ernest J. Gaines (b. 1933)
Just Like a Tree

I shall not;
   I shall not be moved.
I shall not;
   I shall not be moved.
Just like a tree that's
planted 'side the water.
   Oh, I shall not be moved.

I made my home in glory;
   I shall not be moved.
Made my home in glory;
   I shall not be moved.
Just like a tree that's
planted 'side the water.
   Oh, I shall not be moved.

         (from an old Negro spiritual)

Chuckkie

Pa hit him on the back and he jeck in them chains like he pulling, but ever'body in the wagon know he ain't, and Pa hit him on the back again. He jeck again like he pulling, but even Big Red know he ain't doing a thing.

"That's why I'm go'n get a horse," Pa say. "He'll kill that other mule. Get up there, Mr. Bascom."

"Oh, let him alone," Gran'mon say. "How would you like it if you was pulling a wagon in all that mud?"

Pa don't answer Gran'mon; he just hit Mr. Bascom on the back again.

"That's right, kill him," Gran'mon say. "See where you get mo' money to buy another one."

"Get up there, Mr. Bascom," Pa say.

"You hear me talking to you, Emile?" Gran'mon say. "You want me hit you with something?"

"Ma, he ain't pulling," Pa say.

"Leave him alone," Gran'mon say.

Pa shake the lines little bit, but Mr. Bascom don't even feel it, and you can see he letting Big Red do all the pulling again. Pa say something kind o' low to hisself, and I can't make out what it is.

I low' my head little bit, 'cause that wind and fine rain was hitting me in the face, and I can feel Mama pressing close to me to keep me warm. She sitting on one side o' me and Pa sitting on the other side o' me, and Gran'mon in the back o' me in her setting chair. Pa didn't want bring the setting chair, telling Gran'mon there was two boards in that wagon already and she could sit on one of 'em all by herself if she wanted to, but Gran'mon say she was taking her setting chair with her if Pa liked it or not. She say she didn't ride in no wagon on nobody board, and if Pa liked it or not, that setting chair was going.

"Let her take her setting chair," Mama say. "What's wrong with taking her setting chair."

"Ehhh, Lord," Pa say, and picked up the setting chair and took it out to the wagon. "I guess I'll have to bring it back in the house, too, when we come back from there."

Gran'mon went and clambed in the wagon and moved her setting chair back little bit and sat down and folded her arms, waiting for us to get in, too. I got in and knelt down 'side her, but Mama told me to come up there and sit on the board 'side her and Pa so I could stay warm. Soon 's I sat down, Pa hit Mr. Bascom on the back, saying what a trifling thing Mr. Bascom was, and soon 's he got some mo' money he was getting rid o' Mr. Bascom and getting him a horse.

I raise my head to look see how far we is.

"That's it, yonder," I say.

"Stop pointing," Mama say, "and keep your hand in your pocket."

"Where?" Gran'mon say, back there in her setting chair.

"'Cross the ditch, yonder," I say.

"Can't see a thing for this rain," Gran'mon say.

"Can't hardly see it," I say. "But you can see the light little bit. That chinaball tree[1] standing in the way."

"Poor soul," Gran'mon say. "Poor soul."

I know Gran'mon was go'n say "poor soul, poor soul," 'cause she had been saying "poor soul, poor soul," ever since she heard Aunt Fe was go'n leave from back there.

Emile

Darn cane crop to finish getting in and only a mule and a half to do it. If I had my way I'd take that shotgun and a load o' buckshots and—but what's the use.

"Get up, Mr. Bascom—please," I say to that little dried-up, long-eared, tobacco-color thing. "Please, come up. Do your share for God sake—if you don't mind. I know it's hard pulling in all that mud, but if you don't do your share, then Big Red'll have to do his and yours, too. So, please, if it ain't asking you too much to—"

"Oh, Emile, shut up," Leola say.

"I can't hit him," I say, "or Mama back there'll hit me. So I have to talk to him. Please, Mr. Bascom, if you don't mind it. For my sake. No, not for mine; for God sake. No, not even for His'n; for Big Red sake. A fellow mule just like yourself is. Please, come up."

"Now, you hear that boy blaspheming God right in front o' me there," Mama say. "Ehhh, Lord—just keep it up. All this bad weather there like this whole world coming apart—a clap o' thunder come there and knock the fool out you. Just keep it up."

Maybe she right, and I stop. I look at Mr. Bascom there doing nothing, and I just give up. That mule know long 's Mama's alive he go'n do just what he

---

1. Chinaberry tree, a small rapid-growing Asiatic tree found in the southern U.S. where it is widely planted for shade and ornamentation.

want to do. He know when Papa was dying he told Mama to look after him, and he know no matter what he do, no matter what he don't do, Mama ain't go'n never let me do him anything. Sometimes I even feel Mama care mo' for Mr. Bascom 'an she care for me her own son.

We come up to the gate and I pull back on the lines.

"Whoa up, Big Red," I say. "You don't have to stop, Mr. Bascom. You never started."

I can feel Mama looking at me back there in that setting chair, but she don't say nothing.

"Here," I say to Chuckkie.

He take the lines and I jump down on the ground to open the old beat-up gate. I see Etienne's horse in the yard, and I see Chris new red tractor 'side the house, shining in the rain. When Mama die, I say to myself, Mr. Bascom, you going. Ever'body getting tractors and horses and I'm still stuck with you. You going, brother.

"Can you make it through?" I ask Chuckkie. "That gate ain't too wide."

"I can do it," he say.

"Be sure to make Mr. Bascom pull," I say.

"Emile, you better get back up here and drive 'em through," Leola say. "Chuckkie might break up that wagon."

"No, let him stay down there and give orders," Mama say, back there in that setting chair.

"He can do it," I say. "Come on, Chuckkie boy."

"Come up, here, mule," Chuckkie say.

And soon 's he say that, Big Red make a lunge for the yard, and Mr. Bascom don't even move, and 'fore I can bat my eyes I hear *pow-wow; sagg-sagg; pow-wow*. But above all that noise, Leola up there screaming her head off. And Mama—not a word; just sitting in that chair, looking at me with her arms still folded.

"Pull Big Red," I say. "Pull Big Red, Chuckkie."

Poor little Chuckkie up there pulling so hard till one of his little arms straight out in back; and Big Red throwing his shoulders and ever'thing else in it, and Mr. Bascom just walking there just 's loose and free, like he's suppose to be there just for his good looks. I move out the way just in time to let the wagon go by me, pulling half o' the fence in the yard behind it. I glance up again, and there's Leola still hollering and trying to jump out, but Mama not saying a word—just sitting there in that setting chair with her arms still folded.

"Whoa," I hear little Chuckkie saying. "Whoa up, now."

Somebody open the door and a bunch o' people come out on the gallery.

"What the world—?" Etienne say. "Thought the whole place was coming to pieces there."

"Chuckkie had a little trouble coming in the yard," I say.

"Goodness," Etienne say. "Anybody hurt?"

Mama just sit there about ten seconds, then she say something to herself and start clambing out the wagon.

"Let me help you there, Aunt Lou," Etienne say, coming down the steps.

"I can make it," Mama say. When she get on the ground she look up at Chuckkie. "Hand me my chair there, boy."

Poor little Chuckkie, up there with the lines in one hand, get the chair and hold it to the side, and Etienne catch it just 'fore it hit the ground. Mama start looking at me again, and it look like for at least a' hour she stand there looking at nobody but me. Then she say, "Ehhh, Lord," like that again, and go inside with Leola and the rest o' the people.

I look back at half o' the fence laying there in the yard, and I jump back on the wagon and guide the mules to the side o' the house. After unhitching 'em and tying 'em to the wheels, I look at Chris pretty red tractor again, and me and Chuckkie go inside: I make sure he kick all that mud off his shoes 'fore he go in the house.

Leola

Sitting over there by that fireplace, trying to look joyful when ever'body there know she ain't. But she trying, you know; smiling and bowing when people say something to her. How can she be joyful, I ask you; how can she be? Poor thing, she been here all her life—or the most of it, let's say. 'Fore they moved in this house, they lived in one back in the woods 'bout a mile from here. But for the past twenty-five or thirty years, she been right in this one house. I know ever since I been big enough to know people I been seeing her right here.

Aunt Fe, Aunt Fe, Aunt Fe, Aunt Fe; the name's been 'mongst us just like us own family name. Just like the name o' God. Like the name of town—the city. Aunt Fe, Aunt Fe, Aunt Fe, Aunt Fe.

Poor old thing; how many times I done come here and washed clothes for her when she couldn't do it herself. How many times I done hoed in that garden, ironed her clothes, wrung a chicken neck for her. You count the days in the year and you'll be pretty close. And I didn't mind it a bit. No, I didn't mind it a bit. She there trying to pay me. Proud—Lord, talking 'bout pride. "Here." "No, Aunt Fe; no." "Here, here; you got a child there, you can use it." "No, Aunt Fe. No. No. What would Mama think if she knowed I took money from you? Aunt Fe, Mama would never forgive me. No. I love doing these thing for you. I just wish I could do more."

And there, now, trying to make 'tend she don't mind leaving. Ehhh, Lord.

I hear a bunch o' rattling round in the kitchen and I go back there. I see Louise stirring this big pot o' eggnog.

"Louise," I say.

"Leola," she say.

We look at each other and she stir the eggnog again. She know what I'm go'n say next, and she can't even look in my face.

"Louise, I wish there was some other way."

"There's no other way," she say.

"Louise, moving her from here's like moving a tree you been used to in your front yard all your life."

"What else can I do?"

"Oh, Louise, Louise."

"Nothing else but that."

"Louise, what people go'n do without her here?"

She stir the eggnog and don't answer.

"Louise, us'll take her in with us."

"You all no kin to Auntie. She go with me."

"And us'll never see her again."

She stir the eggnog. Her husband come back in the kitchen and kiss her on the back o' the neck and then look at me and grin. Right from the start I can see I ain't go'n like that nigger.

"Almost ready, honey?" he say.

"Almost."

He go to the safe and get one o' them bottles of whiskey he got in there and come back to the stove.

"No," Louise say. "Everybody don't like whiskey in it. Add the whiskey after you've poured it up."

"Okay, hon."

He kiss her on the back o' the neck again. Still don't like that nigger. Something 'bout him ain't right.

"You one o' the family?" he say.

"Same as one," I say. "And you?"

He don't like the way I say it, and I don't care if he like it or not. He look at me there a second, and then he kiss her on the ear.

"Un-unnn," she say, stirring the pot.

"I love your ear, baby," he say.

"Go in the front room and talk with the people," she say.

He kiss her on the other ear. A nigger do all that front o' public got something to hide. He leave the kitchen. I look at Louise.

"Ain't nothing else I can do," she say.

"You sure, Louise? You positive?"

"I'm positive," she say.

The front door open and Emile and Chuckkie come in. A minute later Washington and Adrieu come in, too. Adrieu come back in the kitchen, and I can see she been crying. Aunt Fe is her godmother, you know.

"How you feel, Adrieu?"

"That weather out there," she say.

"Y'all walked?"

"Yes."

"Us here in the wagon. Y'all can go back with us."

"Y'all the one tore the fence down?" she ask.

"Yes, I guess so. That brother-in-law o' yours in there letting Chuckkie drive that wagon."

"Well, I don't guess it'll matter too much. Nobody go'n be here, anyhow."

And she start crying again. I take her in my arms and pat her on the shoulder, and I look at Louise stirring the eggnog.

"What I'm go'n do and my nan-nane gone? I love her so much."

"Ever'body love her."

"Since my mama died, she been like my mama."

"Shhh," I say. "Don't let her hear you. Make her grieve. You don't want her grieving, now, do you?"

She sniffs there 'gainst my dress few times.

"Oh, Lord," she say. "Lord, have mercy."

"Shhh," I say. "Shhh. That's what life's 'bout."

"That ain't what life's 'bout," she say. "It ain't fair. This been her home all her life. These the people she know. She don't know them people she going to. It ain't fair."

"Shhh, Adrieu," I say. "Now, you saying things that ain't your business."
She cry there some mo'.

"Oh, Lord, Lord," she say.

Louise turn from the stove.

"About ready now," she say, going to the middle door. "James, tell everybody to come back and get some."

James

Let me go on back here and show these country niggers how to have a good time. All they know is talk, talk, talk. Talk so much they make me buggy round here. Damn this weather—wind, rain. Must be a million cracks in this old house.

I go to that old beat-up safe in that corner and get that fifth of Mr. Harper (in the South now; got to say Mister), give the seal one swipe, the stopper one jerk, and head back to that old wood stove. (Man, like, these cats are primitive—goodness. You know what I mean? I mean like wood stoves. Don't mention TV, man, these cats here never heard of that.) I start to dump Mr. Harper in the pot and Baby catches my hand again and say not all of them like it. You ever heard of anything like that? I mean a stud's going to drink eggnog, and he's not going to put whiskey in it. I mean he's going to drink it straight. I mean, you ever heard anything like that? Well, I wasn't pressing none of them on Mr. Harper. I mean, me and Mr. Harper get along too well together for me to go around there pressing.

I hold my cup there and let Baby put a few drops of this egg stuff in it; then I jerk my cup back and let Mr. Harper run a while. Couple of these cats come over (some of them aren't so lame) and set their cups, and I let Mr. Harper run for them. Then this cat says he's got 'nough. I let Mr. Harper run for this other stud, and pretty soon he says, "Hold it. Good." Country cat, you know. "Hold it. Good." Real country cat. So I raise the cup to see what Mr. Harper's doing. He's just right. I raise the cup again. Just right, Mr. Harper; just right.

I go to the door with Mr. Harper under my arm and the cup in my hand and I look into the front room where they all are. I mean, there's about ninety-nine of them in there. Old ones, young ones, little ones, big ones, yellow ones, black ones, brown ones—you name them, brother, and they were there. And what for? Brother, I'll tell you what for. Just because me and Baby are taking this old chick out of these sticks. Well, I'll tell you where I'd be at this moment if I was one of them. With that weather out there like it is, I'd be under about five blankets with some little warm belly pressing against mine. Brother, you can bet your hat I wouldn't be here. Man, listen to that thing out there. You can hear that rain beating on that old house like grains of rice; and that wind coming through them cracks like it does in those old Charlie Chaplin movies. Man, like you know—like *whooo-ee; whooo-ee.* Man, you talking about some weird cats.

I can feel Mr. Harper starting to massage my wig and I bat my eyes twice and look at the old girl over there. She's still sitting in that funny-looking little old rocking chair, and not saying a word to anybody. Just sitting there looking into the fireplace at them two pieces of wood that aren't giving out enough heat to warm a baby, let alone ninety-nine grown people. I mean, you know, like that sleet's falling out there like all get-up-and-go, and them two pieces of wood are lying there just as dead as the rest of these way-out cats.

One of the old cats—I don't know which one he is—Mose, Sam, or something like that—leans over and pokes in the fire a minute; then a little blaze shoots up, and he raises up, too, looking as satisfied as if he'd just sent a rocket into orbit. I mean, these cats are like that. They do these little bitty things, and they feel like they've really done something. Well, back in these sticks, I guess there just isn't nothing big to do.

I feel Mr. Harper touching my skull now—and I notice this little chick passing by me with these two cups of eggnog. She goes over to the fireplace and gives one to each of these old chicks. The one sitting in that setting chair she brought with her from God knows where, and the other cup to the old chick that Baby and I are going to haul from here sometime tomorrow morning. Wait, man, I mean like, you ever heard of anybody going to somebody else's house with a chair? I mean, wouldn't you call that an insult at the basest point? I mean, now, like tell me what you think of that? I mean—dig—here I am at my pad, and in you come with your own stool. I mean, now, like man, you know. I mean that's an insult at the basest point. I mean, you know . . . you know, like way out. . . .

Mr. Harper, what you trying to do, boy?—I mean, *sir*. (Got to watch myself, I'm in the South. Got to keep watching myself.)

This stud touches me on the shoulder and raise his cup and say, "How 'bout a taste?" I know what the stud's talking about, so I let Mr. Harper run for him. But soon 's I let a drop get in, the stud say, " 'Nough." I mean I let about two drops get in, and already the stud's got enough. Man, I mean, like you know. I mean these studs are 'way out. I mean like 'way back there.

This stud takes a swig of his eggnog and say, "Ahhh." I mean this real down-home way of saying "Ahhhh." I mean, man, like these studs—I notice this little chick passing by me again, and this time she's crying. I mean weeping, you know. And just because this old ninety-nine-year-old chick's packing up and leaving. I mean, you ever heard of anything like that? I mean, here she is pretty as the day is long and crying because Baby and I are hauling this old chick away. Well, I'd like to make her cry. And I can assure you, brother, it wouldn't be from leaving her.

I turn and look at Baby over there by the stove, pouring eggnog in all these cups. I mean, there're about twenty of these cats lined up there. And I bet you not half of them will take Mr. Harper along. Some way-ernest cats, man. Some way-out cats.

I go up to Baby and kiss her on the back of the neck and give her a little pat where she likes for me to pat her when we're in the bed. She say, "Uh-uh," but I know she likes it anyhow.

Ben O

I back under the bed and touch the slop jar, and I pull back my leg and back somewhere else, and then I get me a good sight on it. I spin my aggie couple times and sight again and then I shoot. I hit it right square in the middle and it go flying over the fireplace. I crawl over there to get it and I see 'em all over there drinking they eggnog and they didn't even offer me and Chuckkie none. I find my marble on the bricks, and I go back and tell Chuckkie they over there drinking eggnog.

"You want some?" I say.

"I want shoot marble," Chuckkie say. "Yo' shot. Shoot up."

"I want some eggnog," I say.

"Shoot up, Ben O," he say. "I'm getting cold staying in one place so long. You feel that draft?"

"Coming from that crack under that bed," I say.

"Where?" Chuckkie say, looking for the crack.

"Over by that bedpost over there," I say.

"This sure's a beat-up old house," Chuckkie say.

"I want me some eggnog," I say.

"Well, you ain't getting none," Gran'mon say, from the fireplace. "It ain't good for you."

"I can drink eggnog," I say. "How come it ain't good for me? It ain't nothing but eggs and milk. I eat chicken, don't I? I eat beef, don't I?"

Gran'mon don't say nothing.

"I want me some eggnog," I say.

Gran'mon still don't say no more. Nobody else don't say nothing, neither.

"I want me some eggnog," I say.

"You go'n get a eggnog," Gran'mon say. "Just keep that noise up."

"I want me some eggnog," I say; "and I 'tend to get me some eggnog tonight."

Next thing I know, Gran'mon done picked up a chip out o' that corner and done sailed it back there where me and Chuckkie is. I duck just in time, and the chip catch old Chuckkie side the head.

"Hey, who that hitting me?" Chuckkie say.

"Move, and you won't get hit," Gran'mon say.

I laugh at old Chuckkie over there holding his head, and next thing I know here's Chuckkie done haul back there and hit me in my side. I jump up from there and give him two just to show him how it feel, and he jump and hit me again. Then we grab each other and start tussling on the floor.

"You, Ben O," I hear Gran'mon saying. "You, Ben O, cut that out. Y'all cut that out."

But we don't stop, 'cause neither one o' us want be first. Then I feel somebody pulling us apart.

"What I ought to do is whip both o' you," Mrs. Leola say. "Is that what y'all want?"

"No'm," I say.

"Then shake hand."

Me and Chuckkie shake hand.

"Kiss," Mrs. Leola say.

"No, ma'am," I say. "I ain't kissing no boy. I ain't that crazy."

"Kiss him, Chuckkie," she say.

Old Chuckkie kiss me on the jaw.

"Now, kiss him, Ben O."

"I ain't kissing no Chuckkie," I say. "No'm. Uh-uh. You kiss girls."

And the next thing I know, Mama done tipped up back o' me and done whop me on the leg with Daddy belt.

"Kiss Chuckkie," she say.

Chuckkie turn his jaw to me and I kiss him. I almost wipe my mouth. I even feel like spitting.

"Now, come back here and get you some eggnog," Mama say.

"That's right, spoil 'em," Gran'mon say. "Next thing you know, they be drinking from bottles."

"Little eggnog won't hurt 'em, Mama," Mama say.

"That's right, never listen," Gran'mon say. "It's you go'n suffer for it. I be dead and gone, me."

Aunt Clo

Be just like wrapping a chain round a tree and jecking and jecking, and then shifting the chain little bit and jecking and jecking some in that direction, and then shifting it some mo' and jecking and jecking in that direction. Jecking and jecking till you get it loose, and then pulling with all your might. Still it might not be loose enough and you have to back the tractor up some and fix the chain round the tree again and start jecking all over. Jeck, jeck, jeck. Then you hear the roots crying, and then you keep on jecking, and then it give, and you jeck some mo', and then it falls. And not till then that you see what you done done. Not till then you see the big hole in the ground and piece of the taproot[2] still way down in it—a piece you won't never get out no matter if you dig till doomsday. Yes, you got the tree—least got it down on the ground, but did you get the taproot? No. No, sir, you didn't get the taproot. You stand there and look down in this hole at it and you grab yo' axe and jump down in it and start chopping at the taproot, but do you get the taproot? No. You don't get the tap-root, sir. You never get the taproot. But, sir, I tell you what you do get. You get a big hole in the ground, sir; and you get another big hole in the air where the lovely branches been all these years. Yes, sir, that's what you get. The holes, sir, the holes. Two holes, sir, you can't never fill no matter how hard you try.

So you wrap yo' chain round yo' tree again, sir, and you start dragging it. But the dragging ain't so easy, sir, 'cause she's a heavy old tree—been there a long time, you know—heavy. And you make yo' tractor strain, sir, and the ele-ments work 'gainst you, too, sir, 'cause the elements, they on her side, too, 'cause she part o' the elements, and the elements, they part o' her. So the ele-ments, they do they little share to discourage you—yes, sir, they does. But you will not let the elements stop you. No, sir, you show the elements that they just elements, and man is stronger than elements, and you jeck and jeck on the chain, and soon she start to moving with you, sir, but if you look over yo' shoulder one second you see her leaving a trail—a trail, sir, that can be seen from miles and miles away. You see her trying to hook her little fine branches in different little cracks, in between pickets, round hills o' grass, round any-

---

2. Primary root.

thing they might brush 'gainst. But you is a determined man, sir, and you jeck and you jeck, and she keep on grabbing and trying to hold, but you stronger, sir—course you the strongest—and you finally get her out on the pave road. But what you don't notice, sir, is just 'fore she get on the pave road she leave couple her little branches to remind the people that it ain't her that want leave, but you, sir, that think she ought to. So you just drag her and drag her, sir, and the folks that live in the houses 'side the pave road, they come out on they gallery and look at her go by, and then they go back in they house and sit by the fire and forget her. So you just go on, sir, and you just go and you go—and for how many days? I don't know. I don't have the least idea. The North to me, sir, is like the elements. It mystify me. But never mind, you finally get there, and then you try to find a place to set her. You look in this corner and you look in that corner, but no corner is good. She kind o' stand in the way no matter where you set her. So finally, sir, you say, "I just stand her up here a little while and see, and if it don't work out, if she keep getting in the way, I guess we'll just have to take her to the dump."

Chris

Just like him, though, standing up there telling them lies when everybody else feeling sad. I don't know what you do without people like him. And, yet, you see him there, he sad just like the rest. But he just got to be funny. Crying on the inside, but still got to be funny.

He didn't steal it, though; didn't steal it a bit. His grandpa was just like him. Mat? Mat Jefferson? Just like that. Mat could make you die laughing. 'Member once at a wake. Who was dead? Yes—Robert Lewis. Robert Lewis laying up in his coffin dead as a door nail. Everybody sad and droopy. Mat look at that and start his lying. Soon, half o' the place laughing. Funniest wake I ever went to, and yet—

Just like now. Look at 'em. Look at 'em laughing. Ten minutes ago you would 'a' thought you was at a funeral. But look at 'em now. Look at her there in that little old chair. How long she had it? Fifty years—a hundred? It ain't a chair no mo', it's little bit o' her. Just like her arm, just like her leg.

You know, I couldn't believe it. I couldn't. Emile passed the house there the other day, right after the bombing,[3] and I was in my yard digging a water drain to let the water run out in the ditch. Emile, he stopped the wagon there 'fore the door. Little Chuckkie, he in there with him with that little rain cap buckled up over his head. I go out to the gate and I say, "Emile, it's the truth?"

"The truth," he say. And just like that he say it. "The truth."

I look at him there, and he looking up the road to keep from looking back at me. You know, they been pretty close to Aunt Fe ever since they was children coming up. His own mon, Aunt Lou, and Aunt Fe, they been like sisters, there, together.

Me and him, we talk there little while 'bout the cane cutting, then he say he got to get on to the back. He shake the lines and drive on.

---

3. During the 1950s and 1960s, numerous bombings occurred in the South as a reaction to initial attempts to achieve racial integration of public facilities.

Inside me, my heart feel like it done swole up ten times the size it ought to be. Water come in my eyes, and I got to 'mit I cried right there. Yes sir, I cried right there by that front gate.

Louise come in the room and whisper something to Leola, and they go back in the kitchen. I can hear 'em moving things round back there, still getting things together they go'n be taking along. If they offer me anything, I'd like that big iron pot out there in the back yard. Good for boiling water when you killing hog, you know.

You can feel the sadness in the room again. Louise brought it in when she come in and whispered to Leola. Only, she didn't take it out when her and Leola left. Every pan they move, every pot they unhook keep telling you she leaving, she leaving.

Etienne turn over one o' them logs to make the fire pick up some, and I see that boy, Lionel, spreading out his hands over the fire. Watch out, I think to myself, here come another lie. People, he just getting started.

Anne-Marie Duvall

"You're not going?"

"I'm not going," he says, turning over the log with the poker. "And if you were in your right mind, you wouldn't go, either."

"You just don't understand, do you?"

"Oh, I understand. She cooked for your daddy. She nursed you when your mama died."

"And I'm trying to pay her back with a seventy-nine-cents scarf. Is that too much?"

He is silent, leaning against the mantel, looking down at the fire. The fire throws strange shadows across the big, old room. Father looks down at me from against the wall. His eyes do not say go nor stay. But I know what he would do.

"Please go with me, Edward."

"You're wasting your breath."

I look at him a long time, then I get the small package from the coffee table.

"You're still going?"

"I am going."

"Don't call for me if you get bogged down anywhere back there."

I look at him and go out to the garage. The sky is black. The clouds are moving fast and low. A fine drizzle is falling, and the wind coming from the swamps blows in my face. I cannot recall a worse night in all my life.

I hurry into the car and drive out of the yard. The house stands big and black in back of me. Am I angry with Edward? No, I'm not angry with Edward. He's right. I should not go out into this kind of weather. But what he does not understand is I must. Father definitely would have gone if he were alive. Grandfather definitely would have gone, also. And, therefore, I must. Why? I cannot answer why. Only, I must go.

As soon as I turn down that old muddy road, I begin to pray. Don't let me go into that ditch, I pray. Don't let me go into that ditch. Please, don't let me go into that ditch.

The lights play on the big old trees along the road. Here and there the lights hit a sagging picket fence. But I know I haven't even started yet. She lives far back into the fields. Why? God, why does she have to live so far back? Why couldn't she have lived closer to the front? But the answer to that is as hard for me as is the answer to everything else. It was ordained before I—before father—was born—that she should live back there. So why should I try to understand it now?

The car slides towards the ditch, and I stop it dead and turn the wheel, and then come back into the road again. Thanks, father. I know you're with me. Because it was you who said that I must look after her, didn't you? No, you did not say it directly, father. You said it only with a glance. As grandfather must have said it to you, and as his father must have said it to him.

But now that she's gone, father, now what? I know. I know. Aunt Lou, Aunt Clo, and the rest.

The lights shine on the dead, wet grass along the road. There's an old pecan tree, looking dead and all alone. I wish I was a little nigger gal so I could pick pecans and eat them under the big old dead tree.

The car hits a rut, but bounces right out of it. I am frightened for a moment, but then I feel better. The windshield wipers are working well, slapping the water away as fast as it hits the glass. If I make the next half mile all right, the rest of the way will be good. It's not much over a mile now.

That was too bad about that bombing—killing that woman and her two children. That poor woman; poor children. What is the answer? What will happen? What do they want? Do they know what they want? Do they really know what they want? Are they positively sure? Have they any idea? Money to buy a car, is that it? If that is all, I pity them. Oh, how I pity them.

Not much farther. Just around that bend and—there's a water hole. Now what?

I stop the car and just stare out at the water a minute; then I get out to see how deep it is. The cold wind shoots through my body like needles. Lightning comes from towards the swamps and lights up the place. For a split second the night is as bright as day. The next second it is blacker than it has ever been.

I look at the water, and I can see that it's too deep for the car to pass through. I must turn back or I must walk the rest of the way. I stand there a while wondering what to do. Is it worth it all? Can't I simply send the gift by someone tomorrow morning? But will there be someone tomorrow morning? Suppose she leaves without getting it, then what? What then? Father would never forgive me. Neither would grandfather or great-grandfather, either. No, they wouldn't.

The lightning flashes again and I look across the field, and I can see the tree in the yard a quarter of a mile away. I have but one choice: I must walk. I get the package out of the car and stuff it in my coat and start out.

I don't make any progress at first, but then I become a little warmer and I find I like walking. The lightning flashes just in time to show up a puddle of water, and I go around it. But there's no light to show up the second puddle, and I fall flat on my face. For a moment I'm completely blind, then I get slowly to my feet and check the package. It's dry, not harmed. I wash the mud off my raincoat, wash my hands, and I start out again.

The house appears in front of me, and as I come into the yard, I can hear the people laughing and talking. Sometimes I think niggers can laugh and joke even if they see somebody beaten to death. I go up on the porch and knock and an old one opens the door for me. I swear, when he sees me he looks as if he's seen a ghost. His mouth drops open, his eyes bulge—I swear.

I go into the old crowded and smelly room, and every one of them looks at me the same way the first one did. All the joking and laughing has ceased. You would think I was the devil in person.

"Done, Lord," I hear her saying over by the fireplace. They move to the side and I can see her sitting in that little rocking chair I bet you she's had since the beginning of time. "Done, Master," she says. "Child, what you doing in weather like this? Y'all move; let her get to that fire. Y'all move. Move, now. Let her warm herself."

They start scattering everywhere.

"I'm not cold, Aunt Fe," I say. "I just brought you something—something small—because you're leaving us. I'm going right back."

"Done, Master," she says. Fussing over me just like she's done all her life. "Done, Master. Child, you ain't got no business in a place like this. Get close to this fire. Get here. Done, Master."

I move closer, and the fire does feel warm and good.

"Done, Lord," she says.

I take out the package and pass it to her. The other niggers gather around with all kinds of smiles on their faces. Just think of it—a white lady coming through all of this for one old darky. It is all right for them to come from all over the plantation, from all over the area, in all kinds of weather: this is to be expected of them. But a white lady, a white lady. They must think we white people don't have their kind of feelings.

She unwraps the package, her bony little fingers working slowly and deliberately. When she sees the scarf—the seventy-nine-cents scarf—she brings it to her mouth and kisses it.

"Y'all look," she says. "Y'all look. Ain't it the prettiest little scarf y'all ever did see? Y'all look."

They move around her and look at the scarf. Some of them touch it.

"I go'n put it on right now," she says. "I go'n put it on right now, my lady."

She unfolds it and ties it round her head and looks up at everybody and smiles.

"Thank you, my lady," she says. "Thank you, ma'am, from the bottom of my heart."

"Oh, Aunt Fe," I say, kneeling down beside her. "Oh, Aunt Fe."

But I think about the other niggers there looking down at me, and I get up. But I look into that wrinkled old face again, and I must go back down again. And I lay my head in that bony old lap, and I cry and I cry—I don't know how long. And I feel those old fingers, like death itself, passing over my hair and my neck. I don't know how long I kneel there crying, and when I stop, I get out of there as fast as I can.

Etienne

The boy come in, and soon, right off, they get quiet, blaming the boy. If people could look little farther than the tip of they nose—No, they blame the boy. Not that they ain't behind the boy, what he doing, but they blame him for what she must do. What they don't know is that the boy didn't start it, and the people that bombed the house didn't start it, neither. It started a million years ago. It started when one man envied another man for having a penny mo' 'an he had, and then the man married a woman to help him work the field so he could get much 's the other man, but when the other man saw the man had married a woman to get much 's him, he, himself, he married a woman, too, so he could still have mo'. Then they started having children—not from love; but so the children could help 'em work so they could have mo'. But even with the children one man still had a penny mo' 'an the other, so the other man went and bought him a ox, and the other man did the same—to keep ahead of the other man. And soon the other man had bought him a slave to work the ox so he could get ahead of the other man. But the other man went out and bought him two slaves so he could stay ahead of the other man, and the other man went out and bought him three slaves. And soon they had a thousand slaves apiece, but they still wasn't satisfied. And one day the slaves all rose and kill the masters, but the masters (knowing slaves was men just like they was, and kind o' expected they might do this) organized theyself a good police force, and the police force, they come out and killed the two thousand slaves.

So it's not this boy you see standing here 'fore you, 'cause it happened a million years ago. And this boy here's just doing something the slaves done a million years ago. Just that this boy here ain't doing it they way. 'Stead of raising arms 'gainst the masters, he bow his head.

No, I say; don't blame the boy 'cause she must go. 'Cause when she's dead, and that won't be long after they get her up there, this boy's work will still be going on. She's not the only one that's go'n die from this boy's work. Many mo' of 'em go'n die 'fore it's over with. The whole place—everything. A big wind is rising, and when a big wind rise, the sea stirs, and the drop o' water you see laying on top the sea this day won't be there tomorrow. 'Cause that's what wind do, and that's what life is. She ain't nothing but one little drop o' water laying on top the sea, and what this boy's doing is called the wind . . . and she must be moved. No, don't blame the boy. Go out and blame the wind. No, don't blame him, 'cause tomorrow, what he's doing today, somebody go'n say he ain't done a thing. 'Cause tomorrow will be his time to be turned over just like it's hers today. And after that, be somebody else time to turn over. And it keep going like that till it ain't nothing left to turn—and nobody left to turn it.

"Sure, they bombed the house," he say; "because they want us to stop. But if we stopped today, then what good would we have done? What good? Those who have already died for the cause would have just died in vain."

"Maybe if they had bombed your house you wouldn't be so set on keeping this up."

"If they had killed my mother and my brothers and sisters, I'd press just that much harder. I can see you all point. I can see it very well. But I can't agree with you. You blame me for their being bombed. You blame me for Aunt Fe's leaving. They died for you and for your children. And I love Aunt Fe as much as anybody in here does. Nobody in here loves her more than I do. Not one of you." He looks at her. "Don't you believe me, Aunt Fe?"

She nods—that little white scarf still tied round her head.

"How many times have I eaten in your kitchen, Aunt Fe? A thousand times? How many times have I eaten tea cakes and drank milk on the back steps, Aunt Fe? A thousand times? How many times have I sat at this same fireplace with you, just the two of us, Aunt Fe? Another thousand times—two thousand times? How many times have I chopped wood for you, chopped grass for you, ran to the store for you? Five thousand times? How many times have we walked to church together, Aunt Fe? Gone fishing at the river together—how many times? I've spent as much time in this house as I've spent in my own. I know every crack in the wall. I know every corner. With my eyes shut, I can go anywhere in here without bumping into anything. How many of you can do that? Not many of you." He looks at her. "Aunt Fe?"

She looks at him.

"Do you think I love you, Aunt Fe?"

She nods.

"I love you, Aunt Fe, much as I do my own parents. I'm going to miss you much as I'd miss my own mother if she were to leave me now. I'm going to miss you, Aunt Fe, but I'm not going to stop what I've started. You told me a story once, Aunt Fe, about my great-grandpa. Remember? Remember how he died?"

She looks in the fire and nods.

"Remember how they lynched him—chopped him into pieces?"

She nods.

"Just the two of us were sitting here beside the fire when you told me that. I was so angry I felt like killing. But it was you who told me get killing out of my mind. It was you who told me I would only bring harm to myself and sadness to the others if I killed. Do you remember that, Aunt Fe?"

She nods, still looking in the fire.

"You were right. We cannot raise our arms. Because it would mean death for ourselves, as well as for the others. But we will do something else—and that's what we will do." He looks at the people standing round him. "And if they were to bomb my own mother's house tomorrow, I would still go on."

"I'm not saying for you not to go on," Louise says. "That's up to you. I'm just taking Auntie from here before hers is the next house they bomb."

The boy look at Louise, and then at Aunt Fe. He go up to the chair where she sitting.

"Good-bye, Aunt Fe," he say, picking up her hand. The hand done shriveled up to almost nothing. Look like nothing but loose skin's covering the bones. "I'll miss you," he say.

"Good-bye, Emmanuel," she say. She look at him a long time. "God be with you."

He stand there holding the hand a while longer, then he nods his head, and leaves the house. The people stir round little bit, but nobody say anything.

Aunt Lou

They tell her good-bye, and half of 'em leave the house crying, or want cry, but she just sit there 'side the fireplace like she don't mind going at all. When Leola ask me if I'm ready to go, I tell her I'm staying right there till Fe leave that house. I tell her I ain't moving one step till she go out that door. I been knowing her for the past fifty some years now, and I ain't 'bout to leave her on her last night here.

That boy, Chuckkie, want stay with me, but I make him go. He follow his mon and paw out the house and soon I hear that wagon turning round. I hear Emile saying something to Mr. Bascom even 'fore that wagon get out the yard. I tell myself, well, Mr. Bascom, you sure go'n catch it, and me not there to take up for you—and I get up from my chair and go to the door.

"Emile?" I call.

"Whoa," he say.

"You leave that mule 'lone, you hear me?"

"I ain't done Mr. Bascom a thing, Mama," he say.

"Well, you just mind you don't," I say. "I'll sure find out."

"Yes'm," he say. "Come up here, Mr. Bascom."

"Now, you hear that boy. Emile?" I say.

"I'm sorry, Mama," he say. "I didn't mean no harm."

They go out in the road, and I go back to the fireplace and sit down again. Louise stir round in the kitchen a few minutes, then she come in the front where we at. Everybody else gone. That husband o' hers, there, got drunk long 'fore midnight, and Emile and them had to put him to bed in the other room.

She come there and stand by the fire.

"I'm dead on my feet," she say.

"Why don't you go to bed," I say. "I'm go'n be here."

"You all won't need anything?"

"They got wood in that corner?"

"Plenty."

"Then we won't need a thing."

She stand there and warm, and then she say good night and go round the other side.

"Well, Fe?" I say.

"I ain't leaving here tomorrow, Lou," she say.

"'Course you is," I say. "Up there ain't that bad."

She shake her head. "No, I ain't going nowhere."

I look at her over in her chair, but I don't say nothing. The fire pops in the fireplace, and I look at the fire again. It's a good little fire—not too big, not too little. Just 'nough there to keep the place warm.

"You want sing, Lou?" she say, after a while. "I feel like singing my 'termination song."

"Sure," I say.

She start singing in that little light voice she got there, and I join with her. We sing two choruses, and then she stop.

"My 'termination for Heaven," she say. "Now—now—"

"What's the matter, Fe?" I say.

"Nothing," she say. "I want get in my bed. My gown hanging over there."

I get the gown for her and bring it back to the firehalf. She get out of her dress slowly, like she don't even have 'nough strength to do it. I help her on with her gown, and she kneel down there 'side the bed and say her prayers. I sit in my chair and look at the fire again.

She pray there a long time—half out loud, half to herself. I look at her kneeling down there, little like a little old girl. I see her making some kind o' jecking motion there, but I feel she crying 'cause this her last night here, and 'cause she got to go and leave ever'thing behind. I look at the fire.

She pray there ever so long, and then she start to get up. But she can't make it by herself. I go to help her, and when I put my hand on her shoulder, she say, "Lou? Lou?"

I say, "What's the matter, Fe?"

"Lou?" she say. "Lou?"

I feel her shaking in my hand with all her might. Shaking, shaking, shaking—like a person with the chill. Then I hear her take a long breath, longest I ever heard anybody take before. Then she ease back on the bed—calm, calm, calm.

"Sleep on, Fe," I tell her. "When you get up there, tell 'em all I ain't far behind."

Questions for Study

1. This is a story that makes the reader put all the pieces of the narrative together. What does a writer gain by setting out a story this way? What does he lose?
2. Why is Aunt Fe leaving? Is there more than one reason?
3. How would you describe the general mood of this story?
4. Setting is important in this story. Does the weather, for instance, provide an appropriate background for the narrative? How is the location of the house appropriate? Why does Gaines describe different approaches to the house? How do several items in and around the house become especially significant?
5. The characters express radically different opinions about everything from mules to people. Are there any discrepancies in their accounts of events? Can we trust any one character's view more than another's?
6. Imagine how the story would have changed if it had been told exclusively from James' point of view. Why did Gaines include James? Why did he not give us one sequence from Emmanuel's point of view?
7. Why does Gaines make several references to a bombing? Do these references strengthen or weaken the impact of the story? How do they relate to Gaines' meaning?
8. Is the story's ending believable? Overdone? Appropriate? Has Gaines prepared us for this ending in any way? Explain your responses.
9. What is the significance of the poem at the beginning? How does it fit in with the story?

Sherwood Anderson   (1876–1941)
Death in the Woods

I

She was an old woman and lived on a farm near the town in which I lived.
All country and small-town people have seen such old women, but no one
knows much about them. Such an old woman comes into town driving an old
worn-out horse or she comes afoot carrying a basket. She may own a few hens
and have eggs to sell. She brings them in a basket and takes them to a grocer.
There she trades them in. She gets some salt pork and some beans. Then she
gets a pound or two of sugar and some flour.

Afterwards she goes to the butcher's and asks for some dog-meat. She may
spend ten or fifteen cents, but when she does she asks for something. Formerly
the butchers gave liver to anyone who wanted to carry it away. In our family
we were always having it. Once one of my brothers got a whole cow's liver at
the slaughterhouse near the fair grounds in our town. We had it until we were
sick of it. It never cost a cent. I have hated the thought of it ever since.

The old farm woman got some liver and a soup-bone. She never visited with
anyone, and as soon as she got what she wanted she lit out for home. It made
quite a load for such an old body. No one gave her a lift. People drive right
down a road and never notice an old woman like that.

There was such an old woman who used to come into town past our house
one summer and fall when I was a young boy and was sick with what was called
inflammatory rheumatism. She went home later carrying a heavy pack on her
back. Two or three large gaunt-looking dogs followed at her heels.

The old woman was nothing special. She was one of the nameless ones that
hardly anyone knows, but she got into my thoughts. I have just suddenly now,
after all these years, remembered her and what happened. It is a story. Her
name was Grimes, and she lived with her husband and son in a small unpainted
house on the bank of a small creek four miles from town.

The husband and son were a tough lot. Although the son was but twenty-
one, he had already served a term in jail. It was whispered about that the
woman's husband stole horses and ran them off to some other county. Now
and then, when a horse turned up missing, the man had also disappeared. No
one ever caught him. Once, when I was loafing at Tom Whitehead's livery-
barn, the man came there and sat on the bench in front. Two or three other men
were there, but no one spoke to him. He sat for a few minutes and then got up
and went away. When he was leaving he turned around and stared at the men.
There was a look of defiance in his eyes. "Well, I have tried to be friendly.
You don't want to talk to me. It has been so wherever I have gone in this town.
If, some day, one of your fine horses turns up missing, well, then what?" He
did not say anything actually. "I'd like to bust one of you on the jaw," was
about what his eyes said. I remember how the look in his eyes made me shiver.

The old man belonged to a family that had had money once. His name was
Jake Grimes. It all comes back clearly now. His father, John Grimes, had owned
a sawmill when the country was new, and had made money. Then he got to

drinking and running after women. When he died there wasn't much left.

Jake blew in the rest. Pretty soon there wasn't any more lumber to cut and his land was nearly all gone.

He got his wife off a German farmer, for whom he went to work one June day in the wheat harvest. She was a young thing then and scared to death. You see, the farmer was up to something with the girl—she was, I think, a bound girl and his wife had her suspicions. She took it out on the girl when the man wasn't around. Then, when the wife had to go off to town for supplies, the farmer got after her. She told young Jake that nothing really ever happened, but he didn't know whether to believe it or not.

He got her pretty easy himself, the first time he was out with her. He wouldn't have married her if the German farmer hadn't tried to tell him where to get off. He got her to go riding with him in his buggy one night when he was threshing on the place, and then he came for her the next Sunday night.

She managed to get out of the house without her employer's seeing, but when she was getting into the buggy he showed up. It was almost dark, and he just popped up suddenly at the horse's head. He grabbed the horse by the bridle and Jake got out his buggy-whip.

They had it out all right! The German was a tough one. Maybe he didn't care whether his wife knew or not. Jake hit him over the face and shoulders with the buggy-whip, but the horse got to acting up and he had to get out.

Then the two men went for it. The girl didn't see it. The horse started to run away and went nearly a mile down the road before the girl got him stopped. Then she managed to tie him to a tree beside the road. (I wonder how I know all this. It must have stuck in my mind from small-town tales when I was a boy.) Jake found her there after he got through with the German. She was huddled up in the buggy seat, crying, scared to death. She told Jake a lot of stuff, how the German had tried to get her, how he chased her once into the barn, how another time, when they happened to be alone in the house together, he tore her dress open clear down the front. The German, she said, might have got her that time if he hadn't heard his old woman drive in at the gate. She had been off to town for supplies. Well, she would be putting the horse in the barn. The German managed to sneak off to the fields without his wife seeing. He told the girl he would kill her if she told. What could she do? She told a lie about ripping her dress in the barn when she was feeding the stock. I remember now that she was a bound girl and did not know where her father and mother were. Maybe she did not have any father. You know what I mean.

Such bound children were often enough cruelly treated. They were children who had no parents, slaves really. There were very few orphan homes then. They were legally bound into some home. It was a matter of pure luck how it came out.

II

She married Jake and had a son and daughter, but the daughter died.

Then she settled down to feed stock. That was her job. At the German's place she had cooked the food for the German and his wife. The wife was a strong woman with big hips and worked most of the time in the fields with her husband. She fed them and fed the cows in the barn, fed the pigs, the horses and the chickens. Every moment of every day, as a young girl, was spent feeding something.

Then she married Jake Grimes and he had to be fed. She was a slight thing, and when she had been married for three or four years, and after the two children were born, her slender shoulders became stooped.

Jake always had a lot of big dogs around the house, that stood near the unused sawmill near the creek. He was always trading horses when he wasn't stealing something and had a lot of poor bony ones about. Also he kept three or four pigs and a cow. They were all pastured in the few acres left of the Grimes place and Jake did little enough work.

He went into debt for a threshing outfit and ran it for several years, but it did not pay. People did not trust him. They were afraid he would steal the grain at night. He had to go a long way off to get work and it cost too much to get there. In the winter he hunted and cut a little firewood, to be sold in some nearby town. When the son grew up he was just like the father. They got drunk together. If there wasn't anything to eat in the house when they came home the old man gave his old woman a cut over the head. She had a few chickens of her own and had to kill one of them in a hurry. When they were all killed she wouldn't have any eggs to sell when she went to town, and then what would she do?

She had to scheme all her life about getting things fed, getting the pigs fed so they would grow fat and could be butchered in the fall. When they were butchered her husband took most of the meat off to town and sold it. If he did not do it first the boy did. They fought sometimes and when they fought the old woman stood aside trembling.

She had got the habit of silence anyway—that was fixed. Sometimes, when she began to look old—she wasn't forty yet—and when the husband and son were both off, trading horses or drinking or hunting or stealing, she went around the house and the barnyard muttering to herself.

How was she going to get everything fed?—that was her problem. The dogs had to be fed. There wasn't enough hay in the barn for the horses and the cow. If she didn't feed the chickens how could they lay eggs? Without eggs to sell how could she get things in town, things she had to have to keep the life of the farm going? Thank heaven, she did not have to feed her husband—in a certain way. That hadn't lasted long after their marriage and after the babies came. Where he went on his long trips she did not know. Sometimes he was gone from home for weeks, and after the boy grew up they went off together.

They left everything at home for her to manage and she had no money. She knew no one. No one ever talked to her in town. When it was winter she had to gather sticks of wood for her fire, had to try to keep the stock fed with very little grain.

The stock in the barn cried to her hungrily, the dogs followed her about. In the winter the hens laid few enough eggs. They huddled in the corners of the barn and she kept watching them. If a hen lays an egg in the barn in the winter and you do not find it, it freezes and breaks.

One day in winter the old woman went off to town with a few eggs and the dogs followed her. She did not get started until nearly three o'clock and the snow was heavy. She hadn't been feeling very well for several days and so she went muttering along, scantily clad, her shoulders stooped. She had an old grain bag in which she carried her eggs, tucked away down in the bottom. There weren't many of them, but in winter the price of eggs is up. She would get a little meat in exchange for the eggs, some salt pork, a little sugar, and some coffee perhaps. It might be the butcher would give her a piece of liver.

When she had got to town and was trading in her eggs the dogs lay by the door outside. She did pretty well, got the things she needed, more than she had hoped. Then she went to the butcher and he gave her some liver and some dog-meat.

It was the first time anyone had spoken to her in a friendly way for a long time. The butcher was alone in his shop when she came in and was annoyed by the thought of such a sick-looking old woman out on such a day. It was bitter cold and the snow, that had let up during the afternoon, was falling again. The butcher said something about her husband and her son, swore at them, and the old woman stared at him, a look of mild surprise in her eyes as he talked. He said that if either the husband or the son were going to get any of the liver or the heavy bones with scraps of meat hanging to them that he had put into the grain bag, he'd see him starve first.

Starve, eh? Well, things had to be fed. Men had to be fed, and the horses that weren't any good but maybe could be traded off, and the poor thin cow that hadn't given any milk for three months.

Horses, cows, pigs, dogs, men.

III

The old woman had to get back before darkness came if she could. The dogs followed at her heels, sniffing at the heavy grain bag she had fastened on her back. When she got to the edge of town she stopped by a fence and tied the bag on her back with a piece of rope she had carried in her dress-pocket for just that purpose. That was an easier way to carry it. Her arms ached. It was hard when she had to crawl over fences and once she fell over and landed in the snow. The dogs went frisking about. She had to struggle to get to her feet again, but she made it. The point of climbing over the fences was that there was a short cut over a hill and through a woods. She might have gone around by the road, but it was a mile farther that way. She was afraid she couldn't make it. And then, besides, the stock had to be fed. There was a little hay left and a little corn. Perhaps her husband and son would bring some home when they came. They had driven off in the only buggy the Grimes family had, a rickety thing, a rickety horse hitched to the buggy, two other rickety horses led by halters. They were going to trade horses, get a little money if they could. They might come home drunk. It would be well to have something in the house when they came back.

The son had an affair on with a woman at the county seat, fifteen miles away. She was a rough enough woman, a tough one. Once, in the summer, the son had brought her to the house. Both she and the son had been drinking. Jake Grimes was away and the son and his woman ordered the old woman about like a servant. She didn't mind much; she was used to it. Whatever happened she never said anything. That was her way of getting along. She had managed that way when she was a young girl at the German's and ever since she had married

Jake. That time her son brought his woman to the house they stayed all night, sleeping together just as though they were married. It hadn't shocked the old woman, not much. She had got past being shocked early in life.

With the pack on her back she went painfully along across an open field, wading in the deep snow, and got into the woods.

There was a path, but it was hard to follow. Just beyond the top of the hill, where the woods was thickest, there was a small clearing. Had someone once thought of building a house there? The clearing was as large as a building lot in town, large enough for a house and a garden. The path ran along the side of the clearing, and when she got there the old woman sat down to rest at the foot of a tree.

It was a foolish thing to do. When she got herself placed, the pack against the tree's trunk, it was nice, but what about getting up again? She worried about that for a moment and then quietly closed her eyes.

She must have slept for a time. When you are about so cold you can't get any colder. The afternoon grew a little warmer and the snow came thicker than ever. Then after a time the weather cleared. The moon even came out.

There were four Grimes dogs that had followed Mrs. Grimes into town, all tall gaunt fellows. Such men as Jake Grimes and his son always keep just such dogs. They kick and abuse them, but they stay. The Grimes dogs, in order to keep from starving, had to do a lot of foraging for themselves, and they had been at it while the old woman slept with her back to the tree at the side of the clearing. They had been chasing rabbits in the woods and in adjoining fields and in their ranging had picked up three other farm dogs.

After a time all the dogs came back to the clearing. They were excited about something. Such nights, cold and clear and with a moon, do things to dogs. It may be that some old instinct, come down from the time when they were wolves and ranged the woods in packs on winter nights, comes back into them.

The dogs in the clearing, before the old woman, had caught two or three rabbits and their immediate hunger had been satisfied. They began to play, running in circles in the clearing. Round and round they ran, each dog's nose at the tail of the next dog. In the clearing, under the snow-laden trees and under the wintry moon they made a strange picture, running thus silently, in a circle their running had beaten in the soft snow. The dogs made no sound. They ran around and around in the circle.

It may have been that the old woman saw them doing that before she died. She may have awakened once or twice and looked at the strange sight with dim old eyes.

She wouldn't be very cold now, just drowsy. Life hangs on a long time. Perhaps the old woman was out of her head. She may have dreamed of her girlhood, at the German's, and before that, when she was a child and before her mother lit out and left her.

Her dreams couldn't have been very pleasant. Not many pleasant things had happened to her. Now and then one of the Grimes dogs left the running circle and came to stand before her. The dog thrust his face close to her face. His red tongue was hanging out.

The running of the dogs may have been a kind of death ceremony. It may have been that the primitive instinct of the wolf, having been aroused in the dogs by the night and the running, made them somehow afraid.

"Now we are no longer wolves. We are dogs, the servants of men. Keep alive, man! When man dies we become wolves again."

When one of the dogs came to where the old woman sat with her back against the tree and thrust his nose close to her face he seemed satisfied and went back to run with the pack. All the Grimes dogs did it at some time during the evening, before she died. I knew all about it afterward, when I grew to be a man, because once in a woods in Illinois, on another winter night, I saw a pack of dogs act just like that. The dogs were waiting for me to die as they had waited for the old woman that night when I was a child, but when it happened to me I was a young man and had no intention whatever of dying.

The old woman died softly and quietly. When she was dead and when one of the Grimes dogs had come to her and had found her dead all the dogs stopped running.

They gathered about her.

Well, she was dead now. She had fed the Grimes dogs when she was alive, what about now?

There was the pack on her back, the grain bag containing the piece of salt pork, the liver the butcher had given her, the dog-meat, the soup bones. The butcher in town, having been suddenly overcome with a feeling of pity, had loaded her grain bag heavily. It had been a big haul for the old woman.

It was a big haul for the dogs now.

IV

One of the Grimes dogs sprang suddenly out from among the others and began worrying[1] the pack on the old woman's back. Had the dogs really been wolves that one would have been the leader of the pack. What he did, all the others did.

All of them sank their teeth into the grain bag the old woman had fastened with ropes to her back.

They dragged the old woman's body out into the open clearing. The worn-out dress was quickly torn from her shoulders. When she was found, a day or two later, the dress had been torn from her body clear to the hips, but the dogs had not touched her body. They had got the meat out of the grain bag, that was all. Her body was frozen stiff when it was found, and the shoulders were so narrow and the body so slight that in death it looked like the body of some charming young girl.

Such things happened in towns of the Middle West, on farms near town, when I was a boy. A hunter out after rabbits found the old woman's body and did not touch it. Something, the beaten round path in the little snow-covered clearing, the silence of the place, the place where the dogs had worried the body trying to pull the grain bag away or tear it open—something startled the man and he hurried off to town.

I was in Main Street with one of my brothers who was town newsboy and who was taking the afternoon papers to the stores. It was almost night.

---

1. I.e., tearing at.

The hunter came into a grocery and told his story. Then he went to a hardware shop and into a drugstore. Men began to gather on the sidewalks. Then they started out along the road to the place in the woods.

My brother should have gone on about his business of distributing papers but he didn't. Everyone was going to the woods. The undertaker went and the town marshal. Several men got on a dray and rode out to where the path left the road and went into the woods, but the horses weren't very sharply shod and slid about on the slippery roads. They made no better time than those of us who walked.

The town marshal was a large man whose leg had been injured in the Civil War. He carried a heavy cane and limped rapidly along the road. My brother and I followed at his heels, and as we went other men and boys joined the crowd.

It had grown dark by the time we got to where the old woman had left the road but the moon had come out. The marshal was thinking there might have been a murder. He kept asking the hunter questions. The hunter went along with his gun across his shoulders, a dog following at his heels. It isn't often a rabbit hunter has a chance to be so conspicuous. He was taking full advantage of it, leading the procession with the town marshal. "I didn't see any wounds. She was a beautiful young girl. Her face was buried in the snow. No, I didn't know her." As a matter of fact, the hunter had not looked closely at the body. He had been frightened. She might have been murdered and someone might spring out from behind a tree and murder him. In a woods, in the late afternoon, when the trees are all bare and there is white snow on the ground, when all is silent, something creepy steals over the mind and body. If something strange or uncanny has happened in the neighborhood all you think about is getting away from there as fast as you can.

The crowd of men and boys had got to where the old woman had crossed the field and went, following the marshal and the hunter, up the slight incline and into the woods.

My brother and I were silent. He had his bundle of papers in a bag slung across his shoulder. When he got back to town he would have to go on distributing his papers before he went home to supper. If I went along, as he had no doubt already determined I should, we would both be late. Either mother or our older sister would have to warm our supper.

Well, we would have something to tell. A boy did not get such a chance very often. It was lucky we just happened to go into the grocery when the hunter came in. The hunter was a country fellow. Neither of us had ever seen him before.

Now the crowd of men and boys had got to the clearing. Darkness comes quickly on such winter nights, but the full moon made everything clear. My brother and I stood near the tree, beneath which the old woman had died.

She did not look old, lying there in that light, frozen and still. One of the men turned her over in the snow and I saw everything. My body trembled with some strange mystical feeling and so did my brother's. It might have been the cold.

Neither of us had ever seen a woman's body before. It may have been the snow, clinging to the frozen flesh, that made it look so white and lovely, so like marble. No woman had come with the party from town; but one of the men, he was the town blacksmith, took off his overcoat and spread it over her. Then he gathered her into his arms and started off to town, all the others following silently. At that time no one knew who she was.

V

I had seen everything, had seen the oval in the snow, like a miniature race track, where the dogs had run, had seen how the men were mystified, had seen the white bare young-looking shoulders, had heard the whispered comments of the men.

The men were simply mystified. They took the body to the undertaker's, and when the blacksmith, the hunter, the marshal and several others had got inside they closed the door. If father had been there perhaps he could have got in, but we boys couldn't.

I went with my brother to distribute the rest of his papers and when we got home it was my brother who told the story.

I kept silent and went to bed early. It may have been I was not satisfied with the way he told it.

Later, in the town, I must have heard other fragments of the old woman's story. She was recognized the next day and there was an investigation.

The husband and son were found somewhere and brought to town and there was an attempt to connect them with the woman's death, but it did not work. They had perfect enough alibis.

However, the town was against them. They had to get out. Where they went I never heard.

I remember only the picture there in the forest, the men standing about, the naked girlish-looking figure, face down in the snow, the tracks made by the running dogs and the clear cold winter sky above. White fragments of clouds were drifting across the sky. They went racing across the little open space among the trees.

The scene in the forest had become for me, without my knowing it, the foundation for the real story I am now trying to tell. The fragments, you see, had to be picked up slowly, long afterwards.

Things happened. When I was a young man I worked on the farm of a German. The hired-girl was afraid of her employer. The farmer's wife hated her.

I saw things at that place. Once later, I had a half-uncanny, mystical adventure with dogs in an Illinois forest on a clear, moonlit winter night. When I was a schoolboy, and on a summer day, I went with a boy friend out along a creek some miles from town and came to the house where the old woman had lived. No one had lived in the house since her death. The doors were broken from the hinges; the window lights were all broken. As the boy and I stood in the road outside, two dogs, just roving farm dogs no doubt, came running around the corner of the house. The dogs were tall, gaunt fellows and came down to the fence and glared through at us, standing in the road.

The whole thing, the story of the old woman's death, was to me as I grew older like music heard from far off. The notes had to be picked up slowly one at a time. Something had to be understood.

The woman who died was one destined to feed animal life. Anyway, that is all she ever did. She was feeding animal life before she was born, as a child, as a young woman working on the farm of the German, after she married, when she grew old and when she died. She fed animal life in cows, in chickens, in pigs, in horses, in dogs, in men. Her daughter had died in childhood and with her one son she had no articulate relations. On the night when she died she was hurrying homeward, bearing on her body food for animal life.

She died in the clearing in the woods and even after her death continued feeding animal life.

You see it is likely that, when my brother told the story, that night when we got home and my mother and sister sat listening, I did not think he got the point. He was too young and so was I. A thing so complete has its own beauty.

I shall not try to emphasize the point. I am only explaining why I was dissatisfied then and have been ever since. I speak of that only that you may understand why I have been impelled to try to tell the simple story over again.

Questions for Study

1. In the initial paragraphs, why does Anderson speak of "such old women" whom "all country and small-town people have seen" before he begins telling about this specific woman?

2. Anderson's narrator tells us that he has "just remembered her" and that hers "is a story." What does this approach tell us about the narrator? Why does he say, "It all comes back clearly now"? Find other sentences and phrases that establish that we are not just reading about certain events but rather about a character trying to understand those events.

3. Is the narrator's detailed knowledge of the events in this woman's life plausible? How would he know these things? Do we have any reminders that he often is speculating about these events?

4. The emphasis throughout is upon things, including men, being fed. What does this emphasis imply? How is the woman's death especially appropriate in relationship to things being fed. Relate this idea to the fact that Anderson said that the story was about the animal hunger in humans.

5. Both the narrator and his brother go into the woods out of curiosity and desire to have "something to tell" similar to the rabbit hunter's tale. Does the narrator then tell his tale for the same reasons?

6. Why was the narrator dissatisfied with the story his brother told? Does his dissatisfaction reveal anything about him?

7. The story focuses, as the narrator says, on the "scene in the forest." How does he work up to that scene? Can you imagine other ways of telling the story, arriving at that scene by other means?

8. What does the narrator mean when he writes, "A thing so complete has its own beauty"? Why is it "like music heard from far off"? Relate these answers to what you believe is the meaning of the story.

Chapter 6
Theme

We remember a piece of music by humming its melody, its theme. That brief musical phrase is not the whole symphony or the whole song, but it represents what the symphony or song is trying to convey. In storytelling, theme functions in much the same way. On one hand, theme could be viewed as the unconscious or conscious assumption from which the storyteller works. In that broad sense, we could say that someone whose tales are consistently about war, murders, auto accidents, airplane crashes, and the like, employs the general theme of violence and destruction in his stories. In that same broad sense, we could say that the general theme of much of Ernest Hemingway's fiction, for example, is the need to strive for individual courage in a modern world devoid of meaning.

On the other hand, theme may consist of the particular point or the concept the storyteller wishes to convey. Every time we repeat incidents or anecdotes to one another we intend that what we say be about something. Although we may ramble or become distracted or get so wrapped up in detail that we forget what we meant to say, we do not begin to speak without first having a point or a concept, however vague, in mind. That concept or point should be the glue which holds our narrative together. And in that same sense much of our casual conversation has a theme. Likewise, behind any piece of effective fiction there is a coherent and identifiable theme. It may simply be the unconscious or the conscious assumptions out of which an author writes or it may be a particular idea that he wishes his story to illustrate. Nevertheless, what he writes is supported by a particular and identifiable point or concept that his materials and art reveal.

Yet in the well-crafted story theme is not merely an assumption or an intention. Instead **theme** is the central idea or understanding around which a story is constructed. It sets up a pattern the author traces throughout the work. Thematically central to Maxim Gorky's

"Twenty-Six Men and a Girl," for instance, is the inevitable frustration of excessive idealism. A basic thematic statement might read: "When brutish men who embody no ideals in their own lives project ideals on others, such a transference of idealization destroys itself and dooms the men to bitterness and further brutalization."

That theme resounds through the contrasts between the nameless, almost faceless men and the seemingly splendid humans Tanya and the soldier, between darkness and sunshine, disease and health, dirt and cleanliness, depth and height, sameness and diversity. The first-person plural point of view underscores the men's lack of individuality. Their idealistic projections are represented by the songs, gifts, advice, love, and religious devotion the men give out. The plot itself depends upon their idealization: Tanya's seduction by the soldier, who has almost supplanted her as an idol, is a direct result of the men's idealization.

In literature, as in music, there are variations on a theme, and such variations echo throughout Gorky's story. Theme unifies and makes the work artistically pleasing. Even if we had not formulated a statement of theme, we would have the satisfied sense that the story is thematically controlled. Elements combine and cohere as they would not if the bakery had been upstairs, if Tanya had darned clothes for the men, or if one of the twenty-six men had seduced Tanya. We are pleased, furthermore, to see how variations on the theme are reflected by every incident in the story. For instance, the men's idealizing of the soldier is a variation on the major theme of idealizing Tanya. Gorky achieves a unified piece of fiction because he can vary the theme without altering the direction of his story. He balances, as a musical composer does, the many and the one, preserving the tension between a multitude of characters and incidents and a single theme.

A coherent theme also is pleasing to us in that it clarifies experiences common to all humanity. It reveals to us the meaning of something that we did not know so well or so intensely before. "Twenty-Six Men and a Girl" invites our participation in the sufferings, longings, and disappointments of men who might otherwise have seemed revolting to us. It further invites us to connect their lives with our own and to recognize how people need ideals as much as bread. In this sense, theme serves as a revelation. There is moral as well as aesthetic balance in Gorky's presentation of a web of suggestive situations, characters, and events. Without distorting or oversimplifying the idea he wishes to convey, Gorky has woven the story's variations into a controlled and cohesive theme.

Theme should always maintain a balance, as it does in "Twenty-Six Men and a Girl," between what is artistically and what is humanly pleasing. Doing so, it confirms that the task of the artist today remains essentially what it was 2000 years ago when the Roman poet Horace spoke of the artist as one *qui miscuit utile dulci*—that is, one who mingles the useful with the sweet. To the writer, the useful is not necessarily immediately practical. Fiction is ultimately valuable in that it imparts to us worthwhile experiences and understandings. It is useful because it humanizes us.

Fiction intended for such limited ends as getting people to go to church or to join the communist party is not usually art at all, but **propaganda.** Because propaganda tends to restrict itself to a single idea, it is useful only in achieving immediate, short-term, or limited purposes. Stories designed with such ends in mind, such as those contrived solely to exemplify an idea or teach a lesson tend to ignore, distort, or oversimplify human experience. By contrast, good fiction is ultimately useful because it illuminates, clarifies, and expands our understanding of human experience. In presenting few variations on or echoes of a theme and in stressing its major point again and again, propaganda usually does not lend itself to various interpretations. The propagandist often fails to present the rich implications of a complex situation and instead relies upon explanation, theory, and instruction. He makes blunt statements that tend to lessen the force of the story, reduce its complexity, and perhaps insult the reader's intelligence.

In many stories theme remains implicit or unstated. The fiction writer often works through *indirect* presentation; he chooses to show, not to tell. Gorky does not explain to us that obsessive idealism can destroy ideals—he shows it. We come to feel and to understand this idea as we would not if we were only given direct statements on the subject.

Inexperienced readers sometimes do not understand that stories are not sermons or editorials. Such readers fault the author for dealing with subjects that seem unpleasant or amoral, or for failing to condemn such situations. Answering such an attack, Russian author Anton Chekhov wrote:

> *You abuse me for objectivity, calling it indifference to good and evil, lack of ideals and ideas, and so on. You would have me, when I describe horse-thieves, say: "Stealing horses is an evil." But that has been known for ages without my saying so. Let the jury judge them; it's my job simply to show what sort of people they are.*

Whatever the author's subject and theme, he must present both to us imaginatively and fully. Although a story does not preach against theft, for example, the fictional presentation of the crime is useful because it brings us to understand the situation. Chekhov in "An Upheaval" writes about a man who steals from his wife; and Joyce Carol Oates in "How I Contemplated My Life . . ." writes about a rich girl who steals for fun. Neither author approves of theft, but neither uses the story to lecture on the subject. Instead, each presents a situation with such sensitivity and insight that we understand how and why those thefts were committed.

Yet our concern is not that an author treat approved subjects in approved ways. Nor is it that he choose acceptable, older themes. When an author takes a familiar idea like God or religious faith and treats it in a shopworn manner, we may like the idea but are bored with the story. Or he may treat that same idea with imaginative freshness and skill, as Philip Roth does in "The Conversion of the Jews." Roth's story provides us with new and even startling insights into an old theme.

Although an author will rarely make an overt statement of theme within the story, a reader should formulate such a statement. Doing so provides a check against misreading and a way of discovering the author's skill in devising a pattern and its variations. A statement of theme must be just that—a statement delivered as a complete thought. It is not enough to say that the theme of "Sredni Vashtar" is revenge, or that of Roth's story is religion, or that of Gorky's story is human brutalization. A thematic statement about Saki's story should take into account, for instance, the issues of life and death, or of the imagination and respectability. One possible statement of Saki's theme might be the following: "If the forces of life in a sensitive, ten-year-old boy are blunted and frustrated by the forces of death and respectability, they will seek other outlets which may be fantastic, bizarre, or cruel and may in the end destroy that which suppressed them." This formulation of Saki's theme is not the only one possible, but it is at least a viable one that expresses the narrative's central issues. Such a statement is generalized—a statement of theme is *never* a plot summary—but it is not *too* generalized. The statement does not say that Conradin rebelled, since that would be too specific. Nor does it say that the forces of life always rebel against the forces of death and suppression, since that would be too general. But it does say that with a certain type of person, such as a sensitive young boy, a genuine rebellion may be expected. In rendering theme it is necessary to avoid blanket generalizations or truisms. The statement should be closely measured against the story itself to make certain that there are no inconsistencies or falsifications between our rendering of theme and what the story says.

Yet thematic statements cannot replace the complexity and richness of the story itself. Flannery O'Connor writes:

> *People talk about the theme of a story as if the theme were like a string that a sack of chicken feed is tied with. They think that if you can pick out the theme, the way you pick the right thread in the chicken-feed sack, you can rip the story open and feed the chickens. But this is not the way meaning works in fiction . . . . The meaning of a story has to be embodied in it, has to be made concrete in it. A story is a way to say something that can't be said*

*in any other way, and it takes every word in the story to say what
the meaning is.*

A statement of theme will not open up the story so completely that we
can digest the statement and spit out the story. But like a knife cutting
into a melon, it opens the story so that we can get inside. Inside, we see
in terms of both technique and meaning how the story, with all its variations, focuses upon and develops a single theme.

Maxim Gorky (1868–1936)
Twenty-Six Men and a Girl

There were six-and-twenty of us;—six-and-twenty living machines in a
damp, underground cellar, where from morning till night we kneaded dough
and rolled it into kringels.[1] Opposite the underground window of our cellar was
a bricked area, green and mouldy with moisture. The window was protected
from outside with a close iron grating, and the light of the sun could not pierce
through the window panes, covered as they were with flour dust.

Our employer had bars placed in front of the windows, so that we should
not be able to give a bit of his bread to passing beggars, or to any of our fellows
who were out of work and hungry. Our employer called us rogues, and gave us
half-rotten tripe to eat for our mid-day meal, instead of meat. It was swel-
teringly close for us cooped up in that stone underground chamber, under the
low, heavy, soot-blackened, cobwebby ceiling. Dreary and sickening was our
life between its thick, dirty, mouldy walls.

Unrefreshed, and with a feeling of not having had our sleep out, we used to
get up at five o'clock in the morning; and before six, we were already seated,
worn out and apathetic, at the table, rolling out the dough which our mates had
already prepared whilst we slept. The whole day, from ten in the early morning
until ten at night, some of us sat round that table, working up in our hands the
yielding paste, rolling it to and fro so that it should not get stiff; whilst the
others kneaded the swelling mass of dough. And the whole day the simmering
water in the kettle, where the kringels were being cooked, sang low and sadly;
and the baker's shovel scraped harshly over the oven floor, as he threw the
slippery bits of dough out of the kettle on to the heated bricks.

From morning till evening wood was burning in the oven, and the red glow
of the fire gleamed and flickered over the walls of the bake-shop, as if silently
mocking us. The giant oven was like the misshapen head of a monster in a fairy
tale; it thrust itself up out of the floor, opened wide jaws, full of glowing fire,
and blew hot breath upon us; it seemed to be ever watching out of its black air-

---

1. Loop-shaped bread rolls.

holes our interminable work. Those two deep holes were like eyes—the cold, pitiless eyes of a monster. They watched us always with the same darkened glance, as if they were weary of seeing before them such eternal slaves, from whom they could expect nothing human, and therefore scorned them with the cold scorn of wisdom.

In meal dust, in the mud which we brought in from the yard on our boots, in the hot, sticky atmosphere, day in, day out, we rolled the dough into kringels, which we moistened with our own sweat. And we hated our work with a glowing hatred; we never ate what had passed through our hands, and preferred black bread to kringels. Sitting opposite each other, at a long table—nine facing nine—we moved our hands and fingers mechanically during endlessly long hours, till we were so accustomed to our monotonous work that we ceased to pay any attention to it.

We had all studied each other so constantly, that each of us knew every wrinkle of his mates' faces. It was not long also before we had exhausted almost every topic of conversation; that is why we were most of the time silent, unless we were chaffing each other; but one cannot always find something about which to chaff another man, especially when that man is one's mate. Neither were we much given to finding fault with one another; how, indeed, could one of us poor devils be in a position to find fault with another, when we were all of us half dead and, as it were, turned to stone? For the heavy drudgery seemed to crush all feeling out of us. But silence is only terrible and fearful for those who have said everything and have nothing more to say to each other; for men, on the contrary, who have never begun to communicate with one another, it is easy and simple.

Sometimes, too, we sang; and this is how it happened that we began to sing: one of us would sigh deeply in the midst of our toil, like an overdriven horse, and then we would begin one of those songs whose gentle swaying melody seems always to ease the burden on the singer's heart.

At first one sang by himself, and we others sat in silence listening to his solitary song, which, under the heavy vaulted roof of the cellar, died gradually away, and became extinguished, like a little fire in the steppes,[2] on a wet autumn night, when the grey heaven hangs like a heavy mass over the earth. Then another would join in with the singer, and now two soft, sad voices would break into song in our narrow, dull hole of a cellar. Suddenly others would join in, and the song would roll forward like a wave, would grow louder and swell upwards, till it would seem as if the damp, foul walls of our stone prison were widening out and opening. Then, all six-and-twenty of us would be singing; our loud, harmonious song would fill the whole cellar, our voices would travel outside and beyond, striking, as it were, against the walls in moaning sobs and sighs, moving our hearts with soft, tantalizing ache, tearing open old wounds, and awakening longings.

The singers would sigh deeply and heavily; suddenly one would become silent and listen to the others singing, then let his voice flow once more in the common tide. Another would exclaim in a stifled voice, "Ah!" and would shut his eyes, whilst the deep, full sound waves would show him, as it were, a road,

---

2. Vast, level, treeless tracts in southeastern Russia.

in front of him—a sunlit, broad road in the distance, which he himself, in thought, wandered along.

But the flame flickers once more in the huge oven, the baker scrapes incessantly with his shovel, the water simmers in the kettle, and the flicker of the fire on the wall dances as before in silent mockery. While in other men's words we sing out our dumb grief, the weary burden of live men robbed of the sunlight, the burden of slaves.

So we lived, we six-and-twenty, in the vaultlike cellar of a great stone house, and we suffered each one of us, as if we had to bear on our shoulders the whole three storeys of that house.

But we had something else good, besides the singing—something we loved, that perhaps took the place of the sunshine.

In the second storey of our house there was established a gold-embroiderer's shop, and there, living amongst the other embroidery girls, was Tanya, a little maid-servant of sixteen. Every morning there peeped in through the glass door a rosy little face, with merry blue eyes; while a ringing, tender voice called out to us:

"Little prisoners! Have you any kringels, please, for me?"

At that clear sound, we knew so well, we all used to turn round, gazing with simple-hearted joy at the pure girlish face which smiled at us so sweetly. The sight of the small nose pressed against the window-pane, and of the white teeth gleaming between the half-open lips, had become for us a daily pleasure. Tumbling over each other we used to jump up to open the door, and she would step in, bright and cheerful, holding out her apron, with her head thrown on one side, and a smile on her lips. Her thick, long chestnut hair fell over her shoulder and across her breast. But we, ugly, dirty and misshapen as we were, looked up at her—the threshold door was four steps above the floor—looked up at her with heads thrown back, wishing her good morning, and speaking strange unaccustomed words, which we kept for her only. Our voices became softer when we spoke to her, our jests were lighter. For her—everything was different with us. The baker took from his oven a shovel of the best and the brownest kringels, and threw them deftly into Tanya's apron.

"Be off with you now, or the boss will catch you!" we warned her each time. She laughed roguishly, called out cheerfully: "Good bye, poor prisoners!" and slipped away as quick as a mouse.

That was all. But long after she had gone we talked about her to one another with pleasure. It was always the same thing as we had said yesterday and the day before, because everything about us, including ourselves and her, remained the same—as yesterday—and as always.

Painful and terrible it is when a man goes on living, while nothing changes around him; and when such an existence does not finally kill his soul, then the monotony becomes with time, even more and more painful. Generally we spoke about women in such a way, that sometimes it was loathsome to us ourselves to hear our rude, shameless talk. The women whom we knew deserved perhaps nothing better. But about Tanya we never let fall an evil word; none of us ever ventured so much as to lay a hand on her, even too free a jest she never heard from us. Maybe this was so because she never remained for long with us; she flashed on our eyes like a star falling from the sky, and vanished; and maybe because she was little and very beautiful, and everything beautiful calls forth respect, even in coarse people. And besides—though our life of penal labour had made us dull beasts, oxen, we were still men, and, like all men, could not live without worshipping something or other. Better than her we had none, and none but she took any notice of us, living in the cellar—no one, though there were dozens of people in the house. And then, too—most likely, this was the chief thing—we all regarded her as something of our own, something existing as it were only by virtue of our kringels. We took on ourselves in turns the duty of providing her with hot kringels, and this became for us like a daily sacrifice to our idol, it became almost a sacred rite, and every day it bound us more closely to her. Besides kringels, we gave Tanya a great deal of advice—to wear warmer clothes, not to run upstairs too quickly, not to carry heavy bundles of wood. She listened to all our counsels with a smile, answered them by a laugh, and never took our advice, but we were not offended at that; all we wanted was to show how much care we bestowed upon her.

Often she would apply to us with different requests, she asked us for instance to open the heavy door into the store-cellar, and to chop wood: with delight and a sort of pride, we did this for her and everything else she wanted.

But when one of us asked her to mend his solitary shirt for him, she said, with a laugh of contempt:

"What next! A likely idea!"

We made great fun of the queer fellow who could entertain such an idea, and—never asked her to do anything else. We loved her—all is said in that. Man always wants to lay his love on someone, though sometimes he crushes, sometimes he sullies, with it; he may poison another life because he loves without respecting the beloved. We were bound to love Tanya, for we had no one else to love.

At times one of us would suddenly begin to reason like this:

"And why do we make so much of the wench? What is there in her? eh? What a to-do we make about her!"

The man who dared to utter such words we promptly and coarsely cut short—we wanted something to love: we had found it and loved it, and what we twenty-six loved must be for each of us unalterable, as a holy thing, and anyone who acted against us in this was our enemy. We loved, maybe, not what was really good, but you see there were twenty-six of us, and so we always wanted to see what was precious to us held sacred by the rest.

Our love is not less burdensome than hate, and maybe that is just why some proud souls maintain that our hate is more flattering than our love. But why do they not run away from us, if it is so?

Besides our department our employer had also a bread-bakery; it was in the same house, separated from our hole only by a wall; but the bakers—there were four of them—held aloof from us, considering their work superior to ours, and therefore themselves better than us; they never used to come into our workroom, and laughed contemptuously at us when they met us in the yard. We, too, did not go to see them; this was forbidden by our employer, from fear that we should steal the fancy bread. We did not like the bakers, because we envied them; their work was lighter than ours, they were paid more, and were better fed; they had a light, spacious workroom, and they were all so clean and healthy—and that made them hateful to us. We all looked grey and yellow;

three of us had syphilis, several suffered from skin diseases, one was completely crippled by rheumatism. On holidays and in their leisure time the bakers wore pea-jackets and creaking boots, two of them had accordions, and they all used to go for strolls in the town gardens,—we wore filthy rags and leather clogs or plaited shoes on our feet, the police would not let us into the town gardens—could we possibly like the bakers?

And one day we learned that their chief baker had been drunk, the master had sacked him and had already taken on another, and that this other was a soldier, wore a satin waistcoat and a watch and gold chain. We were inquisitive to get a sight of such a dandy, and in the hope of catching a glimpse of him we kept running one after another out into the yard.

But he came of his own accord into our room. Kicking at the door, he pushed it open, and leaving it ajar, stood in the doorway smiling, and said to us:

"God help the work! Good morning, mates!"

The ice-cold air, which streamed in through the open door, curled in streaks of vapour round his feet. He stood on the threshold, looked us up and down, and under his fair, twisted moustache gleamed big yellow teeth. His waistcoat was really something quite out of the common, blue-flowered, brilliant with shining little buttons of red stones. He also wore a watch chain.

He was a fine fellow, this soldier; tall, healthy, rosy-cheeked, and his big, clear eyes had a friendly, cheerful glance. He wore on his head a white starched cap, and from under his spotlessly clean apron peeped the pointed toes of fashionable, well-blacked boots.

Our baker asked him politely to shut the door. The soldier did so without hurrying himself, and began to question us about the master. We explained to him, all speaking together, that our employer was a thorough-going brute, a rogue, a knave, and a slave-driver; in a word we repeated to him all that can and must be said about an employer, but cannot be repeated here. The soldier listened to us, twisted his moustache, and watched us with a friendly, open-hearted look.

"But haven't you got a lot of girls here?" he asked, suddenly.

Some of us began to laugh deferentially, others put on a meaning expression, and one of us explained to the soldier that there were nine girls here.

"You make the most of them?" asked the soldier, with a wink.

We laughed, but not so loudly, and with some embarrassment. Many of us would have liked to have shown the soldier that we also were tremendous fellows with the girls, but not one of us could do so; and one of our number confessed as much, when he said in a low voice:

"That sort of thing is not in our line."

"Well no, it wouldn't quite do for you," said the soldier with conviction, after having looked us over. "There is something wanting about you all. You don't look the right sort. You've no sort of appearance; and the women, you see, they like a bold appearance, they will have a well set up body. Everything has to be tip-top for them. That's why they respect strength. They want an arm like that!"

The soldier drew his right hand, with its turned-up shirt sleeve, out of his pocket, and showed us his bare arm. It was white and strong, and covered with shining yellow hairs.

"Leg and chest, all must be strong. And then a man must be dressed in the latest fashion, so as to show off his looks to advantage. Yes, all the women take to me. Whether I call to them, or whether I beckon them, they with one accord, five at a time, throw themselves at my head."

He sat down on a flour sack, and told at length all about the way women loved him, and how bold he was with them. Then he left, and after the door had creaked to behind him, we sat for a long time silent, and thought about him and his talk. Then we all suddenly broke silence together, and it became apparent that we were all equally pleased with him. He was such a nice, open-hearted fellow; he came to see us without any stand-offishness, sat down and chatted. No one else came to us like that, and no one else talked to us in that friendly sort of way. And we continued to talk of him and his coming triumph among the embroidery girls, who passed us by with contemptuous sniffs when they saw us in the yard, or who looked straight through us as if we had been air. But we admired them always when we met them outside, or when they walked past our windows; in winter, in fur jackets and toques[3] to match; in summer, in hats trimmed with flowers, and with coloured parasols in their hands. We talked, however, about these girls in a way that would have made them mad with shame and rage, if they could have heard us.

"If only he does not get hold of little Tanya!" said the baker, suddenly, in an anxious tone of voice.

We were silent, for these words troubled us. Tanya had quite gone out of our minds, supplanted, put on one side by the strong, fine figure of the soldier.

Then began a lively discussion; some of us maintained that Tanya would never lower herself so; others thought she would not be able to resist him, and the third group proposed to give him a thrashing if he should try to annoy Tanya. And, finally, we all decided to watch the soldier and Tanya, and to warn the girl against him. This brought the discussion to an end.

Four weeks had passed by since then; during this time the soldier baked white bread, walked about with the gold-embroidery girls, visited us often, but did not talk any more about his conquests; only twisted his moustache, and licked his lips lasciviously.

Tanya called in as usual every morning for "little kringels," and was as gay and as nice and friendly with us as ever. We certainly tried once or twice to talk to her about the soldier, but she called him a "goggle-eyed calf," and made fun of him all round, and that set our minds at rest. We saw how the gold-embroidery girls carried on with the soldier, and we were proud of our girl; Tanya's behaviour reflected honour on us all; we imitated her, and began in our talks to treat the soldier with small consideration. She became dearer to us, and we greeted her with more friendliness and kindliness every morning.

One day the soldier came to see us, a bit drunk, and sat down and began to laugh. When we asked him what he was laughing about, he explained to us:

"Why two of them—that Lydka girl and Grushka—have been clawing each other on my account. You should have seen the way they went for each other! Ha! ha! One got hold of the other one by the hair, threw her down on the floor of the passage, and sat on her! Ha! ha! ha! They scratched and tore each others' faces. It was enough to make one die with laughter! Why is it women can't fight fair? Why do they always scratch one another, eh?"

---

3. Small, close-fitting, brimless hats.

He sat on the bench, healthy, fresh and jolly he sat there and went on laughing. We were silent. This time he made an unpleasant impression on us.

"Well, it's a funny thing what luck I have with the women-folk! Eh? I've laughed till I'm ill! One wink, and it's all over with them! It's the d-devil!"

He raised his white hairy hands, and slapped them down on his knees. And his eyes seem to reflect such frank astonishment, as if he were himself quite surprised at his good luck with women. His fat red face glistened with delight and self satisfaction, and he licked his lips more than ever.

Our baker scraped the shovel violently and angrily along the oven floor, and all at once he said sarcastically:

"There's no great strength needed to pull up fir saplings, but try a real pine-tree."

"Why—what do you mean by saying that to me?" asked the soldier.

"Oh, well . . ."

"What is it?"

"Nothing—it slipped out!"

"No, wait a minute! What's the point? What pine-tree?"

Our baker did not answer, working rapidly away with the shovel at the oven; flinging into it the half-cooked kringels, taking out those that were done, and noisily throwing them on the floor to the boys who were stringing them on bast. He seemed to have forgotten the soldier and his conversation with him. But the soldier had all at once dropped into a sort of uneasiness. He got up on to his feet, and went to the oven, at the risk of knocking against the handle of the shovel, which was waving spasmodically in the air.

"No, tell me, do—who is it? You've insulted me. I? There's not one could withstand me, n-no! And you say such insulting things to me?"

He really seemed genuinely hurt. He must have had nothing else to pride himself on except his gift for seducing women; maybe, except for that, there was nothing living in him, and it was only that by which he could feel himself a living man.

There are men to whom the most precious and best thing in their lives appears to be some disease of their soul or body. They spend their whole life in relation to it, and only living by it, suffering from it, they sustain themselves on it, they complain of it to others, and so draw the attention of their fellows to themselves. For that they extract sympathy from people, and apart from it they have nothing at all. Take from them that disease, cure them, and they will be miserable, because they have lost their one resource in life—they are left empty then. Sometimes a man's life is so poor, that he is driven instinctively to prize his vice and to live by it; one may say for a fact that often men are vicious from boredom.

The soldier was offended, he went up to our baker and roared:

"No, tell me do—who?"

"Tell you?" the baker turned suddenly to him.

"Well?"

"You know Tanya?"

"Well?"

"Well, there then! Only try."

"I?"

"You!"

"Her? Why that's nothing to me—pooh!"

"We shall see!"

"You will see! Ha! ha!"

"She'll——"

"Give me a month!"

"What a braggart you are, soldier!"

"A fortnight! I'll prove it! Who is it? Tanya! Pooh!"

"Well, get out. You're in my way!"

"A fortnight—and it's done! Ah, you——"

"Get out, I say!"

Our baker, all at once, flew into a rage and brandished his shovel. The soldier staggered away from him in amazement, looked at us, paused, and softly, malignantly said, "Oh, all right, then!" and went away.

During the dispute we had all sat silent, absorbed in it. But when the soldier had gone, eager, loud talk and noise arose among us.

Some one shouted to the baker: "It's a bad job that you've started, Pavel!"

"Do your work!" answered the baker, savagely.

We felt that the soldier had been deeply aggrieved, and that danger threatened Tanya. We felt this, and at the same time we were all possessed by a burning curiosity, most agreeable to us. What would happen? Would Tanya hold out against the soldier? And almost all cried confidently: "Tanya! She'll hold out! You won't catch her with your bare arms!"

We longed terribly to test the strength of our idol; we forcibly proved to each other that our divinity was a strong divinity and would come victorious out of this ordeal. We began at last to fancy that we had not worked enough on the soldier, that he would forget the dispute, and that we ought to pique his vanity more keenly. From that day we began to live a different life, a life of nervous tension, such as we had never known before. We spent whole days in arguing together; we all grew, as it were, sharper; and got to talk more and better. It seemed to us that we were playing some sort of game with the devil, and the stake on our side was Tanya. And when we learnt from the bakers that the soldier had begun "running after our Tanya," we felt a sort of delighted terror, and life was so interesting that we did not even notice that our employer had taken advantage of our pre-occupation to increase our work by fourteen pounds of dough a day. We seemed, indeed, not even tired by our work. Tanya's name was on our lips all day long. And every day we looked for her with a certain special impatience. Sometimes we pictured to ourselves that she would come to us, and it would not be the same Tanya as of old, but somehow different. We said nothing to her, however, of the dispute regarding her. We asked her no questions, and behaved as well and affectionately to her as ever. But even in this a new element crept in, alien to our old feeling for Tanya—and that new element was keen curiosity, keen and cold as a steel knife.

"Mates! To-day the time's up!" our baker said to us one morning, as he set to work.

We were well aware of it without his reminder; but still we were thrilled.

"Look at her. She'll be here directly," suggested the baker.

One of us cried out in a troubled voice, "Why! as though one could notice anything!"

And again an eager, noisy discussion sprang up among us. To-day we were about to prove how pure and spotless was the vessel into which we had poured all that was best in us. This morning, for the first time, it became clear to us, that we really were playing a great game; that we might, indeed, through the exaction of this proof of purity, lose our divinity altogether.

During the whole of the intervening fortnight we had heard that Tanya was persistently followed by the soldier, but not one of us had thought of asking her how she had behaved towards him. And she came every morning to fetch her kringels, and was the same towards us as ever.

This morning, too, we heard her voice outside: "You poor prisoners! Here I am!"

We opened the door, and when she came in we all remained, contrary to our usual custom, silent. Our eyes fixed on her, we did not know how to speak to her, what to ask her. And there we stood in front of her, a gloomy, silent crowd. She seemed to be surprised at this unusual reception; suddenly we saw her turn white, and become uneasy, then she asked, in a choking voice: "Why are you—like this?"

"And you?" the baker flung at her, grimly, never taking his eyes off her.

"What am I?"

"N—nothing."

"Well, then, give me quickly the little kringels."

Never before had she bidden us hurry.

"There's plenty of time," said the baker, not stirring, and not removing his eyes from her face.

Then, suddenly, she turned round and disappeared through the door.

The baker took his shovel and said, calmly turning away towards the oven:

"Well, that settles it! But a soldier! a common beast like that—a low cur!"

Like a flock of sheep we all pressed round the table, sat down silently, and began listlessly to work. Soon, however, one of us remarked:

"Perhaps, after all—"

"Shut up!" shouted the baker.

We were all convinced that he was a man of judgment, a man who knew more than we did about things. And at the sound of his voice we were convinced of the soldier's victory, and our spirits became sad and downcast.

At twelve o'clock—whilst we were eating our dinners—the soldier came in. He was as clean and as smart as ever, and looked at us—as usual—straight in the eyes. But we were all awkward in looking at him.

"Now then, honoured sirs, would you like me to show you a soldier's quality?" he said, chuckling proudly.

"Go out into the passage, and look through the crack—do you understand?"

We went into the passage, and stood all pushing against one another, squeezed up to the cracks of the wooden partition of the passage that looked into the yard. We had not to wait long. Very soon Tanya, with hurried footsteps and a careworn face, walked across the yard, jumping over the puddles of melting snow and mud: she disappeared into the store cellar. Then whistling, and not hurrying himself, the soldier followed in the same direction. His hands were thrust in his pockets; his moustaches were quivering.

Rain was falling, and we saw how its drops fell into the puddles, and the puddles were wrinkled by them. The day was damp and grey—a very dreary day. Snow still lay on the roofs, but on the ground dark patches of mud had begun to appear. And the snow on the roofs too was covered by a layer of brownish dirt. The rain fell slowly with a depressing sound. It was cold and disagreeable for us waiting.

The first to come out of the store cellar was the soldier; he walked slowly across the yard, his moustaches twitching, his hands in his pockets—the same as always.

Then—Tanya, too, came out. Her eyes—her eyes were radiant with joy and happiness, and her lips—were smiling. And she walked as though in a dream, staggering, with unsteady steps.

We could not bear this quietly. All of us at once rushed to the door, dashed out into the yard and—hissed at her, reviled her viciously, loudly, wildly.

She started at seeing us, and stood as though rooted in the mud under her feet. We formed a ring round her; and malignantly, without restraint, abused her with vile words, said shameful things to her.

We did this not loudly, not hurriedly, seeing that she could not get away, that she was hemmed in by us, and we could deride her to our hearts' content. I don't know why, but we did not beat her. She stood in the midst of us, and turned her head this way and that, as she heard our insults. And we—more and more violently flung at her the filth and venom of our words.

The colour had left her face. Her blue eyes, so happy a moment before, opened wide, her bosom heaved, and her lips quivered.

We in a ring round her avenged ourselves on her as though she had robbed us. She belonged to us, we had lavished on her our best, and though that best was a beggar's crumb, still we were twenty-six, she was one, and so there was no pain we could give her equal to her guilt! How we insulted her! She was still mute, still gazed at us with wild eyes, and a shiver ran all over her.

We laughed, roared, yelled. Other people ran up from somewhere and joined us. One of us pulled Tanya by the sleeve of her blouse.

Suddenly her eyes flashed; deliberately she raised her hands to her head and straightening her hair she said loudly but calmly, straight in our faces:

"Ah, you miserable prisoners!"

And she walked straight at us, walked as directly as though we had not been before her, as though we were not blocking her way.

And hence it was that no one did actually prevent her passing.

Walking out of our ring, without turning round, she said loudly and with indescribable contempt:

"Ah you scum—brutes."

And—was gone.

We were left in the middle of the yard, in the rain, under the grey sky without the sun.

Then we went mutely away to our damp stone cellar. As before—the sun never peeped in at our windows, and Tanya came no more!

Questions for Study

1. Describe in detail the setting of this story. How important is setting? The story manages to make extremely dreary surroundings somehow dramatic. How is this achieved?

2. This story is included in a collection entitled *Creatures That Once Were Men.* How is this grim title reflected in the characterization of the twenty-six men? How would you describe their collective character?
3. This story is told by what can be called a collective narrator, a single voice speaking on behalf of twenty-six men. How would you describe this voice?
4. Why would Tanya not mend one of the men's shirts? Why do the twenty-six men make a "holy thing" of Tanya? Why do they admire the soldier? Why do they not admire the other bakers? Why do they finally deride Tanya so viciously?
5. Formulate a statement of theme for this story. Does your statement differ from the one on p. 150?
6. What part do references to religion play in the story?
7. Why is life more miserable at the story's end than at its beginning? Is this decline consistent with Gorky's theme?

Philip Roth (b. 1933)
The Conversion of the Jews

"You're a real one for opening your mouth in the first place," Itzie said. "What do you open your mouth all the time for?"

"I didn't bring it up, Itz, I didn't," Ozzie said.

"What do you care about Jesus Christ for anyway?"

"I didn't bring up Jesus Christ. He did. I didn't even know what he was talking about. Jesus is historical, he kept saying. Jesus is historical." Ozzie mimicked the monumental voice of Rabbi Binder.

"Jesus was a person that lived like you and me," Ozzie continued. "That's what Binder said—"

"Yeah? . . . So what! What do I give two cents whether he lived or not. And what do you gotta open your mouth!" Itzie Lieberman favored closed-mouthedness, especially when it came to Ozzie Freedman's questions. Mrs. Freedman had to see Rabbi Binder twice before about Ozzie's questions and this Wednesday at four-thirty would be the third time. Itzie preferred to keep *his* mother in the kitchen; he settled for behind-the-back subtleties such as gestures, faces, snarls and other less delicate barnyard noises.

"He was a real person, Jesus, but he wasn't like God, and we don't believe he is God." Slowly, Ozzie was explaining Rabbi Binder's position to Itzie, who had been absent from Hebrew School the previous afternoon.

"The Catholics," Itzie said helpfully, "they believe in Jesus Christ, that he's God." Itzie Lieberman used "the Catholics" in its broadest sense—to include the Protestants.

Ozzie received Itzie's remark with a tiny head bob, as though it were a footnote, and went on. "His mother was Mary, and his father probably was Joseph," Ozzie said. "But the New Testament says his real father was God."

"His *real* father?"

"Yeah," Ozzie said, "that's the big thing, his father's supposed to be God."

"Bull."

"That's what Rabbi Binder says, that it's impossible—"

"Sure it's impossible. That stuff's all bull. To have a baby you gotta get laid," Itzie theologized. "Mary hadda get laid."

"That's what Binder says: 'The only way a woman can have a baby is to have intercourse with a man.'"

"He said *that*, Ozz?" For a moment it appeared that Itzie had put the theological question aside. "He said that, intercourse?" A little curled smile shaped itself in the lower half of Itzie's face like a pink mustache. "What you guys do, Ozz, you laugh or something?"

"I raised my hand."

"Yeah? Whatja say?"

"That's when I asked the question."

Itzie's face lit up. "Whatja ask about—intercourse?"

"No, I asked the question about God, how if He could create the heaven and earth in six days, and make all the animals and the fish and the light in six days—the light especially, that's what always gets me, that He could make the light. Making fish and animals, that's pretty good—"

"That's damn good." Itzie's appreciation was honest but unimaginative: it was as though God had just pitched a one-hitter.

"But making light . . . I mean when you think about it, it's really something," Ozzie said. "Anyway, I asked Binder if He could make all that in six days, and He could *pick* the six days he wanted right out of nowhere, why couldn't He let a woman have a baby without having intercourse."

"You said intercourse, Ozz, to Binder?"

"Yeah."

"Right in class?"

"Yeah."

Itzie smacked the side of his head.

"I mean, no kidding around," Ozzie said, "that'd really be nothing. After all that other stuff, that'd practically be nothing."

Itzie considered a moment. "What'd Binder say?"

"He started all over again explaining how Jesus was historical and how he lived like you and me but he wasn't God. So I said I under*stood* that. What I wanted to know was different."

What Ozzie wanted to know was always different. The first time he had wanted to know how Rabbi Binder could call the Jews "The Chosen People" if the Declaration of Independence claimed all men to be created equal. Rabbi Binder tried to distinguish for him between political equality and spiritual legitimacy, but what Ozzie wanted to know, he insisted vehemently, was different. That was the first time his mother had to come.

Then there was the plane crash. Fifty-eight people had been killed in a plane crash at La Guardia. In studying a casualty list in the newspaper his mother had discovered among the list of those dead eight Jewish names (his grandmother had nine but she counted Miller as a Jewish name); because of the eight she said the plane crash was "a tragedy." During free-discussion time on Wednesday Ozzie had brought to Rabbi Binder's attention this matter of "some of his relations" always picking out the Jewish names. Rabbi Binder had begun to explain cultural unity and some other things when Ozzie stood up at his seat and said that what he wanted to know was different. Rabbi Binder insisted that he sit down and it was then that Ozzie shouted that he wished all fifty-eight were Jews. That was the second time his mother came.

"And he kept explaining about Jesus being historical, and so I kept asking him. No kidding, Itz, he was trying to make me look stupid."

"So what he finally do?"

"Finally he starts screaming that I was deliberately simple-minded and a wise guy, and that my mother had to come, and this was the last time. And that I'd never get bar-mitzvahed[1] if he could help it. Then, Itz, then he starts talking in that voice like a statue, real slow and deep, and he says that I better think over what I said about the Lord. He told me to go to his office and think it over." Ozzie leaned his body towards Itzie. "Itz, I thought it over for a solid hour, and now I'm convinced God could do it."

Ozzie had planned to confess his latest transgression to his mother as soon as she came home from work. But it was a Friday night in November and already dark, and when Mrs. Freedman came through the door she tossed off her coat, kissed Ozzie quickly on the face, and went to the kitchen table to light the three yellow candles, two for the Sabbath and one for Ozzie's father.

When his mother lit the candles she would move her two arms slowly towards her, dragging them through the air, as though persuading people whose minds were half made up. And her eyes would get glassy with tears. Even when his father was alive Ozzie remembered that her eyes had gotten glassy, so it didn't have anything to do with his dying. It had something to do with lighting the candles.

As she touched the flaming match to the unlit wick of a Sabbath candle, the phone rang, and Ozzie, standing only a foot from it, plucked it off the receiver and held it muffled to his chest. When his mother lit candles Ozzie felt there should be no noise; even breathing, if you could manage it, should be softened. Ozzie pressed the phone to his breast and watched his mother dragging whatever she was dragging, and he felt his own eyes get glassy. His mother was a round, tired, gray-haired penguin of a woman whose gray skin had begun to feel the tug of gravity and the weight of her own history. Even when she was dressed up she didn't look like a chosen person. But when she lit candles she looked like something better; like a woman who knew momentarily that God could do anything.

After a few mysterious minutes she was finished. Ozzie hung up the phone and walked to the kitchen table where she was beginning to lay the two places for the four-course Sabbath meal. He told her that she would have to see Rabbi Binder next Wednesday at four-thirty, and then he told her why. For the first time in their life together she hit Ozzie across the face with her hand.

All through the chopped liver and chicken soup part of the dinner Ozzie cried; he didn't have any appetite for the rest.

---

1. A bar mitzvah is a Jewish religious ceremony celebrating a thirteen-year-old boy's passage into manhood.

On Wednesday, in the largest of the three basement classrooms of the synagogue, Rabbi Marvin Binder, a tall, handsome, broad-shouldered man of thirty with thick strong-fibered black hair, removed his watch from his pocket and saw that it was four o'clock. At the rear of the room Yakov Blotnik, the seventy-one-year-old custodian, slowly polished the large window, mumbling to himself, unaware that it was four o'clock or six o'clock, Monday or Wednesday. To most of the students Yakov Blotnik's mumbling, along with his brown curly beard, scythe nose, and two heel-trailing black cats, made of him an object of wonder, a foreigner, a relic, towards whom they were alternately fearful and disrespectful. To Ozzie the mumbling had always seemed a monotonous, curious prayer; what made it curious was that old Blotnik had been mumbling so steadily for so many years, Ozzie suspected he had memorized the prayers and forgotten all about God.

"It is now free-discussion time," Rabbi Binder said. "Feel free to talk about any Jewish matter at all—religion, family, politics, sports—"

There was silence. It was a gusty, clouded November afternoon and it did not seem as though there ever was or could be a thing called baseball. So nobody this week said a word about that hero from the past, Hank Greenberg[2]—which limited free discussion considerably.

And the soul-battering Ozzie Freedman had just received from Rabbi Binder had imposed its limitation. When it was Ozzie's turn to read aloud from the Hebrew book the rabbi had asked him petulantly why he didn't read more rapidly. He was showing no progress. Ozzie said he could read faster but that if he did he was sure not to understand what he was reading. Nevertheless, at the rabbi's repeated suggestion Ozzie tried, and showed a great talent, but in the midst of a long passage he stopped short and said he didn't understand a word he was reading, and started in again at a drag-footed pace. Then came the soul-battering.

Consequently when free-discussion time rolled around none of the students felt too free. The rabbi's invitation was answered only by the mumbling of feeble old Blotnik.

"Isn't there anything at all you would like to discuss?" Rabbi Binder asked again, looking at his watch. "No questions or comments?"

There was a small grumble from the third row. The rabbi requested that Ozzie rise and give the rest of the class the advantage of his thought.

Ozzie rose. "I forget it now," he said, and sat down in his place.

Rabbi Binder advanced a seat towards Ozzie and poised himself on the edge of the desk. It was Itzie's desk and the rabbi's frame only a dagger's-length away from his face snapped him to sitting attention.

"Stand up again, Oscar," Rabbi Binder said calmly, "and try to assemble your thoughts."

Ozzie stood up. All his classmates turned in their seats and watched as he gave an unconvincing scratch to his forehead.

"I can't assemble any," he announced, and plunked himself down.

"Stand up!" Rabbi Binder advanced from Itzie's desk to the one directly in front of Ozzie; when the rabbinical back was turned Itzie gave it five-fingers off

---

2. Major-league baseball player from 1933 to 1940; he was twice voted the American League's Most Valuable Player.

the tip of his nose, causing a small titter in the room. Rabbi Binder was too absorbed in squelching Ozzie's nonsense once and for all to bother with titters. "Stand up, Oscar. What's your question about?"

Ozzie pulled a word out of the air. It was the handiest word. "Religion."

"Oh, now you remember?"

"Yes."

"What is it?"

Trapped, Ozzie blurted the first thing that came to him. "Why can't He make anything He wants to make!"

As Rabbi Binder prepared an answer, a final answer, Itzie, ten feet behind him, raised one finger on his left hand, gestured it meaningfully towards the rabbi's back, and brought the house down.

Binder twisted quickly to see what had happened and in the midst of the commotion Ozzie shouted into the rabbi's back what he couldn't have shouted to his face. It was a loud, toneless sound that had the timbre of something stored inside for about six days.

"You don't know! You don't know anything about God!"

The rabbi spun back towards Ozzie. "What?"

"You don't know—you don't—"

"Apologize, Oscar, apologize!" It was a threat.

"You don't—"

Rabbi Binder's hand flicked out at Ozzie's cheek. Perhaps it had only been meant to clamp the boy's mouth shut, but Ozzie ducked and the palm caught him squarely on the nose.

The blood came in a short, red spurt on to Ozzie's shirt front.

The next moment was all confusion. Ozzie screamed, "You bastard, you bastard!" and broke for the classroom door. Rabbi Binder lurched a step backwards, as though his own blood had started flowing violently in the opposite direction, then gave a clumsy lurch forward and bolted out the door after Ozzie. The class followed after the rabbi's huge blue-suited back, and before old Blotnik could turn from his window, the room was empty and everyone was headed full speed up the three flights leading to the roof.

If one should compare the light of day to the life of man: sunrise to birth; sunset—the dropping down over the edge—to death; then as Ozzie Freedman wiggled through the trapdoor of the synagogue roof, his feet kicking backwards bronco-style at Rabbi Binder's outstretched arms—at that moment the day was fifty years old. As a rule, fifty or fifty-five reflects accurately the age of late afternoons in November, for it is in that month, during those hours, that one's awareness of light seems no longer a matter of seeing, but of hearing: light begins clicking away. In fact, as Ozzie locked shut the trapdoor in the rabbi's face, the sharp click of the bolt into the lock might momentarily have been mistaken for the sound of the heavier gray that had just throbbed through the sky.

With all his weight Ozzie kneeled on the locked door; any instant he was certain that Rabbi Binder's shoulder would fling it open, splintering the wood into shrapnel and catapulting his body into the sky. But the door did not move and below him he heard only the rumble of feet, first loud then dim, like thunder rolling away.

A question shot through his brain. "Can this be *me?*" For a thirteen-year-old who had just labeled his religious leader a bastard, twice, it was not an improper question. Louder and louder the question came to him—"Is it me? Is it me?"—until he discovered himself no longer kneeling, but racing crazily towards the edge of the roof, his eyes crying, his throat screaming, and his arms flying everywhichway as though not his own.

"Is it me? Is it me ME ME ME ME! It has to be me—but is it!"

It is the question a thief must ask himself the night he jimmies open his first window, and it is said to be the question with which bridegrooms quiz themselves before the altar.

In the few wild seconds it took Ozzie's body to propel him to the edge of the roof, his self-examination began to grow fuzzy. Gazing down at the street, he became confused as to the problem beneath the question: was it, is-it-me-who-called-Binder-a-bastard? or, is-it-me-prancing-around-on-the-roof? However, the scene below settled all, for there is an instant in any action when whether it is you or somebody else is academic. The thief crams the money in his pockets and scoots out the window. The bridegroom signs the hotel register for two. And the boy on the roof finds a streetful of people gaping at him, necks stretched backwards, faces up, as though he were the ceiling of the Hayden Planetarium. Suddenly you know it's you.

"Oscar! Oscar Freedman!" A voice rose from the center of the crowd, a voice that, could it have been seen, would have looked like the writing on scroll.[3] "Oscar Freedman, get down from there. Immediately!" Rabbi Binder was pointing one arm stiffly up at him; and at the end of that arm, one finger aimed menacingly. It was the attitude of a dictator, but one—the eyes confessed all—whose personal valet had spit neatly in his face.

Ozzie didn't answer. Only for a blink's length did he look towards Rabbi Binder. Instead his eyes began to fit together the world beneath him, to sort out people from places, friends from enemies, participants from spectators. In little jagged starlike clusters his friends stood around Rabbi Binder, who was still pointing. The topmost point on a star compounded not of angels but of five adolescent boys was Itzie. What a world it was, with those stars below, Rabbi Binder below . . . Ozzie, who a moment earlier hadn't been able to control his own body, started to feel the meaning of the word control: he felt Peace and he felt Power.

"Oscar Freedman, I'll give you three to come down."

Few dictators give their subjects three to do anything; but, as always, Rabbi Binder only looked dictatorial.

"Are you ready, Oscar?"

Ozzie nodded his head yes, although he had no intention in the world—the lower one of the celestial one he'd just entered—of coming down even if Rabbi Binder should give him a million.

"All right then," said Rabbi Binder. He ran a hand through his black Samson hair as though it were the gesture prescribed for uttering the first digit. Then, with his other hand cutting a circle out of the small piece of sky around him, he spoke. "One!"

There was no thunder. On the contrary, at that moment, as though "one" was the cue for which he had been waiting, the world's least thunderous person appeared on the synagogue steps. He did not so much come out the synagogue

---

3. The Torah, the first five books of the Old Testament, central to Jewish religious beliefs.

door as lean out, onto the darkening air. He clutched at the doorknob with one hand and looked up at the roof.

"Oy!"

Yakov Blotnik's old mind hobbled slowly, as if on crutches, and though he couldn't decide precisely what the boy was doing on the roof, he knew it wasn't good—that is, it wasn't-good-for-the-Jews. For Yakov Blotnik life had fractioned itself simply: things were either good-for-the-Jews or no-good-for-the-Jews.

He smacked his free hand to his in-sucked cheek, gently. "Oy, Gut!"[4]And then quickly as he was able, he jacked down his head and surveyed the street. There was Rabbi Binder (like a man at an auction with only three dollars in his pocket, he had just delivered a shaky "Two!"); there were the students, and that was all. So far it-wasn't-so-bad-for-the-Jews. But the boy had to come down immediately, before anybody saw. The problem: how to get the boy off the roof?

Anybody who has ever had a cat on the roof knows how to get him down. You call the fire department. Or first you call the operator and you ask her for the fire department. And the next thing there is great jamming of brakes and clanging of bells and shouting of instructions. And then the cat is off the roof. You do the same thing to get a boy off the roof.

That is, you do the same thing if you are Yakov Blotnik and you once had a cat on the roof.

When the engines, all four of them, arrived, Rabbi Binder had four times given Ozzie the count of three. The big hook-and-ladder swung around the corner and one of the firemen leaped from it, plunging headlong towards the yellow fire hydrant in front of the synagogue. With a huge wrench he began to unscrew the top nozzle. Rabbi Binder raced over to him and pulled at his shoulder.

"There's no fire . . ."

The fireman mumbled back over his shoulder and, heatedly, continued working at the nozzle.

"But there's no fire, there's no fire . . ." Binder shouted. When the fireman mumbled again, the rabbi grasped his face with both his hands and pointed it up at the roof.

To Ozzie it looked as though Rabbi Binder was trying to tug the fireman's head out of his body, like a cork from a bottle. He had to giggle at the picture they made: it was a family portrait—rabbi in black skullcap, fireman in red fire hat, and the little yellow hydrant squatting beside like a kid brother, bare-headed. From the edge of the roof Ozzie waved at the portrait, a one-handed, flapping, mocking wave; in doing it his right foot slipped from under him. Rabbi Binder covered his eyes with his hands.

Firemen work fast. Before Ozzie had even regained his balance, a big, round, yellowed net was being held on the synagogue lawn. The firemen who held it looked up at Ozzie with stern, feelingless faces.

One of the firemen turned his head towards Rabbi Binder. "What, is the kid nuts or something?"

Rabbi Binder unpeeled his hands from his eyes, slowly, painfully, as if they

---

4. Loosely translated, "Oh, goodness!"

were tape. Then he checked: nothing on the sidewalk, no dents in the net.

"Is he gonna jump, or what?" the fireman shouted.

In a voice not at all like a statue, Rabbi Binder finally answered. "Yes. Yes, I think so . . . He's been threatening to . . ."

Threatening to? Why, the reason he was on the roof, Ozzie remembered, was to get away; he hadn't even thought about jumping. He had just run to get away, and the truth was that he hadn't really headed for the roof as much as he'd been chased there.

"What's his name, the kid?"

"Freedman," Rabbi Binder answered. "Oscar Freedman."

The fireman looked up at Ozzie. "What is it with you, Oscar? You gonna jump, or what?"

Ozzie did not answer. Frankly, the question had just arisen.

"Look, Oscar, if you're gonna jump, jump—and if you're not gonna jump, don't jump. But don't waste our time, willya?"

Ozzie looked at the fireman and then at Rabbi Binder. He wanted to see Rabbi Binder cover his eyes one more time.

"I'm going to jump."

And then he scampered around the edge of the roof to the corner, where there was no net below, and he flapped his arms at his sides, swishing the air and smacking his palms to his trousers on the downbeat. He began screaming like some kind of engine, "Wheeeee . . . wheeeee," and leaning way out over the edge with the upper half of his body. The firemen whipped around to cover the ground with the net. Rabbi Binder mumbled a few words to Somebody and covered his eyes. Everything happened quickly, jerkily, as in a silent movie. The crowd, which had arrived with the fire engines, gave out a long, Fourth-of-July fireworks oooh-aahhh. In the excitement no one had paid the crowd much heed, except, of course, Yakov Blotnik, who swung from the doorknob counting heads. "Fier und tsvansik . . . finf und tsvantsik[5] . . . Oy, Gut!" It wasn't like this with the cat.

Rabbi Binder peeked through his fingers, checked the sidewalk and net. Empty. But there was Ozzie racing to the other corner. The fireman raced with him but were unable to keep up. Whenever Ozzie wanted to he might jump and splatter himself upon the sidewalk, and by the time the firemen scooted to the spot all they could do with their net would be to cover the mess.

"Wheeeee . . . wheeeee . . ."

"Hey, Oscar," the winded fireman yelled. "What the hell is this, a game or something?"

"Wheeeee . . . wheeeee . . ."

"Hey, Oscar—"

But he was off now to the other corner, flapping his wings fiercely. Rabbi Binder couldn't take it any longer—the fire engines from nowhere, the screaming suicidal boy, the net. He fell to his knees, exhausted, and with his hands curled together in front of his chest like a little dome, he pleaded, "Oscar, stop it, Oscar. Don't jump, Oscar. Please come down . . . Please don't jump."

---

5. "Four and twenty . . . five and twenty."

And further back in the crowd a single voice, a single young voice, shouted a lone word to the boy on the roof.

"Jump!"

It was Itzie. Ozzie momentarily stopped flapping.

"Go ahead, Ozz—jump!" Itzie broke off his point of the star and courageously, with the inspiration not of a wise-guy but of a disciple, stood alone. "Jump, Ozz, jump!"

Still on his knees, his hands still curled, Rabbi Binder twisted his body back. He looked at Itzie, then, agonizingly, back to Ozzie.

"OSCAR, DON'T JUMP! PLEASE, DON'T JUMP . . . please please . . ."

"Jump!" This time it wasn't Itzie but another point of the star. By the time Mrs. Freedman arrived to keep her four-thirty appointment with Rabbi Binder, the whole little upside down heaven was shouting and pleading for Ozzie to jump, and Rabbi Binder no longer was pleading with him not to jump, but was crying into the dome of his hands.

Understandably Mrs. Freedman couldn't figure out what her son was doing on the roof. So she asked.

"Ozzie, my Ozzie, what are you doing? My Ozzie, what is it?"

Ozzie stopped wheeeeeing and slowed his arms down to a cruising flap, the kind birds use in soft winds, but he did not answer. He stood against the low, clouded, darkening sky—light clicked down swiftly now, as on a small gear—flapping softly and gazing down at the small bundle of a woman who was his mother.

"What are you doing, Ozzie?" She turned towards the kneeling Rabbi Binder and rushed so close that only a paper-thickness of dusk lay between her stomach and his shoulders.

"What is my baby doing?"

Rabbi Binder gaped up at her but he too was mute. All that moved was the dome of his hands; it shook back and forth like a weak pulse.

"Rabbi, get him down! He'll kill himself. Get him down, my only baby . . ."

"I can't," Rabbi Binder said, "I can't . . ." and he turned his handsome head towards the crowd of boys behind him. "It's them. Listen to them."

And for the first time Mrs. Freedman saw the crowd of boys, and she heard what they were yelling.

"He's doing it for them. He won't listen to me. It's them." Rabbi Binder spoke like one in a trance.

"For them?"

"Yes."

"Why for them?"

"They want him to . . ."

Mrs. Freedman raised her two arms upward as though she were conducting the sky. "For them he's doing it!" And then in a gesture older than pyramids, older than prophets and floods, her arms came slapping down to her sides. "A martyr I have. Look!" She tilted her head to the roof. Ozzie was still flapping softly. "My martyr."

"Oscar, come down, *please*," Rabbi Binder groaned.

In a startlingly even voice Mrs. Freedman called to the boy on the roof.

"Ozzie, come down, Ozzie. Don't be a martyr, my baby."

As though it were a litany, Rabbi Binder repeated her words. "Don't be a martyr, my baby. Don't be a martyr."

"Gawhead, Ozz—*be* a Martin!" It was Itzie. "Be a Martin, be a Martin," and all the voices joined in singing for Martindom, whatever *it* was. "Be a Martin, be a Martin . . ."

Somehow when you're on a roof the darker it gets the less you can hear. All Ozzie knew was that two groups wanted two new things: his friends were spirited and musical about what they wanted; his mother and the rabbi were even-toned, chanting, about what they didn't want. The rabbi's voice was without tears now and so was his mother's.

The big net stared up at Ozzie like a sightless eye. The big, clouded sky pushed down. From beneath it looked like a gray corrugated board. Suddenly, looking up into that unsympathetic sky, Ozzie realized all the strangeness of what these people, his friends, were asking: they wanted him to jump, to kill himself; they were singing about it now—it made them that happy. And there was an even greater strangeness: Rabbi Binder was on his knees, trembling. If there was a question to be asked now it was not "Is it me?" but rather "Is it us? . . . Is it us?"

Being on the roof, it turned out, was a serious thing. If he jumped would the singing become dancing? Would it? What would jumping stop? Yearningly, Ozzie wished he could rip open the sky, plunge his hands through, and pull out the sun; and on the sun, like a coin, would be stamped JUMP or DON'T JUMP.

Ozzie's knees rocked and sagged a little under him as though they were setting him for a dive. His arms tightened, stiffened, froze, from shoulders to fingernails. He felt as if each part of his body were going to vote as to whether he should kill himself or not—and each part as though it were independent of *him*.

The light took an unexpected click down and the new darkness, like a gag, hushed the friends singing for this and the mother and rabbi chanting for that.

Ozzie stopped counting votes, and in a curiously high voice, like one who wasn't prepared for speech, he spoke.

"Mamma?"

"Yes, Oscar."

"Mamma, get down on your knees, like Rabbi Binder."

"Oscar—"

"Get down on your knees," he said, "or I'll jump."

Ozzie heard a whimper, then a quick rustling, and when he looked down where his mother had stood he saw the top of a head and beneath that a circle of dress. She was kneeling beside Rabbi Binder.

He spoke again. "Everybody kneel." There was the sound of everybody kneeling.

Ozzie looked around. With one hand he pointed towards the synagogue entrance. "Make *him* kneel."

There was a noise, not of kneeling, but of body-and-cloth stretching. Ozzie could hear Rabbi Binder saying in a gruff whisper, ". . . or he'll *kill* himself," and when next he looked there was Yakov Blotnik off the doorknob and for the first time in his life upon his knees in the Gentile posture of prayer.

As for the firemen—it is not as difficult as one might imagine to hold a net taut while you are kneeling.

Ozzie looked around again; and then he called to Rabbi Binder.

"Rabbi?"

"Yes, Oscar."

"Rabbi Binder, do you believe in God?"

"Yes."

"Do you believe God can do Anything?" Ozzie leaned his head out into the darkness. "Anything?"

"Oscar, I think—"

"Tell me you believe God can do Anything."

There was a second's hesitation. Then: "God can do Anything."

"Tell me you believe God can make a child without intercourse."

"He can."

"Tell me!"

"God," Rabbi Binder admitted, "can make a child without intercourse."

"Mamma, you tell me."

"God can make a child without intercourse," his mother said.

"Make *him* tell me." There was no doubt who *him* was.

In a few moments Ozzie heard an old comical voice say something to the increasing darkness about God.

Next, Ozzie made everybody say it. And then he made them all say they believed in Jesus Christ—first one at a time, then all together.

When the catechizing was through it was the beginning of evening. From the street it sounded as if the boy on the roof might have sighed.

"Ozzie?" A woman's voice dared to speak. "You'll come down now?"

There was no answer, but the woman waited, and when a voice finally did speak it was thin and crying, and exhausted as that of an old man who has just finished pulling the bells.

"Mamma, don't you see—you shouldn't hit me. He shouldn't hit me. You shouldn't hit me about God, Mamma. You should never hit anybody about God—"

"Ozzie, please come down now."

"Promise me, promise me you'll never hit anybody about God."

He had asked only his mother, but for some reason everyone kneeling in the street promised he would never hit anybody about God.

Once again there was silence.

"I can come down now, Mamma," the boy on the roof finally said. He turned his head both ways as though checking the traffic lights. "Now I can come down . . ."

And he did, right into the center of the yellow net that glowed in the evening's edge like an overgrown halo.

Questions for Study

1. State the essential incidents of the plot in your own words. Is suspense an important element in this plot?
2. Roth emphasizes throughout the latter part of the story the growing darkness of

the evening. What does this emphasis suggest to you? Why does Roth compare the sunset to a "dropping down over the edge"?

3. Religion, tradition, and authority are all issues in this story. Can you devise a thematic statement dealing with all of them? How are plot and characterization related to theme?

4. When does Ozzie begin to give orders to the Rabbi? Is his change justified? What is the significance of the word *catechizing* (p. 173)?

5. Why does Ozzie make the firemen chase him back and forth? Why does Itzie tell Ozzie to jump? Why do the other boys, the "whole little upside-down heaven," also plead with him to jump? Why do they happily sing urging him to "Be a Martin, be a Martin . . ."? Why does Ozzie jump?

6. Roth often takes a traditional religious symbol or emblem, such as the Star of David or the halo, and uses it in fresh new ways. Cite examples of such uses. What is their effect?

7. What thematic implications are there in Ozzie's statement, "You should never hit anybody about God"?

8. Ozzie's questions, "Is it me?" and "Is it us?" are, Roth tells us in his own voice, familiar ones. How do they relate to the theme of the story? Are these questions universal ones?

9. This is a story that deals with a minor, local event, yet one that seems to have significant implications. How does Roth move from the particular to the general? How does he manage to suggest those large implications?

Chapter 7
Style and Tone

Communicating exactly what we want to say is never simple. When we try to express our joy or misery, love or pain, we often get frustrated because words seem inadequate. So we rely upon facial expressions, body gestures, and voice inflections to convey and emphasize what our words seem incapable of handling. And we may finally resort to an acknowledgment of failure: "I really can't put it into the right words, but you know what I mean!" Our problem usually is not the inadequacy of words but our own difficulties in using them. Few of us have a very clear sense of which words are right at which times or of how they might best be put together.

The effective storyteller, however, whether he is speaking or writing, knows what words to use and what to do with them. He has a sensitivity to **style,** which is his use and arrangement of language, his selection of words, and the pacing and the patterning with which he puts them together. Since an author cannot compel our attention by walking the floor or pounding on the table or grasping our shoulders and staring into our eyes, he must convey the meaning and force of his story by means of his written style. An effective written style is appropriate to and in harmony with the materials and methods of a particular story. No single style is "good" anywhere, anytime. It is good because it is the style a particular story calls for.

Recognizing that words do not just happen but rather are chosen and arranged by an author permits us to evaluate the appropriateness and effectiveness of his style. Several formal elements of style that need to be considered are diction, imagery, and syntax. **Diction** is simply the author's choice of words. We do not have to examine every word the author uses, but rather we need to analyze the types of words he uses and then to consider the appropriateness of the type. For example, diction may be characterized by formal usage: "The experience was quite pleasant''; or by informal usage: ''It was a lot of fun''; or by slang: ''It was groovy, man!'' The words used may be complex or simple, long or short, and their origins and accumulated associations may give them particular meanings. All of these factors make some words appropriate in one context but inappropriate in others.

In ''Sredni Vashtar,'' for example, the diction is rather formal and elevated, sometimes even a bit pompous. Words like *succumbed, paean, lavished,* and *ejaculations* serve a definite purpose by softening and obscuring the horror of the events of the story. Saki's formal description of the toolshed as having ''respectable proportions'' and the chicken as being a ''ragged-plumaged hen'' makes the bizarre and horrid situation seem almost proper. ''The Capital of the World'' too ends with a horrid occurrence. But Hemingway's diction—blunt, concrete, and factual—is radically different from Saki's. Saki uses formal words to make a gruesome incident seem unreal, while Hemingway uses plain words to make a similar incident seem terribly real.

With a first-person narrator, diction must not only be appropriate to the author's intended effect but it must also be consistent with the narrator's character. In ''The Angel of the Bridge,'' John Cheever's narrator, who is quite a sophisticated adult, may speak of the ''incandescence of the sky'' and ''an ecstatic sereneness.'' These are words that Joyce Carol Oates' teen-aged narrator in ''How I Contemplated the World . . .'' probably would not know. When she describes, or tries to describe, Raymond Forrest as ''A handsome man? An ugly man?'' Oates' narrator reveals the limitations of her vocabulary. Her diction not only shows her inability, or her unwillingness, to commit herself to an opinion but it also conveys the sense that the characters she mentions, like the words that describe them, are faceless and interchangeable.

In examining the appropriateness of an author's diction, we should also be aware of the suggestive meanings of the words he uses. Dictionaries are of great help in determining a word's **denotation,** or its exact, literal meaning. Dictionaries do not precisely convey, however, a word's **connotations,** or the suggested or implied meanings which have become associated with it. We can know a word's connotations only through our familiarity with language and through our awareness of how a word is used in a particular context. Although the denotation of *house, home, dwelling, domicile,* and *abode,* for example, is the same, their connotations are quite different and we use them in different contexts. Oates' narrator describes her family residence as a ''classic contemporary'' and a ''traditional modern'' house. Yet at various times she calls it ''home.'' By being aware of the narrator's various shifts between the neutral word *house* and the richly suggestive *home,* we feel her ambivalent and ever changing attitude toward her family life.

By making ourselves conscious of the words we read and of their effect upon us, we can learn to distinguish between kinds of diction and to see how words function in changing situations. We will also discover that abstract language that appeals chiefly to our minds leaves us relatively unmoved, while concrete language that appeals to our senses forcefully moves us. A word or phrase that conveys a sensory impression, that appeals to our sense of seeing, hearing, smelling, tasting, or touching, is called an **image.** Cheever's "The Angel of the Bridge" is filled with images of roads, bridges, and passageways, which become associated with movement, travel, and change. Taken individually or in logical patterns, such images contribute to and illuminate the meaning of the story. Yet the bridges in the story are *literal* images—actual modern and old-fashioned structures the narrator rides over in his travels. They also function as *figurative* images, which signify to us the major and difficult transitions the narrator makes as he travels into middle age and a contemporary world he is reluctant to face. Such figurative language depicts one thing through another. Something abstract, such as a life transition, is seen through something tangible, such as a bridge, and thus is made more concrete, immediate, and vivid.

The simplest and most frequently used kind of figurative language is the simile. A **simile** is an expressed comparison using *like* or *as* that links something unfamiliar or abstract with something familiar or concrete. In "The Capital of the World" Hemingway helps us see the picador by telling us that his legs and arms are "like iron." And he helps us feel the matador's sword thrust by saying that it entered the bull "as easy as into a mound of stiff butter." Oates' narrator's fatigue is realized in the image of her head hanging "heavy as a pumpkin." And Cheever's narrator's disgust with the California landscape is conveyed through the image of palm trees "stuck up . . . like rank upon rank of wet mops."

Such comparisons are explicitly stated. An implied comparison between something unfamiliar or abstract and something familiar or tangible is called a **metaphor.** If the narrator in Oates' story had said her head "was a heavy pumpkin," she would have used a metaphor, not a simile. In "The Angel of the Bridge" Cheever speaks of the "edge of night," a "hoop of light," and "blue-sky courage." These are metaphors that imply a comparison of night, light, and courage with more concrete things. Cheever is able to convey his meaning more vividly and concisely, as he does through the principal metaphor in that story: the implicit comparison between literal bridges and psychological bridges.

Once we recognize how much diction and figurative language affect the impact of a tale, we may further realize that style is not only a matter of word choice but also of word order; that style is a function of both diction and syntax. **Syntax** is the arrangement of words within a sentence to achieve a particular effect. For example, placing a word or a phrase at the beginning of a sentence, immediately before a comma, or at the end of a sentence calls special attention to that word or phrase. In "The Angel of the Bridge," Cheever begins a typically long and involved sentence with a matter-of-fact description of his narrator's brother and finishes it on a dramatic note: "He appeared to be an intelligent, civilized, and well-dressed man, and I wondered how many of the men waiting with him to cross the street made their way as he did through a ruin of absurd delusions, in which the street might appear to be a torrent and the approaching cab driven by the angel of death." The phrase *angel of death* ends the sentence on a note of quiet terror—a condition the urban dwellers, including the narrator, constantly feel. More importantly, the cab-driving angel of death serves as an ironic contrast to the benign hitchhiker-angel who brings salvation and courage to the narrator at the end of the story. This contrast would not have been as forceful (or even apparent) had Cheever chosen to bury the reference to the angel of death in the middle of the sentence. Appearing at the end of the last sentence of the paragraph, his angel both sums up what has preceded it and suggests events to come.

Another method the fiction writer uses to achieve emphasis through syntax is the arrangement of **loose sentences,** which follow a normal subject-verb-modifier pattern, and **periodic sentences,** in which a word or phrase essential to the meaning is withheld until near the sentence's end. In "The Capital of the World," for instance, the second paragraph includes a sequence of loose clauses: "he was a well built boy"; "he had a ready and unpuzzled smile"; "he was fast on his feet"; "he loved his sisters"; "he loved Madrid"; "he loved his work." The sequence of straightforward phrases describes the boy's rather commonplace interests and character. This pattern is radically altered in the next paragraph, which consists of a periodic sentence that clearly emphasizes the boy's consuming passion: ". . . but for Paco, the youngest of the three waiters who served at table, the only ones who really existed were the bullfighters." Only the bullfighters are important to Paco.

Syntax is quite different in Joyce Carol Oates' story, since the narrator many times does not use full sentences. The narrator calls her story "Notes" and expresses herself a great deal in sentence fragments, so that her normal sentences carry a special force. Revealing her weak grasp of reality, the girl asks numerous questions about simple matters: "Day or night?" "What room is this?" And some of her utterances are statements and questions at the same time (Clarita "is twenty, twenty-five, she is thirty or more?"). Such constructions establish her indecisiveness. Similarly, when she describes Sioux Drive, we know by the breathless, lengthy, unpunctuated catalog of items, as well as by her diction, that she is more confident of herself and of her words—perhaps because she gets them from realtors' classified ads in the local newspaper. Because examining syntax helps us characterize a narrator, we can see the differences in Oates' story between a psychological state that produces halting fragments and one that produces long, smooth, intricately constructed sentences.

When a particular pattern of syntax is repeated several times, it sets up a rhythm that leads us to expect its continued repetition. Any break in the pattern calls attention to itself. In "The Capital of the World," for instance, after Paco has been stabbed, the syntax of two long and involved sentences suggests the quick ebbing-away of his life: "But Enrique was running down the Carrera San Jeromino to the all-night first-aid station and Paco was alone, first sitting up, then huddled over, then slumped on the floor, until it was over, feeling his life go out of him as dirty water empties from a bathtub when the plug is drawn. He was frightened and he felt faint and he tried to say an act of contrition and he remembered how it started . . . ." The rhythm here leads us to expect a continuing sequence of action. We are startled and shocked to find that the short last sentence of the paragraph abruptly breaks the pattern and ends the scene on a matter-of-fact—even clinical—note: "A severed femoral artery empties itself faster than you can believe."

In an interview the contemporary American writer Truman Capote spoke of narrative control in terms of "maintaining a stylistic and emotional upper hand over your material." He went on to say: "Call it precious and go to hell, but I believe a story can be wrecked by a faulty rhythm in a sentence . . . ." We may not agree that rhythm alone can make or break a story, but we can sense how much a contribution it makes. When we read Hemingway's description of Paco's bullfighting demonstration—"Standing slim and straight he made four more perfect passes, smooth, elegant and graceful"—the rhythm as well as the words makes us feel Paco's ease and grace. When Enrique explains to Paco that "The bull has such force that the horns rip like a knife, they stab like a bayonet, and they kill like a club" we sense an abrupt, violent force in both the diction and the syntax.

Rhythm and sound convey meaning in fiction as well as in poetry. An author may employ a pattern of harsh, grating sounds to make a fictional situation seem especially disagreeable. For example, Oates' narrator describes Clarita as having "unwashed underclothes, or no underclothes, unwashed skin, gritty toes; hair long and falling into strands, not recently washed." The subject matter here is unpleasant enough, but the very sounds themselves and the jerky rhythm of the fragmented phrases amplify the unsavory impression of the words. An author may also use a rhythmic blend of pleasant-sounding words to make his fictional situation seem especially agreeable. Consider Cheever's description of his narrator's "angel": "Her straight light-brown hair was brushed and brushed and grained with blondness and spread in a kind of cape over her shoulders.'' Our impression of the angel is far more pleasing than that of Clarita not only because her hair is cleaner, but also because the description contains words which flow in a delicate, rhythmic pattern.

We can generalize about a writer's style by describing the way he chooses words and by categorizing the way he puts them together in a particular manner. We may call the style journalistic or poetic, formal or informal, dignified or casual, and so on. We may also speak of its effect upon us. Nevertheless, no matter how subtle, subjective, and indefinable a written style may seem to be, it is composed of objective factors. These measurable elements of style can be put on a computer in order to determine, for example, the number of times a certain image is used or how frequently loose and periodic sentences are employed. A computer can even analyze the rhythm and the prevalence of pleasant or unpleasant sounds. But it cannot analyze a story's tone, for there is nothing objective or verifiable about tone.

In *The Rhetoric of Fiction,* Wayne Booth defines **tone** as the "implicit evaluation which the author manages to convey behind his explicit presentation." As the author's unstated evaluation of or attitude toward his subject matter, tone in fiction shapes and influences meaning just as the tone of our voice colors and controls the implications of our spoken language.

To understand tone better we might imagine the author reading his story aloud to us. Through the quality, pitch, and duration of his pronunciation and through his overall delivery, he conveys to us, for example, a solemn or a light tone, a pleased or an angry tone, a sympathetic or a reserved tone, a matter-of-fact or an ecstatic tone. In reading his story, of course, we cannot literally "hear" the author's voice, but we can become conscious of the implications of his style. Thus we have a sense of what the author's attitude toward his subject matter and audience is. We should, in other words, take into account his tone in order to increase our understanding of the story and to sharpen our appreciation of his artistic presentation. We should be able to recognize, for instance, that the attitude of Cheever's narrator is flippant and that Cheever's tone seems to be lighthearted. The story has something significant to say about the stresses and terror of contemporary urban life. Yet at the moment of crisis in the story, when the "angel" is getting into the car, Cheever cannot resist adding that she is carrying—"believe me"—a small harp wrapped in a crushed raincoat. Behind the detached and world-weary attitude of the girl in Oates' story, we sense a deeply disturbed, even frantic, authorial tone. Similarly, the tone in "The Capital of the World" may at first seem to be matter-of-fact and detached. Yet as we reread the story and become conscious of Hemingway's style we see that his tone is actually laced with compassion and touched occasionally with bitterness.

Hemingway's tone reflects his sense of injustice and his concern for the isolation and the ignorance of the Spanish poor. He sympathizes with their yearning to fulfill their dreams, yet he also sees the pathos of their illusions. And his tone invites us to understand and to share his attitude. When a story's tone is calculated to convey a sense of frustration over human isolation, for example, it simultaneously and paradoxically counters our sense of that isolation by supposing and creating a human community. Even a bitter tone tries to establish between writer and reader a sense of outrage at human failings and weaknesses. For tone finally not only depends upon but also reminds us of the human condition and of the world in which we live.

John Cheever (b. 1912)
The Angel of the Bridge

You may have seen my mother waltzing on ice skates in Rockefeller Center. She's seventy-eight years old now but very wiry, and she wears a red velvet costume with a short skirt. Her tights are flesh-colored, and she wears spectacles and a red ribbon in her white hair, and she waltzes with one of the rink attendants. I don't know why I should find the fact that she waltzes on ice skates so disconcerting, but I do. I avoid that neighborhood whenever I can during the winter months, and I never lunch in the restaurants on the rink. Once when I was passing that way, a total stranger took me by the arm and, pointing to Mother, said, "Look at that crazy old dame." I was very embarrassed. I suppose I should be grateful for the fact that she amuses herself and is not a burden to me, but I sincerely wish she had hit on some less conspicuous recreation. Whenever I see gracious old ladies arranging chrysanthemums and pouring tea, I think of my own mother, dressed like a hat-check girl, pushing some paid rink attendant around the ice, in the middle of the third-biggest city of the world.

My mother learned to figure-skate in the little New England village of St. Botolphs, where we come from, and her waltzing is an expression of her attachment to the past. The older she grows, the more she longs for the vanishing and provincial world of her youth. She is a hardy woman, as you can imagine, but she does not relish change. I arranged one summer for her to fly to Toledo and visit friends. I drove her to the Newark airport. She seemed troubled by the airport waiting room, with its illuminated advertisements, vaulted ceiling, and touching and painful scenes of separation played out to an uproar of continuous tango music. She did not seem to find it in any way interesting or beautiful, and compared to the railroad station in St. Botolphs it was indeed a strange background against which to take one's departure. The flight was delayed for an hour, and we sat in the waiting room. Mother looked tired and old. When we had been waiting half an hour, she began to have some noticeable difficulty in breathing. She spread a hand over the front of her dress and began to gasp deeply, as if she was in pain. Her face got mottled and red. I pretended not to notice this. When the plane was announced, she got to her feet and exclaimed, ''I want to go home! If I have to die suddenly, I don't want to die in a flying machine.'' I cashed in her ticket and drove her back to her apartment, and I have never mentioned this seizure to her or to anyone, but her capricious, or perhaps neurotic, fear of dying in a plane crash was the first insight I had into how, as she grew older, her way was strewn with invisible rocks and lions and how eccentric were the paths she took, as the world seemed to change its boundaries and become less and less comprehensible.

At the time of which I'm writing, I flew a great deal myself. My business was in Rome, New York, San Francisco, and Los Angeles, and I sometimes traveled as often as once a month between these cities. I liked the flying. I liked the incandescence of the sky at high altitudes. I liked all eastward flights where you can see from the ports the edge of night move over the continent and where, when it is four o'clock by your California watch, the housewives of Garden City are washing up the supper dishes and the stewardess in the plane is passing a second round of drinks. Toward the end of the flight, the air is stale. You are tired. The gold thread in the upholstery scratches your cheek, and there is a momentary feeling of forlornness, a sulky and childish sense of estrangement. You find good companions, of course, and bores, but most of the errands we run at such high altitudes are humble and terrestrial. That old lady, flying over the North Pole, is taking a jar of calf's-foot jelly to her sister in Paris, and the man beside her sells imitation-leather inner soles. Flying westward one dark night—we had crossed the Continental Divide, but we were still an hour out of Los Angeles and had not begun our descent, and were at such an altitude that the sense of houses, cities, and people below us was lost—I saw a formation, a trace of light, like the lights that burn along a shore. There was no shore in that part of the world, and I knew I would never know if the edge of the desert or some bluff or mountain accounted for this hoop of light, but it seemed, in its obscurity—and at that velocity and height—like the emergence of a new world, a gentle hint at my own obsolescence, the lateness of my time of life, and my inability to understand the things I often see. It was a pleasant feeling, completely free of regret, of being caught in some observable mid-passage, the farther reaches of which might be understood by my sons.

I liked to fly, as I say, and had none of my mother's anxieties. It was my older brother—her darling—who was to inherit her resoluteness, her stubbornness, her table silver, and some of her eccentricities. One evening, my brother—I had not seen him for a year or so—called and asked if he could come for dinner. I was happy to invite him. We live on the eleventh floor of an apartment house, and at seven-thirty he telephoned from the lobby and asked me to come down. I thought he must have something to tell me privately, but when we met in the lobby he got into the automatic elevator with me and we started up. As soon as the doors closed, he showed the same symptoms of fear I had seen in my mother. Sweat stood out on his forehead, and he gasped like a runner.

''What in the world is the matter?'' I asked.

''I'm afraid of elevators,'' he said miserably.

''But what are you afraid of?''

"I'm afraid the building will fall down."

I laughed—cruelly, I guess. For it all seemed terribly funny, his vision of the buildings of New York banging against one another like ninepins as they fell to the earth. There has always been a strain of jealousy in our feelings about one another, and I am aware, at some obscure level, that he makes more money and has more of everything than I, and to see him humiliated—crushed—saddened me but at the same time and in spite of myself made me feel that I had taken a stunning lead in the race for honors that is at the bottom of our relationship. He is the oldest, he is the favorite, but watching his misery in the elevator I felt that he was merely my poor old brother, overtaken by his worries. He stopped in the hallway to recover his composure, and explained that he had been suffering from this phobia for over a year. He was going to a psychiatrist, he said. I couldn't see that it had done him any good. He was all right once he got out of the elevator, but I noticed that he stayed away from the windows. When it was time to go, I walked him out to the corridor. I was curious. When the elevator reached our floor, he turned to me and said, "I'm afraid I'll have to take the stairs." I led him to the stairway, and we climbed slowly down the eleven flights. He clung to the railing. We said goodbye in the lobby, and I went up in the elevator, and told my wife about his fear that the building might fall down. It seemed strange and sad to her, and it did to me, too, but it also seemed terribly funny.

It wasn't terribly funny when, a month later, the firm he worked for moved to the fifty-second floor of a new office building and he had to resign. I don't know what reasons he gave. It was another six months before he could find a job in a third-floor office. I once saw him on a winter dusk at the corner of Madison Avenue and Fifty-ninth Street, waiting for the light to change. He appeared to be an intelligent, civilized, and well-dressed man, and I wondered how many of the men waiting with him to cross the street made their way as he did through a ruin of absurd delusions, in which the street might appear to be a torrent and the approaching cab driven by the angel of death.

He was quite all right on the ground. My wife and I went to his house in New Jersey, with the children, for a weekend, and he looked healthy and well. I didn't ask about his phobia. We drove back to New York on Sunday afternoon. As we approached the George Washington Bridge, I saw a thunderstorm over the city. A strong wind struck the car the moment we were on the bridge, and nearly took the wheel out of my hand. It seemed to me that I could feel the huge structure swing. Halfway across the bridge, I thought I felt the roadway begin to give. I could see no signs of collapse, and yet I was convinced that in another minute the bridge would split in two and hurl the long lines of Sunday traffic into the dark water below us. This imagined disaster was terrifying. My legs got so weak that I was not sure I could brake the car if I needed to. Then it became difficult for me to breathe. Only by opening my mouth and gasping did I seem able to take in any air. My blood pressure was affected and I began to feel a darkening of my vision. Fear has always seemed to me to run a course, and at its climax the body and perhaps the spirit defend themselves by drawing on some new and fresh source of strength. Once over the center of the bridge, my pain and terror began to diminish. My wife and the children were admiring the storm, and they did not seem to have noticed my spasm. I was afraid both that the bridge would fall down and that they might observe my panic.

I thought back over the weekend for some incident that might account for my preposterous fear that the George Washington Bridge would blow away in a thunderstorm, but it had been a pleasant weekend, and even under the most exaggerated scrutiny I couldn't uncover any source of morbid nervousness or anxiety. Later in the week, I had to drive to Albany, and, although the day was clear and windless, the memory of my first attack was too keen; I hugged the east bank of the river as far north as Troy, where I found a small, old-fashioned bridge that I could cross comfortably. This meant going fifteen or twenty miles out of my way, and it is humiliating to have your travels obstructed by barriers that are senseless and invisible. I drove back from Albany by the same route, and next morning I went to the family doctor and told him I was afraid of bridges.

He laughed. "You, of all people," he said scornfully. "You'd better take hold of yourself."

"But Mother is afraid of airplanes," I said. "And Brother hates elevators."

"Your mother is past seventy," he said, "and one of the most remarkable women I've ever known. I wouldn't bring *her* into this. What *you* need is a little more backbone."

This was all he had to say, and I asked him to recommend an analyst. He does not include psychoanalysis in medical science, and told me I would be wasting my time and money, but, yielding to his obligation to be helpful, he gave me the name and address of a psychiatrist, who told me that my fear of bridges was the surface manifestation of a deep-seated anxiety and that I would have to have a full analysis. I didn't have the time, or the money, or, above all, the confidence in the doctor's methods to put myself in his hands, and I said I would try and muddle through.

There are obviously areas of true and false pain, and my pain was meretricious, but how could I convince my lights and vitals of this? My youth and childhood had their deeply troubled and their jubilant years, and could some repercussions from this past account for my fear of heights? The thought of a life determined by hidden obstacles was unacceptable, and I decided to take the advice of the family doctor and ask more of myself. I had to go to Idlewild later in the week, and, rather than take a bus or a taxi, I drove the car myself. I nearly lost consciousness on the Triborough Bridge. When I got to the airport I ordered a cup of coffee, but my hand was shaking so I spilled the coffee on the counter. The man beside me was amused and said that I must have put in quite a night. How could I tell him that I had gone to bed early and sober but that I was afraid of bridges?

I flew to Los Angeles late that afternoon. It was one o'clock by my watch when we landed. It was only ten o'clock in California. I was tired and took a taxi to the hotel where I always stay, but I couldn't sleep. Outside my hotel window was a monumental statue of a young woman, advertising a Las Vegas night club. She revolves slowly in a beam of light. At 2 A.M. the light is extinguished, but she goes on restlessly turning all through the night. I have never seen her cease her turning, and I wondered, that night, when they greased her axle and washed her shoulders. I felt some affection for her, since neither of us could rest, and I wondered if she had a family—a stage mother, perhaps, and a compromised and broken-spirited father who drove a municipal bus on the West Pico line? There was a restaurant across the street, and I watched a drunken woman in a sable cape being led out to a car. She twice nearly fell. The crosslights from the open door, the lateness, her drunkenness, and the solicitude of the man with her made the scene, I thought, worried and lonely. Then two cars that seemed to be racing down Sunset Boulevard pulled up at a traffic light under my window. Three men piled out of each car and began to slug one another. You could hear the blows land on bone and cartilage. When the light changed, they got back into their cars and raced off..The fight, like the hoop of light I had seen from the plane, seemed like the signs of a new world, but in this case an emergence of brutality and chaos. Then I remembered that I was to go to San Francisco on Thursday, and was expected in Berkeley for lunch. This meant crossing the San Francisco–Oakland Bay Bridge, and I reminded myself to take a cab both ways and leave the car I rented in San Francisco in the hotel garage. I tried again to reason out my fear that the bridge would fall. Was I the victim of some sexual dislocation? My life has been promiscuous, carefree, and a source of immense pleasure, but was there some secret here that would have to be mined by a professional? Were all my pleasures impostures and evasions, and was I really in love with my old mother in her skating costume?

Looking at Sunset Boulevard at three in the morning, I felt that my terror of bridges was an expression of my clumsily concealed horror of what is becoming of the world. I can drive with composure through the outskirts of Cleveland and Toledo—past the birthplace of the Polish Hot Dog, the Buffalo Burger stands, the used-car lots, and the architectural monotony. I claim to enjoy walking down Hollywood Boulevard on a Sunday afternoon. I have cheerfully praised the evening sky hanging beyond the disheveled and expatriated palm trees on Doheny Boulevard, stuck up against the incandescence, like rank upon rank of wet mops. Duluth and East Seneca are charming, and if they aren't, just look away. The hideousness of the road between San Francisco and Palo Alto is nothing more than the search of honest men and women for a decent place to live. The same thing goes for San Pedro and all that coast. But the height of bridges seemed to be one link I could not forge or fasten in this hypocritical chain of acceptances. The truth is, I hate freeways and Buffalo Burgers. Expatriated palm trees and monotonous housing developments depress me. The continuous music on special-fare trains exacerbates my feelings. I detest the destruction of familiar landmarks, I am deeply troubled by the misery and drunkenness I find among my friends, I abhor the dishonest practices I see. And it was at the highest point in the arc of a bridge that I became aware suddenly of the depth and bitterness of my feelings about modern life, and of the profoundness of my yearning for a more vivid, simple, and peaceable world.

But I couldn't reform Sunset Boulevard, and until I could, I couldn't drive across the San Francisco–Oakland Bay Bridge. What *could* I do? Go back to St. Botolphs, wear a Norfolk jacket, and play cribbage in the firehouse? There was only one bridge in the village, and you could throw a stone across the river there.

I got home from San Francisco on Saturday, and found my daughter back from school for the weekend. On Sunday morning, she asked me to drive her to the convent school in Jersey where she is a student. She had to be back in time for nine-o'clock Mass, and we left our apartment in the city a little after seven. We were talking and laughing, and I had approached and was in fact on the George Washington Bridge without having remembered my weakness. There were no preliminaries this time. The seizure came with a rush. The strength went out of my legs, I gasped for breath, and felt the terrifying loss of sight. I was, at the same time, determined to conceal these symptoms from my daughter. I made the other side of the bridge, but I was violently shaken. My daughter didn't seem to have noticed. I got her to school in time, kissed her goodbye, and started home. There was no question of my crossing the George Washington Bridge again, and I decided to drive north to Nyack and cross on the Tappan Zee Bridge. It seemed, in my memory, more gradual and more securely anchored to its shores. Driving up the parkway on the west shore, I decided that oxygen was what I needed, and I opened all the windows of the car. The fresh air seemed to help, but only momentarily. I could feel my sense of reality ebbing. The roadside and the car itself seemed to have less substance than a dream. I had some friends in the neighborhood, and I thought of stopping and asking them for a drink, but it was only a little after nine in the morning, and I could not face the embarrassment of asking for a drink so early in the day, and of explaining that I was afraid of bridges. I thought I might feel better if I talked to someone, and I stopped at a gas station and bought some gas, but the attendant was laconic and sleepy, and I couldn't explain to him that his conversation might make the difference between life and death. I had got onto the Thruway by then, and I wondered what alternatives I had if I couldn't cross the bridge. I could call my wife and ask her to make some arrangements for removing me, but our relationship involves so much self-esteem and face that to admit openly to this foolishness might damage our married happiness. I could call the garage we use and ask them to send up a man to chauffeur me home. I could park the car and wait until one o'clock, when the bars opened, and fill up on whiskey, but I had spent the last of my money for gasoline. I decided to take a chance, and turned onto the approach to the bridge.

All the symptoms returned, and this time they were much worse than ever. The wind was knocked out of my lungs as by a blow. My equilibrium was so shaken that the car swerved from one lane into another. I drove to the side and pulled on the hand brake. The loneliness of my predicament was harrowing. If I had been miserable with romantic love, racked with sickness, or beastly drunk, it would have seemed more dignified. I remembered my brother's face, sallow and greasy with sweat in the elevator, and my mother in her red skirt, one leg held gracefully aloft as she coasted backward in the arms of a rink attendant, and it seemed to me that we were all three characters in some bitter and sordid tragedy, carrying impossible burdens and separated from the rest of mankind by our misfortunes. My life was over, and it would never come back, everything that I loved—blue-sky courage, lustiness, the natural grasp of things. It would never come back. I would end up in the psychiatric ward of the county hospital, screaming that the bridges, all the bridges in the world, were falling down.

Then a young girl opened the door of the car and got in. "I didn't think anyone would pick me up on the bridge," she said. She carried a cardboard suitcase and—believe me—a small harp in a cracked waterproof. Her straight light-brown hair was brushed and brushed and grained with blondness and spread in a kind of cape over her shoulders. Her face seemed full and merry.

"Are you hitchhiking?" I asked.

"Yes."

"But isn't it dangerous for a girl your age?"

"Not at all."

"Do you travel much?"

"All the time. I sing a little. I play the coffeehouses."

"What do you sing?"

"Oh, folk music, mostly. And some old things—Purcell and Dowland.[1] But mostly folk music. . . . 'I gave my love a cherry that had no stone,'" she sang in a true and pretty voice. "'I gave my love a chicken that had no bone/I told my love a story that had no end/I gave my love a baby with no cryin'.'"[2]

She sang me across a bridge that seemed to be an astonishingly sensible, durable, and even beautiful construction designed by intelligent men to simplify my travels, and the water of the Hudson below us was charming and tranquil. It all came back—blue-sky courage, the high spirits of lustiness, an ecstatic sereneness. Her song ended as we got to the toll station on the east bank, and she thanked me, said goodbye, and got out of the car. I offered to take her wherever she wanted to go, but she shook her head and walked away, and I drove on toward the city through a world that, having been restored to me, seemed marvelous and fair. When I got home, I thought of calling my brother and telling him what had happened, on the chance that there was also an angel of the elevator banks, but the harp—that single detail—threatened to make me seem ridiculous or mad, and I didn't call.

I wish I could say that I am convinced that there will always be some merciful intercession to help me with my worries, but I don't believe in rushing my luck, so I will stay off the George Washington Bridge, although I can cross the Triborough and the Tappan Zee with ease. My brother is still afraid of elevators, and my mother, although she's grown quite stiff, still goes around and around and around on the ice.

Questions for Study

1. A seventy-eight-year-old woman wearing a red costume with flesh-colored tights and waltzing on ice skates at Rockefeller Center in New York City creates quite a spectacle. What other elements in the narrative are similar to this flamboyant opening image? What is the overall contribution of such images?
2. Describe the point of view of this story. Is the narrator a reliable narrator?
3. Why does the story begin and end with a description of the narrator's mother? Are the narrator and his brother like their mother? If so, in what ways?
4. In the second sentence of paragraph four, Cheever's narrator lists the things his brother inherits from their mother. Why does he arrange the items in this particular order?
5. Cheever's narrator learns that he too has a phobia. Do you accept the narrator's own view of what his problem is? What alternative explanations are there?
6. During the narrator's initial seizure of panic on the bridge, what happens to the sentence structure? Why are the long sentences at the ends of the second and third

---

1. Henry Purcell (1659–95), noted English composer of a variety of musical forms, including religious music and vocal and instrumental chamber music; John Dowland (1562–1626), English Renaissance lutenist and the foremost composer of his time.
2. From "The Riddle Song," a traditional American folk-ballad of unknown origin.

paragraphs of the story broken up into phrases? Can you find other instances where the syntax helps characterize the narrator?

7. How does the diction change when the narrator refers to the psychiatrist's advice? How does it change at other times? Look closely at each change and comment on its effectiveness.

8. Why does Cheever have his narrator describe in such detail the scenes viewed from his Los Angeles hotel room? How do these details contribute to the narrative? What are the associations of the narrator with these places?

9. Why do you suppose Cheever describes the "angel" as a folksinger? How does her song affect the narrator? What associations does he make with it, and why does he respond as he does?

Joyce Carol Oates (b. 1938)
How I Contemplated the World from the Detroit House of Correction and Began My Life Over Again

Notes for an essay for an English class at Baldwin Country Day School; poking around in debris; disgust and curiosity; a revelation of the meaning of life; a happy ending. . . .

I Events

1. The girl (myself) is walking through Branden's, that excellent store. Suburb of a large famous city that is a symbol for large famous American cities. The event sneaks up on the girl, who believes she is herding it along with a small fixed smile, a girl of fifteen, innocently experienced. She dawdles in a certain style by a counter of costume jewelry. Rings, earrings, necklaces. Prices from $5 to $50, all within reach. All ugly. She eases over to the glove counter, where everything is ugly too. In her close-fitted coat with its black fur collar she contemplates the luxury of Branden's, which she has known for many years: its many mild pale lights, easy on the eye and the soul, its elaborate tinkly decorations, its women shoppers with their excellent shoes and coats and hairdos, all dawdling gracefully, in no hurry.

Who was ever in a hurry here?

2. The girl seated at home. A small library, paneled walls of oak. Someone is talking to me. An earnest husky female voice drives itself against my ears, nervous, frightened, groping around my heart, saying, "If you wanted gloves why didn't you say so? Why didn't you ask for them?" That store, Branden's,

is owned by Raymond Forrest who lives on DuMaurier Drive. We live on Sioux Drive. Raymond Forrest. A handsome man? An ugly man? A man of fifty or sixty, with gray hair, or a man of forty with earnest courteous eyes, a good golf game, who is Raymond Forrest, this man who is my salvation? Father has been talking to him. Father is not his physician; Dr. Berg is his physician. Father and Dr. Berg refer patients to each other. There is a connection. Mother plays bridge with. . . . On Mondays and Wednesdays our maid Billie works at. . . . The strings draw together in a cat's cradle,[1] making a net to save you when you fall. . . .

3. *Harriet Arnold's.* A small shop, better than Branden's. Mother in her black coat, I in my close-fitted blue coat. Shopping. Now look at this, isn't this cute, do you want this, why don't you want this, try this on, take this with you to the fitting room, take this also, what's wrong with you, what can I do for you, why are you so strange . . . ? "I wanted to steal but not to buy," I don't tell her. The girl droops along in her coat and gloves and leather boots, her eyes scan the horizon which is pastel pink and decorated like Branden's, tasteful walls and modern ceilings with graceful glimmering lights.

4. Weeks later, the girl at a bus-stop. Two o'clock in the afternoon, a Tuesday, obviously she has walked out of school.

5. The girl stepping down from a bus. Afternoon, weather changing to colder. Detroit. Pavement and closed-up stores; grill work over the windows of a pawnshop. What is a pawnshop, exactly?

II Characters

1. The girl stands five feet five inches tall. An ordinary height. Baldwin Country Day School draws them up to that height. She dreams along the corridors and presses her face against the Thermoplex Glass. No frost or steam can ever form on that glass. A smudge of grease from her forehead . . . could she be boiled down to grease? She wears her hair loose and long and straight in suburban teenage style, 1968. Eyes smudged with pencil, dark brown. Brown hair. Vague green eyes. A pretty girl? An ugly girl? She sings to herself under her breath, idling in the corridor, thinking of her many secrets (the thirty dollars she once took from the purse of a friend's mother, just for fun, the basement window she smashed in her own house just for fun) and thinking of her brother who is at Susquehanna Boys' Academy, an excellent preparatory school in Maine, remembering him unclearly . . . he has long manic hair and a squeaking voice and he looks like one of the popular teenage singers of 1968, one of those in a group, *The Certain Forces, The Way Out, The Maniacs Responsible.* The girl in her turn looks like one of those fieldsful of girls who

---

1. The figure formed in the game of cat's cradle, in which a string looped in a pattern like a cradle on the fingers of one person's hands is transferred to the hands of another so as to form a different figure.

listen to the boys' singing, dreaming and mooning restlessly, breaking into high sullen laughter, innocently experienced.

2. The mother. A midwestern woman of Detroit and suburbs. Belongs to the Detroit Athletic Club. Also the Detroit Golf Club. Also the Bloomfield Hills Country Club. The Village Women's Club at which lectures are given each winter on Genet and Sartre and James Baldwin, by the Director of the Adult Education Program at Wayne State University. . . . The Bloomfield Art Association. Also the Founders Society of the Detroit Institute of Arts. Also. . . . Oh, she is in perpetual motion, this lady, hair like blown-up gold and finer than gold, hair and fingers and body of inestimable grace. Heavy weighs the gold on the back of her hairbrush and hand mirror. Heavy heavy the candlesticks in the dining room. Very heavy is the big car, a Lincoln, long and black, that on one cool autumn day split a squirrel's body in two unequal parts.

3. The father. Dr. ———. He belongs to the same clubs as # 2. A player of squash and golf; he has a golfer's umbrella of stripes. Candy stripes. In his mouth nothing turns to sugar, however, saliva works no miracles here. His doctoring is of the slightly sick. The sick are sent elsewhere (to Dr. Berg?), the deathly sick are sent back for more tests and their bills are sent to their homes, the unsick are sent to Dr. Coronet (Isabel, a lady), an excellent psychiatrist for unsick people who angrily believe they are sick and want to do something about it. If they demand a male psychiatrist, the unsick are sent by Dr. ——— (my father) to Dr. Lowenstein, a male psychiatrist, excellent and expensive, with a limited practice.

4. Clarita. She is twenty, twenty-five, she is thirty or more? Pretty, ugly, what? She is a woman lounging by the side of a road, in jeans and a sweater, hitch-hiking, or she is slouched on a stool at a counter in some roadside diner. A hard line of jaw. Curious eyes. Amused eyes. Behind her eyes processions move, funeral pageants, cartoons. She says, "I never can figure out why girls like you bum around down here. What are you looking for anyway?" An odor of tobacco about her. Unwashed underclothes, or no underclothes, unwashed skin, gritty toes, hair long and falling into strands, not recently washed.

5. Simon. In this city the weather changes abruptly, so Simon's weather changes abruptly. He sleeps through the afternoon. He sleeps through the morning. Rising he gropes around for something to get him going, for a cigarette or a pill to drive him out to the street, where the temperature is hovering around 35°. Why doesn't it drop? Why, why doesn't the cold clean air come down from Canada, will he have to go up into Canada to get it, will he have to leave the Country of his Birth and sink into Canada's frosty fields . . . ? Will the F.B.I. (which he dreams about constantly) chase him over the Canadian border on foot, hounded out in a blizzard of broken glass and horns . . . ?

"Once I was Huckleberry Finn," Simon says, "but now I am Roderick Usher."[2] Beset by frenzies and fears, this man who makes my spine go cold, he

---

2. Melancholic and mentally deranged character in Edgar Allan Poe's short story "The Fall of the House of Usher" (1839).

takes green pills, yellow pills, pills of white and capsules of dark blue and green . . . he takes other things I may not mention, for what if Simon seeks me out and climbs into my girl's bedroom here in Bloomfield Hills and strangles me, what then . . . ? (As I write this I begin to shiver. Why do I shiver? I am now sixteen and sixteen is not an age for shivering.) It comes from Simon, who is always cold.

III World Events

Nothing.

IV People and Circumstances Contributing
to This Delinquency

Nothing.

V Sioux Drive

George, Clyde G. 240 Sioux. A manufacturer's representative; children, a dog; a wife. Georgian with the usual columns. You think of the White House, then of Thomas Jefferson, then your mind goes blank on the white pillars and you think of nothing. Norris, Ralph W. 246 Sioux. Public relations. Colonial. Bay window, brick, stone, concrete, wood, green shutters, sidewalk, lantern, grass, trees, black-top drive, two children, one of them my classmate Esther (Esther Norris) at Baldwin. Wife, cars. Ramsey, Michael D. 250 Sioux. Colonial. Big living room, thirty by twenty-five, fireplaces in living room library recreation room, paneled walls wet bar five bathrooms five bedrooms two lavatories central air conditioning automatic sprinkler automatic garage door three children one wife two cars a breakfast room a patio a large fenced lot fourteen trees a front door with a brass knocker never knocked. Next is our house. Classic contemporary. Traditional modern. Attached garage, attached Florida room, attached patio, attached pool and cabana, attached roof. A front door mailslot through which pour *Time Magazine, Fortune, Life, Business Week, The Wall Street Journal, The New York Times, The New Yorker, The Saturday Review, M.D., Modern Medicine, Disease of the Month* . . . and also. . . . And in addition to all this a quiet sealed letter from Baldwin saying: *Your daughter is not doing work compatible with her performance on the Stanford-Binet.*[3] . . . And your son is not doing well, not well at all, very sad. Where is your son anyway? Once he stole trick-and-treat candy from some six-year-old kids, he himself being a robust ten. The beginning. Now your daughter steals. In the Village Pharmacy she made off with, yes she did, don't deny it, she made off with a copy of *Pageant Magazine* for no reason, she swiped a roll of lifesavers in a green wrapper and was in no need of saving her life or even in

---

3. A set of standardized tests for measuring intellectual aptitude in terms of "IQ."

need of sucking candy, when she was no more than eight years old she stole, don't blush, she stole a package of *Tums* only because it was out on the counter and available, and the nice lady behind the counter (now dead) said nothing. . . . Sioux Drive. Maples, oaks, elms. Diseased elms cut down. Sioux Drive runs into Roosevelt Drive. Slow turning lanes, not streets, all drives and lanes and ways and passes. A private police force. Quiet private police, in unmarked cars. Cruising on Saturday evenings with paternal smiles for the residents who are streaming in and out of houses, going to and from parties, a thousand parties, slightly staggering, the women in their furs alighting from automobiles bought of Ford and General Motors and Chrysler, very heavy automobiles. No foreign cars. Detroit. In 275 Sioux, down the block, in that magnificent French Normandy mansion, lives ———— ———— himself, who has the C———— account itself, imagine that! Look at where he lives and look at the enormous trees and chimneys, imagine his many fireplaces, imagine his wife and children, imagine his wife's hair, imagine her fingernails, imagine her bathtub of smooth clean glowing pink, imagine their embraces, his trouser pockets filled with odd coins and keys and dust and peanuts, imagine their ecstasy on Sioux Drive, imagine their income tax returns, imagine their little boy's pride in his experimental car, a scaled-down C————, as he roars around the neighborhood on the sidewalks frightening dogs and Negro maids, oh imagine all these things, imagine everything, let your mind roar out all over Sioux Drive and DuMaurier Drive and Roosevelt Drive and Ticonderoga Pass and Burning Bush Way and Lincolnshire Pass and Lois Lane.

When spring comes its winds blow nothing to Sioux Drive, no odors of hollyhocks or forsythia, nothing Sioux Drive doesn't already possess, everything is planted and performing. The weather vanes, had they weather vanes, don't have to turn with the wind, don't have to contend with the weather. There is no weather.

VI Detroit

There is always weather in Detroit. Detroit's temperature is always 32°. Fast falling temperatures. Slow rising temperatures. Wind from the north northeast four to forty miles an hour, small craft warnings, partly cloudy today and Wednesday changing to partly sunny through Thursday . . . small warnings of frost, soot warnings, traffic warnings, hazardous lake conditions for small craft and swimmers, restless Negro gangs, restless cloud formations, restless temperatures aching to fall out the very bottom of the thermometer or shoot up over the top and boil everything over in red mercury.

Detroit's temperature is 32°. Fast falling temperatures. Slow rising temperatures. Wind from the north northeast four to forty miles an hour. . . .

VII Events

1. The girl's heart is pounding. In her pocket is a pair of gloves! In a plastic bag! Airproof breathproof plastic bag, gloves selling for twenty-five dollars on Branden's counter! In her pocket! Shoplifted! . . . In her purse is a blue

comb, not very clean. In her purse is a leather billfold (a birthday present from her grandmother in Philadelphia) with snapshots of the family in clean plastic windows, in the billfold are bills, she doesn't know how many bills. . . . In her purse is an ominous note from her friend Tykie *What's this about Joe H. and the kids hanging around at Louise's Sat. night? You heard anything?* . . . passed in French class. In her purse is a lot of dirty yellow Kleenex, her mother's heart would break to see such very dirty Kleenex, and at the bottom of her purse are brown hairpins and safety pins and a broken pencil and a ballpoint pen (blue) stolen from somewhere forgotten and a purse-size compact of Cover Girl Make-Up, Ivory Rose. . . . Her lipstick is Broken Heart, a corrupt pink; her fingers are trembling like crazy; her teeth are beginning to chatter; her insides are alive; her eyes glow in her head; she is saying to her mother's astonished face *I want to steal but not to buy.*

2. At Clarita's. Day or night? What room is this? A bed, a regular bed, and a mattress on the floor nearby. Wallpaper hanging in strips. Clarita says she tore it like that with her teeth. She was fighting a barbaric tribe that night, high from some pills she was battling for her life with men wearing helmets of heavy iron and their faces no more than Christian crosses to breathe through, every one of those bastards looking like her lover Simon, who seems to breathe with great difficulty through the slits of mouth and nostrils in his face. Clarita has never heard of Sioux Drive. Raymond Forrest cuts no ice with her, nor does the C—— account and its millions; Harvard Business School could be at the corner of Vernor and 12th Street for all she cares, and Vietnam might have sunk by now into the Dead Sea under its tons of debris, for all the amazement she could show . . . her face is overworked, overwrought, at the age of twenty (thirty?) it is already exhausted but fanciful and ready for a laugh. Clarita says mournfully to me *Honey somebody is going to turn you out let me give you warning.* In a movie shown on late television Clarita is not a mess like this but a nurse, with short neat hair and a dedicated look, in love with her doctor and her doctor's patients and their diseases, enamored of needles and sponges and rubbing alcohol. . . . Or no: she is a private secretary. Robert Cummings[4] is her boss. She helps him with fantastic plots, the canned audience laughs, no, the audience doesn't laugh because nothing is funny, instead her boss is Robert Taylor and they are not boss and secretary but husband and wife, she is threatened by a young starlet, she is grim, handsome, wifely, a good companion for a good man. . . . She is Claudette Colbert. Her sister too is Claudette Colbert. They are twins, identical. Her husband Charles Boyer[5] is a very rich handsome man and her sister, Claudette Colbert, is plotting her death in order to take her place as the rich man's wife, no one will know because they are *twins.* . . . All these marvelous lives Clarita might have lived, but she fell out the bottom at the age of thirteen. At the age when I was packing my overnight case for a slumber party at Toni Deshield's she was tearing filthy sheets off a bed and scratching up a rash on her arms. . . . Thirteen is uncom-

---

4. Stage, screen, and television actor (b. 1910) whose TV comedy series was popular in the mid- and late-1950s.

5. Robert Taylor (1911–69); Claudette Colbert (b. 1905); Charles Boyer (b. 1899), popular film stars of the 1930s and '40s whose movies are frequently shown on television.

monly young for a white girl in Detroit, Miss Brook of the Detroit House of Correction said in a sad newspaper interview for the *Detroit News;* fifteen and sixteen are more likely. Eleven, twelve, thirteen are not surprising in colored . . . they are more precocious. What can we do? Taxes are rising and the tax base is falling. The temperature rises slowly but falls rapidly. Everything is falling out the bottom, Woodward Avenue is filthy, Livernois Avenue is filthy! Scraps of paper flutter in the air like pigeons, dirt flies up and hits you right in the eye, oh Detroit is breaking up into dangerous bits of newspaper and dirt, watch out. . . .

Clarita's apartment is over a restaurant. Simon her lover emerges from the cracks at dark. Mrs. Olesko, a neighbor of Clarita's, an aged white wisp of a woman, doesn't complain but sniffs with contentment at Clarita's noisy life and doesn't tell the cops, hating cops, when the cops arrive. I should give more fake names, more blanks, instead of telling all these secrets. I myself am a secret; I am a minor.

3. My father reads a paper at a medical convention in Los Angeles. There he is, on the edge of the North American continent, when the unmarked detective put his hand so gently on my arm in the aisle of Branden's and said, "Miss, would you like to step over here for a minute?"

And where was he when Clarita put her hand on my arm, that wintry dark sulphurous aching day in Detroit, in the company of closed-down barber shops, closed-down diners, closed-down movie houses, homes, windows, basements, faces . . . she put her hand on my arm and said, "Honey, are you looking for somebody down here?"

And was he home worrying about me, gone for two weeks solid, when they carried me off . . . ? It took three of them to get me in the police cruiser, so they said, and they put more than their hands on my arm.

4. I work on this lesson. My English teacher is Mr. Forest, who is from Michigan State. Not handsome, Mr. Forest, and his name is plain unlike Raymond Forrest's, but he is sweet and rodent-like, he has conferred with the principal and my parents, and everything is fixed . . . treat her as if nothing has happened, a new start, begin again, only sixteen years old, what a shame, how did it happen?—nothing happened, nothing could have happened, a slight physiological modification known only to a gynecologist or to Dr. Coronet. I work on my lesson. I sit in my pink room. I look around the room with my sad pink eyes. I sigh, I dawdle, I pause, I eat up time, I am limp and happy to be home, I am sixteen years old suddenly, my head hangs heavy as a pumpkin on my shoulders, and my hair has just been cut by Mr. Faye at the Crystal Salon and is said to be very becoming.

(Simon too put his hand on my arm and said, "Honey, you have got to come with me," and in his six-by-six room we got to know each other. Would I go back to Simon again? Would I lie down with him in all that filth and craziness? Over and over again.

a Clarita is being betrayed as in front of a Cunningham Drug Store she is nervously eyeing a colored man who may or may not have money, or a nervous white boy of twenty with sideburns and an Appalachian look, who may or may not have a knife hidden in his jacket pocket, or a husky red-faced man of friendly countenance who may or may not be a member of the Vice Squad out for an early twilight walk.)

I work on my lesson for Mr. Forest. I have filled up eleven pages. Words pour out of me and won't stop. I want to tell everything . . . what was the song Simon was always humming, and who was Simon's friend in a very new trench coat with an old high school graduation ring on his finger . . . ? Simon's bearded friend? When I was down too low for him Simon kicked me out and gave me to him for three days, I think, on Fourteenth Street in Detroit, an airy room of cold cruel drafts with newspapers on the floor. . . . Do I really remember that or am I piecing it together from what they told me? Did they tell the truth? Did they know much of the truth?

VIII Characters

1. Wednesdays after school, at four; Saturday mornings at ten. Mother drives me to Dr. Coronet. Ferns in the office, plastic or real, they look the same. Dr. Coronet is queenly, an elegant nicotine-stained lady who would have studied with Freud had circumstances not prevented it, a bit of a Catholic, ready to offer you some mystery if your teeth will ache too much without it. Highly recommended by Father! Forty dollars an hour, Father's forty dollars! Progress! Looking up! Looking better! That new haircut is so becoming, says Dr. Coronet herself, showing how normal she is for a woman with an I.Q. of 180 and many advanced degrees.

2. Mother. A lady in a brown suede coat. Boots of shiny black material, black gloves, a black fur hat. She would be humiliated could she know that of all the people in the world it is my ex-lover Simon who walks most like her . . . self-conscious and unreal, listening to distant music, a little bow-legged with craftiness. . . .

3. Father. Tying a necktie. In a hurry. On my first evening home he put his hand on my arm and said, "Honey, we're going to forget all about this."

4. Simon. Outside a plane is crossing the sky, in here we're in a hurry. Morning. It must be morning. The girl is half out of her mind, whimpering and vague, Simon her dear friend is wretched this morning . . . he is wretched with morning itself . . . he forces her to give him an injection, with that needle she knows is filthy, she has a dread of needles and surgical instruments and the odor of things that are to be sent into the blood, thinking somehow of her father. . . . This is a bad morning, Simon says that his mind is being twisted out of shape, and so he submits to the needle which he usually scorns and bites his lip with his yellowish teeth, his face going very pale. *Ah baby!* he says in his soft mocking voice, which with all women is a mockery of love, *do it like this—Slowly—*And the girl, terrified, almost drops the precious needle but manages to turn it up to the light from the window . . . it is an extension of herself, then? She can give him this gift, then? *I wish you wouldn't do this to me,* she says, wise in her terror, because it seems to her that Simon's

danger—in a few minutes he might be dead—is a way of pressing her against him that is more powerful than any other embrace. She has to work over his arm, the knotted corded veins of his arm, her forehead wet with perspiration as she pushes and releases the needle, staring at that mixture of liquid now stained with Simon's bright blood. . . . When the drug hits him she can feel it herself, she feels that magic that is more than any woman can give him, striking the back of his head and making his face stretch as if with the impact of a terrible sun. . . . She tries to embrace him but he pushes her aside and stumbles to his feet. *Jesus Christ,* he says. . . .

5. Princess, a Negro girl of eighteen. What is her charge? She is close-mouthed about it, shrewd and silent, you know that no one had to wrestle her to the sidewalk to get her in here; she came with dignity. In the recreation room she sits reading *Nancy Drew and the Jewel Box Mystery,* which inspires in her face tiny wrinkles of alarm and interest: what a face! Light brown skin, heavy shaded eyes, heavy eyelashes, a serious sinister dark brow, graceful fingers, graceful wristbones, graceful legs, lips, tongue, a sugarsweet voice, a leggy stride more masculine than Simon's and my mother's, decked out in a dirty white blouse and dirty white slacks; vaguely nautical is Princess's style. . . . At breakfast she is in charge of clearing the table and leans over me, saying, *Honey you sure you ate enough?*

6. The girl lies sleepless, wondering. Why here, why not there? Why Bloomfield Hills and not jail? Why jail and not her pink room? Why downtown Detroit and not Sioux Drive? What is the difference? Is Simon all the difference? The girl's head is a parade of wonders. She is nearly sixteen, her breath is marvelous with wonders, not long ago she was coloring with crayons and now she is smearing the landscape with paints that won't come off and won't come off her fingers either. She says to the matron *I am not talking about anything,* not because everyone has warned her not to talk but because, because she will not talk, because she won't say anything about Simon who is her secret. And she says to the matron *I won't go home* up until that night in the lavatory when everything was changed. . . . "No, I won't go home I want to stay here," she says, listening to her own words with amazement, thinking that weeds might climb everywhere over that marvelous $86,000 house and dinosaurs might return to muddy the beige carpeting, but never never will she reconcile four o'clock in the morning in Detroit with eight o'clock breakfasts in Bloomfield Hills . . . oh, she aches still for Simon's hands and his caressing breath, though he gave her little pleasure, he took everything from her (five-dollar bills, ten-dollar bills, passed into her numb hands by men and taken out of her hands by Simon) until she herself was passed into the hands of other men, police, when Simon evidently got tired of her and her hysteria. . . . *No, I won't go home, I don't want to be bailed out,* the girl thinks as a *Stubborn and Wayward Child* (one of several charges lodged against her) and the matron understands her crazy white-rimmed eyes that are seeking out some new violence that will keep her in jail, should someone threaten to let her out. Such children try to strangle the matrons, the attendants, or one another . . . they want the locks locked forever, the doors nailed shut . . . and this girl is no different up until that night her mind is changed for her. . . .

IX   That Night

Princess and Dolly, a little white girl of maybe fifteen, hardy however as a sergeant and in the House of Correction for armed robbery, corner her in the lavatory at the farthest sink and the other girls look away and file out to bed, leaving her. God how she is beaten up! Why is she beaten up? Why do they pound her, why such hatred? Princess vents all the hatred of a thousand silent Detroit winters on her body, this girl whose body belongs to me, fiercely she rides across the midwestern plains on this girl's tender bruised body . . . revenge on the oppressed minorities of America! revenge on the slaughtered Indians! revenge on the female sex, on the male sex, revenge on Bloomfield Hills, revenge revenge. . . .

X   Detroit

In Detroit weather weighs heavily upon everyone. The sky looms large. The horizon shimmers in smoke. Downtown the buildings are imprecise in the haze. Perpetual haze. Perpetual motion inside the haze. Across the choppy river is the city of Windsor, in Canada. Part of the continent has bunched up here and is bulging outward, at the tip of Detroit, a cold hard rain is forever falling on the expressways . . . shoppers shop grimly, their cars are not parked in safe places, their windshields may be smashed and graceful ebony hands may drag them out through their shatterproof smashed windshields crying *Revenge for the Indians!* Ah, they all fear leaving Hudson's[6] and being dragged to the very tip of the city and thrown off the parking roof of Cobo Hall,[7] that expensive tomb, into the river. . . .

XI   Characters We Are Forever
Entwined With

1. Simon drew me into his tender rotting arms and breathed gravity into me. Then I came to earth, weighted down. He said *You are such a little girl,* and he weighed me down with his delight. In the palms of his hands were teeth marks from his previous life experiences. He was thirty-five, they said. Imagine Simon in this room, in my pink room: he is about six feet tall and stoops slightly, in a feline cautious way, always thinking, always on guard, with his scuffed light suede shoes and his clothes which are anyone's clothes, slightly rumpled ordinary clothes that ordinary men might wear to not-bad jobs. Simon has fair, long hair, curly hair, spent languid curls that are like . . . exactly like the curls of wood shavings to the touch, I am trying to be exact . . . and he smells of unheated mornings and coffee and too many pills coating his tongue with a faint green-white scum. . . . Dear Simon, who would be panicked in this room and in this house (right now Billie is vacuuming next door in my parents' room: a vacuum cleaner's roar is a sign of all good things), Simon who is said to have come from a home not much different from this, years ago, fleeing all the

---

6. A department store in downtown Detroit.
7. A convention and exhibition center.

carpeting and the polished banisters . . . Simon has a deathly face, only desperate people fall in love with it. His face is bony and cautious, the bones of his cheeks prominent as if with the rigidity of his ceaseless thinking, plotting, for he has to make money out of girls to whom money means nothing, they're so far gone they can hardly count it, and in a sense money means nothing to him either except as a way of keeping on with his life. *Each Day's Proud Struggle,*[8] the title of a novel we could read at jail. . . . Each day he needs a certain amount of money. He devours it. It wasn't love he uncoiled in me with his hollowed-out eyes and his courteous smile, that remnant of a prosperous past, but a dark terror that needed to press itself flat against him, or against another man . . . but he was the first, he came over to me and took my arm, a claim. We struggled on the stairs and I said, "Let me loose, you're hurting my neck, my face," it was such a surprise that my skin hurt where he rubbed it, and afterward we lay face to face and he breathed everything into me. In the end I think he turned me in.

2. Raymond Forrest. I just read this morning that Raymond Forrest's father, the chairman of the board at ———, died of a heart attack on a plane bound for London. I would like to write Raymond Forrest a note of sympathy. I would like to thank him for not pressing charges against me one hundred years ago, saving me, being so generous . . . well, men like Raymond Forrest are generous men, not like Simon. I would like to write him a letter telling of my love, or of some other emotion that is positive and healthy. Not like Simon and his poetry, which he scrawled down when he was high and never changed a word . . . but when I try to think of something to say it is Simon's language that comes back to me, caught in my head like a bad song, it is always Simon's language:

There is no reality only dreams
Your neck may get snapped when you wake
My love is drawn to some violent end
She keeps wanting to get away
My love is heading downward
And I am heading upward
She is going to crash on the sidewalk
And I am going to dissolve into the clouds

XII Events

1. Out of the hospital, bruised and saddened and converted, with Princess's grunts still tangled in my hair . . . and Father in his overcoat looking like a Prince himself, come to carry me off. Up the expressway and out north to home. Jesus Christ but the air is thinner and cleaner here. Monumental houses. Heartbreaking sidewalks, so clean.

---

8. Unidentified; apparently, a nonexistent work.

2. Weeping in the living room. The ceiling is two storeys high and two chandeliers hang from it. Weeping, weeping, though Billie the maid is *probably listening*. I will never leave home again. Never. Never leave home. Never leave this home again, never.

3. Sugar doughnuts for breakfast. The toaster is very shiny and my face is distorted in it. Is that my face?

4. The car is turning in the driveway. Father brings me home. Mother embraces me. Sunlight breaks in movieland patches on the roof of our traditional contemporary home, which was designed for the famous automotive stylist whose identity, if I told you the name of the famous car he designed, you would all know, so I can't tell you because my teeth chatter at the thought of being sued . . . or having someone climb into my bedroom window with a rope to strangle me. . . . The car turns up the black-top drive. The house opens to me like a doll's house, so lovely in the sunlight, the big living room beckons to me with its walls falling away in a delirium of joy at my return, Billie the maid is *no doubt* listening from the kitchen as I burst into tears and the hysteria Simon got so sick of. Convulsed in Father's arms I say I will never leave again, never, why did I leave, where did I go, what happened, my mind is gone wrong, my body is one big bruise, my backbone was sucked dry, it wasn't the men who hurt me and Simon never hurt me but only those girls . . . my God how they hurt me . . . I will never leave home again. . . . The car is perpetually turning up the drive and I am perpetually breaking down in the living room and we are perpetually taking the right exit from the expressway (Lahser Road) and the wall of the restroom is perpetually banging against my head and perpetually are Simon's hands moving across my body and adding everything up and so too are Father's hands on my shaking bruised back, far from the surface of my skin on the surface of my good blue cashmere coat (drycleaned for my release). . . . I weep for all the money here, for God in gold and beige carpeting, for the beauty of chandeliers and the miracle of a clean polished gleaming toaster and faucets that run both hot and cold water, and I tell them *I will never leave home, this is my home, I love everything here, I am in love with everything here.* . . .
I am home.

Questions for Study

1. Describe the style of the story, mentioning in particular diction, connotation, and sentence structure.
2. Consider the fragmented structure of the narrative. Why are sentence fragments appropriate here? When does the narrator use complete sentences? What is the significance of these changes in structural patterning?
3. Why is nothing listed under "World Events"? What does the fact that there is no weather on Sioux Drive mean? How do the images of weather relate to the theme?
4. Why is it that "her insides are alive" when the narrator steals? What other experiences offer her similar thrills?

5. Someone's hand on the girl's arm becomes a repeated image. What is its significance? What are the implications of the images of rising and falling?
6. What happens in the lavatory at the Detroit House of Correction? How is this related to the story's theme?
7. Why is it that in the last sequence of events even sidewalks in Bloomfield Hills are "heartbreaking"? Why does the girl weep?
8. Oates' narrator is not a very traditional protagonist. Do you nevertheless understand and empathize with her? If you do, explain how the author generates this understanding and empathy.
9. How would you describe the point of view? Why does the narrator sometimes refer to herself as "me," sometimes as "the girl"?
10. How would you describe the tone of the story?

Ernest Hemingway (1898–1961)
The Capital of the World

Madrid is full of boys named Paco, which is the diminutive of the name Francisco, and there is a Madrid joke about a father who came to Madrid and inserted an advertisement in the personal columns of *El Liberal* which said: Paco meet me at Hotel Montana noon Tuesday all is forgiven Papa and how a squadron of Guardia Civil had to be called out to disperse the eight hundred young men who answered the advertisement. But this Paco, who waited on table at the Pension[1] Luarca, had no father to forgive him, nor anything for the father to forgive. He had two older sisters who were chambermaids at the Luarca, who had gotten their place through coming from the same small village as a former Luarca chambermaid who had proven hardworking and honest and hence given her village and its products a good name; and these sisters had paid his way on the auto-bus to Madrid and gotten him his job as an apprentice waiter. He came from a village in a part of Extramadura[2] where conditions were incredibly primitive, food scarce, and comforts unknown and he had worked hard ever since he could remember.

He was a well built boy with very black, rather curly hair, good teeth and a skin that his sisters envied, and he had a ready and unpuzzled smile. He was fast on his feet and did his work well and he loved his sisters, who seemed beautiful and sophisticated; he loved Madrid, which was still an unbelievable place, and he loved his work which, done under bright lights, with clean linen, the wearing of evening clothes, and abundant food in the kitchen, seemed romantically beautiful.

There were from eight to a dozen other people who lived at the Luarca and ate in the dining room but for Paco, the youngest of the three waiters who served at table, the only ones who really existed were the bull fighters.

Second-rate matadors lived at that pension because the address in the Calle

---

1. Boardinghouse.
2. A region in western Spain, once economically important because of its rich winter pastures.

San Jeronimo was good, the food was excellent and the room and board was cheap. It is necessary for a bull fighter to give the appearance, if not of prosperity, at least of respectability, since decorum and dignity rank above courage as the virtues most highly prized in Spain, and bull fighters stayed at the Luarca until their last pesetas[3] were gone. There is no record of any bull fighter having left the Luarca for a better or more expensive hotel; second-rate bull fighters never became first rate; but the descent from the Luarca was swift since any one could stay there who was making anything at all and a bill was never presented to a guest unasked until the woman who ran the place knew that the case was hopeless.

At this time there were three full matadors living at the Luarca as well as two very good picadors, and one excellent banderillero.[4] The Luarca was luxury for the picadors and the banderilleros who, with their families in Seville, required lodging in Madrid during the Spring season; but they were well paid and in the fixed employ of fighters who were heavily contracted during the coming season and the three of these subalterns would probably make much more apiece than any of the three matadors. Of the three matadors one was ill and trying to conceal it; one had passed his short vogue as a novelty; and the third was a coward.

The coward had at one time, until he had received a peculiarly atrocious horn wound in the lower abdomen at the start of his first season as a full matador, been exceptionally brave and remarkably skillful and he still had many of the hearty mannerisms of his days of success. He was jovial to excess and laughed constantly with and without provocation. He had, when successful, been very addicted to practical jokes but he had given them up now. They took an assurance that he did not feel. This matador had an intelligent, very open face and he carried himself with much style.

The matador who was ill was careful never to show it and was meticulous about eating a little of all the dishes that were presented at the table. He had a great many handkerchiefs which he laundered himself in his room and, lately, he had been selling his fighting suits. He had sold one, cheaply, before Christmas and another in the first week of April. They had been very expensive suits, had always been well kept and he had one more. Before he had become ill he had been a very promising, even a sensational, fighter and, while he himself could not read, he had clippings which said that in his debut in Madrid he had been better than Belmonte.[5] He ate alone at a small table and looked up very little.

The matador who had once been a novelty was very short and brown and very dignified. He also ate alone at a separate table and he smiled very rarely and never laughed. He came from Valladolid, where the people are extremely serious, and he was a capable matador; but his style had become old-fashioned before he had ever succeeded in endearing himself to the public through his virtues, which were courage and a calm capability, and his name on a poster

---

3. The basic monetary unit of Spain, roughly equivalent to our dollar.

4. A matador is a bullfighter who has the principal role in a bullfight and who is responsible for killing the bull; a picador is a mounted assistant to a matador who opens the bullfight by enraging the bull and by weakening its shoulder muscles with a lance; a banderillero is a matador's assistant who sticks banderillas (ornamented darts with barbs) into the bull in preparation for the kill.

5. Juan Belmonte (1892–1962), one of the greatest matadors of all times; he revolutionized modern bullfighting by his use of skillful capework instead of footwork to divert the bull.

would draw no one to a bull ring. His novelty had been that he was so short that he could barely see over the bull's withers, but there were other short fighters, and he had never succeeded in imposing himself on the public's fancy.

Of the picadors one was a thin, hawk-faced, gray-haired man, lightly built but with legs and arms like iron, who always wore cattle-men's boots under his trousers, drank too much every evening and gazed amorously at any woman in the pension. The other was huge, dark, brown-faced, good-looking, with black hair like an Indian and enormous hands. Both were great picadors although the first was reputed to have lost much of his ability through drink and dissipation, and the second was said to be too headstrong and quarrelsome to stay with any matador more than a single season.

The banderillero was middle-aged, gray, cat-quick in spite of his years and, sitting at the table he looked a moderately prosperous business man. His legs were still good for this season, and when they should go he was intelligent and experienced enough to keep regularly employed for a long time. The difference would be that when his speed of foot would be gone he would always be frightened where now he was assured and calm in the ring and out of it.

On this evening every one had left the dining room except the hawk-faced picador who drank too much, the birthmarked-faced auctioneer of watches at the fairs and festivals of Spain, who also drank too much, and two priests from Galicia who were sitting at a corner table and drinking if not too much certainly enough. At that time wine was included in the price of the room and board at the Luarca and the waiters had just brought fresh bottles of Valdepeñas[6] to the tables of the auctioneer, then to the picador and, finally, to the two priests.

The three waiters stood at the end of the room. It was the rule of the house that they should all remain on duty until the diners whose tables they were responsible for should all have left, but the one who served the table of the two priests had an appointment to go to an Anarcho-Syndicalist[7] meeting and Paco had agreed to take over his table for him.

Upstairs the matador who was ill was lying face down on his bed alone. The matador who was no longer a novelty was sitting looking out of his window preparatory to walking out to the café. The matador who was a coward had the older sister of Paco in his room with him and was trying to get her to do something which she was laughingly refusing to do. This matador was saying "Come on, little savage."

"No," said the sister. "Why should I?"

"For a favor."

"You've eaten and now you want me for dessert."

"Just once. What harm can it do?"

"Leave me alone. Leave me alone, I tell you."

"It is a very little thing to do."

"Leave me alone, I tell you."

Down in the dining room the tallest of the waiters, who was overdue at the meeting, said "Look at those black pigs drink."

"That's no way to speak," said the second waiter. "They are decent clients. They do not drink too much."

6. Rich red wine, named after the town in south-central Spain in which it is made.
7. Militant labor movement, popular in Spain from about 1910 to 1936, which advocated the violent destruction of capitalism and of the state.

"For me it is a good way to speak," said the tall one. "There are the two curses of Spain, the bulls and the priests."

"Certainly not the individual bull and the individual priest," said the second waiter.

"Yes," said the tall waiter. "Only through the individual can you attack the class. It is necessary to kill the individual bull and the individual priest. All of them. Then there are no more."

"Save it for the meeting," said the other waiter.

"Look at the barbarity of Madrid," said the tall waiter. "It is now half-past eleven o'clock and these are still guzzling."

"They only started to eat at ten," said the other waiter. "As you know there are many dishes. That wine is cheap and these have paid for it. It is not a strong wine."

"How can there be solidarity of workers with fools like you?" asked the tall waiter.

"Look," said the second waiter who was a man of fifty. "I have worked all my life. In all that remains of my life I must work. I have no complaints against work. To work is normal."

"Yes, but the lack of work kills."

"I have always worked," said the older waiter. "Go on to the meeting. There is no necessity to stay."

"You are a good comrade," said the tall waiter. "But you lack all ideology."

"Mejor si me falta eso que el otro," said the older waiter (meaning it is better to lack that than work). "Go on to the *mitin.*"

Paco had said nothing. He did not yet understand politics but it always gave him a thrill to hear the tall waiter speak of the necessity for killing the priests and the Guardia Civil. The tall waiter represented to him revolution and revolution also was romantic. He himself would like to be a good catholic, a revolutionary, and have a steady job like this, while, at the same time, being a bullfighter.

"Go on to the meeting, Ignacio," he said. "I will respond for your work."

"The two of us," said the older waiter.

"There isn't enough for one," said Paco. "Go on to the meeting."

"Pues, me voy,"[8] said the tall waiter. "And thanks."

In the meantime, upstairs, the sister of Paco had gotten out of the embrace of the matador as skilfully as a wrestler breaking a hold and said, now angry, "These are the hungry people. A failed bullfighter. With your ton-load of fear. If you have so much of that, use it in the ring."

"That is the way a whore talks."

"A whore is also a woman, but I am not a whore."

"You'll be one."

"Not through you."

"Leave me," said the matador who, now, repulsed and refused, felt the nakedness of his cowardice returning.

"Leave you? What hasn't left you?" said the sister. "Don't you want me to make up the bed? I'm paid to do that."

---

8. Roughly, "Well then, I'll go."

"Leave me," said the matador, his broad good-looking face wrinkled into a contortion that was like crying. "You whore. You dirty little whore."

"Matador," she said, shutting the door. "My matador."

Inside the room the matador sat on the bed. His face still had the contortion which, in the ring, he made into a constant smile which frightened those people in the first rows of seats who knew what they were watching. "And this," he was saying aloud. "And this. And this."

He could remember when he had been good and it had only been three years before. He could remember the weight of the heavy gold-brocaded fighting jacket on his shoulders on that hot afternoon in May when his voice had still been the same in the ring as in the café, and how he sighted along the point-dipping blade at the place in the top of the shoulders where it was dusty in the short-haired black hump of muscle above the wide, wood-knocking, splintered-tipped horns that lowered as he went in to kill, and how the sword pushed in as easy as into a mound of stiff butter with the palm of his hand pushing the pommel, his left arm crossed low, his left shoulder forward, his weight on his left leg, and then his weight wasn't on his leg. His weight was on his lower belly and as the bull raised his head the horn was out of sight in him and he swung over on it twice before they pulled him off it. So now when he went in to kill, and it was seldom, he could not look at the horns and what did any whore know about what he went through before he fought? And what had they been through that laughed at him? They were all whores and they knew what they could do with it.

Down in the dining room the picador sat looking at the priests. If there were women in the room he stared at them. If there were no women he would stare with enjoyment at a foreigner, *un inglés,*[9] but lacking women or strangers, he now stared with enjoyment and insolence at the two priests. While he stared the birth-marked auctioneer rose and folding his napkin went out, leaving over half the wine in the last bottle he had ordered. If his accounts had been paid up at the Luarca he would have finished the bottle.

The two priests did not stare back at the picador. One of them was saying, "It is ten days since I have been here waiting to see him and all day I sit in the ante-chamber and he will not receive me."

"What is there to do?"

"Nothing. What can one do? One cannot go against authority."

"I have been here for two weeks and nothing. I wait and they will not see me."

"We are from the abandoned country. When the money runs out we can return."

"To the abandoned country. What does Madrid care about Galicia? We are a poor province."

"One understands the action of our brother Basilio."

"Still I have no real confidence in the integrity of Basilio Alvarez."

"Madrid is where one learns to understand. Madrid kills Spain."

"If they would simply see one and refuse."

"No. You must be broken and worn out by waiting."

"Well, we shall see. I can wait as well as another."

At this moment the picador got to his feet, walked over to the priests' table

---

9. An Englishman.

and stood, gray-headed and hawk-faced, staring at them and smiling.

"A torero," said one priest to the other.

"And a good one," said the picador and walked out of the dining room, gray-jacketed, trim-waisted, bow-legged, in tight breeches over his high-heeled cattleman's boots that clicked on the floor as he swaggered quite steadily, smiling to himself. He lived in a small, tight, professional world of personal efficiency, nightly alcoholic triumph, and insolence. Now he lit a cigar and tilting his hat at an angle in the hallway went out to the café.

The priests left immediately after the picador, hurriedly conscious of being the last people in the dining room, and there was no one in the room now but Paco and the middle-aged waiter. They cleared the tables and carried the bottles into the kitchen.

In the kitchen was the boy who washed the dishes. He was three years older than Paco and was very cynical and bitter.

"Take this," the middle-aged waiter said, and poured out a glass of the Valdepeñas and handed it to him.

"Why not?" the boy took the glass.

"Tu, Paco?" the older waiter asked.

"Thank you," said Paco. The three of them drank.

"I will be going," said the middle-aged waiter.

"Good night," they told him.

He went out and they were alone. Paco took a napkin one of the priests had used and standing straight, his heels planted, lowered the napkin and with head following the movement, swung his arms in the motion of a slow sweeping veronica.[10] He turned and advancing his right foot slightly, made the second pass, gained a little terrain on the imaginary bull and made a third pass, slow, perfectly timed and suave, then gathered the napkin to his waist and swung his hips away from the bull in a media-veronica.

The dishwasher, whose name was Enrique, watched him critically and sneeringly.

"How is the bull?" he said.

"Very brave," said Paco. "Look."

Standing slim and straight he made four more perfect passes, smooth, elegant and graceful.

"And the bull?" asked Enrique standing against the sink, holding his wine glass and wearing his apron.

"Still has lots of gas," said Paco.

"You make me sick," said Enrique.

"Why?"

"Look."

Enrique removed his apron and citing the imaginary bull he sculptured four perfect, languid gypsy veronicas and ended up with a rebolera[11] that made the apron swing in a stiff arc past the bull's nose as he walked away from him.

"Look at that," he said. "And I wash dishes."

"Why?"

---

10. A basic pass in bullfighting in which the matador keeps his feet in the same position while slowly swinging the open cape away from the charging bull.

11. A pass ending a series of veronicas in which one end of the cape is released and swung in a graceful arc around the bullfighter's waist.

"Fear," said Enrique. "*Miedo*.[12] The same fear you would have in a ring with a bull."

"No," said Paco. "I wouldn't be afraid."

"*Leche!*"[13] said Enrique. "Every one is afraid. But a torero can control his fear so that he can work the bull. I went in an amateur fight and I was so afraid I couldn't keep from running. Every one thought it was very funny. So would you be afraid. If it wasn't for fear every bootblack in Spain would be a bullfighter. You, a country boy, would be frightened worse than I was."

"No," said Paco.

He had done it too many times in his imagination. Too many times he had seen the horns, seen the bull's wet muzzle, the ear twitching, then the head go down and the charge, the hoofs thudding and the hot bull pass him as he swung the cape, to re-charge as he swung the cape again, then again, and again, and again, to end winding the bull around him in his great media-veronica, and walk swingingly away, with bull hairs caught in the gold ornaments of his jacket from the close passes; the bull standing hypnotized and the crowd applauding. No, he would not be afraid. Others, yes. Not he. He knew he would not be afraid. Even if he ever was afraid he knew that he could do it anyway. He had confidence. "I wouldn't be afraid," he said.

Enrique said, "*Leche*," again.

Then he said, "If we should try it?"

"How?"

"Look," said Enrique. "You think of the bull but you do not think of the horns. The bull has such force that the horns rip like a knife, they stab like a bayonet, and they kill like a club. Look," he opened a table drawer and took out two meat knives. "I will bind these to the legs of a chair. Then I will play bull for you with the chair held before my head. The knives are the horns. If you make those passes then they mean something."

"Lend me your apron," said Paco. "We'll do it in the dining room."

"No," said Enrique, suddenly not bitter. "Don't do it, Paco."

"Yes," said Paco. "I'm not afraid."

"You will be when you see the knives come."

"We'll see," said Paco. "Give me the apron."

At this time, while Enrique was binding the two heavy-bladed razor-sharp meat knives fast to the legs of the chair with two soiled napkins holding the half of each knife, wrapping them tight and then knotting them, the two chamber-maids, Paco's sisters, were on their way to the cinema to see Greta Garbo in "Anna Christie."[14] Of the two priests, one was sitting in his underwear reading his breviary and the other was wearing a nightshirt and saying the rosary. All the bullfighters except the one who was ill had made their evening appearance at the Café Fornos, where the big, dark-haired picador was playing billiards, the short, serious matador was sitting at a crowded table before a coffee and milk, along with the middle-aged banderillero and other serious workmen.

The drinking, gray-headed picador was sitting with a glass of cazalas brandy before him staring with pleasure at a table where the matador whose

---

12. Spanish word for *fear*.
13. Literally, "milk"; used here as a colloquial exclamation of scorn.
14. 1930 film adaptation of a play by Eugene O'Neill. In it the immensely popular silent-film star Greta Garbo (b. 1905) made her "talking" debut, uncharacteristically playing a lowly ex-prostitute.

courage was gone sat with another matador who had renounced the sword to become a banderillero again, and two very houseworn-looking prostitutes.

The auctioneer stood on the street corner talking with friends. The tall waiter was at the Anarcho-Syndicalist meeting waiting for an opportunity to speak. The middle-aged waiter was seated on the terrace of the Café Alvarez drinking a small beer. The woman who owned the Luarca was already asleep in her bed, where she lay on her back with the bolster between her legs; big, fat, honest, clean, easy-going, very religious and never having ceased to miss or pray daily for her husband, dead, now, twenty years. In his room, alone, the matador who was ill lay face down on his bed with his mouth against a handkerchief.

Now, in the deserted dining room, Enrique tied the last knot in the napkins that bound the knives to the chair legs and lifted the chair. He pointed the legs with the knives on them forward and held the chair over his head with the two knives pointing straight ahead, one on each side of his head.

"It's heavy," he said. "Look, Paco. It is very dangerous. Don't do it." He was sweating.

Paco stood facing him, holding the apron spread, holding a fold of it bunched in each hand, thumbs up, first finger down, spread to catch the eye of the bull.

"Charge straight," he said. "Turn like a bull. Charge as many times as you want."

"How will you know when to cut the pass?" asked Enrique. "It's better to do three and then a media."

"All right," said Paco. "But come straight. Huh, torito! Come on, little bull!"

Running with head down Enrique came toward him and Paco swung the apron just ahead of the knife blade as it passed close in front of his belly and as it went by it was, to him, the real horn, white-tipped, black, smooth, and as Enrique passed him and turned to rush again it was the hot, blood-flanked mass of the bull that thudded by, then turned like a cat and came again as he swung the cape slowly. Then the bull turned and came again and, as he watched the onrushing point, he stepped his left foot two inches too far forward and the knife did not pass, but had slipped in as easily as into a wineskin and there was a hot scalding rush above and around the sudden inner rigidity of steel and Enrique shouting. "Ay! Ay! Let me get it out! Let me get it out!" and Paco slipped forward on the chair, the apron cape still held, Enrique pulling on the chair as the knife turned in him, in him, Paco.

The knife was out now and he sat on the floor in the widening warm pool.

"Put the napkin over it. Hold it!" said Enrique. "Hold it tight. I will run for the doctor. You must hold in the hemorrhage."

"There should be a rubber cup," said Paco. He had seen that used in the ring.

"I came straight," said Enrique, crying. "All I wanted was to show the danger."

"Don't worry," said Paco, his voice sounding far away. "But bring the doctor."

In the ring they lifted you and carried you, running with you, to the operating room. If the femoral artery emptied itself before you reached there they called the priest.

"Advise one of the priests," said Paco, holding the napkin tight against his lower abdomen. He could not believe that this had happened to him.

But Enrique was running down the Carrera San Jeromino to the all-night first-aid station and Paco was alone, first sitting up, then huddled over, then slumped on the floor, until it was over, feeling his life go out of him as dirty water empties from a bathtub when the plug is drawn. He was frightened and he felt faint and he tried to say an act of contrition and he remembered how it started but before he had said, as fast as he could, "Oh, my God, I am heartily sorry for having offended Thee who art worthy of all my love and I firmly resolve . . . ," he felt too faint and he was lying face down on the floor and it was over very quickly. A severed femoral artery empties itself faster than you can believe.

As the doctor from the first-aid station came up the stairs accompanied by a policeman who held on to Enrique by the arm, the two sisters of Paco were still in the moving-picture palace of the Gran Via, where they were intensely disappointed in the Garbo film, which showed the great star in miserable low surroundings when they had been accustomed to see her surrounded by great luxury and brilliance. The audience disliked the film thoroughly and were protesting by whistling and stamping their feet. All the other people from the hotel were doing almost what they had been doing when the accident happened, except that the two priests had finished their devotions and were preparing for sleep, and the gray-haired picador had moved his drink over to the table with the two houseworn prostitutes. A little later he went out of the café with one of them. It was the one for whom the matador who had lost his nerve had been buying drinks.

The boy Paco had never known about any of this nor about what all these people would be doing on the next day and on other days to come. He had no idea how they really lived nor how they ended. He did not even realize they ended. He died, as the Spanish phrase has it, full of illusions. He had not had time in his life to lose any of them, nor even, at the end, to complete an act of contrition.

He had not even had time to be disappointed in the Garbo picture which disappointed all Madrid for a week.

Questions for Study

1. Why does Hemingway begin the story with a discussion of the name *Paco*? Why is Enrique named when, apart from Paco, the other characters are not?
2. Why does Hemingway devote so much time to a description of the residents of the hotel? What seem to be his criteria for devoting more space to some residents than to others?
3. We are told that "decorum and dignity rank above courage as the virtues most highly prized in Spain." What evidence in the story supports that generalization? Be sure to consider small, as well as large, details.
4. Examine the many images of animals in the story. How do they contribute to the meaning?
5. Why does Hemingway tell us about the politics of the tall waiter? Why does the waiter think bulls and priests are the curse of Spain? Why is Paco pleased with such talk? Why does one priest say that "Madrid kills Spain"?

6. Why does Hemingway describe what all the other characters are doing both before and after the stabbing? Why does the story end with a reference to illusions?

7. Describe the syntax in the passage in which Paco is stabbed. How does the following one-sentence paragraph differ syntactically from the preceding paragraph? What is the effect of this change in syntax?

8. How would you characterize Hemingway's diction? What kinds of similes does he use? Does he use any metaphors?

9. What does Hemingway's title imply about his tone? How does his tone relate to his style?

Chapter 8
Form and Conflict

In Chapter 2 we described the traditional plot as a sequence of events ordered by their connections and relationships. In such a plot, A causes B, B causes C, C causes D, and so on, with the end being a logical outcome of the story's beginning and middle. The conventional plot assumes, for example, that if two men are captured as spies behind enemy lines while on a fishing excursion, as in Maupassant's story, they will either escape, be spared, or be executed. Regardless of the outcome, any one of these endings will resolve the preceding events in a logical, believable manner. Such plotting supposes that a fictional event has definite causes and generates consequences that are identifiable and reasonable.

For many modern writers, however, the traditional plot does not adequately reflect the structure of actual experience, which often seems chaotic and disjointed. In *A Story Teller's Story* (1924), the American writer Sherwood Anderson wrote: "It was certain that there were no plot stories in any life I had known anything about." In his own fiction Anderson sought "form, not plot," form being to him "an altogether more elusive and difficult thing to come at." In declaring that fiction should more closely approximate the movement of actual happenings, however, Anderson was not suggesting that stories should be haphazard accumulations of events exactly as they occur in real life. Imagine that instead of writing "A & P," Updike had recorded on film or tape everything that Sammy saw and heard and said and did while working behind the counter in the A & P. Such a tape or film would be realistic but it would not have a plot. And it would not have what Anderson calls "form," but only the random flow of real-life events. The essential question for Anderson was how to get into his fiction this "flow of real-life events" without the chaotic formlessness of actual experience. In other words, Anderson wanted to write stories that have an artistic structure but that are still honest and true to life.

As employed here, **form** refers to the organization of a story in relation to the ways various elements shape and determine its total effect. Many elements of a narrative may contribute to its form—for example, the point and counterpoint of its plot actions, the patterns of images and symbols, the arrangement of scenes and details, the development and revelation of its conflict. To Anderson, form is a method of organizing a story not by the cause-and-effect sequence of occurrences but by the suggestion of indirect connections between events. Rather than developing a steadily mounting conflict, many twentieth-century writers arrange their stories by a principle of form other than a logical sequence of events. They may employ characters who represent opposing or complementary ideas and values and who interact in several apparently unrelated incidents which, taken together, serve to reveal meaning. Occasionally they use a pattern of variations on a single theme or a repetition of certain phrases, images, symbols, or situations. And rather than working out a definite, logical dénouement, modern writers usually leave the conclusions of their stories open-ended or unresolved in the conventional sense of tieing together all the diverse elements.

In avoiding the traditional plot structure, many modern writers have refined the uses of **conflict,** which is the struggle between opposing forces in a story. So important in fact is conflict to twentieth-century stories that in this chapter form is considered in relation to the ways conflict determines and shapes the overall organization of a particular narrative. Conflict animates characters and events; it makes the story move, regardless of how static it appears to be. No matter how independent of a normal plot a modern, experimental story may be, it cannot properly be called fiction unless it presents and develops some kind of conflict.

While the traditional plot presents conflict in a rising and a falling pattern, with the conclusion logically growing out of the preceding events, modern fiction often concentrates more on describing and exploring the intricacies and implications of the conflict itself. Many times the story ends and the conflict remains unresolved. In "How I Contemplated the World . . . ," for example, the narrator is in conflict with a host of opposing forces: her parents, her boyfriend Simon, various figures of authority, her environment, and ultimately herself. These conflicts are not presented in logical order, but are gradually unfolded in piecemeal fashion. As readers, we have to fit together these fragments in order to comprehend the mosaic of people, places, and actions that Oates presents. And the narrator's concluding statement, "I am home," can be interpreted more as a suggestion of doubt and irresolution than as an indication that the conflict has been firmly settled.

D. H. Lawrence's "The White Stocking" exhibits more qualities of the traditional plot story than Oates' narrative does. Yet instead of presenting a clearly defined conflict between protagonist and antagonist, Lawrence gives us a complex triangle in which conflicts exist among the husband, the wife, and the wife's flirtatious boss. These conflicts, especially the love-hate relationship between husband and wife, are developed and examined, but they are never thoroughly resolved. Similarly, in William Faulkner's "That Evening Sun," we cannot simply say that the only conflict occurs between the black servant Nancy and her husband, who she believes will eventually kill her. In this story conflicts between husbands and wives, sisters and brothers, blacks and whites, civilized decency and human abuse are overlaid, one on top of the other. The narrative structure is organized around several related oppositions, not merely around one clear conflict. Lawrence and Faulkner place several contrasting elements together and allow them to play against one another. Because both stories are structured by means of the tension created among various opposing characters, the conflicts in each function as the prime method of organization. Conflict, in other words, is instrumental in giving form to each story.

Taken as a whole, "The White Stocking" does not conform to the pattern of the traditional plot, with its rising and falling action. Instead, this design is repeated in each of the three sections, which are not arranged chronologically but rather by a pattern of mounting intensities. The structure of the story is reinforced by images of color, of melting and flowing, of freedom and containment. These images function as continuous strands which serve to unify the three sections of the narrative.

In the Lawrence story there are three separate peaks and dénouements, but in "That Evening Sun" there is no conventional dénouement. That is, Faulkner's ending does not close or round off the story by resolving the conflict but rather repeats structurally the beginning section. In the first section the Compson children and their father are walking toward Nancy's cabin; in the last they are walking away from it. In the first, Nancy's self-control is so firm that she is able to crawl through a fence with a bundle on her head without dropping it. In the last, despite her feeling that her husband is going to murder her, she regains her bravery and composure. Yet in the middle sections Nancy grows increasingly uncontrolled and fearful. She makes an eerie sound that is "not singing" and "not crying," sloshes her coffee and then drops the cup, places her hand on the lantern globe and then in the fire, and at last cries silently. In these scenes Nancy becomes more and more beside herself so that the entire sequence forms a recurrent pattern bringing her closer and closer to the breaking point. These sections do not progress directly so much as they reveal in ever widening circles the extent of Nancy's fear. The reader's participation in her terror is reinforced by Faulkner's breaking off each section just as something is about to happen.

Nancy's behavior is contrasted with patterns of images which organize the narrative by suggesting that the world is so severely split into radically opposed sides that there is no solution to fear and hostility. Faulkner sets next to each other images such as house/cabin, bedroom/kitchen, street/land, white/black, men/women, light/dark, confidence/fear, control/violence. These contrasting images suggest that no matter how the reader may identify with Nancy, the white people who control her existence can never understand the emotions and actions of blacks like her.

In modern stories such as the two in this chapter, conflict functions as an important means of organizing and structuring a narrative. Whether between opposed elements in nature or in society, between people, or within one character, the tensions generated in each story amplify, reinforce, and intensify one another. In *Aspects of the Novel* E. M. Forster observed that "expansion . . . is the idea the novelist must cling to. Not completion. Not rounding off but opening out." Fiction of this type leads first into the very heart of character and event. Then it moves outward to the larger world and the reader. Modern fiction stresses the close involvement of the reader in the story so that he gains an insight into the complexities of life the author is presenting. The impact and value of modern stories depend upon the writers' effective use of organizational methods other than the strictly cause-and-effect plot and the tidy, rigorously logical ending. The issues and concerns of twentieth-century fiction are never easily "rounded off." And conflict is usually at the center of what gives these narratives their overall form.

D. H. Lawrence (1885–1930)
The White Stocking

I

"I'm getting up, Teddilinks," said Mrs. Whiston, and she sprang out of bed briskly.

"What the Hanover's got you?"[1] asked Whiston.

"Nothing. Can't I get up?" she replied animatedly.

It was about seven o'clock, scarcely light yet in the cold bedroom. Whiston lay still and looked at his wife. She was a pretty little thing, with her fleecy, short black hair all tousled. He watched her as she dressed quickly, flicking her small, delightful limbs, throwing her clothes about her. Her slovenliness and un-

---

1. Polite, even overpolite, form of "What the hell's got you?"

tidiness did not trouble him. When she picked up the edge of her petticoat, ripped off a torn string of white lace, and flung it on the dressing-table, her careless abandon made his spirit glow. She stood before the mirror and roughly scrambled together her profuse little mane of hair. He watched the quickness and softness of her young shoulders, calmly, like a husband, and apprecia-tively.

"Rise up," she cried, turning to him with a quick wave of her arm—"and shine forth."

They had been married two years. But still, when she had gone out of the room, he felt as if all his light and warmth were taken away, he became aware of the raw, cold morning. So he rose himself, wondering casually what had roused her so early. Usually she lay in bed as late as she could.

Whiston fastened a belt round his loins and went downstairs in shirt and trousers. He heard her singing in her snatchy fashion. The stairs creaked under his weight. He passed down the narrow little passage, which she called a hall, of the seven and sixpenny house[2] which was his first home.

He was a shapely young fellow of about twenty-eight, sleepy now and easy with well-being. He heard the water drumming into the kettle, and she began to whistle. He loved the quick way she dodged the supper cups under the tap to wash them for breakfast. She looked an untidy minx, but she was quick and handy enough.

"Teddilinks," she cried.

"What?"

"Light a fire, quick."

She wore an old, sack-like dressing-jacket of black silk pinned across her breast. But one of the sleeves, coming unfastened, showed some delightful pink upper-arm.

"Why don't you sew your sleeve up?" he said, suffering from the sight of the exposed soft flesh.

"Where?" she cried, peering round. "Nuisance," she said, seeing the gap, then with light fingers went on drying the cups.

The kitchen was of fair size, but gloomy. Whiston poked out the dead ashes.

Suddenly a thud was heard at the door down the passage.

"I'll go," cried Mrs. Whiston, and she was gone down the hall.

The postman was a ruddy-faced man who had been a soldier. He smiled broadly, handing her some packages.

"They've not forgot you," he said impudently.

"No—lucky for them," she said, with a toss of the head. But she was inter-ested only in her envelopes this morning. The postman waited inquisitively, smiling in an ingratiating fashion. She slowly, abstractedly, as if she did not know anyone was there, closed the door in his face, continuing to look at the addresses on her letters.

She tore open the thin envelope. There was a long, hideous, cartoon valen-tine. She smiled briefly and dropped it on the floor. Struggling with the string of a packet, she opened a white cardboard box, and there lay a white silk hand-kerchief packed neatly under the paper lace of the box, and her initial, worked in heliotrope, fully displayed. She smiled pleasantly, and gently put the box

---

2. House which rents for seven shillings and sixpence per week—about a dollar.

aside. The third envelope contained another white packet—apparently a cotton handkerchief neatly folded. She shook it out. It was a long white stocking, but there was a little weight in the toe. Quickly she thrust down her arm, wriggling her fingers into the toe of the stocking, and brought out a small box. She peeped inside the box, then hastily opened a door on her left hand, and went into the little cold sitting-room. She had her lower lip caught earnestly between her teeth.

With a little flash of triumph, she lifted a pair of pearl ear-rings from the small box, and she went to the mirror. There, earnestly, she began to hook them through her ears, looking at herself sideways in the glass. Curiously concentrated and intent she seemed as she fingered the lobes of her ears, her head bent on one side.

Then the pearl ear-rings dangled under her rosy, small ears. She shook her head sharply, to see the swing of the drops. They went chill against her neck, in little, sharp touches. Then she stood still to look at herself, bridling her head in the dignified fashion. Then she simpered at herself. Catching her own eye, she could not help winking at herself and laughing.

She turned to look at the box. There was a scrap of paper with this posy:

"Pearls may be fair, but thou are fairer.
Wear these for me, and I'll love the wearer."

She made a grimace and a grin. But she was drawn to the mirror again, to look at her ear-rings.

Whiston had made the fire burn, so he came to look for her. When she heard him, she started round quickly, guiltily. She was watching him with intent blue eyes when he appeared.

He did not see much, in his morning-drowsy warmth. He gave her, as ever, a feeling of warmth and slowness. His eyes were very blue, very kind, his manner simple.

"What ha' you got?" he asked.

"Valentines," she said briskly, ostentatiously turning to show him the silk handkerchief. She thrust it under his nose. "Smell how good," she said.

"Who's that from?" he replied, without smelling.

"It's a valentine," she cried. "How do I know who it's from?"

"I'll bet you know," he said.

"Ted!—I don't!" she cried, beginning to shake her head, then stopping because of the ear-rings.

He stood still a moment, displeased.

"They've no right to send you valentines now," he said.

"Ted!—Why not? You're not jealous, are you? I haven't the least idea who it's from. Look—there's my initial"—she pointed with an emphatic finger at the heliotrope embroidery——

"E for Elsie,
Nice little gelsie,"

she sang.

"Get out," he said. "You know who it's from."

"Truth, I don't," she cried.

He looked round, and saw the white stocking lying on a chair.

"Is this another?" he said.

"No, that's a sample," she said. "There's only a comic." And she fetched in the long cartoon.

He stretched it out and looked at it solemnly.

"Fools!" he said, and went out of the room.

She flew upstairs and took off the ear-rings. When she returned, he was crouched before the fire blowing the coals. The skin of his face was flushed, and slightly pitted, as if he had had small-pox. But his neck was white and smooth and goodly. She hung her arms round his neck as he crouched there, and clung to him. He balanced on his toes.

"This fire's a slow-coach,"[3] he said.

"And who else is a slow-coach?" she said.

"One of us two, I know," he said, and he rose carefully.

She remained clinging round his neck, so that she was lifted off her feet.

"Ha!—swing me," she cried.

He lowered his head, and she hung in the air, swinging from his neck, laughing. Then she slipped off.

"The kettle is singing," she sang, flying for the teapot. He bent down again to blow the fire. The veins in his neck stood out, his shirt collar seemed too tight.

> *"Doctor Wyer,*
> *Blow the fire,*
> *Puff! puff! puff!"*

she sang, laughing.

He smiled at her.

She was so glad because of her pearl ear-rings.

Over the breakfast she grew serious. He did not notice. She became portentous in her gravity. Almost it penetrated through his steady good-humour to irritate him.

"Teddy!" she said at last.

"What?" he asked.

"I told you a lie," she said, humbly tragic.

His soul stirred uneasily.

"Oh aye?" he said casually.

She was not satisfied. He ought to be more moved.

"Yes," she said.

He cut a piece of bread.

"Was it a good one?" he asked.

She was piqued. Then she considered—*was* it a good one? Then she laughed.

"No," she said, "it wasn't up to much."

"Ah!" he said easily, but with a steady strength of fondness for her in his tone. "Get it out then."

---

3. Someone or something that moves or thinks slowly.

It became a little more difficult.

"You know that white stocking," she said earnestly. "I told you a lie. It wasn't a sample. It was a valentine."

A little frown came on his brow.

"Then what did you invent it as a sample for?" he said. But he knew this weakness of hers. The touch of anger in his voice frightened her.

"I was afraid you'd be cross," she said pathetically.

"I'll bet you were vastly afraid," he said.

"I *was*, Teddy."

There was a pause. He was resolving one or two things in his mind.

"And who sent it?" he asked.

"I can guess," she said, "though there wasn't a word with it—except——"

She ran to the sitting-room and returned with a slip of paper.

"Pearls may be fair, but thou art fairer.
Wear these for me, and I'll love the wearer."

He read it twice, then a dull red flush came on his face.

"And *who* do you guess it is?" he asked, with a ringing of anger in his voice.

"I suspect it's Sam Adams," she said, with a little virtuous indignation.

Whiston was silent for a moment.

"Fool!" he said. "An' what's it got to do with pearls?—and how can he say 'wear these for me' when there's only one? He hasn't got the brain to invent a proper verse."

He screwed the slip of paper into a ball and flung it into the fire.

"I suppose he thinks it'll make a pair with the one last year," she said.

"Why, did he send one then?"

"Yes. I thought you'd be wild if you knew."

His jaw set rather sullenly.

Presently he rose, and went to wash himself, rolling back his sleeves and pulling open his shirt at the breast. It was as if his fine, clear-cut temples and steady eyes were degraded by the lower, rather brutal part of his face. But she loved it. As she whisked about, clearing the table, she loved the way in which he stood washing himself. He was such a man. She liked to see his neck glistening with water as he swilled it. It amused her and pleased her and thrilled her. He was so sure, so permanent, he had her so utterly in his power. It gave her a delightful, mischievous sense of liberty. Within his grasp, she could dart about excitingly.

He turned round to her, his face red from the cold water, his eyes fresh and very blue.

"You haven't been seeing anything of him, have you?" he asked roughly.

"Yes," she answered, after a moment, as if caught guilty. "He got into the tram[4] with me, and he asked me to drink a coffee and a Benedictine[5] in the Royal."

---

4. Streetcar.
5. A sweet, brown liqueur.

"You've got it off fine and glib," he said sullenly. "And did you?"

"Yes," she replied, with the air of a traitor before the rack.

The blood came up into his neck and face, he stood motionless, dangerous.

"It was cold, and it was such fun to go into the Royal," she said.

"You'd go off with a nigger for a packet of chocolate," he said, in anger and contempt, and some bitterness. Queer how he drew away from her, cut her off from him.

"Ted—how beastly!" she cried. "You know quite well——" She caught her lip, flushed, and the tears came to her eyes.

He turned away, to put on his neck-tie. She went about her work, making a queer pathetic little mouth, down which occasionally dripped a tear.

He was ready to go. With his hat jammed down on his head, and his overcoat buttoned up to his chin, he came to kiss her. He would be miserable all the day if he went without. She allowed herself to be kissed. Her cheek was wet under his lip, and his heart burned. She hurt him so deeply. And she felt aggrieved, and did not quite forgive him.

In a moment she went upstairs to her ear-rings. Sweet they looked nestling in the little drawer—sweet! She examined them with voluptuous pleasure, she threaded them in her ears, she looked at herself, she posed and postured and smiled and looked sad and tragic and winning and appealing, all in turn before the mirror. And she was happy, and very pretty.

She wore her ear-rings all morning, in the house. She was self-conscious, and quite brilliantly winsome, when the baker came, wondering if he would notice. All the tradesmen left her door with a glow in them, feeling elated, and unconsciously favouring the delightful little creature, though there had been nothing to notice in her behaviour.

She was stimulated all the day. She did not think about her husband. He was the permanent basis from which she took these giddy little flights into nowhere. At night, like chickens and curses, she would come home to him, to roost.

Meanwhile Whiston, a traveller and confidential support of a small firm, hastened about his work, his heart all the while anxious for her, yearning for surety, and kept tense by not getting it.

II

She had been a warehouse girl in Adams's lace factory before she was married. Sam Adams was her employer. He was a bachelor of forty, growing stout, a man well dressed and florid, with a large brown moustache and thin hair. From the rest of his well-groomed, showy appearance, it was evident his baldness was a chagrin to him. He had a good presence, and some Irish blood in his veins.

His fondness for the girls, or the fondness of the girls for him, was notorious. And Elsie, quick, pretty, almost witty little thing—she *seemed* witty, although, when her sayings were repeated, they were entirely trivial—she had a great attraction for him. He would come into the warehouse dressed in a rather sporting reefer coat, of fawn colour, and trousers of fine black-and-white check, a cap with a big peak and scarlet carnation in his button-hole, to impress her. She was only half impressed. He was too loud for her good taste. Instinctively perceiving this, he sobered down to navy blue. Then a well-built man, florid, with large brown whiskers, smart navy blue suit, fashionable boots, and manly hat, he was the irreproachable. Elsie was impressed.

But meanwhile Whiston was courting her and she made splendid little gestures, before her bedroom mirror, of the constant-and-true sort.

"True, true till death——"

That was her song. Whiston was made that way, so there was no need to take thought for him.

Every Christmas Sam Adams gave a party at his house, to which he invited his superior work-people—not factory hands and labourers, but those above. He was a generous man in his way, with a real warm feeling for giving pleasure.

Two years ago Elsie had attended this Christmas-party for the last time. Whiston had accompanied her. At that time he worked for Sam Adams.

She had been very proud of herself, in her close-fitting, full-skirted dress of blue silk. Whiston called for her. Then she tripped beside him, holding her large cashmere shawl across her breast. He strode with long strides, his trousers handsomely strapped under his boots, and her silk shoes bulging the pocket of his full-skirted overcoat.

They passed through the park gates, and her spirits rose. Above them the Castle Rock loomed grandly in the night, the naked trees stood still and dark in the frost, along the boulevard.

They were rather late. Agitated with anticipation, in the cloak-room she gave up her shawl, donned her silk shoes, and looked at herself in the mirror. The loose bunches of curls on either side her face danced prettily, her mouth smiled.

She hung a moment in the door of the brilliantly lighted room. Many people were moving within the blaze of lamps, under the crystal chandeliers, the full skirts of the women balancing and floating, the side-whiskers and white cravats of the men bowing above. Then she entered the light.

In an instant Sam Adams was coming forward, lifting both his arms in boisterous welcome. There was a constant red laugh on his face.

"Come late, would you," he shouted, "like royalty."

He seized her hands and led her forward. He opened his mouth wide when he spoke, and the effect of the warm, dark opening behind the brown whiskers was disturbing. But she was floating into the throng on his arm. He was very gallant.

"Now then," he said, taking her card to write down the dances, "I've got *carte blanche,*[6] haven't I?"

"Mr. Whiston doesn't dance," she said.

"I am a lucky man!" he said, scribbling his initials. "I was born with an *amourette*[7] in my mouth."

He wrote on, quietly. She blushed and laughed, not knowing what it meant.

"Why, what is that?" she said.

---

6. Literally, "a blank card."
7. Casual love affair.

"It's you, even littler than you are, dressed in little wings," he said.

"I should have to be pretty small to get in your mouth," she said.

"You think you're too big, do you!" he said easily.

He handed her her card, with a bow.

"Now I'm set up, my darling, for this evening," he said.

Then, quick, always at his ease, he looked over the room. She waited in front of him. He was ready. Catching the eye of the band, he nodded. In a moment, the music began. He seemed to relax, giving himself up.

"Now then, Elsie," he said, with a curious caress in his voice that seemed to lap the outside of her body in a warm glow, delicious. She gave herself to it. She liked it.

He was an excellent dancer. He seemed to draw her close in to him by some male warmth of attraction, so that she became all soft and pliant to him, flowing to his form, whilst he united her with him and they lapsed along in one movement. She was just carried in a kind of strong, warm flood, her feet moved of themselves, and only the music threw her away from him, threw her back to him, to his clasp, in his strong form moving against her, rhythmically, deliciously.

When it was over, he was pleased and his eyes had a curious gleam which thrilled her and yet had nothing to do with her. Yet it held her. He did not speak to her. He only looked straight into her eyes with a curious, gleaming look that disturbed her fearfully and deliciously. But also there was in his look some of the automatic irony of the *roué*.[8] It left her partly cold. She was not carried away.

She went, driven by an opposite, heavier impulse, to Whiston. He stood looking gloomy, trying to admit that she had a perfect right to enjoy herself apart from him. He received her with rather grudging kindliness.

"Aren't you going to play whist?" she asked.

"Aye," he said. "Directly."

"I do wish you could dance."

"Well, I can't," he said. "So you enjoy yourself."

"But I should enjoy it better if I could dance with you."

"Nay, you're all right," he said. "I'm not made that way."

"Then you ought to be!" she cried.

"Well, it's my fault, not yours. You enjoy yourself," he bade her. Which she proceeded to do, a little bit irked.

She went with anticipation to the arms of Sam Adams, when the time came to dance with him. It *was* so gratifying, irrespective of the man. And she felt a little grudge against Whiston, soon forgotten when her host was holding her near to him, in a delicious embrace. And she watched his eyes, to meet the gleam in them, which gratified her.

She was getting warmed right through, the glow was penetrating into her, driving away everything else. Only in her heart was a little tightness, like conscience.

When she got a chance, she escaped from the dancing-room to the card-room. There, in a cloud of smoke, she found Whiston playing cribbage. Radiant, roused, animated, she came up to him and greeted him. She was too

8. High-living womanizer.

strong, too vibrant a note in the quiet room. He lifted his head, and a frown knitted his gloomy forehead.

"Are you playing cribbage? Is it exciting? How are you getting on?" she chattered.

He looked at her. None of these questions needed answering, and he did not feel in touch with her. She turned to the cribbage-board.

"Are you white or red?" she asked.

"He's red," replied the partner.

"Then you're losing," she said, still to Whiston. And she lifted the red peg from the board. "One—two—three—four—five—six—seven—eight—— Right up there you ought to jump——"

"Now put it back in its right place," said Whiston.

"Where was it?" she asked gaily, knowing her transgression. He took the little red peg away from her and stuck it in its hole.

The cards were shuffled.

"What a shame you're losing," said Elsie.

"You'd better cut for him," said the partner.

She did so hastily. The cards were dealt. She put her hand on his shoulder, looking at his cards.

"It's good," she cried, "isn't it?"

He did not answer, but threw down two cards. It moved him more strongly than was comfortable, to have her hand on his shoulder, her curls dangling and touching his ears, whilst she was roused to another man. It made the blood flame over him.

At that moment Sam Adams appeared, florid and boisterous, intoxicated more with himself, with the dancing, than with wine. In his eye the curious, impersonal light gleamed.

"I thought I should find you here, Elsie," he cried boisterously, a disturbing, high note in his voice.

"What made you think so?" she replied, the mischief rousing in her.

The florid, well-built man narrowed his eyes to a smile.

"I should never look for you among the ladies," he said, with a kind of intimate, animal call to her. He laughed, bowed, and offered her his arm.

"Madam, the music waits."

She went almost helplessly, carried along with him, unwilling, yet delighted.

That dance was an intoxication to her. After the first few steps, she felt herself slipping away from herself. She almost knew she was going, she did not even want to go. Yet she must have chosen to go. She lay in the arm of the steady, close man with whom she was dancing, and she seemed to swim away out of contact with the room, into him. She had passed into another, denser element of him, an essential privacy. The room was all vague around her, like an atmosphere, like under sea, with a flow of ghostly, dumb movements. But she herself was held real against her partner, and it seemed she was connected with him, as if the movements of his body and limbs were her own movements, yet not her own movements—and oh, delicious! He also was given up, oblivious, concentrated, into the dance. His eye was unseeing. Only his large, voluptuous body gave off a subtle activity. His fingers seemed to search into her flesh. Every moment, and every moment, she felt she would give way utterly, and sink molten: the fusion point was coming when she would fuse down into perfect unconsciousness at his feet and knees. But he bore her round the room in the dance, and he seemed to sustain all her body with his limbs, his body, and his warmth seemed to come closer into her, nearer, till it would fuse right through her, and she would be as liquid to him as an intoxication only.

It was exquisite. When it was over, she was dazed, and was scarcely breathing. She stood with him in the middle of the room as if she were alone in a remote place. He bent over her. She expected his lips on her bare shoulder, and waited. Yet they were not alone, they were not alone. It was cruel.

"'Twas good, wasn't it, my darling?" he said to her, low and delighted. There was a strange impersonality about his low, exultant call that appealed to her irresistibly. Yet why was she aware of some part shut off in her? She pressed his arm, and he led her towards the door.

She was not aware of what she was doing, only a little grain of resistant trouble was in her. The man, possessed, yet with a superficial presence of mind, made way to the dining-room, as if to give her refreshment, cunningly working to his own escape with her. He was molten hot, filmed over with presence of mind, and bottomed with cold disbelief. In the dining-room was Whiston, carrying coffee to the plain, neglected ladies. Elsie saw him, but felt as if he could not see her. She was beyond his reach and ken. A sort of fusion existed between her and the large man at her side. She ate her custard, but an incomplete fusion all the while sustained and contained within the being of her employer.

But she was growing cooler. Whiston came up. She looked at him, and saw him with different eyes. She saw his slim, young man's figure real and enduring before her. That was he. But she was in the spell with the other man, fused with him, and she could not be taken away.

"Have you finished your cribbage?" she asked, with hasty evasion of him.

"Yes," he replied. "Aren't you getting tired of dancing?"

"Not a bit," she said.

"Not she," said Adams heartily. "No girl with any spirit gets tired of dancing. Have something else, Elsie. Come—sherry. Have a glass of sherry with us, Whiston."

Whilst they sipped the wine, Adams watched Whiston almost cunningly, to find his advantage.

"We'd better be getting back—there's the music," he said. "See the women get something to eat, Whiston, will you, there's a good chap."

And he began to draw away. Elsie was drifting helplessly with him. But Whiston put himself beside them, and went along with them. In silence they passed through to the dancing-room. There Adams hesitated, and looked round the room. It was as if he could not see.

A man came hurrying forward, claiming Elsie, and Adams went to his other partner. Whiston stood watching during the dance. She was conscious of him standing there observant of her, like a ghost, or a judgment, or a guardian angel. She was also conscious, much more intimately and impersonally, of the body of the other man moving somewhere in the room. She still belonged to him, but a feeling of distraction possessed her, and helplessness. Adams danced on, adhering to Elsie, waiting his time, with the persistence of cynicism.

The dance was over. Adams was detained. Elsie found herself beside Whiston. There was something shapely about him as he sat, about his knees and his distinct figure, that she clung to. It was as if he had enduring form. She put her hand on his knee.

"Are you enjoying yourself?" he asked.

"*Ever* so," she replied, with a fervent, yet detached tone.

"It's going on for one o'clock," he said.

"Is it?" she answered. It meant nothing to her.

"Should we be going?" he said.

She was silent. For the first time for an hour or more an inkling of her normal consciousness returned. She resented it.

"What for?" she said.

"I thought you might have had enough," he said.

A slight soberness came over her, an irritation at being frustrated of her illusion.

"Why?" she said.

"We've been here since nine," he said.

That was no answer, no reason. It conveyed nothing to her. She sat detached from him. Across the room Sam Adams glanced at her. She sat there exposed for him.

"You don't want to be too free with Sam Adams," said Whiston cautiously, suffering. "You know what he is."

"How, free?" she asked.

"Why—you don't want to have too much to do with him."

She sat silent. He was forcing her into consciousness of her position. But he could not get hold of her feelings, to change them. She had a curious, perverse desire that he should not.

"I like him," she said.

"What do you find to like in him?" he said, with a hot heart.

"I don't know—but I like him," she said.

She was immutable. He sat feeling heavy and dulled with rage. He was not clear as to what he felt. He sat there unliving whilst she danced. And she, distracted, lost to herself between the opposing forces of the two men, drifted. Between the dances, Whiston kept near to her. She was scarcely conscious. She glanced repeatedly at her card, to see when she would dance again with Adams, half in desire, half in dread. Sometimes she met his steady, glaucous eye as she passed him in the dance. Sometimes she saw the steadiness of his flank as he danced. And it was always as if she rested on his arm, were borne along, up-borne by him, away from herself. And always there was present the other's antagonism. She was divided.

The time came for her to dance with Adams. Oh, the delicious closing of contact with him, of his limbs touching her limbs, his arm supporting her. She seemed to resolve. Whiston had not made himself real to her. He was only a heavy place in her consciousness.

But she breathed heavily, beginning to suffer from the closeness of strain. She was nervous. Adams also was constrained. A tightness, a tension was coming over them all. And he was exasperated, feeling something counteracting physical magnetism, feeling a will stronger with her than his own, intervening in what was becoming a vital necessity to him.

Elsie was almost lost to her own control. As she went forward with him to take her place at the dance, she stooped for her pocket handkerchief. The music sounded for quadrilles.[9] Everybody was ready. Adams stood with his body near her, exerting his attraction over her. He was tense and fighting. She stooped for her pocket handkerchief, and shook it as she rose. It shook out and fell from her hand. With agony, she saw she had taken a white stocking instead of a handkerchief. For a second it lay on the floor, a twist of white stocking. Then, in an instant, Adams picked it up, with a little, surprised laugh of triumph.

"That'll do for me," he whispered—seeming to take possession of her. And he stuffed the stocking in his trousers pocket, and quickly offered her his handkerchief.

The dance began. She felt weak and faint, as if her will were turned to water. A heavy sense of loss came over her. She could not help herself any more. But it was peace.

When the dance was over, Adams yielded her up. Whiston came to her.

"What was it as you dropped?" Whiston asked.

"I thought it was my handkerchief—I'd taken a stocking by mistake," she said, detached and muted.

"And he's got it?"

"Yes."

"What does he mean by that?"

She lifted her shoulders.

"Are you going to let him keep it?" he asked.

"I don't let him."

There was a long pause.

"Am I to go and have it out with him?" he asked, his face flushed, his blue eyes going hard with opposition.

"No," she said, pale.

"Why?"

"No—I don't want you to say anything about it."

He sat exasperated and nonplussed.

"You'll let him keep it, then?" he asked.

She sat silent and made no form of answer.

"What do you mean by it?" he said, dark with fury. And he started up.

"No!" she cried. "Ted!" And she caught hold of him, sharply detaining him.

It made him black with rage.

"Why?" he said.

The something about her mouth was pitiful to him. He did not understand, but he felt she must have her reasons.

"Then I'm not stopping here," he said. "Are you coming with me?"

She rose mutely, and they went out of the room. Adams had not noticed. In a few moments they were in the street.

"What the hell do you mean?" he said, in a black fury.

She went at his side, in silence, neutral.

"That great hog, an' all," he added.

---

9. Dances for four couples.

Then they went a long time in silence through the frozen, deserted darkness of the town. She felt she could not go indoors. They were drawing near her house.

"I don't want to go home," she suddenly cried in distress and anguish. "I don't want to go home."

He looked at her.

"Why don't you?" he said.

"I don't want to go home," was all she could sob.

He heard somebody coming.

"Well, we can walk a bit farther," he said.

She was silent again. They passed out of the town into the fields. He held her by the arm—they could not speak.

"What's a-matter?" he asked at length, puzzled.

She began to cry again.

At last he took her in his arms, to soothe her. She sobbed by herself, almost unaware of him.

"Tell me what's a-matter, Elsie," he said. "Tell me what's a-matter—my dear—tell me, then——"

He kissed her wet face, and caressed her. She made no response. He was puzzled and tender and miserable.

At length she became quiet. Then he kissed her, and she put her arms round him, and clung to him very tight, as if for fear and anguish. He held her in his arms, wondering.

"Ted!" she whispered, frantic. "Ted!"

"What, my love?" he answered, becoming also afraid.

"Be good to me," she cried. "Don't be cruel to me."

"No, my pet," he said, amazed and grieved. "Why?"

"Oh, be good to me," she sobbed.

And he held her very safe, and his heart was white-hot with love for her. His mind was amazed. He could only hold her against his chest that was white-hot with love and belief in her. So she was restored at last.

III

She refused to go to her work at Adams's any more. Her father had to submit and she sent in her notice—she was not well. Sam Adams was ironical. But he had a curious patience. He did not fight.

In a few weeks, she and Whiston were married. She loved him with passion and worship, a fierce little abandon of love that moved him to the depths of his being, and gave him a permanent surety and sense of realness in himself. He did not trouble about himself any more: he felt he was fulfilled and now he had only the many things in the world to busy himself about. Whatever troubled him, at the bottom was surety. He had found himself in this love.

They spoke once or twice of the white stocking.

"Ah!" Whiston exclaimed. "What does it matter?"

He was impatient and angry, and could not bear to consider the matter. So it was left unresolved.

She was quite happy at first, carried away by her adoration of her husband.

Then gradually she got used to him. He always was the ground of her happiness, but she got used to him, as to the air she breathed. He never got used to her in the same way.

Inside of marriage she found her liberty. She was rid of the responsibility of herself. Her husband must look after that. She was free to get what she could out of her time.

So that, when, after some months, she met Sam Adams, she was not quite as unkind to him as she might have been. With a young wife's new and exciting knowledge of men, she perceived he was in love with her, she knew he had always kept an unsatisfied desire for her. And, sportive, she could not help playing a little with this, though she cared not one jot for the man himself.

When Valentine's day came, which was near the first anniversary of her wedding day, there arrived a white stocking with a little amethyst brooch. Luckily Whiston did not see it, so she said nothing of it to him. She had not the faintest intention of having anything to do with Sam Adams, but once a little brooch was in her possession, it was hers, and she did not trouble her head for a moment how she had come by it. She kept it.

Now she had the pearl ear-rings. They were a more valuable and a more conspicuous present. She would have to ask her mother to give them to her, to explain their presence. She made a little plan in her head. And she was extraordinarily pleased. As for Sam Adams, even if he saw her wearing them, he would not give her away. What fun, if he saw her wearing his ear-rings! She would pretend she had inherited them from her grandmother, her mother's mother. She laughed to herself as she went down-town in the afternoon, the pretty drops dangling in front of her curls. But she saw no one of importance.

Whiston came home tired and depressed. All day the male in him had been uneasy, and this had fatigued him. She was curiously against him, inclined, as she sometimes was nowadays, to make mock of him and jeer at him and cut him off. He did not understand this, and it angered him deeply. She was uneasy before him.

She knew he was in a state of suppressed irritation. The veins stood out on the backs of his hands, his brow was drawn stiffly. Yet she could not help goading him.

"What did you do wi' that white stocking?" he asked, out of a gloomy silence, his voice strong and brutal.

"I put it in a drawer—why?" she replied flippantly.

"Why didn't you put it on the fire-back?"[10] he said harshly. "What are you hoarding it up for?"

"I'm not hoarding it up," she said. "I've got a pair."

He relapsed into gloomy silence. She, unable to move him, ran away upstairs, leaving him smoking by the fire. Again she tried on the ear-rings. Then another little inspiration came to her. She drew on the white stockings, both of them.

Presently she came down in them. Her husband still sat immovable and glowering by the fire.

"Look!" she said. "They'll do beautifully."

And she picked up her skirts to her knees, and twisted round, looking at her pretty legs in the neat stockings.

---

10. I.e., throw it on the back of the fire.

He filled with unreasonable rage, and took the pipe from his mouth.

"Don't they look nice?" she said. "One from last year and one from this, they just do. Save you buying a pair."

And she looked over her shoulders at her pretty calves, and at the dangling frills of her knickers.

"Put your skirts down and don't make a fool of yourself," he said.

"Why a fool of myself?" she asked.

And she began to dance slowly round the room, kicking up her feet half reckless, half jeering, in ballet-dancer's fashion. Almost fearful, yet in defiance, she kicked up her legs at him, singing as she did so. She resented him.

"You little fool, ha' done with it," he said. "And you'll back-fire them stockings, I'm telling you." He was angry. His face flushed dark, he kept his head bent. She ceased to dance.

"I shan't," she said. "They'll come in very useful."

He lifted his head and watched her, with lighted, dangerous eyes.

"You'll put 'em on the fire-back, I tell you," he said.

It was a war now. She bent forward, in a ballet-dancer's fashion, and put her tongue between her teeth.

"I shan't back-fire them stockings," she sang, repeating his words, "I shan't, I shan't, I shan't."

And she danced round the room doing a high kick to the tune of her words. There was a real biting indifference in her behaviour.

"We'll see whether you will or not," he said, "trollops!¹¹ You'd like Sam Adams to know you was wearing 'em, wouldn't you? That's what would please you."

"Yes, I'd like him to see how nicely they fit me, he might give me some more then."

And she looked down at her pretty legs.

He knew somehow that she *would* like Sam Adams to see how pretty her legs looked in the white stockings. It made his anger go deep, almost to hatred.

"Yer nasty trolley," he cried. "Put yer petticoats down, and stop being so foul-minded."

"I'm not foul-minded," she said. "My legs are my own. And why shouldn't Sam Adams think they're nice?"

There was a pause. He watched her with eyes glittering to a point.

"Have you been havin' owt to do with him?" he asked.

"I've just spoken to him when I've seen him," she said. "He's not as bad as you would make out."

"Isn't he?" he cried, a certain wakefulness in his voice. "Them who has anything to do wi' him is too bad for me, I tell you."

"Why, what are you frightened of him for?" she mocked.

She was rousing all his uncontrollable anger. He sat glowering. Every one of her sentences stirred him up like a red-hot iron. Soon it would be too much. And she was afraid herself; but she was neither conquered nor convinced.

A curious little grin of hate came on his face. He had a long score against her.

"What am I frightened of him for?" he repeated automatically. "What am I frightened of him for? Why, for you, you stray-running little bitch."

She flushed. The insult went deep into her, right home.

---

11. Loose women.

"Well, if you're so dull——" she said, lowering her eyelids, and speaking coldly, haughtily.

"If I'm so dull I'll break your neck the first word you speak to him," he said, tense.

"Pf!" she sneered. "Do you think I'm frightened of you?" She spoke coldly, detached.

She was frightened, for all that, white round the mouth.

His heart was getting hotter.

"You *will* be frightened of me, the next time you have anything to do with him," he said.

"Do you think *you'd* ever be told—ha!"

Her jeering scorn made him go white-hot, molten. He knew he was incoherent, scarcely responsible for what he might do. Slowly, unseeing, he rose and went out of doors, stifled, moved to kill her.

He stood leaning against the garden fence, unable either to see or hear. Below him, far off, fumed the lights of the town. He stood still, unconscious with a black storm of rage, his face lifted to the night.

Presently, still unconscious of what he was doing, he went indoors again. She stood, a small, stubborn figure with tight-pressed lips and big, sullen, childish eyes, watching him, white with fear. He went heavily across the floor and dropped into his chair.

There was a silence.

"*You're* not going to tell me everything I shall do, and everything I shan't," she broke out at last.

He lifted his head.

"I tell you *this,*" he said, low and intense. "Have anything to do with Sam Adams, and I'll break your neck."

She laughed, shrill and false.

"How I hate your word 'break your neck'," she said, with a grimace of the mouth. "It sounds so common and beastly. Can't you say something else—"

There was a dead silence.

"And besides," she said, with a queer chirrup of mocking laughter, "what do you know about anything? He sent me an amethyst brooch and a pair of pearl ear-rings."

"He what?" said Whiston, in a suddenly normal voice. His eyes were fixed on her.

"Sent me a pair of pearl ear-rings, and an amethyst brooch," she repeated, mechanically, pale to the lips.

And her big, black, childish eyes watched him, fascinated, held in her spell.

He seemed to thrust his face and his eyes forward at her, as he rose slowly and came to her. She watched transfixed in terror. Her throat made a small sound, as she tried to scream.

Then, quick as lightning, the back of his hand struck her with a crash across the mouth, and she was flung back blinded against the wall. The shock shook a queer sound out of her. And then she saw him still coming on, his eyes holding her, his fist drawn back, advancing slowly. At any instant the blow might crash into her.

Mad with terror, she raised her hands with a queer clawing movement to cover her eyes and her temples, opening her mouth in a dumb shriek. There was no sound. But the sight of her slowly arrested him. He hung before her, looking at her fixedly, as she stood crouched against the wall with open, bleeding mouth, and wide-staring eyes, and two hands clawing over her temples. And his lust to see her bleed, to break her and destroy her, rose from an old source against her. It carried him. He wanted satisfaction.

But he had seen her standing there, a piteous, horrified thing, and he turned his face aside in shame and nausea. He went and sat heavily in his chair, and a curious ease, almost like sleep, came over his brain.

She walked away from the wall towards the fire, dizzy, white to the lips, mechanically wiping her small, bleeding mouth. He sat motionless. Then, gradually, her breath began to hiss, she shook, and was sobbing silently, in grief for herself. Without looking, he saw. It made his mad desire to destroy her come back.

At length he lifted his head. His eyes were glowing again, fixed on her.

"And what did he give them you for?" he asked, in a steady, unyielding voice.

Her crying dried up in a second. She also was tense.

"They came as valentines," she replied, still not subjugated. Even if beaten.

"When, to-day?"

"The pearl ear-rings to-day—the amethyst brooch last year."

"You've had it a year?"

"Yes."

She felt that now nothing would prevent him if he rose to kill her. She could not prevent him any more. She was yielded up to him. They both trembled in the balance, unconscious.

"What have you had to do with him?" he asked, in a barren voice.

"I've not had anything to do with him," she quavered.

"You just kept 'em because they were jewellery?" he said.

A weariness came over him. What was the worth of speaking any more of it? He did not care any more. He was dreary and sick.

She began to cry again, but he took no notice. She kept wiping her mouth on her handkerchief. He could see it, the blood-mark. It made him only more sick and tired of the responsibility of it, the violence, the shame.

When she began to move about again, he raised his head once more from his dead, motionless position.

"Where are the things?" he said.

"They are upstairs," she quavered. She knew the passion had gone down in him.

"Bring them down," he said.

"I won't," she wept, with rage. "You're not going to bully me and hit me like that on the mouth."

And she sobbed again. He looked at her in contempt and compassion and in rising anger.

"Where are they?" he said.

"They're in the little drawer under the looking-glass," she sobbed.

He went slowly upstairs, struck a match, and found the trinkets. He brought them downstairs in his hand.

"These?" he said, looking at them as they lay in his palm.

She looked at them without answering. She was not interested in them any more.

He looked at the little jewels. They were pretty.

"It's none of their fault," he said to himself.

And he searched round slowly, persistently, for a box. He tied the things up and addressed them to Sam Adams. Then he went out in his slippers to post the little package.

When he came back she was still sitting crying.

"You'd better go to bed," he said.

She paid no attention. He sat by the fire. She still cried.

"I'm sleeping down here," he said. "Go you to bed."

In a few moments she lifted her tear-stained, swollen face and looked at him with eyes all forlorn and pathetic. A great flash of anguish went over his body. He went over, slowly, and very gently took her in his hands. She let herself be taken. Then as she lay against his shoulder, she sobbed aloud:

"I never meant——"

"My love—my little love——" he cried, in anguish of spirit, holding her in his arms.

Questions for Study

1. How do the everyday details of their early-morning routine serve to characterize Whiston and Elsie? In what way does Whiston suffer when he notices the rip in her sleeve and her general slovenliness? How would you describe his love for her?

2. How would you describe Elsie's love for Whiston? How does she feel about his constancy and devotion? Why does she lie to Whiston about the valentines? Why does she tell him that she has lied?

3. How do setting and social class play significant roles in the story?

4. Lawrence insists that human relationships shift and reorient themselves in each encounter according to a pattern he terms "subpersonal flux." What examples of such flux do you see in this story? Find instances in which Lawrence's language supports these examples.

5. Elsie and Whiston, and to some extent Sam Adams, are bewildered by what is happening to them. Does Lawrence use direct statement, indirect statement, or a combination of both to convey their bewilderment?

6. How are the colors red and white used in the story? How do they relate to various instances of anger in the narrative and to the cribbage game?

7. What elements of the traditional plot structure does Lawrence make use of? How does he use conflict to work out the plot structure?

8. Why does Lawrence put the party sequence second even though it happened two years before the first and the third sequences?

9. What does the story imply about relations between men and women?

William Faulkner (1897–1962)
That Evening Sun[1]

I

Monday is no different from any other weekday in Jefferson now. The streets are paved now, and the telephone and electric companies are cutting down more and more of the shade trees—the water oaks, the maples and locusts and elms—to make room for iron poles bearing clusters of bloated and ghostly and bloodless grapes, and we have a city laundry which makes the rounds on Monday morning, gathering the bundles of clothes into bright-colored, specially-made motor cars: the soiled wearing of a whole week now flees apparitionlike behind alert and irritable electric horns, with a long diminishing noise of rubber and asphalt like tearing silk, and even the Negro women who still take in white people's washing after the old custom, fetch and deliver it in automobiles.

But fifteen years ago, on Monday morning the quiet, dusty, shady streets would be full of Negro women with, balanced on their steady, turbaned heads, bundles of clothes tied up in sheets, almost as large as cotton bales, carried so without touch of hand between the kitchen door of the white house and the blackened washpot beside a cabin door in Negro Hollow.

Nancy would set her bundle on the top of her head, then upon the bundle in turn she would set the black straw sailor hat which she wore winter and summer. She was tall, with a high, sad face sunken a little where her teeth were missing. Sometimes we would go a part of the way down the lane and across the pasture with her, to watch the balanced bundle and the hat that never bobbed nor wavered, even when she walked down into the ditch and up the other side and stooped through the fence. She would go down on her hands and knees and crawl through the gap, her head rigid, uptilted, the bundle steady as a rock or a balloon, and rise to her feet again and go on.

Sometimes the husbands of the washing women would fetch and deliver the clothes, but Jesus never did that for Nancy, even before father told him to stay away from our house, even when Dilsey was sick and Nancy would come to cook for us.

And then about half the time we'd have to go down the lane to Nancy's cabin and tell her to come on and cook breakfast. We would stop at the ditch, because father told us to not have anything to do with Jesus—he was a short black man, with a razor scar down his face—and we would throw rocks at Nancy's house until she came to the door, leaning her head around it without any clothes on.

"What yawl mean, chunking my house?" Nancy said. "What you little devils mean?"

"Father says for you to come on and get breakfast," Caddy said. "Father

---

1. The title is taken from "St. Louis Blues" by W. C. Handy (1873–1958), in which a woman laments her unfaithful lover. The first three lines are: "I hate to see de evenin' sun go down./ Hate to see de evenin' sun go down,/ Cause my baby, he done lef' dis town."

says it's over a half an hour now, and you've got to come this minute.''

"I aint studying no breakfast," Nancy said. "I going to get my sleep out."

"I bet you're drunk," Jason said. "Father says you're drunk. Are you drunk, Nancy?"

"Who says I is?" Nancy said. "I got to get my sleep out. I aint studying no breakfast."

So after a while we quit chunking the cabin and went back home. When she finally came, it was too late for me to go to school. So we thought it was whisky until that day they arrested her again and they were taking her to jail and they passed Mr Stovall. He was the cashier in the bank and a deacon in the Baptist church, and Nancy began to say:

"When you going to pay me, white man? When you going to pay me, white man? It's been three times now since you paid me a cent—" Mr Stovall knocked her down, but she kept on saying, "When you going to pay me, white man? It's been three times now since—" until Mr Stovall kicked her in the mouth with his heel and the marshal caught Mr Stovall back, and Nancy lying in the street, laughing. She turned her head and spat out some blood and teeth and said, "It's been three times now since he paid me a cent."

That was how she lost her teeth, and all that day they told about Nancy and Mr Stovall, and all that night the ones that passed the jail could hear Nancy singing and yelling. They could see her hands holding to the window bars, and a lot of them stopped along the fence, listening to her and to the jailer trying to make her stop. She didn't shut up until almost daylight, when the jailer began to hear a bumping and scraping upstairs and he went up there and found Nancy hanging from the window bar. He said that it was cocaine and not whisky, because no nigger would try to commit suicide unless he was full of cocaine, because a nigger full of cocaine wasn't a nigger any longer.

The jailer cut her down and revived her; then he beat her, whipped her. She had hung herself with her dress. She had fixed it all right, but when they arrested her she didn't have on anything except a dress and so she didn't have anything to tie her hands with and she couldn't make her hands let go of the window ledge. So the jailer heard the noise and ran up there and found Nancy hanging from the window, stark naked, her belly already swelling out a little, like a little balloon.

When Dilsey was sick in her cabin and Nancy was cooking for us, we could see her apron swelling out; that was before father told Jesus to stay away from the house. Jesus was in the kitchen, sitting behind the stove, with his razor scar on his black face like a piece of dirty string. He said it was a watermelon that Nancy had under her dress.

"It never come off of your vine, though," Nancy said.

"Off of what vine?" Caddy said.

"I can cut down the vine it did come off of," Jesus said.

"What makes you want to talk like that before these chillen?" Nancy said. "Whyn't you go on to work? You done et. You want Mr Jason to catch you hanging around his kitchen, talking that way before these chillen?"

"Talking what way?" Caddy said. "What vine?"

"I cant hang around white man's kitchen," Jesus said. "But white man can hang around mine. White man can come in my house, but I cant stop him. When white man want to come in my house, I aint got no house. I cant stop him, but he cant kick me outen it. He cant do that."

Dilsey was still sick in her cabin. Father told Jesus to stay off our place. Dilsey was still sick. It was a long time. We were in the library after supper.

"Isn't Nancy through in the kitchen yet?" mother said. "It seems to me that she has had plenty of time to have finished the dishes."

"Let Quentin go and see," father said. "Go and see if Nancy is through, Quentin. Tell her she can go on home."

I went to the kitchen. Nancy was through. The dishes were put away and the fire was out. Nancy was sitting in a chair, close to the cold stove. She looked at me.

"Mother wants to know if you are through," I said.

"Yes," Nancy said. She looked at me. "I done finished." She looked at me.

"What is it?" I said. "What is it?"

"I aint nothing but a nigger," Nancy said. "It aint none of my fault."

She looked at me, sitting in the chair before the cold stove, the sailor hat on her head. I went back to the library. It was the cold stove and all, when you think of a kitchen being warm and busy and cheerful. And with a cold stove and the dishes all put away, and nobody wanting to eat at that hour.

"Is she through?" mother said.

"Yessum," I said.

"What is she doing?" mother said.

"She's not doing anything. She's through."

"I'll go and see," father said.

"Maybe she's waiting for Jesus to come and take her home," Caddy said.

"Jesus is gone," I said. Nancy told us how one morning she woke up and Jesus was gone.

"He quit me," Nancy said. "Done gone to Memphis, I reckon. Dodging them city *po*-lice for a while, I reckon."

"And a good riddance," father said. "I hope he stays there."

"Nancy's scaired of the dark," Jason said.

"So are you," Caddy said.

"I'm not," Jason said.

"Scairy cat," Caddy said.

"I'm not," Jason said.

"You, Candace!" mother said. Father came back.

"I am going to walk down the lane with Nancy," he said. "She says that Jesus is back."

"Has she seen him?" mother said.

"No. Some Negro sent her word that he was back in town. I wont be long."

"You'll leave me alone, to take Nancy home?" mother said. "Is her safety more precious to you than mine?"

"I wont be long," father said.

"You'll leave these children unprotected, with that Negro about?"

"I'm going too," Caddy said. "Let me go, father."

"What would he do with them, if he were unfortunate enough to have them?" father said.

"I want to go, too," Jason said.

"Jason!" mother said. She was speaking to father. You could tell that by the way she said the name. Like she believed that all day father had been trying to think of doing the thing she wouldn't like the most, and that she knew all the time that after a while he would think of it. I stayed quiet, because father and I both knew that mother would want him to make me stay with her if she just thought of it in time. So father didn't look at me. I was the oldest. I was nine and Caddy was seven and Jason was five.

"Nonsense," father said. "We wont be long."

Nancy had her hat on. We came to the lane. "Jesus always been good to me," Nancy said. "Whenever he had two dollars, one of them was mine." We walked in the lane. "If I can just get through the lane," Nancy said, "I be all right then."

The lane was always dark. "This is where Jason got scared on Hallowe'en," Caddy said.

"I didn't," Jason said.

"Cant Aunt Rachel do anything with him?" father said. Aunt Rachel was old. She lived in a cabin beyond Nancy's, by herself. She had white hair and she smoked a pipe in the door, all day long; she didn't work any more. They said she was Jesus' mother. Sometimes she said she was and sometimes she said she wasn't any kin to Jesus.

"Yes, you did," Caddy said. "You were scairder than Frony. You were scairder than T.P. even. Scairder than niggers."

"Cant nobody do nothing with him," Nancy said. "He say I done woke up the devil in him and aint but one thing going to lay it down again."

"Well, he's gone now," father said. "There's nothing for you to be afraid of now. And if you'd just let white men alone."

"Let what white men alone?" Caddy said. "How let them alone?"

"He aint gone nowhere," Nancy said. "I can feel him. I can feel him now, in this lane. He hearing us talk, every word, hid somewhere, waiting. I aint seen him, and I aint going to see him again but once more, with that razor in his mouth. That razor on that string down his back, inside his shirt. And then I aint going to be even surprised."

"I wasn't scaired," Jason said.

"If you'd behave yourself, you'd have kept out of this," father said. "But it's all right now. He's probably in St. Louis now. Probably got another wife by now and forgot all about you."

"If he has, I better not find out about it," Nancy said. "I'd stand there right over them, and every time he wropped her, I'd cut that arm off. I'd cut his head off and I'd slit her belly and I'd shove—"

"Hush," father said.

"Slit whose belly, Nancy?" Caddy said.

"I wasn't scaired," Jason said. "I'd walk right down this lane by myself."

"Yah," Caddy said. "You wouldn't dare to put your foot down in it if we were not here too."

II

Dilsey was still sick, so we took Nancy home every night until mother said, "How much longer is this going on? I to be left alone in this big house while you take home a frightened Negro?"

We fixed a pallet in the kitchen for Nancy. One night we waked up, hearing the sound. It was not singing and it was not crying, coming up the dark stairs.

There was a light in mother's room and we heard father going down the hall, down the back stairs, and Caddy and I went into the hall. The floor was cold. Our toes curled away from it while we listened to the sound. It was like singing and it wasn't like singing, like the sounds that Negroes make.

Then it stopped and we heard father going down the back stairs, and we went to the head of the stairs. Then the sound began again, in the stairway, not loud, and we could see Nancy's eyes halfway up the stairs, against the wall. They looked like cat's eyes do, like a big cat against the wall, watching us. When we came down the steps to where she was, she quit making the sound again, and we stood there until father came back up from the kitchen, with his pistol in his hand. He went back down with Nancy and they came back with Nancy's pallet.

We spread the pallet in our room. After the light in mother's room went off, we could see Nancy's eyes again. "Nancy," Caddy whispered, "are you asleep, Nancy?"

Nancy whispered something. It was oh or no, I dont know which. Like nobody had made it, like it came from nowhere and went nowhere, until it was like Nancy was not there at all; that I had looked so hard at her eyes on the stairs that they had got printed on my eyeballs, like the sun does when you have closed your eyes and there is no sun. "Jesus," Nancy whispered. "Jesus."

"Was it Jesus?" Caddy said. "Did he try to come into the kitchen?"

"Jesus," Nancy said. Like this: Jeeeeeeeeeeeeeeeeesus, until the sound went out, like a match or a candle does.

"It's the other Jesus she means," I said.

"Can you see us, Nancy?" Caddy whispered. "Can you see our eyes too?"

"I aint nothing but a nigger," Nancy said. "God knows. God knows."

"What did you see down there in the kitchen?" Caddy whispered. "What tried to get in?"

"God knows," Nancy said. We could see her eyes. "God knows."

Dilsey got well. She cooked dinner. "You'd better stay in bed a day or two longer," father said.

"What for?" Dilsey said. "If I had been a day later, this place would be to rack and ruin. Get on out of here now, and let me get my kitchen straight again."

Dilsey cooked supper too. And that night, just before dark, Nancy came into the kitchen.

"How do you know he's back?" Dilsey said. "You aint seen him."

"Jesus is a nigger," Jason said.

"I can feel him," Nancy said. "I can feel him laying yonder in the ditch."

"Tonight?" Dilsey said. "Is he there tonight?"

"Dilsey's a nigger too," Jason said.

"You try to eat something," Dilsey said.

"I dont want nothing," Nancy said.

"I aint a nigger," Jason said.

"Drink some coffee," Dilsey said. She poured a cup of coffee for Nancy. "Do you know he's out there tonight? How come you know it's tonight?"

"I know," Nancy said. "He's there, waiting. I know. I done lived with him too long. I know what he is fixing to do fore he know it himself."

"Drink some coffee," Dilsey said. Nancy held the cup to her mouth and blew into the cup. Her mouth pursed out like a spreading adder's, like a rubber mouth, like she had blown all the color out of her lips with blowing the coffee.

"I aint a nigger," Jason said. "Are you a nigger, Nancy?"

"I hellborn, child," Nancy said. "I wont be nothing soon. I going back where I come from soon."

III

She began to drink the coffee. While she was drinking, holding the cup in both hands, she began to make the sound again. She made the sound into the cup and the coffee splashed out onto her hands and her dress. Her eyes looked at us and she sat there, her elbows on her knees, holding the cup in both hands, looking at us across the wet cup, making the sound. "Look at Nancy," Jason said. "Nancy cant cook for us now. Dilsey's got well now."

"You hush up," Dilsey said. Nancy held the cup in both hands, looking at us, making the sound, like there were two of them: one looking at us and the other making the sound. "Whyn't you let Mr Jason telefoam the marshal?" Dilsey said. Nancy stopped then, holding the cup in her long brown hands. She tried to drink some coffee again, but it splashed out of the cup, onto her hands and her dress, and she put the cup down. Jason watched her.

"I cant swallow it," Nancy said. "I swallows but it wont go down me."

"You go down to the cabin," Dilsey said. "Frony will fix you a pallet and I'll be there soon."

"Wont no nigger stop him," Nancy said.

"I aint a nigger," Jason said. "Am I, Dilsey?"

"I reckon not," Dilsey said. She looked at Nancy. "I dont reckon so. What you going to do, then?"

Nancy looked at us. Her eyes went fast, like she was afraid there wasn't time to look, without hardly moving at all. She looked at us, at all three of us at one time. "You member that night I stayed in yawls' room?" she said. She told about how we waked up early the next morning, and played. We had to play quiet, on her pallet, until father woke up and it was time to get breakfast. "Go and ask your maw to let me stay here tonight," Nancy said. "I wont need no pallet. We can play some more."

Caddy asked mother. Jason went too. "I cant have Negroes sleeping in the bedrooms," mother said. Jason cried. He cried until mother said he couldn't have any dessert for three days if he didn't stop. Then Jason said he would stop if Dilsey would make a chocolate cake. Father was there.

"Why dont you do something about it?" mother said. "What do we have officers for?"

"Why is Nancy afraid of Jesus?" Caddy said. "Are you afraid of father, mother?"

"What could the officers do?" father said. "If Nancy hasn't seen him, how could the officers find him?"

"Then why is she afraid?" mother said.

"She says he is there. She says she knows he is there tonight."

"Yet we pay taxes," mother said. "I must wait here alone in this big house while you take a Negro woman home."

"You know that I am not lying outside with a razor," father said.

"I'll stop if Dilsey will make a chocolate cake," Jason said. Mother told us to go out and father said he didn't know if Jason would get a chocolate cake or not, but he knew what Jason was going to get in about a minute. We went back to the kitchen and told Nancy.

"Father said for you to go home and lock the door, and you'll be all right," Caddy said. "All right from what, Nancy? Is Jesus mad at you?" Nancy was holding the coffee cup in her hands again, her elbows on her knees and her hands holding the cup between her knees. She was looking into the cup. "What have you done that made Jesus mad?" Caddy said. Nancy let the cup go. It didn't break on the floor, but the coffee spilled out, and Nancy sat there with her hands still making the shape of the cup. She began to make the sound again, not loud. Not singing and not unsinging. We watched her.

"Here," Dilsey said. "You quit that, now. You get aholt of yourself. You wait here. I going to get Versh to walk home with you." Dilsey went out.

We looked at Nancy. Her shoulders kept shaking, but she quit making the sound. We watched her. "What's Jesus going to do to you?" Caddy said. "He went away."

Nancy looked at us. "We had fun that night I stayed in yawls' room, didn't we?"

"I didn't," Jason said. "I didn't have any fun."

"You were asleep in mother's room," Caddy said. "You were not there."

"Let's go down to my house and have some more fun," Nancy said.

"Mother wont let us," I said. "It's too late now."

"Dont bother her," Nancy said. "We can tell her in the morning. She wont mind."

"She wouldn't let us," I said.

"Dont ask her now," Nancy said. "Dont bother her now."

"She didn't say we couldn't go," Caddy said.

"We didn't ask," I said.

"If you go, I'll tell," Jason said.

"We'll have fun," Nancy said. "They wont mind, just to my house. I been working for yawl a long time. They won't mind."

"I'm not afraid to go," Caddy said. "Jason is the one that's afraid. He'll tell."

"I'm not," Jason said.

"Yes, you are," Caddy said. "You'll tell."

"I won't tell," Jason said. "I'm not afraid."

"Jason aint afraid to go with me," Nancy said. "Is you, Jason?"

"Jason is going to tell," Caddy said. The lane was dark. We passed the pasture gate. "I bet if something was to jump out from behind that gate, Jason would holler."

"I wouldn't," Jason said. We walked down the lane. Nancy was talking loud.

"What are you talking so loud for, Nancy?" Caddy said.

"Who; me?" Nancy said. "Listen at Quentin and Caddy and Jason saying I'm talking loud."

"You talk like there was five of us here," Caddy said. "You talk like father was here too."

"Who; me talking loud, Mr Jason?" Nancy said.

"Nancy called Jason 'Mister,'" Caddy said.

"Listen how Caddy and Quentin and Jason talk," Nancy said.

"We're not talking loud," Caddy said. "You're the one that's talking like father—"

"Hush," Nancy said; "hush, Mr Jason."

"Nancy called Jason 'Mister' aguh—"

"Hush," Nancy said. She was talking loud when we crossed the ditch and stooped through the fence where she used to stoop through with the clothes on her head. Then we came to her house. We were going fast then. She opened the door. The smell of the house was like the lamp and the smell of Nancy was like the wick, like they were waiting for one another to begin to smell. She lit the lamp and closed the door and put the bar up. Then she quit talking loud, looking at us.

"What're we going to do?" Caddy said.

"What do yawl want to do?" Nancy said.

"You said we would have some fun," Caddy said.

There was something about Nancy's house; something you could smell besides Nancy and the house. Jason smelled it, even. "I dont want to stay here," he said. "I want to go home."

"Go home, then," Caddy said.

"I dont want to go by myself," Jason said.

"We're going to have some fun," Nancy said.

"How?" Caddy said.

Nancy stood by the door. She was looking at us, only it was like she had emptied her eyes, like she had quit using them. "What do you want to do?" she said.

"Tell us a story," Caddy said. "Can you tell a story?"

"Yes," Nancy said.

"Tell it," Caddy said. We looked at Nancy. "You dont know any stories."

"Yes," Nancy said. "Yes, I do."

She came and sat in a chair before the hearth. There was a little fire there. Nancy built it up, when it was already hot inside. She built a good blaze. She told a story. She talked like her eyes looked, like her eyes watching us and her voice talking to us did not belong to her. Like she was living somewhere else, waiting somewhere else. She was outside the cabin. Her voice was inside and the shape of her, the Nancy that could stoop under a barbed wire fence with a bundle of clothes balanced on her head as though without weight, like a balloon, was there. But that was all. "And so this here queen come walking up to the ditch, where that bad man was hiding. She was walking up to the ditch, and she say, 'If I can just get past this here ditch,' was what she say . . ."

"What ditch?" Caddy said. "A ditch like that one out there? Why did a queen want to go into a ditch?"

"To get to her house," Nancy said. She looked at us. "She had to cross the ditch to get into her house quick and bar the door."

"Why did she want to go home and bar the door?" Caddy said.

IV

Nancy looked at us. She quit talking. She looked at us. Jason's legs stuck straight out of his pants where he sat on Nancy's lap. "I dont think that's a good story," he said. "I want to go home."

"Maybe we had better," Caddy said. She got up from the floor. "I bet they are looking for us right now." She went toward the door.

"No," Nancy said. "Dont open it." She got up quick and passed Caddy. She didn't touch the door, the wooden bar.

"Why not?" Caddy said.

"Come back to the lamp," Nancy said. "We'll have fun. You dont have to go."

"We ought to go," Caddy said. "Unless we have a lot of fun." She and Nancy came back to the fire, the lamp.

"I want to go home," Jason said. "I'm going to tell."

"I know another story," Nancy said. She stood close to the lamp. She looked at Caddy, like when your eyes look up at a stick balanced on your nose. She had to look down to see Caddy, but her eyes looked like that, like when you are balancing a stick.

"I wont listen to it," Jason said. "I'll bang on the floor."

"It's a good one," Nancy said. "It's better than the other one."

"What's it about?" Caddy said. Nancy was standing by the lamp. Her hand was on the lamp, against the light, long and brown.

"Your hand is on that hot globe," Caddy said. "Don't it feel hot to your hand?"

Nancy looked at her hand on the lamp chimney. She took her hand away, slow. She stood there, looking at Caddy, wringing her long hand as though it were tied to her wrist with a string.

"Let's do something else," Caddy said.

"I want to go home," Jason said.

"I got some popcorn," Nancy said. She looked at Caddy and then at Jason and then at me and then at Caddy again. "I got some popcorn."

"I don't like popcorn," Jason said. "I'd rather have candy."

Nancy looked at Jason. "You can hold the popper." She was still wringing her hand; it was long and limp and brown.

"All right," Jason said. "I'll stay a while if I can do that. Caddy cant hold it. I'll want to go home again if Caddy holds the popper."

Nancy built up the fire. "Look at Nancy putting her hands in the fire," Caddy said. "What's the matter with you, Nancy?"

"I got popcorn," Nancy said. "I got some." She took the popper from under the bed. It was broken. Jason began to cry.

"Now we cant have any popcorn," he said.

"We ought to go home, anyway," Caddy said. "Come on, Quentin."

"Wait," Nancy said; "wait. I can fix it. Dont you want to help me fix it?"

"I dont think I want any," Caddy said. "It's too late now."

"You help me, Jason," Nancy said. "Dont you want to help me?"

"No," Jason said. "I want to go home."

"Hush," Nancy said; "hush. Watch. Watch me. I can fix it so Jason can hold it and pop the corn." She got a piece of wire and fixed the popper.

"It wont hold good," Caddy said.

"Yes, it will," Nancy said. "Yawl watch. Yawl help me shell some corn."

The popcorn was under the bed too. We shelled it into the popper and Nancy helped Jason hold the popper over the fire.

"It's not popping," Jason said. "I want to go home."

"You wait," Nancy said. "It'll begin to pop. We'll have fun then." She was sitting close to the fire. The lamp was turned up so high it was beginning to smoke.

"Why dont you turn it down some?" I said.

"It's all right," Nancy said. "I'll clean it. Yawl wait. The popcorn will start in a minute."

"I dont believe it's going to start," Caddy said. "We ought to start home, anyway. They'll be worried."

"No," Nancy said. "It's going to pop. Dilsey will tell um yawl with me. I been working for yawl long time. They won't mind if yawl at my house. You wait, now. It'll start popping any minute now."

Then Jason got some smoke in his eyes and he began to cry. He dropped the popper into the fire. Nancy got a wet rag and wiped Jason's face, but he didn't stop crying.

"Hush," she said. "Hush." But he didn't hush. Caddy took the popper out of the fire.

"It's burned up," she said. "You'll have to get some more popcorn, Nancy."

"Did you put all of it in?" Nancy said.

"Yes," Caddy said. Nancy looked at Caddy. Then she took the popper and opened it and poured the cinders into her apron and began to sort the grains, her hands long and brown, and we watching her.

"Haven't you got any more?" Caddy said.

"Yes," Nancy said; "yes. Look. This here aint burnt. All we need to do is—"

"I want to go home," Jason said. "I'm going to tell."

"Hush," Caddy said. We all listened. Nancy's head was already turned toward the barred door, her eyes filled with red lamplight. "Somebody is coming," Caddy said.

Then Nancy began to make that sound again, not loud, sitting there above the fire, her long hands dangling between her knees; all of a sudden water began to come out on her face in big drops, running down her face, carrying in each one a little turning ball of firelight like a spark until it dropped off her chin. "She's not crying," I said.

"I aint crying," Nancy said. Her eyes were closed. "I aint crying. Who is it?"

"I dont know," Caddy said. She went to the door and looked out. "We've got to go now," she said. "Here comes father."

"I'm going to tell," Jason said. "Yawl made me come."

The water still ran down Nancy's face. She turned in her chair. "Listen. Tell him. Tell him we going to have fun. Tell him I take good care of yawl until in the morning. Tell him to let me come home with yawl and sleep on the floor. Tell him I wont need no pallet. We'll have fun. You member last time how we had so much fun?"

"I didn't have fun," Jason said. "You hurt me. You put smoke in my eyes. I'm going to tell."

V

Father came in. He looked at us. Nancy did not get up.

"Tell him," she said.

"Caddy made us come down here," Jason said. "I didn't want to."

Father came to the fire. Nancy looked up at him. "Cant you go to Aunt Rachel's and stay?" he said. Nancy looked up at father, her hands between her knees. "He's not here," father said. "I would have seen him. There's not a soul in sight."

"He in the ditch," Nancy said. "He waiting in the ditch yonder."

"Nonsense," father said. He looked at Nancy. "Do you know he's there?"

"I got the sign," Nancy said.

"What sign?"

"I got it. It was on the table when I come in. It was a hogbone, with blood meat still on it, laying by the lamp. He out there. When yawl walk out that door, I gone."

"Gone where, Nancy?" Caddy said.

"I'm not a tattletale," Jason said.

"Nonsense," father said.

"He out there," Nancy said. "He looking through that window this minute, waiting for yawl to go. Then I gone."

"Nonsense," father said. "Lock up your house and we'll take you on to Aunt Rachel's."

"'Twont do no good," Nancy said. She didn't look at father now, but he looked down at her, at her long, limp, moving hands. "Putting it off wont do no good."

"Then what do you want to do?" father said.

"I dont know," Nancy said. "I cant do nothing. Just put it off. And that don't do no good. I reckon it belong to me. I reckon what I going to get aint no more than mine."

"Get what?" Caddy said. "What's yours?"

"Nothing," father said. "You all must get to bed."

"Caddy made me come," Jason said.

"Go on to Aunt Rachel's," father said.

"It wont do no good," Nancy said. She sat before the fire, her elbows on her knees, her long hands between her knees. "When even your own kitchen wouldn't do no good. When even if I was sleeping on the floor in the room with your chillen, and the next morning there I am, and blood—"

"Hush," father said. "Lock the door and put out the lamp and go to bed."

"I scared of the dark," Nancy said. "I scared for it to happen in the dark."

"You mean you're going to sit right here with the lamp lighted?" father said. Then Nancy began to make the sound again, sitting before the fire, her long hands between her knees. "Ah, damnation," father said. "Come along, chillen. It's past bedtime."

"When yawl go home, I gone," Nancy said. She talked quieter now, and her face looked quiet, like her hands. "Anyway, I got my coffin money saved up with Mr. Lovelady." Mr. Lovelady was a short, dirty man who collected the Negro insurance, coming around to the cabins or the kitchens every Saturday morning, to collect fifteen cents. He and his wife lived at the hotel. One morning his wife committed suicide. They had a child, a little girl. He and the child went away. After a week or two he came back alone. We would see him going along the lanes and the back streets on Saturday mornings.

"Nonsense," father said. "You'll be the first thing I'll see in the kitchen tomorrow morning."

"You'll see what you'll see, I reckon," Nancy said. "But it will take the Lord to say what that will be."

VI

We left her sitting before the fire.

"Come and put the bar up," father said. But she didn't move. She didn't look at us again, sitting quietly there between the lamp and the fire. From some distance down the lane we could look back and see her through the open door.

"What, father?" Caddy said. "What's going to happen?"

"Nothing," father said. Jason was on father's back, so Jason was the tallest of all of us. We went down into the ditch. I looked at it, quiet. I couldn't see much where the moonlight and the shadows tangled.

"If Jesus is hid here, he can see us, cant he?" Caddy said.

"He's not there," father said. "He went away a long time ago."

"You made me come," Jason said, high; against the sky it looked like father had two heads, a little one and a big one. "I didn't want to."

We went up out of the ditch. We could still see Nancy's house and the open door, but we couldn't see Nancy now, sitting before the fire with the door open, because she was tired. "I just done got tired," she said. "I just a nigger. It aint no fault of mine."

But we could hear her, because she began just after we came up out of the ditch, the sound that was not singing and not unsinging. "Who will do our washing now, father?" I said.

"I'm not a nigger," Jason said, high and close above father's head.

"You're worse," Caddy said, "you are a tattletale. If something was to jump out, you'd be scairder than a nigger."

"I wouldn't," Jason said.

"You'd cry," Caddy said.

"Caddy," father said.

"I wouldn't!" Jason said.

"Scairy cat," Caddy said.

"Candace!" father said.

Questions for Study

1. Examine each section of the story and list what happens in each. What structural patterns are repeated? What patterns are varied or reversed? What is the effect of the structuring devices Faulkner uses here?
2. Although the first paragraph tells us that Quentin is remembering the events of the story, the narrative seems to unfold in the present. What aspects of Quentin's speech and mental process recapture the perspective of a nine-year-old boy? Why does Faulkner use this point of view? What does the author gain or lose by having his tale told from the point of view of a child who does not really understand all that is going on?
3. Figurative language plays an important role in this story. Find as many examples of similes as you can and point out how each is effective or ineffective within the narrative. Do these contribute to or detract from the impression that we are seeing events through a young boy's eyes?

4. Describe the behavior of Mr. Stovall, Mr. Lovelady, and the jailor toward Nancy. How do their attitudes toward blacks in general and Nancy in particular contribute to the story?
5. Characterization in this story is indirect. What details *show* us how frightened Nancy is? What details effectively characterize each of the other characters?
6. How does conflict in this story differ from conflict in a traditionally plotted narrative? Why does Faulkner fail to tell us what happens to Nancy? Can we guess what happens?

Chapter 9
Irony, Humor, and Paradox

Human beings have always been unsettled, bewildered, and fascinated by the discrepancy between the assumed and the actual, between expectation and fulfillment, between what is supposed to happen and what actually happens. Our everyday lives would be far less interesting if we did not occasionally come across, directly or indirectly, an incongruous situation. It might involve, for example, a respected banker embezzling $20,000 to pay off a gambling debt, an old woman riding a motorcycle, or a man biting a dog. Such situations, involving an incongruous matching of people, objects, and circumstances, may startle or even delight us. Yet these unusual events also jolt our expectations and preconceptions out of their normal pattern and give us a heightened sense of the unpredictable side of human nature.

Fiction writers employ similar situations to achieve the same effect. Flannery O'Connor, for example, in "Good Country People" shocks and upsets us when she has a Bible salesman carry a hollow Bible containing a flask of whiskey, a deck of cards, and a package of condoms. In order to portray similar absurd and inharmonious facets of human existence, writers have at their disposal a number of techniques for exposing human follies and shaping our responses to them. The three chief methods are irony, humor, and paradox.

Probably the most common method is **irony,** which expresses a disparity between what is said and what is meant, between what is presented and what actually is revealed—and thus between appearance and reality. Irony invites us to do a "double take" as we discover that what seems to be a happy event is after all sad, that what apparently is good fortune actually results in a string of bad luck, and that what is an expression of joy is really one of regret.

Essentially there are three types of irony in fiction: verbal, dramatic, and situational. Usually the simplest kind to detect is **verbal irony,** in which a character says one thing and means another. We derive pleasure from making ironic statements ourselves—exclaiming, for example, that it has been a "great day" when, in fact, we failed an exam, got a parking ticket, and lost ten dollars. Describing such a day as "great" is more effective than saying it was a disaster. Part of the effectiveness of verbal irony is inviting our listeners to see how wide is the discrepancy between the word *great* and the actually dreadful day. In this way our listeners share with us an awareness of what really happened and how we feel about it. Verbal irony is an effective device for aligning speaker and hearer, writer and reader, in a shared vision of the disparity between apparent and real meaning. When Christian Darling in "The Eighty-Yard Run" objects to Louise's coming home from her job on a fashion magazine wearing a chic hat and smelling of liquor, Shaw uses verbal irony in having Louise say that she is "the same simple little wife under the hat." And when Louise adds, with a touch of sarcasm, that she is "Homebody Number One," it is apparent she is becoming just the opposite.

Related to verbal irony is **sarcasm.** We make sarcastic remarks essentially to ridicule or to injure, as when we tell someone how nice he looks when actually his clothes are torn, his hair is filthy, and his eyes are bleary. In "Good Country People" Hulga uses sarcasm when she asks her mother to dismiss the Bible salesman: "Get rid of the salt of the earth . . . and let's eat." Neither her mother nor the salesman, however, senses the sarcasm, which echoes an earlier statement made by her mother that good country people, like the salesman, are the salt of the earth. And so Hulga shares the joke with herself.

Another form of verbal irony is **understatement,** which involves the conscious representation of something as less significant than it really is. For example, in Heinrich Böll's "Christmas Every Day," a story filled with understatement, the narrator describes the wildly manic events at his Uncle Franz's as being just slightly "out of the ordinary." Using understatement in this way actually allows the writer of fiction an opportunity to emphasize, rather than to diminish, the significance of a situation. There is, for example, a certain subtle force in a statement like, "World War III began today at 6:47 A.M.; but I was more worried about catching the train to work."

The opposite form of verbal irony is **overstatement** or **hyperbole,** which is the conscious exaggeration of something so that it is represented as more significant than it really is. In "How I Contemplated the World . . ." Oates' narrator says that "There is no weather" in the wealthy suburb in which she lives. This is her exaggerated way of saying that the area is monotonously regular and bland and cut off from the strife and turmoil of the "real" world represented by Detroit. Such a statement not only adds to the dramatic effect of the story but also indicates the narrator's frame of mind. The narrator's overstatement and Böll's understatement are forms of verbal irony since in both there is a wide discrepancy between what is said and what is really meant.

Closely related to verbal irony is ambiguity. In our everyday lives when we give directions, record experiments, or argue points, ambiguity is a major flaw. Statements that try to clarify whether one should turn left or right, add two or three parts of sodium to a chemical solution, or vote *yes* or *no* but that fail to do so are worthless. Such statements require precision and clarity. They are crippled by imprecision and ambiguity. In fiction, however, ambiguity may be a strength. Authors may consciously employ verbal **ambiguity,** or the capacity of words for suggesting several meanings at once. Ambiguity may enrich the implications of a piece of writing and illustrate the depth, intensity, and complexity of human experience.

Ambiguity in fiction may also arrest our attention and arouse our curiosity. It may enhance a short story because it compels the reader to ask questions. In ''Christmas Every Day,'' for example, Böll calls attention to the narrator's ambiguous state of mind when that character remarks: ''Fortunately—or should I say unfortunately?—this was almost the only aspect of the war that was brought home to my aunt.'' Such an admission provokes the reader's curiosity. He too wonders whether it is fortunate or unfortunate that ladies like Aunt Milla could remain oblivious to a war raging around them. Similarly, at the close of ''Astronomer's Wife'' (Chapter 10), Kay Boyle says that Mrs. Ames takes the plumber's arm ''knowing that what he said was true.'' Just before this, the plumber said that he made his cow a new cud after she lost her old one—a statement we have already rejected as untrue. Thus the word *true* applied to the plumber is startlingly ambiguous, and we now think more carefully about Mrs. Ames' statements. Ambiguity causes us to look more closely at what is said and done, as well as to consider more thoughtfully the implications of what the story actually presents.

Dramatic irony expresses a disparity between what a character says or does and what the reader understands to be true. Such irony is called ''dramatic'' because often in the theater the audience has access to knowledge that the characters on stage lack. A fine example of dramatic irony occurs at the end of ''Good Country People.'' When the malicious and conniving Bible salesman runs off with Hulga's wooden leg after her distasteful attempt to seduce him, the naive Mrs. Hopewell calls him ''so simple,'' adding that ''the world would be better off if we were all that simple.'' To this, Mrs. Freeman, equally unaware and artless, answers, ''Some can't be that simple''; ''I know I never could.'' Not only are they completely blind to the salesman's true character but they also reveal their total lack of self-awareness. Because we have been let in on the true circumstances of the situation, the force and meaning of Hulga's confrontation with the Bible salesman have an even more vivid and dramatic impact on us. Verbal irony is conscious and intended by the speaker. It invites the reader to align himself with the speaker. But with dramatic irony the speaker is unconscious of any irony. The reader is aligned with the author in understanding the discrepancies and absurdities that the characters are unaware of.

In **situational irony** there is a discrepancy between appearance and reality, between expectation and fulfillment. In Böll's story, Aunt Milla's enjoyment of "the best of health" after she has driven her family to exasperation and madness is an instance of irony of situation. Her circumstances are contrary to what we expect and think would be fair and reasonable. O'Connor's story is full of instances of situational irony. There are discrepancies between what people appear to be and actually are, as well as between what we expect to happen and what actually happens. The prime example of an ironic situation is Hulga's attempt to seduce the Bible salesman. Instead, he steals her wooden leg and leaves her stranded in the hayloft.

In fiction the writer can treat such an absurd situation best with irony, just as in life we sometimes cope with a frustrating experience better with a shrug of our shoulders than with tears. An ironic approach guards against careless overindulgence in emotions. And because it guards against the display of painful emotions, an ironic approach is often a function of point of view. In a first-person narrative such as "Christmas Every Day," for example, the narrator's understated casual tone is directly at odds with the bizarre situation. Thus the point of view itself is ironic. Similarly, a third-person objective point of view often uses its natural characteristics of detachment and restraint as a defense against a too painful disclosure of emotion. In "The Children's Campaign" and "The Capital of the World," for example, basically objective points of view are at ironic odds with basically gruesome situations. In both stories, matter-of-fact, utterly cold accounts of the deaths of children paradoxically shock us by their restraint. And when we discover that the situations are not what they first seem—when we discover that the writers' apparent detachment may indicate an actual involvement—then we are jolted out of our apathy and detachment and begin to care what happens to the characters.

Both the Lagerkvist and the Hemingway stories are deeply disturbing. The Böll story is highly comic while O'Connor's contains elements of grotesque humor. Yet all four narratives are ironic. Irony is an essentially intellectual apprehension of a discrepancy which, though serving as a safeguard against emotional indulgence, may make us either frown in horror or laugh in delight. Humor too emerges from a sense of the incongruous and checks emotional indulgence. Yet humor provokes laughter that need not be intellectualized.

It is difficult to say why some situations are funny and some are not—after all, each of us has a different "sense" of humor. But we can say that **humor** involves a reversal: something first seems incongruous and then somehow it makes sense. Humor is delight in the discovery of how appropriate the seemingly inappropriate really is. If a well-dressed snob falls in a mud puddle, we laugh—and we do so because mud on fancy clothes is inappropriate. But we also laugh because it seems fitting that a person's pretensions should be splattered in mud. If, however, a disheveled and pathetic old man falls in the mud, we probably would not laugh. We would probably feel embarrassed and sympathetic because such a fall would be neither totally unexpected nor incongruous. Without a discrepancy or a reversal of expectations, there would be no humor.

Humor emerges from a sense of the human community and its shared, collective values. People like Aunt Milla in "Christmas Every Day," who react to every situation in the same inflexible way, are funny to us. Aunt Milla's rigid belief that every night of the year is Christmas Eve is comic. Her attitude is absurd, and in itself it is relatively harmless. If it resulted in disaster, her rigidity would of course not be comic but disturbing, even tragic. To laugh we must suspend a part of our sympathy for her strange behavior, yet we do not condemn Aunt Milla. We are simply amused by her. Humor is basically tolerant and indulgent of the follies and irrationalities of human actions.

Satire, on the other hand, is not at all tolerant and indulgent. Like humor, **satire** emerges from a sense of discrepancy and incongruity. But unlike humor, satire finds the discrepancy between what is and what ought to be neither appropriate nor tolerable. Satire supposes an ideal of human behavior and exposes distortions of and departures from that ideal. It does so in the hope of correcting these situations. Whatever laughter satire provokes is usually bitter.

There is no hard-and-fast distinction between humor and satire, but they may be differentiated by their tone. Humor is pleased, satire displeased; humor is tolerant, satire critical; humor is indulgent, satire indignant; humor seeks to amuse, satire to reform. In addition, satire lacks that reversal which makes the inappropriate somehow appropriate. Finally, satire is closer to tragedy than to comedy. Although the distinctions may be blurred, it is safe to say that Böll's story is more humorous than O'Connor's; that O'Connor's is more satiric than Böll's.

Irony, ambiguity, humor, and satire first allow us to pretend that things are what they seem and then show us that they are not what they appear to be. **Paradox,** however, attempts to show us that things which seem contradictory *are* indeed the same or at least that they are intimately related. In other words, paradox shows that opposites may be joined and resolved in ways that often defy explanation. Paradox is an apparent contradiction that actually is true, though at another level or in a certain way. In O'Connor's story we find verbal paradox in such statements as "She was brilliant but she didn't have a grain of sense." Yet in its broadest implications, paradox is not just a play on words but a reconciliation of opposites on some other level. In Singer's "Gimpel the Fool," Gimpel is both a fool and a wise man. Gullible and naive nearly beyond belief, he is regarded as a fool by everyone in the story, including himself at times. Yet he is, paradoxically, wiser than anyone imagines because in his tolerance of such indignities as his wife's absurdly blatant infidelities, he recognizes the essential unreality and impermanence of what other people see as the real and permanent world. Because of his belief in an afterlife that he regards as real and infinite, such mundane problems mean little to him. And it is precisely because such things are regarded as important by others that he is thought of as a fool. He is not only a fool and a wise man, he is also a fool because of his wisdom in recognizing other levels of being. Through the use of this paradox, Singer reveals the discrepancy between the physical and the spiritual world. Writers of fiction use similar inharmonious situations to move from a familiar to an unfamiliar level of meaning which is accessible only through the technique of paradox.

Irony, humor, and paradox reveal many levels of meaning in a narrative. By being aware of these verbal techniques, we discover similarities in dissimilarities, dissimilarities in similarities. We must not read them *into* the narrative. Instead, we read them *out of* the words the author has put upon the page and the techniques he has employed. We should not read between the lines, but rather on the lines so that our readings are parallel with and appropriate to the words on the page.

Flannery O'Connor (1925–1964)
Good Country People

Besides the neutral expression that she wore when she was alone, Mrs. Freeman had two others, forward and reverse, that she used for all her human dealings. Her forward expression was steady and driving like the advance of a heavy truck. Her eyes never swerved to left or right but turned as the story turned as if they followed a yellow line down the center of it. She seldom used the other expression because it was not often necessary for her to retract a statement, but when she did, her face came to a complete stop, there was an almost imperceptible movement of her black eyes, during which they seemed to be receding, and then the observer would see that Mrs. Freeman, though she might stand there as real as several grain sacks thrown on top of each other, was no longer there in spirit. As for getting anything across to her when this was the case, Mrs. Hopewell had given it up. She might talk her head off. Mrs. Freeman could never be brought to admit herself wrong on any point. She would stand there and if she could be brought to say anything, it was something like, "Well, I wouldn't of said it was and I wouldn't of said it wasn't" or letting her gaze range over the top kitchen shelf where there was an assortment of dusty bottles, she might remark, "I see you ain't ate many of them figs you put up last summer."

They carried on their most important business in the kitchen at breakfast. Every morning Mrs. Hopewell got up at seven o'clock and lit her gas heater and Joy's. Joy was her daughter, a large blonde girl who had an artificial leg. Mrs. Hopewell thought of her as a child though she was thirty-two years old and highly educated. Joy would get up while her mother was eating and lumber into the bathroom and slam the door, and before long, Mrs. Freeman would arrive at the back door. Joy would hear her mother call, "Come on in," and then they would talk for a while in low voices that were indistinguishable in the bathroom. By the time Joy came in, they had usually finished the weather report and were on one or the other of Mrs. Freeman's daughters, Glynese or Carramae. Joy called them Glycerin and Caramel. Glynese, a redhead, was eighteen and had many admirers; Carramae, a blonde, was only fifteen but already married and pregnant. She could not keep anything on her stomach. Every morning Mrs. Freeman told Mrs. Hopewell how many times she had vomited since the last report.

Mrs. Hopewell liked to tell people that Glynese and Carramae were two of the finest girls she knew and that Mrs. Freeman was a *lady* and that she was never ashamed to take her anywhere or introduce her to anybody they might meet. Then she would tell how she had happened to hire the Freemans in the first place and how they were a godsend to her and how she had had them four years. The reason for her keeping them so long was that they were not trash. They were good country people. She had telephoned the man whose name they had given as reference and he had told her that Mr. Freeman was a good farmer but that his wife was the nosiest woman ever to walk the earth. "She's got to be into everything," the man said. "If she don't get there before the dust settles, you can bet she's dead, that's all. She'll want to know all your business. I can stand him real good," he had said, "but me nor my wife neither could have stood that woman one more minute on this place." That had put Mrs. Hopewell off for a few days.

She had hired them in the end because there were no other applicants but she had made up her mind beforehand exactly how she would handle the woman. Since she was the type who had to be into everything, then, Mrs. Hopewell had decided, she would not only let her be into everything, she would *see to it* that she was into everything—she would give her the responsibility of everything, she would put her in charge. Mrs. Hopewell had no bad qualities of her own but she was able to use other people's in such a constructive way that she had kept them four years.

Nothing is perfect. This was one of Mrs. Hopewell's favorite sayings. Another was: that is life! And still another, the most important, was: well, other people have their opinions too. She would make these statements, usually at the table, in a tone of gentle insistence as if no one held them but her, and the large hulking Joy, whose constant outrage had obliterated every expression from her face, would stare just a little to the side of her, her eyes icy blue, with the look of someone who has achieved blindness by an act of will and means to keep it.

When Mrs. Hopewell said to Mrs. Freeman that life was like that, Mrs. Freeman would say, "I always said so myself." Nothing had been arrived at by anyone that had not first been arrived at by her. She was quicker than Mr. Freeman. When Mrs. Hopewell said to her after they had been on the place a while, "You know, you're the wheel behind the wheel," and winked. Mrs. Freeman had said, "I know it. I've always been quick. It's some that are quicker than others."

"Everybody is different," Mrs. Hopewell said.

"Yes, most people is," Mrs. Freeman said.

"It takes all kinds to make the world."

"I always said it did myself."

The girl was used to this kind of dialogue for breakfast and more of it for dinner; sometimes they had it for supper too. When they had no guest they ate in the kitchen because that was easier. Mrs. Freeman always managed to arrive at some point during the meal and to watch them finish it. She would stand in the doorway if it were summer but in the winter she would stand with one elbow on top of the refrigerator and look down on them, or she would stand by the gas heater, lifting the back of her skirt slightly. Occasionally she would stand against the wall and roll her head from side to side. At no time was she in any hurry to leave. All this was very trying on Mrs. Hopewell but she was a woman of great patience. She realized that nothing is perfect and that in the Freemans she had good country people and that if, in this day and age, you get good country people, you had better hang onto them.

She had had plenty of experience with trash. Before the Freemans she had averaged one tenant family a year. The wives of these farmers were not the kind you would want to be around you for very long. Mrs. Hopewell, who had divorced her husband long ago, needed someone to walk over the fields with her; and when Joy had to be impressed for these services, her remarks were usually so ugly and her face so glum that Mrs. Hopewell would say, "If you can't come pleasantly, I don't want you at all," to which the girl, standing square and rigid-shouldered with her neck thrust slightly forward, would reply, "If you want me, here I am—LIKE I AM."

Mrs. Hopewell excused this attitude because of the leg (which had been shot off in a hunting accident when Joy was ten). It was hard for Mrs. Hopewell to realize that her child was thirty-two now and that for more than twenty years she had had only one leg. She thought of her still as a child because it tore her heart to think instead of the poor stout girl in her thirties who had never danced a step or had any *normal* good times. Her name was really Joy but as soon as she was twenty-one and away from home, she had had it legally changed. Mrs. Hopewell was certain that she had thought and thought until she had hit upon the ugliest name in any language. Then she had gone and had the beautiful name, Joy, changed without telling her mother until after she had done it. Her legal name was Hulga.

When Mrs. Hopewell thought the name, Hulga, she thought of the broad blank hull of a battleship. She would not use it. She continued to call her Joy to which the girl responded but in a purely mechanical way.

Hulga had learned to tolerate Mrs. Freeman who saved her from taking walks with her mother. Even Glynese and Carramae were useful when they occupied attention that might otherwise have been directed at her. At first she had thought she could not stand Mrs. Freeman for she had found that it was not possible to be rude to her. Mrs. Freeman would take on strange resentments and for days together she would be sullen but the source of her displeasure was always obscure; a direct attack, a positive leer, blatant ugliness to her face—these never touched her. And without warning one day, she began calling her Hulga.

She did not call her that in front of Mrs. Hopewell who would have been incensed but when she and the girl happened to be out of the house together, she would say something and add the name Hulga to the end of it, and the big spectacled Joy-Hulga would scowl and redden as if her privacy had been intruded upon. She considered the name her personal affair. She had arrived at it first purely on the basis of its ugly sound and then the full genius of its fitness had struck her. She had a vision of the name working like the ugly sweating Vulcan[1] who stayed in the furnace and to whom, presumably, the goddess had to come when called. She saw it as the name of her highest creative act. One of her major triumphs was that her mother had not been able to turn her dust into Joy, but the greater one was that she had been able to turn it herself into Hulga. However, Mrs. Freeman's relish for using the name only irritated her. It was as if Mrs. Freeman's beady steel-pointed eyes had penetrated far enough behind her face to reach some secret fact. Something about her seemed to fascinate Mrs. Freeman and then one day Hulga realized that it was the artificial leg. Mrs. Freeman had a special fondness for the details of secret infections, hidden deformities, assaults upon children. Of diseases, she preferred the lingering or incurable. Hulga had heard Mrs. Hopewell give her the details of the hunting accident, how the leg had been literally blasted off, how she had never lost consciousness. Mrs. Freeman could listen to it any time as if it had happened an hour ago.

When Hulga stumped into the kitchen in the morning (she could walk without making the awful noise but she made it—Mrs. Hopewell was certain—because it was ugly-sounding), she glanced at them and did not speak. Mrs. Hopewell would be in her red kimono with her hair tied around her head in rags. She would be sitting at the table, finishing her breakfast and Mrs. Freeman would be hanging by her elbow outward from the refrigerator, looking down at the table. Hulga always put her eggs on the stove to boil and then stood over them with her arms folded, and Mrs. Hopewell would look at her—a kind of indirect gaze divided between her and Mrs. Freeman—and would think that if she would only keep herself up a little, she wouldn't be so bad looking. There was nothing wrong with her face that a pleasant expression wouldn't help. Mrs. Hopewell said that people who looked on the bright side of things would be beautiful even if they were not.

Whenever she looked at Joy this way, she could not help but feel that it

---

1. Roman god sometimes identified with Hephaestus, who in Greek mythology was the divine blacksmith forging arms and various artifacts of metal. Although lame and ugly, he was the husband of the beautiful Aphrodite.

would have been better if the child had not taken the Ph.D. It had certainly not brought her out any and now that she had it, there was no more excuse for her to go to school again. Mrs. Hopewell thought it was nice for girls to go to school to have a good time but Joy had "gone through." Anyhow, she would not have been strong enough to go again. The doctors had told Mrs. Hopewell that with the best of care, Joy might see forty-five. She had a weak heart. Joy had made it plain that if it had not been for this condition, she would be far from these red hills and good country people. She would be in a university lecturing to people who knew what she was talking about. And Mrs. Hopewell could very well picture her there, looking like a scarecrow and lecturing to more of the same. Here she went about all day in a six-year-old skirt and a yellow sweat shirt with a faded cowboy on a horse embossed on it. She thought this was funny; Mrs. Hopewell thought it was idiotic and showed simply that she was still a child. She was brilliant but she didn't have a grain of sense. It seemed to Mrs. Hopewell that every year she grew less like other people and more like herself—bloated, rude, and squint-eyed. And she said such strange things! To her own mother she had said—without warning, without excuse, standing up in the middle of a meal with her face purple and her mouth half full—"Woman! do you ever look inside? Do you ever look inside and see what you are *not?* God!" she had cried sinking down again and staring at her plate, "Malebranche[2] was right: we are not our own light. We are not our own light!" Mrs. Hopewell had no idea to this day what brought that on. She had only made the remark, hoping Joy would take it in, that a smile never hurt anyone.

The girl had taken the Ph.D. in philosophy and this left Mrs. Hopewell at a complete loss. You could say, "My daughter is a nurse," or "My daughter is a school teacher," or even, "My daughter is a chemical engineer." You could not say, "My daughter is a philosopher." That was something that had ended with the Greeks and Romans. All day Joy sat on her neck in a deep chair, reading. Sometimes she went for walks but she didn't like dogs or cats or birds or flowers or nature or nice young men. She looked at nice young men as if she could smell their stupidity.

One day Mrs. Hopewell had picked up one of the books the girl had just put down and opening it at random, she read, "Science, on the other hand, has to assert its soberness and seriousness afresh and declare that it is concerned solely with what-is. Nothing—how can it be for science anything but a horror and a phantasm? If science is right, then one thing stands firm: science wishes to know nothing of nothing. Such is after all the strictly scientific approach to Nothing. We know it by wishing to know nothing of Nothing."[3] These words had been underlined with a blue pencil and they worked on Mrs. Hopewell like some evil incantation in gibberish. She shut the book quickly and went out of the room as if she were having a chill.

This morning when the girl came in, Mrs. Freeman was on Carramae. "She thrown up four times after supper," she said, "and was up twict in the night after three o'clock. Yesterday she didn't do nothing but ramble in the bureau drawer. All she did. Stand up there and see what she could run up on."

---

2. Nicolas Malebranche (1638–1715), French philosopher who held that the mind and the body cannot possibly interact and that human knowledge can be arrived at only through God.

3. From the essay "What Is Metaphysics?" by the German philosopher Martin Heidegger (1889–1976); its English translation first appeared in *Existence and Being* (1949).

"She's got to eat," Mrs. Hopewell muttered, sipping her coffee, while she watched Joy's back at the stove. She was wondering what the child had said to the Bible salesman. She could not imagine what kind of a conversation she could possibly have had with him.

He was a tall gaunt hatless youth who had called yesterday to sell them a Bible. He had appeared at the door, carrying a large black suitcase that weighted him so heavily on one side that he had to brace himself against the door facing. He seemed on the point of collapse but he said in a cheerful voice, "Good morning, Mrs. Cedars!" and set the suitcase down on the mat. He was not a bad-looking young man though he had on a bright blue suit and yellow socks that were not pulled up far enough. He had prominent face bones and a streak of sticky-looking brown hair falling across his forehead.

"I'm Mrs. Hopewell," she said.

"Oh!" he said, pretending to look puzzled but with his eyes sparkling, "I saw it said 'The Cedars,' on the mailbox so I thought you was Mrs. Cedars!" and he burst out in a pleasant laugh. He picked up the satchel and under cover of a pant, he fell forward into her hall. It was rather as if the suitcase had moved first, jerking him after it. "Mrs. Hopewell!" he said and grabbed her hand. "I hope you are well!" and he laughed again and then all at once his face sobered completely. He paused and gave her a straight earnest look and said, "Lady, I've come to speak of serious things."

"Well, come in," she muttered, none too pleased because her dinner was almost ready. He came into the parlor and sat down on the edge of a straight chair and put the suitcase between his feet and glanced around the room as if he were sizing her up by it. Her silver gleamed on the two sideboards; she decided he had never been in a room as elegant as this.

"Mrs. Hopewell," he began, using her name in a way that sounded almost intimate, "I know you believe in Chrustian service."

"Well yes," she murmured.

"I know," he said and paused, looking very wise with his head cocked on one side, "that you're a good woman. Friends have told me."

Mrs. Hopewell never liked to be taken for a fool. "What are you selling?" she asked.

"Bibles," the young man said and his eye raced around the room before he added, "I see you have no family Bible in your parlor, I see that is the one lack you got!"

Mrs. Hopewell could not say, "My daughter is an atheist and won't let me keep the Bible in the parlor." She said, stiffening slightly, "I keep my Bible by my bedside." This was not the truth. It was in the attic somewhere.

"Lady," he said, "the word of God ought to be in the parlor."

"Well, I think that's a matter of taste," she began. "I think . . ."

"Lady," he said, "for a Chrustian, the word of God ought to be in every room in the house besides in his heart. I know you're a Chrustian because I can see it in every line of your face."

She stood up and said, "Well, young man, I don't want to buy a Bible and I smell my dinner burning."

He didn't get up. He began to twist his hands and looking down at them, he said softly, "Well lady, I'll tell you the truth—not many people want to buy one nowadays and besides, I know I'm real simple. I don't know how to say a thing but to say it. I'm just a country boy.'' He glanced up into her unfriendly face. ''People like you don't like to fool with country people like me!''

''Why!'' she cried, ''good country people are the salt of the earth!⁴ Besides, we all have different ways of doing, it takes all kinds to make the world go 'round. That's life!''

''You said a mouthful,'' he said.

''Why, I think there aren't enough good country people in the world!'' she said, stirred. ''I think that's what's wrong with it!''

His face had brightened. ''I didn't inraduce myself,'' he said. ''I'm Manley Pointer from out in the country around Willohobie, not even from a place, just from near a place.''

''You wait a minute,'' she said. ''I have to see about my dinner.'' She went out to the kitchen and found Joy standing near the door where she had been listening.

''Get rid of the salt of the earth,'' she said, ''and let's eat.''

Mrs. Hopewell gave her a pained look and turned the heat down under the vegetables. ''*I* can't be rude to anybody,'' she murmured and went back into the parlor.

He had opened the suitcase and was sitting with a Bible on each knee. ''You might as well put those up,'' she told him. ''I don't want one.''

''I appreciate your honesty,'' he said. ''You don't see any more real honest people unless you go way out in the country.''

''I know,'' she said, ''real genuine folks!'' Through the crack in the door she heard a groan.

''I guess a lot of boys come telling you they're working their way through college,'' he said, ''but I'm not going to tell you that. Somehow,'' he said, ''I don't want to go to college. I want to devote my life to Chrustian service. See,'' he said, lowering his voice, ''I got this heart condition. I may not live long. When you know it's something wrong with you and you may not live long, well then, lady . . .'' He paused, with his mouth open, and stared at her.

He and Joy had the same condition! She knew that her eyes were filling with tears but she collected herself quickly and murmured, ''Won't you stay for dinner? We'd love to have you!'' and was sorry the instant she heard herself say it.

''Yes mam,'' he said in an abashed voice, ''I would sher love to do that!''

Joy had given him one look on being introduced to him and then throughout the meal had not glanced at him again. He had addressed several remarks to her, which she had pretended not to hear. Mrs. Hopewell could not understand deliberate rudeness, although she lived with it, and she felt she had always to overflow with hospitality to make up for Joy's lack of courtesy. She urged him to talk about himself and he did. He said he was the seventh child of twelve and that his father had been crushed under a tree when he himself was eight year old. He had been crushed very badly, in fact, almost cut in two and was practically not recognizable. His mother had got along the best she could by hard working and she had always seen that her children went to Sunday School and

---

4. From Christ's Sermon on the Mount: ''You are the salt of the earth; but if salt has lost its taste, how shall its saltness be restored? It is no longer good for anything except to be thrown out and trodden under foot by men'' (Matt. 5:13).

that they read the Bible every evening. He was now nineteen years old and he had been selling Bibles for four months. In that time he had sold seventy-seven Bibles and had the promise of two more sales. He wanted to become a missionary because he thought that was the way you could do most for people. "He who losest his life shall find it,"[5] he said simply and he was so sincere, so genuine and earnest that Mrs. Hopewell would not for the world have smiled. He prevented his peas from sliding onto the table by blocking them with a piece of bread which he later cleaned his plate with. She could see Joy observing sidewise how he handled his knife and fork and she saw too that every few minutes, the boy would dart a keen appraising glance at the girl as if he were trying to attract her attention.

After dinner Joy cleared the dishes off the table and disappeared and Mrs. Hopewell was left to talk with him. He told her again about his childhood and his father's accident and about various things that had happened to him. Every five minutes or so she would stifle a yawn. He sat for two hours until finally she told him she must go because she had an appointment in town. He packed his Bibles and thanked her and prepared to leave, but in the doorway he stopped and wrung her hand and said that not on any of his trips had he met a lady as nice as her and he asked if he could come again. She had said she would always be happy to see him.

Joy had been standing in the road, apparently looking at something in the distance, when he came down the steps toward her, bent to the side with his heavy valise. He stopped where she was standing and confronted her directly. Mrs. Hopewell could not hear what he said but she trembled to think what Joy would say to him. She could see that after a minute Joy said something and that then the boy began to speak again, making an excited gesture with his free hand. After a minute Joy said something else at which the boy began to speak once more. Then to her amazement, Mrs. Hopewell saw the two of them walk off together, toward the gate. Joy had walked all the way to the gate with him and Mrs. Hopewell could not imagine what they had said to each other, and she had not yet dared to ask.

Mrs. Freeman was insisting upon her attention. She had moved from the refrigerator to the heater so that Mrs. Hopewell had to turn and face her in order to seem to be listening. "Glynese gone out with Harvey Hill again last night," she said. "She had this sty."

"Hill," Mrs. Hopewell said absently, "is that the one who works in the garage?"

"Nome, he's the one that goes to chiropracter school," Mrs. Freeman said. "She had this sty. Been had it two days. So she says when he brought her in the other night he says, 'Lemme get rid of that sty for you,' and she says, 'How?' and he says, 'You just lay yourself down acrost the seat of that car and I'll show you.' So she done it and he popped her neck. Kept on a-popping it several times until she made him quit. This morning," Mrs. Freeman said, "she ain't got no sty. She ain't got no traces of a sty."

"I never heard of that before," Mrs. Hopewell said.

"He ast her to marry him before the Ordinary,"[6] Mrs. Freeman went on,

---

5. In several places in the New Testament are recorded Christ's words to his disciples: "He that findeth his life shall lose it; and he that loseth his life for my sake shall find it."
6. A civil judge.

"and she told him she wasn't going to be married in no *office*."

"Well, Glynese is a fine girl," Mrs. Hopewell said. "Glynese and Carramae are both fine girls."

"Carramae said when her and Lyman was married Lyman said it sure felt sacred to him. She said he said he wouldn't take five hundred dollars for being married by a preacher."

"How much would he take?" the girl asked from the stove.

"He said he wouldn't take five hundred dollars," Mrs. Freeman repeated.

"Well we all have work to do," Mrs. Hopewell said.

"Lyman said it just felt more sacred to him," Mrs. Freeman said. "The doctor wants Carramae to eat prunes. Says instead of medicine. Says them cramps is coming from pressure. You know where I think it is?"

"She'll be better in a few weeks," Mrs. Hopewell said.

"In the tube," Mrs. Freeman said. "Else she wouldn't be as sick as she is."

Hulga had cracked her two eggs into a saucer and was bringing them to the table along with a cup of coffee that she had filled too full. She sat down carefully and began to eat, meaning to keep Mrs. Freeman there by questions if for any reason she showed an inclination to leave. She could perceive her mother's eye on her. The first round-about question would be about the Bible salesman and she did not wish to bring it on. "How did he pop her neck?" she asked.

Mrs. Freeman went into a description of how he had popped her neck. She said he owned a '55 Mercury but that Glynese said she would rather marry a man with only a '36 Plymouth who would be married by a preacher. The girl asked what if he had a '32 Plymouth and Mrs. Freeman said what Glynese had said was a '36 Plymouth.

Mrs. Hopewell said there were not many girls with Glynese's common sense. She said what she admired in those girls was their common sense. She said that reminded her that they had had a nice visitor yesterday, a young man selling Bibles. "Lord," she said, "he bored me to death but he was so sincere and genuine I couldn't be rude to him. He was just good country people, you know," she said, "—just the salt of the earth."

"I seen him walk up," Mrs. Freeman said, "and then later—I seen him walk off," and Hulga could feel the slight shift in her voice, the slight insinuation, that he had not walked off alone, had he? Her face remained expressionless but the color rose into her neck and she seemed to swallow it down with the next spoonful of egg. Mrs. Freeman was looking at her as if they had a secret together.

"Well, it takes all kinds of people to make the world go 'round," Mrs. Hopewell said. "It's very good we aren't all alike."

"Some people are more alike than others," Mrs. Freeman said.

Hulga got up and stumped, with about twice the noise that was necessary, into her room and locked the door. She was to meet the Bible salesman at ten o'clock at the gate. She had thought about it half the night. She had started thinking of it as a great joke and then she had begun to see profound implications in it. She had lain in bed imagining dialogues for them that were insane on the surface but that reached below to depths that no Bible salesman would be aware of. Their conversation yesterday had been of this kind.

He had stopped in front of her and had simply stood there. His face was bony and sweaty and bright, with a little pointed nose in the center of it, and his look was different from what it had been at the dinner table. He was gazing at her with open curiosity, with fascination, like a child watching a new fantastic animal at the zoo, and he was breathing as if he had run a great distance to reach her. His gaze seemed somehow familiar but she could not think where she had been regarded with it before. For almost a minute he didn't say anything. Then on what seemed an insuck of breath, he whispered, "You ever ate a chicken that was two days old?"

The girl looked at him stonily. He might have just put this question up for consideration at the meeting of a philosophical association. "Yes," she presently replied as if she had considered it from all angles.

"It must have been mighty small!" he said triumphantly and shook all over with little nervous giggles, getting very red in the face, and subsiding finally into his gaze of complete admiration, while the girl's expression remained exactly the same.

"How old are you?" he asked softly.

She waited some time before she answered. Then in a flat voice she said, "Seventeen."

His smiles came in succession like waves breaking on the surface of a little lake. "I see you got a wooden leg," he said. "I think you're real brave. I think you're real sweet."

The girl stood blank and solid and silent.

"Walk to the gate with me," he said. "You're a brave sweet little thing and I liked you the minute I seen you walk in the door."

Hulga began to move forward.

"What's your name?" he asked, smiling down on the top of her head.

"Hulga," she said.

"Hulga," he murmured, "Hulga. Hulga. I never heard of anybody name Hulga before. You're shy, aren't you, Hulga?" he asked.

She nodded, watching his large red hand on the handle of the giant valise.

"I like girls that wear glasses," he said. "I think a lot. I'm not like these people that a serious thought don't ever enter their heads. It's because I may die."

"I may die too," she said suddenly and looked up at him. His eyes were very small and brown, glittering feverishly.

"Listen," he said, "don't you think some people was meant to meet on account of what all they got in common and all? Like they both think serious thoughts and all?" He shifted the valise to his other hand so that the hand nearest her was free. He caught hold of her elbow and shook it a little. "I don't work on Saturday," he said. "I like to walk in the woods and see what Mother Nature is wearing. O'er the hills and far away. Pic-nics and things. Couldn't we go on a pic-nic tomorrow? Say yes, Hulga," he said and gave her a dying look as if he felt his insides about to drop out of him. He had even seemed to sway slightly toward her.

During the night she had imagined that she seduced him. She imagined that the two of them walked on the place until they came to the storage barn beyond the two back fields and there, she imagined, that things came to such a pass that she very easily seduced him and that then, of course, she had to reckon with his remorse. True genius can get an idea across even to an inferior mind. She imagined that she took his remorse in hand and changed it into a deeper understanding of life. She took all his shame away and turned it into something useful.

She set off for the gate at exactly ten o'clock, escaping without drawing Mrs. Hopewell's attention. She didn't take anything to eat, forgetting that food is usually taken on a picnic. She wore a pair of slacks and a dirty white shirt, and as an afterthought, she had put some Vapex on the collar of it since she did not own any perfume. When she reached the gate no one was there.

She looked up and down the empty highway and had the furious feeling that she had been tricked, that he had only meant to make her walk to the gate after the idea of him. Then suddenly he stood up, very tall, from behind a bush on the opposite embankment. Smiling, he lifted his hat which was new and wide-brimmed. He had not worn it yesterday and she wondered if he had bought it for the occasion. It was toast-colored with a red and white band around it and was slightly too large for him. He stepped from behind the bush still carrying the black valise. He had on the same suit and the same yellow socks sucked down in his shoes from walking. He crossed the highway and said, "I knew you'd come!"

The girl wondered acidly how he had known this. She pointed to the valise and asked, "Why did you bring your Bibles?"

He took her elbow, smiling down on her as if he could not stop. "You can never tell when you'll need the word of God, Hulga," he said. She had a moment in which she doubted that this was actually happening and then they began to climb the embankment. They went down into the pasture toward the woods. The boy walked lightly by her side, bouncing on his toes. The valise did not seem to be heavy today; he even swung it. They crossed half the pasture without saying anything and then, putting his hand easily on the small of her back, he asked softly, "Where does your wooden leg join on?"

She turned an ugly red and glared at him and for an instant the boy looked abashed. "I didn't mean you no harm," he said. "I only meant you're so brave and all. I guess God takes care of you."

"No," she said, looking forward and walking fast, "I don't even believe in God."

At this he stopped and whistled. "No!" he exclaimed as if he were too astonished to say anything else.

She walked on and in a second he was bouncing at her side, fanning with his hat. "That's very unusual for a girl," he remarked, watching her out of the corner of his eye. When they reached the edge of the wood, he put his hand on her back again and drew her against him without a word and kissed her heavily.

The kiss, which had more pressure than feeling behind it, produced that extra surge of adrenalin in the girl that enables one to carry a packed trunk out of a burning house, but in her, the power went at once to the brain. Even before he released her, her mind, clear and detached and ironic anyway, was regarding him from a great distance, with amusement but with pity. She had never been kissed before and she was pleased to discover that it was an unexceptional experience and all a matter of the mind's control. Some people might enjoy drain water if they were told it was vodka. When the boy, looking expectant but uncertain, pushed her gently away, she turned and walked on, saying nothing as if such business, for her, were common enough.

He came along panting at her side, trying to help her when he saw a root that she might trip over. He caught and held back the long swaying blades of thorn vine until she had passed beyond them. She led the way and he came breathing heavily behind her. Then they came out on a sunlit hillside, sloping softly into another one a little smaller. Beyond, they could see the rusted top of the old barn where the extra hay was stored.

The hill was sprinkled with small pink weeds. "Then you ain't saved?" he asked suddenly, stopping.

The girl smiled. It was the first time she had smiled at him at all. "In my economy," she said, "I'm saved and you are damned but I told you I didn't believe in God."

Nothing seemed to destroy the boy's look of admiration. He gazed at her now as if the fantastic animal at the zoo had put its paw through the bars and given him a loving poke. She thought he looked as if he wanted to kiss her again and she walked on before he had the chance.

"Ain't there somewheres we can sit down sometime?" he murmured, his voice softening toward the end of the sentence.

"In that barn," she said.

They made for it rapidly as if it might slide away like a train. It was a large two-story barn, cool and dark inside. The boy pointed up the ladder that led into the loft and said, "It's too bad we can't go up there."

"Why can't we?" she asked.

"Yer leg," he said reverently.

The girl gave him a contemptuous look and putting both hands on the ladder, she climbed it while he stood below, apparently awestruck. She pulled herself expertly through the opening and then looked down at him and said, "Well, come on if you're coming," and he began to climb the ladder, awkwardly bringing the suitcase with him.

"We won't need the Bible," she observed.

"You never can tell," he said, panting. After he had got into the loft, he was a few seconds catching his breath. She had sat down in a pile of straw. A wide sheath of sunlight, filled with dust particles, slanted over her. She lay back against a bale, her face turned away, looking out the front opening of the barn where hay was thrown from a wagon into the loft. The two pink-speckled hillsides lay back against a dark ridge of woods. The sky was cloudless and cold blue. The boy dropped down by her side and put one arm under her and the other over her and began methodically kissing her face, making little noises like a fish. He did not remove his hat but it was pushed far enough back not to interfere. When her glasses got in his way, he took them off of her and slipped them into his pocket.

The girl at first did not return any of the kisses but presently she began to and after she had put several on his cheek, she reached his lips and remained there, kissing him again and again as if she were trying to draw all the breath out of him. His breath was clear and sweet like a child's and the kisses were sticky like a child's. He mumbled about loving her and about knowing when he first seen her that he loved her, but the mumbling was like the sleepy fretting of a child being put to sleep by his mother. Her mind, throughout this, never stopped or lost itself for a second to her feelings. "You ain't said you loved me none," he whispered finally, pulling back from her. "You got to say that."

She looked away from him off into the hollow sky and then down at a black ridge and then down farther into what appeared to be two green swelling lakes.

She didn't realize he had taken her glasses but this landscape could not seem exceptional to her for she seldom paid any close attention to her surroundings.

"You got to say it," he repeated. "You got to say you love me."

She was always careful how she committed herself. "In a sense," she began, "if you use the word loosely, you might say that. But it's not a word I use. I don't have illusions. I'm one of those people who see *through* to nothing."

The boy was frowning. "You got to say it. I said it and you got to say it," he said.

The girl looked at him almost tenderly. "You poor baby," she murmured. "It's just as well you don't understand," and she pulled him by the neck, face-down, against her. "We are all damned," she said, "but some of us have taken off our blindfolds and see that there's nothing to see. It's a kind of salvation."

The boy's astonished eyes looked blankly through the ends of her hair. "Okay," he almost whined, "but do you love me or don'tcher?"

"Yes," she said and added, "in a sense. But I must tell you something. There mustn't be anything dishonest between us." She lifted his head and looked him in the eye. "I am thirty years old," she said. "I have a number of degrees."

The boy's look was irritated but dogged. "I don't care," he said. "I don't care a thing about what all you done. I just want to know if you love me or don'tcher?" and he caught her to him and wildly planted her face with kisses until she said, "Yes, yes."

"Okay then," he said, letting her go. "Prove it."

She smiled, looking dreamily out on the shifty landscape. She had seduced him without even making up her mind to try. "How?" she asked, feeling that he should be delayed a little.

He leaned over and put his lips to her ear. "Show me where your wooden leg joins on," he whispered.

The girl uttered a sharp little cry and her face instantly drained of color. The obscenity of the suggestion was not what shocked her. As a child she had sometimes been subject to feelings of shame but education had removed the last traces of that as a good surgeon scrapes for cancer; she would no more have felt it over what he was asking than she would have believed in his Bible. But she was as sensitive about the artificial leg as a peacock about his tail. No one ever touched it but her. She took care of it as someone else would his soul, in private and almost with her own eyes turned away. "No," she said.

"I known it," he muttered, sitting up. "You're just playing me for a sucker."

"Oh no no!" she cried. "It joins on at the knee. Only at the knee. Why do you want to see it?"

The boy gave her a long penetrating look. "Because," he said, "it's what makes you different. You ain't like anybody else."

She sat staring at him. There was nothing about her face or her round freezing-blue eyes to indicate that this had moved her; but she felt as if her heart had stopped and left her mind to pump her blood. She decided that for the first time in her life she was face to face with real innocence. This boy, with an instinct that came from beyond wisdom, had touched the truth about her. When after a minute, she said in a hoarse high voice, "All right," it was like surrendering to him completely. It was like losing her own life and finding it again, miraculously, in his.

Very gently he began to roll the slack leg up. The artificial limb, in a white sock and brown flat shoe, was bound in a heavy material like canvas and ended in an ugly jointure where it was attached to the stump. The boy's face and his voice were entirely reverent as he uncovered it and said, "Now show me how to take it off and on."

She took it off for him and put it back on again and then he took it off himself, handling it as tenderly as if it were a real one. "See!" he said with a delighted child's face. "Now I can do it myself!"

"Put it back on," she said. She was thinking that she would run away with him and that every night he would take the leg off and every morning put it back on again. "Put it back on," she said.

"Not yet," he murmured, setting it on its foot out of her reach. "Leave it off for awhile. You got me instead."

She gave a little cry of alarm but he pushed her down and began to kiss her again. Without the leg she felt entirely dependent on him. Her brain seemed to have stopped thinking altogether and to be about some other function that it was not very good at. Different expressions raced back and forth over her face. Every now and then the boy, his eyes like two steel spikes, would glance behind him, where the leg stood. Finally she pushed him off and said, "Put it back on me now."

"Wait," he said. He leaned the other way and pulled the valise toward him and opened it. It had a pale blue spotted lining and there were only two Bibles in it. He took one of these out and opened the cover of it. It was hollow and contained a pocket flask of whiskey, a pack of cards, and a small blue box with printing on it. He laid these out in front of her one at a time in an evenly-spaced row, like one presenting offerings at the shrine of a goddess. He put the blue box in her hand. THIS PRODUCT TO BE USED ONLY FOR THE PREVENTION OF DISEASE, she read, and dropped it. The boy was unscrewing the top of the flask. He stopped and pointed, with a smile, to the deck of cards. It was not an ordinary deck but one with an obscene picture on the back of each card. "Take a swig," he said, offering her the bottle first. He held it in front of her, but like one mesmerized, she did not move.

Her voice when she spoke had an almost pleading sound. "Aren't you," she murmured, "aren't you just good country people?"

The boy cocked his head. He looked as if he were just beginning to understand that she might be trying to insult him. "Yeah," he said, curling his lip slightly, "but it ain't held me back none. I'm as good as you any day in the week."

"Give me my leg," she said.

He pushed it farther away with his foot. "Come on now, let's begin to have us a good time," he said coaxingly. "We ain't got to know one another good yet."

"Give me my leg!" she screamed and tried to lunge for it but he pushed her down easily.

"What's the matter with you all of a sudden?" he asked, frowning as he screwed the top on the flask and put it quickly back inside the Bible. "You just a while ago said you didn't believe in nothing. I thought you was some girl!"

Her face was almost purple. "You're a Christian!" she hissed. "You're a fine Christian! You're just like them all—say one thing and do another. You're a perfect Christian, you're . . ."

The boy's mouth was set angrily. "I hope you don't think," he said in a lofty indignant tone, "that I believe in that crap! I may sell Bibles but I know which end is up and I wasn't born yesterday and I know where I'm going!"

"Give me my leg!" she screeched. He jumped up so quickly that she barely saw him sweep the cards and the blue box back into the Bible and throw the Bible into the valise. She saw him grab the leg and then she saw it for an instant slanted forlornly across the inside of the suitcase with a Bible at either side of its opposite ends. He slammed the lid shut and snatched up the valise and swung it down the hole and then stepped through himself.

When all of him had passed but his head, he turned and regarded her with a look that no longer had any admiration in it. "I've gotten a lot of interesting things," he said. "One time I got a woman's glass eye this way. And you needn't to think you'll catch me because Pointer ain't really my name. I use a different name at every house I call at and don't stay nowhere long. And I'll tell you another thing, Hulga," he said, using the name as if he didn't think much of it, "you ain't so smart. I been believing in nothing ever since I was born!" and then the toast-colored hat disappeared down the hole and the girl was left, sitting on the straw in the dusty sunlight. When she turned her churning face toward the opening, she saw his blue figure struggling successfully over the green speckled lake.

Mrs. Hopewell and Mrs. Freeman, who were in the back pasture, digging up onions, saw him emerge a little later from the woods and head across the meadow toward the highway. "Why, that looks like that nice dull young man that tried to sell me a Bible yesterday," Mrs. Hopewell said, squinting. "He must have been selling them to the Negroes back in there. He was so simple," she said, "but I guess the world would be better off if we were all that simple."

Mrs. Freeman's gaze drove forward and just touched him before he disappeared under the hill. Then she returned her attention to the evil-smelling onion shoot she was lifting from the ground. "Some can't be that simple," she said. "I know I never could."

Questions for Study

1. Why does O'Connor begin and end the story with the two mothers? How does she characterize them? Why is Mrs. Freeman emphasized so much when she does not seem to play a very prominent part in events? How are the stories of her daughters pertinent?
2. How do names function in this story? Why did Hulga change her name?
3. How many examples of platitudes can you find in this story? Are there instances in which characters are trapped precisely because of the platitudes by which they live? Find and explain such instances.
4. What has Hulga's education taught her? Why is Mrs. Hopewell so distressed over the strange things Hulga says? Why is she unhappy because her daughter is a philosopher? Why does she shut Hulga's book and leave the room "as if she were having a chill"?
5. When Mrs. Hopewell tells the Bible salesman, "I keep my Bible at my bedside,"

there is a discrepancy between statement and truth. Is that statement therefore an example of verbal irony? Of any other kind of irony?

6. What are Hulga's intentions with the salesman? How does she react to his kiss? How does she use her mind in their meeting? What religious images are used ironically with Hulga?

7. Hulga's "smartness" has consisted of her belief in nothing. Why does the Bible salesman say, "You ain't so smart"? How does he outdo her?

8. This story abounds with both dramatic and situational irony. Point out as many examples of each as you can find. Is there also paradox in this story? Identify it.

Heinrich Böll (b. 1917)
Christmas Every Day

I

Symptoms of decline have become evident in our family. For a time we were at pains to disregard them, but now we have resolved to face the danger. I dare not, as yet, use the word breakdown, but disturbing facts are piling up at such a rate as to constitute a menace and to compel me to report things that will sound disagreeable to my contemporaries; no one, however, can dispute their reality. The minute fungi of destruction have found lodgement beneath the hard, thick crust of respectability; colonies of deadly parasites that proclaim the end of a whole tribe's irreproachable correctness. Today we must deplore our disregard of Cousin Franz, who began long ago to warn us of the dreadful consequences that would result from an event that was harmless enough in itself. So insignificant indeed was the event that the disproportion of the consequences now terrifies us. Franz warned us betimes. Unfortunately he had too little standing. He had chosen a calling that no member of the family had ever followed before, and none ever should have: he was a boxer. Melancholy even in youth and possessed by a devoutness that was always described as "pious fiddle-faddle," he early adopted ways that worried my Uncle Franz, that good, kind man. He was wont to neglect his schoolwork to a quite abnormal degree. He used to meet disreputable companions in the thickets and deserted parks of the suburbs, and there practice the rough discipline of the prize fight, with no thought for his neglected humanistic heritage. These youngsters early revealed the vices of their generation, which, as has since become abundantly evident, is really worthless. The exciting spiritual combats of earlier centuries simply did not interest them; they were far too concerned with the dubious excitements of their own. At first I thought Franz's piety in contradiction to his systematic exercises in passive and active brutality. But today I begin to suspect a connection. This is a subject I shall have to return to.

And so it was Franz who warned us in good time, who refused above all to have anything to do with certain celebrations, calling the whole thing a folly and a disgrace, and later on declined to participate in those measures that proved necessary for the continuance of what he considered evil. But, as I have said, he had too little standing to get a hearing in the family circle.

Now, to be sure, things have gone so far that we stand helpless, not knowing how to call a halt.

Franz has long since become a famous boxer, but today he rejects the praises that the family lavishes on him with the same indifference he once showed toward their criticism.

His brother, however—my Cousin Johannes, a man for whom I would at any time have walked through fire, the successful lawyer and favorite son of my Uncle—Johannes is said to have struck up relations with the Communist Party, a rumor I stubbornly refuse to believe. My Cousin Lucie, hitherto a normal woman, is said to frequent disreputable nightclubs, accompanied by her helpless husband, and to engage in dances that I can only describe as existential. Even Uncle Franz, that good, kind man, is reported to have remarked that he is weary of life, he whom the whole family considered a paragon of vitality and the very model of what we were taught to call a Christian businessman.

Doctors' bills are piling up, psychiatrists and analysts are being called in. Only my Aunt Milla, who must be considered the cause of it all, enjoys the best of health, smiling, well and cheerful, as she has been almost all her life. Her liveliness and cheerfulness are slowly beginning to get on our nerves after our very serious concern about the state of her health. For there was a crisis in her life that threatened to be serious. It is just this that I must explain.

II

In retrospect it is easy enough to determine the source of a disquieting series of events, but only now, when I regard the matter dispassionately, do the things that have been taking place in our family for almost two years appear out of the ordinary.

We might have surmised earlier that something was not quite right. Something in fact was not, and if things ever were quite right—which I doubt—events are now taking place that fill me with consternation.

For a long time Aunt Milla has been famous in our family for her delight in decorating the Christmas tree, a harmless though particularized weakness which is fairly widespread in our country. This weakness of hers was indulgently smiled at by one and all, and the resistance that Franz showed from his earliest days to this "nonsense" was treated with indignation, especially since Franz was in other respects a disturbing young man. He refused to take part in the decoration of the tree. Up to a certain point all this was taken in stride. My aunt had become accustomed to Franz's staying away from the preparations at Advent and also from the celebration itself and only putting in an appearance for the meal. It was not even mentioned.

At the risk of making myself unpopular, I must here mention a fact in defense of which I can only say that it really is a fact. In the years 1939 to 1945 we were at war. In war there is singing, shooting, oratory, fighting, starvation and death—and bombs are dropped. These are thoroughly disagreeable subjects, and I have no desire to bore my contemporaries by dwelling on them. I must only mention them because the war had an influence on the story I am about to tell. For the war registered on my aunt simply as a force that, as early as Christmas 1939, began to threaten her Christmas tree. To be sure, this tree of hers was peculiarly sensitive.

As its principal attraction my Aunt Milla's Christmas tree was furnished with glass gnomes that held cork hammers in their upraised hands. At their feet were bell-shaped anvils, and under their feet candles were fastened. When the heat rose to a certain degree, a hidden mechanism went into operation, imparting a hectic movement to the gnomes' arms; a dozen in number, they beat like mad on the bell-shaped anvils with their cork hammers, thus producing a concerted, high-pitched, elfin tinkling. And at the top of the tree stood a red-cheeked angel, dressed in silver, who at certain intervals opened his lips and whispered "Peace, peace." The mechanical secret of the angel was strictly guarded, and I only learned about it later, when as it happened I had the opportunity of admiring it almost weekly. Naturally in addition to this my aunt's Christmas tree was decorated with sugar rings, cookies, angel hair, marzipan figures and, not to be forgotten, strands of tinsel. I still remember that the proper preparation of these varied decorations cost a good deal of trouble, demanding the help of all, and the whole family on Christmas Eve was too nervous to be hungry. The mood, as people say, was simply terrible, and the one exception was my Cousin Franz, who of course had taken no part in the preparations and was the only one to enjoy the roasts, asparagus, creams and ices. If after that we came for a call on the day after Christmas and ventured the bold conjecture that the secret of the speaking angel resided in the same sort of mechanism that makes certain dolls say "Mama" or "Papa," we were simply greeted by derisive laughter.

Now it is easy to understand that in the neighborhood of falling bombs such a sensitive tree would be in great danger. There were terrible times when the gnomes pitched down from the tree, and once even the angel fell. My aunt was inconsolable. She went to endless pains to restore the tree completely after each air raid so as to preserve it at least through the Christmas holidays. But by 1940 it was out of the question. Once more at the risk of making myself unpopular I must briefly mention here that the number of air raids on our city was considerable, to say nothing of their severity. In any case my aunt's Christmas tree fell victim to the modern art of war (regulations forbid me to say anything about other victims); foreign ballistics experts temporarily extinguished it.

We all sympathized with our aunt, who was an amiable and charming woman, and pretty into the bargain. It pained us that she was compelled, after bitter struggles, endless disputes, scenes and tears, to agree to forego her tree for the duration.

Fortunately—or should I say unfortunately?—this was almost the only aspect of the war that was brought home to my aunt. The bunker my uncle built was really bombproof; in addition a car was always ready to whisk my Aunt Milla away to places where nothing was to be seen of the immediate effects of war. Everything was done to spare her the sight of the horrible ruins. My two cousins had the good fortune not to see military service in its harshest form. Johannes at once entered my uncle's firm, which played an essential part in the wholesale grocery business of our city. Besides, he suffered from gall bladder trouble. Franz on the other hand became a soldier, but he was only engaged in guarding prisoners, a post which he exploited to the extent of making himself unpopular with his military superiors by treating Russians and Poles like human beings. My Cousin Lucie was not yet married at that time and helped with the business. One afternoon a week she did voluntary war work, embroidering swastikas. But this is not the place to recite the political sins of my relations.

On the whole, then, there was no lack of money or food or reasonable safety, and my aunt's only sorrow was the absence of her tree. My Uncle Franz, that good, kind man, had for almost fifty years rendered invaluable service by purchasing oranges and lemons in tropical and subtropical countries and selling them at an appropriate profit. During the war he extended his business to less valuable fruits and to vegetables. After the war, however, the principal objects of his interest became popular once more under the name of citrus fruits and caused sharp competition in business circles. Here Uncle Franz succeeded once more in playing a decisive role by introducing the populace to a taste for vitamins and himself to a sizable fortune. He was almost seventy by that time, however, and wanted to retire and leave the business to his son-in-law. It was then that the event took place which made us smile at the time but which we now recognize as the cause of the whole affair.

My Aunt Milla began again with her Christmas tree. That was harmless in itself; even the tenacity with which she insisted that everything should be "as it used to be" only caused us to smile. At first there was really no reason to take the matter too seriously. To be sure, the war had caused much havoc which it was our duty to put right, but why—so we asked ourselves—deprive a charming old lady of this small joy?

Everyone knows how hard it was at that time to get butter and bacon. And even for my Uncle Franz, who had the best connections, it was impossible in the year 1945 to procure marzipan figures and chocolate rings. It was not until 1946 that everything could be made ready. Fortunately a complete set of gnomes and anvils as well as an angel had been preserved.

I still clearly remember the day on which we were invited. It was in January '47 and it was cold outside. But at my uncle's it was warm and there was no lack of delicacies. When the lights were turned out and the candles lighted, when the gnomes began to hammer and the angel whispered "Peace, peace," I had a vivid feeling of being restored to a time that I had assumed was gone forever.

This experience, however, though surprising was not extraordinary. The extraordinary thing was what happened three months later. My mother—it was now the middle of March—sent me over to find out whether "there was anything doing" with Uncle Franz. She needed fruit. I wandered into the neighboring quarter—the air was mild and it was twilight. Unsuspecting, I walked past the overgrown piles of ruins and the untended parks, turned in at the gate to my uncle's garden and suddenly stopped in amazement. In the evening quiet I could distinctly hear someone singing in my uncle's living room. Singing is a good old German custom, and there are lots of spring songs—but here I clearly heard:

Unto us a child is born!
The King of all creation . . .

I must admit I was confused. Slowly I approached and waited for the end of the song. The curtains were drawn and so I bent down to the keyhole. At that moment the tinkling of the gnomes' bells reached my ear, and I distinctly heard the angel whispering.

I did not have the courage to intrude, and walked slowly home. My report caused general merriment in the family, and it was not until Franz turned up and told us the details that we discovered what had happened.

In our region Christmas trees are dismantled at Candlemas[1] and are then thrown on the rubbish heap where good-for-nothing children pick them up, drag them through ashes and other debris and play all sorts of games with them. This was the time when the dreadful thing happened. On Candlemas Eve after the tree had been lighted for the last time, and Cousin Johannes began to unfasten the gnomes from their clamps, my aunt who had hitherto been so gentle set up a dreadful screaming, so loud and sudden that my cousin was startled, lost control of the swaying tree, and in an instant it was all over; there was a tinkling and ringing; gnomes and bells, anvils and angel, everything pitched down; and my aunt screamed.

She screamed for almost a week. Neurologists were summoned by telegram, psychiatrists came rushing up in taxicabs—but all of them, even the specialists, left with a shrug of the shoulders and a faint expression of dread.

No one could put an end to this shrill and maddening concert. Only the strongest drugs provided a few hours' rest, and the dose of Luminal that one can daily prescribe for a woman in her sixties without endangering her life is, alas, slight. But it is anguish to have a woman in the house screaming with all her might: on the second day the family was completely disorganized. Even the consolation of the priest, who was accustomed to attend the celebration on Holy Eve, remained unavailing: my aunt screamed.

Franz made himself particularly unpopular by advising that a regular exorcism be performed. The minister rebuked him, the family was alarmed by his medieval views, and his reputation for brutality eclipsed for several weeks his reputation as a boxer.

Meanwhile everything was tried to cure my aunt's ailment. She refused nourishment, did not speak, did not sleep; cold water was tried, hot water, foot baths, alternate cold and hot baths; the doctors searched the lexicons for the name of this complex but could not find it. And my aunt screamed. She screamed until my Uncle Franz—that really kind, good man—hit on the idea of putting up a new Christmas tree.

III

The idea was excellent, but to carry it out proved extremely hard. It was now almost the middle of February, and to find a presentable fir tree in the market at that time is naturally difficult. The whole business world has long since turned with happy alacrity to other things. Carnival time[2] is near: masks, pistols,

---

1. February 2, the feast celebrating the presentation of the infant Christ in the temple and the purification of the Virgin Mary.
2. Short period of merrymaking prior to Lent.

cowboy hats and fanciful gypsy headgear fill the shop windows where angels and angel hair, candles and mangers, were formerly on view. In the candy stores Christmas items have long since gone back to the storeroom, while fireworks now adorn the windows. Nowhere in the regular market is a fir tree to be found.

Finally an expedition of rapacious grandchildren was fitted out with pocket money and a sharp hatchet. They rode to the state forest and came back toward evening, obviously in the best of spirits, with a silver fir. But meanwhile it was discovered that four gnomes, six bell-shaped anvils and the crowning angel had been completely destroyed. The marzipan figures and the cookies had fallen victim to the rapacious grandchildren. This coming generation, too, is worthless, and if any generation was ever of any worth—which I doubt—I am slowly coming to the belief that it was the generation of our fathers.

Although there was no lack of cash or the necessary connections, it took four days more before the decorations were complete. Meanwhile my aunt screamed uninterruptedly. Messages to the German centers of the toy business, which were just then resuming operations, were dispatched by wireless, hurried telephone conversations were carried on, packages were delivered in the night by heated young postal employees, an import license from Czechoslovakia was obtained, by bribery, without delay.

These days will stand out in the chronicle of my uncle's family by reason of the extraordinary consumption of coffee, cigarettes, and nervous energy. Meanwhile my aunt fell into a decline: her round face became harsh and angular, her expression of kindliness changed to one of unalterable severity, she did not eat, she did not drink, she screamed constantly, she was attended by two nurses, and the dose of Luminal had to be increased daily.

Franz told us that the whole family was in the grip of a morbid tension when finally, on the twelfth of February, the decoration of the Christmas tree was at last completed. The candles were lighted, the curtains were drawn, my aunt was brought out from her sickroom, and in the family circle there was only the sound of sobs and giggles. My aunt's expression relaxed at the sight of the candles, and when the heat had reached the proper point and the glass gnomes began to pound like mad and finally the angel, too, whispered "Peace, peace," a beautiful smile illuminated her face. Shortly thereafter everyone began to sing "O Tannenbaum."[3] To complete the picture, they had invited the minister, whose custom it was to spend Christmas Eve at my Uncle Franz's; he, too, smiled, he too was relieved and joined in the singing.

What no test, no psychological opinion, no expert search for hidden traumas had succeeded in doing, my uncle's sympathetic heart had accomplished. This good, kind man's Christmas-tree therapy had saved the situation.

My aunt was reassured and almost—so they hoped at the time—cured. After more songs had been sung and several plates of cookies had been emptied, everyone was tired and went to bed. And, imagine my aunt slept without sedatives. The two nurses were dismissed, the doctors shrugged their shoulders, and everything seemed in order. My aunt ate again, drank again, was once more kind and amiable.

---

3. Traditional German Christmas song; literally "Fir Tree."

But the following evening at twilight, when my uncle was reading his newspaper beside his wife under the tree, she suddenly touched him gently on the arm and said: "Now we will call the children for the celebration. I think it's time." My uncle admitted to us later that he was startled, but he got up and hastily summoned his children and grandchildren and dispatched a messenger for the minister. The latter appeared, somewhat distraught and amazed; the candles were lighted, the gnomes hammered away, the angel whispered, there was singing and eating—and everything seemed in order.

Now all vegetation is subject to certain biological laws, and fir trees torn from the soil have a well-known tendency to wilt and lose their needles, especially if they are kept in a warm room, and in my uncle's house it was warm. The life of the silver fir is somewhat longer than that of the common variety, as the well-known work *Abies Vulgaris and Abies Nobilis*[4] by Doctor Hergenring has shown. But even the life of the silver fir is not unlimited. As Carnival approached it became clear that my aunt would have to be prepared for a new sorrow: the tree was rapidly losing its needles, and at the evening singing a slight frown appeared on her forehead. On the advice of a really outstanding psychologist an attempt was made in light, casual conversation to warn her of the possible end of the Christmas season, especially as the trees outside were now covered with leaves, which is generally taken as a sign of approaching spring whereas in our latitudes the word Christmas connotes wintry scenes. My resourceful uncle proposed one evening that the songs "All the birds are now assembled" and "Come Lovely May" should be sung, but at the first verse of the former such a scowl appeared on my aunt's face that the singers quickly broke off and intoned "O Tannenbaum." Three days later my cousin Johannes was instructed to undertake a quiet dismantling operation, but as soon as he stretched out his hand and took the cork hammer from one of the gnomes my aunt broke into such violent screaming that the gnome was immediately given back his implement, the candles were lighted and somewhat hastily but very loudly everyone began to sing "Silent Night."

But the nights were no longer silent; groups of singing, youthful revelers streamed through the city with trumpets and drums, everything was covered with streamers and confetti, masked children crowded the streets, fired guns, screamed, some sang as well, and a private investigation showed that there were at least sixty thousand cowboys and forty thousand gypsy princesses in our city: in short it was Carnival, a holiday that is celebrated in our neighborhood with as much enthusiasm as Christmas or even more. But my aunt seemed blind and deaf: she deplored the carnival costumes that inevitably appeared at this time in the wardrobes of our household; in a sad voice she lamented the decline of morals that caused people even at Christmas to indulge in such disgraceful practices, and when she discovered a toy balloon in Lucie's bedroom, a balloon that had, to be sure, collapsed but nevertheless clearly showed a white fool's cap painted on it, she broke into tears and besought my uncle to put an end to these unholy activities.

They were forced to realize with horror that my aunt actually believed it was still Christmas Eve. My uncle called a family council, requested consider-

---

4. Literally, *Common and Noble Fir Trees*, a nonexistent work.

ation for his wife in view of her extraordinary state of mind, and at once got together an expedition to insure that at least the evening celebration would be peacefully maintained.

While my aunt slept the decorations were taken down from the old tree and placed on a new one, and her state of health continued to be satisfactory.

Carnival, too, went by, spring came for fair; instead of "Come Lovely May" one might properly have sung "Lovely May, Thou Art Here." June arrived. Four Christmas trees had already been discarded and none of the newly summoned doctors could hold out hope of improvement. My aunt remained firm. Even that internationally famous authority, Doctor Bless, had returned to his study, shrugging his shoulders, after having pocketed an honorarium in the sum of 1365 marks,[5] thereby demonstrating once more his complete unworldliness. A few tentative attempts to put an end to the celebration or to intermit it were greeted with such outcries from my aunt that these sacrileges had to be abandoned once and for all.

The dreadful thing was that my aunt insisted that all those closest to her must be present. Among these were the minister and the grandchildren. Even the members of the family could only be compelled by extreme severity to appear punctually; with the minister it was even more difficult. For some weeks he kept it up without protest, out of consideration for his aged pensioner, but then he attempted, clearing his throat in embarrassment, to make it clear to my uncle that this could not go on. The actual celebration was short—it lasted only about thirty-eight minutes—but even this brief ceremonial, the minister maintained, could not be kept up indefinitely. He had other obligations, evening conferences with his confratres, duties connected with his cure of souls, not to mention his regular Saturday confessional. He agreed, however, to some weeks' continuance; but toward the end of May, he began energetic attempts to escape. Franz stormed about, seeking accomplices in the family for his plan to have his mother put in an institution. Everyone turned him down.

And yet difficulties continued. One evening the minister was missing and could not be located either telephonically or by messenger, and it became evident that he had simply skipped out. My uncle swore horribly and took the occasion to describe the servants of the Church in words I must decline to repeat. In this extremity one of the chaplains, a man of humble origin, was requested to help out. He did so, but behaved so abominably that it almost resulted in a catastrophe. However, one must bear in mind that it was June and therefore hot; nevertheless the curtains were drawn to give at least an illusion of wintry twilight and in addition the candles had been lighted. Then the celebration began. The chaplain had, to be sure, heard of this extraordinary event but had no proper idea of it. There was general apprehension when he was presented to my aunt as the minister's substitute. Unexpectedly she accepted this change in the program. Well then, the gnomes hammered, the angel whispered, "O Tannenbaum" was sung, then there was the eating of cookies, more singing, and suddenly the chaplain was overcome by a paroxysm of laughter. Later he admitted that it was the line ". . . in winter, too, when snow is falling" that had been too much for him to endure without laughing. He burst out with clerical

---

5. Roughly equivalent to $300.

tactlessness, left the room and was seen no more. All looked at my aunt apprehensively, but she only murmured resignedly something about "proletarians in priest's robes" and put a piece of marzipan in her mouth. We too deplored this event at this time—but today I am inclined to regard it as an outbreak of quite natural hilarity.

Here I must remark, if I am to be true to the facts, that my uncle exploited his connection with the highest Church authorities to lodge a complaint against both the minister and the chaplain. The matter was taken up with utmost correctness, proceedings were instituted on the grounds of neglect of pastoral duty, and in the first instance the two clergymen were exonerated. Further proceedings are in preparation.

Fortunately a pensioned prelate was found in the neighborhood. This charming old gentleman agreed, with amiable matter-of-factness, to hold himself in readiness daily for the evening celebration. But I am anticipating. My Uncle Franz, who was sensible enough to realize that no medical aid would be of avail and who stubbornly refused to try exorcism, was also a good enough businessman to plan economies for the long haul. First of all, by mid-June, the grandchildren's expeditions were stopped, because they proved too expensive. My resourceful Cousin Johannes, who was on good terms with all branches of the business world, discovered that Söderbaum and Company were in a position to provide fresh fir trees. For almost two years now this firm has done noble service in sparing my relations' nerves. At the end of six months Söderbaum and Company substantially reduced their charges and agreed to have the period of delivery determined most precisely by their conifer[6] specialist Doctor Alfast, so that three days before the old tree became unpresentable a new one would be delivered and could be decorated at leisure. As an additional precaution two dozen gnomes and three crowning angels were kept constantly in reserve.

To this day the candles remain a sore point. They show a disturbing tendency to melt and drip down from the tree more quickly and completely than wax, at any rate in the summer months. Every effort to preserve them by carefully concealed refrigeration has thus far come to grief, as has a series of attempts to substitute artificial decorations. The family remains, however, gratefully receptive toward any proposal that might result in reducing the costs of this continuing festival.

IV

Meanwhile the daily celebrations in my uncle's house have taken on an almost professional regularity. People assemble under the tree or around the tree. My aunt comes in, the candles are lighted, the gnomes begin to hammer and the angel whispers "Peace, peace," songs are sung, cookies are nibbled, there is a little conversation and then everyone retires, yawning and murmuring "Merry Christmas to you, too." The young people turn to the forms of diversion dictated by the season, while my good, kind Uncle Franz goes to bed when Aunt Milla does. The smoke of the candles lingers in the room, there is the mild aroma of heated fir needles and the smell of spices. The gnomes,

---

6. Evergreen tree.

slightly phosphorescent, remain motionless in the darkness, their arms raised threateningly, and the angel can be seen in his silvery robes which are obviously phosphorescent too.

Perhaps it is superfluous to state that in our whole family circle the enjoyment of the real Christmas Eve has suffered a considerable diminution: we can, if we like, admire a classical Christmas tree at our uncle's at any time—and it often happens when we are sitting on the veranda in summertime after the toil and trouble of the day, pouring my uncle's mild orange punch down our throats, that the soft tinkling of glass bells comes to us and we can see in the twilight the gnomes hammering away like spry little devils while the angel whispers "Peace, peace." And it is still disconcerting to hear my uncle in midsummer suddenly whisper to his children: "Please light the tree, Mother will be right out." Then, usually on the dot, the prelate enters, a kindly old gentleman whom we have all taken to our hearts because he plays his role so admirably, if indeed he knows that he is playing one. But no matter: he plays it, white-haired, smiling, with the violet band beneath his collar giving his appearance the final touch of distinction. And it gives one an extraordinary feeling on a mild summer evening to hear the excited cry: "The snuffer, quick, where is the snuffer?" It has even happened during severe thunderstorms that the gnomes have been suddenly impelled to lift their arms without the agency of heat and swing them wildly as though giving a special performance—a phenomenon that people have tried, rather unimaginatively, to explain by the prosaic word "electricity."

A by no means inessential aspect of this arrangement is the financial one. Even though in general our family suffers no lack of cash, such extraordinary expenses upset all calculations. For naturally, despite precautions, the breakage of gnomes, anvils, and hammers is enormous, and the delicate mechanism that causes the angel to speak requires constant care and attention and must now and again be replaced. I have, incidentally, discovered its secret: the angel is connected by a cable with a microphone in the adjoining room, in front of whose metal snout there is a constantly rotating phonograph record which, at proper intervals, whispers "Peace, peace." All these things are the more costly because they are designed for use on only a few occasions during the year, whereas with us they are subjected to daily wear and tear. I was astounded when my uncle told me one day that the gnomes actually had to be replaced every three months, and that a complete set of them cost no less than 128 marks.[7] He said he had requested an engineering friend of his to try strengthening them by a rubber covering without spoiling the beauty of the tone. This experiment was unsuccessful. The consumption of candles, butter-and-almond cookies, marzipan, the regular payments for the trees, doctor's bills and the quarterly honorarium that has to be given to the prelate, altogether, said my uncle, come to an average daily expense of 11 marks, not to mention the nervous wear and tear and other disturbances of health that began to appear in the fall of the first year. These upsets were generally ascribed, at the time, to that autumnal sensibility that is always noticeable.

The real Christmas celebration went off quite normally. Something like a sigh of relief ran through my uncle's family when other families could be seen

---

7. About $25.

gathered under Christmas trees, others too had to sing and eat butter-and-almond cookies. But the relief lasted only as long as the Christmas holidays. By the middle of January my Cousin Lucie began to suffer from a strange ailment: at the sight of Christmas trees lying on the streets and on rubbish heaps she broke into hysterical sobs. Then she had a real attack of insanity which the family tried to discount as a nervous breakdown. At a coffee party in a friend's house she struck a dish out of her hostess' hand as the latter was smilingly offering her butter-and-almond cookies. My cousin is, to be sure, what is called a temperamental woman: and so she struck the dish from her friend's hand, went up to the Christmas tree, tore it from its stand and trampled on the glass balls, the artificial mushrooms, the candles and the stars, the while emitting a continuous roar. The assembled ladies fled, including the hostess. They let Lucie rage, and stood waiting for the doctor in the vestibule, forced to give ear to the sound of crashing china within. Painful though it is for me, I must report that Lucie was taken away in a straightjacket.

Sustained hypnotic treatment checked her illness, but the actual cure proceeded very slowly. Above all, release from the evening celebration, which the doctor demanded, seemed to do her visible good; after a few days she began to brighten. At the end of ten days the doctor could risk at least talking to her about butter-and-almond cookies, although she stubbornly persisted in refusing to eat them. The doctor then struck on the inspired idea of feeding her some sour pickles and offering her salads and nourishing meat dishes. That was poor Lucie's real salvation. She laughed once more and began to interject ironic observations into the endless therapeutic interview she had with her doctor.

To be sure, the vacancy caused by her absence from the evening celebration was painful to my aunt, but it was explained to her by a circumstance that is an adequate excuse in any woman's eyes—pregnancy.

But Lucie had created what is called a precedent: she had proved that although my aunt suffered when someone was absent, she did not immediately begin to scream, and now my Cousin Johannes and his brother-in-law Carl attempted to infringe on the severe regulations, giving sickness as excuse or business appointments or some other quite transparent pretext. But here my uncle remained astonishingly inflexible: with iron severity he decreed that only in exceptional cases upon presentation of acceptable evidence could very short leaves of absence be permitted. For my aunt noticed every further dereliction at once and broke into silent but continuing tears, which gave rise to the most serious apprehensions.

At the end of four weeks Lucie, too, returned and said she was ready to take part once more in the daily ceremony, but her doctor had insisted that a jar of pickles and a platter of nourishing sandwiches should be held in readiness, since her butter-and-almond trauma had proved incurable. Thus for a time, through my uncle's unexpected severity, all breaches of discipline were suppressed.

Shortly after the first anniversary of the daily Christmas celebration, disquieting rumors began to circulate: my Cousin Johannes was said to have consulted a doctor friend of his about my aunt's life expectancy, a truly sinister rumor which throws a disturbing light on a peaceful family's evening gatherings. The doctor's opinion is said to have been crushing for Johannes. All my aunt's vital organs, which had always been sound, were in perfect condition; her father's age at the time of his death had been seventy-eight, and her mother's eighty-six. My aunt herself is sixty-two, and so there is no reason to prophesy an early passing. Still less reason, I consider, to wish for one. After this when my aunt fell ill in midsummer—the poor woman suffered from vomiting and diarrhea—it was hinted that she had been poisoned, but I expressly declare here and now that this rumor was simply the invention of evil-minded relations. The trouble was clearly shown to have been caused by an infection brought into the house by one of the grandchildren. Moreover, analyses that were made of my aunt's stools showed not the slightest traces of poison.

That same summer Johannes gave the first evidences of antisocial inclinations: he resigned from the singing circle and gave notice in writing that he planned to take no further part in the cultivation of the German song. It is only fair for me to add, however, that, despite the academic distinctions he had won, he was always an uncultivated man. For the "Virhymnia"[8] the loss of his bass voice was a serious matter.

My brother-in-law Carl began secretly to consult travel agencies. The land of his dreams had to have unusual characteristics: no fir trees must grow there and their importation must be forbidden or rendered unfeasible by a high tariff; besides—on his wife's account—the secret of preparing butter-and-almond cookies must be unknown and the singing of German Christmas songs forbidden by law. Carl declared himself ready to undertake hard physical labor.

Since then he has been able to dispense with secrecy because of a complete and very sudden change which has taken place in my uncle. This happened at such a disagreeable level that we have really had cause to be disconcerted. The sober citizen, of whom it could be said that he was as stubborn as he was good and kind, was observed performing actions that are neither more nor less than immoral and will remain so as long as the world endures. Things became known about him, testified to by witnesses, that can only be described by the word adultery. And the most dreadful thing is that he no longer denies them, but claims for himself the right to live in circumstances and in relationships that make special legislation seem justifiable. Awkwardly enough, this sudden change became evident just at the time when the second hearing of the two parish priests was called. My Uncle Franz seems to have made such a deplorable impression as a witness, as disguised plaintiff indeed, that it must be ascribed to him alone that the second hearing turned out favorably for the two priests. But in the meantime all this had become a matter of indifference to Uncle Franz: his downfall is complete, already accomplished.

He too was the first to hit upon the shocking idea of having himself represented by an actor at the evening celebration. He had found an unemployed *bon vivant*,[9] who for two weeks imitated him so admirably that not even his wife noticed the impersonation. Nor did his children notice it either. It was one of the grandchildren who, during a pause in the singing, suddenly shouted: "Grandpapa has on socks with rings," and triumphantly raised the *bon vivant*'s trouser leg. This scene must have been terrifying for the poor artist; the family, too, was upset and to avoid disaster struck up a song, as they had done

8. From *vir* ("man") and *hymnos* ("song"); hence a "male chorus."
9. One fond of good living.

so often before in critical situations. After my aunt had gone to bed, the identity of the artist was quickly established. It was the signal for almost complete collapse.

However one must bear in mind that a year and a half is a long time, and it was midsummer again, the time when participation in the play is hardest on my relations. Listless in the heat, they nibble at sand tarts and ginger cookies, smile vacantly while they crack dried-out nuts, listen to the indefatigable hammering of the gnomes and wince when the rosy-cheeked angel above their heads whispers "Peace, peace." But they carry on while, despite their summer clothing, sweat streams down their cheeks and necks and soaks their shirts. Or rather: they have carried on so far.

For the moment money plays no part—almost the reverse. People are beginning to whisper that Uncle Franz has adopted business methods, too, which can hardly be described as those of a "Christian businessman." He is determined not to allow any material lessening of the family fortune, a resolution that both calms and alarms us.

The unmasking of the *bon vivant* led to a regular mutiny, as a result of which a compromise was reached: Uncle Franz agreed to pay the expenses of a small theatrical troupe which would replace him, Johannes, my brother-in-law Carl, and Lucie, and it was further understood that one of the four would always take part in person in the evening celebration in order to keep the children in check. Up till now the prelate has not noticed this deception, which can hardly be described as pious. Aside from my aunt and the children, he is the only original figure still in the play.

An exact schedule has been worked out which, in the family circle, is known as the operational program, and thanks to the provision that one of them is always present in person, the actors too are allowed certain vacations. Meanwhile it was observed that the latter were not averse to the celebration and were glad to earn some additional money; thus it was possible to reduce their wages, since fortunately there is no lack of unemployed actors. Carl tells me that there is reason to hope that these "salaries" can be reduced still more, especially as the actors are given a meal and it is well known that art becomes cheaper when food is involved.

I have already briefly mentioned Lucie's unhappy history: now she spends almost all her time in night spots and, on those days when she is compelled to take part in the household celebration, she is beside herself. She wears corduroy britches, colored pullovers, runs around in sandals and she has cut off her splendid hair in order to wear unbecoming bangs and a coiffure that I only recently discovered was once considered modern—it is known as a pony-tail. Although I have so far been unable to observe any overt immorality on her part, but only a kind of exultation, which she herself describes as existentialism, nevertheless I cannot regard this development as desirable; I prefer quiet women, who move decorously to the rhythm of the waltz, know how to recite agreeable verses and whose nourishment is not exclusively sour pickles and goulash seasoned with paprika. My brother-in-law Carl's plans to emigrate seem on the point of becoming a reality: he has found a country, not far from the equator, which seems to answer his requirements, and Lucie is full of enthusiasm; in this country people wear clothes not unlike hers, they love sharp spices and they dance to those rhythms without which she maintains life is no longer possible for her. It is a little shocking that these two do not plan to obey the command "Abide in the land I have given you,"[10] but on the other hand I can understand their desire to flee.

Things are worse with Johannes. Unfortunately the evil rumor has proved true: he has become a Communist. He has broken off all relations with the family, pays no attention to anything and takes part in the evening celebration only in the person of his double. His eyes have taken on a fanatical expression, he makes public appearances behaving like a dervish at party meetings, neglects his practice and writes furious articles in the appropriate journals. Strangely enough he now sees more of Franz, who is vainly trying to convert him—and vice versa. Despite all their spiritual estrangement, they seem personally to have grown somewhat closer.

Franz I have not seen in a long time, but I have had news of him. He is said to have fallen into a profound depression, to spend his time in dim churches, and I believe that his piety can be fairly described as exaggerated. After the family misfortunes began he started to neglect his calling, and recently I saw on the wall of a ruined house a faded poster saying: "Last Battle of our Veteran Lenz against Lecoq. Lenz is Hanging up the Gloves." The date on the poster was March, and now we are well into August. Franz is said to have fallen on bad times. I believe he finds himself in a situation which has never before occurred in our family: he is poor. Fortunately he has remained single, and so the social consequences of his irresponsible piety harm only him. He has tried with amazing perseverance to have a guardian appointed for Lucie's children because he considers they are endangered by the daily celebration. But his efforts have remained fruitless; thank God, the children of wealthy people are not exposed to the interference of social institutions.

The one least removed from the rest of the family circle is, for all his deplorable actions, Uncle Franz. To be sure, despite his advanced years, he has a mistress. And his business practices, too, are of a sort that we admire, to be sure, but cannot at all approve. Recently he has appointed an unemployed stage manager to supervise the evening celebration and see that everything runs like clockwork. Everything does in fact run like clockwork.

V

Almost two years have now gone by—a long time. And I could not resist the temptation, during one of my evening strolls, to stop in at my uncle's house, where no true hospitality is any longer possible, since strange actors wander about every evening and the members of the family have devoted themselves to reprehensible pleasures. It was a mild summer evening, and as I turned into the avenue of chestnut trees I heard the verse:

---

10. In Deut. 3:18–19, Moses says: "And I commanded you at that time, saying, The Lord your God hath given you this land to possess it: ye shall pass over armed before your brethren the children of Israel, all that are meet for the war. But your wives, and your little ones, and your cattle, (for I know that ye have much cattle), shall abide in your cities which I have given you." In Jer. 42:10, God's answer to the Israelites is reported: "If ye will still abide in this land, then will I build you, and not pull you down, and I will plant you, and not pluck you up; for I repent me of the evil that I have done unto you."

The wintry woods are clad in snow . . .

A passing truck made the rest inaudible. Slowly and softly I approached the house and looked through a crack in the curtains. The similarity of the actors who were present to those of my relations whom they represented was so startling that for an instant I could not recognize which one this evening was the superintendent, as they called him. I could not see the gnomes but I could hear them. Their chirping tinkle has a wave length that can penetrate any wall. The whispering of the angel was inaudible. My aunt seemed to be really happy: she was chatting with the prelate, and it was only later that I recognized my brother-in-law as the one real person present—if that is the right word. I recognized him by the way he rounded and pointed his lips as he blew out a match. Apparently there are unchangeable individual traits. This led me to reflect that the actors, too, were obviously treated to cigars and wine—in addition there was asparagus every evening. If their appetites were shameless—and what artist's is not?—this meant a considerable additional expense for my uncle. The children were playing with dolls and wooden wagons in a corner of the room. They looked pale and tired. Perhaps one really ought to have some consideration for them. I was struck by the idea that they might perhaps be replaced by wax dolls of the kind one sees in the windows of drugstores as advertisements for powdered milk and skin lotions. It seems to me those look quite natural.

As a matter of fact I intend to call the family's attention to the possible effect on the children's temperament of this unnatural daily excitement. Although a certain amount of discipline does no harm, it seems to me that they are being subjected to excessive demands.

I left my observation post when the people inside began to sing: "Silent Night." I simply could not bear the song. The air was so mild—and for an instant I had the feeling that I was watching an assembly of ghosts. Suddenly I had a craving for sour pickles and this gave me some inkling of how very much Lucie must have suffered.

I have now succeeded in having the children replaced by wax dolls. Their procurement was costly—Uncle Franz hesitated for some time—but one really could not go on irresponsibly feeding the children on marzipan every day and making them sing songs which in the long run might cause them psychic injury. The procurement of the dolls proved to be useful because Carl and Lucie really emigrated and Johannes also withdrew his children from his father's household. I bade farewell to Carl and Lucie and the children as they stood amid large traveling trunks. They seemed happy, if a little worried. Johannes, too, has left our town. Somewhere or other he is engaged in reorganizing a Communist cell.

Uncle Franz is weary of life. Recently he complained to me that people are always forgetting to dust off the dolls. His servants in particular cause him difficulties, and the actors seem inclined to be undisciplined. They drink more than they ought, and some of them have been caught filling their pockets with cigars and cigarettes. I advised my uncle to provide them with colored water and cardboard cigars.

The only reliable ones are my aunt and the prelate. They chat together about the good old times, giggle and seem to enjoy themselves, interrupting their conversation only when a song is struck up.

In any event, the celebration goes on.

My cousin Franz has taken an amazing step. He has been accepted as a lay brother in a nearby monastery. When I saw him for the first time in a cowl I was startled: that large figure, with broken nose, thickened lips and melancholy expression, reminded me more of a prisoner than a monk. He seemed almost to have read my thoughts. "Life is a prison sentence," he said softly. I followed him into the interview room. We conversed haltingly, and he was obviously relieved when the bell summoned him to the chapel for prayers. I remained behind, thoughtful, as he departed: he went in a great hurry, and his haste seemed genuine.

Questions for Study

1. Describe the time and place of the story. How does setting function in it?
2. What is the point of view of the story? How involved is the narrator? Why is the choice of point of view appropriate?
3. Describe the significance of the Christmas tree. Explain your reaction to it and to the "red-cheeked angel, dressed in silver," who says, "Peace, peace."
4. Point out at least three instances of irony in the story. Explain the implications of the title itself as an example of irony. What is the effect of Böll's use of irony?
5. Is irony always humorous here? Describe the story's humor.
6. Characterize Aunt Milla. Is she a dynamic or a static character? What is her role in the story?
7. What parts of the story are realistic? What ones are fantastic? How and why does Böll mix realism and fantasy?
8. On one level, the story suggests a great deal about Nazi Germany and the behavior of the German people in the years before the outbreak of World War II. How does Böll seem to feel about this situation? How does the narrator feel? What does the story suggest about the causes of war?

Chapter 10
Symbol and Allegory

Before beginning a discussion of literary symbolism we should recognize that symbols are not unique to literature. They are familiar staples of our everyday lives. Religious, patriotic, advertising, graphic, and instructional symbols offer a kind of shorthand to living: a diploma is a symbol of a certain kind of achievement; a uniform represents a specific profession; Santa Claus signifies the spirit of Christmas giving; a siren usually indicates a warning or danger. Even clothes, cars, and houses function not only as things but also as symbols of economic and social status. Indeed, our very language permits us to talk or write about people, objects, and concepts because words symbolize these things and represent them in their absence.

In our everyday world symbols are all around us. We may use them to simplify our lives—crosses can tell us which buildings are churches; wedding rings can tell us which people are married. Symbols also function in richer and more significant ways—crosses not only suggest much about Christ's death, redemption, and resurrection but also stand for the entire body of Christian doctrine; wedding rings suggest much about love, commitment, unity, and permanence. In literature symbols function in much the same ways, except that a writer is usually more conscious of how a particular symbol will achieve a certain effect. A **symbol** in literature is a concrete element which suggests a range of meanings and associations in rich, deep, and suggestive ways. If a writer can use snow, for example, to suggest a whole complex of associations such as cold, ice, frigidity, sleep, peacefulness, innocence, and death, the snow no longer just means frozen, wet, white stuff. It is a symbol of all these many associations. Using snow as a symbol rather than explicitly describing these associations is economical, evocative, and also effective because we respond to representations of snow much more immediately than to the idea of innocence, for example. Symbols expand and intensify the reach of art while at the same time they compress its materials.

Symbols may be roughly categorized as conventional, literary, or natural. The **conventional symbol** has its meaning established by a particular tradition and is acknowledged among people familiar with a particular culture. Flags and uniforms are such symbols because they refer to something larger than themselves whose identity is established by convention. Flannery O'Connor employs the Bible in "Good Country People" as a symbol for the entire body of Christian belief, which she expects her readers to be somewhat familiar with. Similarly, Christmas in Böll's "Christmas Every Day" is a conventional symbol, representing a time of great joy and holiday festivities.

The second type of symbol is the **literary symbol** whose meaning is located in or defined by the work in which it appears. Although its meaning is limited to a particular story, a literary symbol usually pervades the narrative so thoroughly that its association can often be readily perceived. In itself, a white stocking, for example, symbolizes little or nothing. It is not a conventional symbol in the same sense that the Bible or Christmas are. And it is hardly a universal symbol. In Lawrence's story, however, a white stocking has symbolic meaning central to the theme of the narrative: the love-hate relationship between Whiston and Elsie. In Kay Boyle's "Astronomer's Wife," plumbing—an even more unlikely candidate for symbolic treatment—represents the life of the human body. Outside the context of these two stories, white stockings and plumbing signify almost nothing other than themselves. Within these stories, however, the authors have skillfully used them to convey some rather complex emotions and abstract ideas.

The third type of symbol carries meanings which belong not to a particular civilization or to a particular work of literature but which seem to be shared by the whole human race. Such a **natural symbol** appears to elicit similar responses wherever it appears. Swiss psychiatrist and philosopher Carl Gustav Jung (1875–1961) described such symbols as "natural and spontaneous products," since as he believed: "No genius has ever sat down with a pen or a brush in his hand and said: 'Now I am going to invent a symbol.'" To Jung these natural symbols are the only true symbols. The meanings that snow carries, for example, cannot be invented by a particular author. Nor could Kay Boyle in "Astronomer's Wife" avoid certain associations for earth and sky—the earth suggests the body; the sky, the mind.

One literary device used in much the same way as a conventional symbol is **allusion,** or a reference to another source with which the reader is usually expected to be familiar. Allusions most often refer to figures and events in the Bible, in mythology, in history, and in other works of literature. For example, in "The Secret Miracle" (in "Stories for Further Study''), Jorge Luis Borges alludes to such things as the Koran, the Third Reich, the *Sepher Yezirah,* and to such men as Jakob Böhme, Maimonides, and Vergil. These allusions extend and enrich Borges' story, and readers need to be familiar with or to look up such references in order to understand fully their significance in the narrative. Like a symbol, an allusion stands for itself but also carries additional implications within the context in which it appears.

It is convenient to arrange symbols into the three classifications discussed above, but we need to remind ourselves that these divisions are far from absolute and exclusive. A star, for example, may have symbolic associations decreed by a particular organization, country, religion, or work of literature. Yet stars can also be seen as natural symbols for human dreams and longings.

In searching for the associations suggested by a symbol, we must remember that we first encounter the concrete thing itself. A symbol in literature is first of all itself, then something else besides. In other words, a sunrise may symbolize a great many ideas and qualities and experiences, but it also stands for a real sunrise in a particular work. "Astronomer's Wife" is vastly enriched because the toilet bowl and the pipes become associated with larger concepts and even come to represent those concepts. Yet the toilet bowl and the pipes still stand for actual plumbing equipment in the story. In Richard Brautigan's "Homage to the San Francisco YMCA," however, a toilet bowl, sink, tub, and pipes function less as real and literal bathroom equipment than as representations of ideas. Thus we may characterize Brautigan's story as more allegorical than symbolic.

In **allegory** objects and characters are less important in themselves than as concrete illustrations of abstract ideas whose meaning is not as open-ended as that of a symbol. Allegory conveys meaning by using concrete objects, characters, and events to stand for abstract ideas, qualities, and concepts. If, for example, we read about a character named Everyman who is approached by a man named Death and who later meets other characters with such names as Fellowship, Good Deeds, and Knowledge, we know immediately that the piece is a straightforward allegory. Clearly the method employed is the presentation of the qualities and ideas embodied in these characters rather than the development of their personalities. We are unlikely to encounter this form of allegory in modern fiction. Modern narratives prefer to use allegory or allegorical patterns as possible subelements or implied extensions of a work which stresses character development and detailed actions. In "Good Country People," for example, characters with such suggestively allegorical names as Mrs. Hopewell, Hulga (originally named Joy), and Manley Pointer are not simply one-dimensional figures who embody a single abstract quality or concept. Rather the personality and actions of these characters are more extensively developed and complex than their names imply.

In allegory there are two separate but important levels of meaning: one concrete, one abstract; one on the surface, one independent of the surface. A symbol, on the one hand, exists on many different planes and suggests multiple meanings that cluster about an object. In allegory, on the other hand, the two levels of meaning are overlaid separately, one upon the other. Perhaps the two diagrams below will help to clarify the difference between symbol and allegory. In "Astronomer's Wife" earth carries many implications on various levels best represented in this manner:

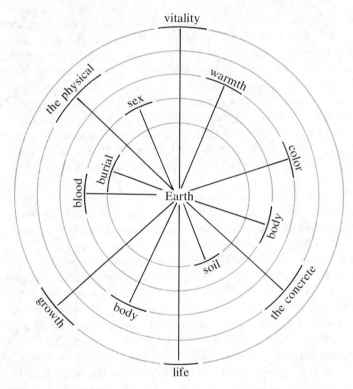

In allegory, by contrast, objects exist on essentially only two levels:

Concrete   pipes (in "Homage")   bread (in "Beggar My Neighbor")

⇕   ⇕

Abstract   practical necessities   basic sustenance

Furthermore, allegory presents a connected, interrelated pattern of events which correlate on a one-to-one basis with abstract ideas and meanings. For example, "Beggar My Neighbor" depicts, on the concrete level, the white boy Michael giving bread to the black African children and his smug sense of generosity. On the abstract level, this act represents white colonialists everywhere who bring what they consider basic necessities to the native people. On the concrete level, Michael's gift of a flashlight to the children becomes an exercise of his power over them. On the abstract level it represents the colonialists' token attempts to grant the natives limited power and enlightenment. On the concrete level, Michael's refusal to give the children the pen-and-pencil set indicates his abuse of power; on the abstract level this act signifies the colonialists' refusal to grant the natives true power and independence.

The meaning of many narratives can be uncovered by dual-level allegorical statements such as these. Jacobson's story invites such an interpretation, but Brautigan's demands it because it makes no sense on its literal level. We are invited to make an allegorical interpretation of a story anytime the narrative technique seems less particular and actual and more representational and abstract. Mrs. Ames in "Astronomer's Wife" is representative of neglected and unappreciated women, and Michael in "Beggar My Neighbor" is representative of people in power. Because the method of characterization suggests representative types, these stories are overlaid with possible allegorical meanings that point to what may happen to anyone in similar circumstances.

One word of caution is needed, however, lest we turn every object into a symbol, every narrative into an allegory. We should remember that representative figures in an allegory must be typical and that symbols in a story are first of all concrete. An interpretation of allegorical meanings or symbols must fit the story *as a whole,* not merely some part of it that we may fancy is allegorical or symbolic. Sunrise, for example, usually suggests rebirth, but in one story it might be associated consistently with pain and anguish, in another story with renewal and joy. Our interpretation would have to take into account these associations. Symbolic objects ultimately represent something different from themselves; a door *is* a door, but it might symbolize opportunity or temptation, escape or entrapment, depending upon how it is used in the story. Finally, we should take care that we understand that symbols function to intensify the narrative, not to exhibit the author's (or the reader's) cleverness. Our understanding of symbols and allegory helps uncover, rather than obscure, the meaning of a narrative. An author may inform the breadth, weight, and force of his implications with symbolic and allegorical patterns which the reader may uncover. Yet an effective short story ultimately consists of well-drawn characters whose specific actions occur in a particular time and place.

Kay Boyle (b. 1903)
Astronomer's Wife

There is an evil moment on awakening when all things seem to pause. But for women, they only falter and may be set in action by a single move: a lifted hand and the pendulum will swing, or the voice raised and through every room the pulse takes up its beating. The astronomer's wife felt the interval gaping and at once filled it to the brim. She fetched up her gentle voice and sent it warily down the stairs for coffee, swung her feet out upon the oval mat, and hailed the morning with her bare arms' quivering flesh drawn taut in rhythmic exercise: left, left, left my wife and fourteen children, right, right, right in the middle of the dusty road.

The day would proceed from this, beat by beat, without reflection, like every other day. The astronomer was still asleep, or feigning it, and she, once out of bed, had come into her own possession. Although scarcely ever out of sight of the impenetrable silence of his brow, she would be absent from him all the day in being clean, busy, kind. He was a man of other things, a dreamer. At times he lay still for hours, at others he sat upon the roof behind his telescope, or wandered down the pathway to the road and out across the mountains. This day, like any other, would go on from the removal of the spot left there from dinner on the astronomer's vest to the severe thrashing of the mayonnaise for lunch. That man might be each time the new arching wave, and woman the undertow that sucked him back, were things she had been told by his silence were so.

In spite of the earliness of the hour, the girl had heard her mistress's voice and was coming up the stairs. At the threshold of the bedroom she paused, and said: "Madame, the plumber is here."

The astronomer's wife put on her white and scarlet smock very quickly and buttoned it at the neck. Then she stepped carefully around the motionless spread of water in the hall.

"Tell him to come right up," she said. She laid her hands on the bannisters and stood looking down the wooden stairway. "Ah, I am Mrs. Ames," she said softly as she saw him mounting. "I am Mrs. Ames," she said softly, softly down the flight of stairs. "I am Mrs. Ames," spoken soft as a willow weeping. "The professor is still sleeping. Just step this way."

The plumber himself looked up and saw Mrs. Ames with her voice hushed, speaking to him. She was a youngish woman, but this she had forgotten. The mystery and silence of her husband's mind lay like a chiding finger on her lips. Her eyes were gray, for the light had been extinguished in them. The strange dim halo of her yellow hair was still uncombed and sideways on her head.

For all of his heavy boots, the plumber quieted the sound of his feet, and together they went down the hall, picking their way around the still lake of water that spread as far as the landing and lay docile there. The plumber was a tough, hardy man; but he took off his hat when he spoke to her and looked her fully, almost insolently in the eye.

"Does it come from the wash-basin," he said, "or from the other . . . ?"

"Oh, from the other," said Mrs. Ames without hesitation.

In this place the villas were scattered out few and primitive, and although beauty lay without there was no reflection of her face within. Here all was awkward and unfit; a sense of wrestling with uncouth forces gave everything an austere countenance. Even the plumber, dealing as does a woman with matters under hand, was grave and stately. The mountains round about seemed to have cast them into the shadow of great dignity.

Mrs. Ames began speaking of their arrival that summer in the little villa, mourning each event as it followed on the other.

"Then, just before going to bed last night," she said, "I noticed something was unusual."

The plumber cast down a folded square of sackcloth on the brimming floor and laid his leather apron on it. Then he stepped boldly onto the heart of the island it shaped and looked long into the overflowing bowl.

"The water should be stopped from the meter in the garden," he said at last.

"Oh, I did that," said Mrs. Ames, "the very first thing last night. I turned it off at once, in my nightgown, as soon as I saw what was happening. But all this had already run in."

The plumber looked for a moment at her red kid slippers. She was standing just at the edge of the clear, pure-seeming tide.

"It's no doubt the soil lines," he said severely. "It may be that something has stopped them, but my opinion is that the water seals aren't working. That's the trouble often enough in such cases. If you had a valve you wouldn't be caught like this."

Mrs. Ames did not know how to meet this rebuke. She stood, swaying a little, looking into the plumber's blue relentless eye.

"I'm sorry—I'm sorry that my husband," she said, "is still—resting and cannot go into this with you. I'm sure it must be very interesting. . . ."

"You'll probably have to have the traps sealed," said the plumber grimly, and at the sound of this Mrs. Ames' hand flew in dismay to the side of her face. The plumber made no move, but the set of his mouth as he looked at her seemed to soften. "Anyway, I'll have a look from the garden end," he said.

"Oh, do," said the astronomer's wife in relief. Here was a man who spoke of action and object as simply as women did! But however hushed her voice had been, it carried clearly to Professor Ames who lay, dreaming and solitary, upon his bed. He heard their footsteps come down the hall, pause, and skip across the pool of overflow.

"Katherine!" said the astronomer in a ringing tone. "There's a problem worthy of your mettle!"

Mrs. Ames did not turn her head, but led the plumber swiftly down the stairs. When the sun in the garden struck her face, he saw there was a wave of color in it, but this may have been anything but shame.

"You see how it is," said the plumber, as if leading her mind away. "The drains run from these houses right down the hill, big enough for a man to stand upright in them, and clean as a whistle too." There they stood in the garden with the vegetation flowering in disorder all about. The plumber looked at the astronomer's wife. "They come out at the torrent on the other side of the forest beyond there," he said.

But the words the astronomer had spoken still sounded in her in despair.

The mind of man, she knew, made steep and sprightly flights, pursued illusion, took foothold in the nameless things that cannot pass between the thumb and finger. But whenever the astronomer gave voice to the thoughts that soared within him, she returned in gratitude to the long expanses of his silence. Desert-like they stretched behind and before the articulation of his scorn.

Life, life is an open sea, she sought to explain it in sorrow, and to survive women cling to the floating débris on the tide. But the plumber had suddenly fallen upon his knees in the grass and had crooked his fingers through the ring of the drains' trap-door. When she looked down she saw that he was looking up into her face, and she saw too that his hair was as light as gold.

"Perhaps Mr. Ames," he said rather bitterly, "would like to come down with me and have a look around?"

"Down?" said Mrs. Ames in wonder.

"Into the drains," said the plumber brutally. "They're a study for a man who likes to know what's what."

"Oh, Mr. Ames," said Mrs. Ames in confusion. "He's still—still in bed, you see."

The plumber lifted his strong, weathered face and looked curiously at her. Surely it seemed to him strange for a man to linger in bed, with the sun pouring yellow as wine all over the place. The astronomer's wife saw his lean cheeks, his high, rugged bones, and the deep seams in his brow. His flesh was as firm and clean as wood, stained richly tan with the climate's rigor. His fingers were blunt, but comprehensible to her, gripped in the ring and holding the iron door wide. The backs of his hands were bound round and round with ripe blue veins of blood.

"At any rate," said the astronomer's wife, and the thought of it moved her lips to smile a little, "Mr. Ames would never go down there alive. He likes going up," she said. And she, in turn, pointed, but impudently, towards the heavens. "On the roof. Or on the mountains. He's been up on the tops of them many times."

"It's matter of habit," said the plumber, and suddenly he went down the trap. Mrs. Ames saw a bright little piece of his hair still shining, like a star, long after the rest of him had gone. Out of the depths, his voice, hollow and dark with foreboding, returned to her. "I think something has stopped the elbow," was what he said.

This was speech that touched her flesh and bone and made her wonder. When her husband spoke of height, having no sense of it, she could not picture it nor hear. Depth or magic passed her by unless a name were given. But madness in a daily shape, as elbow stopped, she saw clearly and well. She sat down on the grasses, bewildered that it should be a man who had spoken to her so.

She saw the weeds springing up, and she did not move to tear them up from life. She sat powerless, her senses veiled, with no action taking shape beneath her hands. In this way some men sat for hours on end, she knew, tracking a single thought back to its origin. The mind of man could balance and divide, weed out, destroy. She sat on the full, burdened grasses, seeking to think, and dimly waiting for the plumber to return.

Whereas her husband had always gone up, as the dead go, she knew now that there were others who went down, like the corporeal being of the dead.

That men were then divided into two bodies now seemed clear to Mrs. Ames. This knowledge stunned her with its simplicity and took the uneasy motion from her limbs. She could not stir, but sat facing the mountains' rocky flanks, and harking in silence to lucidity. Her husband was the mind, this other man the meat, of all mankind.

After a little, the plumber emerged from the earth: first the light top of his head, then the burnt brow, and then the blue eyes fringed with whitest lash. He braced his thick hands flat on the pavings of the garden-path and swung himself completely from the pit.

"It's the soil lines," he said pleasantly. "The gases," he said as he looked down upon her lifted face, "are backing up the drains."

"What in the world are we going to do?" said the astronomer's wife softly. There was a young and strange delight in putting questions to which true answers would be given. Everything the astronomer had ever said to her was a continuous query to which there could be no response.

"Ah, come, now," said the plumber, looking down and smiling. "There's a remedy for every ill, you know. Sometimes it may be that," he said as if speaking to a child, "or sometimes the other thing. But there's always a help for everything a-miss."

Things come out of herbs and make you young again, he might have been saying to her; or the first good rain will quench any drought; or time of itself will put a broken bone together.

"I'm going to follow the ground pipe out right to the torrent," the plumber was saying. "The trouble's between here and there and I'll find it on the way. There's nothing at all that can't be done over for the caring," he was saying, and his eyes were fastened on her face in insolence, or gentleness, or love.

The astronomer's wife stood up, fixed a pin in her hair, and turned around towards the kitchen. Even while she was calling the servant's name, the plumber began speaking again.

"I once had a cow that lost her cud," the plumber was saying. The girl came out on the kitchen-step and Mrs. Ames stood smiling at her in the sun.

"The trouble is very serious, very serious," she said across the garden. "When Mr. Ames gets up, please tell him I've gone down."

She pointed briefly to the open door in the pathway, and the plumber hoisted his kit on his arm and put out his hand to help her down.

"But I made her another in no time," he was saying, "out of flowers and things and what-not."

"Oh," said the astronomer's wife in wonder as she stepped into the heart of the earth. She took his arm, knowing that what he said was true.

Questions for Study

1. Why has Mrs. Ames forgotten that she is "youngish"? What has happened to the light in her eyes?
2. Point out some details of speech and action which seem especially effective in characterizing Mrs. Ames, the plumber, and Mr. Ames. What role does point of view play in establishing these characters?
3. Boyle often generalizes about "man" and "woman." Do her statements constitute the story's theme? Do they suggest that the astronomer and his wife are

representative of men and women in general instead of being mere individuals? Explain why or why not.

4. Why does Mrs. Ames prefer her husband's silence to his speech? What are the implications of Mrs. Ames' remark that her husband "likes going up"?

5. Why does Mrs. Ames delight in asking "questions to which true answers would be given"? Is the plumber's story about the cow "true"? What is the significance of *true* as the final word in the story?

6. What are the symbolic implications of Mrs. Ames' saying, "When Mr. Ames gets up, please tell him that I've gone down"? What do the heavens and the earth symbolize in the story? Remember that each should suggest a whole complex of meanings and associations. Are these symbols natural or literary? Are there other symbols in the story?

7. "Life, life is an open sea," thinks Mrs. Ames. How do you fit this image into the pattern made up by the astronomer's sky and the plumber's sewers? What finally do you make of the "desert-like" quality of the astronomer's silences?

Richard Brautigan (b. 1935)

Homage to the
San Francisco YMCA

Once upon a time in San Francisco there was a man who really liked the finer things in life, especially poetry. He liked good verse.

He could afford to indulge himself in this liking, which meant that he didn't have to work because he was receiving a generous pension that was the result of a 1920s investment that his grandfather had made in a private insane asylum that was operating quite profitably in Southern California.

In the black, as they say and located in the San Fernando Valley, just outside of Tarzana. It was one of those places that do not look like an insane asylum. It looked like something else with flowers all around it, mostly roses.

The checks always arrived on the 1st and the 15th of every month, even when there was not a mail delivery on that day. He had a lovely house in Pacific Heights and he would go out and buy more poetry. He of course had never met a poet in person. That would have been a little too much.

One day he decided that his liking for poetry could not be fully expressed in just reading poetry or listening to poets reading on phonograph records. He decided to take the plumbing out of his house and completely replace it with poetry, and so he did.

He turned off the water and took out the pipes and put in John Donne[1] to replace them. The pipes did not look too happy. He took out his bathtub and

---

1. A number of literary figures are alluded to in the narrative: John Donne (1572–1631), most celebrated of the so-called metaphysical poets; William Shakespeare (1564–1616), world-renowned English playwright and poet; Emily Dickinson (1830–86), American poet; Vladimir Mayakovsky (1893–1930), Russian poet, dramatist, and champion of the Bolshevik Revolution; Michael McClure (b. 1932), American poet and dramatist.

put in William Shakespeare. The bathtub did not know what was happening.

He took out his kitchen sink and put in Emily Dickinson. The kitchen sink could only stare back in wonder. He took out his bathroom sink and put in Vladimir Mayakovsky. The bathroom sink, even though the water was off, broke out into tears.

He took out his hot water heater and put in Michael McClure's poetry. The hot water heater could barely contain its sanity. Finally he took out his toilet and put in the minor poets. The toilet planned on leaving the country.

And now the time had come to see how it all worked, to enjoy the fruit of his amazing labor. Christopher Columbus' slight venture sailing West was merely the shadow of a dismal event in the comparison. He turned the water back on again and surveyed the countenance of his vision brought to reality. He was a happy man.

"I think I'll take a bath," he said, to celebrate. He tried to heat up some Michael McClure to take a bath in some William Shakespeare and what happened was not actually what he had planned on happening.

"Might as well do the dishes, then," he said. He tried to wash some plates in "I taste a liquor never brewed," and found there was quite a difference between that liquid and a kitchen sink. Despair was on its way.

He tried to go to the toilet and the minor poets did not do at all. They began gossiping about their careers as he sat there trying to take a shit. One of them had written 197 sonnets about a penguin he had once seen in a travelling circus. He sensed a Pulitzer Prize in this material.

Suddenly the man realized that poetry could not replace plumbing. It's what they call seeing the light. He decided immediately to take the poetry out and put the pipes back in, along with the sinks, the bathtub, the hot water heater and the toilet.

"This just didn't work out the way I planned it," he said. "I'll have to put the plumbing back. Take the poetry out." It made sense standing there naked in the total light of failure.

But then he ran into more trouble than there was in the first place. The poetry did not want to go. It liked very much occupying the positions of the former plumbing.

"I look great as a kitchen sink," Emily Dickinson's poetry said.

"We look wonderful as a toilet," the minor poets said.

"I'm grand as pipes," John Donne's poetry said.

"I'm a perfect hot water heater," Michael McClure's poetry said.

Vladimir Mayakovsky sang new faucets from the bathroom, there are faucets beyond suffering, and William Shakespeare's poetry was nothing but smiles.

"That's well and dandy for you," the man said. "But I have to have plumbing, *real* plumbing in this house. Did you notice the emphasis I put on *real?* Real! Poetry just can't handle it. Face up to reality," the man said to the poetry.

But the poetry refused to go. "We're staying." The man offered to call the police. "Go ahead and lock us up, you illiterate," the poetry said in one voice.

"I'll call the fire department!"

"Book burner!" the poetry shouted.

The man began to fight the poetry. It was the first time he had ever been in a fight. He kicked the poetry of Emily Dickinson in the nose.

Of course the poetry of Michael McClure and Vladimir Mayakovsky walked over and said in English and in Russian, "That won't do at all," and threw the man down a flight of stairs. He got the message.

That was two years ago. The man is now living in the YMCA in San Francisco and loves it. He spends more time in the bathroom than everybody else. He goes in there at night and talks to himself with the light out.

Questions for Study

1. Why does this story begin, "Once upon a time . . ."? How would you describe Brautigan's tone and style?
2. Does this story have a plot? A conflict? A climax? A dénouement?
3. What happens in the story? What exactly is the man trying to do?
4. What connections does this story make between plumbing and poetry? Why do they seem to go together? What other comparable ways might the man have of trying to fit his liking for poetry into his life?
5. Brautigan refers to light several times. Is light then employed as a symbol? Is poetry? Is plumbing? What do they represent?
6. Certainly this narrative is not realistic. Try to reconstruct the entire narrative in abstract statements to determine whether or not the story is an allegory. Does this story seem to be trying to put across a message? If so, what is the message? If not, what is it trying to do?

Dan Jacobson (b. 1929)
Beggar My Neighbor

Michael saw them for the first time when he was coming home from school one day. One moment the street had been empty, glittering in the light from the sun behind Michael's back, with no traffic on the roadway and apparently no pedestrians on the broad sandy pavement; the next moment these two were before him, their faces raised to his. They seemed to emerge directly in front of him, as if the light and shade of the glaring street had suddenly condensed itself into two little piccanins[1] with large eyes in their round, black faces.

"*Stukkie brood?*"[2] the elder, a boy, said in a plaintive voice. A piece of bread. At Michael's school the slang term for any African child was just that: *stukkie brood.* That was what African children were always begging for.

"*Stukkie brood?*" the little girl said. She was wearing a soiled white dress that was so short it barely covered her loins; there seemed to be nothing at all

---

1. Native South African children (variation of *pickaninnies*).
2. The language used here is Afrikaans, a version of Dutch spoken in South Africa.

beneath the dress. She wore no socks, no shoes, no cardigan, no cap or hat. She must have been about ten years old. The boy, who wore a torn khaki shirt and a pair of gray shorts much too large for him, was about Michael's age, about twelve, though he was a little smaller than the white boy. Like the girl, the African boy had no shoes or socks. Their limbs were painfully thin; their wrists and ankles stood out in knobs, and the skin over these protruding bones was rougher than elsewhere. The dirt on their skin showed up as a faint grayness against the black.

"I've got no bread," the white boy said. He had halted in his surprise at the suddenness of their appearance before him. They must have been hiding behind one of the trees that were planted at intervals along the pavement. "I don't bring bread from school."

They did not move. Michael shifted his school case from one hand to the other and took a pace forward. Silently, the African children stood aside. As he passed them, Michael was conscious of the movement of their eyes; when he turned to look back he saw that they were standing still to watch him go. The boy was holding one of the girl's hands in his.

It was this that made the white child pause. He was touched by their dependence on one another, and disturbed by it too, as he had been by the way they had suddenly come before him, and by their watchfulness and silence after they had uttered their customary, begging request. Michael saw again how ragged and dirty they were, and thought of how hungry they must be. Surely he could give them a piece of bread. He was only three blocks from home.

He said, "I haven't got any bread here. But if you come home with me, I'll see that you get some bread. Do you understand?"

They made no reply; but they obviously understood what he had said. The three children moved down the pavement, their shadows sliding over the rough sand ahead of them. The Africans walked a little behind Michael, and to one side of him. Once Michael asked them if they went to school, and the boy shook his head; when Michael asked them if they were brother and sister, the boy nodded.

When they reached Michael's house, he went inside and told Dora, the cook-girl, that there were two piccanins in the lane outside, and that he wanted her to cut some bread and jam for them. Dora grumbled that she was not supposed to look after every little beggar in town, and Michael answered her angrily, "We've got lots of bread. Why shouldn't we give them some?" He was particularly indignant because he felt that Dora, being of the same race as the two outside, should have been readier than he was to help them. When Dora was about to take the bread out to the back gate, where the piccanins waited, Michael stopped her. "It's all right, Dora," he said in a tone of reproof, "I'll take it," and he went out into the sunlight, carrying the plate in his hand.

"*Stukkie brood*," he called out to them. "Here's your *stukkie brood*."

The two children stretched their hands out eagerly, and Michael let them take the inch-thick slices from the plate. He was pleased to see that Dora had put a scraping of apricot jam on the bread. Each of the piccanins held the bread in both hands, as if afraid of dropping it. The girl's mouth worked a little, but she kept her eyes fixed on the white boy.

"What do you say?" Michael asked.

They replied in high, clear voices, "Thank you, baas."[3]

"That's better. Now you can eat." He wanted to see them eat it; he wanted to share their pleasure in satisfying their strained appetites. But without saying a word to him, they began to back away, side by side. They took a few paces, and then they turned and ran along the land toward the main road they had walked down earlier. The little girl's dress fluttered behind her, white against her black body. At the corner they halted, looked back once, and then ran on, out of sight.

A few days later, at the same time and in the same place, Michael saw them again, on his way home from school. They were standing in the middle of the pavement, and he saw them from a long way off. They were obviously waiting for him to come. Michael was the first to speak, as he approached them.

"What? Another piece of bread?" he called out from a few yards away.

"Yes, baas," they answered together. They turned immediately to join him as he walked by. Yet they kept a respectful pace or two behind.

"How did you know I was coming?"

"We know the baas is coming from school."

"And how do you know that I'm going to give you bread?"

There was no reply; not even a smile from the boy, in response to Michael's. They seemed to Michael, as he glanced casually at them, identical in appearance to a hundred, a thousand, other piccanins, from the peppercorns[4] on top of their heads to their wide, callused, sand-gray feet.

When they reached the house, Michael told Dora, "Those *stukkie broods* are waiting outside again. Give them something, and then they can go."

Dora grumbled once again, but did as she was told. Michael did not go out with the bread himself; he was in a hurry to get back to work on a model car he was making, and was satisfied to see, out of his bedroom window, Dora coming from the back gate a few minutes later with an empty plate in her hand. Soon he had forgotten all about the two children. He did not go out of the house until a couple of hours had passed; by then it was dusk, and he took a torch[5] with him to help him find a piece of wire for his model in the darkness of the lumber shed. Handling the torch gave Michael a feeling of power and importance, and he stepped into the lane with it, intending to shine it about like a policeman on his beat. Immediately he opened the gate, he saw the two little children standing in the half-light, just a few paces away from him.

"What are you doing here?" Michael exclaimed in surprise.

The boy answered, holding his hand up, as if warning Michael to be silent. "We were waiting to say thank you to the baas."

"What!" Michael took a step toward them both, and they stood their ground, only shrinking together slightly.

For all the glare and glitter there was in the streets of Lyndhurst[6] by day, it was winter, midwinter; and once the sun had set, a bitter chill came into the air, as swiftly as the darkness. The cold at night wrung deep notes from the con-

---

3. Literally, "boss" or "master"; thus *kleinbaas,* used later in the narrative, means little boss.
4. Tightly fashioned curls in kinky hair.
5. Flashlight.
6. Suburb of Johannesburg, South Africa, located northeast of the city.

tracting iron roofs of the houses and froze the fish ponds in all the fine gardens of the white suburbs. Already Michael could feel its sharp touch on the tips of his ears and fingers. And the two African children stood there barefoot, in a flimsy dress and torn shirt, waiting to thank him for the bread he had had sent out to them.

"You mustn't wait," Michael said. In the half-darkness he saw the white dress on the girl more clearly than the boy's clothing; and he remembered the nakedness and puniness of her black thighs. He stretched his hand out, with the torch in it. "Take it," he said. The torch was in his hand, and there was nothing else that he could give to them. "It's nice," he said. "It's a torch. Look." He switched it on and saw in its beam of light a pair of startled eyes, darting desperately from side to side. "You see how nice it is," Michael said, turning the beam upward, where it lost itself against the light that lingered in the sky. "If you don't want it, you can sell it. Go on, take it."

A hand came up and took the torch from him. Then the two children ran off, in the same direction they had taken on the first afternoon. When they reached the corner all the street lights came on, as if at a single touch, and the children stopped and stared at them, before running on. Michael saw the torch glinting in the boy's hand, and only then did it occur to him that despite their zeal to thank him for the bread they hadn't thanked him for the torch. The size of the gift must have surprised them into silence, Michael decided; and the thought of his own generosity helped to console him for the regret he couldn't help feeling when he saw the torch being carried away from him.

Michael was a lonely child. He had neither brothers nor sisters; both his parents worked during the day, and he had made few friends at school. But he was not by any means unhappy in his loneliness. He was used to it, in the first place; and then, because he was lonely, he was all the better able to indulge himself in his own fantasies. He played for hours, by himself, games of his own invention—games of war, of exploration, of seafaring, of scientific invention, of crime, of espionage, of living in a house beneath or above his real one. It was not long before the two African children, who were now accosting him regularly, appeared in some of his games, for their weakness, poverty, and dependence gave Michael ample scope to display in fantasy his kindness, generosity, courage and decisiveness. Sometimes in his games Michael saved the boy's life, and was thanked for it in broken English. Sometimes he saved the girl's, and then she humbly begged his pardon for having caused him so much trouble. Sometimes he was just too late to save the life of either, though he tried his best, and then there were affecting scenes of farewell.

But in real life, Michael did not play with the children at all: they were too dirty, too ragged, too strange, too persistent. Their persistence eventually drove Dora to tell Michael's mother about them; and his mother did her duty by telling Michael that on no account should he play with the children, nor should he give them anything of value.

"Play with them!" Michael laughed at the idea. And apart from bread and the torch he had given them nothing but a few old toys, a singlet[7] or two, a pair

---

7. Boy's undershirt.

of old canvas shoes. No one could begrudge them those gifts. The truth was that Michael's mother begrudged the piccanins neither the old toys and clothes not the bread. What she was anxious to do was simply to prevent her son playing with the piccanins, fearing that he would pick up germs, bad language, and "kaffir[8] ways" generally from them, if he did. Hearing both from Michael and Dora that he did not play with them at all, and that he had never even asked them into the backyard, let alone the house, Michael's mother was satisfied.

They came to Michael about once a week, meeting him as he walked back from school, or simply waiting for him outside the back gate. The spring winds had already blown the cold weather away, almost overnight, and still the children came. Their words of thanks varied neither in tone nor length, whatever Michael gave them; but they had revealed, in response to his questions, that the boy's name was Frans and the girl's name was Annie, that they lived in Green Point Location, and that their mother and father were both dead. During all this time Michael had not touched them, except for the fleeting contact of their hands when he passed a gift to them. Yet sometimes Michael wished that they were more demonstrative in their expressions of gratitude to him; he thought that they could, for instance, seize his hand and embrace it; or go down on their knees and weep, just once. As it was, he had to content himself with fantasies of how they spoke of him among their friends, when they returned to the tumbled squalor of Green Point Location; of how incredulous their friends must be to hear their stories about the kind white *kleinbaas* who gave them food and toys and clothing.

One day Michael came out to them carrying a possession he particularly prized—an elaborate pen and pencil set which had been given to him for a recent birthday. He had no intention of giving the outfit to the African children, and he did not think that he would be showing off with it in front of them. He merely wanted to share his pleasure in it with someone who had not already seen it. But as soon as he noticed the way the children were looking at the open box, Michael knew the mistake he had made. "This isn't for you," he said abruptly. The children blinked soundlessly, staring from the box to Michael and back to the box again. "You can just look at it," Michael said. He held the box tightly in his hand, stretching it forward, the pen and the propelling[9] pencils shining inside the velvet-lined case. The two heads of the children came together over the box; they stared deeply into it.

At last the boy lifted his head. "It's beautiful," he breathed out. As he spoke, his hand slowly came up toward the box.

"No," Michael said, and snatched the box away.

"Baas?"

"No." Michael retreated a little, away from the beseeching eyes, and the uplifted hand.

"Please, baas, for me?"

And his sister said, "For me also, baas."

"No, you can't have this." Michael attempted to laugh, as if at the absurdity of the idea. He was annoyed with himself for having shown them the box, and at the same time shocked at them for having asked for it. It was the first time they had asked for anything but bread.

---

8. A term of derision for South African blacks.
9. Mechanical.

"Please, baas. It's nice." The boy's voice trailed away on the last word, in longing; and then his sister repeated the word, like an echo, her own voice trailing away too. "Ni-ice."

"No! I won't give it to you! I won't give you anything if you ask for this. Do you hear?"

Their eyes dropped, their hands came together, they lowered their heads. Being sure now that they would not again ask for the box, Michael relented. He said, "I'm going in now, and I'll tell Dora to bring you some bread."

But Dora came to him in his room a few minutes later. "The little kaffirs are gone." She was holding the plate of bread in her hand. Dora hated the two children, and Michael thought there was some kind of triumph in her voice and manner as she made the announcement.

He went outside to see if she was telling the truth. The lane was empty. He went to the street, and looked up and down its length, but there was no sign of them there either. They were gone. He had driven them away. Michael expected to feel guilty; but to his own intense surprise he felt nothing of the kind. He was relieved that they were gone, and that was all.

When they reappeared a few days later, Michael felt scorn toward them for coming back after what had happened on the last occasion. He felt they were in his power. "So you've come back?" he greeted them. "You like your *stukkies brood,* hey? You're hungry, so today you'll wait, you won't run away."

"Yes, baas," they said, in their low voices.

Michael brought the bread out of them; when they reached for it he jokingly pulled the plate back and laughed at their surprise. Then only did he give them the bread.

"Thank you, baas."

"Thank you, baas."

They ate the bread in Michael's presence; watching them, he felt a little more kindly disposed toward them. "All right, you can come another day, and there'll be come more bread for you."

"Thank you, baas."

"Thank you, baas."

They came back sooner than Michael had expected them to. He gave them their bread and told them to go. They went off, but again did not wait for the usual five or six days to pass before approaching him once more. Only two days had passed, yet here they were with their eternal request—"*Stukkie brood,* baas?"

Michael said, "Why do you get hungry so quickly now?" But he gave them their bread.

When they appeared in his games and fantasies, Michael no longer rescued them, healed them, casually presented them with kingdoms and motor cars. Now he ordered them about, sent them away on disastrous missions, picked them out to be shot for cowardice in the face of the enemy. And because something similar to these fantasies was easier to enact in the real world than his earlier fantasies, Michael soon was ordering them about unreasonably in fact. He deliberately left them waiting; he sent them away and told them to come back on days when he knew he would be in town; he told them there was no bread in the house. And when he did give them anything, it was bread only now; never old toys or articles of clothing.

So, as the weeks passed, Michael's scorn gave way to impatience and irritation, irritation to anger. What angered him most was that the two piccanins seemed too stupid to realize what he now felt about them, and instead of coming less frequently, continued to appear more often than ever before. Soon they were coming almost every day, though Michael shouted at them and teased them, left them waiting for hours, and made them do tricks and sing songs for their bread. They did everything he told them to do; but they altogether ignored his instructions as to which days they should come. Invariably, they would be waiting for him, in the shade of one of the trees that grew alongside the main road from school, or standing at the gate behind the house with sand scuffed up about their bare toes. They were as silent as before; but more persistent, inexorably persistent. Michael took to walking home by different routes, but they were not to be so easily discouraged. They simply waited at the back gate, and whether he went into the house by the front or the back gate he would not avoid seeing their upright, unmoving figures.

Finally, he told them to go and never come back at all. Often he had been tempted to do this, but some shame or pride had always prevented him from doing it; he had always weakened previously, and named a date, a week or two weeks ahead, when they could come again. But now he shouted at them, "It's finished! No more bread—nothing! Come on, *voetsak!*[10] If you come back I'll tell the garden boy to chase you away."

From then on they came every day. They no longer waited right at the back gate, but squatted in the sand across the lane. Michael was aware of their eyes following him when he went by, but they did not approach him at all. They did not even get up from the ground when he passed. A few times he shouted at them to go, and stamped his foot, but he shrank from hitting them. He did not want to touch them. Once he sent out Jan, the garden boy, to drive them away; but Jan, who had hitherto always shared Dora's views on the piccanins, came back muttering angrily and incomprehensibly to himself; and when Michael peeped into the lane he saw that they were still there. Michael tried to ignore them, to pretend he did not see them. He hated them now; even more, he began to dread them.

But he did not how much he hated and feared the two children until he fell ill with a cold, and lay feverish in bed for a few days. During those days the two children were constantly in his dreams, or in his half-dreams, for even as he dreamed he knew he was turning on his bed; he was conscious of the sun shining outside by day, and at night of the passage light that had been left on inside the house. In these dreams he struck and struck again at the children with weapons he found in his hands; he fled in fear from them down lanes so thick with sand his feet could barely move through it; he committed lewd, cruel acts upon the bare-thighed girl and her brother shrieked to tell the empty street of what he was doing. Michael struck out at him with a piece of heavy cast-iron guttering. Its edge dug sharply into Michael's hands as the blow fell, and when he lifted the weapon he saw the horror he had made of the side of the boy's head, and how the one remaining eyeball still stared unwinkingly at him.

Michael thought he was awake, and suddenly calm. The fever seemed to

---

10. Literally, *Voertsek*—"Go away!"

have left him. It was as though he had slept deeply, for days, after that last dream of violence; yet his impression was that he had woken directly from it. The bedclothes felt heavy on him, and he threw them off. The house was silent. He got out of bed and went to look at the clock in the kitchen: it was early afternoon. Dora and Jan were resting in their rooms across the yard, as they always did after lunch. Outside, the light of the sun was unremitting, a single golden glare. He walked back to his bedroom; there, he put on his dressing gown and slippers, feeling the coolness inside his slippers on his bare feet. He went through the kitchen again, quietly, and onto the back stoep,[11] and then across the backyard. The sun seemed to seize his neck as firmly as a hand grasping, and its light was so bright he was aware of it only as a darkness beyond the little stretch of ground he looked down upon. He opened the back gate. Inevitably, as he had known they would be, the two were waiting.

He did not want to go beyond the gate in his pajamas and dressing gown, so, shielding his eyes from the glare with one hand, he beckoned them to him with the other. Together, in silence, they rose and crossed the lane. It seemed to take them a long time to come to him, but at last they stood in front of him, with their hands interlinked. Michael stared into their dark faces, and they stared into his.

"What are you waiting for?" he asked.

"For you." First the boy answered; then the girl repeated, "For you."

Michael looked from the one to the other; and he remembered what he had been doing to them in his dreams. Their eyes were black to look into. Staring forward, Michael understood what he should have understood long before: that they came to him not in hope or appeal or even in reproach, but in hatred. What he felt toward them, they felt toward him; what he had done to them in his dreams, they did to him in theirs.

The sun, their staring eyes, his own fear came together in a sound that seemed to hang in the air of the lane—a cry, the sound of someone weeping. Then Michael knew that is was he who was crying. He felt the heat of the tears in his eyes, he felt moisture running down his cheeks. With the same fixity of decision that had been his in his dreams of violence and torture, Michael knew what he must do. He beckoned them forward, closer. They came. He stretched out his hands, he felt under his fingers the springy hair he had looked at so often before from the distance between himself and them; he felt the smooth skin of their faces; their frail, rounded shoulders, their hands. Their hands were in his, and he led them inside the gate.

He led them into the house, through the kitchen, down the passage, into his room where they had never been before. They looked about at the pictures on the walls, the toys on top of the low cupboard, the twisted white sheets and tumbled blankets on the bed. They stood on both sides of him, and for the first time since he had met them, their lips parted into slow, grave smiles. Michael knew that what he had to give them was not toys or clothes or bread, but something more difficult. Yet it was not difficult at all, for there was nothing else he could give them. He took the girl's face in his hands and pressed his lips to hers. He was aware of the darkness of her skin, and of the smell of it, and of the faint movement of her lips, a single pulse that beat momentarily against his

---

11. Covered porch.

own. Then it was gone. He kissed the boy, too, and let them go. They came together, and grasped each other by the hand, staring at him.

"What do you want now?" he asked.

A last anxiety flickered in Michael and left him, as the boy slowly shook his head. He began to step back, pulling his sister with him; when he was through the door he turned his back on Michael and they walked away down the passage. Michael watched them go. At the door of the kitchen, on their way out of the house, they paused, turned once more, and lifted their hands, the girl copying the boy, in a silent, tentative gesture of farewell.

Michael did not follow them. He heard the back gate swing open and then bang when it closed. He went wearily back to his bed, and as he fell upon it, his relief and gratitude that the bed should be there to receive him, changed suddenly into grief at the knowledge that he was already lying upon it—that he had never left it.

His cold grew worse, turned into bronchitis, kept him in bed for several weeks. But his dreams were no longer of violence; they were calm, spacious, and empty of people. As empty as the lane was, when he was at last allowed out of the house, and made his way there immediately, to see if the children were waiting for him.

He never saw them again, though he looked for them in the streets and lanes of the town. He saw a hundred, a thousand, children like them; but not the two he hoped to find.

Questions for Study

1. Why does Jacobson make Michael an only child? What are Michael's reasons for not playing with the native children? How does his touching or not touching them become a symbolic act?
2. Why does Michael reverse his original intentions and give the children bread? Why does Michael want to see them eat the bread?
3. Does Michael's explanation for the children's failure to thank him for the flashlight seem adequate? How in fact does Michael wish to be thanked?
4. Why does Michael show them the pen-and-pencil set? Why is he surprised at their reactions? How does their relationship change after that event? Why does it change?
5. Why does Jacobson sometimes blur the distinctions between fantasy and reality? Specifically, what happens in each of Michael's fantasies or wish fulfillments? What sort of progression is found in them? How are they related to actual events?
6. This story was originally titled "A Gift Too Late." Why do you suppose Jacobson changed its name to "Beggar My Neighbor"? Which title do you think is more appropriate to the story? Explain your choice.
7. How would you describe Jacobson's tone, particularly in regard to Michael?
8. This is a realistic story which achieves a considerable amount of mystery and suspense. How does it do this? Give your explanation of the last twist of the story: Michael's dream of making peace with the children. What has happened to Michael and why have his dreams changed and become "calm, spacious, and empty of people"?

Chapter 11
Fantasy and Myth

Some stories such as "A & P" and "The Eighty-Yard Run" seem so familiar and true-to-life that we do not question the events they portray. We may even forget that such stories are "made-up" fictions. Whether or not we know anything about the South African setting of "The Old Chief Mshlanga" or about the Russian setting of "An Upheaval," we accept as realistic such stories because the manner in which they are told establishes for us their credibility. Similarly, realistic presentation in "Sredni Vashtar" and "Death in the Woods" brings us to accept as true-to-life even these rather bizarre tales of violence and death. Though we probably never before have heard of a pet ferret killing a woman or of dogs racing in a circle about a dying woman, we feel that such things could happen in the world.

Other stories, however, defy the boundaries of possibility and contradict not only our personal experience but certain of our assumptions about the nature of reality. We usually call these stories fantasies. Among such pieces are "August 2002: Night Meeting," "The Children's Campaign," and "Homage to the San Francisco YMCA." These stories intentionally contradict our experience by presenting not only what is improbable but what is, as far as we know, impossible. **Fantasy** is a highly imaginative fictional creation which defies the limits of any known reality. And fantasy often does so by placing apparently real characters in an unrealistic setting, as Ray Bradbury does by using the planet Mars as the locale for "August 2002: Night Meeting." Bradbury has written that "fantasy assaults and breaks a particular law" of the culture from which it comes. Other writers create fantasy by making the distinction between reality and unreality intentionally ambiguous. Langston Hughes achieves this effect in "On the Road" by relating the story of a black vagrant who single-handedly pulls down a church building and afterwards meets Christ walking beside him. Similarly, Donald Barthelme in "The Balloon" blurs the distinction between reality and unreality when he depicts a giant balloon settling over a large part of New York City.

We study fantasy, just as we study realistic stories, by examining the basic elements of fiction: plot, character, setting, point of view, theme, and style. We also judge realistic stories by their credibility. Yet we do not consider credibility in evaluating fantasy. That is, we accept as realistic a story like "A & P" because Updike seems to "tell it like it is." But we should not reject "August 2002" solely because it defies the prevailing scientific notion that life cannot exist on Mars. Such stories assume conditions of existence different from our own. No matter how apparently unrealistic or unbelievable fantasies may be, we must be willing to grant their basic assumptions. And we can then delight in their imaginativeness and perhaps learn from their vision.

Because it is not judged on the basis of its realism or believability, fantasy may seem unpredictable and freewheeling—unlimited by anything but the author's imaginativeness. But fantasy is limited, as all fiction must be, by an internal standard of coherence. However farfetched fantasy may be, once an author has set up the terms of a narrative, he must be true to them. In "The Balloon," for example, Donald Barthelme's basic assumption is that a strange and inexplicable giant balloon settles over an urban area, which he depicts in a familiar, matter-of-fact way. As readers we grant Barthelme the right to introduce into a familiar and realistic setting a single wild and fanciful element. But once Barthelme has set the terms, he remains true to them. Midway in the story he does not shift and make the familiar residents of New York City turn into talking rodents or animated computers or moon-creatures in disguise.

When we settle the question of credibility and grant the basic assumptions of a particular fantasy, we may discover that fantasy delights because it offers us, for example, a way of traveling imaginatively beyond the galaxy or outside of the conventional limitations of time. We even like sometimes to imagine ourselves as godlike creatures who can alter the nature of the universe. We may enjoy fantasy for its sheer whimsy. If an author creates ghosts, monsters, witches, living mutations, talking vegetables, self-propelled machines, or weird creatures from outer space and puts them in situations which defy our experiences and understanding, we are delighted with his inventiveness and daring.

The appeal of that type of fantasy known as science fiction lies first of all in its escapism and its inventiveness. We are initially pleased with Bradbury's "August 2002: Night Meeting" because it takes us to Mars and into the future and startles us by implying, for instance, that time can be smelled and heard and touched. But science fiction appeals not only as a diversion but also as a projection of ideas. **Science fiction** is a form of fantasy story based on scientific knowledge—or facts, assumptions, and hypotheses which are logically projected beyond the world as we know it. "August 2002," for example, is a fantasy based on current scientific speculation about interrelations between space and time and about time-traveling. However escapist it may seem in going beneath the earth or to another planet or into another dimension of time, science fiction remains a technological fantasy which is as idea-oriented as it is diverting. But no matter how distant it may seem, it should have relevance to the here and now. In presenting a conversation between a Martian and an earthling, Bradbury creates a scene that has absolutely no basis in fact. Yet the subject of the conversation —the meaning of time and the perception of reality—is an actual scientific and philosophic question that thinkers have pondered for centuries. Even though it is arbitrary, largely incredible and speculative, science fiction offers us understanding as well as entertainment.

Fantasy is limited not only by standards of internal coherence and consistency but also by some standard of reference to our own existence. As an imaginative creation, fantasy must maintain its connections with and also say something about the human situation. Fantasy exaggerates and distorts familiar and everyday aspects of the world in order to make us see and understand more dramatically the point the author is making about the human condition. In "On the Road" Hughes' presentation of a vagrant who destroys a church and meets Christ startles us into seeing that modern Christianity must be revitalized because it has lost touch with the basic teachings of its founder. Similarly, in "The Balloon," Barthelme shows the citizens' fascination with the giant balloon that hovers over New York City in order to suggest that something is missing from their lives.

Like fantasy, myth defies the laws of experienced reality, but myth is unlike fantasy in the ways it originates and is accepted. Both fantasy and myth present outsized and unreal events, characters, and situations. But fantasy is consciously contrived by a single author while myth is not. Fantasy is private; myth is public, or at least shared among people related by culture and history. Though we can learn from the world of fantasy we cannot always enter or understand that world since it is an intentionally subjective and personal fabrication. Myth, on the other hand, is a narrative which shapes a view of the world for an entire culture. In our rationalistic age, we might think it a fantasy to believe that winter comes because a goddess of a cornfield is in mourning. For the ancient Greeks the story of how Demeter, the goddess of growth and fertility, refuses to let anything grow while her daughter remains for three months with the god of the underworld, was a myth that offered an explanation for one aspect of the yearly seasons. Myths such as this one gave the Greeks a way of interpreting otherwise unexplainable occurrences

The word *myth* carries various associations ranging from the false to the ultimately true. It is an elusive term to explain. Nevertheless, because myth informs so much of our literature we need to understand what it is and how it functions. In the simplest sense **myth** is a story—the term in Greek means "tale" or "narrative"—or an interrelated cluster of stories relating the activities of gods and goddesses and god-like beings. It is set in the remote past and usually deals with the origins of the universe, gods, and human beings. Myths do not exist as unique phenomena but rather are part of a fully developed, elaborate construction of myths, or a **mythology.** Many cultures—Egyptian, Celtic, Icelandic, African, Polynesian, Chinese, American Indian, for example —possessed or possess their own mythologies. Each of these mythologies constitutes a special class of stories that are vivid, concrete, and thus intelligible to all the people in a particular culture. These stories are rendered in prose or in verse and are embodied in the rites, ceremonies, and symbols of the culture.

Originally myth was regarded by its believers as stating an important truth about the nature of the universe. In *Myth and Reality* (1963), Mircea Eliade argues that "myth narrates a sacred history; it relates an event that took place in primordial Time, the fabled time of the 'beginnings.'" The central fact in understanding the origin and nature of myth, Eliade feels, is to recognize that it is a supreme, enduring "model" for those who believe. Mythology serves then as an entrance into the nature, order, and purpose of a specific culture.

The mythologies of all cultures, however much their surfaces differ, appear to repeat essentially many of the same patterns, suggesting that there are collective elements common to all humankind from which these timeless myths emerge in different times and places. Though in our rationalistic age we are less inclined than our ancestors to acknowledge in myth a valid and compelling basis for our existence, mythic patterns nevertheless remain deeply imprinted in the human psyche. And these patterns emerge in dreams and in art and literature.

A term frequently employed in discussing this collective element is **archetype.** To the Swiss psychiatrist Carl Gustav Jung (1875–1961), archetypes are inborn and unconscious patterns which contain the collective memory of humankind. Admitting that an archetype is a psychic phenomenon and thus not visible in itself, Jung maintained that archetypes such as the savior-redeemer, the hero, the mother, the father, the miraculous child, the shadow, the old wise man, and the self reveal themselves in apprehensible images, which Jung labelled "the images of the archetypes." In literature these images call up patterns from our unconscious memory and thus evoke in us deep and powerful emotions. The soldier in "A Mystery of Heroism," for example, can be said to exemplify the archetype of the hero; and Young Goodman Brown in Nathaniel Hawthorne's story (see "Stories for Further Study") can be identified with the archetype of the would-be true believer.

Jung understood these images and the patterns to which they refer as all-important indications of the channels in which human nature moves and develops. In addition to the working of the human intellect, Jung insisted that "there is a thinking in primordial images, in symbols which are older than the historical man, which are inborn in him from the earliest times, and, eternally living, outlasting all generations, [which] still make up the groundwork of the human psyche. It is only possible to live the fullest life when we are in harmony with these symbols; wisdom is a return to them."

As a psychiatrist, Jung saw the personally therapeutic value of a re-enactment of these old patterns. And he also felt that literature which reenacts the old patterns has a supreme validity and power. If an author, consciously or unconsciously, taps the vein of myth, his work gains a crucial dimension. Such work is empowered by what cultural anthropologist Lucien Lévy-Bruhl (1857–1939) calls a *participation mystique,* or an identification and cross-fertilization between the temporary and the permanent, the personal and the universal, the individual and the archetypal. In this way, myth may serve as an allegorical substructure which connects an individual narrative with the eternal patterns of human behavior and belief.

One example of an archetypal narrative, for example, is the hero quest, in which a warrior, leader, or savior sets out to perform tasks in order to win a coveted prize—a precious gift, a beautiful princess, salvation for his village or people. In *The Hero with a Thousand Faces* (1949), Joseph Campbell shows that a "monomyth" of the hero exists and that its essential features are common to stories as seemingly different as those of Abraham and Davy Crockett, the Buddha and King Arthur. We speak therefore of a particular story or an aspect of a story as demonstrating qualities or as having remnants of the hero quest.

In "On the Road" the vagrant does not act out of a conscious sense of mission when he destroys the church and is subsequently jailed for vandalism, so he hardly seems an archetypal hero. Nevertheless, his humiliating end is especially poignant because it is played off against our conscious or unconscious expectations about the hero myth. The elements of fantasy in the story call to mind the biblical hero-archetype Samson, who pulled down the temple of the Philistines, only to destroy himself in the act; or the tale of Hercules, who performed twelve super-human labors only to be tricked into putting on a garment which burned and seared his flesh until he begged to die. In Jorge Luis Borges' "The Secret Miracle" (see "Stories for Further Reading"), Hladik's fear of death is intensified because he so badly wants to be a hero to his people and thus redeem his own life and justify God's trust in him. In these stories, the hero-archetype may function ironically, but the mythic element nevertheless adds an important dimension to each narrative.

Modern short stories are not myths as such. Fiction is written by an individual, not by a people. But any number of short stories may be, or may include, reenactments of such mythological patterns as the hero quest. In such stories, myth is a substructure conveying authority and power. When we read these stories we sense that power. Usually we identify mythological patterns and try to see what these patterns mean within a specific story.

Neither fantasy nor myth can have meaning without reference to the concrete world. In fact, the strength of the best fantasies, like that of the most effective employment of myth, lies in the tension between the abstract and the concrete or between the unreal and the real. Fantasies and myths distort or abandon the world of experience. Yet they do so in order to represent crucial elements of the human experience. Although fantasies and myths may seem unrelated to our everyday world, they are, on a deeper level, a manifestation of the important aspects of that world.

Langston Hughes (1902–1967)
On the Road

He was not interested in the snow. When he got off the freight, one early evening during the depression, Sargeant never even noticed the snow. But he must have felt it seeping down his neck, cold, wet, sopping in his shoes. But if you had asked him, he wouldn't have known it was snowing. Sargeant didn't see the snow, not even under the bright lights of the main street, falling white and flaky against the night. He was too hungry, too sleepy, too tired.

The Reverend Mr. Dorset, however, saw the snow when he switched on his porch light, opened the front door of his parsonage, and found standing there before him a big black man with snow on his face, a human piece of night with snow on his face—obviously unemployed.

Said the Reverend Mr. Dorset before Sargeant even realized he'd opened his mouth: "I'm sorry. No! Go right on down this street four blocks and turn to your left, walk up seven and you'll see the Relief Shelter. I'm sorry. No!" He shut the door.

Sargeant wanted to tell the holy man that he had already been to the Relief Shelter, been to hundreds of relief shelters during the depression years, the beds were always gone and supper was over, the place was full, and they drew the color line anyhow. But the minister said, "No," and shut the door. Evidently he didn't want to hear about it. And he *had* a door to shut.

The big black man turned away. And even yet he didn't see the snow, walking right into it. Maybe he sensed it, cold, wet sticking to his jaws, wet on his black hands, sopping in his shoes. He stopped and stood on the sidewalk hunched over—hungry, sleepy, cold—looking up and down. Then he looked right where he was—in front of a church. Of course! A church! Sure, right next to a parsonage, certainly a church.

It had *two* doors.

Broad, white steps in the night all snowy white. Two high arched doors with slender stone pillars on either side. And way up, a round lacy window with a stone crucifix in the middle and Christ on the crucifix in stone. All this was pale in the street lights, solid and stony pale in the snow.

Sargeant blinked. When he looked up the snow fell into his eyes. For the first time that night he *saw* the snow. He shook his head. He shook the snow from his coat sleeves, felt hungry, felt lost, felt not lost, felt cold. He walked up the steps of the church. He knocked at the door. No answer. He tried the handle. Locked. He put his shoulder against the door and his long black body slanted like a ramrod. He pushed. With loud rhythmic grunts, like the grunts in a chain-gang song, he pushed against the door.

"I'm   tired . . . Huh! . . . Hongry . . . Uh! . . . I'm   sleepy . . . Huh! I'm cold . . . I got to sleep somewheres," Sargeant said. "This here is a church, ain't it? Well, uh!"

He pushed against the door.

Suddenly, with an undue cracking and squeaking, the door began to give way to the tall black Negro who pushed ferociously against the door.

By now two or three white people had stopped in the street, and Sargeant was vaguely aware of some of them yelling at him concerning the door. Three or four more came running, yelling at him.

"Hey!" they said. "Hey!"

"Un-huh," answered the big tall Negro, "I know it's a white folks' church, but I got to sleep somewhere." He gave another lunge at the door. "Huh!"

And the door broke open.

But just when the door gave way, two white cops arrived in a car, ran up the steps with their clubs and grabbed Sargeant. But Sargeant for once had no intention of being pulled or pushed away from the door.

Sargeant grabbed, but not for anything so weak as a broken door. He grabbed for one of the tall stone pillars beside the door, grabbed at it and caught it. And held it. The cops pulled and Sargeant pulled. Most of the people in the street got behind the cops and helped them pull.

"A big black unemployed Negro holding onto our church!" thought the people. "The idea!"

The cops began to beat Sargeant over the head, and nobody protested. But he held on.

And then the church fell down.

Gradually, the big stone front of the church fell down, the walls and the rafters, the crucifix and the Christ. Then the whole thing fell down, covering the cops and the people with bricks and stones and debris. The whole church fell down in the snow.

Sargeant got out from under the church and went walking on up the street with the stone pillar on his shoulder. He was under the impression that he had buried the parsonage and the Reverend Mr. Dorset who said, "No!" So he laughed, and threw the pillar six blocks up the street and went on.

Sargeant thought he was alone, but listening to the crunch, crunch, crunch on the snow of his own footsteps, he heard other footsteps, too, doubling his own. He looked around and there was Christ walking along beside him,[1] the same Christ that had been on the cross on the church—still stone with a rough stone surface, walking along beside him just like he was broken off the cross when the church fell down.

"Well, I'll be dogged," said Sargeant. "This here's the first time I ever seed you off the cross."

"Yes," said Christ, crunching his feet in the snow. "You had to pull the church down to get me off the cross."

"You glad?" said Sargeant.

"I sure am," said Christ.

They both laughed.

"I'm a hell of a fellow, ain't I?" said Sargeant. "Done pulled the church down!"

"You did a good job," said Christ. "They have kept me nailed on a cross for nearly two thousand years."

"Whee-ee-e!" said Sargeant. "I know you are glad to get off."

"I sure am," said Christ.

They walked on in the snow. Sargeant looked at the man of stone.

"And you been up there two thousand years?"

"I sure have," Christ said.

"Well, if I had a little cash," said Sargeant, "I'd show you around a bit."

"I been around," said Christ.

"Yeah, but that was a long time ago."

"All the same," said Christ, "I've been around."

They walked on in the snow until they came to the railroad yards. Sargeant was tired, sweating and tired.

"Where you goin'?" Sargeant said, stopping by the tracks. He looked at Christ. Sargeant said, "I'm just a bum on the road. How about you? Where you goin'?"

"God knows," Christ said, "but I'm leavin' here."

They saw the red and green lights of the railroad yard half veiled by the snow that fell out of the night. Away down the track they saw a fire in a hobo jungle.

"I can go there and sleep," Sargeant said.

"You can?"

"Sure," said Sargeant. "That place ain't got no doors."

Outside the town, along the tracks, there were barren trees and bushes below the embankment, snow-gray in the dark. And down among the trees and bushes there were makeshift houses made out of boxes and tin and old pieces of wood and canvas. You couldn't see them in the dark, but you knew they were there if you'd ever been on the road, if you had ever lived with the homeless and hungry in a depression.

"I'm side-tracking," Sargeant said. "I'm tired."

"I'm gonna make it on to Kansas City," said Christ.

"O.K.," Sargeant said. "So long!"

---

1. The third day following the Crucifixion of Christ was the day of his Resurrection. Several of his disciples discovered him walking beside them as they journeyed to the village of Emmaus, near Jerusalem. See Luke 24:13–32.

He went down into the hobo jungle and found himself a place to sleep. He never did see Christ no more. About six A.M. a freight came by. Sargeant scrambled out of the jungle with a dozen or so hoboes and ran along the track, grabbing at the freight. It was dawn, early dawn, cold and gray.

"Wonder where Christ is by now?" Sargeant thought. "He must-a gone on way on down the road. He didn't sleep in this jungle."

Sargeant grabbed the train and started to pull himself up into a moving coal car, over the edge of a wheeling coal car. But strangely enough, the car was full of cops. The nearest cop rapped Sargeant soundly across the knuckles with his night stick. Wham! Rapped his big black hands for clinging to the top of the car. Wham! But Sargeant did not turn loose. He clung on and tried to pull himself into the car. He hollered at the top of his voice, "Damn it, lemme in this car!"

"Shut up," barked the cop. "You crazy coon!" He rapped Sargeant across the knuckles and punched him in the stomach. "You ain't out in no jungle now. This ain't no train. You in jail."

Wham! across his bare black fingers clinging to the bars of his cell. Wham! between the steel bars low down against his shins.

Suddenly Sargeant realized that he really was in jail. He wasn't on no train. The blood of the night before had dried on his face, his head hurt terribly, and a cop outside in the corridor was hitting him across the knuckles for holding onto the door, yelling and shaking the cell door.

"They must-a took me to jail for breaking down the door last night," Sargeant thought, "that church door."

Sargeant went over and sat on a wooden bench against the cold stone wall. He was emptier than ever. His clothes were wet, clammy cold wet, and shoes sloppy with snow water. It was just about dawn. There he was, locked up behind a cell door, nursing his bruised fingers.

The bruised fingers were his, but not the *door.*

Not the *club,* but the fingers.

"You wait," mumbled Sargeant, black against the jail wall. "I'm gonna break down this door, too."

"Shut up—or I'll paste you one," said the cop.

"I'm gonna break down this door," yelled Sargeant as he stood up in his cell.

Then he must have been talking to himself because he said, "I wonder where Christ's gone? I wonder if he's gone to Kansas City?"

Questions for Study

1. This story is at once a highly realistic, vivid piece of social criticism and also a fantasy. At what point does it become fantasy? Are there any elements in the story's realistic framework which prepare us for the author's shift into fantasy?

2. What are the implications of doors, bars, stone, coldness, blackness, and whiteness in the story? How do these elements serve as symbols? Are there other symbolic details in the story?

3. Why are we told that it is the "same Christ that had been on the cross on the church" that now walks along with Sargeant? Why does Christ only appear *after* the church falls down? Your responses should take into account both a literal and a symbolic interpretation of the narrative.

4. Sargeant's conversation with Christ seems very casual and inconsequential. Why is this? Why does Hughes not have Christ say something more significant than he does? What is the effect of the underplaying of this encounter?
5. Does Sargeant dream most of the story? Which parts of the story are real and which are dream fantasies? Find other parts of the story which blur the lines between realism and fantasy, such as the "crunching" of the feet of the stone Christ in the snow.
6. What is the significance of Hughes' associating the black protagonist with the figure of the crucified Christ? What political and social implications can you see in the meaning of the story?

Donald Barthelme (b. 1933)
The Balloon

The balloon, beginning at a point on Fourteenth Street,[1] the exact location of which I cannot reveal, expanded northward all one night, while people were sleeping, until it reached the Park. There, I stopped it; at dawn the northernmost edges lay over the Plaza; the free-hanging motion was frivolous and gentle. But experiencing a faint irritation at stopping, even to protect the trees, and seeing no reason the balloon should not be allowed to expand upward, over the parts of the city it was already covering, into the "air space" to be found there, I asked the engineers to see to it. This expansion took place throughout the morning, soft imperceptible sighing of gas through the valves. The balloon then covered forty-five blocks north-south and an irregular area east-west, as many as six crosstown blocks on either side of the Avenue in some places. That was the situation, then.

But it is wrong to speak of "situations," implying sets of circumstances leading to some resolution, some escape of tension; there were no situations, simply the balloon hanging there—muted heavy grays and browns for the most part, contrasting with walnut and soft yellows. A deliberate lack of finish, enhanced by skillful installation, gave the surface a rough, forgotten quality; sliding weights on the inside, carefully adjusted, anchored the great, varishaped mass at a number of points. Now we have had a flood of original ideas in all media, works of singular beauty as well as significant milestones in the history of inflation, but at that moment there was only *this balloon,* concrete particular, hanging there.

There were reactions. Some people found the balloon "interesting." As a response this seemed inadequate to the immensity of the balloon, the suddenness of its appearance over the city; on the other hand, in the absence of hysteria or other societally-induced anxiety, it must be judged a calm, "mature" one. There was a certain amount of initial argumentation about the "meaning" of the balloon; this subsided, because we have learned not to insist on meanings, and they are rarely even looked for now, except in cases in-

---

1. The narrative takes place in New York City.

volving the simplest, safest phenomena. It was agreed that since the meaning of the balloon could never be known absolutely, extended discussion was pointless, or at least less purposeful than the activities of those who, for example, hung green and blue paper lanterns from the warm gray underside, in certain streets, or seized the occasion to write messages on the surface, announcing their availability for the performance of unnatural acts, or the availability of acquaintances.

Daring children jumped, especially at those points where the balloon hovered close to a building, so that the gap between balloon and building was a matter of a few inches, or points where the balloon actually made contact, exerting an ever-so-slight pressure against the side of a building, so that balloon and building seemed a unity. The upper surface was so structured that a "landscape" was presented, small valleys as well as slight knolls, or mounds; once atop the balloon, a stroll was possible, or even a trip, from one place to another. There was pleasure in being able to run down an incline, then up the opposing slope, both gently graded, or in making a leap from one side to the other. Bouncing was possible, because of the pneumaticity of the surface, and even falling, if that was your wish. That all these varied motions, as well as others, were within one's possibilities, in experiencing the "up" side of the balloon, was extremely exciting for children, accustomed to the city's flat, hard skin. But the purpose of the balloon was not to amuse children.

Too, the number of people, children and adults, who took advantage of the opportunities described was not so large as it might have been: a certain timidity, lack of trust in the balloon, was seen. There was, furthermore, some hostility. Because we had hidden the pumps, which fed helium to the interior, and because the surface was so vast that the authorities could not determine the point of entry—that is, the point at which the gas was injected—a degree of frustration was evidenced by those city officers into whose province such manifestations normally fell. The apparent purposelessness of the balloon was vexing (as was the fact that it was "there" at all). Had we painted, in great letters, "LABORATORY TESTS PROVE" or "18% MORE EFFECTIVE" on the sides of the balloon, this difficulty would have been circumvented. But I could not bear to do so. On the whole, these officers were remarkably tolerant, considering the dimensions of the anomaly, this tolerance being the result of, first, secret tests conducted by night that convinced them that little or nothing could be done in the way of removing or destroying the balloon, and secondly, a public warmth that arose (not uncolored by touches of the aforementioned hostility) toward the balloon, from ordinary citizens.

As a single balloon must stand for a lifetime of thinking about balloons, so each citizen expressed, in the attitude he chose, a complex of attitudes. One man might consider that the balloon had to do with the notion *sullied,* as in the sentence *The big balloon sullied the otherwise clear and radiant Manhattan sky.* That is, the balloon was, in this man's view, an imposture, something inferior to the sky that had formerly been there, something interposed between the people and their "sky." But in fact it was January, the sky was dark and ugly; it was not a sky you could look up into, lying on your back in the street, with pleasure, unless pleasure, for you, proceeded from having been threatened, from having been misused. And the underside of the balloon was a pleasure to look up into, we had seen to that, muted grays and browns for the most part, contrasted with walnut and soft, forgotten yellows. And so, while this man was thinking *sullied,* still there was an admixture of pleasurable cognition in his thinking, struggling with the original perception.

Another man, on the other hand, might view the balloon as if it were part of a system of unanticipated rewards, as when one's employer walks in and says, "Here, Henry, take this package of money I have wrapped for you, because we have been doing so well in the business here, and I admire the way you bruise the tulips, without which bruising your department would not be a success, or at least not the success that it is." For this man the balloon might be a brilliantly heroic "muscle and pluck" experience, even if an experience poorly understood.

Another man might say, "Without the example of——, it is doubtful that——would exist today in its present form," and find many to agree with him, or to argue with him. Ideas of "bloat" and "float" were introduced, as well as concepts of dream and responsibility. Others engaged in remarkably detailed fantasies having to do with a wish either to lose themselves in the balloon, or to engorge it. The private character of these wishes, of their origins, deeply buried and unknown, was such that they were not much spoken of; yet there is evidence that they were widespread. It was also argued that what was important was what you felt when you stood under the balloon; some people claimed that they felt sheltered, warmed, as never before, while enemies of the balloon felt, or reported feeling, constrained, a "heavy" feeling.

Critical opinion was divided:

"monstrous pourings"

"harp"

XXXXXXX "certain contrasts with darker portions"

"inner joy"

"large, square corners"

"conservative eclecticism that has so far governed modern balloon design"

::::::: "abnormal vigor"

"warm, soft, lazy passages"

"Has unity been sacrificed for a sprawling quality?"

"*Quelle catastrophe!*"[2]

"munching"

---

2. "What a disaster!"

People began, in a curious way, to locate themselves in relation to aspects of the balloon: "I'll be at that place where it dips down into Forty-seventh Street almost to the sidewalk, near the Alamo Chile House," or, "Why don't we go stand on top, and take the air, and maybe walk about a bit, where it forms a tight, curving line with the façade of the Gallery of Modern Art—" Marginal intersections offered entrances within a given time duration, as well as "warm, soft, lazy passages" in which . . . But it is wrong to speak of "marginal intersections," each intersection was crucial, none could be ignored (as if, walking there, you might not find someone capable of turning your attention, in a flash, from old exercises to new exercises, risks and escalations). Each intersection was crucial, meeting of balloon and building, meeting of balloon and man, meeting of balloon and balloon.

It was suggested that what was admired about the balloon was finally this: that it was not limited, or defined. Sometimes a bulge, blister, or sub-section would carry all the way east to the river on its own initiative, in the manner of an army's movements on a map, as seen in a headquarters remote from the fighting. Then that part would be, as it were, thrown back again, or would withdraw into new dispositions; the next morning, that part would have made another sortie, or disappeared altogether. This ability of the balloon to shift its shape, to change, was very pleasing, especially to people whose lives were rather rigidly patterned, persons to whom change, although desired, was not available. The balloon, for the twenty-two days of its existence, offered the possibility, in its randomness, of mislocation of the self, in contradistinction to the grid of precise, rectangular pathways under our feet. The amount of specialized training currently needed, and the consequent desirability of long-term commitments, has been occasioned by the steadily growing importance of complex machinery, in virtually all kinds of operations; as this tendency increases, more and more people will turn, in bewildered inadequacy, to solutions for which the balloon may stand as a prototype, or "rough draft."

I met you under the balloon, on the occasion of your return from Norway; you asked if it was mine; I said it was. The balloon, I said, is a spontaneous autobiographical disclosure, having to do with the unease I felt at your absence, and with sexual deprivation, but now that your visit to Bergen[3] has been terminated, it is no longer necessary or appropriate. Removal of the balloon was easy; trailer trucks carried away the depleted fabric, which is now stored in West Virginia, awaiting some other time of unhappiness, sometime, perhaps when we are angry with one another..

Questions for Study

1. This story is presented through a narrator who "cannot reveal" certain facts about the balloon; yet it is he who controls the balloon's expansion. What is his attitude toward what happens? Why is he speaking to us? Why does he experience a "faint" irritation "at stopping the ballon's expansion"? Why does he dwell on the balloon's attractiveness?

2. Why does Barthelme in the second paragraph contrast the "concrete particular"

---

3. Norway's second-largest city, a leading cultural and educational center.

balloon with the "flood of original ideas" on inflation? Why is discussion of the balloon's meaning or purpose avoided?

3. Summarize and try to find a pattern in the kinds of reactions Barthelme tells us the balloon *might* provoke in people. May we generalize about each type of reaction, seeing something significant about the individual who experiences it?

4. Identify instances in the story where fantasy often depends on the use of realistic detail.

5. Why is each intersection of balloon and building, balloon and man, or balloon and balloon crucial? What does Barthelme show by these intersections?

6. Try to formulate an interpretation of the balloon's meaning which will be consistent with the basic narrative "facts," remembering that the balloon's presence is at once pleasurable, vexing, and threatening.

7. Does the ending leave us up in the air (like the balloon)? Or can you integrate the final paragraph into a basic understanding of the balloon's meaning?

A Note on Folklore

Earlier we said that myth is a narrative or cluster of stories that imparts collective wisdom about the human condition by depicting superhuman characters and events. Myths that have been transmitted orally down through the ages are examples of folklore. The study of folklore combines the approaches of the sociologist, anthropologist, theologian, and literary critic. Although we have not examined folklore as a part of the craft or the content of literature, this note attempts a brief explanation of the term.

In his study of American folklore Jan Harold Brunvand defines **folklore** as "those materials in culture that circulate traditionally among members of any group in different versions, whether in oral form or by means of customary example." Folklore may include orally transmitted information about such things as folk arts, crafts, cooking, and architecture. Also it may include references to such partly verbal lore as beliefs, games, dances, and customs. Yet verbal folklore is essentially oral literature. It consists of proverbs, sayings, riddles, rhymes, folk songs, and ballads, and such folk narratives as anecdotes, fables, tall tales, ghost stories, fairy tales, legends, and some forms of myth. In order to clarify further the nature of folklore, we offer the following example of an American Indian folktale, along with a brief commentary.

Cherokee Indian
Bear Man

A man went hunting in the mountains and came across a black bear, which he wounded with an arrow. The bear turned and started to run the other way, and the hunter followed, shooting one arrow after another into it without bringing it down. Now, this was a medicine bear, and could talk or read the thoughts of people without their saying a word. At last he stopped and pulled the arrows out of his side and gave them to the man, saying, "It is of no use for you to shoot at me, for you cannot kill me. Come to my house and let us live together." The hunter thought to himself, "He may kill me"; but the bear read his thoughts and said, "No, I won't hurt you." The man thought again, "How can I get anything to eat?" but the bear knew his thoughts, and said, "There shall be plenty." So the hunter went with the bear.

They went on together until they came to a hole in the side of the mountain, and the bear said, "This is not where I live, but there is going to be a council here and we will see what they do." They went in, and the hole widened as they went, until they came to a large cave like a townhouse. It was full of bears—old bears, young bears, and cubs, white bears, black bears, and brown bears—and a large white bear was the chief. They sat down in a corner, but soon the bears scented the hunter and began to ask, "What is it that smells bad?" The chief said, "Don't talk so; it is only a stranger come to see us. Let him alone." Food was getting scarce in the mountains, and the council was to decide what to do about it. They had sent out messengers all over, and while they were talking two bears came in and reported that they had found a country in the low grounds where there were so many chestnuts and acorns that mast was knee deep. Then they were all pleased, and got ready for a dance, and the dance leader was the one the Indians call Kalas-gunahita, "Long Hams," a great black bear that is always lean. After the dance the bears noticed the hunter's bow and arrows, and one said, "This is what men use to kill us. Let us see if we can manage them, and maybe we can fight man with his own weapons." So they took the bow and arrows from the hunter to try them. They fitted the arrow and drew back the string, but when they let go it caught in their long claws and the arrows dropped to the ground. They saw that they could not use the bow and arrows and gave them back to the man. When the dance and the council were over, they began to go home, excepting the White Bear chief, who lived there, and at last the hunter and the bear went out together.

They went on until they came to another hole in the side of the mountain, when the bear said, "This is where I live," and they went in. By this time the hunter was very hungry and was wondering how he could get something to eat. The other knew his thoughts, and sitting up on his hind legs he rubbed his stomach with his forepaws—*so*—and at once he had both paws full of chestnuts and gave them to the man. He rubbed his stomach again—*so*—and had his paws full of huckleberries, and gave them to the man. He rubbed again—*so*—and had his paws full of acorns, but the man said that he could not eat them, and that he had enough already.

The hunter lived in the cave with the bear all winter, until long hair like that of a bear began to grow all over his body and he began to act like a bear; but he still walked like a man. One day in early spring the bear said to him, "Your people down in the settlement are getting ready for a grand hunt in these mountains, and they will come to this cave and kill me and take these clothes from me"—he meant his skin—"but they will not hurt you and will take you home with them." The bear knew what the people were doing down in the settlement just as he always knew what the man was thinking about. Some days passed and the bear said again, "This is the day when the Topknots will come to kill me, but the Split-noses will come first and find us. When they have killed me they will drag me outside the cave and take off my clothes and cut me in pieces. You must cover the blood with leaves, and when they are taking you away look back after you have gone a piece and you will see something."

Soon they heard the hunters coming up the mountain, and then the dogs found the cave and began to bark. The hunters came and looked inside and saw the bear and killed him with their arrows. Then they dragged him outside the cave and skinned the body and cut it in quarters to carry home. The dogs kept on barking until the hunters thought there must be another bear in the cave. They looked in again and saw the man away at the farther end. At first they thought it was another bear on account of his long hair, but they soon saw it was the hunter who had been lost the year before, so they went in and brought him out. Then each hunter took a load of the bear meat and they started home again, bringing the man and the skin with them. Before they left the man piled leaves over the spot where they had cut up the bear, and when they had gone a little way he looked behind and saw the bear rise up out of the leaves, shake himself, and go back into the woods.

In this story we sense the tremendous respect the Cherokee Indians felt toward the bears who inhabited the Appalachian Mountains with them. "Bear Man," in fact, explores the distinction between human beings and beasts. To bears, humans smell bad. The bears, who cannot use weapons, have learned to fear humans. And so in reminding listeners that bears cannot become human, the tale reconfirms human alienation from animals. It suggests, however, that humans need not fear animals, and at the same time it reminds human beings that they must live with the animal kingdom. Yet although he grows long hair and even looks like a bear, the hunter does not eat acorns and still walks on two legs. The tale uses traditional folklore elements such as magical transformations and talking animals to affirm that no matter how alien they are, animals can benefit human beings. The ending of the tale seems to sanction hunting and killing animals for clothing and food in suggesting that the animal kingdom, like nature, is self-perpetuating and eternal.

As folklore, then, this tale may be read as a revelation of a particular culture and as an explanation of the harmony that should exist between humans and animals. As myth, it may be read as a reenactment of an eternal pattern in which a central figure is dismembered or sacrificed voluntarily in order that life itself may be reborn. According to the mythic pattern, the figure descends into the earth or a dark cave in winter and then reappears in spring. His rebirth and renewal exemplify the eternal cycle of nature.

Both the bear and the hunter follow the mythic pattern, and the hunter's descent into the cave and return to the human world is representative of the hero myth which Joseph Campbell calls the central myth of all civilizations. The essential elements of that mythic pattern are the hero's call to adventure, his withdrawal from the human world, his temptation and passing away from life as he had known it, his visit to the underworld, and finally his rebirth and return as a "twice-born" man.

In "Bear Man" the hunter goes alone to the forest and, rather than die, he ceases to be human and lives as a bear. Instead of descending into the underworld, he descends into a bear cave. His return is a rebirth into the human condition.

The connections between myth and folklore are complex and sometimes confusing. The tale "Bear Man" gives one insight into the relationship between myth and folklore. And this brief note may clarify something of their relationship and may suggest the fundamental differences between them as well.

Chapter 12
The Story in Wider Perspective

In Chapter 1 we spoke of the human need to put experience into words, since human beings feel some mastery of a situation as soon as they can express it in language. As we also said, certain particular or universal experiences seem to demand retelling. When put into narrative form by a skilled storyteller, these experiences become more vivid, dramatic, controlled, and unified. The narrative form allows us to see implications in an experience that we may not have been aware of. And so the form itself offers insight, pleasure, and delight.

In this chapter we emphasize the craftsmanship involved in the construction of two complex stories, Leo Tolstoy's "The Death of Ivan Ilych" and Thomas Pynchon's "Entropy." By examining these narratives in terms of many of the elements of fiction discussed in the previous chapters, we can see how the authors have integrated their materials into well-executed tales. The stories in themselves are quite different. "The Death of Ivan Ilych" is written by a nineteenth-century Russian realist, "Entropy" by a twentieth-century American surrealist. One has a more-or-less traditional plot; the second seems to have no plot at all. One traces the life of a single character and at least broaches the question of his afterlife. The other introduces and then abandons a miscellaneous assortment of characters during a few hours in a single day. In one story the subject matter is obvious, while the theme is evasive; in the other, the theme is clearer, but the subject matter itself is difficult to pinpoint. One story carries an illusion of reality; the other pretends to no such illusion. Yet for all their differences the narratives are alike in that both are concerned with particular and universal aspects of the human condition. Each writer has taken the basic elements of the craft of fiction and put them to use in a manner appropriate to his story.

Leo Tolstoy begins "The Death of Ivan Ilych" with the news of Ivan Ilych's death. The black border of the local newspaper and the widow's "profound sorrow," as well as the fact that Ivan Ilych "was liked" by all the gentlemen now present at his funeral, establish his death as an important event and suggest that he will be missed. But Tolstoy undercuts the significance of this event by stating that friends see his death principally in terms of how it will benefit them. The opening section relentlessly details the lack of regret felt by Ivan Ilych's family and his so-called friends.

Beginning a story with a man's funeral is, of course, a radical distortion of chronology. As readers we might ask ourselves why Tolstoy chooses to begin in this way and why his first section places such an emphasis upon greed, ambition, opportunism, propriety, triviality, and even the odor of a decaying body. We might also ask ourselves why Tolstoy chooses to narrate this section from the point of view of a virtual outsider to the life and death of Ivan Ilych.

These are essential questions about the author's craft, but they lead beyond craftsmanship into questions of content and meaning. The question posed by the story is specifically that of the meaning of a man's existence and, by extension, the meaning of the lives of all human beings. Beginning at the end of a life, Tolstoy invites us to review the accomplishments and contributions of one man, something we traditionally do at funerals. But he chooses the most ordinary of names for his protagonist, stressing that this man has done nothing significant or heroic in his entire lifetime.

Why then does Ivan Ilych's life require such a lengthy, carefully written narrative? This question is soon answered, for section 2 begins with a devastating one-sentence paragraph which proclaims the significance of the ordinary: "Ivan Ilych's life had been most simple and most ordinary and therefore most terrible." We do not usually think of ordinariness as significant, much less as terrible. Yet Tolstoy wishes to persuade us that Ivan Ilych's life indicates otherwise. As an omniscient author he begins in section 2 the meticulously detailed, lengthy recapitulation of a life which lacks uniqueness or genuine accomplishment. Armed with certain questions about Tolstoy's craft and theme, let us now turn to the story itself.

Leo Tolstoy (1828–1910)
The Death of Ivan Ilych[1]

I

During an interval in the Melvinski trial in the large building of the Law
Courts, the members and public prosecutor met in Ivan Egorovich Shebek's
private room, where the conversation turned on the celebrated Krasovski case.
Fëdor Vasilievich warmly maintained that it was not subject to their jurisdic-
tion, Ivan Egorovich maintained the contrary, while Peter Ivanovich, not
having entered into the discussion at the start, took no part in it but looked
through the *Gazette* which had just been handed in.

"Gentlemen," he said, "Ivan Ilych has died!"

"You don't say so!"

"Here, read it yourself," replied Peter Ivanovich, handing Fëdor Vasilievich the paper still damp from the press. Surrounded by a black border were
the words: "Praskovya Fëdorovna Golovina, with profound sorrow, informs
relatives and friends of the demise of her beloved husband Ivan Ilych Golovin,
Member of the Court of Justice, which occurred on February the 4th of this
year 1882. The funeral will take place on Friday at one o'clock in the afternoon."

Ivan Ilych had been a colleague of the gentlemen present and was liked by
them all. He had been ill for some weeks with an illness said to be incurable.
His post had been kept open for him, but there had been conjectures that in
case of his death Alexeev might receive his appointment, and that either Vinnikov or Shtabel would succeed Alexeev. So on receiving the news of Ivan
Ilych's death the first thought of each of the gentlemen in that private room was
of the changes and promotions it might occasion among themselves or their
acquaintances.

"I shall be sure to get Shtabel's place or Vinnikov's," thought Fëdor Vasilievich. "I was promised that long ago, and the promotion means an extra eight
hundred rubles[2] a year for me beside the allowance."

"Now I must apply for my brother-in-law's transfer from Kaluga," thought
Peter Ivanovich. "My wife will be very glad, and then she won't be able to say
that I never do anything for her relations."

"I thought he would never leave his bed again," said Peter Ivanovich
aloud. "It's very sad."

"But what really was the matter with him?"

"The doctors couldn't say—at least they could, but each of them said
something different. When last I saw him I thought he was getting better."

"And I haven't been to see him since the holidays. I always meant to go."

"Had he any property?"

---

1. Russians of equal rank and on friendly terms customarily refer to each other by their two
given names. Thus, for example, Ivan Ilych Golovin is not merely Ivan, but Ivan Ilych; the name
suggests about what John Doe does in English—the purely average man.

2. The ruble is the basic monetary unit of Russia. At the time of the narrative, 800 rubles was a
handsome sum; today the ruble is worth a bit more than the U.S. dollar.

"I think his wife had a little—but something quite trifling."

"We shall have to go to see her, but they live so terribly far away."

"Far away from you, you mean. Everything's far away from your place."

"You see, he never can forgive my living on the other side of the river," said Peter Ivanovich, smiling at Shebek. Then, still talking of the distances between different parts of the city, they returned to the Court.

Besides considerations as to the possible transfers and promotions likely to result from Ivan Ilych's death, the mere fact of the death of a near acquaintance aroused, as usual, in all who heard of it the complacent feeling that, "it is he who is dead and not I."

Each one thought or felt, "Well, he's dead but I'm alive!" But the more intimate of Ivan Ilych's acquaintances, his so-called friends, could not help thinking also that they would now have to fulfil the very tiresome demands of propriety by attending the funeral service and paying a visit of condolence to the widow.

Fëdor Vasilievich and Peter Ivanovich had been his nearest acquaintances. Peter Ivanovich had studied law with Ivan Ilych and had considered himself to be under obligations to him.

Having told his wife at dinner-time of Ivan Ilych's death and of his conjecture that it might be possible to get her brother transferred to their circuit, Peter Ivanovich sacrificed his usual nap, put on his evening clothes, and drove to Ivan Ilych's house.

At the entrance stood a carriage and two cabs. Leaning against the wall in the hall downstairs near the cloak-stand was a coffin-lid covered with cloth of gold, ornamented with gold cord and tassels, that had been polished up with metal powder. Two ladies in black were taking off their fur cloaks. Peter Ivanovich recognized one of them as Ivan Ilych's sister, but the other was a stranger to him. His colleague Schwartz was just coming downstairs, but on seeing Peter Ivanovich enter he stopped and winked at him, as if to say: "Ivan Ilych has made a mess of things—not like you and me."

Schwartz's face with his Piccadilly whiskers and his slim figure in evening dress, had as usual an air of elegant solemnity which contrasted with the playfulness of his character and had a special piquancy here, or so it seemed to Peter Ivanovich.

Peter Ivanovich allowed the ladies to precede him and slowly followed them upstairs. Schwartz did not come down but remained where he was, and Peter Ivanovich understood that he wanted to arrange where they should play bridge that evening. The ladies went upstairs to the widow's room, and Schwartz with seriously compressed lips but a playful look in his eyes, indicated by a twist of his eyebrows the room to the right where the body lay.

Peter Ivanovich, like everyone else on such occasions, entered feeling uncertain what he would have to do. All he knew was that at such times it is always safe to cross oneself. But he was not quite sure whether one should make obeisances while doing so. He therefore adopted a middle course. On entering the room he began crossing himself and made a slight movement resembling a bow. At the same time, as far as the motion of his head and arm allowed, he surveyed the room. Two young men—apparently nephews, one of whom was a high-school pupil—were leaving the room, crossing themselves as they did so. An old woman was standing motionless, and a lady with strangely arched eyebrows was saying something to her in a whisper. A vigorous, resolute Church Reader, in a frock-coat, was reading something in a loud voice with an expression that precluded any contradiction. The butler's assistant, Gerasim, stepping lightly in front of Peter Ivanovich, was strewing something on the floor. Noticing this, Peter Ivanovich was immediately aware of a faint odour of a decomposing body.

The last time he had called on Ivan Ilych, Peter Ivanovich had seen Gerasim in the study. Ivan Ilych had been particularly fond of him and he was performing the duty of a sick nurse.

Peter Ivanovich continued to make the sign of the cross slightly inclining his head in an intermediate direction between the coffin, the Reader, and the icons on the table in a corner of the room. Afterwards, when it seemed to him that this movement of his arm in crossing himself had gone on too long, he stopped and began to look at the corpse.

The dead man lay, as dead men always lie, in a specially heavy way, his rigid limbs sunk in the soft cushions of the coffin, with the head forever bowed on the pillow. His yellow waxen brow with bald patches over his sunken temples was thrust up in the way peculiar to the dead, the protruding nose seeming to press on the upper lip. He was much changed and had grown even thinner since Peter Ivanovich had last seen him, but, as is always the case with the dead, his face was handsomer and above all more dignified than when he was alive. The expression on the face said that what was necessary had been accomplished, and accomplished rightly. Besides this there was in that expression a reproach and a warning to the living. This warning seemed to Peter Ivanovich out of place, or at least not applicable to him. He felt a certain discomfort and so he hurriedly crossed himself once more and turned and went out of the door—too hurriedly and too regardless of propriety, as he himself was aware.

Schwartz was waiting for him in the adjoining room with legs spread wide apart and both hands toying with his top-hat behind his back. The mere sight of that playful, well-groomed, and elegant figure refreshed Peter Ivanovich. He felt that Schwartz was above all these happenings and would not surrender to any depressing influences. His very look said that this incident of a church service for Ivan Ilych could not be a sufficient reason for infringing the order of the session—in other words, that it would certainly not prevent his unwrapping a new pack of cards and shuffling them that evening while a footman placed four fresh candles on the table: in fact, that there was no reason for supposing that this incident would hinder their spending the evening agreeably. Indeed he said this in a whisper as Peter Ivanovich passed him, proposing that they should meet for a game at Fëdor Vasilievich's. But apparently Peter Ivanovich was not destined to play bridge that evening. Praskovya Fëdorovna (a short, fat woman who despite all efforts to the contrary had continued to broaden steadily from her shoulders downwards and who had the same extraordinarily arched eyebrows as the lady who had been standing by the coffin), dressed all in black, her head covered with lace, came out of her own room with some other ladies, conducted them to the room where the dead body lay, and said: "The service will begin immediately. Please go in."

Schwartz, making an indefinite bow, stood still, evidently neither accepting nor declining this invitation. Praskovya Fëdorovna, recognizing Peter Ivanovich, sighed, went close up to him, took his hand, and said: "I know you were a true friend to Ivan Ilych . . ." and looked at him awaiting some suitable response. And Peter Ivanovich knew that, just as it had been the right thing to cross himself in that room, so what he had to do here was to press her hand, sigh, and say, "Believe me. . . ." So he did all this and as he did it felt that the desired result had been achieved: that both he and she were touched.

"Come with me. I want to speak to you before it begins," said the widow. "Give me your arm."

Peter Ivanovich gave her his arm and they went to the inner rooms, passing Schwartz, who winked at Peter Ivanovich compassionately.

"That does for our bridge! Don't object if we find another player. Perhaps you can cut in when you do escape," said his playful look.

Peter Ivanovich sighed still more deeply and despondently, and Praskovya Fëdorovna pressed his arm gratefully. When they reached the drawing-room, upholstered in pink cretonne and lighted by a dim lamp, they sat down at the table—she on a sofa and Peter Ivanovich on a low pouffe,[3] the springs of which yielded spasmodically under his weight. Praskovya Fëdorovna had been on the point of warning him to take another seat, but felt that such a warning was out of keeping with her present condition and so changed her mind. As he sat down on the pouffe Peter Ivanovich recalled how Ivan Ilych had arranged this room and had consulted him regarding this pink cretonne with green leaves. The whole room was full of furniture and knickknacks, and on her way to the sofa the lace of the widow's black shawl caught on the carved edge of the table. Peter Ivanovich rose to detach it, and the springs of the pouffe, relieved of his weight, rose also and gave him a push. The widow began detaching her shawl herself, and Peter Ivanovich again sat down, suppressing the rebellious springs of the pouffe under him. But the widow had not quite freed herself and Peter Ivanovich got up again, and again the pouffe rebelled and even creaked. When this was all over she took out a clean cambric handkerchief and began to weep. The episode with the shawl and the struggle with the pouffe had cooled Peter Ivanovich's emotions and he sat there with a sullen look on his face. This awkward situation was interrupted by Sokolov, Ivan Ilych's butler, who came to report that the plot in the cemetery that Praskovya Fëdorovna had chosen would cost two hundred rubles. She stopped weeping and, looking at Peter Ivanovich with the air of a victim, remarked in French that it was very hard for her. Peter Ivanovich made a silent gesture signifying his full conviction that it must indeed be so.

"Please smoke," she said in a magnanimous yet crushed voice, and turned to discuss with Sokolov the price of the plot for the grave.

Peter Ivanovich while lighting his cigarette heard her inquiring very circumstantially into the prices of different plots in the cemetery and finally decide which she would take. When that was done she gave instructions about engaging the choir. Sokolov then left the room.

"I look after everything myself," she told Peter Ivanovich, shifting the albums that lay on the table; and noticing that the table was endangered by his cigarette-ash, she immediately passed him an ash-tray, saying as she did so: "I consider it an affectation to say that my grief prevents my attending to practical affairs. On the contrary, if anything can—I won't say console me, but—dis-

---

3. A rounded ottoman.

tract me, it is seeing to everything concerning him.'' She again took out her handkerchief as if preparing to cry, but suddenly, as if mastering her feeling, she shook herself and began to speak calmly. ''But there is something I want to talk to you about.''

Peter Ivanovich bowed, keeping control of the springs of the pouffe, which immediately began quivering under him.

''He suffered terribly the last few days.''

''Did he?'' said Peter Ivanovich.

''Oh, terribly! He screamed unceasingly, not for minutes but for hours. For the last three days he screamed incessantly. It was unendurable. I cannot understand how I bore it; you could hear him three rooms off. Oh, what I have suffered!''

''Is it possible that he was conscious all that time?'' asked Peter Ivanovich.

''Yes,'' she whispered. ''To the last moment. He took leave of us a quarter of an hour before he died, and asked us to take Volodya away.''

The thought of the sufferings of this man he had known so intimately, first as a merry little boy, then as a school-mate, and later as a grown-up colleague, suddenly struck Peter Ivanovich with horror, despite an unpleasant consciousness of his own and this woman's dissimulation. He again saw that brow, and that nose pressing down on the lip, and felt afraid for himself.

''Three days of frightful suffering and then death! Why, that might suddenly, at any time, happen to me,'' he thought, and for a moment felt terrified. But—he did not himself know how—the customary reflection at once occurred to him that this had happened to Ivan Ilych and not to him, and that it should not and could not happen to him, and to think that it could would be yielding to depression which he ought not to do, as Schwartz's expression plainly showed. After which reflection Peter Ivanovich felt reassured, and began to ask with interest about the details of Ivan Ilych's death, as though death was an accident natural to Ivan Ilych but certainly not to himself.

After many details of the really dreadful physical sufferings Ivan Ilych had endured (which details he learnt only from the effect those sufferings had produced on Praskovya Fëdorovna's nerves) the widow apparently found it necessary to get to business.

''Oh, Peter Ivanovich, how hard it is! How terribly, terribly hard!'' and she again began to weep.

Peter Ivanovich sighed and waited for her to finish blowing her nose. When she had done so he said, ''Believe me . . .'' and she again began talking and brought out what was evidently her chief concern with him—namely, to question him as to how she could obtain a grant of money from the government on the occasion of her husband's death. She made it appear that she was asking Peter Ivanovich's advice about her pension, but he soon saw that she already knew about that to the minutest detail, more even than he did himself. She knew how much could be got out of the government in consequence of her husband's death, but wanted to find out whether she could not possibly extract something more. Peter Ivanovich tried to think of some means of doing so, but after reflecting for a while and, out of propriety, condemning the government for its niggardliness, he said he thought that nothing more could be got. Then she sighed and evidently began to devise means of getting rid of her visitor. Noticing this, he put out his cigarette, rose, pressed her hand, and went out into the anteroom.

In the dining-room where the clock stood that Ivan Ilych had liked so much and had bought at an antique shop, Peter Ivanovich met a priest and a few acquaintances who had come to attend the service, and he recognized Ivan Ilych's daughter, a handsome young woman. She was in black and her slim figure appeared slimmer than ever. She had a gloomy, determined, almost angry expression, and bowed to Peter Ivanovich as though he were in some way to blame. Behind her, with the same offended look, stood a wealthy young man, an examining magistrate, whom Peter Ivanovich also knew and who was her fiancé, as he had heard. He bowed mournfully to them and was about to pass into the death-chamber, when from under the stairs appeared the figure of Ivan Ilych's schoolboy son, who was extremely like his father. He seemed a little Ivan Ilych, such as Peter Ivanovich remembered when they studied law together. His tear-stained eyes had in them the look that is seen in the eyes of boys of thirteen or fourteen who are not pure-minded. When he saw Peter Ivanovich he scowled morosely and shamefacedly. Peter Ivanovich nodded to him and entered the death-chamber. The service began: candles, groans, incense, tears, and sobs. Peter Ivanovich stood looking gloomily down at his feet. He did not look once at the dead man, did not yield to any depressing influence, and was one of the first to leave the room. There was no one in the anteroom, but Gerasim darted out of the dead man's room, rummaged with his strong hands among the fur coats to find Peter Ivanovich's and helped him on with it.

"Well, friend Gerasim," said Peter Ivanovich, so as to say something. "It's a sad affair, isn't it?"

"It's God's will. We shall all come to it some day," said Gerasim, displaying his teeth—the even, white teeth of a healthy peasant—and, like a man in the thick of urgent work, he briskly opened the front door, called the coachman, helped Peter Ivanovich into the sledge,[4] and sprang back to the porch as if in readiness for what he had to do next.

Peter Ivanovich found the fresh air particularly pleasant after the smell of incense, the dead body, and carbolic acid.

"Where to, sir?" asked the coachman.

"It's not too late even now. . . . I'll call round on Fëdor Vasilievich."

He accordingly drove there and found them just finishing the first rubber, so that it was quite convenient for him to cut in.

II

Ivan Ilych's life had been most simple and most ordinary and therefore most terrible.

He had been a member of the Court of Justice, and died at the age of forty-five. His father had been an official who after serving in various ministries and departments in Petersburg had made the sort of career which brings men to positions from which by reason of their long service they cannot be dismissed, though they are obviously unfit to hold any responsible position, and for whom therefore posts are especially created, which though fictitious carry salaries of

---

4. Sleigh.

from six to ten thousand rubles that are not fictitious, and in receipt of which they live on to a great age.

Such was the Privy Councillor and superfluous member of various superfluous institutions, Ilya Epimovich Golovin.

He had three sons, of whom Ivan Ilych was the second. The eldest son was following in his father's footsteps only in another department, and was already approaching that stage in the service at which a similar sinecure would be reached. The third son was a failure. He had ruined his prospects in a number of positions and was now serving in the railway department. His father and brothers, and still more their wives, not merely disliked meeting him, but avoided remembering his existence unless compelled to do so. His sister had married Baron Greff, a Petersburg official of her father's type. Ivan Ilych was *le phénix de la famille*[5] as people said. He was neither as cold and formal as his elder brother nor as wild as the younger, but was a happy mean between them—an intelligent, polished, lively and agreeable man. He had studied with his younger brother at the School of Law, but the latter had failed to complete the course and was expelled when he was in the fifth class. Ivan Ilych finished the course well. Even when he was at the School of Law he was just what he remained for the rest of his life: a capable, cheerful, good-natured, and sociable man, though strict in the fulfilment of what he considered to be his duty: and he considered his duty to be what was so considered by those in authority. Neither as a boy nor as a man was he a toady, but from early youth was by nature attracted to people of high station as a fly is drawn to the light, assimilating their ways and views of life and establishing friendly relations with them. All the enthusiasms of childhood and youth passed without leaving much trace on him; he succumbed to sensuality, to vanity, and latterly among the highest classes to liberalism, but always within limits which his instinct unfailingly indicated to him as correct.

At school he had done things which had formerly seemed to him very horrid and made him feel disgusted with himself when he did them; but when later on he saw that such actions were done by people of good position and that they did not regard them as wrong, he was able not exactly to regard them as right, but to forget about them entirely or not be at all troubled at remembering them.

Having graduated from the School of Law and qualified for the tenth rank of the civil service,[6] and having received money from his father for his equipment, Ivan Ilych ordered himself clothes at Scharmer's, the fashionable tailor, hung a medallion inscribed *respice finem*[7] on his watch-chain, took leave of his professor and the prince who was patron of the school, had a farewell dinner with his comrades at Donon's first-class restaurant, and with his new and fashionable portmanteau, linen, clothes, shaving and other toilet appliances, and a travelling rug, all purchased at the best shops, he set off for one of the provinces where, through his father's influence, he had been attached to the Governor as an official for special service.

In the province Ivan Ilych soon arranged as easy and agreeable a position for himself as he had had at the School of Law. He performed his official tasks,

---

5. "The model of the family." Many educated Russians of the period knew French; hence, the many French expressions and idioms in the story.
6. A very respectable position in the Russian civil service.
7. "Regard the end" (a Latin motto).

made his career, and at the same time amused himself pleasantly and decorously. Occasionally he paid official visits to country districts, where he behaved with dignity both to his superiors and inferiors, and performed the duties entrusted to him, which related chiefly to the sectarians,[8] with an exactness and incorruptible honesty of which he could not but feel proud.

In official matters, despite his youth and taste for frivolous gaiety, he was exceedingly reserved, punctilious, and even severe; but in society he was often amusing and witty, and always good-natured, correct in his manner, and *bon enfant,*[9] as the governor and his wife—with whom he was like one of the family—used to say of him.

In the province he had an affair with a lady who made advances to the elegant young lawyer, and there was also a milliner; and there were carousals with aides-de-camp who visited the district, and after-supper visits to a certain outlying street of doubtful reputation; and there was too some obsequiousness to his chief and even to his chief's wife, but all this was done with such a tone of good breeding that no hard names could be applied to it. It all came under the heading of the French saying: *"Il faut que jeunesse se passe."*[10] It was all done with clean hands, in clean linen, with French phrases, and above all among people of the best society and consequently with the approval of people of rank.

So Ivan Ilych served for five years and then came a change in his official life. The new and reformed judicial institutions were introduced, and new men were needed. Ivan Ilych became such a new man. He was offered the post of examining magistrate, and he accepted it though the post was in another province and obliged him to give up the connexions he had formed and to make new ones. His friends met to give him a send-off; they had a group-photograph taken and presented him with a silver cigarette-case, and he set off to his new post.

As examining magistrate Ivan Ilych was just as *comme il faut*[11] and decorous a man, inspiring general respect and capable of separating his official duties from his private life, as he had been when acting as an official on special service. His duties now as examining magistrate were far more interesting and attractive than before. In his former position it had been pleasant to wear an undress uniform made by Scharmer, and to pass through the crowd of petitioners and officials who were timorously awaiting an audience with the governor, and who envied him as with free and easy gait he went straight into his chief's private room to have a cup of tea and cigarette with him. But not many people had then been directly dependent on him—only police officials and the sectarians when he went on special missions—and he liked to treat them politely, almost as comrades, as if he were letting them feel that he who had the power to crush them was treating them in this simple, friendly way. There were then but few such people. But now, as an examining magistrate, Ivan Ilych felt that everyone without exception, even the most important and self-satisfied, was in his power, and that he need only write a few words on a sheet of paper

---

8. Old Believers or "Dissenters" from the seventeenth-century reforms instituted in the Eastern Orthodox Church. Many legal restrictions were placed upon them.
9. "A good child."
10. "Youth must have its fling."
11. "As it should be"; proper.

with a certain heading, and this or that important, self-satisfied person would be brought before him in the role of an accused person or a witness, and if he did not choose to allow him to sit down, would have to stand before him and answer his questions. Ivan Ilych never abused his power; he tried on the contrary to soften its expression, but the consciousness of it and of the possibility of softening its effect, supplied the chief interest and attraction of his office. In his work itself, especially in his examinations, he very soon acquired a method of eliminating all considerations irrelevant to the legal aspect of the case, and reducing even the most complicated case to a form in which it would be presented on paper only in its externals, completely excluding his personal opinion of the matter, while above all observing every prescribed formality. The work was new and Ivan Ilych was one of the first men to apply the new Code of 1864.[12]

On taking up the post of examining magistrate in a new town, he made new acquaintances and connexions, placed himself on a new footing, and assumed a somewhat different tone. He took up an attitude of rather dignified aloofness towards the provincial authorities, but picked out the best circle of legal gentlemen and wealthy gentry living in the town and assumed a tone of slight dissatisfaction with the government, of moderate liberalism, and of enlightened citizenship. At the same time, without at all altering the elegance of his toilet, he ceased shaving his chin and allowed his beard to grow as it pleased.

Ivan Ilych settled down very pleasantly in this new town. The society there, which inclined towards opposition to the Governor, was friendly, his salary was larger, and he began to play *vint*,[13] which he found added not a little to the pleasure of life, for he had a capacity for cards, played good-humouredly, and calculated rapidly and astutely, so that he usually won.

After living there for two years he met his future wife, Praskovya Fëdorovna Mikhel, who was the most attractive, clever, and brilliant girl of the set in which he moved, and among other amusements and relaxations from his labours as examining magistrate, Ivan Ilych established light and playful relations with her.

While he had been an official on special service he had been accustomed to dance, but now as an examining magistrate it was exceptional for him to do so. If he danced now, he did it as if to show that though he served under the reformed order of things, and had reached the fifth official rank, yet when it came to dancing he could do it better than most people. So at the end of an evening he sometimes danced with Praskovya Fëdorovna, and it was chiefly during these dances that he captivated her. She fell in love with him. Ivan Ilych had at first no definite intention of marrying, but when the girl fell in love with him he said to himself: "Really, why shouldn't I marry?"

Praskovya Fëdorovna came of a good family, was not bad looking, and had some little property. Ivan Ilych might have aspired to a more brilliant match, but even this was good. He had his salary, and she, he hoped, would have an equal income. She was well connected, and was a sweet, pretty, and thoroughly correct young woman. To say that Ivan Ilych married because he

---

12. A general term referring to the legal and judicial reforms that resulted from the emancipation of the Russian serfs in 1861.

13. A card game resembling whist and similar in bidding to auction bridge.

fell in love with Praskovya Fëdorovna and found that she sympathized with his views of life would be as incorrect as to say that he married because his social circle approved of the match. He was swayed by both these considerations: the marriage gave him personal satisfaction, and at the same time it was considered the right thing by the most highly placed of his associates.

So Ivan Ilych got married.

The preparations for marriage and the beginning of married life, with its conjugal caresses, the new furniture, new crockery, and new linen, were very pleasant until his wife became pregnant—so that Ivan Ilych had begun to think that marriage would not impair the easy, agreeable, gay and always decorous character of his life, approved of by society and regarded by himself as natural, but would even improve it. But from the first months of his wife's pregnancy, something new, unpleasant, depressing, and unseemly, and from which there was no way of escape, unexpectedly showed itself.

His wife, without any reason—*de gaieté de coeur*[14] as Ivan Ilych expressed it to himself—began to disturb the pleasure and propriety of their life. She began to be jealous without any cause, expected him to devote his whole attention to her, found fault with everything, and made coarse and ill-mannered scenes.

At first Ivan Ilych hoped to escape from the unpleasantness of this state of affairs by the same easy and decorous relation to life that had served him heretofore: he tried to ignore his wife's disagreeable moods, continued to live in his usual easy and pleasant way, invited friends to his house for a game of cards, and also tried going out to his club or spending his evenings with friends. But one day his wife began upbraiding him so vigorously, using such coarse words, and continued to abuse him every time he did not fulfil her demands, so resolutely and with such evident determination not to give way till he submitted —that is, till he stayed at home and was bored just as she was—that he became alarmed. He now realized that matrimony—at any rate with Praskovya Fëdorovna—was not always conducive to the pleasures and amenities of life, but on the contrary often infringed both comfort and propriety, and that he must therefore entrench himself against such infringement. And Ivan Ilych began to seek for means of doing so. His official duties were the one thing that imposed upon Praskovya Fëdorovna, and by means of his official work and the duties attached to it he began struggling with his wife to secure his own independence.

With the birth of their child, the attempts to feed it and the various failures in doing so, and with the real and imaginary illnesses of mother and child, in which Ivan Ilych's sympathy was demanded but about which he understood nothing, the need of securing for himself an existence outside his family life became still more imperative.

As his wife grew more irritable and exacting and Ivan Ilych transferred the centre of gravity of his life more and more to his official work, so did he grow to like his work better and became more ambitious than before.

Very soon, within a year of his wedding, Ivan Ilych had realized that marriage, though it may add some comforts to life, is in fact a very intricate and difficult affair towards which in order to perform one's duty, that is, to lead a dec-

---

14. "Out of sheer wantonness."

orous life approved of by society, one must adopt a definite attitude just as towards one's official duties.

And Ivan Ilych evolved such an attitude towards married life. He only required of it those conveniences—dinner at home, housewife, and bed—which it could give him, and above all that propriety of external forms required by public opinion. For the rest he looked for light-hearted pleasure and propriety, and was very thankful when he found them, but if he met with antagonism and querulousness he at once retired into his separate fenced-off world of official duties, where he found satisfaction.

Ivan Ilych was esteemed a good official, and after three years was made Assistant Public Prosecutor. His new duties, their importance, the possibility of indicting and imprisoning anyone he chose, the publicity his speeches received, and the success he had in all these things, made his work still more attractive.

More children came. His wife became more and more querulous and ill-tempered, but the attitude Ivan Ilych had adopted towards his home life rendered him almost impervious to her grumbling.

After seven years' service in that town he was transferred to another province as Public Prosecutor. They moved, but were short of money and his wife did not like the place they moved to. Though the salary was higher the cost of living was greater, besides which two of their children died and family life became still more unpleasant for him.

Praskovya Fëdorovna blamed her husband for every inconvenience they encountered in their new home. Most of the conversations between husband and wife, especially as to the children's education, led to topics which recalled former disputes, and those disputes were apt to flare up again at any moment. There remained only those rare periods of amorousness which still came to them at times but did not last long. These were islets at which they anchored for a while and then again set out upon that ocean of veiled hostility which showed itself in their aloofness from one another. This aloofness might have grieved Ivan Ilych had he considered that it ought not to exist, but he now regarded the position as normal, and even made it the goal at which he aimed in family life. His aim was to free himself more and more from those unpleasantnesses and to give them a semblance of harmlessness and propriety. He attained this by spending less and less time with his family, and when obliged to be at home he tried to safeguard his position by the presence of outsiders. The chief thing however was that he had his official duties. The whole interest of his life now centred in the official world and that interest absorbed him. The consciousness of his power, being able to ruin anybody he wished to ruin, the importance, even the external dignity of his entry into court, or meetings with his subordinates, his success with superiors and inferiors, and above all his masterly handling of cases, of which he was conscious—all this gave him pleasure and filled his life, together with chats with his colleagues, dinners, and bridge. So that on the whole Ivan Ilych's life continued to flow as he considered it should do—pleasantly and properly.

So things continued for another seven years. His eldest daughter was already sixteen, another child had died, and only one son was left, a schoolboy and a subject of dissension. Ivan Ilych wanted to put him in the School of Law, but to spite him Praskovya Fëdorovna entered him at the High School. The daughter had been educated at home and had turned out well: the boy did not learn badly either.

III

So Ivan Ilych lived for seventeen years after his marriage. He was already a Public Prosecutor of long standing, and had declined several proposed transfers while awaiting a more desirable post, when an unanticipated and unpleasant occurrence quite upset the peaceful course of his life. He was expecting to be offered the post of presiding judge in a University town, but Happe somehow came to the front and obtained the appointment instead. Ivan Ilych became irritable, reproached Happe, and quarrelled both with him and with his immediate superiors—who became colder to him and again passed him over when other appointments were made.

This was in 1880, the hardest year of Ivan Ilych's life. It was then that it became evident on the one hand that his salary was insufficient for them to live on, and on the other hand that he had been forgotten, and not only this, but that what was for him the greatest and most cruel injustice appeared to others a quite ordinary occurrence. Even his father did not consider it his duty to help him. Ivan Ilych felt himself abandoned by everyone, and that they regarded his position with a salary of 3,500 rubles as quite normal and even fortunate. He alone knew that with the consciousness of the injustices done him, with his wife's incessant nagging, and with the debts he had contracted by living beyond his means, his position was far from normal.

In order to save money that summer he obtained leave of absence and went with his wife to live in the country at her brother's place.

In the country, without his work, he experienced *ennui*[15] for the first time in his life, and not only *ennui* but intolerable depression, and he decided that it was impossible to go on living like that, and that it was necessary to take energetic measures.

Having passed a sleepless night pacing up and down the veranda, he decided to go to Petersburg[16] and bestir himself, in order to punish those who had failed to appreciate him and to get transferred to another ministry.

Next day, despite many protests from his wife and her brother, he started for Petersburg with the sole object of obtaining a post with a salary of five thousand rubles a year. He was no longer bent on any particular department or tendency, or kind of activity. All he now wanted was an appointment to another post with a salary of five thousand rubles, either in the administration, in the banks, with the railways, in one of the Empress Marya's Institutions,[17] or even in the customs—but it had to carry with it a salary of five thousand rubles and be in a ministry other than that in which they had failed to appreciate him.

And this quest of Ivan Ilych's was crowned with remarkable and unexpected success. At Kursk an acquaintance of his, F. I. Ilyin, got into the first-class carriage, sat down beside Ivan Ilych, and told him of a telegram just re-

---

15. Boredom.

16. Czarist capital of Imperial Russia until 1918. During the time of the story, it was Russia's cultural and educational center; renamed Leningrad in 1924.

17. Around 1830, a state ministry was created to administer the charitable institutions and women's schools established by Empress Marya Feodorovna (1759–1828), wife of Czar Paul I.

ceived by the Governor of Kursk announcing that a change was about to take place in the ministry: Peter Ivanovich was to be superseded by Ivan Seménovich.

The proposed change, apart from its significance for Russia, had a special significance for Ivan Ilych, because by bringing forward a new man, Peter Petrovich, and consequently his friend Zachar Ivanovich, it was highly favourable for Ivan Ilych, since Zachar Ivanovich was a friend and colleague of his.

In Moscow this news was confirmed, and on reaching Petersburg Ivan Ilych found Zachar Ivanovich and received a definite promise of an appointment in his former department of Justice.

A week later he telegraphed to his wife: "Zachar in Miller's place. I shall receive appointment on presentation of report."

Thanks to this change of personnel, Ivan Ilych had unexpectedly obtained an appointment in his former ministry which placed him two stages above his former colleagues besides giving him five thousand rubles salary and three thousand five hundred rubles for expenses connected with his removal. All his ill humour towards his former enemies and the whole department vanished, and Ivan Ilych was completely happy.

He returned to the country more cheerful and contented than he had been for a long time. Praskovya Fëdorovna also cheered up and a truce was arranged between them. Ivan Ilych told of how he had been fêted by everybody in Petersburg, how all those who had been his enemies were put to shame and now fawned on him, how envious they were of his appointment, and how much everybody in Petersburg had liked him.

Praskovya Fëdorovna listened to all this and appeared to believe it. She did not contradict anything, but only made plans for their life in the town to which they were going. Ivan Ilych saw with delight that these plans were his plans, that he and his wife agreed, and that, after a stumble, his life was regaining its due and natural character of pleasant lightheartedness and decorum.

Ivan Ilych had come back for a short time only, for he had to take up his new duties on the 10th of September. Moreover, he needed time to settle into the new place, to move all his belongings from the province, and to buy and order many additional things: in a word, to make such arrangements as he had resolved on, which were almost exactly what Praskovya Fëdorovna too had decided on.

Now that everything had happened so fortunately, and that he and his wife were at one in their aims and moreover saw so little of one another, they got on together better than they had done since the first years of marriage. Ivan Ilych had thought of taking his family away with him at once, but the insistence of his wife's brother and her sister-in-law, who had suddenly become particularly amiable and friendly to him and his family, induced him to depart alone.

So he departed, and the cheerful state of mind induced by his success and by the harmony between his wife and himself, the one intensifying the other, did not leave him. He found a delightful house, just the thing both he and his wife had dreamt of. Spacious, lofty reception rooms in the old style, a convenient and dignified study, rooms for his wife and daughter, a study for his son—it might have been specially built for them. Ivan Ilych himself superintended the arrangements, chose the wallpapers, supplemented the furniture (preferably with antiques which he considered particularly *comme il faut*), and supervised the upholstering. Everything progressed and progressed and approached the ideal he had set himself: even when things were only half completed they exceeded his expectations. He saw what a refined and elegant character, free from vulgarity, it would all have when it was ready. On falling asleep he pictured to himself how the reception-room would look. Looking at the yet unfinished drawing-room he could see the fireplace, the screen, the what-not, the little chairs dotted here and there, the dishes and plates on the walls, and the bronzes, as they would be when everything was in place. He was pleased by the thought of how his wife and daughter, who shared his taste in this matter, would be impressed by it. They were certainly not expecting as much. He had been particularly successful in finding, and buying cheaply, antiques which gave a particularly aristocratic character to the whole place. But in his letters he intentionally understated everything in order to be able to surprise them. All this so absorbed him that his new duties—though he liked his official work—interested him less than he had expected. Sometimes he even had moments of absentmindedness during the Court Sessions, and would consider whether he should have straight or curved cornices for his curtains. He was so interested in it all that he often did things himself, rearranging the furniture, or rehanging the curtains. Once when mounting a step-ladder to show the upholsterer, who did not understand, how he wanted the hangings draped, he made a false step and slipped, but being a strong and agile man he clung on and only knocked his side against the knob of the window frame. The bruised place was painful but the pain soon passed, and he felt particularly bright and well just then. He wrote: "I feel fifteen years younger." He thought he would have everything ready by September, but it dragged on till mid-October. But the result was charming not only in his eyes but to everyone who saw it.

In reality it was just what is usually seen in the houses of people of moderate means who want to appear rich, and therefore succeed only in resembling others like themselves: there were damasks, dark wood, plants, rugs, and dull and polished bronzes—all the things people of a certain class have in order to resemble other people of that class. His house was so like the others that it would never have been noticed, but to him it all seemed to be quite exceptional. He was very happy when he met his family at the station and brought them to the newly furnished house all lit up, where a footman in a white tie opened the door into the hall decorated with plants, and when they went on into the drawing-room and the study uttering exclamations of delight. He conducted them everywhere, drank in their praises eagerly, and beamed with pleasure. At tea that evening, when Praskovya Fëdorovna among other things asked him about his fall, he laughed and showed them how he had gone flying and had frightened the upholsterer.

"It's a good thing I'm a bit of an athlete. Another man might have been killed, but I merely knocked myself, just here; it hurts when it's touched, but it's passing off already—it's only a bruise."

So they began living in their new home—in which, as always happens, when they got thoroughly settled in they found they were just one room short—and with the increased income, which as always was just a little (some five hundred rubles) too little, but it was all very nice.

Things went particularly well at first, before everything was finally arranged and while something had still to be done: this thing bought, that thing ordered, another thing moved, and something else adjusted. Though there were some disputes between husband and wife, they were both so well satisfied and had so much to do that it all passed off without any serious quarrels. When nothing was left to arrange it became rather dull and something seemed to be lacking, but they were then making acquaintances, forming habits, and life was growing fuller.

Ivan Ilych spent his mornings at the law court and came home to dinner, and at first he was generally in a good humour, though he occasionally became irritable just on account of his house. (Every spot on the tablecloth or the upholstery, and every broken window-blind string, irritated him. He had devoted so much trouble to arranging it all that every disturbance of it distressed him.) But on the whole his life ran its course as he believed life should do: easily, pleasantly, and decorously.

He got up at nine, drank his coffee, read the paper, and then put on his undress uniform and went to the law courts. There the harness in which he worked had already been stretched to fit him and he donned it without a hitch: petitioners, inquiries at the chancery, the chancery itself, and the sittings public and administrative. In all this the thing was to exclude everything fresh and vital, which always disturbs the regular course of official business, and to admit only official relations with people, and then only on official grounds. A man would come, for instance, wanting some information. Ivan Ilych, as one in whose sphere the matter did not lie, would have nothing to do with him: but if the man had some business with him in his official capacity, something that could be expressed on officially stamped paper, he would do everything, positively everything he could within the limits of such relations, and in doing so would maintain the semblance of friendly human relations, that is, would observe the courtesies of life. As soon as the official relations ended, so did everything else. Ivan Ilych possessed this capacity to separate his real life from the official side of affairs and not mix the two, in the highest degree, and by long practice and natural aptitude had brought it to such a pitch that sometimes, in the manner of a virtuoso, he would even allow himself to let the human and official relations mingle. He let himself do this just because he felt that he could at any time he chose resume the strictly official attitude again and drop the human relation. And he did it all easily, pleasantly, correctly, and even artistically. In the intervals between the sessions he smoked, drank tea, chatted a little about politics, a little about general topics, a little about cards, but most of all about official appointments. Tired, but with the feelings of a virtuoso—one of the first violins who has played his part in an orchestra with precision—he would return home to find that his wife and daughter had been out paying calls, or had a visitor, and that his son had been to school, had done his homework with his tutor, and was duly learning what is taught at High Schools. Everything was as it should be. After dinner, if they had no visitors, Ivan Ilych sometimes read a book that was being much discussed at the time, and in the evening settled down to work, that is, read official papers, compared the depositions of witnesses, and noted paragraphs of the Code applying to them. This was neither dull nor amusing. It was dull when he might have been playing bridge, but if no bridge was available it was at any rate better than doing nothing or sitting with his wife. Ivan Ilych's chief pleasure was giving little dinners to which he invited men and women of good social position, and just as his drawing-room resembled all other drawing-rooms so did his enjoyable little parties resemble all other such parties.

Once they even gave a dance. Ivan Ilych enjoyed it and everything went off well, except that it led to a violent quarrel with his wife about the cakes and sweets. Praskovya Fëdorovna had made her own plans, but Ivan Ilych insisted on getting everything from an expensive confectioner and ordered too many cakes, and the quarrel occurred because some of those cakes were left over and the confectioner's bill came to forty-five rubles. It was a great and disagreeable quarrel. Praskovya Fëdorovna called him "a fool and an imbecile," and he clutched at his head and made angry allusions to divorce.

But the dance itself had been enjoyable. The best people were there, and Ivan Ilych had danced with Princess Trufonova, a sister of the distinguished founder of the Society "Bear my Burden."

The pleasures connected with his work were pleasures of ambition; his social pleasures were those of vanity; but Ivan Ilych's greatest pleasure was playing bridge. He acknowledged that whatever disagreeable incident happened in his life, the pleasure that beamed like a ray of light above everything else was to sit down to bridge with good players, not noisy partners, and of course to four-handed bridge (with five players it was annoying to have to stand out, though one pretended not to mind), to play a clever and serious game (when the cards allowed it) and then to have supper and drink a glass of wine. After a game of bridge, especially if he had won a little (to win a large sum was unpleasant), Ivan Ilych went to bed in specially good humour.

So they lived. They formed a circle of acquaintances among the best people and were visited by people of importance and by young folk. In their views as to their acquaintances, husband, wife and daughter were entirely agreed, and tacitly and unanimously kept at arm's length and shook off the shabby friends and relations who, with much show of affection, gushed into the drawing-room with its Japanese plates on the walls. Soon these shabby friends ceased to obtrude themselves and only the best people remained in the Golovins' set.

Young men made up to Lisa, and Petrishchev, an examining magistrate and Dmitri Ivanovich Petrishchev's son and sole heir, began to be so attentive to her that Ivan Ilych had already spoken to Praskovya Fëdorovna about it, and considered whether they should not arrange a party for them, or get up some private theatricals.

So they lived, and all went well, without change, and life flowed pleasantly.

IV

They were all in good health. It could not be called ill health if Ivan Ilych sometimes said that he had a queer taste in his mouth and felt some discomfort in his left side.

But this discomfort increased and, though not exactly painful, grew into a sense of pressure in his side accompanied by ill humour. And his irritability became worse and worse and began to mar the agreeable, easy, and correct life that had established itself in the Golovin family. Quarrels between husband and wife became more and more frequent, and soon the ease and amenity disappeared and even the decorum was barely maintained. Scenes again became frequent, and very few of those islets remained on which husband and wife could meet without an explosion. Praskovya Fëdorovna now had good reason to say that her husband's temper was trying. With characteristic exaggeration she said he had always had a dreadful temper, and that it had needed all her good nature to put up with it for twenty years. It was true that now the quarrels were started by him. His bursts of temper always came just before dinner, often just as he began to eat his soup. Sometimes he noticed that a plate or dish was chipped, or the food was not right, or his son put his elbow on the table, or his daughter's hair was not done as he liked it, and for all this he blamed Praskovya Fëdorovna. At first she retorted and said disagreeable things to him, but once or twice he fell into such a rage at the beginning of dinner that she realized it was due to some physical derangement brought on by taking food, and so she restrained herself and did not answer, but only hurried to get the dinner over. She regarded this self-restraint as highly praiseworthy. Having come to the conclusion that her husband had a dreadful temper and made her life miserable, she began to feel sorry for herself, and the more she pitied herself the more she hated her husband. She began to wish he would die; yet she did not want him to die because then his salary would cease. And this irritated her against him still more. She considered herself dreadfully unhappy just because not even his death could save her, and though she concealed her exasperation, that hidden exasperation of hers increased his irritation also.

After one scene in which Ivan Ilych had been particularly unfair and after which he had said in explanation that he certainly was irritable but that it was due to his not being well, she said that if he was ill it should be attended to, and insisted on his going to see a celebrated doctor.

He went. Everything took place as he had expected and as it always does. There was the usual waiting and the important air assumed by the doctor, with which he was so familiar (resembling that which he himself assumed in court), and the sounding and listening, and the questions which called for answers that were foregone conclusions and were evidently unnecessary, and the look of importance which implied that "if only you put yourself in our hands we will arrange everything—we know indubitably how it has to be done, always in the same way for everybody alike." It was all just as it was in the law courts. The doctor put on just the same air towards him as he himself put on towards an accused person.

The doctor said that so-and-so indicated there was so-and-so inside the patient, but if the investigation of so-and-so did not confirm this, then he must assume that and that. If he assumed that and that, then . . . . and so on. To Ivan Ilych only one question was important: was his case serious or not? But the doctor ignored that inappropriate question. From his point of view it was not the one under consideration, the real question was to decide between a floating kidney, chronic catarrh,[18] or appendicitis. It was not a question of Ivan Ilych's life or death, but one between a floating kidney and appendicitis. And that question the doctor solved brilliantly, as it seemed to Ivan Ilych, in favour of the appendix, with the reservation that should an examination of the urine give fresh indications the matter would be reconsidered. All this was just what

---

18. Inflammation and congestion of an intestinal mucous membrane.

Ivan Ilych had himself brilliantly accomplished a thousand times in dealing with men on trial. The doctor summed up just as brilliantly, looking over his spectacles triumphantly and even gaily at the accused. From the doctor's summing up Ivan Ilych concluded that things were bad, but that for the doctor, and perhaps for everybody else, it was a matter of indifference, though for him it was bad. And this conclusion struck him painfully, arousing in him a great feeling of pity for himself and of bitterness towards the doctor's indifference to a matter of such importance.

He said nothing of this, but rose, placed the doctor's fee on the table, and remarked with a sigh: "We sick people probably often put inappropriate questions. But tell me, in general, is this complaint dangerous, or not? . . ."

The doctor looked at him sternly over his spectacles with one eye, as if to say: "Prisoner, if you will not keep to the questions put to you, I shall be obliged to have you removed from the court."

"I have already told you what I consider necessary and proper. The analysis may show something more." And the doctor bowed.

Ivan Ilych went out slowly, seated himself disconsolately in his sledge, and drove home. All the way home he was going over what the doctor had said, trying to translate those complicated, obscure, scientific phrases into plain language and find in them an answer to the question: "Is my condition bad? Is it very bad? Or is there as yet nothing much wrong?" And it seemed to him that the meaning of what the doctor had said was that it was very bad. Everything in the streets seemed depressing. The cabmen, the houses, the passers-by, and the shops, were dismal. His ache, this dull gnawing ache that never ceased for a moment, seemed to have acquired a new and more serious significance from the doctor's dubious remarks. Ivan Ilych now watched it with a new and oppressive feeling.

He reached home and began to tell his wife about it. She listened, but in the middle of his account his daughter came in with her hat on, ready to go out with her mother. She sat down reluctantly to listen to this tedious story, but could not stand it long, and her mother too did not hear him to the end.

"Well, I am very glad," she said. "Mind now to take your medicine regularly. Give me the prescription and I'll send Gerasim to the chemist's." And she went to get ready to go out.

While she was in the room Ivan Ilych had hardly taken time to breathe, but he sighed deeply when she left it.

"Well," he thought, "perhaps it isn't so bad after all."

He began taking his medicine and following the doctor's directions, which had been altered after the examination of the urine. But then it happened that there was a contradiction between the indications drawn from the examination of the urine and the symptoms that showed themselves. It turned out that what was happening differed from what the doctor had told him, and that he had either forgotten, or blundered, or hidden something from him. He could not, however, be blamed for that, and Ivan Ilych still obeyed his orders implicitly and at first derived some comfort from doing so.

From the time of his visit to the doctor, Ivan Ilych's chief occupation was the exact fulfilment of the doctor's instructions regarding hygiene and the taking of medicine, and the observation of his pain and his excretions. His chief interests came to be people's ailments and people's health. When sickness, deaths, or recoveries were mentioned in his presence, especially when the illness resembled his own, he listened with agitation which he tried to hide, asked questions, and applied what he heard to his own case.

The pain did not grow less, but Ivan Ilych made efforts to force himself to think that he was better. And he could do this so long as nothing agitated him. But as soon as he had any unpleasantness with his wife, or a lack of success in his official work, or held bad cards at bridge, he was at once acutely sensible of his disease. He had formerly borne such mischances, hoping soon to adjust what was wrong, to master it and attain success, or make a grand slam. But now every mischance upset him and plunged him into despair. He would say to himself: ''There now, just as I was beginning to get better and the medicine had begun to take effect, comes this accursed misfortune, or unpleasantness . . .'' And he was furious with the mishap, or with the people who were causing the unpleasantness and killing him, for he felt that this fury was killing him but could not restrain it. One would have thought that it should have been clear to him that this exasperation with circumstances and people aggravated his illness, and that he ought therefore to ignore unpleasant occurrences. But he drew the very opposite conclusion: he said that he needed peace, and he watched for everything that might disturb it and became irritable at the slightest infringement of it. His condition was rendered worse by the fact that he read medical books and consulted doctors. The progress of his disease was so gradual that he could deceive himself when comparing one day with another—the difference was so slight. But when he consulted the doctors it seemed to him that he was getting worse, and even very rapidly. Yet despite this he was continually consulting them.

That month he went to see another celebrity, who told him almost the same as the first had done but put his questions rather differently, and the interview with this celebrity only increased Ivan Ilych's doubts and fears. A friend of a friend of his, a very good doctor, diagnosed his illness again quite differently from the others, and though he predicted recovery, his questions and suppositions bewildered Ivan Ilych still more and increased his doubts. A homeopathist diagnosed the disease in yet another way, and prescribed medicine which Ivan Ilych took secretly for a week. But after a week, not feeling any improvement and having lost confidence both in the former doctor's treatment and in this one's, he became still more despondent. One day a lady acquaintance mentioned a cure effected by a wonder-working icon. Ivan Ilych caught himself listening attentively and beginning to believe that it had occurred. This incident alarmed him. ''Has my mind really weakened to such an extent?'' he asked himself. ''Nonsense! It's all rubbish. I mustn't give way to nervous fears but having chosen a doctor must keep strictly to his treatment. That is what I will do. Now it's all settled. I won't think about it, but will follow the treatment seriously till summer, and then we shall see. From now there must be no more of this wavering!'' This was easy to say but impossible to carry out. The pain in his side oppressed him and seemed to grow worse and more incessant, while the taste in his mouth grew stranger and stranger. It seemed to him that his breath had a disgusting smell, and he was conscious of a loss of appetite and strength. There was no deceiving himself: something terrible, new, and more important than anything before in his life, was taking place within him of which he alone was aware. Those about him did not understand or would not understand it, but thought everything in the world was going on as usual. That tormented Ivan Ilych more than anything. He saw that his household, especially his wife and daughter who were in a perfect whirl of visiting, did not understand anything of it and were annoyed that he was so depressed and so exacting, as if he were to blame for it. Though they tried to disguise it he saw that he was an obstacle in their path, and that his wife had adopted a definite line in regard to his illness and kept to it regardless of anything he said or did. Her attitude was this: "You know," she would say to her friends, "Ivan Ilych can't do as other people do, and keep to the treatment prescribed for him. One day he'll take his drops and keep strictly to his diet and go to bed in good time, but the next day unless I watch him he'll suddenly forget his medicine, eat sturgeon—which is forbidden—and sit up playing cards till one o'clock in the morning."

"Oh, come, when was that?" Ivan Ilych would ask in vexation. "Only once at Peter Ivanovich's."

"And yesterday with Shebek."

"Well, even if I hadn't stayed up, this pain would have kept me awake."

"Be that as it may you'll never get well like that, but will always make us wretched."

Praskovya Fëdorovna's attitude to Ivan Ilych's illness, as she expressed it both to others and to him, was that it was his own fault and was another of the annoyances he caused her. Ivan Ilych felt that this opinion escaped her involuntarily—but that did not make it easier for him.

At the law courts too, Ivan Ilych noticed, or thought he noticed, a strange attitude towards himself. It sometimes seemed to him that people were watching him inquisitively as a man whose place might soon be vacant. Then again, his friends would suddenly begin to chaff him in a friendly way about his low spirits, as if the awful, horrible, and unheard-of thing that was going on within him, incessantly gnawing at him and irresistibly drawing him away, was a very agreeable subject for jests. Schwartz in particular irritated him by his jocularity, vivacity, and *savoir-faire,*[19] which reminded him of what he himself had been ten years ago.

Friends came to make up a set and they sat down to cards. They dealt, bending the new cards to soften them, and he sorted the diamonds in his hand and found he had seven. His partner said "No trumps" and supported him with two diamonds. What more could be wished for? It ought to be jolly and lively. They would make a grand slam. But suddenly Ivan Ilych was conscious of that gnawing pain, that taste in his mouth, and it seemed ridiculous that in such circumstances he should be pleased to make a grand slam.

He looked at his partner Mikhail Mikhaylovich, who rapped the table with his strong hand and instead of snatching up the tricks pushed the cards courteously and indulgently towards Ivan Ilych that he might have the pleasure of gathering them up without the trouble of stretching out his hand for them. "Does he think I am too weak to stretch out my arm?" thought Ivan Ilych, and forgetting what he was doing he over-trumped his partner, missing the grand slam by three tricks. And what was most awful of all was that he saw how upset

---

19. Knowing just the right thing to do and say.

Mikhail Mikhaylovich was about it but did not himself care. And it was dreadful to realize why he did not care.

They all saw that he was suffering, and said: "We can stop if you are tired. Take a rest." Lie down? No, he was not at all tired, and he finished the rubber. All were gloomy and silent. Ivan Ilych felt that he had diffused this gloom over them and could not dispel it. They had supper and went away, and Ivan Ilych was left alone with the consciousness that his life was poisoned and was poisoning the lives of others, and that this poison did not weaken but penetrated more and more deeply into his whole being.

With this consciousness, and with physical pain besides that terror, he must go to bed, often to lie awake the greater part of the night. Next morning he had to get up again, dress, go to the law courts, speak, and write; or if he did not go out, spend at home those twenty-four hours a day each of which was a torture. And he had to live thus all alone on the brink of an abyss, with no one who understood or pitied him.

V

So one month passed and then another. Just before the New Year his brother-in-law came to town and stayed at their house. Ivan Ilych was at the law courts and Praskovya Fëdorovna had gone shopping. When Ivan Ilych came home and entered his study he found his brother-in-law there—a healthy, florid man—unpacking his portmanteau himself. He raised his head on hearing Ivan Ilych's footsteps and looked up at him for a moment without a word. That stare told Ivan Ilych everything. His brother-in-law opened his mouth to utter an exclamation of surprise but checked himself, and that action confirmed it all.

"I have changed, eh?"

"Yes, there is a change."

And after that, try as he would to get his brother-in-law to return to the subject of his looks, the latter would say nothing about it. Praskovya Fëdorovna came home and her brother went out to her. Ivan Ilych locked the door and began to examine himself in the glass, first full face, then in profile. He took up a portrait of himself taken with his wife, and compared it with what he saw in the glass. The change in him was immense. Then he bared his arms to the elbow, looked at them, drew the sleeves down again, sat down on an ottoman, and grew blacker than night.

"No, no, this won't do!" he said to himself, and jumped up, went to the table, took up some law papers and began to read them, but could not continue. He unlocked the door and went into the reception-room. The door leading to the drawing-room was shut. He approached it on tiptoe and listened.

"No, you are exaggerating!" Praskovya Fëdorovna was saying.

"Exaggerating! Don't you see it? Why, he's a dead man! Look at his eyes—there's no light in them. But what is it that is wrong with him?"

"No one knows. Nikolaevich [that was another doctor] said something, but I don't know what. And Leshchetitsky [this was the celebrated specialist] said quite the contrary . . ."

Ivan Ilych walked away, went to his own room, lay down, and began musing: ''The kidney, a floating kidney.'' He recalled all the doctors had told him of how it detached itself and swayed about. And by an effort of imagination he tried to catch that kidney and arrest it and support it. So little was needed for this, it seemed to him. ''No, I'll go to see Peter Ivanovich again.'' [That was the friend whose friend was a doctor.] He rang, ordered the carriage, and got ready to go.

''Where are you going, Jean?'' asked his wife, with a specially sad and exceptionally kind look.

This exceptionally kind look irritated him. He looked morosely at her. ''I must go to see Peter Ivanovich.''

He went to see Peter Ivanovich, and together they went to see his friend, the doctor. He was in, and Ivan Ilych had a long talk with him.

Reviewing the anatomical and physiological details of what in the doctor's opinion was going on inside him, he understood it all.

There was something, a small thing, in the vermiform appendix. It might all come right. Only stimulate the energy of one organ and check the activity of another, then absorption would take place and everything would come right. He got home rather late for dinner, ate his dinner, conversed cheerfully, but could not for a long time bring himself to go back to work in his room. At last, however, he went to his study and did what was necessary, but the consciousness that he had put something aside—an important, intimate matter which he would revert to when his work was done—never left him. When he had finished his work he remembered that this intimate matter was the thought of his vermiform appendix. But he did not give himself up to it, and went to the drawing-room for tea. There were callers there, including the examining magistrate who was a desirable match for his daughter, and they were conversing, playing the piano, and singing. Ivan Ilych, as Praskovya Fëdorovna remarked, spent that evening more cheerfully than usual, but he never for a moment forgot that he had postponed the important matter of the appendix. At eleven o'clock he said good-night and went to his bedroom. Since his illness he had slept alone in a small room next to his study. He undressed and took up a novel by Zola,[20] but instead of reading it fell into thought, and in his imagination that desired improvement in the vermiform appendix occurred. There was the absorption and evacuation and the re-establishment of normal activity. ''Yes, that's it!'' he said to himself. ''One need only assist nature, that's all.'' He remembered his medicine, rose, took it, and lay down on his back watching for the beneficent action of the medicine and for it to lessen the pain. ''I need only take it regularly and avoid all injurious influences. I am already feeling better, much better.'' He began touching his side: it was not painful to the touch. ''There, I really don't feel it. It's much better already.'' He put out the light and turned on his side . . . ''The appendix is getting better, absorption is occurring.'' Suddenly he felt the old, familiar, dull, gnawing pain, stubborn and serious. There was the same familiar loathsome taste in his mouth. His heart sank and he felt dazed. ''My God! My God!'' he muttered. ''Again, again! and it will never cease.'' And suddenly the matter presented itself in a quite different aspect. ''Vermiform appendix! Kidney!'' he said to himself. ''It's not a

---

20. Émile Zola (1840–1902), popular and controversial French novelist, famous for his naturalistic tales of sordid life in Paris; Tolstoy thought him crude and crass.

question of appendix or kidney, but of life and . . . death. Yes, life was there and now it is going, going and I cannot stop it. Yes. Why deceive myself? Isn't it obvious to everyone but me that I'm dying, and that it's only a question of weeks, days . . . it may happen this moment. There was light and now there is darkness. I was here and now I'm going there! Where?'' A chill came over him, his breathing ceased, and he felt only the throbbing of his heart.

''When I am not, what will there be? There will be nothing. Then where shall I be when I am no more? Can this be dying? No, I don't want to!'' He jumped up and tried to light the candle, felt for it with trembling hands, dropped candle and candlestick on the floor, and fell back on his pillow.

''What's the use? It makes no difference,'' he said to himself, staring with wide-open eyes into the darkness. ''Death. Yes, death. And none of them know or wish to know it, and they have no pity for me. Now they are playing.'' (He heard through the door the distant sound of a song and its accompaniment.) ''It's all the same to them, but they will die too! Fools! I first, and they later, but it will be the same for them. And now they are merry . . . the beasts!''

Anger choked him and he was agonizingly, unbearably, miserable. ''It is impossible that all men have been doomed to suffer this awful horror!'' He raised himself.

''Something must be wrong. I must calm myself—must think it all over from the beginning.'' And he again began thinking. ''Yes, the beginning of my illness: I knocked my side, but I was quite well that day and the next. It hurt a little, then rather more. I saw the doctor, then followed despondency and anguish, more doctors, and I drew nearer to the abyss. My strength grew less and I kept coming nearer and nearer, and now I have wasted away and there is no light in my eyes. I think of the appendix—but this is death! I think of mending the appendix, and all the while here is death! Can it really be death?'' Again terror seized him and he gasped for breath. He leant down and began feeling for the matches, pressing with his elbow on the stand beside the bed. It was in the way and hurt him, he grew furious with it, pressed on it still harder, and upset it. Breathless and in despair he fell on his back, expecting death to come immediately.

Meanwhile the visitors were leaving. Praskovya Fëdorovna was seeing them off. She heard something fall and came in.

''What has happened?''

''Nothing. I knocked it over accidentally.''

She went out and returned with a candle. He lay there panting heavily, like a man who has run a thousand yards, and stared upwards at her with a fixed look.

''What is it, Jean?''

''No . . . o . . . thing. I upset it.'' (''Why speak of it? She won't understand,'' he thought.)

And in truth she did not understand. She picked up the stand, lit his candle, and hurried away to see another visitor off. When she came back he still lay on his back, looking upwards.

''What is it? Do you feel worse?''

''Yes.''

She shook her head and sat down.

"Do you know, Jean, I think we must ask Leshchetitsky to come and see you here."

This meant calling in the famous specialist, regardless of expense. He smiled malignantly and said "No." She remained a little longer and then went up to him and kissed his forehead.

While she was kissing him he hated her from the bottom of his soul and with difficulty refrained from pushing her away.

"Good-night. Please God you'll sleep."

"Yes."

VI

Ivan Ilych saw that he was dying, and he was in continual despair.

In the depth of his heart he knew he was dying, but not only was he not accustomed to the thought, he simply did not and could not grasp it.

The syllogism he had learnt from Kiezewetter's Logic:[21] "Caius is a man, men are mortal, therefore Caius is mortal," had always seemed to him correct as applied to Caius, but certainly not as applied to himself. That Caius—man in the abstract—was mortal, was perfectly correct, but he was not Caius, not an abstract man, but a creature quite, quite separate from all others. He had been little Vanya, with a mamma and a papa, with Mitya and Volodya, with the toys, a coachman and a nurse, afterwards with Katenka and with all the joys, griefs, and delights of childhood, boyhood, and youth. What did Caius know of the smell of that striped leather ball Vanya had been so fond of? Had Caius kissed his mother's hand like that, and did the silk of her dress rustle so for Caius? Had he rioted like that at school when the pastry was bad? Had Caius been in love like that? Could Caius preside at a session as he did? "Caius really was mortal, and it was right for him to die; but for me, little Vanya, Ivan Ilych, with all my thoughts and emotions, it's altogether a different matter. It cannot be that I ought to die. That would be too terrible."

Such was his feeling.

"If I had to die like Caius, I should have known it was so. An inner voice would have told me so, but there was nothing of the sort in me and I and all my friends felt that our case was quite different from that of Caius. And now here it is!" he said to himself. "It can't be. It's impossible! But here it is. How is this? How is one to understand it?"

He could not understand it, and tried to drive this false, incorrect, morbid thought away and to replace it by other proper and healthy thoughts. But that thought, and not the thought only but the reality itself, seemed to come and confront him.

And to replace that thought he called up a succession of others, hoping to find in them some support. He tried to get back into the former current of thoughts that had once screened the thought of death from him. But strange to say, all that had formerly shut off, hidden, and destroyed, his consciousness of death, no longer had that effect. Ivan Ilych now spent most of his time in at-

---

21. Karl Kiezewetter (1766–1819), whose text, *Outline of Logic According to Kantian Principles* (1796), was widely used in Russian schools of the time.

tempting to re-establish that old current. He would say to himself: ''I will take up my duties again—after all I used to live by them.'' And banishing all doubts he would go to the law courts, enter into conversation with his colleagues, and sit carelessly as was his wont, scanning the crowd with a thoughtful look and leaning both his emaciated arms on the arms of his oak chair; bending over as usual to a colleague and drawing his papers nearer he would interchange whispers with him, and then suddenly raising his eyes and sitting erect would pronounce certain words and open the proceedings. But suddenly in the midst of those proceedings the pain in his side, regardless of the stage the proceedings had reached, would begin its own gnawing work. Ivan Ilych would turn his attention to it and try to drive the thought of it away, but without success. *It* would come and stand before him and look at him, and he would be petrified and the light would die out of his eyes, and he would again begin asking himself whether *It* alone was true. And his colleagues and subordinates would see with surprise and distress that he, the brilliant and subtle judge, was becoming confused and making mistakes. He would shake himself, try to pull himself together, manage somehow to bring the sitting to a close, and return home with the sorrowful consciousness that his judicial labours could not as formerly hide from him what he wanted them to hide, and could not deliver him from *It*. And what was worst of all was that *It* drew his attention to itself not in order to make him take some action but only that he should look at *It*, look it straight in the face: look at it and without doing anything, suffer inexpressibly.

And to save himself from this condition Ivan Ilych looked for consolations—new screens—and new screens were found and for a while seemed to save him, but then they immediately fell to pieces or rather became transparent as if *It* penetrated them and nothing could veil *It*.

In these latter days he would go into the drawing-room he had arranged—that drawing-room where he had fallen and for the sake of which (how bitterly ridiculous it seemed) he had sacrificed his life—for he knew that his illness originated with that knock. He would enter and see that something had scratched the polished table. He would look for the cause of this and find that it was the bronze ornamentation of an album, that had got bent. He would take up the expensive album which he had lovingly arranged, and feel vexed with his daughter and her friends for their untidiness—for the album was torn here and there and some of the photographs turned upside down. He would put it carefully in order and bend the ornamentation back into position. Then it would occur to him to place all those things in another corner of the room, near the plants. He would call the footman, but his daughter or wife would come to help him. They would not agree, and his wife would contradict him, and he would dispute and grow angry. But that was all right, for then he did not think about *It*. *It* was invisible.

But then, when he was moving something himself, his wife would say: ''Let the servants do it. You will hurt yourself again.'' And suddenly *It* would flash through the screen and he would see it. It was just a flash, and he hoped it would disappear, but he would involuntarily pay attention to his side. ''It sits there as before, gnawing just the same!'' And he could no longer forget *It*, but could distinctly see it looking at him from behind the flowers. ''What is it all for?''

''It really is so! I lost my life over that curtain as I might have done when storming a fort. Is that possible? How terrible and how stupid. It can't be true! It can't, but it is."

He would go to his study, lie down, and again be alone with *It:* face to face with *It.* And nothing could be done with *It* except to look at it and shudder.

VII

How it happened it is impossible to say because it came about step by step, unnoticed, but in the third month of Ivan Ilych's illness, his wife, his daughter, his son, his acquaintances, the doctors, the servants, and above all he himself, were aware that the whole interest he had for other people was whether he would soon vacate his place, and at last release the living from the discomfort caused by his presence and be himself released from his sufferings.

He slept less and less. He was given opium and hypodermic injections of morphine, but this did not relieve him. The dull depression he experienced in a somnolent condition at first gave him a little relief, but only as something new, afterwards it became as distressing as the pain itself or even more so.

Special foods were prepared for him by the doctors' orders, but all those foods became increasingly distasteful and disgusting to him.

For his excretions also special arrangements had to be made, and this was a torment to him every time—a torment from the uncleanliness, the unseemliness, and the smell, and from knowing that another person had to take part in it.

But just through this most unpleasant matter, Ivan Ilych obtained comfort. Gerasim, the butler's young assistant, always came in to carry the things out. Gerasim was a clean, fresh peasant lad, grown stout on town food and always cheerful and bright. At first the sight of him, in his clean Russian peasant costume, engaged in that disgusting task embarrassed Ivan Ilych.

Once when he got up from the commode too weak to draw up his trousers, he dropped into a soft armchair and looked with horror at his bare, enfeebled thighs with the muscles so sharply marked on them.

Gerasim with a firm light tread, his heavy boots emitting a pleasant smell of tar and fresh winter air, came in wearing a clean Hessian apron, the sleeves of his print shirt tucked up over his strong bare young arms; and refraining from looking at his sick master out of consideration for his feelings, and restraining the joy of life that beamed from his face, he went up to the commode.

"Gerasim!" said Ivan Ilych in a weak voice.

Gerasim started, evidently afraid he might have committed some blunder, and with a rapid movement turned his fresh, kind, simple young face which just showed the first downy signs of a beard.

"Yes, sir?"

"That must be very unpleasant for you. You must forgive me. I am helpless."

"Oh, why, sir," and Gerasim's eyes beamed and he showed his glistening white teeth, "what's a little trouble? It's a case of illness with you, sir."

And his deft strong hands did their accustomed task, and he went out of the room stepping lightly. Five minutes later he as lightly returned.

Ivan Ilych was still sitting in the same position in the armchair.

"Gerasim," he said when the latter had replaced the freshly-washed utensil. "Please come here and help me." Gerasim went up to him. "Lift me up. It is hard for me to get up, and I have sent Dmitri away."

Gerasim went up to him, grasped his master with his strong arms deftly but gently, in the same way that he stepped—lifted him, supported him with one hand, and with the other drew up his trousers and would have set him down again, but Ivan Ilych asked to be led to the sofa. Gerasim, without an effort and without apparent pressure, led him, almost lifting him, to the sofa and placed him on it.

"Thank you. How easily and well you do it all!"

Gerasim smiled again and turned to leave the room. But Ivan Ilych felt his presence such a comfort that he did not want to let him go.

"One thing more, please move up that chair. No, the other one—under my feet. It is easier for me when my feet are raised."

Gerasim brought the chair, set it down gently in place, and raised Ivan Ilych's legs on to it. It seemed to Ivan Ilych that he felt better while Gerasim was holding up his legs.

"It's better when my legs are higher," he said. "Place that cushion under them."

Gerasim did so. He again lifted the legs and placed them, and again Ivan Ilych felt better while Gerasim held his legs. When he set them down Ivan Ilych fancied he felt worse.

"Gerasim," he said. "Are you busy now?"

"Not at all, sir," said Gerasim, who had learnt from the townfolk how to speak to gentlefolk.

"What have you still to do?"

"What have I to do? I've done everything except chopping the logs for tomorrow."

"Then hold my legs up a bit higher, can you?"

"Of course I can. Why not?" And Gerasim raised his master's legs higher and Ivan Ilych thought that in that position he did not feel any pain at all.

"And how about the logs?"

"Don't trouble about that, sir. There's plenty of time."

Ivan Ilych told Gerasim to sit down and hold his legs, and began to talk to him. And strange to say it seemed to him that he felt better while Gerasim held his legs up.

After that Ivan Ilych would sometimes call Gerasim and get him to hold his legs on his shoulders, and he liked talking to him. Gerasim did it all easily, willingly, simply, and with a good nature that touched Ivan Ilych. Health, strength, and vitality in other people were offensive to him, but Gerasim's strength and vitality did not mortify but soothed him.

What tormented Ivan Ilych most was the deception, the lie, which for some reason they all accepted, that he was not dying but was simply ill, and that he only need keep quiet and undergo a treatment and then something very good would result. He however knew that do what they would nothing would come of it, only still more agonizing suffering and death. This deception tortured him—their not wishing to admit what they all knew and what he knew, but wanting to lie to him concerning his terrible condition, and wishing and forcing him to participate in that lie. Those lies—lies enacted over him on the eve of his death and destined to degrade this awful, solemn act to the level of their vis-itings, their curtains, their sturgeon for dinner—were a terrible agony for Ivan Ilych. And strangely enough, many times when they were going through their antics over him he had been within a hairbreadth of calling out to them: "Stop lying! You know and I know that I am dying. Then at least stop lying about it!" But he had never had the spirit to do it. The awful, terrible act of his dying was, he could see, reduced by those about him to the level of a casual, unpleas-ant, and almost indecorous incident (as if someone entered a drawing-room dif-fusing an unpleasant odour) and this was done by that very decorum which he had served all his life long. He saw that no one felt for him, because no one even wished to grasp his position. Only Gerasim recognized it and pitied him. And so Ivan Ilych felt at ease only with him. He felt comforted when Gerasim supported his legs (sometimes all night long) and refused to go to bed, saying: "Don't you worry, Ivan Ilych. I'll get sleep enough later on," or when he sud-denly became familiar and exclaimed: "If you weren't sick it would be another matter, but as it is, why should I grudge a little trouble?" Gerasim alone did not lie; everything showed that he alone understood the facts of the case and did not consider it necessary to disguise them, but simply felt sorry for his ema-ciated and enfeebled master. Once when Ivan Ilych was sending him away he even said straight out: "We shall all of us die, so why should I grudge a little trouble?"—expressing the fact that he did not think his work burdensome, be-cause he was doing it for a dying man and hoped someone would do the same for him when his time came.

Apart from this lying, or because of it, what most tormented Ivan Ilych was that no one pitied him as he wished to be pitied. At certain moments after pro-longed suffering he wished most of all (though he would have been ashamed to confess it) for someone to pity him as a sick child is pitied. He longed to be petted and comforted. He knew he was an important functionary, that he had a beard turning grey, and that therefore what he longed for was impossible, but still he longed for it. And in Gerasim's attitude towards him there was some-thing akin to what he wished for, and so that attitude comforted him. Ivan Ilych wanted to weep, wanted to be petted and cried over, and then his colleague Shebek would come, and instead of weeping and being petted, Ivan Ilych would assume a serious, severe, and profound air, and by force of habit would express his opinion on a decision of the Court of Cassation[22] and would stub-bornly insist on that view. This falsity around him and within him did more than anything else to poison his last days.

VIII

It was morning. He knew it was morning because Gerasim had gone, and Peter the footman had come and put out the candles, drawn back one of the curtains, and begun quietly to tidy up. Whether it was morning or evening, Friday or Sunday, made no difference, it was all just the same: the gnawing, unmitigated, agonizing pain, never ceasing for an instant, the consciousness of life inexorably waning but not yet extinguished, the approach of that ever

---

22. The highest court of appeals.

dreaded and hateful Death which was the only reality, and always the same falsity. What were days, weeks, hours, in such a case?

"Will you have some tea, sir?"

"He wants things to be regular, and wishes the gentlefolk to drink tea in the morning," thought Ivan Ilych, and only said "No."

"Wouldn't you like to move onto the sofa, sir?"

"He wants to tidy up the room, and I'm in the way. I am uncleanliness and disorder," he thought, and said only:

"No, leave me alone."

The man went on bustling about. Ivan Ilych stretched out his hand. Peter came up, ready to help.

"What is it, sir?"

"My watch."

Peter took the watch which was close at hand and gave it to his master.

"Half-past eight. Are they up?"

"No, sir, except Vladimir Ivanich" (the son) "who has gone to school. Praskovya Fëdorovna ordered me to wake her if you asked for her. Shall I do so?"

"No, there's no need to." "Perhaps I'd better have some tea," he thought, and added aloud: "Yes, bring me some tea."

Peter went to the door, but Ivan Ilych dreaded being left alone. "How can I keep him here? Oh yes, my medicine." "Peter, give me my medicine." "Why not? Perhaps it may still do me some good." He took a spoonful and swallowed it. "No, it won't help. It's all tomfoolery, all deception," he decided as soon as he became aware of the familiar, sickly, hopeless taste. "No, I can't believe in it any longer. But the pain, why this pain? If it would only cease just for a moment!" And he moaned. Peter turned towards him. "It's all right. Go and fetch me some tea."

Peter went out. Left alone Ivan Ilych groaned not so much with pain, terrible though that was, as from mental anguish. Always and for ever the same, always these endless days and nights. If only it would come quicker! If only *what* would come quicker? Death, darkness? . . . No, no! Anything rather than death!

When Peter returned with the tea on a tray, Ivan Ilych stared at him for a time in perplexity, not realizing who and what he was. Peter was disconcerted by that look and his embarrassment brought Ivan Ilych to himself.

"Oh, tea! All right, put it down. Only help me to wash and put on a clean shirt."

And Ivan Ilych began to wash. With pauses for rest, he washed his hands and then his face, cleaned his teeth, brushed his hair, and looked in the glass. He was terrified by what he saw, especially by the limp way in which his hair clung to his pallid forehead.

While his shirt was being changed he knew that he would be still more frightened at the sight of his body, so he avoided looking at it. Finally he was ready. He drew on a dressing-gown, wrapped himself in a plaid, and sat down in the armchair to take his tea. For a moment he felt refreshed, but as soon as he began to drink the tea he was again aware of the same taste, and the pain also returned. He finished it with an effort, and then lay down stretching out his legs, and dismissed Peter.

Always the same. Now a spark of hope flashes up, then a sea of despair rages, and always pain; always pain, always despair, and always the same. When alone he had a dreadful and distressing desire to call someone, but he knew beforehand that with others present it would be still worse. "Another dose of morphine—to lose consciousness. I will tell him, the doctor, that he must think of something else. It's impossible, impossible, to go on like this."

An hour and another pass like that. But now there is a ring at the door bell. Perhaps it's the doctor? It is. He comes in fresh, hearty, plump, and cheerful, with that look on his face that seems to say: "There now, you're in a panic about something, but we'll arrange it all for you directly!" The doctor knows this expression is out of place here, but he has put it on once for all and can't take it off—like a man who has put on a frock-coat in the morning to pay a round of calls.

The doctor rubs his hands vigorously and reassuringly.

"Brr! How cold it is! There's such a sharp frost; just let me warm myself!" he says, as if it were only a matter of waiting till he was warm, and then he would put everything right.

"Well now, how are you?"

Ivan Ilych feels that the doctor would like to say: "Well, how are your affairs?" but that even he feels that this would not do, and says instead: "What sort of a night have you had?"

Ivan Ilych looks at him as much as to say: "Are you really never ashamed of lying?" But the doctor does not wish to understand this question, and Ivan Ilych says: "Just as terrible as ever. The pain never leaves me and never subsides. If only something . . ."

"Yes, you sick people are always like that . . . There, now I think I am warm enough. Even Praskovya Fëdorovna, who is so particular, could find no fault with my temperature. Well, now I can say good-morning," and the doctor presses his patient's hand.

Then, dropping his former playfulness, he begins with a most serious face to examine the patient, feeling his pulse and taking his temperature, and then begins the sounding and auscultation.

Ivan Ilych knows quite well and definitely that all this is nonsense and pure deception, but when the doctor, getting down on his knee, leans over him, putting the ear first higher then lower, and performs various gymnastic movements over him with a significant expression on his face, Ivan Ilych submits to it all as he used to submit to the speeches of the lawyers, though he knew very well that they were all lying and why they were lying.

The doctor, kneeling on the sofa, is still sounding him when Praskovya Fëdorovna's silk dress rustles at the door and she is heard scolding Peter for not having let her know of the doctor's arrival.

She comes in, kisses her husband, and at once proceeds to prove that she has been up a long time already, and only owing to a misunderstanding failed to be there when the doctor arrived.

Ivan Ilych looks at her, scans her all over, sets against her the whiteness and plumpness and cleanness of her hands and neck, the gloss of her hair, and the sparkle of her vivacious eyes. He hates her with his whole soul. And the thrill of hatred he feels for her makes him suffer from her touch.

Her attitude towards him and his disease is still the same. Just as the doctor had adopted a certain relation to his patient which he could not abandon, so had she formed one towards him—that he was not doing something he ought to do and was himself to blame, and that she reproached him lovingly for this—and she could not now change that attitude.

"You see he doesn't listen to me and doesn't take his medicine at the proper time. And above all he lies in a position that is no doubt bad for him—with his legs up."

She described how he made Gerasim hold his legs up.

The doctor smiled with a contemptuous affability that said: "What's to be done? These sick people do have foolish fancies of that kind, but we must forgive them."

When the examination was over the doctor looked at his watch, and then Praskovya Fëdorovna announced to Ivan Ilych that it was of course as he pleased, but she had sent today for a celebrated specialist who would examine him and have a consultation with Michael Danilovich (their regular doctor).

"Please don't raise any objections. I am doing this for my own sake," she said ironically, letting it be felt that she was doing it all for his sake and only said this to leave him no right to refuse. He remained silent, knitting his brows. He felt that he was so surrounded and involved in a mesh of falsity that it was hard to unravel anything.

Everything she did for him was entirely for her own sake, and she told him she was doing for herself what she actually was doing for herself, as if that was so incredible that he must understand the opposite.

At half-past eleven the celebrated specialist arrived. Again the sounding began and the significant conversations in his presence and in another room, about the kidneys and the appendix, and the questions and answers, with such an air of importance that again, instead of the real question of life and death which now alone confronted him, the question arose of the kidney and appendix which were not behaving as they ought to and would now be attacked by Michael Danilovich and the specialist and forced to mend their ways.

The celebrated specialist took leave of him with a serious though not hopeless look, and in reply to the timid question Ivan Ilych, with eyes glistening with fear and hope, put to him as to whether there was a chance of recovery, said that he could not vouch for it but there was a possibility. The look of hope with which Ivan Ilych watched the doctor out was so pathetic that Praskovya Fëdorovna, seeing it, even wept as she left the room to hand the doctor his fee.

The gleam of hope kindled by the doctor's encouragement did not last long. The same room, the same pictures, curtains, wall-paper, medicine bottles, were all there, and the same aching suffering body, and Ivan Ilych began to moan. They gave him a subcutaneous injection and he sank into oblivion.

It was twilight when he came to. They brought him his dinner and he swallowed some beef tea with difficulty, and then everything was the same again and night was coming on.

After dinner, at seven o'clock, Praskovya Fëdorovna came into the room in evening dress, her full bosom pushed up by her corset, and with traces of powder on her face. She had reminded him in the morning that they were going to the theatre. Sarah Bernhardt[23] was visiting the town and they had a box,

---

23. World-renowned French actress (1844–1923) whose appearance in Petersburg in 1882 was a highly acclaimed success.

which he had insisted on their taking. Now he had forgotten about it and her toilet offended him, but he concealed his vexation when he remembered that he had himself insisted on their securing a box and going because it would be an instructive and aesthetic pleasure for the children.

Praskovya Fëdorovna came in, self-satisfied but yet with a rather guilty air. She sat down and asked how he was, but, as he saw, only for the sake of asking and not in order to learn about it, knowing that there was nothing to learn—and then went on to what she really wanted to say: that she would not on any account have gone but that the box had been taken and Helen and their daughter were going, as well as Petrishchev (the examining magistrate, their daughter's fiancé) and that it was out of the question to let them go alone; but that she would have much preferred to sit with him for a while; and he must be sure to follow the doctor's orders while she was away.

"Oh, and Fëdor Petrovich" (the fiancé) "would like to come in. May he? And Lisa?"

"All right."

Their daughter came in in full evening dress, her fresh young flesh exposed (making a show of that very flesh which in his own case caused so much suffering), strong, healthy, evidently in love, and impatient with illness, suffering, and death, because they interfered with her happiness.

Fëdor Petrovich came in too, in evening dress, his hair curled *à la Capoul,*[24] a tight stiff collar round his long sinewy neck, an enormous white shirt-front and narrow black trousers tightly stretched over his strong thighs. He had one white glove tightly drawn on, and was holding his opera hat in his hand.

Following him the schoolboy crept in unnoticed, in a new uniform, poor little fellow, and wearing gloves. Terribly dark shadows showed under his eyes, the meaning of which Ivan Ilych knew well.

His son had always seemed pathetic to him, and now it was dreadful to see the boy's frightened look of pity. It seemed to Ivan Ilych that Vasya was the only one besides Gerasim who understood and pitied him.

They all sat down and again asked how he was. A silence followed. Lisa asked her mother about the opera-glasses, and there was an altercation between mother and daughter as to who had taken them and where they had been put. This occasioned some unpleasantness.

Fëdor Petrovich inquired of Ivan Ilych whether he had ever seen Sarah Bernhardt. Ivan Ilych did not at first catch the question, but then replied: "No, have you seen her before?"

"Yes, in *Adrienne Lecouvreur.*"[25]

Praskovya Fëdorovna mentioned some rôles in which Sarah Bernhardt was particularly good. Her daughter disagreed. Conversation sprang up as to the elegance and realism of her acting—the sort of conversation that is always repeated and is always the same.

In the midst of the conversation Fëdor Petrovich glanced at Ivan Ilych and became silent. Ivan Ilych was staring with glittering eyes straight before him,

---

24. A popular hair style of the time, named after Victor Capoul (1839–1924), highly acclaimed French operatic tenor.

25. A play by French dramatists Eugène Scribe (1791–1861) and Ernest Legouvé (1807–1903); it is a melodramatic rendering of a true incident involving an actress who dies under mysterious circumstances after being abandoned by her lover. Sarah Bernhardt played the death scene to rave notices.

evidently indignant with them. This had to be rectified, but it was impossible to do so. The silence had to be broken, but for a time no one dared to break it and they all became afraid that the conventional deception would suddenly become obvious and the truth become plain to all. Lisa was the first to pluck up courage and break that silence, but by trying to hide what everybody was feeling, she betrayed it.

"Well, if we are going it's time to start," she said, looking at her watch, a present from her father, and with a faint and significant smile at Fëdor Petrovich relating to something known only to them. She got up with a rustle of her dress.

They all rose, said good-night, and went away.

When they had gone it seemed to Ivan Ilych that he felt better; the falsity had gone with them. But the pain remained—that same pain and that same fear that made everything monotonously alike, nothing harder and nothing easier. Everything was worse.

Again minute followed minute and hour followed hour. Everything remained the same and there was no cessation. And the inevitable end of it all became more and more terrible.

"Yes, send Gerasim here," he replied to a question Peter asked.

IX

His wife returned late at night. She came in on tiptoe, but he heard her, opened his eyes, and made haste to close them again. She wished to send Gerasim away and to sit with him herself, but he opened his eyes and said: "No, go away."

"Are you in great pain?"

"Always the same."

"Take some opium."

He agreed and took some. She went away.

Till about three in the morning he was in a state of stupefied misery. It seemed to him that he and his pain were being thrust into a narrow, deep black sack, but though they were pushed further and further in they could not be pushed to the bottom. And this, terrible enough in itself, was accompanied by suffering. He struggled but yet cooperated. And suddenly he broke through, fell, and regained consciousness. Gerasim was sitting at the foot of the bed dozing quietly, while he himself lay with his emaciated stockinged legs resting on Gerasim's shoulders; the same shaded candle was there and the same unceasing pain.

"Go away, Gerasim," he whispered.

"It's all right, sir. I'll stay a while."

"No. Go away."

He removed his legs from Gerasim's shoulders, turned sideways onto his arm, and felt sorry for himself. He only waited till Gerasim had gone into the next room and then restrained himself no longer but wept like a child. He wept on account of his helplessness, his terrible loneliness, the cruelty of man, the cruelty of God, and the absence of God.

"Why hast Thou done all this? Why hast Thou brought me here? Why, why dost Thou torment me so terribly?"

He did not expect an answer and yet wept because there was no answer and could be none. The pain again grew more acute, but he did not stir and did not call. He said to himself: "Go on! Strike me! But what is it for? What have I done to Thee? What is it for?"

Then he grew quiet and not only ceased weeping but even held his breath and became all attention. It was as though he were listening not to an audible voice but to the voice of his soul, to the current of thoughts arising within him.

"What is it you want?" was the first clear conception capable of expression in words, that he heard.

"What do you want? What do you want?" he repeated to himself.

"What do I want? To live and not to suffer," he answered.

And again he listened with such concentrated attention that even his pain did not distract him.

"To live? How?" asked his inner voice.

"Why, to live as I used to—well and pleasantly."

"As you lived before, well and pleasantly?" the voice repeated.

And in imagination he began to recall the best moments of his pleasant life. But strange to say none of those best moments of his pleasant life now seemed at all what they had then seemed—none of them except the first recollections of childhood. There, in childhood, there had been something really pleasant with which it would be possible to live if it could return. But the child who had experienced that happiness existed no longer, it was like a reminiscence of somebody else.

As soon as the period began which had produced the present Ivan Ilych, all that had then seemed joys now melted before his sight and turned into something trivial and often nasty.

And the further he departed from childhood and the nearer he came to the present the more worthless and doubtful were the joys. This began with the School of Law. A little that was really good was still found there—there was light-heartedness, friendship, and hope. But in the upper classes there had already been fewer of such good moments. Then during the first years of his official career, when he was in the service of the Governor, some pleasant moments again occurred: they were the memories of love for a woman. Then all became confused and there was still less of what was good; later on again there was still less that was good, and the further he went the less there was. His marriage, a mere accident, then the disenchantment that followed it, his wife's bad breath and the sensuality and hypocrisy: then that deadly official life and those preoccupations about money, a year of it, and two, and ten, and twenty, and always the same thing. And the longer it lasted the more deadly it became. "It is as if I had been going downhill while I imagined I was going up. And that is really what it was. I was going up in public opinion, but to the same extent life was ebbing away from me. And now it is all done and there is only death."

"Then what does it mean? Why? It can't be that life is so senseless and horrible. But if it really has been so horrible and senseless, why must I die and die in agony? There is something wrong!"

"Maybe I did not live as I ought to have done," it suddenly occurred to him. "But how could that be, when I did everything properly?" he replied, and immediately dismissed from his mind this, the sole solution of all the riddles of life and death, as something quite impossible.

"Then what do you want now? To live? Live how? Live as you lived in the law courts when the usher proclaimed 'The judge is coming!' The judge is coming, the judge!'' he repeated to himself. ''Here he is, the judge. But I am not guilty!'' he exclaimed angrily. ''What is it for?'' And he ceased crying, but turning his face to the wall continued to ponder on the same question: Why, and for what purpose, is there all this horror? But however much he pondered he found no answer. And whenever the thought occurred to him, as it often did, that it all resulted from his not having lived as he ought to have done, he at once recalled the correctness of his whole life and dismissed so strange an idea.

X

Another fortnight passed. Ivan Ilych now no longer left his sofa. He would not lie in bed but lay on the sofa, facing the wall nearly all the time. He suffered ever the same unceasing agonies and in his loneliness pondered always on the same insoluble question: ''What is this? Can it be that it is Death?'' And the inner voice answered: ''Yes, it is Death.''

''Why these sufferings?'' And the voice answered, ''For no reason—they just are so.'' Beyond and besides this there was nothing.

From the very beginning of his illness, ever since he had first been to see the doctor, Ivan Ilych's life had been divided between two contrary and alternating moods: now it was despair and the expectation of this uncomprehended and terrible death, and now hope and an intently interested observation of the functioning of his organs. Now before his eyes there was only a kidney or an intestine that temporarily evaded its duty, and now only that incomprehensible and dreadful death from which it was impossible to escape.

These two states of mind had alternated from the very beginning of his illness, but the further it progressed the more doubtful and fantastic became the conception of the kidney, and the more real the sense of impending death.

He had but to call to mind what he had been three months before and what he was now, to call to mind with what regularity he had been going downhill, for every possibility of hope to be shattered.

Latterly during that loneliness in which he found himself as he lay facing the back of the sofa, a loneliness in the midst of a populous town and surrounded by numerous acquaintances and relations but that yet could not have been more complete anywhere—either at the bottom of the sea or under the earth—during that terrible loneliness Ivan Ilych had lived only in memories of the past. Pictures of his past rose before him one after another. They always began with what was nearest in time and then went back to what was the most remote—to his childhood—and rested there. If he thought of the stewed prunes that had been offered him that day, his mind went back to the raw shrivelled French plums of his childhood, their peculiar flavour and the flow of saliva when he sucked their stones, and along with the memory of that taste came a whole series of memories of those days: his nurse, his brother, and their toys. ''No, I mustn't think of that . . . It is too painful,'' Ivan Ilych said to himself, and brought himself back to the present—to the button on the back of the sofa and the creases in its morocco.[26] ''Morocco is expensive, but it does not wear

---

26. Moroccan leather, a rare and expensive type.

well: there had been a quarrel about it. It was a different kind of quarrel and a different kind of morocco that time when we tore father's portfolio and were punished, and Mamma brought us some tarts . . ." And again his thoughts dwelt on his childhood, and again it was painful and he tried to banish them and fix his mind on something else.

Then again together with that chain of memories another series passed through his mind—of how his illness had progressed and grown worse. There also the further back he looked the more life there had been. There had been more of what was good in life and more of life itself. The two merged together. "Just as the pain went on getting worse and worse, so my life grew worse and worse," he thought. "There is one bright spot there at the back, at the beginning of life, and afterwards all becomes blacker and blacker and proceeds more and more rapidly—in inverse ratio to the square of the distance from death," thought Ivan Ilych. And the example of a stone falling downwards with increasing velocity entered his mind. Life, a series of increasing sufferings, flies further and further towards its end—the most terrible suffering. "I am flying . . ." He shuddered, shifted himself, and tried to resist, but was already aware that resistance was impossible, and again with eyes weary of gazing but unable to cease seeing what was before them, he stared at the back of the sofa and waited—awaiting that dreadful fall and shock and destruction.

"Resistance is impossible!" he said to himself. "If I could only understand what it is all for! But that too is impossible. An explanation would be possible if it could be said that I have not lived as I ought to. But it is impossible to say that," and he remembered all the legality, correctitude, and propriety of his life. "That at any rate can certainly not be admitted," he thought, and his lips smiled ironically as if someone could see that smile and be taken in by it. "There is no explanation! Agony, death . . . What for?"

XI

Another two weeks went by in this way and during that fortnight an event occurred that Ivan Ilych and his wife had desired. Petrishchev formally proposed. It happened in the evening. The next day Praskovya Fëdorovna came into her husband's room considering how best to inform him of it, but that very night there had been a fresh change for the worse in his condition. She found him still lying on the sofa but in a different position. He lay on his back, groaning and staring fixedly in front of him.

She began to remind him of his medicines, but he turned his eyes towards her with such a look that she did not finish what she was saying; so great an animosity, to her in particular, did that look express.

"For Christ's sake let me die in peace!" he said.

She would have gone away, but just then their daughter came in and went up to say good morning. He looked at her as he had done at his wife, and in reply to her inquiry about his health said dryly that he would soon free them all of himself. They were both silent and after sitting with him for a while went away.

"Is it our fault?" Lisa said to her mother. "It's as if we were to blame! I am sorry for papa, but why should we be tortured?"

The doctor came at his usual time. Ivan Ilych answered "Yes" and "No," never taking his angry eyes from him, and at last said: "You know you can do nothing for me, so leave me alone."

"We can ease your sufferings."

"You can't even do that. Let me be."

The doctor went into the drawing-room and told Praskovya Fëdorovna that the case was very serious and that the only resource left was opium to allay her husband's sufferings, which must be terrible.

It was true, as the doctor said, that Ivan Ilych's physical sufferings were terrible, but worse than the physical sufferings were his mental sufferings, which were his chief torture.

His mental sufferings were due to the fact that that night, as he looked at Gerasim's sleepy, good-natured face with its prominent cheek-bones, the question suddenly occurred to him: "What if my whole life has really been wrong?"

It occurred to him that what had appeared perfectly impossible before, namely that he had not spent his life as he should have done, might after all be true. It occurred to him that his scarcely perceptible attempts to struggle against what was considered good by the most highly placed people, those scarcely noticeable impulses which he had immediately suppressed, might have been the real thing, and all the rest false. And his professional duties and the whole arrangement of his life and of his family, and all his social and official interests, might all have been false. He tried to defend all those things to himself and suddenly felt the weakness of what he was defending. There was nothing to defend.

"But if that is so," he said to himself, "and I am leaving this life with the consciousness that I have lost all that was given me and it is impossible to rectify it—what then?"

He lay on his back and began to pass his life in review in quite a new way. In the morning when he saw first his footman, then his wife, then his daughter, and then the doctor, their every word and movement confirmed to him the awful truth that had been revealed to him during the night. In them he saw himself—all that for which he had lived—and saw clearly that it was not real at all, but a terrible and huge deception which had hidden both life and death. This consciousness intensified his physical suffering tenfold. He groaned and tossed about, and pulled at his clothing which choked and stifled him. And he hated them on that account.

He was given a large dose of opium and became unconscious, but at noon his sufferings began again. He drove everybody away and tossed from side to side.

His wife came to him and said:

"Jean, my dear, do this for me. It can't do any harm and often helps. Healthy people often do it."

He opened his eyes wide.

"What? Take communion? Why? It's unnecessary! However . . ."

She began to cry.

"Yes, do, my dear. I'll send for our priest. He is such a nice man."

"All right. Very well," he muttered.

When the priest came and heard his confession, Ivan Ilych was softened and seemed to feel a relief from his doubts and consequently from his sufferings, and for a moment there came a ray of hope. He again began to think of the vermiform appendix and the possibility of correcting it. He received the sacrament with tears in his eyes.

When they laid him down again afterwards he felt a moment's ease, and the hope that he might live awoke in him again. He began to think of the operation that had been suggested to him. "To live! I want to live!" he said to himself.

His wife came to congratulate him after his communion, and when uttering the usual conventional words she added:

"You feel better, don't you?"

Without looking at her he said "Yes."

Her dress, her figure, the expression of her face, the tone of her voice, all revealed the same thing. "This is wrong, it is not as it should be. All you have lived for and still live for is falsehood and deception, hiding life and death from you." And as soon as he admitted that thought, his hatred and his agonizing physical suffering again sprang up, and with that suffering a consciousness of the unavoidable, approaching end. And to this was added a new sensation of grinding shooting pain and a feeling of suffocation.

The expression of his face when he uttered that "yes" was dreadful. Having uttered it, he looked her straight in the eyes, turned on his face with a rapidity extraordinary in his weak state and shouted:

"Go away! Go away and leave me alone!"

XII

From that moment the screaming began that continued for three days, and was so terrible that one could not hear it through two closed doors without horror. At the moment he answered his wife he realized that he was lost, that there was no return, that the end had come, the very end, and his doubts were still unsolved and remained doubts.

"Oh! Oh! Oh!" he cried in various intonations. He had begun by screaming "I won't!" and continued screaming on the letter *O*.

For three whole days, during which time did not exist for him, he struggled in that black sack into which he was being thrust by an invisible resistless force. He struggled as a man condemned to death struggles in the hands of the executioner, knowing that he cannot save himself. And every moment he felt that despite all his efforts he was drawing nearer and nearer to what terrified him. He felt that his agony was due to his being thrust into that black hole and still more to his not being able to get right into it. He was hindered from getting into it by his conviction that his life had been a good one. That very justification of his life held him fast and prevented his moving forward, and it caused him most torment of all.

Suddenly some force struck him in the chest and side, making it still harder to breathe, and he fell through the hole and there at the bottom was a light. What had happened to him was like the sensation one sometimes experiences in a railway carriage when one thinks one is going backwards while one is really going forwards and suddenly becomes aware of the real direction.

"Yes, it was all not the right thing," he said to himself, "but that's no matter. It can be done. But what *is* the right thing?" he asked himself, and suddenly grew quiet.

This occurred at the end of the third day, two hours before his death. Just then his schoolboy son had crept softly in and gone up to the bedside. The dying man was still screaming and waving his arms. His hand fell on the boy's head, and the boy caught it, pressed it to his lips, and began to cry.

At that very moment Ivan Ilych fell through and caught sight of the light, and it was revealed to him that though his life had not been what it should have been, this could still be rectified. He asked himself, "What *is* the right thing?" and grew still, listening. Then he felt that someone was kissing his hand. He opened his eyes, looked at his son, and felt sorry for him. His wife came up to him and he glanced at her. She was gazing at him openmouthed, with undried tears on her nose and cheek and a despairing look on her face. He felt sorry for her too.

"Yes, I am making them wretched," he thought. "They are sorry, but it will be better for them when I die." He wished to say this but had not the strength to utter it. "Besides, why speak? I must act," he thought. With a look at his wife he indicated his son and said: "Take him away . . . sorry for him . . . sorry for you too . . . " He tried to add, "forgive me," but said "forgo" and waved his hand, knowing that He whose understanding mattered would understand.

And suddenly it grew clear to him that what had been oppressing him and would not leave him was dropping away at once from two sides, from ten sides, and from all sides. He was sorry for them, he must act so as not to hurt them and free himself from these sufferings. "How good and how simple!" he thought. "And the pain?" he asked himself. "What has become of it? Where are you, pain?"

He turned his attention to it.

"Yes, here it is. Well, what of it? Let the pain be."

"And death . . . where is it?"

He sought his former accustomed fear of death and did not find it. "Where is it? What death?" There was no fear because there was no death.

In place of death there was light.

"So that's what it is!" he suddenly exclaimed aloud. "What joy!"

To him all this happened in a single instant, and the meaning of that instant did not change. For those present his agony continued for another two hours. Something rattled in his throat, his emaciated body twitched, then the gasping and rattle became less and less frequent.

"It is finished!" said someone near him.

He heard these words and repeated them in his soul.

"Death is finished," he said to himself. "It is no more!"

He drew in a breath, stopped in the midst of a sigh, stretched out, and died.

"The Death of Ivan Ilych" is more than a chronicle or life-history. It differs from a standard biographical approach in numerous ways, but first of all because it begins with the end of a life. The outcome of Ivan Ilych's life is not an issue and thus suspense is minimized, though interest in the man is not. The structure of the narrative is important, for Tolstoy has arranged his story in twelve sections of unequal length.

Each section is determined essentially by content and theme. Section 2, for instance, ends with the assurance that Ivan Ilych's children have "turned out well"; and section 3 ends with comments on his daughter's suitors. At the end of section 6 Ivan Ilych at last confronts death itself. In section 7 his beneficial relationship with Gerasim begins. Section 9 ends with Ivan Ilych's sense of injustice at having to suffer an agonizing death after a life that he considers to have been proper and "correct." Section 12 ends with his death. Yet there is some indication that the story actually ends with a beginning, that death itself is the way into another life. Framed by the death scenes, the narrative is divided into four parts, each making use of the traditional plot structure.

The essential features of Ivan Ilych's character are not defined in terms of his deeds and accomplishments. We know very little about his actual duties, but we do know something about his opinions. We know his reasons for dancing, for card-playing, for marriage, and for house-decorating. We know why he seeks new jobs and how he goes about getting them. We see how his wife changes, and we understand their mutual disappointment with each other.

Tolstoy extends this realistic presentation of detail to include not only Ivan Ilych's family but also his public life as well. We see Ivan Ilych as the "Everyman" of Russian bureaucratic life in Petersburg during the last era of the Romanov dynasty. The story depicts both a particular social class and a certain historical era. Tolstoy exposes the emptiness of the pretensions of Ivan Ilych and others like him by ironic comparisons between magistrates and physicians. The world Ivan Ilych inhabits and represents is trivial, artificial, and hollow. Authority is a sham. Accomplishments such as promotions and daily pleasures such as card-playing are equally meaningless. Ivan Ilych's house itself, so like all the other houses, suggests his middle-class pretensions. Terrible ordinariness hardly belongs to him alone. In numerous ways Tolstoy establishes how Ivan Ilych's life is typical of his social class and time.

Tolstoy, however, is not only a social but also a psychological realist. He takes us into Ivan Ilych's mind, showing us how inadequate are the consolations in which Ivan Ilych has taken refuge when he is confronted with illness and death. We see him first take comfort in scientific knowledge, in the "ultimate matter" of his appendix. And we see him fabricate a whole pattern of psychological defenses against his knowledge of impending death. Tolstoy describes these defenses as a "mesh of falsity." The epiphany Ivan Ilych experiences in section 5 momentarily ends his self-deception. Tolstoy presents that moment in terms of images of light, while he represents deception and falsity with images of darkness. Here Tolstoy shows symbolically that both outside and inside Ivan Ilych is empty and afraid.

His emotional emptiness comes to represent not only artificiality and hypocrisy but also a kind of death-in-life. Thus in Ivan Ilych's own life, "the further back he looked the more life there had been." Only his young son shows grief; only the peasant Gerasim possesses genuine life and vitality. The adult society Ivan Ilych lives in has destroyed both emotion and life. And so he is forced to recognize how deathlike his existence has been. And now he must confront death itself. In section 6 Ivan Ilych comes to see how meaningless it has been to talk of mortality when humans typically refuse to consider the reality of death. What he (and the reader as well) must confront is "it"—death itself. On his death bed Ivan Ilych screams for three days before he dies.

Themes of life and death have been staples of literature throughout history. But in most literary depictions death is treated heroically, or poignantly, or even casually. Death seldom seems as real or as threatening or as horrible as Tolstoy makes it. He treats death with unsparing honesty and unalleviated grimness. The painful and unpleasant details serve to bring the reader, like Ivan Ilych, face-to-face with the fact of death. Yet death is not the final subject of this narrative. Shortly before his death, Ivan Ilych stops screaming.

If Tolstoy exposes the pretensions of an era and explores the emptiness of a particular consciousness as it faces certain death, he also goes beyond these issues to raise the question of life not only in this but possibly in the next world. As an omniscient author, Tolstoy says in section 9 that Ivan Ilych dismissed what was "the sole solution of all the riddles of life and death." Yet he insists that Ivan Ilych's life can "still be rectified." In order to suggest how this may be done, Tolstoy introduces symbols showing Ivan Ilych falling into a hole which contains a light at its bottom. Ivan Ilych stops screaming and light replaces darkness; joy replaces the agony of dying. Tolstoy allows the end of his story to remain ambiguous. We cannot precisely determine what the images of light and dark indicate here. Ivan Ilych's ceasing to scream and his asking for forgiveness may mean that beyond pain, suffering, and death lies the possibility of immortality.

In interpreting Tolstoy's ending, it is helpful to know that about eight years before writing this story Tolstoy himself experienced a spiritual crisis precipitated by his fear of death. After undergoing a religious conversion, he ceased to live as an aristocratic skeptic and attempted to live as a Christian believer. He came to see that, for him, only faith in an afterlife made existence bearable and the knowledge of death tolerable.

Tolstoy's own experiences influenced "The Death of Ivan Ilych," and his religious conversion in particular seems to be reflected in the story's ending. Knowing such biographical material permits us additional insight into the story, yet such knowledge is not required to understand Ivan Ilych. Realistic and symbolic, psychological and sociological, personal and historical, physical and metaphysical, the story exposes death-in-life and suggests that there can be life-in-death. It reinforces these thematic concerns with paradoxical images of darkness in light and light in darkness. Similarly, plotting and characterization, setting and symbol, work effectively together so that the major themes reverberate throughout minor incidents, heightening our appreciation of Tolstoy's craftsmanship.

Tolstoy makes ''The Death of Ivan Ilych'' believable by his meticulous accumulation of historical, sociological, and psychological details. By contrast, Thomas Pynchon in '' Entropy'' presents an accumulation of disjointed facts, outlandish incidents, and improbable if not impossible situations. Because of the way in which Pynchon presents these materials, his story is not literally believable. Yet in dealing with a story like ''Entropy'' the question of believability is beside the point. As we saw in Chapters 10 and 11, there are different ways in which fiction writers may present reality. Pynchon does so by disregarding many of the conventions of fiction and by upsetting traditional assumptions about what is real.

With Pynchon the connections between fiction and life have little to do with artistically representing ''real life.'' Like Tolstoy, Pynchon sets his story in a specific time and place (Washington, D.C., in February 1957), and he too refers to famous persons, actual events, current fads and theories. Pynchon, however, uses facts for their abstract value and incorporates into his story certain aspects of reality in order to achieve a theoretical, imaginative framework. In ''The Death of Ivan Ilych'' we accept as true to life the picture Tolstoy paints of the mood of Russian middle-class bureaucrats during the last years of a dying monarchy. But in ''Entropy'' we cannot be expected to gauge how accurately the story reflects the mood of Washington in 1957, any more than we can be expected to decide whether or not its improbable characters could exist in ''real life.'' Let us now turn to the story to see how Pynchon achieves these various effects.

Thomas Pynchon (b. 1937)
Entropy[1]

Boris has just given me a summary of his views. He is a weather prophet. The weather will continue bad, he says. There will be more calamities, more death, more despair. Not the slightest indication of a change anywhere. . . . We must get into step, a lockstep toward the prison of death. There is no escape. The weather will not change.—TROPIC OF CANCER[2]

Downstairs, Meatball Mulligan's lease-breaking party was moving into its 40th hour. On the kitchen floor, amid a litter of empty champagne fifths, were Sandor Rojas and three friends, playing spit in the ocean and staying awake on Heidseck and benzedrine pills. In the living room Duke, Vincent, Krinkles and Paco sat crouched over a fifteen-inch speaker which had been bolted into the top of a wastepaper basket, listening to 27 watts' worth of *The Heroes' Gate at Kiev*. They all wore horn-rimmed sunglasses and rapt expressions, and smoked funny-looking cigarettes which contained not, as you might expect, tobacco, but an adulterated form of *cannibis sativa*.[3] This group was the Duke di Angelis quartet. They recorded for a local label called Tambú and had to their credit one 10″ LP entitled *Songs of Outer Space*. From time to time one of them would flick the ashes from his cigarette into the speaker cone to watch them dance around. Meatball himself was sleeping over by the window, holding an empty magnum to his chest as if it were a teddy bear. Several government girls, who worked for people like the State Department and NSA, had passed out on couches, chairs and in one case the bathroom sink.

This was in early February of '57 and back then there were a lot of American expatriates around Washington, D.C., who would talk, every time they met you, about how someday they were going to go over to Europe for real but right now it seemed they were working for the government. Everyone saw a fine irony in this. They would stage, for instance, polyglot parties where the newcomer was sort of ignored if he couldn't carry on simultaneous conversations in three or four languages. They would haunt Armenian delicatessens for weeks at a stretch and invite you over for bulghour and lamb in tiny kitchens whose walls were covered with bullfight posters. They would have affairs with sultry girls from Andalucía or the Midi[4] who studied economics at Georgetown. Their Dôme[5] was a collegiate Rathskeller out on Wisconsin Avenue called the Old Heidelberg and they had to settle for cherry blossoms instead of lime trees

---

1. In physics, the measure of heat in a substance that is lost and no longer available; it is a measure of the disorder in the substance and of the deterioration of the system. In a wider sense, it is also the ultimate state reached in the degradation of the matter and energy of the universe, marked by the inert uniformity of its elements.
2. A novel by Henry Miller (b. 1891), published in France in 1934 and banned in the U.S. until 1961. Narrating the intellectual and sexual life of an American expatriate in Paris, it is animated by the belief that "more obscene than anything is inertia."
3. Hashish.
4. The southern regions of Spain and France, respectively.
5. Famous cafe in Paris.

when spring came, but in its lethargic way their life provided, as they said, kicks.

At the moment, Meatball's party seemed to be gathering its second wind. Outside there was rain. Rain splatted against the tar paper on the roof and was fractured into a fine spray off the noses, eyebrows and lips of wooden gargoyles under the eaves, and ran like drool down the windowpanes. The day before, it had snowed and the day before that there had been winds of gale force and before that the sun had made the city glitter bright as April, though the calendar read early February. It is a curious season in Washington, this false spring. Somewhere in it are Lincoln's Birthday and the Chinese New Year, and a forlornness in the streets because cherry blossoms are weeks away still and, as Sarah Vaughan has put it, spring will be a little late this year. Generally crowds like the one which would gather in the Old Heidelberg on weekday afternoons to drink Würtzburger and to sing "Lili Marlene" (not to mention "The Sweetheart of Sigma Chi") are inevitably and incorrigibly Romantic. And as every good Romantic knows, the soul (*spiritus, ruach, pneuma*)[6] is nothing, substantially, but air; it is only natural that warpings in the atmosphere should be recapitulated in those who breathe it. So that over and above the public components—holidays, tourist attractions—there are private meanderings, linked to the climate as if this spell were a *stretto* passage in the year's fugue:[7] haphazard weather, aimless loves, unpredicted commitments: months one can easily spend *in* fugue,[8] because oddly enough, later on, winds, rains, passions of February and March are never remembered in that city, it is as if they had never been.

The last bass notes of *The Heroes' Gate* boomed up through the floor and woke Callisto[9] from an uneasy sleep. The first thing he became aware of was a small bird he had been holding gently between his hands, against his body. He turned his head sidewise on the pillow to smile down at it, at its blue hunched-down head and sick, lidded eyes, wondering how many more nights he would have to give it warmth before it was well again. He had been holding the bird like that for three days: it was the only way he knew to restore its health. Next to him the girl stirred and whimpered, her arm thrown across her face. Mingled with the sounds of the rain came the first tentative, querulous morning voices of the other birds, hidden in philodendrons and small fan palms: patches of scarlet, yellow and blue laced through this Rousseau-like fantasy,[10] this hot-house jungle it had taken him seven years to weave together. Hermetically sealed, it was a tiny enclave of regularity in the city's chaos, alien to the vagaries of the weather, of national politics, of any civil disorder. Through trial-and-error Callisto had perfected its ecological balance, with the help of the girl its artistic harmony, so that the swayings of its plant life, the stirrings of its

---

6. Latin, Hebrew, and Greek for "soul" or "spirit."

7. A musical composition in which a theme is repeated or imitated by at least two instruments or voices counterpointed against one another and interwoven into a single structure. In a fugue, a *stretto* is the quick succession or overlapping of elements, usually in the closing section.

8. Used here in another sense: a severe form of amnesia in which a person performs conscious acts of which, upon recovery, he has no recollection.

9. In Greek mythology, a nymph loved by Zeus and transformed into a bear by Hera. Zeus placed her among the stars in the constellation Ursa Major, where she endlessly revolves around the Pole Star without setting.

10. Henri Rousseau (1844–1910), French painter known for his brightly colored and meticulously detailed paintings of lush and fantastic jungle scenes.

birds and human inhabitants were all as integral as the rhythms of a perfectly executed mobile. He and the girl could no longer, of course, be omitted from that sanctuary; they had become necessary to its unity. What they needed from outside was delivered. They did not go out.

"Is he all right," she whispered. She lay like a tawny question mark facing him, her eyes suddenly huge and dark and blinking slowly. Callisto ran a finger beneath the feathers at the base of the bird's neck; caressed it gently. "He's going to be well, I think. See: he hears his friends beginning to wake up." The girl had heard the rain and the birds even before she was fully awake. Her name was Aubade:[11] she was part French and part Annamese,[12] and she lived on her own curious and lonely planet, where the clouds and the odor of poincianas, the bitterness of wine and the accidental fingers at the small of her back or feathery against her breasts came to her reduced inevitably to the terms of sound: of music which emerged at intervals from a howling darkness of discordancy. "Aubade," he said, "go see." Obedient, she arose; padded to the window, pulled aside the drapes and after a moment said: "It is 37. Still 37." Callisto frowned. "Since Tuesday, then," he said. "No change." Henry Adams, three generations before his own, had stared aghast at Power;[13] Callisto found himself now in much the same state over Thermodynamics,[14] the inner life of that power, realizing like his predecessor that the Virgin and the dynamo stand as much for love as for power; that the two are indeed identical; and that love therefore not only makes the world go 'round but also makes the boccie ball spin, the nebula precess. It was this latter or sidereal element which disturbed him. The cosmologists had predicted an eventual heat-death for the universe (something like Limbo: form and motion abolished, heat-energy identical at every point in it); the meteorologists, day-to-day, staved it off by contradicting with a reassuring array of varied temperatures.

But for three days now, despite the changeful weather, the mercury had stayed at 37 degrees Fahrenheit. Leery at omens of apocalypse, Callisto shifted beneath the covers. His fingers pressed the bird more firmly, as if needing some pulsing or suffering assurance of an early break in the temperature.

It was that last cymbal crash that did it. Meatball was hurled wincing into consciousness as the synchronized wagging of heads over the wastebasket stopped. The final hiss remained for an instant in the room, then melted into the whisper of rain outside. "Aarrgghh," announced Meatball in the silence, looking at the empty magnum. Krinkles, in slow motion, turned, smiled and held out a cigarette. "Tea time, man," he said. "No, no," said Meatball. "How many times I got to tell you guys. Not at my place. You ought to know, Washington is lousy with Feds." Krinkles looked wistful. "Jeez, Meatball," he said, "you don't want to do nothing no more." "Hair of dog," said Meatball. "Only hope. Any juice left?" He began to crawl toward the kitchen. "No

---

11. French for "dawn song": joyous music for lovers celebrating the morning.
12. I.e., Vietnamese.
13. In *The Education of Henry Adams* (1907), Adams (1838–1918) formulates a dynamic theory of history by his application of the second law of thermodynamics, which holds that all matter in the universe tends to dissipate mechanical energy. For a symbol of twentieth-century power Adams uses the dynamo, which expends energy and thus will eventually run down. By contrast, he believed the thirteenth century was unified by the medieval church and the worship of the Virgin, whom he regards as a symbol of "the ideal of human perfection" and of a power which generated rather than dissipated energy.
14. Branch of physics dealing with heat and energy and with the conversion of one into the other.

champagne, I don't think," Duke said. "Case of tequila behind the icebox." They put on an Earl Bostic side.[15] Meatball paused at the kitchen door, glowering at Sandor Rojas. "Lemons," he said after some thought. He crawled to the refrigerator and got out three lemons and some cubes, found the tequila and set about restoring order to his nervous system. He drew blood once cutting the lemons and had to use two hands squeezing them and his foot to crack the ice tray but after about ten minutes he found himself, through some miracle, beaming down into a monster tequila sour. "That looks yummy," Sandor Rojas said. "How about you make me one." Meatball blinked at him. *"Kitchi lofass a shegitbe,"*[16] he replied automatically, and wandered away into the bathroom. "I say," he called out a moment later to no one in particular. "I say, there seems to be a girl or something sleeping in the sink." He took her by the shoulders and shook. "Wha," she said. "You don't look too comfortable," Meatball said. "Well," she agreed. She stumbled to the shower, turned on the cold water and sat down crosslegged in the spray. "That's better," she smiled.

"Meatball," Sandor Rojas yelled from the kitchen. "Somebody is trying to come in the window. A burglar, I think. A second-story man." "What are you worrying about," Meatball said. "We're on the third floor." He loped back into the kitchen. A shaggy woebegone figure stood out on the fire escape, raking his fingernails down the windowpane. Meatball opened the window. "Saul," he said.

"Sort of wet out," Saul said. He climbed in, dripping. "You heard, I guess."

"Miriam left you," Meatball said, "or something, is all I heard."

There was a sudden flurry of knocking at the front door. "Do come in," Sandor Rojas called. The door opened and there were three coeds from George Washington, all of whom were majoring in philosophy. They were each holding a gallon of Chianti. Sandor leaped up and dashed into the living room. "We heard there was a party," one blonde said. "Young blood," Sandor shouted. He was an ex-Hungarian freedom fighter who had easily the worst chronic case of what certain critics of the middle class have called Don Giovannism in the District of Columbia. *Purche porti la gonnella, voi sapete quel che fa.*[17] Like Pavlov's dog: a contralto voice or a whiff of Arpège and Sandor would begin to salivate. Meatball regarded the trio blearily as they filed into the kitchen; he shrugged. "Put the wine in the icebox," he said, "and good morning."

Aubade's neck made a golden bow as she bent over the sheets of foolscap, scribbling away in the green murk of the room. "As a young man at Princeton," Callisto was dictating, nestling the bird against the gray hairs of his chest, "Callisto had learned a mnemonic device for remembering the Laws of Thermodynamics: you can't win, things are going to get worse before they get better, who says they're going to get better. At the age of 54, confronted with Gibbs' notion of the universe, he suddenly realized that undergraduate cant had been oracle, after all. That spindly maze of equations became, for him, a

---

15. Earl Bostic (1913–65), modern jazz composer and alto saxophonist.

16. A more or less phonetic spelling of an obscene Hungarian phrase meaning roughly "Screw you."

17. As long as she is wearing a skirt, you know what he will do—from Act I of *Don Giovanni* (1787), an opera by Wolfgang Amadeus Mozart (1756–91) which tells the story of Don Juan, legendary womanizer. Hence Don Giovannism is excessive male lust and sexual activity.

vision of ultimate, cosmic heat-death. He had known all along, of course, that nothing but a theoretical engine or system ever runs at 100 per cent efficiency; and about the theorem of Clausius, which states that the entropy of an isolated system always continually increases. It was not, however, until Gibbs and Boltzmann[18] brought to this principle the methods of statistical mechanics that the horrible significance of it all dawned on him: only then did he realize that the isolated system—galaxy, engine, human being, culture, whatever—must evolve spontaneously toward the Condition of the More Probable. He was forced, therefore, in the sad dying fall of middle age, to a radical reëvaluation of everything he had learned up to then; all the cities and seasons and casual passions of his days had now to be looked at in a new and elusive light. He did not know if he was equal to the task. He was aware of the dangers of the reductive fallacy and, he hoped, strong enough not to drift into the graceful decadence of an enervated fatalism. His had always been a vigorous, Italian sort of pessimism: like Machiavelli,[19] he allowed the forces of *virtú* and *fortuna* to be about 50/50; but the equations now introduced a random factor which pushed the odds to some unutterable and indeterminate ratio which he found himself afraid to calculate.'' Around him loomed vague hothouse shapes; the pitifully small heart fluttered against his own. Counterpointed against his words the girl heard the chatter of birds and fitful car honkings scattered along the wet morning and Earl Bostic's alto rising in occasional wild peaks through the floor. The architectonic purity of her world was constantly threatened by such hints of anarchy: gaps and excrescences and skew lines, and a shifting or tilting of planes to which she had continually to readjust lest the whole structure shiver into disarray of discrete and meaningless signals. Callisto had described the process once as a kind of ''feedback'': she crawled into dreams each night with a sense of exhaustion, and a desperate resolve never to relax that vigilance. Even in the brief periods when Callisto made love to her, soaring above the bowing of taut nerves in haphazard double-stops would be the one singing string of her determination.

''Nevertheless,'' continued Callisto, ''he found in entropy or the measure of disorganization for a closed system an adequate metaphor to apply to certain phenomena in his own world. He saw, for example, the younger generation responding to Madison Avenue with the same spleen his own had once reserved for Wall Street, and in American 'consumerism' discovered a similar tendency from the least to the most probable, from differentiation to sameness, from ordered individuality to a kind of chaos. He found himself, in short, restating Gibbs' prediction in social terms, and envisioned a heat-death for his culture in which ideas, like heat-energy, would no longer be transferred, since each point in it would ultimately have the same quantity of energy; and intellec-

---

18. Rudolf J. E. Clausius (1822–88), German mathematician and physicist who introduced the theory that there is an inherent tendency in substances toward disorder or a state of maximum entropy. This tendency actually provides a driving force for many chemical reactions and physical processes. Josiah W. Gibbs (1839–1903), American physicist who applied statistical mechanics to Clausius' theories to show that the idea of entropy could be extended to all heterogeneous substances in the universe. Ludwig Boltzmann (1844–1906), Austrian physicist who associated entropy with probability, identifying the flow of time with an increase in entropy.

19. Niccolò Machiavelli (1469–1527), Italian author and statesman who believed that expediency, cunning, and amorality were necessary for building and maintaining a strong national state; he held that human beings have an innate tendency toward evil. Loosely translated, *virtú* and *fortuna* mean ''action'' and ''luck.''

tual motion would, accordingly, cease." He glanced up suddenly. "Check it now," he said. Again she rose and peered out at the thermometer. "Thirty-seven," she said. "The rain has stopped." He bent his head quickly and held his lips against a quivering wing. "Then it will change soon," he said, trying to keep his voice firm.

Sitting on the stove Saul was like any big rag doll that a kid has been taking out some incomprehensible rage on. "What happened," Meatball said. "If you feel like talking, I mean."

"Of course I feel like talking," Saul said. "One thing I did, I slugged her."

"Discipline must be maintained."

"Ha, ha. I wish you'd been there. Oh Meatball, it was a lovely fight. She ended up throwing a *Handbook of Chemistry and Physics* at me, only it missed and went through the window, and when the glass broke I reckon something in her broke too. She stormed out of the house crying, out in the rain. No raincoat or anything."

"She'll be back."

"No."

"Well." Soon Meatball said: "It was something earth-shattering, no doubt. Like who is better, Sal Mineo or Ricky Nelson."

"What it was about," Saul said, "was communication theory. Which of course makes it very hilarious."

"I don't know anything about communication theory."

"Neither does my wife. Come right down to it, who does? That's the joke."

When Meatball saw the kind of smile Saul had on his face he said: "Maybe you would like tequila or something."

"No. I mean, I'm sorry. It's a field you can go off the deep end in, is all. You get where you're watching all the time for security cops: behind bushes, around corners. MUFFET is top secret."

"Wha."

"Multi-unit factorial field electronic tabulator."

"You were fighting about that."

"Miriam has been reading science-fiction again. That and *Scientific American*. It seems she is, as we say, bugged at this idea of computers acting like people. I made the mistake of saying you can just as well turn that around, and talk about human behavior like a program fed into an IBM machine."

"Why not," Meatball said.

"Indeed, why not. In fact it is sort of crucial to communication, not to mention information theory. Only when I said that she hit the roof. Up went the balloon. And I can't figure out *why*. If anybody should know why, I should. I refuse to believe the government is wasting taxpayers' money on me, when it has so many bigger and better things to waste it on."

Meatball made a moue. "Maybe she thought you were acting like a cold, dehumanized amoral scientist type."

"My god," Saul flung up an arm. "Dehumanized. How much more human can I get? I worry, Meatball, I do. There are Europeans wandering around North Africa these days with their tongues torn out of their heads because those tongues have spoken the wrong words. Only the Europeans thought they were the right words."

"Language barrier," Meatball suggested.

Saul jumped down off the stove. "That," he said, angry, "is a good candidate for sick joke of the year. No, ace, it is *not* a barrier. If it is anything it's a kind of leakage. Tell a girl: 'I love you.' No trouble with two-thirds of that, it's a closed circuit. Just you and she. But that nasty four-letter word in the middle, *that's* the one you have to look out for. Ambiguity. Redundance. Irrelevance, even. Leakage. All this is noise. Noise screws up your signal, makes for disorganization in the circuit."

Meatball shuffled around. "Well, now, Saul," he muttered, "you're sort of, I don't know, expecting a lot from people. I mean, you know. What it is is, most of the things we say, I guess, are mostly noise."

"Ha! Half of what you just said, for example."

"Well, you do it too."

"I know." Saul smiled grimly. "It's a bitch, ain't it."

"I bet that's what keeps divorce lawyers in business. Whoops."

"Oh I'm not sensitive. Besides," frowning, "you're right. You find I think that most 'successful' marriages—Miriam and me, up to last night—are sort of founded on compromises. You never run at top efficiency, usually all you have is a minimum basis for a workable thing. I believe the phrase is Togetherness."

"Aarrgghh."

"Exactly. You find that one a bit noisy, don't you. But the noise content is different for each of us because you're a bachelor and I'm not. Or wasn't. The hell with it."

"Well sure," Meatball said, trying to be helpful, "you were using different words. By 'human being' you meant something that you can look at like it was a computer. It helps you think better on the job or something. But Miriam meant something entirely—"

"The hell with it."

Meatball fell silent. "I'll take that drink," Saul said after a while.

The card game had been abandoned and Sandor's friends were slowly getting wasted on tequila. On the living room couch, one of the coeds and Krinkles were engaged in amorous conversation. "No," Krinkles was saying, "no, I can't put Dave[20] *down*. In fact I give Dave a lot of credit, man. Especially considering his accident and all." The girl's smile faded. "How terrible," she said. "What accident?" "Hadn't you heard?" Krinkles said. "When Dave was in the army, just a private E-2, they sent him down to Oak Ridge on special duty. Something to do with the Manhattan Project.[21] He was handling hot stuff one day and got an overdose of radiation. So now he's got to wear lead gloves all the time." She shook her head sympathetically. "What an awful break for a piano-player."

Meatball had abandoned Saul to a bottle of tequila and was about to go to sleep in a closet when the front door flew open and the place was invaded by five enlisted personnel of the U.S. Navy, all in varying stages of abomination. "This is the place," shouted a fat, pimply seaman apprentice who had lost his white hat. "This here is the hoorhouse that chief was telling us about." A

---

20. Probably Dave Brubeck (b. 1920), modern jazz pianist and composer whose musical innovations were widely influential in the 1950s.

21. The code name for the U.S.'s secret operation to develop the first atomic bomb during World War II.

stringy-looking 3rd class boatswain's mate pushed him aside and cased the living room. "You're right, Slab," he said. "But it don't look like much, even for Stateside. I seen better tail in Naples, Italy." "How much, hey," boomed a large seaman with adenoids, who was holding a Mason jar full of white lightning. "Oh, my god," said Meatball.

Outside the temperature remained constant at 37 degrees Fahrenheit. In the hothouse Aubade stood absently caressing the branches of a young mimosa, hearing a motif of sap-rising, the rough and unresolved anticipatory theme of those fragile pink blossoms which, it is said, insure fertility. That music rose in a tangled tracery: arabesques of order competing fugally with the improvised discords of the party downstairs, which peaked sometimes in cusps and ogees of noise. That precious signal-to-noise ratio, whose delicate balance required every calorie of her strength, seesawed inside the small tenuous skull as she watched Callisto, sheltering the bird. Callisto was trying to confront any idea of the heat-death now, as he nuzzled the feathery lump in his hands. He sought correspondences. Sade,[22] of course. And Temple Drake,[23] gaunt and hopeless in her little park in Paris, at the end of *Sanctuary*. Final equilibrium. *Nightwood*.[24] And the tango. Any tango, but more than any perhaps the sad sick dance in Stravinsky's *L'Histoire du Soldat*.[25] He thought back: what had tango music been for them after the war, what meanings had he missed in all the stately coupled automatons in the *cafés-dansants*,[26] or in the metronomes which had ticked behind the eyes of his own partners? Not even the clean constant winds of Switzerland could cure the *grippe espagnole*:[27] Stravinsky had had it, they all had had it. And how many musicians were left after Passchendaele, after the Marne?[28] It came down in this case to seven: violin, doublebass. Clarinet, bassoon. Cornet, trombone. Tympani. Almost as if any tiny troupe of saltimbanques[29] had set about conveying the same information as a full pit-orchestra. There was hardly a full complement left in Europe. Yet with violin and tympani Stravinsky had managed to communicate in that tango the same exhaustion, the same airlessness one saw in the slicked-down youths who were trying to imitate Vernon Castle,[30] and in their mistresses, who simply did not care. *Ma maitresse*.[31] Celeste. Returning to Nice after the second war he had found that café replaced by a perfume shop which catered to American tourists. And no secret vestige of her in the cobblestones or in the old pension

---

22. The Marquis de Sade (1740–1814), French author of erotic writings which illustrated the concept of "sadism"—sexual gratification resulting from the infliction of pain upon others.

23. The protagonist of William Faulkner's *Sanctuary* (1931). At the close of the novel, Temple sits in a park in Paris looking at herself in a compact mirror, listening to "dying brasses" play somber tunes, and gazing "on into the sky lying prone and vanquished in the embrace of the season of rain and death."

24. A novel published in 1936 by Djuna Barnes (b. 1892); the story, about the relationships among psychopathic people, is pervaded by a sense of doom.

25. *The Soldier's Tale*, a ballet by Igor Stravinsky (1882–1971), first performed in Switzerland in 1918. Stravinsky wrote the music for only seven instruments because World War I had depleted the supply of trained musicians.

26. Cafes for dancing.

27. The Spanish Influenza which, in a worldwide epidemic in 1918, killed about twenty-million people and seriously depleted the fighting forces in the last phase of the war.

28. Two major battles of World War I in which both sides suffered enormous casualties.

29. I.e., Acrobats.

30. With his wife Irene, Vernon Castle (1887–1918) became famous around 1910 for developing and popularizing such dance steps as the one-step and the Turkey Trot.

31. "My mistress."

next door; no perfume to match her breath heavy with the sweet Spanish wine she always drank. And so instead he had purchased a Henry Miller novel and left for Paris, and read the book on the train so that when he arrived he had been given at least a little forewarning. And saw that Celeste and the others and even Temple Drake were not all that had changed. "Aubade," he said, "my head aches." The sound of his voice generated in the girl an answering scrap of melody. Her movement toward the kitchen, the towel, the cold water, and his eyes following her formed a weird and intricate canon; as she placed the compress on his forehead his sigh of gratitude seemed to signal a new subject, another series of modulations.

"No," Meatball was still saying, "no, I'm afraid not. This is not a house of ill repute. I'm sorry, really I am." Slab was adamant. "But the chief said," he kept repeating. The seaman offered to swap the moonshine for a good piece. Meatball looked around frantically, as if seeking assistance. In the middle of the room, the Duke di Angelis quartet were engaged in a historic moment. Vincent was seated and the others standing: they were going through the emotions of a group having a session, only without instruments. "I say," Meatball said. Duke moved his head a few times, smiled faintly, lit a cigarette, and eventually caught sight of Meatball. "Quiet, man," he whispered. Vincent began to fling his arms around, his fists clenched; then, abruptly, was still, then repeated the performance. This went on for a few minutes while Meatball sipped his drink moodily. The navy had withdrawn to the kitchen. Finally at some invisible signal the group stopped tapping their feet and Duke grinned and said, "At least we ended together."

Meatball glared at him. "I say," he said. "I have this new conception, man," Duke said. "You remember your namesake. You remember Gerry."

"No," said Meatball. "I'll remember April, if that's any help."

"As a matter of fact," Duke said, "it was Love for Sale. Which shows how much you know. The point is, it was Mulligan, Chet Baker and that crew,[32] way back then, out yonder. You dig?"

"Baritone sax," Meatball said. "Something about a baritone sax."

"But no piano, man. No guitar. Or accordion. You know what that means."

"Not exactly," Meatball said.

"Well first let me just say, that I am no Mingus, no John Lewis.[33] Theory was never my strong point. I mean things like reading were always difficult for me and all—"

"I know," Meatball said drily. "You got your card taken away because you changed key on Happy Birthday at a Kiwanis Club picnic."

"Rotarian. But it occurred to me, in one of these flashes of insight, that if that first quartet of Mulligan's had no piano, it could only mean one thing."

"No chords," said Paco, the baby-faced bass.

"What he is trying to say," Duke said, "is no root chords. Nothing to listen

---

32. Gerry Mulligan (b. 1927), baritone saxophonist, composer, and leader of a modern-jazz quartet in which Chet Baker (b. 1929) played and which was highly regarded in the early 1950s.
33. Charley Mingus (b. 1922), bass-player and jazz composer whose experiments with atonal and dissonant musical effects were regarded as avant-garde at the time. John Lewis (b. 1920), pianist, composer, and arranger; because of innovations such as his attempt to bridge the gap between classical music and jazz, he is thought to be one of the most influential of modern jazz musicians.

to while you blow a horizontal line. What one does in such a case is, one *thinks* the roots.''

A horrified awareness was dawning on Meatball. ''And the next logical extension,'' he said.

''Is to think everything,'' Duke announced with simple dignity. ''Roots, line, everything.''

Meatball looked at Duke, awed. ''But,'' he said.

''Well,'' Duke said modestly, ''there are a few bugs to work out.''

''But,'' Meatball said.

''Just listen,'' Duke said. ''You'll catch on.'' And off they went again into orbit, presumably somewhere around the asteroid belt. After a while Krinkles made an embouchure[34] and started moving his fingers and Duke clapped his hand to his forehead. ''Oaf!'' he roared. ''The new head we're using, you remember, I wrote last night?'' ''Sure,'' Krinkles said, ''the new head. I come in on the bridge. All your heads I come in then.'' ''Right,'' Duke said. ''So why—'' ''Wha,'' said Krinkles, ''16 bars, I wait, I come in—'' ''16?'' Duke said. ''No. No, Krinkles. Eight you waited. You want me to sing it? A cigarette that bears a lipstick's traces, an airline ticket to romantic places.'' Krinkles scratched his head. ''These Foolish Things, you mean.'' ''Yes,'' Duke said, ''yes, Krinkles. Bravo.'' ''Not I'll Remember April,'' Krinkles said. ''*Minghe morte,*''[35] said Duke. ''I *figured* we were playing it a little slow,'' Krinkles said. Meatball chuckled. ''Back to the old drawing board,'' he said. ''No, man,'' Duke said, ''back to the airless void.'' And they took off again, only it seemed Paco was playing in G sharp while the rest were in E flat, so they had to start all over.

In the kitchen two of the girls from George Washington and the sailors were singing Let's All Go Down and Piss on the Forrestal. There was a two-handed, bilingual *mura* game[36] on over by the icebox. Saul had filled several paper bags with water and was sitting on the fire escape, dropping them on passersby in the street. A fat government girl in a Bennington sweatshirt, recently engaged to an ensign attached to the Forrestal, came charging into the kitchen, head lowered, and butted Slab in the stomach. Figuring this was as good an excuse for a fight as any, Slab's buddies piled in. The *mura* players were nose-to-nose, screaming *trois, sette* at the tops of their lungs. From the shower the girl Meatball had taken out of the sink announced that she was drowning. She had apparently sat on the drain and the water was now up to her neck. The noise in Meatball's apartment had reached a sustained, ungodly crescendo.

Meatball stood and watched, scratching his stomach lazily. The way he figured, there were only about two ways he could cope: (a) lock himself in the closet and maybe eventually they would all go away, or (b) try to calm everybody down, one by one. (a) was certainly the more attractive alternative. But then he started thinking about that closet. It was dark and stuffy and he would be alone. He did not feature being alone. And then this crew off the good ship Lollipop or whatever it was might take it upon themselves to kick down the

---

34. The puckering of the lips when playing a wind instrument.
35. Probably, ''Mingus is dead,'' a reference to the group's abortive attempts to experiment in the manner of Charley Mingus.
36. Actually spelled *mora,* a game of Italian origin in which the players simultaneously display any number of fingers on one hand and try to guess the total shown.

closet door, for a lark. And if that happened he would be, at the very least, embarrassed. The other way was more a pain in the neck, but probably better in the long run.

So he decided to try and keep his lease-breaking party from deteriorating into total chaos: he gave wine to the sailors and separated the *mura* players; he introduced the fat government girl to Sandor Rojas, who would keep her out of trouble; he helped the girl in the shower to dry off and get into bed; he had another talk with Saul; he called a repairman for the refrigerator, which someone had discovered was on the blink. This is what he did until nightfall, when most of the revellers had passed out and the party trembled on the threshold of its third day.

Upstairs Callisto, helpless in the past, did not feel the faint rhythm inside the bird begin to slacken and fail. Aubade was by the window, wandering the ashes of her own lovely world; the temperature held steady, the sky had become a uniform darkening gray. Then something from downstairs—a girl's scream, an over-turned chair, a glass dropped on the floor, he would never know what exactly—pierced that private time-warp and he became aware of the faltering, the constriction of muscles, the tiny tossings of the bird's head; and his own pulse began to pound more fiercely, as if trying to compensate. "Aubade," he called weakly, "he's dying." The girl, flowing and rapt, crossed the hothouse to gaze down at Callisto's hands. The two remained like that, poised, for one minute, and two, while the heartbeat ticked a graceful diminuendo down at last into stillness. Callisto raised his head slowly. "I held him," he protested, impotent with the wonder of it, "to give him the warmth of my body. Almost as if I were communicating life to him, or a sense of life. What has happened? Has the transfer of heat ceased to work? Is there no more . . ." He did not finish.

"I was just at the window," she said. He sank back, terrified. She stood a moment more, irresolute; she had sensed his obsession long ago, realized somehow that that constant 37 was now decisive. Suddenly then, as if seeing the single and unavoidable conclusion to all this she moved swiftly to the window before Callisto could speak; tore away the drapes and smashed out the glass with two exquisite hands which came away bleeding and glistening with splinters; and turned to face the man on the bed and wait with him until the moment of equilibrium was reached, when 37 degrees Fahrenheit should prevail both outside and inside, and forever, and the hovering, curious dominant of their separate lives should resolve into a tonic of darkness and the final absence of all motion.

Although "Entropy" seems to depart radically from more conventional kinds of stories, it uses many of the standard elements of fiction. Actually, we can examine the plot of the story as an ongoing narrative with two settings, two sets of characters, and two conflicts whose resolutions are ambiguous. Setting is important in the story because a sense of discord is established by the apparently arbitrary juxtaposition of the two apartments. Although the two are connected because the ceiling of one is the floor of the other and because noises rise from the lower apartment, the settings are polar opposites, appearing at first glance to have no significant relationship to one another. One depicts the chaos of Meatball's wild party, and the other the balanced order of Callisto's consciously planned interior. And few transitional devices are employed in shifting back and forth between the two.

Pynchon even uses two different styles in presenting the upstairs and the downstairs apartments. For the chaotic scenes in Meatball's apartment, the sentences are often forceful, abrupt, and disjointed. For the placid scenes in Callisto's, the sentences tend to be rhythmical and languid, with phrases and clauses harmoniously blended (compare, for example, the first paragraph describing each setting). Telling his story from the omniscient point of view, Pynchon manipulates events, moves scenes arbitrarily, and enters into several of his characters' minds. He presents facts that no one else in the story could possibly be aware of. Only the author could know, for example, that the three coeds who drop into Meatball's party as total strangers "were majoring in philosophy." And Pynchon uses other conventional techniques of fiction: ambiguity, irony and paradox, symbol and allegory, and fantasy.

Pynchon displays great skill in interweaving two seemingly unrelated scenes containing two sets of characters who apparently have nothing to do with one another. His ability to interrelate such diverse information as the principles of thermodynamics, communication theory, and the many allusions to jazz and popular music is remarkable. An examination of these elements and the various structural parallels in the story reveals the interplay of three central themes: correspondence, order, and communication. Each is mentioned by name and amplified in the story. Each is contrasted with its opposite: *lack of* correspondence, *dis*order, and *failure of* communication. Tracing the way Pynchon presents these concepts helps us understand how the story is put together.

Correspondences are vital to the story, which explores correlations between the climate and human behavior, between hearing and feeling, between mechanical energy and heat energy, between the transfer of heat and the transfer of ideas, between outer space and inner space, between electronic circuits and human minds, between physics and music, between event and mood, between expression and reaction, between situation and response. Such correspondences pervade the tale, yet they fail to answer the questions it poses. In fact Callisto, who desperately seeks correspondences, finds himself "helpless in the past" and tied to a "private time-warp." He is lost because the evidence of correspondences he finds is only a half-truth at best. "Entropy" presents us with discord and disharmony, which Callisto would like to eliminate, or at least to deny.

Callisto attempts to deny discord and disharmony by establishing correspondences between human life and the theory of mechanical entropy, which holds that all matter and energy in the universe will eventually degenerate into an inert state. Callisto sees love, one of the most vital of human emotions, in terms of power—of attraction and repulsion—and concludes that if heat and energy (which is what he would call love) can no longer be transferred on earth, there eventually will be "heat death for the universe." He is pleased to find analogies between humans and machines; and he thinks of disillusioned people dancing like automatons to tango music after World War i. He reminds himself that "nothing but a theoretical engine or system runs at 100% efficiency." Yet there are obvious limitations to the similarities between humans and machines, and machinelike efficiency is hardly a criterion for judging human behavior.

The implication is that the mechanical metaphor dehumanizes people because it denies their capacity for acting like anything other than complex computers. Callisto, however, refuses to see that there is anything lacking in his theory of mechanical correspondence. He rejects humanity and despairingly quests for order by trying to form "a tiny enclave of regularity in the city's chaos." This enclave is a man-made garden, a "perfectly executed mobile" which is designed to be "alien to the vagaries of the weather." In other words, Callisto's self-imposed order alienates him and Aubade from a full existence. Like Meatball's intended trip into the closet, it is a retreat.

Callisto can find order only through isolation and retreat or through reliance upon a schoolbook formula which he himself describes as "undergraduate cant." He attempts to find order in an artificial construct (the hothouse world of his apartment) and through a rigid abstraction (his formula for heat death in the universe). But ironically Callisto ignores the basic premise of the formula—that entropy is maximized only in an isolated system. And so it is complete alienation, not the end of the universe, which really threatens Callisto and Aubade.

Callisto is further alienated because communication in the hothouse is a one-way affair. Aubade, who can *hear* the sap rising in a mimosa tree, takes dictation from Callisto. Whenever he speaks, "The sound of his voice generated in the girl an answering scrap of melody." But we have no indication that Aubade can communicate with Callisto or that he can respond to her. Callisto in fact is very slow in receiving the signals of their small bird's death. Although he dictates theorems about the universe and reflections about himself, he cannot communicate warmth and life to the bird nor, apparently, to Aubade.

In the Meatball sequences, on the other hand, we do see examples of genuine communication. The evidence is that such communication is not accomplished through words, but rather through feeling and action. When Meatball tries to talk to Saul about the inefficiency and imprecision of language, he fails to comfort his companion. But Meatball's concern means something to Saul, who has just fought with his wife about communication theory. Similarly, the "synchronized wagging" of heads among the quartet indicates that communication is possible without words and perhaps without sounds. The best examples of communication in the story are enumerated in the last paragraph of the final Meatball sequence. There Pynchon names the exhausting and irritating but human actions Meatball takes. Ironically, Meatball, not Callisto, achieves order. He does so because he can absorb randomness and because he can act and not merely react.

In presenting the maze of allusions, formulations, memories, incidents, theories, and actions, Pynchon gives us some sense of what works in human existence and what does not. Clearly, retreat and withdrawal do not; nor does letting a formula dictate one's life; nor does total chaos. Instead a willingness to come to terms with chaos seems a useful way to diminish its force. Meatball's final acts allow him to deal with chaos without being overtaken by it. Such an alternative cannot be put into a simple statement because, by its nature, it resists being reduced to a formula. Yet Meatball's behavior signifies his retention of human feelings and a willingness to act or to be involved. Thus "Entropy" provides us with meaningful instances of chaos and alienation which can be overcome only by personal acts, involvement, and genuine human feelings.

In discussing the story in wider perspective we have suggested some of the relationships between life and art. Tolstoy's story faithfully represents life itself, while Pynchon's illustrates ideas and inner contradictions. Yet finally Tolstoy's "life" connects with ideas and Pynchon's "ideas" connect with life. In the following brief illustration entitled "Dreamtigers," Jorge Luis Borges (b. 1899) shows us how inadequate and yet how marvelous are the creations of the human imagination.

In my childhood I was a fervent worshiper of the tiger: not the jaguar, the spotted "tiger" of the Amazonian tangles and the isles of vegetation that float down the Paraná, but that striped, Asiatic, royal tiger, that can be faced only by a man of war, on a castle atop an elephant. I used to linger endlessly before one of the cages at the zoo; I judged vast encyclopedias and books of natural history by the splendor of their tigers. (I still remember those illustrations: I who cannot rightly recall the brow or the smile of a woman.) Childhood passed away, and the tigers and my passion for them grew old, but still they are in my dreams. At that submerged or chaotic level they keep prevailing. And so, as I sleep, some dream beguiles me, and suddenly I know I am dreaming. Then I think: This is a dream, a pure diversion of my will; and now that I have unlimited power, I am going to cause a tiger.

Oh, incompetence! Never can my dreams engender the wild beast I long for. The tiger indeed appears, but stuffed or flimsy, or with impure variations of shape, or of an implausible size, or all too fleeting, or with a touch of the dog or the bird.

The tiger in this passage may suggest life itself in all its indescribable or unknowable majesty. The speaker discovers that he cannot "cause" a tiger, just as no writer can create life itself. The writer can, however, create "dreamtigers." Although these dreamtigers, to be sure, are not so splendid as real tigers, they do exhibit the creative power of the human imagination. We study dreamtigers in order to understand better the imagination which creates them and to appreciate the insights they can give into real tigers. Finally, we read stories in order to understand the human imagination and to appreciate the insights into human experience fiction can provide.

A Note on the Novel

A study of short fiction serves as an excellent introduction to the novel. Although the short story and the novel are distinct types of prose fiction, there are more similarities than differences between the two. Both are prose representations of imaginative, fictionalized experience and both employ plot, characters, and setting in presenting conflicts. Both convey themes, ideas, and complex patterns of human behavior. And both present vivid, dramatic, and unified experiences in order to reveal their particular and universal implications. But if there are many similarities between the short story and the novel, their differences are significant enough to require some clarification.

A **novel** is an extended prose narrative that portrays fictional characters engaging in actions and conflicts which are held together by a plot or by a pattern of themes or ideas. Except for the word *extended*, this definition can also be applied to the short story. Although the most obvious difference between the two forms is that the novel is generally longer than the short story, this generalized distinction needs to be qualified. There are actually no hard-and-fast rules to mark the exact point at which a piece of prose fiction ceases to be a long short story and becomes a short novel. In terms of length, the two forms occasionally overlap. Some narratives which may be designated as short stories are in fact longer and more complex than novels like Ernest Hemingway's *The Old Man and the Sea* (1952) and Eudora Welty's *The Ponder Heart* (1954). Nevertheless, it can be safely said that the novel form is almost always longer than the short story.

Length, however, is dependent upon a more essential distinction between the two forms: an author's conceptualization and treatment of his fictionalized world. A novel is not merely a short story stretched out to 300 or 400 pages. The extensive and intensive treatment the novel gives to such elements of fiction as character, plot, and setting is actually required by the way an author envisions his materials.

Nathaniel Hawthorne (1804–64), for example, set out to write a story about one character, a Puritan woman punished for adultery. He soon recognized that the subject was far too complex for a short story and decided to construct a lengthy narrative with four principal characters instead of one. He created a large background of townspeople representative of seventeenth-century New England, and devised a plot which stressed the conflicts of two of the four central characters. He then employed five, rather than one or two, major scenes, and worked out a number of significant complications and thematic points. Hawthorne wrote *The Scarlet Letter* (1850) as a novel because he realized that the scope and the complexity of his subject matter and theme required extensive development.

The plot of a standard novel contains more events than that of a short story, permitting the novelist to devise a variety of plot complications and even to construct a number of subplots that may embellish or counterpoint the main conflict. A novel progresses more deliberately and unfolds its elements more slowly than does a short story. Usually readers quickly see how the plot is developed in a short story. But in a novel, turns of events and sudden revelations and reversals of character may complicate the action. It is not always easy, in fact, to determine where particular actions are likely to lead. Setting too is usually more varied in a novel, with the action moving over a longer period of time and taking place in a greater variety of locales than in a short story. A short story typically compresses its conflict into a narrow scope of setting, plot, and character, whereas a novel develops its characters and their actions and values much more extensively.

Usually there are more characters in a novel than in a short story. A short story often depicts one character rather fully and extensively, with several others acting as stock characters. More often than not, a novel contains several characters treated in depth, with a larger cast of supporting players, many of whom may be more than cardboard figures. Because characterization is generally regarded as the chief concern of the novel form, the actions and values of several major characters will be developed more fully in order to reveal a greater range of implications. Readers of a novel therefore must observe how action influences character and how character initiates and determines action.

An approach that may prove useful in seeing the distinctions between the short story and the novel is the attempt to imagine each of the stories in this collection rendered into novelistic form. With most, the task would be almost impossible. Because of the subject matter and the limited scope of "A & P," for example, it would be hard to imagine the story expanded into a novel that would be very arresting or effective. Within the context of a novel, however, the incident in the supermarket could form one in a series of events that introduce the young narrator to the harsh adult world. The materials of "Gimpel the Fool," on the other hand, could readily be used as the basis for a novel. As it stands, the story ranges over a long period of time and contains numerous incidents and characters. Yet each element in it contributes to the depiction of Gimpel as both a fool and a wise man. Rendered into novel form, the story would probably contain more incidents and settings, with several treated in depth. The characters, notably Gimpel's wife and children, would be fully delineated. And there would be more emphasis on Gimpel himself, so that his motivations for acting as he does would be more fully developed throughout the narrative. If "Gimpel the Fool" were transformed into a novel, then, it would require not only greater length, but also more details, developments, and scenes.

Traditionally, novelists have made their subjects the exploration of a personality as it emerges from a past to a present time. Details of that past, including physical and social circumstances, are important in tracing a character's development. Less tangible elements such as family influences, memory, and self-awareness also contribute to a novel's representation of a character's personality and behavior.

As novelists became increasingly concerned with establishing the particular and the general circumstances in their characters' development, place became more important than the action depicted. For example, the London of Charles Dickens (1812–70), the Paris of Marcel Proust (1871–1922), and the Dublin of James Joyce (1882–1941) are literal places described and dramatized in many works of these writers. These and other novelists create a convincing illusion of individuality in their fictional characters by portraying them in particular times and in actual places. In many modern novels, place is dramatized not merely in terms of its physical attributes, but also in terms of its social and psychological significance as well. It would be impossible to assess and appreciate, for example, James Joyce's *Ulysses* (1922) or William Faulkner's *Light in August* (1932) without grasping the essential role turn-of-the-century Dublin plays in the former and the function of the rural American South in the latter. By giving their characters specific backgrounds related to actual places, novelists create a convincing illusion of individuality. And readers of novels often feel that what they are experiencing is not an imagined or different reality but the *real* reality. Place in the modern novel therefore has come to represent psychological and social attitudes and, as such, it can reflect the dreams, memories, hopes, and fears of its characters.

Similarly, a great emphasis on time is another vital issue in twentieth-century novels. Northrop Frye argues that the "alliance of time and Western Man" is the defining characteristic of the novel today as compared with other types of literature. A novel such as Ralph Ellison's *Invisible Man* (1952) or J. F. Powers' *Morte D'Urban* (1962) uses time to define the personality of its central character, as well as to intensify the theme of the narrative. And because time is stressed, readers of such fiction have a sense of personal identity with characters who exist within a specific period of time, yet who are changed by the flow of their experiences. Although we should remember that the novel is not a work of psychology or of philosophy, time and place in the modern novel serve to reveal and to dramatize feelings that are reflections of how people actually live.

The major difference between the novel and the short story lies in the novel's ability to treat a greater range of characters, settings, events, and themes. Yet because of its compression of these elements for the purpose of achieving a single effect, a well-crafted short story can be an equally effective fictional medium. The question for us is not whether one form is "better" than the other, but whether each piece of fiction we read gives us, in a unified, dramatic, and vivid way, a deeper understanding of the human condition.

Stories for Further Study

Nathaniel Hawthorne (1804–1864)

Young Goodman Brown

Young Goodman Brown came forth at sunset into the street at Salem village;[1] but put his head back, after crossing the threshold, to exchange a parting kiss with his young wife. And Faith, as the wife was aptly named, thrust her own pretty head into the street, letting the wind play with the pink ribbons of her cap while she called to Goodman Brown.

"Dearest heart," whispered she, softly and rather sadly, when her lips were close to his ear, "prithee put off your journey until sunrise and sleep in your own bed to-night. A lone woman is troubled with such dreams and such thoughts that she's afeard of herself sometimes. Pray tarry with me this night, dear husband, of all nights in the year."

"My love and my Faith," replied young Goodman Brown, "of all nights in the year, this one night must I tarry away from thee. My journey, as thou callest it, forth and back again, must needs be done 'twixt now and sunrise. What, my sweet, pretty wife, dost thou doubt me already, and we but three months married?"

"Then God bless you!" said Faith, with the pink ribbons; "and may you find all well when you come back."

"Amen!" cried Goodman Brown. "Say thy prayers, dear Faith, and go to bed at dusk, and no harm will come to thee."

So they parted; and the young man pursued his way until, being about to

---

1. Salem, Massachusetts, where in 1692 thirty persons were tried and sentenced to death for practicing witchcraft; nineteen were eventually hanged.

turn the corner by the meeting-house, he looked back and saw the head of Faith still peeping after him with a melancholy air, in spite of her pink ribbons.

"Poor little Faith!" thought he, for his heart smote him. "What a wretch am I to leave her on such an errand! She talks of dreams, too. Methought as she spoke there was trouble in her face, as if a dream had warned her what work is to be done to-night. But no, no; 't would kill her to think it. Well, she's a blessed angel on earth; and after this one night I'll cling to her skirts and follow her to heaven."

With this excellent resolve for the future, Goodman Brown felt himself justified in making more haste on his present evil purpose. He had taken a dreary road, darkened by all the gloomiest trees of the forest, which barely stood aside to let the narrow path creep through, and closed immediately behind. It was all as lonely as could be; and there is this peculiarity in such a solitude, that the traveler knows not who may be concealed by the innumerable trunks and the thick boughs overhead; so that with lonely footsteps he may yet be passing through an unseen multitude.

"There may be a devilish Indian behind every tree," said Goodman Brown to himself; and he glanced fearfully behind him as he added, "What if the devil himself should be at my very elbow!"

His head being turned back, he passed a crook of the road, and, looking forward again, beheld the figure of a man, in grave and decent attire, seated at the foot of an old tree. He arose at Goodman Brown's approach and walked onward side by side with him.

"You are late, Goodman Brown," said he. "The clock of the Old South[2] was striking as I came through Boston, and that is full fifteen minutes agone."

"Faith kept me back awhile," replied the young man, with a tremor in his voice, caused by the sudden appearance of his companion, though not wholly unexpected.

It was now deep dusk in the forest, and deepest in that part of it where these two were journeying. As nearly as could be discerned, the second traveler was about fifty years old, apparently in the same rank of life as Goodman Brown, and bearing a considerable resemblance to him, though perhaps more in expression than features. Still they might have been taken for father and son. And yet, though the elder person was as simply clad as the younger, and as simple in manner too, he had an indescribable air of one who knew the world, and who would not have felt abashed at the governor's dinner table or in King William's court,[3] were it possible that his affairs should call him thither. But the only thing about him that could be fixed upon as remarkable was his staff, which bore the likeness of a great black snake, so curiously wrought that it might almost be seen to twist and wriggle itself like a living serpent. This, of course, must have been an ocular deception, assisted by the uncertain light.

"Come, Goodman Brown," cried his fellow-traveler, "this is a dull pace for the beginning of a journey. Take my staff, if you are so soon weary."

"Friend," said the other, exchanging his slow pace for a full stop, "having kept covenant by meeting thee here, it is my purpose now to return whence I came. I have scruples touching the matter thou wot'st of."

---

2. Old South Church, Boston; it was built in 1730, although the events of the story take place around 1690.

3. William III, King of England from 1689 to 1702.

"Sayest thou so?" replied he of the serpent, smiling apart. "Let us walk on, nevertheless, reasoning as we go; and if I convince thee not thou shalt turn back. We are but a little way in the forest yet."

"Too far! too far!" exclaimed the goodman, unconsciously resuming his walk. "My father never went into the woods on such an errand, nor his father before him. We have been a race of honest men and good Christians since the days of the martyrs; and shall I be the first of the name of Brown that ever took his path and kept"—

"Such company, thou wouldst say," observed the elder person, interpreting his pause. "Well said, Goodman Brown! I have been as well acquainted with your family as with ever a one among the Puritans; and that's no trifle to say. I helped your grandfather, the constable, when he lashed the Quaker woman so smartly through the streets of Salem; and it was I that brought your father a pitch-pine knot, kindled at my own hearth, to set fire to an Indian village, in King Philip's war.[4] They were my good friends, both; and many a pleasant walk have we had along this path, and returned merrily after midnight. I would fain be friends with you for their sake."

"If it be as thou sayest," replied Goodman Brown, "I marvel they never spoke of these matters; or, verily, I marvel not, seeing that the least rumor of the sort would have driven them from New England. We are a people of prayer, and good works to boot, and abide no such wickedness."

"Wickedness or not," said the traveler with the twisted staff, "I have a very general acquaintance here in New England. The deacons of many a church have drunk the communion wine with me; the selectmen of divers towns make me their chairman; and a majority of the Great and General Court[5] are firm supporters of my interest. The governor and I, too—But these are state secrets."

"Can this be so?" cried Goodman Brown, with a stare of amazement at his undisturbed companion. "Howbeit, I have nothing to do with the governor and council; they have their own ways, and are no rule for a simple husbandman[6] like me. But, were I to go on with thee, how should I meet the eye of that good old man, our minister, at Salem village? Oh, his voice would make me tremble both Sabbath day and lecture day."[7]

Thus far the elder traveler had listened with due gravity; but now burst into a fit of irrepressible mirth, shaking himself so violently that his snake-like staff actually seemed to wriggle in sympathy.

"Ha! ha! ha!" shouted he again and again; then composing himself, "Well, go on, Goodman Brown, go on; but, prithee, don't kill me with laughing."

"Well, then, to end the matter at once," said Goodman Brown, considerably nettled, "there is my wife, Faith. It would break her dear little heart; and I'd rather break my own."

"Nay, if that be the case," answered the other, "e'en go thy ways,

---

4. King Philip (also called Metacomet) was the leader of the last Indian insurrection (1675–76) against the Puritan settlers in southern New England.
5. The legislature of the Massachusetts colony.
6. Married man of humble social position.
7. Day of the midweek sermon, usually Thursday.

Goodman Brown. I would not for twenty old women like the one hobbling before us that Faith should come to any harm.''

As he spoke he pointed his staff at a female figure on the path, in whom Goodman Brown recognized a very pious and exemplary dame, who had taught him his catechism in youth, and was still his moral and spiritual adviser, jointly with the minister and Deacon Gookin.

"A marvel, truly, that Goody Cloyse[8] should be so far in the wilderness at nightfall," said he. "But with your leave, friend, I shall take a cut through the woods until we have left this Christian woman behind. Being a stranger to you, she might ask whom I was consorting with and whither I was going."

"Be it so," said his fellow-traveler. "Betake you the woods, and let me keep the path."

Accordingly the young man turned aside, but took care to watch his companion, who advanced softly along the road until he had come within a staff's length of the old dame. She, meanwhile, was making the best of her way, with singular speed for so aged a woman, and mumbling some indistinct words—a prayer, doubtless—as she went. The traveler put forth his staff and touched her withered neck with what seemed the serpent's tail.

"The devil!" screamed the pious old lady.

"Then Goody Cloyse knows her old friend?" observed the traveler, confronting her and leaning on his writhing stick.

"Ah, forsooth, and is it your worship indeed?" cried the good dame. "Yea, truly is it, and in the very image of my old gossip,[9] Goodman Brown, the grandfather of the silly fellow that now is. But—would your worship believe it?—my broomstick hath strangely disappeared, stolen, as I suspect, by that unhanged witch, Goody Cory, and that, too, when I was all anointed with the juice of smallage, and cinquefoil, and wolf's bane"[10]—

"Mingled with fine wheat and the fat of a new-born babe," said the shape of old Goodman Brown.

"Ah, your worship knows the recipe," cried the old lady, cackling aloud. "So, as I was saying, being all ready for the meeting, and no horse to ride on, I made up my mind to foot it; for they tell me there is a nice young man to be taken into communion to-night. But now your good worship will lend me your arm, and we shall be there in a twinkling."

"That can hardly be," answered her friend. "I may not spare you my arm, Goody Cloyse; but here is my staff, if you will."

So saying, he threw it down at her feet, where, perhaps, it assumed life, being one of the rods which its owner had formerly lent to the Egyptian magi.[11] Of this fact, however, Goodman Brown could not take cognizance. He had cast up his eyes in astonishment, and, looking down again, beheld neither Goody Cloyse nor the serpentine staff, but this fellow-traveler alone, who waited for him as calmly as if nothing had happened.

---

8. Along with Goody Cory and Martha Carrier (who are mentioned later), Goody Cloyse was among those tried and sentenced in the witchcraft trials of 1692. "Goody" is a contraction of "Goodwife," used in addressing a married woman of modest social position. Likewise, "Goodman" denotes a man, usually married, of similar status.

9. Crony; companion.

10. Plants thought to have the power to ward off evil.

11. The wise men of the Egyptian Pharaoh in the biblical story of Aaron's rod (Exodus 7). Symbolizing Satan and death, their magical rods were transformed into serpents which were swallowed up by Aaron's rod, a symbol of life.

"That old woman taught me my catechism," said the young man; and there was a world of meaning in this simple comment.

They continued to walk onward, while the elder traveler exhorted his companion to make good speed and persevere in the path, discoursing so aptly that his arguments seemed rather to spring up in the bosom of his auditor than to be suggested by himself. As they went, he plucked a branch of maple to serve for a walking stick, and began to strip it of the twigs and little boughs, which were wet with evening dew. The moment his fingers touched them they became strangely withered and dried up as with a week's sunshine. Thus the pair proceeded, at a good free pace, until suddenly, in a gloomy hollow of the road, Goodman Brown sat himself down on the stump of a tree and refused to go any farther.

"Friend," said he, stubbornly, "my mind is made up. Not another step will I budge on this errand. What if a wretched old woman do choose to go to the devil when I thought she was going to heaven: is that any reason why I should quit my dear Faith and go after her?"

"You will think better of this by and by," said his acquaintance, composedly. "Sit here and rest yourself a while; and when you feel like moving again, there is my staff to help you along."

Without more words, he threw his companion the maple stick, and was as speedily out of sight as if he had vanished into the deepening gloom. The young man sat a few moments by the roadside, applauding himself greatly, and thinking with how clear a conscience he should meet the minister in his morning walk, nor shrink from the eye of good old Deacon Gookin. And what calm sleep would be his that very night, which was to have been spent so wickedly, but so purely and sweetly now, in the arms of Faith! Amidst these pleasant and praiseworthy meditations, Goodman Brown heard the tramp of horses along the road, and deemed it advisable to conceal himself within the verge of the forest, conscious of the guilty purpose that had brought him thither, though now so happily turned from it.

On came the hoof tramps and the voices of the riders, two grave old voices, conversing soberly as they drew near. These mingled sounds appeared to pass along the road, within a few yards of the young man's hiding-place; but, owing doubtless to the depth of the gloom at that particular spot, neither the travelers nor their steeds were visible. Though their figures brushed the small boughs by the wayside, it could not be seen that they intercepted, even for a moment, the faint gleam from the strip of bright sky athwart which they must have passed. Goodman Brown alternately crouched and stood on tiptoe, pulling aside the branches and thrusting forth his head as far as he durst without discerning so much as a shadow. It vexed him the more, because he could have sworn, were such a thing possible, that he recognized the voices of the minister and Deacon Gookin, jogging along quietly, as they were wont to do, when bound to some ordination or ecclesiastical council. While yet within hearing, one of the riders stopped to pluck a switch.

"Of the two, reverend sir," said the voice like the deacon's, "I had rather miss an ordination dinner than to-night's meeting. They tell me that some of our community are to be here from Falmouth and beyond, and others from Connecticut and Rhode Island, besides several of the Indian powwows,[12] who,

---

12. Conjurers or medicine men.

after their fashion, know almost as much deviltry as the best of us. Moreover, there is a goodly young woman to be taken into communion.''

"Mighty well, Deacon Gookin!" replied the solemn old tones of the minister, "Spur up, or we shall be late. Nothing can be done, you know, until I get on the ground.''

The hoofs clattered again; and the voices, talking so strangely in the empty air, passed on through the forest, where no church had ever been gathered or solitary Christian prayed. Whither, then, could these holy men be journeying so deep into the heathen wilderness? Young Goodman Brown caught hold of a tree for support, being ready to sink down on the ground, faint and overburdened with the heavy sickness of his heart. He looked up to the sky, doubting whether there really was a heaven above him. Yet there was the blue arch, and the stars brightening in it.

"With heaven above and Faith below, I will yet stand firm against the devil!" cried Goodman Brown.

While he still gazed upward into the deep arch of the firmament and had lifted his hands to pray, a cloud, though no wind was stirring, hurried across the zenith and hid the brightening stars. The blue sky was still visible, except directly overhead, where this black mass of cloud was sweeping swiftly northward. Aloft in the air, as if from the depths of the cloud, came a confused and doubtful sound of voices. Once the listener fancied that he could distinguish the accents of towns-people of his own, men and women, both pious and ungodly, many of whom he had met at the communion table, and had seen others rioting at the tavern. The next moment, so indistinct were the sounds, he doubted whether he had heard aught but the murmur of the old forest, whispering without a wind. Then came a stronger swell of those familiar tones, heard daily in the sunshine at Salem village, but never until now from a cloud of night. There was one voice, of a young woman, uttering lamentations, yet with an uncertain sorrow, and entreating for some favor, which, perhaps, it would grieve her to obtain; and all the unseen multitude, both saints and sinners, seemed to encourage her onward.

"Faith!" shouted Goodman Brown, in a voice of agony and desperation; and the echoes of the forest mocked him, crying, "Faith! Faith!" as if bewildered wretches were seeking her all through the wilderness.

The cry of grief, rage, and terror was yet piercing the night, when the unhappy husband held his breath for a response. There was a scream, drowned immediately in a louder murmur of voices, fading into far-off laughter, as the dark cloud swept away, leaving the clear and silent sky above Goodman Brown. But something fluttered lightly down through the air and caught on the branch of a tree. The young man seized it, and beheld a pink ribbon.

"My Faith is gone!" cried he, after one stupefied moment. "There is no good on earth; and sin is but a name. Come, devil; for to thee is this world given.''

And, maddened with despair, so that he laughed loud and long, did Goodman Brown grasp his staff and set forth again, at such a rate that he seemed to fly along the forest path rather than to walk or run. The road grew wilder and drearier and more faintly traced, and vanished at length, leaving him in the heart of the dark wilderness, still rushing onward with the instinct that guides mortal man to evil. The whole forest was peopled with frightful sounds—the creaking of the trees, the howling of wild beasts, and the yell of Indians; while sometimes the wind tolled like a distant church bell, and sometimes gave a broad roar around the traveler, as if all Nature were laughing him to scorn. But he was himself the chief horror of the scene, and shrank not from its other horrors.

"Ha! ha! ha!" roared Goodman Brown when the wind laughed at him. "Let us hear which will laugh loudest. Think not to frighten me with your deviltry. Come witch, come wizard, come Indian powwow, come devil himself, and here comes Goodman Brown. You may as well fear him as he fear you."

In truth, all through the haunted forest there could be nothing more frightful than the figure of Goodman Brown. On he flew among the black pines, brandishing his staff with frenzied gestures, now giving vent to an inspiration of horrid blasphemy, and now shouting forth such laughter as set all the echoes of the forest laughing like demons around him. The fiend in his own shape is less hideous than when he rages in the breast of man. Thus sped the demoniac on his course, until, quivering among the trees, he saw a red light before him, as when the felled trunks and branches of a clearing have been set on fire, and throw up their lurid blaze against the sky, at the hour of midnight. He paused, in a lull of the tempest that had driven him onward, and heard the swell of what seemed a hymn, rolling solemnly from a distance with the weight of many voices. He knew the tune; it was a familiar one in the choir of the village meeting-house. The verse died heavily away, and was lengthened by a chorus, not of human voices, but of all the sounds of the benighted wilderness pealing in awful harmony together. Goodman Brown cried out, and his cry was lost to his own ear by its unison with the cry of the desert.

In the interval of silence he stole forward until the light glared full upon his eyes. At one extremity of an open space, hemmed in by the dark wall of the forest, arose a rock, bearing some rude, natural resemblance either to an altar or a pulpit, and surrounded by four blazing pines, their tops aflame, their stems untouched, like candles at an evening meeting. The mass of foliage that had overgrown the summit of the rock was all on fire, blazing high into the night and fitfully illuminating the whole field. Each pendent twig and leafy festoon was in a blaze. As the red light arose and fell, a numerous congregation alternately shone forth, then disappeared in shadow, and again grew, as it were, out of the darkness, peopling the heart of the solitary woods at once.

"A grave and dark-clad company," quoth Goodman Brown.

In truth they were such. Among them, quivering to and fro between gloom and splendor, appeared faces that would be seen next day at the council board of the province, and others which, Sabbath after Sabbath, looked devoutly heavenward, and benignantly over the crowded pews, from the holiest pulpits in the land. Some affirm that the lady of the governor was there. At least there were high dames well known to her, and wives of honored husbands, and widows, a great multitude, and ancient maidens, all of excellent repute, and fair young girls, who trembled lest their mothers should espy them. Either the sudden gleams of light flashing over the obscure field bedazzled Goodman Brown, or he recognized a score of the church members of Salem village famous for their especial sanctity. Good old Deacon Gookin had arrived, and waited at the skirts of that venerable saint, his revered pastor. But, irreverently consorting with these grave, reputable, and pious people, these elders of the church, these chaste dames and dewy virgins, there were men of dissolute lives and women of spotted fame, wretches given over to all mean and filthy vice, and suspected even of horrid crimes. It was strange to see that the good shrank not from the wicked, nor were the sinners abashed by the saints. Scattered also among their pale-faced enemies were the Indian priests, or powwows, who had often scared their native forest with more hideous incantations than any known to English witchcraft.

"But where is Faith?" thought Goodman Brown; and, as hope came into his heart, he trembled.

Another verse of the hymn arose, a slow and mournful strain, such as the pious love, but joined to words which expressed all that our nature can conceive of sin, and darkly hinted at far more. Unfathomable to mere mortals is the lore of fiends. Verse after verse was sung; and still the chorus of the desert swelled between like the deepest tone of a mighty organ; and with the final peal of that dreadful anthem there came a sound, as if the roaring wind, the rushing streams, the howling beasts, and every other voice of the unconcerted wilderness were mingling and according with the voice of guilty man in homage to the prince of all. The four blazing pines threw up a loftier flame, and obscurely discovered shapes and visages of horror on the smoke wreaths above the impious assembly. At the same moment the fire on the rock shot redly forth and formed a glowing arch above its base, where now appeared a figure. With reverence be it spoken, the figure bore no slight similitude, both in garb and manner, to some grave divine of the New England churches.

"Bring forth the converts!" cried a voice that echoed through the field and rolled into the forest.

At the word, Goodman Brown stepped forth from the shadow of the trees and approached the congregation, with whom he felt a loathful brotherhood by the sympathy of all that was wicked in his heart. He could have well-nigh sworn that the shape of his own dead father beckoned him to advance, looking downward from a smoke wreath, while a woman, with dim features of despair, threw out her hand to warn him back. Was it his mother? But he had no power to retreat one step, nor to resist, even in thought, when the minister and good old Deacon Gookin seized his arms and led him to the blazing rock. Thither came also the slender form of a veiled female, led between Goody Cloyse, that pious teacher of the catechism, and Martha Carrier, who had received the devil's promise to be queen of hell. A rampant hag was she. And there stood the proselytes beneath the canopy of fire.

"Welcome, my children," said the dark figure, "to the communion of your race. Ye have found thus young your nature and your destiny. My children, look behind you!"

They turned; and flashing forth, as it were, in a sheet of flame, the fiend worshippers were seen; the smile of welcome gleamed darkly on every visage.

"There," resumed the sable form, "are all whom ye have reverenced from youth. Ye deemed them holier than yourselves, and shrank from your own sin, contrasting it with their lives of righteousness and prayerful aspirations heavenward. Yet here are they all in my worshipping assembly. This night it shall be granted you to know their secret deeds: how hoary-bearded elders of the church have whispered wanton words to the young maids of their households; how many a woman, eager for widows' weeds, has given her husband a drink at bedtime and let him sleep his last sleep in her bosom; how beardless youths have made haste to inherit their fathers' wealth; and how fair damsels—blush not, sweet ones—have dug little graves in the garden, and bidden me, the sole guest, to an infant's funeral. By the sympathy of your human hearts for sin ye shall scent out all the places—whether in church, bed-chamber, street, field, or forest—where crime has been committed, and shall exult to behold the whole earth one stain of guilt, one mighty blood spot. Far more than this. It shall be yours to penetrate, in every bosom, the deep mystery of sin, the fountain of all wicked arts, and which inexhaustibly supplies more evil impulses than human power—than my power at its utmost—can make manifest in deeds. And now, my children, look upon each other.''

They did so; and, by the blaze of the hell-kindled torches, the wretched man beheld his Faith, and the wife her husband, trembling before that unhallowed altar.

''Lo, there ye stand, my children,'' said the figure, in a deep and solemn tone, almost sad with its despairing awfulness, as if his once angelic nature could yet mourn for our miserable race. ''Depending upon one another's hearts, ye had still hoped that virtue were not all a dream. Now are ye undeceived. Evil is the nature of mankind. Evil must be your only happiness. Welcome again, my children, to the communion of your race.''

''Welcome,'' repeated the fiend worshippers, in one cry of despair and triumph.

And there they stood, the only pair, as it seemed, who were yet hesitating on the verge of wickedness in this dark world. A basin was hollowed, naturally, in the rock. Did it contain water, reddened by the lurid right? or was it blood? or, perchance, a liquid flame? Herein did the shape of evil dip his hand and prepare to lay the mark of baptism upon their foreheads, that they might be partakers of the mystery of sin, more conscious of the secret guilt of others, both in deed and thought, than they could now be of their own. The husband cast one look at his pale wife, and Faith at him. What polluted wretches would the next glance show them to each other, shuddering alike at what they disclosed and what they saw!

''Faith! Faith!'' cried the husband, ''look up to heaven, and resist the wicked one.''

Whether Faith obeyed he knew not. Hardly had he spoken when he found himself amid calm night and solitude, listening to a roar of the wind which died heavily away through the forest. He staggered against the rock, and felt it chill and damp; while a hanging twig, that had been all on fire, besprinkled his cheek with the coldest dew.

The next morning young Goodman Brown came slowly into the street of Salem village, staring around him like a bewildered man. The good old minister was taking a walk along the graveyard to get an appetite for breakfast and meditate his sermon, and bestowed a blessing, as he passed, on Goodman Brown. He shrank from the venerable saint as if to avoid an anathema. Old Deacon Gooking was at domestic worship, and the holy words of his prayer were heard through the open window. ''What God doth the wizard pray to?'' quoth Goodman Brown. Goody Cloyse, that excellent old Christian, stood in the early sunshine at her own lattice, catechizing a little girl who had brought her a pint of morning's milk. Goodman Brown snatched away the child as from the grasp of the fiend himself. Turning the corner by the meeting-house, he spied the head of Faith, with the pink ribbons, gazing anxiously forth, and bursting into such joy at sight of him that she skipped along the street and almost kissed her husband before the whole village. But Goodman Brown looked sternly and sadly into her face, and passed on without a greeting.

Had Goodman Brown fallen asleep in the forest and only dreamed a wild dream of a witch-meeting?

Be it so if you will; but, alas! it was a dream of evil omen for young Goodman Brown. A stern, a sad, a darkly meditative, a distrustful, if not a desperate man did he become from the night of that fearful dream. On the Sabbath day, when the congregation were singing a holy psalm, he could not listen because an anthem of sin rushed loudly upon his ear and drowned all the blessed strain. When the minister spoke from the pulpit with power and fervid eloquence, and, with his hand on the open Bible, of the sacred truths of our religion, and of saint-like lives and triumphant deaths, and of future bliss or misery unutterable, then did Goodman Brown turn pale, dreading lest the roof should thunder down upon the gray blasphemer and his hearers. Often, awaking suddenly at midnight, he shrank from the bosom of Faith; and at morning or eventide, when the family knelt down at prayer, he scowled and muttered to himself, and gazed sternly at his wife, and turned away. And when he had lived long, and was borne to his grave a hoary corpse, followed by Faith, an aged woman, and children and grandchildren, a goodly procession, besides neighbors not a few, they carved no hopeful verse upon his tombstone, for his dying hour was gloom.

Herman Melville (1819–1891)
Bartleby the Scrivener
A Story of Wall Street

I am a rather elderly man. The nature of my avocations, for the last thirty years, has brought me into more than ordinary contact with what would seem an interesting and somewhat singular set of men, of whom, as yet, nothing, that I know of, has ever been written—I mean, the law-copyists, or scriveners. I have known very many of them, professionally and privately, and, if I pleased, could relate divers histories, at which good-natured gentlemen might smile, and sentimental souls might weep. But I waive the biographies of all other scriveners, for a few passages in the life of Bartleby, who was a scrivener, the strangest I ever saw, or heard of. While, of other law-copyists, I might write the complete life, of Bartleby nothing of that sort can be done. I believe that no materials exist, for a full and satisfactory biography of this man. It is an irreparable loss to literature. Bartleby was one of those beings of whom nothing is ascertainable except from the original sources, and, in his case, those are very small. What my own astonished eyes saw of Bartleby, *that* is all I know of him, except, indeed, one vague report, which will appear in the sequel.

Ere introducing the scrivener, as he first appeared to me, it is fit I make some mention of myself, my *employés,* my business, my chambers and general surroundings; because some such description is indispensable to an adequate understanding of the chief character about to be presented. Imprimis:[1] I am a man who, from his youth upwards, has been filled with a profound conviction that the easiest way of life is the best. Hence, though I belong to a profession proverbially energetic and nervous, even to turbulence, at times, yet nothing of that sort have I ever suffered to invade my peace. I am one of those unambitious lawyers who never addresses a jury, or in any way draws down public applause; but, in the cool tranquillity of a snug retreat, do a snug business among rich men's bonds, and mortgages, and title-deeds. All who know me, consider me an eminently *safe* man. The late John Jacob Astor,[2] a personage little given to poetic enthusiasm, had no hesitation in pronouncing my first grand point to be prudence; my next, method. I do not speak it in vanity, but simply record the fact, that I was not unemployed in my profession by the late John Jacob Astor; a name which, I admit, I love to repeat; for it hath a rounded and orbicular sound to it, and rings like unto bullion. I will freely add, that I was not insensible to the late John Jacob Astor's good opinion.

Some time prior to the period at which this little history begins, my avocations had been largely increased. The good old office, now extinct in the State of New York, of a Master in Chancery,[3] had been conferred upon me. It was not a very arduous office, but very pleasantly remunerative. I seldom lose my temper; much more seldom indulge in dangerous indignation at wrongs and outrages; but I must permitted to be rash here and declare, that I consider the sudden and violent abrogation of the office of Master in Chancery, by the new Constitution, as a ———premature act; inasmuch as I had counted upon a life-lease of the profits, whereas I only received those of a few short years. But this is by the way.

My chambers were up stairs, at No.—Wall Street. At one end, they looked upon the white wall of the interior of a spacious skylight shaft, penetrating the building from top to bottom.

This view might have been considered rather tame than otherwise, deficient in what landscape painters call "life." But, if so, the view from the other end of my chambers offered, at least, a contrast, if nothing more. In that direction, my windows commanded an unobstructed view of a lofty brick wall, black by age and everlasting shade; which wall required no spy-glass to bring out its lurking beauties, but, for the benefit of all near-sighted spectators, was pushed up to within ten feet of my window panes. Owing to the great height of the surroundings buildings, and my chambers being on the second floor, the interval between this wall and mine not a little resembled a huge square cistern.

At the period just preceding the advent of Bartleby, I had two persons as

---

1. "In the first place."

2. Merchant and real-estate investor (1763–1848); his monopolization of the western fur trade and his vast land holdings made him the richest American of his time.

3. An appointed officer of a court of equity who assisted in executing the transfer of property owned by a defendant who has refused to transfer under the decree of the court. The position was abolished by the state Constitutional Convention of 1846.

copyists in my employment, and a promising lad as an office-boy. First, Turkey; second, Nippers; third, Ginger Nut. These may seem names, the like of which are not usually found in the Directory.[4] In truth, they were nicknames, mutually conferred upon each other by my three clerks, and were deemed expressive of their respective persons or characters. Turkey was a short, pursy Englishman, of about my age—that is, somewhere not far from sixty. In the morning, one might say, his face was of a fine florid hue, but after twelve o'clock, meridian—his dinner hour—it blazed like a grate full of Christmas coals; and continued blazing—but, as it were, with a gradual wane—till six o'clock, P.M., or thereabouts; after which, I saw no more of the proprietor of the face, which, gaining its meridian with the sun, seemed to set with it, to rise, culminate, and decline the following day, with the like regularity and undiminished glory. There are many singular coincidences I have known in the course of my life, not the least among which was the fact, that, exactly when Turkey displayed his fullest beams from his red and radiant countenance, just then, too, at that critical moment, began the daily period when I considered his business capacities as seriously disturbed for the remainder of the twenty-four hours. Not that he was absolutely idle, or averse to business, then; far from it. The difficulty was, he was apt to be altogether too energetic. There was a strange, inflamed, flurried, flighty recklessness of activity about him. He would be incautious in dipping his pen into his inkstand. All his blots upon my documents were dropped there after twelve o'clock, meridian. Indeed, not only would he be reckless, and sadly given to making blots in the afternoon, but, some days, he went further, and was rather noisy. At such times, "too, his face flamed with augmented blazonry, as if cannel coal had been heaped on anthracite. He made an unpleasant racket with his chair; spilled his sand-box;[5] in mending his pens, impatiently split them all to pieces, and threw them on the floor in a sudden passion; stood up, and leaned over his table, boxing his papers about in a most indecorous manner, very sad to behold in an elderly man like him. Nevertheless, as he was in many ways a most valuable person to me, and all the time before twelve o'clock meridian, was the quickest, steadiest creature, too, accomplishing a great deal of work in a style not easily to be matched—for these reasons, I was willing to overlook his eccentricities, though, indeed, occasionally, I remonstrated with him. I did this very gently, however, because, though the civilest, nay, the blandest and most reverential of men in the morning, yet, in the afternoon, he was disposed upon provocation, to be slightly rash with his tongue—in fact, insolent. Now, valuing his morning services as I did, and resolved not to lose them—yet, at the same time, made uncomfortable by his inflamed ways after twelve o'clock —and being a man of peace, unwilling by my admonitions to call forth unseemly retorts from him, I took upon me, one Saturday noon (he was always worse on Saturdays) to hint to him, very kindly, that, perhaps, now that he was growing old, it might be well to abridge his labors; in short, he need not come to my chambers after twelve o'clock, but, dinner over, had best go home to his lodgings, and rest himself till tea-time. But no; he insisted upon his afternoon devotions. His countenance became intolerably fervid, as he oratorically assured me—gesticulating with a long ruler at the other end of the room—that if

---

4. Post-office directory.
5. Small box containing sand which was sprinkled on the wet ink of a manuscript.

Herman Melville **391**

his services in the morning were useful, how indispensable, then, in the afternoon?

"With submission, sir," said Turkey, on this occasion, "I consider myself your right-hand man. In the morning I but marshal and deploy my columns; but in the afternoon I put myself at their head, and gallantly charge the foe, thus"—and he made a violent thrust with the ruler.

"But the blots, Turkey," intimated I.

"True; but, with submission, sir, behold these hairs! I am getting old. Surely, sir, a blot or two of a warm afternoon is not to be severely urged against gray hairs. Old age—even if it blot the page—is honorable. With submission, sir, we *both* are getting old."

This appeal to my fellow-feeling was hardly to be resisted. At all events, I saw that go he would not. So I made up my mind to let him stay, resolving, nevertheless, to see to it that, during the afternoon, he had to do with my less important papers.

Nippers, the second on my list, was a whiskered, sallow, and upon the whole, rather piratical-looking young man, of about five-and-twenty. I always deemed him the victim of two evil powers—ambition and indigestion. The ambition was evinced by a certain impatience of the duties of a mere copyist, and unwarrantable usurpation of strictly professional affairs, such as the original drawing up of legal documents. The indigestion seemed betokened in an occasional nervous testiness and grinning irritability, causing the teeth to audibly grind together over mistakes committed in copying; unnecessary maledictions, hissed, rather than spoken, in the heat of business; and especially by a continual discontent with the height of the table where he worked. Though of a very ingenious mechanical turn, Nippers could never get this table to suit him. He put chips under it, blocks of various sorts, bits of pasteboard, and at last went so far as to attempt an exquisite adjustment, by final pieces of folded blotting-paper. But no invention would answer. If, for the sake of easing his back, he brought the table-lid at a sharp angle well up towards his chin, and wrote there like a man using the steep roof of a Dutch house for his desk, then he declared that it stopped the circulation in his arms. If now he lowered the table to his waistbands, and stooped over it in writing, then there was a sore aching in his back. In short, the truth of the matter was, Nippers knew not what he wanted. Or, if he wanted anything, it was to be rid of a scrivener's table altogether. Among the manifestations of his diseased ambition was a fondness he had for receiving visits from certain ambiguous-looking fellows in seedy coats, whom he called his clients. Indeed, I was aware that not only was he, at times, considerable of a ward-politician, but he occasionally did a little business at the Justices' courts, and was not unknown on the steps of the Tombs.[6] I have good reason to believe, however, that one individual who called upon him at my chambers, and who, with a grand air, he insisted was his client, was no other than a dun,[7] and the alleged title-deed, a bill. But, with all his failings, and the annoyances he caused me, Nippers, like his compatriot Turkey, was a very useful man to me; wrote a neat, swift hand; and, when he chose, was not deficient in a gentlemanly sort of deportment. Added to this, he always dressed in a gentlemanly sort of way; and so, incidentally, reflected credit upon my

---

6. New York City prison.
7. Bill collector.

chambers. Whereas, with respect to Turkey, I had much ado to keep him from being a reproach to me. His clothes were apt to look oily, and smell of eating-houses. He wore his pantaloons very loose and baggy in summer. His coats were execrable; his hat not to be handled. But while the hat was a thing of indifference to me, inasmuch as his natural civility and deference, as a dependent Englishman, always led him to doff it the moment he entered the room, yet his coat was another matter. Concerning his coats, I reasoned with him; but with no effect. The truth was, I suppose, that a man with so small an income could not afford to sport such a lustrous face and a lustrous coat at one and the same time. As Nippers once observed, Turkey's money went chiefly for red ink. One winter day, I presented Turkey with a highly respectable-looking coat of my own—a padded gray coat, of a most comfortable warmth, and which buttoned straight up from the knee to the neck. I thought Turkey would appreciate the favor, and abate his rashness and obstreperousness of afternoons. But no; I verily believe that buttoning himself up in so downy and blanketlike a coat had a pernicious effect upon him—upon the same principle that too much oats are bad for horses. In fact, precisely as a rash, restive horse is said to feel his oats, so Turkey felt his coat. It made him insolent. He was a man whom prosperity harmed.

Though, concerning the self-indulgent habits of Turkey, I had my own private surmises, yet, touching Nippers, I was well persuaded that, whatever might be his faults in other respects, he was, at least, a temperate young man. But, indeed, nature herself seemed to have been his vintner, and, at his birth, charged him so thoroughly with an irritable, brandy-like disposition, that all subsequent potations were needless. When I consider how, amid the stillness of my chambers, Nippers would sometimes impatiently rise from his seat, and stooping over his table, spread his arms wide apart, seize the whole desk, and move it, and jerk it, with a grim, grinding motion on the floor, as if the table were a perverse voluntary agent, intent on thwarting and vexing him, I plainly perceive that, for Nippers, brandy-and-water were altogether superfluous.

It was fortunate for me that, owing to its peculiar cause—indigestion—the irritability and consequent nervousness of Nippers were mainly observable in the morning, while in the afternoon he was comparatively mild. So that, Turkey's paroxysms only coming on about twelve o'clock, I never had to do with their eccentricities at one time. Their fits relieved each other, like guards. When Nippers's was on, Turkey's was off; and *vice versa*. This was a good natural arrangement, under the circumstances.

Ginger Nut, the third on my list, was a lad, some twelve years old. His father was a carman, ambitious of seeing his son on the bench instead of a cart, before he died. So he sent him to my office, as student at law, errand-boy, cleaner and sweeper, at the rate of one dollar a week. He had a little desk to himself, but he did not use it much. Upon inspection, the drawer exhibited a great array of the shells of various sorts of nuts. Indeed, to this quick-witted youth, the whole noble science of the law was contained in a nutshell. Not the least among the employments of Ginger Nut, as well as one which he discharged with the most alacrity, was his duty as cake and apple purveyor for Turkey and Nippers. Copying law-papers being proverbially a dry, husky sort of business, my two scriveners were fain to moisten their mouths very often with Spitzenbergs,[8] to be had at the numerous stalls nigh the Custom House and Post Office. Also, they sent Ginger Nut very frequently for that peculiar cake—small, flat, round, and very spicy—after which he had been named by them. Of a cold morning, when business was but dull, Turkey would gobble up scores of these cakes, as if they were mere wafers—indeed, they sell them at the rate of six or eight for a penny—the scrape of his pen blending with the crunching of the crisp particles in his mouth. Rashest of all the fiery afternoon blunders and flurried rashnesses of Turkey, was his once moistening a ginger-cake between his lips, and clapping it on to a mortgage, for a seal. I came within an ace of dismissing him then. But he mollified me by making an oriental bow, and saying—

"With submission, sir, it was generous of me to find you in stationery on my own account."

Now my original business—that of a conveyancer[9] and title hunter, and drawer-up of recondite documents of all sorts—was considerably increased by receiving the master's office. There was now great work for scriveners. Not only must I push the clerks already with me, but I must have additional help.

In answer to my advertisement, a motionless young man one morning stood upon my office threshold, the door being open, for it was summer. I can see that figure now—pallidly neat, pitiably respectable, incurably forlorn! It was Bartleby.

After a few words touching his qualifications, I engaged him, glad to have among my corps of copyists a man of so singularly sedate an aspect, which I thought might operate beneficially upon the flighty temper of Turkey, and the fiery one of Nippers.

I should have stated before that ground-glass folding-doors divided my premises into two parts, one of which was occupied by my scriveners, the other by myself. According to my humor, I threw open these doors, or closed them. I resolved to assign Bartleby a corner by the folding-doors, but on my side of them, so as to have this quiet man within easy call, in case any trifling thing was to be done. I placed his desk close up to a small side-window in that part of the room, a window which originally had afforded a lateral view of certain grimy back-yards and bricks, but which, owing to subsequent erections, commanded at present no view at all, though it gave some light. Within three feet of the panes was a wall, and the light came down from far above, between two lofty buildings, as from a very small opening in a dome. Still further to a satisfactory arrangement, I procured a high green folding screen, which might entirely isolate Bartleby from my sight, though not remove him from my voice. And thus, in a manner, privacy and society were conjoined.

At first, Bartleby did an extraordinary quantity of writing. As if long famishing for something to copy, he seemed to gorge himself on my documents. There was no pause for digestion. He ran a day and night line, copying by sunlight and by candle-light. I should have been quite delighted with his application, had he been cheerfully industrious. But he wrote on silently, palely, mechanically.

---

8. A variety of apple.
9. Lawyer who deals with the transfer of real-estate deeds and mortgages.

It is, of course, an indispensable part of a scrivener's business to verify the accuracy of his copy, word by word. Where there are two or more scriveners in an office, they assist each other in this examination, one reading from the copy, the other holding the original. It is a very dull, wearisome, and lethargic affair. I can readily imagine that, to some sanguine temperaments, it would be altogether intolerable. For example, I cannot credit that the mettlesome poet, Byron,[10] would have contentedly sat down with Bartleby to examine a law document of, say five hundred pages, closely written in a crimpy hand.

Now and then, in the haste of business, it had been my habit to assist in comparing some brief document myself, calling Turkey or Nippers for this purpose. One object I had, in placing Bartleby so handy to me behind the screen, was, to avail myself of his services on such trivial occasions. It was on the third day, I think, of his being with me, and before any necessity had arisen for having his own writing examined, that, being much hurried to complete a small affair I had in hand, I abruptly called to Bartleby. In my haste and natural expectancy of instant compliance, I sat with my head bent over the original on my desk, and my right hand sideways, and somewhat nervously extended with the copy, so that, immediately upon emerging from his retreat, Bartleby might snatch it and proceed to business without the least delay.

In this very attitude did I sit when I called to him, rapidly stating what it was I wanted him to do—namely, to examine a small paper with me. Imagine my surprise, nay, my consternation, when, without moving from his privacy, Bartleby, in a singularly mild, firm voice, replied, "I would prefer not to."

I sat awhile in perfect silence, rallying my stunned faculties. Immediately it occurred to me that my ears had deceived me, or Bartleby had entirely misunderstood my meaning. I repeated my request in the clearest tone I could assume; but in quite as clear a one came the previous reply, "I would prefer not to."

"Prefer not to," echoed I, rising in high excitement, and crossing the room with a stride. "What do you mean? Are you moon-struck? I want you to help me compare this sheet here—take it," and I thrust it towards him.

"I would prefer not to," said he.

I looked at him steadfastly. His face was leanly composed; his gray eye dimly calm. Not a wrinkle of agitation rippled him. Had there been the least uneasiness, anger, impatience or impertinence in his manner; in other words, had there been anything ordinarily human about him, doubtless I should have violently dismissed him from the premises. But as it was, I should have as soon thought of turning my pale plaster-of-paris bust of Cicero[11] out of doors. I stood gazing at him awhile, as he went on with his own writing, and then reseated myself at my desk. This is very strange, thought I. What had one best do? But my business hurried me. I concluded to forget the matter for the present, reserving it for my future leisure. So, calling Nippers from the other room, the paper was speedily examined.

A few days after this, Bartleby concluded four lengthy documents, being quadruplicates of a week's testimony taken before me in my High Court of

---

10. George Gordon, Lord Byron (1788–1824), English Romantic poet whose restless and tempestuous spirit would have ill suited him to the sedate life of a law clerk.

11. Marius Tullius Cicero (106–43 B.C.), Roman statesman, orator, and writer.

Chancery. It became necessary to examine them. It was an important suit, and great accuracy was imperative. Having all things arranged, I called Turkey, Nippers and Ginger Nut, from the next room, meaning to place the four copies in the hands of my four clerks, while I should read from the original. Accordingly, Turkey, Nippers, and Ginger Nut had taken their seats in a row, each with his document in his hand, when I called to Bartleby to join this interesting group.

"Bartleby! quick, I am waiting."

I heard a slow scrape of his chair legs on the uncarpeted floor, and soon he appeared standing at the entrance of his hermitage.

"What is wanted?" said he, mildly.

"The copies, the copies," said I, hurriedly. "We are going to examine them. There"—and I held towards him the fourth quadruplicate.

"I would prefer not to," he said, and gently disappeared behind the screen.

For a few moments I was turned into a pillar of salt,[12] standing at the head of my seated column of clerks. Recovering myself, I advanced towards the screen, and demanded the reason for such extraordinary conduct.

"*Why* do you refuse?"

"I would prefer not to."

With any other man I should have flown outright into a dreadful passion, scorned all further words, and thrust him ignominiously from my presence. But there was something about Bartleby that not only strangely disarmed me, but, in a wonderful manner, touched and disconcerted me. I began to reason with him.

"These are your own copies we are about to examine. It is labor saving to you, because one examination will answer for your four papers. It is common usage. Every copyist is bound to help examine his copy. Is it not so? Will you not speak? Answer!"

"I prefer not to," he replied in a flute-like tone. It seemed to me that, while I had been addressing him, he carefully revolved every statement that I made; fully comprehended the meaning; could not gainsay the irresistible conclusion; but at the same time, some paramount consideration prevailed with him to reply as he did.

"You are decided, then, not to comply with my request—a request made according to common usage and common sense?"

He briefly gave me to understand, that on that point my judgment was sound. Yes: his decision was irreversible.

It is not seldom the case that, when a man is browbeaten in some unprecedented and violently unreasonably way, he begins to stagger in his own plainest faith. He begins, as it were, vaguely to surmise that, wonderful as it may be, all the justice and all the reason is on the other side. Accordingly, if any disinterested persons are present, he turns to them for some reinforcement for his own faltering mind.

"Turkey," said I, "what do you think of this? Am I not right?"

"With submission, sir," said Turkey, in his blandest tone, "I think that you are."

---

12. In Gen. 19:26, Lot's wife was turned into a pillar of salt after she defied God's command not to look back at the destruction of Sodom and Gomorrah.

"Nippers," said I, "what do *you* think of it?"

"I think I should kick him out of the office."

(The reader of nice perceptions will here perceive that, it being morning, Turkey's answer is couched in polite and tranquil terms, but Nippers replies in ill-tempered ones. Or, to repeat a previous sentence, Nippers's ugly mood was on duty, and Turkey's off.)

"Ginger Nut," said I, willing to enlist the smallest suffrage in my behalf, "what do *you* think of it?"

"I think, sir, he's a little *luny*," replied Ginger Nut, with a grin.

"You hear what they say," said I, turning towards the screen, "come forth and do your duty."

But he vouchsafed no reply. I pondered a moment in sore perplexity. But once more business hurried me. I determined again to postpone the consideration of this dilemma to my future leisure. With a little trouble we made out to examine the papers without Bartleby, though at every page or two Turkey deferentially dropped his opinion, that this proceeding was quite out of the common; while Nippers, twitching in his chair with a dyspeptic nervousness, ground out, between his set teeth, occasional hissing maledictions against the stubborn oaf behind the screen. And for his (Nippers's) part, this was the first and the last time he would do another man's business without pay.

Meanwhile Bartleby sat in his hermitage, oblivious to everything but his own peculiar business there.

Some days passed, the scrivener being employed upon another lengthy work. His late remarkable conduct led me to regard his ways narrowly. I observed that he never went to dinner; indeed, that he never went anywhere. As yet I had never, of my personal knowledge, known him to be outside of my office. He was a perpetual sentry in the corner. At about eleven o'clock though, in the morning, I noticed that Ginger Nut would advance toward the opening in Bartleby's screen, as if silently beckoned thither by a gesture invisible to me where I sat. The boy would then leave the office, jingling a few pence, and reappear with a handful of ginger-nuts which he delivered in the hermitage, receiving two of the cakes for his trouble.

He lives, then, on ginger-nuts thought I; never eats a dinner, properly speaking; he must be a vegetarian, then, but no; he never eats even vegetables, he eats nothing but ginger-nuts. My mind then ran on in reveries concerning the probable effects upon the human constitution of living entirely on ginger-nuts. Ginger-nuts are so called, because they contain ginger as one of the peculiar constituents, and the final flavoring one. Now, what was ginger? A hot, spicy thing. Was Bartleby hot and spicy? Not at all. Ginger then, had no effect upon Bartleby. Probably he preferred it should have none.

Nothing so aggravates an earnest person as a passive resistance. If the individual so resisted be of a not inhumane temper, and the resisting one perfectly harmless in his passivity, then, in the better moods of the former, he will endeavor charitably to construe to his imagination what proves impossible to be solved by his judgment. Even so, for the most part, I regarded Bartleby and his ways. Poor fellow! thought I, he means no mischief; it is plain he intends no insolence; his aspect sufficiently evinces that his eccentricities are involuntary. He is useful to me. I can get along with him. If I turn him away, the chances are he will fall in with some less-indulgent employer, and then he will be rudely treated, and perhaps driven forth miserably to starve. Yes. Here I can cheaply purchase a delicious self-approval. To befriend Bartleby; to humor him in his strange willfulness, will cost me little or nothing, while I lay up in my soul what will eventually prove a sweet morsel for my conscience. But this mood was not invariable with me. The passiveness of Bartleby sometimes irritated me. I felt strangely goaded on to encounter him in new opposition—to elicit some angry spark from him answerable to my own. But, indeed, I might as well have essayed to strike fire with my knuckles against a bit of Windsor soap.[13] But one afternoon the evil impulse in me mastered me, and the following little scene ensued:

"Bartleby," said I, "when those papers are all copied, I will compare them with you."

"I would prefer not to."

"How? Surely you do not mean to persist in that mulish vagary?"

No answer.

I threw open the folding-doors near by, and, turning upon Turkey and Nippers, exclaimed:

"Bartleby a second time says, he won't examine his papers. What do you think of it, Turkey?"

It was afternoon, be it remembered. Turkey sat glowing like a brass boiler; his bald head steaming; his hands reeling among his blotted papers.

"Think of it?" roared Turkey. "I think I'll just step behind his screen, and black his eyes for him!"

So saying, Turkey rose to his feet and threw his arms into a pugilistic position. He was hurrying away to make good his promise, when I detained him, alarmed at the effect of incautiously rousing Turkey's combativeness after dinner.

"Sit down, Turkey," said I, "and hear what Nippers has to say. What do you think of it, Nippers? Would I not be justified in immediately dismissing Bartleby?"

"Excuse me, that is for you to decide, sir. I think his conduct quite unusual, and, indeed, unjust, as regards Turkey and myself. But it may only be a passing whim."

"Ah," exclaimed I, "you have strangely changed your mind, then—you speak very gently of him now."

"All beer," cried Turkey; "gentleness is effects of beer—Nippers and I dined together to-day. You see how gentle *I* am, sir. Shall I go and black his eyes?"

"You refer to Bartleby, I suppose. No, not to-day, Turkey," I replied; "pray, put up your fists."

I closed the doors, and again advanced towards Bartleby. I felt additional incentives tempting me to my fate. I burned to be rebelled against again. I remembered that Bartleby never left the office.

"Bartleby," said I, "Ginger Nut is away; just step around to the Post Office, won't you?" (it was but a three minutes' walk) "and see if there is anything for me."

---

13. A kind of scented, brown soap.

"I would prefer not to."

"You *will* not?"

"I *prefer* not."

I staggered to my desk, and sat there in a deep study. My blind inveteracy returned. Was there any other thing in which I could procure myself to be ignominiously repulsed by this lean, penniless wight?[14]—my hired clerk? What added thing is there, perfectly reasonable, that he will be sure to refuse to do?

"Bartleby!"

No answer.

"Bartleby," in a louder tone.

No answer.

"Bartleby," I roared.

Like a very ghost, agreeably to the laws of magical invocation, at the third summons, he appeared at the entrance of his hermitage.

"Go to the next room, and tell Nippers to come to me."

"I prefer not to," he respectfully and slowly said, and mildly disappeared.

"Very good, Bartleby," said I, in a quiet sort of serenely-severe self-possessed tone, intimating the unalterable purpose of some terrible retribution very close at hand. At the moment I half intended something of the kind. But upon the whole, as it was drawing towards my dinner-hour, I thought it best to put on my hat and walk home for the day, suffering much from perplexity and distress of mind.

Shall I acknowledge it? The conclusion of this whole business was, that it soon became a fixed fact of my chambers, that a pale young scrivener, by the name of Bartleby, had a desk there; that he copied for me at the usual rate of four cents a folio (one hundred words); but he was permanently exempt from examining the work done by him, that duty being transferred to Turkey and Nippers, out of compliment, doubtless, to their superior acuteness; moreover, said Bartleby was never, on any account, to be dispatched on the most trivial errand of any sort; and that even if entreated to take upon him such a matter, it was generally understood that he would "prefer not to"—in other words, that he would refuse point-blank.

As days passed on, I became considerably reconciled to Bartleby. His steadiness, his freedom from all dissipation, his incessant industry (except when he chose to throw himself into a standing revery behind his screen), his great stillness, his unalterableness of demeanor under all circumstances, made him a valuable acquisition. One prime thing was this—*he was always there*—first in the morning, continually through the day, and the last at night. I had a singular confidence in his honesty. I felt my most precious papers perfectly safe in his hands. Sometimes, to be sure, I could not, for the very soul of me, avoid falling into sudden spasmodic passions with him. For it was exceeding difficult to bear in mind all the time those strange peculiarities, privileges, and unheard-of-exemptions, forming the tacit stipulations on Bartleby's part under which he remained in my office. Now and then, in the eagerness of dispatching pressing business. I would inadvertently summon Bartleby, in a short, rapid tone, to put his finger, say, on the incipient tie of a bit of red tape with which I was about compressing some papers. Of course, from behind the screen the usual answer,

---

14. Creature.

"I prefer not to," was sure to come; and then, how could a human creature, with the common infirmities of our nature, refrain from bitterly exclaiming upon such perverseness—such unreasonableness? However, every added repulse of this sort which I received only tended to lessen the probability of my repeating the inadvertence.

Here it must be said, that, according to the custom of most legal gentlemen occupying chambers in densely-populated law buildings, there were several keys to my door. One was kept by a woman residing in the attic, which person weekly scrubbed and daily swept and dusted my apartments. Another was kept by Turkey for convenience sake. The third I sometimes carried in my own pocket. The fourth I knew not who had.

Now, one Sunday morning I happened to go to Trinity Church, to hear a celebrated preacher, and finding myself rather early on the ground I thought I would walk round to my chambers for a while. Luckily I had my key with me; but upon applying it to the lock, I found it resisted by something inserted from the inside. Quite surprised, I called out; when to my consternation a key was turned from within; and thrusting his lean visage at me, and holding the door ajar, the apparition of Bartleby appeared, in his shirtsleeves, and otherwise in a strangely tattered *déshabillé*,[15] saying quietly that he was sorry, but he was deeply engaged just then, and—preferred not admitting me at present. In a brief word or two, he moreover added, that perhaps I had better walk round the block two or three times, and by that time he would probably have concluded his affairs.

Now, the utterly unsurmised appearance of Bartleby, tenanting my law-chambers of a Sunday morning, with his cadaverously gentlemanly *nonchalance,* yet withal firm and self-possessed, had such a strange effect upon me, that incontinently I slunk away from my own door, and did as desired. But not without sundry twinges of impotent rebellion against the mild effrontery of this unaccountable scrivener. Indeed, it was his wonderful mildness chiefly, which not only disarmed me, but unmanned me as it were. For I consider that one, for the time, is sort of unmanned when he tranquilly permits his hired clerk to dictate to him, and order him away from his own premises. Furthermore, I was full of uneasiness as to what Bartleby could possibly be doing in my office in his shirt sleeves, and in an otherwise dismantled condition of a Sunday morning. Was anything amiss going on? Nay, that was out of the question. It was not to be thought of for a moment that Bartleby was an immoral person. But what could he be doing there?—copying? Nay again, whatever might be his eccentricities, Bartleby was an eminently decorous person. He would be the last man to sit down to his desk in any state approaching to nudity. Besides, it was Sunday; and there was something about Bartleby that forbade the supposition that he would by any secular occupation violate the proprieties of the day.

Nevertheless, my mind was not pacified; and full of restless curiosity, at last I returned to the door. Without hindrance I inserted my key, opened it, and entered. Bartleby was not to be seen. I looked around anxiously, peeped behind his screen; but it was very plain that he was gone. Upon more closely examining the place, I surmised that for an indefinite period Bartleby must have eaten, dressed, and slept in my office, and that too without plate, mirror, or

---

15. Carelessly dressed condition.

bed. The cushioned seat of a ricketty old sofa in one corner bore the faint impress of a lean, reclining form. Rolled away under his desk, I found a blanket; under the empty grate, a blacking box[16] and brush; on a chair, a tin basin, with soap and a ragged towel; in a newspaper a few crumbs of ginger-nuts and a morsel of cheese. Yes, thought I, it is evident enough that Bartleby has been making his home here, keeping bachelor's hall all by himself. Immediately then the thought came sweeping across me, what miserable friend-lessness and loneliness are here revealed! His poverty is great; but his soli-tude, how horrible! Think of it. Of a Sunday, Wall Street is deserted as Petra;[17] and every night of every day it is an emptiness. This building, too, which of week-days hums with industry and life, at nightfall echoes with sheer vacancy, and all through Sunday is forlorn. And here Bartleby makes his home; sole spectator of a solitude which he has seen all populous—a sort of innocent and transformed Marius brooding among the ruins of Carthage![18]

For the first time in my life a feeling of overpowering stinging melancholy seized me. Before, I had never experienced aught but a not unpleasing sadness. The bond of a common humanity now drew me irresistibly to gloom. A fra-ternal melancholy! For both I and Bartleby were sons of Adam. I remembered the bright silks and sparkling faces I had seen that day, in gala trim, swan-like sailing down the Mississippi of Broadway; and I contrasted them with the pallid copyist, and thought to myself, Ah, happiness courts the light, so we deem the world is gay; but misery hides aloof, so we deem that misery there is none. These sad fancyings—chimeras, doubtless, of a sick and silly brain—led on to other and more special thoughts, concerning the eccentricities of Bart-leby. Presentiments of strange discoveries hovered round me. The scrivener's pale form appeared to me laid out, among uncaring strangers, in its shivering winding-sheet.[19]

Suddenly I was attracted by Bartleby's closed desk, the key in open sight left in the lock.

I mean no mischief, seek the gratification of no heartless curiosity, thought I; besides, the desk is mine, and its contents, too, so I will make bold to look within. Everything was methodically arranged, the papers smoothly placed. The pigeon holes were deep, and removing the files of documents, I groped into their recesses. Presently I felt something there, and dragged it out. It was an old bandana handkerchief heavy and knotted. I opened it, and saw it was a savings' bank.

I now recalled all the quiet mysteries which I had noted in the man. I re-membered that he never spoke but to answer; that, though at intervals he had considerable time to himself, yet I had never seen him reading—no, not even a newspaper; that for long periods he would stand looking out, at his pale window behind the screen, upon the dead brick wall; I was quite sure he never visited any refectory or eating house; while his pale face clearly indicated that he never drank beer like Turkey, or tea and coffee even, like other men; that he

---

16. Box of black shoe polish.
17. Ancient Palestinian city, once a flourishing trade center, whose ruins were discovered in 1812.
18. Gaius Marius (155–86 B.C.), Roman consul and general, was forced to leave Rome because of political strife. He is sometimes pictured sitting in the ruins of Carthage, North African city destroyed by Rome in the third of the Punic Wars (149–146 B.C.).
19. Sheet in which a corpse is wrapped.

never went anywhere in particular that I could learn; never went out for a walk, unless, indeed, that was the case at present; that he had declined telling who he was, or whence he came, or whether he had any relatives in the world; that though so thin and pale, he never complained of ill health. And more than all, I remembered a certain unconscious air of pallid—how shall I call it?—of pallid haughtiness, say, or rather an austere reserve about him, which had positively awed me into my tame compliance with his eccentricities, when I had feared to ask him to do the slightest incidental thing for me, even though I might know, from his long-continued motionlessness, that behind his screen he must be standing in one of those dead-wall reveries of his.

Revolving all these things, and coupling them with the recently discovered fact, that he made my office his constant abiding place and home, and not forgetful of his morbid moodiness; revolving all these things, a prudential feeling began to steal over me. My first emotions had been those of pure melancholy and sincerest pity; but just in proportion as the forlornness of Bartleby grew and grew to my imagination, did that same melancholy merge into fear, that pity into repulsion. So true it is, and so terrible, too, that up to a certain point the thought or sight of misery enlists our best affections; but, in certain special cases, beyond that point it does not. They err who would assert that invariably this is owing to the inherent selfishness of the human heart. It rather proceeds from a certain hopelessness of remedying excessive and organic ill. To a sensitive being, pity is not seldom pain. And when at last it is perceived that such pity cannot lead to effectual succor, common sense bids the soul be rid of it. What I saw that morning persuaded me that the scrivener was the victim of innate and incurable disorder. I might give alms to his body; but his body did not pain him; it was his soul that suffered, and his soul I could not reach.

I did not accomplish the purpose of going to Trinity Church that morning. Somehow, the things I had seen disqualified me for the time from church-going. I walked homeward, thinking what I would do with Bartleby. Finally, I resolved upon this—I would put certain calm questions to him the next morning, touching his history, etc., and if he declined to answer them openly and unreservedly (and I supposed he would prefer not), then to give him a twenty dollar bill over and above whatever I might owe him, and tell him his services were no longer required; but that if in any other way I could assist him, I would be happy to do so, especially if he desired to return to his native place, wherever that might be, I would willingly help to defray the expenses. Moreover, if, after reaching home, he found himself at any time in want of aid, a letter from him would be sure of a reply.

The next morning came.

"Bartleby," said I, gently calling to him behind his screen.

No reply.

"Bartleby," said I, in a still gentler tone, "come here; I am not going to ask you to do anything you would prefer not to do—I simply wish to speak to you."

Upon this he noiselessly slid into view.

"Will you tell me, Bartleby, where you were born?"

"I would prefer not to."

"Will you tell me *anything* about yourself?"

"I would prefer not to."

"But what reasonable objection can you have to speak to me? I feel friendly towards you."

He did not look at me while I spoke, but kept his glance fixed upon my bust of Cicero, which, as I then sat, was directly behind me, some six inches above my head.

"What is your answer, Bartleby?" said I, after waiting a considerable time for a reply, during which his countenance remained immovable, only there was the faintest conceivable tremor of the white attenuated mouth.

"At present I prefer to give no answer," he said, and retired into his hermitage.

It was rather weak in me I confess, but his manner, on this occasion, nettled me. Not only did there seem to lurk in it a certain calm disdain, but his perverseness seemed ungrateful, considering the undeniable good usage and indulgence he had received from me.

Again I sat ruminating what I should do. Mortified as I was at his behavior, and resolved as I had been to dismiss him when I entered my office, nevertheless I strangely felt something superstitious knocking at my heart, and forbidding me to carry out my purpose, and denouncing me for a villian if I dared to breathe one bitter word against this forlornest of mankind. At last, familiarly drawing my chair behind his screen, I sat down and said: "Bartleby, never mind, then, about revealing your history; but let me entreat you, as a friend, to comply as far as may be with the usages of this office. Say now, you will help to examine papers to-morrow or next day: in short, say now, that in a day or two you will begin to be a little reasonable:—say so, Bartleby."

"At present I would prefer not to be a little reasonable," was his mildly cadaverous reply.

Just then the folding-doors opened, and Nippers approached. He seemed suffering from an unusually bad night's rest, induced by severer indigestion than common. He overheard those final words of Bartleby.

"*Prefer not*, eh?" gritted Nippers—"I'd *prefer* him, if I were you, sir," addressing me—"I'd *prefer* him; I'd give him preferences, the stubborn mule! What is it, sir, pray, that he *prefers* not to do now?"

Bartleby moved not a limb.

"Mr. Nippers," said I, "I'd prefer that you would withdraw for the present."

Somehow, of late, I had got into the way of involuntarily using this word "prefer" upon all sorts of not exactly suitable occasions. And I trembled to think that my contact with the scrivener had already and seriously affected me in a mental way. And what further and deeper aberration might it not yet produce? This apprehension had not been without efficacy in determining me to summary measures.

As Nippers, looking very sour and sulky, was departing, Turkey blandly and deferentially approached.

"With submission, sir," said he, "yesterday I was thinking about Bartleby here, and I think that if he would but prefer to take a quart of good ale every day, it would do much towards mending him, and enabling him to assist in examining his papers."

"So you have got the word, too," said I, slightly excited.

"With submission, what word, sir?" asked Turkey, respectfully crowding himself into the contracted space behind the screen, and by so doing, making me jostle the scrivener. "What word, sir?"

"I would prefer to be left alone here," said Bartleby, as if offended at being mobbed in his privacy.

"*That's* the word, Turkey," said I—"*that's* it."

"Oh, *prefer?* oh yes—queer word. I never use it myself. But, sir, as I was saying, if he would but prefer—"

"Turkey," interrupted I, "you will please withdraw."

"Oh certainly, sir, if you prefer that I should."

As he opened the folding-door to retire, Nippers at his desk caught a glimpse of me, and asked whether I would prefer to have a certain paper copied on blue paper or white. He did not in the least roguishly accent the word "prefer." It was plain that it involuntarily rolled from his tongue. I thought to myself, surely I must get rid of a demented man, who already has in some degree turned the tongues, if not the heads, of myself and clerks. But I thought it prudent not to break the dismission at once.

The next day I noticed that Bartleby did nothing but stand at his window in his dead-wall revery. Upon asking him why he did not write he said that he had decided upon doing no more writing.

"Why, how now? what next?" exclaimed I "do no more writing?"

"No more."

"And what is the reason?"

"Do you not see the reason for yourself?" he indifferently replied.

I looked steadfastly at him and perceived that his eyes looked dull and glazed. Instantly it occurred to me, that his unexampled diligence in copying by his dim window for the first few weeks of his stay with me might have temporarily impaired his vision.

I was touched. I said something in condolence with him. I hinted that of course he did wisely in abstaining from writing for a while; and urged him to embrace that opportunity of taking wholesome exercise in the open air. This, however, he did not do. A few days after this, my other clerks being absent, and being in a great hurry to dispatch certain letters by the mail, I thought that, having nothing else earthly to do, Bartleby would surely be less inflexible than usual, and carry these letters to the post-office. But he blankly declined. So, much to my inconvenience, I went myself.

Still added days went by. Whether Bartleby's eyes improved or not, I could not say. To all appearance, I thought they did. But when I asked him if they did, he vouchsafed no answer. At all events, he would do no copying. At last, in reply to my urgings, he informed me that he had permanently given up copying.

"What!" exclaimed I; "suppose your eyes should get entirely well—better than ever before—would you not copy then?"

"I have given up copying," he answered, and slid aside.

He remained as ever, a fixture in my chamber. Nay—if that were possible—he became still more of a fixture than before. What was to be done? He would do nothing in the office; why should he stay there? In plain fact, he had now become a millstone[20] to me, not only useless as a necklace, but afflictive to

---

20. Heavy stone used for grinding grain.

bear. Yet I was sorry for him. I speak less than truth when I say that, on his own account, he occasioned me uneasiness. If he would but have named a single relative or friend. I would instantly have written, and urged their taking the poor fellow away to some convenient retreat. But he seemed alone, absolutely alone in the universe. A bit of wreck in the mid Atlantic. At length, necessities connected with my business tyrannized over all other considerations. Decently as I could, I told Bartleby that in six days' time he must unconditionally leave the office. I warned him to take measures, in the interval, for procuring some other abode. I offered to assist him in this endeavor, if he himself would but take the first step towards a removal. "And when you finally quit me, Bartleby," added I, "I shall see that you go not away entirely unprovided. Six days from this hour, remember."

At the expiration of that period, I peeped behind the screen, and lo! Bartleby was there.

I buttoned up my coat, balanced myself; advanced slowly towards him, touched his shoulder, and said, "The time has come; you must quit this place; I am sorry for you; here is money; but you must go."

"I would prefer not," he replied, with his back still towards me.

"You *must*."

He remained silent.

Now I had an unbounded confidence in this man's common honesty. He had frequently restored to me sixpences and shillings carelessly dropped upon the floor, for I am apt to be very reckless in such shirt-button affairs. The proceeding, then, which followed will not be deemed extraordinary.

"Bartleby," said I, "I owe you twelve dollars on account; here are thirty-two; the odd twenty are yours—Will you take it?" and I handed the bills towards him.

But he made no motion.

"I will leave them here, then," putting them under a weight on the table. Then taking my hat and cane and going to the door, I tranquilly turned and added—"After you have removed your things from these offices, Bartleby, you will of course lock the door—since every one is now gone for the day but you—and if you please, slip your key underneath the mat, so that I may have it in the morning. I shall not see you again; so good-by to you. If, hereafter, in your new place of abode, I can be of any service to you, do not fail to advise me by letter. Good-by, Bartleby, and fare you well."

But he answered not a word; like the last column of some ruined temple, he remained standing mute and solitary in the middle of the otherwise deserted room.

As I walked home in a pensive mood, my vanity got the better of my pity. I could not but highly plume myself on my masterly management in getting rid of Bartleby. Masterly I call it, and such it must appear to any dispassionate thinker. The beauty of my procedure seemed to consist in its perfect quietness. There was no vulgar bullying, no bravado of any sort, no choleric hectoring, and striding to and fro across the apartment, jerking out vehement commands for Bartleby to bundle himself off with his beggarly traps.[21] Nothing of the kind. Without loudly bidding Bartleby depart—as an inferior genius might have

---

21. Personal belongings.

done—I *assumed* the ground that depart he must; and upon that assumption built all I had to say. The more I thought over my procedure, the more I was charmed with it. Nevertheless, next morning, upon awakening, I had my doubts—I had somehow slept off the fumes of vanity. One of the coolest and wisest hours a man has, is just after he awakes in the morning. My procedure seemed as sagacious as ever—but only in theory. How it would prove in practice—there was the rub. It was truly a beautiful thought to have assumed Bartleby's departure; but, after all, that assumption was simply my own, and none of Bartleby's. The great point was, not whether I had assumed that he would quit me, but whether he would prefer so to do. He was more a man of preferences than assumptions.

After breakfast, I walked down town, arguing the probabilities *pro* and *con*. One moment I thought it would prove a miserable failure, and Bartleby would be found all alive at my office as usual; the next moment it seemed certain that I should find his chair empty. And so I kept veering about. At the corner of Broadway and Canal Street, I saw quite an excited group of people standing in earnest conversation.

"I'll take odds he doesn't," said a voice as I passed.

"Doesn't go?—done!" said I, "put up your money."

I was instinctively putting my hand in my pocket to produce my own, when I remembered that this was an election day. The words I had overheard bore no reference to Bartleby, but to the success or non-success of some candidate for the mayoralty. In my intent frame of mind, I had, as it were, imagined that all Broadway shared in my excitement, and were debating the same question with me. I passed on, very thankful that the uproar of the street screened my momentary absent-mindedness.

As I had intended, I was earlier than usual at my office door. I stood listening for a moment. All was still. He must be gone. I tried the knob. The door was locked. Yes, my procedure had worked to a charm; he indeed must be vanished. Yet a certain melancholy mixed with this: I was almost sorry for my brilliant success. I was fumbling under the door mat for the key, which Bartleby was to have left there for me, when accidentally my knee knocked against a panel, producing a summoning sound, and in response a voice came to me from within—"Not yet; I am occupied."

It was Bartleby.

I was thunderstruck. For an instant I stood like the man who, pipe in mouth, was killed one cloudless afternoon long ago in Virginia, by summer lightning; at his own warm open window he was killed, and remained leaning out there upon the dreamy afternoon, till some one touched him, when he fell.

"Not gone!" I murmured at last. But again obeying that wondrous ascendancy which the inscrutable scrivener had over me, and from which ascendancy, for all my chafing, I could not completely escape, I slowly went down stairs and out into the street, and while walking round the block, considered what I should next do in this unheard-of perplexity. Turn the man out by an actual thrusting I could not; to drive away by calling him hard names would not do; calling in the police was an unpleasant idea; and yet, permit him to enjoy his cadaverous triumph over me—this, too, I could not think of. What was to be done? or, if nothing could be done, was there anything further that I could *assume* in the matter? Yes, as before I had prospectively assumed that Bartleby would depart, so now I might retrospectively assume that departed he was. In the legitimate carrying out of this assumption, I might enter my office in a great hurry, and pretending not to see Bartleby at all, walk straight against him as if he were air. Such a proceeding would in a singular degree have the appearance of a home-thrust. It was hardly possible that Bartleby could withstand such an application of the doctrine of assumptions. But upon second thoughts the success of the plan seemed rather dubious. I resolved to argue the matter over with him.

"Bartleby," said I, entering the office, with a quietly severe expression, "I am seriously displeased. I am pained, Bartleby. I had thought better of you. I had imagined you of such a gentlemanly organization, that in any delicate dilemma a slight hint would suffice—in short, an assumption. But it appears I am deceived. Why," I added, unaffectedly starting, "you have not even touched that money yet," pointing to it, just where I had left it the evening previous.

He answered nothing.

"Will you, or will you not, quit me?" I now demanded in a sudden passion, advancing close to him.

"I would prefer *not* to quit you," he replied, gently emphasizing the *not*.

"What earthly right have you to stay here? Do you pay any rent? Do you pay my taxes? Or is this property yours?"

He answered nothing.

"Are you ready to go on and write now? Are your eyes recovered? Could you copy a small paper for me this morning? or help examine a few lines? or step round to the post-office? In a word, will you do anything at all, to give a coloring to your refusal to depart the premises?"

He silently retired into his hermitage.

I was now in such a state of nervous resentment that I thought it but prudent to check myself at present from further demonstrations. Bartleby and I were alone. I remembered the tragedy of the unfortunate Adams and the still more unfortunate Colt[22] in the solitary office of the latter; and how poor Colt, being dreadfully incensed by Adams, and imprudently permitting himself to get wildly excited, was at unawares hurried into his fatal act—an act which certainly no man could possibly deplore more than the actor himself. Often it had occurred to me in my ponderings upon the subject that had that altercation taken place in the public street, or at a private residence, it would not have terminated as it did. It was the circumstance of being alone in a solitary office, up stairs, of a building entirely unhallowed by humanizing domestic associations—an uncarpeted office, doubtless, of a dusty, haggard sort of appearance—this it must have been, which greatly helped to enhance the irritable desperation of the hapless Colt.

But when this old Adam of resentment rose in me and tempted me concerning Bartleby, I grappled him and threw him. How? Why, simply by recalling the divine injunction: "A new commandment give I unto you, that ye love one another."[23] Yes, this it was that saved me. Aside from higher considerations, charity often operates as a vastly wise and prudent principle—a great safeguard to its possessor. Men have committed murder for jealousy's sake,

---

22. A celebrated New York City murder case of 1842, in which John C. Colt unintentionally killed Samuel Adams with a blow to the head during a quarrel. Condemned to death, Colt committed suicide before his execution.
23. Christ's words to his disciples (John 13:34).

and anger's sake, and hatred's sake, and selfishness' sake, and spiritual pride's sake; but no man, that ever I heard of, ever committed a diabolical murder for sweet charity's sake. Mere self-interest, then, if no better motive can be enlisted, should, especially with high-tempered men, prompt all beings to charity and philanthropy. At any rate, upon the occasion in question, I strove to drown my exasperated feelings towards the scrivener by benevolently construing his conduct. Poor fellow, poor fellow! thought I, he don't mean anything; and besides, he has seen hard times, and ought to be indulged.

I endeavored, also, immediately to occupy myself, and at the same time to comfort my despondency. I tried to fancy, that in the course of the morning, at such time as might prove agreeable to him, Bartleby, of his own free accord, would emerge from his hermitage and take up some decided line of march in the direction of the door. But no. Half-past twelve o'clock came; Turkey began to glow in the face, overturn his inkstand, and become generally obstreperous; Nippers abated down into quietude and courtesy; Ginger Nut munched his noon apple; and Bartleby remained standing at his window in one of his profoundest dead-wall reveries. Will it be credited? Ought I to acknowledge it? That afternoon I left the office without saying one further word to him.

Some days now passed, during which, at leisure intervals I looked a little into "Edwards on the Will," and "Priestley on Necessity."[24] Under the circumstances, those books induced a salutary feeling. Gradually I slid into the persuasion that these troubles of mine, touching the scrivener, had been all predestinated from eternity, and Bartleby was billeted upon me for some mysterious purpose of an allwise Providence, which it was not for a mere mortal like me to fathom. Yes, Bartleby, stay there behind your screen, thought I; I shall persecute you no more; you are harmless and noiseless as any of these old chairs; in short, I never feel so private as when I know you are here. At last I see it, I feel it; I penetrate to the predestinated purpose of my life. I am content. Others may have loftier parts to enact; but my mission in this world, Bartleby, is to furnish you with office-room for such period as you may see fit to remain.

I believe that this wise and blessed frame of mind would have continued with me, had it not been for the unsolicited and uncharitable remarks obtruded upon me by my professional friends who visited the rooms. But thus it often is, that the constant friction of illiberal minds wears out at last the best resolves of the more generous. Though to be sure, when I reflected upon it, it was not strange that people entering my office should be struck by the peculiar aspect of the unaccountable Bartleby, and so be tempted to throw out some sinister observations concerning him. Sometimes an attorney, having business with me, and calling at my office, and finding no one but the scrivener there, would undertake to obtain some sort of precise information from him touching my whereabouts; but without heeding his idle talk, Bartleby would remain standing immovable in the middle of the room. So after contemplating him in that position for a time, the attorney would depart, no wiser than he came.

---

24. Jonathan Edwards (1703–58), Calvinist theologian, argued in *Freedom of the Will* that human actions are caused not by the exercise of free will, but by such predetermined conditions as heredity, environment, and character. Joseph Priestley (1733–1804), English scientist and philosopher, in *The Doctrine of Philosophical Necessity Illustrated* argued against the doctrine of free will, believing that humans behave according to the divine will by acting from principles which are conducive to the general happiness.

Also, when a Reference[25] was going on, and the room full of lawyers and witnesses, and business driving fast, some deeply-occupied legal gentleman present, seeing Bartleby wholly unemployed, would request him to run round to his (the legal gentleman's) office and fetch some papers for him. Thereupon, Bartleby would tranquilly decline, and yet remain idle as before. Then the lawyer would give a great stare, and turn to me. And what could I say? At last I was made aware that all through the circle of my professional acquaintance, a whisper of wonder was running round, having reference to the strange creature I kept at my office. This worried me very much. And as the idea came upon me of his possibly turning out a long-lived man, and keep occupying my chambers, and denying my authority; and perplexing my visitors; and scandalizing my professional reputation; and casting a general gloom over the premises; keeping soul and body together to the last upon his savings (for doubtless he spent but half a dime a day), and in the end perhaps outlive me, and claim possession of my office by right of his perpetual occupancy: as all these dark anticipations crowded upon me more and more, and my friends continually intruded their relentless remarks upon the apparition in my room; a great change was wrought in me. I resolved to gather all my faculties together, and forever rid me of this intolerable incubus.

Ere revolving any complicated project, however, adapted to this end, I first simply suggested to Bartleby the propriety of his permanent departure. In a calm and serious tone, I commended the idea to his careful and mature consideration. But, having taken three days to meditate upon it, he apprised me, that his original determination remained the same; in short, that he still preferred to abide with me.

What shall I do? I now said to myself, buttoning up my coat to the last button. What shall I do? what ought I to do? what does conscience say I *should* do with this man, or, rather, ghost. Rid myself of him, I must; go, he shall. But how? You will not thrust him, the poor, pale, passive mortal—you will not thrust such a helpless creature out of your door? you will not dishonor yourself by such cruelty? No, I will not, I cannot do that. Rather would I let him live and die here, and then mason up his remains in the wall. What, then, will you do? For all your coaxing, he will not budge. Bribes he leaves under your own paperweight on your table; in short, it is quite plain that he prefers to cling to you.

Then something severe, something unusual must be done. What! surely you will not have him collared by a constable, and commit his innocent pallor to the common jail? And upon what ground could you procure such a thing to be done?—a vagrant, is he? What! he a vagrant, a wanderer, who refuses to budge? It is because he will *not* be a vagrant, then, that you seek to count him *as* a vagrant. That is too absurd. No visible means of support: there I have him. Wrong again: for indubitably he *does* support himself, and that is the only unanswerable proof that any man can show of his possessing the means so to do. No more, then. Since he will not quit me, I must quit him. I will change my offices; I will move elsewhere, and give him fair notice, that if I find him on my new premises I will then proceed against him as a common trespasser.

Acting accordingly, next day I thus addressed him: "I find these chambers too far from the City Hall; the air is unwholesome. In a word, I propose to re-

---

25. A meeting of the Masters of the Court of Chancery.

move my offices next week, and shall no longer require your services. I tell you this now, in order that you may seek another place.''

He made no reply, and nothing more was said.

On the appointed day I engaged carts and men, proceeded to my chambers, and, having but little furniture, everything was removed in a few hours. Throughout, the scrivener remained standing behind the screen, which I directed to be removed the last thing. It was withdrawn; and, being folded up like a huge folio, left him the motionless occupant of a naked room. I stood in the entry watching him a moment, while something from within me upbraided me.

I re-entered, with my hand in my pocket—and—and my heart in my mouth.

''Good-by, Bartleby; I am going—good-by, and God some way bless you; and take that,'' slipping something in his hand. But it dropped upon the floor, and then—strange to say—I tore myself from him whom I had so longed to be rid of.

Established in my new quarters, for a day or two I kept the door locked, and started at every footfall in the passages. When I returned to my rooms, after any little absence, I would pause at the threshold for an instant, and attentively listen, ere applying my key. But these fears were needless. Bartleby never came nigh me.

I thought all was going well, when a perturbed-looking stranger visited me, inquiring whether I was the person who had recently occupied rooms at No. — Wall Street.

Full of forebodings, I replied that I was.

''Then, sir,'' said the stranger, who proved a lawyer, ''you are responsible for the man you left there. He refuses to do any copying; he refuses to do anything; he says he prefers not to; and he refuses to quit the premises.''

''I am very sorry, sir,'' said I, with assumed tranquillity, but an inward tremor, ''but, really, the man you allude to is nothing to me—he is no relation or apprentice of mine, that you should hold me responsible for him.''

''In mercy's name, who is he?''

''I certainly cannot inform you. I know nothing about him. Formerly I employed him as a copyist; but he has done nothing for me now for some time past.''

''I shall settle him, then—good morning, sir.''

Several days passed, and I heard nothing more; and, though I often felt a charitable prompting to call at the place and see poor Bartleby, yet a certain squeamishness, of I know not what, withheld me.

All is over with him, by this time, thought I, at last, when, through another week, no further intelligence reached me. But, coming to my room the day after, I found several persons waiting at my door in a high state of nervous excitement.

''That's the man—here he comes,'' cried the foremost one, whom I recognized as the lawyer who had previously called upon me alone.

''You must take him away, sir, at once,'' cried a portly person among them, advancing upon me, and whom I knew to be the landlord of No. — Wall Street. ''These gentlemen, my tenants, cannot stand it any longer; Mr. B——,'' pointing to the lawyer, ''has turned him out of his room, and he now persists in haunting the building generally, sitting upon the banisters of the stairs by day, and sleeping in the entry by night. Everybody is concerned;

clients are leaving the offices; some fears are entertained of a mob; something you must do, and that without delay."

Aghast at this torrent, I fell back before it, and would fain have locked myself in my new quarters. In vain I persisted that Bartleby was nothing to me—no more than to any one else. In vain—I was the last person known to have anything to do with him, and they held me to the terrible account. Fearful, then, of being exposed in the papers (as one person present obscurely threatened), I considered the matter, and, at length, said, that if the lawyer would give me a confidential interview with the scrivener, in his (the lawyer's) own room, I would, that afternoon, strive my best to rid them of the nuisance they complained of.

Going up stairs to my old haunt, there was Bartleby silently sitting upon the banister at the landing.

"What are you doing here, Bartleby?" said I.

"Sitting upon the banister," he mildly replied.

I motioned him into the lawyer's room, who then left us.

"Bartleby," said I, "are you aware that you are the cause of great tribulation to me, by persisting in occupying the entry after being dismissed from the office?"

No answer.

"Now one of two things must take place. Either you must do something, or something must be done to you. Now what sort of business would you like to engage in? Would you like to re-engage in copying for some one?"

"No; I would prefer not to make any change."

"Would you like a clerkship in a dry-goods store?"

"There is too much confinement about that. No, I would not like a clerkship; but I am not particular."

"Too much confinement," I cried, "why, you keep yourself confined all the time!"

"I would prefer not to take a clerkship," he rejoined, as if to settle that little item at once.

"How would a bar-tender's business suit you? There is no trying of the eyesight in that."

"I would not like it at all; though, as I said before, I am not particular."

His unwonted wordiness inspirited me. I returned to the charge.

"Well, then, would you like to travel through the country collecting bills for the merchants? That would improve your health."

"No, I would prefer to do something else."

"How, then, would going as a companion to Europe, to entertain some young gentleman with your conversation—how would that suit you?"

"Not at all. It does not strike me that there is anything definite about that. I like to be stationary. But I am not particular."

"Stationary you shall be, then," I cried, now losing all patience, and, for the first time in all my exasperating connection with him, fairly flying into a passion. "If you do not go away from these premises before night, I shall feel bound—indeed, I *am* bound—to—to—to quit the premises myself!" I rather absurdly concluded, knowing not with what possible threat to try to frighten his immobility into compliance. Despairing of all further efforts, I was precipitately leaving him, when a final thought occurred to me—one which had not been wholly unindulged before.

"Bartleby," said I, in the kindest tone I could assume under such exciting circumstances, "will you go home with me now—not to my office, but my dwelling—and remain there till we can conclude upon some convenient arrangement for you at our leisure? Come, let us start now, right away."

"No: at present I would prefer not to make any change at all."

I answered nothing; but, effectually dodging every one by the suddenness and rapidity of my flight, rushed from the building, ran up Wall Street towards Broadway, and, jumping into the first omnibus, was soon removed from pursuit. As soon as tranquillity returned, I distinctly perceived that I had now done all that I possibly could, both in respect to the demands of the landlord and his tenants, and with regard to my own desire and sense of duty, to benefit Bartleby, and shield him from rude persecution. I now strove to be entirely care-free and quiescent; and my conscience justified me in the attempt; though, indeed, it was not so successful as I could have wished. So fearful was I of being again hunted out by the incensed landlord and his exasperated tenants, that, surrendering my business to Nippers, for a few days, I drove about the upper part of the town and through the suburbs, in my rockaway;[26] crossed over to Jersey City and Hoboken, and paid fugitive visits to Manhattanville and Astoria. In fact, I almost lived in my rockaway for the time.

When again I entered my office, lo, a note from the landlord lay upon the desk. I opened it with trembling hands. It informed me that the writer had sent to the police, and had Bartleby removed to the Tombs as a vagrant. Moreover, since I knew more about him than any one else, he wished me to appear at the place, and make a suitable statement of the facts. These tidings had a conflicting effect upon me. At first I was indignant; but, at last, almost approved. The landlord's energetic, summary disposition, had led him to adopt a procedure which I do not think I would have decided upon myself; and yet, as a last resort, under such peculiar circumstances, it seemed the only plan.

As I afterwards learned, the poor scrivener, when told that he must be conducted to the Tombs, offered not the slightest obstacle, but, in his pale, unmoving way, silently acquiesced.

Some of the compassionate and curious bystanders joined the party; and headed by one of the constables arm-in-arm with Bartleby, the silent procession filed its way through all the noise, and heat, and joy of the roaring thoroughfares at noon.

The same day I received the note, I went to the Tombs, or, to speak more properly, the Halls of Justice. Seeking the right officer, I stated the purpose of my call, and was informed that the individual I described was, indeed, within. I then assured the functionary that Bartleby was a perfectly honest man, and greatly to be compassionated, however unaccountably eccentric. I narrated all I knew, and closed by suggesting the idea of letting him remain in as indulgent confinement as possible, till something less harsh might be done—though, indeed, I hardly knew what. At all events, if nothing else could be decided upon, the alms-house must receive him. I then begged to have an interview.

Being under no disgraceful charge, and quite serene and harmless in all his ways, they had permitted him freely to wander about the prison, and, especially, in the inclosed grass-platted yards thereof. And so I found him there,

---

26. Light four-wheeled carriage.

standing all alone in the quietest of the yards, his face towards a high wall, while all around, from the narrow slits of the jail windows, I thought I saw peering out upon him the eyes of murderers and thieves.

"Bartleby!"

"I know you," he said, without looking round—"and I want nothing to say to you."

"It was not I that brought you here, Bartleby," said I, keenly pained at his implied suspicion. "And to you, this should not be so vile a place. Nothing reproachful attaches to you being here. And see, it is not so sad a place as one might think. Look, there is the sky, and here is the grass."

"I know where I am," he replied, but would say nothing more, and so I left him.

As I entered the corridor again, a broad meat-like man, in an apron, accosted me, and, jerking his thumb over his shoulder, said—"Is that your friend?"

"Yes."

"Does he want to starve? If he does, let him live on the prison fare, that's all."

"Who are you?" asked I, not knowing what to make of such an unofficially speaking person in such a place.

"I am the grub-man. Such gentlemen as have friends here, hire me to provide them with something good to eat."

"Is this so?" said I, turning to the turnkey.

He said it was.

"Well, then," said I, slipping some silver into the grub-man's hands (for so they called him), "I want you to give particular attention to my friend there; let him have the best dinner you can get. And you must be as polite to him as possible."

"Introduce me, will you?" said the grub-man, looking at me with an expression which seemed to say he was all impatience for an opportunity to give a specimen of his breeding.

Thinking it would prove of benefit to the scrivener, I acquiesced; and, asking the grub-man his name, went up with him to Bartleby.

"Bartleby, this is a friend; you will find him very useful to you."

"Your sarvant, sir, your sarvant," said the grub-man, making a low salutation behind his apron. "Hope you find it pleasant here, sir; nice grounds—cool apartments—hope you'll stay with us some time—try to make it agreeable. What will you have for dinner today?"

"I prefer not to dine to-day," said Bartleby, turning away. "It would disagree with me; I am unused to dinners." So saying, he slowly moved to the other side of the inclosure, and took up a position fronting the dead-wall.

"How's this?" said the grub-man, addressing me with a stare of astonishment. "He's odd, ain't he?"

"I think he is a little deranged," said I, sadly.

"Deranged? deranged is it? Well, now, upon my word, I thought that friend of yourn was a gentleman forger; they are always pale and genteel-like, them forgers. I can't help pity 'em—can't help it, sir. Did you know Monroe Edwards?" he added, touchingly, and paused. Then, laying his hand piteously on my shoulder, sighed, "he died of consumption at Sing-Sing.[27] So you weren't acquainted with Monroe?"

"No, I was never socially acquainted with any forgers. But I cannot stop longer. Look to my friend yonder. You will not lose by it. I will see you again."

Some few days after this, I again obtained admission to the Tombs, and went through the corridors in quest of Bartleby; but without finding him.

"I saw him coming from his cell not long ago," said a turnkey, "may be he's gone to loiter in the yards."

So I went in that direction.

"Are you looking for the silent man?" said another turnkey, passing me. "Yonder he lies—sleeping in the yard there. 'Tis not twenty minutes since I saw him lie down."

The yard was entirely quiet. It was not accessible to the common prisoners. The surrounding walls, of amazing thickness, kept off all sounds behind them. The Egyptian character of the masonry weighed upon me with its gloom. But a soft imprisoned turf grew under foot. The heart of the eternal pyramids, it seemed, wherein, by some strange magic, through the clefts, grass-seed, dropped by birds, had sprung.

Strangely huddled at the base of the wall, his knees drawn up, and lying on his side, his head touching the cold stones, I saw the wasted Bartleby. But nothing stirred. I paused; then went close up to him; stooped over, and saw that his dim eyes were open; otherwise he seemed profoundly sleeping. Something prompted me to touch him. I felt his hand, when a tingling shiver ran up my arm and down my spine to my feet.

The round face of the grub-man peered upon me now. "His dinner is ready. Won't he dine to-day, either? Or does he live without dining?"

"Lives without dining," said I, and closed the eyes.

"Eh!—He's asleep, ain't he?"

"With kings and counselors,"[28] murmured I.

There would seem little need for proceeding further in this history. Imagination will readily supply the meagre recital of poor Bartleby's interment. But, ere parting with the reader, let me say, that if this little narrative has sufficiently interested him, to awaken curiosity as to who Bartleby was, and what manner of life he led prior to the present narrator's making his acquaintance, I can only reply, that in such curiosity I fully share, but am wholly unable to gratify it. Yet here I hardly know whether I should divulge one little item of rumor, which came to my ear a few months after the scrivener's decease. Upon what basis it rested, I could never ascertain; and hence, how true it is I cannot now tell. But, inasmuch as this vague report has not been without a certain suggestive interest to me, however sad, it may prove the same with some others; and so I will briefly mention it. The report was this: that Bartleby had been a subordinate clerk in the Dead Letter Office at Washington, from which he had been

---

27. State prison near Ossining, New York.
28. In the Bible, Job despairingly wonders why he did not die at birth so that his subsequent miseries would have been prevented: "For now should I have lain still and been quiet, I should have slept; then had I been at peace. With kings and counselors of the earth, which built desolate places for themselves" (Job 3:13–14).

suddenly removed by a change in the administration. When I think over this rumor, hardly can I express the emotions which seize me. Dead letters! does it not sound like dead men? Conceive a man by nature and misfortune prone to a pallid hopelessness, can any business seem more fitted to heighten it than that of continually handling these dead letters, and assorting them for the flames? For by the cartload they are annually burned. Sometimes from out the folded paper the pale clerk takes a ring—the finger it was meant for, perhaps, moulders in the grave; a bank-note sent in swiftest charity—he whom it would relieve, nor eats nor hungers any more; pardon for those who died despairing; hope for those who died unhoping; good tidings for those who died stifled by unrelieved calamities. On errands of life, these letters speed to death.

Ah, Bartleby! Ah, humanity!

James Joyce (1882–1941)
Araby

North Richmond Street, being blind, was a quiet street except at the hour when the Christian Brothers' School set the boys free. An uninhabited house of two storeys stood at the blind end, detached from its neighbours in a square ground. The other houses of the street, conscious of decent lives within them, gazed at one another with brown imperturbable faces.

The former tenant of our house, a priest, had died in the back drawing-room. Air, musty from having been long enclosed, hung in all the rooms, and the waste room behind the kitchen was littered with old useless papers. Among these I found a few paper-covered books, the pages of which were curled and damp: *The Abbot,* by Walter Scott, *The Devout Communicant* and *The Memoirs of Vidocq.*[1] I liked the last best because its leaves were yellow. The wild garden behind the house contained a central apple-tree and a few straggling bushes under one of which I found the late tenant's rusty bicycle-pump. He had been a very charitable priest; in his will he had left all his money to institutions and the furniture of his house to his sister.

When the short days of winter came dusk fell before we had well eaten our dinners. When we met in the street the houses had grown sombre. The space of sky above us was the colour of ever-changing violet and towards it the lamps of the street lifted their feeble lanterns. The cold air stung us and we played till our bodies glowed. Our shouts echoed in the silent street. The career of our play brought us through the dark muddy lanes behind the houses where we ran the gauntlet of the rough tribes from the cottages, to the back doors of the dark dripping gardens where odours arose from the ashpits, to the dark odorous

---

1. *The Abbot* (1820) is a romantic novel about the imprisonment of Mary Queen of Scots and her escape through the help of a page who falls in love with one of her attendants. *The Devout Communicant,* written by the Franciscan friar Pacificus Baker, is a book of religious meditations for Catholics receiving communion. *The Memoirs of Vidocq* recounts the exploits of François Eugène Vidocq (1775–1857), French criminal who joined the Paris police and was later made chief of detectives; as the result of a scandal, he was dismissed and subsequently died in poverty.

stables where a coachman smoothed and combed the horse or shook music from the buckled harness. When we returned to the street, light from the kitchen windows had filled the areas. If my uncle was seen turning the corner we hid in the shadow until we had seen him safely housed. Or if Mangan's sister came out on the doorstep to call her brother in to his tea we watched her from our shadow peer up and down the street. We waited to see whether she would remain or go in and, if she remained, we left our shadow and walked up to Mangan's steps resignedly. She was waiting for us, her figure defined by the light from the half-opened door. Her brother always teased her before he obeyed and I stood by the railings looking at her. Her dress swung as she moved her body and the soft rope of her hair tossed from side to side.

Every morning I lay on the floor in the front parlour watching her door. The blind was pulled down to within an inch of the sash so that I could not be seen. When she came out on the doorstep my heart leaped. I ran to the hall, seized my books and followed her. I kept her brown figure always in my eye and, when we came near the point at which our ways diverged, I quickened my pace and passed her. This happened morning after morning. I had never spoken to her, except for a few casual words, and yet her name was like a summons to all my foolish blood.

Her image accompanied me even in places the most hostile to romance. On Saturday evenings when my aunt went marketing I had to go to carry some of the parcels. We walked through the flaring streets, jostled by drunken men and bargaining women, amid the curses of labourers, the shrill litanies of shop-boys who stood on guard by the barrels of pigs' cheeks, the nasal chanting of street-singers, who sang a *come-all-you* about O'Donovan Rossa,[2] or a ballad about the troubles in our native land. These noises converged in a single sensation of life for me: I imagined that I bore my chalice safely through a throng of foes. Her name sprang to my lips at moments in strange prayers and praises which I myself did not understand. My eyes were often full of tears (I could not tell why) and at times a flood from my heart seemed to pour itself out into my bosom. I thought little of the future. I did not know whether I would ever speak to her or not or, if I spoke to her, how I could tell her of my confused adoration. But my body was like a harp and her words and gestures were like fingers running upon the wires.

One evening I went into the back drawing-room in which the priest had died. It was a dark rainy evening and there was no sound in the house. Through one of the broken panes I heard the rain impinge upon the earth, the fine incessant needles of water playing in the sodden beds. Some distant lamp or lighted window gleamed below me. I was thankful that I could see so little. All my senses seemed to desire to veil themselves and, feeling that I was about to slip from them, I pressed the palms of my hands together until they trembled, murmuring: *"O love! O love!"* many times.

At last she spoke to me. When she addressed the first words to me I was so confused that I did not know what to answer. She asked me was I going to *Araby*.[3] I forgot whether I answered yes or no. It would be a splendid bazaar, she said she would love to go.

---

2. A *come-all-you* is any Irish street ballad beginning with these words. O'Donovan Rossa was the popular name of Jeremiah O'Donovan (1831–1915), Irish nationalist and revolutionary.
3. A bazaar with an oriental theme, held in Dublin on May 14–19, 1894.

"And why can't you?" I asked.

While she spoke she turned a silver bracelet round and round her wrist. She could not go, she said, because there would be a retreat[4] that week in her convent. Her brother and two other boys were fighting for their caps and I was alone at the railings. She held one of the spikes, bowing her head towards me. The light from the lamp opposite our door caught the white curve of her neck, lit up her hair that rested there and, falling, lit up the hand upon the railing. It fell over one side of her dress and caught the white border of a petticoat, just visible as she stood at ease.

"It's well for you," she said.

"If I go," I said, "I will bring you something."

What innumerable follies laid waste my waking and sleeping thoughts after that evening! I wished to annihilate the tedious intervening days. I chafed against the work of school. At night in my bedroom and by day in the classroom her image came between me and the page I strove to read. The syllables of the word *Araby* were called to me through the silence in which my soul luxuriated and cast an Eastern enchantment over me. I asked for leave to go to the bazaar on Saturday night. My aunt was surprised and hoped it was not some Freemason[5] affair. I answered few questions in class. I watched my master's face pass from amiability to sternness; he hoped I was not beginning to idle. I could not call my wandering thoughts together. I had hardly any patience with the serious work of life which, now that it stood between me and my desire, seemed to me child's play, ugly monotonous child's play.

On Saturday morning I reminded my uncle that I wished to go to the bazaar in the evening. He was fussing at the hallstand, looking for the hat-brush, and answered me curtly:

"Yes, boy, I know."

As he was in the hall I could not go into the front parlour and lie at the window. I left the house in bad humour and walked slowly towards the school. The air was pitilessly raw and already my heart misgave me.

When I came home to dinner my uncle had not yet been home. Still it was early. I sat staring at the clock for some time and, when its ticking began to irritate me, I left the room. I mounted the staircase and gained the upper part of the house. The high cold empty gloomy rooms liberated me and I went from room to room singing. From the front window I saw my companions playing below in the street. Their cries reached me weakened and indistinct and, leaning my forehead against the cool glass, I looked over at the dark house where she lived. I may have stood there for an hour, seeing nothing but the brown-clad figure cast by my imagination, touched discreetly by the lamplight at the curved neck, at the hand upon the railings and at the border below the dress.

When I came downstairs again I found Mrs. Mercer sitting at the fire. She was an old garrulous woman, a pawnbroker's widow, who collected used stamps for some pious purpose. I had to endure the gossip of the tea-table. The meal was prolonged beyond an hour and still my uncle did not come. Mrs. Mercer stood up to go: she was sorry she couldn't wait any longer, but it was after eight o'clock and she did not like to be out late, as the night air was bad

---

4. Period of seclusion in which the participants engage in prayer and meditation.
5. The Masonic Order, a secret fraternal society, was thought to be anti-Catholic.

for her. When she had gone I began to walk up and down the room, clenching my fists. My aunt said:

"I'm afraid you may put off your bazaar for this night of Our Lord."

At nine o'clock I heard my uncle's latchkey in the halldoor. I heard him talking to himself and heard the hallstand rocking when it had received the weight of his overcoat. I could interpret these signs. When he was midway through his dinner I asked him to give me the money to go to the bazaar. He had forgotten.

"The people are in bed and after their first sleep now," he said.

I did not smile. My aunt said to him energetically:

"Can't you give him the money and let him go? You've kept him late enough as it is."

My uncle said he was very sorry he had forgotten. He said he believed in the old saying: "All work and no play makes Jack a dull boy." He asked me where I was going and, when I had told him a second time he asked me did I know *The Arab's Farewell to his Steed.*[6] When I left the kitchen he was about to recite the opening lines of the piece to my aunt.

I held a florin[7] tightly in my hand as I strode down Buckingham Street towards the station. The sight of the streets thronged with buyers and glaring with gas recalled to me the purpose of my journey. I took my seat in a third-class carriage of a deserted train. After an intolerable delay the train moved out of the station slowly. It crept onward among ruinous houses and over the twinkling river. At Westland Row Station a crowd of people pressed to the carriage doors; but the porters moved them back, saying that it was a special train for the bazaar. I remained alone in the bare carriage. In a few minutes the train drew up beside an improvised wooden platform. I passed out on to the road and saw by the lighted dial of a clock that it was ten minutes to ten. In front of me was a large building which displayed the magical name.

I could not find any sixpenny entrance, and, fearing that the bazaar would be closed, I passed in quickly through a turnstile, handing a shilling to a weary-looking man. I found myself in a big hall girdled at half its height by a gallery. Nearly all the stalls were closed and the greater part of the hall was in darkness. I recognised a silence like that which pervades a church after a service. I walked into the centre of the bazaar timidly. A few people were gathered about the stalls which were still open. Before a curtain, over which the words *Café Chantant*[8] were written in coloured lamps, two men were counting money on a salver.[9] I listened to the fall of the coins.

Remembering with difficulty why I had come I went over to one of the stalls and examined porcelain vases and flowered tea-sets. At the door of the stall a young lady was talking and laughing with two young gentlemen. I remarked their English accents and listened vaguely to their conversation.

"O, I never said such a thing!"

"O, but you did!"

"O, but I didn't!"

---

6. Once popular sentimental poem by Caroline Norton (1808–77).
7. Silver coin worth two shillings.
8. Literally, "singing cafe," one providing musical entertainment.
9. Tray.

"Didn't she say that?"

"Yes. I heard her."

"O, there's a . . . fib!"

Observing me the young lady came over and asked me did I wish to buy anything. The tone of her voice was not encouraging; she seemed to have spoken to me out of a sense of duty. I looked humbly at the great jars that stood like eastern guards at either side of the dark entrance to the stall and murmured:

"No, thank you."

The young lady changed the position of one of the vases and went back to the two young men. They began to talk of the same subject. Once or twice the young lady glanced at me over her shoulder.

I lingered before her stall, though I knew my stay was useless, to make my interest in her wares seem the more real. Then I turned away slowly and walked down the middle of the bazaar. I allowed the two pennies to fall against the sixpence in my pocket. I heard a voice call from one end of the gallery that the light was out. The upper part of the hall was now completely dark.

Gazing up into the darkness I saw myself as a creature driven and derided by vanity; and my eyes burned with anguish and anger.

Franz Kafka (1883–1924)
Jackals and Arabs

We were camping in the oasis. My companions were asleep. The tall, white figure of an Arab passed by; he had been seeing to the camels and was on his way to his own sleeping place.

I threw myself on my back in the grass; I tried to fall asleep; I could not; a jackal[1] howled in the distance; I sat up again. And what had been so far away was all at once quite near. Jackals were swarming round me, eyes gleaming dull gold and vanishing again, lithe bodies moving nimbly and rhythmically, as if at the crack of a whip.

One jackal came from behind me, nudging right under my arm, pressing against me, as if he needed my warmth, and then stood before me and spoke to me almost eye to eye.

"I am the oldest jackal far and wide. I am delighted to have met you here at last. I had almost given up hope, since we have been waiting endless years for you; my mother waited for you, and her mother, and all our fore-mothers right back to the first mother of all the jackals. It is true, believe me!"

"That is surprising," said I, forgetting to kindle the pile of firewood which lay ready to smoke away jackals, "that is very surprising for me to hear. It is by pure chance that I have come here from the far North, and I am making only a short tour of your country. What do you jackals want, then?"

---

1. Small, wild dog which usually hunts at night, feeding on decaying meat and small animals.

As if emboldened by this perhaps too friendly inquiry the ring of jackals closed in on me; all were panting and open-mouthed.

"We know," began the eldest, "that you have come from the North; that is just what we base our hopes on. You Northerners have the kind of intelligence that is not to be found among Arabs. Not a spark of intelligence, let me tell you, can be struck from their cold arrogance. They kill animals for food, and carrion they despise."

"Not so loud," said I, "there are Arabs sleeping near by."

"You are indeed a stranger here," said the jackal, "or you would know that never in the history of the world has any jackal been afraid of an Arab. Why should we fear them? Is it not misfortune enough for us to be exiled among such creatures?"

"Maybe, maybe," said I, "matters so far outside my province I am not competent to judge; it seems to me a very old quarrel; I suppose it's in the blood, and perhaps will only end with it."

"You are very clever," said the old jackal; and they all began to pant more quickly; the air pumped out of their lungs although they were standing still; a rank smell which at times I had to set my teeth to endure streamed from their open jaws, "you are very clever; what you have just said agrees with our old tradition. So we shall draw blood from them and the quarrel will be over."

"Oh!" said I, more vehemently than I intended, "they'll defend themselves; they'll shoot you down in dozens with their muskets."

"You misunderstand us," said he, "a human failing which persists apparently even in the far North. We're not proposing to kill them. All the water in the Nile couldn't cleanse us of that. Why, the mere sight of their living flesh makes us turn tail and flee into cleaner air, into the desert, which for that very reason is our home."

And all the jackals around, including many newcomers from farther away, dropped their muzzles between their forelegs and wiped them with their paws; it was as if they were trying to conceal a disgust so overpowering that I felt like leaping over their heads to get away.

"Then what are you proposing to do?" I asked, trying to rise to my feet; but I could not get up; two young beasts behind me had locked their teeth through my coat and shirt; I had to go on sitting. "These are your train-bearers,"[2] explained the old jackal, quite seriously, "a mark of honor." "They must let go!" I cried, turning now to the old jackal, now to the youngsters. "They will, of course," said the old one, "if that is your wish. But it will take a little time, for they have got their teeth well in, as is our custom, and must first loosen their jaws bit by bit. Meanwhile, give ear to our petition." "Your conduct hasn't exactly inclined me to grant it," said I. "Don't hold it against us that we are clumsy," said he, and now for the first time had recourse to the natural plaintiveness of his voice, "we are poor creatures, we have nothing but our teeth; whatever we want to do, good or bad, we can tackle it only with our teeth." "Well, what do you want?" I asked, not much mollified.

"Sir," he cried, and all the jackals howled together; very remotely it seemed to resemble a melody. "Sir, we want you to end this quarrel that divides the world. You are exactly the man whom our ancestors foretold as born

---

2. Attendants who hold the trailing part of a robe or gown at a ceremonial event.

to do it. We want to be troubled no more by Arabs; room to breathe; a skyline
cleansed of them; no more bleating of sheep knifed by an Arab; every beast to
die a natural death; no interference till we have drained the carcass empty and
picked its bones clean. Cleanliness, nothing but cleanliness is what we
want"—and now they were all lamenting and sobbing—"how can you bear to
live in such a world, O noble heart and kindly bowels? Filth is their white; filth
is their black; their beards are a horror; the very sight of their eye sockets
makes one want to spit; and when they lift an arm, the murk of hell yawns in
the armpit. And so, sir, and so, dear sir, by means of your all-powerful hands
slit their throats through with these scissors!" And in answer to a jerk of his
head a jackal came trotting up with a small pair of sewing scissors, covered
with ancient rust, dangling from an eyetooth.

"Well, here's the scissors at last, and high time to stop!" cried the Arab
leader of our caravan who had crept upwind towards us and now cracked his
great whip.

The jackals fled in haste, but at some little distance rallied in a close huddle,
all the brutes so tightly packed and rigid that they looked as if penned in a small
fold girt by flickering will-o'-the-wisps.[3]

"So you've been treated to this entertainment too, sir," said the Arab,
laughing as gaily as the reserve of his race permitted. "You know, then, what
the brutes are after?" I asked. "Of course," said he, "it's common knowledge;
so long as Arabs exist, that pair of scissors goes wandering through the desert
and will wander with us to the end of our days. Every European is offered it for
the great work; every European is just the man that Fate has chosen for them.
They have the most lunatic hopes, these beasts; they're just fools, utter fools.
That's why we like them; they are our dogs; finer dogs than any of yours.
Watch this, now, a camel died last night and I have had it brought here."

Four men came up with the heavy carcass and threw it down before us. It
had hardly touched the ground before the jackals lifed up their voices. As if
irresistibly drawn by cords each of them began to waver forward, crawling on
his belly. They had forgotten the Arabs, forgotten their hatred, the all-
obliterating immediate presence of the stinking carrion bewitched them. One
was already at the camel's throat, sinking his teeth straight into an artery. Like a
vehement small pump endeavoring with as much determination as hopefulness
to extinguish some raging fire, every muscle in his body twitched and labored
at the task. In a trice they were all on top of the carcass, laboring in common,
piled mountain-high.

And now the caravan leader lashed his cutting whip crisscross over their
backs. They lifted their heads; half swooning in ecstasy; saw the Arabs
standing before them; felt the sting of the whip on their muzzles; leaped and ran
backwards a stretch. But the camel's blood was already lying in pools, reeking
to heaven, the carcass was torn wide open in many places. They could not resist it; they were back again; once more the leader lifted his whip; I stayed his
arm.

"You are right, sir," said he, "we'll leave them to their business; besides,
it's time to break camp. Well, you've seen them. Marvelous creatures, aren't
they? And how they hate us!"

---

3. Shadowy light seen over open ground at night which is usually caused by the combustion of
natural gas.

Jorge Luis Borges (b. 1899)
The Secret Miracle

And God had him die for a hundred years and then revived him and said:
"How long have you been here?"
"A day or a part of a day," he answered.—KORAN, II, 261[1]

The night of March 14, 1943, in an apartment in the Zeltnergasse[2] of Prague,
Jaromir Hladik, the author of the unfinished drama entitled *The Enemies,* of
Vindication of Eternity and of a study of the indirect Jewish sources of Jakob
Böhme,[3] had a dream of a long game of chess. The players were not two persons,
but two illustrious families; the game had been going on for centuries. Nobody
could remember what the stakes were, but it was rumored that they were enormous, perhaps infinite; the chessmen and the board were in a secret tower.
Jaromir (in his dream) was the first-born of one of the contending families. The
clock struck the hour for the game, which could not be postponed. The dreamer
raced over the sands of a rainy desert, and was unable to recall either the pieces
or the rules of chess. At that moment he awoke. The clangor of the rain and of
the terrible clocks ceased. A rhythmic, unanimous noise, punctuated by shouts
of command, arose from the Zeltnergasse. It was dawn, and the armored
vanguard of the Third Reich[4] was entering Prague.

On the nineteenth the authorities received a denunciation; that same nineteenth, toward evening, Jaromir Hladik was arrested. He was taken to an
aseptic, white barracks on the opposite bank of the Moldau.[5] He was unable to
refute a single one of the Gestapo's charges; his mother's family name was
Jaroslavski, he was of Jewish blood, his study on Böhme had a marked Jewish
emphasis, his signature had been one more on the protest against the
Anschluss. In 1928 he had translated the *Sepher Yezirah*[6] for the publishing
house of Hermann Barsdorf. The fulsome catalogue of the firm had exaggerated, for publicity purposes, the translator's reputation, and the catalogue had
been examined by Julius Rothe, one of the officials who held Hladik's fate in
his hands. There is not a person who, except in the field of his own specializa-
tion, is not credulous; two or three adjectives in Gothic type were enough to
persuade Julius Rothe of Hladik's importance, and he ordered him sentenced
to death *pour encourager les autres.*[7] The execution was set for March 29th,

---

1. Sacred book of the Islamic religion containing the revelations of God to the prophet Mo-
hammed.
2. Zeltner Street, located in the old residential district of Prague, the capital of Czechoslovakia
and its commercial and cultural center.
3. Influential German mystic and philosopher (1575–1624) who held that God represents the ultimate unity in which all the antithetical elements of the universe are integrated and resolved.
4. The Nazi regime in Germany, established by Adolf Hitler in 1933. By means of the principle of
Anschluss (literally, "union" or "annexation"), Nazi forces took over Austria and a part of Czechoslovakia, and on March 15, 1939, marched into Prague. Jews and people suspected of being Jews
were sought out and exterminated by various Nazi agencies, particularly the Gestapo, the infamous
secret police.
5. German name for the Vlatava, the river running through the heart of Prague.
6. Possibly the oldest document in Hebrew mysticism; set down between the third and the sixth
centuries by an unknown author, it treats the emergence of the universe and God's bringing it forth.
7. "To encourage others" (to avoid the same fate).

at 9:00 A.M. This delay (whose importance the reader will grasp later) was owing to the desire on the authorities' part to proceed impersonally and slowly, after the manner of vegetables and plants.

Hladik's first reaction was mere terror. He felt he would not have shrunk from the gallows, the block, or the knife, but that death by a firing squad was unbearable. In vain he tried to convince himself that the plain, unvarnished fact of dying was the fearsome thing, not the attendant circumstances. He never wearied of conjuring up these circumstances, senselessly trying to exhaust all their possible variations. He infinitely anticipated the process of his dying, from the sleepless dawn to the mysterious volley. Before the day set by Julius Rothe he died hundreds of deaths in courtyards whose forms and angles strained geometrical probabilities, machine-gunned by variable soldiers in changing numbers, who at times killed him from a distance, at others from close by. He faced these imaginary executions with real terror (perhaps with real bravery); each simulacrum[8] lasted a few seconds. When the circle was closed, Jaromir returned once more and interminably to the tremulous vespers of his death. Then he reflected that reality does not usually coincide with our anticipation of it; with a logic of his own he inferred that to foresee a circumstantial detail is to prevent its happening. Trusting in this weak magic, he invented, *so that they would not happen,* the most gruesome details. Finally, as was natural, he came to fear that they were prophetic. Miserable in the night, he endeavored to find some way to hold fast to the fleeting substance of time. He knew that it was rushing headlong toward the dawn of the twenty-ninth. He reasoned aloud: "I am now in the night of the twenty-second; while this night lasts (and for six nights more), I am invulnerable, immortal." The nights of sleep seemed to him deep, dark pools in which he could submerge himself. There were moments when he longed impatiently for the final burst of fire that would free him, for better or for worse, from the vain compulsion of his imaginings. On the twenty-eighth, as the last sunset was reverberating from the high barred windows, the thought of his drama, *The Enemies,* deflected him from these abject considerations.

Hladik had rounded forty. Aside from a few friendships and many habits, the problematic exercise of literature constituted his life. Like all writers, he measured the achievements of others by what they had accomplished, asking of them that they measure him by what he envisaged or planned. All the books he had published had left him with a complex feeling of repentance. His studies of the work of Böhme, of Ibn Ezra, and of Fludd[9] had been characterized essentially by mere application; his translation of the *Sepher Yezirah,* by carelessness, fatigue, and conjecture. *Vindication of Eternity* perhaps had fewer shortcomings. The first volume gave a history of man's various concepts of eternity, from the immutable Being of Parmenides to the modifiable Past of Hinton. The second denied (with Francis Bradley)[10] that all the events of the

---

8. Illusion.

9. Ibn Ezra (1090?–1164), Spanish-born Hebrew philosopher and biblical interpreter, Sir Robert Fludd (1574–1637), English physician and mystical philosopher who held that God is an all-pervading entity manifested in all the elements of the universe.

10. Hladik is interested in philosophers who are concerned with questions of the nature of time and of reality: Parmenides, Greek philosopher of the 6th and 5th centuries B.C.; James Hinton (1822–75), British physician and philosopher; and Francis H. Bradley (1846–1924), British philosopher and logician.

universe make up a temporal series, arguing that the number of man's possible experiences is not infinite, and that a single "repetition" suffices to prove that time is a fallacy . . . Unfortunately, the arguments that demonstrate this fallacy are equally fallacious. Hladik was in the habit of going over them with a kind of contemptuous perplexity. He had also composed a series of Expressionist poems;[11] to the poet's chagrin they had been included in an anthology published in 1924, and no subsequent anthology but inherited them. From all this equivocal, uninspired past Hladik had hoped to redeem himself with his drama in verse, *The Enemies*. (Hladik felt the verse form to be essential because it makes it impossible for the spectators to lose sight of irreality, one of art's requisites.)

The drama observed the unities of time, place, and action. The scene was laid in Hradčany,[12] in the library of Baron von Roemerstadt, on one of the last afternoons of the nineteenth century. In the first scene of the first act a strange man visits Roemerstadt. (A clock was striking seven, the vehemence of the setting sun's rays glorified the windows, a passionate, familiar Hungarian music floated in the air.) This visit is followed by others; Roemerstadt does not know the people who are importuning him, but he has the uncomfortable feeling that he has seen them somewhere, perhaps in a dream. They all fawn upon him, but it is apparent—first to the audience and then to the Baron—that they are secret enemies, in league to ruin him. Roemerstadt succeeds in checking or evading their involved schemings. In the dialogue mention is made of his sweetheart, Julia von Weidenau, and a certain Jaroslav Kubin, who at one time pressed his attentions on her. Kubin has now lost his mind, and believes himself to be Roemerstadt. The dangers increase; Roemerstadt, at the end of the second act, is forced to kill one of the conspirators. The third and final act opens. The incoherencies gradually increase; actors who had seemed out of the play reappear; the man Roemerstadt killed returns for a moment. Someone points out that evening has not fallen; the clock strikes seven, the high windows reverberate in the western sun, the air carries an impassioned Hungarian melody. The first actor comes on and repeats the lines he had spoken in the first scene of the first act. Roemerstadt speaks to him without surprise; the audience understands that Roemerstadt is the miserable Jaroslav Kubin. The drama has never taken place; it is the circular delirium that Kubin lives and relives endlessly.

Hladik had never asked himself whether this tragicomedy of errors was preposterous or admirable, well thought out or slipshod. He felt that the plot I have just sketched was best contrived to cover up his defects and point up his abilities and held the possibility of allowing him to redeem (symbolically) the meaning of his life. He had finished the first act and one or two scenes of the third; the metrical nature of the work made it possible for him to keep working it over, changing the hexameters,[13] without the manuscript in front of him. He thought how he still had two acts to do, and that he was going to die very soon. He spoke with God in the darkness: " If in some fashion I exist, if I am not one of Your repetitions and mistakes, I exist as the author of *The Enemies*. To finish this drama, which can justify me and justify You, I need another year.

---

11. Expressionistic poetry relies upon distortions of external reality in order to portray internal or subjective experience.

12. West district of Prague in which the ancient Hradčany Castle stands.

13. Lines of poetry each containing six metrical feet.

Grant me these days, You to whom the centuries and time belong." This was the last night, the most dreadful of all, but ten minutes later sleep flooded over him like a dark water.

Toward dawn he dreamed that he had concealed himself in one of the naves of the Clementine Library. A librarian wearing dark glasses asked him: "What are you looking for?" Hladik answered: "I am looking for God." The librarian said to him: "God is in one of the letters on one of the pages of one of the four hundred thousand volumes of the Clementine. My fathers and the fathers of my fathers have searched for this letter; I have grown blind seeking it." He removed his glasses, and Hladik saw his eyes, which were dead. A reader came in to return an atlas. "This atlas is worthless," he said, and handed it to Hladik, who opened it at random. He saw a map of India as in a daze. Suddenly sure of himself, he touched one of the tiniest letters. A ubiquitous voice said to him: "The time of your labor has been granted," At this point Hladik awoke.

He remembered that men's dreams belong to God, and that Maimonides[14] had written that the words heard in a dream are divine when they are distinct and clear and the person uttering them cannot be seen. He dressed: two soldiers came into the cell and ordered him to follow them.

From behind the door, Hladik had envisaged a labyrinth of passageways, stairs, and separate buildings. The reality was less spectacular: they descended to an inner court by a narrow iron stairway. Several soldiers—some with uniform unbottoned—were examining a motorcycle and discussing it. The sergeant looked at the clock; it was 8:44. They had to wait until it struck nine. Hladik, more insignificant than pitiable, sat down on a pile of wood. He noticed that the soldiers' eyes avoided his. To ease his wait, the sergeant handed him a cigarette. Hladik did not smoke; he accepted it out of politeness or humility. As he lighted it, he noticed that his hands were shaking. The day was clouding over; the soldiers spoke in a low voice as though he were already dead. Vainly he tried to recall the woman of whom Julia von Weidenau was the symbol.

The squad formed and stood at attention. Hladik, standing against the barracks wall, waited for the volley. Someone pointed out that the wall was going to be stained with blood; the victim was ordered to step forward a few paces. Incongruously, this reminded Hladik of the fumbling preparations of photographers. A big drop of rain struck one of Hladik's temples and rolled slowly down his cheek; the sergeant shouted the final order.

The physical universe came to a halt.

The guns converged on Hladik, but the men who were to kill him stood motionless. The sergeant's arm eternized an unfinished gesture. On a paving stone of the courtyard a bee cast an unchanging shadow. The wind had ceased, as in a picture. Hladik attempted a cry, a word, a movement of the hand. He realized that he was paralyzed. Not a sound reached him from the halted world. He thought: "I am in hell, I am dead." He thought: "I am mad." He thought: "Time has stopped." Then he reflected that if that was the case, his mind would have stopped too. He wanted to test this; he repeated (without moving his lips) Vergil's mysterious fourth Eclogue.[15] He imagined that the

---

14. Moses Maimonides (1135–1204), Spanish-born Jewish philosopher who codified the Talmud, the collection of Jewish oral law.

15. Publius Vergilius Maro, or Vergil (70–19 B.C.), Roman epic poet whose fourth Eclogue, written in 40 B.C., is variously interpreted: some regard its depiction of a miraculous baby boy as a reference to Augustus Caesar; others interpret the boy as the Messiah; and others see him as the promise of a new Golden Age on earth.

now remote soldiers must be sharing his anxiety; he longed to be able to communicate with them. It astonished him not to feel the least fatigue, not even the numbness of his protracted immobility. After an indeterminate time he fell asleep. When he awoke the world continued motionless and mute. The drop of water still clung to his cheek, the shadow of the bee to the stone. The smoke from the cigarette he had thrown away had not dispersed. Another "day" went by before Hladik understood.

He had asked God for a whole year to finish his work; His omnipotence had granted it. God had worked a secret miracle for him; German lead would kill him at the set hour, but in his mind a year would go by between the order and its execution. From perplexity he passed to stupor, from stupor to resignation, from resignation to sudden gratitude.

He had no document but his memory; the training he had acquired with each added hexameter gave him a discipline unsuspected by those who set down and forget temporary, incomplete paragraphs. He was not working for posterity or even for God, whose literary tastes were unknown to him. Meticulously, motionlessly, secretely, he wrought in time his lofty, invisible labyrinth. He worked the third act over twice. He eliminated certain symbols as over-obvious, such as the repeated striking of the clock, the music. Nothing hurried him. He omitted, he condensed, he amplified. In certain instances he came back to the original version. He came to feel an affection for the courtyard, the barracks; one of the faces before him modified his conception of Roemerstadt's character. He discovered that the wearying cacophonies that bothered Flaubert[16] so much are mere visual superstitions, weakness and limitation of the written word, not the spoken . . . He concluded his drama. He had only the problem of a single phrase. He found it. The drop of water slid down his cheek. He opened his mouth in a maddened cry, moved his face, dropped under the quadruple blast.

Jaromir Hladik died on March 29, at 9:02 A.M.

Eudora Welty (b. 1909)
Keela, the Outcast Indian Maiden

One morning in summertime, when all his sons and daughters were off picking plums and Little Lee Roy was all alone, sitting on the porch and only listening to the screech owls away down in the woods, he had a surprise.

First he heard white men talking. He heard two white men coming up the path from the highway. Little Lee Roy ducked his head and held his breath; then he patted all around back of him for his crutches. The chickens all came out from under the house and waited attentively on the steps.

The men came closer. It was the young man who was doing all of the talking. But when they got through the fence, Max, the older man, interrupted him. He

---

16. Gustave Flaubert (1821–80), French novelist who practiced his belief that every word and phrase in a work of fiction should be precise and harmonious.

tapped him on the arm and pointed his thumb toward Little Lee Roy.

He said, "Bud? Yonder he is."

But the younger man kept straight on talking, in an explanatory voice.

"Bud?" said Max again. "Look, Bud, yonder's the only little clubfooted nigger man was ever around Cane Springs. Is he the party?"

They came nearer and nearer to Little Lee Roy and then stopped and stood there in the middle of the yard. But the young man was so excited he did not seem to realize that they had arrived anywhere. He was only about twenty years old, very sunburned. He talked constantly, making only one gesture—raising his hand stiffly and then moving it a little to one side.

"They dressed it in a red dress, and it ate chickens alive," he said. "I sold tickets and I thought it was worth a dime, honest. They gimme a piece of paper with the thing wrote off I had to say. That was easy. 'Keela, the Outcast Indian Maiden!' I call it out through a pasteboard megaphone. Then ever' time it was fixin' to eat a live chicken, I blowed the sireen out front."

"Just tell me, Bud," said Max, resting back on the heels of his perforated tan-and-white sport shoes "Is this nigger the one? Is that him sittin' there?"

Little Lee Roy sat huddled and blinking, a smile on his face. . . . But the young man did not look his way.

"Just took the job that time. I didn't mean to—I mean, I meant to go to Port Arthur because my brother was on a boat," he said. "My name is Steve, mister. But I worked with this show selling tickets for three months, and I never would of knowed it was like that if it hadn't been for that man." He arrested his gesture.

"Yeah, what man?" said Max in a hopeless voice.

Little Lee Roy was looking from one white man to the other, excited almost beyond respectful silence. He trembled all over, and a look of amazement and sudden life came into his eyes.

"Two years ago," Steve was saying impatiently. "And we was travelin' through Texas in those ole trucks.—See, the reason nobody ever come clost to it before was they give it a iron bar this long. And tole it if anybody come near, to shake the bar good at 'em, like this. But it couldn't say nothin'. Turned out they'd tole it it couldn't say nothin' to anybody ever, so it just kind of mumbled and growled, like a animal."

"Hee! hee!" This from Little Lee Roy, softly.

"Tell me again," said Max, and just from his look you could tell that everybody knew old Max. "Somehow I can't get it straight in my mind. Is this the boy? Is this little nigger boy the same as this Keela, the Outcast Indian Maiden?"

Up on the porch, above them, Little Lee Roy gave Max a glance full of hilarity, and then bent the other way to catch Steve's next words.

"Why, if anybody was to even come near it or even bresh their shoulder against the rope it'd growl and take on and shake its iron rod. When it would eat the live chickens it'd growl somethin' awful—you ought to heard it."

"Hee! hee!" It was a soft, almost incredulous laugh that began to escape from Little Lee Roy's tight lips, a little mew of delight.

"They'd throw it this chicken, and it would reach out an' grab it. Would sort of rub over the chicken's neck with its thumb an' press on it good, an' then it would bite its head off."

"O.K.," said Max.

"It skint back the feathers and stuff from the neck and sucked the blood. But ever'body said it was still alive." Steve drew closer to Max and fastened his light-colored, troubled eyes on his face.

"O.K."

"Then it would pull the feathers out easy and neat-like, awful fast, an' growl the whole time, kind of moan, an' then it would commence to eat all the white meat. I'd go in an' look at it. I reckon I seen it a thousand times."

"That was you, boy?" Max demanded of Little Lee Roy unexpectedly.

But Little Lee Roy could only say, "Hee! hee!" The little man at the head of the steps where the chickens sat, one on each step, and the two men facing each other below made a pyramid.

Steve stuck his hand out for silence. "They said—I mean, I said it, out front through the megaphone, I said it myself, that it wouldn't eat nothin' but only live meat. It was supposed to be a Indian woman, see, in this red dress an' stockin's. It didn't have on no shoes, so when it drug its foot ever'body could see. . . . When it come to the chicken's heart, it would eat that too, real fast, and the heart would still be jumpin'."

"Wait a second, Bud," said Max briefly. "Say, boy, is this white man here crazy?"

Little Lee Roy burst into hysterical, deprecatory giggles. He said, "Naw suh, don't think so." He tried to catch Steve's eye, seeking appreciation, crying, "Naw suh, don't think he crazy, mista."

Steve gripped Max's arm. "Wait! Wait!" he cried anxiously. "You ain't listenin'. I want to tell you about it. You didn't catch my name—Steve. You never did hear about that little nigger—all that happened to him? Lived in Cane Springs, Miss'ippi?"

"Bud," said Max, disengaging himself, "I don't hear anything. I got a juke box, see, so I don't have to listen."

"Look—I was really the one," said Steve more patiently, but nervously, as if he had been slowly breaking bad news. He walked up and down the bare-swept ground in front of Little Lee Roy's porch, along the row of princess feathers and snow-on-the-mountain.[1] Little Lee Roy's turning head followed him. "I was the one—that's what I'm tellin' you."

"Suppose I was to listen to what every dope comes in Max's Place got to say, *I'd* be nuts," said Max.

"It's all me, see," said Steve. "I know that. I was the one was the cause for it goin' on an' on an' not bein' found out—such an awful thing. It was me, what I said out front through the megaphone."

He stopped still and stared at Max in despair.

"Look," said Max. He sat on the steps, and the chickens hopped off. "I know I ain't nobody but Max. I got Max's Place. I only run a place, understand, fifty yards down the highway. Liquor buried twenty feet from the premises, and no trouble yet. I ain't ever been up here before. I don't claim to been anywhere. People come to my place. Now. You're the hitchhiker. You're tellin' me, see. You claim a lot of information. If I don't get it I don't get it and I

---

1. Princess feathers are a variety of plants that bloom with spectacular red spikes; snow-on-the-mountain is a plant characterized by its clusters of snowy white leaves.

ain't complainin' about it, see. But I think you're nuts, and did from the first. I only come up here with you because I figured you's crazy."

"Maybe you don't believe I remember every word of it even now," Steve was saying gently. "I think about it at night—that an' drums on the midway. You ever hear drums on the midway?" He paused and stared politely at Max and Little Lee Roy.

"Yeh," said Max.

"Don't it make you feel sad. I remember how the drums was goin' and I was yellin', 'Ladies and gents! Do not try to touch Keela, the Outcast Indian Maiden—she will only beat your brains out with her iron rod, and eat them alive!'" Steve waved his arm gently in the air, and Little Lee Roy drew back and squealed. "'Do not go near her, ladies and gents! I'm warnin' you!' So nobody ever did. Nobody ever come near her. Until that man."

"Sure," said Max. "That fella." He shut his eyes.

"Afterwards when he come up so bold, I remembered seein' him walk up an' buy the ticket an' go in the tent. I'll never forget that man as long as I live. To me he's a sort of—well—"

"Hero," said Max.

"I wish I could remember what he looked like. Seem like he was a tallish man with a sort of white face. Seem like he had bad teeth, but I may be wrong. I remember he frowned a lot. Kept frownin'. Whenever he'd buy a ticket, why, he'd frown."

"Ever seen him since?" asked Max cautiously, still with his eyes closed. "Ever hunt him up?"

"No, never did," said Steve. Then he went on. "He'd frown an' buy a ticket ever' day we was in these two little smelly towns in Texas, sometimes three-four times a day, whether it was fixin' to eat a chicken or not."

"O.K., so he gets in the tent," said Max.

"Well, what the man finally done was, he walked right up to the little stand where it was tied up and laid his hand out open on the planks in the platform. He just laid his hand out open there and said, 'Come here,' real low and quick, that-a-way."

Steve laid his open hand on Little Lee Roy's porch and held it there, frowning in concentration.

"I get it," said Max. "He'd caught on it was a fake."

Steve straightened up. "So ever'body yelled to git away, git away," he continued, his voice rising, "because it was growlin' an' carryin' on an' shakin' its iron bar like they tole it. When I heard all that commotion—boy! I was scared."

"You didn't know it was a fake."

Steve was silent for a moment, and Little Lee Roy held his breath, for fear everything was all over.

"Look," said Steve finally, his voice trembling. "I guess I was supposed to feel bad like this, and you wasn't. I wasn't supposed to ship out on that boat from Port Arthur and all like that. This other had to happen to me—not you all. Feelin' responsible. You'll be O.K., mister, but I won't. I feel awful about it. That poor little old thing."

"Look, you got him right here," said Max quickly. "See him? Use your eyes. He's O.K., ain't he? Looks O.K. to me. It's just you. You're nuts, is all."

"You know—when that man laid out his open hand on the boards, why, it just let go the iron bar," continued Steve, "let it fall down like that—bang—and act like it didn't know what to do. Then it drug itself over to where the fella was standin' an' leaned down an' grabbed holt onto that white man's hand as tight as it could an' cried like a baby. It didn't want to hit him!"

"Hee! hee! hee!"

"No sir, it didn't want to hit him. You know what it wanted?"

Max shook his head.

"It wanted him to help it. So the man said, 'Do you wanta get out of this place, whoever you are?' An' it never answered—none of us knowed it could talk—but it just wouldn't let that man's hand a-loose. It hung on, cryin' like a baby. So the man says, 'Well, wait here till I come back.'"

"Uh-huh?" said Max.

"Went off an' come back with the sheriff. Took us all to jail. But just the man owned the show and his son got took to the pen. They said I could go free. I kep' tellin' 'em I didn't know it wouldn't hit me with the iron bar an' kep' tellin' 'em I didn't know it could tell what you was sayin' to it."

"Yeh, guess you told 'em," said Max.

"By that time I felt bad. Been feelin' bad ever since. Can't hold onto a job or stay in one place for nothin' in the world. They made it stay in jail to see if it could talk or not, and the first night it wouldn't say nothin'. Some time it cried. And they undressed it an' found out it wasn't no outcast Indian woman a-tall. It was a little clubfooted nigger man."

"Hee! hee!"

"You mean it was this boy here—yeh. It was him."

"Washed its face, and it was paint all over it made it look red. It all come off. And it could talk—as good as me or you. But they'd tole it not to, so it never did. They'd tole it if anybody was to come near it they was comin' to git it—and for it to hit 'em quick with that iron bar an' growl. So nobody ever come near it—until that man. I was yellin' outside, tellin' 'em to keep away, keep away. You could see where they'd whup it. They had to whup it some to make it eat all the chickens. It was awful dirty. They let it go back home free, to where they got it in the first place. They made them pay its ticket from Little Oil, Texas, to Cane Springs, Miss'ippi."

"You got a good memory," said Max.

"The way it *started* was," said Steve, in a wondering voice, "the show was just travelin' along in ole trucks through the country, and just seen this little deformed nigger man, sittin' on a fence, and just took it. It couldn't help it."

Little Lee Roy tossed his head back in a frenzy of amusement.

"I found it all out later. I was up on the Ferris wheel with one of the boys—got to talkin' up yonder in the peace an' quiet—an' said they just kind of happened up on it. Like a cyclone happens: it wasn't nothin' it could do. It was just took up." Steve suddenly paled through his sunburn. "An' they found out that back in Miss'ippi it had it a little bitty pair of crutches an' could just go runnin' on 'em!"

"And there they are," said Max.

Little Lee Roy held up a crutch and turned it about, and then snatched it back like a monkey.

"But if it hadn't been for that man, I wouldn't of knowed it till yet. If it wasn't for him bein' so bold. If he hadn't knowed what he was doin'.''

"You remember that man this fella's talkin' about, boy?'' asked Max, eying Little Lee Roy.

Little Lee Roy, in reluctance and shyness, shook his head gently.

"Naw suh, I can't say as I remembas that ve'y man, suh,'' he said softly, looking down where just then a sparrow alighted on his child's shoe. He added happily, as if on inspiration, "Now I remembas *this* man.''

Steve did not look up, but when Max shook with silent laughter, alarm seemed to seize him like a spasm in his side. He walked painfully over and stood in the shade for a few minutes, leaning his head on a sycamore tree.

"Seemed like that man just studied it out an' knowed it was somethin' wrong,'' he said presently, his voice coming more remotely than ever. "But I didn't know. I can't look at nothin' an' be sure what it is. Then afterwards I know. Then I see how it was.''

"Yeh, but you're nuts,'' said Max affably.

"You wouldn't of knowed it either!'' cried Steve in sudden boyish, defensive anger. Then he came out from under the tree and stood again almost pleadingly in the sun, facing Max where he was sitting below Little Lee Roy on the steps. "You'd of let it go on an' on when they made it do those things—just like I did.''

"Bet I could tell a man from a woman and an Indian from a nigger though,'' said Max.

Steve scuffed the dust into little puffs with his worn shoe. The chickens scattered, alarmed at last.

Little Lee Roy looked from one man to the other radiantly, his hands pressed over his grinning gums.

Then Steve sighed, and as if he did not know what else he could do, he reached out and without any warning hit Max in the jaw with his fist. Max fell off the steps.

Little Lee Roy suddenly sat as still and dark as a statue, looking on.

"Say! Say!'' cried Steve. He pulled shyly at Max where he lay on the ground, with his lips pursed up like a whistler, and then stepped back. He looked horrified. "How you feel?''

"Lousy,'' said Max thoughtfully. "Let me alone.'' He raised up on one elbow and lay there looking all around, at the cabin, at Little Lee Roy sitting cross-legged on the porch, and at Steve with his hand out. Finally he got up.

"I can't figure out how I could of ever knocked down an athaletic guy like you. I had to do it,'' said Steve. "But I guess you don't understand. I had to hit you. First you didn't believe me, and then it didn't bother you.''

"That's all O.K., only hush,'' said Max, and added, "Some dope is always giving me the lowdown on something, but this is the first time one of 'em ever got away with a thing like this. I got to watch out.''

"I hope it don't stay black long,'' said Steve.

"I got to be going,'' said Max. But he waited. "What you want to transact with Keela? You come a long way to see him.'' He stared at Steve with his eyes wide open now, and interested.

"Well, I was goin' to give him some money or somethin', I guess, if I ever found him, only now I ain't got any,'' said Steve defiantly.

"O.K.,'' said Max. "Here's some change for you, boy. Just take it. Go on back in the house. Go on.''

Little Lee Roy took the money speechlessly, and then fell upon his yellow crutches and hopped with miraculous rapidity away through the door. Max stared after him for a moment.

"As for you"—he brushed himself off, turned to Steve and then said, "When did you eat last?"

"Well, I'll tell you," said Steve.

"Not here," said Max. "I didn't go to ask you a question. Just follow me. We serve eats at Max's Place, and I want to play the juke box. You eat, and I'll listen to the juke box."

"Well . . . ." said Steve. "But when it cools off I got to catch a ride some place."

"Today while all you all was gone, and not a soul in de house," said Little Lee Roy at the supper table that night, "two white mens come heah to de house. Wouldn't come in. But talks to me about de ole times when I use to be wid de circus—"

"Hush up, Pappy," said the children.

Albert Camus (1913–1960)
Return to Tipasa

You have navigated with raging soul far from the paternal home, passing beyond the sea's double rocks, and you now inhabit a foreign land.—MEDEA[1]

For five days rain had been falling ceaselessly on Algiers and had finally wet the sea itself. From an apparently inexhaustible sky, constant downpours, viscous in their density, streamed down upon the gulf. Gray and soft as a huge sponge, the sea rose slowly in the ill-defined bay. But the surface of the water seemed almost motionless under the steady rain. Only now and then a barely perceptible swelling motion would raise above the sea's surface a vague puff of smoke that would come to dock in the harbor, under an arc of wet boulevards. The city itself, all its white walls dripping, gave off a different steam that went out to meet the first steam. Whichever way you turned, you seemed to be breathing water, to be drinking the air.

In front of the soaked sea I walked and waited in that December Algiers, which was for me the city of summers. I had fled Europe's night, the winter of faces. But the summer city herself had been emptied of her laughter and offered me only bent and shining backs. In the evening, in the crudely lighted cafés where I took refuge, I read my age in faces I recognized without being able to name them. I merely knew that they had been young with me and that they were no longer so.

---

1. Greek tragedy by Euripides (480?–406? B.C.). These words are spoken to the sorceress Medea after she has been banished from Corinth because of her anticipated revenge against the king and his daughter, who had married Medea's former husband Jason.

Yet I persisted without very well knowing what I was waiting for, unless perhaps the moment to go back to Tipasa.[2] To be sure, it is sheer madness, almost always punished, to return to the sites of one's youth and try to relive at forty what one loved or keenly enjoyed at twenty. But I was forewarned of that madness. Once already I had returned to Tipasa, soon after those war years that marked for me the end of youth. I hoped, I think, to recapture there a freedom I could not forget. In that spot, indeed, more than twenty years ago, I had spent whole mornings wandering among the ruins, breathing in the wormwood, warming myself against the stones, discovering little roses, soon plucked of their petals, which outlive the spring. Only at noon, at the hour when the cicadas themselves fell silent as if overcome, I would flee the greedy glare of an all-consuming light. Sometimes at night I would sleep open-eyed under a sky dripping with stars. I was alive then. Fifteen years later I found my ruins, a few feet from the first waves, I followed the streets of the forgotten walled city through fields covered with bitter trees, and on the slopes overlooking the bay I still caressed the bread-colored columns. But the ruins were now surrounded with barbed wire and could be entered only through certain openings. It was also forbidden, for reasons which it appears that morality approves, to walk there at night; by day one encountered an official guardian. It just happened, that morning, that it was raining over the whole extent of the ruins.

Disoriented, walking through the wet, solitary countryside, I tried at least to recapture that strength, hitherto always at hand, that helps me to accept *what is* when once I have admitted that I cannot change it. And I could not, indeed, reverse the course of time and restore to the world the appearance I had loved which had disappeared in a day, long before. The second of September 1939, in fact, I had not gone to Greece, as I was to do. War,[3] on the contrary, had come to us, then it had spread over Greece herself. That distance, those years separating the warm ruins from the barbed wire were to be found in me, too, that day as I stood before the sarcophaguses full of black water or under the sodden tamarisks. Originally brought up surrounded by beauty which was my only wealth, I had begun in plenty. Then had come the barbed wire—I mean tyrannies, war, police forces, the era of revolt. One had had to put oneself right with the authorities of night: the day's beauty was but a memory. And in this muddy Tipasa the memory itself was becoming dim. It was indeed a question of beauty, plenty, or youth! In the light from conflagrations the world had suddenly shown its wrinkles and its wounds, old and new. It had aged all at once, and we with it. I had come here looking for a certain "lift"; but I realized that it inspires only the man who is unaware that he is about to launch forward. No love without a little innocence. Where was the innocence? Empires were tumbling down; nations and men were tearing at one another's throats; our hands were soiled. Originally innocent without knowing it, we were now guilty without meaning to be: the mystery was increasing with our knowledge. This is why, O mockery, we were concerned with morality. Weak and disabled, I was dreaming of virtue! In the days of innocence I didn't even know that morality

---

2. Small Algerian village noted for its ancient ruins. First a Phoenician trading center and later a Roman colony, it was destroyed around A.D. 490.

3. On September 1, 1939, the forces of Nazi Germany invaded Poland, precipitating World War II.

existed. I knew it now, and I was not capable of living up to its standard. On the promontory that I used to love, among the wet columns of the ruined temple, I seemed to be walking behind someone whose steps I could still hear on the stone slabs and mosaics but whom I should never again overtake. I went back to Paris and remained several years before returning home.

Yet I obscurely missed something during all those years. When one has once had the good luck to love intensely, life is spent in trying to recapture that ardor and that illumination. Forsaking beauty and the sensual happiness attached to it, exclusively serving misfortune, calls for a nobility I lack. But, after all, nothing is true that forces one to exclude. Isolated beauty ends up simpering; solitary justice ends up oppressing. Whoever aims to serve one exclusive of the other serves no one, not even himself, and eventually serves injustice twice. A day comes when, thanks to rigidity, nothing causes wonder any more, everything is known and life is spent in beginning over again. These are the days of exile, of desiccated life, of dead souls. To come alive again, one needs a special grace, self-forgetfulness, or a homeland. Certain mornings, on turning a corner, a delightful dew falls on the heart and then evaporates. But its coolness remains, and this is what the heart requires always. I had to set out again.

And in Algiers a second time, still walking under the same downpour which seemed not to have ceased since a departure I had thought definitive, amid the same vast melancholy smelling of rain and sea, despite this misty sky, these backs fleeing under the shower, these cafés whose sulphureous light distorted faces, I persisted in hoping. Didn't I know, besides, that Algiers rains, despite their appearance of never meaning to end, nonetheless stop in an instant, like those streams in my country which rise in two hours, lay waste acres of land, and suddenly dry up? One evening, in fact, the rain ceased. I waited one night more. A limpid morning rose, dazzling, over the pure sea. From the sky, fresh as a daisy, washed over and over again by the rains, reduced by these repeated washings to its finest and clearest texture, emanated a vibrant light that gave to each house and each tree a sharp outline, an astonished newness. In the world's morning the earth must have sprung forth in such a light. I again took the road for Tipasa.

For me there is not a single one of those sixty-nine kilometers that is not filled with memories and sensations. Turbulent childhood, adolescent daydreams in the drone of the bus's motor, mornings, unspoiled girls, beaches, young muscles always at the peak of their effort, evening's slight anxiety in a sixteen-year-old heart, lust for life, fame, and ever the same sky throughout the years, unfailing in strength and light, itself insatiable, consuming one by one over a period of months the victims stretched out in the form of crosses on the beach at the deathlike hour of noon. Always the same sea, too, almost impalpable in the morning light, which I again saw on the horizon as soon as the road, leaving the Sahel[4] and its bronze-colored vineyards, sloped down toward the coast. But I did not stop to look at it. I wanted to see again the Chenoua, that solid, heavy mountain cut out of a single block of stone, which borders the bay of Tipasa to the west before dropping down into the sea itself. It is seen from a distance, long before arriving, a light, blue haze still confused with the sky.

---

4. Range of hills running parallel to the Algerian coastline.

But gradually it is condensed, as you advance toward it, until it takes on the color of the surrounding waters, a huge motionless wave whose amazing leap upward has been brutally solidified above the sea calmed all at once. Still nearer, almost at the gates of Tipasa, here is its frowning bulk, brown and green, here is the old mossy god that nothing will ever shake, a refuge and harbor for its sons, of whom I am one.

While watching it I finally got through the barbed wire and found myself among the ruins. And under the glorious December light, as happens but once or twice in lives which ever after can consider themselves favored to the full, I found exactly what I had come seeking, what, despite the era and the world, was offered me, truly to me alone, in that forsaken nature. From the forum strewn with olives could be seen the village down below. No sound came from it; wisps of smoke rose in the limpid air. The sea likewise was silent as if smothered under the unbroken shower of dazzling, cold light. From the Chenoua a distant cock's crow alone celebrated the day's fragile glory. In the direction of the ruins, as far as the eye could see, there was nothing but pock-marked stones and wormwood, trees and perfect columns in the transparence of the crystalline air. It seemed as if the morning were stabilized, the sun stopped for an incalculable moment. In this light and this silence, years of wrath and night melted slowly away. I listened to an almost forgotten sound within myself as if my heart, long stopped, were calmly beginning to beat again. And awake now, I recognized one by one the imperceptible sounds of which the silence was made up: the figured bass of the birds, the sea's faint, brief sighs at the foot of the rocks, the vibration of the trees, the blind singing of the columns, the rustling of the wormwood plants, the furtive lizards. I heard that; I also listened to the happy torrents rising within me. It seemed to me that I had at last come to harbor, for a moment at least, and that henceforth that moment would be endless. But soon after, the sun rose visibly a degree in the sky. A magpie preluded briefly, and at once, from all directions, birds' songs burst out with energy, jubilation, joyful discordance, and infinite rapture. The day started up again. It was to carry me to evening.

At noon on the half-sandy slopes covered with heliotropes like a foam left by the furious waves of the last few days as they withdrew, I watched the sea barely swelling at that hour with an exhausted motion, and I satisfied the two thirsts one cannot long neglect without drying up—I mean loving and admiring. For there is merely bad luck in not being loved; there is misfortune in not loving. All of us, today, are dying of this misfortune. For violence and hatred dry up the heart itself; the long fight for justice exhausts the love that nevertheless gave birth to it. In the clamor in which we live, love is impossible and justice does not suffice. This is why Europe hates daylight and is only able to set injustice up against injustice. But in order to keep justice from shriveling up like a beautiful orange fruit containing nothing but a bitter, dry pulp, I discovered once more at Tipasa that one must keep intact in oneself a freshness, a cool wellspring of joy, love the day that escapes injustice, and return to combat having won that light. Here I recaptured the former beauty, a young sky, and I measured my luck, realizing at last that in the worst years of our madness the memory of that sky had never left me. This was what in the end had kept me from despairing. I had always known that the ruins of Tipasa were younger than our new constructions or our bomb damage. There the world began over again every day in an ever new light. O light! This is the cry of all the characters of ancient drama brought face to face with their fate. This last resort was ours, too, and I knew it now. In the middle of winter I at last discovered that there was in me an invincible summer.

I have again left Tipasa; I have returned to Europe and its struggles. But the memory of that day still uplifts me and helps me to welcome equally what delights and what crushes. In the difficult hour we are living, what else can I desire than to exclude nothing and to learn how to braid with white thread and black thread a single cord stretched to the breaking-point? In everything I have done or said up to now, I seem to recognize these two forces, even when they work at cross-purposes. I have not been able to disown the light into which I was born and yet I have not wanted to reject the servitudes of this time. It would be too easy to contrast here with the sweet name of Tipasa other more sonorous and crueler names. For men of today there is an inner way, which I know well from having taken it in both directions, leading from the spiritual hilltops to the capitals of crime. And doubtless one can always rest, fall asleep on the hilltop or board with crime. But if one forgoes a part of what is, one must forgo being oneself; one must forgo living or loving otherwise than by proxy. There is thus a will to live without rejecting anything of life, which is the virtue I honor most in this world. From time to time, at least, it is true that I should like to have practiced it. Inasmuch as few epochs require as much as ours that one should be equal to the best as to the worst, I should like, indeed, to shirk nothing and to keep faithfully a double memory. Yes, there is beauty and there are the humiliated. Whatever may be the difficulties of the undertaking, I should like never to be unfaithful either to one or to the others.

But this still resembles a moral code, and we live for something that goes farther than morality. If we could only name it, what silence! On the hill of Sainte-Salsa, to the east of Tipasa, the evening is inhabited. It is still light, to tell the truth, but in this light an almost invisible fading announces the day's end. A wind rises, young like the night, and suddenly the waveless sea chooses a direction and flows like a great barren river from one end of the horizon to the other. The sky darkens. Then begins the mystery, the gods of night, the beyond-pleasure. But how to translate this? The little coin I am carrying away from here has a visible surface, a woman's beautiful face which repeats to me all I have learned in this day, and a worn surface which I feel under my fingers during the return. What can that lipless mouth be saying, except what I am told by another mysterious voice, within me, which every day informs me of my ignorance and my happiness:

"The secret I am seeking lies hidden in a valley full of olive trees, under the grass and the cold violets, around an old house that smells of wood smoke. For more than twenty years I rambled over that valley and others resembling it, I questioned mute goatherds, I knocked at the door of deserted ruins. Occasionally, at the moment of the first star in the still bright sky, under a shower of shimmering light, I thought I knew. I did know, in truth. I still know, perhaps. But no one wants any of this secret; I don't want any myself, doubtless; and I cannot stand apart from my people. I live in my family, which thinks it rules over rich and hideous cities built of stones and mists. Day and night it speaks up, and everything bows before it, which bows before nothing: it is deaf to all secrets. Its power that carries me bores me, nevertheless, and on occasion its shouts weary me. But its misfortune is mine, and we are of the same blood. A cripple, likewise, an accomplice and noisy, have I not shouted among the stones? Consequently, I strive to forget, I walk in our cities of iron and fire, I smile bravely at the night, I hail the storms, I shall be faithful. I have forgotten, in truth: active and deaf, henceforth. But perhaps someday, when we are ready to die of exhaustion and ignorance, I shall be able to disown our garish tombs and go and stretch out in the valley, under the same light, and learn for the last time what I know.''

Bernard Malamud (b. 1914)
Take Pity

Davidov, the census-taker, opened the door without knocking, limped into the room and sat wearily down. Out came his notebook and he was on the job. Rosen, the ex-coffee salesman, wasted, eyes despairing, sat motionless, cross-legged, on his cot. The square, clean but cold room, lit by a dim globe, was sparsely furnished: the cot, a folding chair, small table, old unpainted chests—no closets but who needed them?—and a small sink with a rough piece of green, institutional soap on its holder—you could smell it across the room. The worn black shade over the single narrow window was drawn to the ledge, surprising Davidov.

"What's the matter you don't pull the shade up?" he remarked.

Rosen ultimately sighed. "Let it stay."

"Why? Outside is light."

"Who needs light?"

"What then you need?"

"Light I don't need," replied Rosen.

Davidov, sour-faced, flipped through the closely scrawled pages of his note-book until he found a clean one. He attempted to scratch in a word with his fountain pen but it had run dry, so he fished a pencil stub out of his vest pocket and sharpened it with a cracked razor blade. Rosen paid no attention to the feathery shavings falling to the floor. He looked restless, seemed to be listening to or for something, although Davidov was convinced there was absolutely nothing to listen to. It was only when the census-taker somewhat irritably and with increasing loudness repeated a question, that Rosen stirred and identified himself. He was about to furnish an address but caught himself and shrugged.

Davidov did not comment on the salesman's gesture. "So begin," he nodded.

"Who knows where to begin?" Rosen stared at the drawn shade. "Do they know here where to begin?"

"Philosophy we are not interested," said Davidov. "Start in how you met her."

"Who?" pretended Rosen.

"Her," he snapped.

"So if I got to begin, how you know about her already?" Rosen asked triumphantly.

Davidov spoke wearily, "You mentioned before."

Rosen remembered. They had questioned him upon his arrival and he now recalled blurting out her name. It was perhaps something in the air. It did not permit you to retain what you remembered. That was part of the cure, if you wanted a cure.

"Where I met her—?" Rosen murmured. "I met her where she always was—in the back room there in that hole in the wall that it was a waste of time for me I went there. Maybe I sold them a half a bag of coffee a month. This is not business."

"In business we are not interested."

"What then you are interested?" Rosen mimicked Davidov's tone.

Davidov clammed up coldly.

Rosen knew they had him where it hurt, so he went on: "The husband was maybe forty, Axel Kalish, a Polish refugee. He worked like a blind horse when he got to America, and saved maybe two—three thousand dollars that he bought with the money this pisher[1] grocery in a dead neighborhood where he didn't have a chance. He called my company up for credit and they sent me I should see. I recommended okay because I felt sorry. He had a wife, Eva, you know already about her, and two darling girls, one five and one three, little dolls, Fega and Surale, that I didn't want them to suffer. So right away I told him, without tricks, 'Kiddo, this is a mistake. This place is a grave. Here they will bury you if you don't get out quick!'"

Rosen sighed deeply.

"So?" Davidov had thus far written nothing, irking the ex-salesman.

"So?—Nothing. He didn't get out. After a couple months he tried to sell but nobody bought, so he stayed and starved. They never made expenses. Every day they got poorer you couldn't look in their faces. 'Don't be a damn fool,' I told him, 'go in bankruptcy.' But he couldn't stand it to lose all his capital, and he was also afraid it would be hard to find a job. 'My God,' I said, 'do anything. Be a painter, a janitor, a junk man, but get out of here before everybody is a skeleton.'

"This he finally agreed with me, but before he could go in auction he dropped dead."

Davidov made a note. "How did he die?"

"On this I am not an expert," Rosen replied. "You know better than me."

"How did he die?" Davidov spoke impatiently. "Say in one word."

"From what he died?—he died, that's all."

"Answer, please, this question."

"Broke in him something. That's how."

"Broke what?"

"Broke what breaks. He was talking to me how bitter was his life, and he touched me on my sleeve to say something else, but the next minute his face got small and he fell down dead, the wife screaming, the little girls crying that it made in my heart pain. I am myself a sick man and when I saw him laying on

---

1. Piddling; insignificant.

the floor, I said to myself, 'Rosen, say goodbye, this guy is finished.' So I said it.''

Rosen got up from the cot and strayed despondently around the room, avoiding the window. Davidov was occupying the only chair, so the ex-salesman was finally forced to sit on the edge of the bed again. This irritated him. He badly wanted a cigarette but disliked asking for one.

Davidov permitted him a short interval of silence, then leafed impatiently through his notebook. Rosen, to needle the census-taker, said nothing.

''So what happened?'' Davidov finally demanded.

Rosen spoke with ashes in his mouth. ''After the funeral—'' he paused, tried to wet his lips, then went on, '' He belonged to a society that they buried him, and he also left a thousand dollars insurance, but after the funeral I said to her, 'Eva, listen to me. Take the money and your children and run away from here. Let the creditors take the store. What will they get?—Nothing.'

'' But she answered me, 'Where will I go, where, with my two orphans that their father left them to starve?'

'' 'Go anywhere,' I said. 'Go to your relatives.'

''She laughed like laughs somebody who hasn't got no joy. 'My relatives Hitler took away from me.'

'' 'What about Axel—surely an uncle somewheres?'

'' 'Nobody,' she said, 'I will stay here like my Axel wanted. With the insurance I will buy new stock and fix up the store. Every week I will decorate the window, and in this way gradually will come in new customers—'

'' 'Eva, my darling girl—'

'' 'A millionaire I don't expect to be. All I want is I should make a little living and take care on my girls. We will live in the back here like before, and in this way I can work and watch them, too.'

'' 'Eva,' I said, 'you are a nice-looking young woman, only thirty-eight years. Don't throw away your life here. Don't flush in the toilet—you should excuse me—the thousand poor dollars from your dead husband. Believe me, I know from such stores. After thirty-five years' experience I know a graveyard when I smell it. Go better some place and find a job. You're young yet. Sometime you will meet somebody and get married.'

'' 'No, Rosen, not me,' she said. 'With marriage I am finished. Nobody wants a poor widow with two children.'

'' 'This I don't believe it.'

'' 'I know,' she said.

''Never in my life I saw so bitter a woman's face.

'' 'No,' I said. 'No.'

'' 'Yes, Rosen, yes. In my whole life I never had anything. In my whole life I always suffered. I don't expect better. This is my life.'

''I said no and she said yes. What could I do? I am a man with only one kidney, and worse than that, that I won't mention it. When I talked she didn't listen, so I stopped to talk. Who can argue with a widow?''

The ex-salesman glanced up at Davidov but the census-taker did not reply. ''What happened then?'' he asked.

''What happened?'' mocked Rosen. ''Happened what happens.''

Davidov's face grew red.

''What happened, happened,'' Rosen said hastily. '' She ordered from the wholesalers all kinds goods that she paid for them cash. All week she opened boxes and packed on the shelves cans, jars, packages. Also she cleaned, and she washed, and she mopped with oil the floor. With tissue paper she made new decorations in the window, everything should look nice—but who came in? Nobody except a few poor customers from the tenement around the corner. And when they came? When was closed the supermarkets and they needed some little item that they forgot to buy, like a quart milk, fifteen cents' cheese, a small can sardines for lunch. In a few months was again dusty the cans on the shelves, and her thousand was gone. Credit she couldn't get except from me, and from me she got because I paid out of my pocket the company. This she didn't know. She worked, she dressed clean, she waited that the store should get better. Little by little the shelves got empty, but where was the profit? They ate it up. When I looked on the little girls I knew what she didn't tell me. Their faces were white, they were thin, they were hungry. She kept the little food that was left, on the shelves. One night I brought in a nice piece sirloin, but I could see from her eyes that she didn't like that I did it. So what else could I do? I have a heart and I am human.''

Here the ex-salesman wept.

Davidov pretended not to see though once he peeked.

Rosen blew his nose, then went on more calmly, ''When the children were sleeping we sat in the dark there, in the back, and not once in four hours opened the door should come in a customer. 'Eva, for Godsakes, *run away*,' I said.

'' 'I have no place to go,' she said.

'' 'I will give you where you can go, and please don't say to me no. I am a bachelor, this you know. I got whatever I need and more besides. Let me help you and the children. Money don't interest me. Interests me good health, but I can't buy it. I'll tell you what I will do. Let this place go to the creditors and move into a two-family house that I own, which the top floor is now empty. Rent will cost you nothing. In the meantime you can go and find a job. I will also pay the downstairs lady to take care of the girls—God bless them—until you will come home. With your wages you will buy the food, if you need clothes, and also save a little. This you can use when you get married someday. What do you say?'

''She didn't answer me. She only looked on me in such a way, with such burning eyes, like I was small and ugly. For the first time I thought to myself, 'Rosen, this woman don't like you.'

'' 'Thank you very kindly, my friend Mr. Rosen,' she answered me, 'but charity we are not needing. I got yet a paying business, and it will get better when times are better. Now is bad times. When comes again good times will get better the business.'

'' 'Who charity?' I cried to her. 'What charity? Speaks to you your husband's a friend.'

'' 'Mr. Rosen, my husband didn't have no friends.'

'' 'Can't you see that I want to help the children?'

'' 'The children have their mother.'

'' 'Eva, what's the matter with you?' I said. 'Why do you make sound bad something that I mean it should be good?'

''This she didn't answer. I felt sick in my stomach, and was coming also a headache so I left.

'' All night I didn't sleep, and then all of a sudden I figured out a reason why she was worried. She was worried I would ask for some kind payment except cash. She got the wrong man. Anyway, this made me think of something that I didn't think about before. I thought now to ask her to marry me. What did she have to lose? I could take care of myself without any trouble to them. Fega and Surale would have a father he could give them for the movies, or sometime to buy a little doll to play with, and when I died, would go to them my investments and insurance policies.

"The next day I spoke to her.

" 'For myself, Eva, I don't want a thing. Absolutely not a thing. For you and your girls—everything. I am not a strong man, Eva. In fact, I am sick. I tell you this you should understand I don't expect to live long. But even for a few years would be nice to have a little family.'

"She was with her back to me and didn't speak.

"When she turned around again her face was white but the mouth was like iron.

" 'No, Mr. Rosen.'

" 'Why not, tell me?'

" 'I had enough with sick men.' She began to cry. 'Please, Mr. Rosen. Go home.'

"I didn't have strength I should argue with her, so I went home. I went home but hurt me my mind. All day long and all night I felt bad. My back pained me where was missing my kidney. Also too much smoking. I tried to understand this woman but I couldn't. Why should somebody that her two children were starving always say no to a man that he wanted to help her? What did I do to her bad? Am I maybe a murderer she should hate me so much? All that I felt in my heart was pity for her and the children, but I couldn't convince her. Then I went back and begged her she should let me help them, and once more she told me no.

" 'Eva,' I said, 'I don't blame you that you don't want a sick man. So come with me to a marriage broker and we will find you a strong, healthy husband that he will support you and your girls. I will give the dowry.'

"She screamed, 'On this I don't need your help, Rosen!'

"I didn't say no more. What more could I say? All day long, from early in the morning till late in the night she worked like an animal. All day she mopped, she washed with soap and a brush the shelves, the few cans she polished, but the store was still rotten. The little girls I was afraid to look at. I could see in their faces their bones. They were tired, they were weak. Little Surale held with her hand all the time the dress of Fega. Once when I saw them in the street I gave them some cakes, but when I tried the next day to give them something else, the mother shouldn't know, Fega answered me, 'We can't take, Momma says today is a fast day.'

"I went inside. I made my voice soft. 'Eva, on my bended knee, I am a man with nothing in this world. Allow me that I should have a little pleasure before I die. Allow me that I should help you stock up once more the store.'

"So what did she do? She cried, it was terrible to see. And after she cried, what did she say? She told me to go away and I shouldn't come back. I felt like to pick up a chair and break her head.

"In my house I was too weak to eat. For two days I took in my mouth nothing except maybe a spoon of chicken noodle soup, or maybe a glass tea without sugar. This wasn't good for me. My health felt bad.

"Then I made up a scheme that I was a friend of Axel's who lived in Jersey. I said I owed Axel seven hundred dollars that he lent me this money fifteen years ago, before he got married. I said I did not have the whole money now, but I would send her every week twenty dollars till it was paid up the debt. I put inside the letter two tens and gave it to a friend of mine, also a salesman, he should mail it in Newark so she would not be suspicious who wrote the letters."

To Rosen's surprise Davidov had stopped writing. The book was full, so he tossed it onto the table, yawned, but listened amiably. His curiosity had died.

Rosen got up and fingered the notebook. He tried to read the small distorted handwriting but could not make out a single word.

"It's not English and it's not Yiddish," he said. "Could it be in Hebrew?"

"No," answered Davidov. "It's an old-fashioned language that they don't use it nowadays."

"Oh?" Rosen returned to the cot. He saw no purpose to going on now that it was not required, but he felt he had to.

"Came back all the letters," he said dully. "The first she opened it, then pasted back again the envelope, but the rest she didn't even open."

" 'Here,' I said to myself, 'is a very strange thing—a person that you can never give her anything.—*But I will give.*'

"I went then to my lawyer and we made out a will that everything I had—all my investments, my two houses that I owned, also furniture, my car, the checking account—every cent would go to her, and when she died, the rest would be left for the two girls. The same with my insurance. They would be my beneficiaries. Then I signed and went home. In the kitchen I turned on the gas and put my head in the stove.

"Let her say now no."

Davidov, scratching his stubbled cheek, nodded. This was the part he already knew. He got up and before Rosen could cry no, idly raised the window shade.

It was twilight in space but a woman stood before the window.

Rosen with a bound was off his cot to see.

It was Eva, staring at him with haunted, beseeching eyes. She raised her arms to him.

Infuriated, the ex-salesman shook his fist.

"Whore, bastard, bitch," he shouted at her. "Go 'way from here. Go home to your children."

Davidov made no move to hinder him as Rosen rammed down the window shade.

Jean Stafford (b. 1915)
The Maiden

"I bought the pair of them in Berlin for forty marks,"[1] Mrs. Andreas was saying to Dr. Reinmuth, who had admired the twin decanters on her dinner table. "It sickens me, the way they must let their treasures go for nothing. I can take no pride in having got a bargain when I feel like a pirate." Evan Leckie, an American journalist who was the extra man at the party, turned away from the woman on his right to glance at his hostess to see if her face revealed the hypocrisy he had heard, ever so faintly, in her voice, but he could read nothing in her bland eyes, nor could he discover the reaction of her interlocutor, who slightly inclined his head in acknowledgment of her sympathy for his moritified compatriots but said nothing and resumed his affectionate scrutiny of the decanters as Mrs. Andreas went on to enumerate other instances of the victors' gains through the Germans' losses. Evan, just transferred to Heidelberg from the squalor and perdition of Nuremberg,[2] joined in the German's contemplation of these relics of more handsome times. One of the bottles was filled with red wine, which gleamed darkly through the lustrous, sculptured glass, chased with silver, and the other with pale, sunny Chablis. The candlelight invested the wines with a property beyond taste and fluidity, a subtle grace belonging to a world almost imaginary in its elegance, and for a moment Evan warmed toward Mrs. Andreas, who had tried to resuscitate this charming world for her guests by putting the decanters in the becoming company of heavy, florid silverware and Dresden fruit plates and a bowl of immaculate white roses, and by dressing herself, a plump and unexceptional person, in an opulent frock of gold brocade and a little queenly crown of amethysts for her curly, graying hair.

The double doors to the garden were open to admit the moonlight and the summer breeze, and now and again, in the course of the meal, Evan had glanced out and had seen luminous nicotiana and delphiniums growing profusely beside a high stone wall. Here, in the hilly section of the city, it was as quiet as in the country; there was not a sound of jeeps or drunken G.I.s to disturb the light and general conversation of Americans breaking bread with Germans. Only by implication and indirection were the war and the Occupation[3] spoken of, and in this abandonment of the contemporary, the vanquished, these charming Reinmuths, save by their dress and their speech, could not be distinguished from the conquerors. If chivalry, thought Evan, were ever to return to the world, peace would come with it, but evenings like this were isolated, were all but lost in the vast, arid wastes of the present hour within the present decade. And the pity that Mrs. Andreas bestowed upon her German guests would not return to them the decanters they had forfeited, nor would her hospitality obliterate from their hearts the knowledge of their immense dilemma. Paradox-

---

1. The mark is the basic monetary unit of Germany; today the West German mark is worth roughly 40 cents.
2. German city where, in 1945–46, 26 former Nazi leaders were brought to trial as war criminals by the International Military Tribunal; 11 were eventually executed.
3. The military occupation of Germany by the Allied forces following World War II.

ically, it was only upon the highest possible level that Germans and Americans these days could communicate with one another; only a past that was now irretrievable could bring them into harmony.

For the past month in Nuremberg, ever since Evan's wife, Virginia, had left him—left him, as she had put it in a shout, "to stew in his own juice"—Evan had spent his evenings in the bar of his hotel, drinking by himself and listening, in a trance of boredom, to the conversations of the Americans about him. The mirrored walls and mirrored ceilings had cast back the manifold reflections of able-bodied WACs in summer uniforms, who talked of their baseball teams (once he had seen a phalanx of them in the lobby, armed with bats and catchers' mitts, looking no less manly than the Brooklyn Dodgers) and of posts where they had been stationed and of itineraries, past and future. "Where were you in '45?" he had heard one of them cry. "New Caledonia! My God! So was I. Isn't it a riot to think we were both in New Caledonia in '45 and now are here in the Theater?"[4] Things had come to a pretty pass, thought Evan, when *this* was the theater of a young girl's dreams. They did not talk like women and they did not look like women but like a modern mutation, a revision, perhaps more efficient and sturdier, of an old model. Half hypnotized by the signs of the times, he had come almost to believe that the days of men and women were over and that the world had moved into a new era dominated by a neuter body called Personnel, whose only concerns were to make history and to snub the history that had already been made. Miss Sally Dean, who sat across from him tonight, had pleased him at first glance with her bright-blond hair and her alabaster shoulders and the fine length of her legs, but over the cocktails his delight departed when, in the accents of West Los Angeles, she had said she wished General MacArthur were in Germany, since he was, in her opinion, a "real glamour puss." The woman on his right, Mrs. Crowell, the wife of a judge from Ohio in the judiciary of the Occupation, was obsessively loquacious; for a very long time she had been delivering to him a self-sustaining monologue on the effronteries of German servants, announcing once, with all the authority of an anthropologist, that "the Baden mind is *consecrated* to dishonesty." He could not put his finger on it, but, in spite of her familiar housewife's complaints, she did not sound at all like his mother and his aunts in Charlottesville, whose lives, spun out in loving domesticity, would lose their pungency if cooks kept civil tongues in their heads and if upstairs maids were not light-fingered. Mrs. Crowell brought to her housekeeping problems a modern and impersonal intellect. "The Baden mind," "the Franconian[5] mind," "the German character" were phrases that came forth irrefutably. And the bluestocking wife of a Captain McNaughton, who sat on Evan's left and who taught library science to the wives of other Army officers, had all evening lectured Dr. Reinmuth on the faults (remediable, in her opinion) of his generation that had forced the world into war. Dr. Reinmuth was a lawyer. She was herself a warrior; she argued hotly, although the German did not oppose her, and sometimes she threatened him with her spoon.

It was the German woman, Frau Reinmuth, who, although her gray dress was modest and although she wore no jewels and little rouge, captivated Evan

---

4. The European Theater of Operations, the name for the Allied military operations in western Europe in World War II.

5. Baden and Franconia are regions in southern Germany.

with her ineffable femininity; she, of all the women there, had been challenged by violence and she had ignored it, had firmly and with great poise set it aside. To look at her, no one would know that the slightest alteration had taken place in the dignified modus vivendi[6] she must have known all her life. The serenity she emanated touched him so warmly and so deeply that he almost loved her, and upon the recognition of his feeling he was seized with loneliness and with a sort of homesickness that he felt sure she would understand—a longing, it was, for the places that *she* would remember. Suddenly it occurred to him that the only other time he had been in Heidelberg, he had been here with his wife, two years before, and they had gone one afternoon by trolley to Schwetzingen to see the palace gardens. Virginia had always hated history and that day she had looked at a cool Louis Quatorze[7] summerhouse, designed for witty persiflage and premeditated kisses, and had said, "It's so chichi[8] it makes me sick." And she had meant it. How she had prided herself on despising everything that had been made before 1920, the year of her birth! Staring at the wines aglow in their fine vessels, Evan recaptured exactly the feeling he had had that day in Schwetzingen when, very abruptly, he had realized that he was only technically bound for life to this fretful iconoclast; for a short while, there beside the playing fountains, he had made her vanish and in her place there stood a quiet woman, rich in meditations and in fancies. If he had known Frau Reinmuth then, she might have been the one he thought of.

Evan watched Dr. Reinmuth as he poured the gold and garnet liquids, first one and then the other, into the glasses before his plate. The little lawyer closely attended the surge of color behind the radiant crystal and he murmured, in a soft Bavarian voice, "Lovely, lovely. Look, Liselotte, how beautiful Mrs. Andreas' *Karaffen*[9] are!" Frau Reinmuth, wide-faced, twice his size, turned from her talk of the Salzburg Festival with Mr. Andreas and cherished both her husband and the decanters with her broad gray eyes, in whose depths love lay limitlessly. When she praised the design of the cut glass, and the etching of the silver, and the shape of the stoppers, like enormous diamonds, she managed somehow, through the timbre of her voice or its cadences or through the way she looked at him, to proclaim that she loved her husband and that the beauty of the bottles was rivaled and surpassed by the nature of this little man of hers, who, still fascinated, moved his handsome head this way and that, the better to see the prismatic green and violet beams that burst from the shelves and crannies of the glass. His movements were quick and delicately articulated, like a small animal's, and his slender fingers touched and traced the glass as if he were playing a musical instrument that only his ears could hear. He must have been in his middle forties, but he looked like a nervous, gifted boy not twenty yet, he was so slight, his hair was so black and curly, his brown face was so lineless, and there was such candor and curiosity in his dark eyes. He seemed now to want to carry his visual and tactile encounter with the decanters to a further point, to a completion, to bliss. And Evan, arrested by the man's absorption (if it was not that of a child, it was that of an artist bent on abstracting meanings from all the data presented to his senses), found it hard to

---

6. "Manner of living."
7. Louis XIV (1643–1715), French monarch.
8. Excessively ornamental; gaudy.
9. "Decanters."

imagine him arguing in a court of law, where the materials, no matter how one elevated and embellished justice, were not poetry. Equally difficult was it to see him as he had been during the war, in his role of interpreter for the German Army in Italy. Like every German one met in a polite American house, Dr. Reinmuth had been an enemy of the Third Reich;[10] he had escaped concentration camp only because his languages were useful to the Nazis. While Evan, for the most part, was suspicious of these self-named martyrs who seemed always to have fetched up in gentlemanly jobs where their lives were not in the least imperiled, he did believe in Dr. Reinmuth, and was certain that a belligerent ideology could not enlist the tender creature so unaffectedly playing with Mrs. Andreas' toys, so obviously well beloved by his benevolent wife. Everyone, even Mrs. Crowell, paused a second to look from the man to the woman and to esteem their concord.

Frau Reinmuth then returned to Mr. Andreas, but it was plain to see that her mind was only half with him. She said, "I envy you to hear Flagstad.[11] Our pain is that there is no music now," and in a lower voice she added, "I have seen August bite his lip for sorrow when he goes past the opera house in Mannheim. It's nothing now, you know, but a ruin, like everything." Glancing at her, Evan wondered whether she were older than her husband or if this marriage had been entered upon late, and he concluded that perhaps the second was true, for they were childless—the downright Mrs. McNaughton had determined that before the canapés were passed—and Frau Reinmuth looked born to motherhood. But even more telling was the honeymoon inflection in her voice, as if she were still marveling how to say the name "August" as easily as she said "I" and to be able to bestow these limnings of her dearest possession generously on the members of a dinner party. It was not that she spoke of him as if he were a child, as some women do who marry late or marry men younger than themselves, but as if he were a paragon with whom she had the remarkable honor to be associated. She, in her boundless patience, could endure being deprived of music and it was not for herself that she complained, but she could not bear to see August's grief over the hush that lay upon their singing country; she lived not only for, she lived *in*, him. She wore her yellow hair in Germanic braids that coiled around her head, sitting too low to be smart; her hands were soft and large, honestly meriting the wide wedding band on the right one. She was as completely a woman as Virginia, in spite of a kind of ravening femaleness and piquant good looks, had never been one. He shuddered to think how she must be maligning him in Nevada to the other angry petitioners, and then he tried to imagine how Frau Reinmuth would behave under similar circumstances. But it was unthinkable that she should ever be a divorcée; no matter what sort of man she married, this wifely woman would somehow, he was sure, quell all disorder. Again he felt a wave of affection for her; he fancied drinking tea with her in a little crowded drawing room at the end of one of these warm days, and he saw himself walking with both the Reinmuths up through the hills behind the Philosophenweg, proving to the world by their compassionate amity that there was no longer a state of war between their country and his.

But he was prevented from spinning out his fantasy of a friendship with the

---

10. The Nazi regime in Germany (1933–45).
11. Kirsten Flagstad (1895–1962), popular Norwegian operatic soprano.

Reinmuths because Mrs. Crowell was demanding his attention. Her present servant, she told him, was an aristocrat ("as aristocratic as a German can be," she said sotto voce,[12] "which isn't saying much") and might therefore be expected not to steal the spoons; now, having brought him up to date on her belowstairs problems, she changed the subject and drew him into the orbit of her bright-eyed, pervasive bustling. She understood that he had just come from Nuremberg, where she and the Judge had lived for two years. "Isn't it too profoundly *triste?*"[13] she cried. "Where did they billet you, poor thing?"

"At the Grand Hotel," said Evan, recollecting the WACs with their mustaches and their soldierly patois.[14.]

"Oh, no!" protested Mrs. Cromwell. "But it's simply *overrun* with awful Army children! Not children—brats. Brats, I'm sorry to say, is the only word for them. They actually roller-skate through the lobby, you know, to say nothing of the *ghastly* noise they make. I used to go to the hairdresser there and finally had to give up because of the hullabaloo."

At the mention of Nuremberg, Dr. Reinmuth had pivoted around toward them and now, speaking across Mrs. McNaughton, he said dreamily, "Once it was a lovely town. We lived there, my wife and I, all our lives until the war. I understand there is now a French orchestra in the opera house that plays calypso for your soldiers." There sounded in his voice the same note of wonder that he had used when he acclaimed the decanters that he could not own; neither could he again possess the beauties of his birthplace. And Evan Leckie, to whom the genesis of war had always been incomprehensible, looked with astonishment at these two pacific Germans and pondered how the whole hideous mistake had come about, what Eumenides[15] had driven this pair to hardship, humiliation, and exile. Whatever else they were, however alien their values might be, these enemies were, *sub specie aeternitatis,*[16] of incalculable worth if for no other reason than that, in an unloving world, they loved.

Mrs. Andreas, tactfully refusing Dr. Reinmuth's gambit, since she knew that the deterioration of the Nuremberg Opera House into a night club must be a painful subject to him, maneuvered her guests until the talk at the table became general. They all continued the exchange that had begun with Frau Reinmuth and Mr. Andreas on the Salzburg Festival; they went on to speak of Edinburgh, of the *Salome* that someone had heard at La Scala, of a coloratura who had delighted the Reinmuths in Weimar. Dr. Reinmuth then told the story of his having once defended a pianist who had been sued for slander by a violinist; the defendant had been accused of saying publicly that the plaintiff played Mozart as if the music had been written for the barrel organ and that the only thing missing was a monkey to take up a collection. This anecdote, coinciding with the arrival of the dessert, diverted the stream of talk, and Judge Crowell, whose interest in music was perfunctory and social, revived and took the floor. He told of a murder case he had tried the week before in Frankfurt and of a rape case on the docket in Stuttgart. Dr. Reinmuth countered with cases he was pleading; they matched their legal wits, made Latin puns, and so enjoyed their

---

12. Very softly; privately.
13. "Sad."
14. Jargon.
15. In Greek mythology the Eumenides, or Furies, were goddesses of vengeance who punished their victims by driving them insane.
16. "From the point of view of eternity."

game that the others laughed, although they barely understood the meanings of the words.

Dr. Reinmuth, who was again fondling the decanters, said, "I suppose every lawyer is fond of telling the story of his first case. May I tell mine?" He besought his hostess with an endearing smile, and his wife, forever at his side, pleaded for him, "Oh, do!" and she explained, "It's such an extraordinary story of a young lawyer's first case."

He poured himself a little more Chablis and smiled and began. When he was twenty-three, in Nuremberg, just down from Bonn, with no practice at all, he had one day been called upon by the state to defend a man who had confessed to murdering an old woman and robbing her of sixty pfennig.[17] The defense, of course, was purely a convention, and the man was immediately sentenced to death, since there was no question of his guilt or of the enormity of his crime. Some few days after the trial, Dr. Reinmuth had received an elaborate engraved invitation to the execution by guillotine, which was to be carried out in the courtyard of the Justizpalast one morning a day or so later, punctually at seven o'clock. He was instructed, in an accompanying letter, to wear a Prince Albert[18] and a top hat.

Mrs. Andreas was shocked. "Guillotine? Did you *have* to go?"

Dr. Reinmuth smiled and bowed to her. "No, I was not required. It was, you see, my *right* to go, as the advocate of the prisoner."

Judge Crowell laughed deeply. "Your first case, eh, Reinmuth?" And Dr. Reinmuth spread out his hands in a mock gesture of deprecation.

"My fellow-spectators were three judges from the bench," he continued, "who were dressed, like myself, in Prince Alberts and cylinders. We were a little early when we got to the courtyard, so that we saw the last-minute preparations of the stage before the play began. Near the guillotine, with its great knife—that blade, my God in Heaven!—there stood a man in uniform with a drum, ready to drown out the sound if my client should yell."

The dimmest of frowns had gathered on Judge Crowell's forehead. "All this pomp and circumstance for sixty pfennigs?" he said.

"Right you are, sir," replied Dr. Reinmuth. "That is the irony of my story." He paused to eat a strawberry and to take a sip of wine. "Next we watched them test the machine to make sure it was in proper—shall I say decapitating?—condition. When they released it, the cleaver came down with such stupendous force that the earth beneath our feet vibrated and my brains buzzed like a bee.

"As the bells began to ring for seven, Herr Murderer was led out by two executioners, dressed as we were dressed. Their white gloves were spotless! It was a glorious morning in May. The flowers were out, the birds were singing, the sky had not a cloud. To have your head cut off on such a day!"

"For sixty pfennigs!" persisted the judge from Ohio. And Miss Dean, paling, stopped eating her dessert.

"Mein Herr had been confessed and anointed. You could fairly see the holy oil on his forehead as his keepers led him across the paving to the guillotine. The drummer was ready. As the fourth note of the seven struck in the church

---

17. The pfennig is comparable to the U.S. penny; today it is worth a bit less than one-half of a cent.

18. Long double-breasted outer coat named for Prince Albert of England (1841–1910).

towers, they persuaded him to take the position necessary to the success of Dr. Guillotin's invention. One, he was horizontal! Two, the blade descended! Three, the head was off the carcass and the blood shot out from the neck like a volcano, a geyser, the flame from an explosion. No sight I saw in the war was worse. The last stroke of seven sounded. There had been no need for the drum.''

''Great Scott!'' said Mr. Andreas, and flushed.

Captain McNaughton stared at Dr. Reinmuth and said, ''You chaps don't do things by halves, do you?''

Mrs. Andreas, frantic at the dangerous note that had sounded, menacing her party, put her hand lightly on the lawyer's and said, ''I know that then you must have fainted.''

Dr. Reinmuth tilted back his head and smiled at the ceiling. ''No. No, I did not faint. You remember that this was a beautiful day in spring? And that I was a young man, all dressed up at seven in the morning?'' He lowered his head and gave his smile to the whole company. ''Faint! Dear lady, no! I took the tram back to Fürth and I called my sweetheart on the telephone.'' He gazed at his wife. ''Liselotte was surprised, considering the hour. 'What are you thinking of? It's not eight o'clock,' she said. I flustered her then. I said, 'I know it's an unusual time of day to call, but I have something unusual to say. Will you marry me?'''

He clasped his hands together and exchanged with his wife a look as exuberant and shy as if they were in the first rapture of their romance, and, bewitched, she said, ''Twenty years ago next May.''

A silence settled on the room. Whether Evan Leckie was the more dumfounded by Dr. Reinmuth's story of a majestic penalty to fit a sordid crime or by his ostentatious hinting at his connubial delights, he did not know. Evan sought the stunned faces of his countrymen and could not tell in them, either, what feeling was the uppermost. The party suddenly was no longer a whole; it consisted of two parts, the Americans and the Germans, and while the former outnumbered them, the Germans, in a deeper sense, had triumphed. They had joyfully danced a *Totentanz,*[19] had implied all the details of their sixty-pfennig marriage, and they were still, even now, smiling at each other as if there had never been anything untoward in their lives.

''I could take a wife then, you see,'' said Dr. Reinmuth, by way of a dénouement, ''since I was a full-fledged lawyer. And she could not resist me in that finery, which, as a matter of fact, I had had to hire for the occasion.''

Judge Crowell lighted a cigarette, and, snatching at the externals of the tale, he said, ''Didn't know you fellows used the guillotine as late as that. I've never seen one except that one they've got in the antiquarian place in Edinburgh. They call it the Maiden.''

Dr. Reinmuth poured the very last of the Chablis into his glass, and, turning to Mrs. Andreas, he said, ''It was nectar and I've drunk it all. *Sic transit gloria mundi.*''[20]

---

19. Dance of death.
20. ''So passes away the glory of the world.''

Alain Robbe-Grillet (b. 1922)
The Secret Room

The first thing to be seen is a red stain, of a deep, dark, shiny red, with almost black shadows. It is in the form of an irregular rosette, sharply outlined, extending in several directions in wide outflows of unequal length, dividing and dwindling afterward into single sinuous streaks. The whole stands out against a smooth, pale surface, round in shape, at once dull and pearly, a hemisphere joined by gentle curves to an expanse of the same pale color—white darkened by the shadowy quality of the place: a dungeon, a sunken room, or a cathedral—glowing with a diffused brilliance in the semidarkness.

Farther back, the space is filled with the cylindrical trunks of columns, repeated with progressive vagueness in their retreat toward the beginning of a vast stone stairway, turning slightly as it rises, growing narrower and narrower as it approaches the high vaults where it disappears.

The whole setting is empty, stairway and colonnades. Alone, in the foreground, the stretched-out body gleams feebly, marked with the red stain—a white body whose full, supple flesh can be sensed, fragile, no doubt, and vulnerable. Alongside the bloody hemisphere another identical round form, this one intact, is seen at almost the same angle of view; but the haloed point at its summit, of darker tint, is in this case quite recognizable, whereas the other one is entirely destroyed, or at least covered by the wound.

In the background, near the top of the stairway, a black silhouette is seen fleeing, a man wrapped in a long, floating cape, ascending the last steps without turning around, his deed accomplished. A thin smoke rises in twisting scrolls from a sort of incense burner placed on a high stand of ironwork with a silvery glint. Nearby lies the milkwhite body, with wide streaks of blood running from the left breast, along the flank and on the hip.

It is a fully rounded woman's body, but not heavy, completely nude, lying on its back, the bust raised up somewhat by thick cushions thrown down on the floor, which is covered with Oriental rugs. The waist is very narrow, the neck long and thin, curved to one side, the head thrown back into a darker area where, even so, the facial features may be discerned, the partly opened mouth, the wide-staring eyes, shining with a fixed brilliance, and the mass of long, black hair spread out in a complicated wavy disorder over a heavily folded cloth, of velvet perhaps, on which also rest the arm and shoulder.

It is a uniformly colored velvet of dark purple, or which seems so in this lighting. But purple, brown, blue also seem to dominate in the colors of the cushions—only a small portion of which is hidden beneath the velvet cloth, and which protrude noticeably, lower down, beneath the bust and waist—as well as in the Oriental patterns of the rugs on the floor. Farther on, these same colors are picked up again in the stone of the paving and the columns, the vaulted archways, the stairs, and the less discernible surfaces that disappear into the farthest reaches of the room.

The dimensions of this room are difficult to determine exactly; the body of the young sacrificial victim seems at first glance to occupy a substantial portion of it, but the vast size of the stairway leading down to it would imply rather that this is not the whole room, whose considerable space must in reality extend all around, right and left, as it does toward the faraway browns and blues among the columns standing in line, in every direction, perhaps toward other sofas, thick carpets, piles of cushions and fabrics, other tortured bodies, other incense burners.

It is also difficult to say where the light comes from. No clue, on the columns or on the floor, suggests the direction of the rays. Nor is any window or torch visible. The milkwhite body itself seems to light the scene, with its full breasts, the curve of its thighs, the rounded belly, the full buttocks, the stretched-out legs, widely spread, and the black tuft of the exposed sex, provocative, proffered, useless now.

The man has already moved several steps back. He is now on the first steps of the stairs, ready to go up. The bottom steps are wide and deep, like the steps leading up to some great building, a temple or theater; they grow smaller as they ascend, and at the same time describe a wide, helical curve, so gradually that the stairway has not yet made a half-turn by the time it disappears near the top of the vaults, reduced then to a steep, narrow flight of steps without handrail, vaguely outlined, moreover, in the thickening darkness beyond.

But the man does not look in this direction, where his movement nonetheless carries him; his left foot on the second step and his right foot already touching the third, with his knee bent, he has turned around to look at the spectacle for one last time. The long, floating cape thrown hastily over his shoulders, clasped in one hand at his waist, has been whirled around by the rapid circular motion that has just caused his head and chest to turn in the opposite direction, and a corner of the cloth remains suspended in the air as if blown by a gust of wind; this corner, twisting around upon itself in the form of a loose S, reveals the red silk lining with its gold embroidery.

The man's features are impassive, but tense, as if in expectation—or perhaps fear—of some sudden event, or surveying with one last glance the total immobility of the scene. Though he is looking backward, his whole body is turned slightly forward, as if he were continuing up the stairs. His right arm—not the one holding the edge of the cape—is bent sharply toward the left, toward a point in space where the balustrade should be, if this stairway had one, an interrupted gesture, almost incomprehensible, unless it arose from an instinctive movement to grasp the absent support.

As to the direction of his glance, it is certainly aimed at the body of the victim lying on the cushions, its extended members stretched out in the form of a cross, its bust raised up, its head thrown back. But the face is perhaps hidden from the man's eyes by one of the columns, standing at the foot of the stairs. The young woman's right hand touches the floor just at the foot of the column. The fragile wrist is encircled by an iron bracelet. The arm is almost in darkness, only the hand receiving enough light to make the thin, outspread fingers clearly visible against the circular protrusion at the base of the stone column. A black metal chain running around the column passes through a ring affixed to the bracelet, binding the wrist tightly to the column.

At the top of the arm a rounded shoulder, raised up by the cushions, also stands out well lighted, as well as the neck, the throat, and the other shoulder, the armpit with its soft hair, the left arm likewise pulled back with its wrist bound in the same manner to the base of another column, in the extreme foreground; here the iron bracelet and the chain are fully displayed, represented with perfect clarity down to the slightest details.

The same is true, still in the foreground but at the other side, for a similar chain, but not quite as thick, wound directly around the ankle, running twice around the column and terminating in a heavy iron ring embedded in the floor. About a yard further back, or perhaps slightly farther, the right foot is identically chained. But it is the left foot, and its chain, that are the most minutely depicted.

The foot is small, delicate, finely modeled. In several places the chain has broken the skin, causing noticeable if not extensive depressions in the flesh. The chain links are oval, thick, the size of an eye. The ring in the floor resembles those used to attach horses; it lies almost touching the stone pavement to which it is riveted by a massive iron peg. A few inches away is the edge of a rug; it is grossly wrinkled at this point, doubtless as a result of the convulsive, but necessarily very restricted, movements of the victim attempting to struggle.

The man is still standing about a yard away, half leaning over her. He looks at her face, seen upside down, her dark eyes made larger by their surrounding eye-shadow, her mouth wide open as if screaming. The man's posture allows his face to be seen only in a vague profile, but one senses in it a violent exaltation, despite the rigid attitude, the silence, the immobility. His back is slightly arched. His left hand, the only one visible, holds up at some distance from the body a piece of cloth, some dark-colored piece of clothing, which drags on the carpet, and which must be the long cape with its gold-embroidered lining.

This immense silhouette hides most of the bare flesh over which the red stain, spreading from the globe of the breast, runs in long rivulets that branch out, growing narrower, upon the pale background of the bust and the flank. One thread has reached the armpit and runs in an almost straight line along the arm; others have run down toward the waist and traced out, along one side of the belly, the hip, the top of the thigh, a more random network already starting to congeal. Three or four tiny veins have reached the hollow between the legs, meeting in a sinuous line, touching the point of the V formed by the outspread legs, and disappearing into the black tuft.

Look, now the flesh is still intact: the black tuft and the white belly, the soft curve of the hips, the narrow waist, and, higher up, the pearly breasts rising and falling in time with the rapid breathing, whose rhythm grows more accelerated. The man, close to her, one knee on the floor, leans farther over. The head, with its long, curly hair, which alone is free to move somewhat, turns from side to side, struggling; finally the woman's mouth twists open, while the flesh is torn open, the blood spurts out over the tender skin, stretched tight, the carefully shadowed eyes grow abnormally large, the mouth opens wider, the head twists violently, one last time, from right to left, then more gently, to fall back finally and become still, amid the mass of black hair spread out on the velvet.

At the very top of the stone stairway, the little door has opened, allowing a yellowish but sustained shaft of light to enter, against which stands out the dark silhouette of the man wrapped in his long cloak. He has but to climb a few more steps to reach the threshold.

Afterward, the whole setting is empty, the enormous room with its purple shadows and its stone columns proliferating in all directions, the monumental staircase with no handrail that twists upward, growing narrower and vaguer as it rises into the darkness, toward the top of the vaults where it disappears.

Near the body, whose wound has stiffened, whose brilliance is already growing dim, the thin smoke from the incense burner traces complicated scrolls in the still air: first a coil turned horizontally to the left, which then straightens out and rises slightly, then returns to the axis of its point of origin, which it crosses as it moves to the right, then turns back in the first direction, only to wind back again, thus forming an irregular sinusoidal curve, more and more flattened out, and rising vertically, toward the top of the canvas.

II
Poetry

Chapter 1
The Experience
of Poetry

We enjoy poetry for many reasons. We delight in the songs on radio and television, the organized cheers at athletic events, and the slogans of commercial advertising. Even as children we were fascinated by nursery rimes and the songs we learned in school. In all of these instances, the sounds of words, their rhythms and sometimes their rimes, delight us. Yet poetry also stimulates our imaginations by demanding that we visualize events, places, and characters that are often outside the realm of common experience. In this way, we participate in a world not always accessible to us. Poetry appeals to our intellects too. It attempts to register, to organize, and to interpret the nature and the content of human experience. Above all, reading poetry is an activity which demands that we respond not only with our senses and emotions but also with our imaginations and intellects.

We may initially say that poetry concentrates, compresses, and intensifies our oral or written language in order to render a particular experience. It involves us in the sounds of language. Indeed, poetry may have originated in a fascination with the music of words. Our word *lyrical,* for example, is derived from the ancient Greek practice of singing verses to the accompaniment of a lyre. This fact reminds us of the musical possibilities of words, although today only certain kinds of poetry are actually sung. Yet the **song,** or verses adapted to musical expression, continues to be the most commonly known and most popular instance of poetry. Let us begin our study of poetry, then, with two songs—one contemporary, the other almost two centuries old—that illustrate many of the elements of poetry which we will be discussing.

Bob Dylan (b. 1941)
The Times They Are A-Changin'

Come gather 'round people
Wherever you roam
And admit that the waters
Around you have grown
And accept it that soon   5
You'll be drenched to the bone
If your time to you
Is worth savin'.
Then you better start swimmin'
Or you'll sink like a stone   10
For the times they are a-changin'.

Come writers and critics
Who prophesize with your pen
And keep your eyes wide
The chance won't come again   15
And don't speak too soon
For the wheel's still in spin
And there's no tellin' who
That it's namin'.
For the loser now   20
Will be later to win
For the times they are a-changin'.

Come senators, congressmen
Please heed the call
Don't stand in the doorway   25
Don't block up the hall
For he that gets hurt
Will be he who has stalled
There's a battle outside
And it is ragin'.   30
It'll soon shake your windows
And rattle your walls
For the times they are a-changin'.

Come mothers and fathers
Throughout the land   35
And don't criticize
What you can't understand
Your sons and your daughters
Are beyond your command
Your old road is   40

Rapidly agin'.
Please get out of the new one
If you can't lend your hand
For the times they are a-changin'.

The line it is drawn   45
The curse it is cast
The slow one now
Will later be fast
As the present now
Will later be past   50
The order is
Rapidly fadin'.
And the first one now
Will later be last
For the times they are a-changin'.   55

     This contemporary song is written in everyday language. Such colloquialisms as *a-changin'*, *'round*, and *swimmin'*, even a misspelling—*prophesize* (for *prophesy*)—reinforce the oral nature of Dylan's work. Read without its musical accompaniment, the song still develops the idea of time and change, stressing in particular the likely consequences of ignoring that "the times they are a-changin'." Its terse, often short lines are unified by various instances of rimes. In the opening stanza, for example, *roam, grown, bone, stone* emphasize this theme of time and its passing. Each stanza, moreover, focuses upon a different segment of modern-day society. The opening stanza sets the theme, and the following stanzas develop comments about "writers and critics," "senators, congressmen," and "mothers and fathers." The concluding stanza restates the fundamental problem around which the verses are constructed: the present order of things is being reversed, or radically transformed, by an emerging order in which a new generation replaces an older one.

     The typical form of the traditional song is the English ballad. Although composed with many variations, the **ballad** is a narrative in verse written about popular subjects and intended for oral presentation, normally for singing. Such verses were usually anonymous, since they were frequently changed and added to by numerous individuals. The stanzaic form of the **popular** or **folk ballad** consists of four lines of alternating lengths.

     Because of the diversity and the popularity of the ballad, many of the better-known ones are included in various chapters of this anthology. The following verses, written by one of Scotland's most famous poets, illustrate the richness and the vitality of the ballad form.

Robert Burns (1759–1796)
John Barleycorn

There was three kings into the east,
    Three kings both great and high,
And they hae° sworn a solemn oath   *have*
    John Barleycorn should die.

They took a plough and plough'd him down,   5
    Put clods upon his head,
And they hae sworn a solemn oath
    John Barleycorn was dead.

But the cheerful Spring came kindly on,
    And show'rs began to fall;   10
John Barleycorn got up again,
    And sore surpris'd them all.

The sultry suns of Summer came,
    And he grew thick and strong;
His head weel arm'd wi'° pointed spears,   *well armed with* 15
    That no one should him wrong.

The sober Autumn enter'd mild,
    When he grew wan and pale;
His bending joints and drooping head
    Show'd he began to fail.   20

His colour sicken'd more and more,
    He faded into age;
And then his enemies began
    To show their deadly rage.

They've taen° a weapon long and sharp,   *taken* 25
    And cut him by the knee;
Then ty'd° him fast upon a cart,   *tied*
    Like a rogue for forgerie.

They laid him down upon his back,
    And cudgell'd° him full sore;   *beat with sticks* 30
They hung him up before the storm,
    And turn'd him o'er and o'er.

They fillèd up a darksome pit
    With water to the brim,
They heavèd in John Barleycorn—   35
    There, let him sink or swim!

They laid him out upon the floor,
    To work him farther woe;
And still, as signs of life appear'd,
    They toss'd him to and fro.   40

They wasted o'er a scorching flame
    The marrow of his bones;
But a miller us'd him worst of all,
    For he crush'd him between two stones.

And they hae taen his very heart's blood,   45
    And drank it round and round;
And still the more and more they drank,
    Their joy did more abound.

John Barleycorn was a hero bold,
    Of noble enterprise;   50
For if you do but taste his blood,
    'T will° make your courage rise.   *It will*

'T will make a man forget his woe;
    'T will heighten all his joy:
'T will make the widow's heart to sing,   55
    Tho' the tear were in her eye.

Then let us toast John Barleycorn,
    Each man a glass in hand;
And may his great posterity
    Ne'er fail in old Scotlànd!   60

　　The origin and making of whiskey are the subject of this ballad. Although no one really knows how the story of John Barleycorn began, his tale is told by many people in various times and places. What is certain, however, is that John Barleycorn is the personification of grain alcohol. In Burns' version of the story, we learn the general process by which grain yields a drink strong in alcohol. John Barleycorn, Burns says, is "a hero bold," and if you "taste his blood, / 'T will make your courage rise." John Barleycorn makes us forget our "woe," he heightens all of our "joy," and he can even make a "widow's heart to sing." Suggested in this humorous ballad are the very elements of nature and the cycle of the yearly seasons. Although slain (or harvested) each fall, John Barleycorn somehow rises from the earth each spring. And to the poet, he is a necessary and beneficial spirit.

　　The ballad has long been a popular verse form, and it continues to influence popular music. The basic stanzaic patterns of most Protestant hymns, for instance, are derived from the ballad. Similarly, contemporary songwriters have used numerous variations of the ballad form. The story of John Barleycorn, for example, is currently available in several recordings by such groups as Traffic and Steeleye Span.

The ability of poetry to relate an incident, to set a vivid scene, and to describe emotions and ideas accounts for much of its effectiveness and appeal. As stated earlier, poetry concentrates, compresses, and intensifies a particular experience. Thus poets can depict incidents in ways which prose writers cannot. The following two poems are examples of how precisely and descriptively incidents can be presented in verse form.

Thomas Hardy (1840–1928)
The Man He Killed

"Had he and I but met
By some old ancient inn,
We should have sat us down to wet
Right many a nipperkin!° *half-pint of ale*

"But ranged as infantry, 5
And staring face to face,
I shot at him as he at me,
And killed him in his place.

"I shot him dead because—
Because he was my foe, 10
Just so: my foe of course he was;
That's clear enough; although

"He thought he'd 'list,° perhaps, *enlist*
Off-hand like—just as I—
Was out of work—had sold his traps°— *possessions* 15
No other reason why.

"Yes; quaint and curious war is!
You shoot a fellow down
You'd treat if met where any bar is,
Or help to half-a-crown."° *2½-shilling coin* 20

The impersonality of war is a familiar theme of many poets. Here Thomas Hardy dramatizes in a few lines how an individual reacts to the fact that in war one must kill or be killed. The terrible battles of World War I greatly depressed Hardy, who saw in them what he believed to be the beginning of a new kind of savagery and national suicide. In "The

Man He Killed," an infantryman relates how he has shot an enemy soldier. Each joined the army ("perhaps") because he was unemployed, simply thinking that enlisting was a harmless enough thing to do. Mere chance brought the two together at the front. And mere chance also appears in the fact that although both men fired at once, only one has survived. In the final stanza, the speaker observes that "Yes; quaint and curious war is!" Circumstances and the impersonal nature of modern warfare, in which enormous numbers of men and machines are thrown together, have made deadly enemies of two soldiers who might just as easily have exchanged drinks in a bar.

Thom Gunn   (b. 1929)
In the Tank

A man sat in the felon's tank, alone,
Fearful, ungrateful, in a cell for two.
And from his metal bunk, the lower one,
He studied where he was, as felons do.

The cell was clean and cornered, and contained   5
A bowl, grey gritty soap, and paper towels,
A mattress lumpy and not over-stained,
Also a toilet, for the felon's bowels.

He could see clearly all there was to see,
And later when the lights flicked off at nine   10
He saw as clearly all there was to see:
An order without colour, bulk, or line.

And then he knew exactly where he sat.
For though the total riches could not fail
—Red weathered brick, fountains, wisteria—yet   15
Still they contained the silence of a jail,

The jail contained a tank, the tank contained
A box, a mere suspension, at the centre,
Where there was nothing left to understand,
And where he must re-enter and re-enter.   20

The experience of being in jail is the subject of Thom Gunn's poem. And his lines capture with compactness and precision the harrowing realization that the felon experiences. Initially, Gunn describes the physical appearance and the atmosphere of the two-man cell, located within a kind of larger unit (the "tank") of the jail. What the imprisoned man sees, Gunn says, is "An order without colour, bulk, or line." Here is a scene without the motion and color and activity of normal human existence. It is a place silent and frozen, "A box, a mere suspension, at the centre, / Where there was nothing left to understand." The poem effectively communicates not merely the literal place of confinement but also the felon's impressions of it. Vividly and concretely, then, the poem works out what the cell and tank mean to the man imprisoned there.

The presentation of experiences marked by highly personal and emotional impressions is another important aspect of poetry. Naturally, poems of this type vary considerably in style and form since they necessarily characterize the speaker or the subject. The speaker or subject of the poem, however, should not always be identified with the poet. And the meaning of such pieces depends upon the point of view and on what a speaker or a subject maintains. As readers, we enter this kind of poetry by understanding the viewpoint of the speaker or subject. We may do this, of course, and still disagree with what the poem says. The following three poems are examples of how poetry develops subjective experiences.

Maxine Kumin   (b. 1925)
A Family Man

We are talking in bed. You show me snapshots.
Your wallet opens like a salesman's case
on a dog, a frame house hung with shutters
and your eyes reset in a child's face.
Here is your mother standing in full sun   5
on the veranda back home. She is wearing
what we used to call a washdress. Geraniums
flank her as pious in their bearing
as the soap and water she called down on your head.
We carry around our mothers. But mine is dead.   10

Out of the celluloid album, cleverly as a shill
you pull an old snap of yourself squatting beside
a stag you shot early in the war in the Black Hills.
The dog tags dangle on your naked chest.
The rifle, broken, lies across your knees.   15
What do I say to the killer you love best,
that boy-man full of his summer expertise?
I with no place in the file will
wake on dark mornings alone with him in my head.
This is what comes of snapshots. Of talking in bed.   20

"A Family Man" is a dramatization of a man and a woman talking in bed. The point of view is that of the woman; she is reporting how the man shows her photographs from a family album. Yet the true subject of the poem is her personal reaction to these pictures and to the man. Her style is conversational, crisp, dry, and detached. Essentially, she is negative to the man's presentation because she does not see him as he sees himself. To her, his mother seems plain and commonplace, and we can only guess at her suspicions of his lingering attachment to the mother. And the snapshot of him, squatting by a stag he has shot in the Black Hills of South Dakota, provokes her comment that he is a "boy-man full of his summer expertise." This observation indicates her recognition of his immaturity and aggressive tendencies. She herself has "no place in the file" and thus feels excluded from what she sees as very important years of his life. In the final line, she rather dryly concludes that "This is what comes of snapshots. Of talking in bed." Precisely what *this* refers to is somewhat ambiguous. Yet she is apparently referring to the bad impressions and feelings which have resulted from her watching him show the snapshots. From her point of view, their intimate relationship is a disappointment.

Joan Johnson (b. 1953)
Continental Drift

We come to rest in Florence:
an ancient bed. In dreams
I sleep Lucretia to
your Ludovico. At the dark
edge of the world, this sea   5
of sheets, you drift, rolling
and tossing, wrapped in the sea.

We grow old, blind, thirsting,
drifting, crying water, water.

This is our world.   10
You are a dark continent.
I would be Ponce de León
in the new world seeking
water, crying always water.
My calls echo back unheard   15
from your still stones:
how he must have felt
those years gone by with
only the salting sea to drink.

We grow old, blind, thirsting,   20
deaf: so deaf that waking
we can barely hear the sea,
drifting, crying water, water.

"Continental Drift" is another subjective impression of a woman's relationship with a man. Yet this poem is developed even more within the consciousness of the speaker than is "A Family Man." Kumin's lines set a definite scene; Johnson's poem invites readers to imagine the scene and then to listen closely to what the woman says about the man and their relationship. And, too, the speaker in "Continental Drift" alludes to Florence, Italy, and to historical figures such as Lucretia Borgia, Lodovico Sforza, and Ponce de León. The Borgias of Florence were a famous Renaissance family whose intrigues and wars were often the result of marital arrangements and betrayals. The Sforzas were a rival family; and some believe that Lucretia and Lodovico were lovers, although at one time Lucretia was married to Lodovico's brother. Ponce de León, Spanish governor of Puerto Rico, explored Florida, where he searched for the Fountain of Youth.

"Continental Drift" employs images of lovers and of an explorer, of discovery and conquest, to describe a love relationship that, from the woman's point of view, has grown cold and sterile. It is now only "in dreams" that the two are lovers—she, playing Lucretia to his Lodovico. The speaker tells us that the man is "a dark continent" and no longer joined to her. Like Ponce de León, she must seek for that "water" which is necessary for things to grow.

Lucille Clifton (b. 1936)
in the inner city

in the inner city
or
like we call it
home
we think a lot about uptown   5
and the silent nights
and the houses straight as
dead men
and the pastel lights
and we hang on to our no place   10
happy to be alive
and in the inner city
or
like we call it
home   15

The speaker in the poem is an inhabitant of the inner city. It is "home" and therefore a familiar and accepted place. Yet the speaker calls it a "no place." Contrasted with the inner city is "uptown," a place of "silent nights," "pastel lights," and "houses straight as / dead men." Where is this uptown, and why is it alluded to with such a clear sense of deadness and even of fear? Uptown seems to represent all that the inner city is not. Thus the speaker's contrasting descriptions of the two places show why those who live in the inner city "think a lot about uptown."

A Note on Reading Poetry

Given below are suggestions about reading poetry. These points will be useful in helping you understand the poems you will read later in this collection. As you become a more experienced reader, you may want to follow these steps in a slightly different order, or you may want to skip some altogether.

1. Since poetry uses highly compressed and intensified language, you should read a poem through several times. You need to move through your initial reading quickly, attempting to get the "drift" of the poem and to grasp its overall pattern.

2. In your next readings, you may want to read the poem aloud. Poetry makes use of musical elements, which can be better understood if you hear the words spoken aloud. In this oral reading, pronounce the words deliberately, a bit slower than you would normally, and listen to the emerging pattern of sounds and rhythms. If you cannot read the poem aloud, form the words with the tongue and lips and pronounce them silently. In this way, some of the effect of an oral reading will come through. (Reading poetry aloud is discussed in more detail in Chapter 8.)

3. After these initial readings, you should begin to identify specific and prominent features of the poem. You might look up unfamiliar words, phrases, or references, such as biblical, mythological, or historical names, places, and events. Ask yourself some of the following questions. What is the situation in the poem? Is something being described, related, narrated? What is the setting, the time, and the place? Who is speaking and to whom? Or is the speaker unidentified? Are basic contrasts employed, such as different seasons, days, characters, places, or events? Sort out as many of these details and features as you can.

4. Finally, work out a paraphrase of the poem, trying to include the major features and details. Putting the main content of a poem into your own words may be difficult, but it will focus your attention upon concrete details in the poem.

Using the suggestions in "A Note on Reading Poetry," study the following poem. After you have read the selection several times, mark any passages which you do not understand. Some additional questions and a brief discussion are given after the poem.

T. S. Eliot   (1888–1965)
Preludes

I

The winter evening settles down
With smell of steaks in passageways.
Six o'clock.
The burnt-out ends of smoky days.
And now a gusty shower wraps   5
The grimy scraps
Of withered leaves about your feet
And newspapers from vacant lots;
The showers beat
On broken blinds and chimney-pots,   10
And at the corner of the street
A lonely cab-horse steams and stamps.
And then the lighting of the lamps.

II

The morning comes to consciousness
Of faint stale smells of beer   15
From the sawdust-trampled street
With all its muddy feet that press
To early coffee-stands.
With the other masquerades
That time resumes,   20
One thinks of all the hands
That are raising dingy shades
In a thousand furnished rooms.

III

You tossed a blanket from the bed,
You lay upon your back, and waited;   25
You dozed, and watched the night revealing
The thousand sordid images
Of which your soul was constituted;
They flickered against the ceiling.
And when all the world came back   30
And the light crept up between the shutters
And you heard the sparrows in the gutters,
You had such a vision of the street
As the street hardly understands;

Sitting along the bed's edge, where   35
You curled the papers from your hair,
Or clasped the yellow soles of feet
In the palms of both soiled hands.

IV

His soul stretched tight across the skies   40
That fade behind a city block,
Or trampled by insistent feet
At four and five and six o'clock;
And short square fingers stuffing pipes,
And evening newspapers, and eyes   45
Assured of certain certainties,
The conscience of a blackened street
Impatient to assume the world.
I am moved by fancies that are curled
Around these images, and cling:
The notion of some infinitely gentle   50
Infinitely suffering thing.

Wipe your hand across your mouth, and laugh;
The worlds revolve like ancient women
Gathering fuel in vacant lots.

The design or overall structural pattern of Eliot's "Preludes" depends upon several features. By dividing his work into four parts, the poet has indicated the key feature of his structure. Why has he so divided his poem? What contrasts are apparent among the four parts? We note immediately certain differences among these structural parts. Prelude I has for its setting the "winter evening," and Prelude II has the winter "morning." Prelude III directly addresses a "you." Is the "you" a man or a woman? How do you know this? Is the matter of sexual distinction important at this point in the poem? Is this person addressed one of those whose hands will raise "dingy shades"? Finally, in Prelude IV another person is referred to, a man who apparently is very much aware of the life he sees around him. What, in fact, are some details of this life? What really is being described here? Why does he use so many words and terms associated with scenes and aspects taken from the working-class district of a large town or city?

Although born in St. Louis, Missouri, and educated at Harvard University, T. S. Eliot spent his life from just before World War I until his death in London. Looking again at his words, are you aware of the British flavor of several of them? *Cab-horse,* for example, is a British term and indicates a time obviously prior to the general popularity of the automobile. In speaking of himself, Eliot once said that the poet was one who undergoes "the intolerable wrestle with words and meanings." Although Eliot's poetry consistently shows a language largely evolved out of this "intolerable wrestle," the words employed in the "Preludes" are rather ordinary, everyday ones. Yet the words themselves, their specific usage and associations, tell us much about the urban background and somber atmosphere of the work.

In line 48, the poet introduces an "I" into the poem. Henceforth, this "I" is the one who comments upon winter evenings and mornings, dingy rooms and blackened streets. What is the speaker's attitude toward these things? Who then is the "you" that the speaker commands to "wipe your hand across your mouth and laugh" in line 52? The last three lines are important as a final interpretative comment upon the entire work and particularly as an indication of the speaker's view of what the poem means.

It might be useful now to look back over the "Preludes" to see what elements of meaning you can begin putting together in order to answer the question raised in the final lines. Note once more the division into sections and the general pattern of movement in the poem. Investigate the details and the "characters" introduced, and examine the way in which all of these features work together.

At some point in this process, you may have read the poem aloud, or at least certain verses aloud. This will help you considerably because you can hear in its sounds, especially in its rimes and rhythms, the poem's mood, which is one of serious concern and sympathy toward what is being rendered.

The speaker is not a detached reporter. He is apparently distressed at the "grimy scraps," the "dingy shades," and the "sordid images" present in these scenes. He takes little comfort in their "certain certainties," described as the only "conscience of a blackened street," which is itself viewed as forcing its way of life upon everything around it. The speaker is not only involved and distressed but also genuinely concerned about the dull, mechanical existence of those who inhabit the world of the "Preludes." He himself says that he is

> . . . moved by fancies that are curled
> Around these images, and cling:
> The notion of some infinitely gentle
> Infinitely suffering thing.

Here is serious involvement and some degree of personal commitment. But the speaker immediately seems to change his mind, telling the "you"—and presumably himself, too, by implication—"Wipe your hand across your mouth, and laugh." Why, after depicting this grim urban world, does the poet command laughter? The speaker's final statement is that

> The worlds revolve like ancient women
> Gathering fuel in vacant lots.

Does this image show cynicism or a deeper acceptance of life as it is and must be? Has the speaker learned something that he is trying to communicate to readers? The poet describes injustice, sordidness, and the genuine waste of human beings. But does he also believe in an underlying, sustaining life-force—one suggested in the image of "ancient women" gathering sticks and twigs in vacant lots? Is he aware of a power working to preserve and perpetuate human life? Finally, does the poem suggest that the misery of life is inevitable and must therefore be accepted, or does it offer a further solution?

This preliminary investigation of "Preludes" shows some ways in which you can work with particular poems. The kinds of suggestions offered above are ones you can begin with, but only by studying a poem closely and thoughtfully can you grasp its full effects.

Thomas Dekker (1572?–1632)
Golden Slumbers

Golden slumbers kiss your eyes;
Smiles awake you when you rise.
Sleep, pretty wantons, do not cry,
And I will sing a lullaby:
Rock them, rock them, lullaby.   5

Care is heavy, therefore sleep you;
You are care, and care must keep you.
Sleep, pretty wantons, do not cry,
And I will sing a lullaby:
Rock them, rock them, lullaby.   10

Questions for Study

1. Vocabulary: *slumbers, wantons*.
2. This short poem has been adapted for musical expression many times, recently by the Beatles in their *Abbey Road* album. What musical qualities do you find in these lines? What is a lullaby?
3. Describe the attitude of the subject toward the "you." Comment upon who, in your opinion, the "you" might be.

Gordon Lightfoot (b. 1939)
Early Morning Rain

In the early mornin' rain
With a dollar in my hand.
With an achin' in my heart
And my pockets full of sand.

I'm a long way from home
And I miss my loved one so.   5
In the early mornin' rain
And no place to go.

Out on runway number nine
Big seven-o-seven set to go,
Well I'm standin' on the grass   10
Where the cold wind blows.
Well, the liquor tasted good
And the women all were fast,
Well, there she goes, my friend   15
She's rollin' now at last.

Hear the mighty engines roar,
See the silver bird on high,
She's away and westward bound
Far above the clouds she'll fly,   20
Where the mornin' rain don't fall
And the sun always shines,
She'll be flyin' o'er my home
In about three hours time.

Well, this old airport's got me down.   25
It's no earthly good to me,
'Cause I'm stuck here on the ground
As cold and drunk as I can be.
You can't jump a jet plane
Like you can a freight train,   30
So I best be on my way
In the early mornin' rain.

Questions for Study

1. Like "Golden Slumbers," this work is meant to be sung. What features do you find, such as rimes, rhythms, and repetitions, which give this song its musical qualities?
2. Describe the setting. How is it important in this piece?
3. Who is speaking? Briefly describe the incident he is relating.
4. Why is the speaker depressed by watching the jet plane take off? Describe the emotions of the speaker.

Langston Hughes (1902–1967)
Dreams

Hold fast to dreams
For if dreams die
Life is a broken-winged bird
That cannot fly.

Hold fast to dreams   5
For when dreams go
Life is a barren field
Frozen with snow.

Questions for Study

1. The poem compares life without dreams to two different things. What are they? How are they similar?
2. Paraphrase the essential idea in this poem. Comment in your own words on what the poem says.

William Shakespeare   (1564–1616)
Not Marble, nor the Gilded Monuments

Not marble, nor the gilded monuments
Of princes, shall outlive this powerful rhyme;
But you shall shine more bright in these contents
Than unswept stone besmeared with sluttish time.
When wasteful war shall statues overturn,   5
And broils root out the work of masonry,
Nor Mars° his sword nor war's quick fire shall burn   *Roman god of war*
The living record of your memory.
'Gainst death and all-oblivious enmity
Shall you pace forth; your praise shall still find room   10
Even in the eyes of all posterity
That wear this world out to the ending doom.°   *Judgment Day*
   So, till the judgment that yourself arise,
   You live in this, and dwell in lover's eyes.

Questions for Study

1. Vocabulary: *gilded, broils, masonry, enmity, posterity.*
2. Is the subject praising his own abilities as a poet or praising the "you" of the poem? What exactly, in your view, is he saying about both poetry and the "you"?
3. List as many details as you can that are used in the comparisons between poetry and the "you."

Dylan Thomas   (1914–1953)
In My Craft or Sullen Art

In my craft or sullen art
Exercised in the still night
When only the moon rages
And the lovers lie abed

With all their griefs in their arms,   5
I labor by singing light
Not for ambition or bread
Or the strut and trade of charms
On the ivory stages
But for the common wages   10
Of their most secret heart.

Not for the proud man apart
From the raging moon I write
On these spindrift pages
Nor for the towering dead   15
With their nightingales and psalms
But for the lovers, their arms
Round the griefs of the ages,
Who pay no praise or wages
Nor heed my craft or art.   20

Questions for Study

1. Vocabulary: *sullen, spindrift pages, psalms.*
2. Is the theme of this poem concerned with the poet's view of why he writes poetry? Explain.
3. What is the fundamental comparison in this poem? Indicate several lines in which you see this comparison sharply expressed.
4. Shakespeare and Thomas express similar ideas about the enduring place of poetry. What, in your opinion, is Thomas' view of poetry? Do you agree or disagree with this position? Explain your response.

Edwin Arlington Robinson   (1869–1935)
Richard Cory

Whenever Richard Cory went down town,
We people on the pavement looked at him:
He was a gentleman from sole to crown,
Clean favored, and imperially slim.

And he was always quietly arrayed,   5
And he was always human when he talked;
But still he fluttered pulses when he said,
"Good-morning," and he glittered when he walked.

And he was rich—yes, richer than a king—
And admirably schooled in every grace: 10
In fine, we thought that he was everything
To make us wish that we were in his place.

So on we worked, and waited for the light,
And went without the meat, and cursed the bread;
And Richard Cory, one calm summer night,   15
Went home and put a bullet through his head.

Questions for Study

1. Describe Richard Cory in your own words.
2. Describe the "people on the pavement." How are they different from Richard Cory?
3. Why do the townspeople want to be like Richard Cory? What happens to disillusion them?

Paul Simon   (b. 1942)
Richard Cory

They say that Richard Cory owns one-half of this old town,
With political connections to extend his weight around.
Born into society, a banker's only child,
He had everything a man could want: power, grace, and style.

But I work in his factory   5
And I curse the life I'm living, and I curse my poverty,
And I wish that I could be, O I wish that I could be . . .
        Richard Cory

The papers print his picture almost everywhere he goes;
Richard Cory at the opera, Richard Cory at the show.   10
And the rumors of his parties and the orgies on his yachts,
O, he surely must be happy with everything he's got.

But I work in his factory
And I curse the life I'm living, and I curse my poverty,
And I wish that I could be, O I wish that I could be . . .   15
        Richard Cory

He freely gave to charity; he had the common touch,
And they were grateful for his patronage, and they thanked him very much.
So my mind was filled with wonder when the evening papers read:
"Richard Cory went home last night and put a bullet through his head." 20

But I work in his factory,
And I curse the life I'm living, and I curse my poverty,
And I wish that I could be, O I wish that I could be . . .
        Richard Cory

"Richard Cory" © 1966 by Paul Simon. Used with permission of the publisher.

Questions for Study

1. How is this contemporary song version of Richard Cory's tale different from Edwin Arlington Robinson's treatment?
2. Specifically, what details does the Paul Simon version add about Richard Cory's life? Are we also given additional details about the likes and dislikes of the townspeople?
3. Even after Cory kills himself, why does the speaker still wish that he "could be . . . Richard Cory"? How then would you characterize the speaker?

Louis Simpson   (b. 1923)
American Poetry

Whatever it is, it must have
A stomach that can digest
Rubber, coal, uranium, moons, poems.

Like the shark, it contains a shoe.
It must swim for miles through the desert   5
Uttering cries that are almost human.

Questions for Study

1. What is the view of American poetry that emerges from this poem?
2. Comment on why, in your opinion, the poem uses *stomach* and *shark* in talking about American poetry.
3. Explain the phrase "cries that are almost human."

Chapter 2
Language

The American poet Hart Crane once declared that the poet "must be drenched in words, literally soaked in them, to have the right ones form themselves into the proper patterns at the right moment." There is no doubt that in order to give expressive and precise form to what he wishes to say, the poet must be committed to, even obsessed with, words. He must be aware of their roots, their "dictionary" definitions, their various shades of meaning, their intellectual and emotional impact, their relationship to other words in a particular context. Likewise, in studying poetry, we must be sensitive to these various aspects of words in order to grasp what the word-conscious poet is communicating.

One of the most important facets of the study of poetry is **diction,** or the poet's choice and use of words. Diction involves the selection of the "right" or the exact word, the one which most expressively and economically helps both convey the meaning and heighten the effect of the poem. Often the word needed is an old one, such as *blood*. Transmitted through Old High German into English, *blood* is a word whose meaning has been and continues to be quite precise. Occasionally, a poet may require a relatively new word, such as *jeep, high-rise, supermarket,* or *astronaut*. Sometimes a poet may need to use slang words such as *fuzz* (law officer), regional words such as *hoecake* (a fried cornmeal cake), or rather formal and unfamiliar words such as *crepuscular* (relating to or similar to twilight). We should also be aware, especially when reading older poetry, that the meanings of some words have changed from one historical period to another. In sixteenth-century England *hussy,* for example, meant simply "housewife." Such is hardly its meaning today.

Dictionaries are useful in providing us with the meanings of unfamiliar, specialized, or archaic words. Yet even with this knowledge, we really cannot judge the appropriateness of a word unless we know its context, the entire passage or poem of which the word is a part. By itself, *crepuscular* is neither a "right" nor a "wrong" word—it is simply a word with a particular meaning. Only when we see the word in its context can we judge its appropriateness. In the statement, "The vagrant gobbled up his hash, slurped his coffee, plunked down $1.29, and shuffled out into the crepuscular air," *crepuscular* is far too formal a word for the humble circumstances it describes. Yet in other contexts, it may be quite appropriate. As readers, we need to read a poem through several times, noting what it is saying and the direction it is taking. We may then attempt to determine how specific words function within the poem. In this chapter, Lawrence Ferlinghetti's "The World Is a Beautiful Place," for example, contains such familiar words as *hell, priests, patrolmen,* and *constipations*. The "rightness" of these words can only be evaluated by looking at how they contrast with other words in the poem, at the irony they suggest, and at the way they contribute to the total effect and the meaning of the poem.

Along with examining the words the poet uses, we should note the arrangement and the order of the words within a poem. In the nineteenth century, Samuel Taylor Coleridge defined poetry as "the best words in their best order." The "best words" are those that, out of all the choices available to the poet, express his meaning in the most precise, vivid, concrete, and effective way possible. The poet also concerns himself with the "best order" of the words within a line or a stanza of poetry. The ordering of and relationships between words within phrases and sentences is called **syntax.** And we usually speak of poetic syntax when we are distinguishing between the actual words and their patterning within the poem.

The normal syntactical order of an English sentence is subject-verb-object, with adjectives usually preceding nouns. Poets may alter this pattern, even reverse it, to construct statements that stress key words or that suspend a riming word until the end of a line of verse. Frequently **ellipsis** occurs. This is the omission of one or more words of an entire phrase. The following short poem shows instances of these changes in normal English syntax.

James Russell Lowell   (1819–1891)
Sixty-Eighth Birthday

As life runs on, the road grows strange
With faces new, and near the end
The milestones into headstones change,
'Neath every one a friend.

The opening line is regular in its syntax. The second line, however, stresses the adjective *new* by putting it after the noun *faces*. Also in line 2, the poet does not say "near the end of the road" but omits the last qualifying phrase. In normal syntactical order, line 3 would read, "The milestones change into headstones." In order to have *change* rime with *strange,* however, he places the verb at the end of the line, a position which also lends the word added emphasis. The last line has a clipped word—*'neath* for *beneath*—and then omits the verb *is*. Finally, to give strong emphasis to the subject of his statement, the poet places "a friend" at the end of the concluding line. Poets use such deviations from normal English syntax not to confound readers but to achieve the effects of rhythm, emphasis, and freshness in their verse.

Recalling Coleridge's statement that poetry is "the best words in the best order," read the following short poem.

Alfred, Lord Tennyson (1809–1892)
Flower in the Crannied Wall

Flower in the crannied wall,
I pluck you out of the crannies,
I hold you here, root and all, in my hand,
Little flower—but *if* I could understand
What you are, root and all, and all in all,   5
I should know what God and man is.

Sometimes, as with this six-line poem, the best words are the commonly used ones. Similarly, the best order may be the most direct presentation of these words. Although a few of us may need to look up the meaning of *crannied* (or *crannies*), the rest of the poem contains commonly known words arranged in several direct statements. Although subtleties exist, the selection and order of these words convey the poet's inquiry into how and why a flower grows in a small opening in a wall—an inquiry which he says might provide an insight into "what God and man is." The following poem also contains familiar words and direct statements, yet it achieves effects somewhat different from Tennyson's.

William Butler Yeats (1865–1939)
The Old Men Admiring Themselves in the Water

I heard the old, old men say,
"Everything alters,
And one by one we drop away."
They had hands like claws, and their knees

Were twisted like the old thorn-trees   5
By the waters.
I heard the old, old men say,
"All that's beautiful drifts away
Like the waters."

Like Tennyson, Yeats uses ordinary words and straightforward statements, two of which are bits of speech. Yeats, however, involves us
more deeply in the meanings and the implications of words than Tennyson does. First, Yeats compares "hands" to "claws," and "knees" to
"old thorn-trees / By the waters." Such comparisons sharpen and
intensify Yeats' meanings. He also expresses the abstract idea that
"Everything alters" by comparing "All that's beautiful" to "waters"
that drift downstream. Tennyson's language depicts an act of contemplation and makes a statement about it. In Yeats' poem, the language
dramatizes a situation and then renders the emotion contained in it—
specifically, the emotion of the old men "admiring themselves in the
water." Tennyson meditates on the puzzling, mysterious nature of
existence. Yeats involves us in the dramatic and the emotion-filled
experience of the old men.

We frequently hear people say that poetry is written in "flowery"
language. This is a serious misconception of poetry and a carry-over
from the days when English poets attempted to create a poetic language
distinct from everyday speech. If some poems contain "high-flown"
words, many others are written in down-to-earth language. Much contemporary poetry, in fact, is written in familiar language spoken by
average individuals in everyday situations. The following poem illustrates that really it is not the kind but the use of words that distinguishes
poetry from other forms of human expression.

Leonard Cohen (b. 1934)
Story

She tells me a child built her house
one Spring afternoon,
but that the child was killed
crossing the street.

She says she read it in the newspaper,   5
that at the corner of this and this avenue
a child was run down by an automobile.

Of course I do not believe her.
She has built the house herself,
hung the oranges and coloured beads in the doorways,   10
crayoned flowers on the walls.
She has made the paper things for the wind,
collected crooked stones for their shadows in the sun,
fastened yellow and dark balloons to the ceiling.

Each time I visit her   15
she repeats the story of the child to me,
I never question her. It is important
to understand one's part in a legend.

I take my place
among the paper fish and make-believe clocks,   20
naming the flowers she has drawn,
smiling while she paints my head on large clay coins,
and making a sort of courtly love to her
when she contemplates her own traffic death.

The voice in the poem, the narrator, tells about a playhouse and the child who built it. His presentation of these things is direct and condensed, and both his diction and syntax are simple and conversational. Yet in using conversational language, the poet actually heightens the tension between what is said and the emotional impact of the poem—that is, between the claim of the girl that the playhouse was built by another child killed by an automobile and the narrator's gradual involvement in this fantasy.

Some poems whose diction and syntax are quite straightforward may prove troublesome because of such innovations as a lack of punctuation or unusual **typography**—the arrangement of words and lines on a page. The following poem may at first seem confusing. Yet, if you read it slowly, observing the pauses indicated by many of the line breaks, the poem moves along as easily as one printed in a less radical style. And its unusual configuration actually supports and intensifies its meaning, achieving an effect of uninterrupted randomness.

Lawrence Ferlinghetti (b. 1919)
The World Is a Beautiful Place

      The world is a beautiful place
                        to be born into
if you don't mind happiness
                not always being
                        so very much fun   5

if you don't mind a touch of hell
                              now and then
         just when everything is fine
                              because even in heaven
                they don't sing   10
                              all the time

         The world is a beautiful place
                              to be born into
      if you don't mind some people dying
                              all the time   15
                or maybe only starving
                              some of the time
           which isn't half so bad
                              if it isn't you

   Oh the world is a beautiful place   20
                              to be born into
               if you don't much mind
                              a few dead minds
                in the higher places
                              or a bomb or two   25
                now and then
                              in your upturned faces
      or such other improprieties
                              as our Name Brand society
                is prey to   30
                              with its men of distinction
            and its men of extinction
                              and its priests
                and other patrolmen
                              and its various segregations   35
   and congressional investigations
                              and other constipations
             that our fool flesh
                              is heir to

   Yes the world is the best place of all   40
                              for a lot of such things as
                making the fun scene
                              and making the love scene
   and making the sad scene
                              and singing low songs and having inspirations   45
                and walking around
                              looking at everything
                              and smelling flowers
             and goosing statues
                              and even thinking   50

and kissing people and
making babies and wearing pants
and waving hats and
dancing
and going swimming in rivers   55
on picnics
in the middle of the summer
and just generally
'living it up'

Yes   60
but then right in the middle of it
comes the smiling
mortician

Despite the poem's unconventional typography, the words are commonplace and their syntax is, for the most part, straightforward and declarative. Words like *priests, patrolmen,* and *investigations* do not require explanations. Yet their function within the context of the poem becomes more significant once we sense Ferlinghetti's attitude toward his subject. We readily see that his attitude toward life is ironic, essentially bittersweet—saying that "the world is a beautiful place" despite misery, war, injustice, inhumanity, and even the certainty of death. We then recognize that priests, patrolmen, and investigations represent elements of society which, in the poet's opinion, stifle, but do not destroy, an appreciation of life. And the last word in the poem, *mortician,* leaves us with a final ironic reminder of the human predicament. Ferlinghetti reinforces the irony by means of the typography, which emphasizes certain key words and phrases.

The following two poems are examples of the skillful use of diction and syntax to achieve different effects.

John Frederick Nims (b. 1913)
D.O.M., A.D. 2167

When I've outlived three plastic hearts, or four,
Another's kidneys, corneas *(beep!),* with more
Unmentionable rubber, nylon, such—
And when *(beep!)* in a steel drawer (DO NOT TOUCH!),
Mere brain cells in saline wash, I thrive   5
With thousands, taped to quaver out, "Alive!"—
God grant that steel two wee *(beep!)* eyes of glass
To glitter wicked when the nurses pass.

Questions for Study

1. The title consists of an abbreviation and a date. Possible meanings for *D. O. M.* are Digital Ohmmeter, depth of modulation, dirty old man, Division of Overseas Maintenance, and the Latin maxims *Deo Optimo Maximo* ("To God, the best and greatest"), *Datur Omnibus Mori* ("It is alloted to all to die"), and *Dominus Omnium Magister* ("God, the Master and Lord of All"). Choose which of these you feel best fits the poem and give reasons for your choice.
2. The word *beep* interrupts the poem in an apparently random fashion. What function does it serve?
3. What is the speaker's attitude toward the kind of artificially maintained "life" he describes?

Louis MacNeice (1907–1963)
Museums

Museums offer us, running from among the buses,
A centrally heated refuge, parquet floors and sarcophaguses,
Into whose tall fake porches we hurry without a sound
Like a beetle under a brick that lies, useless, on the ground.
Warmed and cajoled by the silence the cowed cipher revives,   5
Mirrors himself in the cases of pots, paces himself by marble lives,
Makes believe it was he that was the glory that was Rome,
Soft on his cheek the nimbus of other people's martyrdom,
And then returns to the street, his mind an arena where sprawls
Any number of consumptive Keatses and dying Gauls.   10

Questions for Study

1. Vocabulary: *parquet, sarcophaguses, cajoled, cipher, nimbus, consumptive.*
2. Why is the poem titled "Museums"? Relate this title to the meaning of the poem.
3. What is the effect of *brick* in line 4? What does it tell you about the speaker's attitude toward his subject? Is his attitude serious or whimsical? What are some other ways in which he establishes this attitude?
4. In his final line, MacNeice mentions "consumptive Keatses and dying Gauls." John Keats (1795–1821) was a British poet who died young of tuberculosis; and Gauls were Germanic tribes living in what later became France. Why does the poet include these two references? How are both related to the poem's meaning?
5. In line 7, MacNeice recalls Edgar Allan Poe's "To Helen" (see Chapter 5) with the phrase "the glory that was Rome." Read Poe's poem and comment on what MacNeice does with this reference.

In order to choose the "best" words out of all those available to him, the poet must be sensitive to two essential features of words—their denotations and connotations. **Denotation** is the literal or dictionary meaning of a word. The word *bridge,* for example, has several denotations: a structure which spans a road, river, or lake; a part of a ship above the main deck from which it is controlled; an artificial device which replaces one or more teeth; a card game; and so on. From the particular context in which a word such as *bridge* is used, there is usually no problem in determining which one of its denotations is intended.

A word like *bridge*, however, has few (if any) **connotations,** which are the associations and overtones of meaning which have become attached to it. Words acquire their connotations by frequent usage and by the way in which they are employed in certain contexts. *Laugh, chuckle, guffaw, snicker, giggle,* for example, all have the same general denotation—the physical exhaling of breath in reaction to something humorous or absurd. Yet these words are not strictly interchangeable because their connotations are quite different. In the statement, "The burly state trooper giggled in my face when I tried to talk my way out of a speeding ticket," *giggled* is inappropriate because its connotations suggest a childlike silliness which does not fit the circumstances. Determining the appropriateness of a word with certain connotations, then, actually depends upon the context in which it is used.

Poets take extraordinary care in selecting words whose connotations suggest as precisely and vividly as possible the overtones of meaning they wish to convey. In "The Second Coming" (Chapter 5), William Butler Yeats envisions the approach of a bestial messiahlike figure whose birth will usher in a long and violent period in human history. In the last line of the poem, the half-human figure "Slouches toward Bethlehem to be born." With its connotations suggesting a slow and stealthy awkwardness, *slouches* captures the humanly sinister quality of the beast. Words with similar denotations but with different connotations—*walks, ambles, marches, strolls,* and so on—would not have expressed as well the quiet horror of the coming event.

The denotations and connotations of many words and phrases in the following poem help convey a certain attitude about the death of a young girl.

John Crowe Ransom (1888–1974)
Bells for John Whiteside's Daughter

There was such speed in her little body,	
And such lightness in her footfall,	
It is no wonder her brown study°	*reverie* or *deep thought*
Astonishes us all.	
Her wars were bruited° in our high window.	*reported* 5
We looked among orchard trees and beyond,	
Where she took arms against her shadow,	
Or harried unto the pond	

The lazy geese, like a snow cloud
Dripping their snow on the green grass,   10
Tricking and stopping, sleepy and proud,
Who cried in goose, Alas,

For the tireless heart within the little
Lady with rod that made them rise
From their noon apple-dreams, and scuttle   15
Goose-fashion under the skies!

But now go the bells, and we are ready,
In one house we are sternly stopped
To say we are vexed at her brown study,
Lying so primly propped.   20

Ransom does not describe the unexpected death of John Whiteside's daughter in a conventional manner by formally praising the accomplishments of her past life. Yet the poet is not impersonal or cold-hearted. The connotative possibilities of Ransom's language intensify and extend the death of a particular individual to express his concern with death in general. He speaks of the "speed" in the girl's body and of the "lightness" of her "footfall," suggesting by the connotations of these words an ironic contrast between her dead and alive. In the second stanza he recalls her vitality and boundless energies. The third and the fourth stanzas show her playing with geese and convey her imagination and her blithe spirit. In each of these instances, Ransom's language is rich in ironic connotations. Her games, for example, are called "wars," and we know the grim, ironic connotations of such "games." She plays with her "shadow," an innocent child's game, but one foreshadowing her death. The poet calls her heart "tireless," creating one of the most effective ironies in the poem, since she unexpectedly dies.

The poet's attitude emerges indirectly through the suggestiveness of his language. Referring to the dead girl laid out for burial as in a contemplative "brown study," he quickly announces that this "astonishes" all who see her. Similarly, alluding once more in the final stanza to her brown study, he confesses that those present "are vexed" at her "lying so primly propped." The connotations in both cases suggest the inability of the spectators to grasp the mysterious reality of death. Those around the dead girl see it as monstrous and puzzling. By his indirect presentation, Ransom avoids the sentimentality that the death of a young girl might easily evoke. Both grief and sadness, surprise and shock, are subordinated and transformed by the inescapable fact of death itself. By implication, moreover, the poem affirms life in resisting its negation in the face of death.

John Keats (1795–1821)
La Belle Dame sans Merci[1]

O what can ail thee, knight at arms,
    Alone and palely loitering?
The sedge° has withered from the lake   *marsh grass*
    And no birds sing!

O what can ail thee, knight at arms,   5
    So haggard and so woe-begone?
The squirrel's granary is full,
    And the harvest's done.

I see a lily on thy brow,
    With anguish moist and fever dew;   10
And on thy cheeks a fading rose
    Fast withereth too.

I met a lady in the meads,°   *meadows*
    Full beautiful, a faery's child;
Her hair was long, her foot was light   15
    And her eyes were wild.

I made a garland for her head,
    And bracelets, too, and fragrant zone;°   *belt of flowers*
She looked at me as she did love
    And made sweet moan.   20

I set her on my pacing steed,
    And nothing else saw, all day long;
For sidelong would she bend, and sing
    A faery's song.

She found me roots of relish sweet,   25
    And honey wild, and manna° dew;   *food derived from the ash plant*
And sure in language strange she said,
    "I love thee true."

She took me to her elfin grot,°   *fairyland grotto*
    And there she wept and sighed full sore;   30
And there I shut her wild, wild eyes
    With kisses four.

---

1. "The beautiful lady without pity." The title was taken from a medieval poem by Alain Chartier, but the subject matter and treatment are Keats'.

And there she lullèd me asleep
    And there I dreamed, Ah woe betide!
The latest dream I ever dreamt   35
    On the cold hill side.

I saw pale kings, and princes too
    Pale warriors, death pale were they all;
They cried, "La belle dame sans merci
    Hath thee in thrall!"   40

I saw their starved lips in the gloam°   *twilight*
    With horrid warning gapèd wide,
And I awoke, and found me here
    On the cold hill's side.

And this is why I sojourn here   45
    Alone and palely loitering;
Though the sedge is withered from the lake
    And no birds sing.

Questions for Study

1. Vocabulary: *loitering, woe-begone, granary, garland, steed, thrall, sojourn.*
2. This poem employs some of the conventions of the folk ballad (see Chapter 1). Identify as many of these conventions as you can.
3. Comment on Keats' choice of specific words and on how they function in the poem. How does word order contribute to the poem's meaning?
4. What are the questions the voice in the poem asks in the first three stanzas? What answers does the "I" give in the stanzas that follow?
5. The theme of a noble individual ruined by love is a familiar one. Describe how Keats uses this theme in his poem. What finally is the outcome of such an adventure?

Al Young (b. 1939)
Birthday Poem

First light of day in Mississippi
son of laborer & of house wife
it says so on the official photostat
not son of fisherman & child fugitive
from cotton fields & potato patches   5
from sugarcane chickens & well-water
from kerosene lamps & watermelons
mules named jack or jenny & wagonwheels,

years of meaningless farm work
work Work WORK WORK *WORK*—   10
"Papa pull you outta school bout March

to stay on the place & work the crop"
—her own earliest knowledge
of human hopelessness & waste

She carried me around nine months   15
inside her fifteen year old self
before here I sit numbering it all

How I got from then to now
is the mystery that could fill a whole library
much less an arbitrary stanza   20

But of course you already know about that
from your own random suffering
& sudden inexplicable bliss

Questions for Study

1. Who is the speaker in the poem? What is his history? How does he view his future?
2. Describe the language in this poem. How do the poet's words define the speaker?
3. Find instances of words that have, in your opinion, significant connotations. Relate these words to the meaning of the poem.
4. Why do you think the poet includes words such as *arbitrary, random,* and *inexplicable?* Is his use of such words effective?

W. H. Auden   (1907–1973)
The Unknown Citizen

(To JS/07/M/378
This Marble Monument
Is Erected by the State)

He was found by the Bureau of Statistics to be
One against whom there was no official complaint,
And all the reports on his conduct agree
That, in the modern sense of an old-fashioned word, he was a saint,
For in everything he did he served the Greater Community.   5
Except for the War till the day he retired
He worked in a factory and never got fired,
But satisfied his employers, Fudge Motors Inc.
Yet he wasn't a scab or odd in his views,
For his Union reports that he paid his dues,   10
(Our report on his Union shows it was sound)
And our Social Psychology workers found
That he was popular with his mates and liked a drink.
The Press are convinced that he bought a paper every day
And that his reactions to advertisements were normal in every way.   15

Policies taken out in his name prove that he was fully insured,
And his Health-card shows he was once in hospital but left it cured.
Both Producers Research and High-Grade Living declare
He was fully sensible to the advantages of the Installment Plan
And had everything necessary to the Modern Man,   20
A phonograph, a radio, a car and a frigidaire.
Our researchers into Public Opinion are content
That he held the proper opinions for the time of year;
When there was peace, he was for peace; when there was war, he went.
He was married and added five children to the population,   25
Which our Eugenist says was the right number for a parent of his
    generation,
And our teachers report that he never interfered with their education.
Was he free? Was he happy? The question is absurd:
Had anything been wrong, we should certainly have heard.

Questions for Study

1. Diction is very important in this poem, especially in two aspects: (1) proper names and technical terms; and (2) dry, matter-of-fact, bureaucratic language. Find instances of both and briefly describe their function.
2. Comment upon the meaning of this poem. Specifically, comment upon the title and relate it to the meaning. Also relate the "data" given just under the title.
3. Point out specific aspects of modern life—in particular, modern organizations—that Auden is critical of here.
4. Is denotation or connotation more important in this poem? Identify several examples in which connotation influences its meaning.
5. How do the last two lines tell us why Auden has written this poem? Does the poem itself answer the questions, "Was he free? Was he happy?"

Robert Graves   (b. 1895)
My Name and I

The impartial Law enrolled a name
    For my especial use:
My rights in it would rest the same
Whether I puffed it into fame
    Or sank it in abuse.   5

Robert was what my parents guessed
    When first they peered at me,
And *Graves* an honourable bequest
With Georgian silver and the rest
    From my male ancestry.   10

They taught me: "You are *Robert Graves*
    (Which you must learn to spell),

But see that *Robert Graves* behaves,
Whether with honest men or knaves,
   Exemplarily well."   15

Then though my I was always I,
   Illegal and unknown,
With nothing to arrest it by—
As will be obvious when I die
   And *Robert Graves* lives on—   20

I cannot well repudiate
   This noun, this natal star,
This gentlemanly self, this mate
So kindly forced on me by fate,
   Time and the registrar;   25

And therefore hurry him ahead
   As an ambassador
To fetch me home my beer and bread
Or commandeer the best green bed,
   As he has done before.   30

Yet, understand, I am not he
   Either in mind or limb;
My name will take less thought for me,
In worlds of men I cannot see,
   Than ever I for him.   35

Questions for Study

1. Describe the words Graves uses in this poem. Are they effective ones for the subject he is writing about?
2. Is denotation or connotation more significant here? Support your response with specific words and phrases from the poem.
3. Why does the poet distinguish in his title between what he calls "I" and his "name"?
4. What implications does Graves suggest are in the name a person is given? Does he accept or reject these?

Anonymous
The Twa Corbies

As I was walking all alane,°   *alone*
I herd twa corbies° making a mane;°   *two ravens / moan*°
The tane° unto the t' other say,   *one*
"Where sall we gang° and dine to-day?"   *shall we go*

"In behint yon auld fail dyke,°   *old turf wall* 5
I wot° there lies a new slain knight;   *know*
And naebody kens° that he lies there,   *knows*
But his hawk, his hound, and lady fair.

"His hound is to the hunting gane,
His hawk to fetch the wild-fowl hame,°   *home* 10
His lady's ta'en another mate,
So we may mak our dinner sweet.

"Ye'll sit on his white hause-bane,°   *neck bone*
And I'll pike out his bonny blue een;°   *eyes*
Wi' ae° lock o' his gowden° hair   *one / golden* 15
We'll theek° our nest when it grows bare.   *thatch*

"Mony a one for him makes mane,
But nane sall ken where he is gane;
O'er his white banes when they are bare,
The wind sall blaw for evermair."   20

Questions for Study

1. Comment on the realism of the diction employed in the poem. What words does the poet use to depict vividly the brutal, horrible fate of the "new-slain knight"? Are his choices effective ones?
2. The poem narrates a situation, but it also implies an action. We are not quite sure what has happened, but the poem suggests enough for us to make some guesses. What, in your view, has indeed happened to the knight?
3. What is the attitude of the "I" in the poem?
4. As a folk ballad, this poem was meant to be sung or recited. If possible, read the poem aloud and comment on how such an oral presentation contributes to its effectiveness.

Robert Bly (b. 1926)
Surprised by Evening

There is unknown dust that is near us,
Waves breaking on shores just over the hill,
Trees full of birds that we have never seen,
Nets drawn down with dark fish.

The evening arrives; we look up and it is there,   5
It has come through the nets of the stars,
Through the tissues of the grass,
Walking quietly over the asylums of the waters.

The day shall never end, we think:
We have hair that seems born for the daylight;   10
But, at last, the quiet waters of the night will rise,
And our skin shall see far off, as it does under water.

Questions for Study

1. What associations does the poet hope to gather around the following words: *dust, nets, tissues, asylums, hair?*
2. Characterize the diction in this poem. Is it serious or casual? Personal or impersonal?
3. What is the theme of this poem?
4. Explain the last two lines.

Chapter 3
Imagery

Language reflects not only our thoughts and emotions but also the experiences of our senses. Day by day, we are involved continuously in the life of the senses—in seeing, feeling, hearing, smelling, and tasting. We see that the sky is clear and blue, or cloudy and gray. The coarse sweater scratches our skin; the acrid chemicals in the lab irritate our noses; the strawberries are sweet and we like their taste. In addition to these five basic senses, two more are important in our everyday lives: the thermal sense of distinguishing between heat and cold; and the kinesthetic sense of motion and muscular tensions. The pizza is too hot to eat; the weather is too cold for us to remain outdoors. Our muscles ache from the strain of climbing a steep hill. By our sensory responses, we immerse ourselves in life itself. In these acts, we relate to our environment and to ourselves.

More than the fiction writer or the dramatist, certainly more than any of us in normal conversation, the poet wants to distill sensory experience into language. And the primary way the poet accomplishes this is by means of images. Essentially, it is the poet's skill with images that transforms the world of direct experience into artistic meanings.

We may define **image** as any word or group of words that renders sensory experience. **Imagery** consists of all the images in a poem or in a section of a poem. Because images can be grouped, we speak of the pattern of images or of imagery.

We should point out, first of all, that an image may be literal or figurative. We must determine whether a poet has employed a certain image or pattern of imagery in a literal or a figurative way. If we say that "the white orchid sits in the round bowl," we are employing a literal image. But if we compare our loved one to a white orchid, we are using nonliteral or figurative language. We are letting one object (the orchid) suggest something else (our loved one). Specifically, we might say that our loved one is "*like* an orchid" (a *simile*) or that our loved one "*is* an orchid" (a *metaphor*). In both cases, *orchid* remains an image, yet it has also taken on the function of a figurative expression. Both simile and metaphor are discussed in the next chapter; other figures of speech are considered in later chapters. Here, however, we will explore image and imagery without distinguishing between their literal and figurative use.

An image is familiarly thought of as "a picture in words." That is, we have the sensation of an actual object being created before us through the use of words. Through *visual* images we seem to "see" what the poet presents. Such images are by far the most frequently used, but a poet may also wish us to think we are hearing or smelling or even touching something. Memory has a lot to do with the way we respond to images. We can imagine a rainbow or a thunderstorm because we have actually seen one. But can we imagine how a yak looks or how it feels to ride one? The poet can help us with unfamiliar experiences by employing familiar words or known objects to represent or suggest unfamiliar sensory experiences.

Images and imagery present concrete elements of experience in fresh and intense ways. British poet and critic T. E. Hulme (1883–1917) observed that poetry "always endeavors to arrest you, and to make you continuously see a physical thing, to prevent you gliding through an abstract process." It does so through new images because, in Hulme's words, "the old [images] cease to convey a physical thing and become abstract counters." An effective image is always much more incisive, more forceful than a concept. It is concrete and precise while achieving all manner of suggestiveness. An old man's face, for example, is better seen if we speak of the many deep lines in it and the sunburned color of the skin than if we merely report the face as "old." Poetic images seem to give us an object instantly and sensuously. At the same time, images focus and concentrate what is being said.

Because images and imagery are important to poetry, numerous classifications and approaches have been devised. Let us here classify images rather simply by their relationship to the familiar senses of seeing, hearing, touching, smelling, and tasting. Illustrations of thermal and kinesthetic images are also included.

The opening lines of William Wordsworth's "I Wandered Lonely As a Cloud" consist of highly effective visual images, with motion and color animating the scene:

> I wandered lonely as a cloud
> That floats on high o'er vales and hills,
> When all at once I saw a crowd,
> A host, of golden daffodils;
> Beside the lake, beneath the trees,
> Fluttering and dancing in the breeze.

In the following stanza from *The Rime of the Ancient Mariner,* Samuel Taylor Coleridge gives us an excellent example of how poetry can effectively present images of hearing.

> The ice was here, the ice was there,
> The ice was all around:
> It cracked and growled, and roared and howled,
> Like noises in a swound!

Robert Frost appeals to our sense of touch in four lines from his "Birches":

> And life is too much like a pathless wood
> Where your face burns and tickles with the cobwebs
> Broken across it, and one eye is weeping
> From a twig's having lashed across it open.

John Keats offers us a fine illustration of images that appeal to our senses of smell and taste in these lines from "The Eve of St. Agnes":

> Of candied apple, quince, and plum, and gourd;
> With jellies soother than the creamy curd,
> And lucent syrups, tinct with cinnamon;
> Manna and dates, in argosy transferred
> From Fez; and spicéd dainties, every one,
> From silken Samarcand to cedared Lebanon.

The opening stanza of the same poem provides us with an example of images of biting cold (thermal images):

> St. Agnes' Eve—Ah, bitter chill it was!
> The owl, for all his feathers, was a-cold;
> The hare limped trembling through the frozen grass,
> And silent was the flock in woolly fold:
> Numb were the Beadsman's fingers, while he told
> His rosary, and while his frosted breath,
> Like pious incense from a censer old,
> Seemed taking flight for heaven, without a death,
> Past the sweet Virgin's picture, while his prayer he saith.

In "After Apple-Picking," Robert Frost employs the sense of muscular tension (kinesthetic images) to convey the weariness of the speaker:

> My instep arch not only keeps the ache,
> It keeps the pressure of a ladder-round.
> I feel the ladder sway as the boughs bend.

The basis of an image may be the expression of a relationship between two commonly known, but dissimilar things. Through a single visual image, the following poem associates fog and a cat in a particularly apt and delightful manner.

Carl Sandburg (1878–1967)
Fog

The fog comes
on little cat feet.

It sits looking
over harbor and city
on silent haunches   5
and then moves on.

Given below is another short poem structured around a single image. But here the sense of sight is reinforced by the senses of touch and taste.

William Carlos Williams (1883–1963)
This Is Just to Say

I have eaten
the plums
that were in
the icebox

and which   5
you were probably
saving
for breakfast

Forgive me   10
they were delicious
so sweet
and so cold.

Each of the images in these two poems—the fog as a cat and the cold, sweet plums—is conveyed with as few words as possible. Each is delivered in precise, direct, concrete language. Our pleasure in both poems lies in the illusion they create of an immediate experience of the objects themselves. We are pleased by the delicacy of the little cat feet;

and we sense the shy, timid attitude suggested in the act of stealing the tasty plums. In trying to convey these same feelings in our own words, we would have to employ many more words than do Sandburg and Williams. Such an attempt can illustrate to us the use and power of poetic imagery—specifically, the brevity and intensity of its language.

Images and imagery constitute one aspect of poetry. Few poems are written merely for the sake of creating images. Yet the range and the effectiveness of the imagery are often considerable and even crucial. Read the following poem, looking specifically at its images in order to determine what role imagery plays in its overall meaning.

Louis Simpson (b. 1923)
The Battle

Helmet and rifle, pack and overcoat
Marched through a forest. Somewhere up ahead
Guns thudded. Like the circle of a throat
The night on every side was turning red.

They halted and they dug. They sank like moles   5
Into the clammy earth between the trees.
And soon the sentries, standing in their holes,
Felt the first snow. Their feet began to freeze.

At dawn the first shell landed with a crack.
Then shells and bullets swept the icy woods.   10
This lasted many days. The snow was black.
The corpses stiffened in their scarlet hoods.

Most clearly of that battle I remember
The tiredness in eyes, how hands looked thin
Around a cigarette, and the bright ember   15
Would pulse with all the life there was within.

The subject of this poem is war, specifically the feeling one gets in a battle. The images present the scene as awesome and horrible. Such images as the "red" night (from the flare of the artillery), "the clammy earth," "the icy woods," and the "black" snow tell us something of the speaker's perception of how the landscape looked and felt. Similarly, the soldiers—now burdened with helmets, rifles, packs, and overcoats—act like "moles" who burrow into the earth. Sentries stand in holes—"their feet began to freeze." The corpses lie "stiffened in their scarlet hoods," an image that depicts their bloody helmets. In the final stanza, the speaker uses images to picture "the tiredness in eyes" and "how hands looked thin / Around a cigarette." In the battle, only the burning cigarette pulses "with all the life there was within," suggesting that the inner spirit of the men is focused and concentrated in the simple pleasure of smoking. The controlling images of "The Battle" establish the context and mood. They convey, in fact, the very feeling of what it means to be in a military battle.

Imagery brings together with precision and economy the many rich associations a poet may wish to convey in depicting feelings and ideas. Rather than explicitly stating these associations, the poet uses various images in novel combinations to suggest different facets of a central issue. The following poem shows how images can communicate feelings and ideas through multiple associations.

Langston Hughes   (1902–1967)
Dream Deferred

What happens to a dream deferred?

> Does it dry up
> like a raisin in the sun?
> Or fester like a sore—
> And then run?   5
> Does it stink like rotten meat?
> Or crust and sugar over—
> like a syrupy sweet?
>
> Maybe it just sags
> like a heavy load.   10
>
> *Or does it explode?*

We recognize that the "dream deferred" of the poem generally denotes thwarted human aspirations. It is not beside the point, however, to mention that the poem was originally entitled "Harlem" and that the frustration suggested in it applies specifically to blacks struggling to survive and achieve dignity in an urban ghetto. Whatever way we read the poem, though, we see that the central issue is presented in the initial question. The answers, most in the form of other questions, are conveyed in terms of sharp, suggestive images: a dried raisin, a festering sore, rotting meat, a sugary syrup, a heavy load, and finally an image asking whether the dream will "explode." It is important that Hughes does not tell us how a dream is like an explosion. He leaves the final image open-ended so that we may wonder how the aspirations of human beings can in fact explode.

Poets often extend an image in such a way that it forms the

framework for an entire poem. As the image unfolds it reveals the content and the meaning of the poem. The following short poem provides an excellent example of this use of an image.

Walt Whitman (1819–1892)
Cavalry Crossing a Ford

A line in long array where they wind betwixt green islands,
They take a serpentine course, their arms flash in the sun—hark to the
    musical clank,
Behold the silvery river, in it the splashing horses loitering stop to drink,
Behold the brown-faced men, each group, each person a picture, the
    negligent rest on the saddles,
Some emerge on the opposite bank, others are just entering the ford—
    while,   5
Scarlet and blue and snowy white,
The guidon flags flutter gayly in the wind.

The content and the meaning of the poem are shown in the dominant image of "cavalry crossing a ford." The image also includes the various parts of a cavalry unit, the scene at the ford, and the actual event of crossing. The image is not static; it unfolds with motion and action. The point to stress is that Whitman employs really only one central visual image and that, by working out its aspects, he depicts his military scene.

    There are at least four ways an image or a pattern of imagery may function in poetry. First, it establishes the context and the mood of a poem, as we saw in "The Battle" and in "Dream Deferred." Second, it provides the structural organization of a poem, as in "Cavalry Crossing a Ford." Third, it supports or contributes to the movement and action, as well as to the theme and the meaning, of a given work. Fourth, it may suggest deeper levels of awareness and meaning, evoking primordial, archetypal, or mythic elements embodied within a poem.

    With these four major functions of images in mind, let us read and analyze the following short poem.

Howard Nemerov (b. 1920)
The Vacuum

The house is so quiet now
The vacuum cleaner sulks in the corner closet,
Its bag limp as a stopped lung, its mouth
Grinning into the floor, maybe at my
Slovenly life, my dog-dead youth.   5

I've lived this way long enough,
But when my old woman died her soul
Went into that vacuum cleaner, and I can't bear
To see the bag swell like a belly, eating the dust
And the woolen mice, and begin to howl   10

Because there is old filth everywhere
She used to crawl, in the corner and under the stair.
I know now how life is cheap as dirt,
And still the hungry, angry heart
Hangs on and howls, biting at air.   15

Nemerov's poem depends heavily upon a pattern of interrelated images
for its structure and meaning. The image of the vacuum cleaner sets the
physical and also the psychological context of the poem, depicting the
home and the function of the woman within the home. Now that "my old
woman died," the speaker relates, he experiences a terrible sense of
anxiety and loss, a feeling of emptiness (thus, by analogy, a "vacuum")
at the sight of the idle vacuum cleaner. He associates the household
appliance with the role of woman, ranging from its "sulking" in the
corner, to its "grinning" and "howling," to its belly "swelling" with
dust and woolen mice (perhaps also swelling as if with child). Nemerov's
images operate at several levels, and do so more or less at once, establishing the concrete idea of home and also suggesting the speaker's
bereavement and anger at his lost mate. Without the woman, the man
finds only a "vacuum" in his life, and he now understands that her life
was also a vacuum.

The following poem will serve as a final illustration of how imagery
organizes and integrates subject matter.

Norman Russell (b. 1921)
indian school

in the darkness
of the house of the white brother
i go alone and am frightened
strange things touch me
i cannot breathe his air   5
or eat his tasteless food

on his walls
are pictures of the world
that his walls shut out
in his hands are leaves of words   10
from dead mens mouths

he speaks to me with only
the sounds of his mouth
for he is dumb and blind
as the staggering old bear   15
filled with many arrows
as the rocks that lie on the mountain

and in his odd robes
uglier
than any other creature i have ever seen   20

i am not wise enough to know
gods purpose in him.

Here the speaker is "not wise enough to know" what purpose the
"gods" have in creating the white man and his civilization. This proposition is explored by means of images which depict white civilization as
insensitive, ugly, and sterile. The central or structural image of this
poem, as of "The Vacuum" above, is that of "house"—literally, the
Indian school. This visual image is used in the sense of a physical
dwelling but also in the sense of the larger world and of the white man's
civilization. The speaker is puzzled by the white man's habit of shutting
out the natural world and he sees him as "dumb and blind," comparing
him with a useless old bear and with rocks. In the final descriptive image,
the speaker finds the dress (the "odd robes") of the white man ugly and
unnatural. Throughout the poem, the imagery suggests, either directly
or by implication, a fundamental contrast between the natural world of
the Indian and the artificial world of the white man. In "indian school,"
as in any successful poem, the effectiveness of the imagery depends
upon how well it represents what the poet is trying to say.

Emily Dickinson   (1830–1886)
I Taste a Liquor Never Brewed

I taste a liquor never brewed—
From Tankards scooped in Pearl—
Not all the Frankfort Berries[1]
Yield such an Alcohol!

Inebriate of Air—am I—   5
And Debauchee of Dew—

----
1. Wine grapes from the region of the Rhine River near Frankfort, Germany.

Reeling—thro endless summer days—
From inns of Molten Blue—

When "Landlords" turn the drunken Bee
Out of the Foxglove's door—   10
When Butterflies—renounce their "drams"—
I shall but drink the more!

Till Seraphs swing their snowy Hats—
And Saints—to windows run—
To see the little Tippler   15
From Manzanilla² come!

Questions for Study

1. Identify the images in this poem. How does alcohol in its various forms control many of the images? Is this pattern of images effective?
2. How does the love of nature reveal itself in the poem?
3. Describe the speaker, drawing support for your comments directly from elements within the poem.
4. In earlier versions, line 3 read, "Not all the Vats upon the Rhine." Line 16 had two versions: "Leaning against the—Sun—"; and "Come staggering toward the sun." Examine these variations and determine, in your view, the most effective images for what the poem says.

Arna Bontemps (1902–1973)
Southern Mansion

Poplars are standing there still as death
And ghosts of dead men
Meet their ladies walking
Two by two beneath the shade
And standing on the marble steps.   5

There is a sound of music echoing
Through the open door
And in the field there is
Another sound tinkling in the cotton:
Chains of bondmen dragging on the ground.   10

The years go back with an iron clank,
A hand is on the gate,
A dry leaf trembles on the wall.
Ghosts are walking.
They have broken roses down   15
And poplars stand there still as death.

---

2. A dry sherry wine from Spain.

Questions for Study

1. What is the speaker's attitude toward the southern mansion? How can we determine this attitude?
2. Identify as many images as you can. Is there a pattern of images? What is the central, controlling image?
3. Certain images in the poem are highly suggestive. What, in your view, do figures such as "chains" and "ghosts" suggest?
4. Comment on what you feel Bontemps is saying in "Southern Mansion."
5. What is meant by "A hand is on the gate" and the idea that ghosts have "broken roses down"? Are these images effective ones or are they merely obscure? Explain your answer.

William Shakespeare (1564–1616)
Fear No More the Heat o' the Sun

Fear no more the heat o' the sun,
    Nor the furious winter's rages;
Thou thy worldly task hast done,
    Home art gone, and ta'en thy wages;
Golden lads and girls all must,   5
As chimney-sweepers, come to dust.

Fear no more the frown o' the great,
    Thou art past the tyrant's stroke;
Care no more to clothe and eat;
    To thee the reed is as the oak;
The sceptre,° learning, physic,° must   10   *law / medical arts*
All follow this, and come to dust.

Fear no more the lightning-flash,
    Nor the all-dreaded thunder-stone;[1]
Fear not slander, censure rash;   15
    Thou hast finished joy and moan;
All lovers young, all lovers must
Consign° to thee, and come to dust.   *Join in signing the contract*

No exorciser harm thee!
Nor no witchcraft charm thee!   20
Ghost unlaid forbear thee!
Nothing ill come near thee!
Quiet consummation have;
And renownèd be thy grave!

---

1. People in Shakespeare's time commonly thought that thunder was caused by falling stones or meteorites.

Questions for Study

1. These lines are written as a *dirge,* or a lyric of protestation and lamentation for a dead person. What structural role does the similarity of statement in the initial line of the first three stanzas suggest? How do you interpret the change in pattern in the last stanza?
2. What types of things is the person instructed not to "fear"? Is there a pattern implied in these instructions?
3. Describe three images in the poem which you regard as striking and effective, pointing out how they are so.
4. Characterize the mood of the poem. Is it consistent throughout?
5. Are the implications contained in the poem appropriate to one thought to be dead? Point out several images which support these implications.

Gerard Manley Hopkins   (1844–1889)
Spring and Fall:
To a Young Child

Márgarét, are you gríeving
Over Goldengrove unleaving?°   *shedding leaves*
Leáves, líke the things of man, you
With your fresh thoughts care for, can you?
Áh! ás the heart grows older   5
It will come to such sights colder
By and by, nor spare a sigh
Though worlds of wanwood leafmeal¹ lie;
And yet you wíll weep and know why.
Now no matter, child, the name: 10
Sórrow's spríngs áre the same.
Nor mouth had, no nor mind, expressed
What heart heard of, ghost° guessed: *spirit*
It ís the blight man was born for,
It is Margaret you mourn for.   15

Questions for Study

1. What is the speaker in this poem actually saying to Margaret? What is the speaker's attitude toward her?
2. In the poem, Margaret is sad at the falling of the leaves. What then is suggested in the image of falling leaves and the coming of the fall season? Why should Margaret, only a young child, be saddened by this passing?
3. Identify several images which you regard as effective and characterize each, pointing out its function.
4. What is the effectiveness of such an unusual word as *leafmeal?* What connota-

---

1. I.e., the leaves in the pale woods ("wanwood") fall one by one and form mealy fragments.

tions does its association with *piecemeal* and with the fallen leaves convey?

5. Interpret the following: "Sórrow's spríngs" and "It ís the blight man was born for."

6. What do you think Hopkins means by the last line? How does this line support the meaning in line 9?

Samuel Taylor Coleridge (1772–1834)
Kubla Khan

Or, a Vision in a Dream. A Fragment

In Xanadu did Kubla Khan[1]
A stately pleasure dome decree:
Where Alph, the sacred river, ran
Through caverns measureless to man
    Down to a sunless sea.   5
So twice five miles of fertile ground
With walls and towers were girdled round:
And there were gardens bright with sinuous rills,
Where blossomed many an incense-bearing tree;
And here were forests ancient as the hills,   10
Enfolding sunny spots of greenery.

But oh! that deep romantic chasm which slanted
Down the green hill athwart a cedarn cover!°   *cover of cedar trees*
A savage place! as holy and enchanted
As e'er beneath a waning moon was haunted   15
By woman wailing for her demon lover!
And from this chasm, with ceaseless turmoil seething,
As if this earth in fast thick pants were breathing,
A mighty fountain momently was forced:
Amid whose swift half-intermitted burst   20
Huge fragments vaulted like rebounding hail,
Or chaffy grain beneath the thresher's flail:
And 'mid these dancing rocks at once and ever
It flung up momently the sacred river.
Five miles meandering with a mazy motion   25
Through wood and dale the sacred river ran,
Then reached the caverns measureless to man,
And sank in tumult to a lifeless ocean:
And 'mid this tumult Kubla heard from far
Ancestral voices prophesying war!   30
    The shadow of the dome of pleasure

---

1. There was an actual thirteenth-century Mongol emperor named Kublai Khan who built a royal palace in a region of China called Xandu. Coleridge freely incorporated elements from other exotic places into the dream imagery of his poem. For example, in line 3, the river Alph is Alpheus, actually located in Greece and mentioned in Greek mythology.

Floated midway on the waves;
Where was heard the mingled measure
From the fountain and the caves.
It was a miracle of rare device,   35
A sunny pleasure dome with caves of ice!

A damsel with a dulcimer
In a vision once I saw:
It was an Abyssinian maid,
And on her dulcimer she played,   40
Singing of Mount Abora.[2]
Could I revive within me
Her symphony and song,
To such a deep delight 'twould win me,
That with music loud and long,   45
I would build that dome in air,
That sunny dome! those caves of ice!
And all who heard should see them there,
And all should cry, Beware! Beware!
His flashing eyes, his floating hair!   50
Weave a circle round him thrice,[3]
And close your eyes with holy dread,
For he on honeydew hath fed,
And drunk the milk of Paradise.

Questions for Study

1. Study the imagery of this poem. Is there a pattern evident? What are the dominant images Coleridge employs and how, in your view, do these support what he says is the reason Kubla Khan built his "stately pleasure dome"?
2. Point out words and phrases which to you seem unusual and exotic. Is there a pattern to any of these?
3. Do you detect any differences between the first and the second part of the poem? Do the language and the imagery change? Justify your responses.
4. Coleridge terms this work "a fragment," explaining that he wrote it from a partially recollected dream. Do you feel that it is a fragment or a finished, complete poem?

William Blake (1757–1827)
Ah Sun-Flower

Ah Sun-flower! weary of time,
Who countest the steps of the Sun,
Seeking after that sweet golden clime
Where the traveler's journey is done:

---

2. Identified by some scholars as Mount Amara in Abyssinia (Ethiopia).
3. A magic rite to protect one from evil spirits.

Where the Youth pined away with desire,   5
And the pale Virgin shrouded in snow
Arise from their graves, and aspire
Where my Sun-flower wishes to go.

Questions for Study

1. What associations does Blake suggest by the image of the Sun-flower? Is the image effective? Identify and comment upon other images in the poem.
2. How has Blake organized his poem? How, for example, does he work the element of time into his lines?
3. What do the Youth and the Virgin have to do with the Sun-flower? Why are they in their graves? Is the Sun-flower in the last line the same flower as in the first line? Why does Blake say "my Sun-flower"?

A Note on Haiku

Haiku is a traditional form of Japanese poetry. It has influenced modern poetry, which has come to rely heavily upon imagery. Consisting usually of seventeen syllables, normally arranged in three lines of five, seven, and five syllables respectively, haiku strives, through one striking image, to paint a vivid and sharp picture that suggests an insight into nature or human existence.

Matsuo Bashō (1644–1694)
Coolness

How very cool it feels:
    taking a noonday nap, to have
        this wall against my heels.

Kobayashi Issa (1763–1828)
The Place Where I Was Born

The place where I was born:
    All I come to—all I touch—
        blossoms of the thorn!

Characteristically, both of these haiku demonstrate the close attention given to the physical object and to the phenomena of interaction with the object. As the master Bashō put it: "The Way of Haiku arises from concentration and lack of distractions. / Look well within yourself." Haiku leads to a perception that changes and enriches the way we see ourselves and our world. Because of the differences between the Japanese and the English languages, the exact structural effects of haiku can only be approximated. Here are more examples rendered into modern English.

Matsuo Bashō (1644–1694)
The Unknown Flower

To bird and butterfly
    it is unknown, this flower here:
      the autumn sky.

Kobayashi Issa (1763–1828)
Contentment in Poverty

A one-foot waterfall
    it too makes noises, and at night
      the coolness of it all!

Kyoshi Tkkahama (1874–1959)
A Butterfly's Noises

A butterfly's
    noises while eating something—
      such quietness.

Hakyō Ishida (1913–1969)
The Captive Eagle

The captive eagle
    because of loneliness is
      flapping his wings—oh!

The economy, clarity, and sharp images of haiku make it an appealing form to imitate. Ezra Pound said that the Japanese form influenced him a great deal. This influence is especially evident in his early poetry, particularly in this lovely two-line poem.

Ezra Pound   (1885–1972)
In a Station of the Metro[1]

The apparition of these faces in the crowd;
Petals on a wet, black bough.

The haiku form is also apparent in the following lines written by a contemporary American poet.

Gary Snyder   (b. 1930)
The Roof Leak

After weeks of watching the roof leak
   I fixed it tonight
by moving a single board.

---

1. The Paris subway.

Chapter 4
Metaphor and Simile

We need to distinguish between the literal and the figurative uses of language. We must explore the second use in some detail because our understanding and enjoyment of poetry depend upon our ability to perceive figurative language and to recognize what it does in a particular poem. When we say, "Janet is pretty as a picture" or "My car is a tired, old dog," we are making nonliteral statements—we are employing figurative language. Figurative expressions present one thing in terms of another with the intention of communicating something that cannot be said, or said as well, literally. We may wish to make the vague clear, the general precise, or the abstract concrete. Perhaps we feel a need to be original, colorful, or extravagant—"The party was a real bomb" or "The liquor tasted like fire" or "As the band played, I saw reds and greens and yellows rush around in my brain."

We must be careful not to confuse literal and figurative statements, or we may find ourselves behaving like the horse in the following poem.

Anonymous (18th century)
On a Horse Who Bit a Clergyman

The steed bit his master;
  How came this to pass?
He heard the good pastor
  Say, "All flesh is grass."

The horse is literal-minded. Fortunately, we understand that the phrase "All flesh is grass" is not literal but figurative. In this chapter and in later ones, the distinctive features and uses of figurative language are explored and discussed.

Viewed in the broadest terms, **figurative language** (also referred to as **tropes,** or **figures of speech)** is an imaginative departure from straightforward statements. In poetry, we restrict the definition to specific types of nonliteral expressions. In this chapter, we intend to examine five commonly employed figures of speech, classifying them in two ways. The first group, "figures of comparison," consists of *metaphor, simile,* and *personification;* the second, "figures of association," includes *metonymy* and *synecdoche.* All figurative language relates two things that essentially are dissimilar. Any figure of speech, moreover, contains two parts or "terms": (1) the central term or subject; and (2) the second term or element introduced by comparison or by association with the subject. In the statement "Death is sleep," the first term or subject is *death,* and the second term or element introduced by comparison is *sleep.* The peaceful associations of sleep are used to create a reassuring impression of death. The effectiveness and the appeal of figurative language lie in our being able to sense the aptness of the compared or associated terms. Robert Burns says that "Love's the cloudless summer sun," but Samuel Daniel remarks that "Love is a sickness full of woes." In both lines, we understand why love might be compared with the sun or with a disease.

In examining figures of speech, we always begin by identifying the two terms of a particular figure. But often one of the terms is merely implied, not stated. If, for example, we say that "the majestic ship plows the waves," we are implying a comparison between the sea and a cultivated field. Similarly, when we are speaking of "shooting a motion picture," we are suggesting a comparison between the camera and a gun. It is not always easy to identify the implied—usually the second—term. Yet if we hope to understand the figure we must identify both terms.

Every figurative expression establishes a likeness or an approximation between two seemingly dissimilar things. If we say "Her eyes shine as brightly as Mary's eyes," we do not have a figure of speech, only a literal comparison. The two objects must be fundamentally different before we can have a proper figurative expression.

By far the most common figures of speech are metaphor and simile. A **simile** is a directly expressed comparison usually introduced by the words *like* or *as.* It shows similarity between two dissimilar things by relating them in specific ways. A famous simile occurs in the opening lines of "The Love Song of J. Alfred Prufrock" by T. S. Eliot:

> Let us go then, you and I,
> When the evening is spread out against the sky
> Like a patient etherized upon a table;

The expressed comparison of the evening "spread out against the sky / Like a patient etherized upon a table" is striking and unusual, suggesting both the inert, seemingly lifeless quality and the sickly, deteriorating condition of the evening.

A **metaphor** is an implied comparison between two dissimilar things. It relates and fuses two unlike things by expressing an identity between them. If a simile points to specific similarities, a metaphor suggests in its comparison multiple associations and identities. Aptness and precision are the virtues of effective similes, but intuitive freshness and intensity are those of successful metaphors. The beauty and power of metaphor led the Greek philosopher Aristotle (384–322 B.C.) to observe that the ability to construct these figures of speech is "a sign of genius, since it implies an intuitive perception of the similarity in dissimilars."

The following poem shows the power of metaphor.

William Blake (1757–1827)
To See a World

To see a world in a grain of sand
And a heaven in a wild flower,
Hold infinity in the palm of your hand
And eternity in an hour.

The terms of the metaphors in these lines are controlled by verbs denoting sensuous activities—*see* and *hold*. Thus, *a world* and *a heaven* are the first terms or subjects and *a grain of sand* and *a wild flower* are the second terms or elements introduced by comparison in lines 1 and 2. In lines 3 and 4, the verb *to hold* controls the subjects *infinity* and *eternity*. The powerful suggestiveness of these constructions is clear if, for example, we grasp the many ways in which "a grain of sand" is both like our world and a piece of that world. How are "heaven" and "wild flower" alike? And what identities are suggested by holding infinity in the palm of our hand and compressing eternity into an hour?

Poets sometimes extend a figure of speech throughout several lines, occasionally throughout a stanza or a poem. We call this kind of figure an **extended figure** (or an **extended simile** or **extended metaphor**). Shelley begins "The Moon" with an extended simile:

And, like a dying lady lean and pale,
Who totters forth, wrapp'd in a gauzy veil,
Out of her chamber, led by the insane
And feeble wanderings of her fading brain,
The moon arose up in the murky east
A white and shapeless mass.

The first term or subject is *moon,* and the second term is *a dying lady lean and pale.* Shelley employs the extended simile to establish precisely the "white and shapeless mass" of the moon and also to set the languid, melancholy mood of the poem. The terms of such figures are not always easy to identify. The following extended metaphor, from the opening lines of Sir Walter Raleigh's "What Is Our Life?" illustrates this difficulty:

What is our life? A play of passion;
Our mirth, the music of division;
Our mothers' wombs the tiring-houses° be   *dressing rooms*
Where we are dressed for this short comedy.   *for actors*

Raleigh identifies "life" with a play and compares features of the latter to it, concluding that although life may be "a play of passion" it finally is only "this short comedy."

In the same general category as metaphor and simile is the poetic **conceit,** any figure of speech that is especially ingenious and farfetched in its terms. Sir Thomas Wyatt, in "My Galley Charged with Forgetfulness" (see "Poems for Further Study"), employs a conceit when he identifies his frustrated love for a lady with a storm-tossed ship loaded with a cargo of that which must, but cannot be, forgotten—namely, the recollections of his lost love. He says, for example, that "every oar [is] a thought in readiness" and that his reason, which should comfort him, is "drowned." Perhaps the most famous conceit in English literature occurs in John Donne's "A Valediction: Forbidding Mourning." In it, the speaker says at one point that his and the soul of his beloved react as "twin compasses":

> If they be two, they are two so
> As stiff twin compasses are two,
> Thy soul the fixt foot makes no show
> To move, but doth, if the other do.
>
> And though it in the center sit,
> Yet when the other far doth roam,
> It leans, and hearkens after it,
> And grows erect, as that comes home.

Called a **metaphysical conceit,** the figure employed here appeals more to the intellect than to the senses or the emotions. The first term, the lovers' souls, is compared to two linked compasses (the V-shaped device for drawing circles). The brilliance of the figure lies in the unexpected view of one lover circling the other like the arm of a compass on a piece of paper.

A third important figure of comparison is personification. As the name suggests, **personification** attributes human characteristics to objects, animals, natural events, or abstract ideas. (Some scholars insist upon a clear distinction between personification and **animation,** which is giving lifelike—but not specifically human—traits to nonhuman objects, events, and the like. Here animation is included with personification.) In a broadly defined sense, personification is a metaphor, since it suggests an identity between two different objects. When we say "Time stands still" or "Money talks," we are employing personifications. Yet we see how each is also a metaphor. We commonly personify automobiles, ships, trains, airplanes, and many other objects and events in an effort to bring these things into closer view and to make our relations with them more intimate. An anonymous lyric from the sixteenth century opens with a typical personification:

> Love winged my hopes and taught me how to fly
> Far from base earth, but not to mount too high.

Here the abstract term *love* is animated, in that it has fixed "wings" to the speaker's hopes and "taught" him to fly. Similarly, James Thomson, in *The Seasons,* uses a personification in the line "The meek-eyed Morn appears, mother of dews." The personification is direct, obvious: the morning is a mother. In this way, personification brings the object close to us. At the same time, it invites countless associations because the object is animated and thus given traits with which we can identify.

A figure of speech usually associated with personification is **apostrophe,** or directly addressing someone or something absent as if present, dead as if living, or inanimate as if animate. We see, particularly in this last category, the close relationship between apostrophe and personification. Apostrophe is employed to generate the sense of someone or something being directly addressed *and* listening to what is being said. This function of apostrophe is exemplified by William Wordsworth in the opening lines of his sonnet "London, 1802":

> Milton! thou shouldst be living at this hour:
> England hath need of thee . . . .

Similarly, Robert Frost begins his short poem "Tree at My Window" with an apostrophe, organizing his entire poem as a kind of dialog between himself and the tree:

> Tree at my window, window tree,
> My sash is lowered when night comes on;
> But let there never be curtain drawn
> Between you and me.

In the twentieth-century lyric given below, the author begins with a series of apostrophes, each of which is also a personification:

Anonymous
Thus Passeth

Oh Nature! World! Oh Life! Oh Time!
Why aren't you always in your prime?
Why doesn't summer always stay?
Why aren't the flowers always gay?
Why is love's song so short a tune?   5
Why isn't January June?
I sigh to see all young girls grow
Older and older, their hair like snow.
All things on earth thus pass away:
Nothing save virtue lasts for aye.°   *ever*   10

These definitions and illustrations of the "figures of comparison" —metaphor, simile, personification—show us something of the way in which figurative language works and also indicate its power in conveying meaning. We need now to look closely at a few poems and to study the figures they contain. As stressed above, we must be able to distinguish figurative from literal statement. We must also be able to grasp the terms of the figures that are being used.

The following short poem is about war in the twentieth century.

Randall Jarrell   (1914–1965)
The Death of the Ball Turret Gunner

From my mother's sleep I fell into the State,
And I hunched in its belly till my wet fur froze.
Six miles from earth, loosed from its dreams of life,
I woke to black flak and the nightmare fighters.
When I died they washed me out of the turret with a hose.   5

Jarrell attached the following explanatory note to his poem.

"A ball turret was a plexiglass sphere set into the belly of a B-17 or B-24, and inhabited by two .50-caliber machine guns and one man, a short small man. When this gunner tracked with his machine guns a fighter attacking his bomber from below, he revolved with the turret; hunched upside-down in his little sphere, he looked like the fetus in the womb. The fighters which attacked him were armed with cannon firing explosive shells. The hose was a steam hose.''

This five-line poem gives us a first-person account of the life and death of an air-force gunner in World War II. The poem opens with a metaphor, the birth of the "I" of the poem as a "falling" from his "mother's sleep" into the State. *State* is also figurative, a personification, since in line 2 the "I" says that he "hunched in its belly" as an unborn child lies in the mother's womb. Line 3 contains a second personification—the earth is said to possess a "dream of life." The hose in line 5 is technically a synecdoche, a figure of speech in which the container (hose) is employed for the thing contained (steam). (Synecdoche is examined more thoroughly on p. 518.) But the line strikes us with the force of a literal statement, as the dead gunner, now in pieces, is washed from the turret with steam from a hose. The description "nightmare fighters" suggests a frightening view of the attacking planes, and may be termed *overstatement* (see p. 556). Yet we may also see the description as only a statement of fact, though a grim one. In line 2, "my wet fur froze" may be a literal statement—the fur-lined jacket of the gunner, wet with perspiration, would freeze at high altitudes. Or we may see the statement as a metaphor, an implicit comparison to a furry animal.

Each of these figures is drawn from the idea of mother and offspring: the connection between mother and child in line 1 and between the individual and the State in line 2; between the earth and the gunner in line 3, who is "loosed" from earth as an infant is separated from its mother at birth. Similarly, the washing-out of the gunner's remains with a hose suggests abortion. Throughout the poem the "belly" position of the gunner reminds us of mother and unborn child.

If these figures evoke the idea of mother and child, the implications are clearly ironic and grim. The individual in the twentieth century is depicted as only an impersonal part or functionary of the State, which here denotes not only the government but also society and the system under which people live. In their antiwar theme and in the raw impersonality of the life they evoke, Jarrell's lines are a bitter indictment of the fate of many modern individuals.

Lawrence Ferlinghetti (b. 1919)
Constantly Risking Absurdity

Constantly risking absurdity
           and death
  whenever he performs
        above the heads
           of his audience   5

the poet like an acrobat
climbs on rime
to a high wire of his own making
and balancing on eyebeams
above a sea of faces   10
paces his way
to the other side of day
performing entrechats°   *ballet leaps*
and sleight-of-foot tricks
and other high theatrics   15
and all without mistaking
any thing
for what it may not be

For he's the super realist
who must perforce perceive   20
taut truth
before the taking of each stance or step
in his supposed advance
toward that still higher perch
where Beauty stands and waits   25
with gravity
to start her death-defying leap

And he
a little charleychaplin man
who may or may not catch   30
her fair eternal form
spreadeagled in the empty air
of existence

Ferlinghetti has organized his poem around a comparison between the poet and a high-wire acrobat. In line 6, he explicitly states the comparison with a simile. Like the acrobat, the poet "climbs on rime / to a high wire of his own making." Each figure in the poem then discloses its meaning by reference to the high-wire acrobat: the absurdity of the poet's role, the fact of both his working "above the heads / of his audience" and his being "the super realist" who "perceives / taut truth," and his determination to achieve elusive beauty in his work. We are also introduced to the famous movie comic Charlie Chaplin who, like the poet-as-acrobat, must entertain and win over his audiences while trying to capture artistic beauty.

Ferlinghetti makes the central figure of his poem explicit. Occasionally, a poet only implies the full terms of such a figure, leaving to the reader the task of determining by the language and its connotations what this all-important figure actually is.

Emily Dickinson (1830–1886)
Because I Could Not Stop for Death

Because I could not stop for Death—
He kindly stopped for me—
The Carriage held by just Ourselves—
And Immortality.

We slowly drove—He knew no haste   5
And I had put away
My labor and my leisure too,
For His Civility—

We passed the School, where Children strove
At Recess—in the Ring—   10
We passed the Fields of Gazing Grain—
We passed the Setting Sun—

Or rather—He passed Us—
The Dews drew quivering and chill—
For only Gossamer,° my Gown—   *a soft, sheer fabric* 15
My Tippet°—only Tulle°—   *cape / a thin net fabric*

We paused before a House that seemed
A Swelling of the Ground—
The Roof was scarcely visible—
The Cornice—in the Ground—   20

Since then—'tis Centuries—and yet
Feels shorter than the Day
I first surmised the Horses' Heads
Were toward Eternity—

This poem introduces a number of personifications which are worked
out in highly striking ways. The first stanza personifies Death as one who
stops his carriage for the "I" of the poem. Immortality, also personified,
is the only other occupant. The remaining five stanzas describe the
journey of these figures to the cemetery. Additional personifications are
the "Gazing Grain," the "Setting Sun" (the "He" who passes them),
and the "Dews" that "grew quivering and chill." The grave is identified in lines 17–20 by a metaphor—"a House that seemed / A Swelling
of the Ground." We cannot catch the subtlety and the effectiveness of
these figures unless we understand that Death is portrayed as a courteous gentleman who takes the "I" for a carriage ride. This image of Death
is supported throughout by the language and the figures of the poem—he
"kindly" stops for the "I" and exhibits "Civility." Yet Dickinson never

explicitly identifies Death as a gentleman caller. We must discover this figure from a close examination of the poem.

Two other important kinds of figurative language, mentioned earlier as "figures of association," are metonymy and synecdoche. Sometimes these two are simply called metonymy, but for our purposes a distinction between them is useful. **Synecdoche** is a figure of speech that substitutes the part for the whole or the contained for the container. When we say "Give me a cup" (a cup of coffee) or "He loves the bottle" (the liquor inside), we are employing the container for the thing contained. Similarly, when we say "Get your wheels" (your car) or "He had six hands working his farm" (six workers), we are using the part for the whole. **Metonymy,** by contrast, substitutes a thing or a quality attributed to or closely associated with it for that thing. When we say "He attempted to usurp the crown" (the monarchy) or "She left to have a smoke" (cigarette), we are replacing a thing with something attributed to or associated with it.

Because synecdoche and metonymy are really extensions of the essentially comparative nature of all figurative language, it is occasionally difficult to distinguish them from metaphors. When we say "He is a limey" (a slang term for an Englishman, derived from the early practice of British sailors eating limes to prevent scurvy on long voyages) or "How much loot have you got?" (money, by association with valuables "looted" or taken as treasure), we are not sure if these figures are examples of metonymy or metaphor. Perhaps it is not finally necessary to know. A thin line exists between the need to understand the kind and function of a particular figure and an overly narrow concern with technicalities.

Nevertheless, in studying poetry, the essential kinds of figurative language need to be examined and understood. Perhaps it is a good idea to state briefly the four principal uses poems make of figures of speech: (1) to say what usually cannot be expressed literally; (2) to make the abstract concrete, the vague clear, the general precise; (3) to achieve emotional intensity and to convey strong attitudes and feelings; and (4) to concentrate thoughts and patterns of meanings.

The following two poems contain many examples of metonymy and synecdoche, in addition to other effective figures of speech.

James Shirley   (1596–1666)
The Glories of Our Blood and State

The glories of our blood and state
  Are shadows, not substantial things;

There is no armor against fate,
> Death lays his icy hand on kings:
>> Scepter and crown
>> Must tumble down,

And in the dust be equal made
With the poor crooked scythe and spade.

Some men with swords may reap the field,
> And plant fresh laurels where they kill;

But their strong nerves at last must yield,
> They tame but one another still:
>> Early or late,
>> They stoop to fate,

And must give up their murmuring breath,
When they, pale captives, creep to death.

The garlands wither on your brow,
> Then boast no more your mighty deeds;

Upon Death's purple altar now,
> See where the victor-victim bleeds:
>> Your heads must come
>> To the cold tomb;

Only the actions of the just
Smell sweet, and blossom in their dust.

The theme of this poem is a familiar one—death comes to all, to kings and to commoners alike. Shirley states this theme in a fresh and powerful way by devising striking figures of speech. He uses many examples of metonymy, with five or six occurring in the first stanza, depending upon how one reads the figure in the opening line.

The poem begins with a metonymy: *blood* (for ancestral heritage). We might read *blood* as a synecdoche, the part (blood) for the whole (people). Yet the sense of the figure indicates that it probably refers to the aristocratic bloodline, not merely to individuals as ancestors. Perhaps the most memorable examples of metonymy in the poem are the two pairs in the opening stanza: *scepter* and *crown* (badges of royalty) in line 5; and *scythe* and *spade* (farm tools) in line 8. Shirley contrasts the life of royalty with that of the commoner or peasant, but he uses these figures as ironic reminders that death makes all classes "equal" in the "dust" (the grave). *Dust* is a metonymy, associating the remains of the dead (dust) with their living selves. In another sense, the dust may be also seen as literal dust.

The second and third stanzas also contain examples of metonymy and synecdoche. In lines 9 and 10, *men with swords* and *laurels* (for triumphs in battle, by association with the wreaths of laurel branches given to heroes) are examples of metonymy. Similarly, in line 11, Shirley employs a metonymy, *strong nerves* (courage), and a synecdoche, *murmuring breath* (life) in line 15. The final stanza contains a synecdoche in line 17, *brow* (the entire head); and another in line 21, *heads* (persons). The final line of the poem repeats the metonymy of *dust* (the grave).

Other figures of speech occur in the poem. A metaphor, for example, is used in lines 1 and 2, "The glories . . . are shadows." A personification turns up in line 4, "Death lays his icy hand on kings." Shirley uses an implied metaphor in line 19 when he speaks of "Death's purple altar," implying a comparison with a place of sacrifice. In the last two lines, he makes an implied comparison between actions and flowers, saying that actions "smell sweet" and "blossom" in the grave. Although each of the figures in the poem is vivid and striking, their effectiveness depends ultimately upon the skillful manner in which each serves to support and convey the poem's meaning.

Richard Lovelace (1618–1658)
To Lucasta, Going to the Wars

Tell me not, Sweet, I am unkind
That from the nunnery
Of thy chaste breast and quiet mind,
To war and arms I fly.

True, a new mistress now I chase,   5
The first foe in the field;
And with a stronger faith embrace
A sword, a horse, a shield.

Yet this inconstancy is such
As you too shall adore;   10
I could not love thee, Dear, so much,
Loved I not honor more.

This seventeenth-century poem contains several notable figures of speech. Written to Lucasta, who is addressed in an apostrophe in line 1, the poem offers a paradox—that the speaker cannot love her unless he leaves her to fight as a soldier. The figures Lovelace employs support this paradox. Metonymy occurs in line 4 in the use of *arms* for the act of bearing arms (and Lovelace may be punning on the word *arms*); and in line 8 in the use of *sword, horse,* and *shield* for the profession of the soldier. Several effective metaphors occur. Lines 2 and 3 contain a metaphor comparing the "chaste breast" of Lucasta to a "nunnery" (another possible pun, since in Renaissance England *nunnery* was sometimes vulgarly used to refer to a brothel). And in lines 5 and 6, Lovelace identifies his "new mistress" with the first enemy soldier he meets. The final two lines introduce a personification of honor as a thing that the poet loves more than he loves the lady. Lovelace manages to praise Lucasta and still leave her, but he does so without seeming to deny his love for her.

Paul Lawrence Dunbar (1872–1906)
We Wear the Mask

We wear the mask that grins and lies,
It hides our cheeks and shades our eyes,—
This debt we pay to human guile;
With torn and bleeding hearts we smile,
And mouth with myriad subtleties.   5

Why should the world be overwise,
In counting all our tears and sighs?
Nay, let them only see us, while
   We wear the mask.

We smile, but, O great Christ, our cries   10
To thee from tortured souls arise.
We sing, but oh the clay is vile
Beneath our feet, and long the mile;
But let the world dream otherwise,
   We wear the mask!   15

Questions for Study

1. What is the meaning of the mask Dunbar speaks of? What kind of figure of speech is *mask?*
2. Find examples of personification in the poem.
3. Comment on the effectiveness of the figures employed in lines 4 and 5.
4. What do you think the "we" and the "them" in the poem represent?
5. Read the final stanza carefully and identify any figurative language you find.

George Gordon, Lord Byron (1788–1824)
She Walks in Beauty

She walks in beauty, like the night
   Of cloudless climes and starry skies;
And all that's best of dark and bright

Meet in her aspect and her eyes:
Thus mellowed to that tender light   5
    Which heaven to gaudy day denies.

One shade the more, one ray the less,
    Had half impaired the nameless grace
Which waves in every raven tress,
    Or softly lightens o'er her face;   10
Where thoughts serenely sweet express
    How pure, how dear their dwelling place.

And on that cheek, and o'er that brow,
    So soft, so calm, yet eloquent,
The smiles that win, the tints that glow,   15
    But tell of days in goodness spent,
A mind at peace with all below,
    A heart whose love is innocent!

Questions for Study

1. We are told that these lines were written in honor of Mrs. Robert John Wilmot, whom Byron had met only the night before; she was wearing a black mourning gown decorated with bright spangles. How does the poet see this lady who "walks in beauty"? Try to construct an impression of her from your reading of the poem.
2. The theme of the poem is the beauty of the lady. Identify as many references to this beauty as you can. How many of these references employ figurative language?
3. Can you discover a central figure of speech in the poem? If so, describe it and show how it is implied in the other figures.
4. Why does Byron employ three stanzas to describe the lady? Is there a pattern to his description? Is there some type of progression in the development of the poem?

Stephen Spender (b. 1909)
An Elementary School Classroom in a Slum

Far far from gusty waves these children's faces.
Like rootless weeds, the hair torn round their pallor.
The tall girl with her weighed-down head. The paper-
seeming boy, with rat's eyes. The stunted, unlucky heir
Of twisted bones, reciting a father's gnarled disease,   5
His lesson from his desk. At back of the dim class
One unnoted, sweet and young. His eyes live in a dream
Of squirrel's game, in tree room, other than this.

On sour cream walls, donations. Shakespeare's head,
Cloudless at dawn, civilized dome riding all cities.   10
Belled, flowery, Tyrolese valley.[1] Open-handed map

---

1. The Tyrol, a province in the Alpine region of western Austria, is noted for its scenic and pastoral beauty.

Awarding the world its world. And yet, for these
Children, these windows, not this world, are world,
Where all their future's painted with a fog,
A narrow street sealed in with a lead sky,   15
Far far from rivers, capes, and stars of words.

Surely, Shakespeare is wicked, the map a bad example
With ships and sun and love tempting them to steal—
For lives that slyly turn in their cramp*e*d holes
From fog to endless night? On their slag heap, these children   20
Wear skins peeped through by bones and spectacles of steel
With mended glass, like bottle bits on stones.
All of their time and space are foggy slum.
So blot their maps with slums as big as doom.

Unless, governor, teacher, inspector, visitor,   25
This map becomes their window and these windows
That shut upon their lives like catacombs,
Break O break open till they break the town
And show the children to green fields, and make their world
Run azure on gold sands, and let their tongues   30
Run naked into books, the white and green leaves open
History theirs whose language is the sun.

Questions for Study

1. The children in the poem are, each in his or her own way, victims of poverty, disease, parental and social indifference. Identify as many figures of speech as you can which depict these conditions, pointing out how each figure describes its subject.
2. In addition to figurative language, the poet employs vivid, often striking language. Identify as many of these nonfigurative instances of striking language as you can, pointing out how each depicts its subject.
3. Interpret the lines, "Surely, Shakespeare is wicked, the map a bad example / With ships and sun and love tempting them to steal—." Relate your response to what the poet continues to say in the stanza.
4. Why does the poet employ four apostrophes in line 25? Do you think he is trying to get these people to listen? Why? What does he hope will happen to these children?

Sir Philip Sidney (1554–1586)
With How Sad Steps, O Moon, Thou Climb'st the Skies

With how sad steps, O Moon, thou climb'st the skies!
    How silently, and with how wan a face!
    What! may it be that even in heavenly place
    That busy archer his sharp arrows tries?
Sure, if that long-with-love-acquainted eyes   5
    Can judge of love, thou feel'st a lover's case.

I read it in thy looks; thy languished grace
To me, that feel the like, thy state descries.
Then, even of fellowship, O Moon, tell me:
Is constant love deemed there but want of wit?
Are beauties there as proud as here they be?
Do they above love to be loved, and yet
Those lovers scorn whom that love doth possess?
Do they call virtue there ungratefulness?

10

Questions for Study

1. This poem is organized around what central figure? Explain how this figure controls the thought pattern of the entire poem.
2. Traditionally, the moon is associated with love (as well as with chastity), particularly with love-sickness and love-madness. Does this fact explain any of the figures in the poem? If so, which ones?
3. Who or what is "that busy archer"? What figure of speech is this?
4. Explain the line, "Is constant love deemed there but want of wit?" How is this line indicative of the general meaning of the poem?

Sylvia Plath   (1932–1963)
Metaphors

I'm a riddle in nine syllables,
An elephant, a ponderous house,
A melon strolling on two tendrils.
O red fruit, ivory, fine timbers!
This loaf's big with its yeasty rising.
Money's new-minted in this fat purse.
I'm a means, a stage, a cow in calf.
I've eaten a bag of green apples,
Boarded the train there's no getting off.

5

Questions for Study

1. As the poet says, the poem is a riddle; and its solution depends upon our ability to analyze the terms of the metaphors she employs, beginning with the metaphor in line 1. Such words as *elephant, house, melon, loaf, purse, stage, cow* are our initial clues. Can you solve the riddle?
2. The last two lines are crucial to the poem. Comment on them and on how they work out what you believe is the meaning of the poem.

Chapter 5
Symbol and Allegory

Figures of speech are often referred to collectively as *metaphorical language*. The Greek word *metapherein,* from which the word *metaphor* comes, means "to bring over" or "to carry beyond." And so metaphorical language is concerned with meanings that are carried beyond literal statements. The richest and, at the same time, the most troublesome example of metaphorical language is the symbol. In the broadest sense, a **symbol,** like other figures of speech, consists of using one thing to suggest another. But it is more than an image or a metaphor. A symbol remains itself and yet stands for or suggests something else. Its function is illustrated by the Christian cross, the Star of David, and the crescent of Islam. These symbols not only *stand for* Christianity, Judaism, and the Islamic religion but also *embody* a complex of meanings, emotions, and attitudes clustered about the histories of these religions. As symbols, the cross, the star, and the crescent point to much more than can be reduced to a simple statement. In the end, we cannot exhaust or empty these symbols of their rich meanings and significance.

The Swiss psychiatrist Carl G. Jung (1875–1961) had the living power of certain symbols in mind when, in *Man and His Symbols* (1964), he insisted upon a distinction between a sign and a symbol: "The sign is always less than the concept it represents, while a symbol always stands for something more than its obvious and immediate meaning." A sign is one object substituted for another; a symbol is something which is itself and yet which represents, suggests, and embodies an intricate system of feelings, ideas, values, attitudes, and meanings. A sign is exhausted when it has pointed to something else, but the implications of a true symbol are never exhausted. It always suggests more than can be grasped or fitted neatly into words.

This distinction is useful in considering symbols in poetry. Such symbols are not solely objects presented in the work. They also may be characters, situations, actions, even verbal patterns or ideas. Thus it is best to approach symbols with a view toward their function within a particular work and to recognize that symbols must emerge from their contexts. These points need emphasis to rid us of the notion that poetry is merely a network of symbols and "hidden meanings," a coded message which can be totally and immediately grasped only after we have "cracked" the code. Symbols do not yield their meanings in this way. By its nature, a symbol embodies such a rich complex of things, qualities, feelings, and ideas that all its implications can never be completely comprehended.

Recognizing that symbols emerge from a work makes it easier to identify and interpret them, as well as to distinguish between them and other figures of speech. A symbol differs from other figures in basic ways. First, unlike other figures of speech, a symbol usually points to what is unnamed. Second, a symbol, though concrete in itself, suggests a meaning that is often complex and abstract. A circle, for example, is frequently a symbol of perfection, completion, unity, or the integrity of the self. When employed in this way in poetry, a circle calls up a concrete image. Yet it is also a symbolic reference to one or more of these universal meanings. However, such abstractions as love, honor, justice, and truth are not symbols, which are always concrete and exist in and for themselves. A circle, after all, *is* a physical representation. Only as themselves and in a context do symbols emerge with the power to suggest and embody other things such as love, honor, justice, and truth.

An examination of a symbol in several poems should make this discussion clearer. Consider the following poem and examine what we may call the three-part symbol of the spider, the flower, and the moth.

Robert Frost (1874–1963)
Design

I found a dimpled spider, fat and white,
On a white heal-all, holding up a moth
Like a white piece of rigid satin cloth—
Assorted characters of death and blight
Mixed ready to begin the morning right,   5
Like the ingredients of a witches' broth—
A snow-drop spider, a flower like a froth,
And dead wings carried like a paper kite.

What had that flower to do with being white,
The wayside blue and innocent heal-all?   10

What brought the kindred spider to that height,
Then steered the white moth thither in the night?
What but design of darkness to appall?—
If design govern in a thing so small.

The scene Frost draws is a simple one: a white spider sits atop a white flower and holds a white moth. However, the poet, using two graphic similes (lines 6 and 7), sees in this event more than a scene in nature. In line 9, Frost introduces a series of inquiries or propositions regarding this event, looking beyond it to discover what, if any, force or purpose made things as they are. Further, he asks what possibly brought these three—flower, spider, moth—together in such a deadly way. He offers his own speculations in the last two lines: "What but [i.e., except] design of darkness to appall" has accomplished these things. In the last line, however, he qualifies this statement, wondering if the principle of "design govern in a thing so small." The word *design* (significantly the poem's title) suggests a pattern or shape that perhaps operates throughout nature. Yet "design of darkness" clearly "appalls"—it astonishes and fills the speaker in the poem with dismay. Frost employs his symbol, in other words, to raise the question of "design," but he leaves its answer open-ended.

An effective symbol in poetry fits the content from which it emerges. Its value is the deepening and the enriching of the meaning the poet hopes to convey. The following poem shows how a symbol grows out of the way a poem presents a particular subject.

Edna St. Vincent Millay (1892–1950)
God's World

O world, I cannot hold thee close enough!
  Thy winds, thy wide grey skies!
  Thy mists, that roll and rise!
Thy woods, this autumn day, that ache and sag
And all but cry with colour! That gaunt crag   5
To crush! To lift the lean of that black bluff!
World, World, I cannot get thee close enough!

Long have I known a glory in it all,
  But never knew I this:
  Here such a passion is   10
As stretcheth me apart,—Lord, I do fear
Thou'st made the world too beautiful this year;
My soul is all but out of me,—let fall
No burning leaf; prithee, let no bird call.

The two-part division of this poem is important. If it had ended with the first stanza, *world,* here an apostrophe, would have been merely the central figure of the piece. And wind, sky, mist, and so on would have been only physical attributes of the figure itself. But in the second stanza, the poet suggests much more in the use of *world,* speaking of experiences with the world that evoke "a passion" which "stretcheth me apart." The world emerges as a symbol of the forces that animate human existence and inform our lives—the physical scenes around us, the passions we experience, and our hopes for grace and beauty. Although expressing the planet earth, world as symbol embodies much more than the poet can put into the few words of her poem. The speaker in these lines is unable to express in any other way what that world actually means to him or her.

Poets create symbols, as we have said, to deepen and to enrich a particular work. They also employ symbols to intensify and to extend experiences, as in "Design" and "God's World." Often a poet will use as his subject a topic or an event that is already highly symbolic. He does this in order to associate his own thoughts and emotions with a known symbol. In this way, the symbol supports and strengthens his meaning. The following poem offers a personalized interpretation of a recognized symbolic event.

William Butler Yeats   (1865–1939)
The Second Coming[1]

Turning and turning in the widening gyre[2]
The falcon cannot hear the falconer;
Things fall apart; the center cannot hold;
Mere anarchy is loosed upon the world,
The blood-dimmed tide is loosed, and everywhere   5
The ceremony of innocence is drowned;
The best lack all conviction, while the worst
Are full of passionate intensity.

Surely some revelation is at hand;
Surely the Second Coming is at hand.   10
The Second Coming! Hardly are those words out
When a vast image out of *Spiritus Mundi*[3]

---

1. The return of Christ, which signifies for Yeats the end of the 2000-year Christian cycle of history. See Matt. 24:29–44.
2. Literally, the spiral turning of the falcon in flight. Yeats uses *gyre* figuratively to suggest a cycle of history.
3. "Soul of the Universe," one of Yeats' private symbols. All individuals are connected to it by means of what he called the "Great Memory," another of his symbols and an idea closely associated with Jung's "collective unconscious"—a universal unconscious which holds and preserves the earlier memories of the human race. Out of this Great Memory, Yeats believed, the poet drew his true images and symbols.

Troubles my sight: somewhere in sands of the desert
A shape with lion body and the head of a man,[4]
A gaze blank and pitiless as the sun,   15
Is moving its slow thighs, while all about it
Reel shadows of the indignant desert birds.
The darkness drops again; but now I know
That twenty centuries of stony sleep
Were vexed to nightmare by a rocking cradle,[5]   20
And what rough beast, its hour come round at last,
Slouches towards Bethlehem to be born?

Yeats has constructed his poem around a well-known prophecy,
though he employs specific symbols as well. In approaching this complex work, let us initially identify certain symbols and see how the poet
uses them. In doing this, we may find clues to other symbols and levels of
meaning.

Yeats divides his poem into two unequal parts. The second, longer
part begins in line 9 with references to the Second Coming. In Christian
doctrine, the Second Coming is the key event marking the end of the
world and world history. Christ, who was crucified, buried, and arose
from the dead, will return to earth to judge the living and the dead, after
which the millennial reign of God will begin. This act of Christ's Second
Coming provides the central figure of the poem and gives Yeats his title.
But Yeats offers no literal rendition of Christian prophecy. Rather he
adapts the event to his own view of the world, employing the Second
Coming to suggest that the disorder, upheaval, and cataclysmic changes
taking place during and after World War I indicate that this event is at
hand. The poem appeared in fact in 1921.

The opening figure of the poem shows a falconer losing contact with
his falcon, which flies ever higher in a widening spiral. This movement
away from a center accords with Yeats' next image—"Things fall apart;
the center cannot hold." It is now a time of falling away from the
"center" that, according to Yeats, every civilization must have. Yeats
believed that history moves in cycles of birth-growth-decline-death. The
image of the falconer and his falcon suggests Yeats' idea that the twentieth century will see the collapse of Western civilization.

Lines 4 through 8 introduce the idea of decay and dissolution in no
uncertain terms. In the civil war in his native Ireland, in the Russian
Revolution of 1917, and in World War I, Yeats saw "mere anarchy"
loosed upon the world.

---

4. The sphinx, a mythical beast of Egypt with the head of a man and the body of a lion. In Greek
mythology, the sphinx is a winged monster with a woman's head and a lion's body that destroyed all
who could not answer its riddle. To Yeats, the figure suggested an enigmatic force anticipating great
change.
5. The cradle of the infant Jesus whose birth, Yeats believed, signalled the end of the Greco-
Roman cycle of history.

> The blood-dimmed tide is loosed, and everywhere
> The ceremony of innocence is drowned;
> The best lack all conviction, while the worst
> Are full of passionate intensity.

Yeats felt that true ritual growing out of a spiritual center might redeem the flood of irrationality and reinstate "the ceremony of innocence," which "is drowned" in the mounting chaos. He saw "the blood-dimmed tide" of horror succeeding horror and could only conclude sorrowfully that the leaders and the intellectuals ("the best" of modern men) today "lack all conviction" and that others, those who seem to speak for mankind ("the worst") offer nothing but "passionate intensity." For Yeats, this situation meant only hatred and violence.

The opening stanza of the poem is dominated by symbols of dissolution, irrationality, and death, while the second is characterized by the figure of the Second Coming—that is, by the symbolic end of the present era, which also signals the birth of a new order of life. Yet what alarms Yeats is that, in the place of the infant Christ who in time transformed the Greco-Roman civilization, only a "rough beast" appears, arising "somewhere in sands of the desert." It even now "Slouches towards Bethlehem to be born." Sphinxlike, with the head of a man and the body of a lion, this figure is an enigmatic and crucial symbol, suggesting many kinds of associations and implications. The possibilities of interpretation are rich and diverse. Yet the coming of the "rough beast" symbolizes for Yeats both an end and a beginning—a time of vast and monumental change in Western civilization. Whether the new era will be one of nightmare and destruction or creative vision and a new civilization, the poem does not say.

In poetry, symbols are usually classified into two types: *conventional symbols* and *literary* (or *personal*) *symbols*. A third category, *natural symbols*, is also explained below.

Conventional symbols are objects and the like that, through time and usage, have taken on a customary significance or meaning. These range from flags, uniforms, and insignias, to objects such as red roses (romantic love), altars (sacrifice or worship), and mansions (social status). Since many of these symbols are stale because of overuse, poets employ them sparingly.

Literary symbols are by far the most frequently employed kind. They result either from an author's explicit use and from the context within which they appear or, less likely, from an author's private system of philosophical ideas. As we saw in "The Second Coming," Yeats employs this latter kind of symbolic figure. William Blake is another poet who has his own system of symbols. Usually, however, the power and meaning of symbols depend upon the context and way in which an author treats a subject.

Natural symbols are objects and patterns that suggest meanings, associations, and implications without reference to any particular work or conventional usage. The sun, for example, is an accepted symbol for light, energy, power, rejuvenation, and so on. Yet any use of the sun within a particular work is not necessarily a symbolic one. The sun is itself a prominent natural object, and such a reference may be literal. Natural symbols, unlike conventional symbols, are "open-ended"— that is, the sun as symbol suggests much more than can be fixed and literally expressed. Other natural symbols are the earth, the moon, the sea, summer and winter, day and night. C. G. Jung has argued that such figures as the mother, the father, the virgin, the hero, the guide, the antagonist, and similar human types often manifest themselves as "images of the archetypes." Later in this chapter, "A Note on Myth and Archetypes" explores Jung's meaning.

Symbols and symbolic patterns in poetry cause difficulties. You may ask, "How can I tell what is and what is not a symbol in this poem?" There is no simple or sure method. Only through practice and study can you gain confidence and skill in reading and analyzing poetry—for its symbols, as well as for its other features. Here, nevertheless, are three rules of thumb to follow in exploring a poem for its possible symbols.

1. Read carefully and closely, looking for the repetition of words, phrases, ideas, and especially verbal patterns. Remember that symbols do not so much "stick out" as *emerge* from the body of a poem.

2. Paraphrase the poem, or at least its notable parts, seeing if objects and the like suggest more than what at first they appear to. Oddly enough, paraphrasing often reveals in surprising ways a symbol or the likelihood of a symbolic element.

3. Observe in particular biblical, mythological, and historical references, or any pattern of seasonal and daily repetitions. These frequently point to additional implications and meanings which often are symbolic.

A word of caution: in reading poetry, it is better to find too few symbols than too many. The impulse to read too much into a poem, to project one's personal views or prejudices, and to confuse vivid, colorful images and figures of speech with symbols is great and should be counterbalanced with thoughtfulness. Every red rose does not have to mean love and romance; every conflict between persons, an Oedipal or a Faustian struggle; every unfortunate victim, a crucified Jesus. Most poems will yield their meanings, or at least much of their meaning, even if you miss a symbol or two.

Closely related to symbolism is allegory. Like the symbol, allegory uses one thing to suggest another and thus in form resembles an extended metaphor. But there are also marked differences. In poetry, **allegory** is a narrative or descriptive technique in which objects, names, and qualities are employed in a more or less interrelated pattern which points beyond the poem to other meanings. Allegory concerns itself less with objects and their surface meanings than with representing something to which these concrete figures refer, usually issues of a moral, religious, historical, or philosophical nature. Dante's *Divine Comedy* and Edmund Spenser's *The Faerie Queene* are masterworks in the technique of poetic allegory. The following short poem is an example of allegory in verse:

Stephen Crane   (1871–1900)
The Wayfarer

The wayfarer,
Perceiving the pathway to truth,
Was struck with astonishment.
It was thickly grown with weeds.
"Ha," he said,   5
"I see that none has passed here
In a long time."
Later he saw that each weed
Was a singular knife.
"Well," he mumbled at last,   10
"Doubtless there are other roads."

Such elements as "the wayfarer" who perceives the "pathway to truth," which is "thickly grown with weeds," and the "other roads" of the final line establish that the poem is allegorical. Let us paraphrase Crane's lines: the individual, journeying through this world, discovers that the pursuit of truth is attempted by few and that the way is difficult and painful ("each weed" is "a singular knife"). Understanding this, the individual may choose another path. On the surface level, the tale of the wayfarer is not important or even interesting. It is only after we recognize and explore the secondary or allegorical level that the poem's true meaning emerges.

Allegory, at least in a pure or consistent form, is seldom employed today. But short narrative or lyric poems often contain allegorical elements. A part or several aspects of a poem might employ allegorical techniques in developing its overall meaning. The following poem lends itself to an allegorical interpretation.

William Blake   (1757–1827)
A Poison Tree

I was angry with my friend:
I told my wrath, my wrath did end.
I was angry with my foe:
I told it not, my wrath did grow.

And I water'd it in fears,   5
Night and morning with my tears:
And I sunnèd it with smiles,
And with soft deceitful wiles.

And it grew both day and night,
Till it bore an apple bright;   10
And my foe beheld it shine,
And he knew that it was mine,

And into my garden stole
When the night had veil'd the pole:
In the morning glad I see   15
My foe outstretch'd beneath the trée.

One of the principal features of allegory is that characters, objects, and
situations are one-to-one representations of abstract qualities. The action takes place on both the surface and the allegorical levels. In Blake's
poem, each element may be interpreted on the allegorical level: "I" is
any person angry with a friend or foe; unconfessed "wrath" is a "poison
tree" which the "I" waters at night by "fears" and in the morning by
"tears." This allegorical poison tree is then "sunnèd" with "smiles"
and "soft deceitful wiles." In time it produces an "apple" which
poisons the foe. Moral of the narrative: unconfessed anger can cause
irreparable damage to ourselves and to others.

Read in this way, each component of the poem is thoroughly allegorical and is related to an abstract framework. We might also read the
poem as an allegorical treatment of the fall of man in the Garden of Eden.
This reading is suggested by the implication of envy (associated with the
envy of Adam and Eve toward God's knowledge), by references to the
tree (the tree of knowledge of good and evil), to the apple (which,
according to some accounts, was the fruit Eve took from the tree), and
even to the death of the foe (the introduction of death into the world by
eating the forbidden fruit).

Symbolism and allegory, although different, are often found together
in the same work. The following popular American folk song is a delightful mixture of symbols and allegorical elements.

Anonymous (c. 1910)
The Big Rock Candy Mountains

One evening when the sun was low
And the jungle fires were burning
Down the track came a hobo hamming°   *overacting*
And he said, "Boys, I'm not turning;

I'm headed for a land that's far away
Beside the crystal fountains.
So come with me, we'll go and see
The Big Rock Candy Mountains.''

In the Big Rock Candy Mountains
There's a land that's fair and bright,
Where the handouts grow on bushes
And you sleep out every night,
Where the boxcars all are empty
And the sun shines every day
On the birds and the bees
And the cigarette trees,
The rock-and-rye° springs   *drink made from rye whiskey*
Where the whangdoodle° sings,   *imaginary bird*
In the Big Rock Candy Mountains.

In the Big Rock Candy Mountains
All the cops have wooden legs
And the bulldogs all have rubber teeth
And the hens lay hard-boiled eggs;
The farmers' trees are full of fruit
And the barns are full of hay:
O I'm bound to go
Where there ain't no snow,
And the rain don't fall,
And the wind don't blow,
In the Big Rock Candy Mountains.

In the Big Rock Candy Mountains
You never change your socks
And the little streams of alkyhol
Come a-trickling down the rocks;
The shacks all have to tip their hats
And the railroad bulls° are blind;   *detectives*
There's a lake of stew,
You can paddle all around
In a big canoe,
In the Big Rock Candy Mountains.

In the Big Rock Candy Mountains
The jails are made of tin
And you can bust right out again
As soon as they put you in;
There ain't no short-handled shovels,
No axes, saws or picks:
O I'm going to stay
Where you sleep all day,
Where they hung the Turk
That invented work,

5

10

15

20

25

30

35

40

45

50

In the Big Rock Candy Mountains.
I'll see you all
This coming fall
In the Big Rock Candy Mountains.

The Big Rock Candy Mountains are at once a symbol of what the speaker fantasies an earthly paradise would be like and also an allegorical element upon which the poet bases other elements: e.g., "handouts grow on bushes"; "the cops have wooden legs"; and there are "little streams of alkyhol." Although the images and figures are wonderfully exaggerated, they suggest several levels of meaning and various implications. What, for example, is meant by the lines, "There ain't no short-handled shovels, / No axes, saws or picks"? Similarly, what associations can be made between the descriptive details, even the overall outline, of this would-be paradise and other idyllic lands of fable and myth?

Another poetic device closely related to symbol is **allusion,** or a reference, either direct or indirect, to something real or fictitious outside of the work. Usually the reference is taken from history, literature, the Bible, mythology, or other sources. If we say, "Like Caesar, the politician believed in power," we are making a historical allusion to Julius Caesar, general and statesman who became the first dictator of Rome. If we say, "The new playwright is certainly no Tennessee Williams," we are employing an allusion to one of the most successful dramatists in American stage history. Allusions introduce significant additional materials that support and intensify the emotion or idea of a particular line of verse or poem. In his long poem *Hugh Selwyn Mauberly,* Ezra Pound wrote that "His true Penelope was Flaubert," creating a double allusion—first, to the faithful wife of Odysseus in Homer's *Odyssey* and, second, to Gustave Flaubert, French novelist noted for the precision of his written style. Pound's allusions vividly emphasize that the true "wife" of the artist is a craft as precise and exact as Flaubert's style.

In the following poem, allusions help the poet organize and intensify his meaning.

Edgar Allan Poe (1809–1849)
To Helen

Helen, thy beauty is to me
   Like those Nicèan barks of yore,
That gently, o'er a perfumed sea,
   The weary, way-worn wanderer bore
   To his own native shore.   5

On desperate seas long wont to roam,
    Thy hyacinth hair, thy classic face,
Thy Naiad airs have brought me home
    To the glory that was Greece
And the grandeur that was Rome.   10

Lo! in yon brilliant window-niche
    How statue-like I see thee stand,
    The agate lamp within thy hand!
Ah, Psyche, from the regions which
    Are Holy Land!   15

   These lines in praise of feminine beauty are developed largely by
means of allusions to ancient Greece and Rome, particularly to mythology and the Trojan War. The title is itself an allusion to Helen, wife of the
king of Sparta; her abduction by Paris began the Trojan War. The first
stanza is dominated by allusions to the war and to exotic places associated with it. The beauty of Helen is directly compared to those
"Nicèan barks of yore." Scholars are not agreed on the source of this
allusion. It clearly refers to ships, but also to trees taken from around the
ancient city of Nicaea (an area in what is now Turkey and not far from
the site of ancient Troy). The indirect allusion to "the perfumed sea" is a
further linking of Helen's beauty with the seas Odysseus traveled in
attempting to return to his native Ithaca after the Trojan War.
   The second stanza continues this association with the Trojan legend
with the mention of the "desperate seas" which caused the Greeks such
difficulties in traveling to and from Troy. The references to Helen's
"hyacinth hair" and to her "classic face" might be seen as indirect
allusions to the mythological story of Apollo's love for the dead youth
Hyacinthus, preserved by Apollo in a beautiful flower bearing the
youth's name. Lines 9 and 10 allude to the Hellenic and the Roman
civilizations—to the "glory" of Greece and the "grandeur" of Rome.
The last stanza draws upon the myth of Psyche, who loved the beautiful
Cupid so much that she lit a lamp in order to see him as he slept. Some
readers also see in these lines a hint of the Greek legend of Leander, who
nightly swam the Hellespont to his beloved Hero, who guided him
across by a lamp. (Poe's lamp is made of agate stone, in ancient times
thought to have magical powers that imparted immortality.) The last line
connects Psyche, in a final allusion, with the Holy Land of Palestine.
   It is difficult to imagine Poe's achieving either the intensity or the
striking, effective associations in "To Helen" without these allusions.
At the same time, the lines are largely unintelligible to readers who do
not recognize the allusions. And so we must look up all unfamiliar
allusions if we are to appreciate and employ the rich and complex

suggestiveness of a great deal of poetry.

Not all poems depend upon allusions as heavily as Poe's "To Helen." Here is a poem by a contemporary poet that contains one literary allusion. Even if we fail to recognize it, we should still be able to understand the overall direction and meaning of these lines.

Imamu Amiri Baraka [Leroi Jones] (b. 1934)
A Poem for Speculative Hipsters

He had got, finally,
to the forest
of motives. There were no
owls, or hunters. No Connie Chatterleys
resting beautifully   5
on their backs, having casually
brought socialism
To England.
            Only ideas,
and their opposites.   10
                  Like,
            he was *really*
            nowhere.

The literary allusion (line 4) is to the heroine of D. H. Lawrence's novel, *Lady Chatterley's Lover* (1928), in which she is sexually and spiritually awakened by a liaison with her husband's gamekeeper. The reference suggests that in the "forest / of motives" there are no "Connie Chatterleys," only speculative possibilities. Yet the poem can be read without identifying or interpreting this allusion. Baraka organizes his lines around the image of a journey or quest. In the opening lines, the speaker observes that he has come to the point of trying to understand why he or others do what they do. Regardless of how we interpret his internal references—"owls," "hunters," "Connie Chatterleys"—we can grasp in the closing lines that the speaker has discovered "Only ideas, / and their opposites" and that this discovery has gotten him "nowhere." For whatever reasons, which the poem does not explore, the speaker is aware of the futility of mere "speculation." There is perhaps in the title a warning to would-be "hipsters" not to indulge in speculations but, by inference, to act. And the poem suggests that we should act rather than ask, like the owl, "why" or "who."

A Note on Myth and Archetypes

Two terms frequently used today in discussing poetry are *myth* and *archetype*. In the popular mind, a myth is something that is not true, a description which does not explain the full meaning of the term. In a narrow sense, myths are tales about gods and heroes and the supernatural worlds in which they live. Traditional folk narratives and the rites of primitive or preliterate societies employ myths in this way. Viewed more comprehensively, **myth** is a story or a group of interrelated stories—the Greek *mythos* means "tale" or "story"—that people accept, for various reasons, as making important statements about the universe and human life that could not be made in any other way. Stories of pre-Hellenic Greek gods and goddesses are examples of myths. These tales constitute a developed pattern of myths, or a **mythology.**

Myth or mythic elements occur in related types of literature. A **legend** is a tale more historical in origin and tied more closely to an actual time and place than a myth. A legend is usually less cosmic and sweeping in intention and implications than a myth. The legends surrounding the life of the American frontiersman Davy Crockett are typical of the form. By contrast, a **fable** is a short tale, in verse or in prose, that contains a moral. The fables of Aesop, a Greek slave living about 600 B.C., are the most famous. The Uncle Remus stories by Joel Chandler Harris (1848–1908) are a more recent illustration of how fables are constructed. A **fairy tale** relates the lives and adventures of supernatural spirits, or at least of mysterious creatures endowed with unusual powers, whose behavior and actions are often playful and benevolent, but also sometimes sinister and wicked. Fairy tales vary widely in manner and form. The collections by the brothers Grimm (Jakob, 1785–1863, and Wilhelm, 1786–1859) and by Hans Christian Andersen (1805–1875) provide notable examples of the genre. A **folktale** is yet another type often highly saturated with mythic elements. This literary subtype is usually placed within the larger framework of **folklore,** which is itself made up of sayings, tales, superstitions, records, diaries, songs, proverbs, customs, even actual objects believed to belong to the life and times of a particular group, race, geographical region, or culture. Folklore comprises a vast and diverse store of materials that, if not always literary in nature and form, are important as sources of literary subjects, themes, and works.

The nature and function of myth are still disputed and debated. In *Myth and Reality* (1963), Mircea Eliade argues that

> myth narrates a sacred history; it relates an event that took place in primordial Time, the fabled time of the "beginnings." In other words, myth tells how, through the deeds of Supernatural Beings, a reality came into exis-

tence, be it the whole of reality, the Cosmos, or only a fragment of reality—
an island, a species of plant, a particular kind of human behavior, or an
institution. Myth, then, is always an account of a "creation"; it relates how
something was produced, began *to be*.

In short, Eliade concludes, "myths reveal that the World, man, and life
have a supernatural origin and history, and that this history is significant,
precious, and exemplary."

Many writers believe that myth is, as René Wellek and Austin
Warren once observed, "the common denominator between poetry and
religion." Yet poets are concerned primarily with the function of myth,
not with its definitions. What is useful for them is that myth belongs to a
"collective" body of shared ideas, emotions, attitudes, forms, and even
cultural tendencies. A poet successful or lucky enough to tap the vein of
living myths gains an all-important dimension, enriching the personal
with collective associations and meanings.

The term *archetype* (literally, "initial imprint") is now used frequently in discussing poetry. There are two perfectly valid but widely
differing meanings of this term, and it is important to understand each.
First, **archetype** may signify merely a representative type, as when we
say that Franklin Delano Roosevelt, for example, was the "archetype"
of the modern American president. A second meaning of the term, one
more relevant to literary studies, derives from the Jungian theory of
archetypes. To the late Swiss psychiatrist Carl Gustav Jung, archetypes
are ancient patterns in which the very energies of human life flow. To
Jung, an archetype is a psychic phenomenon, not a visible, tangible
thing. Jung maintained that archetypes such as God, the savior-
redeemer, the hero, the mother, the father, the miraculous child, the
shadow, the old wise man, and the self—to name the notable ones—
manifest themselves in sensuously apprehensible images, which he
labeled "images of the archetypes." These images are revealed in such
diverse forms as dreams, literature, and even different types of popular
culture. Snakes and wild beasts in dreams, heroes and heroines in
literature, and figures such as Tarzan and Superman in popular culture
are instances of what Jung termed images of archetypal activity.

If we say that President Roosevelt exemplifies the archetype of the
father, we are now employing *archetype* in its Jungian context. Here we
are saying something far different about Roosevelt from what we said
above when we used the term to mean "representative type." Jung
understood the images and the patterns to which they refer as indications of the channels in which human nature moves and develops. In addition to human intellect, Jung insisted that

there is a thinking in primordial images, in symbols which are older than the
historical man, which are inborn in him from the earliest times, and [which],

eternally living, outlasting all generations, still make up the groundwork of the human psyche. It is only possible to live the fullest life when we are in harmony with these symbols; wisdom is a return to them.

These symbols are manifestly the images of the archetypes. And Jung regarded the appearance of an archetype, arranged in appropriate images, as a highly significant indication of what was taking place within an individual. Jung felt that these patterns are the purposeful, restorative, and empowering agents of human life itself, since they refer specifically to "collective" and thus to universal characteristics of human existence.

We may now return to myth, seeing it as a widely dispersed and a generally accepted "model." In this sense, myths are "exemplary." Here many writers and critics find useful means by which to compose and to interpret certain literary works. A notable model is, for example, the hero quest: a warrior, leader, or would-be savior sets out to perform tasks in order to win a boon—some precious gift, a beautiful princess, salvation for his village or people, even immortality. In *The Hero with a Thousand Faces* (1949), Joseph Campbell shows that a "monomyth" of the hero exists and that its essential features are common to stories as different as those of Beowulf and Paul Bunyan, the Buddha and King Arthur. Literary critic Northrop Frye, writing in *Fables of Identity: Studies in Poetic Mythology* (1963), goes beyond Campbell and says that "all literary genres are derived from the quest myth." Many poems offer support to these views; John Keats' "La Belle Dame sans Merci" (Chapter 2) and W. B. Yeats' "Leda and the Swan" (Chapter 11) are notable examples. And the larger framework of many poems employs elements of the quest myth. T. S. Eliot's "The Love Song of J. Alfred Prufrock" (Chapter 12) is structured around a quest for the meaning of human existence. Similarly, Samuel Taylor Coleridge's "Kubla Khan" (Chapter 3) contains mythic elements which undergird and shape the poet's verses.

Archibald MacLeish (b. 1892)
Dr. Sigmund Freud Discovers the Sea Shell

Science, that simple saint, cannot be bothered
Figuring what anything is for:
Enough for her devotions that things are
And can be contemplated soon as gathered.

She knows how every living thing was fathered,   5
She calculates the climate of each star,

She counts the fish at sea, but cannot care
Why any one of them exists, fish, fire or feathered.

Why should she? Her religion is to tell
By rote her rosary of perfect answers.   10
Metaphysics she can leave to man:
She never wakes at night in heaven or hell

Staring at darkness. In her holy cell
There is no darkness ever: the pure candle
Burns, the beads drop briskly from her hand.   15

Who dares to offer Her the curled sea shell!
She will not touch it!—knows the world she sees
Is all the world there is! Her faith is perfect!

Questions for Study

1. Why does the poet personify science? MacLeish calls her, in fact, "that simple saint" and concludes that "Her faith is perfect." What does he suggest by presenting science in religious terms?
2. Identify as many figures of speech as you can in the poem and explain the function of each.
3. How does MacLeish use the "sea shell"? Is it a symbol? If it is a symbol, comment on its implications.
4. Dr. Sigmund Freud (1856–1939), an Austrian physician and neurologist by training, is the founder of psychoanalysis. Why does MacLeish use his name in the title? Does MacLeish allude favorably or unfavorably to Freud?
5. Describe the language employed in the poem. Is it, for instance, essentially denotative or connotative? Point out at least three instances of both types of language and try to explain why, in your view, the poet has used his words in the way he does.

Langston Hughes   (1902–1967)
I, Too, Sing America

I, too, sing America.

I am the darker brother.
They send me to eat in the kitchen
When company comes,
But I laugh,   5
And eat well,
And grow strong.

Tomorrow,
I'll sit at the table

When company comes.   10
Nobody'll dare
Say to me,
"Eat in the kitchen,"
Then.

Besides,   15
They'll see how beautiful I am
And be ashamed—

I, too, am America.

Questions for Study

1. Would you call this poem symbolic or allegorical? Look carefully at its meaning and determine what Hughes is trying to say.
2. What is the thematic relationship between the first and the last lines? Why does the "I" say that "They'll see how beautiful I am / And be ashamed—"?
3. Today, he eats in the kitchen; tomorrow, at the main table with the "company." Explain the meaning of these two statements.
4. Identify the figures of speech you find in the poem and comment on their function.
5. Paraphrase the poem, drawing out as many of the implications Hughes develops as you can.

Robert Frost (1874–1963)
Stopping by Woods on a Snowy Evening

Whose woods these are I think I know.
His house is in the village, though;
He will not see me stopping here
To watch his woods fill up with snow.

My little horse must think it queer   5
To stop without a farmhouse near
Between the woods and frozen lake
The darkest evening of the year.

He gives his harness bells a shake
To ask if there is some mistake.   10
The only other sound's the sweep
Of easy wind and downy flake.

The woods are lovely, dark, and deep,
But I have promises to keep,
And miles to go before I sleep,   15
And miles to go before I sleep.

Questions for Study

1. This familiar poem has been variously interpreted, usually by means of the numerous symbols in the work: e.g., the woods, the horse, miles, and sleep. What other symbols can you find? Interpret the poem in terms of all its notable symbols.
2. What relationships do you find among the four stanzas?
3. Describe the language of the poem. Is the language composed largely of simple, everyday words? Is it largely denotative or connotative? What figures of speech do you find in Frost's lines?
4. Paraphrase the poem and state what you believe to be its theme. What universal implications do you see in Frost's account of a simple event?

William Wordsworth   (1770–1850)
The Solitary Reaper[1]

Behold her, single in the field,
Yon solitary Highland lass!
Reaping and singing by herself;
Stop here, or gently pass!
Alone she cuts and binds the grain,   5
And sings a melancholy strain;
O listen! for the vale profound
Is overflowing with the sound.

No nightingale did ever chaunt
More welcome notes to weary bands   10
Of travelers in some shady haunt,
Among Arabian sands:
A voice so thrilling ne'er was heard
In springtime from the cuckoo-bird,
Breaking the silence of the seas   15
Among the farthest Hebrides.[2]

Will no one tell me what she sings?—
Perhaps the plaintive numbers flow
For old, unhappy, far-off things,
And battles long ago: 20
Or is it some more humble lay,
Familiar matter of today?
Some natural sorrow, loss, or pain,
That has been, and may be again?

Whate'er the theme, the maiden sang   25

---

1. In a note, Wordsworth explains that this poem grew out of a passage in Thomas Wilkinson's *Tour of Scotland* (1824): "Passed by a female who was reaping alone; she sung in Erse [Gaelic language in Scotland] as she bended over her sickle, the sweetest human voice I ever heard. Her strains were tenderly melancholy, and felt delicious long after they were heard no more."
2. Islands off the coast of western Scotland.

As if her song could have no ending;
I saw her singing at her work,
And o'er the sickle bending;—
I listened, motionless and still;
And, as I mounted up the hill,   30
The music in my heart I bore,
Long after it was heard no more.

Questions for Study

1. Given that Wordsworth is not writing from direct experience, what is there in this
   figure of the Scottish reaper that attracts him? Is she then a symbol and, if so,
   of what?
2. Wordsworth believed that vital experiences and memorable impressions made
   deep "imprints" in the imagination and that often these returned, much later,
   to minister spiritually and psychologically to the individual. Consider the final
   stanza in light of this belief and explain any ways the content supports it.
3. Identify as many figures of speech in this poem as you can. Be sure to describe
   each one by reference to both of its terms.
4. To whom is this poem addressed? What is the relationship between its theme
   and Wordsworth's method of narration?
5. What allusions can you find in the poem?

Anne Sexton   (1928–1974)
The Moss of His Skin

Young girls in old Arabia were often buried alive
next to their dead fathers, apparently as sacrifice
to the goddesses of the tribes . . . .
HAROLD FELDMAN, "Children of the Desert"
Psychoanalysis and Psychoanalytic Review, Fall 1958

It was only important
to smile and hold still,
to lie down beside him
and to rest awhile,
to be folded up together   5
as if we were silk,
to sink from the eyes of mother
and not to talk.
The black room took us
like a cave or a mouth   10
or an indoor belly.
I held my breath
and daddy was there,
his thumbs, his fat skull,
his teeth, his hair growing   15

like a field or a shawl.
I lay by the moss
of his skin until
it grew strange. My sisters
will never know that I fall   20
out of myself and pretend
that Allah[1] will not see
how I hold my daddy
like an old stone tree.

Questions for Study

1. The title of this poem is unusual. Why does the voice in the poem refer to "the moss" of her father's skin? Further, what does she mean by speaking of "his thumbs, his fat skull, / his teeth, his hair growing / like a field or a shawl"? Clearly the relationship between the voice and her father is central to the meaning of this poem. What is that relationship?
2. In line 19, the voice in the poem mentions her "sisters." Are these literal or symbolic "sisters"? What is the meaning of the last six lines?
3. The quotation under the title mentions an ancient custom of "old Arabia." How does this information help us understand the poem? Is this custom given as a hint of what happens, or may happen, to modern-day daughters? Try to clarify the function of the quotation.
4. Look closely at the diction in the poem. What words do you think have been selected with particular associations in mind? What controlling idea seems to determine the diction in this poem?

Norman Cameron   (1903–1953)
Lucifer

Lucifer did not wish to murder God,
But only to reduce His Self-esteem.
Weary of brightness where no shadow showed,
What took the rebel's fancy was a dream

Of God bewildered, angered out of measure   5
And driven, almost weeping, to implore,
"I built this Heaven for My angels' pleasure,
And yet you like it not. What would you more?"

At this, of course, with most Divine compassion,
Lucifer, all forgiving and adept,   10
Would soon have taught his Master how to fashion
A Heaven such as angels could accept.

---

1. The Arabic name for God.

Questions for Study

1. According to Cameron, why did Lucifer rebel? Refer to specific lines in the poem to support your answer.
2. List and describe all the figures of speech you can find in the poem.
3. From the poem, what kind of Heaven do you think there could be "such as angels could accept"?

Chapter 6
Irony and Paradox

Because our language is so rich and suggestive, we sometimes use words and phrases that convey a meaning different from the one we intended to express. Poetry, however, often contains language that is intentionally designed to express meanings that are different from what at first they seem. Poetry achieves this effect by employing two devices in particular: *irony* and *paradox*. This chapter examines these and touches upon three related ones: *ambiguity, understatement,* and *overstatement* (or *hyperbole*).

In poetry, **ambiguity** is the deliberate use of a word or a statement in order to suggest more than one meaning. If the ambiguity is unintentional, it signals the failure of an author to be clear and precise. Correctly utilized, however, ambiguity performs several important functions. The first of these is humor, as in the following four-line verse, said to be anonymous but sometimes attributed to English critic Sir Edmund Gosse (1849–1928).

O Moon

O Moon, when I gaze on thy beautiful face,
Careering along through the boundaries of space,
The thought has often come into my mind
If I ever shall see thy glorious behind.

A second function of ambiguity is the creation of additional implications and meanings, essentially by deepening and extending what is said. Alfred, Lord Tennyson gives us a brilliant instance of ambiguity when in "Ulysses" he has the old mariner say, "I am a part of all that I have met." The line suggests: (1) that what Ulysses has absorbed from his travels has contributed to what he now is; and (2) that he has given some part of himself to everything he has experienced. The double meaning is entirely plausible, and it is artistically and thematically important in the poem. Tennyson gains by this ambiguity significant associations and implications in his portrayal of the aging Ulysses. Similarly, the ambiguous statement arouses our curiosity and involves us more intensely in the poem.

A third function of ambiguity is that it provides a way of articulating the view that life is often two-edged and self-contradictory. Edwin Arlington Robinson, for example, employs ambiguity in "Richard Cory" (Chapter 1) in order to suggest that people like the title character, who seems to have everything, may in fact lack something vital, an inadequacy which leads them to self-destruction. A poet's desire to express the unknown or the multifaceted aspects of life many times accounts for his use of ambiguity. As a result, a particular situation or event in a poem may suggest many possible meanings and implications. In this process of leaving matters open-ended, however, ambiguity shades into irony; and many poets prefer the various degrees and kinds of irony to the methods of ambiguity.

Irony consists of rendering meanings that are not what at first they seem. Specifically, **irony** suggests an intended discrepancy between what is said and what is meant, between what is revealed and what is actually so. Irony, however, must not be confused with sarcasm or with satire. **Sarcasm** is an ironic statement that is deeply cutting and mocking: "I see that Pringle has lost some weight—he's now down to a slim and trim 288 pounds." **Satire** is a way of ridiculing human follies and vices, with the expressed purpose of reforming objectionable, even contemptible, behavior and values. Although people claim that satire is therapeutic, Jonathan Swift once observed that it, unfortunately, does not always fulfill that function: "Satire is a sort of glass wherein beholders do generally discover everybody's face but their own." Yet Swift, the preeminent satirist in the English language, was uncompromising in holding up the glass of satire to human foibles. (See his "A Description of a City Shower" in "Poems for Further Study.")

Irony is never so blunt as sarcasm, nor so therapeutic in its intention as satire. We experience a genuine pleasure in irony—both in creating it ourselves and in discovering it in a piece of literature. And that pleasure consists of our recognizing the difference between an apparent reality and an actual one.

The simplest and most frequently used form of irony is **verbal irony**, which says one thing when another—usually the opposite—thing is meant. If someone says, "We sure worked hard to drink the rest of that beer," he is declaring that drinking the beer was difficult, but also at the same time suggesting that the act was pleasurable. Both meanings are true, but the second implication of *worked* is clearly ironic. Much of the effectiveness of verbal irony lies in its ability to achieve such related, if opposed, meanings.

The following poem illustrates how verbal irony includes two points of view at once.

John Berryman (1914–1972)
Dream Song: 14

Life, friends, is boring. We must not say so.
After all, the sky flashes, the great sea yearns,
we ourselves flash and yearn,
and moreover my mother told me as a boy
(repeatingly) "Ever to confess you're bored   5
means you have no

Inner Resources." I conclude now I have no
inner resources, because I am heavy bored.
Peoples bore me,
literature bores me, especially great literature,   10
Henry[1] bores me, with his plights & gripes
as bad as achilles,[2]

who loves people and valiant art, which bores me.
And the tranquil hills, & gin, look like a drag
and somehow a dog   15
has taken itself & its tail considerably away
into mountains or sea or sky, leaving
behind: me, wag.

Here verbal irony results principally from the linking or juxtaposition of unequal things. For example, Henry, a professor of English, is compared with the fiercely heroic Achilles. The words *Inner Resources* are capitalized in the mother's quotation, but are not capitalized in the speaker's own statement. Similarly, *boring* is emphasized by its repetition and variation throughout the poem.

The levels of language in the poem are also contrasted. It begins with a proposition stated in everyday language: "Life, friends, is boring."

---

1. Imaginary character who appears throughout Berryman's *The Dream Songs* (1969), the volume from which this poem is taken.
2. One of the Greek heroes of the Trojan War; because of his petty quarrel with the leader of the Greek forces, he temporarily withdrew from the fighting.

This declaration is followed by the phrases "the sky flashes" and "the great sea yearns," which are undercut by the flat statement "after all." This kind of verbal irony continues throughout Berryman's lines with such phrases as "great literature," "valiant art," "tranquil hills, & gin"—all aspects of life which, to the speaker, "look like a drag." The poem closes with the sharp image of a dog wagging its tail, suggesting to the speaker that he is as inconsequential as the left-over "wag" of a dog's tail.

Verbal irony often occurs in connection with **situational irony,** which expresses a discrepancy between what is normally appropriate and what actually takes place, or between what is anticipated and what finally happens. While verbal irony is concerned with words, situational irony is concerned with events, so that what appears to be happening is not what is actually happening. For example, if a fellow stands up his date in order to go to a bar with his friends, only to discover the girl there, then we have an ironic situation. Situational irony makes it possible for a poet to work out many effects and themes. He can, for instance, create humorous situations by giving us absurd and unexpected incongruities. Geoffrey Chaucer's *Canterbury Tales* (begun in 1386) are filled with extraordinary illustrations of situational irony: liars trapped by their deceptions, adulterers caught amusingly in the act, good men and women tricked through their own honesty and decency, and many more. The power of situational irony is that it carries us behind the scenes and beyond appearances in order to convey to us realities we did not know existed.

Both of the following poems employ forms of situational irony in revealing subtle realities that, from the circumstances, are not immediately apparent.

James Dickey (b. 1923)
Deer Among Cattle

Here and there in the searing beam
Of my hand going through the night meadow
They all are grazing

With pins of human light in their eyes.
A wild one also is eating   5
The human grass,

Slender, graceful, domesticated
By darkness, among the bred-
for-slaughter,

Having bounded their paralyzed fence   10
And inclined his branched forehead onto
Their green frosted table,

The only live thing in this flashlight
Who can leave whenever he wishes,
Turn grass into forest,   15

Foreclose inhuman brightness from his eyes
But stands here still, unperturbed,
In their wide-open country,

The sparks from my hand in his pupils
Unmatched anywhere among cattle,   20

Grazing with them the night of the hammer
As one of their own who shall rise.

Standing at night with a flashlight in his hand, the speaker is looking at
cattle in a meadow. The situation is ironic, however, since the cattle,
now grazing serenely, are destined to be slaughtered. Furthermore, it is
"the night of the hammer"—an allusion to the slaughterhouse method
(now rarely used) of stunning an animal with a sledgehammer prior to
slitting its throat. The principal situational irony, however, is introduced
by the presence of the deer. It is like the cattle in many ways, but unlike
them in one very crucial aspect—it can jump over the fence at will.
Dickey reinforces and extends these two instances of irony with images
and figures of speech that express the differences between the free, wild
deer and the confined, stupid cattle. The deer is "domesticated / By
darkness"; it can "turn grass into forest" and leave. Also it can "Foreclose inhuman brightness" from its eyes (that is, leave the beam of the
flashlight). In the final line, Dickey says that the deer alone "shall rise,"
an image that emphasizes the marked difference between animal life in
its natural, wild state and the timid, domesticated cattle.

Gwendolyn Brooks (b. 1917)
Of De Witt Williams on His Way to Lincoln Cemetery[1]

He was born in Alabama.
He was bred in Illinois.
He was nothing but a
Plain black boy.

---

1. A black cemetery in Chicago.

Swing low swing low sweet sweet chariot.   5
Nothing but a plain black boy.

Drive him past the Pool Hall.
Drive him past the Show.
Blind within his casket,
But maybe he will know.   10

Down through Forty-seventh Street:[2]
Underneath the L,[3]
And Northwest Corner, Prairie,
That he loved so well.

Don't forget the Dance Halls—   15
Warwick and Savoy,
Where he picked his women, where
He drank his liquid joy.

Born in Alabama.
Bred in Illinois.   20
He was nothing but a
Plain black boy.

Swing low swing low sweet sweet chariot.
Nothing but a plain black boy.

This poem describes the funeral procession of De Witt Williams, an individual who lived a faceless existence in a black, urban ghetto. No facts about him, not even about the cause of his death, are given. Yet the sights and sounds of his ghetto environment are vividly described: the pool hall, the movie theater, the elevated train, the dance halls, the liquor, and the easy women. The ironic tone is conveyed largely by the poet's voice and by the adaptation of a line from the spiritual "Swing Low, Sweet Chariot" in this statement about ghetto life. In the song, the "chariot" is the chariot of God that comes to take his "children" to heaven. The situation of De Witt Williams—his environment and his funeral—stands in ironic contrast to the expectations expressed in the spiritual. He is represented, in other words, as anything *but* "a plain black boy," and so what is said in the poem is not what is actually meant. Through irony, the poem constructs an indictment of the way of life individuals such as De Witt Williams are forced to lead.

The following poem illustrates how verbal irony and situational irony can be effectively combined.

---

2. One of the main streets in Chicago's South Side black ghetto; it crosses Prairie Avenue.
3. Chicago's elevated railway.

Thomas Hardy (1840–1928)

The Convergence of the Twain

Lines on the Loss of the Titanic[1]

    In a solitude of the sea
    Deep from human vanity,
And the Pride of Life that planned her, stilly couches she.

    Steel chambers, late the pyres
    Of her salamandrine[2] fires,   5
Cold currents thrid,° and turn to rhythmic tidal lyres   *thread*

    Over the mirrors meant
    To glass the opulent
The sea-worm crawls—grotesque, slimed, dumb, indifferent.

    Jewels in joy designed   10
    To ravish the sensuous mind
Lie lightless, all their sparkles bleared and black and blind.

    Dim moon-eyed fishes near
    Gaze at the gilded gear
And query: "What does this vaingloriousness down here?" . . .   15

    Well: while was fashioning
    This creature of cleaving wing,
The Immanent Will[3] that stirs and urges everything

    Prepared a sinister mate
    For her—so gaily great—   20
A Shape of Ice, for the time far and dissociate.

    And as the smart ship grew
    In stature, grace, and hue,
In shadowy silent distance grew the Iceberg too.

    Alien they seemed to be: 25
    No mortal eye could see
The intimate welding of their later history,

---

    1. The British luxury liner *Titanic,* the largest ship of its day and supposedly unsinkable, sank on its maiden voyage after striking an iceberg in the North Atlantic on the night of April 12, 1912; of the 2206 people aboard, 1517 were lost.
    2. The salamander is a lizardlike animal once thought to be able to live in or to withstand fire.
    3. Hardy's term for what he regarded as the dominant force that capriciously activates and controls the events of the world.

Or sign that they were bent
By paths coincident
On being anon twin halves of one august event,   30

Till the Spinner of the Years
Said "Now!" And each one hears,
And consummation comes, and jars two hemispheres.

Irony exists in this poem on several levels. First, the opening stanza declares that the mightiest ship of its time now lies on the bottom of the ocean. Second, the poem hints that the great vessel was considered unsinkable by many people: those who designed and built it; those who christened and manned it; and those who sailed and sank with it. And finally, nature's creation of the iceberg parallels man's construction of the ship. Hardy's voice is present in the poem, putting forth his philosophy about the Immanent Will, which from a timeless past created and fixed the iceberg and the ship for a "convergence" in the North Atlantic. Time and fate (suggested in the figure of "the Spinner of the Years") respond to this Immanent Will. For Hardy, the supreme irony in the sinking of the *Titanic* is a cosmic irony which creates and moves without any thought of individuals and of their goals and wishes. The actual sinking, therefore, provides Hardy with an occasion for expressing his view of the forces that underlie human existence.

A third notable type of irony is **dramatic irony,** which expresses a discrepancy between what a character says and does and what the reader knows to be true. A character may be blind to the true significance or to the full implications of a particular situation; but readers, if they understand what is taking place, are not. A further refinement of dramatic irony in poetry—the term is derived from its use in plays—is a discrepancy between what a speaker or voice in a poem says and does and what the poet is actually attempting to express. Often a poet takes on what critics call a **mask** (or a **persona**) through which he speaks. In many cases, the thoughts, feelings, and actions of this voice or mask or persona are in opposition to what the poet is actually saying. Robert Browning's "My Last Duchess" (Chapter 11) illustrates how this kind of dramatic irony works. Although the speaker, the Duke of Ferrara, reveals himself as an archvillain whose egotism and arrogance compel him to have his young wife done away with, these feelings and acts are scarcely those which the poet is in sympathy with. Dramatic irony is a particularly valuable, if sometimes complex, form of irony which allows the reader to see the discrepancy between the true implications of a situation and what the character or voice in the poem believes to be taking place.

The following poem presents a conversation between two people. Only one of them, however, actually knows the facts of the situation.

A. E. Housman   (1859–1936)
Is My Team Ploughing

"Is my team ploughing,
    That I was used to drive
And hear the harness jingle
    When I was man alive?"

Ay, the horses trample,   5
    The harness jingles now;
No change though you lie under
    The land you used to plough.

"Is football° playing   *soccer*
    Along the river shore,   10
With lads to chase the leather,
    Now I stand up no more?"

Ay, the ball is flying,
    The lads play heart and soul;
The goal stands up, the keeper   15
    Stands up to keep the goal.

"Is my girl happy,
    That I thought hard to leave,
And has she tired of weeping
    As she lies down at eve?"   20

Ay, she lies down lightly,
    She lies not down to weep:
Your girl is well contented.
    Be still, my lad, and sleep.

"Is my friend hearty,   25
    Now I am thin and pine,
And has he found to sleep in
    A better bed than mine?"

Yes, lad, I lie easy,
    I lie as lads would choose;   30
I cheer a dead man's sweetheart,
    Never ask me whose.

Here is an imaginary dialog between two men, one dead and the other
alive. To the dead man's questions, his friend replies with answers that
reveal many ironic facts. The living speaker affirms that the dead man's
passing has not altered daily affairs: horses still plough the fields, "lads"

still play soccer by the river, and his former sweetheart is now beyond any grief over losing him. The closing stanza, in fact, reveals that his friend has replaced the dead speaker in the girl's affections. Throughout the poem, moreover, the dialog between a dead and a living man implies more than either speaker states—namely, that these facts of life and death not only apply to these two but to all individuals as well.

Closely related to irony are understatement and overstatement (or hyperbole). Whereas verbal irony expresses in words a meaning opposite to what is actually said, **understatement** intentionally expresses less than what is actually the case in order to achieve a subtle effect. Understatement is used skillfully in Robert Browning's "My Last Duchess" when, at one point, the Duke of Ferrara, reporting the fate of his recent wife, says to his guest:

> Oh Sir, she smiled, no doubt,
> Whene'er I passed her; but who passed without
> Much the same smile? This grew; I gave commands;
> Then all smiles stopped together.

Understatement is used here to express the fact that the Duchess' flirtatious smiles have indeed stopped not because the Duke had scolded her, but because he had issued "commands" to have her permanently removed.

Overstatement (sometimes called **hyperbole**) is the deliberate expression of something as more than it actually is. Like understatement, overstatement is employed for emphasis and for establishing a point or creating an effect. Andrew Marvell provides an excellent illustration of these functions in "To His Coy Mistress," in which the speaker tells his beloved that if he had the time he would love her in this way:

> I would
> Love you ten years before the Flood;
> And you should, if you please, refuse
> Till the conversion of the Jews.°   *i.e., the end of the world*

Overstatement in poetry is not mere exaggeration. It is a means of making a point by cleverly overstating the case. In "Richard Cory" (Chapter 1), for instance, the townspeople see the wealthy Richard Cory as their ideal. It seems to them quite natural that "he glittered when he walked." The associations between their ideal of riches and the word *glittered* contribute to the mood and overall effect of the poem. Effective overstatement and understatement retain this connection between the terms of their figurative expressions and the context and theme of the individual work.

The following poem skillfully employs both overstatement and understatement.

Sir John Suckling   (1609–1642)
The Constant Lover

Out upon it!° I have lov'd   *Be done with it!*
   Three whole days together;
And am like to love three more,
   If it prove fair weather.

Time shall moult away his wings,   5
   Ere he shall discover
In the whole wide world again
   Such a constant lover.

But the spite on't is, no praise
   Is due at all to me: 10
Love with me had made no stays,°   *standstill*
   Had it any been but she.

Had it any been but she,
   And that very face,
There had been at least ere this   15
   A dozen dozen in her place.

The poem is framed as an ironic jest concerning the speaker's pride in having been "constant" (faithful) to one woman for "three whole days." To him, this is an act of incredible devotion made possible *only* because of the very special woman involved. His overstatement of constancy is as ironic as his compliment to the woman for keeping such a man as himself for three days. He expands the fanciful overstatement by commenting in the final stanza that, if it were not for her "face," he would have loved "a dozen dozen in her place." The entire third stanza, by contrast, is delivered as an understatement. The speaker, who has declared himself an exceptional man, now emphasizes his compliment to the woman by understating his own worth: it is only because of her rare qualities that his love has been so devotedly won. This reversal of the sentiments expressed in the opening stanzas is effective irony.

Paradox is an expression in which an apparent contradiction turns out to be plausible or even true. Irony often shows us that things are not what they seem. Paradox endeavors to reveal to us that things which seem contradictory are indeed the same. It joins and resolves opposites in ways that are not always precisely logical or fully explained. A paradox is expressed in each of the following statements: "He that findeth his life shall lose it; and he that loseth his life for My sake shall find it" (Matt. 10:39), and "The way up and the way down are the same." An especially clear illustration of how paradox frames contradictory elements in life was given by the Cretan prophet Epimenides in the observation, "If I say that I am lying, am I telling the truth?" It seems initially that if the assertion is true it is definitely false, and that if false it is certainly true.

An amusing pun on liars is provided in the following two-line poem.

John Donne (1572–1631)
A Lame Beggar

"I am unable," yonder beggar cries,
"To stand or move!" If he say true, he lies.

A **pun** is a deliberate confusion of words that sound alike but are different in meaning. In Donne's lines, the pun results from the use of **lies,** which here means not only telling a falsehood but also reclining—a witty comment on the beggar who neither "stands" nor "moves." Punning is the play on different meanings of words, as in "The metric system is the *weigh* to go," or " 'When he asked for my hand,' sighed the maiden, 'I could not *bear* it.' " Not all puns, fortunately, are as contemptible as these.

Paradox causes us to look again and perhaps to rethink what is said, to analyze more carefully assumptions and circumstances, and thus to come to a new insight. When William Wordsworth writes in "My Heart Leaps Up" that "the Child is father to the Man," we are compelled to stop and examine the proposition, thereby recognizing that the statement, if properly viewed, is after all quite plausible and accurate. Similarly, when Emily Dickinson in "My Life Closed Twice" offers these lines, "Parting is all we know of heaven, / And all we need of hell," we must work out their meaning in terms of the entire poem. Only then do we see that the departure of a loved one usually stirs contradictory, or paradoxical, emotions within us.

The following short poem is constructed around a paradox that offers a significant insight.

William Butler Yeats (1865–1939)
The Choice

The intellect of man is forced to choose
Perfection of the life, or of the work,
And if it take the second must refuse
A heavenly mansion, raging in the dark.

When all that story's finished, what's the news?   5
In luck or out the toil has left its mark:
That old perplexity an empty purse,
Or the day's vanity, the night's remorse.

By framing his statements in ironic terms, Yeats is able to compress a
philosophical dilemma into eight lines of verse. In the first four lines, he
observes that an individual must choose to expend his energies on
perfecting either his life or his work. The last four lines examine what
this choice will bring. Line 5 poses the question facing the individual
who chooses and finishes the work—what then are the results of this
labor? The answer to this question is given in the final three lines, which
contain the ironic resolution that regardless of what route the person
chooses, his life will remain unfulfilled.

Archibald MacLeish (b. 1892)
The Snowflake Which Is Now and Hence Forever

Will it last? he says.
Is it a masterpiece?
Will generation after generation
Turn with reverence to the page?

Birdseye scholar of the frozen fish,   5
What would he make of the sole, clean, clear
Leap of the salmon that has disappeared?

To *be,* yes!—whether they like it or not!
But not to last when leap and water are forgotten,
A plank of standard pinkness in the dish.   10

They also live
Who swerve and vanish in the river.

Questions for Study

1. Who is the "he" in the first line? What is his definition of a "masterpiece"? What
   does the title suggest about this definition of a "masterpiece"?
2. Does the poem as a whole agree with the "he" and with his definition?
3. Explain the irony in the poem's distinction between the leaping "salmon" and the
   "plank of standard pinkness in the dish."
4. Is the poet's use of *Birdseye* and *frozen* an example of punning?
5. John Milton concluded his sonnet "When I Consider How My Light Is Spent"

with the line, "They also serve who only stand and wait." MacLeish parodies
Milton in the last line of this poem. How are the two lines similar and how are
they different?

Anonymous
Lord Randal

"O where hae° ye been, Lord Randal, my son?   *have*
   O where hae ye been, my handsome young man?"
"I hae been to the wild wood; mother, make my bed soon,
   For I'm weary wi' hunting, and fain wald° lie down."   *would like to*

"Where gat ye° your dinner, Lord Randal, my son?   *did you get* 5
   Where gat ye your dinner, my handsome young man?"
"I din'd wi' my true-love; mother, make my bed soon,
   For I'm weary wi' hunting, and fain wald lie down."

"What gat ye to your dinner, Lord Randal, my son?
   What gat ye to your dinner, my handsome young man?"   10
"I gat eels boil'd in broth; mother, make my bed soon,
   For I'm weary wi' hunting, and fain wald lie down."

"What became of your bloodhounds, Lord Randal, my son?
   What became of your bloodhounds, my handsome young man?"
"O they swell'd and they died; mother, make my bed soon,   15
   For I'm weary wi' hunting, and fain wald lie down."

"O I fear ye are poisoned, Lord Randal, my son!
   O I fear ye are poisoned, my handsome young man!"
"O yes! I am poison'd; mother, make my bed soon,
   For I'm sick at the heart, and fain wald lie down."   20

Questions for Study

1. Several types of irony are employed in this poem. Identify as many as you can.
2. "Lord Randal" is a folk ballad (see Chapter 1), essentially intended for reciting
   or singing. What features in it are appropriate for such an oral rendition? (Read
   the poem aloud, if possible, before you answer.)
3. The composition of such pieces as "Lord Randal" depends upon effect, in this
   case the revelation in the final stanza that Lord Randal has been poisoned by his
   lover. How is this revelation prepared for?
4. The story of Lord Randal occurs in more than one rendition. One version relates
   that the dying Lord Randal leaves some of his possessions to various members
   of his family; in the final stanza, however, he tells his mother that he will leave
   her "hell and fire." His hostility toward his mother suggests a connection between her and the poisoning by his lover. Do you see any of this hostility in the
   version reprinted here? Why, for instance, does the mother ask probing questions?
   Why, similarly, does she seem apprehensive? She guesses, perhaps before we do,
   that her son has been poisoned. What does this insight tell us?

Richard Eberhart (b. 1904)
The Fury of Aerial Bombardment[1]

You would think the fury of aerial bombardment
Would rouse God to relent; the infinite spaces
Are still silent. He looks on shock-pried faces.
History, even, does not know what is meant.

You would feel that after so many centuries   5
God would give man to repent; yet he can kill
As Cain[2] could, but with multitudinous will,
No farther advanced than in his ancient furies.

Was man made stupid to see his own stupidity?
Is God by definition indifferent, beyond us all?   10
Is the eternal truth man's fighting soul
Wherein the beast ravens in his own avidity?

Of Van Wettering I speak, and Averill,
Names on a list whose faces I do not recall.
But they are gone to early death, who late in school   15
Distinguished the belt feed lever from the belt holding pawl.[3]

Questions for Study

1. Explain the irony of the speaker's reference to Cain in lines 6–8.
2. Van Wettering and Averill are names on the gunnery class rolls. What is ironic
   about the fact that the speaker cannot remember their faces? Does this fact suggest a similarity between the speaker and the "indifferent" God of line 10?
3. Comment upon how Eberhart's lines suggest the murderous capacities of human
   beings. Does the speaker regard men as stupid who unthinkingly and indifferently kill each other?
4. After writing the first three stanzas, Eberhart later revised them and added a
   fourth. Can you find a reversal or change in tone between the first three stanzas
   and the fourth? How does the diction in the fourth stanza affect the tone?

E. E. Cummings (1894–1962)
when serpents bargain for the right to squirm

when serpents bargain for the right to squirm
and the sun strikes to gain a living wage—
when thorns regard their roses with alarm
and rainbows are insured against old age

---

1. Most of the poem was written in 1944 while Eberhart was a Naval Reserve officer teaching aerial
gunnery in Virginia.
2. In Genesis, Cain killed his brother Abel.
3. Parts of the .50-caliber Browning machine gun.

when every thrush may sing no new moon in   5
if all screech-owls have not okayed his voice
—and any wave signs on the dotted line
or else an ocean is compelled to close

when the oak begs permission of the birch
to make an acorn—valleys accuse their   10
mountains of having altitude—and march
denounces april as a saboteur

then we'll believe in that incredible
unanimal mankind (and not until)

Questions for Study

1. Who is the "we" in the poem?
2. What view of human beings is Cummings expressing here? With what does he
   compare them? Explain the words *incredible* and *unanimal* in terms of your
   initial response to Cummings' comparison.
3. Each of the first three stanzas is introduced by an exaggerated proposition. Identify the figure of speech in each of these propositions.
4. What symbols do you find in the poem? What are their implications?
5. The poem is a Shakespearean sonnet (see Chapter 10). In what ways does the
   poem follow the conventions of this type of sonnet? How does it depart from
   them?

Robert Frost (1874–1963)
The Road Not Taken

Two roads diverged in a yellow wood,
And sorry I could not travel both
And be one traveler, long I stood
And looked down one as far as I could
To where it bent in the undergrowth;   5

Then took the other, as just as fair,
And having perhaps the better claim,
Because it was grassy and wanted wear;
Though as for that, the passing there
Had worn them really about the same,   10

And both that morning equally lay
In leaves no step had trodden black.
Oh, I kept the first for another day!
Yet knowing how way leads on to way,
I doubted if I should ever come back.   15

I shall be telling this with a sigh
Somewhere ages and ages hence:
Two roads diverged in a wood, and I—
I took the one less traveled by,
And that has made all the difference.   20

Questions for Study

1. In the light of the entire poem, is the road in the title symbolic? If so, of what? Is the title ironic? Explain.
2. What precisely are the similarities between the two roads? What are the differences? Why does the speaker take the road he does? Is his answer ambiguous? Is it ironic? Explain.
3. Frost is skillful at using verse that is conversational in tone in order to present subtle and often complex kinds of poetic devices. Try to find in the poem examples of the following: overstatement, understatement, and symbol.
4. In your view, precisely *where* is this "somewhere" that the speaker will be "telling this with a sigh"?
5. Has the fact that the speaker took one road and not another actually made any difference in his life? Did he *really* take "the one less traveled by"? What then is the thematic point of the poem?

Robert Creeley   (b. 1926)
Joy

I could look at
an empty hole for hours
thinking it will
get something in it,
will collect   5
things. There is
an infinite emptiness
placed there.

Questions for Study

1. This poem focuses on a single, seemingly meaningless act: looking at "an empty hole for hours." What do you feel is the point of this act?
2. What is "an infinite emptiness"? Is it a literal statement, a figure of speech, or a symbol?

Chapter 7
Tone

Tone is the attitude of an author, as expressed in a poem, toward his subject, theme, and audience. Various features and qualities of a poem work together to establish tone. In one sense, it is controlled by the manner of expression of a particular work. In another sense, it is determined by both the content and the manner of expression. Because there are, unfortunately, no rules or precise guidelines for recognizing it, tone in a particular poem is sometimes difficult to describe exactly. In speaking, we perceive tone largely by the speaker's vocal inflections, gestures, facial expressions, and the like. In poetry, we must depend exclusively upon the words on the page.

The most obvious indication of a poem's tone is the level of language used. Words, their ordering in patterns and sentences, their figurative possibilities, and their sounds and rhythms function together to produce tone. The language level in a particular poem may vary from formal to informal, dignified to casual, eloquent to colloquial, and so on. Similarly, emotional and intellectual attitudes expressed within a poem contribute to its tone. An emotional attitude may be happy or sad, friendly or belligerent, solemn or playful, humorous or bitter. An intellectual attitude may be thoughtful or unconcerned, philosophical or superficial, skeptical or credulous. Poets use gradations and combinations of several levels of language, as well as of several different emotional and intellectual attitudes.

Two additional features of a work can help us discover its tone. First, the point of view of a poem, represented by either a character or a voice *within* the work, usually expresses the presumed attitude of the poet toward his subject, theme, and audience. The speaker in a poem may be, for example, involved or detached, friendly or hostile, familiar or aloof. Also, the character or the voice may stand in opposition to the overall meaning or implications of a poem. These various possibilities involving point of view sometimes indicate the presence of irony—a second factor that may establish tone. Still, tone is not easy to determine. We usually need several close readings of a poem in order to grasp and describe its tone.

The following short poem exemplifies how tone contributes to the overall meaning and effect of a particular work.

Theodore Roethke (1908–1963)
My Papa's Waltz

The whiskey on your breath
Could make a small boy dizzy;
But I hung on like death:
Such waltzing was not easy.

We romped until the pans   5
Slid from the kitchen shelf;
My mother's countenance
Could not unfrown itself.

The hand that held my wrist
Was battered on one knuckle;   10
At every step you missed
My right ear scraped a buckle.

You beat time on my head
With a palm caked hard by dirt,
Then waltzed me off to bed   15
Still clinging to your shirt.

The point of view in "My Papa's Waltz" is the first person. The poem, in fact, is a reminiscence, and the "I" is sorting out as best he can what the scene meant to him when he was a child and what, indeed, it means to him now as an adult. His father's drunken dancing frightens the boy. When the man misses a step, the youth suffers a scrape on the ear from the man's belt buckle. The father even keeps time to the music by tapping out the rhythm on the boy's head. Yet the boy wants to dance with him, despite the mother's disapproval. And at last the father carries the boy off to bed with the youth "clinging" to the father's shirt. The tone of the piece is controlled by the distance of the speaker from these past events. The experience itself displays emotional ambiguity—both fear and love, both distaste and joy. As an event from the past, however, the experience is recalled with a sense of detached interest. Thus the contrast between the actual experience and the recollection gives this reminiscence an ironic flavor. Time has irrevocably separated past from present.

Sylvia Plath   (1932–1963)
The Rival

If the moon smiled, she would resemble you.
You leave the same impression
Of something beautiful, but annihilating.
Both of you are great light borrowers.
Her O-mouth grieves at the world; yours is unaffected,   5

And your first gift is making stone out of everything.
I wake to a mausoleum; you are here,
Ticking your fingers on the marble table, looking for cigarettes,
Spiteful as a woman, but not so nervous,
And dying to say something unanswerable.   10

The moon, too, abases her subjects,
But in the daytime she is ridiculous.
Your dissatisfactions, on the other hand,
Arrive through the mailslot with loving regularity,
White and blank, expansive as carbon monoxide.   15

No day is safe from news of you,
Walking about in Africa maybe, but thinking of me.

If a poem begins with the line, "If the moon smiled, she would resemble you," we might expect the comparison to continue in the same positive manner. Plath's verses, however, express negative, hostile attitudes. The tone of the poem is bitter and highly critical of the "you" to whom it is addressed. And this tone is conveyed through the first-person point of view. Plath also employs irony and language with highly emotional connotations to work out this tone. The comparison of the "you" with the moon provides the central irony of "The Rival." Usually associated with romantic thoughts and feelings, the moon is here depicted in unattractive terms. Its "smile" seems "beautiful" but is really "annihilating," its "light" is "borrowed," and it "abases" (or diminishes and humiliates) its "subjects" by night, only to turn "ridiculous" in the daytime. Everything the speaker says about the "you" reveals her repugnance—for example, "I wake to a mausoleum; you are here" and "No day is safe from news of you." Such language, although measured and calm, conceals bitterness and rage. To the speaker, the "you" has no redeeming, beneficial qualities. The tone of Plath's lines, in fact, is hardly less than quietly nasty.

The following poem conveys a tone that is more subtle and indirectly worked out than that of Plath's work.

William Heyen (b. 1940)
Driving at Dawn

Driving at dawn past Buffalo
we point to steel mills' stacks
reddening the sky as though
they threaten to set it afire. Hereabouts
soot rains steadily on the shacks   5
of steelmen and their ashen wives,
once sparks themselves in other lives
that burned a while, but then went out.

A limbo of gray trees and grass, then
a few miles more   10
and roadsides are green again
under the sun. This arsonist,
rising with matches in his fist,
glaring our windshield's ash on fire,
burns again for the steelmen   15
who burned like hell for their women.

Throughout the first stanza and in part of the second, the scene is one of industrial pollution and desolation—a landscape the "steelmen and their ashen wives" inhabit and "a limbo of gray trees and grass." The language is disturbing, even frightening, in its vivid descriptions of a world of desolate, violent forces which consume both inhabitants and nature. The imagery of these lines—the stacks of fire-reddened chimneys rising toward the dawn sky—is especially effective in creating the tone.

    In the second stanza, the speaker reports driving out of this area and into country that is "green again / under the sun." We might now expect the tone, certainly grim and harsh thus far, to change. But actually it is sustained and reinforced, even intensified, by the spectral figure of an "arsonist, / rising with matches in his fist, / glaring our windshield's ash on fire." This fantasy figure is symbolic, an evocation of those forces which create and control the steel mills. Yet the associations with arson are appropriate and support the tone of the poem. Further, as the image of an arsonist seeks the steelmen, they in turn burn "like hell for their women." This closing simile emphasizes the slight but constant irony of the speaker's voice—an irony suggesting the far-reaching, the almost more-than-human implications of this profoundly disturbing scene.

The tone of many poems depends almost exclusively upon the sound and rhythms of the language used, as in the following work.

Walt Whitman   (1819–1892)
Whispers of Heavenly Death

Whispers of heavenly death murmur'd I hear,
Labial gossip of night, sibilant chorals,
Footsteps gently ascending, mystical breezes wafted soft and low,
Ripples of unseen rivers, tides of a current flowing, forever flowing,
(Or is it the plashing of tears? the measureless waters of human tears?)   5

I see, just see skyward, great cloud-masses,
Mournfully slowly they roll, silently swelling and mixing,
With at times a half-dimm'd sadden'd far-off star,
Appearing and disappearing.

(Some parturition rather, some solemn immortal birth;   10
On the frontiers to eyes impenetrable,
Some soul is passing over.)

Whitman associates death, first in stanza 1, with various night sounds: breezes, ripples of "unseen rivers," tides, even possible human tears lightly falling. In stanza 2, he links death with what he sees in the sky: "great cloud-masses" and "a half-dimm'd sadden'd far-off star." In the final stanza, Whitman speculates that these "whispers" are of "some soul" that has just died and "is passing over" to what, implicitly, is the next world. The tone here depends upon the sounds of the words and the slow, rhythmical, and mellow quality of the long poetic lines. If read aloud, the poem clearly establishes its tone: a subdued and quiet acceptance, even perhaps a subtle anticipation, of the reality of death.

Allen Ginsberg   (b. 1926)
A Supermarket in California

What thoughts I have of you tonight, Walt Whitman, for I walked down the sidestreets under the trees with a headache self-conscious looking at the full moon.
In my hungry fatigue, and shopping for images, I went into the neon fruit supermarket, dreaming of your enumerations!
What peaches and what penumbras! Whole families shopping at night!

Aisles full of husbands! Wives in the avocados, babies in the tomatoes!—
and you, Garcia Lorca,[1] what were you doing down by the watermelons?

I saw you, Walt Whitman, childless, lonely old grubber, poking among
the meats in the refrigerator and eyeing the grocery boys.

I heard you asking questions of each: Who killed the pork chops? What
price bananas? Are you my Angel? 5

I wandered in and out of the brilliant stacks of cans following you, and
followed in my imagination by the store detective.

We strode down the open corridors together in our solitary fancy
tasting artichokes, possessing every frozen delicacy, and never passing
the cashier.

Where are we going, Walt Whitman? The doors close in an hour.
Which way does your beard point tonight?

(I touch your book and dream of our odyssey in the supermarket and
feel absurd.)

Will we walk all night through solitary streets? The trees add shade to
shade, lights out in the houses, we'll both be lonely. 10

Will we stroll dreaming of the lost America of love past blue automobiles in driveways, home to our silent cottage?

Ah, dear father, graybeard, lonely old courage-teacher, what America
did you have when Charon[2] quit poling his ferry and you got out on a
smoking bank and stood watching the boat disappear on the black waters
of Lethe?

These lines pay homage to Walt Whitman by employing the free verse
(see Chapter 10) Whitman wrote and also by reference to him as "dear
father, graybeard, lonely old courage-teacher." Thinking of Whitman
and "shopping for images" in a California supermarket, the voice in the
poem is amused and disturbed by the chaotic scene he describes in the
opening lines. He asks, "Where are we going, Walt Whitman?"
Ginsberg's lines speculate on what America now is, suggesting that, as
in Whitman's day, the poet is alienated from society. In the night walk
with Whitman, who was a fervent advocate of American democracy and
poetry, the voice says that the two can only dream "of the lost America
of love" as they pass "blue automobiles in driveways." The final lines
suggest that today we can neither know nor guess what that earlier
American dream of love (if it, in fact, ever existed) truly meant. The tone
mixes amusement with sadness, humor with frustration, loneliness with

---

1. Federico García Lorca (1898–1936), Spanish poet and dramatist, whose poetry is similar to
Whitman's in its sensuously concrete imagery.
2. In Greek mythology, the boatman who ferries the dead across the "black waters of Lethe,"
the River of Forgetfulness in Hades.

a sense of satisfaction at carrying on Whitman's fight for individual freedom and expression. Furthermore, Ginsberg employs irony in his contention that, given America's earlier dream of love, the country today is a nightmarish supermarket in California.

A Note on Sentimentality

The presence of irony in poems that express intense emotions is often highly useful in redeeming these works from possible sentimentality. In poetry, **sentimentality** is an attempt to draw from the reader a greater emotional response than is warranted by the subject and by its artistic treatment. We should not, however, confuse this fault with the expression of genuine and appropriate emotions and feelings, which should elicit from readers genuine and appropriate reactions. If we read the following short poem without the two concluding lines, it is merely a sentimental piece about dying swans. Yet with the last two lines it becomes an appropriate comment, not on swans, but on vainglorious, insensitive, pompous individuals.

Anonymous (16th-century English song)
The Silver Swan

The silver swan, who living had no note,
When death approached, unlocked her silent throat;
Leaning her breast against the reedy shore,
Thus sung her first and last, and sung no more.
Farewell, all joys; O death, come close mine eyes;   5
More geese than swans now live, more fools than wise.

We need to stress that sentimentality results not so much from the subject itself but from the poet's failure to treat the subject properly. Given below are four poems for reading and analysis. Look closely at their treatment of love, noting in particular the language and the figures employed. Then determine if any of the four contains instances of sentimentality. (For impartiality, the names of the authors are not given. In class discussion, the instructor can supply the names as he or she wishes.)

I Have Loved You in So Many Ways

I have loved you
in so many ways
in crowds or all alone.
When you were sleeping beside me.
When you were away   5
and I imagined others watching you in the street
or worse—you in other people's arms.

I have seen the march of beach birds and loved you.
I have lent myself to summer sun and loved you.
And seeing naked trees
         and raising my collar to the wind   10
and counting minutes till chartered hours were there
I have loved you.

And the questions never asked.
The answers learned at love's expense.
I've promised myself.   15
I will not ask where you have been tonight
I'll only say hello
             and hope.

You

You touched me last night
and awakened the insides of my mind.
Your words
written on paper
gently engulfed me,   5
my kind.

I waited so long to hear from you
yet I don't know what I expected
to hear.
I guess, I was just hoping   10
somehow,
to have you near,
to have you close,
to me.

The Weary Year His Race Now Having Run

The weary year his race now having run,
The new begins his compast° course anew,   *encompassing*
With show of morning mild he hath begun,
Betokening peace and plenty to ensue.

So let us, which this change of weather view,
Change eke° our minds, and former lives amend;   5
The old year's sins forepast let us eschew,   *also*
And fly the faults with which we did offend.
Then shall the new year's joy forth freshly send
Into the glooming world his gladsome ray,   10
And all these storms, which now his beauty blend,
Shall turn to calms and timely clear away.
So, likewise, Love, cheer you your heavy sprite,
And change old year's annoy° to new delight.   *annoyance*

Old Ladies

In every old lady I chance to meet
      Whoever, wherever she be,
From her snow-crowned head to her patient feet
      My own brave mother I see.

In every old lady whose patient eyes   5
      Are deeps of a fathomless sea,
So patient and tender and kind and wise
      My mother looks out at me.

In every old lady in silent prayer
      To God on her bended knee,   10
I vision my own mother kneeling there
      Praying a prayer for me.

In every old lady I bend above,
      Asleep in death's mystery,
I whisper, "Please carry my lone heart's love   15
      To my angel mother for me."

In every old lady I meet each day,
      The humble, or lofty and fine,
I see an angel stand, guarding the way,
      Somebody's mother and mine.   20

Nikki Giovanni (b. 1943)
For Saundra

i wanted to write
a poem
that rhymes
but revolution doesn't lend
itself to be-bopping   5

then my neighbor
who thinks i hate
asked—do you ever write
tree poems—i like trees
so i thought   10
i'll write a beautiful green tree poem
peeked from my window
to check the image
noticed the school yard was covered
with asphalt   15
no green—no trees grow
in manhattan

then, well, i thought the sky
i'll do a big blue sky poem
but all the clouds have winged   20
low since no-Dick was elected

so i thought again
and it occurred to me
maybe i shouldn't write
at all   25
but clean my gun
and check my kerosene supply

perhaps these are not poetic
times
at all   30

Questions for Study

1. Paraphrase the poem and state its theme. Is it about "revolution"? About poetry? About Manhattan?
2. Is the second stanza a comment on the poet's environment? Is it more than this? Explain.
3. Interpret the last two stanzas. What does the poet mean when she says that "perhaps these are not poetic times"?
4. Describe the tone of the poem. What notable features determine the tone?
5. Indicate at least two significant examples of irony in the poem.

Robert Bly (b. 1926)
When the Dumb Speak

There is a joyful night in which we lose
Everything, and drift
Like a radish
Rising and falling, and the ocean

At last throws us into the ocean,   5
And on the water we are sinking
As if floating on darkness.
The body raging
And driving itself, disappearing in smoke,
Walks in large cities late at night,   10
Or reading the Bible in Christian Science[1] windows,
Or reading a history of Bougainville.[2]
Then the images appear:
Images of death,
Images of the body shaken in the grave,   15
And the graves filled with seawater;
Fires in the sea,
The ships smoldering like bodies,
Images of wasted life,
Life lost, imagination ruined,   20
The house fallen,
The gold sticks broken,
Then shall the talkative be silent,
And the dumb shall speak.

Questions for Study

1. We might expect a poem that begins, "There is a joyful night . . . ." to be joyful. But is this poem joyful? What is its tone? Support your answer with examples from the poem.
2. What is the function of the allusions to Christian Science and to Bougainville?
3. Figurative language is important in this poem. Identify as many figures as you can and point out their function.
4. Why has Bly introduced into his poem "images of death"? Is death his theme or an aspect of his theme?
5. Bly's lines read (especially if read orally) like conversational statements. How is this quality important to the tone of the poem?
6. Interpret the last two lines and relate your interpretation to the poem as a whole.

John Crowe Ransom   (1888–1974)
Dead Boy

The little cousin is dead, by foul subtraction,
A green bough from Virginia's aged tree,
And none of the county kin like the transaction,
Nor some of the world of outer dark, like me.

---

1. Founded by Mary Baker Eddy (1821–1910), Christian Science emphasizes healing through spiritual means as one notable aspect of the divine goodness of Christianity, proof that it is the foundation of scientific reality.
2. Louis Antoine de Bougainville (1729–1811), French diplomat, explorer, and soldier. Bougainville Island, largest of the Solomon Islands in the southwest Pacific, is named for him; it was the scene of bloody battles between the U.S. and Japan in World War II.

A boy not beautiful, nor good, nor clever,   5
A black cloud full of storms too hot for keeping,
A sword beneath his mother's heart—yet never
Woman bewept her babe as this is weeping.

A pig with a pasty face, so I had said,
Squealing for cookies, kinned by poor pretense   10
With a noble house. But the little man quite dead,
I see the forbears' antique lineaments.

The elder men have strode by the box of death
To the wide flag porch, and muttering low send round
The bruit° of the day. O friendly waste of breath!   *news* 15
Their hearts are hurt with a deep dynastic wound.

He was pale and little, the foolish neighbors say;
The first-fruits, saith the Preacher, the Lord hath taken;
But this was the old tree's late branch wrenched away,
Grieving the sapless limbs, the shorn and shaken.   20

Questions for Study

1. What was the speaker's attitude toward the boy before he died? How has his attitude changed since the boy's death?
2. Comment on the diction of the poem. Examine in particular such phrases as "foul subtraction," "green bough," "antique lineaments," and "deep dynastic wound." Are these effectively employed or are they merely unusual?
3. Describe the tone of the poem. Is it one of involvement or detachment, humor or grief, or a mixture of all these?
4. Interpret the poem, commenting upon the role of tone in developing its meaning.

William Carlos Williams (1883–1963)
The Pause

Values are split, summer, the fierce
jet an axe would not sever, spreads out
at length, of its own weight, a rainbow
over the lake of memory—the hard
stem of pure speed broken. Autumn   5
comes, fruit of many contours, that
glistening tegument painters love hiding
the soft pulp of the insidious reason,
dormant, for worm to nibble or for woman.
But there, within the seed, shaken by   10
fear as by a sea, it wakes again! to
drive upward, presently, from that soft
belly such a stem as will crack quartz.

Questions for Study

1. What is the significance of the title? How do summer and autumn function within the poem? Determine the tone of the poem and try to point out what elements contribute to establishing the tone.
2. Identify and relate the following to the poem: "the lake of memory"; "the hard / stem of pure speed"; "fruit of many contours"; "glistening tegument"; "the soft pulp of the insidious reason."
3. What is the "it" in line 11?
4. What is the significance of the connection between "worm" and "woman" in line 9?

Henry Reed (b. 1914)
Naming of Parts

Today we have naming of parts. Yesterday,
We had daily cleaning. And tomorrow morning,
We shall have what to do after firing. But today,
Today we have naming of parts. Japonica
Glistens like coral in all of the neighbouring gardens,   5
    And today we have naming of parts.

This is the lower sling swivel. And this
Is the upper sling swivel, whose use you will see,
When you are given your slings. And this is the piling swivel
Which in your case you have not got. The branches   10
Hold in the gardens their silent, eloquent gestures,
    Which in our case we have not got.

This is the safety-catch, which is always released
With an easy flick of the thumb. And please do not let me
See anyone using his finger. You can do it quite easy   15
If you have any strength in your thumb. The blossoms
Are fragile and motionless, never letting anyone see
    Any of them using their finger.

And this you can see is the bolt. The purpose of this
Is to open the breech, as you see. We can slide it   20
Rapidly backwards and forwards: we call this
Easing the spring. And rapidly backwards and forwards
The early bees are assaulting and fumbling the flowers:
    They call it easing the Spring.

They call it easing the Spring: it is perfectly easy   25
If you have any strength in your thumb; like the bolt,
And the breech, and the cocking-piece, and the point of balance,

Which in our case we have not got; and the almond-blossom
Silent in all of the gardens and the bees going backwards and forwards,
    For today we have naming of parts.   30

Questions for Study

1. What is the tone of this poem? Do you think that the speaker is expressing the point of view or the attitude of the poem? Explain your response.
2. Is there a pun on the word *spring?*
3. Why has the poet employed various contrasts between the rifle drill and nature? What is achieved by these contrasts? How does the language change in these contrasts?
4. Why are certain phrases in the poem repeated? What is the effect of such repetitions?

James Wright (b. 1927)
The Jewel

There is this cave
In the air behind my body
That nobody is going to touch:
A cloister, a silence
Closing around a blossom of fire.   5
When I stand upright in the wind,
My bones turn to dark emeralds.

Questions for Study

1. What is the "cave"?
2. What is the significance of the connection between "cloister" and "silence" in line 4?
3. What is the "blossom of fire"? Is this a symbol and, if so, of what?
4. What is the connection between the title and the "dark emeralds" in the last line? How does this connection relate to the meaning of the poem?

Frank Daniel (b. 1900)
Salve

Most of the night and most of the day,
I'm thinking of you since you went on your way,
But in between throes, when the pain's less acute,
I plan to start seeking a substitute.

Question for Study

What is the tone of this poem? What elements in these lines most notably contribute to the tone?

Chapter 8
Sound

Without the music of words there would be no poetry. Because of this quality, it is always helpful to read poems aloud. Even if we read poems silently, the qualities and elements of sound still govern our perceptions of the verse. The poet creates musical effects in poetry by the selection and arrangement of sound and of syllabic accents. The various aspects of sound are considered in this chapter. Syllabic accents and their arrangement into patterns are discussed in Chapter 9.

Our delight in the sound of poetry can be evoked by such nursery rimes as the following:

Anonymous
High Diddle Diddle

High diddle diddle
   The cat and the fiddle
The cow jumped over the moon;
   The little dog laughed
   To see such craft   5
And the dish ran away with the spoon.

The three musical elements at work here are the sounds of words, the repetition of words, and the rhythm generated by their arrangement. The sense (or the nonsense) in these lines is integrated with these sounds and with this particular rhythm. Like a musical composer, a poet understands our delight in sound and uses repetition and variation to create sound patterns with words. Listen to the sounds in the following short song:

William Shakespeare   (1564–1616)
Winter

When icicles hang by the wall,
   And Dick the shepherd blows his nail,°   *blows on his fingers*
And Tom bears logs into the hall,   *to warm them*
   And milk comes frozen home in pail,
When blood is nipp'd, and ways° be foul,   *roads* 5
Then nightly sings the staring owl,
          Tu-who;
Tu-whit, tu-who—a merry note,
While greasy Joan doth keel° the pot.   *cool by stirring*

When all aloud the wind doth blow,   10
   And coughing drowns the parson's saw,°   *wise saying*
And birds sit brooding in the snow,
   And Marian's nose looks red and raw,
When roasted crabs° hiss in the bowl,   *crab apples*
Then nightly sings the staring owl,   15
          Tu-who;
Tu-whit, tu-who—a merry note,
While greasy Joan doth keel the pot.

The harsh winter in sixteenth-century England is the subject of Shakespeare's song. The weather is miserably cold—milk freezes in the pail, one's blood is "nipp'd," roads are foul, colds and coughing spoil the parson's sermon, birds "sit brooding in the snow," noses are red and raw. Nevertheless, there is some pleasant activity, with bowls of hot ale to drink. In selecting and arranging his concrete details, Shakespeare keeps in mind the music of his words, which have the effect of compensating for the cheerless scene. Sounds support the details and the meaning of his poem. Reading it aloud, we hear directly and clearly the strong role sound plays in the lines. The use of the owl, a night bird often associated with omens and hidden messages, is especially effective because Shakespeare places it in the refrain. A **refrain** is a word, a group of words, or verses repeated at intervals throughout a poem, often at the end of a stanza. The last four lines of each of the two stanzas of "Winter" constitute Shakespeare's refrain. In these lines, moreover, Shakespeare's language approximates the hooting of an owl in "Tu-who, Tu-whit, tu-who," another excellent illustration of how sound functions in poetry.

    Other properties and functions of sound in poetry, some of which we find in Shakespeare's lines, need to be mentioned. When a sound pattern is pleasing to the ear, we say it is an example of **euphony.** Such pleasant-sounding phrases as "sweet music of moaning doves" and "low-lying neath the pale moon" are euphonious. Shakespeare's "birds sit brood-ing in the snow" is similarly euphonious, though certainly the scene is not very soothing. Sound patterns that are harsh and displeasing to the ear are examples of **cacophony.** A line from Robert Browning's "Rabbi Ben Ezra" illustrates the intentional use of cacophonous sounds to reinforce a particularly unpleasant scene: "Irks care the crop-full bird? Frets doubt the maw-crammed beast?" Like harmony and dissonance in musical compositions, euphony and cacophony in poetry support mean-ings and work out variations of the sound patterns.

Another sound effect in poetry is **onomatopoeia,** or the suggestion of a word's meaning by its actual sound. Such words as *buzz, crash, hiss, sneeze,* and *squeak* approximate in sound their meanings. A close rela-tionship between sound and sense, not always the case with euphony and cacophony, always exists with onomatopoeia. Incidentally, many names, such as *chickadee* and *whippoorwill,* are onomatopoetic in origin and show clearly the widespread use of this device.

Each of these three sound effects—euphony, cacophony, and onomatopoeia—is more than a game played with words. When used effectively, these devices are essential to the meaning and the effect of a poem.

John Updike   (b. 1932)
Player Piano

My stick fingers click with a snicker
And, chuckling, they knuckle the keys;
Light-footed, my steel feelers flicker
And pluck from these keys melodies.

My paper can caper; abandon   5
Is broadcast by dint of my din,
And no man or band has a hand in
The tones I turn on from within.

At times I'm a jumble of rumbles,
At others I'm light like the moon,   10
But never my numb plunker fumbles,
Misstrums me, or tries a new tune.

The poem, first of all, is about an instrument that makes sounds—a player piano. Through the device of personification, Updike has the piano itself describe how it works. Such onomatopoetic words as *click, chuckling, flicker, plunk* evoke the actual sounds a player piano makes. Instances of euphony occur in such phrases as "The tones I turn on" and "I'm light like the moon." Examples of cacophony are "chuckling, they knuckle the keys" and "my numb plunker fumbles, / Misstrums me." Like elements in a musical piece, one line uses a key sound that contrasts with the key sound in another. In the opening stanza, for example, "stick"/"click"/"snicker" contrast with "chuckling"/"knuckle"/"keys" in the following line. Each stanza establishes dominant sounds which are then played off against other sounds. Updike's patterning of sounds, in fact, provides the overall organization, as it determines the light-hearted meaning of the poem. These lines present Updike's gently mocking view of the role of sound in poetry.

The functions of sound in poetry depend not only upon harmonic or dissonant patterns but also upon repetitions of identical or closely related sounds. Two important types of repetition often used in poetry (and in prose as well) are alliteration and assonance. **Alliteration** is the repetition of identical or nearly identical consonant sounds. Alliteration is further described as **initial** and **internal** (or **hidden**). The following two lines by Samuel Taylor Coleridge show examples of both kinds:

> The fair breeze blew, the white foam flew,
> The furrow followed free.

Not only the initial *f*'s and *b*'s but also the internal *r*'s are examples of alliteration.[1] Perhaps it should be noted here that alliteration depends solely upon sound, not upon spelling; for example, *know* and *pneumatic* are alliterative, *church* and *circle* are not.

The following line from John Keats' "The Eve of St. Agnes" employs alliteration in several ways: "And still she slept an azure-lidded sleep." We easily note the alliterative initial *s*'s in "*s*till *s*he *s*lept" and "*s*leep." We also need to recognize the use, first, of internal *l*'s in "sti*ll* she s*l*ept an azure-*l*idded s*l*eep" and, second, of internal *p*'s in "sle*p*t" and "slee*p*." Alliteration contributes noticeably to the subtle qualities and associations Keats wishes to stress—essentially, the peaceful, soothing, innocent sleep of a young girl.

Assonance is the repetition of identical or related vowel sounds. Like alliteration, assonance can occur initially or internally within a word. Such combinations as *each* and *every, ill* and *idle, owl* and *otter* show initial assonance. In "Ode on a Grecian Urn," John Keats provides an illustration: "Thou foster-ch*i*ld of s*i*lence and slow T*i*me."

While you need to recognize and understand these and other elements of sound, you must keep the poem as a whole in mind. By answering the questions following each of the next four poems, you should be able to determine not only how sound and sound patterns but also how other elements contribute to the meaning and effect of each.

---

1. Some critics prefer to call this poetic device **consonance,** which is the use of words having identical or related consonants, but different vowels.

Walter de la Mare (1873–1956)
Silver

Slowly, silently, now the moon
Walks the night in her silver shoon;°   *shoe*
This way, and that, she peers, and sees
Silver fruit upon silver trees;
One by one the casements catch   5
Her beams beneath the silvery thatch;
Couched in his kennel, like a log,
With paws of silver sleeps the dog;
From their shadowy cote the white breasts peep
Of doves in a silver-feathered sleep;   10
A harvest mouse goes scampering by,
With silver claws and a silver eye;
And moveless fish in the water gleam,
By silver reeds in a silver stream.

Questions for Study

1. The poet creates specific effects by the sound patterns in this short poem. Describe these effects, citing specific words and lines, as well as pertinent details, to support your comments.
2. Repetition is essential to de la Mare's poem. Find examples of different kinds of repetition in the work and show how these function to create and sustain the overall effect and meaning.
3. The basic image in the poem is *silver,* used in the sense of a metal, a color, a texture. Interpret the poem by commenting upon the various ways in which this image functions in the overall meaning.

Philip Larkin (b. 1922)
Wedding-Wind

The wind blew all my wedding-day,
And my wedding-night was the night of the high wind;
And a stable door was banging, again and again,
That he must go and shut it, leaving me
Stupid in candlelight, hearing rain,   5
Seeing my face in the twisted candlestick,
Yet seeing nothing. When he came back
He said the horses were restless, and I was sad
That any man or beast that night should lack
The happiness I had.   10

              Now in the day
All's ravelled under the sun by the wind's blowing.
He has gone to look at the floods, and I
Carry a chipped pail to the chicken-run,
Set it down, and stare. All is the wind   15
Hunting through clouds and forests, thrashing
My apron and the hanging cloths on the line.
Can it be borne, this bodying-forth by wind
Of joy my actions turn on, like a thread
Carrying beads? Shall I be let to sleep   20
Now this perpetual morning shares my bed?
Can even death dry up
These new delighted lakes, conclude
Our kneeling as cattle by all-generous waters?

Questions for Study

1. W. H. Auden said that poetry is "the clear expression of mixed feelings." Could this description be applied to "Wedding-Wind"? In trying out Auden's comment, first establish what feelings in the poem may or may not be "mixed."
2. Who is the speaker, or voice, in the poem? State the theme and then examine how the speaker is related to it.
3. Alliterative effects abound in the poem. Identify representative instances and comment on the functions of each.
4. The poet structures his work by a basic contrast, with each stanza containing one of the contrasted elements. Identify these and relate each to the theme of the poem.

Denise Levertov (b. 1923)
The Ache of Marriage

The ache of marriage:

thigh and tongue, beloved,
are heavy with it,
it throbs in the teeth

We look for communion   5
and are turned away, beloved,
each and each

It is leviathan and we
in its belly
looking for joy, some joy   10
not to be known outside it

two by two in the ark of
the ache of it.

Questions for Study

1. Like "Wedding-Wind," this poem is about marriage. What is the view of marriage presented here? How does it contrast with the view given in "Wedding-Wind"?
2. A key element in the poem is the statement that marriage "is leviathan." The Book of Job describes leviathan as a sea monster; often it is associated with the fish which swallowed Jonah and kept him in its belly for three days. What does the poet imply by the use of "leviathan" to describe marriage? Is the word *ark* in line 12 related to this use? If so, how and what does the poem gain by such biblical associations?
3. Identify and describe each instance of alliteration and repetition you can find in the poem.
4. Why has Levertov organized her poem into three parts: an initial premise; three statements; and a two-line final stanza which seems judgmental and conclusive? Look closely at the three internal stanzas. Is there a pattern common to each of them? Is there any modulation or movement from one point to another?

Robinson Jeffers (1887–1962)
November Surf

Some lucky day each November great waves awake and are drawn
Like smoking mountains bright from the west
And come and cover the cliff with white violent cleanness: then suddenly
The old granite forgets half a year's filth:
The orange-peel, eggshells, papers, pieces of clothing, the clots   5
Of dung in corners of the rock, and used
Sheaths that make light love safe in the evenings: all the droppings of the
          summer
Idlers washed off in a winter ecstasy:
I think this cumbered continent envies its cliff then. . . . But all seasons
The earth, in her childlike prophetic sleep,   10
Keeps dreaming of the bath of a storm that prepares up the long coast
Of the future to scour more than her sea-lines:
The cities gone down, the people fewer and the hawks more numerous,
The rivers mouth to source pure; when the two-footed
Mammal, being someways one of the nobler animals, regains   15
The dignity of room, the value of rareness.

Questions for Study

1. What is the subject of this poem? Are words such as *ecology* and *overpopulation* appropriate in describing the subject?
2. Jeffers organizes his poem into two distinct parts. Identify these and comment upon the function of each.
3. Jeffers lived on the coast of California, below San Francisco, in a house he himself built. Identify in the poem details which relate to such matters.

The most obvious use of sound in poetry occurs in rime (or rhyme). For many readers rime is the most notable, memorable feature of poetry. It is what is most easily heard and thus what, for many people, most distinguishes poetry from other uses of language. Along with rhythm and meter, rime is one of the three traditional building stones of poetry. Defined broadly, **rime** is the repetition of similar or identical sounds. Viewed in this way, alliteration might be considered as a kind of rime. A more specific definition, however, is needed for the study of poetry. Rime is the repetition, usually at the end of a line, of similar or identical vowel sounds in accented syllables which are *preceded* by unlike consonants. If a consonant follows the accented vowel, it must be the same consonant for rime to occur. Two lines from Alexander Pope's *An Essay on Man* contain a clear rime:

> Know then thyself, presume not God to scan;
> The proper study of Mankind is Man.

True rime, *scan* and *Man,* exists only when the riming sounds occur in words in which the final accented vowel sounds are the same. For example, *chews* and *re-FUSE* rime, but not *chews* and *REF-use*. True rime depends solely upon the accented identical sounds, not upon spelling.

Rimes are classified in two basic ways: first, by the number and kind of syllables having similar or identical sounds; and, second, by the position of a rime in one line or more of verse. When a correspondence of sound exists in the final accented syllables of two or more words, we call this **masculine rime:** *bed* with *head, St. Ives* with *wives, shot* with *pot*. When a correspondence of sound exists in two final syllables, an accented one followed by an unaccented one, we call this **feminine rime:** *miser* with *wiser, decaying* with *saying,* even *know it* with *show it*. Occasionally, a poet uses **triple rime,** or a correspondence of sound in three syllables, one accented followed by two unaccented ones, as in *vainglorious* and *meritorious*. This rime is so pronounced and melodious that it is usually reserved for light and even humorous verse, as in these two lines from W. S. Gilbert's *The Pirates of Penzance:*

> I'm very good at integral and differential *calculus,*
> I know the scientific names of beings *animalculous* . . . .

Looking at the position of rimes in a poem, we see that rimes at the end of two or more lines, or **end rimes,** are the most familiar and frequent kinds. **Internal rime** occurs within a line of verse. Sometimes poets emploly **beginning rime,** with a correspondence of sound existing in the first word of two or more lines. The following short poem illustrates internal rime, as well as end rime.

Anonymous
I Cannot Eat But Little Meat

I cannot eat but little meat,
    My stomach is not good;
But sure I think that I can drink
    With him that wears a hood.
Though I go bare, take ye no care,   5
    I am nothing a-cold;
I stuff my skin so full within
    Of jolly good ale and old.

You might identify the rimes by underscoring each of them. If you have
any difficulty, simply read the poem aloud.

   Some poetry, contemporary poetry in particular, contains variations
of true or exact rime. Some of these variations need to be briefly
mentioned. First, **slant rime** (or **off rime**) occurs when final consonant
sounds that are alike are preceded by vowel sounds that are different.
Typical examples are *dear* and *dare*, *early* and *barley*, *tune* and *phone*.
We should note here that some of what seem imperfect rimes today
once were true rimes. Here is an illustration from Christopher Marlowe's "The Passionate Shepherd to His Love":

> Come live with me and be my *love,*
> And we will all the pleasures *prove.*

In sixteenth-century England, the vowel sound in *love* was similar to
that in *prove*. Not so today; the centuries have changed many of our
English pronunciations.

   A second variation is **consonantal rime,** or a correspondence (sometimes merely a resemblance) of sound between consonants: *matter* and
mutter, simple and *supple, floor* and *flair*. The consonant sounds are
similar, but the vowel sounds are different. This variation has become
increasingly popular in this century. Here is a stanza from Wilfred
Owen's "Strange Meeting," which makes strong use of consonantal
rime:

> It seemed that out of battle I *escaped*
> Down some profound dull tunnel, long since *scooped*
> Through granites which titanic wars had *groined.*
> Yet also there encumbered sleepers *groaned.*

Another variant is **sight rime** (also called **eye rime**), in which the correspondence is simply in the spelling: *head* with *bead, death* with *wreath,*

dew with *sew*. Variations of rime patterns such as these can be found in early poetry, but they are much more prevalent in poems written in this century. In addition, a great deal of modern poetry does not even use any rime at all.

The pattern or order in which rimes occur in a poem, or in a part or in a stanza of a poem, is called its **rime scheme.** In marking the rime scheme of a poem, a letter of the alphabet is given to each end rime with the same sound. Such a method allows a quick and easy identification of the pattern used. The rime scheme of one stanza of Robert Herrick's "To the Virgins, to Make Much of Time" looks like this:

> That age is best which is the first,   *a*
>   When youth and blood are warmer;   *b*
> But being spent, the worse, and worst   *a*
>   Times still succeed the former.   *b*

Additional examples and further practice in working with rime schemes will be given in Chapters 9 and 10. Rime scheme is only briefly examined here because it bears upon the following discussion of the functions of rime.

The functions of rime in poetry are many and varied. One of the most basic is the chance it affords us to delight in sound and in the patterns of repeated sounds. Nursery rimes such as the following provide the most obvious examples of how rime can produce delightful effects.

Anonymous
Jack Sprat

Jack Sprat could eat no fat,
    His wife could eat no lean,
And so betwixt them both, you see,
    They licked the platter clean.

The appeal of these lines depends heavily upon rime—in this instance, on both end rimes and internal rimes. We might say, in fact, that in these lines rime is *the* poetic device that essentially carries off the whole affair, since it generates most of the "fun" in these verses.

Similarly, we enjoy hearing new, often odd combinations made by means of rime. We are delighted by such combinations and even commit them to memory.

Ogden Nash   (1902–1971)
Reflections on Ice-Breaking

Candy
Is dandy
But liquor
Is quicker.

The usefulness of rime in conveying a humorous but pointed message is
apparent in the following poem.

Robert Frost   (1874–1963)
The Span of Life

The old dog barks backward without getting up.
I can remember when he was a pup.

Another important function of rime is to give emphasis to the riming
words and to compress and intensify the meaning and effect of the poem.
The following poem shows how rime functions in this way.

William Blake   (1757–1827)
The Lamb

   Little Lamb, who made thee?
   Dost thou know who made thee?
Gave thee life and bid thee feed,
By the stream and o'er the mead;
Gave thee clothing of delight,   5
Softest clothing wooly bright;
Gave thee such a tender voice,
Making all the vales rejoice?
   Little Lamb, who made thee?
   Dost thou know who made thee?   10

   Little Lamb, I'll tell thee,
   Little Lamb, I'll tell thee:
He is callèd by thy name,
For He calls Himself a Lamb:
He is meek, and He is mild;   15
He became a little child:
I a child, and thou a lamb,

We are callèd by His name.
    Little Lamb, God bless thee.
    Little Lamb, God bless thee.   20

Blake utilizes rime (and sometimes repetitions of words) to give emphasis, first, to his question, who made the lamb? and, second, to his answer, God made the lamb. Repeating in the last two lines of stanza 1 the question asked in the opening two lines like a refrain, Blake brings into sharp focus the thematic proposition of his poem. Rime here is used to give further stress to the question he is asking. In the first stanza, three pairs of lines having corresponding end rimes depict the innocence of the lamb and its harmonious relationship with nature: "feed"/"mead," "delight"/"bright," and "voice"/"rejoice." Blake moves from the question to an affirmation in the opening lines of stanza 2 and then to a benediction in the closing two lines. Here only one set of end-rimed lines is used, but it is a crucial one:

> He is meek, and He is *mild;*
> He became a little *child.*

Here rime plays a key thematic role in linking Jesus with the child and both with the lamb.

    In the following poem, rime gives these rather short lines an emphatic, if poignant, quality.

Countee Cullen   (1903–1946)
Incident

Once riding in old Baltimore,
    Heart-filled, head-filled with glee,
I saw a Baltimorean
    Keep looking straight at me.

Now I was eight and very small,   5
    And he was no whit bigger,
And so I smiled, but he poked out
    His tongue and called me, "Nigger."

I saw the whole of Baltimore
    From May until December: 10
Of all the things that happened there
    That's all that I remember.

Rime is employed at key points in these lines to emphasize and intensify the ugly incident the child experiences. The riming words are actually the key ones in the poem. We see in each pair of rimes the central issue of the poem: "glee"/"me," "bigger"/"Nigger," "December"/"remember." The "glee" of a day in Baltimore—and much else in this boy's life—is forever ruined by another boy who senselessly and viciously insults him.

Rime also serves to establish and order relationships among elements in a poem. We often hear it said that poetry is compressed language in its most concise, intensive state. And rime is a key device in organizing the diverse aspects of this compressed language into meaningful poetic form. The following poem well illustrates this function of rime.

Peter La Farge (b. 1931)
Vision of a Past Warrior

I have within me such a dream of pain
That all my silver horseman hopes rust still—
Beyond quick silver mountains, on the plain,
The buffalo are gone, none left to kill.

I see the plains grow blackened with that dawn,   5
No robes for winter warmth, no meat to eat—
The ghost white buffalos' medicine[1] gone,
No hope for Indians then; I see defeat.

Then there will be changes to another way,
We will fight battles that are legends long.   10
But of all our glory none will stay—
Who will remember that I sang this song?

There is nothing unusual about the rime employed here. All are masculine end rimes, in a standard pattern of alternating lines riming *abab, cdcd, efef.* The rime here is important precisely because of its conventionality. The meaning and thematic emphasis of the poem require rimes and a rime scheme which do not call attention to themselves. The poem, in its solid but unobtrusive structure, presents the vision of an Indian warrior lamenting the triumph of the white man's civilization over his own: "No hope for Indians then; I see defeat." The speaker thinks of what has been, of what is now, and of what will be. And the warrior's inner pain and loss are the elements La Farge portrays in the poem, disciplined by the formality of rime.

---

1. The North American Plains Indians attached special significance to the rare white buffalo. Whenever one was caught, it was sacrificed in order to bring good fortune ("good medicine") to the tribe.

In shaping and ordering his lines by means of rime, a poet often employs it as an effective means of "punctuating" his verse. Used in this way, rimes may indicate the end of a line or may perhaps round off a structural unit of a piece. Even if there is no definite pattern of rimes, they may be arranged in ways which contribute to the progression of the lines. In the following poem, rime is used in working out some of these problems.

Robert Frost (1874–1963)
After Apple-Picking

My long two-pointed ladder's sticking through a tree
Toward heaven still,
And there's a barrel that I didn't fill
Beside it, and there may be two or three
Apples I didn't pick upon some bough.   5
But I am done with apple-picking now.
Essence of winter sleep is on the night,
The scent of apples: I am drowsing off.
I cannot rub the strangeness from my sight
I got from looking through a pane of glass   10
I skimmed this morning from the drinking trough
And held against the world of hoary grass.
It melted, and I let it fall and break.
But I was well
Upon my way to sleep before it fell,   15
And I could tell
What form my dreaming was about to take.
Magnified apples appear and disappear,
Stem end and blossom end,
And every fleck of russet showing clear.   20
My instep arch not only keeps the ache,
It keeps the pressure of a ladder-round.
I feel the ladder sway as the boughs bend.
And I keep hearing from the cellar bin
The rumbling sound   25
Of load on load of apples coming in.
For I have had too much
Of apple-picking: I am overtired
Of the great harvest I myself desired.
There were ten thousand thousand fruit to touch,   30
Cherish in hand, lift down, and not let fall.
For all
That struck the earth,
No matter if not bruised or spiked with stubble,
Went surely to the cider-apple heap   35
As of no worth.

One can see what will trouble
This sleep of mine, whatever sleep it is.
Were he not gone,
The woodchuck could say whether it's like his   40
Long sleep, as I describe its coming on,
Or just some human sleep.

The language of Frost's poem is conversational and informal. His tone is consistently that of a country man musing about his work, his increasing age, and his discontent with his labors. Although the effect Frost achieves throughout is one of simplicity and apparent ease, "After Apple-Picking" is a complex poem. Without attempting a comprehensive analysis, we can note the care with which he arranges the lengths of his lines and the way rime functions as an ordering device. By using rime, Frost is indicating that these musings are not prose but poetry. Yet there is no definite pattern of rimes or rime scheme. Rather, Frost uses rimes to end his verse lines and, in some instances, to round off his thoughts, as in "I am overtired / Of the great harvest I myself desired." All of the rimes are end rimes, but they are variously arranged throughout the verses, some in alternating lines and some in couplets. There is even one three-line rime, in "well"/"fell"/"tell." Frost's rimes organize his thoughts, emphasize important words, and thus convey the speaker's view of his own existence and of life in general.

W. H. Auden (1907–1973)
It's No Use Raising a Shout

It's no use raising a shout.
No, Honey, you can cut that right out.
I don't want any more hugs;
Make me some fresh tea, fetch me some rugs.
Here am I, here are you: 5
But what does it mean? What are we going to do?

A long time ago I told my mother
I was leaving home to find another:
I never answered her letter
But I never found a better.   10
Here am I, here are you:
But what does it mean? What are we going to do?

In my spine there was a base;
And I knew the general's face:

But they've severed all the wires, 15
And I can't tell what the general desires.
Here am I, here are you:
But what does it mean? What are we going to do?

In my veins there is a wish,
And a memory of fish: 20
When I lie crying on the floor,
It says, "You've often done this before."
Here am I, here are you:
But what does it mean? What are we going to do?

A bird used to visit this shore: 25
It isn't going to come any more.
I've come a very long way to prove
No land, no water, and no love.
Here am I, here are you:
But what does it mean? What are we going to do? 30

Questions for Study

1. There is considerable humor in this poem. What devices does Auden use to create the humor?
2. In each of the five stanzas, Auden uses a refrain. What is its function? Is it effective and, if so, why?
3. The theme of this poem might be suggested in the lines "I've come a very long way to prove / No land, no water, and no love." What is meant here? Relate these lines to the entire poem. How does the poem's humor seem to support this rather solemn theme?
4. Identify the rimes in this poem and mark the rime scheme.

Gwendolyn Brooks (b. 1917)
We Real Cool

The Pool Players.
Seven at the Golden Shovel.

We real cool. We
Left school. We

Lurk late. We
Strike straight. We

Sing sin. We 5
Thin gin. We

Jazz June. We
Die soon.

Questions for Study

1. The biting, sarcastic humor in this short poem is created largely by diction and rime. Comment on both of these elements, in particular upon the use of slang.
2. Why does each line, except the last, end with the pronoun *We?*
3. Identify and comment upon the function of musical elements other than rime in the poem.

Thomas Carew   (1594?–1639?)
Song

Give me more love, or more disdain;
   The torrid or the frozen zone
Bring equal ease unto my pain;
   The temperate affords me none:
Either extreme, of love or hate,   5
Is sweeter than a calm estate.

Give me a storm; if it be love,
   Like Danaë in that golden shower,[1]
I swim in pleasure; if it prove
   Disdain, that torrent will devour   10
My vulture hopes; and he's possessed
Of heaven that's but from hell released.
   Then crown my joys, or cure my pain;
   Give me more love or more disdain.

Questions for Study

1. Who is speaking and what is the situation in this poem?
2. Mark the rime scheme Carew uses. Classify the rimes according to their place in the line and to their type.
3. Underlying the speaker's pleas there is a tone of firmness, even of toughness. Identify those poetic devices which suggest this tone—for example, "My vulture hopes."

A Note on Reading Poems Aloud

The music of words, the marvelous sound patterns the poet has created, are best heard and appreciated by reading poems aloud. An oral rendition conveys much more than many silent readings and a close

---

1. In Greek mythology, Danaë, imprisoned in a tower by her father, was visited by Zeus in a shower of gold; consequently, she gave birth to Perseus.

analysis can give. Reading poetry aloud offers much more than a useful way of understanding a poem; it provides an enriching experience which cannot be gained or even approximated by any other means.

Here are two important guidelines to keep in mind when reading poetry aloud.

1. Before your oral reading of a poem, go through it once or twice. Note its language and punctuation, underscore important elements you want to emphasize or take special care with, and familiarize yourself with any special features of the work.

2. In reading aloud, let your voice strike its normal, natural pitch; avoid false or assumed speech patterns. Read slowly, certainly more slowly than when you read most kinds of prose. And read deliberately, maintaining an even tempo in your delivery. Observe punctuation, pausing at a comma, a little longer at a semicolon or a period, and so on. Allow the sense of the verse to determine the rhythm. Especially avoid always stopping at the end of a verse line; if not punctuated, the line usually runs on directly to the following line. As we have seen, many poems are conversational in style and need to be read that way.

Perhaps a reminder is in order: many contemporary poets have recorded some of their poetry, and often such recordings are useful in helping us read and understand a particular work. Also available are numerous recordings of poetry readings done by professional actors and actresses.

The following poems lend themselves especially well to oral reading. Such devices of sound as alliteration, assonance, onomatopoeia, and rime are prominent in each. Examples of euphony and cacophony also occur. After reading each poem, identify and classify notable elements of sound you find.

William Shakespeare (1564–1616)
Full Fathom Five

Full fathom five thy father lies:
  Of his bones are coral made;
Those are pearls that were his eyes:
  Nothing of him that doth fade,
But doth suffer a sea-change   5
Into something rich and strange.
Sea-nymphs hourly ring his knell:
  Hark! now I hear them,—
    Ding, dong, Bell.

Ben Jonson   (1573?–1637)
It Was a Beauty That I Saw

It was a beauty that I saw,
So pure, so perfect, as the frame
Of all the universe was lame
To that one figure, could I draw
Or give least line of it a law.   5
A skein of silk without a knot,
A fair march made without a halt,
A curious° form without a fault,   *elaborate*
A printed book without a blot:
All beauty, and without a spot.   10

Anonymous   (traditional Scottish folk ballad)
Sir Patrick Spens

The King sits in Dumferling town,
    Drinking the blood-red wine:
"O where will I get good sailors
    To sail this ship of mine?"

Up and spoke an old knight,   5
    Sat at the King's right knee:
"Sir Patrick Spens is the best sailor
    That sails upon the sea."

The King has written a broad letter,
    And signed it with his hand,   10
And sent it to Sir Patrick Spens,
    Was walking on the sand.

The first line that Sir Patrick read
    A loud laugh laughed he:
The next line that Sir Patrick read,   15
    A tear blinded his ee.°   *eye*

"O who is this has done this deed,
    This ill deed done to me,
To send me out this time of the year
    To sail upon the sea?   20

Make haste, make haste, my merry men all,
    Our good ship sails at morn."
"O say not so, my master dear,
    For I fear a deadly storm.

Late, late last night I saw the new moon 25
  With the old moon in her arm,
And I fear, I fear, my master dear,
  That we will come to harm."

O our Scots nobles were right loth°   *very reluctant*
  To wet their cork-heeled shoon;°   *shoes* 30
But long ere all the play was played,
  Their hats they swam aboon.°   *above*

O long, long will their ladies sit
  With their fans into their hand,
Before they see Sir Patrick Spens
  Come sailing to the land. 35

O long, long will the ladies stand
  With their gold combs in their hair,
Waiting for their own dear lords,
  For they'll see them no mair.°   *more* 40

Half-o'er,° half-o'er to Abadour   *halfway over*
  'Tis fifty fathoms deep,
And there lies good Sir Patrick Spens
  With the Scots lords at his feet.

Chapter 9
Rhythm and Meter

In using language for most purposes, we usually do not pay much attention to the rhythm of our speech. We are concerned more with getting our message across clearly than with consciously arranging words and phrases in order to convey a heightened musical effect. A crucial aspect of poetry, however, is its ability to achieve such an effect by the use of **rhythm,** which is the repetition at measured intervals of stressed (accented) and unstressed (unaccented) syllables.

The process of analyzing the rhythmic pattern and determining the kinds and the number of stressed and unstressed syllables in a line of poetry is called **scansion.** By "scanning" lines of verse, we determine the rhythm and the meter. From a Greek word meaning "to measure," meter (discussed later in this chapter) is the more or less regular pattern of rhythms contained in a line, a stanza, or in an entire poem. The following lines from Alexander Pope's *An Essay on Criticism* have been scanned to show how rhythm and meter function in poetry.

> True ease | in writ | ing comes | from art, ‖ not chance,
>
> As those | move eas | iest who | have learned | to dance.
>
> 'Tis not | enough ‖ no harsh | ness gives | offence,
>
> The sound | must seem | an ech | o to | the sense.

In marking lines of verse such as these, we use a thin perpendicular line (|) to set off each poetic foot. The basic unit of English verse is the **foot** (the plural, not surprisingly, is **feet**), which normally consists of one stressed and one or more unstressed syllables. Within the foot, we use a short, slanted mark (′) to indicate a stressed syllable and a curved line

(˘) to show an unstressed one. Two perpendicular lines (‖) indicate a **caesura,** or a pause within a verse line. Such pauses are frequently indicated by the poet's use of punctuation; but at other times, a pause will occur even though no punctuation mark is present. The method for marking scansion varies slightly from critic to critic, but the system offered here is one many use. At the moment, however, rhythm is our chief concern; meter and scansion are examined more closely later in this chapter.

The following short poem provides several good instances of how rhythm functions in poetry.

Gwendolyn Brooks (b. 1917)
Old Mary

Mȳ lást │ defénse	*a*
Ĭs thĕ prés │ ĕnt teńse.	*a*
Ĭt lít │ tlĕ húrts │ mĕ nów │ tŏ knów	*b*
Ĭ shall │ nŏt gó	*b*
Căthéd │ răl-húnt │ ĭng ĭn Spáin	*c*
Nŏr chér │ rўĭng │ ĭn Mích │ ĭgán │ ŏr Maíne.	*c*

5

The poem has a strong rhythmic pattern. By looking closely at the stressed syllables, which are fairly obvious throughout the lines, then at the unstressed ones, we note that the dominant rhythmic pattern is an unstressed syllable, followed by a stressed one. The poem also contains three variations from this pattern. Line 2 begins with two unstressed syllables and one stressed syllable; line 5 ends with the same variation; and line 6 contains three unstressed syllables in a row. If we count the number of feet in the poem, we find a total of eighteen. Each of the three stanzas contains two lines having the same end rime, a form that is known as the *couplet* (see Chapter 10). The first ("defense"/"tense") has four feet, the middle one ("know"/"go") six, and the final one ("Spain"/"Maine") eight. These variations in line length illustrate what Pope meant, that the sound of poetry "must seem an echo to the sense," or to the meaning. The opening couplet is the shortest and the most emphatic, stating the speaker's proposition that she must live in the present. She later says that she cannot expect to travel and to enjoy the cathedrals of Spain or the countryside of Michigan or Maine. As the poem explains the proposition, the lines get longer, the rhythms are less emphatic, and the actual pace of the lines slows. She is traveling in her words in "the present tense."

Pauses, either punctuated or unpunctuated, help express rhythmic patterns in a poem. When a line of verse ends in a full pause, either punctuated or dictated by the natural rhythm of the language, we say that the line is **end-stopped.** Some lines are heavily end-stopped, while others are lightly end-stopped. In the following short poem, each line is heavily end-stopped with a period.

Robert Bly (b. 1926)
In a Train

There has been a light snow.
Dark car tracks move in out of the darkness.
I stare at the train window marked with soft dust.
I have awakened at Missoula, Montana, utterly happy.

The poem consists of four emphatic propositions—hence the need for each line to be end-stopped. The final line contains the resolution, expressing the speaker's surprising reaction to what seemingly are very ordinary circumstances.

When a line stops without either punctuation or a natural pause in the thought, we say that the line is **run-on**—that it moves directly into the next line without a noticeable stop. The continuation of the thought from one line to the next is called **enjambement.** Obviously, the arrangement of poetic lines on a printed page suggests a kind of visual pause after each line. Yet the rhythmic pattern and the sense of the run-on lines demand that we read them without pausing at the end.

Theodore Roethke (1908–1963)
Night Crow

When I saw that clumsy crow
Flap from a wasted tree,
A shape in the mind rose up:
Over the gulps of dream
Flew a tremendous bird   5
Further and further away
Into a moonless black,
Deep in the brain, far back.

Lines 2, 3, 7, and the final one are end-stopped, creating a jerky effect which mirrors the action of the "clumsy crow." Run-on lines occur in the initial line, as well as in 4, 5, and 6. Their rhythmic effect supports the linking of the crow and his actions to the image of something similarly black and elusive in the speaker's mind.

The following poem makes effective use of the rhythm of ordinary speech and of clichés. In helping you see how this rhythm functions, we have added stressed and unstressed marks which, of course, do not appear in the original poem.

E. E. Cummings   (1894–1962)
next to of course god

"next to of course god america i

love you land of the pilgrims' and so forth oh

say can you see by the dawn's early my

country 'tis of centuries come and go

and are no more what of it we should worry   5

in every language even deafanddumb

thy sons acclaim your glorious name by gorry

by jingo by gee by gosh by gum

why talk of beauty what could be more beautiful

than these heroic happy dead   10

who rushed like lions to the roaring slaughter

they did not stop to think they died instead

then shall the voice of liberty be mute?"

He spoke. And drank rapidly a glass of water

The absence of punctuation, except (meaningfully enough) in the final two lines, makes it difficult at first to read this poem. It seems a jumble of run-together bits and pieces. Yet these seemingly incoherent and disjointed statements achieve a definite effect. In using them, Cummings is suggesting that the typical expression of patriotism is a grab bag of clichés and thoughtless sentiments. The ironic culmination of the speech in lines 1–13 is fittingly interpreted by the intrusion of an objective authorial voice in the final line. Cummings mocks the speaker by the formal declaration, "He spoke." And the empty phrase-making of the speaker is further emphasized by the terse addition, "And drank rapidly a glass of water." Furthermore, Cummings leaves the end of the poem unpunctuated, suggesting both the incompletion of the speech and the continuation of such empty sentiments among the citizenry.

This poem is a variation of the sonnet form (see Chapter 10). The rhythm of the lines is consistently irregular—yet Cummings employs this irregularity to organize the content of the poem. Here rhythmic stresses shape and manage the content. The first four lines, for example, mix fragments of patriotic songs with the speaker's garbled, rambling thoughts. And these lines depend upon stressed syllables to indicate the end of one fragment and the beginning of a new statement; for example,

> and so forth oh

> say can you see by the dawn's early my

> country

The stressed syllables reinforce the meaning, permitting us to read the poem intelligently. Similarly, further along in the poem the rhythmic patterns convey the disjointed, inane sentiments of the speaker:

> they died instead

> then shall the voice

No genuine understanding or actual relationship exists in stringing together such patriotic sentiments.

Closely related in function to rhythm is **meter,** the more or less regular pattern of stressed and unstressed syllables in a line, a stanza, or an entire poem. Meter, then, is the measure of poetic rhythm. All poems have rhythm, but not all have meter, or a regular pattern of rhythms. And we scan a poem to determine the kind of meter it has. Once the stressed and the unstressed syllables in a line or more of poetry have been marked, the next step is to determine the kinds and the number of feet in each line and in each stanza. In identifying the kinds of feet, we need to include both the dominant and the variant feet in the line and the stanza. In determining the number of feet, we mark them in the poem by means of a thin perpendicular line. With practice, both operations are soon easily performed.

In poetry, the most commonly employed types of feet are the four listed below.

Kind of foot		Markings	Examples
iamb	(iambic)	˘ ´	recéive | destróy
trochee	(trochaic)	´ ˘	wáiting | sláughter
anapest	(anapestic)	˘ ˘ ´	seventéen | interlóck
dactyl	(dactylic)	´ ˘ ˘	nóthingness | mérrily

Iambic and trochaic feet consist of two syllables, and are called *duple meters*. Anapestic and dactylic feet consist of three syllables, and are called *triple meters*. It is also common to refer to iambic and anapestic feet as *rising* meters, since the movement is from unstressed to stressed units. Trochaic and dactylic feet are often referred to as *falling* meters, since the movement is from stressed to unstressed units.

Here are examples of each of the four principal types of poetic feet, scanned for close study.

iambs

> Ĭ táste | ă líqu | ŏr név | ĕr bréwed,
>
> Frŏm tánk | ărds scóoped | ĭn péarl;
>
> Nŏt áll | thĕ váts | ŭpón | thĕ Rhíne
>
> Yíeld sŭch | ăn ál | cŏhól!
>
> (*Emily Dickinson*)

trochees

> Týger! | Týger! | búrnĭng | bríght
>
> Ín thĕ | fórĕsts | óf thĕ | níght,
>
> Whát ĭm | mórtăl | hánd ŏr | éye
>
> Cóuld fráme | thy féarful | sýmmĕt | rý?
>
> (*William Blake*)

An alternate scanning of the last line above would treat it as a regular iambic line in this fashion:

Could frame | thy fear | ful sym | metry?

anapests

For the moon | never beams | without bring | ing me dreams

Of the beaut | iful Ann | abel Lee;

And the stars | never rise | but I see | the bright eyes

Of the beaut | iful Ann | abel Lee.

(Edgar Allan Poe)

dactyls

Just for a | handful of | silver he | left us,

Just for a | riband to | stick in his | coat—

Found the one | gift of which | fortune be | reft us,

Lost all the | others she | let us de | vote . . . .

(Robert Browning)

Although not used in poetry for creating sustained rhythmic patterns, the following types of poetic feet are used as variations of and as substitutions for dominant feet.

monosyllable   only one stressed syllable: | ´ |

Out, | damned | spot! | out | I say!

spondee   two stressed syllables: | ´ ´ |

Dark car | tracks move | in out | of the | darkness.

pyrrhic   two unstressed syllables: | ˘ ˘ |

Tomor | row and | tomor | row and | tomorrow.

amphibrach   an unstressed, a stressed, and another unstressed syllable: | ˘ ´ ˘ |

He dis | appeared | in the dead | of winter.

The next step in examining meter is to determine the length of the line (or lines) by counting the number of feet. The names below identify the line lengths most commonly employed in poetry.

monometer	one foot
dimeter	two feet
trimeter	three feet
tetrameter	four feet
pentameter	five feet
hexameter	six feet
heptameter	seven feet
octameter	eight feet

Lines of more than six feet are rare in poetry because they are difficult to manage and because the ear often does not seem to pick them up as coherent units of verse. It is probably more natural to have poetic lines broken into three, four, or five feet. Edgar Allan Poe's famous poem "The Raven" offers an example. The opening line.

> Once upon a midnight dreary, while I pondered weak and weary,

might be broken into two lines, in this manner:

> Once upon a midnight dreary,
> While I pondered weak and weary.

No doubt this changes Poe's effect, but the illustration gives some notion of what the ear might actually hear.

Scanning poetry is a matter not only of terminology and skill—the ability to distinguish between stressed and unstressed syllables, for example—but also of common sense and of interpretation. Few rhythmic patterns occur without some variations, often subtle and difficult ones. Readers must occasionally make a choice between several metrical possibilities. Scansion is not a sure technic for the comprehensive analysis of a poem. It is merely one useful way of making us aware of certain poetic devices employed and of seeing how the poet shaped his materials and worked out his meaning. The temptation to use an analysis of rhythm and meter as the final standard for judging a poem must be resisted. The richness and the power of poetry are what finally matter. And no one analytical approach or method by itself can uncover these qualities.

With these words of caution in mind, read the following poem. It is scanned for close analysis and then discussed in light of its notable metrical features.

Henry Wadsworth Longfellow (1807–1882)
The Tide Rises, the Tide Falls

The tide | rises, | the tide | falls,   *a*

The twi | light dark | ens, | the cur | lew calls   *a*

Along | the sea | sands damp | and brown   *b*

The trav | eller hast | ens toward | the town,   *b*

  And the tide | rises, | the tide | falls.   *a*   5

Darkness | settles | on roofs | and walls,   *a*

But the sea, | the sea | in the dark |ness calls;   *a*

The lit | tle waves, | with their soft, | white hands,   *c*

Efface | the foot | prints in | the sands,   *c*

  And the tide | rises, | the tide | falls.   *a*   10

The morn | ing breaks; | the steeds | in their stalls   *a*

Stamp and | neigh, | as the host | ler calls;   *a*

The day | returns, | but nev | ermore   *d*

Returns | the trav | eller to | the shore,   *d*

  And the tide | rises, | the tide | falls.   *a*   15

The poem's solemn and meditative tone is striking. The scenes and details connected with the ocean imply the drowning of a person journeying to a near-by town. This death may be considered not only as a literal death but also as the close of life itself. The poem laments the passing of the years and the imminent end of life, things which Longfellow associates with the approach of evening and with the sea. He makes a parallel between it and life: the sea is calling the "traveller" toward unknown depths, beckoning him toward whatever lies beyond.

The metrical pattern Longfellow chooses for such thoughts is one frequently employed in English poetry, a four-line stanza, called a *quatrain* (see Chapter 10), modified by a fifth line added as a refrain. The rime scheme, *aabba, aacca, aadda,* shows that there are only four different kinds of rime used and that the initial *a* rime is retained throughout, a pattern that effectively organizes and compresses the three stanzas. The metrical pattern is predominantly iambic tetrameter, with frequent variations, particularly of anapestic feet. All of the lines are end-stopped, except 2, 11, and 13, which are run-on lines.

The metrical effect Longfellow creates is that of the sounds of the ocean along the shore. His refrain is an excellent approximation of the rise and fall of the tide:

$$\text{And the tide} \mid \text{rises,} \mid \text{the tide} \mid \text{falls.}$$

Instead of the iambic feet predominant in the rest of the poem, he uses here an anapestic, next a trochaic, and at the end of the line a monosyllabic foot. These and most of the other variations from the iambic foot result from Longfellow's attempt to simulate ocean sounds. And so he uses many anapestic feet, since this meter naturally produces a rising and a falling sound pattern.

Three spondees occur in the poem, each a matter of emphasis. Two are a necessary consequence of normal pronunciation:

$$\text{sea} \mid \text{sands damp}$$

and

$$\text{foot} \mid \text{prints in.}$$

The third spondee (line 8) serves to emphasize the adjective *white*. Besides the trochees in the refrain and in its variation in line 1, there are three others in the poem. Each gives stress to the thought conveyed— namely, that

$$\text{Darkness} \mid \text{settles}$$

and that steeds

$$\text{Stamp and} \mid \text{neigh.}$$

All of these spondees and trochees, however, are variations that alter the rhythmic flow of the iambic and the anapestic feet, thereby preventing a sing-song effect in the lines.

In many of the lines, caesuras work with stressed and unstressed syllables and with pauses at the ends of lines to create effective rhythms. Some caesural pauses are heavy, as in line 7, in which the caesura emphasizes the repetition of *sea*. In line 11, the caesura, reinforced by a semicolon, stresses the image of the quick arrival of dawn. And so we can see that, whether punctuated or not, caesuras are devices with which a poet can vary and control his rhythms. They are, we might say, the "fine tuning" a poet gives to his sound patterns.

At this point, several guidelines for scanning poetry are in order:

1. Read through the poem several times in order to get an idea of its subject matter and tone. Listen to dominant rhythmic elements that emerge. (An oral reading generates these rhythms more quickly than a silent reading.)

2. Begin your marking of stressed syllables by labeling only those that clearly take the accent. Do not worry if these syllables are scattered about, perhaps from stanza to stanza; in time a pattern will appear. Then you can begin to mark those unstressed syllables that are easily recognized. Soon the basic foot and perhaps even the line length will become apparent.

3. Read aloud the lines you have some doubt about, pronouncing each syllable clearly and slowly. Doing so should bring out the more difficult stressed and unstressed elements. Reading aloud also helps determine internal pauses. Finally, mark the rime scheme, if there is one. Only occasionally is it necessary to pronounce rimes orally to hear their exact sounds.

Again, remember that scansion is not a method that ensures either a thorough understanding or an enjoyment of poetry. Its purposes are served when it helps one gain additional insight into the artistry and the meaning of a particular poem.

Exercise

Before proceeding with additional analysis of rhythmic patterns, try your hand at scanning poetry. Mark each of the following passages to show, when possible, these metrical features: (1) the basic poetic foot and the length of each line; (2) the caesuras; and (3) the rime scheme.

1. The Frost performs its secret ministry,

   Unhelped by any wind. The owlet's cry

   Came loud—and hark, again! loud as before.
   (Samuel Taylor Coleridge)

2. Out upon it! I have loved

   Three whole days together;

> And am like to love three more,
>
> > If it prove fair weather.
> >
> > > *(John Sucking)*

3. Oft I had heard of Lucy Gray:

   And, when I crossed the wild,

   I chanced to see at break of day

   The solitary child.

   > > > *(William Wordsworth)*

4. Of man's first disobedience, and the fruit

   Of that forbidden tree, whose mortal taste

   Brought death into the world, and all our woe,

   With loss of Eden . . . .

   > > > *(John Milton)*

5. Among the smoke and fog of a December afternoon

   You have the scene arrange itself—as it will seem to do—

   With "I have saved this afternoon for you";

   And four wax candles in the darkened room.

   > > > *(T. S. Eliot)*

6. St. Agnes' Eve—Ah, bitter chill it was!

   The owl, for all his feathers, was a-cold;

   The hare limp'd trembling through the frozen grass,

   And silent was the flock in woolly fold.

   > > > *(John Keats)*

7. From too much love of living,

   > From hope and fear set free,

   We thank with brief thanksgiving

   > Whatever gods may be

   That no life lives for ever;

   That dead men rise up never;

5

That even the weariest river

    Winds somewhere safe to sea.
               (Algernon Charles Swinburne)

8. Sleep after toil, ports after stormy seas,

    Ease after war, death after life does greatly please.
               (Edmund Spenser)

9. The Lord is my shepherd;

  I shall not want.

  He maketh me to lie down in green pastures;

  He leadeth me beside the still waters;

  He restoreth my soul.   5
              (Psalm 23)

10. Captain Carpenter rose up in his prime

  Put on his pistols and went riding out

  But he got wellnigh nowhere at that time

  Till he fell in with ladies in a rout.
              (John Crowe Ransom)

It may be a commonplace to say that the meter is made for the poem, not the poem for the meter. Yet this point should be kept clearly in mind. Meter is not only a *means* but also a part of the *meaning* of a poem. It must be fitted, varied, adapted in many ways to sustain the poetic materials and to generate meaning. The following short poem provides several illustrations of how this process works.

A. E. Housman   (1859–1936)
They Say My Verse Is Sad: No Wonder

They say | my verse | is sad: ‖ no wonder;   *a*

  Its nar | row meas | ure spans   *b*

Tears of | eter | nity, ‖ and sorrow,   *c*

  Not mine, ‖ but man's.   *b*

This is | for all | ill-treat | ed fellows   *d*   5

  Unborn | and un | begot,   *e*

For them | to read | when they're | in trouble   *f*

  And I | am not.   *e*

In this eight-line poem, Housman answers those critics who say that his poetry is too sad. His poetry is indeed sad, but this is because of his sympathy for the human condition, rather than because of any immediate personal sorrow. The manner of the poem is direct and sincere, but its tone is lightly caustic and pointed. The metrical pattern Housman chooses for these thoughts is a standard one in English poetry—two quatrains of alternating lines of iambic tetrameter, iambic trimeter, riming *abcb, defe*. His metrical variations show how skillfully he adapts this pattern to his poetic needs. The poem has seven substitutions, the most noticeable being the four amphibrachs at the end of lines 1, 3, 5, and 7. Housman uses amphibrachs to lighten and soften his iambic line and to introduce just a touch of gentle wit. One spondee occurs in the poem, in the third foot of line 5. The effect is a slowing of the line, thus stressing the meaning of

ill-treated fellows.

Trochees occur at the beginning of lines 3 and 5. In line 3, the trochaic foot alters and slows the rhythm so that the implications of

spans

Tears of eternity

will receive due attention. Housman also supports the thought here by means of a run-on line with enjambement. The trochee in line 5 appropriately emphasizes *This,* which begins a new quatrain and which refers to the poem itself. The remaining lines are end-stopped, either by punctuation or, in lines 5 and 7, by slight pauses. The last two lines contain regular iambic feet, except that an amphibrach occurs at the end of line 7 and the last line has only two iambs. This causes the final two lines to skip along, heightening the tongue-in-cheek implications of the closing remark:

when they're in trouble

And I am not.

Variations in the dominant metrical foot are often introduced for rhetorical purposes. Rhetoric suggests in poetry, as it does in prose, a way of saying a thing persuasively and of using devices to get it said effectively. The following poem, scanned for analysis and study, shows variations that are employed largely for rhetorical reasons.

Thomas Hardy (1840–1928)
I Look into My Glass

I look | into | my glass,   *a*

And view | my wast | ing skin,   *b*

And say, ‖ "Would God | it came | to pass   *a*

My heart | had shrunk | as thin!"   *b*

For then, ‖ I, un | distressed   *c*   5

By hearts | grown cold | to me,   *d*

Could lone | ly wait | my end | less rest   *c*

With equ | anim | ity.   *d*

But Time, ‖ to make | me grieve,   *e*

Part steals, ‖ lets part | abide;   *f*   10

And shakes | this frag | ile frame | at eve   *e*

With throbb | ings of | noontide.   *f*

The poem treats the familiar theme of growing old, but it does so with an insight that is rather unusual. For the speaker, the experience of physical aging has become all the more poignant because it has not been accompanied by a lessening of youthful desires, a sentiment that is reinforced by the deeply melancholic tone of these lines. The metrical patterns are in general quite regular. Iambic trimeter is the dominant meter, with the third line of each stanza in iambic tetrameter. The poem has a standard rime scheme for the quatrain, *abab, cdcd, efef*. The six substitutions for the regular iambic foot are important in loosening the rhythms of the short lines. Hardy substitutes four spondaic feet and two pyrrhic feet for iambic feet. Stanza 1 has two variations, a pyrrhic in the first line, and a spondee in line 3, variations which emphasize what is being said. Line 5 also contains a spondee, which stresses the "I" in the poem. The last stanza has three substitutions, a spondee at the beginning of line 10, and a pyrrhic and a spondee in line 12. Here again, the substitutions emphasize important elements and slow the rhythm of an otherwise regular stanza. Hardy achieves a subtle balance between the first two and the last two lines here by using these two spondaic feet. The theme of an aging person being left with "throbbings of noontide" is rendered more effective because the meter supports Hardy's meaning.

Sometimes a quest for metrical variations spurs a poet to make technical innovations that are truly radical, even revolutionary. A notable illustration occurs in the work of Victorian poet Gerard Manley Hopkins. His interest in folk speech and idioms led him to devise what he called **sprung rhythm,** essentially a way of organizing sounds in poetry by stressed syllables regardless of the number of unstressed syllables. Each accented syllable, in other words, controls the number of metrical feet; the number of unaccented syllables does not matter. Usually, the accented element is the initial syllable of the metrical foot. At first sight, these metrical units look like monosyllabic, trochaic, and dactylic feet. Hopkins also devised a foot made up of a stressed syllable followed by three unstressed ones, which he called the "First Pæon." The effect of sprung rhythm is often fascinating and certainly unusual, with the highly irregular patterns somewhat compensated for by fresh words and hyphenated combinations of words that reinforce the rhythms. The following poem is written in sprung rhythm. The first stanza is scanned for analysis and study.

Gerard Manley Hopkins   (1844–1889)
Felix Randal

Félix | Rándal the | fárrier, ‖ Ó he is | deád then? my | dúty all | énded,

Who have | watched his | mould of | mán, | big- | boned and | hárdy-
    | handsome

Pining, | pining, till | time when | reáson | rambled in | it and some

Fátal | four dis | orders, | fléshed there, ‖ all con | ténded?

Sickness broke him. Impatient he cursed at first, but mended   5
Being anointed and all; though a heavenlier heart began some

Months earlier, since I had our sweet reprieve and ransom
Tendered to him.[1] Ah well, God rest him all road ever[2] he offended!

This seeing the sick endears them to us, us too it endears.
My tongue had taught thee comfort, touch had quenched thy tears,   10
Thy tears that touched my heart, child, Felix, poor Felix Randal;

How far from then forethought of, all thy more boisterous years,
When thou at the random grim forge, powerful amidst peers,
Didst fettle° for the great grey drayhorse his bright and battering   *prepare*
   sandal!

As a Jesuit and a parish priest, Hopkins came into contact with many working-class people of England. Here he mourns the death of a blacksmith ("farrier") who was apparently rough and sometimes crude, but also essentially good-hearted and childlike. Hopkins' poem is full of powerful emotions: sadness at seeing the once vigorous man wasting away; a sense of inadequacy in ministering to him; and pain in struggling with the problem of life and death.

Hopkins said that sprung rhythm closely approximates "the native and natural rhythm of speech." "Felix Randal" shows how sprung rhythm can convey powerful emotions through the natural rhythms of speech. The first stanza contains lines of seven, eight, six, and six metrical feet, respectively. Except for the two monosyllables in line 2, these feet appear to be quite regular. If, however, we read the poem with a slight emphasis on the stressed syllables, it is easy to hear the unusual sound patterning of sprung rhythm. Particularly noticeable is the relationship between Hopkins' rhythms and certain unusual words and word combinations. A splendid illustration of how Hopkins has rhythm and language work together is the phrase in stanza 1:

mould of man, big-boned and hardy-handsome.

The precise effect is difficult to describe, yet we feel here and elsewhere in the poem the strong emotions conveyed by such phrases. Alliteration and assonance obviously contribute to this effect, and Hopkins makes fine use of other musical devices. But the sensuous and emotion-charged effect of his lines results from his radical alterations of stressed and unstressed patterns of syllables. If these features of sprung rhythm are not yet clear, perhaps scanning the rest of the poem and studying the lines will provide additional instances of how this meter works.

---

1. I.e., had heard his confession and had given him absolution and communion.
2. In whatever manner.

Robert Herrick (1591–1674)
To the Virgins, to Make Much of Time

Gather ye rosebuds while ye may,
    Old time is still a-flying;
And this same flower that smiles today
    Tomorrow will be dying.

The glorious lamp of heaven, the sun,   5
    The higher he's a-getting,
The sooner will his race be run,
    And nearer he's to setting.

That age is best which is the first,
    When youth and blood are warmer;   10
But being spent, the worse, and worst
    Times still succeed the former.

Then be not coy, but use your time,
    And, while ye may, go marry;
For, having lost but once your prime,   15
    You may forever tarry.°   *linger*

Questions for Study

  1. The theme of this poem, as of many in the sixteenth and the seventeenth centuries, is often identified with the phrase attributed to the Roman poet Horace, *Carpe diem* ("Seize the day")—an admonition to enjoy one's life since it is so uncertain and short. How does Herrick express this idea in his poem?

  2. Examine the third stanza:

That age | is best | which is | the first,   *e*

    When youth | and blood | are warmer;   *f*

But be | ing spent, | the worse, | and worst   *e*

    Times still | succeed | the former.   *f*

What is the dominant foot? What is the length of each line? Name the metrical foot which ends lines 2 and 4. How would you classify these two rimes? Why has the poet substituted a spondaic for an iambic foot at the beginning of the last line? Identify the run-on line in this stanza.

  3. Study the metrical pattern of the other three stanzas for variations. Identify these and explain why you think the poet has employed them as he does.

  4. Point out instances of alliteration and assonance in the poem, explaining the function of each.

Alfred, Lord Tennyson   (1809–1892)
Break, Break, Break

Break, break, break,
   On thy cold gray stones, O Sea!
And I would that my tongue could utter
   The thoughts that arise in me.

O, well for the fisherman's boy,   5
   That he shouts with his sister at play!
O, well for the sailor lad,
   That he sings in his boat on the bay!

And the stately ships go on
   To their haven under the hill;   10
But O for the touch of a vanished hand,
   And the sound of a voice that is still!

Break, break, break,
   At the foot of thy crags, O Sea!
But the tender grace of a day that is dead   15
   Will never come back to me.

Questions for Study

1. What is the dominant foot in these lines? Scan the entire poem, recopying it if you need to.
2. What is the relationship between the rhythmic patterns and the subject matter of these lines? Where is "the sound an echo to the sense"?
3. Look closely for musical elements, identifying and classifying them. Mark the rime scheme and comment on its contribution to the poem.

Carl Sandburg   (1878–1967)
Prayers of Steel

Lay me on an anvil, O God.
Beat me and hammer me into a crowbar.
Let me pry loose old walls.
Let me lift and loosen old foundations.

Lay me on an anvil, O God.   5
Beat me and hammer me into a steel spike.
Drive me into the girders that hold a skyscraper together.
Take red-hot rivets and fasten me into the central girders.
Let me be the great nail holding a skyscraper through blue nights into
    white stars.

Questions for Study

1. Why do you think Sandburg entitled this short poem "Prayers of Steel"? How does he support this title in the organization and structure of the poem?
2. Sandburg's metrical pattern, though without rimes or definite meter, does have strong rhythmic properties. Here is the first stanza scanned for analysis:

Láy mé | on an | anvíl, | Ō Gód.

Beát mé | and hammér | mé in | tó a | crówbár.

Lét mē | pry loóse | óld walls.

Lét mē | líft and | loósēn | óld foūn | dátiōns.

How are these metrical patterns appropriate to Sandburg's subject and purpose?
3. Try your hand at scanning the second stanza.

Anonymous (19th-century American folk ballad)
The Housewife's Lament

One day I was walking, I heard a complaining,
And saw an old woman the picture of gloom.
She gazed at the mud on her doorstep ('twas raining)
And this was her song as she wielded her broom.

Chorus:
Oh, life is a toil and love is a trouble,   5
Beauty will fade and riches will flee,
Pleasures they dwindle and prices they double,
And nothing is as I would wish it to be.

There's too much of worriment goes to a bonnet,
There's too much of ironing goes to a shirt,   10
There's nothing that pays for the time you waste on it,
There's nothing that lasts us but trouble and dirt.

In March it is mud, it is slush in December,
The midsummer breezes are loaded with dust,
In fall the leaves litter, in muddy September   15
The wallpaper rots and the candlesticks rust.

There are worms on the cherries and slugs on the roses,
And ants in the sugar and mice in the pies,
The rubbish of spiders no mortal supposes
And ravaging roaches and damaging flies.   20

With grease and with grime from corner to centre,
Forever at war and forever alert,

No rest for a day lest the enemy enter,
I spend my whole life in a struggle with dirt.

Last night in my dreams I was stationed forever   25
On a far little rock in the midst of the sea,
My one chance of life was a ceaseless endeavor
To sweep off the waves as they swept over me.

Alas! 'Twas no dream; ahead I behold it,
I see I am helpless my fate to avert.—   30
She lay down her broom, her apron she folded,
She lay down and died and was buried in dirt.

Questions for Study

1. This anonymous American folk ballad, originating in the middle of the nineteenth century, has a certain contemporary flavor to it. Specifically, what does the housewife object to and why? Is the narrator of the poem sympathetic to her? How can you determine this?
2. This ballad has marked musical devices. Identify as many as you can and describe their function in the piece.
3. Pick out one stanza and scan it thoroughly, identifying its rime scheme. What notable metrical characteristics do you find? How regular is the rhythm? What is its effect?
4. Consider the implied comparison in "To sweep off the waves as they swept over me" (line 28) and comment upon its effectiveness.

Walt Whitman (1819–1892)
When I Heard the Learn'd Astronomer

When I heard the learn'd astronomer,
When the proofs, the figures, were ranged in columns before me,
When I was shown the charts and diagrams, to add, divide, and measure
    them,
When I sitting heard the astronomer where he lectured with much
    applause in the lecture-room,
How soon unaccountable I became tired and sick,   5
Till rising and gliding out I wander'd off by myself,
In the mystical moist night-air, and from time to time,
Look'd up in perfect silence at the stars.

Questions for Study

1. Rhythm is crucial in this poem. There are no rimes and the lines vary in length. Structure depends heavily upon the rhythmic patterns. Mark each line to determine the dominant metrical foot and to calculate the number of feet in each line.

Can you find any emerging pattern? What, for example, are the differences between lines 1 through 4 and lines 5 through 8?

2. What is the structural function of the phrase *When I* with which Whitman opens three of his lines?

3. What is the subject of this poem? Clarify and support your answer by references to specific lines.

Chapter 10
Form and Pattern

In talking about poetry, the term *form* may be employed to mean several different things. It is frequently used to indicate the larger, overall artistic design of a work. This meaning of form is considered in the discussion of structure in Chapter 11. In this chapter, **form** is employed, first, to designate the commonly used verse forms and stanzaic forms of poetry. Second, it indicates a particular kind of poem, such as epic, ballad, ode, or sonnet.

A clear distinction should be made between verse and stanza. **Verse** refers to one line or more of poetry. A verse line is usually defined according to the kind and the number of stressed and unstressed syllables it contains—as, for example, iambic pentameter or anapestic tetrameter or trochaic trimeter. The term *verse* is not to be used as a synonym for *stanza,* as when we say, ''Sing the second verse,'' meaning the second stanza. A **stanza** is a group of two or more lines of poetry that have a demonstrated integrity of metrical or of some other organizational pattern. Divisions into stanzas are normally indicated in print by an extra line or two of space and in oral poetry by a heavy pause, or occasionally (as in a song) by a chorus or a refrain. In the technical sense, the term *stanza* is correctly employed only when the pattern of the verse lines is repeated in a poem. Such units of poetry as terza rima, the quatrain, and the Spenserian stanza are examples of some basic stanzaic forms.

The verse and the stanza are basic units of poetic composition. Together they inform the meaning of a poem. Quite literally, that is, verse and stanza work by means of particular forms to render meaning. Look at the following short poem to get a basic idea of how this process operates.

Sir Thomas Wyatt (1503–1542)
Throughout the World, If It Were Sought

Throughout the world, if it were sought,
Fair words enough a man shall find:
They be good cheap,° they cost right nought,   *inexpensive*
Their substance is but only wind;
 But well to say and so to mean,   5
 That sweet accord is seldom seen.

In a few lines, the poet expresses an important truth: words of praise are easily given, but it is difficult to find those that are truly and deeply meant. The verse form is iambic tetrameter, and the poem consists of six lines rimed *ababcc*. Yet form is more substantial than it at first appears. The poet uses the arrangement of his rimes to create a four-line unit, followed by a two-line unit, a grouping which gives a two-part movement to his thought. The initial four lines state the proposition that "fair words" are easy to find and inexpensive by any standard. The last two lines add the comment that it is nevertheless difficult to find sincere praise because the "sweet accord" between words and realities is "seldom seen."

 A familiar and commonly used verse form is **blank verse,** or lines of unrimed iambic pentameter. The actual rhythms of the English language seem most at home in the iambic foot, and the five-stress or pentameter line is an appropriate line length for a number of purposes. Blank verse, for example, is used in dramatic poetry and in many notable nondramatic works, such as Milton's *Paradise Lost* and Wordsworth's *The Prelude*.

 The master of dramatic blank verse is William Shakespeare. The following is an example taken from *Richard II*. Here King Richard of England, soon after returning from Ireland, speaks to a group of supporters.

William Shakespeare (1564–1616)
from *Richard II*

And nothing can we call our own but death
And that small model° of the barren earth   *shape*
Which serves as paste° and cover to our bones.   *a covering like a piecrust*
For God's sake, let us sit upon the ground
And tell sad stories of the death of kings: 5
How some have been deposed; some slain in war;
Some haunted by the ghosts they have deposed;
Some poison'd by their wives; some sleeping kill'd;

All murder'd: for within the hollow crown
That rounds the mortal temples of a king   10
Keeps Death his court and there the antic° sits   *buffoon*
Scoffing his state and grinning at his pomp,
Allowing him a breath, a little scene,
To monarchize,° be fear'd and kill with looks,   *play the monarch*
Infusing him with self and vain conceit,   15
As if this flesh which walls about our life
Were brass impregnable, and humour'd thus
Comes at the last and with a little pin
Bores through his castle wall, and farewell king!

By carefully combining end-stopped lines with run-on lines and by using
caesuras, Shakespeare creates a highly dramatic effect that is appropriate to the return of King Richard. The range and flexibility achieved
here are what make blank verse so useful in dramatic poetry.

   Because of the considerable power and versatility of blank verse, the
form was a favorite not only of dramatic but also of narrative poets. We
can see something of the possibilities of the form in the contrast between
Shakespeare's lines and these.

John Milton   (1608–1674)
from *Paradise Lost*

   Say first (for Heaven hides nothing from thy[1] view,
Nor the deep tract of Hell), say first what cause
Moved our grand[2] parents, in that happy state,
Favored of Heaven so highly, to fall off
From their Creator, and transgress his will   5
For° one restraint, lords of the world besides?°   *Because of / in every*
Who first seduced them to that foul revolt?   *other respect*
   Th' infernal serpent; he it was, whose guile,
Stirred up with envy and revenge, deceived
The mother of mankind, what time° his pride   *at the time when*   10
Had cast him out from Heaven, with all his host
Of rebel angels, by whose aid, aspiring
To set himself in glory above his peers,
He trusted to have equaled the Most High,
If he opposed; and with ambitious aim   15
Against the throne and monarchy of God,
Raised impious war in Heaven and battle proud,
With vain attempt. Him the Almighty Power
Hurled headlong flaming from th' ethereal sky,

---

1. The Holy Spirit of the Bible, from which Moses received inspiration to write Genesis.
2. Adam and Eve.

With hideous ruin and combustion, down   20
To bottomless perdition, there to dwell
In adamantine[3] chains and penal fire,
Who durst defy th' Omnipotent to arms.

Taken from early in Book I, these lines exhibit a tone that is clearly
grand and noble. The lines rise and fall with a deliberate sweep and force
indicative of the high drama of this scene in Hell. As the Archfiend,
Lucifer is depicted as mighty but evil—a figure of enormous proportions
and strengths. The final six lines here demonstrate a strong rhythmic
pattern that illustrates how blank verse is an excellent vehicle for the
poetical expression of epic themes.

    Another unit of verse popular in English poetry is the **couplet,** two
successive lines of verse usually of the same metrical length and with the
same end rime. Here are a few examples of the couplet form. Each
four-line excerpt contains two couplets.

> An ant on the table cloth
> Ran into a dormant moth
> Of many times his size.
> He showed not the least surprise.
> *(Robert Frost)*

> Had we but world enough, and time,
> This coyness, Lady, were no crime.
> We would sit down and think which way
> To walk and pass our long love's day.
> *(Andrew Marvell)*

> Let observation, with extensive view,
> Survey mankind, from China to Peru;
> Remark each anxious toil, each eager strife,
> And watch the busy scenes of crowded life.
> *(Samuel Johnson)*

The couplets are in, first, trimeter, then tetrameter, and finally pentameter line lengths. The couplet is a convenient and useful verse
pattern, obviously effective for closely controlled expressions,
thoughts, and proposals. It is usually employed in lines having at least
four stresses. As the lines from Frost show, the tightly organized riming
couplet in the three-stress line achieves a humorous effect.

    In English poetry, the most notable variation of the couplet is the
heroic (or **closed**) **couplet.** Here the metrical pattern completes its

---

3. Unbreakable; adamant was an imaginary mineral thought to be the hardest substance in the
universe.

thought and its grammatical structure within two lines. (When the second line is run-on, we have an **open couplet**.) Used by Geoffrey Chaucer and many poets after him, the heroic couplet was popular during the second half of the seventeenth and throughout the eighteenth century. John Dryden and Alexander Pope are considered masters of the form. The following lines exemplify the strengths of the heroic couplet.

Alexander Pope (1688–1744)

from *An Essay on Man*

> Know then thyself, presume not God to scan;°   *examine; judge*
> The proper study of mankind is Man.
> Placed on this isthmus of a middle state,
> A being darkly wise, and rudely great:
> With too much knowledge for the skeptic side,   5
> With too much weakness for the Stoic's[1] pride,
> He hangs between; in doubt to act, or rest,
> In doubt to deem himself a god, or beast;
> In doubt his mind or body to prefer,
> Born but to die, and reasoning but to err;   10
> Alike in ignorance, his reason such,
> Whether he thinks too little, or too much:
> Chaos of thought and passion, all confused;
> Still by himself abused, or disabused;
> Created half to rise, and half to fall;   15
> Great lord of all things, yet a prey to all;
> Sole judge of truth, in endless error hurled:
> The glory, jest, and riddle of the world!

As a verse form, the couplet can render statements with clarity and precision. Pope's theme is clearly expressed in the initial couplet, with the rest of the lines expanding on his view of the human condition. Pope also uses the couplet for emphasizing key words and phrases and then for contrasting these with other words and phrases expressed in similar grammatical structures. A line such as "Born but to die, and reasoning but to err" strikes us as pleasant in sound and exact in sense. When employed by less skillful a poet than Pope, however, the couplet form may emerge as stilted and pompous. Obviously, it is not suited to the expression of a wide range of emotions.

Although not as popular as the couplet, another unit of verse often employed is the **tercet** (also called the **triplet**). It consists of three lines, usually of the same metrical length and frequently with the same end rime. Here are some examples, along with a few variations, of this form.

---

1. One of the tenets of the Stoic philosophy holds that human beings should be free from passion and the expression of emotion.

Whereas in silks my Julia goes,
Then, then methinks how sweetly flows
That liquefaction of her clothes.
(Robert Herrick)

O, wild West Wind, thou breath of Autumn's being,
Thou, from whose unseen presence the leaves dead
Are driven, like ghosts from an enchanter fleeing.
(Percy Bysshe Shelley)

And as the smart ship grew
In stature, grace, and hue,
In shadowy silent distance grew the Iceberg too.
(Thomas Hardy)

The first example is perfectly regular—three lines of similar length with the same end rime. The second tercet, however, with a rime scheme *aba,* employs an unrimed sound in the second line. Actually, Shelley is here using an adaptation of **terza rima,** the three-line stanza used by Dante in *The Divine Comedy.* Each tercet is tied into the next one by rime, in the rime scheme *aba, bcb, cdc,* and so on. The last example maintains only one end rime but employs two line lengths. The first two lines are iambic trimeter and the final one is iambic hexameter—a considerable variation. In the strength of the tercet, its compression and tight organization, also lies its weakness, the tendency to become monotonous and stiff. Hardy's variation is an attempt to open up the form and give it more flexibility.

The most popular and commonly employed unit of verse in English poetry is the **quatrain,** or the four-line stanza. Because this verse form is so widespread, we probably do not notice that many nursery rimes, proverbs, hymns, and popular songs are composed in this form. Its use has been so prevalent that the quatrain is what most people have in mind when poetry is mentioned.

The basic form of the quatrain is utilized in the **ballad stanza,** which usually contains lines of alternating iambic tetrameter and iambic trimeter, riming *abcb.* The poem below is a very early example that shows the strengths of the ballad stanza.

Anonymous (14th century)
Western Wind

Western wind, when will thou blow,
The° small rain down can rain?   *So that the*
Christ, if my love were in my arms,
And I in my bed again!

Although the poem has considerable metrical sophistication, its subject is directly stated in a two-part movement. The initial two lines set the mood and the last two express the wanderer's longing for his home and his loved one.

A common variation of the ballad stanza is illustrated in the following:

Oliver Goldsmith (1728–1774)
When Lovely Woman

When lovely woman stoops to folly,
    And finds too late that men betray,
What charm can soothe her melancholy,
    What art can wash her guilt away?

The only art her guilt to cover,   5
    To hide her shame from every eye,
To give repentance to her lover,
    And wring his bosom—is to die.

The poet has added one foot to the second and the fourth lines of each quatrain, making each of the lines iambic tetrameter. He has also altered the rime scheme from the ballad pattern of *abcb* to *abab,* a tighter, more compact four-line pattern. In addition, Goldsmith has also alternated masculine and feminine end rimes. This variation in rime scheme is common to countless poems in English.

The quatrain appears with two- or three-foot lines, but the most frequently used lengths are lines of four and five feet. And the most familiar of the five-foot adaptations is called the **elegiac quatrain,** following Thomas Gray's employment of it in his famous "Elegy Written in a Country Churchyard" (1751). The initial quatrain illustrates the form.

    The curfew tolls the knell of parting day,
    The lowing herd wind slowly o'er the lea,
    The plowman homeward plods his weary way,
    And leaves the world to darkness and to me.

This quatrain, as well as the others in the poem, contains alternately rimed lines of iambic pentameter. What is gained by the addition of a foot to each line and by the use of alternate rimes is, first, a weightiness and a tightness that contribute to the poem's solemn and dignified tone. Second, these variations enable the form to carry and to emphasize a greater amount of materials. After Gray, this variation of the quatrain was often used as a vehicle for expressions of sorrow.

Alfred, Lord Tennyson employs an adaptation of the quatrain in his long elegy, *In Memoriam*. Usually occasioned by the death of a specific person, the **elegy** expresses the pensive thoughts of the poet as he reflects on death and on other solemn subjects. Here is an excerpt from Tennyson's poem honoring the memory of his deceased friend, Arthur Hallam.

Alfred, Lord Tennyson (1809–1892)
In Memoriam: 5

I sometimes hold it half a sin
    To put in words the grief I feel;
    For words, like Nature, half reveal
And half conceal the Soul within.

But for the unquiet heart and brain,   5
    A use in measured language lies;
    The sad mechanic exercise,
Like dull narcotics, numbing pain.

In words, like weeds,° I'll wrap me o'er,   *mourning clothes*
    Like coarsest clothes against the cold;   10
    But that large grief which these enfold
Is given in outline and no more.

This particular variation of the standard quatrain depends for its distinctiveness and effectiveness upon two metrical features. First, an entire thought is enclosed within each stanza, especially by means of the rime scheme *abba, cddc, effe*. Second, the thought pattern of each stanza is usually arranged so that the major point is expressed in the first three lines, with the fourth line used for comment, contrast, or summary.

One humorous variation of the quatrain is the **clerihew,** named for its originator, Edmund Clerihew Bentley (1875–1956). Similar in effect to the limerick, discussed later in this chapter, the clerihew is, unfortunately, not as well known. Here is an example by its inventor.

John Stuart Mill
By a might effort of will
Overcame his natural bonhomie°   *geniality*
And wrote *Principles of Political Economy*.[1]

---

1. A ponderous, but highly influential work published in 1848 which outlines Mill's socialistic theories on population and on the production and distribution of goods.

The clerihew is a rigid form, consisting of two couplets, rimed for a whimsical, humorous effect. The line lengths increase, with the fourth line the longest. An additional challenge to anyone attempting a clerihew is that its subject must be a famous person, whose name must appear in the first line. Here are two more examples; the first is anonymous, the second is by Maurice Sagoff.

Cecil B. deMille,[1]
Much against his will,
Was persuaded to keep Moses
Out of the Wars of the Roses.

Monet[1]
Liked an occasional roll in the hay.
After resting his back,
He would then paint the stack.

Occasionally poets arrange verse lines on a page in visual patterns that approximate the shape of the poem's subject. Here is a one-stanza poem that shows how a visual pattern may reinforce meaning.

George Herbert (1593–1633)
The Altar

A broken ALTAR, Lord, thy servant rears,
Made of a heart, and cemented with tears:
  Whose parts are as thy hand did frame;
  No workman's tool hath touched the same.
          A HEART alone   5
          Is such a stone,
          As nothing but
          Thy power doth cut.
          Wherefore each part
          Of my hard heart   10
          Meets in this frame,
          To praise thy Name:
  That, if I chance to hold my peace,
  These stones to praise thee may not cease.
Oh let thy blessed SACRIFICE be mine,   15
And sanctify this ALTAR to be thine.

1. Hollywood motion-picture producer, renowned for his biblical epics which took great liberties with historical fact.

1. Claude Monet (1840–1926), leading French Impressionist painter; one of his most famous works is a series of paintings entitled *Haystacks*.

In its visual shape, this poem resembles a church altar. Here poetic form is rendered both as language and as visual pattern. If we object that this sort of thing is merely clever, a reading of the lines should convince us that the rhythmic patterns of the varied lines and the organization by couplets and rimes are highly effective. It has been said that Herbert also meant for the visual image of the poem to represent a capital *I,* suggesting that the persona or the "I" of the poem is God's altar. Regardless of how we interpret its physical shape, however, "The Altar" integrates verbal and visual form in an unusual way.

A significant verse form that displays few of the conventions of the other forms is **free verse** (sometimes called *"vers libre"*). Technically, free verse does not have a regular metrical pattern or a definite rime scheme. It substitutes for meter various rhythmic effects or **cadences** that are usually so irregular that they are noticeable only within larger units of a poem—within, for example, a stanza or a verse paragraph. Although a **verse paragraph** is, in general, any marked division or section of poetry not ordered by a regular scheme of lines or rimes, the term refers more specifically to units of free verse. The poet relies upon sound and rhythms, together with rich and novel figures of speech, in working out his lines and stanzas. Such poetry is at once a problem and a challenge. Robert Frost is said to have remarked once that "writing free verse is like playing tennis without a net." Yet if free verse omits many conventions of poetry, it also brings to the craft of poetry an exhilarating sense of experimentation. Many poets find with free verse countless opportunities to express their meanings in innovative ways. And so, in the twentieth century, it has become the most frequently employed verse form in our language.

William Carlos Williams (1883–1963)
The Red Wheelbarrow

so much depends
upon

a red wheel
barrow

glazed with rain   5
water

beside the white
chickens.

Here is a poem in free-verse that lacks many things upon which poetry traditionally depends—rime and regular meter, for example. Yet it has a formal shape. Although containing only one sentence, the poem is divided into four verse paragraphs. Suspended precisely within a spatial frame, the red wheelbarrow is depicted as "glazed with rain / water / beside the white / chickens." By means of this image expressed in free verse, the poem integrates meaning and form. Here is a more contemporary example of free verse which achieves effects different from those of Williams' poem.

Frank O'Hara   (1926–1966)
Poem

Lana Turner has collapsed!
I was trotting along and suddenly
it started raining and snowing
and you said it was hailing
but hailing hits you on the head   5
hard so it was really snowing and
raining and I was in such a hurry
to meet you but the traffic
was acting exactly like the sky
and suddenly I see a headline   10
LANA TURNER HAS COLLAPSED!
there is no snow in Hollywood
there is no rain in California
I have been to lots of parties
and acted perfectly disgraceful   15
but I never actually collapsed
oh Lana Turner we love you get up

The free verse here results in a language and a style that are direct, even breezy. The verse lines, in other words, read and sound much like a prose rendition might. Although neither regular meter nor rime is used, the poet has carefully organized his lines by other principles. Sounds and rhythmic effects are clearly evident in the frequency of the -*ing* words and in the repetition of certain words and phrases. He also employs a parallel in lines 12 and 13, contrasting the weather in Hollywood with his earlier description of the rain and snow he experiences. Here he suggests humorously that Lana Turner and Hollywood are nothing like his own urban existence. The free verse, in fact, conveys the speaker's disturbed equilibrium at the news of Lana Turner—after all, *he* has "never actually collapsed."

T. S. Eliot once said that the term *free verse* was imprecise, since "no *vers* is *libre* for the man who wants to do a good job." Eliot's comment and O'Hara's poem show us that free verse, like more structured forms, has its rules and requires a disciplined approach in utilizing them.

We turn now from verse forms and stanzaic forms to what are often called **fixed forms,** a term frequently applied to specific types of poems that have traditionally accepted structures and conventions of composition. Although we shall limit the discussion to the sonnet and the limerick, there are other fixed forms, like the sestina, and there are forms with looser but nevertheless clearly recognizable conventions, like the ode.

A Note on the Sonnet

The most esteemed of the fixed forms of English poetry is the sonnet. Developed in Italy around the thirteenth century, the sonnet form was brought to England by Sir Thomas Wyatt (1503–1542) who, with Henry Howard, Earl of Surrey (1517–1547), began to adapt it to English meter. Soon after, the sonnet acquired great popularity. Although the form is difficult to execute, poets from the time of the Renaissance right up until today have been continually fascinated and challenged by its economy and the subtleties of its tight unity. Specifically, the **sonnet** (from the Italian *sonnetto:* "little song") is a lyric poem of fourteen lines, usually of iambic pentameter. There are two major types, which differ from one another in organization and in rime: the Italian or Petrarchan sonnet; and the English or Shakespearean sonnet.

The original form is the **Italian sonnet,** which takes its other name from Petrarch (1304–1374), Italian poet who had a great influence on its development. It has a two-part organization: eight lines riming *abbaabba,* followed by six lines riming *cdecde.* But the rime scheme of the final six lines may vary—for example, *cdeced* or *cdcdcd.* The organization of the **octave** or first eight lines and the **sestet** or last six lines is established not only by the metrics but also by the content. The octave presents a situation, sets a problem, or gives an observation. The sestet usually offers a response, resolution, or closing appropriate to the subject. Here is an Italian sonnet for study and analysis.

John Keats (1795–1821)
On First Looking into Chapman's Homer[1]

Much have I traveled in the realms of gold,
And many goodly states and kingdoms seen;
Round many western islands have I been
Which bards in fealty[2] to Apollo hold.
Oft of one wide expanse had I been told   5
That deep-browed Homer ruled as his demesne;°   *domain*
Yet did I never breathe its pure serene°   *air*
Till I heard Chapman speak out loud and bold:
Then felt I like some watcher of the skies
When a new planet swims into his ken;°   *range of vision* 10
Or like stout Cortez[3] when with eagle eyes
He stared at the Pacific—and all his men
Looked at each other with a wild surmise—
Silent, upon a peak in Darien.

The success of the Italian sonnet depends largely upon generating effective correspondences between the two parts of the poem's structure. The logic of this form, in fact, is that of an intimate relationship between the situation presented in the octave and the response given in the sestet. In Keats' poem, there is an emphatic "turn" at the end of line eight as the poet moves from the general proposition of the octave, the matter of familiarity with poets and poetry, to the specific resolution in the sestet, the introduction of concrete images of explorers. The poem effectively illustrates the idea of related movement, of point-counterpoint, which is the hallmark of the Italian sonnet.

The second general type of sonnet is the **English** or **Shakespearean sonnet** (so named because of Shakespeare's consummate skill with the form). This sonnet has three quatrains and a couplet, with a rime scheme *abab, cdcd, efef, gg*. This organization, in contrast to the tight, two-part order of the Italian sonnet, gives the English form a greater flexibility, allowing the poet to treat different aspects of a situation, problem, or experience. He may, in fact, utilize the three quatrains to offer a variety of impressions and images. The resolution in the final two lines is limited by the couplet form and thus tends to be pointed and succinct. Here the poet usually presents summary and judgmental propositions, often in witty and ironic fashion. The following exemplifies many of the features of the English sonnet.

---

1. George Chapman (1559?–1634) was an English poet and dramatist who translated Homer's *Iliad* and *Odyssey* in rimed verse.
2. Allegiance; Apollo was the Greek god of poetry and music.
3. Hernando Cortez (1485–1547), Spanish conqueror of Mexico. It was actually Balboa who first viewed the Pacific from Darien, in Panama.

William Shakespeare   (1564–1616)
When in Disgrace with Fortune and Men's Eyes

When in disgrace with fortune and men's eyes,	
I all alone beweep my outcast state,	
And trouble deaf heaven with my bootless° cries,	*useless*
And look upon myself and curse my fate,	
Wishing me like to one more rich in hope,	5
Featur'd like him, like him with friends possess'd,	
Desiring this man's art, and that man's scope,°	*power or opportunity*
With what I most enjoy contented least,	
Yet in these thoughts myself almost despising,	
Haply° I think on thee, and then my state,	*By chance* 10
Like to the lark at break of day arising,	
From sullen° earth sings hymns at heaven's gate,	*dull; heavy*
For thy sweet love rememb'red such wealth brings,	
That when I scorn to change my state with kings.	

In the English sonnet, there is a progression from one quatrain to the next that must relate logically and aesthetically to the overall pattern of the poem. Each four-line unit functions as an extension and presents a slightly different aspect of a central, dominant image or theme, the integrity and movement of which are crucial to the success of the sonnet. Its outer form must reflect its inner progression in order for the poet's meaning to be expressed. And this is what Shakespeare is able to accomplish in the sonnet above. The first two quatrains explore the speaker's sense of despair with his situation in life. The third quatrain presents a radical shift in attitude as thoughts of his beloved rescue the speaker from his gloom. And the image of a lark singing at daybreak reinforces this change. The couplet ties up matters nicely by presenting a contrast between the speaker's refusal to trade places with kings and his former despair. By skillfully integrating images that establish and sustain his form and his theme, Shakespeare surmounts two of the dangers of the English sonnet—repetition and a lack of progression from quatrain to quatrain.

In addition to the two major types of sonnets, there are numerous variations, usually modeled on either the Italian or the English forms. There are three variations which need to be mentioned.

1. The **Spenserian sonnet,** named for its originator Edmund Spenser (1552?–1599), is a version of the English sonnet. The only difference is its use of just five interrelated rimes, *abab, bcbc, cdcd, ee,* which link various elements of the poem more closely together. An example is Spenser's sonnet sequence *Amoretti.* A **sonnet sequence** consists of a number of sonnets joined by a common purpose and a unified subject.

Other significant sonnet sequences in English poetry are Sir Philip Sidney's *Astrophel and Stella* (which sometimes employs hexameter for pentameter meter) and Elizabeth Barrett Browning's *Sonnets from the Portuguese.*

2. The **curtal sonnet** is a distinct variation devised by Gerard Manley Hopkins. It is a "curtailed" sonnet, consisting of ten lines plus—in most cases—a fraction of a line. An example is his "Pied Beauty" (see "Poems for Further Study").

3. The third variation is found in many of the poems of George Meredith (1828–1909). Although these "sonnets" have sixteen lines, they manifest a sonnetlike logic of organization and development and so are considered to be an adaptation of the form. For an example, see Meredith's sonnet taken from his sonnet sequence *Modern Love* in "Poems for Further Study."

Exercise

In examining each of the sonnets below for form and content, answer the following questions. (Some of them may not apply to each poem.)

1. *Form and pattern.* What is the meter employed? What is the rime scheme? Is it entirely regular in verse form? Is it an Italian or an English sonnet? Does it contain any notable variations from the standard form of either type? If Italian, how does the poet handle the "turn" or break after the eighth line? Is the shift clearly indicated or do the line and the thought run on from octave to sestet? If the sonnet is English, how do the three quatrains present various aspects of the situation? What is the function of the couplet?

2. *Subject and theme.* What is the situation? Is something happening, being described, or narrated? Or does the poem present an attitude or an emotion? Who is speaking and to whom? What is the theme? What meaning do you find in the poem?

3. *Language.* Pick out unfamiliar words and allusions, define and identify them, and determine what associations and implications they have in the poem. Identify the significant images; do these have a general pattern or purpose in the poem? Frequently, a poet will take his images from nature, common occupations, and familiar happenings. How would you characterize the patterns of images you find?

William Shakespeare (1564–1616)
That Time of Year Thou Mayst in Me Behold

That time of year thou mayst in me behold,
When yellow leaves, or none, or few, do hang
Upon those boughs which shake against the cold,
Bare ruin'd choirs,[1] where late the sweet birds sang.

---

1. The image is that of a choir loft or that part of a church or cathedral where the choir sat. The forest is compared to a ruined church, so the birds become choir singers.

In me thou see'st the twilight of such day,   5
As after sunset fadeth in the west,
Which by and by° black night doth take away,   *shortly*
Death's second self,° that seals up all in rest.   *i.e., sleep*
In me thou see'st the glowing of such fire,
That on the ashes of his° youth doth lie,   *its* 10
As the death-bed whereon it must expire,
Consum'd with that which it was nourish'd by.[2]
    This thou perceiv'st, which makes thy love more strong,
    To love that well, which thou must leave ere long.

John Donne (1572–1631)
Batter My Heart

Batter my heart, three-personed God; for You
As yet but knock, breathe, shine, and seek to mend;
That I may rise and stand, o'erthrow me, and bend
Your force to break, blow, burn, and make me new.
I, like an usurped town, to another due,   5
Labor to admit You, but O, to no end;
Reason, Your viceroy[1] in me, me should defend,
But is captived, and proves weak or untrue.
Yet dearly I love You, and would be loved fain,°   *gladly*
But am bethrothed unto Your enemy.   10
Divorce me, untie or break that knot again;
Take me to You, imprison me, for I,
Except You enthrall me,° never shall be free,   *hold me prisoner*
Nor ever chaste, except You ravish me.

John Milton (1608–1674)
How Soon Hath Time

How soon hath Time, the subtle thief of youth,
    Stoln on his wing my three and twentieth year!
    My hasting days fly on with full career,°   *speed*
    But my late spring no bud or blossom show'th.
Perhaps my semblance° might deceive the truth,   *appearance* 5
    That I to manhood am arrived so near,
    And inward ripeness doth much less appear,

---

2. The sense of this line is that his life, now advanced, is choked by the ashes of that which in him formerly nourished its flame.

1. One who rules on behalf of a superior power.

That some more timely-happy spirits endu'th.°   *endows*
Yet be it less or more, or soon or slow,
   It shall be still in strictest measure even   10
   To that same lot, however mean or high,
Toward which Time leads me, and the will of Heaven;
   All is, if I have grace to use it so,
   As ever in my great Taskmaster's eye.

William Wordsworth   (1770–1850)
London, 1802

Milton! thou should'st be living at this hour:
England hath need of thee: she is a fen°   *marsh*
Of stagnant waters: altar, sword, and pen,
Fireside, the heroic wealth of hall and bower,
Have forfeited their ancient English dower°   *inheritance* 5
Of inward happiness. We are selfish men:
Oh! raise us up, return to us again;
And give us manners, virtue, freedom, power.
Thy soul was like a Star, and dwelt apart:
Thou hadst a voice whose sound was like the sea,   10
Pure as the naked heavens, majestic, free,
So didst thou travel on life's common way,
In cheerful godliness; and yet thy heart
The lowliest duties on herself did lay.

Percy Bysshe Shelley   (1792–1822)
Ozymandias[1]

I met a traveller from an antique land
Who said: Two vast and trunkless legs of stone
Stand in the desert. Near them, on the sand,
Half sunk, a shattered visage lies, whose frown,
And wrinkled lip, and sneer of cold command,   5
Tell that its sculptor well those passions read
Which yet survive, stamped on these lifeless things,
The hand that mocked them and the heart that fed;
And on the pedestal these words appear:
"My name is Ozymandias, king of kings: 10

---

1. Rameses ii, pharaoh of Egypt (13th century b.c.). One account reports that his statue at Thebes was the largest in Egypt and that it bore the inscription: "I am Ozymandias, king of kings; if anyone wishes to know what I am and where I lie, let him surpass me in some of my exploits."

Look on my works, ye Mighty, and despair!"
Nothing beside remains. Round the decay
Of that colossal wreck, boundless and bare
The lone and level sands stretch far away.

Ezra Pound (1885–1972)
A Virginal[1]

No, no! Go from me. I have left her lately.
I will not spoil my sheath with lesser brightness,
For my surrounding air hath a new lightness;
Slight are her arms, yet they have bound me straitly
And left me cloaked as with a gauze of æther;°   *rarefied air* 5
As with sweet leaves; as with subtle clearness.
Oh, I have picked up magic in her nearness
To sheathe me half in half the things that sheathe her.
No, no! Go from me. I have still the flavour,
Soft as spring wind that's come from birchen bowers.   10
Green come the shoots, aye April in the branches,
As winter's wound with her sleight hand she staunches,[2]
Hath of the trees a likeness of the savour:
As white their bark, so white this lady's hours.[3]

Robert Frost (1874–1963)
The Silken Tent

She is as in a field a silken tent
At midday when a sunny summer breeze
Has dried the dew and all its ropes relent,
So that in guys it gently sways at ease,
And its supporting central cedar pole,   5
That is its pinnacle to heavenward
And signifies the sureness of the soul,
Seems to owe naught to any single cord,
But strictly held by none, is loosely bound
By countless silken ties of love and thought   10
To everything on earth the compass round,
And only by one's going slightly taut
In the capriciousness of summer air
Is of the slightest bondage made aware.

---

1. The virginal was a Renaissance keyboard instrument having only one wire to a note.
2. I.e., she heals "winter's wound" by staunching (stopping the flow of blood).
3. Hours given to daily liturgical devotion, which are now "white" or empty.

Robert Lowell   (b. 1917)
France
(From the Gibbet)[1]

My human brothers who live after me,
See how I hang. My bones eat through the skin
And flesh they carried here upon the chin
And lipping clutch of their cupidity;
And here, now here, the starling and the sea   5
Gull splinter the groined eyeball of my sin,
Brothers, more beaks of birds than needles in
The fathoms of the Bayeux Tapestry:[2]
"God wills it, wills it, wills it: it is blood."
My brothers, if I call you brothers, see: 10
The blood of Abel[3] crying from the dead
Sticks to my blackened skull and eyes. What good
Are *lebensraum*[4] and bread to Abel dead
And rotten on the cross-beams of the tree?[5]

A Note on Limericks, Epigrams and Epitaphs

The **limerick** is another of the fixed forms of English poetry. Consisting usually of five short lines of anapests, riming *aabba,* limericks are humorous and frequently satiric exercises in verse. Not seriously literary in content and subject, they nevertheless require a certain skill and ingenuity in the use of rhythm and rime.

There was a young fellow named Dice
Who remarked, "They say bigamy's nice.
    Even two are a bore,
    I'd prefer three or four,
For the plural of spouse, it is spice."

---

1. The arm or that part of a gallows from which the rope hangs. Lowell takes the first lines and several images from a poem written by François Villon (1431–1463?) when he was expecting to be hanged.
2. Intricately woven, medieval French tapestry which depicts the Norman Conquest of England in 1066.
3. In Genesis, Cain killed his brother Abel out of jealousy.
4. German for "living space." Adolf Hitler used it as a catchphrase in attempting to justify the Nazi take-over of Europe.
5. A reference to the gallows; also, indirectly to the crucifixion.

Although the origins and the originator—if indeed there was only one—of the limerick are obscure, Edward Lear (1812–1888), a British painter and humorist, popularized the form in the late nineteenth century. Since then, limericks have been favorites of children and adults, as well as of notable poets and mediocre versifiers.

There once was an artist named Lear
Who wrote verses to make children cheer.
  Though they never made sense,
  Their success was immense;
And the Queen thought that Lear was a dear.

Lear liked to have his last line recall the first one, and typical of his limericks—his "Learicks," or "Lazy-Liners"—is the following.

There was an old man with a beard
Who said, "It is just as I feared!
  Two Owls and a Hen,
  Four Larks and a Wren
Have built their nests in my beard."

For various reasons, including frequent oral transmission and numerous spontaneous adaptations, limericks are usually anonymous. Here are two more selections to illustrate the humor, sense, and nonsense of this poetic form.

A limerick packs laughs anatomical
Into space that is quite economical.
  But the good ones I've seen,
  So seldom are clean,
And the clean ones so seldom are comical.

There was a young man of Westphalia
Who yearly got tail-ier and tail-ier
  Till he took on the shape
  Of a Barbary ape
With the consequent paraphernalia.

Exercise

Try your hand at some limericks. Here are some possible first lines.
There once was a man from Nantucket

A tutor who danced to a lute
When a jolly old man named Bisher
A nice old lady from Cerruchos
Said an ardent young bridegroom from Kent

In their general meaning, an *epigram* is a concise and pointed statement, and an *epitaph* is an inscription on a monument or a tombstone. In poetry, an **epigram** is a type of very short poem that strives to capture in summary or to render a personal judgment on an act, event, or thought, often in a humorous or satiric manner. An **epitaph** is a short commemorative poem used to mark burial places or at least written as if this were the intention. Both usually consist of rimed verses with various patterns of metrical arrangements. Here is an example of an epigram and an epitaph.

John Donne   (1572–1631)
Antiquary

If in his study he hath so much care
To hang all old strange things, let his wife beware.

John Gay   (1685–1732)
My Own Epitaph

Life is a jest; and all things show it.
I thought so once; but now I know it.

These two pieces are obviously humorous and satiric. Yet the two forms traditionally have also been used for serious subjects and purposes—for philosophic statements, eulogies, personal reflections, compliments, and expressions of friendship and tribute.

Here are a handful of epigrams and epitaphs which show something of the variety and vigor of these two poetic forms.

Theodore Roethke   (1908–1963)
The Mistake

He left his pants upon a chair;
She was a widow, so she said:
But he was apprehended, bare,
By one who rose up from the dead.

A. R. Ammons (b. 1926)
Hippie Hop

I have no program for
saving this world or scuttling
the next: I know no political,
sexual, racial cures: I make
analogies, my bucketful of   5
flowers: I give flowers to people
of all policies, sexes, and races
including the vicious, the
uncertain, and the white.

Anonymous
Epitaph on an Infant Eight Months Old

Since I have been so quickly done for,
I wonder what I was begun for.

Ben Jonson (1572–1637)
Epitaph on Elizabeth, L. H.

Wouldst thou hear what man can say
In a little? Reader, stay.
Underneath this stone doth lie
As much beauty as could die;
Which in life did harbor give   5
To more virtue than doth live.
If at all she had a fault,
Leave it buried in this vault.
One name was Elizabeth;
Th' other, let it sleep with death: 10
Fitter, where it died, to tell,
Than that it lived at all. Farewell.

X. J. Kennedy (b. 1929)
Epitaph for a Postal Clerk

Here lies wrapped up tight in sod
Henry Harkins c/o God.
On the day of Resurrection
May be opened for inspection.

Exercise

The sheer delight of nailing down a person or a perception in a tight formulation is what makes epigrams and epitaphs enjoyable. To get a different perspective on how these forms work, try to rewrite several of the epigrams and epitaphs above by changing words and phrases, especially by altering the rimes. Then try to compose several of your own from scratch.

John Dryden (1631–1700)
To the Memory of Mr. Oldham[1]

Farewell, too little and too lately known,
Whom I began to think and call my own;
For sure our souls were near allied, and thine
Cast in the same poetic mold with mine.
One common note on either lyre did strike,   5
And knaves and fools we both abhorr'd alike:
To the same goal did both our studies drive;
The last set out the soonest did arrive.[2]
Thus Nisus[3] fell upon the slippery place,
Whilst his young friend perform'd and won the race.   10
O early ripe! to thy abundant store
What could advancing age have added more?
It might (what nature never gives the young)
Have taught the numbers° of thy native tongue.   *rhythm*
But satire needs not those, and wit will shine   15
Through the harsh cadence of a rugged line.
A noble error, and but seldom made,
When poets are by too much force betray'd.
Thy generous fruits, though gather'd ere their prime,
Still show'd a quickness;° and maturing time   *acuteness of feeling* 20
But mellows what we write to the dull sweets of rhyme.
Once more, hail, and farewell; farewell, thou young,
But ah too short, Marcellus[4] of our tongue;
Thy brows with ivy and with laurels bound;
But Fate and gloomy night encompass thee around.   25

---

1. John Oldham (1653–1683), English satirist, whom Dryden admired.
2. Although Oldham was born twenty-two years after Dryden, he died before him, at the age of thirty.
3. In Virgil's *Aeneid*, Nisus, running in a footrace, slipped on a spot where steers had been slaughtered; realizing he would lose, he threw himself in front of another runner so that his friend Euryalus could win.
4. The nephew and potential successor of the Roman emperor Augustus, he died at age twenty. Virgil in the *Aeneid* celebrates his youthful military fame.

Questions for Study

1. What is the form of the verse? Comment on significant metrical features that contribute to the solemn tone of this elegy. Note in particular the final line.
2. Dryden is particularly skillful in using the caesura to achieve certain effects. Point out instances where these internal pauses vary the rhythms and reinforce the meaning.
3. In praising the dead Oldham, Dryden is specific in his remarks. What are those qualities in the man and in his poetry that Dryden cites as especially notable?
4. Is it possible to mark off any overall structural pattern in this poem? How is it organized and how does it move from line to line? Can you identify any thematic subdivisions or emphases?

E. E. Cummings   (1894–1962)
if everything happens that can't be done

if everything happens that can't be done
(and anything's righter
than books
could plan)
the stupidest teacher will almost guess   5
(with a run
skip
around we go yes)
there's nothing as something as one

one hasn't a why or because or although   10
(and buds know better
than books
don't grow)
one's anything old being everything new
(with a what   15
which
around we come who)
one's everyanything so

so world is a leaf so tree is a bough
(and birds sing sweeter   20
than books
tell how)
so here is away and so your is a my
(with a down
up   25
around again fly)
forever was never till now

now i love you and you love me
(and books are shuter

than books   30
can be)
and deep in the high that does nothing but fall
(with a shout
each
around we go all)   35
there's somebody calling who's we

we're anything brighter than even the sun
(we're everything greater
than books
might mean)   40
we're everyanything more than believe
(with a spin
leap
alive we're alive)
we're wonderful one times one   45

Questions for Study

1. What is the kind of verse employed here? How can you determine it? Mention
   several specific poetic devices used in the poem. What effects do they achieve?
2. Why do you think Cummings has arranged his poem in five verse paragraphs?
   What is the theme and the emphasis of each one?
3. Mark each line and each rime. Can you detect a pattern in either of the verse
   paragraphs? What does scanning this poem indicate? Is scansion actually useful
   here?
4. What is the meaning of *one* as Cummings uses it in the poem?

Anonymous   (Scottish folk ballad)
Edward

"Why does your brand sae drap wi' bluid,[1]
    Edward, Edward?
Why does your brand sae drap wi' bluid,
    And why sae sad gang° ye, O?"   *go*
"O I ha'e killed my hawk sae guid,   5
    Mither, mither,
O I ha'e killed my hawk sae guid,
    And I had nae mair° but he, O."   *more*

"Your hawkes bluid was never sae reid,°   *red*
    Edward, Edward.   10
Your hawkes bluid was never sae reid,
    My dear son I tell thee, O."
"O I ha'e killed my reid-roan° steed,   *chestnut*
    Mither, mither,

---

1. "Why does your sword so drip with blood."

O I ha'e killed my reid-roan steed,   15
    That erst° was sae fair and free, O.''   *once*

''Your steed was auld° and ye ha'e gat mair,   *old*
    Edward, Edward.
Your steed was auld and ye ha'e gat mair:
    Som other dule° ye dree,° O.''   *grief* / *suffer* 20
''O I ha'e killed my fader dear,
    Mither, mither,
O I ha'e killed my fader dear,
    Alas and wae° is me, O!''   *woe*

''And whatten° penance wul ye dree for that,   *what* 25
    Edward, Edward?
And whatten penance wul ye dree for that,
    My dear son, now tell me, O?''
''I'll set my feet in yonder boat,
    Mither, mither,   30
I'll set my feet in yonder boat,
    And I'll fare over the sea, O.''

''And what wul ye do wi' your towers and your ha',°   *hall*
    Edward, Edward?
And what wul ye do wi' your towers and your ha',   35
    That were sae fair to see, O?''
''I'll let thame stand til they down fa',
    Mither, mither,
I'll let thame stand til they down fa',
    For here never mair maun° I be, O.''   *must* 40

''And what wul ye leave to your bairns° and your wife,   *children*
    Edward, Edward,
And what wul ye leave to your bairns and your wife,
    Whan ye gang over the sea, O?''
''The warldes room, late them beg thrae life,[2]   45
    Mither, mither,
The warldes room, late them beg thrae life,
    For thame never mair wul I see, O.''

''And what wul ye leave to your ain° mither dear,   *own*
    Edward, Edward?   50
And what wul ye leave to your ain mither dear,
    My dear son, now tell me, O?''
''The curse of hell frae° me sal° ye bear,   *from* / *shall*
    Mither, mither,
The curse of hell frae me sal ye bear,   55
    Sic° counseils ye gave to me, O.''   *such*

---

2. ''The world's room, let them beg through life.''

Questions for Study

1. "Edward" is a ballad, a form of poetry intended for singing or reciting, and concerned with narrating in a simple style a dramatic situation or an exciting (even supernatural) episode. Identify the verse form, the stanzaic form, and the rime scheme. Point out other metrical effects. What is gained, for example, in the repetition of *Edward, Edward* and *Mither, mither?* Why is the final *O* employed in lines 4 and 8 of each stanza? What other repetitions can you find in the poem? Why are they effective?

2. The entire narrative is presented in the form of the mother's questions and Edward's responses. From these, we learn by implication what has happened. Is this method of narration successful? Explain.

3. Many ballads are constructed so that some stanzas can be interchanged or removed without detracting from the overall meaning of the piece. Clearly, such is not the case here. Try rearranging or omitting any one or two of these stanzas. What is the effect?

4. What do we know about Edward and about his mother? Describe their relationship. Why does Edward hesitate before he tells her what he has actually done? Does she already know? The theme of this ballad concerns Edward's murder of his father. Elaborate on this theme and examine its implications.

Chapter 11
Structure and Types

In this chapter we want to consider some of the ways in which poets organize and control the content of their poems. Louis MacNeice once said that "In any poet's poem the shape is half the meaning." A poem's meaning, of course, depends upon many features. But certainly its design or **structure** is crucial in integrating various materials, ideas, and emotions into a unified pattern.

Often poetic structure depends largely upon those informing principles discussed in earlier chapters. Such devices, for example, as a central image or an idea, a controlling allusion or an extended analogy, even the tone or the point of view shape a poem's meaning. In addition, structure may also result from the scene a poem develops or from the situation it describes. The implications of scene and situation are usually highly significant, and we must look closely at these. Similarly, the type of poetry to which a poem belongs also influences its design or structure. Later in this chapter we look at several types of poetry—narrative, dramatic, and lyric—to see how these modes work.

The structure of each of the two short poems below depends on a situation which must be comprehended in order for the meaning to emerge.

A. E. Housman (1859–1936)
When I Was One-and-Twenty

When I was one-and-twenty
  I heard a wise man say,
"Give crowns and pounds and guineas
  But not your heart away;
Give pearls away and rubies   5

But keep your fancy free."
But I was one-and-twenty,
 No use to talk to me.

When I was one-and-twenty
 I heard him say again,   10
"The heart out of the bosom
 Was never given in vain;
'Tis paid with sighs a plenty
 And sold for endless rue."°   *regret*
And I am two-and-twenty,   15
 And oh, 'tis true, 'tis true.

The speaker in this poem reports the words of "a wise man." We must imagine this situation and how the speaker, at twenty-one, does not heed the man's advice. Actually, the man's two statements comment on the same proposition: give your money but not your heart away, and the loss of money will not prove as troublesome as the loss of one's heart. The wise man's words refer to emotional entanglements and caution that such involvements are paid for with "sighs" and "endless rue." At twenty-one, the speaker has not understood what at twenty-two he now understands. Having given his heart away, he can now admit the truth of the wise man's advice.

Gary Snyder (b. 1930)
Looking at Pictures to Be Put Away

Who was this girl
In her white night gown
Clutching a pair of jeans

On a foggy redwood deck.
She looks up at me tender,   5
Calm, surprised,

What will we remember
Bodies thick with food and lovers
After twenty years.

We might say that in this short poem two different times are suggested. First, we need to see that the speaker is looking at photographs "to be put away." Second, we need to imagine the particular photograph described here, that of a young girl "In her white night gown / Clutching a pair of jeans / On a foggy redwood deck." Apparently he has taken the picture, for he remarks that she "looks up at me tender, / Calm, surprised." It is important for us to imagine both of these scenes because of the final three lines, in which the speaker comments on the girl and on himself, wondering what indeed the two will remember after twenty years.

The short poem below indirectly asks us to imagine not so much a scene as an intimate situation between the speaker and a loved one.

Nikki Giovanni   (b. 1943)
Balances

in life
one is always
balancing

like we juggle our mothers
against our fathers   5

or one teacher
against another
(only to balance our grade average)

3 grains salt
to one ounce truth   10

our sweet black essence
or the funky honkies down the street

and lately i've begun wondering
if you're trying to tell me something

we used to talk all night   15
and do things alone together

and i've begun
(as a reaction to a feeling)
to balance
the pleasure of loneliness   20
against the pain
of loving you

The theme of this poem may be taken from the opening stanza: "in life / one is always / balancing." And the recurrence of the idea of "balancing" develops this theme. Yet the proposition Giovanni works out in these lines is subtle. The poem's overall integrity depends not simply upon such internal devices as repetition but also upon the situation suggested in the poem. The meaning and implications of the piece are clarified only if we are able to see what this situation is. We should recognize that the speaker is referring to an intimate relationship with someone that apparently is about to end. And so we understand that the speaker, "as a reaction to a feeling" about the lover's loss of interest, is now trying "to balance / the pleasure of loneliness / against the pain / of loving" that person. Within the implied situation, then, the reaction to a *feeling*—not to the *fact* of loss—requires the speaker to resort to a compensatory act. This act is an attempt to balance the anticipation of losing the loved one with the speaker's present plight of loving but not being loved. We might, in fact, imagine that the speaker is thinking of breaking off the relationship first.

Occasionally, a poem depicts a scene that is so vivid and rich in implications that we must understand it in order to grasp the meaning of the poem. The following poem, a sonnet, presents such an scene.

William Butler Yeats (1865–1939)
Leda and the Swan

A sudden blow: the great wings beating still
Above the staggering girl, her thighs caressed
By the dark webs, her nape caught in his bill,
He holds her helpless breast upon his breast.

How can those terrified vague fingers push   5
The feathered glory from her loosening thighs?
And how can body, laid in that white rush,
But feel the strange heart beating where it lies?

A shudder in the loins engenders there
The broken wall, the burning roof and tower   10
And Agamemnon dead.
              Being so caught up,
So mastered by the brute blood of the air,
Did she put on his knowledge with his power
Before the indifferent beak could let her drop?

The background and the structure of this poem are drawn from the story of Leda and the swan. According to Greek mythology, Zeus, king of the Olympian gods, took the form of a swan and impregnated Leda, who gave birth to four children, including Helen, who became the wife of Menelaus, and Clytemnestra, wife of Agamemnon (brother of Menelaus). Menelaus and Agamemnon were kings of pre-Hellenic Greece. Helen's abduction by the Trojan prince Paris occasioned the long and bloody Trojan War, an event alluded to in line 10. Clytemnestra and her lover killed Agamemnon upon his victorious return from the war. Thus a "shudder" in Leda's loins engenders the ruin of Troy and the death of a hero: "The broken wall, the burning roof and tower / And Agamemnon dead."

We can read Yeats' poem with considerably more understanding if we have this mythological story in mind. The poem concerns itself primarily with the rape of Leda and with her feelings. Yeats' lines dramatize the sudden descent of the bird/god, Leda's terror, and the consummation. But the lines also contain speculations about what Leda's thoughts might have been. For example, did she in that brief moment foresee, with Zeus, the immense consequences of the act? By implication, the poem asks if Zeus thereby unwittingly passed on to mankind qualities and knowledge he originally did not wish mortals to have. Here various individual interpretations are possible. But each interpretation should result from the reader's understanding of how Yeats has adapted the materials of the original story to his poem.

The following poem does not employ materials from other sources as a basis for its structure. But it does use an important allusion in presenting its theme. Similar to Yeats' use of a mythological story, Auden's reference to a specific painting has a crucial function in the poem.

W. H. Auden   (1907–1973)
Musée des Beaux Arts[1]

About suffering they were never wrong,
The Old Masters: how well they understood
Its human position; how it takes place
While someone else is eating or opening a window or just walking dully
     along;
How, when the aged are reverently, passionately waiting   5
For the miraculous birth, there always must be
Children who did not specially want it to happen, skating
On a pond at the edge of the wood:
They never forgot
That even the dreadful martyrdom must run its course   10
Anyhow in a corner, some untidy spot
Where the dogs go on with their doggy life and the torturer's horse
Scratches its innocent behind on a tree.

In Brueghel's *Icarus,* for instance: how everything turns away
Quite leisurely from the disaster; the plowman may   15
Have heard the splash, the forsaken cry,
But for him it was not an important failure; the sun shone

---

1. Literally, "Museum of the Beautiful Arts"; actually, the *Palais des Musées Royaux de Peinture et de Sculpture* (the Palace Museum of Royal Painting and Sculpturing), located in Brussels, Belgium. It contains *The Fall of Icarus* by Pieter Brueghel, the Elder (1525?–1569).

As it had to on the white legs disappearing into the green
Water; and the expensive delicate ship that must have seen
Something amazing, a boy falling out of the sky,   20
Had somewhere to get to and sailed calmly on.

The first thirteen lines present a scene in which the speaker is musing on the human indifference to suffering, a theme which is treated by many works of the "Old Masters" hanging in the museum. He recognizes that most of the people in these pictures (and, by implication, people in general) go about their everyday affairs without noticing the tragedy and suffering about them. To emphasize his point, the speaker alludes to Brueghel's *The Fall of Icarus* in line 14. Thereafter, the subject matter of this work becomes part of the poem, and we must consider this painting and how Auden has used it.

Brueghel's painting is based on the story of Icarus. In Greek mythology, Icarus escaped from a labyrinth in which he was imprisoned by using wings created by his father Daedalus. Although warned not to do so by Daedalus, the youth flew so near the sun that the wax bindings of the wings melted, and he fell into the sea. Only one small portion of Brueghel's painting takes up Icarus' drowning, with only his legs visible as he disappears headfirst into the sea. The rest of the painting shows a farmer and shepherd unconcernedly going about their duties, while various ships sail by. Clearly, the fall of Icarus goes unnoticed by the world, a subject Auden incorporates into his lines about the world's indifference to tragedy and suffering. In "Musée des Beaux Arts," the situation of the speaker, the paintings by the Old Masters, and specifically Brueghel's work are integrated into the overall structure. And the poem cannot be fully appreciated unless each of these elements is understood.

We have been talking thus far about how internal elements determine the structure of a poem. There are also numerous external elements or conventions, some of which are determined by the type of poem employed. The three types of poems to be considered are narrative, dramatic, and lyric.

A **narrative poem** tells a story. Like prose fiction, it has characters, setting, and various elements of plot: a rising action (in which the conflict develops toward a climax) and a falling action (in which the conflict reaches its climax and is then resolved). In poetry the best-known narratives are folk or popular ballads which, in their origins, were intended for oral presentation and which are usually anonymous. "Bonny Barbara Allen," included later in this chapter, is an instance of a folk ballad. When a ballad is consciously written for a literary effect, the form is called a **literary ballad.** John Keats' "La Belle Dame sans Merci" (Chapter 2) illustrates the form. Other kinds of narrative poetry are the epic and the metrical romance. An **epic** is a poem of considerable length written in a serious style and concerned with heroic characters and situations that illustrate the origins, history, and destiny of a race, people, or nation. Homer's *Iliad* and Virgil's *Aeneid* are particularly noteworthy examples. **Metrical romances,** also of considerable length, present tales of love, intrigue, and chivalric adventures and romances. *Sir Gawain and the Green Knight* and Lord Byron's *The Bride of Abydos* are examples of the form.

Here are two short poems, both written in this century, that illustrate how the narrative method provides a structure for poetic materials.

Robert Frost   (1874–1963)
"Out, Out—"

The buzz saw snarled and rattled in the yard
And made dust and dropped stove-length sticks of wood,
Sweet-scented stuff when the breeze drew across it.
And from there those that lifted eyes could count
Five mountain ranges one behind the other   5
Under the sunset far into Vermont.
And the saw snarled and rattled, snarled and rattled,
As it ran light, or had to bear a load.
And nothing happened: day was all but done.
Call it a day, I wish they might have said   10
To please the boy by giving him the half hour
That a boy counts so much when saved from work.
His sister stood beside them in her apron
To tell them "Supper." At the word, the saw,
As if to prove saws knew what supper meant,   15
Leaped out at the boy's hand, or seemed to leap—
He must have given the hand. However it was,
Neither refused the meeting. But the hand!
The boy's first outcry was a rueful laugh,
As he swung toward them holding up the hand,   20
Half in appeal, but half as if to keep
The life from spilling. Then the boy saw all—
Since he was old enough to know, big boy
Doing a man's work, though a child at heart—
He saw all spoiled. "Don't let him cut my hand off—   25
The doctor, when he comes. Don't let him, sister!"
So. But the hand was gone already.
The doctor put him in the dark of ether.
He lay and puffed his lips out with his breath.
And then—the watcher at his pulse took fright.   30

No one believed. They listened at his heart.
Little—less—nothing!—and that ended it.
No more to build on there. And they, since they
Were not the one dead, turned to their affairs.

Questions for Study

1. What is the plot of this poem? Break the plot down into its basic components: rising action, conflict, climax, falling action, and resolution.
2. Describe the point of view of the outside narrator. Why, in your opinion, is this point of view effective?
3. What is the narrator's attitude toward his story? Specifically, what is the attitude toward life and death that he expresses in the poem? Cite details from the poem in giving your answers.
4. Frost's title is taken from Shakespeare's *Macbeth,* specifically from a speech made by Macbeth in which he laments the death of his wife. Read the speech (p. 656) and then explain how Shakespeare's lines support the theme of Frost's poem.

Edwin Arlington Robinson (1869–1935)
The Mill

The miller's wife had waited long,
    The tea was cold, the fire was dead;
And there might yet be nothing wrong
    In how he went and what he said:
"There are no millers any more,"   5
    Was all that she had heard him say;
And he had lingered at the door
    So long that it seemed yesterday.

Sick with a fear that had no form
    She knew that she was there at last;   10
And in the mill there was a warm
    And mealy fragrance of the past.
What else there was would only seem
    To say again what he had meant;
And what was hanging from a beam   15
    Would not have heeded where she went.

And if she thought it followed her,
    She may have reasoned in the dark
That one way of the few there were
    Would hide her and would leave no mark: 20
Black water, smooth above the weir°   *pond*
    Like starry velvet in the night,
Though ruffled once, would soon appear
    The same as ever to the sight.

Questions for Study

1. The organization of this poem is chronological, with the sequence of events moving directly from one point to the next. This is usually, if not always, the progress of a narrative poem. What benefit does Robinson achieve by organizing his poem as a narrative rather than, say, as a mere description of the scene at the mill? What, in other words, are the positive features of this poem as a narrative?
2. What has happened to the miller and what then does his wife do? How can you be sure of these events?
3. Robinson implies specific acts in this poem. Would the poem have been more effective if Robinson had stated explicitly what happened? Is something gained by his manner of implying and suggesting?
4. Explain lines 13 and 14, and the reference to the "ruffled water" in the final stanza. Are these effective in contributing to the theme of the poem?

Dramatic poetry is a broadly used literary term. As the name suggests, dramatic poetry clearly refers to the use of poetry in some dramatic form or, at least, in a form that utilizes elements of dramatic technique. The following lines, taken from the last act of *Macbeth,* comprise one of the most famous speeches in English drama.

William Shakespeare   (1564–1616)
from *Macbeth*

She should have died hereafter;
There would have been a time for such a word.
Tomorrow, and tomorrow, and tomorrow,
Creeps in this petty pace from day to day,
To the last syllable of recorded time;   5
And all our yesterdays have lighted fools
The way to dusty death. Out, out, brief candle!
Life's but a walking shadow, a poor player
That struts and frets his hour upon the stage,
And then is heard no more. It is a tale   10
Told by an idiot, full of sound and fury,
Signifying nothing.

Questions for Study

1. Macbeth speaks these lines after he has learned of his wife's death. What do they tell us about his view of life? Try to describe the attitudes and emotions you find expressed here.
2. An uninvolved narrator speaks in Frost's " 'Out, Out—.' " But Macbeth is very much involved in what he says—in fact, his kingdom is being lost and he is about to die. Describe the tone of these lines in terms of his involvement in what he is saying.

3. Frost and Shakespeare are writing about death. How are their attitudes similar? How are they different?

The term *dramatic poetry* may also refer to poems whose method of presentation is partly or largely dramatic. The most notable illustration of this method occurs in the **dramatic monolog**. An intricate and sophisticated form, the dramatic monolog contains several essential features: first, a central character speaking to a listener (who may also speak but who often remains silent); second, a physical setting in which speaker and listener confront each other; and, third, a situation which presents the gradual self-revelation of the speaker, typically about something highly significant in his life. Poets as different as Tennyson, Frost, Eliot, and Allen Tate have written dramatic monologs. The example below is perhaps the most famous of all dramatic monologs, by the acknowledged master of the form.

Robert Browning (1812–1889)
My Last Duchess

Ferrara[1]

That's my last Duchess painted on the wall,
Looking as if she were alive. I call
That piece a wonder, now: Frà Pandolf's[2] hands
Worked busily a day, and there she stands.
Will't please you sit and look at her? I said   5
"Frà Pandolf" by design, for never read
Strangers like you that pictured countenance,
The depth and passion of its earnest glance,
But to myself they turned (since none puts by
The curtain I have drawn for you, but I)   10
And seemed as they would ask me, if they durst,
How such a glance came there; so, not the first
Are you to turn and ask thus. Sir, 'twas not
Her husband's presence only, called that spot
Of joy into the Duchess' cheek: perhaps   15
Frà Pandolf chanced to say "Her mantle laps
Over my lady's wrist too much," or "Paint
Must never hope to reproduce the faint
Half-flush that dies along her throat": such stuff

---

1. The speaker in the poem is thought to have been based on Alfonso II, Duke of Ferrara in Renaissance Italy. After three years of marriage, his young wife died in 1561 under mysterious circumstances. Working through an agent, the Duke later arranged another marriage to the niece of the Count of Tyrol. Here Browning has his ficticious Duke talking to the agent about a marriage to the daughter of the agent's master.
2. Fra (Brother) Pandolf and Claus of Innsbruck (mentioned in line 56) are both ficticious artisans. Innsbruck served as the capital for the Duke of Tyrol.

Was courtesy, she thought, and cause enough   20
For calling up that spot of joy. She had
A heart—how shall I say?—too soon made glad,
Too easily impressed; she liked whate'er
She looked on, and her looks went everywhere.
Sir, 'twas all one! My favor at her breast,   25
The dropping of the daylight in the West,
The bough of cherries some officious fool
Broke in the orchard for her, the white mule
She rode with round the terrace—all and each
Would draw from her alike the approving speech,   30
Or blush, at least. She thanked men,—good! but thanked
Somehow—I know not how—as if she ranked
My gift of a nine-hundred-years-old name
With anybody's gift. Who'd stoop to blame
This sort of trifling? Even had you skill   35
In speech—which I have not—to make your will
Quite clear to such an one, and say, "Just this
Or that in you disgust me; here you miss,
Or there exceed the mark"—and if she let
Herself be lessoned so, nor plainly set   40
Her wits to yours, forsooth, and made excuse,
—E'en then would be some stooping; and I choose
Never to stoop. Oh sir, she smiled, no doubt,
Whene'er I passed her; but who passed without
Much the same smile? This grew; I gave commands   45
Then all smiles stopped together. There she stands
As if alive. Will't please you rise? We'll meet
The company below, then. I repeat,
The Count your master's known munificence
Is ample warrant that no just pretense   50
Of mine for dowry will be disallowed;
Though his fair daughter's self, as I avowed
At starting, is my object. Nay, we'll go
Together down, sir. Notice Neptune,[3] though,
Taming a sea-horse, thought a rarity,   55
Which Claus of Innsbruck cast in bronze for me!

Questions for Study

1. The dramatic monolog organizes content by means of a speaker. Here, the Duke of Ferrara and his listener walk along an upper floor, sit down to observe the portrait, then begin to go downstairs. How does this scene control the principal content of the poem? Explain how this dramatic framework contributes to the meaning of the poem.
2. This is a poem in which the speaker reveals himself through what he says and the

---

3. The Roman god of the sea.

way he says it. How does he do this? Specifically, what statements does the Duke make that constitute self-admissions? Does he intend to tell such things about himself? How does the Duke see himself?

3. Characterize the Duke, supporting your description with evidence from the poem. Is he arrogant? Evil? Vainglorious? What effect does the setting in Renaissance Italy have upon him and upon your view of him?

4. What precisely has the Duchess actually done to offend the Duke? What, in fact, can be inferred about her life and personality from the Duke's remarks?

5. Browning constructs the Duke's remarks so that at no point in the poem does he actually declare what has happened to the Duchess. What do you think has happened? Is this use of suggestion and implication an effective device? Would the poem have been improved if Browning had simply stated the facts of the story through the Duke?

Taking its name from the ancient Greek practice of singing to the music of the lyre, the term **lyric poetry** refers to any poem that expresses the feelings, attitudes, and thoughts of the poet or the persona. Usually written in the first person, lyrics treat a nearly limitless range of subjects—a rose, a landscape, a military battle, the idea of God, and so on. Lyric poetry relies upon description and evocative statement rather than upon the presentation of narrative events or the revelation of character.

Many of the varieties of lyric poetry have been discussed in previous chapters. The song, the elegy, the sonnet, as well as many additional subclassifications, have been defined according to their verse forms and their subject matter. The three lyric poems which follow show the continuing popularity and vigor of this form in English.

Anonymous (13th century)
The Cuckoo Song

Sing cuccu nu!° Sing cuccu!   *cuckoo now*
Sing cuccu! Sing cuccu nu!

Sumer is icumen in,
    Lhude° sing cuccu;   *loud*
Groweth sed° and bloweth med°   *seed / meadow blossoms* 5
    And springth the wude° nu.   *wood*
      Sing cuccu!
Awe bleteth after lomb,°   *ewe bleats after lamb*
    Lhouth after calve cu;°   *cow lows after calf*
Bulluc sterteth, bucke verteth;°   *bullock leaps, buck breaks wind* 10
    Murie sing° cuccu.   *merrily sing*
      Cuccu, cuccu,
    Wel singes thu,° cuccu,   *thou*
      Ne swik thu naver nu.°   *Cease thou never now*

Questions for Study

1. What is the basic attitude expressed toward the spring? What details convey this attitude?
2. What significance does the cuckoo have for the voice in the song? What associations does the cuckoo have for this voice?
3. What features of the organization of these lines shape and control the poem's meaning?

William Wordsworth (1770–1850)
My Heart Leaps Up

My heart leaps up when I behold
  A rainbow in the sky:
So was it when my life began;
So is it now I am a man;
So be it when I shall grow old.   5
  Or let me die!
The Child is father of the Man;
And I could wish my days to be
Bound each to each by natural piety.

Questions for Study

1. What is the subject of this poem? What are the details the poet uses in working out his subject?
2. Describe the tone of "My Heart Leaps Up."
3. Relate the proposition "The Child is father of the Man" to the theme of the poem.

John Crowe Ransom (1888–1974)
Blue Girls

Twirling your blue skirts, traveling the sward°   *sod*
Under the towers of your seminary,
Go listen to your teachers old and contrary
Without believing a word.

Tie the white fillets then about your lustrous hair   5
And think no more of what will come to pass
Than bluebirds that go walking on the grass
And chattering on the air.

Practice your beauty, blue girls, before it fail;
And I will cry with my loud lips and publish   10
Beauty which all our power shall never establish,
It is so frail.

For I could tell you a story which is true:
I know a lady with a terrible tongue,
Blear eyes fallen from blue,   15
All her perfections tarnished—and yet it is not long
Since she was lovelier than any of you.

Questions for Study

1. The scene here is one in which the speaker is musing about young ladies, dressed in blue outfits, casually indifferent to their education and to the significant issues of life. What is the speaker's attitude toward these "blue girls"? What specific details express the speaker's attitude?
2. One structural device of this poem consists of several contrasts. Identify these and relate them to the speaker's idea of "beauty."
3. In selecting several of his words, Ransom has a keen sense of their original or root meaning. He uses *publish* in its original sense of "making public" and *establish* in its logical sense of "making stable and bringing into balance." What are the meanings of the following words as Ransom uses them: *practice, travel, terrible, walk?*
4. Scan at least one stanza of this poem. Are Ransom's metrics regular or irregular?

Ted Hughes (b. 1930)
Secretary

If I should touch her she would shriek and weeping
Crawl off to nurse the terrible wound: all
Day like a starling under the bellies of bulls
She hurries among men, ducking, peeping,

Of in a whirl at the first move of a horn.   5
At dusk she scuttles down the gauntlet of lust
Like a clockwork mouse. Safe home at last
She mends socks with holes, shirts that are torn,

For father and brother, and a delicate supper cooks:
Goes to bed early, shuts out with the light   10
Her thirty years, and lies with buttocks tight,
Hiding her lovely eyes until day break.

Questions for Study

1. Here Hughes draws a portrait of a modern-day secretary. Is the description sympathetic, flattering, favorable? Explain your response, citing evidence from the poem to support your remarks.

2. What structural devices are evident in the poem? Attempt to characterize its organization.
3. Certain images seem highly significant for Hughes' meaning. Identify at least three and explain their function in the poem and their contribution to its meaning.

Alfred, Lord Tennyson   (1809–1892)
The Eagle

He clasps the crag with crooked hands;
Close to the sun in lonely lands,
Ringed with the azure world, he stands.

The wrinkled sea beneath him crawls;
He watches from his mountain walls,   5
And like a thunderbolt he falls.

Questions for Study

1. What is the scene depicted here? In fact, what two views of the eagle do you get? How does this shift in visual perspective contribute to Tennyson's description of the eagle?
2. What is the tone of "The Eagle"?
3. Try to describe the emotional qualities which this lyric expresses.

Theodore Roethke   (1908–1963)
I Knew a Woman

I knew a woman, lovely in her bones,
When small birds sighed, she would sigh back at them;
Ah, when she moved, she moved more ways than one:
The shapes a bright container can contain!
Of her choice virtues only gods should speak,   5
Or English poets who grew up on Greek
(I'd have them sing in chorus, cheek to cheek).

How well her wishes went! She stroked my chin,
She taught me Turn, and Counter-turn, and Stand;[1]
She taught me Touch, that undulant white skin;   10
I nibbled meekly from her proffered hand;
She was the sickle; I, poor I, the rake,
Coming behind her for her pretty sake
(But what prodigious mowing we did make).

Love likes a gander, and adores a goose: 15
Her full lips pursed, the errant note to seize;

---

1. Parts of a Pindaric ode.

She played it quick, she played it light and loose;
My eyes, they dazzled at her flowing knees;
Her several parts could keep a pure repose,
Or one hip quiver with a mobile nose   20
(She moved in circles, and those circles moved).

Let seed be grass, and grass turn into hay:
I'm martyr to a motion not my own;
What's freedom for? To know eternity.
I swear she cast a shadow white as stone.   25
But who would count eternity in days?
These old bones live to learn her wanton ways:
(I measure time by how a body sways).

Questions for Study

1. Describe the speaker's tone. Is it light, serious, humorous, sad? Support your
   answer with specific details from the poem.
2. Roethke's poem contains several instances of overstatement and understatement.
   Identify these and describe what effect these devices create.
3. "I Knew a Woman" is an **ode,** a poetic form which originated in ancient Greece as
   verse spoken aloud by a chorus and accompanied by music. Traditionally, the ode
   has treated dignified, serious themes within a complex metrical framework. How
   does Roethke adapt this form in conveying his meaning?
4. Scan the poem for its meter and rime scheme. Why does Roethke deal with the
   subject of motion and the process of change within such a formal structure?

Anonymous   (Scottish folk ballad)
Bonny Barbara Allan

It was in and about the Martinmas[1] time,
    When the green leaves were a falling,
That Sir John Graeme, in the West Country,
    Fell in love with Barbara Allan.

He sent his man down through the town,   5
    To the place where she was dwelling:
"O haste and come to my master dear,
    Gin° ye be Barbara Allan."   *if*

O hooly,° hooly rose she up,   *slowly*
    To the place where he was lying,   10
And when she drew the curtain by:
    "Young man, I think you're dying."

"O it's I'm sick, and very, very sick,
    And 'tis a' for Barbara Allan."

---
1. St. Martin's Day, November 11.

"O the better for me ye s'° never be,   *shall* 15
 Though your heart's blood were a-spilling.

"O dinna ye mind, young man," said she,
 "When ye was in the tavern a drinking,
That ye made the healths gae° round and round,   *toasts go*
 And slighted Barbara Allan?"   20

He turned his face unto the wall,
 And death was with him dealing:
"Adieu, adieu, my dear friends all,
 And be kind to Barbara Allan."

And slowly, slowly raise she up,   25
 And slowly, slowly left him,
And sighing said, she could not stay,
 Since death of life had reft° him.   *deprived*
She had not gane° a mile but twa,°   *gone / two*
 When she heard the dead-bell ringing,   30
And every jow° that the dead-bell geid,° *stroke / gave*
 It cry'd, Woe to Barbara Allan!

"O Mother, mother, make my bed!
 O make it saft° and narrow!   *soft*
Since my love died for me to-day,   35
 I'll die for him to-morrow."

Questions for Study

 1. This narrative poem has a rising action and a climax. Describe the climax of the action. Do we expect it? Is it justified by what we know from the poem?

 2. Is Barbara Allan kind or cruel? How do we discover her nature? At what point does she have a change of heart?

 3. Although the narrative manner is simple and direct, the action has its subtle aspects. What, for example, is the reason for the slighting of Barbara Allan when the drinking toasts were going around? Why does Sir John Graeme turn his face to the wall? What is the significance of the ringing of the bell? And why is the bed to be made "saft and narrow"?

 4. Like most folk ballads, "Bonny Barbara Allan" has other versions, some of which have additional stanzas. In the American adaptation, Sir John becomes a common citizen and the following two stanzas are added at the end:

   They buried Willie in the old churchyard
    And Barbara in the choir;
   And out of his grave grew a red, red rose,
    And out of hers a briar.

   They grew and grew to the steeple top
    Till they could grow no higher;
   And there they locked in a true love's knot,
    The red rose round the briar.

Are these stanzas effective as an ending? Are the sentiments expressed identical with those of the Scottish version? Why are the rose and the briar introduced into these lines?

Robert Hayden (b. 1913)
Frederick Douglass[1]

When it is finally ours, this freedom, this liberty, this beautiful
and terrible thing, needful to man as air,
usable as earth; when it belongs at last to all,
when it is truly instinct, brain matter, diastole, systole,
reflex action; when it is finally won; when it is more   5
than the gaudy mumbo jumbo of politicians:
this man, this Douglass, this former slave, this Negro
beaten to his knees, exiled, visioning a world
where none is lonely, none hunted, alien,
this man, superb in love and logic, this man   10
shall be remembered. Oh, not with statues' rhetoric,
not with legends and poems and wreaths of bronze alone,
but with the lives grown out of his life, the lives
fleshing his dream of the beautiful, needful thing.

Questions for Study

1. What is the attitude expressed here toward Douglass? In particular, what qualities of this nineteenth-century man are emphasized in this contemporary poem?
2. Vocabulary: *diastole, systole, mumbo jumbo, statues' rhetoric, wreaths of bronze.*
3. The structure of this poem uses syntactical and grammatical parallelisms for its organization. Identify several instances of these and comment briefly on how each works as a structuring element.
4. Hayden describes liberty as "this beautiful / and terrible thing." What other pointed references to liberty are there in the poem? From these, try to construct a definition of liberty as it is presented in the poem.

Frank Daniel (b. 1900)
Tom Tom

The piper's son was Tom, and aye,
Another Tom so featly° won   *adroitly*
By heart that he, too, is (I say)
      The piper's son.

---

1. Born a slave, Frederick Douglass (1817–1895) won his legal freedom when he was 29. An influential abolitionist orator, newspaper editor and publisher, and poet, Douglass came to believe that only a truly unified America of complete equality could guarantee the fact of liberty.

Impetuously, half in fun,   5
This son of Pan[1] would have his way
With me before the chase was run.

My heart is giddy-glad today,
And yet already I've begun
To wonder if a girl must pay   10
        The piper's son.

Questions for Study

  1. Describe the tone of this poem. Support your answer with examples.
  2. Interpret the final stanza. Is the speaker of the poem male or female?
  3. This poem draws upon a familiar nursery rhyme, the opening stanza of which
     reads:

     Tom, Tom, the Piper's son,
     Stole a pig, and away he run!
     The pig was eat, and Tom was beat,
     And Tom went roaring down the street.

     What possible relationship do you see between this nursery rhyme and Daniel's
     poem?

Carl Sandburg   (1878–1967)
Washerwoman

The washerwoman is a member of the Salvation Army.
And over the tub of suds rubbing underwear clean
She sings that Jesus will wash her sins away
And the red wrongs she has done God and man
Shall be white as driven snow.   5
Rubbing underwear she sings of the Last Great Washday.

Questions for Study

  1. What use does Sandburg make of the image of washing? How does he use colors in
     the poem? Are these effective? Explain.
  2. What is the speaker's attitude toward the washerwoman? Provide details from the
     poem in your answer.

---

    1. In Greek mythology, the god of pastures and fertility; he is often pictured as pursuing young
girls for amorous purposes.

Chapter 12
The Poem in Wider Perspective

In studying poetry, we cannot ask questions about the meaning of a poem without asking questions about its form. The poet and critic John Ciardi phrases the problem in this way: "How does a poem mean?" Ciardi is saying that in poetry form *and* meaning fuse in the completed work.

This concluding chapter focuses on three ambitious poems which try both to capture a larger moment of a particular historical era or culture and to see human existence within a definite social time and place. "The grand power of poetry," Matthew Arnold wrote, "is its interpretive power, by which I mean, not the power of drawing out in black and white an explanation of the mystery of the universe, but the power of so dealing with things as to awaken in us a wonderfully full, new and intimate sense of them." The larger, wider implications of poetry are clearly for Arnold its power to organize and intensify and thus to interpret the world in which men and women live. In this way, poetry extends human consciousness.

Challenging and exciting poems are often difficult to understand. Yet in studying them, we are compelled to examine their ideas and attitudes in terms of our own. In this process, our consciousness is thoroughly engaged and our close attention is required. Even if we fail to grasp everything contained or suggested in such works, the very fact of our serious involvement provides us with a valuable experience. We are likely, in fact, to understand more than we may realize at the time.

How then are we to approach a poem that is difficult in subject matter and complex in treatment? In concluding a study of certain basic forms and techniques of poetry, we need to bring the knowledge and the skills we have gained to any investigation of such a poem. Actually, the problem is still the one faced in reading and analyzing pieces in the other chapters—that of answering certain basic questions. In the first chapter, we outlined four "rules of thumb" for reading a poem: (1) read the poem several times; (2) read the poem aloud, if possible; (3) look for notable features and patterns; and (4) accurately determine the contents.

Keeping these points in mind, consider the following poem, the subject matter and form of which are difficult and elusive. It is also regarded as one of the most influential poems of the twentieth century.

T. S. Eliot (1888–1965)
The Love Song of J. Alfred Prufrock

S'io credesse che mia risposta fosse
A persona che mai tornasse al mondo,
Questa fiamma staria senza piu scosse.
Ma perciocche giammai di questo fondo
Non torno vivo alcun, s'i'odo il vero,
Senza tema d'infamia ti rispondo.[1]

Let us go then, you and I,
When the evening is spread out against the sky
Like a patient etherized upon a table;
Let us go, through certain half-deserted streets,
The muttering retreats   5
Of restless nights in one-night cheap hotels
And sawdust restaurants with oyster-shells:
Streets that follow like a tedious argument
Of insidious intent
To lead you to an overwhelming question . . .   10
Oh, do not ask, "What is it?"
Let us go and make our visit.

In the room the women come and go
Talking of Michelangelo.[2]

The yellow fog that rubs its back upon the window-panes,   15
The yellow smoke that rubs its muzzle on the window-panes
Licked its tongue into the corners of the evening,
Lingered upon the pools that stand in drains,

---

1. The epigraph is from Dante's *Inferno* (Canto 27, lines 61–66): "If I believed that my answer were to a person who could ever return to the world, this flame would quiver [i.e., 'I would speak'] no longer; but since, if what I hear is true, no one ever returned from this abyss, I answer you without fear of infamy." It is spoken to the poet by Guido da Montefeltro, who was promised absolution by Pope Boniface VIII but who died without repentance for telling the latter how to destroy the powerful Colonna family or Palestrina.
2. Michelangelo Buonarroti (1475–1564), Italian painter, sculptor, poet, and architect; alluded to here ironically to suggest superficial conversation about the arts.

Let fall upon its back the soot that falls from chimneys,
Slipped by the terrace, made a sudden leap, 20
And seeing that it was a soft October night,
Curled once about the house, and fell asleep.

    And indeed there will be time
For the yellow smoke[3] that slides along the street,
Rubbing its back upon the window-panes; 25
There will be time, there will be time
To prepare a face to meet the faces that you meet;
There will be time to murder and create,
And time for all the works and days[4] of hands
That lift and drop a question on your plate; 30
Time for you and time for me,
And time yet for a hundred indecisions,
And for a hundred visions and revisions,
Before the taking of a toast and tea.

    In the room the women come and go 35
Talking of Michelangelo.

    And indeed there will be time
To wonder, "Do I dare?" and, "Do I dare?"
Time to turn back and descend the stair,
With a bald spot in the middle of my hair— 40
(They will say: "How his hair is growing thin!")
My morning coat, my collar mounting firmly to the chin,
My necktie rich and modest, but asserted by a simple pin—
(They will say: "But how his arms and legs are thin!")
Do I dare 45
Disturb the universe?
In a minute there is time
For decisions and revisions which a minute will reverse.

    For I have known them all already, known them all:—
Have known the evenings, mornings, afternoons, 50
I have measured out my life with coffee spoons;
I know the voices dying with a dying fall[5]
Beneath the music from a farther room.
    So how should I presume?

    And I have known the eyes already, known them all— 55
The eyes that fix you in a formulated phrase,
And when I am formulated, sprawling on a pin,

---

    3. The extended image of yellow fog is a figure which the French symbolists associated with the ugly and unpleasant aspects of the city.
    4. Probably a literary allusion to *Works and Days* by Hesiod (8th century B.C.), a poem celebrating daily farm life and expressing numerous moral precepts and maxims.
    5. Shakespeare's *Twelfth Night* opens with the lines: "If music be the food of love, play on; / Give me excess of it, that, surfeiting / The appetite may sicken, and so die. / That strain again! it had a dying fall."

When I am pinned and wriggling on the wall,
Then how should I begin
To spit out all the butt-ends of my days and ways?   60
    And how should I presume?

    And I have known the arms already, known them all—
Arms that are braceleted and white and bare
(But in the lamplight, downed with light brown hair!)
Is it perfume from a dress   65
That makes me so digress?
Arms that lie along a table, or wrap about a shawl.
    And should I then presume?
    And how should I begin?

          . . . . .

Shall I say, I have gone at dusk through narrow streets   70
And watched the smoke that rises from the pipes
Of lonely men in shirt-sleeves, leaning out of windows? . . .

    I should have been a pair of ragged claws
Scuttling across the floors of silent seas.

          . . . . .

And the afternoon, the evening, sleeps so peacefully!   75
Smoothed by long fingers,
Asleep . . . tired . . . or it malingers,
Stretched on the floor, here beside you and me.
Should I, after tea and cakes and ices,
Have the strength to force the moment to its crisis?   80
But though I have wept and fasted, wept and prayed,
Though I have seen my head (grown slightly bald) brought in upon a
        platter,
I am no prophet[6]—and here's no great matter;
I have seen the moment of my greatness flicker,
And I have seen the eternal Footman hold my coat, and snicker,   85
And in short, I was afraid.

    And would it have been worth it, after all,
After the cups, the marmalade, the tea,
Among the porcelain, among some talk of you and me,
Would it have been worth while,   90
To have bitten off the matter with a smile,
To have squeezed the universe into a ball[7]
To roll it toward some overwhelming question,

---

6. At the request of Salome, King Herod had the prophet John the Baptist beheaded. Salome was then presented with the head on a silver dish (Matt. 14:3–11).
7. See the last six lines of Andrew Marvell's "To His Coy Mistress" (in "Poems for Further Study").

To say: "I am Lazarus,[8] come from the dead,
Come back to tell you all, I shall tell you all"—   95
If one, settling a pillow by her head,
    Should say: "That is not what I meant at all.
    That is not it, at all."

    And would it have been worth it, after all,
Would it have been worth while,   100
After the sunsets and the dooryards and the sprinkled streets,
After the novels, after the teacups, after the skirts that trail along the
    floor—
And this, and so much more?—
It is impossible to say just what I mean!
But as if a magic lantern[9] threw the nerves in patterns on a screen: 105
Would it have been worth while
If one, settling a pillow or throwing off a shawl,
And turning toward the window, should say:
    "That is not it at all,
    That is not what I meant, at all."   110

    . . . . .

No! I am not Prince Hamlet, nor was meant to be;
Am an attendant lord,[10] one that will do
To swell a progress,° start a scene or two,   *royal procession*
Advise the prince; no doubt, an easy tool,
Deferential, glad to be of use,   115
Politic, cautious, and meticulous;
Full of high sentence,[11] but a bit obtuse;
At times, indeed, almost ridiculous—
Almost, at times, the Fool.[12]

    I grow old . . . I grow old . . .   120
I shall wear the bottoms of my trousers rolled.

    Shall I part my hair behind? Do I dare to eat a peach?
I shall wear white flannel trousers, and walk upon the beach.
I have heard the mermaids singing, each to each.

    I do not think that they will sing to me.   125

---

    8. Either the Lazarus whom Christ raised from the dead (John 11:1–44) or the beggar Lazarus, who was not allowed to return to earth from heaven in order to warn the rich man's brothers of the torments of hell (Luke 16:19–31). Perhaps Eliot means to suggest both men.

    9. Early nonelectric device that projected images from a transparent slide.

    10. The noble and tragic hero of Shakespeare's *Hamlet.* In the next line, Prufrock considers himself "an attendant lord," suggesting Polonius, or even Rosencrantz or Guildenstern, other characters in the play.

    11. Geoffrey Chaucer, in the Prologue to his *Canterbury Tales* (l. 308), says that the speech of the scholarly Clerk of Oxford is terse and "full of high sentence" (weighty thoughts).

    12. In English Renaissance drama, the court "Fool" was a stock character who often knew and spoke the truth although few believed him.

I have seen them riding seaward on the waves
Combing the white hair of the waves blown back
When the wind blows the water white and black.

We have lingered in the chambers of the sea
By sea-girls wreathed with seaweed red and brown   130
Till human voices wake us, and we drown.[13]

Eliot's poem immediately presents several difficulties. To the inexperienced reader, many of the items alluded to are unfamiliar. And so several explanatory notes are needed that identify the principal allusions or refer to sources which will clarify them. Works like "Prufrock" require such notes because the poet has included materials which many readers simply cannot, or can no longer, be expected to know. Similarly, words such as *malingers, deferential,* or *meticulous* may be unfamiliar ones, and their meanings must be looked up in a dictionary. Another difficulty of Eliot's poem is that it seems at first a collection of disconnected statements and scenes. Yet several readings, including an oral one, should reveal recurring features of the poem's overall design and general meaning.

In spite of its variations in diction and tone, "The Love Song of J. Alfred Prufrock" is actually the utterance of a single speaker. Formally, the poem is a dramatic monolog, in which one person reveals certain things about himself to a listener in the work. Some critics have suggested that the poem is a **soliloquy,** a monolog delivered while the speaker is alone, seeing the "I" and the "you" as merely different aspects of the speaker. In either case, two features of the "I" soon become clear. First, because each part of the poem is an expression of the speaker, he provides the connection between all its diverse elements. Second, each part consists of either what he experiences—details of a scene, a conversation, an event—or what he himself is thinking. And occasionally his experiences and his thoughts blend so that it is difficult to distinguish between the two. Thus the shape and the direction of the poem emerge dramatically from what the "I" is saying. The effect of this technique resembles a stream of thoughts, impressions, sensations, associations, memories, and reflections.

A closer examination of the "I," whom we may identify with the J. Alfred Prufrock of the title, reveals the poem's subject matter and theme. Prufrock complains that his head is "grown slightly bald," and he worries about his age (see, for example, lines 41–44, 84–86, 120–121). Generalizations about his age can be made on the basis of some of his expressed interests. He is not likely younger than, say, twenty-five or

---

13. In Greek and Roman mythology, the Sirens lured men into caverns beneath the sea by their enchanting songs; when the songs ended, the men drowned.

thirty, and not older than about fifty. He definitely has women very much on his mind. In fact, the "you" he frequently addresses may be a woman who is either physically present or a product of his imagination.

The time is evening and the place is a large city such as the London Eliot was familiar with. Prufrock may be going to a social event and musing about it as he walks through "Streets that follow like a tedious argument / Of insidious intent." What we definitely know about him, however, is that he is obsessed with certain questions, yet unable either to ask these directly or to discover satisfactory answers to them. In the opening stanza, Prufrock invites the "you" to "make a visit," which he says will lead to "an overwhelming question." At this point he declines to identify or to characterize this question. Yet this invitation serves as the dramatic framework within which he recalls scenes and introduces subjects throughout the rest of the poem.

What then is this "overwhelming question" which Prufrock initially asks? It is never precisely expressed, and it may be that he himself is uncertain of its exact nature. Yet it can be associated with the subject matter he introduces: "The muttering retreats / Of restless nights in one-night cheap hotels / And sawdust restaurants with oyster-shells," women superficially talking of Michelangelo, women whose arms are "braceleted and white and bare," the sordid "yellow fog" of the working-class districts of a large city, the "lonely men in shirt-sleeves, leaning out of windows," and the endless socializing—"the taking of a toast and tea" during "the evenings, mornings, afternoons," the "tea and cakes and ices," and "the cups, the marmalade, the tea."

From these vivid, often brilliantly constructed images, specific contrasts emerge. First, a contrast is drawn between the city's working classes—the "lonely men in shirt-sleeves"—and the affluent upper classes—the women and their arty talk about Michelangelo. Prufrock certainly belongs to the latter group. As he recounts his wanderings through the "half-deserted streets" and city slums, however, he is very much concerned with this other world. Second, there is a marked contrast between Prufrock's mood and thoughts and the men and women with whom he seems constantly to be socializing. This contrast is established by the vivid and clear imagery. It depicts an external world of "evenings, mornings, afternoons," of "coffee spoons" and "marmalade" and "porcelain," and of "tea and cakes and ices." Contrasted with such scenes is the internal world of Prufrock's mind, a region best described as resembling "twilight" and filled with mazelike images, fears, anxieties, and doubts. His momentary wish to become "a pair of ragged claws / Scuttling across the floors of silent seas" hardly suggests a man living contentedly in a fashionable world.

J. Alfred Prufrock, then, comes to a difficult, crucial moment. Obsessed with his "visit" and his "overwhelming question"—a question that clearly is much more than a limited, personal one—he struggles to identify, organize, and then to act upon what he truly feels and senses he must do. Throughout the poem, however, his nagging doubts haunt him. Can he frame the precise question, ask it, and make himself understood? Can he communicate with those around him, people who are his friends and associates? And so how is he to "presume" upon them by forcing the question and involving them in it?

Near the end of the poem (lines 111–119) Prufrock's inner resolve collapses. He gives up his efforts to phrase and ask his all-important question. In the remaining lines, he rationalizes that he himself is not heroic ("not Prince Hamlet") but merely an attendant (as are Polonius, or Rosencrantz and Guildenstern), finally perhaps only a "Fool" (a literal one and also a court jester or clown). The concluding images of the poem capture the terms of his personal failure, rendering brilliantly Prufrock's likely fate. Unable to assert and thus to renew himself, he will enter "the chambers of the sea" and drown. That is, he will be drawn back into the "human" sterility of the world he inhabits and perish amid its chatter and meaninglessness. His attempts to assert himself are over and he sinks into a state resembling despair.

An examination of Prufrock leads to a consideration of the poem's theme and overall meaning. Obviously, both are contained in the figure of Prufrock, in his self-dramatization, and in the implications of the "overwhelming question" he proposes to ask. And some informed guesses can be made at this point about the question and its relationship to Prufrock and to the meaning of the work. Prufrock believes that the question, when framed and asked, is likely to "disturb the universe." Furthermore, allusions to religious figures such as John the Baptist and to either one or both of the Lazaruses suggest momentous issues hovering around Prufrock. Similarly, the work of Dante, Michelangelo, and Shakespeare offer dominant contrasts to the triviality and the mindlessness of Prufrock's world. The sustained irony of Prufrock's intelligent and perceptive, but indecisive, statements further sharpens the focus on the implicit issues clustering around this question. Whatever it is, its implications concern self-assertiveness versus timidity, a life authentically lived versus one mired in inconclusive acts and thoughts, and a society vital and creative versus one aimless and purposeless. Although Prufrock cannot phrase or ask his "overwhelming question," the poem itself suggests that it would involve the deepest elements of his life and the lives of those around him.

Through allusions and imagery, and the working out of scenes and descriptions, the poem depicts urban life in this century as harsh, sterile, and anxiety-ridden. Traditional religious and historical figures suggest by implication the absence of any redeeming, creative beliefs and values. The pervading tone of the poem is somber, even melancholic. The world of Prufrock suggests twilight and the etherized conditions of the hospital—images with which the poem opens. But if he recognizes his own situation, Prufrock also understands that many individuals, both rich and poor, are like him. Whether or not they are also like him in being unable to ask or to confront the "overwhelming question," Eliot's poem never says.

"The Love Song of J. Alfred Prufrock" presents numerous additional facets which could be explored profitably: the ironic implications of love; the use of historical, mythological, and literary materials; its patterns of images; its sustained irony; its metrics. Also relevant to a discussion of the poem is Eliot's idea that a serious poet works within a tradition, from which his work takes its meaning and relative significance. Although offering numerous insights into the poem, however, an examination of these and other elements would not serve the immediate purpose of this chapter. Rather than providing a comprehensive and exhaustive analysis, this discussion has only attempted to suggest some of the wider implications of this important poem.

The following poem, although far shorter, is probably even more difficult and elusive than Eliot's. It too should be read closely and carefully in terms of its form and meaning. The discussion that follows it provides general suggestions about how one might approach the poem, rather than an in-depth treatment of all its complex elements.

William Butler Yeats (1865–1939)
Sailing to Byzantium[1]

That[2] is no country for old men. The young
In one another's arms, birds in the trees,
—Those dying generations—at their song,
The salmon-falls, the mackerel-crowded seas,
Fish, flesh, or fowl, commend all summer long   5
Whatever is begotten, born, and dies.
Caught in that sensual music all neglect
Monuments of unaging intellect.

An aged man is but a paltry thing,
A tattered coat upon a stick, unless   10
Soul clap its hands and sing,[3] and louder sing
For every tatter in its mortal dress,
Nor is there singing school but° studying   *except for*

---

1. Ancient city in Asia Minor, later named Constantinople and today known as Istanbul. From the fourth century until 1453, it was the capital of the Roman Empire and then of Christendom. It was famous for its arts and crafts, as well as for its ornate mosaics and the stylized facades of its buildings. To Yeats, Byzantium was a symbol of the spiritual perfection achieved by great art, of timelessness, and of escape from the decay of the physical world.
2. Ireland, which Yeats associated with the physical world and its sensuous longings.
3. Perhaps an allusion to the English poet William Blake, who envisioned his dead brother's soul "clapping his hands for joy" as it ascended to heaven.

Monuments of its own magnificence;
And therefore I have sailed the seas and come   15
To the holy city of Byzantium.

O sages standing in God's holy fire
As in the gold mosaic of a wall,[4]
Come from the holy fire, perne in a gyre,[5]
And be the singing-masters of my soul.   20
Consume my heart away, sick with desire
And fastened to a dying animal
It knows not what it is; and gather me
Into the artifice of eternity.

Once out of nature I shall never take   25
My bodily form from any natural thing.
But such a form as Grecian goldsmiths make
Of hammered gold and gold enamelling
To keep a drowsy Emperor awake;[6]
Or set upon a golden bough[7] to sing   30
To lords and ladies of Byzantium
Of what is past, or passing, or to come.

"Sailing to Byzantium" is a complex poem. It operates on various
levels and develops more than one thematic concern. One useful way of
approaching it, however, is to recognize and examine the central symbol, Byzantium, and a less prominent one, Ireland. In addition to mentioning Byzantium by name in the title and in lines 16 and 31, Yeats
indirectly alludes to it by referring to the mosaic adornments in the
cathedral of St. Sophia which depict the figures of saints (lines 17–18),
and to the golden bough and bird in the last stanza. Although Yeats
never mentions Ireland by name, we may infer from statements in the
opening stanza that he has his native land in mind. The possibility also
exists that, on another level, he is suggesting life in general, with its
cycle of "Whatever is begotten, born, and dies."

An initial recognition of Byzantium and Ireland as symbols should
then lead to an understanding of how each functions in the poem.
Furthermore we should explore how the two are contrasted with one
another and what this contrast signifies and implies.

---

4. I.e., the sages in the holy fire look like figures in a gold mosaic.

5. "Perne" suggests the winding and unwinding of a thread on a bobbin or spool. The figure
indicates a whirling down in a spiral motion, with the result that the soul merges with its motion as
eternity pervades history and nature. Specifically, Yeats here requests the sages to spin down to his
time.

6. Yeats' note to this line reads: "I have read somewhere that in the Emperor's palace at
Byzantium was a tree made of gold and silver, and artificial birds that sang."

7. A familiar image (and symbol) in literature and in numerous mythologies. For example, in Book
VI of the *Aeneid*, Aeneas is told by the sybil that if he intends to descend into the underworld, he must
pluck a golden bough from a tree. When it is taken, however, an identical one appears in its place.

One useful approach to these two symbols is an examination of the images which cluster around each. Ireland, for example, is associated with "The young / In one another's arms, birds in the trees" and with "The salmon-falls, the mackerel-crowded seas"; Byzantium, with "sages standing in God's holy fire" and with "such a form as Grecian goldsmiths make / Of hammered gold and gold enamelling." Images not only define and enrich Yeats' associations with Byzantium and Ireland but they also establish relationships between what the speaker knows and what he can imagine—between the actual and the ideal. Here we need also to identify other images and to describe briefly how these are used. For instance, what is suggested by "Those dying generations," and how does this image contrast with "Monuments of unaging intellect"? Yeats uses the word *monuments* twice. What does it mean? Are its connotations in the poem good, bad, or mixed? Similarly, what is the relationship between the "birds in the trees" in the first stanza and the golden bird in the last? Finally, is there a connection, a parallel, between "Whatever is begotten, born, and dies" and the bird's singing "Of what is past, or passing, or to come"? Answering such questions should clarify Yeats' two symbols and his pattern of images. It should also suggest other thematic aspects of the poem.

Yeats' imagery, in fact, establishes a sharp contrast between natural, sensuous forms and those of a timeless, perfected order. One statement of the theme of the poem might be the speaker's desire for perfection and eternity—for immortality. The images the speaker uses to describe himself—"An aged man," "a paltry thing, / A tattered coat upon a stick," "fastened to a dying animal"—suggest the decay of the physical body. He prefers to be "out of nature" and given such "bodily form . . . as Grecian goldsmiths make / Of hammered gold and gold enamelling"—that is, to be given a form which is artistically whole, beautiful, and imperishable. At this point, we might ask several important questions. What is the relationship between Byzantium / Ireland and the speaker in the poem? In what ways does he identify with both? In what ways does he prefer the one to the other?

Yeats' poem is also concerned with the role of poetry and the poet. To Yeats, the poet is the master "singer" whose only true school is the "singing school." We need to look closely at this metaphor of singer and singing. How precisely does the figure relate to Byzantium and Ireland? Similarly, does the poem suggest that, because a great poem is a "monument" of the soul's "magnificence," a great poet achieves immortality through his work? What other qualities does Yeats associate with a poet and his art? Why, for instance, is an invocation to the "sages" in line 18 introduced?

In addition to these concerns and questions, we could explore many other facets of this poem. One might, for example, examine what many people consider to be its near-perfect integration of image and idea, symbol and thought. Similarly, we need to determine the metrical pattern and identify the dominant foot and line length. How does Yeats vary the stanzaic pattern? What, for instance, is the effect of the couplets which end each stanza?

Although other features of the poem offer opportunities for study and comment, it can be said here that "Sailing to Byzantium" is at once a remarkable statement and a very personal poem. Yeats wrote it in his early sixties, conscious of his advancing age. He confessed that he hated to grow old, and he knew full well that "An aged man is but a paltry thing." Does this poem present an alternative to growing old? In this connection, W. H. Auden once said that Yeats was "lying" in the poem because no one could possibly want to be a mechanical bird. Was Auden right, or are there additional significant implications in the figure of the golden bird on the golden bough which Auden did not take into account?

The final selection is Auden's tribute to Yeats. Let us keep Auden's remarks in mind when reading it.

W. H. Auden   (1907–1973)
In Memory of W. B. Yeats
(d. Jan. 1939)

I

He disappeared in the dead of winter:[1]
The brooks were frozen, the airports almost deserted,
And snow disfigured the public statues;
The mercury sank in the mouth of the dying day.
What instruments we have agree   5
The day of his death was a dark cold day.

Far from his illness
The wolves ran on through the evergreen forests,
The peasant river was untempted by the fashionable quays;
By mourning tongues   10
The death of the poet was kept from his poems.

But for him it was his last afternoon as himself,
An afternoon of nurses and rumors;
The provinces of his body revolted,
The squares of his mind were empty,   15
Silence invaded the suburbs,
The current of his feeling failed; he became his admirers.

---

1. Yeats died in southern France on January 28, 1939.

Now he is scattered among a hundred cities
And wholly given over to unfamiliar affections,
To find his happiness in another kind of wood[2]   20
And be punished under a foreign code of conscience.[3]
The words of a dead man
Are modified in the guts of the living.

But in the importance and noise of tomorrow
When the brokers are roaring like beasts on the floor of the Bourse,[4]   25
And the poor have the sufferings to which they are fairly accustomed,
And each in the cell of himself is almost convinced of his freedom,
A few thousand will think of this day
As one thinks of a day when one did something slightly unusual.
What instruments we have agree   30
The day of his death was a dark cold day.

                    II

            You were silly like us; your gift survived it all:
            The parish of rich women,[5] physical decay,
            Yourself. Mad Ireland hurt you into poetry.
            Now Ireland has her madness and her weather still,   35
            For poetry makes nothing happen: it survives
            In the valley of its making where executives
            Would never want to tamper, flows on south
            From ranches of isolation and the busy griefs,
            Raw towns that we believe and die in; it survives,   40
            A way of happening, a mouth.

                    III

            Earth, receive an honored guest:
            William Yeats is laid to rest.
            Let the Irish vessel lie
            Emptied of its poetry.   45

            Time[6] that is intolerant
            Of the brave and innocent,
            And indifferent in a week
            To a beautiful physique,

---

   2. An allusion to the opening of Dante's *Inferno,* where the speaker is alone in the middle of his life "in a dark wood."
   3. I.e., Yeats is now to be judged by the living.
   4. The Paris stock exchange.
   5. An allusion to the fact that in his early years, and extending even into his later life, Yeats counted wealthy women among his patrons.
   6. This and the next two stanzas were deleted from Auden's 1966 edition of his *Collected Poems.* They are retained here for examination and perhaps for speculative interest as to why they were omitted.

Worships language and forgives   50
Everyone by whom it lives;
Pardons cowardice, conceit,
Lays its honours at their feet.

Time that with this strange excuse
Pardoned Kipling and his views,   55
And will pardon Paul Claudel,[7]
Pardons him for writing well.[8]

In the nightmare of the dark
All the dogs of Europe bark,[9]
And the living nations wait,   60
Each sequestered in its hate;

Intellectual disgrace
Stares from every human face,
And the seas of pity lie
Locked and frozen in each eye.   65

Follow, poet, follow right
To the bottom of the night,
With your unconstraining voice
Still persuade us to rejoice;

With the farming of a verse   70
Make a vineyard of the curse,
Sing of human unsuccess
In a rapture of distress;

In the deserts of the heart
Let the healing fountain start,   75
In the prison of his days
Teach the free man how to praise.

Many of the initial difficulties of this ambitious poem are clarified by
the poet's arrangement of it into three parts and by the sustained presence of his voice in the verse. In the first section, Auden employs
winter to symbolize the loss of the famous Irish poet and to suggest the
situation in Europe at the opening of World War II. European civilization, the poem suggests, is also in the "winter" or dying phase of its life.
Section II distinguishes between Yeats the poet and Yeats the man and,

---

7. Many people, including Auden, were hostile to the imperialistic sentiments of Rudyard Kipling
(1865–1936), British poet and fiction writer, and to the extreme political conservatism of Paul Louis
Charles Claudel (1868–1955), French author and diplomat.
8. Auden also looked with disfavor on Yeats' frequently antidemocratic politics.
9. World War II was to begin in September 1939.

at the same time, praises the art of poetry, identified as "a way of happening, a mouth," that speaks to all mankind. The third section employs traditional English quatrains in a kind of deliberate cadence or, better, a meter familiarly used in many nursery rhymes. The tone here is elegaic, but the diction is somewhat direct and even colloquial.

Metrics are especially important in Auden's poem. He employs in fact three different metrical patterns, one for each of the three sections. Examine and describe the pattern of each section and comment upon the relationship between the form and the content of each section. Which form is the most successful in expressing the thought? Which form is the least successful?

Like "Sailing to Byzantium," this poem is also concerned with poetry and with the role of the poet. Study closely the lines in section II which proclaim that

> . . . poetry makes nothing happen: it survives
> In the valley of its making where executives
> Would never want to tamper . . . .

What is the poem suggesting as the role or the function of poetry? There are other places in the poem in which the subject of poetry is mentioned. Identify these and also interpret what the poem says about poetry, the poet, and the significance of both.

Auden once said that there were two principal questions he liked to ask when first reading a poem: "(1) Here is a verbal contraption, how does it work? and; (2) What kind of a guy inhabits this poem?" We too are interested in these two questions. They deal with technique and with the intellectual—perhaps with what we should term the psychological—dimension of a poem. After examining certain technical characteristics of his poem, perhaps we ought to turn Auden's second question back on him and simply ask "What kind of a guy inhabits this poem"?

"Sailing to Byzantium" contains both a particular, personal view and a general, universal application. Well-crafted poems often achieve these dimensions. How then would you characterize "In Memory of W. B. Yeats"? Identify its personal and its universal implications. Finally, determine which poem, in your opinion, is the more successful one, Auden's or Yeats'.

Poems for Further Study

Geoffrey Chaucer (1340?–1400)
Gentilesse

The firste fader and findere° of gentilesse,	*founder*
What° man desireth gentil for to be	*whatever*
Moste folwe his traas,° and alle his wittes dresse°	*path / direct*
Vertu to sue,° and vices for to flee:	*follow*
For unto vertu longeth dignitee,°	*belongs honor* 5
And nought the revers, saufly° dar I deeme,	*safely*
Al were he° mitre, crowne, or diademe.	*Although he wears*
This firste stok was ground of rightwisnesse,°	*righteousness*
Trewe of his word, sobre, pietous,° and free,°	*merciful / generous*
Clene of his gost,° and loved bisinesse	*pure in spirit* 10
Against the vice of slouthe,° in honestee;	*sloth*
And but° his heir love vertu as dide he,	*unless*
He is nat gentil, though he riche° seeme,	*noble*
Al were he mitre, crowne, or diademe.	
Vice may wel be heir to old richesse,	15
But ther may no man, as ye may wel see,	
Biquethe his heir his vertuous noblesse:	
That is appropred° unto no degree	*assigned*
But to the firste fader in majestee,	
That maketh his heir him that wol him queme,°	*please* 20
Al were he mitre, crowne, or diademe.	

Geoffrey Chaucer (1340?–1400)
Lak of Stedfastnesse

Balade[1]

Sometyme the world was so stedfast and stable
That mannes word was obligacioun;
And now it is so fals and deceivable
That word and deed, as in conclusioun,
Ben nothing lyk, for turned up-so-doun   5
Is al this world for mede° and wilfulnesse,   *gain*
That al is lost for lak of stedfastnesse.

What maketh this world to be so variable
But lust° that folk have in dissensioun?   *desire*
For among us now a man is holde unable,   10
But if he can, by som collusioun,
Don his neighbour wrong or oppressioun.
What causeth this but wilful wrecchednesse,
That al is lost for lak of stedfastnesse?

Trouthe is put doun, resoun is holden fable;°   *false* 15
Vertu hath now no dominacioun;
Pitee exyled, no man is merciable;
Through covetyse is blent° discrecioun.   *blended*
The world hath mad a permutacioun
Fro right to wrong, fro trouthe to fikelnesse,   20
That al is lost for lak of stedfastnesse.

Lenvoy to King Richard[2]

O prince, desyre to be honourable,
Cherish thy folk and hate extorcioun!
Suffre nothing that may be reprevable°   *deserving of reproof*
To thyn estat don in thy regioun.   25
Shew forth thy swerd of castigacioun,
Dred God, do law, love trouthe and worthinesse,
And wed thy folk agein to stedfastnesse.

Sir Thomas Wyatt (1503–1542)
My Galley Chargéd with Forgetfulness

My galley chargéd with forgetfulness[1]
Thorough sharp seas, in winter nights doth pass

---

1. The *ballade* is an old French verse form that usually consists of three stanzas and an *envoy,* a fourth stanza directly addressed to an important personage.
2. Richard II (1367–1400), king of England whose reign was beset by internal strife and rebellion.

1. I.e., my ship is so loaded with love that all else is forgotten.

'Tween rock and rock; and eke mine° enemy, alas,   *also my*
That is my lord,[2] steereth with cruelness.
And every oar a thought in readiness,   5
As though that death were light in such a case.
An endless wind doth tear the sail apace
Of forcéd sighs and trusty fearfulness.
A rain of tears, a cloud of dark disdain,
Hath done the wearied cords great hinderance,   10
Wreathéd with error and eke with ignorance.
The stars be hid that led me to this pain,
Drownéd is reason that should me consort,°   *accompany*
And I remain despairing of the port.

Sir Thomas Wyatt (1503–1542)
They Flee from Me

They flee from me that sometime did me seek
   With naked foot, stalking in my chamber.
I have seen them gentle, tame, and meek,
   That now are wild, and do not remember
   That sometime they did put themselves in danger   5
To take bread at my hand; and now they range
Busily seeking with a continual change.

Thankèd be fortune, it hath been otherwise
   Twenty times better; but once in special,
In thin array, after a pleasant guise,   10
   When her loose gown from her shoulders did fall
   And she me caught in her arms long and small°   *slender*
Therewith all sweetly did me kiss
And softly said, "Dear heart how like you this?"

It was no dream; I lay broad waking: 15
   But all is turned, thorough° my gentleness,   *through*
Into a strange fashion of forsaking;
   And I have leave to go of her goodness,
   And she also to use newfangleness.°   *fashionable novelty*
But since that I so kindely° am served,   *in a way natural to women* 20
I would fain° know what she hath deserved.   *eagerly*

Michael Drayton (1563–1631)
Since There's No Help

Since there's no help, come, let us kiss and part.
Nay, I have done; you get no more of me.

---

2. Love is both his "enemy" and his "lord."

And I am glad, yea, glad with all my heart
That thus so cleanly I myself can free.
Shake hands for ever; cancel all our vows;   5
And when we meet at any time again,
Be it not seen in either of our brows
That we one jot of former love retain.
Now at the last gasp of Love's latest breath,
When, his pulse failing, Passion speechless lies,   10
When Faith is kneeling by his bed of death,
And Innocence is closing up his eyes—
   Now, if thou wouldst, when all have given him over,
   From death to life thou might'st him yet recover.

Christopher Marlowe   (1564–1593)
The Passionate Shepherd to His Love

Come live with me and be my love,
And we will all the pleasures prove,°   *experience*
That valleys, groves, hills and fields,
Woods or steepy mountain yields.

And we will sit upon the rocks,   5
Seeing the shepherds feed their flocks
By shallow rivers, to whose falls
Melodious birds sing madrigals.

And I will make thee beds of roses,
And a thousand fragrant posies,   10
A cap of flowers and a kirtle°   *skirt*
Embroidered all with leaves of myrtle;

A gown made of the finest wool,
Which from our pretty lambs we pull;
Fair-linèd slippers for the cold,   15
With buckles of the purest gold;

A belt of straw and ivy buds,
With coral clasps and amber studs;
And if these pleasures may thee move,
Come live with me and be my love.   20

The shepherd swains° shall dance and sing   *attendants*
For thy delight each May morning;
If these delights thy mind may move,
Then live with me and be my love.

William Shakespeare (1564–1616)
How Like a Winter Hath My Absence Been

How like a winter hath my absence been
From thee, the pleasure of the fleeting year!
What freezings have I felt, what dark days seen!
What old December's bareness every where!
And yet this time remov'd° was summer's time,   *absence* 5
The teeming autumn, big with rich increase,
Bearing the wanton burthen° of the prime,°   *plentiful crops / spring*
Like widow'd wombs after their lords' decease:
Yet this abundant issue seem'd to me
But hope of orphans and unfathered fruit;   10
For summer and his pleasures wait on thee,
And, thou away, the very birds are mute;
    Or, if they sing, 'tis with so dull a cheer
    That leaves look pale, dreading the winter's near.

William Shakespeare (1564–1616)
When I Have Seen by Time's Fell Hand Defaced

When I have seen by Time's fell° hand defaced   *cruel*
The rich proud cost of outworn buried age;
When sometime lofty towers I see down-razed
And brass eternal slave to mortal rage;
When I have seen the hungry ocean gain   5
Advantage on the kingdom of the shore,
And the firm soil win of the wat'ry main,
Increasing store° with loss and loss with store;   *abundance*
When I have seen such interchange of state,°   *condition*
Or state° itself confounded to decay;   *grandeur* 10
Ruin hath taught me thus to ruminate,
That Time will come and take my love away.
    This thought is as a death, which cannot choose
    But weep to have° that which it fears to lose.   *because now it has*

John Donne (1572–1631)
The Good-Morrow

I wonder, by my troth,° what thou and I   *word*
Did, till we loved? Were we not weaned till then,
But sucked on country pleasures, childishly?
Or snorted° we in the seven sleepers' den?[1]   *snored*

---

1. According to legend, seven Christian youths escaped Roman persecution by hiding in a cave,
where they slept for 187 years.

'Twas so; But° this, all pleasures fancies be.   *Except for* 5
If ever any beauty I did see,
Which I desired, and got, 'twas but a dream of thee.

And now good morrow to our waking souls,
Which watch not one another out of fear;
For love all love of other sights controls,   10
And makes one little room an everywhere.
Let sea-discoverers to new worlds have gone,
Let maps to other,° worlds on worlds have shown,   *others*
Let us possess one world; each hath one, and is one.

My face in thine eye, thine in mine appears,[2]   15
And true plain hearts do in the faces rest;
Where can we find two better hemispheres
Without sharp North, without declining West?
Whatever dies was not mixed equally;[3]
If our two loves be one, or thou and I   20
Love so alike that none do slacken, none can die.

John Donne (1572–1631)
A Valediction:[1] Forbidding Mourning

As virtuous men pass mildly away,
    And whisper to their souls to go,
Whilst some of their sad friends do say,
    "The breath goes now," and some say, "No":

So let us melt, and make no noise,   5
    No tear-floods nor sigh-tempests move;
'Twere profanation of our joys
    To tell the laity our love.

Moving of the earth° brings harms and fears;   *earthquake*
    Men reckon what it did, and meant;   10
But trepidation of the spheres,
    Though greater far, is innocent.[2]

Dull sublunary[3] lovers' love
    —Whose soul is sense—cannot admit

---

2. The images of the lovers are reflected in one another's eyes.
3. A theory of the time held that elements which were improperly mixed resulted in matter that was changeable and mortal.

1. A Farewell.
2. In Ptolemaic astronomy, any variation ("trepidation") in the circular motion of the nine spheres surrounding the earth, although of great magnitude, was considered harmless ("innocent") to the earth.
3. Beneath the moon; therefore mundane and mutable.

Absence, because it doth remove   15
   Those things which elemented° it.   *composed*

But we by a love so far refined
   That ourselves know not what it is,
Inter-assurèd of the mind,
   Care less eyes, lips, and hands to miss.   20

Our two souls therefore, which are one,
   Though I must go, endure not yet
A breach, but an expansion,
   Like gold to airy thinness beat.

If they be two, they are two so   25
   As stiff twin compasses are two;
Thy soul, the fixed foot, makes no show
   To move, but doth if the other do.[4]

And though it in the center sit,
   Yet, when the other far doth roam,   30
It leans, and hearkens after it,
   And grows erect as that comes home.

Such wilt thou be to me, who must,
   Like the other foot, obliquely run;
Thy firmness makes my circle just,°   *perfect* 35
   And makes me end where I begun.

Ben Jonson   (1572?–1637)
On My First Son

Farewell, thou child of my right hand,[1] and joy;
My sin was too much hope of thee, loved boy:
Seven years thou'wert lent to me, and I thee pay,
Exacted by thy fate, on the just° day.   *exact*
O could I lose all father[2] now! for why   5
Will man lament the state he should envý,
To have so soon 'scaped world's and flesh's rage,
And, if no other misery, yet age?
Rest in soft peace, and asked, say, "Here doth lie
Ben Jonson his best piece of poetry."   10
For whose sake henceforth all his vows be such
As what he loves may never like too much.

---

4. See p. 512 for a discussion of this complex figure.

1. Jonson's son, who died on his seventh birthday, was named Benjamin, which in Hebrew means "child of the right hand."
2. I.e., all thoughts of acting like a father.

Ben Jonson (1572?–1637)
Though I Am Young and Cannot Tell

Though I am young, and cannot tell
  Either what Death or Love is well,
Yet I have heard they both bear darts,
  And both do aim at human hearts.
And then again, I have been told   5
  Love wounds with heat, as Death with cold;
So that I fear they do but bring
  Extremes to touch, and mean one thing.

As in a ruin we it call
  One thing to be blown up, or fall;   10
Or to our end like way may have
  By a flash of lightning, or a wave;
So Love's inflaméd shaft or brand
  May kill as soon as Death's cold hand;
Except Love's fires the virtue have   15
  To fright the frost out of the grave.

George Herbert (1593–1633)
Redemption

Having been tenant long to a rich Lord,
  Not thriving, I resolved to be bold,
  And make a suit° unto him, to afford   *legal appeal*
A new small-rented lease, and cancel th' old.

In heaven at his manor I him sought: 5
  They told me there, that he was lately gone
  About some land, which he had dearly bought
Long since on earth, to take possession.

I straight returned, and knowing his great birth,
  Sought him accordingly in great resorts;   10
  In cities, theaters, gardens, parks and courts:
At length I heard a ragged noise and mirth

  Of thieves and murderers: there° I him espied,   *at the Crucifixion*
  Who straight, *Your suit is granted,* said, and died.

Andrew Marvell (1621–1678)
To His Coy Mistress

  Had we but world enough, and time,
This coyness,° lady, were no crime.   *modesty*

We would sit down, and think which way
To walk, and pass our long love's day.
Thou by the Indian Ganges' side   5
Should'st rubies find: I by the tide
Of Humber[1] would complain.° I would   *sing sad love songs*
Love you ten years before the Flood,
And you should, if you please, refuse
Till the conversion of the Jews.[2]   10
My vegetable° love should grow   *slow-growing*
Vaster than empires, and more slow.
An hundred years should go to praise
Thine eyes, and on thy forehead gaze:
Two hundred to adore each breast: 15
But thirty thousand to the rest;
An age at least to every part,
And the last age should show your heart.
For, lady, you deserve this state,
Nor would I love at lower rate.   20
    But at my back I always hear
Time's wingéd chariot hurrying near:
And yonder all before us lie
Deserts of vast eternity.
Thy beauty shall no more be found;   25
Nor, in thy marble vault, shall sound
My echoing song: then worms shall try
That long-preserved virginity,
And your quaint honor turn to dust,
And into ashes all my lust.   30
The grave's a fine and private place,
But none, I think, do there embrace.
    Now, therefore, while the youthful hue
Sits on thy skin like morning dew,
And while thy willing soul transpires°   *gives forth* 35
At every pore with instant fires,
Now let us sport us while we may;
And now, like amorous birds of prey,
Rather at once our Time devour,
Than languish in his slow-chapt° power.   *slow-jawed*   40
Let us roll all our strength and all
Our sweetness up into one ball,
And tear our pleasures with rough strife
Thorough° the iron gates of life.   *Through*
Thus, though we cannot make our Sun   45
Stand still, yet we will make him run.

---

    1. A small river that flows through Marvell's hometown of Hull; it is contrasted with the exotic and holy Ganges River of India.
    2. An event that, according to a popular belief of the time, will occur just before the end of the world.

Jonathan Swift (1667–1745)
A Description of a City Shower

Careful observers may foretell the hour
(By sure prognostics) when to dread a shower:
While rain depends,° the pensive cat gives o'er   *threatens*
Her frolics, and pursues her tail no more.
Returning home at night, you'll find the sink°   *sewer* 5
Strike your offended sense with double stink.
If you be wise, then go not far to dine;
You'll spend in coach hire more than save in wine.
A coming shower your shooting corns presage,
Old achés throb, your hollow tooth will rage.   10
Sauntering in coffeehouse is Dulman seen;
He damns the climate and complains of spleen.°   *melancholy*
   Meanwhile the South, rising with dabbled wings,
A sable cloud athwart the welkin° flings,   *across the sky*
That swilled more liquor than it could contain,   15
And, like a drunkard, gives it up again.
Brisk Susan whips her linen from the rope,
While the first drizzling shower is borne aslope:
Such is that sprinkling which some careless quean°   *wench*
Flirts on you from her mop, but not so clean: 20
You fly, invoke the gods; then turning, stop
To rail; she singing, still whirls on her mop.
Not yet the dust had shunned the unequal strife,
But, aided by the wind, fought still for life,
And wafted with its foe by violent gust,   25
'Twas doubtful which was rain and which was dust.
Ah! where must needy poet seek for aid,
When dust and rain at once his coat invade?
Sole coat, where dust cemented by the rain
Erects the nap, and leaves a mingled stain.   30
   Now in contiguous drops the flood comes down,
Threatening with deluge this devoted town.
To shops in crowds the daggled° females fly,   *wet and muddy*
Pretend to cheapen° goods, but nothing buy.   *bargain for*
The Templar¹ spruce, while every spout's abroach,°   *spewing water* 35
Stays till 'tis fair, yet seems to call a coach.
The tucked-up sempstress walks with hasty strides,
While streams run down her oiled umbrella's sides.
Here various kinds, by various fortunes led,
Commence acquaintance underneath a shed.   40
Triumphant Tories and desponding Whigs
Forget their feuds,² and join to save their wigs.

---

1. A law student.
2. At the time (1710), the Tory party had just gained control of the government from the Whigs.

Boxed in a chair[3] the beau impatient sits,
While spouts run clattering o'er the roof by fits,
And ever and anon with frightful din   45
The leather sounds; he trembles from within.
So when Troy chairmen bore the wooden steed,
Pregnant with Greeks impatient to be freed[4]
(Those bully Greeks, who, as the moderns do,
Instead of paying chairmen, run them through°),   *stab them* 50
Laocoön struck the outside with his spear,
And each imprisoned hero quaked for fear.
　　Now from all parts the swelling kennels° flow,   *gutters*
And bear their trophies with them as they go:
Filth of all hues and odors seem to tell   55
What street they sailed from, by their sight and smell.
They, as each torrent drives with rapid force,
From Smithfield or St. Pulchre's[5] shape their course,
And in huge confluence joined at Snow Hill ridge,
Fall from the conduit prone to Holborn Bridge.   60
Sweepings from butchers' stalls, dung, guts, and blood,
Drowned puppies, stinking sprats,° all drenched in mud, *small herrings*
Dead cats, and turnip tops, come tumbling down the flood.

Jonathan Swift (1667–1745)
On Stella's Birthday

Stella this day is thirty-four,[1]
(We won't dispute a year or more:)
However, Stella, be not troubled,
Although thy size and years are doubled
Since first I saw thee at sixteen,   5
The brightest virgin on the green;
So little is thy form declined,
Made up so largely in thy mind.
　　O, would it please the gods to split
Thy beauty, size, and years, and wit,   10
No age could furnish out a pair
Of nymphs so graceful, wise, and fair;
With half the lustre of your eyes,
With half your wit, your years, and size.

---

3. A portable and enclosed chair carried by two men; its roof was made of leather.
　　4. In the Trojan War of classical mythology, the Greeks built a huge hollow wooden horse in which a small group of soldiers was hidden. After the Greeks persuaded the Trojans to take the horse into Troy as a gift, the concealed soldiers crept out, opened the gates to the main Greek force, and overwhelmed the city. In emphasizing his warning to the Trojans not to accept the horse, Laocoön struck its side with a spear (lines 51–52).
　　5. The church of St. Sepulchre. Smithfield, Snow Hill, and Holborn Bridge were all within London's city limits.

1. Hester Johnson, for whom the poem was written, was in fact thirty-eight at the time.

And then, before it grew too late, 15
How should I beg of gentle fate,
(That either nymph might have her swain,°) *suitor*
To split my worship too in twain.

Thomas Gray (1716–1771)
Elegy Written in a Country Churchyard

The curfew[1] tolls the knell of parting day,
    The lowing herd wind slowly o'er the lea,° *meadow*
The plowman homeward plods his weary way,
    And leaves the world to darkness and to me.

Now fades the glimmering landscape on the sight, 5
    And all the air a solemn stillness holds,
Save where the beetle wheels his droning flight,
    And drowsy tinklings lull the distant folds;

Save that from yonder ivy-mantled tower
    The moping owl does to the moon complain 10
Of such, as wand'ring near her secret bower,
    Molest her ancient solitary reign.

Beneath those rugged elms, that yew tree's shade,
    Where heaves the turf in many a mold'ring heap,
Each in his narrow cell forever laid, 15
    The rude° forefathers of the hamlet sleep. *uneducated; simple*

The breezy call of incense-breathing morn,
    The swallow twittering from the straw-built shed,
The cock's shrill clarion, or the echoing horn,° *hunter's horn*
    No more shall rouse them from their lowly bed. 20

For them no more the blazing hearth shall burn,
    Or busy housewife ply her evening care;
No children run to lisp their sire's return,
    Or climb his knees the envied kiss to share.

Oft did the harvest to their sickle yield, 25
    Their furrow oft the stubborn glebe° has broke; *sod*
How jocund did they drive their team afield!
    How bowed the woods beneath their sturdy stroke!

Let not Ambition mock their useful toil,
    Their homely joys, and destiny obscure; 30

---

1. The practice of ringing a bell in the evening to signal the end of the workday.

Nor Grandeur hear with a disdainful smile
    The short and simple annals of the poor.

The boast of heraldry,° the pomp of power,   *noble ancestors*
    And all that beauty, all that wealth e'er gave,
Awaits alike the inevitable hour.   35
    The paths of glory lead but to the grave.

Nor you, ye proud, impute to these the fault,
    If Memory o'er their tomb no trophies° raise,   *memorial ornamentation*
Where through the long-drawn aisle and fretted° vault   *decorated*
    The pealing anthem swells the note of praise.   40

Can storied° urn or animated° bust   *inscribed with epitaphs / lifelike*
    Back to its mansion call the fleeting breath?
Can Honor's voice provoke° the silent dust,   *call forth*
    Or Flattery soothe the dull cold ear of Death?

Perhaps in this neglected spot is laid   45
    Some heart once pregnant with celestial fire;
Hands that the rod of empire might have swayed,
    Or waked to ecstasy the living lyre.

But Knowledge to their eyes her ample page
    Rich with the spoils of time did ne'er unroll;   50
Chill Penury repressed their noble rage,°   *fervor*
    And froze the genial current of the soul.

Full many a gem of purest ray serene,
    The dark unfathomed caves of ocean bear:
Full many a flower is born to blush unseen,   55
    And waste its sweetness on the desert air.

Some village Hampden,[2] that with dauntless breast
    The little tyrant of his fields withstood;
Some mute inglorious Milton here may rest,
    Some Cromwell[3] guiltless of his country's blood.   60

Th' applause of listening senates to command,
    The threats of pain and ruin to despise,
To scatter plenty o'er a smiling land,
    And read their history in a nation's eyes

Their lot forbade: nor circumscribed alone   65
    Their growing virtues, but their crimes confined;

---

2. John Hampden (1594–1643) was a leader of the public opposition to the taxation policies of Charles I of England.

3. After figuring prominently in the insurrection against Charles I, Oliver Cromwell (1599–1658) became Lord Protector of the Commonwealth, the regime that was established after the dissolution of the monarchy. John Milton (1608–1674), English poet, defended the Commonwealth in many of his writings.

Forbade to wade through slaughter to a throne,
    And shut the gates of mercy on mankind,

The struggling pangs of conscious truth to hide,
    To quench the blushes of ingenuous shame,   70
Or heap the shrine of Luxury and Pride
    With incense kindled at the Muse's flame.

Far from the madding° crowd's ignoble strife,   *tumultuous*
    Their sober wishes never learned to stray;
Along the cool sequestered° vale of life   *secluded* 75
    They kept the noiseless tenor° of their way.   *course*

Yet ev'n these bones from insult to protect
    Some frail memorial still erected nigh,
With uncouth° rhymes and shapeless sculpture decked,   *unpolished*
    Implores the passing tribute of a sigh.   80

Their name, their years, spelt by th' unlettered Muse,
    The place of fame and elegy supply:
And many a holy text around she strews,
    That teach the rustic moralist to die.

For who to dumb Forgetfulness a prey,   85
    This pleasing anxious being e'er resigned,
Left the warm precincts of the cheerful day,
    Nor cast one longing lingering look behind?

On some fond breast the parting soul relies,
    Some pious drops the closing eye requires;   90
Ev'n from the tomb the voice of Nature cries,
    Ev'n in our ashes live their wonted° fires.   *customary*

For thee, who mindful of the unhonored dead
    Dost in these lines their artless tale relate;
If chance, by lonely contemplation led,   95
    Some kindred spirit shall inquire thy fate,

Haply some hoary-headed swain° may say,   *gray-haired peasant*
    "Oft have we seen him at the peep of dawn
Brushing with hasty steps the dews away
    To meet the sun upon the upland lawn.   100

"There at the foot of yonder nodding beech
    That wreathes its old fantastic roots so high,
His listless length at noontide would he stretch.
    And pore upon the brook that babbles by.

"Hard by yon wood, now smiling as in scorn,   105
    Mutt'ring his wayward fancies he would rove,

Now drooping, woeful wan, like one forlorn,
    Or crazed with care, or crossed in hopeless love.

"One morn I missed him on the customed hill,
    Along the heath and near his favorite tree;
Another came; nor yet beside the rill,   110
    Nor up the lawn, nor at the wood was he;

"The next with dirges due in sad array
    Slow through the churchway path we saw him borne.
Approach and read (for thou canst read) the lay,   115
    Graved on the stone beneath yon aged thorn."

The Epitaph

Here rests his head upon the lap of Earth
    A youth to Fortune and to Fame unknown,
Fair Science° frowned not on his humble birth,   *Learning*
    And Melancholy marked him for her own.   120

Large was his bounty, and his soul sincere,
    Heaven did a recompense as largely send:
He gave to Misery all he had, a tear,
    He gained from Heaven ('twas all he wished) a friend.

No farther seek his merits to disclose,   125
    Or draw his frailties from their dread abode
(There they alike in trembling hope repose),
    The bosom of his Father and his God.

William Blake   (1757–1827)
The Tyger

Tyger! Tyger! burning bright
In the forests of the night,
What immortal hand or eye
Could frame thy fearful symmetry?

In what distant deeps or skies   5
Burnt the fire of thine eyes?
On what wings dare he aspire?
What the hand dare seize the fire?

And what shoulder, and what art,
Could twist the sinews of thy heart?   10
And when thy heart began to beat,
What dread hand? and what dread feet?

What the hammer? what the chain?
In what furnace was thy brain?
What the anvil? what dread grasp   15
Dare its deadly terrors clasp?

When the stars threw down their spears,
And watered heaven with their tears,
Did he smile his work to see?
Did he who made the Lamb make thee?   20

Tyger! Tyger! burning bright
In the forests of the night,
What immortal hand or eye,
Dare frame thy fearful symmetry?

William Wordsworth (1770–1850)
Composed upon Westminster Bridge

Earth has not anything to show more fair:
Dull would he be of soul who could pass by
A sight so touching in its majesty:
This City now doth like a garment wear
The beauty of the morning; silent, bare,   5
Ships, towers, domes, theaters, and temples lie
Open unto the fields, and to the sky;
All bright and glittering in the smokeless air.
Never did sun more beautifully steep
In his first splendor valley, rock, or hill;   10
Ne'er saw I, never felt, a calm so deep!
The river glideth at his own sweet will:
Dear God! the very houses seem asleep;
And all that mighty heart is lying still!

William Wordsworth (1770–1850)
Lucy Gray
or Solitude

Oft I had heard of Lucy Gray:
And, when I crossed the wild,
I chanced to see at break of day
The solitary child.

No mate, no comrade Lucy knew;   5
She dwelt on a wide moor,
—The sweetest thing that ever grew
Beside a human door!

You yet may spy the fawn at play,
The hare upon the green;   10
But the sweet face of Lucy Gray
Will never more be seen.

"Tonight will be a stormy night—
You to the town must go;
And take a lantern, Child, to light   15
Your mother through the snow."

"That, Father! will I gladly do:
'Tis scarcely afternoon—
The minster° clock has just struck two,   *church*
And yonder is the moon!"   20

At this the Father raised his hook,
And snapped a faggot band;[1]
He plied his work—and Lucy took
The lantern in her hand.

Not blither° is the mountain roe;   *merrier* 25
With many a wanton stroke
Her feet disperse the powdery snow,
That rises up like smoke.

The storm came on before its time;
She wandered up and down;   30
And many a hill did Lucy climb,
But never reached the town.

The wretched parents all that night
Went shouting far and wide;
But there was neither sound nor sight   35
To serve them for a guide.

At daybreak on a hill they stood
That overlooked the moor;
And thence they saw the bridge of wood,
A furlong° from their door.   *one eighth of a mile* 40

They wept—and, turning homeward, cried,
"In heaven we all shall meet";
—When in the snow the mother spied
The print of Lucy's feet.

Then downwards from the steep hill's edge   45
They tracked the footmarks small;

---

1. A cord binding a bundle of sticks ("faggot").

And through the broken hawthorn hedge,
And by the long stone wall;

And then an open field they crossed:
The marks were still the same;   50
They tracked them on, nor ever lost;
And to the bridge they came.

They followed from the snowy bank
Those footmarks, one by one,
Into the middle of the plank;   55
And further there were none!

—Yet some maintain that to this day
She is a living child;
That you may see sweet Lucy Gray   60
Upon the lonesome wild.

O'er rough and smooth she trips along,
And never looks behind;
And sings a solitary song
That whistles in the wind.

John Keats   (1795–1821)
Ode to a Nightingale

I

My heart aches, and a drowsy numbness pains
   My sense, as though of hemlock° I had drunk,   *a poisonous drug*
Or emptied some dull opiate to the drains
   One minute past, and Lethe-wards[1] had sunk:
'Tis not through envy of thy happy lot,   5
   But being too happy in thine happiness—
      That thou, light-wingéd Dryad° of the trees,   *nymph*
        In some melodious plot
   Of beechen green, and shadows numberless,
      Singest of summer in full-throated ease.   10

II

O, for a draught of vintage! that hath been
   Cooled a long age in the deep-delvéd earth,
Tasting of Flora[2] and the country green,

---

1. In Greek mythology, Lethe is the river of forgetfulness in Hades.
2. Roman goddess of flowers.

Dance, and Provençal song,³ and sunburnt mirth!
O for a beaker full of the warm South,   15
    Full of the true, the blushful Hippocrene,⁴
        With beaded bubbles winking at the brim,
            And purple-stainéd mouth;
    That I might drink, and leave the world unseen,
        And with thee fade away into the forest dim: 20

III

Fade far away, dissolve, and quite forget
    What thou among the leaves hast never known,
The weariness, the fever, and the fret
    Here, where men sit and hear each other groan;
Where palsy shakes a few, sad, last gray hairs,   25
    Where youth grows pale, and specter-thin, and dies;
        Where but to think is to be full of sorrow
            And leaden-eyed despairs,
    Where Beauty cannot keep her lustrous eyes,
        Or new Love pine at them beyond tomorrow.   30

IV

Away! away! for I will fly to thee,
    Not charioted by Bacchus and his pards,⁵
But on the viewless° wings of Poesy,   *invisible*
    Though the dull brain perplexes and retards:
Already with thee! tender is the night,   35
    And haply the Queen-Moon is on her throne,
        Clustered around by all her starry Fays;°   *Fairies*
            But here there is no light,
    Save what from heaven is with the breezes blown
        Through verdurous glooms and winding mossy ways.   40

V

I cannot see what flowers are at my feet,
    Nor what soft incense hangs upon the boughs,
But, in embalméd° darkness, guess each sweet   *fragrant*
    Wherewith the seasonable month endows
The grass, the thicket, and the fruit tree wild;   45
    White hawthorn, and the pastoral eglantine;
        Fast fading violets covered up in leaves;
            And mid-May's eldest child,
    The coming musk-rose, full of dewy wine,
        The murmurous haunt of flies on summer eves.   50

---

3. Provence, in southern France, was famous for the love songs written and sung by its medieval troubadours.
    4. In Greek mythology, the fountain on Mount Helicon whose waters were a source of poetic inspiration.
    5. Bacchus, the Roman god of wine, was sometimes depicted riding in a chariot pulled by leopards ("pards").

VI

Darkling° I listen; and for many a time   *in darkness*
 I have been half in love with easeful Death,
Called him soft names in many a muséd° rhyme,   *meditative*
 To take into the air my quiet breath;
Now more than ever seems it rich to die,   55
 To cease upon the midnight with no pain,
  While thou art pouring forth thy soul abroad
   In such an ecstasy!
 Still wouldst thou sing, and I have ears in vain—
  To thy high requiem become a sod.   60

VII

Thou wast not born for death, immortal Bird!
 No hungry generations tread thee down;
The voice I hear this passing night was heard
 In ancient days by emperor and clown:
Perhaps the selfsame song that found a path   65
 Through the sad heart of Ruth,[6] when, sick for home,
  She stood in tears amid the alien corn;°   *wheat*
   The same that ofttimes hath
 Charmed magic casements, opening on the foam
  Of perilous seas, in faery lands forlorn.   70

VIII

Forlorn! the very word is like a bell
 To toll me back from thee to my sole self!
Adieu! the fancy cannot cheat so well
 As she is famed to do, deceiving elf.
Adieu! adieu! thy plaintive anthem fades   75
 Past the near meadows, over the still stream,
  Up the hillside; and now 'tis buried deep
   In the next valley-glades:
 Was it a vision, or a waking dream?
  Fled is that music:—Do I wake or sleep?   80

John Keats (1795–1821)
To Autumn

I

Season of mists and mellow fruitfulness,
 Close bosom-friend of the maturing sun;
Conspiring with him how to load and bless
 With fruit the vines that round the thatch-eaves run;

---

6. In the Bible, the widow Ruth of Moab faithfully labored in the wheat fields of Bethlehem and was subsequently rewarded with marriage to Boaz.

To bend with apples the mossed cottage-trees,   5
   And fill all fruit with ripeness to the core;
     To swell the gourd, and plump the hazel shells
With a sweet kernel; to set budding more,
   And still more, later flowers for the bees,
   Until they think warm days will never cease,   10
     For summer has o'er-brimmed their clammy cells.

II

Who hath not seen thee oft amid thy store?
   Sometimes whoever seeks abroad may find
Thee sitting careless on a granary floor,
   Thy hair soft-lifted by the winnowing wind;   15
Or on a half-reaped furrow sound asleep,
   Drowsed with the fume of poppies, while thy hook°   *scythe*
     Spares the next swath and all its twined flowers:
And sometime like a gleaner° thou dost keep   *reaper*
   Steady thy laden head across a brook;   20
   Or by a cider-press, with patient look,
     Thou watchest the last oozings hours by hours.

III

Where are the songs of Spring? Ay, where are they?
   Think not of them, thou hast thy music too—
While barred clouds bloom the soft-dying day,   25
   And touch the stubble-plains with rosy hue;
Then in a wailful choir the small gnats mourn
   Among the river sallows,° borne aloft   *willows*
     Or sinking as the light wind lives or dies;
And full-grown lambs loud bleat from hilly bourn;°   *field* 30
   Hedge-crickets sing; and now with treble soft
   The red-breast whistles from a garden-croft;°   *enclosed garden*
     And gathering swallows twitter in the skies.

Alfred, Lord Tennyson   (1809–1892)
Ulysses[1]

   It little profits that an idle king,
By this still hearth, among these barren crags,
Matched with an aged wife, I mete and dole
Unequal laws unto a savage race,
That hoard, and sleep, and feed, and know not me.   5
   I cannot rest from travel; I will drink

---

1. Also called Odysseus, Ulysses was one of the Greek heroes of the Trojan War; after a ten-year voyage filled with adventure, he returned to rule his island kingdom. His exploits are recounted in Homer's *Odyssey*, but his characterization here is based on that in Dante's *Inferno*, Canto XXVI.

Life to the lees.° All times I have enjoyed   *dregs*
Greatly, have suffered greatly, both with those
That loved me, and alone; on shore, and when
Through scudding drifts the rainy Hyades[2]   10
Vexed the dim sea. I am become a name;
For always roaming with a hungry heart
Much have I seen and known—cities of men
And manners, climates, councils, governments,
Myself not least, but honored of them all—   15
And drunk delight of battle with my peers,
Far on the ringing plains of windy Troy.
I am a part of all that I have met;
Yet all experience is an arch wherethrough
Gleams that untraveled world, whose margin fades   20
For ever and for ever when I move.
How dull it is to pause, to make an end,
To rust unburnished, not to shine in use!
As though to breathe were life. Life piled on life
Were all too little, and of one to me   25
Little remains; but every hour is saved
From that eternal silence, something more,
A bringer of new things; and vile it were
For some three suns to store and hoard myself,
And this gray spirit yearning in desire   30
To follow knowledge like a sinking star,
Beyond the utmost bound of human thought.
　　　This is my son, mine own Telemachus,
To whom I leave the scepter and the isle—
Well-loved of me, discerning to fulfill   35
This labor by slow prudence to make mild
A rugged people, and through soft degrees
Subdue them to the useful and the good.
Most blameless is he, centered in the sphere
Of common duties, decent not to fail   40
In offices of tenderness, and pay
Meet adoration to my household gods,
When I am gone. He works his work, I mine.
　　　There lies the port; the vessel puffs her sail:
There gloom the dark, broad seas. My mariners,   45
Souls that have toiled, and wrought, and thought with me—
That ever with a frolic welcome took
The thunder and the sunshine, and opposed
Free hearts, free foreheads—you and I are old;
Old age hath yet his honor and his toil.   50
Death closes all; but something ere the end,
Some work of noble note, may yet be done,

---

2. A group of stars whose simultaneous rising with the sun was thought to signal the coming of rain.

Not unbecoming men that strove with Gods.
The lights begin to twinkle from the rocks;
The long day wanes; the slow moon climbs; the deep   55
Moans round with many voices. Come, my friends.
'Tis not too late to seek a newer world.
Push off, and sitting well in order smite
The sounding furrows; for my purpose holds
To sail beyond the sunset, and the baths   60
Of all the western stars, until I die.
It may be that the gulfs will wash us down;[3]
It may be we shall touch the Happy Isles,[4]
And see the great Achilles, whom we knew.
Though much is taken, much abides; and though   65
We are not now that strength which in old days
Moved earth and heaven, that which we are, we are:
One equal temper of heroic hearts,
Made weak by time and fate, but strong in will
To strive, to seek, to find, and not to yield.   70

Matthew Arnold   (1822–1888)
Dover Beach[1]

The sea is calm to-night.
The tide is full, the moon lies fair
Upon the straits;—on the French coast the light
Gleams and is gone; the cliffs of England stand,
Glimmering and vast, out in the tranquil bay.   5
Come to the window, sweet is the night-air!
Only, from the long line of spray
Where the sea meets the moon-blanched land,
Listen! you hear the grating roar
Of pebbles which the waves draw back, and fling,   10
At their return, up the high strand,
Begin, and cease, and then again begin,
With tremulous cadence slow, and bring
The eternal note of sadness in.

Sophocles[2] long ago   15
Heard it on the Ægean, and it brought
Into his mind the turbid ebb and flow
Of human misery; we

---

3. It was believed that the world was surrounded by an ocean which carried ships over its edge.
4. Elysium, or the Islands of the Blessed, where heroes such as Achilles, slain in the Trojan War, were thought to lead a blissful afterlife.

1. Point on the southeast coast of England lying closest to France, about twenty miles away.
2. Greek tragic dramatist of the fifth century B.C. The indirect allusion in these lines is to his *Antigone*, Ode II, lines 1–9.

Find also in the sound a thought,
Hearing it by this distant northern sea.   20
The Sea of Faith
Was once, too, at the full, and round earth's shore
Lay like the folds of a bright girdle furled.
But now I only hear
Its melancholy, long, withdrawing roar,   25
Retreating, to the breath
Of the night-wind, down the vast edges drear
And naked shingles° of the world.   *pebble-covered beaches*

Ah, love, let us be true
To one another! for the world, which seems   30
To lie before us like a land of dreams,
So various, so beautiful, so new,
Hath really neither joy, nor love, nor light,
Nor certitude, nor peace, nor help for pain;
And we are here as on a darkling plain   35
Swept with confused alarms of struggle and flight,
Where ignorant armies clash by night.

George Meredith   (1828–1909)
from *Modern Love:* Sonnet 48

Their sense is with their senses all mixed in,
Destroyed by subtleties these women are!
More brain, O Lord, more brain! or we shall mar
Utterly this fair garden we might win.
Behold! I looked for peace, and thought it near.   5
Our inmost hearts had opened, each to each
We drank the pure daylight of honest speech.
Alas! that was the fatal draft, I fear.
For when of my lost Lady came the word,
This woman, O this agony of flesh!   10
Jealous devotion bade her break the mesh,
That I might seek that other like a bird.
I do adore the nobleness! despise
The act! She has gone forth, I know not where.
Will the hard world my sentience of her share?   15
I feel the truth; so let the world surmise.

Emily Dickinson   (1830–1886)
After Great Pain, a Formal Feeling Comes

After great pain, a formal feeling comes—
The Nerves sit ceremonious, like Tombs—

The stiff Heart questions was it He, that bore,
And Yesterday, or Centuries before?

The Feet, mechanical, go round—   5
Of Ground, or Air, or Ought°—   *nothing*
A Wooden way
Regardless grown,
A Quartz contentment, like a stone—

This is the Hour of Lead—   10
Remembered, if outlived,
As Freezing Persons recollect the Snow—
First—Chill—then Stupor—then the letting go—

Emily Dickinson   (1830–1886)
I Heard a Fly Buzz—When I Died

I heard a Fly buzz—when I died—
The Stillness in the Room
Was like the Stillness in the Air—
Between the Heaves of Storm—

The Eyes around—had wrung them dry—   5
And Breaths were gathering firm
For that last Onset—when the King
Be witnessed—in the Room—

I willed my Keepsakes—Signed away
What portion of me be   10
Assignable—and then it was
There interposed a Fly—

With Blue—uncertain stumbling Buzz—
Between the light—and me—
And then the Windows failed—and then   15
I could not see to see—

Emily Dickinson   (1830–1886)
I Never Saw a Moor

I never saw a Moor,
I never saw the Sea;
Yet know I how the Heather looks,
And what a Billow be.

I never spoke with God,   5
Nor visited in Heaven;

Yet certain am I of the spot
As if the Checks were given.

Emily Dickinson   (1830–1886)
My Life Had Stood—a Loaded Gun

My Life had stood—a Loaded Gun—
In Corners—till a Day
The Owner passed—identified—
And carried Me away—

And now We roam the Sovereign Woods—   5
And now We hunt the Doe—
And every time I speak for Him
The Mountains straight reply—

And do I smile, such cordial light
Upon the Valley glow—   10
It is as a Vesuvian[1] face
Had let its pleasure through—

And when at Night—Our good Day done—
I guard My Master's Head—
'Tis better than the Eider-Duck's   15
Deep Pillow—to have shared—

To foe of His—I'm deadly foe—
None stir the second time—
On whom I lay a Yellow Eye°—   *i.e., the "eye" of the gun barrel*
Or an emphatic Thumb—   20

Though I than He—may longer live
He longer must—than I—
For I have but the power to kill,
Without—the power to die—

Emily Dickinson   (1830–1886)
The Soul Selects Her Own Society

The Soul selects her own Society—
Then—shuts the Door—
To her divine Majority—
Present no more—

---

1. Vesuvius is a volcano in southern Italy.

Unmoved—she notes the Chariots—pausing—   5
At her low Gate—
Unmoved—an Emperor be kneeling
Upon her Mat—

I've known her—from an ample nation—
Choose One—   10
Then—close the Valves of her attention—
Like Stone—

Gerard Manley Hopkins   (1844–1889)
No Worst, There Is None

No worst, there is none. Pitched past pitch of grief,
More pangs will, schooled at forepangs, wilder wring.
Comforter, where, where is your comforting?
Mary, mother of us, where is your relief?
My cries heave, herds-long;[1] huddle in a main, a chief   5
Woe, world-sorrow; on an age-old anvil wince and sing—
Then lull, then leave off. Fury had shrieked "No ling-
ering! Let me be fell:° force° I must be brief."   *cruel / perforce (by necessity)*

   O the mind, mind has mountains; cliffs of fall
Frightful, sheer, no-man-fathomed. Hold them cheap   10
May who ne'er hung there. Nor does long our small
Durance° deal with that steep or deep. Here! creep,   *endurance*
Wretch, under a comfort serves in a whirlwind: all
Life death does end and each day dies with sleep.

Gerard Manley Hopkins   (1844–1889)
Pied[1] Beauty

Glory be to God for dappled things—
   For skies of couple-colour as a brinded° cow;   *streaked*
     For rose-moles all in stipple° upon trout that swim;   *spots*
Fresh-firecoal chestnut-falls;[2] finches' wings;
   Landscape plotted and pieced—fold, fallow,[3] and plough;   5
     And áll trádes, their gear and tackle and trim.°   *equipment*

All things counter,° original, spare, strange;   *in opposition; contrasting*
   Whatever is fickle, freckled (who knows how?)

---

1. Like herds of cattle.

1. Multicolored.
2. Fallen chestnuts as red as fresh-burning coals.
3. A fold is an enclosed piece of land; a fallow is a ploughed field left unplanted for a year.

With swift, slow; sweet, sour; adazzle, dim;
He fathers-forth whose beauty is past change: 10
        Praise him.

A. E. Housman   (1859–1936)
Loveliest of Trees

Loveliest of trees, the cherry now
Is hung with bloom along the bough,
And stands about the woodland ride
Wearing white for Eastertide.

Now, of my threescore years and ten,   5
Twenty will not come again,
And take from seventy springs a score,
It only leaves me fifty more.

And since to look at things in bloom
Fifty springs are little room,   10
About the woodlands I will go
To see the cherry hung with snow.

A. E. Housman   (1859–1936)
Terence, This Is Stupid Stuff

  "Terence, this is stupid stuff:
You eat your victuals fast enough;
There can't be much amiss, 'tis clear,
To see the rate you drink your beer.
But oh, good Lord, the verse you make,   5
It gives a chap the belly-ache.
The cow, the old cow, she is dead;
It sleeps well, the horned head:
We poor lads, 'tis our turn now
To hear such tunes as killed the cow.   10
Pretty friendship 'tis to rhyme
Your friends to death before their time
Moping melancholy mad:
Come, pipe a tune to dance to, lad."

  Why, if 'tis dancing you would be,   15
There's brisker pipes than poetry.
Say, for what were hop-yards meant,
Or why was Burton[1] built on Trent?

---

1. Burton-on-Trent is a town in England known for its breweries, many of whose owners became peers (members of the nobility).

Oh many a peer of England brews
Livelier liquor than the Muse,   20
And malt does more than Milton can
To justify God's ways to man.[2]
Ale, man, ale's the stuff to drink
For fellows whom it hurts to think:
Look into the pewter pot   25
To see the world as the world's not.
And faith, 'tis pleasant till 'tis past:
The mischief is that 'twill not last.
Oh I have been to Ludlow[3] fair
And left my necktie God knows where,   30
And carried half-way home, or near,
Pints and quarts of Ludlow beer:
Then the world seemed none so bad,
And I myself a sterling lad;
And down in lovely muck I've lain,   35
Happy till I woke again.
Then I saw the morning sky:
Heigho, the tale was all a lie;
The world, it was the old world yet,
I was I, my things were wet,   40
And nothing now remained to do
But begin the game anew.

Therefore, since the world has still
Much good, but much less good than ill,
And while the sun and moon endure   45
Luck's a chance, but trouble's sure,
I'd face it as a wise man would,
And train for ill and not for good.
'Tis true, the stuff I bring for sale
Is not so brisk a brew as ale: 50
Out of a stem that scored° the hand   *cut*
I wrung it in a weary land.
But take it: if the smack is sour,
The better for the embittered hour;
It should do good to heart and head   55
When your soul is in my soul's stead;°   *place*
And I will friend you, if I may,
In the dark and cloudy day.

There was a king reigned in the East:
There, when kings will sit to feast,   60
They get their fill before they think

---

2. English poet John Milton said that his purpose in writing *Paradise Lost* was to "justify the ways of God to man."
3. A town in Shropshire known for its commercial markets.

With poisoned meat and poisoned drink:
He gathered all that springs to birth
From the many-venomed earth;
First a little, thence to more,   65
He sampled all her killing store;
And easy, smiling, seasoned sound,
Sate the king when healths° went round.   *toasts*
They put arsenic in his meat
And stared aghast to watch him eat;   70
They poured strychnine in his cup
And shook to see him drink it up:
They shook, they stared as white's their shirt:
Them it was their poison hurt.
—I tell the tale that I heard told.   75
Mithridates,[4] he died old.

Rudyard Kipling (1865–1936)
Danny Deever

"What are the bugles blowin' for?" said Files-on-Parade.[1]
"To turn you out, to turn you out," the Color-Sergeant[2] said.
"What makes you look so white, so white?" said Files-on-Parade.
"I'm dreadin' what I've got to watch," the Color-Sergeant said.
    For they're hangin' Danny Deever, you can hear the Dead March play,   5
    The regiment's in 'ollow square[3]—they're hangin' him today;
    They've taken of his buttons off an' cut his stripes away,
    An' they're hangin' Danny Deever in the mornin'.

"What makes the rear rank breathe so 'ard?" said Files-on-Parade.
"It's bitter cold, it's bitter cold," the Color-Sergeant said.   10
"What makes that front-rank man fall down?" said Files-on-Parade.
"A touch o' sun, a touch o' sun," the Color-Sergeant said.
    They are hangin' Danny Deever, they are marchin' of 'im round,
    They 'ave 'alted Danny Deever by 'is coffin on the ground;
    An' 'e'll swing in 'arf a minute for a sneakin' shootin' hound—   15
    O they're hangin' Danny Deever in the mornin'!

" 'Is cot was right-'and cot to mine," said Files-on-Parade.
" 'E's sleepin' out an' far tonight," the Color-Sergeant said.
"I've drunk 'is beer a score o' times," said Files-on-Parade.
" 'E's drinkin' bitter beer alone," the Color-Sergeant said.   20

---

4. Mithridates VI (133?–63 B.C.), King of Pontus in Asia Minor, was said to have developed an immunity to poison by taking gradually stronger doses.

1. Soldier assigned to close up the files or ranks.
2. Noncommissioned officer who carried the regimental colors.
3. The soldiers form the four sides of a square, a formation used on ceremonial occasions.

They are hangin' Danny Deever, you must mark 'im to 'is place,
For 'e shot a comrade sleepin'—you must look 'im in the face;
Nine 'undred of 'is county an' the Regiment's disgrace,
While they're hangin' Danny Deever in the mornin'.

"What's that so black agin the sun?" said Files-on-Parade.   25
"It's Danny fightin' 'ard for life," the Color-Sergeant said.
"What's that that whimpers over'ead?" said Files-on-Parade.
"It's Danny's soul that's passin' now," the Color-Sergeant said.
    For they're done with Danny Deever, you can 'ear the quickstep[4] play,
    The regiment's in column, an' they're marchin' us away;   30
    Ho! the young recruits are shakin', an' they'll want their beer today,
    After hangin' Danny Deever in the mornin'.

William Butler Yeats (1865–1939)
Long-Legged Fly

That civilisation may not sink,
Its great battle lost,
Quiet the dog, tether the pony
To a distant post;
Our master Caesar[1] is in the tent   5
Where the maps are spread,
His eyes fixed upon nothing,
A hand under his head.
Like a long-legged fly upon the stream
His mind moves upon silence.   10

That the topless towers be burnt
And men recall that face,[2]
Move most gently if move you must
In this lonely place.
She thinks, part woman, three parts a child,   15
That nobody looks; her feet
Practise a tinker shuffle°   *gypsy dance*
Picked up on a street.
Like a long-legged fly upon the stream
His mind moves upon silence.   20

That girls at puberty may find
The first Adam in their thought,

---

4. A lively march tune.

1. Julius Caesar (102?–44 B.C.), Roman general and emperor; his military conquests extended the Roman Empire throughout most of western Europe.
2. The face of Helen of Troy, whose abduction precipitated the Trojan War. Yeats' description of her is based on the one given by Christopher Marlowe in his play *The Tragical History of Dr. Faustus* (1604): "Was this the face that launched a thousand ships / And burnt the topless towers of Ilium?"

Shut the door of the Pope's chapel,
Keep those children out.
There on that scaffolding reclines   25
Michael Angelo.[3]
With no more sound than the mice make
His hand moves to and fro.
Like a long-legged fly upon the stream
His mind moves upon silence.   30

William Butler Yeats (1865–1939)
That the Night Come

She lived in storm and strife,
Her soul had such desire
For what proud death may bring
That it could not endure
The common good of life,   5
But lived as 'twere a king
That packed his marriage day
With banneret° and pennon,°   *small banner / pennant*
Trumpet and kettle drum,
And the outrageous cannon   10
To bundle time away
That the night come.

William Butler Yeats (1865–1939)
The Wild Swans at Coole[1]

The trees are in their autumn beauty,
The woodland paths are dry;
Under the October twilight the water
Mirrors a still sky.
Upon the brimming water among the stones   5
Are nine and fifty swans.

The nineteenth autumn has come upon me
Since I first made my count.
I saw, before I had well finished,
All suddenly mount   10
And scatter wheeling in great broken rings
Upon their clamorous wings.

---

3. Michelangelo Buonarroti (1475–1564) painted the frescoes on the ceiling of the Sistine Chapel in the Vatican while lying on his back.

1. Coole Park, the country estate of Lady Gregory, which Yeats frequently visited.

I have looked upon those brilliant creatures,
And now my heart is sore.
All's changed since I, hearing at twilight,   15
The first time on this shore,
The bell-beat of their wings above my head,
Trod with a lighter tread.

Unwearied still, lover by lover,
They paddle in the cold   20
Companionable streams, or climb the air.
Their hearts have not grown old;
Passion or conquest, wander where they will,
Attend upon them still.

But now they drift on the still water   25
Mysterious, beautiful.
Among what rushes will they build,
By what lake's edge or pool
Delight men's eyes, when I awake some day
To find they have flown away?   30

Edwin Arlington Robinson (1869–1935)
Mr. Flood's Party

Old Eben Flood, climbing alone one night
Over the hill between the town below
And the forsaken upland hermitage
That held as much as he should ever know
On earth again of home, paused warily.   5
The road was his with not a native near;
And Eben, having leisure, said aloud,
For no man else in Tilbury Town to hear:

"Well, Mr. Flood, we have the harvest moon
Again, and we may not have many more;   10
The bird is on the wing, the poet says,
And you and I have said it here before.
Drink to the bird." He raised up to the light
The jug that he had gone so far to fill,
And answered huskily: "Well, Mr. Flood,   15
Since you propose it, I believe I will."

Alone, as if enduring to the end
A valiant armor of scarred hopes outworn,
He stood there in the middle of the road
Like Roland's ghost winding a silent horn.[1]   20

---

1. Roland, the hero of the medieval French poem *Chanson de Roland,* proudly refused to sound his horn for help at the battle of Roncesvalles until his troops were overwhelmed and he was near death.

Below him, in the town among the trees,
Where friends of other days had honored him,
A phantom salutation of the dead
Rang thinly till old Eben's eyes were dim.

Then, as a mother lays her sleeping child   25
Down tenderly, fearing it may awake,
He set the jug down slowly at his feet
With trembling care, knowing that most things break;
And only when assured that on firm earth
It stood, as the uncertain lives of men   30
Assuredly did not, he paced away,
And with his hand extended paused again:

"Well, Mr. Flood, we have not met like this
In a long time; and many a change has come
To both of us, I fear, since last it was   35
We had a drop together. Welcome home!"
Convivially returning with himself,
Again he raised the jug up to the light;
And with an acquiescent quaver said:
"Well, Mr. Flood, if you insist, I might.   40

"Only a very little, Mr. Flood—
For auld lang syne. No more, sir; that will do."
So, for the time, apparently it did,
And Eben evidently thought so too;
For soon amid the silver loneliness   45
Of night he lifted up his voice and sang,
Secure, with only two moons listening,
Until the whole harmonious landscape rang—

"For auld lang syne." The weary throat gave out,
The last word wavered; and the song being done,   50
He raised again the jug regretfully
And shook his head, and was again alone.
There was not much that was ahead of him,
And there was nothing in the town below—
Where strangers would have shut the many doors   55
That many friends had opened long ago.

Robert Frost   (1874–1963)
A Considerable Speck

(Microscopic)

A speck that would have been beneath my sight
On any but a paper sheet so white
Set off across what I had written there.

And I had idly poised my pen in air
To stop it with a period of ink,   5
When something strange about it made me think.
This was no dust speck by my breathing blown,
But unmistakably a living mite
With inclinations it could call its own.
It paused as with suspicion of my pen,   10
And then came racing wildly on again
To where my manuscript was not yet dry;
Then paused again and either drank or smelt—
With loathing, for again it turned to fly.
Plainly with an intelligence I dealt.   15
It seemed too tiny to have room for feet,
Yet must have had a set of them complete
To express how much it didn't want to die.
It ran with terror and with cunning crept.
It faltered: I could see it hesitate;   20
Then in the middle of the open sheet
Cower down in desperation to accept
Whatever I accorded it of fate.
I have none of the tenderer-than-thou
Collectivistic regimenting love   25
With which the modern world is being swept.
But this poor miscroscopic item now!
Since it was nothing I knew evil of
I let it lie there till I hope it slept.

I have a mind myself and recognize   30
Mind when I meet with it in any guise.
No one can know how glad I am to find
On any sheet the least display of mind.

Robert Frost (1874–1963)
Departmental

An ant on the tablecloth
Ran into a dormant moth
Of many times his size.
He showed not the least surprise.
His business wasn't with such.   5
He gave it scarcely a touch,
And was off on his duty run.
Yet if he encountered one
Of the hive's enquiry squad
Whose work is to find out God   10
And the nature of time and space,
He would put him onto the case.
Ants are a curious race;
One crossing with hurried tread
The body of one of their dead   15

Isn't given a moment's arrest—
Seems not even impressed.
But he no doubt reports to any
With whom he crosses antennae,
And they no doubt report   20
To the higher-up at court.
Then word goes forth in Formic:
"Death's come to Jerry McCormic,
Our selfless forager Jerry.
Will the special Janizary[1]   25
Whose office it is to bury
The dead of the commissary
Go bring him home to his people.
Lay him in state on a sepal.°   *leaf*
Wrap him for shroud in a petal.   30
Embalm him with ichor of nettle.°   *fluid from a prickly plant*
This is the word of your Queen."
And presently on the scene
Appears a solemn mortician;
And taking formal position,   35
With feelers calmly atwiddle,
Seizes the dead by the middle,
And heaving him high in air,
Carries him out of there.
No one stands round to stare.   40
It is nobody else's affair.

It couldn't be called ungentle.
But how thoroughly departmental.

Robert Frost   (1874–1963)
Fire and Ice

Some say the world will end in fire,
Some say in ice.
From what I've tasted of desire
I hold with those who favor fire.
But if it had to perish twice,   5
I think I know enough of hate
To say that for destruction ice
Is also great
And would suffice.

Robert Frost   (1874–1963)
Tree at My Window

Tree at my window, window tree,
My sash is lowered when night comes on;

---

1. Elite soldier of the Ottoman Empire.

But let there never be curtain drawn
Between you and me.

Vague dream-head lifted out of the ground,   5
And thing next most diffuse to cloud,
Not all your light tongues talking aloud
Could be profound.

But, tree, I have seen you taken and tossed,
And if you have seen me when I slept,   10
You have seen me when I was taken and swept
And all but lost.

That day she put our heads together,
Fate had her imagination about her,
Your head so much concerned with outer,   15
Mine with inner, weather.

Wallace Stevens   (1879–1955)
The Candle a Saint

Green is the night, green kindled and apparelled.
It is she that walks among astronomers.

She strides above the rabbit and the cat,
Like a noble figure, out of the sky,

Moving among the sleepers, the men,   5
Those that lie chanting *green is the night*.

Green is the night and out of madness woven,
The self-same madness of the astronomers

And of him that sees, beyond the astronomers,
The topaz rabbit and the emerald cat,   10

That sees above them, that sees rise up above them,
The noble figure, the essential shadow,

Moving and being, the image at its source,
The abstract, the archaic queen. Green is the night.

Wallace Stevens   (1879–1955)
A High-Toned Old Christian Woman

Poetry is the supreme fiction, madame.
Take the moral law and make a nave[1] of it

---
1. The main section of the interior of a Christian church.

And from the nave build haunted heaven. Thus,
The conscience is converted into palms,
Like windy citherns[2] hankering for hymns.   5
We agree in principle. That's clear. But take
The opposing law and make a peristyle,[3]
And from the peristyle project a masque[4]
Beyond the planets. Thus, our bawdiness,°   *boldness*
Unpurged by epitaph, indulged at last,   10
Is equally converted into palms,
Squiggling like saxophones. And palm for palm,
Madame, we are where we began. Allow,
Therefore, that in the planetary scene
Your disaffected flagellants,[5] well studied,   15
Smacking their muzzy° bellies in parade,   *dulled*
Proud of such novelties of the sublime,
Such tink and tank and tunk-a-tunk-tunk,
May, merely may, madame, whip from themselves
A jovial hullabaloo among the spheres.   20
This will make widows wince: But fictive things
Wink as they will. Wink most when widows wince.

Wallace Stevens   (1879–1955)
Of Modern Poetry

The poem of the mind in the act of finding
What will suffice. It has not always had
To find: the scene was set; it repeated what
Was in the script.
                          Then the theatre was changed   5
To something else. Its past was a souvenir.
It has to be living, to learn the speech of the place.
It has to face the men of the time and to meet
The women of the time. It has to think about war
And it has to find what will suffice. It has   10
To construct a new stage. It has to be on that stage
And, like an insatiable actor, slowly and
With meditation speak words that in the ear,
In the delicatest ear of the mind, repeat,
Exactly, that which it wants to hear, at the sound   15
Of which, an invisible audience listens,
Not to the play, but to itself, expressed
In an emotion as of two people, as of two
Emotions becoming one. The actor is

---

2. Small, pear-shaped guitars popular in Renaissance England.
3. A series of columns surrounding a building or courtyard; a peristyle is usually associated with classical Greek temples and is contrasted here with the nave of the Christian church.
4. An elaborate form of Renaissance entertainment in which the participants danced, sang, and acted out dramatic scenes.
5. People who punish themselves in religious ceremonies in order to do penance.

A metaphysician in the dark, twanging   20
An instrument, twanging a wiry string that gives
Sounds passing through sudden rightnesses, wholly
Containing the mind, below which it cannot descend,
Beyond which it has no will to rise.
                            It must   25
Be the finding of a satisfaction, and may
Be of a man skating, a woman dancing, a woman
Combing. The poem of the act of the mind.

Wallace Stevens   (1879–1955)
The Snow Man

One must have a mind of winter
To regard the frost and the boughs
Of the pinetrees crusted with snow;

And have been cold a long time
To behold the junipers shagged with ice,   5
The spruces rough in the distant glitter

Of the January sun; and not to think
Of any misery in the sound of the wind,
In the sound of a few leaves,

Which is the sound of the land   10
Full of the same wind
That is blowing in the same bare place

For the listener, who listens in the snow,
And, nothing himself, beholds
Nothing that is not there and the nothing that is.   15

D. H. Lawrence   (1885–1930)
Bavarian Gentians[1]

Not every man has gentians in his house
in Soft September, at slow, sad Michaelmas.[2]

Bavarian gentians, big and dark, only dark
darkening the day-time, torch-like with the smoking blueness of Pluto's
       gloom,[3]

---

   1. A family of flowers, usually fall-blooming and blue in color.
   2. September 29, feast celebrated in honor of Michael the Archangel.
   3. In classical mythology, Pluto (also called Dis) was the god of the underworld. He abducted Persephone and made her his queen. The daughter of Demeter, goddess of fruitfulness, Persephone was allowed to return to earth each spring but she had to rejoin her husband each fall.

ribbed and torch-like, with their blaze of darkness spread blue   5
down flattening into points, flattened under the sweep of white day
torch-flower of the blue-smoking darkness, Pluto's dark-blue daze,
black lamps from the halls of Dis, burning dark blue,
giving off darkness, blue darkness, as Demeter's pale lamps give off light,
lead me then, lead the way.   10

Reach me a gentian, give me a torch!
let me guide myself with the blue, forked torch of this flower
down the darker and darker stairs, where blue is darkened on blueness
even where Persephone goes, just now, from the frosted September
to the sightless realm where darkness is awake upon the dark   15
and Persephone herself is but a voice
or a darkness invisible enfolded in the deeper dark
of the arms Plutonic, and pierced with the passion of dense gloom,
among the splendour of torches of darkness, shedding darkness on the lost
     bride and her groom.

D. H. Lawrence   (1885–1930)
Piano

Softly, in the dusk, a woman is singing to me;
Taking me back down the vista of years, till I see
A child sitting under the piano, in the boom of the tingling strings
And pressing the small, poised feet of a mother who smiles as she sings.

In spite of myself, the insidious mastery of song   5
Betrays me back, till the heart of me weeps to belong
To the old Sunday evenings at home, with winter outside
And hymns in the cosy parlour, the tinkling piano our guide.

So now it is vain for the singer to burst into clamour
With the great black piano appassionato.[1] The glamour   10
Of childish days is upon me, my manhood is cast
Down in the flood of remembrance, I weep like a child for the past.

Ezra Pound   (1885–1972)
Portrait d'une Femme[1]

Your mind and you are our Sargasso Sea,[2]
London has swept about you this score years
And bright ships left you this or that in fee:

---

1. "Impassioned," a musical direction.

1. "Portrait of a Woman" (Fr.).
2. Area of the north Atlantic having large accumulations of seaweed, which at one time was thought to entrap ships.

Ideas, old gossip, oddments of all things,
Strange spars of knowledge and dimmed wares of price.   5
Great minds have sought you—lacking someone else.
You have been second always. Tragical?
No. You preferred it to the usual thing:
One dull man, dulling and uxorious,
One average mind—with one thought less, each year.   10
Oh, you are patient, I have seen you sit
Hours, where something might have floated up.
And now you pay one. Yes, you richly pay.
You are a person of some interest, one comes to you
And takes strange gain away: 15
Trophies fished up; some curious suggestion;
Fact that leads nowhere; and a tale or two,
Pregnant with mandrakes,³ or with something else
That might prove useful and yet never proves,
That never fits a corner or shows use,   20
Or finds its hour upon the loom of days:
The tarnished, gaudy, wonderful old work;
Idols and ambergris⁴ and rare inlays,
These are your riches, your great store; and yet
For all this sea-hoard of deciduous things,   25
Strange woods half sodden, and new brighter stuff:
In the slow float of differing light and deep,
No! there is nothing! In the whole and all,
Nothing that's quite your own.
          Yet this is you.   30

Marianne Moore   (1887–1972)
The Mind Is an Enchanting Thing

is an enchanted thing
   like the glaze on a
katydid-wing
      subdivided by sun
        till the nettings are legion.   5
Like Gieseking playing Scarlatti;¹

like the apteryx-awl²
   as a beak, or the

---

3. The roots of the mandrake plant were once thought to have magical properties, including the ability to promote conception.
4. A highly valuable waxlike substance originating in the intestines of the sperm whale; it is used in making perfumes.

1. Walter Gieseking (1895–1956), German pianist; Alessandro Scarlatti (1660?–1725), Italian composer.
2. A nearly extinct flightless bird (also called the kiwi) with a long, pointed bill and hairless plummage.

kiwi's rain-shawl
  of haired feathers, the mind   10
  feeling its way as though blind,
walks along with its eyes on the ground.

It has memory's ear
  that can hear without
having to hear.   15
  Like the gyroscope's fall,
  truly unequivocal
because trued by regnant° certainty,   *ruling*

it is a power of
  strong enchantment. It   20
is like the dove-
  neck animated by
  sun; it is memory's eye;
it's conscientious inconsistency.

It tears off the veil; tears   25
  the temptation, the
mist the heart wears,
  from its eyes,—if the heart
  has a face; it takes apart
dejection. It's fire in the dove-neck's   30
iridescence; in the
  inconsistencies
of Scarlatti.
  Unconfusion submits
  its confusion to proof; it's   35
not a Herod's oath[3] that cannot change.

Marianne Moore (1887–1972)
No Swan So Fine

"No water so still as the
  dead fountains of Versailles."[1] No swan,
with swart° blind look askance   *malignant*
and gondoliering legs,[2] so fine
  as the chintz china one with fawn-   5

---

 3. King Herod was so pleased with Salome's dance that "he promised with an oath" to grant her any wish. When she asked for the head of John the Baptist on a silver dish, Herod, "for the oath's sake," fulfilled his promise (Matt. 14:6–11).

 1. The author has stated that this quote is from the *New York Times Magazine,* May 10, 1931. Versailles is the site of the opulent French royal palace built in the seventeenth century by Louis XIV. It became the principal residence of the French kings and the seat of government for more than 100 years.
 2. I.e., legs that paddle like a gondolier propelling his craft.

brown eyes and toothed gold
collar on to show whose bird it was.

Lodged in the Louis Fifteenth
    candelabrum-tree[3] of cockscomb-
tinted buttons, dahlias,   10
sea-urchins, and everlastings,[4]
    it perches on the branching foam
of polished sculptured
flowers—at ease and tall. The king is dead.

John Crowe Ransom   (1888–1974)
Piazza Piece

—I am a gentleman in a dustcoat trying
To make you hear. Your ears are soft and small
And listen to an old man not at all,
They want the young men's whispering and sighing.
But see the roses on your trellis dying   5
And hear the spectral singing of the moon;
For I must have my lovely lady soon,
I am a gentleman in a dustcoat trying.

—I am a lady young in beauty waiting
Until my truelove comes, and then we kiss.   10
But what gray man among the vines is this
Whose words are dry and faint as in a dream?
Back from my trellis, Sir, before I scream!
I am a lady young in beauty waiting.

Conrad Aiken   (1889–1973)
Sound of Breaking

Why do you cry out, why do I like to hear you
Cry out, here in the dewless evening, sitting
Close, close together, so close that the heart stops beating
And the brain its thought? Wordless, worthless mortals
Stumbling, exhausted, in this wilderness   5
Of our conjoint destruction! Hear the grass
Raging about us! Hear the worms applaud!
Hear how the ripples make a sound of chaos!
Hear now, in these and the other sounds of evening,
The first brute step of God!   10

---

    3. Moore has said that this is "a pair of Louis xv candelabra with Dresden figures of swans." The reign of Louis xv (1710–1774) saw a style of art that was heavily, sometimes excessively, ornate.
    4. Flowers which retain their form and color when dried.

About your elbow,
Making a ring of thumb and finger, I
Slide the walled blood against the less-walled blood,
Move down your arm, surmount the wrist-bone, shut
Your long slim hand in mine. Each finger-tip   15
Is then saluted by a finger-tip;
The hands meet back to back, then face to face;
Then lock together. And we, with eyes averted,
Smile at the evening sky of alabaster,
See nothing, lose our souls in the maelstrom, turning   20
Downward in rapid circles.

              Bitter woman,
Bitter of heart and brain and blood, bitter as I
Who drink your bitterness—can this be beauty?
Do you cry out because the beauty is cruel?   25
Terror, because we downward sweep so swiftly?
Terror of darkness?

              It is a sound of breaking,
The world is breaking, the world is a sound of breaking,
Many-harmonied, diverse, profound,   30
A shattering beauty. See, how together we break,
Hear what a crashing of disordered chords and discords
Fills the world with falling, when we thus lean
Our two mad bodies together!

              It is a sound   35
Of everlasting grief, the sound of weeping,
The sound of disaster and misery, the sound
Of passionate heartbreak at the centre of the world.

Archibald MacLeish (b. 1892)
Ars Poetica[1]

A poem should be palpable and mute
As a globed fruit

Dumb
As old medallions to the thumb

Silent as the sleeve-worn stone   5
Of casement ledges where the moss has grown—

A poem should be wordless
As the flight of birds

---

1. "The Art of Poetry" (Lat.).

A poem should be motionless in time
As the moon climbs   10

Leaving, as the moon releases
Twig by twig the night-entangled trees,

Leaving, as the moon behind the winter leaves,
Memory by memory the mind—

A poem should be motionless in time   15
As the moon climbs

A poem should be equal to:
Not true

For all the history of grief
An empty doorway and a maple leaf   20

For love
The leaning grasses and two lights above the sea—

A poem should not mean
But be

E. E. Cummings   (1894–1962)
(ponder,darling,these busted statues

(ponder,darling,these busted statues
of yon motheaten forum be aware
notice what hath remained
—the stone cringes
clinging to the stone,how obsolete   5

lips utter their extant smile . . . .
remark

a few deleted of texture
or meaning monuments and dolls

resist Them Greediest Paws of careful   10
time all of which is extremely
unimportant) whereas Life

matters if or

when the your- and my-
idle vertical worthless   15
self unite in a peculiarly
momentary

partnership(to instigate
constructive
                Horizontal   20
business . . . . even so,let us make haste
—consider well this ruined aqueduct

lady,
which used to lead something into somewhere)

Hart Crane   (1899–1932)
At Melville's Tomb[1]

Often beneath the wave, wide from this ledge
The dice of drowned men's bones he saw bequeath
An embassy. Their numbers as he watched,
Beat on the dusty shore and were obscured.

And wrecks passed without sound of bells,   5
The calyx[2] of death's bounty giving back
A scattered chapter, lived hieroglyph,[3]
The portent wound in corridors of shells.

Then in the circuit calm of one vast coil,
Its lashings charmed and malice reconciled,   10
Frosted eyes there were that lifted altars;
And silent answers crept across the stars.

Compass, quadrant and sextant[4] contrive
No farther tides . . . High in the azure steeps
Monody[5] shall not wake the mariner.   15
This fabulous shadow only the sea keeps.

Hart Crane   (1899–1932)
from *The Bridge*
Proem:[1] *To Brooklyn Bridge*

How many dawns, chill from his rippling rest
The seagull's wings shall dip and pivot him,

---

1. Herman Melville (1819–1891), American writer, is buried in New York City's Woodlawn Cemetery.
2. Crane said that this "refers in a double ironic sense both to a cornucopia and the vortex made by a sinking vessel."
3. A system of writing in pictorial characters.
4. Various navigational instruments.
5. A dirge or song of mourning sung by one person; it is also the title of a poem by Melville.

1. Preface. These lines comprise the opening section of *The Bridge*, Crane's epic poem which he said "concerns a mystical synthesis of 'America.'" Brooklyn Bridge was to him a symbol of the country's unity, diversity, and movement through time.

Shedding white rings of tumult, building high
Over the chained bay waters Liberty²—

Then, with inviolate curve, forsake our eyes   5
As apparitional as sails that cross
Some page of figures to be filed away;
—Till elevators drop us from our day . . .

I think of cinemas, panoramic sleights
With multitudes bent toward some flashing scene   10
Never disclosed, but hastened to again,
Foretold to other eyes on the same screen;

And Thee,³ across the harbor, silver-paced
As though the sun took step of thee, yet left
Some motion ever unspent in thy stride,—   15
Implicitly thy freedom staying thee!

Out of some subway scuttle, cell or loft
A bedlamite⁴ speeds to thy parapets,
Tilting there momently, shrill shirt ballooning,
A jest falls from the speechless caravan.   20

Down Wall,⁵ from girder into street noon leaks,
A rip-tooth of the sky's acetylene;⁶
All afternoon the cloud-flown derricks turn . . .
Thy cables breathe the North Atlantic still.

And obscure as that heaven of the Jews,   25
Thy guerdon° . . . Accolade thou dost bestow   *reward*
Of anonymity time cannot raise:
Vibrant reprieve and pardon thou dost show.

O harp and altar, of the fury fused,
(How could mere toil align thy choiring strings!)   30
Terrific threshold of the prophet's pledge,
Prayer of pariah,° and the lover's cry,—   *outcast*

Again the traffic lights that skim thy swift
Unfractioned idiom, immaculate sigh of stars,
Beading thy path—condense eternity: 35
And we have seen night lifted in thine arms.

Under thy shadow by the piers I waited;

---

2. The Statue of Liberty, in Upper New York Bay.
3. Brooklyn Bridge.
4. A madman, intent on suicide.
5. Wall Street, the financial district of New York City.
6. A gas that, when stored under pressure, mixed with air, and ignited, is used in welding and
cutting metal.

Only in darkness is thy shadow clear.
The City's fiery parcels all undone,
Already snow submerges an iron year . . .   40

O Sleepless as the river under thee,
Vaulting the sea, the prairies' dreaming sod,
Unto us lowliest sometime sweep, descend
And of the curveship lend a myth to God.

Allen Tate   (b. 1899)
Sonnets at Christmas
1934

I

This is the day His hour of life draws near,
Let me get ready from head to foot for it
Most handily with eyes to pick the year
For small feed to reward a feathered wit.
Some men would see it an epiphany[1]   5
At ease, at food and drink, others at chase
Yet I, stung lassitude, with ecstasy
Unspent argue with the season's difficult case
So: Man, dull critter of enormous head,
What would he look at in the coiling sky?   10
But I must kneel again unto the Dead
While Christmas bells of paper white and red,
Figured with boys and girls spilt from a sled,
Ring out the silence I am nourished by.

II

Ah, Christ, I love you rings to the wild sky
And I must think a little of the past:
When I was ten I told a stinking lie
That got a black boy whipped; but now at last
The going years, caught in an accurate glow,   5
Reverse like balls englished upon green baize—
Let them return, let the round trumpets blow
The ancient crackle of the Christ's deep gaze.
Deafened and blind, with senses yet unfound,
Am I, untutored to the after-wit   10
Of knowledge, knowing a nightmare has no sound;
Therefore with idle hands and head I sit
In late December before the fire's daze
Punished by crimes of which I would be quit.

---

1. The appearance of a divine being.

Theodore Roethke (1908–1963)
Elegy for Jane

My Student, Thrown by a Horse

I remember the neckcurls, limp and damp as tendrils;
And her quick look, a sidelong pickerel[1] smile;
And how, once startled into talk, the light syllables leaped for her,
And she balanced in the delight of her thought,
A wren, happy, tail into the wind,   5
Her song trembling the twigs and small branches.
The shade sang with her;
The leaves, their whispers turned to kissing;
And the mold sang in the bleached valleys under the rose.

Oh, when she was sad, she cast herself down into such a pure depth,   10
Even a father could not find her:
Scraping her cheek against straw;
Stirring the clearest water.

My sparrow, you are not here,
Waiting like a fern, making a spiny shadow.   15
The sides of wet stones cannot console me,
Nor the moss, wound with the last light.

If only I could nudge you from this sleep,
My maimed darling, my skittery pigeon.
Over this damp grave I speak the words of my love: 20
I, with no rights in this matter,
Neither father nor lover.

John Berryman (1914–1972)
Dream Song: 266

Dinch me,[1] dark God, having smoked me out.
Let Henry's[2] ails fail, pennies on his eyes
never to open more,
the shires are voting him out of time & place,
they'll drop his bundle, drunkard & Boy Scout,   5
where he was once before:

nowhere, nowhere. Was then the thing all planned?
I mention what I do not understand.

---

1. A young pike, a variety of fish having a wide, elongated mouth.

1. I.e., snuff me out like a cigarette; *dinch* is a slang term for the unused portion of a cigarette.
2. Henry is an imaginary character who appears throughout Berryman's 385 Dream Songs; he is continually haunted by personal doubts, anxieties, and thoughts of death.

I mention for instance Love:
God loves his creatures when he treats them so? 10
Surely one grand *exception* here below
his presidency of

the widespread galaxies might once be made
for perishing Henry, whom let not then die.
He can advance no claim, 15
save that he studied thy Word & grew afraid,
work & fear be the basis for his terrible cry
not to forget his name.

John Berryman (1914–1972)
Dream Song: 382

At Henry's bier[1] let some thing fall out well:
enter there none who somewhat has to sell,
the music ancient & gradual,
the voices solemn but the grief subdued,
no hairy jokes but everybody's mood 5
subdued, subdued,

until the Dancer comes, in a short short dress
hair black & long & loose, dark dark glasses,
uptilted face,
pallor & strangeness, the music changes 10
to "Give!" & "Ow!" and how! the music changes,
she kicks a backward limb

on tiptoe, pirouettes, & she is free
to the knocking music, sails, dips, & suddenly
returns to the terrible gay 15
occasion hopeless & mad, she weaves, it's hell,
she flings to her head a leg, bobs, all is well,
she dances Henry away.

Randall Jarrell (1914–1965)
Eighth Air Force[1]

If, in an odd angle of the hutment,°   *military camp*
A puppy laps the water from a can
Of flowers, and the drunk sergeant shaving

---

1. See footnote 2 for *Dream Song: 266.* A bier is a stand upon which a coffin or a corpse is placed.

1. Principal American Air Force unit in the bombing of Europe in World War II.

Whistles *O Paradiso!*² —shall I say that man
Is not as men have said: a wolf to man?   5

The other murderers troop in yawning;
Three of them play Pitch,³ one sleeps, and one
Lies counting missions, lies there sweating
Till even his heart beat: One; One; One.
O murderers! . . . Still, this is how it's done: 10

This is a war. . . . But since these play, before they die,
Like puppies with their puppy; since, a man,
I did as these have done, but did not die—
I will content the people as I can
And give up these to them: Behold the man!⁴   15

I have suffered, in a dream, because of him,
Many things; for this last saviour, man,
I have lied as I lie now. But what is lying?
Men wash their hands, in blood, as best they can:
I find no fault in this just man.⁵   20

Dylan Thomas (1914–1953)
Fern Hill¹

Now as I was young and easy under the apple boughs
About the lilting house and happy as the grass was green,
    The night above the dingle° starry,   *wooded valley*
        Time let me hail and climb
        Golden in the heydays of his eyes,   5
And honoured among wagons I was prince of the apple towns
And once below a time I lordly had the trees and leaves
        Trail with daisies and barley
    Down the rivers of the windfall light.

And as I was green and carefree, famous among the barns   10
About the happy yard and singing as the farm was home,
    In the sun that is young once only,
        Time let me play and be
        Golden in the mercy of his means,

---

2. An operatic aria.
3. Card game similar to seven-up.
4. When Pilate asked the people to chose whether Christ or Barabbas should be released, they chose Barabbas. "Pilate therefore went forth again, and saith unto them, Behold, I bring him forth to you, that ye may know that I find no fault in him. Then came Jesus forth, wearing the crown of thorns, and the purple robe. And Pilate saith unto them, Behold the man!" (John 19:4–5.)
5. "When Pilate saw that he could prevail nothing, but that rather a tumult was made, he took water, and washed his hands before the multitude, saying, I am innocent of the blood of this just person: see ye to it." (Matt. 27:24.)

1. A farm where the poet spent many of his summer holidays as a boy.

And green and golden I was huntsman and herdsman, the calves   15
Sang to my horn, the foxes on the hills barked clear and cold,
    And the sabbath rang slowly
  In the pebbles of the holy streams.

All the sun long it was running, it was lovely, the hay-
Fields high as the house, the tunes from the chimneys, it was air   20
    And playing, lovely and watery
      And fire green as grass.
    And nightly under the simple stars
As I rode to sleep the owls were bearing the farm away,
All the moon long I heard, blessed among stables, the night-jars°   *birds* 25
    Flying with the ricks,° and the horses   *haystacks*
      Flashing into the dark.

And then to awake, and the farm, like a wanderer white
With the dew, come back, the cock on his shoulder: it was all
    Shining, it was Adam and maiden,   30
      The sky gathered again
    And the sun grew round that very day.
So it must have been after the birth of the simple light
In the first, spinning place, the spellbound horses walking warm
    Out of the whinnying green stable   35
      On to the fields of praise.

And honoured among foxes and pheasants by the gay house
Under the new made clouds and happy as the heart was long,
    In the sun born over and over,
      I ran my heedless ways,   40
    My wishes raced through the house-high hay
And nothing I cared, at my sky blue trades, that time allows
In all his tuneful turning so few and such morning songs
    Before the children green and golden
      Follow him out of grace,   45

Nothing I cared, in the lamb white days, that time would take me
Up to the swallow thronged loft by the shadow of my hand,
    In the moon that is always rising,
      Nor that riding to sleep
    I should hear him fly with the high fields   50
And wake to the farm forever fled from the childless land.
Oh as I was young and easy in the mercy of his means,
    Time held me green and dying
  Though I sang in my chains like the sea.

Dylan Thomas (1914–1953)
A Refusal to Mourn the Death, by Fire, of a Child in London

Never until the mankind making
Bird beast and flower

Fathering and all humbling darkness
Tells with silence the last light breaking
And the still hour   5
Is come of the sea tumbling in harness

And I must enter again the round
Zion[1] of the water bead
And the synagogue of the ear of corn°   *wheat*
Shall I let pray the shadow of a sound   10
Or sow my salt seed
In the least valley of sackcloth to mourn

The majesty and burning of the child's death.
I shall not murder
The mankind of her going with a grave truth   15
Nor blaspheme down the stations of the breath
With any further
Elegy of innocence and youth.

Deep with the first dead lies London's daughter,
Robed in the long friends,   20
The grains beyond age, the dark veins of her mother
Secret by the unmourning water
Of the riding Thames.
After the first death, there is no other.

Robert Lowell (b. 1917)
Christmas Eve under Hooker's Statue[1]

Tonight in a blackout. Twenty years ago
I hung my stocking on the tree, and hell's
Serpent entwined the apple in the toe
To sting the child with knowledge. Hooker's heels
Kicking at nothing in the shifting snow,   5
A cannon and a cairn° of cannon balls   *pile*
Rusting before the blackened Statehouse, know
How the long horn of plenty broke like glass
In Hooker's gauntlets. Once I came from Mass;
Now storm-clouds shelter Christmas, once again   10
Mars[2] meets his fruitless star with open arms,
His heavy sabre flashes with the rime,°   *frost*

---

1. The Promised Land of the Old Testament.

1. Located on the lawn of the Massachusetts State House in Boston. Joseph Hooker (1814–1879) was a Union general in the Civil War. Under his brief command, the Army of the Potomac was soundly defeated at the Battle of Chancellorsville (1863) by a Confederate force with less than half the number of men.
2. The Roman god of war.

The war-god's bronzed and empty forehead forms
Anonymous machinery from raw men;
The cannon on the Common cannot stun   15
The blundering butcher as he rides on Time—
The barrel clinks with holly. I am cold:
I ask for bread, my father gives me mould;

His stocking is full of stones. Santa in red
Is crowned with wizened° berries. Man of war,   *withered* 20
Where is the summer's garden? In its bed
The ancient speckled serpent will appear,
And black-eyed susan with her frizzled head.
When Chancellorsville mowed down the volunteer,
"All wars are boyish," Herman Melville said;[3]   25
But we are old, our fields are running wild:
Till Christ again turn wanderer and child.

Robert Lowell   (b. 1917)
The Mouth of the Hudson[1]

(for Esther Brooks)

A single man stands like a bird-watcher,
and scuffles the pepper and salt snow
from a discarded, gray
Westinghouse Electric cable drum.
He cannot discover America by counting   5
the chains of condemned freight-trains
from thirty states. They jolt and jar
and junk in the siding below him.
He has trouble with his balance.
His eyes drop,   10
and he drifts with the wild ice
ticking seaward down the Hudson,
like the blank sides of a jig-saw puzzle.

The ice ticks seaward like a clock.
A Negro toasts   15
Wheat-seeds over the coke-fumes
of a punctured barrel.
Chemical air
sweeps in from New Jersey,
and smells of coffee.   20

---

3. In his poem "The March into Virginia" (1861), Melville said "All wars are boyish, and are fought by boys, / The champions and enthusiasts of the state."

1. The Hudson River; at its mouth, it flows between New York City and New Jersey.

Across the river,
ledges of suburban factories tan
in the sulphur-yellow sun
of the unforgivable landscape.

Richard Wilbur   (b. 1921)
A Dubious Night

A bell diphthonging[1] in an atmosphere
Of shying night air summons some to prayer
Down in the town, two deep lone miles from here,

Yet wallows faint or sudden everywhere,
In every ear, as if the twist wind wrung   5
Some ten years' tangled echoes from the air.

What kyries[2] it says are mauled among
The queer elisions[3] of the mist and murk,
Of lights and shapes; the senses were unstrung,

Except that one star's synecdochic[4] smirk   10
Burns steadily to me, that nothing's odd
And firm as ever is the masterwork.

I weary of the confidence of God.

Richard Wilbur   (b. 1921)
A Simile for Her Smile

Your smiling, or the hope, the thought of it,
Makes in my mind such pause and abrupt ease
As when the highway bridgegates fall,
Balking the hasty traffic, which must sit
On each side massed and staring, while   5
Deliberately the drawbridge starts to rise:

Then horns are hushed, the oilsmoke rarefies,
Above the idling motors one can tell
The packet's smooth approach, the slip,

---

1. A diphthong is a unit of speech in which the sound glides from one vowel to the next, as in the *ou* of *loud* and the *oi* of *spoil*.
2. In the liturgy of various Christian denominations, a kyrie is a short prayer that begins "Kyrie eleison" ("Lord, have mercy").
3. In speech or writing, elisions are deliberate omissions of syllables from words, usually for poetic effect, e.g., *'tis* for *it is, e'er* for *ever*.
4. I.e., functioning as a synecdoche, a figure of speech in which a part of something is used to signify the whole; in "she had six mouths to feed," *mouths* (for *persons*) is a synecdoche.

Slip of the silken river past the sides,   10
The ringing of clear bells, the dip
And slow cascading of the paddle wheel.

James Dickey (b. 1923)
The Heaven of Animals

Here they are. The soft eyes open.
If they have lived in a wood
It is a wood.
If they have lived on plains
It is grass rolling   5
Under their feet forever.

Having no souls, they have come,
Anyway, beyond their knowing.
Their instincts wholly bloom
And they rise.   10
The soft eyes open.

To match them, the landscape flowers,
Outdoing, desperately
Outdoing what is required:
The richest wood,   15
The deepest field.

For some of these,
It could not be the place
It is, without blood.
These hunt, as they have done,   20
But with claws and teeth grown perfect,

More deadly than they can believe.
They stalk more silently,
And crouch on the limbs of trees,
And their descent   25
Upon the bright backs of their prey

May take years
In a sovereign floating of joy.
And those that are hunted
Know this as their life,   30
Their reward: to walk

Under such trees in full knowledge
Of what is in glory above them,
And to feel no fear,

But acceptance, compliance.   35
Fulfilling themselves without pain

At the cycle's center,
They tremble, they walk
Under the tree,
They fall, they are torn,   40
They rise, they walk again.

Mari Evans (b. 1923)
When in Rome

Mattie dear
the box is full . . .
take
whatever you like
to eat . . .   5

       (an egg
       or soup
       . . . there ain't no meat.)

there's endive there
and   10
cottage cheese . . .

       (whew! if I had some
       black-eyed peas . . .)

there's sardines
on the shelves   15
and such . . .
but
don't
get my anchovies . . .
they cost   20
too much!

       (me get the
       anchovies indeed!
       what she think, she got—
       a bird to feed?)   25

there's plenty in there
to fill you up . . .

       (yes'm. just the
       sight's
       enough!   30

Hope I lives till I get
home
I'm tired of eatin'
what they eats in Rome . . .)

Anthony Hecht (b. 1923)
The Dover Bitch

A Criticism of Life

So there stood Matthew Arnold and this girl[1]
With the cliffs of England crumbling away behind them,
And he said to her, "Try to be true to me,
And I'll do the same for you, for things are bad
All over, etc., etc."   5
Well now, I knew this girl. It's true she had read
Sophocles in a fairly good translation
And caught that bitter allusion to the sea,
But all the time he was talking she had in mind
The notion of what his whiskers would feel like   10
On the back of her neck. She told me later on
That after a while she got to looking out
At the lights across the channel, and really felt sad,
Thinking of all the wine and enormous beds
And blandishments in French and the perfumes.   15
And then she got really angry. To have been brought
All the way down from London, and then be addressed
As sort of a mournful cosmic last resort
Is really tough on a girl, and she was pretty.
Anyway, she watched him pace the room   20
And finger his watch-chain and seem to sweat a bit,
And then she said one or two unprintable things.
But you mustn't judge her by that. What I mean to say is,
She's really all right. I still see her once in a while
And she always treats me right. We have a drink   25
And I give her a good time, and perhaps it's a year
Before I see her again, but there she is,
Running to fat, but dependable as they come,
And sometimes I bring her a bottle of *Nuit d'Amour*.[2]

A. R. Ammons (b. 1926)
Cascadilla Falls

I went down by Cascadilla
Falls this
evening, the

---

1. See Matthew Arnold's "Dover Beach" (p 704).
2. "Night of Love."

stream below the falls,
and picked up a   5
handsized stone
kidney-shaped, testicular, and

thought all its motions into it,
the 800 mph earth spin,
the 190-million-mile yearly   10
displacement around the sun,
the overriding
grand
haul

of the galaxy with the 30,000   15
mph of where
the sun's going:
thought all the interweaving
motions
into myself: dropped   20

the stone to dead rest:
the stream from other motions
broke
rushing over it:
shelterless,   25
I turned

to the sky and stood still:
Oh
I do
not know where I am going   30
that I can live my life
by this single creek.

Frank O'Hara   (1926–1966)

Steps

How funny you are today New York
like Ginger Rogers in *Swingtime*[1]
and St. Bridget's steeple leaning a little to the left

here I have just jumped out of a bed full of V-days
(I got tired of D-days) and blue .you there still   5
accepts me foolish and free
all I want is a room up there
and you in it

---

1. Ginger Rogers and Fred Astaire were the stars of the film *Swing Time* (1936), which featured the
kinds of dance routines that made them so popular in the 1930s.

and even the traffic halt so thick is a way
for people to rub up against each other 10
and when their surgical appliances lock
they stay together
for the rest of the day (what a day)
I go by to check a slide and I say
that painting's not so blue 15

where's Lana Turner
she's out eating
and Garbo's backstage at the Met[2]
everyone's taking their coat off
so they can show a rib-cage to the rib-watchers 20
and the park's full of dancers with their tights and shoes
in little bags
who are often mistaken for worker-outers at the West Side Y
why not
the Pittsburgh Pirates shout because they won 25
and in a sense we're all winning
we're alive

the apartment was vacated by a gay couple
who moved to the country for fun
they moved a day too soon 30
even the stabbings are helping the population explosion
though in the wrong country
and all those liars have left the UN
and Seagram Building's no longer rivalled in interest
not that we need liquor (we just like it) 35

and the little box is out on the sidewalk
next to the delicatessen
so the old man can sit on it and drink beer
and get knocked off it by his wife later in the day
while the sun is still shining 40

oh god it's wonderful
to get out of bed
and drink too much coffee
and smoke too many cigarettes
and love you so much 45

W. D. Snodgrass (b. 1926)
April Inventory

The green catalpa tree has turned
All white; the cherry blooms once more.

---

2. The Metropolitan Opera House in New York City.

In one whole year I haven't learned
A blessed thing they pay you for.
The blossoms snow down in my hair;   5
The trees and I will soon be bare.

The trees have more than I to spare.
The sleek, expensive girls I teach,
Younger and pinker every year,
Bloom gradually out of reach.   10
The pear tree lets its petals drop
Like dandruff on a tabletop.

The girls have grown so young by now
I have to nudge myself to stare.
This year they smile and mind me how   15
My teeth are falling with my hair.
In thirty years I may not get
Younger, shrewder, or out of debt.

The tenth time, just a year ago,
I made myself a little list   20
Of all the things I'd ought to know,
Then told my parents, analyst,
And everyone who's trusted me
I'd be substantial, presently.

I haven't read one book about   25
A book or memorized one plot.
Or found a mind I did not doubt.
I learned one date. And then forgot.
And one by one the solid scholars
Get the degrees, the jobs, the dollars.   30

And smile above their starchy collars.
I taught my classes Whitehead's[1] notions;
One lovely girl, a song of Mahler's.[2]
Lacking a source-book or promotions,
I showed one child the colors of   35
A luna moth and how to love.

I taught myself to name my name,
To bark back, loosen love and crying;
To ease my woman so she came,
To ease an old man who was dying.   40
I have not learned how often I
Can win, can love, but choose to die.

---

1. Alfred North Whitehead (1861–1947), British philosopher and mathematician.
2. Gustav Mahler (1860–1911), Austrian composer and conductor.

I have not learned there is a lie
Love shall be blonder, slimmer, younger;
That my equivocating eye   45
Loves only by my body's hunger;
That I have poems, true to feel,
Or that the lovely world is real.

While scholars speak authority
And wear their ulcers on their sleeves,   50
My eyes in spectacles shall see
These trees procure and spend their leaves.
There is a value underneath
The gold and silver in my teeth.

Though trees turn bare and girls turn wives,   55
We shall afford our costly seasons;
There is a gentleness survives
That will outspeak and has its reasons.
There is a loveliness exists,
Preserves us. Not for specialists.   60

W. D. Snodgrass (b. 1926)
from *Heart's Needle:* 4

    No one can tell you why
  the season will not wait;
    the night I told you I
must leave, you wept a fearful rate
     to stay up late.   5

    Now that it's turning Fall,
  we go to take our walk
    among municipal
flowers, to steal one off its stalk,
     to try and talk.   10

    We huff like windy giants
  scattering with our breath
    grey-headed dandelions;
Spring is the cold Wind's aftermath.
     The poet saith.   15

    But the asters, too, are grey,
  ghost-grey. Last night's cold
    is sending on their way
petunias and dwarf marigold,
     hunched sick and old.   20

Like nerves caught in a graph,
　the morning-glory vines
　　frost has erased by half
still crawl over their rigid twines.
　　　Like broken lines   25

　of verses I can't make.
In its unravelling loom
　　we find a flower to take,
with some late buds that might still bloom
　　　back to your room.   30

　Night comes and the stiff dew.
I'm told a friend's child cried
　　because a cricket, who
had minstrelled every night outside
　　　her window, died.   35

John Ashbery   (b. 1927)
These Lacustrine[1] Cities

These lacustrine cities grew out of loathing
Into something forgetful, although angry with history.
They are the product of an idea: that man is horrible, for instance,
Though this is only one example.

They emerged until a tower   5
Controlled the sky, and with artifice dipped back
Into the past for swans and tapering branches,
Burning, until all that hate was transformed into useless love.

Then you are left with an idea of yourself
And the feeling of ascending emptiness of the afternoon   10
Which must be charged to the embarrassment of others
Who fly by you like beacons.

The night is a sentinel.
Much of your time has been occupied by creative games
Until now, but we have all-inclusive plans for you.   15
We had thought, for instance, of sending you to the middle of the desert,

To a violent sea, or of having the closeness of the others be air
To you, pressing you back into a startled dream
As sea-breezes greet a child's face.
But the past is already here, and you are nursing some private project.   20

---

1. Of, or relating to, lakes.

The worst is not over, yet I know
You will be happy here. Because of the logic
Of your situation, which is something no climate can outsmart.
Tender and insouciant by turns, you see,

You have built a mountain of something,   25
Thoughtfully pouring all your energy into this single monument,
Whose wind is desire starching a petal,
Whose disappointment broke into a rainbow of tears.

Donald Hall   (b. 1928)
My Son, My Executioner

My son, my executioner,
    I take you in my arms,
Quiet and small and just astir,
    And whom my body warms.

Sweet death, small son, our instrument   5
    Of immortality,
Your cries and hungers document
    Our bodily decay.

We twenty-five and twenty-two,
    Who seemed to live forever,   10
Observe enduring life in you
    And start to die together.

Donald Hall   (b. 1928)
Six Poets in Search of a Lawyer

Finesse be first, whose elegance deplores
All things save beauty, and the swinging doors;
Whose cleverness in writing verse is just
Exceeded by his lack of taste and lust;
Who lives off lady lovers of his verse   5
And thanks them by departing with their purse;
Who writes his verse in order to amaze,
To win the Pulitzer,[1] or *Time*'s sweet praise;
Who will endure a moment, and then pass,
As hopeless as an olive in his glass.   10

Dullard be second, as he always will,
From lack of brains as well as lack of skill.

---

1. The Pulitzer Prizes are awarded annually in the United States to honor distinguished work in various categories of journalism and literature, including poetry.

Expert in some, and dilettante in all
The ways of making poems gasp and fall,
He teaches at a junior college where   15
He's recognized as Homer's[2] son and heir.
Respectable, brown-suited, it is he
Who represents on forums poetry,
And argues to protect the libeled Muse,
Who'd tear his flimsy tongue out, could she choose.   20

His opposite is anarchistic *Bomb*,
Who writes a manifesto with aplomb.
Revolt! Revolt! No matter why or when,
It's novelty, old novelty again.
Yet *Bomb* if read intently may reveal   25
A talent not to murder but to steal;
First from old *Gone,* whose fragmentary style
Disguised his sawdust Keats a little while;
And now from one who writes at very best
What ne'er was thought and much the less expressed.[3]   30

Lucre be next, who takes to poetry
The businessman he swore he would not be.
Anthologies and lecture tours and grants
Create a solvency which disenchants.
He writes his poems now to suit his purse,   35
Short-lined and windy, and reserves his curse
For all the little magazines so fine
That offer only fifty cents a line.
He makes his money, certainly, to write,
But writes for money. Such is appetite.   40

Of *Mucker* will I tell, who tries to show
He is a kind of poet men don't know.
To shadow box at literary teas
And every girl at Bennington[4] to seize,
To talk of baseball rather than of Yeats,   45
To drink straight whisky while the bard creates—
This is his pose, and so his poems seem
Incongruous in proving life a dream.
Some say, with Freud, that *Mucker* has a reason
For acting virile in and out of season.   50

Scoundrel be last. Be deaf, be dumb, be blind,
Who writes satiric verses on his kind.

---

2. Homer, ancient Greek poet traditionally thought to be the author of the *Iliad* and the *Odyssey*.
3. This line is a humorous paraphrase of Alexander Pope's description of wit in his *Essay on Criticism:* "What oft was thought, but ne'er so well expressed."
4. Bennington College.

Anne Sexton   (b. 1928)
The Truth the Dead Know

for my mother, born March 1902, died March 1959
and my father, born February 1900, died June 1959

Gone, I say, and walk from church,
refusing the stiff procession to the grave,
letting the dead ride alone in the hearse.
It is June. I am tired of being brave.

We drive to The Cape. I cultivate   5
myself where the sun gutters from the sky,
where the sea swings in like an iron gate
and we touch. In another country people die.

My darling, the wind falls in like stones
from the whitehearted water and when we touch   10
we enter touch entirely. No one's alone.
Men kill for this, or for as much.

And what of the dead? They lie without shoes
in their stone boats. They are more like stone
than the sea would be if it stopped. They refuse   15
to be blessed, throat, eye, and knucklebone.

X. J. Kennedy   (b. 1929)
Nude Descending a Staircase[1]

Toe upon toe, a snowing flesh,
A gold of lemon, root and rind,
She sifts in sunlight down the stairs
With nothing on. Nor on her mind.

We spy beneath the banister   5
A constant thresh of thigh on thigh—
Her lips imprint the swinging air
That parts to let her parts go by.

One-woman waterfall, she wears
Her slow descent like a long cape   10
And pausing, on the final stair
Collects her motions into shape.

---

1. Painting by Marcel Duchamp (1887–1968); combining techniques of cubism and futurism, it
depicts successive stages of motion through a series of overlapping images.

Adrienne Rich (b. 1929)
Face to Face

Never to be lonely like that—
the Early American figure on the beach
in black coat and knee-breeches
scanning the didactic storm in privacy,

never to hear the prairie wolves   5
in their lunar hilarity
circling one's little all, one's claim
to be Law and Prophets

for all that lawlessness,
never to whet the appetite   10
weeks early, for a face, a hand
longed-for and dreaded—

How people used to meet!
starved, intense, the old
Christmas gifts saved up till spring,   15
and the old plain words,

and each with his God-given secret,
spelled out through months of snow and silence,
burning under the bleached scalp; behind dry lips
a loaded gun.   20

Sylvia Plath (1932–1963)
The Stones

This is the city where men are mended.
I lie on a great anvil.
The flat blue sky-circle

Flew off like the hat of a doll
When I fell out of the light. I entered   5
The stomach of indifference, the wordless cupboard.

The mother of pestles diminished me.
I became a still pebble.
The stones of the belly were peaceable,

The head-stone quiet, jostled by nothing.   10
Only the mouth-hole piped out,
Importunate cricket

In a quarry of silences.
The people of the city heard it.
They hunted the stones, taciturn and separate,   15

The mouth-hole crying their locations.
Drunk as a fetus
I suck at the paps of darkness.

The food tubes embrace me. Sponges kiss my lichens away.
The jewelmaster drives his chisel to pry   20
Open one stone eye.

This is the after-hell: I see the light.
A wind unstoppers the chamber
Of the ear, old worrier.

Water mollifies the flint lip,   25
And daylight lays its sameness on the wall.
The grafters are cheerful,

Heating the pincers, hoisting the delicate hammers.
A current agitates the wires
Volt upon volt. Catgut stitches my fissures.   30

A workman walks by carrying a pink torso.
The storerooms are full of hearts.
This is the city of spare parts.

My swaddled legs and arms smell sweet as rubber.
Here they can doctor heads, or any limb.   35
On Fridays the little children come

To trade their hooks for hands.
Dead men leave eyes for others.
Love is the uniform of my bald nurse.

Love is the bone and sinew of my curse.   40
The vase, reconstructed, houses
The elusive rose.

Ten fingers shape a bowl for shadows.
My mendings itch. There is nothing to do.
I shall be good as new.   45

William Heyen (b. 1940)

In Memoriam: Theodore Roethke[1]

I

A gourd like Jonah's,[2] brimming with dark, still water,
hangs from a rafter. No wind quickening
to sway it loose from its shade.
Becoming, it is breathing
only mosquitoes rising   5
from small fish.

Nothing has moved for so long,
his flowers are drowsing in my house of bones.
I need his river's undersong.

The wind is trapped in the mouths of flowers.   10
The morning glory folds its victrola shape.
The dog sniffing the vines dies among the briars.

O Lord, send
your worm,
a storm.   15

II

If the stations are dark,
the porters gone,
the platforms deserted in the dead of morning,
the rails flowering with rust,
the trains gathering cobwebs in their sheds;   20

If the busses are lost in the woods,
the roads pitted and crossed with fallen poles;

If poisonous fogs settle in empty hangars,
the planes all abandoned in far fields;

Whatever cripple seeks a Lord,   25
however slowly,
a Lord finds.

III

Theodore Roethke, once locked
in a glass house, is dead.
He heard a low sobbing in the veins   30

---

1. Contemporary American poet who died in 1963; several of his poems appear in this collection.
2. After Jonah had delivered God's word to the city of Nineveh, God ordered that a gourd (large plant) grow over the prophet's head to protect him from the sun. The next day, at God's command, a worm destroyed the gourd and a strong wind began to blow, causing Jonah to despair (Jon. 4:5–9). The story of Jonah and the "whale" is alluded to in lines 58–59.

of small things, a sucking to live.
A trapped lark cried love, love,
from a dripping pipe.

Overhead, over the flats of roses
(his blood warming with the breathing dirt),   35
over the slanted panes (the first eyes
of a child's adoration), the great bear
of heaven[3] danced a dance for the fled sun.

Dark light dissatisfies. I know
his impure joy, the luminous darkness   40
of rubbed eyes: feeling I know,
knowing I can only feel.
Momentarily, the heart seems to stop.

The motion begins again, muffled, insistent, a train
seeking its own horizon, but making its journey mean.   45

IV

If a house consumes the spirit,
dust spiraling downward from stair to stair,
windows shutting with ivy and tall weeds,
ceiling so low we must fall to all four legs,
faucets drawing stagnant green water from the well;   50

If the potted nasturtiums are swarming with aphids,
the geraniums flecked with smuts on the darkening sills;

If with each step the floor creaks
as though a bit of muscle is torn from bone;

Whatever cripple seeks a Lord,   55
however slowly,
a Lord finds.

V

I swear, use witchcraft, deceive,
am vomited forth from the whale's mouth.
I walk the sands of the desert watching   60
for the rough sage, perhaps a cactus, to bloom.

There shall be pure water in the wind, a Lord says.

The heavy man clumping beside me stands,
holds me in his sweating paws and whispers
in a fervor of knowing: "It is enough.   65
We have come far enough, watched long enough, to die."

3. The constellation *Ursa Major*.

Shall we not, gladly, give up our flesh
to the shredding wind?

We shall stretch out our blistered arms to touch
the water that shimmers in a cloud   70
over the far dunes, blowing closer and closer.
The wind shall shake loose a lightning of thorns,
the sky open like the mouth of a rose.
Adoring, we shall draw near.
In need, we choose a Lord.   75
We welcome the winds.
A Lord finds.

John Lennon   (b. 1940)
Paul McCartney   (b. 1942)
A Day in the Life

I read the news today oh boy
About a lucky man who made the grade
And though the news was rather sad
Well I just had to laugh
I saw the photograph.   5
He blew his mind out in a car
He didn't notice that the light had changed
A crowd of people stood and stared
They'd seen his face before
Nobody was really sure   10
If he was from the House of Lords.
I saw a film today oh boy
The English Army had just won the war
A crowd of people turned away
But I just had to look   15
Having read the book.
I'd love to turn you on
Woke up, fell out of bed,
Dragged a comb across my head
Found my way downstairs and drank a cup,   20
And looking up I noticed I was late.
Found my coat and grabbed my hat
Made the bus in seconds flat
Found my way upstairs and had a smoke,
Somebody spoke and I went into a dream.   25
I read the news today oh boy
Four thousand holes in Blackburn, Lancashire,
And though the holes were rather small
They had to count them all
Now they know how many holes it takes to fill the Albert Hall.   30
I'd love to turn you on

III

Drama

Chapter 1
The Classical Forms:
Tragedy and Comedy

Fiction and poetry are written primarily for reading, an experience which is usually private and individual. Drama, in contrast, is mainly intended for public performance. Although **closet dramas**—plays intended solely for reading—have been written, especially during the last century, it can be argued that drama has not fulfilled its true function unless it is enacted before an audience. This view is defended on the grounds that, from its inception in ancient Greece, drama has been a communal or social form.

Both the classical theater of ancient Greece and the medieval theater of Christian Europe developed from religious ritual. Classical drama began as part of the festival of Dionysus in Athens, and the religious plays of medieval Europe grew out of the celebration of the Mass. For example, the *Quem Quaeritis*, dating from the tenth century, is a reenactment of the scene at the empty tomb of the risen Christ. Three priests playing the part of the three Marys approach a representation of the Holy Sepulchre and are asked by a fourth priest dressed as an angel, "Whom do you seek?" Then, using lines taken from the New Testament books of Matthew and Mark, he informs them and the congregation that Christ has arisen. Greek tragedy evidently developed in similar fashion from the hymns connected with the sacrificial rites of Dionysus. Both the Dionysus cult and Christianity are death-and-rebirth religions. And the drama that evolved from them was intended to cleanse and renew the community through ritual reenactments.

Drama is a communal event in another sense as well. Besides a dramatist, a few actors, and an audience, a director, designers, and often musicians and choreographers are needed to bring a play to life. This latter group is responsible for all the nonverbal aspects of drama, such as the positioning of actors, the costumes, the sets, the music, and the dancing.

The dramatist often includes **stage directions,** or instructions about the setting, as well as about the physical features, actions, and emotional responses of the actors. Printed in italics and sometimes set off in brackets, stage directions range from a mere indication of entrances and exits to detailed descriptions of character and scene. In *The Hairy Ape* (Chapter 3), Eugene O'Neill begins the first scene with a detailed description of his main character and explicit instructions about how the set should look. Shakespeare, in contrast, provided few stage directions in his plays, many having been added later on by theater managers and editors of his works. But no matter how complete the stage directions are, the performance of a play is ultimately shaped by the ability of the actors, designers, and director to create a coherent stage presentation from the written play itself.

Stage directions are the dramatist's sole opportunity in the play to comment directly on his characters. **Characterization,** or the presentation of a coherent human identity, is particularly difficult for the dramatist. Unlike the fiction writer, who can tell us what his characters are thinking and feeling, the dramatist can only represent speech and action without direct interpretive comment. He cannot *tell* us about his characters. He must show us their natures through what they say and what they do. Before the nineteenth century, dramatists regularly used a **soliloquy,** a speech in which a character speaks his inner thoughts while alone on stage. A similar technique often used was the **aside,** a brief statement which is overheard by the audience but supposedly imperceptible to the other characters on stage. Following the nineteenth-century movement toward greater dramatic realism, modern playwrights, however, have largely eliminated these artificial modes of dramatization. Except in rare instances, they have retained only the **monolog,** a long, uninterrupted speech addressed to one or more characters, and **dialog,** the speech exchanged between two or more characters. When limited to these two basic techniques, the dramatist must create situations in which characters will reveal themselves naturally to one another.

In our modern view of drama, a great deal of emphasis is placed on character transformation and motivation. Dynamic characters, whose attitudes and beliefs are affected by their situation, usually provide exciting drama. To seem psychologically plausible, character transformations must be revealed slowly through a series of speeches and actions. For example, in Shakespeare's play, Othello's rapid transformation from noble warrior and loving bridegroom to vengeful, jealous murderer has raised many a critical eyebrow. Similarly, a character's motivation must be plausible so that his temperament and situation result in specific actions. Although Shakespeare allows Iago to soliloquize about his motivation for ensnaring Othello, his explanations have struck some as too many and too glib. The Romantic poet and critic Samuel Taylor Coleridge concluded that Iago's actions are the "machinations of a motiveless malignancy." The questions involved in Othello's transformation and Iago's motivation will probably be debated as long as the play is performed or read.

The modern audience, however, looks for balance: character defined by action and action arising plausibly out of character. In a discussion of drama, *action* can mean several things. It may mean a particular event ("an action") or the whole sequence of events which comprise the drama ("the action"). Action manifests itself in plot, or the selecting, ordering, and arranging of events in order to suggest their importance and relationship. Traditionally, the plot of a drama has five parts: exposition, rising action, climax, falling action, and dénouement.

Exposition is the presentation of background material—events which occurred before the drama begins and which are relevant to an understanding of what happens in the play. It should blend as naturally as possible into the **rising action,** or the sequence of events which complicate the original situation. The plot rises toward the **climax,** in which the fate of the major characters is firmly established. The **falling action** ensues as the major character in a tragedy gradually loses control, or in a comedy gradually gains control, of the situation. The **dénouement** (literally, the "untying") is the final outcome or resolution of the plot complications.

Any drama with a clearly defined plot can be described in these terms. In *Othello,* for instance, the exposition is spread through Act I. The dialog between Iago and Roderigo in the first scene represents formal exposition, in which the immediate circumstances are revealed. The rest of the act consists of a preliminary action through which the characters of Othello, Desdemona, and Iago are established. The rising action begins in Act II and continues through Act III as Iago's scheme unfolds step by step. First, he provokes Cassio to behavior which angers Othello. He next suggests that Cassio enlist the aid of Desdemona in regaining favor, and he makes certain that Othello notices their meeting. He then begins to hint that Cassio and Desdemona are lovers. Throughout this sequence of events, the **suspense,** or the uncertainty of the plot's outcome, builds as Othello wavers between belief in Iago or in Desdemona. The climax occurs in Act III, scene iii, when Othello swears a quick and violent revenge. During the falling action in Act IV, Othello, completely overwhelmed by jealousy, orders the murder of Cassio and plans the death of Desdemona. The introduction of Lodovico, the messenger from Venice, at this point helps us measure how much Othello has been transformed. The dénouement comes when Emilia discloses Iago's treachery and when Othello, dying by his own hand, comes to understand how he has been tricked.

The plot of *Othello* is relatively straightforward and unified. In other dramas, however, the plot is often more complex. The obstacles to satisfactory resolution may be multipled, and a series of crises required before the dénouement. **Subplots,** or secondary sequences of actions which mirror the main plot, may be introduced. Regardless of how complex the plot may be, the dramatist's object is to create **conflict,** the opposition between forces which grows in intensity before it is resolved. The **protagonist,** or the chief figure in the play, struggles against opposing forces, which are often personified by the **antagonist.** In Shakespeare's play, Othello is clearly the protagonist, Iago the antagonist. In Richard Sheridan's *The Rivals,* Jack Adverse is clearly the protagonist and faces several antagonists, including Sir Anthony, Mrs. Malaprop, and the romantic attitudes of Lydia Languish. In other plays, the antagonist may consist of more impersonal forces such as an institution, society, or even nature. It is the conflict between mighty—or in comedy, not so mighty—opponents which holds the attention of the audience and which constitutes the life of the play.

We all recognize tragedy or comedy when we find one or the other in pure form. *Othello* is clearly a tragedy; *The Rivals* is just as clearly a comedy. Stating just what qualities make *Othello* a tragedy and *The Rivals* a comedy is, however, another problem.

In his *Poetics,* Aristotle (384–322 B.C.) examined the nature of tragedy and introduced terms which critics and scholars have studied and discussed ever since. The precise meaning of his key statements has been the subject of much controversy, and the general applicability of his terminology to all but a few plays has been questioned. (He seems to have had Sophocles' *Oedipus Rex* in mind through most of his discussion.) Yet his definitions and terms are still worth a brief examination.

Aristotle defined **tragedy** as the "imitation of an action of high importance." In his view, the protagonist in tragedy is neither completely virtuous nor completely evil, but rather a noble figure who experiences great suffering through **hamartia.** Often translated as "tragic flaw," this term literally means "missing the mark," as in archery or, more simply, "error." Hamartia has often been identified with **hubris,** or excessive pride, although Aristotle does not in fact use that term in the *Poetics.* Tragedy moves steadily toward **peripeteia** (often anglicized as **peripity**), a reversal or change in fortune. Oedipus in Sophocles' play sets out to find the slayer of his father King Laiös, only to discover that he himself is the murderer. The seeker is the sought. As in this instance, the reversal often involves **irony,** or a sharp discrepancy between what is expected and what actually happens. The tragedy is near completion at the **anagnorisis,** the recognition of the real situation and its implications.

Naturally, Aristotle's terms apply most readily to classical drama. Nevertheless, they can be applied to *Othello* as long as we do not allow Greek terminology to obscure Elizabethan preoccupations. The "action of high importance" in Shakespeare's tragedy is the preservation of the existing Christian, civilized order. The Venetian senate commissions Othello to defend Cyprus, an outpost of civilization, against non-Christian, barbarian forces identified as "the general enemy Ottoman." Yet the real enemy turns out to be the barbarian within. At the first civil disturbance provoked by Iago in Cyprus, Othello exclaims:

> Are we turn'd Turks, and to ourselves do that
> Which heaven hath forbid the Ottomites?
> For Christian shame, put by this barbarous brawl.

Under Iago's influence, Othello gradually becomes a "Turk," unable to distinguish between the evil and the falsehood of Iago and the goodness and purity of Desdemona. In the ironic reversal, the noble general and governor proves incapable of ruling his own passions. His hamartia is his susceptibility to jealousy, a powerful passion which destroys his capacity to act in a reasonable, civilized manner. In his final moments, he comes to full self-recognition *(anagnorisis)* and identifies himself as

> . . . one whose hand,
> Like the base Judean, threw a pearl away
> Richer than all his tribe . . . .

He recognizes that the infidel actually lies in himself and, by implication, in all of us.

As this discussion of *Othello* suggests, tragedy usually involves some conception of a cosmic order, and that conception will vary with different historical periods. For the Greek dramatists, this order is identified with fate or the will of the gods. The problem is for human beings to recognize that order, which occasionally seems obscure or arbitrary. For the Elizabethan dramatists, that order is identified with the laws of nature and of the state and is discovered through reason and revelation. Thus, the problem becomes the capacity of humanity to act in harmony with that order. By the time Shakespeare wrote *Othello,* tragedy seems much less concerned with defining the cosmic order than with defining the nature of humanity and the relationships among people.

An examination of the best-known examples of Greek and Elizabethan tragedy would reveal one common feature: they depict a world in which knowledge is acquired through suffering. In his *Philosophy of Literary Form* (1941), Kenneth Burke isolates three moments in the rhythm of tragic action: purpose, suffering, and perception. The three seem to be present in all tragedies. For example, Othello's purpose is to maintain the rational order of Christian civilization. Since he cannot control his passion, he suffers the loss of self-respect, position, and wife. Through his suffering, he comes to a clearer perception of the disharmony between human passion and the divine order.

Purpose, suffering, perception. Human beings have the hubris—the overreaching pride or presumptuousness—to act. They suffer as a result of their action and gain wisdom as a result of their suffering. Their final perception lends dignity to their pain. It is typical of tragedy that this perception leads to the establishment or restoration of the proper social order at the end of the play. This renewal of society is achieved through the protagonist's suffering and often through his death. This common characteristic of tragedy suggests both the communal nature of drama and the relation of tragedy to death-rebirth religions. The tragic protagonist corresponds to the god who suffers and dies to ensure the rebirth of nature and the spiritual renovation of humanity. The audience which participates vicariously in his ordeal experiences what Aristotle called **catharsis,** or an individual emotional purgation. Tragedy, then, can be seen as a ritual death through which the community is reborn.

Considered in this same context, **comedy** can be regarded as the celebration of rebirth. Comedy, which takes its name from the Greek *komos* (meaning "revel") derives from the ritual rejoicing over the resurrection of Dionysus and the simultaneous renewal of nature in the spring. Ancient comedy invariably ended with a feast or dance celebrating a wedding. This conventional conclusion has been retained through the centuries. Shakespeare's *As You Like It* (1599) ends with no fewer than four marriages. And in our own day, many motion-picture comedies end with the kiss of hero and heroine indicating a prospective marriage. This pairing-off of couples at the end of a comedy suggests the proper reordering of society for the raising of a new generation. It suggests, that is, renewal.

Derived from the comedies of ancient Greece, the standard plot has remained, until the modern period, essentially very simple. An attractive young man desires an attractive young woman but is prevented from winning her by an older man, usually father, uncle, or guardian. Near the end of the play, a discovery is made which allows the young man to overcome all obstacles and to win his bride. Allowing for slight variations, this plot can be found in comedies ranging from *Dyskolos* ("the Grouch") written by Menander in the third century B.C. to Beaumarchais' *The Barber of Seville* (1775) and Gilbert and Sullivan's *The Mikado* (1885).

Since plot and character are so closely related, the standard plot entails certain **stock characters,** or stereotypes, who appear in slightly varied forms in many plays. First, of course, are the young lovers. Usually, but not always, they are remarkably normal, and their one-dimensional characterization allows the audience easily to identify with them. They are opposed by the *senex,* the old man who prevents their union for a variety of selfish reasons. He is usually characterized as absurd in some way. During the Renaissance, he became a **humour character,** one completely overpowered by a single obsessive emotion like greed, jealousy, anger, or even sensitivity to noise. In terms of Renaissance physiology, one of his humours, or bodily fluids—blood, phlegm, choler, or bile—is overly predominant, thus upsetting the balance of his personality. The laughter provoked by the humour character can be explained by more recent theories. The French philosopher Henri Bergson (1859–1941) writes: "Any arrangement of acts and events is comic which gives us, in a single combination, the illusion of life and the distinct impression of a mechanical arrangement." This is the principle behind the humour character, who responds to every situation in the same mechanical manner.

Part of the action of the conventional comedy is designed to expose the *senex'* absurdity and often to free him from his obsessive trait. The lovers are aided in this endeavor by the wiley servant, who is often the one who actually outwits the *senex.* The dramatist may also supply one of the lovers with a **confidant,** a character in whom he or she can confide without resorting to soliloquy. There may also be a **foil,** a character whose main purpose is to set off through contrast the qualities of one of the major characters. Another stock character, who often complicates the plot is the *miles gloriosus,* or the military braggart, who proves to be a coward and thus loses his dubious claim to the heroine.

Of course, if this same plot and these same characters had appeared in play after play, comedy would soon have lost its audience. One of the essential ingredients in traditional comedy is the subtle variation and complication of the familiar comic situation. In *The Rivals,* for instance, Sheridan varies and complicates the standard plot until it is nearly unrecognizable.

Jack Absolute is the young man who, under the assumed name of Ensign Beverley, is courting Lydia Languish. He is apparently prevented from winning her by his father, Sir Anthony, and by her aunt, Mrs. Malaprop, who wish to force him into an arranged match with a lady of their choosing. Sir Anthony, the *senex,* is whimsical and inconsistent. Mrs. Malaprop, a feminine variation of the *senex,* is even more absurd in her pretensions to learning. It is clear from the beginning—as it always is in comedy—that the lovers will eventually overcome the opposition of their elders. But the situation is complicated by an unusual variation on the standard plot: the other lady whom Sir Anthony and Mrs. Malaprop have chosen for Absolute is his own choice, Lydia Languish.

The real obstacle to a happy ending in *The Rivals* is Lydia herself. In another variation on the standard plot, Sheridan depicts his heroine as a humour character. Completely obsessed with romantic notions of elopement with a penniless ensign, Lydia refuses to marry Absolute, who comes with a fortune, a good name, and the blessing of her aunt. The plot is further complicated by the intrigues of Lucy, a variation on the wiley servant, and by the antics of Bob Acres and Sir Lucius O'Trigger, variations on the *miles gloriosus*. As a final touch, Sheridan adds a mirroring subplot in which Faulkland, an overly romantic young man, is blocked by his humour from marrying Julia.

Certainly, much of the laughter in comedy is provoked by such variations on the standard plot. The plot of *The Rivals* allows room for many comic misunderstandings and a great deal of irony, particularly dramatic irony. In comedy, **dramatic irony** elicits laughter because the audience, having knowledge which a character does not have, sees the disparity between what a character believes to be occurring and what is actually taking place. A good example of dramatic irony is found in Act II, scene i, when Absolute, in his ignorance, defies his father's attempts to force him into a match with a lady whom the audience knows is his own Lydia. In fact, almost every scene of the first four acts of the play utilizes some character's ignorance to create dramatic irony.

Misunderstandings and dramatic irony cannot, however, account for all the laughter provoked by comedy. Much of the fun derives directly from the verbal texture of the play. In Shakespeare's *Twelfth Night* (1600), Feste the fool defines the role of jester as being a "corrupter of words." He reminds us that misuse of language, deliberate or otherwise, is usually comic. Mrs. Malaprop's mechanical misuse of long, Latinate words has, in fact, added a new word to the dictionary—*malapropism,* meaning the humorous misapplication of words. Her description of Lydia as being as headstrong "as an allegory on the banks of the Nile" will probably get a laugh until alligators are extinct and forgotten.

Deliberate and artful misuse of language has an important place in comedy. When the overly romantic Faulkland complains that his Julia has been in good health instead of suffering during their separation, Absolute responds: "Oh, it was very unkind of her to be well in your absence, to be sure." Absolute, who does not share Faulkland's sentimental notions of love, is using **verbal irony**—which is saying one thing and meaning quite another. When Lydia discovers that her marriage to Absolute will involve a dowry and marriage contracts, she exclaims that she feels like "a mere Smithfield bargain." She is comparing a blushing bride to a piece of merchandise obtained after hard bargaining in the Smithfield marketplace. The yoking of bride and merchandise, things which are different in all respects except one—both are purchased after haggling—accounts for several witty statements in the play. Much of the fun in comedy derives from wit and verbal irony, especially when the performers establish a brisk pace by speaking their lines with crispness and verve.

Yet most of the laughter in comedy is provoked by a more general activity—the display and the exposure of human folly. **Satire,** or the ridiculing of absurd behavior, is usually present to some degree in comedy. Acres, the country squire in *The Rivals,* attempts to achieve the polish of the swaggering sophisticate by learning the latest dance steps, by swearing fashionably, and by engaging his supposed rival in a duel. His kind of pretentious behavior is what comedy excels at satirizing. More central to the play is the exposure of the faddish, sentimental notions of love which Lydia and Faulkland no doubt acquired from the popular fiction of the day. Through ridiculing this type of absurdity, comedy gets a laugh and makes a serious comment on the foolishness of many social attitudes and the folly of human nature.

The Rivals contains many important elements of satire. In some comedies, however, the exposure of absurd behavior is the very essence of the comic action. In **satiric comedy,** the foibles of human nature are grossly exaggerated and often cruelly exposed. In this type of comedy, the humour characters who separate the lovers get most of the attention and all of the abuse. Their folly is displayed and held up to ridicule until they are finally outwitted and driven from the stage. The assumption of satiric comedy is that human nature is essentially ridiculous and can never measure up to the ideal implied by the dramatist.

Romantic comedy, in contrast, deals more gently with human weakness. Often set in some isolated never-never land, this type of comedy focuses more closely on the lovers in their struggle to achieve happiness. "The course of true love never did run smooth," as Shakespeare writes in *A Midsummer-Night's Dream* (1595), a typical romantic comedy. Yet the course of true love will be run and all obstacles finally overcome. Romantic comedy exposes human folly and often leads to character reform. But, in the end, it usually unites all the characters in the celebration which concludes the action. Romantic comedy seems to suggest that human nature must finally be accepted as it is.

The various types of comedy all have one thing in common: each ends with the lovers triumphing over all obstructions and obstructing characters. It is this direct triumph which distinguishes comedy from tragedy. In tragedy, the protagonist is pitted against a *cosmic* order, a rhythm of things, which is beyond him and to which he must conform or perish. He and society gain clearer insights into the human condition through his inevitable defeat. In comedy, the young lovers are pitted against a *social* order, usually a whimsical human order imposed by an irrational, older generation. By the dénouement of comedy, the lovers have triumphed over the irrational order, and a new social structure is formed around the now-united couple.

Northrop Frye has written in *The Anatomy of Criticism* (1957) that "comedy sets up an arbitrary law and then organizes the action to break or evade it." Tragedy, in contrast, treats the relationship between humanity and an absolute, unavoidable law. With this distinction between comedy and tragedy in mind, it would be pleasant if we could say that all dramas fall into one category or the other. Unfortunately, they do not. Shakespeare, for example, wrote several **tragicomedies,** which utilize elements of both comedy and tragedy. And modern playwrights have certainly not felt obliged to write plays that can be easily classified. In all forms of literature, the tendency in the last two hundred years has been toward mixed types and forms. Drama is no exception. An understanding of the traditional distinctions between comedy and tragedy, however, will help us understand the great classics of the stage. It should also aid us in coming to terms with the new forms which modern dramatists are constantly creating.

William Shakespeare (1564–1616)
Othello

The Names of the Actors

OTHELLO, *the Moor.*
BRABANTIO, *[a senator,] father to Desdemona.*
CASSIO, *an honourable lieutenant [to Othello].*
IAGO, *[Othello's ancient,] a villain.*
RODERIGO, *a gulled gentleman.*
DUKE OF VENICE.
Senators [of Venice].
MONTANO, *governor of Cyprus.*
LODOVICO *and* GRATIANO, *[kinsmen to Brabantio,] two noble Venetians.*
Sailors.
Clown.
DESDEMONA, *[daughter to Brabantio and] wife to Othello.*
EMILIA, *wife to Iago.*
BIANCA, *courtezan [and mistress to Cassio].*
[Messenger, Herald, Officers, Gentlemen, Musicians, and Attendants.]

[SCENE: *Venice: a Sea-port in Cyprus.*]

ACT I.

Scene I. [*Venice. A street.*]

    Enter RODERIGO *and* IAGO.

    ROD.   Tush! never tell me; I take it much unkindly
That thou, Iago, who hast had my purse
As if the strings were thine, shouldst know of this.
    IAGO.   'Sblood, but you'll not hear me:
If ever I did dream of such a matter,
Abhor me.
    ROD.   Thou told'st me thou didst hold him in thy hate.
    IAGO.   Despise me, if I do not. Three great ones of the city,
In personal suit to make me his lieutenant,

Act I. Scene I. 4. **'Sblood,** an oath, "by God's blood." 8. **great ones of the city.** Iago means to indicate his importance in the community; this is suggested also by his use of the word *worth* in line 11.

Off-capp'd to him: and, by the faith of man,   10
I know my price, I am worth no worse a place:
But he, as loving his own pride and purposes,
Evades them, with a bombast circumstance
Horribly stuff'd with epithets of war;
And, in conclusion,
Nonsuits my mediators; for, 'Certes,' says he,
'I have already chose my officer.'
And what was he?
Forsooth, a great arithmetician,
One Michael Cassio, a Florentine,   20
A fellow almost damn'd in a fair wife;
That never set a squadron in the field,
Nor the division of a battle knows
More than a spinster; unless the bookish theoric,
Wherein the toged consuls can propose
As masterly as he: mere prattle, without practice,
Is all his soldiership. But he, sir, had th' election:
And I, of whom his eyes had seen the proof
At Rhodes, at Cyprus and on other grounds
Christian and heathen, must be be-lee'd and calm'd   30
By debitor and creditor: this counter-caster,
He, in good time, must his lieutenant be,
And I—God bless the mark!—his Moorship's ancient.
    Rod.   By heaven, I rather would have been his hangman.
    Iago.   Why, there's no remedy; 'tis the curse of service,
Preferment goes by letter and affection,
And not by old gradation, where each second
Stood heir to th' first. Now, sir, be judge yourself,
Whether I in any just term am affin'd
To love the Moor.
    Rod.   I would not follow him then.   40
    Iago.   O, sir, content you;
I follow him to serve my turn upon him:
We cannot all be masters, nor all masters
Cannot be truly follow'd. You shall mark
Many a duteous and knee-crooking knave,
That, doting on his own obsequious bondage,
Wears out his time, much like his master's ass,
For nought but provender, and when he's old, cashier'd:
Whip me such honest knaves. Others there are
Who, trimm'd in forms and visages of duty,   50

10. **him**, Othello. 16. **Nonsuits,** rejects. 19. **arithmetician,** a man whose military knowledge was merely theoretical, based on books of tactics. 21. **A . . . wife.** Cassio does not seem to be married, but his counterpart in Shakespeare's source did have a wife. 23. **division,** disposition of a battle line. 24. **theoric,** theory. 25. **toged,** wearing the toga. **propose,** discuss. 29. **Rhodes, Cyprus,** islands in the Mediterranean south of Asia Minor, long subject to contention between the Venetians and the Turks. 31. **counter-caster,** a sort of bookkeeper; contemptuous term. 32. **in good time,** forsooth. 33. **God bless the mark,** anciently, a pious interjection to avert evil omens. **ancient,** standardbearer, ensign. 37. **old gradation,** seniority. Iago here expresses a characteristic prejudice of professional soldiers. 39. **affin'd,** bound.

Keep yet their hearts attending on themselves,
And, throwing but shows of service on their lords,
Do well thrive by them and when they have lin'd their coats
Do themselves homage: these fellows have some soul;
And such a one do I profess myself. For, sir,
It is as sure as you are Roderigo,
Were I the Moor, I would not be Iago:
In following him, I follow but myself;
Heaven is my judge, not I for love and duty,
But seeming so, for my peculiar end: 60
For when my outward action doth demonstrate
The native act and figure of my heart
In compliment extern, 'tis not long after
But I will wear my heart upon my sleeve
For daws to peck at: I am not what I am.
     Rod.   What a full fortune does the thick-lips owe,
If he can carry 't thus!
     Iago.   Call up her father,
Rouse him: make after him, poison his delight,
Proclaim him in the streets; incense her kinsmen,
And, though he in a fertile climate dwell,   70
Plague him with flies: though that his joy be joy,
Yet throw such changes of vexation on 't,
As it may lose some colour.
     Rod.   Here is her father's house; I'll call aloud.
     Iago.   Do, with like timorous accent and dire yell
As when, by night and negligence, the fire
Is spied in populous cities.
     Rod.   What, ho, Brabantio! Signior Brabantio, ho!
     Iago.   Awake! what, ho, Brabantio! thieves! thieves! thieves!
Look to your house, your daughter and your bags!   80
Thieves! Thieves!

     Brabantio [*appears*] *above* [*at a window*].

     Bra.   What is the reason of this terrible summons?
What is the matter there?
     Rod.   Signior, is all your family within?
     Iago.   Are your doors lock'd?
     Bra.   Why, wherefore ask you this?
     Iago.   'Zounds, sir, y' are robb'd; for shame, put on your gown;
Your heart is burst, you have lost half your soul;
Even now, now, very now, an old black ram
Is tupping your white ewe. Arise, arise;
Awake the snorting citizens with the bell,   90
Or else the devil will make a grandsire of you:

---

57. **Were . . . Iago.** Were I in the position of the Moor, I should not feel as Iago feels.   63.
compliment extern, outward civility. 66. **thick-lips.** Elizabethans often applied the term "Moor"
to Negroes. 75. **timorous,** frightening. 90. **snorting,** snoring.

Arise, I say.

BRA. What, have you lost your wits?

ROD. Most reverend signior, do you know my voice?

BRA. Not I: what are you?

ROD. My name is Roderigo.

BRA.   The worser welcome:
I have charg'd thee not to haunt about my doors:
In honest plainness thou hast heard me say
My daughter is not for thee; and now, in madness,
Being full of supper and distemp'ring draughts,
Upon malicious bravery, dost thou come   100
To start my quiet.

ROD. Sir, sir, sir,—

BRA.   But thou must needs be sure
My spirit and my place have in them power
To make this bitter to thee.

ROD.   Patience, good sir.

BRA. What tell'st thou me of robbing? this is Venice;
My house is not a grange.

ROD.   Most grave Brabantio,
In simple and pure soul I come to you.

IAGO. 'Zounds, sir, you are one of those that will not serve God, if the
devil bid you. Because we come to do you service and you think we are ruffians,
you'll have your daughter covered with a Barbary horse; you'll have your
nephews neigh to you; you'll have coursers for cousins and gennets for
germans.   112

BRA. What profane wretch art thou?

IAGO. I am one, sir, that comes to tell you your daughter and the Moor
are now making the beast with two backs.

BRA. Thou art a villain.

IAGO.   You are—a senator.

BRA. This thou shalt answer; I know thee, Roderigo.

ROD. Sir, I will answer any thing. But, I beseech you,
If 't be your pleasure and most wise consent,
As partly I find it is, that your fair daughter,   120
At this odd-even and dull watch o' th' night,
Transported, with no worse nor better guard
But with a knave of common hire, a gondolier,
To the gross clasps of a lascivious Moor,—
If this be known to you and your allowance,
We then have done you bold and saucy wrongs;
But if you know not this, my manners tell me
We have your wrong rebuke. Do not believe
That, from the sense of all civility,
I thus would play and trifle with your reverence: 130

---

100. **bravery**, defiance, bravado.   101. **start**, disrupt.   106. **grange**, isolated farmhouse.   111.
nephews, grandsons.   112. **gennets**, small Spanish horses.   **germans**, near relatives.   121. **odd-even**,
between night and morning.   125. **allowance**, permission.   129. **from**, contrary to.

Your daughter, if you have not given her leave,
I say again, hath made a gross revolt;
Tying her duty, beauty, wit and fortunes
In an extravagant and wheeling stranger
Of here and every where. Straight satisfy yourself:
If she be in her chamber or your house,
Let loose on me the justice of the state
For thus deluding you.
      Bra.   Strike on the tinder, ho!
Give me a taper! call up all my people!
This accident is not unlike my dream: 140
Belief of it oppresses me already.
Light, I say! light!   *Exit* [*above*].
      Iago.   Farewell; for I must leave you:
It seems not meet, nor wholesome to my place,
To be produc'd—as, if I stay, I shall—
Against the Moor: for, I do know, the state,
However this may gall him with some check,
Cannot with safety cast him, for he's embark'd
With such loud reason to the Cyprus wars,
Which even now stand in act, that, for their souls,
Another of his fathom they have none,   150
To lead their business: in which regard,
Though I do hate him as I do hell-pains,
Yet, for necessity of present life,
I must show out a flag and sign of love,
Which is indeed but sign. That you shall surely find him,
Lead to the Sagittary the raised search;
And there will I be with him. So, farewell.   *Exit*.

     Enter [*below*]
     Brabantio, *with* Servants *and torches*.

      Bra. It is too true an evil: gone she is;
And what's to come of my despised time
Is nought but bitterness. Now, Roderigo,
Where didst thou see her? O unhappy girl!   160
With the Moor, say'st thou? Who would be a father!
How didst thou know 'twas she? O, she deceives me
Past thought! What said she to you? Get moe tapers:
Raise all my kindred. Are they married, think you?
      Rod. Truly, I think they are.
      Bra. O heaven! How got she out? O treason of the blood!
Fathers, from hence trust not your daughters' minds
By what you see them act. Is there not charms

---

    134. **extravagant,** wandering. **wheeling,** vagabond.   138. **tinder,** charred linen kept in a metal box, and ignited by a spark from flint and steel.   140. **accident,** occurrence.   146. **check,** rebuke. 147. **cast,** dismiss.   149. **stand in act,** are going on.   150. **fathom,** ability.   156. **Sagittary,** probably an inn.   164. **moe,** more.

By which the property of youth and maidhood   170
May be abus'd? Have you not read, Roderigo,
Of some such thing?
    Rod.   Yes, sir, I have indeed.
    Bra.   Call up my brother. O, would you had had her!
Some one way, some another. Do you know
Where we may apprehend her and the Moor?
    Rod.   I think I can discover him, if you please
To get good guard and go along with me.
    Bra.   Pray you, lead on. At every house I'll call;
I may command at most. Get weapons, ho!
And raise some special officers of night.   180
On, good Roderigo: I will deserve your pains.   *Exeunt.*

Scene II. [*Another street.*]

    Enter Othello, Iago, Attendants *with torches.*

    Iago.   Though in the trade of war I have slain men,
Yet do I hold it very stuff o' th' conscience
To do no contriv'd murder: I lack iniquity
Sometime to do me service: nine or ten times
I had thought t' have yerk'd him here under the ribs.
    Oth.   'Tis better as it is.
    Iago.   Nay, but he prated,
And spoke such scurvy and provoking terms
Against your honour
That, with the little godliness I have,
I did full hard forbear him. But, I pray you, sir,   10
Are you fast married? Be assur'd of this,
That the magnifico is much belov'd,
And hath in his effect a voice potential
As double as the duke's: he will divorce you;
Or put upon you what restraint and grievance
The law, with all his might to enforce it on,
Will give him cable.
    Oth.   Let him do his spite;
My services which I have done the signiory
Shall out-tongue his complaints. 'Tis yet to know,—
Which, when I know that boasting is an honour,   20
I shall promulgate—I fetch my life and being
From men of royal siege, and my demerits
May speak unbonneted to as proud a fortune
As this that I have reach'd: for know, Iago,

---

    170. **property,** special quality.   173. **you,** Roderigo.   180. **officers of night,** police.
    Scene II.   5. **yerk'd,** stabbed.   12. **magnifico,** Venetian grandee (i.e., Brabantio).   13. **effect,**
influence.   **potential,** powerful.   14. **double,** twice as influential as most men's.   18. **signiory,** Venetian government.   22. **siege,** rank.   **demerits,** deserts.   23. **unbonneted,** on equal terms.

But that I love the gentle Desdemona,
I would not my unhoused free condition
Put into circumscription and confine
For the sea's worth. But, look! what lights come yond?
    Iago.   Those are the raised father and his friends:
You were best go in.
    Oth.   Not I; I must be found: 30
My parts, my title and my perfect soul
Shall manifest me rightly. Is it they?
    Iago.   By Janus, I think no.

Enter Cassio [*and certain* Officers] *with torches.*

    Oth.   The servants of the duke, and my lieutenant.
The goodness of the night upon you, friends!
What is the news?
    Cas.   The duke does greet you, general,
And he requires your haste-post-haste appearance,
Even on the instant.
    Oth.   What is the matter, think you?
    Cas.   Something from Cyprus, as I may divine:
It is a business of some heat: the galleys   40
Have sent a dozen sequent messengers
This very night at one another's heels,
And many of the consuls, rais'd and met,
Are at the duke's already: you have been hotly call'd for;
When, being not at your lodging to be found,
The senate hath sent about three several quests
To search you out.
    Oth.   'Tis well I am found by you.
I will but spend a word here in the house,
And go with you.   [*Exit.*]
    Cas.   Ancient, what makes he here?
    Iago.   'Faith, he to-night hath boarded a land carack: 50
If it prove lawful prize, he's made for ever.
    Cas. I do not understand.
    Iago.   He's married.
    Cas.   To who?

[*Enter* Othello.]

    Iago.   Marry, to—Come, captain, will you go?
    Oth.   Have with you.
    Cas.   Here comes another troop to seek for you.

Enter Brabantio, Roderigo, *with* Officers *and torches.*

---

    31. **perfect soul,** unflawed conscience. 41. **sequent,** successive. 43. **consuls,** senators. 46. **several,** separate. 50. **carack,** large merchant ship.

IAGO.   It is Brabantio. General, be advis'd;
He comes to bad intent.
OTH.   Holla! stand there!
ROD.   Signior, it is the Moor.
BRA.   Down with him, thief!

[*They draw on both sides.*]

IAGO.   You, Roderigo! come, sir, I am for you.
OTH.   Keep up your bright swords, for the dew will rust them.
Good signior, you shall more command with years   60
Than with your weapons.
BRA.   O thou foul thief, where hast thou stow'd my daughter?
Damn'd as thou art, thou hast enchanted her;
For I'll refer me to all things of sense,
If she in chains of magic were not bound,
Whether a maid so tender, fair and happy,
So opposite to marriage that she shunn'd
The wealthy curled darlings of our nation,
Would ever have, t' incur a general mock,
Run from her guardage to the sooty bosom   70
Of such a thing as thou, to fear, not to delight.
Judge me the world, if 'tis not gross in sense
That thou hast practis'd on her with foul charms,
Abus'd her delicate youth with drugs or minerals
That weaken motion: I'll have 't disputed on;
'Tis probable and palpable to thinking.
I therefore apprehend and do attach thee
For an abuser of the world, a practiser
Of arts inhibited and out of warrant.
Lay hold upon him: if he do resist,   80
Subdue him at his peril.
OTH.   Hold your hands,
Both you of my inclining, and the rest:
Were it my cue to fight, I should have known it
Without a prompter. Wither will you that I go
To answer this your charge?
BRA.   To prison, till fit time
Of law and course of direct session
Call thee to answer.
OTH.   What if I do obey?
How may the duke be therewith satisfied,
Whose messengers are here about my side,
Upon some present business of the state   90
To bring me to him?
FIRST OFF.   'Tis true, most worthy signior;

---

63. **things of sense,** commonsense understandings of the natural order.   70. **guardage,** guardian-
ship.   72. **gross in sense,** easily discernible in apprehension or perception.   74. **minerals,** medicine,
poison.   75. **motion,** thought, reason.   **disputed on,** argued in court by professional counsel.   78.
abuser of the world, corrupter of society.   79. **inhibited,** prohibited.   82. **inclining,** following, party.
86. **course of direct session,** regular legal proceedings.

The duke's in council, and your noble self,
I am sure, is sent for.
    BRA   How! the duke in council!
In this time of the night! Bring him away:
Mine's not an idle cause: the duke himself,
Or any of my brothers of the state,
Cannot but feel this wrong as 'twere their own;
For if such actions may have passage free,
Bond-slaves and pagans shall our statesmen be.   *Exeunt.*

Scene III.   [*A council-chamber.*]

    Enter DUKE, Senators, *and* Officers [*set at a table, with lights and* Attendants].

    DUKE.   There is no composition in these news
That gives them credit.
    FIRST SEN.   Indeed, they are disproportion'd;
My letters say a hundred and seven galleys.
    DUKE.   And mine, a hundred forty.
    SEC. SEN.   And mine, two hundred:
But though they jump not on a just account,—
As in these cases, where the aim reports,
'Tis oft with difference—yet do they all confirm
A Turkish fleet, and bearing up to Cyprus.
    DUKE.   Nay, it is possible enough to judgement:
I do not so secure me in the error,   10
But the main article I do approve
In fearful sense.
    SAILOR.   [*Within*] What, ho! what, ho! what, ho!
    FIRST OFF.   A messenger from the galleys.

    Enter Sailor.

    DUKE.   Now, what's the business?
    SAIL.   The Turkish preparation makes for Rhodes;
So was I bid report here to the state
By Signior Angelo.
    DUKE.   How say you by this change?
    FIRST SEN.   This cannot be,
By no assay of reason: 'tis a pageant,
To keep us in false gaze. When we consider
Th' importancy of Cyprus to the Turk,   20
And let ourselves again but understand,
That as it more concerns the Turk than Rhodes,
So may he with more facile question bear it,

---

    99. **Bond-slaves and pagans,** contemptuous references to Othello's past history.
    Scene III.   2. **disproportion'd,** inconsistent.   5. **jump,** agree.   6. **aim,** conjecture.   10. **secure me,** feel myself secure.   11. **main article,** i.e., that the Turkish fleet is threatening.   **approve,** accept.
    18. **assay,** test.   23. **more facile question,** greater facility of effort.

For that it stands not in such warlike brace,
But altogether lacks th' abilities
That Rhodes is dress'd in: if we make thought of this,
We must not think the Turk is so unskilful
To leave that latest which concerns him first,
Neglecting an attempt of ease and gain,
To wake and wage a danger profitless.   30
    DUKE. Nay, in all confidence, he's not for Rhodes.
    FIRST OFF. Here is more news.

    Enter a Messenger.

    MESS. The Ottomites, reverend and gracious,
Steering with due course toward the isle of Rhodes,
Have there injointed them with an after fleet.
    FIRST SEN. Ay, so I thought. How many, as you guess?
    MESS. Of thirty sail: and now they do re-stem
Their backward course, bearing with frank appearance
Their purposes toward Cyprus. Signior Montano,
Your trusty and most valiant servitor,   40
With his free duty recommends you thus,
And prays you to believe him.
    DUKE. 'Tis certain, then, for Cyprus.
Marcus Luccicos, is not he in town?
    FIRST SEN. He's now in Florence.
    DUKE. Write from us to him; post-post-haste dispatch.
    FIRST SEN. Here comes Brabantio and the valiant Moor.

    Enter BRABANTIO, OTHELLO, CASSIO, IAGO, RODERIGO, *and* Officers.

    DUKE. Valiant Othello, we must straight employ you
Against the general enemy Ottoman.
[*To Brabantio*] I did not see you; welcome, gentle signior;   50
We lack'd your counsel and your help to-night.
    BRA. So did I yours. Good your grace, pardon me;
Neither my place nor aught I heard of business
Hath rais'd me from my bed, nor doth the general care
Take hold on me, for my particular grief
Is of so flood-gate and o'erbearing nature
That it engluts and swallows other sorrows
And it is still itself.
    DUKE.   Why, what's the matter?
    BRA. My daughter! O, my daughter!
    DUKE AND SEN.   Dead?
    BRA.   Ay, to me;
She is abus'd, stol'n from me, and corrupted   60
By spells and medicines bought of mountebanks;

---

    24. **brace,** state of defense. 37. **re-stem,** steer again. 57. **engluts,** engulfs.

For nature so preposterously to err,
Being not deficient, blind, or lame of sense,
Sans witchcraft could not.
    DUKE. Whoe'er he be that in this foul proceeding
Hath thus beguil'd your daughter of herself
And you of her, the bloody book of law
You shall yourself read in the bitter letter
After your own sense, yea, though our proper son
Stood in your action.
    BRA.   Humbly I thank your grace.   70
Here is the man, this Moor, whom now, it seems,
Your special mandate for the state-affairs
Hath hither brought.
    DUKE AND SEN. We are very sorry for 't.
    DUKE. [*To Othello*] What, in your own part, can you say to this?
    BRA. Nothing, but this is so.
    OTH. Most potent, grave, and reverend signiors,
My very noble and approv'd good masters,
That I have ta'en away this old man's daughter,
It is most true; true, I have married her:
The very head and front of my offending   80
Hath this extent, no more. Rude am I in my speech,
And little bless'd with the soft phrase of peace;
For since these arms of mine had seven years' pith,
Till now some nine moons wasted, they have us'd
Their dearest action in the tented field,
And little of this great world can I speak,
More than pertains to feats of broil and battle,
And therefore little shall I grace my cause
In speaking for myself. Yet, by your gracious patience,
I will a round unvarnish'd tale deliver   90
Of my whole course of love; what drugs, what charms,
What conjuration and what mighty magic,
For such proceeding I am charg'd withal,
I won his daughter.
    BRA.   A maiden never bold;
Of spirit so still and quiet, that her motion
Blush'd at herself; and she, in spite of nature,
Of years, of country, credit, every thing,
To fall in love with what she fear'd to look on!
It is a judgement maim'd and most imperfect
That will confess perfection so could err   100
Against all rules of nature, and must be driven
To find out practices of cunning hell,
Why this should be. I therefore vouch again

---

70. **Stood . . . action,** was under your accusation. 83. **pith,** strength, vigor. 89. **patience,** sufferance, permission. 95–96. **motion . . . herself,** inward impulses blushed at themselves. 103. **vouch,** assert.

That with some mixtures pow'rful o'er the blood,
Or with some dram conjur'd to this effect,
He wrought upon her.
    DUKE.   To vouch this, is no proof,
Without more wider and more overt test
Than these thin habits and poor likelihoods
Of modern seeming do prefer against him.
    FIRST SEN. But, Othello, speak: 110
Did you by indirect and forced courses
Subdue and poison this young maid's affections?
Or came it by request and such fair question
As soul to soul affordeth?
    OTH.   I do beseech you,
Send for the lady to the Sagittary,
And let her speak of me before her father:
If you do find me foul in her report,
The trust, the office I do hold of you,
Not only take away, but let your sentence
Even fall upon my life.
    DUKE.   Fetch Desdemona hither. 120
    OTH. Ancient, conduct them; you best know the place.

                     [Exeunt Iago and Attendants.]

And, till she come, as truly as to heaven
I do confess the vices of my blood,
So justly to your grave ears I'll present
How I did thrive in this fair lady's love,
And she in mine.
    DUKE. Say it, Othello.
    OTH. Her father lov'd me; oft invited me;
Still question'd me the story of my life,
From year to year, the battles, sieges, fortunes, 130
That I have pass'd.
I ran it through, even from my boyish days,
To th' very moment that he bade me tell it;
Wherein I spake of most disastrous chances,
Of moving accidents by flood and field,
Of hair-breadth scapes i' th' imminent deadly breach,
Of being taken by the insolent foe
And sold to slavery, of my redemption thence
And portance in my travels' history:
Wherein of antres vast and deserts idle, 140
Rough quarries, rocks and hills whose heads touch heaven,
It was my hint to speak,—such was the process;
And of the Cannibals that each other eat,
The Anthropophagi and men whose heads

---

136. **imminent,** i.e., impending parts when a gap has been made in a fortification.   139. **portance,** conduct.   140. **antres,** caverns.   **idle,** barren, unprofitable.   142. **hint,** occasion.   144. **Anthropophagi,** man-eaters.

Do grow beneath their shoulders. This to hear
Would Desdemona seriously incline:
But still the house-affairs would draw her thence:
Which ever as she could with haste dispatch,
She 'ld come again, and with a greedy ear
Devour up my discourse: which I observing, 150
Took once a pliant hour, and found good means
To draw from her a prayer of earnest heart
That I would all my pilgrimage dilate,
Whereof by parcels she had something heard,
But not intentively: I did consent,
And often did beguile her of her tears,
When I did speak of some distressful stroke
That my youth suffer'd. My story being done,
She gave me for my pains a world of sighs:
She swore, in faith, 'twas strange, 'twas passing strange, 160
'Twas pitiful, 'twas wondrous pitiful:
She wish'd she had not heard it, yet she wish'd
That heaven had made her such a man: she thank'd me,
And bade me, if I had a friend that lov'd her,
I should but teach him how to tell my story,
And that would woo her. Upon this hint I spake:
She lov'd me for the dangers I had pass'd,
And I lov'd her that she did pity them.
This only is the witchcraft I have us'd:
Here comes the lady; let her witness it. 170

    Enter DESDEMONA, IAGO, [*and*] Attendants.

    DUKE. I think this tale would win my daughter too.
Good Brabantio,
Take up this mangled matter at the best:
Men do their broken weapons rather use
Than their bare hands.
    BRA.   I pray you, hear her speak:
If she confess that she was half the wooer,
Destruction on my head, if my bad blame
Light on the man! Come hither, gentle mistress:
Do you perceive in all this noble company
Where most you owe obedience?
    DES.   My noble father, 180
I do perceive here a divided duty:
To you I am bound for life and education;
My life and education both do learn me
How to respect you; you are the lord of duty;
I am hitherto your daughter: but here's my husband,

---

    153. **dilate,** relate in detail. 155. **intentively,** with full attention. 181. **divided duty.** Desdemona recognizes that she still owes a duty to her father even after marriage.

And so much duty as my mother show'd
To you, preferring you before her father,
So much I challenge that I may profess
Due to the Moor my lord.
    BRA.   God be with you! I have done.
Please it your grace, on to the state-affairs: 190
I had rather to adopt a child than get it.
Come hither, Moor:
I here do give thee that with all my heart
Which, but thou hast already, with all my heart
I would keep from thee. For your sake, jewel,
I am glad at soul I have no other child;
For thy escape would teach me tyranny,
To hang clogs on them. I have done, my lord.
    DUKE. Let me speak like yourself, and lay a sentence,
Which, as a grise or step, may help these lovers   200
Into your favour.
When remedies are past, the griefs are ended
By seeing the worst, which late on hopes depended.
To mourn a mischief that is past and gone
Is the next way to draw new mischief on.
What cannot be preserv'd when fortune takes,
Patience her injury a mock'ry makes.
The robb'd that smiles steals something from the thief;
He robs himself that spends a bootless grief.
    BRA. So let the Turk of Cyprus us beguile;   210
We lose it not, so long as we can smile.
He bears the sentence well that nothing bears
But the free comfort which from thence he hears,
But he bears both the sentence and the sorrow
That, to pay grief, must of poor patience borrow.
These sentences, to sugar, or to gall,
Being strong on both sides, are equivocal:
But words are words; I never yet did hear
That the bruis'd heart was pierced through the ear.
I humbly beseech you, proceed to th' affairs of state.   220
    DUKE. The Turk with a most mighty preparation makes for Cyprus.
Othello, the fortitude of the place is best known to you; and though we have there
a substitute of most allowed sufficiency, yet opinion, a sovereign mistress of
effects, throws a more safer voice on you: you must therefore be content to
slubber the gloss of your new fortunes with this more stubborn and boisterous
expedition.
    OTH. The tyrant custom, most grave senators,
Hath made the flinty and steel couch of war

---

190. **on to,** i.e., proceed with. 191. **get,** beget. 195. **For your sake,** on your account. 199.
like yourself, i.e., as you would, in your proper temper. **sentence,** maxim. 200. **grise,** step. 205.
next, nearest. 213. **comfort,** i.e., the consolation that it may be borne with patience. 222. **fortitude,**
strength. 223. **allowed,** acknowledged. 223–224. **opinion . . . on you,** public opinion, an important
determiner of affairs, chooses you as the best man. 225. **slubber,** sully, soil.

My thrice-driven bed of down: I do agnize
A natural and prompt alacrity   230
I find in hardness, and do undertake
These present wars against the Ottomites.
Most humbly therefore bending to your state,
I crave fit disposition for my wife,
Due reference of place and exhibition,
With such accommodation and besort
As levels with her breeding.
      DUKE.   If you please,
Be 't at her father's.
      BRA.   I'll not have it so.
      OTH. Nor I.
      DES.   Nor I; I would not there reside,
To put my father in impatient thoughts   240
By being in his eye. Most gracious duke,
To my unfolding lend your prosperous ear;
And let me find a charter in your voice,
T' assist my simpleness.
      DUKE. What would you, Desdemona?
      DES. That I did love the Moor to live with him,
My downright violence and storm of fortunes
May trumpet to the world: my heart's subdu'd
Even to the very quality of my lord:
I saw Othello's visage in his mind,   250
And to his honours and his valiant parts
Did I my soul and fortunes consecrate.
So that, dear lords, if I be left behind,
A moth of peace, and he go to the war,
The rites for why I love him are bereft me,
And I a heavy interim shall support
By his dear absence. Let me go with him.
      OTH. Let her have your voices.
Vouch with me, heaven, I therefore beg it not,
To please the palate of my appetite,   260
Nor to comply with heat—the young affects
In me defunct—and proper satisfaction,
But to be free and bounteous to her mind:
And heaven defend your good souls, that you think
I will your serious and great business scant
When she is with me: no, when light-wing'd toys
Of feather'd Cupid seel with wanton dullness
My speculative and offic'd instruments,
That my disports corrupt and taint my business,

---

229. **thrice-driven,** thrice-sifted. **agnize,** know in myself. 231. **hardness,** hardship. 235. **exhibition,** allowance. 236. **besort,** suitable company. 242. **prosperous,** propitious. 243. **charter,** privilege. 261. **affects,** inclinations. 267. **seel,** in falconry, to make blind by sewing up the eyes of the hawk in training. 268. **speculative . . . instruments,** ability to see and reason clearly. 269. **That,** so that. **disports,** pastime. **taint,** impair.

Let housewives make a skillet of my helm,   270
And all indign and base adversities
Make head against my estimation!
      DUKE. Be it as you shall privately determine,
Either for her stay or going: th' affair cries haste,
And speed must answer it.
      FIRST SEN. You must away to-night.
      OTH.   With all my heart.
      DUKE. At nine i' th' morning here we'll meet again.
Othello, leave some officer behind,
And he shall our commission bring to you;
With such things else of quality and respect   280
As doth import you.
      OTH.   So please your grace, my ancient;
A man he is of honesty and trust:
To his conveyance I assign my wife,
With what else needful your good grace shall think
To be sent after me.
      DUKE.   Let it be so.
Good night to every one. [*To Bra.*] And, noble signior,
If virtue no delighted beauty lack,
Your son-in-law is far more fair than black.
      FIRST SEN. Adieu, brave Moor; use Desdemona well.
      BRA. Look to her. Moor, if thou hast eyes to see: 290
She has deceiv'd her father, and may thee.
                     Exeunt [*Duke, Senators, Officers, &c.*].
      OTH. My life upon her faith! Honest Iago,
My Desdemona must I leave to thee:
I prithee, let thy wife attend on her;
And bring them after in the best advantage.
Come, Desdemona; I have but an hour
Of love, of worldly matters and direction,
To spend with thee: we must obey the time.   *Exit* [*with Desdemona*].
      ROD. Iago,—
      IAGO. What say'st thou, noble heart?   300
      ROD. What will I do, thinkest thou?
      IAGO. Why, go to bed, and sleep.
      ROD. I will incontinently drown myself.
      IAGO. If thou dost, I shall never love thee after.
Why, thou silly gentleman!
      ROD. It is silliness to live when to live is torment; and then have we a
prescription to die when death is our physician.
      IAGO. O villanous! I have looked upon the world for four times seven
years; and since I could distinguish betwixt a benefit and an injury, I never found
man that knew how to love himself. Ere I would say, I would drown myself for
the love of a guinea-hen, I would change my humanity with a baboon.   312

---

     271. **indign,** unworthy, shameful.   272. **estimation,** reputation.   281. **import,** concern.   287.
delighted, delightful.   292. **Honest Iago,** an evidence of Iago's carefully built reputation.   303. **incontinently,** immediately.

ROD.   What should I do? I confess it is my shame to be so fond; but it is not in my virtue to amend it.

IAGO.   Virtue! a fig! 'tis in ourselves that we are thus or thus. Our bodies are our gardens, to the which our wills are gardeners; so that if we will plant nettles, or sow lettuce, set hyssop and weed up thyme, supply it with one gender of herbs, or distract it with many, either to have it sterile with idleness, or manured with industry, why, the power and corrigible authority of this lies in our wills. If the balance of our lives had not one scale of reason to poise another of sensuality, the blood and baseness of our natures would conduct us to most preposterous conclusions: but we have reason to cool our raging motions, our carnal stings, our unbitted lusts, whereof I take this that you call love to be a sect or scion.   325

ROD.   It cannot be.

IAGO.   It is merely a lust of the blood and a permission of the will. Come, be a man. Drown thyself! drown cats and blind puppies. I have professed me thy friend and I confess me knit to thy deserving with cables of perdurable toughness; I could never better stead thee than now. Put money in thy purse; follow thou the wars; defeat thy favour with an usurped beard; I say, put money in thy purse. It cannot be that Desdemona should long continue her love to the Moor,—put money in thy purse,—nor he his to her: it was a violent commencement in her, and thou shalt see an answerable sequestration:—put but money in thy purse. These Moors are changeable in their wills:—fill thy purse with money:—the food that to him now is as luscious as locusts, shall be to him shortly as bitter as coloquintida. She must change for youth: when she is sated with his body, she will find the error of her choice: she must have change, she must: therefore put money in thy purse. If thou wilt needs damn thyself, do it a more delicate way than drowning. Make all the money thou canst: if sanctimony and a frail vow betwixt an erring barbarian and a super-subtle Venetian be not too hard for my wits and all the tribe of hell, thou shalt enjoy her; therefore make money. A pox of drowning thyself! it is clean out of the way: seek thou rather to be hanged in compassing thy joy than to be drowned and go without her.   345

ROD.   Wilt thou be fast to my hopes, if I depend on the issue?

IAGO.   Thou art sure of me:—go, make money:—I have told thee often, and I re-tell thee again and again, I hate the Moor: my cause is hearted; thine hath no less reason. Let us be conjunctive in our revenge against him; if thou canst cuckold him, thou dost thyself a pleasure, me a sport. There are many events in the womb of time which will be delivered. Traverse! go, provide thy money. We will have more of this to-morrow. Adieu.   352

ROD.   Where shall we meet i' the morning?

IAGO.   At my lodging.

ROD.   I'll be with thee betimes.

---

314. **virtue,** strength. 317. **hyssop,** an herb of the mint family. 318. **gender,** kind. 319. **corrigible authority,** the power to correct. 321–323. **reason . . . motions,** Iago understands the warfare between reason and sensuality, but his ethics are totally inverted; reason works in him not good, as it should according to natural law, but evil, which he has chosen for his good. 323. **motions,** appetites. . 324. **unbitted,** uncontrolled. **sect,** cutting. 331. **defeat thy favour,** disguise and disfigure thy face. 334. **answerable sequestration,** a separation corresponding. 336. **locusts,** of doubtful meaning; defined as fruit of the carob tree, as honeysuckle, and as lollipops or sugar-sticks. **coloquintida,** colocynth, a purgative. 341. **erring,** wandering. 348. **hearted,** fixed in the heart. 349. **conjunctive,** united.

IAGO.   Go to; farewell. Do you hear, Roderigo?
ROD.   What say you?
IAGO.   No more of drowning, do you hear?
ROD.   I am changed: I'll go sell all my land.   *Exit.*
IAGO.   Thus do I ever make my fool my purse;   360
For I mine own gain'd knowledge should profane,
If I would time expend with such a snipe,
But for my sport and profit. I hate the Moor;
And it is thought abroad, that 'twixt my sheets
H' as done my office: I know not if't be true;
But I, for mere suspicion in that kind,
Will do as if for surety. He holds me well;
The better shall my purpose work on him.
Cassio's a proper man: let me see now:
To get his place and to plume up my will   370
In double knavery—How, how?—Let's see:—
After some time, to abuse Othello's ears
That he is too familiar with his wife.
He hath a person and a smooth dispose
To be suspected, fram'd to make women false.
The Moor is of a free and open nature,
That thinks men honest that but seem to be so,
And will as tenderly be led by th' nose
As asses are.
I have't. It is engend'red. Hell and night   380
Must bring this monstrous birth to the world's light.   [*Exit.*]

ACT II.

Scene I.   [*A Sea-port in Cyprus. An open place near the quay.*]

Enter MONTANO *and two* Gentlemen.

MON.   What from the cape can you discern at sea?
FIRST GENT.   Nothing at all: it is a high-wrought flood;
I cannot, 'twixt the heaven and the main,
Descry a sail.
MON.   Methinks the wind hath spoke aloud at land;
A fuller blast ne'er shook our battlements:
If it hath ruffian'd so upon the sea,
What ribs of oak, when mountains melt on them,
Can hold the mortise? What shall we hear of this?
SEC. GENT.   A segregation of the Turkish fleet: 10
For do but stand upon the foaming shore,

---

370. **plume up,** glorify, gratify.   373. **he,** i.e., Cassio.   374. **dispose,** external manner.
    Act II. Scene I.   7. **ruffian'd,** raged.   9. **mortise,** the socket hollowed out in fitting timbers.
10. **segregation,** dispersion.

The chidden billow seems to pelt the clouds:
The wind-shak'd surge, with high and monstrous mane,
Seems to cast water on the burning bear,
And quench the guards of th' ever-fixed pole:
I never did like molestation view
On the enchafed flood.
      MON.   If that the Turkish fleet
Be not enshelter'd and embay'd, they are drown'd;
It is impossible they bear it out.

    Enter a [*third*] *Gentleman.*

    THIRD GENT.   News, lads! our wars are done.   20
The desperate tempest hath so bang'd the Turks,
That their designment halts: a noble ship of Venice
Hath seen a grievous wrack and sufferance
On most part of their fleet.
      MON. How! is this true?
    THIRD GENT.   The ship is here put in,
A Veronesa; Michael Cassio,
Lieutenant to the warlike Moor Othello,
Is come on shore: the Moor himself at sea,
And is in full commission here for Cyprus.
      MON. I am glad on 't; 'tis a worthy governor.   30
    THIRD GENT.   But this same Cassio, though he speak of comfort
Touching the Turkish loss, yet he looks sadly,
And prays the Moor be safe; for they were parted
With foul and violent tempest.
      MON.   Pray heavens he be;
For I have serv'd him, and the man commands
Like a full soldier. Let's to the seaside, ho!
As well to see the vessel that's come in
As to throw out our eyes for brave Othello,
Even till we make the main and th' aerial blue
An indistinct regard.
    THIRD GENT. Come, let's do so;   40
For every minute is expectancy
Of more arrivance.

    Enter CASSIO.

    CAS. Thanks, you the valiant of this warlike isle,
That so approve the Moor! O, let the heavens
Give him defence against the elements,
For I have lost him on a dangerous sea.

---

14. **bear,** a constellation. 15. **quench the guards,** overwhelm the stars near the polestar. 17.
enchafed, angry. 22. **designment,** enterprise. 23. **sufferance,** disaster. 36. **full,** perfect. 39–40.
make . . . regard, cause the blue of the sea and the air to grow indistinguishable in our view. 42.
arrivance, arrival.

MON.   Is he well shipp'd?
CAS.   His bark is stoutly timber'd, and his pilot
Of very expert and approv'd allowance;
Therefore my hopes, not surfeited to death,   50
Stand in bold cure. [*A cry*] *within* 'A sail, a sail, a sail!'

[*Enter a fourth* Gentleman.]

CAS.   What noise?
FOURTH GENT.   The town is empty; on the brow o' th' sea
Stand ranks of people, and they cry 'A sail!'
CAS.   My hopes do shape him for the governor.   [*Guns heard.*]
SEC. GENT.   They do discharge their shot of courtesy:
Our friends at least.
CAS.   I pray you, sir, go forth,
And give us truth who 'tis that is arriv'd.
SEC. GENT.   I shall.   *Exit.*
MON.   But, good lieutenant, is your general wiv'd?   60
CAS.   Most fortunately: he hath achiev'd a maid
That paragons description and wild fame;
One that excels the quirks of blazoning pens,
And in th' essential vesture of creation
Does tire the ingener.

Enter [*second*] Gentleman.

              How now! who has put in?
SEC. GENT.   'Tis one Iago, ancient to the general.
CAS.   Has had most favourable and happy speed:
Tempests themselves, high seas and howling winds,
The gutter'd rocks and congregated sands,—
Traitors ensteep'd to clog the guiltless keel,—   70
As having sense of beauty, do omit
Their mortal natures, letting go safely by
The divine Desdemona.
MON.   What is she?
CAS.   She that I spake of, our great captain's captain,
Left in the conduct of the bold Iago,
Whose footing here anticipates our thoughts
A se'nnight's speed. Great Jove, Othello guard,
And swell his sail with thine own pow'rful breath,
That he may bless this bay with his tall ship,
Make love's quick pants in Desdemona's arms,   80
Give renew'd fire to our extincted spirits,
And bring all Cyprus comfort!

---

49. **allowance,** reputation.   62. **paragons,** surpasses.   63. **quirks,** witty conceits.   **blazoning,**
setting forth honorably in words.   64. **vesture of creation,** the real qualities with which creation has
invested her.   65. **ingener,** inventor, praiser.   69. **gutter'd,** jagged, trenched.   70. **ensteep'd,** lying
under water.   72. **mortal,** deadly.   77. **se'nnight's,** week's.

Enter DESDEMONA, IAGO, RODERIGO, *and* EMILIA, [*with* Attendants].

                           O, behold,
The riches of the ship is come on shore!
You men of Cyprus, let her have your knees.
Hail to thee, lady! and the grace of heaven,
Before, behind thee and on every hand,
Enwheel thee round!
    DES.   I thank you, valiant Cassio.
What tidings can you tell me of my lord?
    CAS. He is not yet arriv'd: nor know I aught
But that he's well and will be shortly here.   90
    DES. O, but I fear—How lost you company?
    CAS. The great contention of the sea and skies
Parted our fellowship—But, hark! a sail.
                      [*Within*] 'A sail, a sail!' [*Guns heard.*]
    SEC. GENT. They give their greeting to the citadel:
This likewise is a friend.
    CAS.   See for the news.   [*Exit Gentleman.*]
Good ancient, you are welcome. [*To Emilia*] Welcome, mistress:
Let it not gall your patience, good Iago,
That I extend my manners; 'tis my breeding   99
That gives me this bold show of courtesy.   [*Kissing her.*]
    IAGO. Sir, would she give you so much of her lips
As of her tongue she oft bestows on me,
You would have enough.
    DES.   Alas, she has no speech.
    IAGO. In faith, too much;
I find it still, when I have list to sleep:
Marry, before your ladyship, I grant,
She puts her tongue a little in her heart,
And chides with thinking.
    EMIL. You have little cause to say so.
    IAGO. Come on, come on; you are pictures out of doors,   110
Bells in your parlours, wild-cats in your kitchens,
Saints in your injuries, devils being offended,
Players in your housewifery, and housewives in your beds.
    DES. O, fie upon thee, slanderer!
    IAGO. Nay, it is true, or else I am a Turk:
You rise to play and go to bed to work.
    EMIL. You shall not write my praise.
    IAGO.   No, let me not.
    DES. What wouldst thou write of me, if thou shouldst praise me?
    IAGO. O gentle lady, do not put me to 't;
For I am nothing, if not critical.   120
    DES. Come on, assay. There's one gone to the harbour?
    IAGO. Ay, madam.

---

113. **housewives,** huzzies.   120. **critical,** censorious.

DES. I am not merry; but I do beguile
The thing I am, by seeming otherwise.
Come, how wouldst thou praise me?
    IAGO. I am about it; but indeed my invention
Comes from my pate as birdlime does from frieze;
It plucks out brains and all: but my Muse labours,
And thus she is deliver'd.
If she be fair and wise, fairness and wit,   130
The one's for use, the other useth it.
    DES. Well praised! How if she be black and witty?
    IAGO. If she be black, and thereto have a wit,
She'll find a white that shall her blackness fit.
    DES. Worse and worse.
    EMIL. How if fair and foolish?
    IAGO. She never yet was foolish that was fair;
For even her folly help'd her to an heir.
    DES. These are old fond paradoxes to make fools laugh i' the alehouse.
What miserable praise hast thou for her that's foul and foolish?   140
    IAGO. There's none so foul and foolish thereunto,
But does foul pranks which fair and wise ones do.
    DES. O heavy ignorance! thou praisest the worst best. But what praise
couldst thou bestow on a deserving woman indeed, one that, in the authority of
her merit, did justly put on the vouch of very malice itself?
    IAGO. She that was ever fair and never proud,
Had tongue at will and yet was never loud,
Never lack'd gold and yet went never gay,
Fled from her wish and yet said 'Now I may,'   150
She that being ang'red, her revenge being nigh,
Bade her wrong stay and her displeasure fly,
She that in wisdom never was so frail
To change the cod's head for the salmon's tail,
She that could think and ne'er disclose her mind,
See suitors following and not look behind,
She was a wight, if ever such wight were,—
    DES. To do what?
    IAGO. To suckle fools and chronicle small beer.
    DES. O most lame and impotent conclusion! Do not learn of him, Emilia,
though he be thy husband. How say you, Cassio? is he not a most profane and
liberal counsellor?   162
    CAS. He speaks home, madam: you may relish him more in the soldier
than in the scholar.
    IAGO. [*Aside*] He takes her by the palm: ay, well said, whisper: with as
little a web as this will I ensnare as great a fly as Cassio. Ay, smile upon her, do;
I will gyve thee in thine own courtship. You say true; 'tis so, indeed: if such

---

127. **birdlime,** sticky substance smeared on twigs to catch small birds. **frieze,** coarse woolen
cloth. 134. **white,** a fair person, with word-play on "wight." 139. **fond,** foolish. 145. **put on the
vouch,** compel the approval. 154. **To change . . . tail,** to exchange a delicacy for mere refuse.
159. **chronicle small beer,** keep petty household accounts. 162. **liberal,** licentious. 163. **speaks home,**
i.e., without reserve. 167. **gyve,** shackle. **courtship,** courtesy.

tricks as these strip you out of your lieutenantry, it had been better you had not kissed your three fingers so oft, which now again you are most apt to play the sir in. Very good; well kissed! an excellent courtesy! 'tis so, indeed. Yet again your fingers to your lips? would they were clyster-pipes for your sake! [*Trumpet within.*] The Moor! I know his trumpet.   173

    CAS. 'Tis truly so.

    DES. Let's meet him and receive him.

    CAS. Lo, where he comes!

Enter OTHELLO *and* Attendants.

    OTH. O my fair warrior!

    DES.   My dear Othello!

    OTH. It gives me wonder great as my content

To see you here before me. O my soul's joy!

If after every tempest come such calms,   180

May the winds blow till they have waken'd death!

And let the labouring bark climb hills of seas

Olympus-high and duck again as low

As hell 's from heaven! If it were now to die,

'Twere now to be most happy; for, I fear,

My soul hath her content so absolute

That not another comfort like to this

Succeeds in unknown fate.

    DES.   The heavens forbid.

But that our loves and comforts should increase,

Even as our days do grow!

    OTH.   Amen to that, sweet powers!   190

I cannot speak enough of this content;

It stops me here; it is too much of joy:

And this, and this, the greatest discords be   [*Kissing her.*]

That e'er our hearts shall make!

    IAGO.   [*Aside*] O, you are well tun'd now!

But I'll set down the pegs that make this music,

As honest as I am.

    OTH.   Come, let us to the castle.

News, friends; our wars are done, the Turks are drown'd.

How does my old acquaintance of this isle?

Honey, you shall be well desir'd in Cyprus;

I have found great love amongst them. O my sweet,   200

I prattle out of fashion, and I dote

In mine own comforts. I prithee, good Iago,

Go to the bay and disembark my coffers:

Bring thou the master to the citadel;

He is a good one, and his worthiness

---

169. **kissed your three fingers.** He kisses his own hand as a token of reverence. 170. **the sir,** i.e., the fine gentleman. 172. **clyster-pipes,** tubes used for enemas. 195. **set down the pegs,** lower the pitch of the strings, i.e., disturb the harmony.

Does challenge much respect. Come, Desdemona,
Once more, well met at Cyprus.

        Exeunt Othello and Desdemona [and all but Iago and Roderigo].

    IAGO. [*To an Attendant*] Do thou meet me presently at the harbour. [*To Rod.*] Come hither. If thou be'st valiant,—as, they say, base men being in love have then a nobility in their natures more than is native to them,—list me. The lieutenant tonight watches on the court of guard:—first, I must tell thee this— Desdemona is directly in love with him.   212

    ROD. With him! why, 'tis not possible.

    IAGO. Lay thy finger thus, and let thy soul be instructed. Mark me with what violence she first loved the Moor, but for bragging and telling her fantastical lies: and will she love him still for prating? let not thy discreet heart think it. Her eye must be fed; and what delight shall she have to look on the devil? When the blood is made dull with the act of sport, there should be, again to inflame it and to give satiety a fresh appetite, loveliness in favour, sympathy in years, manners and beauties; all which the Moor is defective in: now, for want of these required conveniences, her delicate tenderness will find itself abused, begin to heave the gorge, disrelish and abhor the Moor; very nature will instruct her in it and compel her to some second choice. Now, sir, this granted,—as it is a most pregnant and unforced position—who stands so eminent in the degree of this fortune as Cassio does? a knave very voluble; no further conscionable than in putting on the mere form of civil and humane seeming, for the better compassing of his salt and most hidden loose affection? why, none; why, none: a slipper and subtle knave, a finder of occasions, that has an eye can stamp and counterfeit advantages, though true advantage never present itself; a devilish knave. Besides, the knave is handsome, young, and hath all those requisites in him that folly and green minds look after: a pestilent complete knave; and the woman hath found him already.   233

    ROD. I cannot believe that in her; she's full of most blessed condition.

    IAGO. Blessed fig's-end! the wine she drinks is made of grapes: if she had been blessed, she would never have loved the Moor. Blessed pudding! Didst thou not see her paddle with the palm of his hand? didst not mark that?

    ROD. Yes, that I did; but that was but courtesy.   239

    IAGO. Lechery, by this hand; an index and obscure prologue to the history of lust and foul thoughts. They met so near with their lips that their breaths embraced together. Villanous thoughts, Roderigo! when these mutualities so marshal the way, hard at hand comes the master and main exercise, the incorporate conclusion, Pish! But, sir, be you ruled by me: I have brought you from Venice. Watch you to-night; for the command, I'll lay't upon you. Cassio knows you not. I'll not be far from you: do you find some occasion to anger Cassio, either by speaking too loud, or tainting his discipline; or from what other course you please, which the time shall more favourably minister.

    ROD. Well.   249

    IAGO. Sir, he is rash and very sudden in choler, and haply may strike at you: provoke him, that he may; for even out of that will I cause these of Cyprus to mutiny; whose qualification shall come into no true taste again but by the

---

211. **court of guard,** guardhouse. 226. **conscionable,** conscientious. 227. **salt,** licentious. 228. **slipper,** slippery. 247. **tainting,** disparaging. 252. **qualification,** appeasement.

displanting of Cassio. So shall you have a shorter journey to your desires by the means I shall then have to prefer them; and the impediment most profitably removed, without the which there were no expectation of our prosperity.

ROD. I will do this, if I can bring it to any opportunity.

IAGO. I warrant thee. Meet me by and by at the citadel: I must fetch his necessaries ashore. Farewell.   260

ROD. Adieu.   *Exit.*

IAGO. That Cassio loves her, I do well believe 't;
That she loves him, 'tis apt and of great credit:
The Moor, howbeit that I endure him not,
Is of a constant, loving, noble nature,
And I dare think he'll prove to Desdemona
A most dear husband. Now, I do love her too;
Not out of absolute lust, though peradventure
I stand accountant for as great a sin,
But partly led to diet my revenge,   270
For that I do suspect the lusty Moor
Hath leap'd into my seat; the thought whereof
Doth, like a poisonous mineral, gnaw my inwards;
And nothing can or shall content my soul
Till I am even'd with him, wife for wife,
Or failing so, yet that I put the Moor
At least into a jealousy so strong
That judgement cannot cure. Which thing to do,
If this poor trash of Venice, whom I trash
For his quick hunting, stand the putting on,   280
I'll have our Michael Cassio on the hip,
Abuse him to the Moor in the rank garb—
For I fear Cassio with my night-cap too—
Make the Moor thank me, love me and reward me,
For making him egregiously an ass
And practising upon his peace and quiet
Even to madness. 'Tis here, but yet confus'd:
Knavery's plain face is never seen till us'd.   *Exit.*

Scene II. [*A street.*]

Enter Othello's Herald *with a proclamation.*

HER. It is Othello's pleasure, our noble and valiant general, that, upon certain tidings now arrived, importing the mere perdition of the Turkish fleet, every man put himself into triumph; some to dance, some to make bonfires, each man to what sport and revels his addiction leads him: for, besides these beneficial news, it is the celebration of his nuptial. So much was his pleasure should

---

259. **by and by,** immediately. 263. **apt,** probable. **credit,** credibility. 279. **trash,** worthless thing (Roderigo). **trash,** hold in check. 280. **putting on,** incitement to quarrel. 281. **on the hip,** at my mercy (wrestling term).
Scene II. 2. **mere perdition,** complete destruction.

be proclaimed. All offices are open, and there is full liberty of feasting from this present hour of five till the bell have told eleven. Heaven bless the isle of Cyprus and our noble general Othello!   *Exit.*

[**Scene III.** *A hall in the castle.*]

   Enter OTHELLO, DESDEMONA, CASSIO, *and* Attendants.

  OTH. Good Michael, look you to the guard to-night:
Let's teach ourselves that honourable stop,
Not to outsport discretion.
  CAS. Iago hath direction what to do;
But, notwithstanding, with my personal eye
Will I look to 't.
  OTH. Iago is most honest.
Michael, good night: to-morrow with your earliest
Let me have speech with you. [*To Desdemona*] Come, my dear love,
The purchase made, the fruits are to ensue;
That profit's yet to come 'tween me and you.   10
Good night.   *Exit* [*Othello, with Desdemona and Attendants*].

  Enter IAGO.

  CAS. Welcome, Iago; we must to the watch.
  IAGO. Not this hour, lieutenant; 'tis not yet ten o' the clock. Our general cast us thus early for the love of his Desdemona; who let us not therefore blame: he hath not yet made wanton the night with her; and she is sport for Jove.
  CAS. She's a most exquisite lady.
  IAGO. And, I'll warrant her, full of game.
  CAS. Indeed, she's a most fresh and delicate creature.
  IAGO. What an eye she has! methinks it sounds a parley of provoca-
tion.   20
  CAS. An inviting eye; and yet methinks right modest.
  IAGO. And when she speaks, is it not an alarum to love?
  CAS. She is indeed perfection.
  IAGO. Well, happiness to their sheets! Come, lieutenant, I have a stoup of wine; and here without are a brace of Cyprus gallants that would fain have a measure to the health of black Othello.
  CAS. Not to-night, good Iago: I have very poor and unhappy brains for drinking: I could well wish courtesy would invent some other custom of enter-
tainment.
  IAGO. O, they are our friends; but one cup: I'll drink for you. 30
  CAS. I have drunk but one cup to-night, and that was craftily qualified too, and, behold, what innovation it makes here: I am unfortunate in the infirmity, and dare not task my weakness with any more.

---

  6. **offices,** rooms where food and drink were kept.
  Scene III. 2. **stop,** restraint. 14. **cast,** dismissed. 25. **stoup,** measure of liquor, two quarts.
31. **qualified,** diluted. 32. **innovation,** disturbance. **here,** i.e., in Cassio's head.

IAGO.   What, man! 'tis a night of revels: the gallants desire it.

CAS.   Where are they?

IAGO.   Here at the door; I pray you, call them in.

CAS.   I'll do 't; but it dislikes me.   *Exit.*

IAGO.   If I can fasten but one cup upon him,
With that which he hath drunk to-night already,
He'll be as full of quarrel and offence   40
As my young mistress' dog. Now, my sick fool Roderigo,
Whom love hath turn'd almost the wrong side out,
To Desdemona hath to-night carous'd
Potations pottle-deep; and he's to watch:
Three lads of Cyprus, noble swelling spirits,
That hold their honours in a wary distance,
The very elements of this warlike isle,
Have I to-night fluster'd with flowing cups,
And they watch too. Now, 'mongst this flock of drunkards,
Am I to put our Cassio in some action   50
That may offend the isle.—But here they come:

Enter CASSIO, MONTANO, *and* Gentlemen [; *servants following with wine*].

If consequence do but approve my dream,
My boat sails freely, both with wind and stream.

CAS.   'Fore God, they have given me a rouse already.

MON.   Good faith, a little one; not past a pint, as I am a soldier.

IAGO.   Some wine, ho!

[*Sings*]   And let me the canakin clink, clink;
               And let me the canakin clink:
                  A soldier's a man;
                  A life's but a span;   60
               Why, then, let a soldier drink.
Some wine, boys!

CAS.   'Fore God, an excellent song.

IAGO.   I learned it in England, where, indeed, they are most potent in
potting: your Dane, your German, and your swag-bellied Hollander—Drink,
ho!—are nothing to your English.

CAS.   Is your Englishman so expert in his drinking?

IAGO.   Why, he drinks you, with facility, your Dane dead drunk; he
sweats not to overthrow your Almain; he gives your Hollander a vomit, ere the
next pottle can be filled.   70

CAS.   To the health of our general!

MON.   I am for it, lieutenant; and I'll do you justice.

IAGO.   O sweet England! [*Sings.*]
               King Stephen was a worthy peer,

---

44. **pottle-deep,** to the bottom of the tankard.   46. **hold . . . distance,** i.e., are extremely sensitive of their honor.   47. **very elements,** true representatives.   49. **watch,** are members of the guard.   52. **approve,** confirm.   54. **rouse,** full draft of liquor.   57. **canakin,** small drinking vessel.   69. **Almain,** German.   72. **I'll . . . justice,** i.e., drink as much as you.

His breeches cost him but a crown;
He held them sixpence all too dear,
With that he call'd the tailor lown.

He was a wight of high renown,
  And thou art but of low degree:
'Tis pride that pulls the country down;   80
  Then take thine auld cloak about thee.
Some wine, ho!
CAS.   Why, this is a more exquisite song than the other.
IAGO.   Will you hear 't again?
CAS.   No; for I hold him to be unworthy of his place that does those
things. Well, God's above all; and there be souls must be saved, and there be
souls must not be saved.
IAGO.   It's true, good lieutenant.
CAS.   For mine own part,—no offence to the general, nor any man of
quality,—I hope to be saved.   90
IAGO.   And so do I too, lieutenant.
CAS.   Ay, but, by your leave, not before me; the lieutenant is to be saved
before the ancient. Let's have no more of this; let's to our affairs.—God forgive
us our sins!—Gentlemen, let's look to our business. Do not think, gentlemen, I
am drunk: this is my ancient; this is my right hand, and this is my left: I am not
drunk now; I can stand well enough, and speak well enough.
ALL.   Excellent well.
CAS.   Why, very well then; you must not think then that I am drunk.
                                                        Exit.

MON.   To th' platform, masters; come, let's set the watch.   100
IAGO.   You see this fellow that is gone before;
He's a soldier fit to stand by Cæsar
And give direction: and do but see his vice;
'Tis to his virtue a just equinox,
The one as long as th' other: 'tis pity of him.
I fear the trust Othello puts him in,
On some odd time of his infirmity,
Will shake this island.
MON.   But is he often thus?
IAGO.   'Tis evermore the prologue to his sleep:
He'll watch the horologe a double set,   110
If drink rock not his cradle.
MON.   It were well
The general were put in mind of it.
Perhaps he sees it not; or his good nature
Prizes the virtue that appears in Cassio,
And looks not on his evils: is not this true?

Enter RODERIGO.

----

77. **lown,** lout, loon.   104. **equinox,** equal length of days and nights; used figuratively to mean
"counterpart."   110. **horologe,** clock.   **double set,** twice around.

Iago. [*Aside to him*] How now, Roderigo!
I pray you, after the lieutenant; go.   [*Exit Roderigo.*]
    Mon. And 'tis great pity that the noble Moor
Should hazard such a place as his own second
With one of an ingraft infirmity: 120
It were an honest action to say
So to the Moor.
    Iago.   Not I, for this fair island:
I do love Cassio well; and would do much
To cure him of this evil—But, hark! what noise?
                    [*Cry within:* 'Help! help!']

    Enter Cassio, *pursuing* Roderigo.

    Cas. 'Zounds, you rogue! you rascal!
    Mon.   What's the matter, lieutenant?
    Cas. A knave teach me my duty!
I'll beat the knave into a twiggen bottle.
    Rod. Beat me!
    Cas.   Dost thou prate, rogue?   [*Striking Roderigo.*]
    Mon.   Nay, good lieutenant; [*Staying him.*]
I pray you, sir, hold your hand.
    Cas.   Let me go, sir,   130
Or I'll knock you o'er the mazzard.
    Mon.   Come, come, you're drunk.
    Cas. Drunk!   [*They fight.*]
    Iago. [*Aside to Roderigo*] Away, I say; go out, and cry a mutiny.
                    [*Exit Roderigo.*]
Nay, good lieutenant,—God's will, gentlemen;—
Help, ho!—Lieutenant,—sir,—Montano,—sir;—
Help, masters!—Here's a goodly watch indeed!   [*Bell rings.*]
Who's that which rings the bell?—Diablo, ho!
The town will rise: God's will, lieutenant, hold!
You'll be asham'd for ever.

    Enter Othello *and* Attendants.

    Oth.   What is the matter here?   140
    Mon. 'Zounds, I bleed still; I am hurt to th' death.
He dies!   [*Thrusts at Cassio.*]
    Oth. Hold, for your lives!
    Iago. Hold, ho! Lieutenant,—sir,—Montano,—gentlemen,—
Have you forgot all sense of place and duty?
Hold! the general speaks to you; hold, for shame!
    Oth. Why, how now, ho! from whence ariseth this?
Are we turn'd Turks, and to ourselves do that

---

128. **twiggen,** covered with woven twigs. 137. **Diablo,** the Devil. 148. **turn'd Turks,** changed
completely for the worse.

Which heaven hath forbid the Ottomites?
For Christian shame, put by this barbarous brawl: 150
He that stirs next to carve for his own rage
Holds his soul light; he dies upon his motion.
Silence that dreadful bell: it frights the isle
From her propriety. What is the matter, masters?
Honest Iago, that looks dead with grieving,
Speak, who began this? on thy love, I charge thee.
    IAGO.   I do not know: friends all but now, even now,
In quarter, and in terms like bride and groom
Devesting them for bed; and then, but now—
As if some planet had unwitted men—   160
Swords out, and tilting one at other's breast,
In opposition bloody. I cannot speak
Any beginning to this peevish odds;
And would in action glorious I had lost
Those legs that brought me to a part of it!
    OTH.   How comes it, Michael, you are thus forgot?
    CAS.   I pray you, pardon me; I cannot speak.
    OTH.   Worthy Montano, you were wont be civil;
The gravity and stillness of your youth
The world hath noted, and your name is great   170
In mouths of wisest censure: what's the matter,
That you unlace your reputation thus
And spend your rich opinion for the name
Of a night-brawler? give me answer to it.
    MON.   Worthy Othello, I am hurt to danger:
Your officer, Iago, can inform you,—
While I spare speech, which something now offends me,—
Of all that I do know: nor know I aught
By me that's said or done amiss this night;
Unless self-charity be sometimes a vice,   180
And to defend ourselves it be a sin
When violence assails us.
    OTH.   Now, by heaven,
My blood begins my safer guides to rule;
And passion, having my best judgement collied,
Assays to lead the way: if I once stir,
Or do but lift this arm, the best of you
Shall sink in my rebuke. Give me to know
How this foul rout began, who set it on;
And he that is approv'd in this offence,
Though he had twinn'd with me, both at a birth,   190
Shall lose me. What! in a town of war,
Yet wild, the people's hearts brimful of fear,
To manage private and domestic quarrel,

---

    151. **carve for,** indulge.   154. **propriety,** proper state or condition.   158. **In quarter,** on terms.
163. **peevish odds,** childish quarrel.   171. **censure,** judgment.   172. **unlace,** degrade.   184. **collied,**
darkened.   189. **approv'd in,** found guilty of.

In night, and on the court and guard of safety!
'Tis monstrous, Iago, who began 't?
   Mon. If partially affin'd, or leagu'd in office,
Thou dost deliver more or less than truth,
Thou art no soldier.
   Iago.   Touch me not so near:
I had rather have this tongue cut from my mouth
Than it should do offence to Michael Cassio;   200
Yet, I persuade myself, to speak the truth
Shall nothing wrong him. Thus it is, general.
Montano and myself being in speech,
There comes a fellow crying out for help;
And Cassio following him with determin'd sword,
To execute upon him. Sir, this gentleman
Steps in to Cassio, and entreats his pause:
Myself the crying fellow did pursue,
Lest by his clamour—as it so fell out—
The town might fall in fright: he, swift of foot,   210
Outran my purpose; and I return'd the rather
For that I heard the clink and fall of swords,
And Cassio high in oath; which till to-night
I ne'er might say before. When I came back—
For this was brief—I found them close together,
At blow and thrust; even as again they were
When you yourself did part them.
More of this matter cannot I report:
But men are men; the best sometimes forget:
Though Cassio did some little wrong to him,   220
As men in rage strike those that wish them best,
Yet surely Cassio, I believe, receiv'd
From him that fled some strange indignity,
Which patience could not pass.
   Oth.   I know, Iago,
Thy honesty and love doth mince this matter,
Making it light to Cassio. Cassio, I love thee;
But never more be officer of mine.

   Enter Desdemona, *attended.*

Look, if my gentle love be not rais'd up!
I'll make thee an example.
   Des.   What's the matter?
   Oth. All's well now, sweeting; come away to bed. 230
Sir, for your hurts, myself will be your surgeon:
Lead him off.   *[To Montano, who is led off.]*
Iago, look with care about the town,
And silence those whom this vile brawl distracted.

---

194. **court and guard,** i.e., the main guardhouse. 196. **affin'd,** bound by a tie.

Come, Desdemona: 'tis the soldiers' life
To have their balmy slumbers wak'd with strife.

Exit [with all but Iago and Cassio].

IAGO. What, are you hurt, lieutenant?

CAS. Ay, past all surgery.

IAGO. Marry, God forbid!

CAS. Reputation, reputation, reputation! O, I have lost my reputation! I have lost the immortal part of myself, and what remains is bestial. My reputation, Iago, my reputation! 242

IAGO. As I am an honest man, I thought you had received some bodily wound; there is more sense in that than in reputation. Reputation is an idle and most false imposition; oft got without merit, and lost without deserving: you have lost no reputation at all, unless you repute yourself such a loser. What, man! there are ways to recover the general again: you are but now cast in his mood, a punishment more in policy than in malice; even so as one would beat his offenceless dog to affright an imperious lion: sue to him again, and he's yours. 250

CAS. I will rather sue to be despised than to deceive so good a commander with so slight, so drunken, and so indiscreet an officer. Drunk? and speak parrot? and squabble? swagger? swear? and discourse fustian with one's own shadow? O thou invisible spirit of wine, if thou hast no name to be known by, let us call thee devil!

IAGO. What was he that you followed with your sword? What had he done to you?

CAS. I know not.

IAGO. Is 't possible?

CAS. I remember a mass of things, but nothing distinctly; a quarrel, but nothing wherefore. O God, that men should put an enemy in their mouths to steal away their brains! that we should, with joy, pleasance, revel and applause, transform ourselves into beasts! 263

IAGO. Why, but you are now well enough: how came you thus recovered?

CAS. It hath pleased the devil drunkenness to give place to the devil wrath: one unperfectness shows me another, to make me frankly despise myself.

IAGO. Come, you are too severe a moraler: as the time, the place, and the condition of this country stands, I could heartily wish this had not befallen; but, since it is as it is, mend it for your own good. 270

CAS. I will ask him for my place again; he shall tell me I am a drunkard! Had I as many mouths as Hydra, such an answer would stop them all. To be now a sensible man, by and by a fool, and presently a beast! O strange! Every inordinate cup is unblessed and the ingredient is a devil.

IAGO. Come, come, good wine is a good familiar creature, if it be well used: exclaim no more against it. And, good lieutenant, I think you think I love you.

---

253. **speak parrot,** talk nonsense; *discourse fustian,* below, has the same meaning. 266. **unperfectness,** imperfection. 272. **Hydra,** a monster with many heads, slain by Hercules as the second of his twelve labors.

CAS.   I have well approved it, sir. I drunk!

IAGO.   You or any man living may be drunk at a time, man. I'll tell you what you shall do. Our general's wife is now the general: I may say so in this respect, for that he hath devoted and given up himself to the contemplation, mark, and denotement of her parts and graces: confess yourself freely to her; importune her help to put you in your place again: she is of so free, so kind, so apt, so blessed a disposition, she holds it a vice in her goodness not to do more than she is requested: this broken joint between you and her husband entreat her to splinter; and, my fortunes against any lay worth naming, this crack of your love shall grow stronger than it was before.   288

CAS.   You advise me well.

IAGO.   I protest, in the sincerity of love and honest kindness.

CAS.   I think it freely; and betimes in the morning I will beseech the virtuous Desdemona to undertake for me: I am desperate of my fortunes if they check me here.

IAGO.   You are in the right. Good night, lieutenant; I must to the watch.

CAS.   Good night, honest Iago.   *Exit Cassio.*

IAGO.   And what's he then that says I play the villain?
When this advice is free I give and honest,
Probal to thinking and indeed the course
To win the Moor again? For 'tis most easy   300
Th' inclining Desdemona to subdue
In any honest suit: she's fram'd as fruitful
As the free elements. And then for her
To win the Moor—were 't to renounce his baptism,
All seals and symbols of redeemed sin,
His soul is so enfetter'd to her love,
That she may make, unmake, do what she list,
Even as her appetite shall play the god
With his weak function. How am I then a villain
To counsel Cassio to this parallel course,   310
Directly to his good? Divinity of hell!
When devils will the blackest sins put on,
They do suggest at first with heavenly shows,
As I do now: for whiles this honest fool
Plies Desdemona to repair his fortunes
And she for him pleads strongly to the Moor,
I'll pour this pestilence into his ear,
That she repeals him for her body's lust;
And by how much she strives to do him good,
She shall undo her credit with the Moor.   320
So will I turn her virtue into pitch,
And out of her own goodness make the net
That shall enmesh them all.

---

278. **approved,** proved.   286. **splinter,** bind with splints.   287. **lay,** wager.   299. **Probal,** probable.   301. **inclining,** favorably disposed.   **subdue,** persuade.   310. **parallel,** probably, corresponding to his best interest.   313. **suggest,** tempt.   318. **repeals him,** i.e., attempts to get him restored.

Enter RODERIGO.

How now, Roderigo!

ROD.   I do follow here in the chase, not like a hound that hunts, but one that fills up the cry. My money is almost spent; I have been to-night exceedingly well cudgelled; and I think the issue will be, I shall have so much experience for my pains, and so, with no money at all and a little more wit, return again to Venice.

IAGO.   How poor are they that have not patience!
What wound did ever heal but by degrees?   330
Thou know'st we work by wit, and not by witchcraft;
And wit depends on dilatory time.
Does 't not go well? Cassio hath beaten thee,
And thou, by that small hurt, hast cashier'd Cassio:
Though other things grow fair against the sun,
Yet fruits that blossom first will first be ripe:
Content thyself awhile. By th' mass, 'tis morning;
Pleasure and action make the hours seem short.
Retire thee; go where thou art billeted:
Away, I say; thou shalt know more hereafter: 340
Nay, get thee gone.   *Exit Roderigo.*
                    Two things are to be done:
My wife must move for Cassio to her mistress;
I'll set her on;
Myself the while to draw the Moor apart,
And bring him jump when he may Cassio find
Soliciting his wife: ay, that's the way:
Dull not device by coldness and delay.   *Exit.*

ACT III.

Scene I. [*Before the castle.*]

Enter CASSIO [*and*] Musicians.

CAS.   Masters, play here; I will content your pains; Something that's brief; and bid 'Good morrow, general.'   [*They play.*]

[*Enter*] Clown.

CLO.   Why, masters, have your instruments been in Naples, that they speak i' the nose thus?
FIRST MUS.   How, sir, how!
CLO.   Are these, I pray you, wind-instruments?

---

325. **cry,** pack.   334. **cashier'd,** dismissed from service.   345. **jump,** precisely.
Act III. Scene I. 1. **content,** reward.   4. **speak i' the nose,** i.e., like Neapolitans, who spoke a nasal dialect (with a joke on syphilis, which attacks the nose).

FIRST MUS. Ay, marry, are they, sir.

CLO. O, thereby hangs a tail.

FIRST MUS. Whereby hangs a tale, sir?   9

CLO. Marry, sir, by many a wind-instrument that I know. But, masters, here's money for you: and the general so likes your music, that he desires you, for love's sake, to make no more noise with it.

FIRST MUS. Well, sir, we will not.

CLO. If you have any music that may not be heard, to 't again: but, as they say, to hear music the general does not greatly care.

FIRST MUS. We have none such, sir.

CLO. Then put up your pipes in your bag, for I'll away: go; vanish into air; away!   *Exeunt Musicians.*

CAS. Dost thou hear, my honest friend?

CLO. No, I hear not your honest friend; I hear you.   20

CAS. Prithee, keep up thy quillets. There's a poor piece of gold for thee: if the gentlewoman that attends the general's wife be stirring, tell her there's one Cassio entreats her a little favour of speech: wilt thou do this?

CLO. She is stirring, sir: if she will stir hither, I shall seem to notify unto her.

CAS. Do, good my friend.   *Exit Clown.*

Enter IAGO.

In happy time, Iago.

IAGO. You have not been a-bed, then?

CAS. Why, no; the day had broke
Before we parted. I have made bold, Iago,
To send in to your wife: my suit to her   30
Is, that she will to virtuous Desdemona
Procure me some access.

IAGO.   I'll send her to you presently;
And I'll devise a mean to draw the Moor
Out of the way, that your converse and business
May be more free.

CAS. I humbly thank you for 't.   *Exit [Iago].*

I never knew
A Florentine more kind and honest.

Enter EMILIA.

EMIL. Good morrow, good lieutenant: I am sorry
For your displeasure; but all will sure be well.
The general and his wife are talking of it;   40
And she speaks for you stoutly: the Moor replies,
That he you hurt is of great fame in Cyprus
And great affinity and that in wholesome wisdom
He might not but refuse you, but he protests he loves you

---

43. **affinity,** family connection.

And needs no other suitor but his likings
To take the safest occasion by the front
To bring you in again.
    Cas.   Yet, I beseech you,
If you think fit, or that it may be done,
Give me advantage of some brief discourse
With Desdemona alone.
    Emil.   Pray you, come in: 50
I will bestow you where you shall have time
To speak your bosom freely.
    Cas. I am much bound to you.   *[Exeunt.]*

Scene II.   [*A room in the castle.*]

    Enter OTHELLO, IAGO, *and* Gentlemen.

    Oth. These letters give, Iago, to the pilot;
And by him do my duties to the senate:
That done, I will be walking on the works;
Repair there to me.
    Iago.   Well, my good lord, I'll do 't.
    Oth. This fortification, gentlemen, shall we see 't?
    Gent. We'll wait upon your lordship.   *Exeunt.*

Scene III.   [*The garden of the castle.*]

    Enter DESDEMONA, CASSIO, *and* EMILIA.

    Des. Be thou assur'd, good Cassio, I will do
All my abilities in thy behalf.
    Emil. Good madam, do: I warrant it grieves my husband,
As if the case were his.
    Des. O, that's an honest fellow. Do not doubt, Cassio,
But I will have my lord and you again
As friendly as you were.
    Cas.   Bounteous madam,
Whatever shall become of Michael Cassio,
He's never any thing but your true servant.
    Des. I know 't; I thank you. You do love my lord: 10
You have known him long; and be you well assur'd
He shall in strangeness stand no farther off
Than in a politic distance.
    Cas.   Ay, but, lady,
That policy may either last so long,
Or feed upon such nice and waterish diet,

---

    46. **by the front,** i.e., by the forelock.
    Scene II. 3. **works,** earthworks, fortifications.
    Scene III. 12. **strangeness,** distant behavior. 16. **breed . . . circumstance,** increase itself so
on account of accidents.

Or breed itself so out of circumstance,
That, I being absent and my place supplied,
My general will forget my love and service.
    DES. Do not doubt that; before Emilia here
I give thee warrant of thy place: assure thee,   20
If I do vow a friendship, I'll perform it
To the last article: my lord shall never rest;
I'll watch him tame and talk him out of patience;
His bed shall seem a school, his board a shrift;
I'll intermingle every thing he does
With Cassio's suit: therefore be merry, Cassio;
For thy solicitor shall rather die
Than give thy cause away.

      Enter OTHELLO *and* IAGO [*at a distance*].

    EMIL. Madam, here comes my lord.
    CAS. Madam, I'll take my leave.   30
    DES. Why, stay, and hear me speak.
    CAS. Madam, not now: I am very ill at ease,
Unfit for mine own purposes.
    DES. Well, do your discretion.   *Exit Cassio.*
    IAGO. Ha! I like not that.
    OTH.   What dost thou say?
    IAGO. Nothing, my lord: or if—I know not what.
    OTH. Was not that Cassio parted from my wife?
    IAGO. Cassio, my lord! No, sure, I cannot think it,
That he would steal away so guilty-like,
Seeing you coming.
    OTH.   I do believe 'twas he.   40
    DES. How now, my lord!
I have been talking with a suitor here,
A man that languishes in your displeasure.
    OTH. Who is 't you mean?
    DES. Why, your lieutenant, Cassio. Good my lord,
If I have any grace or power to move you,
His present reconciliation take;
For if he be not one that truly loves you,
That errs in ignorance and not in cunning,
I have no judgement in an honest face: 50
I prithee, call him back.
    OTH.   Went he hence now?
    DES. Ay, sooth; so humbled
That he hath left part of his grief with me,
To suffer with him. Good love, call him back.
    OTH. Not now, sweet Desdemon; some other time.

---

    19. **doubt,** fear.   23. **watch him tame,** tame him by keeping him from sleeping (a term from falconry).   24. **shrift,** confessional.   28. **away,** up.

DES. But shall 't be shortly?

OTH.   The sooner, sweet, for you.

DES. Shall 't be to-night at supper?

OTH.   No, not to-night.

DES. To-morrow dinner, then?

OTH.   I shall not dine at home;
I meet the captains at the citadel.

DES. Why, then, to-morrow night; or Tuesday morn;   60
On Tuesday noon, or night; on Wednesday morn:
I prithee, name the time, but let it not
Exceed three days: in faith, he 's penitent;
And yet his trespass, in our common reason—
Save that, they say, the wars must make examples
Out of their best—is not almost a fault
T' incur a private check. When shall he come?
Tell me, Othello: I wonder in my soul,
What you would ask me, that I should deny,
Or stand so mamm'ring on. What! Michael Cassio,   70
That came a-wooing with you, and so many a time,
When I have spoke of you dispraisingly,
Hath ta'en your part; to have so much to do
To bring him in! Trust me, I could do much,—

OTH. Prithee, no more: let him come when he will;
I will deny thee nothing.

DES.   Why, this is not a boon;
'Tis as I should entreat you wear your gloves,
Or feed on nourishing dishes, or keep you warm,
Or sue to you to do a peculiar profit
To your own person: nay, when I have a suit   80
Wherein I mean to touch your love indeed,
It shall be full of poise and difficult weight
And fearful to be granted.

OTH.   I will deny thee nothing:
Whereon, I do beseech thee, grant me this,
To leave me but a little to myself.

DES. Shall I deny you? no: farewell, my lord.

OTH. Farewell, my Desdemona: I'll come to thee straight.

DES. Emilia, come. Be as your fancies teach you;
Whate'er you be, I am obedient.   *Exit* [*with Emilia*].

OTH. Excellent wretch! Perdition catch my soul,   90
But I do love thee! and when I love thee not,
Chaos is come again.

IAGO. My noble lord,—

OTH.   What dost thou say, Iago?

IAGO. Did Michael Cassio, when you woo'd my lady, Know of your
love?

---

64. **common reason,** everyday judgments. 70. **mamm'ring on,** wavering. 82. **poise,** weight,
heaviness. 90. **wretch,** term of affectionate endearment with a connotation of pity.

OTH.   He did, from first to last: why dost thou ask?

IAGO.   But for a satisfaction of my thought;
No further harm.

OTH.   Why of thy thought, Iago?

IAGO.   I did not think he had been acquainted with her.

OTH.   O, yes; and went between us very oft.   100

IAGO.   Indeed!

OTH.   Indeed! ay, indeed: discern'st thou aught in that?
Is he not honest?

IAGO.   Honest, my lord!

OTH.   Honest! ay, honest.

IAGO.   My lord, for aught I know.

OTH.   What dost thou think?

IAGO.   Think, my lord!

OTH.   Think, my lord!
By heaven, he echoes me,
As if there were some monster in his thought
Too hideous to be shown. Thou dost mean something:
I heard thee say even now, thou lik'st not that,
When Cassio left my wife: what didst not like?   110
And when I told thee he was of my counsel
In my whole course of wooing, thou criedst 'Indeed!'
And didst contract and purse thy brow together,
As if thou then hadst shut up in thy brain
Some horrible conceit: if thou dost love me,
Show me thy thought.

IAGO.   My lord, you know I love you.

OTH.   I think thou dost;
And, for I know thou 'rt full of love and honesty,
And weigh'st thy words before thou giv'st them breath,
Therefore these stops of thine fright me the more: 120
For such things in a false disloyal knave
Are tricks of custom, but in a man that 's just
They 're close delations, working from the heart
That passion cannot rule.

IAGO.   For Michael Cassio,
I dare be sworn I think that he is honest.

OTH.   I think so too.

IAGO.   Men should be what they seem;
Or those that be not, would they might seem none!

OTH.   Certain, men should be what they seem.

IAGO.   Why, then, I think Cassio's an honest man.

OTH.   Nay, yet there's more in this: 130
I prithee, speak to me as to thy thinkings,
As thou dost ruminate, and give thy worst of thoughts
The worst of words.

IAGO.   Good my lord, pardon me:

---

123. **close delations,** secret or involuntary accusations.

Though I am bound to every act of duty,
I am not bound to that all slaves are free to.
Utter my thoughts? Why, say they are vile and false;
As where's that palace whereinto foul things
Sometimes intrude not? who has a breast so pure,
But some uncleanly apprehensions
Keep leets and law-days and in sessions sit   140
With meditations lawful?
      OTH.   Thou dost conspire against thy friend, Iago,
If thou but think'st him wrong'd and mak'st his ear
A stranger to thy thoughts.
      IAGO.   I do beseech you—
Though I perchance am vicious in my guess,
As, I confess, it is my nature's plague
To spy into abuses, and oft my jealousy
Shapes faults that are not—that your wisdom yet,
From one that so imperfectly conceits,
Would take no notice, nor build yourself a trouble   150
Out of his scattering and unsure observance.
It were not for your quiet nor your good,
Nor for my manhood, honesty, or wisdom,
To let you know my thoughts.
      OTH.   What dost thou mean?
      IAGO.   Good name in man and woman, dear my lord,
Is the immediate jewel of their souls:
Who steals my purse steals trash; 'tis something, nothing;
'Twas mine, 'tis his, and has been slave to thousands;
But he that filches from me my good name
Robs me of that which not enriches him   160
And makes me poor indeed.
      OTH.   By heaven, I'll know thy thoughts.
      IAGO.   You cannot, if my heart were in your hand;
Nor shall not, whilst 'tis in my custody.
      OTH.   Ha!
      IAGO.   O, beware, my lord, of jealousy;
It is the green-ey'd monster which doth mock
The meat it feeds on: that cuckold lives in bliss
Who, certain of his fate, loves not his wronger;
But, O, what damned minutes tells he o'er
Who dotes, yet doubts, suspects, yet strongly loves!   170
      OTH.   O misery!
      IAGO.   Poor and content is rich and rich enough,
But riches fineless is as poor as winter
To him that ever fears he shall be poor.
Good God, the souls of all my tribe defend
From jealousy!

---

    140. **Keep leets,** hold courts. **law-days,** court-days.   145. **vicious,** wrong.   147. **jealousy,** suspicion of evil.   149. **conceits,** judges.   173. **fineless,** boundless.

OTH.   Why, why is this?
Think'st thou I 'ld make a life of jealousy,
To follow still the changes of the moon
With fresh suspicions? No; to be once in doubt
Is once to be resolv'd: exchange me for a goat,   180
When I shall turn the business of my soul
To such exsufflicate and blown surmises,
Matching thy inference. 'Tis not to make me jealous
To say my wife is fair, feeds well, loves company,
Is free of speech, sings, plays and dances well;
Where virtue is, these are more virtuous:
Nor from mine own weak merits will I draw
The smallest fear or doubt of her revolt;
For she had eyes, and chose me. No, Iago;
I'll see before I doubt; when I doubt, prove;   190
And on the proof, there is no more but this,—
Away at once with love or jealousy!
        IAGO.   I am glad of this; for now I shall have reason
To show the love and duty that I bear you
With franker spirit: therefore, as I am bound,
Receive it from me. I speak not yet of proof.
Look to your wife; observe her well with Cassio;
Wear your eye thus, not jealous nor secure:
I would not have your free and noble nature,
Out of self-bounty, be abus'd; look to 't: 200
I know our country disposition well;
In Venice they do let heaven see the pranks
They dare not show their husbands; their best conscience
Is not to leave 't undone, but keep 't unknown.
        OTH.   Dost thou say so?
        IAGO.   She did deceive her father, marrying you;
And when she seem'd to shake and fear your looks,
She lov'd them most.
        OTH.   And so she did.
        IAGO.   Why, go to then;
She that, so young, could give out such a seeming,
To seel her father's eyes up close as oak—   210
He thought 'twas witchcraft—but I am much to blame;
I humbly do beseech you of your pardon
For too much loving you.
        OTH.   I am bound to thee for ever.
        IAGO.   I see this hath a little dash'd your spirits.
        OTH.   Not a jot, not a jot.
        IAGO.   I' faith, I fear it has.
I hope you will consider what is spoke
Comes from my love. But I do see y' are mov'd:

----

182. **exsufflicate and blown,** unsubstantial and inflated, flyblown.   198. **secure,** free from uneasiness.   200. **self-bounty,** inherent or natural goodness.   209. **seeming,** false appearance.   210. **seel,** blind (a term from falconry).

I am to pray you not to strain my speech
To grosser issues nor to larger reach
Than to suspicion.   220
    OTH. I will not.
    IAGO.   Should you do so, my lord,
My speech should fall into such vile success
As my thoughts aim not at. Cassio's my worthy friend—
My lord, I see y' are mov'd.
    OTH.   No, not much mov'd:
I do not think but Desdemona's honest.
    IAGO. Long live she so! and long live you to think so!
    OTH. And yet, how nature erring from itself,—
    IAGO. Ay, there's the point: as—to be bold with you—
Not to affect many proposed matches
Of her own clime, complexion, and degree,   230
Whereto we see in all things nature tends—
Foh! one may smell in such a will most rank,
Foul disproportion, thoughts unnatural.
But pardon me; I do not in position
Distinctly speak of her; though I may fear
Her will, recoiling to her better judgement,
May fall to match you with her country forms
And happily repent.
    OTH.   Farewell, farewell:
If more thou dost perceive, let me know more;
Set on thy wife to observe: leave me, Iago.   240
    IAGO. [*Going*] My lord, I take my leave.
    OTH. Why did I marry? This honest creature doubtless
Sees and knows more, much more, than he unfolds.
    IAGO. [*Returning*] My Lord, I would I might entreat your honour
To scan this thing no farther; leave it to time:
Although 'tis fit that Cassio have his place,
For, sure, he fills it up with great ability,
Yet, if you please to hold him off awhile,
You shall by that perceive him and his means:
Note, if your lady strain his entertainment   250
With any strong or vehement importunity;
Much will be seen in that. In the mean time,
Let me be thought too busy in my fears—
As worthy cause I have to fear I am—
And hold her free, I do beseech your honour.
    OTH. Fear not my government.
    IAGO. I once more take my leave.   *Exit.*
    OTH. This fellow 's of exceeding honesty,

---

219. **reach**, meaning.   232. **will**, sensuality.   233. **disproportion**, abnormality.   234. **position**, general argument.   236. **recoiling to**, falling back upon, or recoiling against.   237. **fall . . . forms**, happen to compare you with Venetian norms of handsomeness.   238. **repent**, i.e., of her marriage. 250. **strain his entertainment**, urge his reinstatement.   255. **hold her free**, regard her as innocent. 256. **government**, self-control.

And knows all qualities, with a learned spirit,
Of human dealings. If I do prove her haggard, 260
Though that her jesses were my dear heartstrings,
I 'ld whistle her off and let her down the wind,
To prey at fortune. Haply, for I am black
And have not those soft parts of conversation
That chamberers have, or for I am declin'd
Into the vale of years,—yet that's not much—
She's gone. I am abus'd: and my relief
Must be to loathe her. O curse of marriage,
That we can call these delicate creatures ours,
And not their appetites! I had rather be a toad, 270
And live upon the vapour of a dungeon,
Than keep a corner in the thing I love
For others' uses. Yet, 'tis the plague of great ones;
Prerogativ'd are they less than the base;
'Tis destiny unshunnable, like death:
Even then this forked plague is fated to us
When we do quicken. Look where she comes:

  Enter DESDEMONA *and* EMILIA.

If she be false, O, then heaven mocks itself!
I'll not believe 't.
  DES. How now, my dear Othello!
Your dinner, and the generous islanders 280
By you invited, do attend your presence.
  OTH. I am to blame.
  DES.   Why do you speak so faintly?
Are you not well?
  OTH. I have a pain upon my forehead here.
  DES. 'Faith, that 's with watching; 'twill away again:
Let me but bind it hard, within this hour
It will be well.
  OTH. Your napkin is too little:
    [*He puts the handkerchief from him; and it drops.*]
Let it alone. Come, I'll go in with you.
  DES. I am very sorry that you are not well. *Exit* [*with Othello*].
  EMIL. I am glad I have found this napkin: 290
This was her first remembrance from the Moor:
My wayward husband hath a hundred times
Woo'd me to steal it; but she so loves the token,
For he conjur'd her she should ever keep it,
That she reserves it evermore about her
To kiss and talk to. I'll have the work ta'en out,
And give 't Iago: what he will do with it

---

  260. **haggard,** a wild female duck. 261. **jesses,** straps fastened around the legs of a trained hawk.
263. **at fortune,** at random. 265. **chamberers,** gallants. 274. **Prerogativ'd,** privileged. 276. **forked,**
an allusion to the horns of the cuckold. 277. **quicken,** receive life. 280. **generous,** noble. 285.
watching, working late. 296. **work ta'en out,** design copied.

Heaven knows, not I;
I nothing but to please his fantasy.

> *Enter* IAGO.

    IAGO. How now! what do you here alone?   300
    EMIL. Do not you chide; I have a thing for you.
    IAGO. A thing for me? it is a common thing—
    EMIL. Ha!
    IAGO. To have a foolish wife.
    EMIL. O, is that all? What will you give me now
For that same handkerchief?
    IAGO.   What handkerchief?
    EMIL. What handkerchief!
Why, that the Moor first gave to Desdemona;
That which so often you did bid me steal.
    IAGO. Hast stol'n it from her?   310
    EMIL. No, 'faith; she let it drop by negligence,
And, to th' advantage, I, being here, took 't up.
Look, here it is.
    IAGO.   A good wench; give it me.
    EMIL. What will you do with 't, that you have been so earnest
To have me filch it?
    IAGO.   [*Snatching it*] Why, what is that to you?
    EMIL. If it be not for some purpose of import,
Give 't me again: poor lady, she'll run mad
When she shall lack it.
    IAGO. Be not acknown on 't; I have use for it.
Go, leave me.   *Exit Emilia.* 320
I will in Cassio's lodging lose this napkin,
And let him find it. Trifles light as air
Are to the jealous confirmations strong
As proofs of holy writ: this may do something.
The Moor already changes with my poison:
Dangerous conceits are, in their natures, poisons,
Which at the first are scarce found to distaste,
But with a little act upon the blood,
Burn like the mines of sulphur. I did say so:

> *Enter* OTHELLO.

Look, where he comes! Not poppy, nor mandragora,   330
Nor all the drowsy syrups of the world,
Shall ever medicine thee to that sweet sleep
Which thou owedst yesterday.
    OTH.   Ha! ha! false to me?

---

302. **common thing** (with bawdy suggestion). 319. **Be . . . on 't,** do not confess knowledge of
it. 328. **act,** action, working.

IAGO. Why, how now, general! no more of that.

OTH. Avaunt! be gone! thou hast set me on the rack;
I swear 'tis better to be much abus'd
Than but to know 't a little.

IAGO. How now, my lord!

OTH. What sense had I of her stol'n hours of lust?
I saw 't not, thought it not, it harm'd not me:
I slept the next night well, fed well, was free and merry;　　　340
I found not Cassio's kisses on her lips:
He that is robb'd, not wanting what is stol'n,
Let him not know 't, and he's not robb'd at all.

IAGO. I am sorry to hear this.

OTH. I had been happy, if the general camp,
Pioners and all, had tasted her sweet body,
So I had nothing known. O, now, for ever
Farewell the tranquil mind! farewell content!
Farewell the plumed troop, and the big wars,
That make ambition virtue! O, farewell!　　　350
Farewell the neighing steed, and the shrill trump,
The spirit-stirring drum, th' ear-piercing fife,
The royal banner, and all quality,
Pride, pomp and circumstance of glorious war!
And, O you mortal engines, whose rude throats
Th' immortal Jove's dread clamours counterfeit,
Farewell! Othello's occupation's gone!

IAGO. Is 't possible, my lord?

OTH. Villain, be sure thou prove my love a whore,
Be sure of it; give me the ocular proof;　　　360
Or, by the worth of mine eternal soul,
Thou hadst been better have been born a dog
Than answer my wak'd wrath!

IAGO. Is 't come to this?

OTH. Make me to see 't; or, at the least, so prove it,
That the probation bear no hinge nor loop
To hang a doubt on; or woe upon thy life!

IAGO. My noble lord,—

OTH. If thou dost slander her and torture me,
Never pray more; abandon all remorse;
On horror's head horrors accumulate;　　　370
Do deeds to make heaven weep, all earth amaz'd;
For nothing canst thou to damnation add
Greater than that.

IAGO. O grace! O heaven forgive me!
Are you a man? have you a soul or sense?
God be wi' you; take mine office. O wretched fool,
That liv'st to make thine honesty a vice!

---

346. **Pioners,** sappers, a low grade of soldiers.　354. **circumstance,** attendant fact; here, formal display.　355. **mortal engines,** i.e., cannon.　370. **horrors,** object of *accumulate*.

O monstrous world! Take note, take note, O world,
To be direct and honest is not safe.
I thank you for this profit; and from hence
I'll love no friend, sith love breeds such offence.   380
    OTH.   Nay, stay: thou shouldst be honest.
    IAGO.   I should be wise, for honesty's a fool
And loses that it works for.
    OTH.   By the world,
I think my wife be honest and think she is not;
I think that thou art just and think thou art not.
I'll have some proof. Her name, that was as fresh
As Dian's visage, is now begrim'd and black
As mine own face. If there be cords, or knives,
Poison, or fire, or suffocating streams,
I'll not endure it. Would I were satisfied!   390
    IAGO.   I see, sir, you are eaten up with passion:
I do repent me that I put it to you.
You would be satisfied?
    OTH.   Would! nay, I will.
    IAGO.   And may: but, how? how satisfied, my lord?
Would you, the supervisor, grossly gape on—
Behold her topp'd?
    OTH.   Death and damnation! O!
    IAGO.   It were a tedious difficulty, I think,
To bring them to that prospect: damn them then,
If ever mortal eyes do see them bolster
More than their own! What then? how then?   400
What shall I say? Where's satisfaction?
It is impossible you should see this,
Were they as prime as goats, as hot as monkeys,
As salt as wolves in pride, and fools as gross
As ignorance made drunk. But yet, I say,
If imputation and strong circumstances,
Which lead directly to the door of truth,
Will give you satisfaction, you may have 't.
    OTH.   Give me a living reason she's disloyal.
    IAGO.   I do not like the office: 410
But, sith I am ent'red in this cause so far,
Prick'd to 't by foolish honesty and love,
I will go on. I lay with Cassio lately;
And, being troubled with a raging tooth,
I could not sleep.
There are a kind of men so loose of soul,
That in their sleeps will mutter their affairs:
One of this kind is Cassio:
In sleep I heard him say 'Sweet Desdemona,

---

    399. **bolster,** lie together. 404. **salt,** wanton, sensual. 406. **imputation,** i.e., opinion founded
on strong circumstantial evidence.

Let us be wary, let us hide our loves;'   420
And then, sir, would he gripe and wring my hand,
Cry 'O sweet creature!' and then kiss me hard,
As if he pluck'd up kisses by the roots
That grew upon my lips: then laid his leg
Over my thigh, and sigh'd, and kiss'd; and then
Cried 'Cursed fate that gave thee to the Moor!'
      OTH. O monstrous! monstrous!
      IAGO.   Nay, this was but his dream.
      OTH. But this denoted a foregone conclusion:
'Tis a shrewd doubt, though it be but a dream.
      IAGO. And this may help to thicken other proofs   430
That do demonstrate thinly.
      OTH.   I'll tear her all to pieces.
      IAGO. Nay, but be wise: yet we see nothing done;
She may be honest yet. Tell me but this,
Have you not sometimes seen a handkerchief
Spotted with strawberries in your wife's hand?
      OTH. I gave her such a one; 'twas my first gift.
      IAGO. I know not that: but such a handkerchief—
I am sure it was your wife's—did I to-day
See Cassio wipe his beard with.
      OTH.   If it be that,—
      IAGO. If it be that, or any that was hers,   440
It speaks against her with the other proofs.
      OTH. O, that the slave had forty thousand lives!
One is too poor, too weak for my revenge.
Now do I see 'tis true. Look here, Iago;
All my fond love thus do I blow to heaven.
'Tis gone.
Arise, black vengeance, from the hollow hell!
Yield up, O love, thy crown and hearted throne
To tyrannous hate! Swell, bosom, with thy fraught,
For 'tis of aspics' tongues!
      IAGO.   Yet be content.   450
      OTH. O, blood, blood, blood!
      IAGO. Patience, I say; your mind perhaps may change.
      OTH. Never, Iago. Like to the Pontic sea,
Whose icy current and compulsive course
Ne'er feels retiring ebb, but keeps due on
To the Propontic and the Hellespont,
Even so my bloody thoughts, with violent pace,
Shall ne'er look back, ne'er ebb to humble love,
Till that a capable and wide revenge
Swallow them up. Now, by yond marble heaven,   460

---

428. **foregone conclusion,** previous trial or experience (not used in our sense). 448. **hearted,**
fixed in the heart. 449. **fraught,** freight, burden. 450. **aspics',** venomous serpents'. 460. **marble,**
i.e., gleaming like marble.

[*Kneels*] In the due reverence of a sacred vow
I here engage my words.
    IAGO.   Do not rise yet.
[*Kneels*] Witness, you ever-burning lights above,
You elements that clip us round about,
Witness that here Iago doth give up
The execution of his wit, hands, heart,
To wrong'd Othello's service! Let him command,
And to obey shall be in me remorse,
What bloody business ever.   [*They rise.*]
    OTH.   I greet thy love,
Not with vain thanks, but with acceptance bounteous,   470
And will upon the instant put thee to 't:
Within these three days let me hear thee say
That Cassio's not alive.
    IAGO.   My friend is dead; 'tis done at your request:
But let her live.
    OTH.   Damn her, lewd minx! O, damn her! damn her!
Come, go with me apart; I will withdraw,
To furnish me with some swift means of death
For the fair devil. Now art thou my lieutenant.
    IAGO.   I am your own for ever.   *Exeunt.* 480

Scene IV. [*Before the castle.*]

Enter DESDEMONA, EMILIA, *and* Clown.

    DES.   Do you know, sirrah, where Lieutenant Cassio lies?
    CLO.   I dare not say he lies any where.
    DES.   Why, man?
    CLO.   He's a soldier, and for one to say a soldier lies, is stabbing.
    DES.   Go to: where lodges he?
    CLO.   To tell you where he lodges, is to tell you where I lie.
    DES.   Can any thing be made of this?
    CLO.   I know not where he lodges, and for me to devise a lodging and say
he lies here or he lies there, were to lie in mine own throat.
    DES.   Can you inquire him out, and be edified by report?   10
    CLO.   I will catechize the world for him; that is, make questions, and by
them answer.
    DES.   Seek him, bid him come hither: tell him I have moved my lord on his
behalf, and hope all will be well.
    CLO.   To do this is within the compass of man's wit; and therefore I will
attempt the doing it.   *Exit Clo.*
    DES.   Where should I lose that handkerchief, Emilia?
    EMIL.   I know not, madam.
    DES.   Believe me, I had rather have lost my purse
Full of crusadoes: and, but my noble Moor   20

---

466. **execution,** exercise. 468. **remorse,** pity for Othello's wrongs.
Scene IV. 20. **crusadoes,** Portuguese gold coins.

Is true of mind and made of no such baseness
As jealous creatures are, it were enough
To put him to ill thinking.
     EMIL.   Is he not jealous?
     DES.   Who, he? I think the sun where he was born
Drew all such humours from him.
     EMIL.   Look, where he comes.

    Enter OTHELLO.

     DES.   I will not leave him now till Cassio
Be call'd to him.—How is 't with you, my lord?
     OTH.   Well, my good lady. [*Aside*] O, hardness to dissemble!—
How do you, Desdemona?
     DES.   Well, my good lord.
     OTH.   Give me your hand: this hand is moist, my lady.   30
     DES.   It yet hath felt no age nor known no sorrow.
     OTH.   This argues fruitfulness and liberal heart:
Hot, hot, and moist: this hand of yours requires
A sequester from liberty, fasting and prayer,
Much castigation, exercise devout;
For here 's a young and sweating devil here,
That commonly rebels. 'Tis a good hand,
A frank one.
     DES.   You may, indeed, say so;
For 'twas that hand that gave away my heart.
     OTH.   A liberal hand: the hearts of old gave hands;   40
But our new heraldry is hands, not hearts.
     DES.   I cannot speak of this. Come now, your promise.
     OTH.   What promise, chuck?
     DES.   I have sent to bid Cassio come speak with you.
     OTH.   I have a salt and sorry rheum offends me;
Lend me thy handkerchief.
     DES.   Here, my lord.
     OTH.   That which I gave you.
     DES.   I have it not about me.
     OTH.   Not?
     DES.   No, indeed, my lord.
     OTH.   That's a fault.
That handkerchief
Did an Egyptian to my mother give;   50
She was a charmer, and could almost read
The thoughts of people: she told her, while she kept it,
'Twould make her amiable and subdue my father
Entirely to her love, but if she lost it
Or made a gift of it, my father's eye
Should hold her loathed and his spirits should hunt

---

    34. **sequester,** separation.   41. **new . . . hearts,** a current expression referring to marriages in
which there is a joining of hands without the giving of hearts.   45. **sorry rheum,** distressful head cold.
50. **Egyptian,** gypsy.

After new fancies: she, dying, gave it me;
And bid me, when my fate would have me wive,
To give it her. I did so: and take heed on 't;
Make it a darling like your precious eye;　　　　　　　60
To lose 't or give 't away were such perdition
As nothing else could match.
　　　　Des.　　　　　　　Is 't possible?
　　　　Oth.　'Tis true: there's magic in the web of it:
A sibyl, that had numb'red in the world
The sun to course two hundred compasses,
In her prophetic fury sew'd the work;
The worms were hallow'd that did breed the silk;
And it was dy'd in mummy which the skilful
Conserv'd of maidens' hearts.
　　　　Des.　　　　　　　Indeed! is 't true?
　　　　Oth.　Most veritable; therefore look to 't well.　　70
　　　　Des.　Then would to God that I had never seen 't!
　　　　Oth.　Ha! wherefore?
　　　　Des.　Why do you speak so startingly and rash?
　　　　Oth.　Is 't lost? is 't gone? speak, is it out o' th' way?
　　　　Des.　Heaven bless us!
　　　　Oth.　Say you?
　　　　Des.　It is not lost; but what an if it were?
　　　　Oth.　How!
　　　　Des.　I say, it is not lost.
　　　　Oth.　　　　　　　Fetch 't, let me see 't.
　　　　Des.　Why, so I can, sir, but I will not now.　　　80
This is a trick to put me from my suit:
Pray you, let Cassio be receiv'd again.
　　　　Oth.　Fetch me the handkerchief: my mind misgives.
　　　　Des.　Come, come;
You'll never meet a more sufficient man.
　　　　Oth.　The handkerchief!
　　　　Des.　　　　　　　I pray, talk me of Cassio.
　　　　Oth.　The handkerchief!
　　　　Des.　　　　　　　A man that all his time
Hath founded his good fortunes on your love,
Shar'd dangers with you,—
　　　　Oth.　The handkerchief!　　　　　　　　　90
　　　　Des.　In sooth, you are to blame.
　　　　Oth.　Away!　　　　　　　　　　　*Exit Othello.*
　　　　Emil.　Is not this man jealous?
　　　　Des.　I ne'er saw this before.
Sure, there's some wonder in this handkerchief:
I am most unhappy in the loss of it.
　　　　Emil.　'Tis not a year or two shows us a man:

---

68. **mummy,** medicinal or magical preparation drained from the flesh of mummified bodies.　69. **Conserv'd of,** preserved out of.

They are all but stomachs, and we all but food;
They eat us hungerly, and when they are full,
They belch us.

Enter IAGO *and* CASSIO.

Look you, Cassio and my husband! 100
IAGO.   There is no other way; 'tis she must do 't:
And, lo, the happiness! go, and importune her.
DES.   How now, good Cassio! what's the news with you?
CAS.   Madam, my former suit: I do beseech you
That by your virtuous means I may again
Exist, and be a member of his love
Whom I with all the office of my heart
Entirely honour: I would not be delay'd.
If my offence be of such mortal kind
That nor my service past, nor present sorrows, 110
Nor purpos'd merit in futurity,
Can ransom me into his love again,
But to know so must be my benefit;
So shall I clothe me in a forc'd content,
And shut myself up in some other course,
To fortune's alms.
DES.   Alas, thrice-gentle Cassio!
My advocation is not now in tune;
My lord is not my lord; nor should I know him,
Were he in favour as in humour alter'd.
So help me every spirit sanctified, 120
As I have spoken for you all my best
And stood within the blank of his displeasure
For my free speech! you must awhile be patient:
What I can do I will; and more I will
Than for myself I dare: let that suffice you.
IAGO.   Is my lord angry?
EMIL.   He went hence but now,
And certainly in strange unquietness.
IAGO.   Can he be angry? I have seen the cannon,
When it hath blown his ranks into the air,
And, like the devil, from his very arm 130
Puff'd his own brother:—and can he be angry?
Something of moment then: I will go meet him:
There's matter in 't indeed, if he be angry.
DES.   I prithee, do so.   *Exit* [*Iago*].
Something, sure, of state,
Either from Venice, or some unhatch'd practice
Made demonstrable here in Cyprus to him,

---

113. **to know . . . benefit,** to know that my case is hopeless will end my vain endeavor.   117. **advocation,** advocacy.   122. **blank,** white spot in the center of a target; here, range.

Hath puddled his clear spirit; and in such cases
Men's natures wrangle with inferior things,
Though great ones are their object. 'Tis even so;
For let our finger ache, and it indues   140
Our other healthful members even to a sense
Of pain: nay, we must think men are not gods,
Nor of them look for such observancy
As fits the bridal. Beshrew me much, Emilia,
I was, unhandsome warrior as I am,
Arraigning his unkindness with my soul;
But now I find I had suborn'd the witness,
And he's indicted falsely.
      EMIL. Pray heaven it be state-matters, as you think,
And no conception nor no jealous toy   150
Concerning you.
      DES. Alas the day! I never gave him cause.
      EMIL. But jealous souls will not be answer'd so;
They are not ever jealous for the cause,
But jealous for they are jealous: 'tis a monster
Begot upon itself, born on itself.
      DES. Heaven keep that monster from Othello's mind!
      EMIL. Lady, amen.
      DES. I will go seek him. Cassio, walk here about:
If I do find him fit, I'll move your suit   160
And seek to effect it to my uttermost.
      CAS. I humbly thank your ladyship.   *Exit [Desdemona with Emilia].*

Enter BIANCA.

      BIAN. Save you, friend Cassio!
      CAS.   What make you from home?
How is 't with you, my most fair Bianca?
I' faith, sweet love, I was coming to your house.
      BIAN. And I was going to your lodging, Cassio.
What, keep a week away? seven days and nights?
Eight score eight hours? and lovers' absent hours,
More tedious than the dial eight score times?
O weary reck'ning!
      CAS.   Pardon me, Bianca: 170
I have this while with leaden thoughts been press'd;
But I shall, in a more continuate time,
Strike off this score of absence. Sweet Bianca,
             [Giving her Desdemona's handkerchief.]
Take me this work out.
      BIAN.   O Cassio, whence came this?

---

    137. **puddled,** sullied the purity of.   140. **indues,** brings to the same condition.   145. **unhandsome,** unfair.   150. **conception,** mere fancy.   172. **continuate,** uninterrupted.   174. **Take . . . out,** i.e., copy this embroidery for me.

This is some token from a newer friend:
To the felt absence now I feel a cause:
Is 't come to this? Well, well.

CAS.   Go to, woman!
Throw your vile guesses in the devil's teeth,
From whence you have them. You are jealous now
That this is from some mistress, some remembrance: 180
No, in good troth, Bianca.

BIAN.   Why, whose is it?

CAS.   I know not, sweet: I found it in my chamber.
I like the work well: ere it be demanded—
As like enough it will—I would have it copied:
Take it, and do 't; and leave me for this time.

BIAN.   Leave you! wherefore?

CAS.   I do attend here on the general;
And think it no addition, nor my wish,
To have him see me woman'd.

BIAN.   Why, I pray you?

CAS.   Not that I love you not.

BIAN.   But that you do not love me.   190
I pray you, bring me on the way a little,
And say if I shall see you soon at night.

CAS.   'Tis but a little way that I can bring you;
For I attend here: but I'll see you soon.

BIAN.   'Tis very good; I must be circumstanc'd.   *Exeunt omnes.*

ACT IV.

Scene I. [*Cyprus. Before the castle.*]

     Enter OTHELLO *and* IAGO.

IAGO.   Will you think so?

OTH.   Think so, Iago!

IAGO.   What,
To kiss in private?

OTH.   An unauthoriz'd kiss.

IAGO.   Or to be naked with her friend in bed
An hour or more, not meaning any harm?

OTH.   Naked in bed, Iago, and not mean harm!
It is hypocrisy against the devil:
They that mean virtuously, and yet do so,
The devil their virtue tempts, and they tempt heaven.

IAGO.   So they do nothing, 'tis a venial slip:
But if I give my wife a handkerchief,—   10

---

195. **circumstanc'd,** governed by circumstances.
Act IV. Scene I.   9. **So,** so long as.

OTH. What then?

IAGO. Why, then, 'tis hers, my lord; and, being hers,
She may, I think, bestow 't on any man.

OTH. She is protectress of her honour too:
May she give that?

IAGO. Her honour is an essence that 's not seen;
They have it very oft that have it not:
But, for the handkerchief,—

OTH. By heaven, I would most gladly have forgot it.
Thou said'st—O, it comes o'er my memory,   20
As doth the raven o'er the infected house,
Boding to all—he had my handkerchief.

IAGO. Ay, what of that?

OTH.   That's not so good now.

IAGO.   What,
If I had said I had seen him do you wrong?
Or heard him say,—as knaves be such abroad,
Who having, by their own importunate suit,
Or voluntary dotage of some mistress,
Convinced or supplied them, cannot choose
But they must blab—

OTH.   Hath he said any thing?

IAGO. He hath, my lord; but be you well assur'd,   30
No more than he'll unswear.

OTH.   What hath he said?

IAGO. 'Faith, that he did—I know not what he did.

OTH. What? what?

IAGO. Lie—

OTH.   With her?

IAGO.   With her, on her; what you will.

OTH. Lie with her! lie on her! We say lie on her, when they belie her. Lie
with her! that's fulsome.—Handkerchief—confessions—handkerchief!—To
confess, and be hanged for his labour;—first, to be hanged, and then to
confess.—I tremble at it. Nature would not invest herself in such shadowing
passion without some instruction. It is not words that shakes me thus. Pish!
Noses, ears, and lips.—Is 't possible?—Confess—handerchief!—O devil!

                                        Falls in a trance.

IAGO. Work on,
My medicine, work! Thus credulous fools are caught;
And many worthy and chaste dames even thus,
All guiltless, meet reproach. What, ho! my lord!
My lord, I say! Othello!

Enter CASSIO.

                    How now, Cassio!

---

21. **raven . . . house,** allusion to the belief that the raven hovered over a house of sickness or
infection.   28. **Convinced or supplied,** i.e., mistresses gained by importunity and those who doted
voluntarily.   38–39. **Nature . . . instruction,** i.e., my jealousy cannot be merely the result of natural
imagination, but must have some foundation in fact.

Cas. What's the matter?

Iago. My lord is fall'n into an epilepsy:
This is his second fit; he had one yesterday.

Cas. Rub him about the temples.

Iago.   No, forbear;   50
The lethargy must have his quiet course:
If not, he foams at mouth and by and by
Breaks out to savage madness. Look, he stirs:
Do you withdraw yourself a little while,
He will recover straight: when he is gone,
I would on great occasion speak with you.   [*Exit Cassio*].
How is it, general? have you not hurt your head?

Oth. Dost thou mock me?

Iago.   I mock you! no, by heaven.
Would you would bear your fortune like a man!

Oth. A horned man 's a monster and a beast.   60

Iago. There's many a beast then in a populous city,
And many a civil monster.

Oth. Did he confess it?

Iago.   Good sir, be a man;
Think every bearded fellow that 's but yok'd
May draw with you: there 's millions now alive
That nightly lie in those unproper beds
Which they dare swear peculiar: your case is better.
O, 'tis the spite of hell, the fiend's arch-mock,
To lip a wanton in a secure couch,
And to suppose her chaste! No, let me know;   70
And knowing what I am, I know what she shall be.

Oth. O, thou art wise; 'tis certain.

Iago.   Stand you awhile apart;
Confine yourself but in a patient list.
Whilst you were here o'erwhelmed with your grief—
A passion most unsuiting such a man—
Cassio came hither: I shifted him away,
And laid good 'scuse upon your ecstasy,
Bade him anon return and here speak with me;
The which he promis'd. Do but encave yourself,
And mark the fleers, the gibes, and notable scorns,   80
That dwell in every region of his face;
For I will make him tell the tale anew,
Where, how, how oft, how long ago, and when
He hath, and is again to cope your wife:
I say, but mark his gesture. Marry, patience;
Or I shall say y' are all in all in spleen,
And nothing of a man.

Oth.   Dost thou hear, Iago?

---

51. **lethargy,** unconscious condition.   62. **civil,** i.e., in civilized society.   65. **draw with you,** i.e., share your fate as cuckold.   66. **unproper,** not belonging exclusively to an individual.   67. **peculiar,** private, one's own.   73. **patient list,** within the bounds of patience.   79. **encave,** conceal.   80. **fleers,** sneers.

I will be found most cunning in my patience;
But—dost thou hear?—most bloody.
    IAGO.   That's not amiss;
But yet keep time in all. Will you withdraw?   [*Othello retires.*] 90
Now will I question Cassio of Bianca,
A housewife that by selling her desires
Buys herself bread and clothes: it is a creature
That dotes on Cassio; as 'tis the strumpet's plague
To beguile many and be beguil'd by one:
He, when he hears of her, cannot refrain
From the excess of laughter. Here he comes:

    Enter CASSIO.

As he shall smile, Othello shall go mad;
And his unbookish jealousy must conster
Poor Cassio's smiles, gestures and light behaviour,   100
Quite in the wrong. How do you now, lieutenant?
    CAS.   The worser that you give me the addition
Whose want even kills me.
    IAGO.   Ply Desdemona well, and you are sure on 't.
[*Speaking lower*] Now, if this suit lay in Bianca's power,
How quickly should you speed!
    CAS.   Alas, poor caitiff!
    OTH.   Look, how he laughs already!
    IAGO.   I never knew woman love man so.
    CAS.   Alas, poor rogue! I think, i' faith, she loves me.
    OTH.   Now he denies it faintly, and laughs it out.   110
    IAGO.   Do you hear, Cassio?
    OTH.   Now he importunes him
To tell it o'er: go to; well said, well said.
    IAGO.   She gives it out that you shall marry her:
Do you intend it?
    CAS.   Ha, ha, ha!
    OTH.   Do you triumph, Roman? do you triumph?
    CAS.   I marry her! what? a customer! Prithee, bear some charity to my
wit; do not think it so unwholesome. Ha, ha, ha!
    OTH.   So, so, so, so: they laugh that win.
    IAGO.   'Faith, the cry goes that you shall marry her.   120
    CAS.   Prithee, say true.
    IAGO.   I am a very villain else.
    OTH.   Have you scored me? Well.
    CAS.   This is the monkey's own giving out: she is persuaded I will marry
her, out of her own love and flattery, not out of my promise.

---

    90. **keep time,** use judgment and order.   99. **unbookish,** uninstructed. **conster,** construe. 102.
addition, title. 116. **Roman.** The epithet arises from the association of the Romans with the
idea of triumph. 117. **customer,** prostitute. 123. **scored me,** made up my reckoning, or brand-
ed me.

Oth.   Iago beckons me; now he begins the story.

Cas.   She was here even now; she haunts me in every place. I was the other day talking on the sea-bank with certain Venetians; and thither comes the bauble, and, by this hand, she falls me thus about my neck—

Oth.   Crying, 'O dear Cassio!' as it were: his gesture imports it.   130

Cas.   So hangs, and lolls, and weeps upon me; so shakes, and pulls me: ha, ha, ha!

Oth.   Now he tells how she plucked him to my chamber. O, I see that nose of yours, but not that dog I shall throw it to.

Cas.   Well, I must leave her company.

Iago.   Before me! look, where she comes.

Enter Bianca.

Cas.   'Tis such another fitchew! marry, a perfumed one.—What do you mean by this haunting of me?

Bian.   Let the devil and his dam haunt you! What did you mean by that same handkerchief you gave me even now? I was a fine fool to take it. I must take out the work?—A likely piece of work, that you should find it in your chamber, and not know who left it there! This is some minx's token, and I must take out the work? There; give it your hobby-horse: wheresoever you had it, I'll take out no work on 't.   144

Cas.   How now, my sweet Bianca! how now! how now!

Oth.   By heaven, that should be my handkerchief!

Bian.   An you'll come to supper to-night, you may; an you will not, come when you are next prepared for.   *Exit.*

Iago.   After her, after her.

Cas.   'Faith, I must; she'll rail in the street else.   150

Iago.   Will you sup there?

Cas.   Yes, I intend so.

Iago.   Well, I may chance to see you; for I would very fain speak with you.

Cas.   Prithee, come; will you?

Iago.   Go to; say no more.   [*Exit Cassio.*]

Oth.   [*Advancing*] How shall I murder him, Iago?

Iago.   Did you perceive how he laughed at his vice?

Oth.   O Iago!

Iago.   And did you see the handkerchief?   160

Oth.   Was that mine?

Iago.   Yours, by this hand: and to see how he prizes the foolish woman your wife! she gave it him, and he hath given it his whore.

Oth.   I would have him nine years a-killing. A fine woman! a fair woman! a sweet woman!

Iago.   Nay, you must forget that.

Oth.   Ay, let her rot, and perish, and be damned to-night; for she shall not live: no, my heart is turned to stone; I strike it, and it hurts my hand. O, the world

---

129. **bauble**, plaything.   136. **Before me!** On my soul!   137. **fitchew**, polecat (because of her strong perfume; also, slang word for a prostitute).   143. **hobby-horse**, harlot.

hath not a sweeter creature: she might lie by an emperor's side and command
him tasks.   170

IAGO.   Nay, that 's not your way.

OTH.   Hang her! I do but say what she is: so delicate with her needle: an
admirable musician: O! she will sing the savageness out of a bear: of so high and
plenteous wit and invention:—

IAGO.   She 's the worse for all this.

OTH.   O, a thousand thousand times: and then, of so gentle a condition!

IAGO.   Ay, too gentle.

OTH.   Nay, that 's certain: but yet the pity of it, Iago! O Iago, the pity of it,
Iago!   180

IAGO.   If you are so fond over her iniquity, give her patent to offend; for,
if it touch not you, it comes near nobody.

OTH.   I will chop her into messes: cuckold me!

IAGO.   O, 'tis foul in her.

OTH.   With mine officer!

IAGO.   That 's fouler.

OTH.   Get me some poison, Iago; this night: I'll not expostulate with her,
lest her body and beauty unprovide my mind again: this night, Iago.

IAGO.   Do it not with poison, strangle her in her bed, even the bed she hath
contaminated.   190

OTH.   Good, good: the justice of it pleases: very good.

IAGO.   And for Cassio, let me be his undertaker: you shall hear more by
midnight.

OTH.   Excellent good. [*A trumpet within.*] What trumpet is that same?

IAGO.   I warrant something from Venice.

Enter LODOVICO, DESDEMONA, *and* Attendants.

                                                    'Tis Lodovico.
This comes from the duke: and, see, your wife's with him.

LOD.   God save you, worthy general!

OTH.   With all my heart, sir.

LOD.   The duke and the senators of Venice greet you.
                                                    [*Gives him a letter.*]

OTH.   I kiss the instrument of their pleasures.   200
                                                    [*Opens the letter, and reads.*]

DES.   And what's the news, good cousin Lodovico?

IAGO.   I am very glad to see you, signior;
Welcome to Cyprus.

LOD.   I thank you. How does Lieutenant Cassio?

IAGO.   Lives, sir.

DES.   Cousin, there 's fall'n between him and my lord
An unkind breach: but you shall make all well.

OTH.   Are you sure of that?

---

171. **your way,** i.e., the way you should think of her.   181. **patent,** license.   183. **messes,** dishes
of food.   188. **unprovide,** weaken.   192. **let . . . undertaker,** i.e., let me settle with him.

Des. My lord?

Oth. [*Reads*] 'This fail you not to do, as you will—' 210

Lod. He did not call; he 's busy in the paper.
Is there division 'twixt my lord and Cassio?

Des. A most unhappy one: I would do much
T' atone them, for the love I bear to Cassio.

Oth. Fire and brimstone!

Des. My lord?

Oth. Are you wise?

Des. What, is he angry?

Lod. May be the letter mov'd him;
For, as I think, they do command him home,
Deputing Cassio in his government.

Des. Trust me, I am glad on 't.

Oth. Indeed!

Des. My lord?

Oth. I am glad to see you mad.

Des. Why, sweet Othello,— 220

Oth. [*Striking her*] Devil!

Des. I have not deserv'd this.

Lod. My lord, this would not be believ'd in Venice,
Though I should swear I saw 't: 'tis very much:
Make her amends; she weeps.

Oth. O devil, devil!
If that the earth could teem with woman's tears,
Each drop she falls would prove a crocodile.
Out of my sight!

Des. I will not stay to offend you. [*Going*].

Lod. Truly, an obedient lady:
I do beseech your lordship, call her back. 230

Oth. Mistress!

Des. My lord?

Oth. What would you with her, sir?

Lod. Who, I, my lord?

Oth. Ay; you did wish that I would make her turn:
Sir, she can turn, and turn, and yet go on,
And turn again; and she can weep, sir, weep;
And she 's obedient, as you say, obedient,
Very obedient. Proceed you in your tears.
Concerning this, sir,—O well-painted passion!—
I am commanded home. Get you away;
I'll send for you anon. Sir, I obey the mandate, 240
And will return to Venice. Hence, avaunt! [*Exit Desdemona.*]
Cassio shall have my place. And, sir, to-night,
I do entreat that we may sup together:

---

218. **government,** office. 227. **prove a crocodile,** i.e., by weeping crocodile tears; it was believed the crocodile shed tears over the body of the man he was eating. 238. **well-painted passion,** well-simulated emotion.

You are welcome, sir, to Cyprus.—Goats and monkeys!   *Exit.*
    Lod.   Is this the noble Moor whom our full senate
Call all in all sufficient? Is this the nature
Whom passion could not shake? whose solid virtue
The shot of accident, nor dart of chance,
Could neither graze nor pierce?
    Iago.   He is much chang'd.
    Lod.   Are his wits safe? is he not light of brain?   250
    Iago.   He 's that he is: I may not breathe my censure
What he might be: if what he might he is not,
I would to heaven he were!
    Lod.   What, strike his wife!
    Iago.   'Faith, that was not so well; yet would I knew
That stroke would prove the worst!
    Lod.   Is it his use?
Or did the letters work upon his blood,
And new-create this fault?
    Iago.   Alas, alas!
It is not honesty in me to speak
What I have seen and known. You shall observe him,
And his own courses will denote him so   260
That I may save my speech: do but go after,
And mark how he continues.
    Lod.   I am sorry that I am deceiv'd in him.   *Exeunt.*

Scene II.   [*A room in the castle.*]

Enter Othello *and* Emilia.

    Oth.   You have seen nothing then?
    Emil.   Nor ever heard, nor ever did suspect.
    Oth.   Yes, you have seen Cassio and she together.
    Emil.   But then I saw no harm, and then I heard
Each syllable that breath made up between them.
    Oth.   What, did they never whisper?
    Emil.   Never, my lord.
    Oth.   Nor send you out o' th' way?
    Emil.   Never.
    Oth.   To fetch her fan, her gloves, her mask, nor nothing?
    Emil.   Never, my lord.   10
    Oth.   That 's strange.
    Emil.   I durst, my lord, to wager she is honest,
Lay down my soul at stake: if you think other,
Remove your thought; it doth abuse your bosom.
If any wretch have put this in your head,
Let heaven requite it with the serpent's curse!
For, if she be not honest, chaste, and true,
There 's no man happy; the purest of their wives
Is foul as slander.

OTH.   Bid her come hither: go.   *Exit Emilia.*
She says enough; yet she 's a simple bawd   20
That cannot say as much. This is a subtle whore,
A closet lock and key of villanous secrets:
And yet she'll kneel and pray; I have seen her do 't.

   Enter DESDEMONA *and* EMILIA.

DES.   My lord, what is your will?
OTH.   Pray, chuck, come hither.
DES.   What is your pleasure?
OTH.   Let me see your eyes;
Look in my face.
DES.   What horrible fancy 's this?
OTH. [*To Emilia*] Some of your function, mistress;
Leave procreants alone and shut the door;
Cough, or cry 'hem', if any body come:
Your mystery, your mystery: nay, dispatch.   *Exit Emilia*   30
DES.   Upon my knees, what doth your speech import?
I understand a fury in your words,
But not the words.
OTH.   Why, what are thou?
DES.   Your wife, my lord; your true
And loyal wife.
OTH.   Come, swear it, damn thyself;
Lest, being like one of heaven, the devils themselves
Should fear to seize thee: therefore be double damn'd:
Swear thou art honest.
DES.   Heaven doth truly know it.
OTH.   Heaven truly knows that thou art false as hell.
DES.   To whom, my lord? with whom? how am I false?   40
OTH.   O Desdemon! away! away! away!
DES.   Alas the heavy day! Why do you weep?
Am I the motive of these tears, my lord?
If haply you my father do suspect
An instrument of this your calling back,
Lay not your blame on me: if you have lost him,
Why, I have lost him too.
OTH.   Had it pleas'd heaven
To try me with affliction; had they rain'd
All kinds of sores and shames on my bare head,
Steep'd me in poverty to the very lips,   50
Given to captivity me and my utmost hopes,
I should have found in some place of my soul
A drop of patience: but, alas, to make me

   Scene II.   22. **closet lock and key,** complete storeroom.   27. **Some . . . function,** i.e., set to work
in your chosen profession, that of bawd.   28. **procreants,** mating couples.   30. **mystery,** trade, occupation.   48. **they,** heavenly powers.

A fixed figure for the time of scorn
To point his slow unmoving finger at!
Yet could I bear that too; well, very well:
But there, where I have garner'd up my heart,
Where either I must live, or bear no life;
The fountain from the which my current runs,
Or else dries up; to be discarded thence!   60
Or keep it as a cistern for foul toads
To knot and gender in! Turn thy complexion there,
Patience, thou young and rose-lipp'd cherubin,—
Ay, there, look grim as hell!
    DES. I hope my noble lord esteems me honest.
    OTH. O, ay; as summer flies are in the shambles,
That quicken even with blowing. O thou weed,
Who art so lovely fair and smell'st so sweet
That the sense aches at thee, would thou hadst ne'er been born!
    DES. Alas, what ignorant sin have I committed?   70
    OTH. Was this fair paper, this most goodly book,
Made to write 'whore' upon? What committed!
Committed! O thou public commoner!
I should make very forges of my cheeks,
That would to cinders burn up modesty,
Did I but speak thy deeds. What committed!
Heaven stops the nose at it and the moon winks,
The bawdy wind that kisses all it meets
Is hush'd within the hollow mine of earth,
And will not hear it. What committed!   80
Impudent strumpet!
    DES.   By heaven, you do me wrong.
    OTH. Are not you a strumpet?
    DES.   No, as I am a Christian:
If to preserve this vessel for my lord
From any other foul unlawful touch
Be not to be a strumpet, I am none.
    OTH. What, not a whore?
    DES.   No, as I shall be sav'd.
    OTH. Is 't possible?
    DES. O, heaven forgive us!
    OTH.   I cry you mercy, then:
I took you for that cunning whore of Venice
That married with Othello. [*Raising his voice*] You, mistress,   90
That have the office opposite to Saint Peter,
And keep the gate of hell!

    54–55. **A . . . at.** Othello possibly thinks of himself as a man set in a pillory at whom the scornful world points in mockery. There seems to be a comparison with the sundial, whose gnomon, or indicator, becomes the finger of scornful time. 62. **gender,** engender. **Turn thy complexion,** grow pale. 66. **shambles,** slaughterhouse. 67. **quicken,** come to life. 73. **commoner,** prostitute. 83. **vessel,** body.

Enter EMILIA.

       You, you, ay, you!
We have done our course; there 's money for your pains:
I pray you, turn the key and keep our counsel.   *Exit.*
  EMIL. Alas, what does this gentleman conceive?
How do you, madam? how do you, my good lady?
  DES. 'Faith, half asleep.
  EMIL. Good madam, what 's the matter with my lord?
  DES. With who?
  EMIL. Why, with my lord, madam.   100
  DES. Who is thy lord?
  EMIL.   He that is yours, sweet lady.
  DES. I have none: do not talk to me, Emilia;
I cannot weep; nor answers have I none,
But what should go by water. Prithee, tonight
Lay on my bed my wedding sheets: remember;
And call thy husband hither.
  EMIL.   Here's a change indeed!   *Exit.*
  DES. 'Tis meet I should be us'd so, very meet.
How have I been behav'd, that he might stick
The small'st opinion on my least misuse?

Enter IAGO *and* EMILIA.

  IAGO. What is your pleasure, madam? How is 't with you? 110
  DES. I cannot tell. Those that do teach young babes
Do it with gentle means and easy tasks:
He might have chid me so; for, in good faith,
I am a child to chiding.
  IAGO.   What is the matter, lady?
  EMIL. Alas, Iago, my lord hath so bewhor'd her,
Thrown such despite and heavy terms upon her,
As true hearts cannot bear.
  DES. Am I that name, Iago?
  IAGO.   What name, fair lady?
  DES. Such as she said my lord did say I was.
  EMIL. He call'd her whore: a beggar in his drink   120
Could not have laid such terms upon his callet.
  IAGO. Why did he so?
  DES. I do not know; I am sure I am none such.
  IAGO. Do not weep, do not weep. Alas the day!
  EMIL. Hath she forsook so many noble matches,
Her father and her country and her friends,
To be call'd whore? would it not make one weep?

---

104. **go by water,** be expressed by tears. 109. **misuse,** evil conduct. 116. **despite,** contempt.
121. **callet,** lewd woman.

DES.   It is my wretched fortune.

IAGO.   Beshrew him for 't!
How comes this trick upon him?

DES.   Nay, heaven doth know.

EMIL.   I will be hang'd, if some eternal villain,   130
Some busy and insinuating rogue,
Some cogging, cozening slave, to get some office,
Have not devis'd this slander; I will be hang'd else.

IAGO.   Fie, there is no such man; it is impossible.

DES.   If any such there be, heaven pardon him!

EMIL.   A halter pardon him! and hell gnaw his bones!
Why should he call her whore? who keeps her company?
What place? what time? what form? what likelihood?
The Moor 's abus'd by some most villanous knave,
Some base notorious knave, some scurvy fellow.   140
O heaven, that such companions thou 'ldst unfold,
And put in every honest hand a whip
To lash the rascals naked through the world
Even from the east to th' west!

IAGO.   Speak within door.

EMIL.   O, fie upon them! Some such squire he was
That turn'd your wit the seamy side without,
And made you to suspect me with the Moor.

IAGO.   You are a fool; go to.

DES.   Alas, Iago,
What shall I do to win my lord again?
Good friend, go to him; for, by this light of heaven,   150
I know not how I lost him. Here I kneel:
If e'er my will did trespass 'gainst his love,
Either in discourse of thought or actual deed,
Or that mine eyes, mine ears, or any sense,
Delighted them in any other form;
Or that I do not yet, and ever did,
And ever will—though he do shake me off
To beggarly divorcement—love him dearly,
Comfort forswear me! Unkindness may do much;
And his unkindness may defeat my life,   160
But never taint my love. I cannot say 'whore:'
It doth abhor me now I speak the word;
To do the act that might the addition earn
Not the world's mass of vanity could make me.

IAGO.   I pray you, be content; 'tis but his humour:
The business of the state does him offence,
And he does chide with you.

DES.   If 'twere no other,—

IAGO.   'Tis but so, I warrant. [*Trumpets within.*]

---

132. **cogging,** cheating.   144. **Speak . . . door,** i.e., not so loud.   163. **addition,** title.

Hark, how these instruments summon to supper!
The messengers of Venice stay the meat: 170
Go in, and weep not; all things shall be well.

> *Exeunt Desdemona and Emilia.*

Enter RODERIGO.

How now, Roderigo!

ROD.   I do not find that thou dealest justly with me.

IAGO.   What in the contrary?

ROD.   Every day thou daffest me with some device, Iago; and rather, as
it seems to me now, keepest from me all conveniency than suppliest me with
the least advantage of hope. I will indeed no longer endure it, nor am I yet persuaded to put up in peace what already I have foolishly suffered.

IAGO.   Will you hear me, Roderigo?

ROD.   'Faith, I have heard too much, for your words and performances
are no kin together.   181

IAGO.   You charge me most unjustly.

ROD.   With nought but truth. I have wasted myself out of my means. The
jewels you have had from me to deliver to Desdemona would half have corrupted a votarist: you have told me she hath received them and returned me expectations and comforts of sudden respect and acquaintance, but I find none.

IAGO.   Well; go to; very well.

ROD.   Very well! go to! I cannot go to, man; nor 'tis not very well: nay, I
think it is scurvy, and begin to find myself fopped in it.

IAGO.   Very well.   190

ROD.   I tell you 'tis not very well. I will make myself known to Desdemona: if she will return me my jewels, I will give over my suit and repent my
unlawful solicitation; if not, assure yourself I will seek satisfaction of you.

IAGO.   You have said now.

ROD.   Ay, and said nothing but what I protest intendment of doing.

IAGO.   Why, now I see there 's mettle in thee, and even from this instant
do build on thee a better opinion than ever before. Give me thy hand, Roderigo:
thou hast taken against me a most just exception; but yet, I protest, I have dealt
most directly in thy affair.

ROD.   It hath not appeared.   200

IAGO.   I grant indeed it hath not appeared, and your suspicion is not
without wit and judgement. But, Roderigo, if thou hast that in thee indeed, which
I have greater reason to believe now than ever, I mean purpose, courage and
valour, this night show it: if thou the next night following enjoy not Desdemona,
take me from this world with treachery and devise engines for my life.

ROD.   Well, what is it? is it within reason and compass?

IAGO.   Sir, there is especial commission come from Venice to depute

---

170. **stay the meat,** are waiting for supper.   175. **daffest me,** puttest me off with an excuse.   176.
conveniency, advantage, opportunity.   178. **put up,** submit to.   185. **votarist,** nun.   189. **fopped,**
fooled.   194. **You . . . now,** well said, quite right.   195. **intendment,** intention.   205. **engines for,**
plots against.

Cassio in Othello's place.

ROD.   Is that true? why, then Othello and Desdemona return again to Venice.   210

IAGO.   O, no; he goes into Mauritania and takes away with him the fair Desdemona, unless his abode be lingered here by some accident: wherein none can be so determinate as the removing of Cassio.

ROD.   How do you mean, removing of him?

IAGO.   Why, by making him uncapable of Othello's place; knocking out his brains.

ROD.   And that you would have me to do?

IAGO.   Ay, if you dare do yourself a profit and a right. He sups to-night with a harlotry, and thither will I go to him: he knows not yet of his honourable fortune. If you will watch his going thence, which I will fashion to fall out between twelve and one, you may take him at your pleasure: I will be near to second your attempt, and he shall fall between us. Come, stand not amazed at it, but go along with me; I will show you such a necessity in his death that you shall think yourself bound to put it on him. It is now high supper-time, and the night grows to waste: about it.   225

ROD.   I will hear further reason for this.

IAGO.   And you shall be satisfied.   *Exeunt.*

Scene III. [*Another room in the castle.*]

Enter OTHELLO, LODOVICO, DESDEMONA, EMILIA, *and* Attendants.

LOD.   I do beseech you, sir, trouble yourself no further.

OTH.   O, pardon me; 'twill do me good to walk.

LOD.   Madam, good night; I humbly thank your ladyship.

DES.   Your honour is most welcome.

OTH.   Will you walk, sir?
O,—Desdemona,—

DES.   My lord?

OTH.   Get you to bed on th' instant; I will be returned forthwith: dismiss your attendant there: look 't be done.

DES.   I will, my lord.   *Exit* [*Othello, with Lodovico and Attendants*].

EMIL.   How goes it now? he looks gentler than he did.   10

DES.   He says he will return incontinent:
He hath commanded me to go to bed,
And bade me to dismiss you.

EMIL.   Dismiss me!

DES.   It was his bidding; therefore, good Emilia,
Give me my nightly wearing, and adieu:
We must not now displease him.

EMIL.   I would you had never seen him!

---

211. **Mauritania,** Roman name of northwest Africa, supposed land of the Moors.   213. **determinate,** decisive.   219. **harlotry,** courtesan.
    Scene III.   11. **incontinent,** immediately.

DES. So would not I: my love doth so approve him,
That even his stubbornness, his checks, his frowns,—
Prithee, unpin me,—have grace and favour in them.   20
    EMIL. I have laid those sheets you bade me on the bed.
    DES. All 's one. Good faith, how foolish are our minds!
If I do die before thee, prithee, shroud me
In one of those same sheets.
    EMIL.   Come, come, you talk.
    DES. My mother had a maid call'd Barbary:
She was in love, and he she lov'd prov'd mad
And did forsake her: she had a song of 'willow;'
An old thing 'twas, but it express'd her fortune,
And she died singing it: that song to-night
Will not go from my mind; I have much to do,   30
But to go hang my head all at one side,
And sing it like poor Barbary. Prithee, dispatch.
    EMIL. Shall I go fetch your night-gown?
    DES.   No, unpin me here.
This Lodovico is a proper man.
    EMIL. A very handsome man.
    DES. He speaks well.
    EMIL. I know a lady in Venice would have walked barefoot to Palestine
for a touch of his nether lip.
    DES. [*Singing*] The poor soul sat sighing by a sycamore tree,
    Sing all a green willow;   40
Her hand on her bosom, her head on her knee,
    Sing willow, willow, willow:
The fresh streams ran by her, and murmur'd her moans;
    Sing willow, willow, willow;
Her salt tears fell from her, and soft'ned the stones;—
Lay by these:—
[*Singing*] Sing willow, willow, willow;
Prithee, hie thee; he'll come anon:—
[*Singing*] Sing all a green willow must be my garland.
Let nobody blame him; his scorn I approve,—   50
Nay, that 's not next.—Hark! who is 't that knocks?
    EMIL. It 's the wind.
    DES. [*Singing*] I call'd my love false love; but what said he then?
    Sing willow, willow, willow:
If I court moe women, you'll couch with moe men.—
So, get thee gone; good night. Mine eyes do itch;
Doth that bode weeping?
    EMIL.   'Tis neither here nor there.
    DES. I have heard it said so. O, these men, these men!
Dost thou in conscience think,—tell me, Emilia,—
That there be women do abuse their husbands   60
In such gross kind?

---

19. **stubbornness,** harshness. **checks,** rebukes. 31. **But to,** not to.

EMIL.   There be some such, no question.

DES. Wouldst thou do such a deed for all the world?

EMIL. Why, would not you?

DES.   No, by this heavenly light!

EMIL. Nor I neither by this heavenly light; I might do 't as well i' the dark.

DES. Wouldst thou do such a deed for all the world?

EMIL. The world 's a huge thing: it is a great price
For a small vice.

DES. In troth, I think thou wouldst not.

EMIL. In troth, I think I should; and undo 't when I had done. Marry, I would not do such a thing for a joint-ring, nor for measures of lawn, nor for gowns, petticoats, nor caps, nor any petty exhibition; but, for all the whole world,—why, who would not make her husband a cuckold to make him a monarch? I should venture purgatory for 't.   74

DES. Beshrew me, if I would do such a wrong
For the whole world.

EMIL. Why, the wrong is but a wrong i' the world; and having the world for your labour, 'tis a wrong in your own world, and you might quickly make it right.

DES. I do not think there is any such woman.   80

EMIL. Yes, a dozen; and as many to the vantage as would store the world they played for.
But I do think it is their husbands' faults
If wives do fall: say that they slack their duties,
And pour our treasures into foreign laps,
Or else break out in peevish jealousies,
Throwing restraint upon us; or say they strike us,
Or scant our former having in despite;
Why, we have galls, and though we have some grace,
Yet have we some revenge. Let husbands know   90
Their wives have sense like them: they see and smell
And have their palates both for sweet and sour,
As husbands have. What is it that they do
When they change us for others? Is it sport?
I think it is: and doth affection breed it?
I think it doth: is 't frailty that thus errs?
It is so too: and have not we affections,
Desires for sport, and frailty, as men have?
Then let them use us well: else let them know,
The ills we do, their ills instruct us so.   100

DES. Good night, good night: heaven me such uses send,
Not to pick bad from bad, but by bad mend!   *Exeunt.*

---

71. **joint-ring,** a ring made in separable halves as a lover's token. 72. **exhibition,** gift. 81. **to
the vantage,** in addition. 85. **pour . . . laps,** i.e., are unfaithful. 88. **scant . . . despite,** reduce
our allowance to spite us. 89. **have galls,** are capable of resenting injury and insult. **grace,** i.e., to
forgive.

ACT V.

Scene I. [*Cyprus. A street.*]

Enter IAGO *and* RODERIGO.

IAGO.   Here stand behind this bulk; straight will he come:
Wear thy good rapier bare, and put it home:
Quick, quick; fear nothing; I'll be at thy elbow:
It makes us, or it mars us; think on that,
And fix most firm thy resolution.
    ROD.   Be near at hand; I may miscarry in 't.
    IAGO.   Here, at thy hand: be bold, and take thy stand.   [*Retires.*]
    ROD.   I have no great devotion to the deed;
And yet he hath given me satisfying reasons:
'Tis but a man gone. Forth, my sword: he dies.   10
    IAGO.   I have rubb'd this young quat almost to the sense,
And he grows angry. Now, whether he kill Cassio,
Or Cassio him, or each do kill the other,
Every way makes my gain: live Roderigo,
He calls me to a restitution large
Of gold and jewels that I bobb'd from him,
As gifts to Desdemona;
It must not be: if Cassio do remain,
He hath a daily beauty in his life
That makes me ugly; and, besides, the Moor   20
May unfold me to him; there stand I in much peril:
No, he must die. But so: I hear him coming.

Enter CASSIO.

    ROD.   I know his gait, 'tis he.—Villain, thou diest!
                    [*Makes a pass at Cassio.*]
    CAS.   That thrust had been mine enemy indeed,
But that my coat is better than thou know'st:
I will make proof of thine.   [*Draws, and wounds Roderigo.*]
    ROD.   O, I am slain!
       [*Iago from behind wounds Cassio in the leg, and exit.*]
    CAS.   I am maim'd for ever. Help, ho! murder!   [*Falls.*]

Enter OTHELLO.

    OTH.   The voice of Cassio: Iago keeps his word.
    ROD.   O, villain that I am!
    OTH.   It is even so.

    Act V. Scene I. 1. **bulk,** framework projecting from the front of a shop. 11. **quat,** pimple, pustule; used contemptuously. **to the sense,** to the quick. 16. **bobb'd,** filched cunningly. 25. **coat,** coat of mail.

Cas. O, help, ho! light! a surgeon!   30
Oth. 'Tis he:—O brave Iago, honest and just,
That hast such noble sense of thy friend's wrong!
Thou teachest me. Minion, your dear lies dead,
And your unblest fate hies: strumpet, I come.
Forth of my heart those charms, thine eyes, are blotted;
Thy bed, lust-stain'd, shall with lust's blood be spotted.   *Exit Othello.*

    Enter Lodovico *and* Gratiano.

Cas. What, ho! no watch? no passage? murder! murder!
Gra. 'Tis some mischance; the cry is very direful.
Cas. O, help!
Lod. Hark!   40
Rod. O wretched villain!
Lod. Two or three groan: it is a heavy night:
These may be counterfeits; let's think 't unsafe
To come in to the cry without more help.
Rod. Nobody come? then shall I bleed to death.
Lod. Hark!

    Enter Iago [*with a light*].

Gra. Here 's one comes in his shirt, with light and weapons.
Iago. Who 's there? whose noise is this that cries on murder?
Lod. We do not know.
Iago.   Did not you hear a cry?
Cas. Here, here! for heaven's sake, help me!
Iago.   What 's the matter?   50
Gra. This is Othello's ancient, as I take it.
Lod. The same indeed; a very valiant fellow.
Iago. What are you here that cry so grievously?
Cas. Iago? O, I am spoil'd, undone by villains!
Give me some help.
Iago. O me, lieutenant! what villains have done this?
Cas. I think that one of them is hereabout,
And cannot make away.
Iago.   O treacherous villains!
What are you there? come in, and give some help.
                              [To Lodovico and Gratiano.]
Rod. O, help me here!   60
Cas. That 's one of them.
Iago.   O murd'rous slave! O villain!
                                      [Stabs Roderigo.]
Rod. O damn'd Iago! O inhuman dog!
Iago. Kill men i' th' dark!—Where be these bloody thieves?—
How silent is this town!—Ho! murder! murder!—

---

37. **passage,** people passing. 48. **cries on,** cries out.

What may you be? are you of good or evil?

LOD. As you shall prove us, praise us.

IAGO. Signior Lodovico?

LOD. He, sir.

IAGO. I cry you mercy. Here 's Cassio hurt by villains.

GRA. Cassio!   70

IAGO. How is 't, brother!

CAS. My leg is cut in two.

IAGO.   Marry, heaven forbid!

Light, gentlemen: I'll bind it with my shirt.

Enter BIANCA.

BIAN. What is the matter, ho? who is 't that cried?

IAGO. Who is 't that cried?

BIAN. O my dear Cassio! my sweet Cassio!

O Cassio, Cassio, Cassio!

IAGO. O notable strumpet! Cassio, may you suspect

Who they should be that have thus mangled you?

CAS. No.   80

GRA. I am sorry to find you thus: I have been to seek you.

IAGO. Lend me a garter. So. O, for a chair,

To bear him easily hence!

BIAN. Alas, he faints! O Cassio, Cassio, Cassio!

IAGO. Gentlemen all, I do suspect this trash

To be a party in this injury.

Patience awhile, good Cassio. Come, come;

Lend me a light. Know we this face or no?

Alas, my friend and my dear countryman

Roderigo! no:—yes, sure:—O heaven! Roderigo.   90

GRA. What, of Venice?

IAGO. Even he, sir: did you know him?

GRA.   Know him! ay.

IAGO. Signior Gratiano? I cry your gentle pardon;

These bloody accidents must excuse my manners,

That so neglected you.

GRA.   I am glad to see you.

IAGO. How do you, Cassio? O, a chair, a chair!

GRA. Roderigo!

IAGO. He, he, 'tis he. [*A chair brought in.*] O, that's well said; the chair.

Some good man bear him carefully from hence;

I'll fetch the general's surgeon. [*To Bianca*] For you, mistress,   100

Save you your labour. He that lies slain here, Cassio,

Was my dear friend: what malice was between you?

CAS. None in the world; nor do I know the man.

IAGO. [*To Bian.*] What, look you pale? O, bear him out o' th' air.

        [*Cassio and Roderigo are borne off.*]

---

65. **What,** who.   82. **chair,** sedan chair.   85. **trash,** worthless thing, i.e., Bianca.

Stay you, good gentlemen. Look you pale, mistress?
Do you perceive the gastness of her eye?
Nay, if you stare, we shall hear more anon.
Behold her well; I pray you, look upon her:
Do you see, gentlemen? nay, guiltiness will speak,
Though tongues were out of use.   110

> [*Enter* EMILIA.]

    EMIL.   'Las, what 's the matter? what 's the matter, husband?
    IAGO.   Cassio hath here been set on in the dark
By Roderigo and fellows that are scap'd:
He 's almost slain, and Roderigo dead.
    EMIL.   Alas, good gentleman! alas, good Cassio!
    IAGO.   This is the fruit of whoring. Prithee, Emilia,
Go know of Cassio where he supp'd to-night.
[*To Bianca*] What, do you shake at that?
    BIAN.   He supp'd at my house; but I therefore shake not.
    IAGO.   O, did he so? I charge you, go with me.   120
    EMIL.   Fie, fie upon thee, strumpet!
    BIAN.   I am no strumpet; but of life as honest
As you that thus abuse me.
    EMIL.   As I! foh! fie upon thee!
    IAGO.   Kind gentlemen, let 's go see poor Cassio dress'd.
Come, mistress, you must tell 's another tale.
Emilia, run you to the citadel,
And tell my lord and lady what hath happ'd.
Will you go on afore? [*Aside*] This is the night
That either makes me or fordoes me quite.   *Exeunt.*

Scene II. [*A bedchamber in the castle.*]

> *Enter* OTHELLO [*with a light*]; DESDEMONA *in her bed.*

    OTH.   It is the cause, it is the cause, my soul,—
Let me not name it to you, you chaste stars!—
It is the cause. Yet I'll not shed her blood;
Nor scar that whiter skin of hers than snow,
And smooth as monumental alabaster.
Yet she must die, else she'll betray more men.
Put out the light, and then put out the light:
If I quench thee, thou flaming minister,
I can again thy former light restore,
Should I repent me: but once put out thy light,   10
Thou cunning'st pattern of excelling nature,

---

106. **gastness,** terror, ghastliness.   129. **fordoes,** undoes, ruins. Iago's uneasiness is again apparent in this scene.
    Scene II.   1. **It is the cause,** i.e., the cause of justice on which Othello must act, Desdemona's deed, which is too unmentionable to be named to the chaste stars.

I know not where is that Promethean heat
That can thy light relume. When I have pluck'd the rose,
I cannot give it vital growth again,
It needs must wither: I'll smell thee on the tree.   [*Kissing her.*]
O balmy breath, that dost almost persuade
Justice to break her sword! One more, one more.
Be thus when thou art dead, and I will kill thee,
And love thee after. One more, and that 's the last:
So sweet was ne'er so fatal. I must weep,   20
But they are cruel tears: this sorrow 's heavenly;
It strikes where it doth love. She wakes.
  DES. Who 's there? Othello?
  OTH.   Ay, Desdemona.
  DES. Will you come to bed, my lord?
  OTH. Have you pray'd to-night, Desdemona?
  DES.   Ay, my lord.
  OTH. If you bethink yourself of any crime
Unreconcil'd as yet to heaven and grace,
Solicit for it straight.
  DES. Alack, my lord, what may you mean by that?
  OTH. Well, do it, and be brief; I will walk by: 30
I would not kill thy unprepared spirit;
No; heaven forfend! I would not kill thy soul.
  DES. Talk you of killing?
  OTH.   Ay, I do.
  DES.   Then heaven
Have mercy on me!
  OTH.   Amen, with all my heart!
  DES. If you say so, I hope you will not kill me.
  OTH. Hum!
  DES. And yet I fear you; for you 're fatal then
When your eyes roll so: why I should fear I know not,
Since guiltiness I know not; but yet I feel I fear.
  OTH. Think on thy sins.
  DES.   They are loves I bear to you. 40
  OTH. Ay, and for that thou diest.
  DES. That death 's unnatural that kills for loving.
Alas, why gnaw you so your nether lip?
Some bloody passion shakes your very frame:
These are portents; but yet I hope, I hope,
They do not point on me.
  OTH.   Peace, and be still!
  DES. I will so. What 's the matter?
  OTH. That handkerchief which I so lov'd and gave thee
Thou gav'st to Cassio.

---

12. **Promethean heat,** divine fire; allusion to the theft of fire from heaven by Prometheus. 13.
relume, rekindle. 21. **this . . . heavenly,** this tenderness, with which I lament the punishment which
justice compels me to inflict, is a holy passion.

DES.   No, by my life and soul!
Send for the man, and ask him.
OTH.   Sweet soul, take heed,   50
Take heed of perjury; thou art on thy deathbed.
DES.   Ay, but not yet to die.
OTH.   Yes, presently:
Therefore confess thee freely of thy sin;
For to deny each article with oath
Cannot remove nor choke the strong conception
That I do groan withal. Thou art to die.
DES.   Then Lord have mercy on me!
OTH.   I say, amen.
DES.   And have you mercy too! I never did
Offend you in my life; never lov'd Cassio
But with such general warranty of heaven   60
As I might love; I never gave him token.
OTH.   By heaven, I saw my handkerchief in 's hand.
O perjur'd woman! thou dost stone my heart,
And makes me call what I intend to do
A murder, which I thought a sacrifice:
I saw the handkerchief.
DES.   He found it then;
I never gave it him: send for him hither;
Let him confess a truth.
OTH.   He hath confess'd.
DES.   What, my lord?
OTH.   That he hath us'd thee.
DES.   How? unlawfully?
OTH.   Ay.   70
DES.   He will not say so.
OTH.   No, his mouth is stopp'd;
Honest Iago hath ta'en order for 't.
DES.   O! my fear interprets: what, is he dead?
OTH.   Had all his hairs been lives, my great revenge
Had stomach for them all.
DES.   Alas! he is betray'd and I undone.
OTH.   Out, strumpet! weep'st thou for him to my face?
DES.   O, banish me, my lord, but kill me not!
OTH.   Down, strumpet!
DES.   Kill me to-morrow: let me live to-night!   80
OTH.   Nay, if you strive,—
DES.   But half an hour!
OTH.   Being done, there is no pause.
DES.   But while I say one prayer!
OTH.   It is too late.   *Smothers her.*

---

55. **conception,** plan, intention.   63. **stone,** turn to stone, harden; Othello means that he will
be tempted to kill her in sheer anger because of her perjury.   72. **ta'en order,** taken measures.   82.
Being . . . pause, i.e., when the execution of the deed has once begun, there is no stopping.

EMIL. [*At the door*]   My lord, my lord! what, ho! my lord, my lord!
OTH.   What noise is this? Not dead? not yet quite dead?
I that am cruel am yet merciful;
I would not have thee linger in thy pain:
So, so.
    EMIL. [*Within*]   What, ho! my lord, my lord!
    OTH.   Who 's there?
    EMIL. [*Within*]   O, good my lord, I would speak a word with you! 90
    OTH.   Yes: 'tis Emilia. By and by. She 's dead.
'Tis like she comes to speak of Cassio's death.—
The noise was here. Ha! no more moving?
Still as the grave. Shall she come in? were 't good?—
I think she stirs again:—no. What 's best to do?
If she come in, she'll sure speak to my wife:
My wife! my wife! what wife? I have no wife.
O, insupportable! O heavy hour!
Methinks it should be now a huge eclipse
Of sun and moon, and that th' affrighted globe   100
Should yawn at alteration.
    EMIL.   [*Within*] I do beseech you
That I may speak with you, O, good my lord!
    OTH.   I had forgot thee: O, come in, Emilia:
Soft; by and by. Let me the curtains draw.
Where art thou?   [*Closes bed-curtains and opens door.*]

Enter EMILIA.

              What 's the matter with thee now?
    EMIL.   O, my good lord, yonder 's foul murders done!
    OTH.   What, now?
    EMIL.   But now, my lord.
    OTH.   It is the very error of the moon;
She comes more nearer earth than she was wont,   110
And makes men mad.
    EMIL.   Cassio, my lord, hath kill'd a young Venetian
Call'd Roderigo.
    OTH.   Roderigo kill'd!
And Cassio kill'd!
    EMIL.   No, Cassio is not kill'd.
    OTH.   Not Cassio kill'd! then murder 's out of tune,
And sweet revenge grows harsh.
    DES.   O, falsely, falsely murder'd!
    EMIL.   Alas, what cry is that?
    OTH.   That! what?
    EMIL.   Out, and alas! that was my lady's voice.
Help! help, ho! help! O lady, speak again!   120
Sweet Desdemona! O sweet mistress, speak!

---

101. **yawn,** gape in amazement. **at alteration,** at the change.   109. **error,** irregularity.

DES. A guiltless death I die.

EMIL. O, who hath done this deed?

DES. Nobody; I myself. Farewell:
Commend me to my kind lord: O, farewell! *[Dies.]*

OTH. Why, how should she be murd'red?

EMIL.   Alas, who knows?

OTH. You heard her say herself, it was not I.

EMIL. She said so: I must needs report the truth.

OTH. She 's, like a liar, gone to burning hell:
'Twas I that kill'd her.

EMIL.   O, the more angel she,   130
And you the blacker devil!

OTH. She turn'd to folly, and she was a whore.

EMIL. Thou dost belie her, and thou art a devil.

OTH. She was false as water.

EMIL.   Thou art rash as fire, to say
That she was false: O, she was heavenly true!

OTH. Cassio did top her; ask thy husband else.
O, I were damn'd beneath all depth in hell,
But that I did proceed upon just grounds
To this extremity. Thy husband knew it all.

EMIL. My husband!   140

OTH. Thy husband.

EMIL. That she was false to wedlock?

OTH. Ay, with Cassio. Nay, had she been true,
If heaven would make me such another world
Of one entire and perfect chrysolite,
I 'ld not have sold her for it.

EMIL. My husband!

OTH.   Ay, 'twas he that told me first:
An honest man he is, and hates the slime
That sticks on filthy deeds.

EMIL.   My husband!

OTH. What needs this iterance, woman? I say thy husband.   150

EMIL. O mistress, villany hath made mocks with love!
My husband say that she was false!

OTH.   He, woman;
I say thy husband: dost understand the word?
My friend, thy husband, honest, honest Iago.

EMIL. If he say so, may his pernicious soul
Rot half a grain a day! he lies to th' heart:
She was too fond of her most filthy bargain.

OTH. Ha!

EMIL. Do thy worst:
This deed of thine is no more worthy heaven   160
Than thou wast worthy her.

---

132. **folly,** unchastity. 145. **chrysolite,** the golden stone; a name given to various precious stones of green color. 150. **iterance,** iteration, repetition. 151. **made mocks with,** made sport of.

OTH.   Peace, you were best.
EMIL.   Thou hast not half that power to do me harm
As I have to be hurt. O gull! O dolt!
As ignorant as dirt! thou hast done a deed—
I care not for thy sword; I'll make thee known,
Though I lost twenty lives.—Help! help, ho! help!
The Moor hath kill'd my mistress! Murder! murder!

Enter MONTANO, GRATIANO, *and* IAGO [*with others*].

MON.   What is the matter? How now, general!
EMIL.   O, are you come, Iago? you have done well,
That men must lay their murders on your neck.   170
GRA.   What is the matter?
EMIL.   Disprove this villain, if thou be'st a man:
He says thou told'st him that his wife was false:
I know thou didst not, thou 'rt not such a villain:
Speak, for my heart is full.
IAGO.   I told him what I thought, and told no more
Than what he found himself was apt and true.
EMIL.   But did you ever tell him she was false?
IAGO.   I did.
EMIL.   You told a lie; an odious, damned lie;   180
Upon my soul, a lie, a wicked lie.
She false with Cassio!—did you say with Cassio?
IAGO.   With Cassio, mistress. Go to, charm your tongue.
EMIL.   I will not charm my tongue; I am bound to speak:
My mistress here lies murdered in her bed,—
ALL.   O heavens forfend!
EMIL.   And your reports have set the murder on.
OTH.   Nay, stare not, masters: it is true, indeed.
GRA.   'Tis a strange truth.
MON.   O monstrous act!
EMIL.   Villany, villany, villany!   190
I think upon 't, I think: I smell 't: O villany!—
I thought so then:—I'll kill myself for grief:—
O villany, villany!
IAGO.   What, are you mad? I charge you, get you home.
EMIL.   Good gentlemen, let me have leave to speak:
'Tis proper I obey him, but not now.
Perchance, Iago, I will ne'er go home.
OTH.   O! O! O!   [*He falls on the bed.*]
EMIL.   Nay, lay thee down and roar;
For thou hast kill'd the sweetest innocent
That e'er did lift up eye.

---

163. **to be hurt,** i.e., to endure hurting.   177. **apt,** natural, likely.   183. **charm,** keep silent.   192.
then, i.e., at some earlier time, probably IV, ii, 130–144, when she suspected the machinations of
some eternal villain: she did not, however, know that villain to be Iago until this moment.

OTH.   [*Rising*] O, she was foul!   200
I scarce did know you, uncle: there lies your niece,
Whose breath, indeed, these hands have newly stopp'd:
I know this act shows horrible and grim.
        GRA.   Poor Desdemon! I am glad thy father 's dead:
Thy match was mortal to him, and pure grief
Shore his old thread in twain: did he live now,
This sight would make him do a desperate turn,
Yea, curse his better angel from his side,
And fall to reprobation.
        OTH.   'Tis pitiful; but yet Iago knows   210
That she with Cassio hath the act of shame
A thousand times committed; Cassio confess'd it:
And she did gratify his amorous works
With that recognizance and pledge of love
Which I first gave her; I saw it in his hand:
It was a handkerchief, an antique token
My father gave my mother.
        EMIL.   O heaven! O heavenly pow'rs!
        IAGO.   Come, hold your peace.
        EMIL.   •   'Twill out, 'twill out: I peace!
No, I will speak as liberal as the north: 220
Let heaven and men and devils, let them all,
All, all, cry shame against me, yet I'll speak.
        IAGO.   Be wise, and get you home.
        EMIL.   I will not.
                    [*Iago offers to stab Emilia.*]
        GRA.   Fie!
Your sword upon a woman?
        EMIL.   O thou dull Moor! that handkerchief thou speak'st of
I found by fortune and did give my husband;
For often, with a solemn earnestness,
More than indeed belong'd to such a trifle,
He begg'd of me to steal it.
        IAGO.   Villanous whore!
        EMIL.   She give it Cassio! no, alas! I found it,   230
And I did give 't my husband.
        IAGO.   Filth, thou liest!
        EMIL.   By heaven, I do not, I do not, gentlemen.
O murd'rous coxcomb! what should such a fool
Do with so good a wife?
        OTH.   Are there no stones in heaven
But what serves for the thunder?—Precious villain!
            [*He runs at Iago: Iago, from behind, stabs Emilia, and exit.*]
        GRA.   The woman falls; sure, he hath kill'd his wife.

---

206. **Shore**, cut.   209. **reprobation**, damnation, rejection by God.   214. **recognizance**, token.
220. **liberal as the north**, freely as the north wind.   226. **fortune**, chance.   233. **coxcomb**, fool; addressed to Othello.   234. **stones in heaven**, thunderbolts. It was supposed that real stones fell with
the thunder and caused the damage.

EMIL.   Ay, ay: O, lay me by my mistress' side.

GRA.   He 's gone, but his wife 's kill'd.

MON.   'Tis a notorious villain. Take you this weapon,
Which I have here recover'd from the Moor: 240
Come, guard the door without; let him not pass,
But kill him rather. I'll after that same villain,
For 'tis a damned slave.   *Exit [with all but Othello and Emilia].*

OTH.   I am not valiant neither,
But every puny whipster gets my sword:
But why should honour outlive honesty?
Let it go all.

EMIL.   What did thy song bode, lady?
Hark, canst thou hear me? I will play the swan,
And die in music. [*Singing*] Willow, willow, willow.—
Moor, she was chaste; she lov'd thee, cruel Moor;
So come my soul to bliss, as I speak true;   250
So speaking as I think, I die, I die.   [*Dies.*]

OTH.   I have another weapon in this chamber;
It is a sword of Spain, the ice-brook's temper:—
O, here it is. Uncle, I must come forth.

GRA. [*Within*]   If thou attempt it, it will cost thee dear:
Thou hast no weapon, and perforce must suffer.

OTH.   Look in upon me then and speak with me,
Or, naked as I am, I will assault thee.

[*Enter* GRATIANO.]

GRA.   What is the matter?

OTH.   Behold, I have a weapon;
A better never did itself sustain   260
Upon a soldier's thigh: I have seen the day,
That, with this little arm and this good sword,
I have made my way through more impediments
Than twenty times your stop: but, O vain boast!
Who can control his fate? 'tis not so now.
Be not afraid, though you do see me weapon'd;
Here is my journey's end, here is my butt,
And very sea-mark of my utmost sail.
Do you go back dismay'd? 'tis a lost fear;
Man but a rush against Othello's breast,   270
And he retires. Where should Othello go?
Now, how dost thou look now? O ill-starr'd wench!
Pale as thy smock! when we shall meet at compt,
This look of thine will hurl my soul from heaven,

---

244. **whipster,** contemptible fellow.   245. **honour outlive honesty.** Othello realizes that he has
done a shameful deed; he asks why his reputation for valor should endure.   253. **ice-brook's temper,**
usually defined as "tempered in ice-cold water."   258. **naked,** unarmed.   264. **stop,** power.   267.
butt, mark for archery, goal, limit.   268. **sea-mark,** beacon (marking his destination or limit).   270.
Man, provide, as in manning a gun.   **rush,** reed.   273. **compt,** account, judgment day.

And fiends will snatch at it. Cold, cold, my girl!
Even like thy chastity. O cursed, cursed slave!
Whip me, ye devils,
From the possession of this heavenly sight!
Blow me about in winds! roast me in sulphur!
Wash me in steep-down gulfs of liquid fire!   280
O Desdemon! Dead Desdemon! dead!
Oh! Oh!

    Enter Lodovico, Cassio [*carried in a chair*], Montano, *and* Iago [*prisoner*], *with* Officers.

    Lod.   Where is this rash and most unfortunate man?
    Oth.   That 's he that was Othello: here I am.
    Lod.   Where is that viper? bring the villain forth.
    Oth.   I look down towards his feet; but that 's a fable.
If that thou be'st a devil, I cannot kill thee.   [*Wounds Iago.*]
    Lod.   Wrench his sword from him.
    Iago.   I bleed, sir; but not kill'd.
    Oth.   I am not sorry neither: I 'ld have thee live;
For, in my sense, 'tis happiness to die.   290
    Lod.   O thou Othello, that wert once so good,
Fall'n in the practice of a damned slave,
What shall be said to thee?
    Oth.   Why, any thing:
An honourable murderer, if you will;
For nought I did in hate, but all in honour.
    Lod.   This wretch hath part confess'd his villany:
Did you and he consent in Cassio's death?
    Oth.   Ay.
    Cas.   Dear general, I never gave you cause.
    Oth.   I do believe it, and I ask you pardon.   300
Will you, I pray, demand that demi-devil
Why he hath thus ensnar'd my soul and body?
    Iago.   Demand me nothing: what you know, you know:
From this time forth I never will speak word.
    Lod.   What, not to pray?
    Gra.   Torments will ope your lips.
    Oth.   Well, thou dost best.
    Lod.   Sir, you shall understand what hath befall'n,
Which, as I think, you know not. Here is a letter
Found in the pocket of the slain Roderigo;
And here another: the one of them imports   310
The death of Cassio to be undertook
By Roderigo.
    Oth.   O villain!
    Cas.   Most heathenish and most gross!

---

    286. **towards his feet,** i.e., to see if they were cloven like a devil's.

Lod.   Now here 's another discontented paper,
Found in his pocket too; and this, it seems,
Roderigo meant t' have sent this damned villain;
But that belike Iago in the interim
Came in and satisfied him.
    Oth.   O thou pernicious caitiff!—
How came you, Cassio, by that handkerchief
That was my wife's?
    Cas.   I found it in my chamber: 320
And he himself confess'd but even now
That there he dropp'd it for a special purpose
Which wrought to his desire.
    Oth.   O fool! fool! fool!
    Cas.   There is besides in Roderigo's letter,
How he upbraids Iago, that he made him
Brave me upon the watch; whereon it came
That I was cast: and even but now he spake,
After long seeming dead, Iago hurt him,
Iago set him on.
    Lod.   You must forsake this room, and go with us: 330
Your power and your command is taken off,
And Cassio rules in Cyprus. For this slave,
If there be any cunning cruelty
That can torment him much and hold him long,
It shall be his. You shall close prisoner rest,
Till that the nature of your fault be known
To the Venetian state. Come, bring him away.
    Oth.   Soft you; a word or two before you go.
I have done the state some service, and they know 't.
No more of that. I pray you, in your letters,   340
When you shall these unlucky deeds relate,
Speak of me as I am; nothing extenuate,
Nor set down aught in malice: then must you speak
Of one that lov'd not wisely but too well;
Of one not easily jealous, but being wrought,
Perplex'd in the extreme; of one whose hand,
Like the base Judean, threw a pearl away
Richer than all his tribe; of one whose subdu'd eyes,
Albeit unused to the melting mood,
Drop tears as fast as the Arabian trees   350
Their medicinable gum. Set you down this;
And say besides, that in Aleppo once,
Where a malignant and a turban'd Turk

---

314. **discontented,** expressing dissatisfaction.   318. **caitiff,** wretch.   326. **Brave,** defy.   327. **cast,** dismissed.   331. **taken off,** taken away.   342. **extenuate,** diminish, depreciate; the idea is contrasted with the thought of *malice* in the following line.   346. **Perplex'd,** confounded, distracted.   347. **Judean,** infidel or disbeliever.   352. **Aleppo,** a Turkish city where the Venetians had special trading privileges. It is stated that it was immediate death for a Christian to strike a Turk in Aleppo; Othello risked his life for the honor of Venice.

Beat a Venetian and traduc'd the state,
I took by th' throat the circumcised dog,
And smote him, thus.   [*Stabs himself.*]
        Lod.   O bloody period!
        Gra.   All that is spoke is marr'd.
        Oth.   I kiss'd thee ere I kill'd thee: no way but this;
Killing myself, to die upon a kiss.   [*Falls on the bed, and*] *dies.*
        Cas.   This did I fear, but thought he had no weapon;   360
For he was great of heart.
        Lod.   [*To Iago*] O Spartan dog,
More fell than anguish, hunger, or the sea!
Look on the tragic loading of this bed;
This is thy work: the object poisons sight;
Let it be hid. Gratiano, keep the house,
And seize upon the fortunes of the Moor,
For they succeed on you. To you, lord governor,
Remains the censure of this hellish villain;
The time, the place, the torture: O, enforce it!
Myself will straight aboard; and to the state   370
This heavy act with heavy heart relate.   *Exeunt.*

---

357. **period,** conclusion.   361. **Spartan dog.** Spartan dogs were noted for their savagery.

Questions for Study

1. What plot elements has Shakespeare used in fashioning an astonishingly success-ful theatrical play out of a husband's suspicion and another man's villainy? What function do Roderigo, Bianca, and Emilia have in the play? What then is Cassio's role? How does Desdemona's largely passive attitude contribute to the growing intrigues around her?
2. What motivates Iago's thirst for vengeance? Are his motives in Acts I and II believable for a scheme of such enormous evil? Explain why or why not. How is Iago regarded at the opening of the play? Point out specific instances in which various characters change their attitude toward Iago. How is he finally exposed?
3. Iago uses various techniques of deception in handling people around him. De-scribe how he handles Roderigo, Brabantio, and Cassio. Describe how he handles Othello. How does he deceive Desdemona? How does he manipulate Lodovico? Can you generalize on why Iago's techniques are effective?
4. What is Iago's philosophy of life? How does his view of human nature permit him to manipulate and deceive others?
5. Describe Othello's emotional collapse in Act III under the attacks upon his self-confidence and his wife's faithfulness. What in Othello's background and character makes this collapse likely and believable?
6. Describe Othello on the eve of his murder of Desdemona. Is he now a convincing murderer? How then does he again change after the death of Desdemona, making a final speech that restores him to a position of tragedy? Do you, in fact, see Othello at last as a noble, perhaps even a great figure? Explain.
7. Looking closely at the opening two acts, how would you describe Desdemona? Is she a believable character to you? Explain why or why not. Are there instances when Desdemona might have acted to offset the intrigues growing about her faithfulness to Othello? How do you explain her failures to act? Finally, is she an admirable woman in your view?
8. Emilia has all the pieces of the intrigues against Othello and Desdemona. Why does she not put the puzzle together? Given her position and character, do you see her failure to do so as believable?
9. Why in the end does Emilia turn against her husband? Is her defiance heroic? What have you seen in her before that would lead you to expect her capable of these final words and deeds?
10. Numerous instances of dramatic irony occur in this play. Point out at least five which, in your opinion, are highly effective.
11. Identify several instances in which Shakespeare's poetry strikes you as particu-larly effective. Consider especially the soliloquies of Iago. Compare the speeches of Cassio and Iago, for example, in Act II, scene I, pointing out what the differ-ences in language and style tell us about these two men. Also, examine the opening of Act IV, scene II, and comment on how the language is appropriate to the situation. Then identify instances in which Shakespeare employs prose and rimed couplets. How are these variations from the blank verse employed?
12. In addition to its concern with psychological motivation, *Othello* is a highly visual play. Identify at least four scenes which deliver actions that are visually exciting and effective.
13. What weakness does the character of Othello manifest? Is this weakness only personal or does it have general implications for human nature?

Richard Brinsley Sheridan (1751–1816)
The Rivals

Characters

CAPTAIN ABSOLUTE
LYDIA LANGUISH
SIR ANTHONY ABSOLUTE, *father of Captain Absolute*
MRS. MALAPROP, *aunt of Lydia Languish*
FAULKLAND
JULIA MELVILLE, *cousin of Lydia Languish*
BOB ACRES
SIR LUCIUS O'TRIGGER
FAG, *valet of Captain Absolute*
LUCY, *lady's maid of Lydia Languish*
DAVID, *valet of Bob Acres*
COACHMAN
MAID
BOY
SERVANTS

SCENE: *Bath*[1]
TIME OF ACTION: *Within one day*

ACT I.

Scene I. [*A street in Bath.*]

[COACHMAN *crosses the stage. Enter* FAG, *looking after him.*]

FAG. What!—Thomas!—Sure, 'tis he?—What!—Thomas!—Thomas!
COACHMAN. Hey!—Odd's life![2]—Mr. Fag!—give us your hand, my old fellow-servant.
FAG. Excuse my glove, Thomas:—I'm dev'lish glad to see you, my lad: why, my prince of charioteers, you look as hearty!—but who the deuce thought of seeing you in Bath!

---

1. Fashionable health resort and spa in southwest England; it was a popular gathering-spot for English upper-class society.
2. "God's life," a mild oath whose sounds were slurred in order to avoid profanity or taking the Lord's name in vain. Other examples in the play include *Zounds* ("God's wounds"), *'sdeath* ("God's death"), *Zooks* ("God's hooks"—the nails of the cross).

COACHMAN. Sure, Master, Madam Julia, Harry, Mrs. Kate, and the postilion be all come!

FAG. Indeed!

COACHMAN. Aye! Master thought another fit of the gout was coming to make him a visit: so he'd a mind to gi't the slip, and whip! we were all off at an hour's warning.

FAG. Aye, aye! hasty in everything, or it would not be Sir Anthony Absolute!

COACHMAN. But tell us, Mr. Fag, how does young master? Odd! Sir Anthony will stare to see the Captain here!

FAG. I do not serve Captain Absolute now.

COACHMAN. Why sure!

FAG. At present I am employed by Ensign Beverley.

COACHMAN. I doubt, Mr. Fag, you ha'n't changed for the better.

FAG. I have not changed, Thomas.

COACHMAN. No! why, didn't you say you had left young master?

FAG. No.——Well, honest Thomas, I must puzzle you no farther: briefly then—Captain Absolute and Ensign Beverley are one and the same person.

COACHMAN. The devil they are!

FAG. So it is indeed, Thomas; and the *Ensign*-half of my master being on guard at present—the *Captain* has nothing to do with me.

COACHMAN. So, so!—What, this is some freak, I warrant!——Do tell us, Mr. Fag, the meaning o't—you know I ha' trusted you.

FAG. You'll be secret, Thomas?

COACHMAN. As a coach-horse.

FAG. Why then the cause of all this is—LOVE—Love, Thomas, who (as you may get read to you) has been a masquerader ever since the days of Jupiter.

COACHMAN. Aye, aye;—I guessed there was a lady in the case: but pray, why does your master pass only for *Ensign?* Now if he had shammed *General,* indeed——

FAG. Ah! Thomas, there lies the mystery o' the matter. Hark'ee, Thomas, my master is in love with a lady of a very singular taste: a lady who likes him better as a *half-pay Ensign* than if she knew he was son and heir to Sir Anthony Absolute, a baronet of three thousand a year!

COACHMAN. That is an odd taste indeed!—but has she got the stuff, Mr. Fag? is she rich, hey?

FAG. Rich!—why, I believe she owns half the stocks—Zounds! Thomas, she could pay the national debt as easily as I could my washerwoman! She has a lap-dog that eats out of gold—she feeds her parrot with small pearls— and all her thread-papers[3] are made of bank-notes!

COACHMAN. Bravo!—Faith!—Odd! I warrant she has a set of thousands[4] at least. But does she draw kindly with the Captain?

FAG. As fond as pigeons.

COACHMAN. May one hear her name?

FAG. Miss Lydia Languish. But there is an old tough aunt in the way; though, by the bye, she has never seen my master, for he got acquainted with Miss while on a visit in Gloucestershire.

---

3. Papers on which thread is wound.
4. Team of matched coach horses worth thousands of pounds.

COACHMAN. Well—I wish they were once harnessed together in matrimony.——But pray, Mr. Fag, what kind of a place is this Bath? I ha' heard a deal of it—here's a mort[5] o' merry-making, hey?

FAG. Pretty well, Thomas, pretty well—'tis a good lounge. In the morning we go to the Pump-room[6] (though neither my master nor I drink the waters); after breakfast we saunter on the Parades,[7] or play a game at billiards; at night we dance: but damn the place, I'm tired of it: their regular hours stupefy me—not a fiddle nor a card after eleven! However, Mr. Faulkland's gentleman and I keep it up a little in private parties—I'll introduce you there, Thomas: you'll like him much.

COACHMAN. Sure I know Mr. Du-Peigne—you know his master is to marry Madam Julia.

FAG. I had forgot.——But Thomas, you must polish a little—indeed you must. Here now—this wig! what the devil do you do with a *wig,* Thomas? —none of the London whips[8] of any degree of *ton*[9] wear *wigs* now.

COACHMAN. More's the pity! more's the pity, I say—Odd's life! when I heard how the lawyers and doctors had took to their own hair, I thought how 'twould go next:——Odd rabbit it! when the fashion had got foot on the Bar, I guessed 'twould mount to the Box![10] But 'tis all out of character, believe me, Mr. Fag: and look'ee, I'll never gi' up mine—the lawyers and doctors may do as they will.

FAG. Well, Thomas, we'll not quarrel about that.

COACHMAN. Why, bless you, the gentlemen of they professions ben't all of a mind—for in our village now, tho'ff[11] *Jack Gauge,* the *exciseman,* has ta'en to his carrots,[12] there's little Dick, the farrier, swears he'll never forsake his *bob,*[13] tho' all the college should appear with their own heads!

FAG. Indeed! well said, Dick! But hold—mark! mark! Thomas.

COACHMAN. Zooks! 'tis the Captain!—Is that the lady with him?

FAG. No! no! that is Madam Lucy—my master's mistress's maid. They lodge at that house—but I must after him to tell him the news.

COACHMAN. Odd! he's giving her money!——Well, Mr. Fag——

FAG. Good-bye, Thomas.—I have an appointment in Gyde's Porch this evening at eight; meet me there, and we'll make a little party.

[*Exeunt severally.*]

Scene II. [*A dressing-room in* MRS. MALAPROP'S *lodgings.*]

[LYDIA *sitting on a sofa, with a book in her hand.* LUCY, *as just returned from a message.*]

---

5. Great deal of.
6. Main room where the healthful waters were drunk.
7. Broad walks for promenading.
8. Coachmen.
9. Fashion, style.
10. *had got foot . . . Box,* i.e., had become popular with lawyers, I guessed it would become popular with coachmen.
11. Though.
12. His own red hair.
13. Wig.

LUCY.   Indeed, Ma'am, I traversed half the town in search of it: I don't believe there's a circulating library in Bath I ha'n't been at.

LYDIA.   And could not you get *The Reward of Constancy?*[1]

LUCY.   No, indeed, Ma'am.

LYDIA.   Nor *The Fatal Connection?*

LUCY.   No, indeed, Ma'am.

LYDIA.   Nor *The Mistakes of the Heart?*

LUCY.   Ma'am, as ill-luck would have it, Mr. Bull said Miss Sukey Saunter had just fetched it away.

LYDIA.   Heigh-ho! Did you inquire for *The Delicate Distress?*

LUCY.   Or *The Memoirs of Lady Woodford?* Yes, indeed, Ma'am. I asked everywhere for it; and I might have brought it from Mr. Frederick's, but Lady Slattern Lounger, who had just sent it home, had so soiled and dog's-eared it, it wa'n't fit for a Christian to read.

LYDIA.   Heigh-ho!—Yes, I always know when Lady Slattern has been before me. She has a most observing thumb; and I believe cherishes her nails for the convenience of making marginal notes.——Well, child, what *have* you brought me?

LUCY.   Oh! here, Ma'am [*taking books from under her cloak, and from her pockets*]. This is *The Gordian Knot,* and this *Peregrine Pickle.* Here are *The Tears of Sensibility* and *Humphry Clinker.* This is *The Memoirs of a Lady of Quality, written by herself,* and here the second volume of *The Sentimental Journey.*[2]

LYDIA.   Heigh-ho!—What are those books by the glass?

LUCY.   The great one is only *The Whole Duty of Man*[3]—where I press a few blonds, Ma'am.

LYDIA.   Very well—give me the *sal volatile.*

LUCY.   Is it in a blue cover, Ma'am?

LYDIA.   My smelling bottle, you simpleton!

LUCY.   Oh, the drops!—Here, Ma'am.

LYDIA.   Hold!—here's some one coming——quick! see who it is.

[*Exit* LUCY.]

Surely I heard my cousin Julia's voice!

[*Re-enter* LUCY.]

LUCY.   Lud! Ma'am, here is Miss Melville.

LYDIA.   It is possible!——[*Enter* JULIA.] My dearest Julia, how delighted am I!—[*Embrace.*] How unexpected was this happiness!

JULIA.   True, Lydia—and our pleasure is the greater; but what has been the matter?—you were denied to me at first!

LYDIA.   Ah! Julia, I have a thousand things to tell you! But first inform me what has conjured you to Bath? Is Sir Anthony here?

---

1. Lydia's taste in books is limited to sentimental novels popular in Sheridan's day.

2. Lucy has brought home a hodge-podge of quality fiction and sentimental trash.

3. The most famous and most generally read tract on Christian morals in eighteenth-century England. Lucy uses it only to press "blonds" or silk laces.

JULIA.   He is—we are arrived within this hour, and I suppose he will be here to wait on Mrs. Malaprop as soon as he is dressed.

LYDIA.   Then, before we are interrupted, let me impart to you some of my distress! I know your gentle nature will sympathize with me, though your prudence may condemn me! My letters have informed you of my whole connexion with Beverley—but I have lost him, Julia! My aunt has discovered our intercourse[4] by a note she intercepted, and has confined me ever since! Yet, would you believe it? she has fallen absolutely in love with a tall Irish baronet she met one night since we have been here, at Lady Macshuffle's rout.[5]

JULIA.   You jest, Lydia!

LYDIA.   No, upon my word. She really carries on a kind of correspondence with him, under a feigned name though, till she chooses to be known to him; but it is a *Delia* or a *Celia,* I assure you.

JULIA.   Then surely she is now more indulgent to her niece.

LYDIA.   Quite the contrary. Since she has discovered her own frailty she is become more suspicious of mine. Then I must inform you of another plague! That odious Acres is to be in Bath to-day; so that I protest I shall be teased out of all spirits!

JULIA.   Come, come, Lydia, hope the best. Sir Anthony shall use his interest with Mrs. Malaprop.

LYDIA.   But you have not heard the worst. Unfortunately I had quarreled with my poor Beverley just before my aunt made the discovery, and I have not seen him since to make it up.

JULIA.   What was his offence?

LYDIA.   Nothing at all! But, I don't know how it was, as often as we had been together we had never had a quarrel! And, somehow, I was afraid he would never give me an opportunity. So last Thursday I wrote a letter to myself to inform myself that Beverley was at that time paying his addresses to another woman. I signed it *your friend unknown,* showed it to Beverley, charged him with his falsehood, put myself in a violent passion, and vowed I'd never see him more.

JULIA.   And you let him depart so, and have not seen him since?

LYDIA.   'Twas the next day my aunt found the matter out. I intended only to have teased him three days and a half, and now I've lost him forever!

JULIA.   If he is as deserving and sincere as you have represented him to me, he will never give you up so. Yet consider, Lydia, you tell me he is but an ensign, and you have thirty thousand pounds!

LYDIA.   But you know I lose most of my fortune if I marry without my aunt's consent, till of age; and that is what I have determined to do ever since I knew the penalty. Nor could I love the man who would wish to wait a day for the alternative.

JULIA.   Nay, this is caprice!

LYDIA.   What, does Julia tax me with caprice? I thought her lover Faulkland had enured her to it.

JULIA.   I do not love even *his* faults.

LYDIA.   But a-propos—you have sent to him, I suppose?

JULIA.   Not yet, upon my word, nor has he the least idea of my being in

---

4. Correspondence.
5. Party.

Bath. Sir Anthony's resolution was so sudden I could not inform him of it.

LYDIA.   Well, Julia, you are your own mistress (though under the protection of Sir Anthony), yet have you for this long year been a slave to the caprice, the whim, the jealousy of this ungrateful Faulkland, who will ever delay assuming the right of a husband, while you suffer him to be equally imperious as a lover.

JULIA.   Nay, you are wrong entirely. We were contracted before my father's death. That, and some consequent embarrassments, have delayed what I know to be my Faulkland's most ardent wish. He is too generous to trifle on such a point. And for his character, you wrong him there too. No, Lydia, he is too proud, too noble to be jealous: if he is captious, 'tis without dissembling; if fretful, without rudeness. Unused to the fopperies of love, he is negligent of the little duties expected from a lover—but being unhackneyd in the passion, his affection is ardent and sincere; and as it engrosses his whole soul, he expects every thought and emotion of his mistress to move in unison with his. Yet, though his pride calls for this full return, his humility makes him undervalue those qualities in him which would entitle him to it; and not feeling why he should be loved to the degree he wishes, he still suspects that he is not loved enough. This temper, I must own, has cost me many unhappy hours; but I have learned to think myself his debtor for those imperfections which arise from the ardour of his attachment.

LYDIA.   Well, I cannot blame you for defending him. But tell me candidly, Julia, had he never saved your life, do you think you should have been attached to him as you are? Believe me, the rude blast that overset your boat was a prosperous gale of love to him.

JULIA.   Gratitude may have strengthened my attachment to Mr. Faulkland, but I loved him before he had preserved me; yet surely that alone were an obligation sufficient——

LYDIA.   Obligation! Why, a water-spaniel would have done as much! Well, I should never think of giving my heart to a man because he could swim!

JULIA.   Come, Lydia, you are too inconsiderate.

LYDIA.   Nay, I do but jest.——What's here?

[*Enter* LUCY *in a hurry.*]

LUCY.   O Ma'am, here is Sir Anthony Absolute just come home with your aunt.

LYDIA.   They'll not come here.——Lucy, do you watch.

[*Exit* LUCY.]

JULIA.   Yet I must go. Sir Anthony does not know I am here, and if we meet, he'll detain me, to show me the town. I'll take another opportunity of paying my respects to Mrs. Malaprop, when she shall treat me, as long as she chooses, with her select words so ingeniously *misapplied,* without being *mispronounced.*

[*Re-enter* LUCY.]

LUCY.   O lud! Ma'am, they are both coming upstairs.

LYDIA.   Well, I'll not detain you, coz.[6] Adieu, my dear Julia. I'm sure you are in haste to send to Faulkland. There—through my room you'll find another stair-case.

JULIA.   Adieu.——[*Embrace. Exit* JULIA.]

LYDIA.   Here, my dear Lucy, hide these books. Quick, quick! Fling *Peregrine Pickle* under the toilet[7]—throw *Roderick Random* into the closet—put *The Innocent Adultery* into *The Whole Duty of Man*—thrust *Lord Aimworth* under the sofa—cram *Ovid* behind the bolster—there—put *The Man of Feeling* into your pocket—so, so,—now lay *Mrs. Chapone* in sight, and leave *Fordyce's Sermons* open on the table.

LUCY.   Oh burn it, Ma'am! the hair-dresser has torn away as far as *Proper Pride*.

LYDIA.   Never mind—open at *Sobriety.*—Fling me *Lord Chesterfield's Letters.*—Now for 'em.

[*Enter* MRS. MALAPROP, *and* SIR ANTHONY ABSOLUTE.]

MRS. MALAPROP.   There, Sir Anthony, there sits the deliberate simpleton who wants to disgrace her family, and lavish herself on a fellow not worth a shilling!

LYDIA.   Madam, I thought you once——

MRS. MALAPROP.   You thought, Miss! I don't know any business you have to think at all. Thought does not become a young woman. But the point we would request of you is, that you will promise to forget this fellow—to illiterate[8] him, I say, quite from your memory.

LYDIA.   Ah! Madam! our memories are independent of our wills. It is not so easy to forget.

MRS. MALAPROP.   But I say it is, Miss; there is nothing on earth so easy as to *forget,* if a person chooses to set about it. I'm sure I have as much forgot your poor dear uncle as if he had never existed—and I thought it my duty so to do; and let me tell you, Lydia, these violent memories don't become a young woman.

SIR ANTHONY.   Why sure she won't pretend to remember what she's ordered not!—aye, this comes of her reading!

LYDIA.   What crime, Madam, have I committed to be treated thus?

MRS. MALAPROP.   Now don't attempt to extirpate[9] yourself from the matter; you know I have proof controvertible[10] of it. But tell me, will you promise to do as you're bid? Will you take a husband of your friend's choosing?

LYDIA.   Madam, I must tell you plainly, that had I no preference for anyone else, the choice you have made would be my aversion.

MRS. MALAPROP.   What business have you, Miss, with *preference* and *aversion?* They don't become a young woman; and you ought to know, that as

---

6. Cousin.
7. Dressing table.
8. Mrs. Malaprop means "obliterate." Similar misapplications of words throughout the play characterize her as a pretender to learning. Her idiosyncrasy has since resulted in the term *malapropism* to indicate any similar misuse of words.
9. Extricate.
10. Incontrovertible; indisputable.

both always wear off, 'tis safest in matrimony to begin with a little *aversion*. I am sure I hated your poor dear uncle before marriage as if he'd been a blackamoor—and yet, Miss, you are sensible what a wife I made!—and when it pleased heaven to release me from him, 'tis unknown what tears I shed! But suppose we were going to give you another choice, will you promise us to give up this Beverley?

LYDIA. Could I belie my thoughts so far as to give that promise, my actions would certainly as far belie my words.

MRS. MALAPROP. Take yourself to your room. You are fit company for nothing but your own ill-humours.

LYDIA. Willingly, Ma'am—I cannot change for the worse.   [*Exit.*]

MRS. MALAPROP. There's a little intricate[11] hussy for you!

SIR ANTHONY. It is not to be wondered at, Ma'am—all this is the natural consequence of teaching girls to read. Had I a thousand daughters, by heaven! I'd as soon have them taught the black art as their alphabet!

MRS. MALAPROP. Nay, nay, Sir Anthony, you are an absolute misanthropy.[12]

SIR ANTHONY. In my way hither, Mrs. Malaprop, I observed your niece's maid coming forth from a circulating library! She had a book in each hand—they were half-bound volumes, with marble covers! From that moment I guessed how full of duty I should see her mistress!

MRS. MALAPROP. Those are vile places, indeed!

SIR ANTHONY. Madam, a circulating library in a town is as an evergreen tree of diabolical knowledge! It blossoms through the year! And depend on it, Mrs. Malaprop, that they who are so fond of handling the leaves, will long for the fruit at last.

MRS. MALAPROP. Fie, fie, Sir Anthony, you surely speak laconically![13]

SIR ANTHONY. Why, Mrs. Malaprop, in moderation, now, what would you have a woman know?

MRS. MALAPROP. Observe me, Sir Anthony. I would by no means wish a daughter of mine to be a progeny[14] of learning; I don't think so much learning becomes a young woman; for instance—I would never let her meddle with Greek, or Hebrew, or Algebra, or Simony, or Fluxions, or Paradoxes, or such inflammatory branches of learning—neither would it be necessary for her to handle any of your mathematical, astronomical, diabolical instruments;—but, Sir Anthony, I would send her, at nine years old, to a boarding-school, in order to learn a little ingenuity and artifice.[15] Then, Sir, she should have a supercilious[16] knowledge in accounts—and as she grew up, I would have her instructed in geometry,[17] that she might know something of the contagious[18] countries—but above all, Sir Anthony, she should be mistress of orthodoxy,[19] that she might not misspell, and mispronounce words so shamefully as girls usually do; and

---

11. Probably she means "obstinate."
12. Misanthrope—one who hates mankind.
13. Ironically.
14. Prodigy.
15. Artistry.
16. Superficial.
17. Geography.
18. Contiguous—adjoining.
19. Orthography—the study of writing and spelling.

likewise that she might reprehend[20] the true meaning of what she is saying. This, Sir Anthony, is what I would have a woman know—and I don't think there is a superstitious[21] article in it.

SIR ANTHONY. Well, well, Mrs. Malaprop, I will dispute the point no further with you; though I must confess that you are a truly moderate and polite arguer, for almost every third word you say is on my side of the question. But, Mrs. Malaprop, to the more important point in debate—you say you have no objection to my proposal.

MRS. MALAPROP. None, I assure you. I am under no positive engagement with Mr. Acres, and as Lydia is so obstinate against him, perhaps your son may have better success.

SIR ANTHONY. Well, Madam, I will write for the boy directly. He knows not a syllable of this yet, though I have for some time had the proposal in my head. He is at present with his regiment.

MRS. MALAPROP. We have never seen your son, Sir Anthony; but I hope no objection on his side.

SIR ANTHONY. Objection!—let him object if he dare! No, no, Mrs. Malaprop, Jack knows that the least demur puts me in a frenzy directly. My process was always very simple—in their young days, 'twas "Jack do this";—if he demurred—I knocked him down—and if he grumbled at that—I always sent him out of the room.

MRS. MALAPROP. Aye, and the properest way, o' my conscience!—nothing is so conciliating to young people as severity. Well, Sir Anthony, I shall give Mr. Acres his discharge, and prepare Lydia to receive your son's invocations; and I hope you will represent *her* to the Captain as an object not altogether illegible.[22]

SIR ANTHONY. Madam, I will handle the subject prudently. Well, I must leave you—and let me beg you, Mrs. Malaprop, to enforce this matter roundly to the girl; take my advice—keep a tight hand; if she rejects this proposal—clap her under lock and key—and if you were just to let the servants forget to bring her dinner for three or four days, you can't conceive how she'd come about!

[*Exit.*]

MRS. MALAPROP. Well, at any rate I shall be glad to get her from under my intuition.[23] She has somehow discovered my partiality for Sir Lucius O'Trigger—sure, Lucy can't have betrayed me! No, the girl is such a simpleton, I should have made her confess it.——[*Calls*] Lucy!—Lucy—Had she been one of your artificial[24] ones, I should never have trusted her.

[*Enter* LUCY.]

LUCY. Did you call, Ma'am?

MRS. MALAPROP. Yes, girl. Did you see Sir Lucius while you was out?

LUCY. No, indeed, Ma'am, not a glimpse of him.

MRS. MALAPROP. You are sure, Lucy, that you never mentioned——

---

20. Comprehend.
21. Superfluous.
22. Ineligible.
23. Tuition—care.
24. Artful.

LUCY. O Gemini! I'd sooner cut my tongue out.

MRS. MALAPROP. Well, don't let your simplicity be imposed on.

LUCY. No, Ma'am.

MRS. MALAPROP. So, come to me presently, and I'll give you another letter to Sir Lucius; but mind, Lucy—if ever you betray what you are intrusted with (unless it be other people's secrets to me) you forfeit my malevolence[25] forever, and your being a simpleton shall be no excuse for your locality.

[Exit.]

LUCY. Ha! ha! ha!—So, my dear *simplicity,* let me give you a little respite—[*altering her manner*]—let girls in my station be as fond as they please of appearing expert, and knowing in their trusts—commend me to a mask of *silliness,* and a pair of sharp eyes for my own interest under it! Let me see to what account have I turned my *simplicity* lately—[*Looks at a paper.*] For *abetting Miss Lydia Languish in a design of running away with an Ensign!—in money—sundry times—twelve pound twelve—gowns, five—hats, ruffles, caps, &c., &c.—numberless! From the said Ensign, within this last month, six guineas and a half.*—About a quarter's pay!—Item, *from Mrs. Malaprop, for betraying the young people to her*—when I found matters were likely to be discovered—*two guineas, and a black paduasoy.*[26]—Item, *from Mr. Acres, for carrying divers letters*—which I never delivered—*two guineas, and a pair of buckles.*—Item, *from Sir Lucius O'Trigger—three crowns—two gold pocket-pieces—and a silver snuff-box!*—Well done, *simplicity!*—Yet I was forced to make my Hibernian[27] believe that he was corresponding, not with the *aunt,* but with the *niece:* for, though not overrich, I found he had too much pride and delicacy to sacrifice the feelings of a gentleman to the necessities of his fortune.

[Exit.]

ACT II.

Scene I. [CAPTAIN ABSOLUTE'S *lodgings.*]

[CAPTAIN ABSOLUTE *and* FAG.]

FAG. Sir, while I was there Sir Anthony came in: I told him you had sent me to inquire after his health, and to know if he was at leisure to see you.

ABSOLUTE. And what did he say on hearing I was at Bath?

FAG. Sir, in my life I never saw an elderly gentleman more astonished! He started back two or three paces, rapped out a dozen interjectoral oaths, and asked what the devil had brought you here!

ABSOLUTE. Well, Sir, and what did you say?

FAG. Oh, I lied, Sir—I forget the precise lie; but you may depend on't, he got no truth from me. Yet, with submission, for fear of blunders in future, I should be glad to fix what *has* brought us to Bath, in order that we may lie a little consistently. Sir Anthony's servants were curious, Sir, very curious indeed.

---

25. Benevolence.
26. Silk from the Italian city of Padua.
27. Irishman.

ABSOLUTE.   You have said nothing to them?

FAG.   Oh, not a word, Sir—not a word. Mr. Thomas, indeed, the coachman (whom I take to be the discreetest of whips)——

ABSOLUTE.   'Sdeath!—you rascal! you have not trusted him!

FAG.   Oh, *no*, Sir!—no—no—not a syllable, upon my veracity! He was, indeed, a little inquisitive; but I was sly, Sir—devilish sly!—My master (said I), honest Thomas (you know, Sir, one says *honest* to one's inferiors), is come to Bath to *recruit*—yes, Sir—I said, *to recruit*—and whether for men, money, or constitution, you know, Sir, is nothing to him, nor anyone else.

ABSOLUTE.   Well—*recruit* will do—let it be so——

FAG.   Oh, Sir, recruit will do surprisingly—indeed, to give the thing an air, I told Thomas that your Honour had already enlisted five disbanded chairmen, seven minority waiters, and thirteen billiard markers.[1]

ABSOLUTE.   You blockhead, never say more than is necessary.

FAG.   I beg pardon, Sir—I beg pardon——But with submission, a lie is nothing unless one supports it. Sir, whenever I draw on my invention for a good current lie, I always forge indorsements, as well as the bill.

ABSOLUTE.   Well, take care you don't hurt your credit by offering too much security. Is Mr. Faulkland returned?

FAG.   He is above, Sir, changing his dress.

ABSOLUTE.   Can you tell whether he has been informed of Sir Anthony's and Miss Melville's arrival?

FAG.   I fancy not, Sir; he has seen no one since he came in but his gentleman, who was with him at Bristol.——I think, Sir, I hear Mr. Faulkland coming down——

ABSOLUTE.   Go tell him I am here.

FAG.   Yes, Sir [*going*]. I beg pardon, Sir, but should Sir Anthony call, you will do me the favour to remember that we are *recruiting*, if you please.

ABSOLUTE.   Well, well.

FAG.   And in tenderness to my character, if your Honour could bring in the chairmen and waiters, I shall esteem it as an obligation; for though I never scruple a lie to serve my master, yet it hurts one's conscience to be found out.   [*Exit.*]

ABSOLUTE.   Now for my whimsical friend—if he does not know that his mistress is here, I'll tease him a little before I tell him——[*Enter* FAULKLAND.] Faulkland, you're welcome to Bath again; you are punctual in your return.

FAULKLAND.   Yes; I had nothing to detain me when I had finished the business I went on. Well, what news since I left you? How stand matters between you and Lydia?

ABSOLUTE.   Faith, much as they were; I have not seen her since our quarrel; however, I expect to be recalled every hour.

FAULKLAND.   Why don't you persuade her to go off with you at once?

ABSOLUTE.   What, and lose two-thirds of her fortune? You forget that, my friend. No, no, I could have brought her to that long ago.

FAULKLAND.   Nay then, you trifle too long—if you are sure of *her*,

---

1. *five . . . billiard markers*, i.e., five bearers of sedan chairs who have been fired, seven unemployed waiters, and thirteen men who keep score in billiard rooms.

propose to the aunt *in your own character,* and write to Sir Anthony for his consent.

ABSOLUTE.   Softly, softly, for though I am convinced my little Lydia would elope with me as Ensign Beverley, yet am I by no means certain that she would take me with the impediment of our friend's consent, a regular humdrum wedding, and the reversion of a good fortune on my side; no, no, I must prepare her gradually for the discovery, and make myself necessary to her, before I risk it.——Well, but Faulkland, you'll dine with us to-day at the hotel?

FAULKLAND.   Indeed, I cannot: I am not in spirits to be of such a party.

ABSOLUTE.   By heavens! I shall foreswear your company. You are the most teasing, captious, incorrigible lover! Do love like a man!

FAULKLAND.   I own I am unfit for company.

ABSOLUTE.   Am not *I* a lover; aye, and a romantic one too? Yet do I carry everywhere with me such a confounded farrago[2] of doubts, fears, hopes, wishes, and all the flimsy furniture of a country miss's brain!

FAULKLAND.   Ah! Jack, your heart and soul are not, like mine, fixed immutably on one only object. You throw for a large stake, but losing—you could stake, and throw again. But I have set my sum of happiness on this cast, and not to succeed were to be stripped of all.

ABSOLUTE.   But, for heaven's sake! what grounds for apprehension can your whimsical brain conjure up at present?

FAULKLAND.   What grounds for apprehension did you say? Heavens! are there not a thousand! I fear for her spirits—her health—her life. My absence may fret her; her anxiety for my return, her fears for me, may oppress her gentle temper. And for her health—does not every hour bring me cause to be alarmed? If it rains, some shower may even then have chilled her delicate frame! If the wind be keen, some rude blast may have affected her! The heat of noon, the dews of the evening, may endanger the life of her, for whom only I value mine. O! Jack, when delicate and feeling souls are separated, there is not a feature in the sky, not a movement of the elements, not an aspiration of the breeze, but hints some cause for a lover's apprehension!

ABSOLUTE.   Aye, but we may choose whether we will take the hint or not. So then, Faulkland, if you were convinced that Julia were well and in spirits, you would be entirely content?

FAULKLAND.   I should be happy beyond measure—I am anxious only for that.

ABSOLUTE.   Then to cure your anxiety at once—Miss Melville is in perfect health, and is at this moment in Bath!

FAULKLAND.   Nay, Jack—don't trifle with me.

ABSOLUTE.   She is arrived here with my father within this hour.

FAULKLAND.   Can you be serious?

ABSOLUTE.   I thought you knew Sir Anthony better than to be surprised at a sudden whim of this kind. Seriously then, it is as I tell you—upon my honour.

FAULKLAND.   My dear friend!—Hollo, Du-Peigne! my hat—my dear Jack—now nothing on earth can give me a moment's uneasiness.

---

2. Mixture.

[*Enter* FAG.]

FAG.   Sir, Mr. Acres just arrived is below.

ABSOLUTE.   Stay, Faulkland, this Acres lives within a mile of Sir Anthony, and he shall tell you how your mistress has been ever since you left her.——Fag, show the gentleman up.

[*Exit* FAG.]

FAULKLAND.   What, is he much acquainted in the family?

ABSOLUTE.   Oh, very intimate. I insist on your not going: besides, his character will divert you.

FAULKLAND.   Well, I should like to ask him a few questions.

ABSOLUTE.   He is likewise a rival of mine—that is of my *other self's,* for he does not think his friend Captain Absolute ever saw the lady in question; and it is ridiculous enough to hear him complain to me of *one Beverley,* a concealed skulking rival, who——

FAULKLAND.   Hush! He's here.

[*Enter* ACRES.]

ACRES.   Hah! my dear friend, noble captain, and honest Jack, how dost thou? Just arrived, faith, as you see. Sir, your humble servant. Warm work on the roads, Jack!—Odds whips and wheels! I've travelled like a comet, with a tail of dust all the way as long as the Mall.[3]

ABSOLUTE.   Ah! Bob, you are indeed an eccentric planet, but we know your attraction hither. Give me leave to introduce Mr. Faulkland to you; Mr. Faulkland, Mr. Acres.

ACRES.   Sir, I am most heartily glad to see you: Sir, I solicit your connexions.——Hey, Jack—what—this is Mr. Faulkland, who——?

ABSOLUTE.   Aye, Bob, Miss Melville's Mr. Faulkland.

ACRES.   Odd so! she and your father can be but just arrived before me—I suppose you have seen them. Ah! Mr. Faulkland, you are indeed a happy man.

FAULKLAND.   I have not seen Miss Melville yet, Sir. I hope she enjoyed full health and spirits in Devonshire?

ACRES.   Never knew her better in my life, Sir—never better. Odds blushes and blooms! she has been as healthy as the German Spa.[4]

FAULKLAND.   Indeed! I did hear that she had been a little indisposed.

ACRES.   False, false, Sir—only said to vex you: quite the reverse, I assure you.

FAULKLAND.   There, Jack, you see she has the advantage of me; I had almost fretted myself ill.

ABSOLUTE.   Now are you angry with your mistress for not having been sick.

FAULKLAND.   No, no, you misunderstand me: yet surely a little trifling indisposition is not an unnatural consequence of absence from those we love. Now confess—isn't there something unkind in this violent, robust, unfeeling health?

---

3. Promenade in St. James's Park, London.
4. The original health resort, located in Belgium.

ABSOLUTE. Oh, it was very unkind of her to be well in your absence, to be sure!

ACRES. Good apartments, Jack.

FAULKLAND. Well, Sir, but you were saying that Miss Melville has been so *exceedingly* well—what, then she has been merry and gay, I suppose? Always in spirits—hey?

ACRES. Merry! Odds crickets! she has been the belle and spirit of the company wherever she has been—so lively and entertaining! so full of wit and humour!

FAULKLAND. There, Jack, there! Oh, by my soul! there is an innate levity in woman, that nothing can overcome. What! happy, and I away!

ABSOLUTE. Have done—how foolish this is! Just now you were only apprehensive for your mistress's *spirits*.

FAULKLAND. Why, Jack, have I been the joy and spirit of the company?

ABSOLUTE. No, indeed, you have not.

FAULKLAND. Have I been lively and entertaining?

ABSOLUTE. Oh, upon my word, I acquit you.

FAULKLAND. Have I been full of wit and humour?

ABSOLUTE. No, faith; to do you justice, you have been confoundedly stupid indeed.

ACRES. What's the matter with the gentleman?

ABSOLUTE. He is only expressing his great satisfaction at hearing that Julia has been so well and happy—that's all—hey, Faulkland?

FAULKLAND. Oh! I am rejoiced to hear it—yes, yes, she has a *happy* disposition!

ACRES. That she has indeed. Then she is so accomplished—so sweet a voice—so expert at her harpsichord—such a mistress of flat and sharp, squallante, rumblante, and quiverante![5] There was this time month—Odds minims and crotchets![6] how she did chirrup at Mrs. Piano's concert!

FAULKLAND. There again, what say you to this? You see she has been all mirth and song—not a thought of me!

ABSOLUTE. Pho! man, is not music the food of love?

FAULKLAND. Well, well, it may be so.——Pray, Mr.——what's his damned name? Do you remember what songs Miss Melville sung?

ACRES. Not I, indeed.

ABSOLUTE. Stay now, they were some pretty, melancholy, purling-stream airs, I warrant; perhaps you may recollect; did she sing *"When absent from my soul's delight"*?

ACRES. No, that wa'n't it.

ABSOLUTE. Or "Go, *gentle gales*"?—"*Go, gentle gales!*" [*Sings.*]

ACRES. Oh no! nothing like it. Odds! now I recollect one of them—"*My heart's my own, my will is free.*" [*Sings.*]

FAULKLAND. Fool! fool that I am! to fix all my happiness on such a trifler! 'Sdeath! to make herself the pipe and ballad-monger of a circle! to soothe her light heart with catches and glees![7] What can you say to this, Sir?

---

5. Fictitious musical terms.
6. Half-notes and quarter-notes.
7. Spirited songs.

ABSOLUTE. Why, that I should be glad to hear my mistress had been so merry, *Sir*.

FAULKLAND. Nay, nay, nay—I am not sorry that she has been happy—no, no, I am glad of that—I would not have had her sad or sick—yet surely a sympathetic heart would have shown itself even in the choice of a song: she might have been temperately healthy, and, somehow, plaintively gay; but she has been dancing too, I doubt not!

ACRES. What does the gentleman say about dancing?

ABSOLUTE. He says the lady we speak of dances as well as she sings.

ACRES. Aye, truly, does she—there was at our last race-ball——

FAULKLAND. Hell and the devil! There! there!—I told you so! I told you so! Oh! she thrives in my absence! Dancing! But her whole feelings have been in opposition with mine! I have been anxious, silent, pensive, sedentary—my days have been hours of care, my nights of watchfulness. She has been all Health! Spirit! Laugh! Song! Dance! Oh! damn'd damn'd levity!

ABSOLUTE. For heaven's sake! Faulkland, don't expose yourself so. Suppose she has danced, what then? Does not the ceremony of society often oblige——

FAULKLAND. Well, well, I'll contain myself. Perhaps, as you say, for form sake. What, Mr. Acres, you were praising Miss Melville's manner of dancing a *minuet*—hey?

ACRES. Oh I dare insure her for that—but what I was going to speak of was her *country dancing*. Odds swimmings! she has such an air with her!

FAULKLAND. Now disappointment on her! Defend this, Absolute, why don't you defend this? Country-dances! jigs, and reels! Am I to blame now? A minuet I could have forgiven—I should not have minded that—I say I should not have regarded a minuet—but *country-dances!* Zounds! had she made one in a cotillion—I believe I could have forgiven even that—but to be monkey-led for a night! to run the gauntlet through a string of amorous palming puppies! to show paces like a managed filly! O Jack, there never can be but *one* man in the world whom a truly modest and delicate woman ought to pair with in a *country-dance;* and even then, the rest of the couples should be her great uncles and aunts!

ABSOLUTE. Aye, to be sure!—grandfathers and grandmothers!

FAULKLAND. If there be but one vicious mind in the Set, 'twill spread like a contagion—the action of their pulse beats to the lascivious movement of the jig—their quivering, warm-breathed sighs impregnate the very air—the atmosphere becomes electrical to love, and each amorous spark darts through every link of the chain; I must leave you—I own I am somewhat flurried—and that confounded looby[8] has perceived it [*going*].

ABSOLUTE. Nay, but stay, Faulkland, and thank Mr. Acres for his good news.

FAULKLAND. Damn his news! [*Exit.*]

ABSOLUTE. Ha! ha! ha! Poor Faulkland! Five minutes since—"nothing on earth could give him a moment's uneasiness!"

ACRES. The gentleman wa'n't angry at my praising his mistress, was he?

ABSOLUTE. A little jealous, I believe, Bob.

---

8. Dolt.

ACRES.   You don't say so? Ha! ha! jealous of me?—that's a good joke.

ABSOLUTE.   There's nothing strange in that, Bob: let me tell you, that sprightly grace and insinuating manner of yours will do some mischief among the girls here.

ACRES.   Ah! you joke—ha! ha!—mischief—ha! ha! But you know I am not my own property; my dear Lydia has forestalled me. She could never abide me in the country, because I used to dress so badly—but odds frogs and tambours![9] I shan't take matters so here—now ancient madam has no voice in it. I'll make my old clothes know who's master. I shall straightway cashier the hunting-frock, and render my leather breeches incapable. My hair has been in training some time.

ABSOLUTE.   Indeed!

ACRES.   Aye—and tho'ff the side-curls are a little restive, my hindpart takes to it very kindly.

ABSOLUTE.   O, you'll polish, I doubt not.

ACRES.   Absolutely I propose so. Then if I can find out this Ensign Beverley, odds triggers and flints! I'll make him know the difference o't.

ABSOLUTE.   Spoke like a man—but pray, Bob, I observe you have got an odd kind of a new method of swearing——

ACRES.   Ha! ha! you've taken notice of it? 'Tis genteel, isn't it? I didn't invent it myself, though; but a commander in our militia—a great scholar, I assure you—says that there is no meaning in the common oaths, and that nothing but their antiquity makes them respectable, because, he says, the ancients would never stick to an oath or two, but would say, by Jove! or by Bacchus! or by Mars! or by Venus! or by Pallas! according to the sentiment; so that to swear with propriety, says my little major, the "oath should be an echo to the sense"; and this we call the *oath referential,* or *sentimental swearing*—ha! ha! ha! 'tis genteel, isn't it?

ABSOLUTE.   Very genteel, and very new, indeed—and I dare say will supplant all other figures of imprecation.

ACRES.   Aye, aye, the best terms will grow obsolete. Damns have had their day.

[*Enter* FAG.]

FAG.   Sir, there is a gentleman below desires to see you. Shall I show him into the parlour?

ABSOLUTE.   Aye—you may.

ACRES.   Well, I must be gone——

ABSOLUTE.   Stay; who is it, Fag?

FAG.   Your father, Sir.

ABSOLUTE.   You puppy, why didn't you show him up directly?

[*Exit* FAG.]

ACRES.   You have business with Sir Anthony. I expect a message from

---

9. Ornamental loops for fastening coats and embroidery frames.

Mrs. Malaprop at my lodgings. I have sent also to my dear friend, Sir Lucius O'Trigger. Adieu, Jack! We must meet at night, when you shall give me a dozen bumpers to little Lydia.

ABSOLUTE. That I will, with all my heart.   [*Exit* ACRES.]
Now for a parental lecture. I hope he has heard nothing of the business that has brought me here. I wish the gout had held him fast in Devonshire, with all my soul! [*Enter* SIR ANTHONY.] Sir, I am delighted to see you here; and looking so well! Your sudden arrival at Bath made me apprehensive for your health.

SIR ANTHONY. Very apprehensive, I dare say, Jack. What, you are recruiting here, hey?

ABSOLUTE. Yes, Sir, I am on duty.

SIR ANTHONY. Well, Jack, I am glad to see you, though I did not expect it, for I was going to write to you on a little matter of business. Jack, I have been considering that I grow old and infirm, and shall probably not trouble you long.

ABSOLUTE. Pardon me, Sir, I never saw you look more strong and hearty; and I pray frequently that you may continue so.

SIR ANTHONY. I hope your prayers may be heard with all my heart. Well then, Jack, I have been considering that I am so strong and hearty, I may continue to plague you a long time. Now, Jack, I am sensible that the income of your commission, and what I have hitherto allowed you, is but a small pittance for a lad of your spirit.

ABSOLUTE. Sir, you are very good.

SIR ANTHONY. And it is my wish, while yet I live, to have my boy make some figure in the world. I have resolved, therefore, to fix you at once in a noble independence.

ABSOLUTE. Sir, your kindness overpowers me—such generosity makes the gratitude of reason more lively than the sensations even of filial affection.

SIR ANTHONY. I am glad you are so sensible of my attention—and you shall be master of a large estate in a few weeks.

ABSOLUTE. Let my future life, Sir, speak my gratitude: I cannot express the sense I have of your munificence. Yet, Sir, I presume you would not wish me to quit the army?

SIR ANTHONY. Oh, that shall be as your wife chooses.

ABSOLUTE. My wife, Sir!

SIR ANTHONY. Aye, aye—settle that between you—settle that between you.

ABSOLUTE. A *wife,* Sir, did you say?

SIR ANTHONY. Aye, a wife—why; did not I mention her before?

ABSOLUTE. Not a word of her, Sir.

SIR ANTHONY. Odd so!—I mus'n't forget *her,* though. Yes, Jack, the independence I was talking of is by a marriage—the fortune is saddled with a wife—but I suppose that makes no difference.

ABSOLUTE. Sir! Sir!—you amaze me!

SIR ANTHONY. Why, what the devil's the matter with the fool? Just now you were all gratitude and duty.

ABSOLUTE. I was, Sir—you talked to me of independence and a fortune, but not a word of a wife.

SIR ANTHONY. Why—what difference does that make? Odd's life, Sir! if you have the estate, you must take it with the live stock on it, as it stands.

ABSOLUTE.   If my happiness is to be the price, I must beg leave to decline the purchase. Pray, Sir, who is the lady?

SIR ANTHONY.   What's that to you, Sir? Come, give me your promise to love, and to marry her directly.

ABSOLUTE.   Sure, Sir, this is not very reasonable, to summon my affections for a lady I know nothing of!

SIR ANTHONY.   I am sure, Sir, 'tis more unreasonable in you to *object* to a lady you know nothing of.

ABSOLUTE.   Then, Sir, I must tell you plainly that my inclinations are fixed on another—my heart is engaged to an angel.

SIR ANTHONY.   Then pray let it send an excuse. It is very sorry—but *business* prevents its waiting on her.

ABSOLUTE.   But my vows are pledged to her.

SIR ANTHONY.   Let her foreclose, Jack; let her foreclose, they are not worth redeeming: besides, you have the angel's vows in exchange, I suppose; so there can be no loss there.

ABSOLUTE.   You must excuse me, Sir, if I tell you, once for all, that in this point I cannot obey you.

SIR ANTHONY.   Hark'ee, Jack: I have heard you for some time with patience—I have been cool—quite cool; but take care—you know I am compliance itself when I am not thwarted—no one more easily led when I have my own way; but don't put me in a frenzy.

ABSOLUTE.   Sir, I must repeat it—in this I cannot obey you.

SIR ANTHONY.   Now, damn me! if ever I call you *Jack* again while I live!

ABSOLUTE.   Nay, Sir, but hear me.

SIR ANTHONY.   Sir, I won't hear a word—not a word! not one word! so give me your promise by a nod—and I'll tell you what, Jack—I mean, you dog—if you don't, by——

ABSOLUTE.   What, Sir, promise to link myself to some mass of ugliness! to——

SIR ANTHONY.   Zounds! Sirrah! the lady shall be as ugly as I choose: she shall have a hump on each shoulder; she shall be as crooked as the Crescent;[10] her one eye shall roll like the Bull's in Cox's Museum[11]—she shall have a skin like a mummy, and the beard of a Jew—she shall be all this, Sirrah!— yet I'll make you ogle her all day, and sit up all night to write sonnets on her beauty.

ABSOLUTE.   This is reason and moderation indeed!

SIR ANTHONY.   None of your sneering, puppy! no grinning, jackanapes!

ABSOLUTE.   Indeed, Sir, I never was in a worse humour for mirth in my life.

SIR ANTHONY.   'Tis false, Sir! I know you are laughing in your sleeve; I know you'll grin when I am gone, Sirrah!

ABSOLUTE.   Sir, I hope I know my duty better.

SIR ANTHONY.   None of your passion, Sir! none of your violence! if you please. It won't do with me, I promise you.

ABSOLUTE.   Indeed, Sir, I never was cooler in my life.

---

10. The Royal Crescent, a group of fashionable houses in Bath arranged in the form of a crescent.
11. A mechanical bull, a popular exhibit of the time.

SIR ANTHONY. 'Tis a confounded lie!—I know you are in a passion in your heart; I know you are, you hypocritical young dog! But it won't do.

ABSOLUTE. Nay, Sir, upon my word.

SIR ANTHONY. So you will fly out! Can't you be cool, like me? What the devil good can *passion* do! *Passion* is of no service, you impudent, insolent, overbearing reprobate!—There you sneer again! don't provoke me! But you rely upon the mildness of my temper—you do, you dog! you play upon the meekness of my disposition! Yet take care—the patience of a saint may be overcome at last!—but mark! I give you six hours and a half to consider of this: if you then agree, without any condition, to do everything on earth that I choose, why—confound you! I may in time forgive you. If not, zounds! don't enter the same hemisphere with me! don't dare to breathe the same air, or use the same light with me; but get an atmosphere and a sun of your own! I'll strip you of your commission; I'll lodge a five-and-threepence in the hands of trustees, and you shall live on the interest. I'll disown you, I'll disinherit you, I'll unget you! and—damn me, if ever I call you Jack again! [*Exit.*]

ABSOLUTE. Mild, gentle, considerate Father—I kiss your hands. What a tender method of giving his opinion in these matters Sir Anthony has! I dare not trust him with the truth. I wonder what old wealthy hag it is that he wants to bestow on me! Yet he married himself for love! and was in his youth a bold intriguer, and a gay companion!

[*Enter* FAG.]

FAG. Assuredly, Sir, our father is wrath to a degree; he comes downstairs eight or ten steps at a time—muttering, growling, and thumping the bannisters all the way: I, and the cook's dog, stand bowing at the door—rap! he gives me a stroke on the head with his cane; bids me carry that to my master; then kicking the poor turnspit[12] into the area,[13] damns us all for a puppy triumvirate! Upon my credit, Sir, were I in your place, and found my father such very bad company, I should certainly drop his acquaintance.

ABSOLUTE. Cease your impertinence, Sir, at present. Did you come in for nothing more? Stand out of the way! [*Pushes him aside, and exit.*]

FAG. Soh! Sir Anthony trims[14] my master. He is afraid to reply to his father—then vents his spleen on poor Fag! When one is vexed by one person, to revenge one's self on another who happens to come in the way is the vilest injustice. Ah! it shows the worst temper—the basest——

[*Enter* ERRAND-BOY.]

BOY. Mr. Fag! Mr. Fag! your master calls you.

FAG. Well, you little dirty puppy, you need not bawl so!——The meanest disposition! the——

BOY. Quick, quick, Mr. Fag!

FAG. *Quick, quick,* you impudent jackanapes! am I to be commanded by

---

12. Small dog trained to walk on a treadmill which turned the spit.
13. Sunken area near the basement door.
14. Scolds.

you too? you little, impertinent, insolent, kitchen-bred——[*Exit, kicking and beating him.*]

Scene II. [*The North Parade*]

[*Enter* LUCY.]

LUCY. So—I shall have another rival to add to my mistress's list—Captain Absolute. However, I shall not enter his name till my purse has received notice in form. Poor Acres is dismissed! Well, I have done him a last friendly office in letting him know that Beverley was here before him. Sir Lucius is generally more punctual when he expects to hear from his *dear Delia,* as he calls her: I wonder he's not here! I have a little scruple of conscience from this deceit; though I should not be paid so well, if my hero knew that *Delia* was near fifty, and her own mistress.

[*Enter* SIR LUCIUS O'TRIGGER.]

SIR LUCIUS. Hah! my little embassadress—upon my conscience, I have been looking for you; I have been on the South Parade this half-hour.

LUCY [*speaking simply*]. O Gemini! and I have been waiting for your worship here on the North.

SIR LUCIUS. Faith!—maybe that was the reason we did not meet; and it is very comical, too, how you could go out and I not see you—for I was only taking a nap at the Parade Coffee-house, and I chose the *window* on purpose that I might not miss you.

LUCY. My stars! Now I'd wager a sixpence I went by while you were asleep.

SIR LUCIUS. Sure enough it must have been so—and I never dreamt it was so late, till I waked. Well, but my little girl, have you got nothing for me?

LUCY. Yes, but I have: I've got a letter for you in my pocket.

SIR LUCIUS. Oh faith! I guessed you weren't come empty-handed—well—let me see what the dear creature says.

LUCY. There, Sir Lucius. [*Gives him a letter.*]

SIR LUCIUS [*reads*]. *Sir—there is often a sudden incentive*[1] *impulse in love, that has a greater induction*[2] *than years of domestic combination: such was the commotion I felt at the first superfluous*[3] *view of Sir Lucius O'Trigger.*—Very pretty, upon my word.—*Female punctuation*[4] *forbids me to say more; yet let me add, that it will give me joy infallible*[5] *to find Sir Lucius worthy the last criterion*[6] *of my affections.* DELIA. Upon my conscience! Lucy, your lady is a great mistress of language. Faith, she's quite the queen of the dictionary! —for the devil a word dare refuse coming at her call—though one would think it was quite out of hearing.

LUCY. Aye, Sir, a lady of her experience——

---

1. Instinctive.
2. Seduction.
3. Superficial.
4. Punctilio—proper conduct.
5. Ineffable—indescribable.
6. Degree.

SIR LUCIUS.   Experience! what, at seventeen?

LUCY.   O true, Sir—but then she reads so—my stars! how she will read off-hand!

SIR LUCIUS.   Faith, she must be very deep read to write this way—though she is rather an arbitrary writer too—for here are a great many poor words pressed into the service of this note, that would get their *habeas corpus* from any court in Christendom.[7]

LUCY.   Ah! Sir Lucius, if you were to hear how she talks of you!

SIR LUCIUS.   Oh tell her I'll make her the best husband in the world, and Lady O'Trigger into the bargain! But we must get the old gentlewoman's consent—and do everything fairly.

LUCY.   Nay, Sir Lucius, I thought you wa'n't rich enough to be so nice!

SIR LUCIUS.   Upon my word, young woman, you have hit it: I am so poor that I can't afford to do a dirty action. If I did not want money I'd steal your mistress and her fortune with a great deal of pleasure. However, my pretty girl [*gives her money*], here's a little something to buy you a ribband; and meet me in the evening, and I'll give you an answer to this. So, hussy, take a kiss beforehand to put you in mind. [*Kisses her.*]

LUCY.   O lud! Sir Lucius—I never seed such a gemman! My lady won't like you if you're so impudent.

SIR LUCIUS.   Faith she will, Lucy—That same—pho! what's the name of it?—*Modesty!*—is a quality in a lover more praised by the women than liked; so, if your mistress asks you whether Sir Lucius ever gave you a kiss, tell her *fifty*—my dear.

LUCY.   What, would you have me tell her a lie?

SIR LUCIUS.   Ah, then, you baggage! I'll make it a truth presently.

LUCY.   For shame now; here is someone coming.

SIR LUCIUS.   Oh faith, I'll quiet your conscience. [*Sees* FAG.—*Exit, humming a tune. Enter* FAG.]

FAG.   So, so, Ma'am. I humbly beg pardon.

LUCY.   O lud!—now, Mr. Fag, you flurry one so.

FAG.   Come, come, Lucy, here's no one by—so a little less simplicity, with a grain or two more sincerity, if you please. You play false with us, Madam. I saw you give the baronet a letter. My master shall know this, and if he don't call him out—I will.

LUCY.   Ha! ha! ha! you gentlemen's gentlemen are so hasty. That letter was from Mrs. Malaprop, simpleton. She is taken with Sir Lucius's address.

FAG.   How! what tastes some people have! Why, I suppose I have walked by her window an hundred times. But what says our young lady? Any message to my master?

LUCY.   Sad news, Mr. Fag! A worse rival than Acres! Sir Anthony Absolute has proposed his son.

FAG.   What, Captain Absolute?

LUCY.   Even so. I overheard it all.

---

7. *poor words . . . Christendom,* i.e., many words that could demand and get a fair trial in protest over being drafted and misused by Mrs. Malaprop.

FAG.   Ha! ha! ha!—very good, faith. Good-bye, Lucy, I must away with this news.

LUCY.   Well—you may laugh, but it is true, I assure you [*going*]. But—Mr. Fag—tell your master not to be cast down by this.

FAG.   Oh, he'll be so disconsolate!

LUCY.   And charge him not to think of quarrelling with young Absolute.

FAG.   Never fear!—never fear!

LUCY.   Be sure—bid him keep up his spirits.

FAG.   We will—we will.   [*Exeunt severally.*]

ACT III.

Scene I.   [*The North Parade*]

[*Enter* ABSOLUTE.]

ABSOLUTE.   'Tis just as Fag told me, indeed. Whimsical enough, faith! My father wants to *force* me to marry the very girl I am plotting to run away with! He must not know of my connexion with her yet awhile. He has too summary a method of proceeding in these matters. However, I'll read my recantation instantly. My conversion is something sudden, indeed, but I can assure him it is very *sincere*.——So, so—here he comes. He looks plaguy gruff. [*Steps aside.*]

[*Enter* SIR ANTHONY.]

SIR ANTHONY.   No—I'll die sooner than forgive him. *Die,* did I say? I'll live these fifty years to plague him. At our last meeting, his impudence had almost put me out of temper. An obstinate, passionate, self-willed boy! Who can he take after? This is my return for getting him before all his brothers and sisters!—for putting him, at twelve years old, into a marching regiment, and allowing him fifty pounds a year, beside his pay ever since! But I have done with him; he's anybody's son for me. I never will see him more—never—never—never!

ABSOLUTE.   Now for a penitential face.

SIR ANTHONY.   Fellow, get out of my way.

ABSOLUTE.   Sir, you see a penitent before you.

SIR ANTHONY.   I see an impudent scoundrel before me.

ABSOLUTE.   A sincere penitent. I am come, Sir, to acknowledge my error, and to submit entirely to your will.

SIR ANTHONY.   What's that?

ABSOLUTE.   I have been revolving, and reflecting, and considering on your past goodness, and kindness, and condescension to me.

SIR ANTHONY.   Well, Sir?

ABSOLUTE.   I have been likewise weighing and balancing what you were pleased to mention concerning duty, and obedience, and authority.

SIR ANTHONY.   Well, puppy?

ABSOLUTE. Why, then, Sir, the result of my reflections is—a resolution to sacrifice every inclination of my own to your satisfaction.

SIR ANTHONY. Why, now you talk sense—absolute sense—I never heard anything more sensible in my life. Confound you, you shall be *Jack* again!

ABSOLUTE. I am happy in the appellation.

SIR ANTHONY. Why then, Jack, my dear Jack, I will now inform you who the lady really is. Nothing but your passion and violence, you silly fellow, prevented my telling you at first. Prepare, Jack, for wonder and rapture! prepare!——What think you of Miss Lydia Languish?

ABSOLUTE. Languish! What, the Languishes of Worcestershire?

SIR ANTHONY. Worcestershire! No. Did you never meet Mrs. Malaprop and her niece, Miss Languish, who came into our country just before you were last ordered to your regiment?

ABSOLUTE. Malaprop! Languish! I don't remember ever to have heard the names before. Yet, stay—I think I do recollect something.——*Languish! Languish!* She squints, don't she? A little, red-haired girl?

SIR ANTHONY. Squints? A red-haired girl! Zounds, no!

ABSOLUTE. Then I must have forgot; it can't be the same person.

SIR ANTHONY. Jack! Jack! what think you of blooming, love-breathing seventeen?

ABSOLUTE. As to that, Sir, I am quite indifferent. If I can please you in the matter, 'tis all I desire.

SIR ANTHONY. Nay, but Jack, such eyes! such eyes! so innocently wild! so bashfully irresolute! Not a glance but speaks and kindles some thought of love! Then, Jack, her cheeks! her cheeks, Jack! so deeply blushing at the insinuations of her tell-tale eyes! Then, Jack, her lips!—O Jack, lips smiling at their own discretion; and if not smiling, more sweetly pouting, more lovely in sullenness!

ABSOLUTE [*aside*]. That's she, indeed. Well done, old gentleman!

SIR ANTHONY. Then, Jack, her neck!—O Jack! Jack!

ABSOLUTE. And which is to be mine, Sir, the niece or the aunt?

SIR ANTHONY. Why, you unfeeling, insensible puppy, I despise you! When I was of your age, such a description would have made me fly like a rocket! The *aunt,* indeed! Odd's life! when I ran away with your mother, I would not have touched anything old or ugly to gain an empire.

ABSOLUTE. Not to please your father, Sir?

SIR ANTHONY. To please my father! Zounds! not to please——Oh, my father!—Odd so!—yes—yes!—if my father, indeed, had desired—that's quite another matter. Though he wa'n't the indulgent father that I am, Jack.

ABSOLUTE. I dare say not, Sir.

SIR ANTHONY. But, Jack, you are not sorry to find your mistress is so beautiful?

ABSOLUTE. Sir, I repeat it; if I please you in this affair, 'tis all I desire. Not that I think a woman the worse for being handsome; but, Sir, if you please to recollect, you before hinted something about a hump or two, one eye, and a few more graces of that kind. Now, without being very nice, I own I should rather choose a wife of mine to have the usual number of limbs, and a limited quantity of back: and though *one* eye may be very agreeable, yet as the prejudice has always run in favour of *two,* I would not wish to affect a singularity in that article.

SIR ANTHONY. What a phlegmatic sot it is! Why, Sirrah, you're an anchorite! a vile, insensible stock. You a soldier! you're a walking block, fit only to dust the company's regimentals[1] on! Odd's life! I've a great mind to marry the girl myself!

ABSOLUTE.   I am entirely at your disposal, Sir; if you should think of addressing Miss Languish yourself, I suppose you would have me marry the *aunt;* or if you should change your mind, and take the old lady—'tis the same to me—I'll marry the *niece.*

SIR ANTHONY.   Upon my word, Jack, thou'rt either a very great hypo-crite, or——But come, I know your indifference on such a subject must be all a lie—I'm sure it must—come, now—damn your demure face!—come, confess, Jack—you have been lying—ha'n't you? you have been playing the hypocrite, hey?—I'll never forgive you if you ha'n't been lying and playing the hypocrite.

ABSOLUTE.   I'm sorry, Sir, that the respect and duty which I bear to you should be so mistaken.

SIR ANTHONY.   Hang your respect and duty! But come along with me, I'll write a note to Mrs. Malaprop, and you shall visit the lady directly. Her eyes shall be the Promethean torch to you[2]—come along. I'll never forgive you if you don't come back stark mad with rapture and impatience. If you don't, egad, I'll marry the girl myself!   [*Exeunt.*]

Scene II.   [JULIA'S *dressing-room*]

[FAULKLAND, *alone.*]

FAULKLAND.   They told me Julia would return directly; I wonder she is not yet come! How mean does this captious, unsatisfied temper of mine appear to my cooler judgment! Yet I know not that I indulge it in any other point: but on this one subject, and to this one subject, whom I think I love beyond my life, I am ever ungenerously fretful, and madly capricious! I am conscious of it—yet I cannot correct myself! What tender, honest joy sparkled in her eyes when we met! How delicate was the warmth of her expressions! I was ashamed to appear less happy, though I had come resolved to wear a face of coolness and upbraid-ing. Sir Anthony's presence prevented my proposed expostulations, yet I must be satisfied that she has not been so *very* happy in my absence. She is coming! Yes! I know the nimbleness of her tread when she thinks her impatient Faulkland counts the moments of her stay.

[*Enter* JULIA.]

JULIA.   I had not hoped to see you again so soon.

FAULKLAND.   Could I, Julia, be contented with my first welcome— restrained as we were by the presence of a third person?

JULIA.   O Faulkland, when your kindness can make me thus happy, let me not think that I discovered something of coldness in your first salutation.

FAULKLAND.   'Twas but your fancy, Julia. I *was* rejoiced to see you—to see you in such health. Sure I had no cause for coldness?

---

1. Regimental uniforms.
2. I.e., her eyes shall kindle in you a fire, just as Prometheus stole fire from the gods and gave it to mankind.

JULIA. Nay then, I see you have taken something ill. You must not conceal from me what it is.

FAULKLAND. Well then—shall I own to you—that my joy at hearing of your health and arrival here, by your neighbour Acres, was somewhat damped by his dwelling much on the high spirits you had enjoyed in Devonshire—on your mirth, your singing, dancing, and I know not what! For such is my temper, Julia, that I should regard every mirthful moment in your absence as a treason to constancy. The mutual tear that steals down the cheek of parting lovers is a compact that no smile shall live there till they meet again.

JULIA. Must I never cease to tax my Faulkland with this teasing minute caprice? Can the idle reports of a silly boor weigh in your breast against my tried affection?

FAULKLAND. They have no weight with me, Julia: no, no—I am happy if you have been so—yet only say that you did not sing with *mirth*—say that you *thought* of Faulkland in the dance.

JULIA. I never can be happy in your absence. If I wear a countenance of content, it is to show that my mind holds no doubt of my Faulkland's truth. If I seemed sad, it were to make malice triumph, and say that I had fixed my heart on one who left me to lament his roving, and my own credulity. Believe me, Faulkland, I mean not to upbraid you when I say that I have often dressed sorrow in smiles, lest my friends should guess whose unkindness had caused my tears.

FAULKLAND. You were ever all goodness to me. Oh, I am a brute when I but admit a doubt of your true constancy!

JULIA. If ever, without such cause from you, as I will not suppose possible, you find my affections veering but a point, may I become a proverbial scoff for levity and base ingratitude.

FAULKLAND. Ah! Julia, that last word is grating to me. I would I had no title to your *gratitude!* Search your heart, Julia; perhaps what you have mistaken for love, is but the warm effusion of a too thankful heart!

JULIA. For what quality must I love you?

FAULKLAND. For no quality! To regard me for any quality of mind or understanding were only to *esteem* me. And for person—I have often wished myself deformed, to be convinced that I owed no obligation *there* for any part of your affection.

JULIA. Where Nature has bestowed a show of nice attention in the features of a man, he should laugh at it as misplaced. I have seen men who in *this* vain article perhaps might rank above you; but my heart has never asked my eyes if it were so or not.

FAULKLAND. Now this is not well from *you,* Julia. I despise person in a man. Yet if you loved me as I wish, though I were an Æthiop, you'd think none so fair.

JULIA. I see you are determined to be unkind. The *contract* which my poor father bound us in gives you more than a lover's privilege.

FAULKLAND. Again, Julia, you raise ideas that feed and justify my doubts. I would not have been more free—no—I am proud of my restraint. Yet—yet—perhaps your high respect alone for this solemn compact has fettered your inclinations, which else had made a worthier choice. How shall I be sure, had you remained unbound in thought and promise, that I should still have been the object of your persevering love?

JULIA.   Then try me now. Let us be free as strangers as to what is past: *my heart will not feel more liberty!*

FAULKLAND.   There now! so hasty, Julia! so anxious to be free! If your love for me were fixed and ardent, you would not loose your hold, even though I wished it!

JULIA.   Oh, you torture me to the heart! I cannot bear it.

FAULKLAND.   I do not mean to distress you. If I loved you less I should never give you an uneasy moment. But hear me. All my fretful doubts arise from this: women are not used to weigh, and separate the motives of their affections; the cold dictates of prudence, gratitude, or filial duty, may sometimes be mistaken for the pleadings of the heart. I would not boast—yet let me say that I have neither age, person, or character to found dislike on; my fortune such as few ladies could be charged with *indiscretion* in the match. O Julia! when *Love* receives such countenance from *Prudence,* nice minds will be suspicious of its birth.

JULIA.   I know not whither your insinuations would tend, but as they seem pressing to insult me, I will spare you the regret of having done so. I have given you no cause for this!   [*Exit in tears.*]

FAULKLAND.   In tears! Stay, Julia: stay but for a moment.——The door is fastened! Julia!—my soul—but for one moment. I hear her sobbing! 'Sdeath! what a brute am I to use her thus! Yet stay!——Aye—she is coming now. How little resolution there is in woman! How a few soft words can turn them!——No, faith!—she is *not* coming either! Why, Julia—my love—say but that you forgive me—come but to tell me that. Now, this is being *too* resentful.——Stay! she *is* coming too—I thought she would—no *steadiness* in anything! her going away must have been a mere trick then. She sha'n't see that I was hurt by it. I'll affect indifference. [*Hums a tune: then listens.*]——No—Zounds! she's *not* coming!—nor don't intend it, I suppose. This is not *steadiness,* but *obstinacy!* Yet I deserve it. What, after so long an absence to quarrel with her tenderness!—'twas barbarous and unmanly! I should be ashamed to see her now. I'll wait till her just resentment is abated—and when I distress her so again, may I lose her forever, and be linked instead to some antique virago,[1] whose gnawing passions, and long-hoarded spleen shall make me curse my folly half the day, and all the night!   [*Exit.*]

Scene III.   [MRS. MALAPROP'S *lodgings*]

[MRS. MALAPROP, *with a letter in her hand, and* CAPTAIN ABSOLUTE.]

MRS. MALAPROP.   Your being Sir Anthony's son, Captain, would itself be a sufficient accommodation;[1] but from the ingenuity[2] of your appearance, I am convinced you deserve the character here given of you.

ABSOLUTE.   Permit me to say, Madam, that as I never yet have had the pleasure of seeing Miss Languish, my principal inducement in this affair at present is the honour of being allied to Mrs. Malaprop; of whose intellectual

---

1. Ill-tempered woman.

1. Recommendation.
2. Ingenuousness—straightforwardness.

accomplishments, elegant manners, and unaffected learning, no tongue is silent.

MRS. MALAPROP.   Sir, you do me infinite honour! I beg, Captain, you'll be seated. [*Sit.*] Ah! few gentlemen now-a-days know how to value the ineffectual[3] qualities in a woman! few think how a little knowledge becomes a gentlewoman! Men have no sense now but for the worthless flower of beauty!

ABSOLUTE.   It is but too true, indeed, Ma'am. Yet I fear our ladies should share the blame—they think our admiration of *beauty* so great, that *knowledge* in *them* would be superfluous. Thus, like garden-trees, they seldom show fruit till time has robbed them of the more specious blossom. Few, like Mrs. Malaprop and the orange-tree, are rich in both at once!

MRS. MALAPROP.   Sir—you overpower me with good-breeding. [*Aside.*] He is the very pineapple[4] of politeness!——You are not ignorant, Captain, that this giddy girl has somehow contrived to fix her affections on a beggarly, strolling, eaves-dropping Ensign, whom none of us have seen, and nobody knows anything of.

ABSOLUTE.   Oh, I have heard the silly affair before. I'm not at all prejudiced against her on *that* account.

MRS. MALAPROP.   You are very good, and very considerate, Captain. I am sure I have done everything in my power since I exploded[5] the affair! Long ago I laid my positive conjunctions[6] on her never to think on the fellow again; I have since laid Sir Anthony's preposition[7] before her; but I'm sorry to say, she seems resolved to decline every particle[8] that I enjoin her.

ABSOLUTE.   It must be very distressing, indeed, Ma'am.

MRS. MALAPROP.   Oh! it gives me the hydrostatics[9] to such a degree! I thought she had persisted[10] from corresponding with him; but behold this very day I have interceded[11] another letter from the fellow! I believe I have it in my pocket.

ABSOLUTE [*aside*].   Oh the devil! my last note.

MRS. MALAPROP.   Aye, here it is.

ABSOLUTE [*aside*].   Aye, my note, indeed! Oh the little traitress Lucy!

MRS. MALAPROP.   There; perhaps you may know the writing. [*Gives him the letter.*]

ABSOLUTE.   I think I have seen the hand before—yes, I certainly must have seen this hand before——

MRS. MALAPROP.   Nay, but read it, Captain.

ABSOLUTE [*reads*].   *"My soul's idol, my adored Lydia!"*——Very tender, indeed!

MRS. MALAPROP.   Tender! aye, and profane, too, o' my conscience!

ABSOLUTE.   *"I am excessively alarmed at the intelligence you send me, the more so as my new rival"*——

MRS. MALAPROP.   That's *you,* Sir.

---

3. Intellectual.
4. Pinnacle.
5. Exposed.
6. Injunctions.
7. Proposition.
8. Article.
9. Hysterics.
10. Desisted.
11. Intercepted.

ABSOLUTE. *"Has universally the character of being an accomplished gentleman, and a man of honour."* ——Well, that's handsome enough.

MRS. MALAPROP. Oh, the fellow had some design in writing so.

ABSOLUTE. That he had, I'll answer for him, Ma'am.

MRS. MALAPROP. But go on, Sir—you'll see presently.

ABSOLUTE. *"As for the old weather-beaten she-dragon who guards you"* ——Who can he mean by that?

MRS. MALAPROP. Me! Sir—*me!*—he means *me!* There—what do you think now? But go on a little further.

ABSOLUTE. Impudent scoundrel!—*"it shall go hard but I will elude her vigilance, as I am told that the same ridiculous vanity which makes her dress up her coarse features, and deck her dull chat with hard words which she don't understand"* ——

MRS. MALAPROP. There, Sir! an attack upon my language! What do you think of that?—an aspersion upon my parts of speech! Was ever such a brute! Sure if I reprehend[12] anything in this world, it is the use of my oracular[13] tongue, and a nice derangement of epitaphs![14]

ABSOLUTE. He deserves to be hanged and quartered! Let me see— *"same ridiculous vanity"* ——

MRS. MALAPROP. You need not read it again, Sir.

ABSOLUTE. I beg pardon, Ma'am—*"does also lay her open to the grossest deceptions from flattery and pretended admiration"*—an impudent coxcomb!—*"so that I have a scheme to see you shortly with the old harridan's consent, and even to make her a go-between in our interviews."*—Was ever such assurance!

MRS. MALAPROP. Did you ever hear anything like it? He'll elude my vigilance, will he? Yes, yes! ha! ha! He's very likely to enter these doors! We'll try who can plot best!

ABSOLUTE. So we will, Ma'am—so we will. Ha! ha! ha! A conceited puppy, ha! ha! ha! Well, but Mrs. Malaprop, as the girl seems so infatuated by this fellow, suppose you were to wink at her corresponding with him for a little time—let her even plot an elopement with him—then do you connive at her escape—while *I*, just in the nick, will have the fellow laid by the heels, and fairly contrive to carry her off in his stead.

MRS. MALAPROP. I am delighted with the scheme; never was anything better perpetrated!

ABSOLUTE. But, pray, could not I see the lady for a few minutes now? I should like to try her temper a little.

MRS. MALAPROP. Why, I don't know—I doubt she is not prepared for a visit of this kind. There is a decorum in these matters.

ABSOLUTE. O Lord! she won't mind *me*—only tell her Beverley——

MRS. MALAPROP. Sir!——

ABSOLUTE [*aside*]. Gently, good tongue.

MRS. MALAPROP. What did you say of Beverley?

ABSOLUTE. Oh, I was going to propose that you should tell her, by way of

12. Comprehend.
13. Vernacular.
14. Arrangement of epithets.

jest, that it was Beverley who was below—she'd come down fast enough then—ha! ha! ha!

MRS. MALAPROP. 'Twould be a trick she well deserves. Besides, you know the fellow tells her he'll get my consent to see her—ha! ha! Let him if he can, I say again. [*Calling.*] Lydia, come down here!——He'll make me a *go-between in their interviews!*—ha! ha! ha!—Come down, I say, Lydia!—I don't wonder at your laughing, ha! ha! ha!—his impudence is truly ridiculous.

ABSOLUTE. 'Tis very ridiculous, upon my soul, Ma'am, ha! ha! ha!

MRS. MALAPROP. The little hussy won't hear. Well, I'll go and tell her at once who it is. She shall know that Captain Absolute is come to wait on her. And I'll make her behave as becomes a young woman.

ABSOLUTE. As you please, Ma'am.

MRS. MALAPROP. For the present, Captain, your servant. Ah! you've not done laughing yet, I see—*elude my vigilance!*—yes, yes, ha! ha! ha! [*Exit.*]

ABSOLUTE. Ha! ha! ha! one would think now that I might throw off all disguise at once, and seize my prize with security—but such is Lydia's caprice that to undeceive were probably to lose her. I'll see whether she knows me. [*Walks aside, and seems engaged in looking at the pictures. Enter* LYDIA.]

LYDIA. What a scene am I now to go through! Surely nothing can be more dreadful than to be obliged to listen to the loathsome addresses of a stranger to one's heart. I have heard of girls persecuted as I am, who have appealed in behalf of their favoured lover to the generosity of his rival: suppose I were to try it. There stands the hated rival—an officer, too!—but oh, how unlike my Beverley! I wonder he don't begin. Truly he seems a very negligent wooer! Quite at his ease, upon my word! I'll speak first. [*Aloud.*] Mr. Absolute.

ABSOLUTE. Madam. [*Turns around.*]

LYDIA. O heavens! Beverley!

ABSOLUTE. Hush!—hush, my life! Softly! Be not surprised.

LYDIA. I am so astonished! and so terrified! and so overjoyed! For heaven's sake! how came you here?

ABSOLUTE. Briefly—I have deceived your aunt. I was informed that my new rival was to visit here this evening, and contriving to have him kept away, have passed myself on *her* for Captain Absolute.

LYDIA. Oh, charming! And she really takes you for young Absolute?

ABSOLUTE. Oh, she's convinced of it.

LYDIA. Ha! ha! ha! I can't forbear laughing to think how her sagacity is overreached!

ABSOLUTE. But we trifle with our precious moments. Such another opportunity may not occur. Then let me now conjure my kind, my condescending angel, to fix the time when I may rescue her from undeserved persecution, and with a licensed warmth plead for my reward.

LYDIA. Will you then, Beverley, consent to forfeit that portion of my paltry wealth? that burden on the wings of love?

ABSOLUTE. Oh, come to me—rich only thus—in loveliness. Bring no portion to me but thy love—'twill be generous in you, Lydia—for well you know, it is the only dower your poor Beverley can repay.

LYDIA. How persuasive are his words! How charming will poverty be with him!

ABSOLUTE. Ah! my soul, what a life will we then live! Love shall be our idol and support! We will worship him with a monastic strictness; abjuring all worldly toys, to center every thought and action there. Proud of calamity, we will enjoy the wreck of wealth; while the surrounding gloom of adversity shall make the flame of our pure love show doubly bright. By heavens! I would fling all goods of fortune from me with a prodigal hand to enjoy the scene where I might clasp my Lydia to my bosom, and say, the world affords no smile to me—but here [*embracing her*].——[*Aside.*] If she holds out now the devil is in it!

LYDIA [*aside*]. Now could I fly with him to the Antipodes![15] but my persecution is not yet come to a crisis.

[*Enter* MRS. MALAPROP, *listening.*]

MRS. MALAPROP [*aside*]. I am impatient to know how the little hussy deports herself.

ABSOLUTE. So pensive, Lydia!—is then your warmth abated?

MRS. MALAPROP [*aside*]. *Warmth abated!* So! she has been in a passion, I suppose.

LYDIA. No—nor ever can while I have life.

MRS. MALAPROP [*aside*]. An ill-tempered little devil! She'll be *in a passion all her life*—will she?

LYDIA. Think not the idle threats of my ridiculous aunt can ever have any weight with me.

MRS. MALAPROP [*aside*]. Very dutiful, upon my word!

LYDIA. Let her choice be Captain Absolute, but Beverley is mine.

MRS. MALAPROP [*aside*]. I am astonished at her assurance!—to his face—this is to his face!

ABSOLUTE. Thus then let me enforce my suit [*kneeling*].

MRS. MALAPROP [*aside*]. Aye—poor young man! down on his knees entreating her pity! I can contain no longer.—[*Aloud.*] Why, thou vixen! I have overheard you.

ABSOLUTE [*aside*]. Oh, confound her vigilance!

MRS. MALAPROP. Captain Absolute—I know not how to apologize for her shocking rudeness.

ABSOLUTE [*aside*]. So—all's safe, I find.—[*Aloud.*] I have hopes, Madam, that time will bring the young lady——

MRS. MALAPROP. Oh, there's nothing to be hoped for from her! She's as headstrong as an allegory[15] on the banks of Nile.

LYDIA. Nay, Madam, what do you charge me with now?

MRS. MALAPROP. Why, thou unblushing rebel—didn't you tell this gentleman to his face that you loved another better?—didn't you say you never would be his?

LYDIA. No, Madam—I did not.

MRS. MALAPROP. Good heavens! what assurance! Lydia, Lydia, you ought to know that lying don't become a young woman! Didn't you boast that Beverley—that stroller Beverley—possessed your heart? tell me that, I say.

LYDIA. 'Tis true, Ma'am, and none but Beverley——

---

15. Ends of the earth.
16. Alligator.

MRS. MALAPROP.   Hold—hold, Assurance! you shall not be so rude.

ABSOLUTE.   Nay, pray Mrs. Malaprop, don't stop the young lady's speech: she's very welcome to talk thus—it does not hurt *me* in the least, I assure you.

MRS. MALAPROP.   You are *too* good, Captain—*too* amiably patient—but come with me, Miss. Let us see you again soon, Captain. Remember what we have fixed.

ABSOLUTE.   I shall, Ma'am.

MRS. MALAPROP.   Come, take a graceful leave of the gentleman.

LYDIA.   May every blessing wait on my Beverley, my loved Bev——

MRS. MALAPROP.   Hussy! I'll choke the word in your throat!—come along—come along.

[*Exeunt severally,* ABSOLUTE *kissing his hand to* LYDIA—MRS. MALA-PROP *stopping her from speaking.*]

Scene IV.   [ACRES' *lodgings*]

[ACRES *and* DAVID, ACRES *as just dressed.*]

ACRES.   Indeed, David—do you think I become it so?

DAVID.   You are quite another creature, believe me, master, by the Mass! an' we've any luck we shall see the Devon monkeyrony in all the print-shops in Bath![1]

ACRES.   Dress *does* make a difference, David.

DAVID.   'Tis all in all,[2] I think. Difference! why, an' you were to go now to Clod-Hall, I am certain the old lady wouldn't know you: Master Butler wouldn't believe his own eyes, and Mrs. Pickle would cry, "Lard presarve me!"—our dairy-maid would come giggling to the door, and I warrant Dolly Tester, your Honour's favorite, would blush like my waistcoat. Oons! I'll hold a gallon, there a'n't a dog in the house but would bark, and I question whether *Phillis* would wag a hair of her tail!

ACRES.   Aye, David, there's nothing like polishing.

DAVID.   So I says of your Honour's boots; but the boy never heeds me!

ACRES.   But, David, has Mr. De-la-Grace been here? I must rub up my balancing, and chasing, and boring.[3]

DAVID.   I'll call again, Sir.

ACRES.   Do—and see if there are any letters for me at the post office.

DAVID.   I will. By the Mass, I can't help looking at your head! If I hadn't been by at the cooking, I wish I may die if I should have known the dish again myself!   [*Exit.*]

[ACRES *comes forward, practising a dancing step.*]

ACRES.   Sink, slide—coupee! Confound the first inventors of cotillions!

---

1. *an' we've . . . Bath,* i.e., if we have any luck, we will see pictures of the Devonshire dandy (Acres) in all the printshops of Bath. *Monkeyrony* is a corruption of *macaroni,* a slang term for a dandy.
2. Everything.
3. Anglicized corruptions of French dancing terms.

say I—they are as bad as algebra to us country gentlemen. I can walk a minuet easy enough when I'm forced! and I have been accounted a good stick in a country-dance. Odds jigs and tabours! I never valued your cross-over to couple —figure in—right and left—and I'd foot it with e'er a captain in the county! But these outlandish heathen allemandes and cotillions are quite beyond me! I shall never prosper at 'em, that's sure. Mine are true-born English legs—they don't understand their curst French lingo! their *pas* this, and *pas* that, and *pas* t'other! Damn me! my feet don't like to be called paws! No, 'tis certain I have most anti-Gallican toes!

[*Enter* SERVANT.]

SERVANT. Here is Sir Lucius O'Trigger to wait on you, Sir.
ACRES. Show him in.

[*Enter* SIR LUCIUS.]

SIR LUCIUS. Mr. Acres, I am delighted to embrace you.
ACRES. My dear Sir Lucius, I kiss your hands.
SIR LUCIUS. Pray, my friend, what has brought you so suddenly to Bath?
ACRES. Faith! I have followed Cupid's Jack-a-Lantern,[4] and find myself in a quagmire at last. In short, I have been very ill-used, Sir Lucius. I don't choose to mention names, but look on me as on a very ill-used gentleman.
SIR LUCIUS. Pray, what is the case? I ask no names.
ACRES. Mark me, Sir Lucius, I fall as deep as need be in love with a young lady—her friends take my part—I follow her to Bath—send word of my arrival, and receive answer that the lady is to be otherwise disposed of. This, Sir Lucius, I call being ill-used.
SIR LUCIUS. Very ill, upon my conscience. Pray, can you divine the cause of it?
ACRES. Why, there's the matter: she has another lover, one Beverley, who, I am told, is now in Bath. Odds slanders and lies! he must be at the bottom of it.
SIR LUCIUS. A rival in the case, is there? And you think he has supplanted you unfairly?
ACRES. Unfairly!—to be sure he has. He never could have done it fairly.
SIR LUCIUS. Then sure you know what is to be done!
ACRES. Not I, upon my soul!
SIR LUCIUS. We wear no swords here, but you understand me.
ACRES. What! fight him?
SIR LUCIUS. Aye, to be sure: what can I mean else?
ACRES. But he has given me no provocation.
SIR LUCIUS. Now, I think he has given you the greatest provocation in the world. Can a man commit a more heinous offense against another than to fall in love with the same woman? Oh, by my soul, it is the most unpardonable breach of friendship!

---

4. I.e., the elusive light of love.

ACRES.   Breach of friendship! Aye, aye; but I have no acquaintance with this man. I never saw him in my life.

SIR LUCIUS.   That's no argument at all—he has the less right then to take such a liberty.

ACRES.   'Gad, that's true. I grow full of anger, Sir Lucius! I fire apace! Odds hilts and blades! I find a man may have a deal of valour in him and not know it! But couldn't I contrive to have a little right of my side?

SIR LUCIUS.   What the devil signifies *right* when your *honour* is concerned? Do you think Achilles, or my little Alexander the Great ever inquired where the right lay? No, by my soul, they drew their broadswords, and left the lazy sons of peace to settle the justice of it.

ACRES.   Your words are a grenadier's march to my heart! I believe courage must be catching! I certainly do feel a kind of valour rising, as it were—a kind of courage, as I may say. Odds flints, pans, and triggers! I'll challenge him directly.

SIR LUCIUS.   Ah, my little friend! if we had Blunderbuss-Hall here—I could show you a range of ancestry, in the O'Trigger line, that would furnish the New Room, every one of whom had killed his man! For though the mansion-house and dirty acres have slipped through my fingers, I thank heaven our honour, and the family-pictures, are as fresh as ever.

ACRES.   O Sir Lucius! I have had ancestors too! every man of 'em colonel or captain in the militia! Odds balls and barrels! say no more—I'm braced for it. The thunder of your words has soured the milk of human kindness in my breast! Zounds! as the man in the play says, "I could do such deeds!"

SIR LUCIUS.   Come, come, there must be no passion at all in the case— these things should always be done civilly.

ACRES.   I must be in a passion, Sir Lucius—I must be in a rage. Dear Sir Lucius, let me be in a rage, if you love me. Come, here's pen and paper. [*Sits down to write.*] I would the ink were red! Indite, I say, indite! How shall I begin? Odds bullets and blades! I'll write a good bold hand, however.

SIR LUCIUS.   Pray compose yourself.

ACRES.   Come now, shall I begin with an oath? Do, Sir Lucius, let me begin with a damme.

SIR LUCIUS.   Pho! pho! do the thing decently and like a Christian. Begin now—*"Sir"*——

ACRES.   That's too civil by half.

SIR LUCIUS.   *"To prevent the confusion that might arise"*——

ACRES.   Well——

SIR LUCIUS.   *"From our both addressing the same lady"*——

ACRES.   Aye—there's the reason—*"same lady"*—Well——

SIR LUCIUS.   *"I shall expect the honour of your company"*——

ACRES.   Zounds! I'm not asking him to dinner.

SIR LUCIUS.   Pray be easy.

ACRES.   Well then—*"honour of your company"*——

SIR LUCIUS.   Pray be easy.

ACRES.   Well then—*"honour of your company"*——

SIR LUCIUS.   *"To settle our pretensions"*——

ACRES.   Well——

SIR LUCIUS. Let me see—aye, King's-Mead-Fields[5] will do—*"In King's-Mead-Fields."*

ACRES. So that's done.——Well, I'll fold it up presently; my own crest—a hand and dagger shall be the seal.

SIR LUCIUS. You see now, this little explanation will put a stop at once to all confusion or misunderstanding that might arise between you.

ACRES. Aye, we fight to prevent any misunderstanding.

SIR LUCIUS. Now, I'll leave you to fix your own time. Take my advice, and you'll decide it this evening if you can; then let the worst come of it, 'twill be off your mind to-morrow.

ACRES. Very true.

SIR LUCIUS. So I shall see nothing more of you, unless it be by letter, till the evening. I would do myself the honour to carry your message; but, to tell you a secret, I believe I shall have just such another affair on my own hands. There is a gay captain here who put a jest on me lately at the expense of my country, and I only want to fall in with the gentleman to call him out.

ACRES. By my valour, I should like to see you fight first! Odd's life! I should like to see you kill him, if it was only to get a little lesson.

SIR LUCIUS. I shall be very proud of instructing you. Well for the present—but remember now, when you meet your antagonist, do everything in a mild and agreeable manner. Let your courage be as keen, but at the same time as polished, as your sword. *[Exeunt severally.]*

ACT IV.

Scene I. [ACRES' *lodgings*]

[ACRES *and* DAVID.]

DAVID. Then, by the Mass, Sir! I would do no such thing—ne'er a Sir Lucius O'Trigger in the kingdom should make me fight, when I wa'n't so minded. Oons! What will the old lady say when she hears o't!

ACRES. Ah! David, if you had heard Sir Lucius! Odds sparks and flames! he would have roused your valour.

DAVID. Not he, indeed. I hates such bloodthirsty cormorants.[1] Look'ee, master, if you'd wanted a bout at boxing, quarterstaff, or shortstaff, I should never be the man to bid you cry off: but for your curst sharps and snaps,[2] I never knew any good come of 'em.

ACRES. But my honour, David, my honour! I must be very careful of my honour.

DAVID. Aye, by the Mass! and I would be very careful of it; and I think in return my *honour* couldn't do less than to be very careful of *me*.

---

5. Since dueling and even the wearing of swords were prohibited in Bath, it was necessary to schedule the duel in a spot outside of town.

1. I.e., vultures.
2. Swords and pistols.

ACRES.   Odds blades! David, no gentleman will ever risk the loss of his honour!

DAVID.   I say then, it would be but civil in *honour* never to risk the loss of a *gentleman*. Look'ee, master, this *honour* seems to me to be a marvellous false friend; aye, truly, a very courtier-like servant. Put the case, I was a gentleman (which, thank God, no one can say of me); well—my honour makes me quarrel with another gentleman of my acquaintance. So—we fight. (Pleasant enough that.) Boh!—I kill him (the more's my luck). Now, pray who gets the profit of it? Why, my *honour*. But put the case that he kills me!—by the Mass! I go to the worms, and my honour whips over to my enemy!

ACRES.   No, David—in that case—odds crowns and laurels!—your honour follows you to the grave.

DAVID.   Now, that's just the place where I could make a shift to do without it.

ACRES.   Zounds, David, you're a coward! It doesn't become any valour to listen to you. What, shall I disgrace my ancestors? Think of that, David— think what it would be to disgrace my ancestors!

DAVID.   Under favour, the surest way of not disgracing them is to keep as long as you can out of their company. Look'ee now, master, to go to them in such haste—with an ounce of lead in your brains—I should think might as well be let alone. Our ancestors are very good kind of folks; but they are the last people I should choose to have a visiting acquaintance with.

ACRES.   But David, now, you don't think there is such very, very, *very* great danger, hey? Odd's life! people often fight without any mischief done!

DAVID.   By the Mass, I think 'tis ten to one against you! Oons! here to meet some lion-headed fellow, I warrant, with his damn'd double-barrelled swords, and cut-and-thrust pistols! Lord bless us! it makes me tremble to think o't. Those be such desperate bloody-minded weapons! Well, I never could abide 'em! from a child I never could fancy 'em! I suppose there a'n't so merciless a beast in the world as your loaded pistol!

ACRES.   Zounds! I *won't* be afraid! Odds fire and fury! you sha'n't make me afraid! Here is the challenge, and I have sent for my dear friend Jack Absolute to carry it for me.

DAVID.   Aye, i' the name of mischief, let *him* be the messenger. For my part, I wouldn't lend a hand to it for the best horse in your stable. By the Mass! it don't look like another letter! It is, as I may say, a designing and malicious-looking letter! and I warrant smells of gunpowder, like a soldier's pouch! Oons! I wouldn't swear it mayn't go off!

ACRES.   Out, you poltroon! You ha'n't the valour of a grasshopper.

DAVID.   Well, I say no more—'twill be sad news, to be sure, at Clod-Hall!—but I ha' done. How Phillis will howl when she hears of it! Aye, poor bitch, she little thinks what shooting her master's going after! And I warrant old Crop, who has carried your Honour, field and road, these ten years, will curse the hour he was born [*whimpering*].

ACRES.   It won't do, David—I am determined to fight—so get along, you coward, while I'm in the mind.

[*Enter* SERVANT.]

SERVANT. Captain Absolute, Sir.

ACRES. Oh! show him up.   [*Exit* SERVANT.]

DAVID. Well, heaven send we be all alive this time to-morrow.

ACRES. What's that! Don't provoke me, David!

DAVID. Good-bye, master [*whimpering*].

ACRES. Get along, you cowardly, dastardly, croaking raven.

[*Exit* DAVID.]

[*Enter* ABSOLUTE.]

ABSOLUTE. What's the matter, Bob?

ACRES. A vile, sheep-hearted blockhead! If I hadn't the valour of St. George and the dragon to boot——

ABSOLUTE. But what did you want with me, Bob?

ACRES. Oh! There——[*Gives him the challenge.*]

ABSOLUTE. "*To Ensign Beverley.*" [*Aside.*] So—what's going on now? [*Aloud.*] Well, what's this?

ACRES. A challenge!

ABSOLUTE. Indeed! Why, you won't fight him, will you, Bob?

ACRES. 'Egad, but I will, Jack. Sir Lucius has wrought me to it. He has left me full of rage, and I'll fight this evening, that so much good passion mayn't be wasted.

ABSOLUTE. But what have I to do with this?

ACRES. Why, as I think you know something of this fellow, I want you to find him out for me, and give him this mortal defiance.

ABSOLUTE. Well, give it to me, and trust me he gets it.

ACRES. Thank you, my dear friend, my dear Jack; but it is giving you a great deal of trouble.

ABSOLUTE. Not in the least—I beg you won't mention it. No trouble in the world, I assure you.

ACRES. You are very kind. What it is to have a friend! You couldn't be my second—could you, Jack?

ABSOLUTE. Why no, Bob—not in *this* affair. It would not be quite so proper.

ACRES. Well then, I must get my friend Sir Lucius. I shall have your good wishes, however, Jack.

ABSOLUTE. Whenever he meets you, believe me.

[*Enter* SERVANT.]

SERVANT. Sir Anthony Absolute is below, inquiring for the Captain.

ABSOLUTE. I'll come instantly. Well, my little hero, success attend you [*going*].

ACRES. Stay—stay, Jack. If Beverley should ask you what kind of a man your friend Acres is, do tell him I am a devil of a fellow—will you, Jack?

ABSOLUTE. To be sure I shall. I'll say you are a determined dog—hey, Bob?

ACRES. Aye, do, do—and if that frightens him, 'egad, perhaps he mayn't come. So tell him I generally kill a man a week—will you, Jack?

ABSOLUTE. I will, I will; I'll say you are called in the country *"Fighting Bob!"*

ACRES. Right, right—'tis all to prevent mischief; for I don't want to take his life if I clear my honour.

ABSOLUTE. No!—that's very kind of you.

ACRES. Why, you don't wish me to kill him—do you, Jack?

ABSOLUTE. No, upon my soul, I do not. But a devil of a fellow, hey? [*Going.*]

ACRES. True, true—but stay—stay, Jack. You may add that you never saw me in such a rage before—a most devouring rage!

ABSOLUTE. I will, I will.

ACRES. Remember, Jack—a determined dog!

ABSOLUTE. Aye, aye, *"Fighting Bob!"*   [*Exeunt severally.*]

Scene II. [MRS. MALAPROP'S *lodgings.*]

[MRS. MALAPROP *and* LYDIA.]

MRS. MALAPROP. Why, thou perverse one! tell me what you can object to him? Isn't he a handsome man? tell me that. A genteel man? a pretty figure of a man?

LYDIA [*aside*]. She little thinks whom she is praising!—[*Aloud.*] So is Beverley, Ma'am.

MRS. MALAPROP. No caparisons,[1] Miss, if you please! Caparisons don't become a young woman. No! Captain Absolute is indeed a fine gentleman!

LYDIA [*aside*]. Aye, the Captain Absolute *you* have seen.

MRS. MALAPROP. Then he's *so* well bred; so full of alacrity, and adulation! and has *so much* to say for himself—in such good language, too! His physiognomy[2] so grammatical! Then his presence is so noble! I protest, when I saw him, I thought of what Hamlet says in the play:[3] "Hesperian curls!—the front of *Job* himself! An eye, like *March,* to threaten at command—a station, like Harry Mercury, new"—something about kissing on a hill—however, the similitude struck me directly.

LYDIA [*aside*]. How enraged she'll be presently when she discovers her mistake!

[*Enter* SERVANT.]

SERVANT. Sir Anthony and Captain Absolute are below, Ma'am.

MRS. MALAPROP. Show them up here. [*Exit* SERVANT.] Now, Lydia, I insist on your behaving as becomes a young woman. Show your good breeding at least, though you have forgot your duty.

---

1. Comparisons.

2. Phraseology.

3. One of a number of misquoted lines and phrases from Shakespeare and from other writers scattered throughout the play. The original from *Hamlet* reads: "Hyperion's curls; the front of Jove himself; / An eye like Mars, to threaten and command; / A station like the herald Mercury / New-lighted on a heaven-kissing hill."

LYDIA. Madam, I have told you my resolution; I shall not only give him no encouragement, but I won't even speak to, or look at him.

[*Flings herself into a chair with her face from the door. Enter* SIR ANTHONY *and* ABSOLUTE.]

SIR ANTHONY. Here we are, Mrs. Malaprop, come to mitigate the frowns of unrelenting beauty—and difficulty enough I had to bring this fellow. I don't know what's the matter; but if I hadn't held him by force, he'd have given me the slip.

MRS. MALAPROP. You have infinite trouble, Sir Anthony, in the affair. I am ashamed for the cause!—[*Aside to her.*] Lydia, Lydia, rise, I beseech you!—pay your respects!

SIR ANTHONY. I hope, Madam, that Miss Languish has reflected on the worth of this gentleman, and the regard due to her aunt's choice, and *my* alliance.—[*Aside to him.*] Now, Jack, speak to her!

ABSOLUTE [*aside*]. What the devil shall I do!—[*Aloud.*] You see, Sir, she won't even look at me whilst you are here. I knew she wouldn't! I told you so. Let me entreat you, Sir, to leave us together! [ABSOLUTE *seems to expostulate with his father.*]

LYDIA [*aside*]. I wonder I ha'n't heard my aunt exclaim yet! Sure she can't have looked at him! Perhaps their regimentals are alike, and she is something[4] blind.

SIR ANTHONY. I say, Sir, I won't stir a foot yet!

MRS. MALAPROP. I am sorry to say, Sir Anthony, that my affluence[5] over my niece is very small.—[*Aside to her.*] Turn round, Lydia; I blush for you!

SIR ANTHONY. May I not flatter myself that Miss Languish will assign what cause of dislike she can have to my son! Why don't you begin, Jack?—[*Aside to him.*] Speak, you puppy—speak!

MRS. MALAPROP. It is impossible, Sir Anthony, she can have any. She will not *say* she has.—[*Aside to her.*] Answer, hussy! why don't you answer?

SIR ANTHONY. Then, Madam, I trust that a childish and hasty predilection will be no bar to Jack's happiness.—[*Aside to him.*] Zounds! Sirrah! why don't you speak?

LYDIA [*aside*]. I think my lover seems as little inclined to conversation as myself. How strangely blind my aunt must be!

ABSOLUTE. Hem! hem!—Madam—hem!—[ABSOLUTE *attempts to speak, then returns to* SIR ANTHONY.]—Faith! Sir, I am so confounded! and so—so—confused! I told you I should be so, Sir, I knew it. The —the—tremor of my passion entirely takes away my presence of mind.

SIR ANTHONY. But it don't take away your voice, fool, does it? Go up, and speak to her directly!

[ABSOLUTE *makes signs to* MRS. MALAPROP *to leave them together.*]

---

4. Somewhat.
5. Influence.

MRS. MALAPROP.   Sir Anthony, shall we leave them together?—[*Aside to her.*] Ah! you stubborn little vixen!

SIR ANTHONY.   Not yet, Ma'am, not yet!—[*Aside to him.*] What the devil are you at? Unlock your jaws, Sirrah, or——

[ABSOLUTE *draws near* LYDIA.]

ABSOLUTE [*aside*].   Now heaven send she may be too sullen to look round! I must disguise my voice.—[*Speaks in a low hoarse tone.*] Will not Miss Languish lend an ear to the mild accents of true love? Will not——

SIR ANTHONY.   What the devil ails the fellow? Why don't you speak out?—not stand croaking like a frog in a quinsy!

ABSOLUTE.   The—the—excess of my awe, and my—my—my modesty quite choke me!

SIR ANTHONY.   Ah! your *modesty* again! I'll tell you what, Jack, if you don't speak out directly, and glibly, too, I shall be in such a rage! Mrs. Malaprop, I wish the lady would favour us with something more than a side-front.

[MRS. MALAPROP *seems to chide* LYDIA.]

ABSOLUTE.   So! All will out I see! [*Goes up to* LYDIA, *speaks softly.*] Be not surprised, my Lydia; suppress all surprise at present.

LYDIA [*aside*].   Heavens! 'tis Beverley's voice! Sure he can't have imposed on Sir Anthony, too!—[*Looks round by degrees, then starts up.*] Is this possible—my Beverley!—how can this be?—my Beverley?

ABSOLUTE [*aside*].   Ah! 'tis all over.

SIR ANTHONY.   Beverley!—the devil!—Beverley! What can the girl mean? This is my son, Jack Absolute!

MRS. MALAPROP.   For shame, hussy! for shame! your head runs so on that fellow that you have him always in your eyes! Beg Captain Absolute's pardon directly.

LYDIA.   I see no Captain Absolute, but my loved Beverley!

SIR ANTHONY.   Zounds! the girl's mad!—her brain's turned by reading!

MRS. MALAPROP.   O' my conscience, I believe so! What do you mean by Beverley, hussy? You saw Captain Absolute before to-day; there he is—your husband that shall be.

LYDIA.   With all my soul, Ma'am. When I refuse my Beverley——

SIR ANTHONY.   Oh! she's as mad as Bedlam! Or has this fellow been playing us a rogue's trick! Come here, Sirrah!—who the devil are you?

ABSOLUTE.   Faith, Sir, I am not quite clear myself, but I'll endeavour to recollect.

SIR ANTHONY.   Are you my son, or not? Answer for your mother, you dog, if you won't for me.

MRS. MALAPROP.   Aye, Sir, who are you? Oh mercy! I begin to suspect!——

ABSOLUTE [*aside*].   Ye Powers of Impudence befriend me!—[*Aloud.*] Sir Anthony, most assuredly I am your wife's son; and that I sincerely believe myself to be *yours* also, I hope my duty has always shown.——Mrs. Malaprop, I am your most respectful admirer—and shall be proud to add *affectionate nephew.* ——I need not tell my Lydia, that she sees her faithful Beverley, who, knowing the singular generosity of her temper, assumed that name, and a station which has proved a test of the most disinterested love, which he now hopes to enjoy in a more elevated character.

LYDIA [*sullenly*]. So!—there will be no elopement after all!

SIR ANTHONY. Upon my soul, Jack, thou art a very impudent fellow! to do you justice, I think I never saw a piece of more consummate assurance!

ABSOLUTE. Oh you flatter me, Sir—you compliment—'tis my *modesty* you know, Sir—my *modesty* that has stood in my way.

SIR ANTHONY. Well, I am glad you are not the dull, insensible varlet you pretended to be, however! I'm glad you have made a fool of your father, you dog—I am. So this was your *penitence,* your *duty,* and *obedience!* I thought it was damned sudden! You *never heard their names before,* not you! *What!* The *Languishes of Worcestershire,* hey?—*if you could please me in the affair, 'twas all you desired!*—Ah! you dissembling villain! What!—[*pointing to* LYDIA] *she squints, don't she!—a little red-haired girl!*—hey? Why, you hypocritical young rascal! I wonder you a'n't ashamed to hold up your head!

ABSOLUTE. 'Tis with difficulty, Sir. I *am* confused—very much confused, as you must perceive.

MRS. MALAPROP. O lud! Sir Anthony!—a new light breaks in upon me! Hey! how! what! Captain, did *you* write the letters then? What!—am I to thank you for the elegant compilation[6] of *"an old weatherbeaten she-dragon"*—hey? O mercy! was it *you* that reflected on my parts of speech?

ABSOLUTE. Dear Sir! my modesty will be overpowered at last, if you don't assist me. I shall certainly not be able to stand it!

SIR ANTHONY. Come, come, Mrs. Malaprop, we must forget and forgive. Odd's life! matters have taken so clever a turn.all of a sudden, that I could find in my heart to be so good-humoured! and so gallant!—hey! Mrs. Malaprop!

MRS. MALAPROP. Well, Sir Anthony, since *you* desire it, we will not anticipate the past; so mind, young people: our retrospection[7] will now be all to the future.

SIR ANTHONY. Come, we must leave them together; Mrs. Malaprop, they long to fly into each other's arms. I warrant!—[*Aside.*] Jack—isn't the cheek as I said, hey?—and the eye, you rogue!—and the lip—hey? Come, Mrs. Malaprop, we'll not disturb their tenderness—theirs is the time of life for happiness!—[*Sings.*] *"Youth's the season made for joy"*—hey! Odd's life! I'm in such spirits, I don't know what I couldn't do! Permit me, Ma'am—[*Gives his hand to* MRS. MALAPROP. *Sings.*] Tol-de-rol!—'gad, I should like a little fooling myself. Tol-de-rol! de-rol! [*Exit singing, and handing* MRS. MALAPROP. LYDIA *sits sullenly in her chair.*]

ABSOLUTE [*aside*]. So much thought bodes me no good.——[*Aloud.*] So grave, Lydia!

LYDIA. Sir!

ABSOLUTE [*aside*]. So!—egad! I thought as much! That damned monosyllable has froze me!——[*Aloud.*] What, Lydia, now that we are as happy in our friends' consent, as in our mutual vows——

---

6. Appellation—name.

7. She reverses the meanings of *anticipate* and *retrospection.*

LYDIA [*peevishly*].   *Friends' consent,* indeed!

ABSOLUTE.   Come, come, we must lay aside some of our romance—a little *wealth* and *comfort* may be endured after all. And for your fortune, the lawyers shall make such settlements as——

LYDIA.   *Lawyers!* I *hate* lawyers!

ABSOLUTE.   Nay then, we will not wait for their lingering forms but instantly procure the license, and——

LYDIA.   The *license!* I *hate* license!

ABSOLUTE.   O my love! be not so unkind! Thus let me intreat— [*kneeling*].

LYDIA.   Pshaw! what signifies kneeling when you know I *must* have you?

ABSOLUTE [*rising*].   Nay, Madam, there shall be no constraint upon your inclinations, I promise you. If I have lost your heart, I resign the rest.—[*Aside.*] 'Gad, I must try what a little *spirit* will do.

LYDIA [*rising*].   Then, Sir, let me tell you, the interest you had there was acquired by a mean, unmanly imposition, and deserves the punishment of fraud. What, you have been treating *me* like a child!—humouring my romance! and laughing, I suppose, at your success!

ABSOLUTE.   You wrong me, Lydia, you wrong me. Only hear——

LYDIA.   So, while *I* fondly imagined we were deceiving my relations, and flattered myself that I should outwit and incense them all—behold! my hopes are to be crushed at once, by my aunt's consent and approbation!—and *I* am myself the only dupe at last! [*Walking about in heat.*] But here, Sir, here is the picture—Beverley's picture! [*taking a miniature from her bosom*]—which I have worn, night and day, in spite of threats and entreaties! There, Sir [*flings it to him*]—and be assured I throw the original from my heart as easily.

ABSOLUTE.   Nay, nay, Ma'am, we will not differ as to that. Here [*taking out a picture*], here is Miss Lydia Languish. What a difference! Aye, *there* is the heavenly assenting smile that first gave soul and spirit to my hopes!—those are the lips which sealed a vow, as yet scarce dry in Cupid's calendar!—and *there,* the half resentful blush that *would* have checked the ardour of my thanks. Well, all that's past—all over indeed! There, Madam, in beauty, that copy is not equal to you, but in my mind its merit over the original, in being still the same, in such—that—I cannot find in my heart to part with it. [*Puts it up again.*]

LYDIA [*softening*].   'Tis *your own* doing, Sir. I—I—I suppose you are perfectly satisfied.

ABSOLUTE.   Ah, most certainly. Sure now this is much better than being in love! Ha! ha! ha!—there's some spirit in *this!* What signifies breaking some scores of solemn promises, half an hundred vows, under one's hand, with the marks of a dozen or two angels to witness!—all that's of no consequence, you know. To be sure, people will say that Miss didn't know her own mind—but never mind that: or perhaps they may be ill-natured enough to hint that the gentleman grew tired of the lady and forsook her—but don't let that fret you.

LYDIA.   There's no bearing his insolence. [*Bursts into tears.*]

[*Enter* MRS. MALAPROP *and* SIR ANTHONY.]

MRS. MALAPROP [*entering*].   Come, we must interrupt your billing and cooing a while.

LYDIA.   This is worse than your treachery and deceit, you base ingrate! [*Sobbing.*]

SIR ANTHONY.   What the devil's the matter now! Zounds! Mrs. Malaprop, this is the *oddest billing* and *cooing* I ever heard! But what the deuce is the meaning of it? I'm quite astonished!

ABSOLUTE.   Ask the lady, Sir.

MRS. MALAPROP.   Oh mercy! I'm quite analysed,[8] for my part! Why, Lydia, what is the reason of this?

LYDIA.   Ask the *gentleman,* Ma'am.

SIR ANTHONY.   Zounds! I shall be in a frenzy!——Why, Jack, you are not come out to be anyone else, are you?

MRS. MALAPROP.   Aye, Sir, there's no more *trick,* is there? You are not like Cerberus,[9] *three* gentlemen at once, are you?

ABSOLUTE.   You'll not let me speak. I say the lady can account for this much better than I can.

LYDIA.   Ma'am, you once commanded me never to think of Beverley again. There is the man—I now obey you:—for, from this moment, I renounce him forever.   [*Exit.*]

MRS. MALAPROP.   Oh mercy! and miracles! what a turn here is! Why, sure, Captain, you haven't behaved disrespectfully to my niece?

SIR ANTHONY.   Ha! ha! ha!—ha! ha! ha!—now I see it—ha! ha! ha!—now I see it—you have been too lively, Jack.

ABSOLUTE.   Nay, Sir, upon my word——

SIR ANTHONY.   Come, no lying, Jack—I'm sure *'twas* so.

MRS. MALAPROP.   O lud! Sir Anthony! Oh fie, Captain!

ABSOLUTE.   Upon my soul, Ma'am——

SIR ANTHONY.   Come, no excuses, Jack; why, your father, you rogue, was so before you: the blood of the Absolutes was always impatient. Ha! ha! ha! poor little Lydia!—why, you've frightened her, you dog, you have.

ABSOLUTE.   By all that's good, Sir——

SIR ANTHONY.   Zounds! say no more, I tell you. Mrs. Malaprop shall make your peace.——You must make his peace, Mrs. Malaprop; you must tell her 'tis Jack's way—tell her 'tis all our ways—it runs in the blood of our family! Come, away, Jack—ha! ha! ha! Mrs. Malaprop—a young villain! [*Pushes him out.*]

MRS. MALAPROP.   Oh, Sir Anthony! Oh fie, Captain! [*Exeunt severally.*]

Scene III.   [*The North Parade.*]

[*Enter* SIR LUCIUS O'TRIGGER.]

SIR LUCIUS.   I wonder where this Captain Absolute hides himself. Upon my conscience! these officers are always in one's way in love-affairs. I remember I might have married Lady Dorothy Carmine, if it had not been for a little rogue of a major, who ran away with her before she could get a sight of me! And I wonder too what it is the ladies can see in them to be so fond of them—unless

---

8. Paralyzed.
9. In Greek mythology, the three-headed dog who guarded the entrance to Hades.

it be a touch of the old serpent in 'em, that makes the little creatures be caught, like vipers, with a bit of red cloth.——Hah!—isn't this the Captain coming?—faith it is! There is a probability of succeeding about that fellow that is mighty provoking! Who the devil is he talking to? [*Steps aside. Enter* CAPTAIN ABSOLUTE.]

ABSOLUTE.   To what fine purpose I have been plotting! A noble reward for all my schemes, upon my soul! A little gypsy! I did not think her romance could have made her so damnd absurd either. 'Sdeath, I never was in a worse humour in my life! I could cut my own throat, or any other person's, with the greatest pleasure in the world!

SIR LUCIUS.   Oh, faith! I'm in the luck of it—I never could have found him in a sweeter temper for my purpose—to be sure I'm just come in the nick! Now to enter into conversation with him, and so quarrel genteelly. [SIR LUCIUS *goes up to* ABSOLUTE.]—With regard to that matter, Captain, I must beg leave to differ in opinion with you.

ABSOLUTE.   Upon my word then, you must be a very subtle disputant, because, Sir, I happened just then to be giving no opinion at all.

SIR LUCIUS.   That's no reason. For give me leave to tell you, a man may *think* an untruth as well as *speak* one.

ABSOLUTE.   Very true, Sir, but if a man never utters his thoughts I should think they might stand a chance of escaping controversy.

SIR LUCIUS.   Then, Sir, you differ in opinion with me, which amounts to the same thing.

ABSOLUTE.   Hark'ee, Sir Lucius—if I had not before known you to be a gentleman, upon my soul, I should not have discovered it at this interview, for what you can drive at, unless you mean to quarrel with me, I cannot conceive!

SIR LUCIUS.   I humbly thank you, Sir, for the quickness of your apprehension. [*Bowing.*] You have named the very thing I would be at.

ABSOLUTE.   Very well, Sir—I shall certainly not balk your inclinations but I should be glad you would please to explain your motives.

SIR LUCIUS.   Pray, Sir, be easy: the quarrel is a very pretty quarrel as it stands—we should only spoil it by trying to explain it. However, your memory is very short or you could not have forgot an affront you passed on me within this week. So no more, but name your time and place.

ABSOLUTE.   Well, Sir, since you are so bent on it, the sooner the better; let it be this evening—here, by the Spring-Gardens. We shall scarcely be interrupted.

SIR LUCIUS.   Faith! that same interruption in affairs of this nature shows very great ill-breeding. I don't know what's the reason, but in England, if a thing of this kind gets wind, people make such a pother that a gentleman can never fight in peace and quietness. However, if it's the same to you, Captain, I should take it as a particular kindness if you'd let us meet in King's-Mead-Fields, as a little business will call me there about six o'clock, and I may dispatch both matters at once.

ABSOLUTE.   'Tis the same to me exactly. A little after six, then, we will discuss this matter more seriously.

SIR LUCIUS.   If you please, Sir, there will be very pretty small-sword light, though it won't do for a long shot. So that matter's settled! and my mind's at ease!

[*Exit.*]

[*Enter* FAULKLAND, *meeting* ABSOLUTE.]

ABSOLUTE. Well met. I was going to look for you. O Faulkland! all the dæmons of spite and disappointment have conspired against me! I'm so vexed that if I had not the prospect of a resource in being knocked o' the head by and by, I should scarce have spirits to tell you the cause.

FAULKLAND. What can you mean? Has Lydia changed her mind? I should have thought her duty and inclination would now have pointed to the same object.

ABSOLUTE. Aye, just as the eyes do of a person who squints: when her love-eye was fixed on me—t' other—her eye of duty, was finely obliqued:—but when duty bid her point that the same way—off t'other turned on a swivel, and secured its retreat with a frown!

FAULKLAND. But what's the resource you——

ABSOLUTE. Oh, to wind up the whole, a good-natured Irishman here has [*mimicking* SIR LUCIUS] begged leave to have the pleasure of cutting my throat, and I mean to indulge him—that's all.

FAULKLAND. Prithee, be serious.

ABSOLUTE. 'Tis fact, upon my soul. Sir Lucius O'Trigger—you know him by sight—for some affront, which I am sure I never intended, has obliged me to meet him this evening at six o'clock: 'tis on that account I wished to see you—you must go with me.

FAULKLAND. Nay, there must be some mistake, sure. Sir Lucius shall explain himself—and I dare say matters may be accommodated. But this evening, did you say? I wish it had been any other time.

ABSOLUTE. Why? there will be light enough. There will (as Sir Lucius says) "be very pretty small-sword light, though it won't do for a long shot." Confound his long shots!

FAULKLAND. But I am myself a good deal ruffled by a difference I have had with Julia. My vile tormenting temper has made me treat her so cruelly that I shall not be myself till we are reconciled.

ABSOLUTE. By heavens, Faulkland, you don't deserve her.

[*Enter* SERVANT, *gives* FAULKLAND *a letter.*]

FAULKLAND. O Jack! this is from Julia. I dread to open it. I fear it may be to take a last leave—perhaps to bid me return her letters and restore——Oh! how I suffer for my folly!

ABSOLUTE. Here—let me see. [*Takes the letter and opens it.*] Aye, a final sentence indeed!—'tis all over with you, faith!

FAULKLAND. Nay, Jack—don't keep me in suspense.

ABSOLUTE. Hear then.—"*As I am convinced that my dear* FAULKLAND'S *own reflections have already upbraided him for his last unkindness to me, I will not add a word on the subject. I wish to speak with you as soon as possible.—Yours ever and truly,* JULIA."—There's stubbornness and resentment for you! [*Gives him the letter.*] Why, man, you don't seem one whit happier at this.

FAULKLAND. Oh, yes, I am—but—but——

ABSOLUTE. Confound your *buts.* You never hear anything that would make another man bless himself, but you immediately damn it with a *but*.

FAULKLAND.   Now, Jack, as you are my friend, own honestly—don't you think there is something forward, something indelicate, in this haste to forgive? Women should never sue for reconciliation: that should always come from us. They should retain their coldness till *wooed* to kindness—and their *pardon*, like their *love*, should "not unsought be won."

ABSOLUTE.   I have not patience to listen to you—thou'rt incorrigible!—so say no more on the subject. I must go to settle a few matters. Let me see you before six—remember—at my lodgings. A poor industrious devil like me, who have toiled, and drudged, and plotted to gain my ends, and am at last disappointed by other people's folly, may in pity be allowed to swear and grumble a little; but a captious sceptic in love, a slave to fretfulness and whim, who has no difficulties but of his own creating, is a subject more fit for ridicule than compassion!   [*Exit.*]

FAULKLAND.   I feel his reproaches, yet I would not change this too exquisite nicety for the gross content with which *he* tramples on the thorns of love. His engaging me in this duel has started an idea in my head, which I will instantly pursue. I'll use it as the touchstone of Julia's sincerity and disinterestedness. If her love prove pure and sterling ore, my name will rest on it with honour!—and once I've stamped it there, I lay aside my doubts forever—; but if the dross of selfishness, the alloy of pride predominate, 'twill be best to leave her as a toy for some less cautious fool to sigh for.   [*Exit.*]

ACT V.

Scene I.   [JULIA'S *dressing-room.*]

[JULIA *alone.*]

JULIA.   How his message has alarmed me! What dreadful accident can he mean? why such charge to be alone? O Faulkland! how many unhappy moments, how many tears, have you cost me!

[*Enter* FAULKLAND.]

JULIA.   What means this?—why this caution, Faulkland?
FAULKLAND.   Alas! Julia, I am come to take a long farewell.
JULIA.   Heavens! what do you mean?
FAULKLAND.   You see before you a wretch whose life is forfeited. Nay, start not! the infirmity of my temper has drawn all this misery on me. I left you fretful and passionate—an untoward accident drew me into a quarrel—the event is that I must fly this kingdom instantly. O Julia, had I been so fortunate as to have called you mine entirely before this mischance had fallen on me, I should not so deeply dread my banishment!
JULIA.   My soul is oppressed with sorrow at the nature of your misfortune: had these adverse circumstances arisen from a less fatal cause, I should

have felt strong comfort in the thought that I could now chase from your bosom every doubt of the warm sincerity of my love. My heart has long known no other guardian. I now entrust my person to your honour—we will fly together. When safe from pursuit, my father's will may be fulfilled, and I receive a legal claim to be the partner of your sorrows, and tenderest comforter. Then on the bosom of your wedded Julia, you may lull your keen regret to slumbering; while virtuous love, with a cherub's hand, shall smooth the brow of upbraiding thought, and pluck the thorn from compunction.

FAULKLAND. O Julia! I am bankrupt in gratitude! But the time is so pressing, it calls on you for so hasty a resolution—would you not wish some hours to weigh the advantages you forego, and what little compensation poor Faulkland can make you beside his solitary love?

JULIA. I ask not a moment. No, Faulkland, I have loved you for yourself: and if I now, more than ever, prize the solemn engagement which so long has pledged us to each other, it is because it leaves no room for hard aspersions on my fame, and puts the seal of duty to an act of love——But let us not linger. Perhaps this delay——

FAULKLAND. 'Twill be better I should not venture out again till dark. Yet am I grieved to think what numberless distresses will press heavy on your gentle disposition!

JULIA. Perhaps your fortune may be forfeited by this unhappy act. I know not whether 'tis so, but sure that alone can never make us unhappy. The little I have will be sufficient to support us; and exile never should be splendid.

FAULKLAND. Aye, but in such an abject state of life, my wounded pride perhaps may increase the natural fretfulness of my temper, till I become a rude, morose companion, beyond your patience to endure. Perhaps the recollection of a deed my conscience cannot justify may haunt me in such gloomy and unsocial fits that I shall hate the tenderness that would relieve me, break from your arms, and quarrel with your fondness!

JULIA. If your thoughts should assume so unhappy a bent, you will the more want some mild and affectionate spirit to watch over and console you, one who, by bearing *your* infirmities with gentleness and resignation, may teach you *so* to bear the evils of your fortune.

FAULKLAND. Julia, I have proved you to the quick! and with this useless device I throw away all my doubts. How shall I plead to be forgiven this last unworthy effect of my restless, unsatisfied disposition?

JULIA. Has no such disaster happened as you related?

FAULKLAND. I am ashamed to own that it was all pretended; yet in pity, Julia, do not kill me with resenting a fault which never can be repeated, but sealing, this once, my pardon, let me to-morrow, in the face of heaven, receive my future guide and monitress, and expiate my past folly by years of tender adoration.

JULIA. Hold, Faulkland! That you are free from a crime which I before feared to name, heaven knows how sincerely I rejoice! These are tears of thankfulness for that! But that your cruel doubts should have urged you to an imposition that has wrung my heart, gives me now a pang more keen than I can express!

FAULKLAND. By heavens! Julia——

JULIA. Yet hear me. My father loved you, Faulkland! and you preserved the life that tender parent gave me; in his presence I pledged my hand—joyfully pledged it—where before I had given my heart. When, soon after, I lost that parent, it seemed to me that Providence had, in Faulkland, shown me whither to transfer without a pause my grateful duty, as well as my affection: hence I have been content to bear from you what pride and delicacy would have forbid me from another. I will not upbraid you by repeating how you have trifled with my sincerity.

FAULKLAND. I confess it all! yet hear——

JULIA. After such a year of trial, I might have flattered myself that I should not have been insulted with a new probation of my sincerity, as cruel as unnecessary! I now see it is not in your nature to be content or confident in love. With this conviction, I never will be yours. While I had hopes that my persevering attention and unreproaching kindness might in time reform your temper, I should have been happy to have gained a dearer influence over you; but I will not furnish you with a licensed power to keep alive an incorrigible fault, at the expense of one who never would contend with you.

FAULKLAND. Nay, but Julia, by my soul and honour, if after this——

JULIA. But one word more. As my faith has once been given to you, I never will barter it with another. I shall pray for your happiness with the truest sincerity; and the dearest blessing I can ask of heaven to send you will be to charm you from that unhappy temper which alone has prevented the performance of our solemn engagement. All I request of *you* is that you will yourself reflect upon this infirmity, and when you number up the many true delights it has deprived you of, let it not be your *least* regret that it lost you the love of one, who would have followed you in beggary through the world! [*Exit.*]

FAULKLAND. She's gone!—forever! There was an awful resolution in her manner, that riveted me to my place. O fool!—dolt!—barbarian! Curst as I am with more imperfections than my fellow-wretches, kind Fortune sent a heaven-gifted cherub to my aid, and, like a ruffian, I have driven her from my side! I must now haste to my appointment. Well, my mind is tuned for such a scene. I shall wish only to become a principal in it, and reverse the tale my cursed folly put me upon forging here. O love!—tormentor!—fiend! whose influence, like the moon's, acting on men of dull souls, makes idiots of them, but meeting subtler spirits, betrays their course, and urges sensibility to madness! [*Exit.*]

[*Enter* MAID *and* LYDIA.]

MAID. My mistress, Ma'am, I know, was here just now—perhaps she is only in the next room. [*Exit.*]

LYDIA. Heigh-ho! Though he has used me so, this fellow runs strangely in my head. I believe one lecture from my grave cousin will make me recall him.

[*Enter* JULIA.]

LYDIA. O Julia, I am come to you with such an appetite for consolation. —Lud! child, what's the matter with you? You have been crying! I'll be hanged if that Faulkland has not been tormenting you!

JULIA. You mistake the cause of my uneasiness. Something *has* flurried me a little. Nothing that you can guess at.—[*Aside.*] I would not accuse Faulkland to a sister!

LYDIA. Ah! whatever vexations you may have, I can assure you mine surpass them.——You know who Beverley proves to be?

JULIA. I will now own to you, Lydia, that Mr. Faulkland had before informed me of the whole affair. Had young Absolute been the person you took him for, I should not have accepted your confidence on the subject without a serious endeavour to counteract your caprice.

LYDIA. So, then, I see I have been deceived by everyone! But I don't care—I'll never have him.

JULIA. Nay, Lydia——

LYDIA. Why, is it not provoking? when I thought we were coming to the prettiest distress imaginable, to find myself made a mere Smithfield bargain[1] of at last! There had I projected one of the most sentimental elopements! so becoming a disguise! so amiable a ladder of ropes! Conscious moon—four horses—Scotch parson[2]—with such surprise to Mrs. Malaprop, and such paragraphs in the newspapers! Oh, I shall die with disappointment!

JULIA. I don't wonder at it!

LYDIA. Now—sad reverse!—what have I to expect, but, after a deal of flimsy preparation, with a bishop's license, and my aunt's blessing, to go simpering up to the altar; or perhaps be cried three times in a country-church, and have an unmannerly fat clerk ask the consent of every butcher in the parish to join John Absolute and Lydia Languish, Spinster! Oh, that I should live to hear myself called Spinster!

JULIA. Melancholy, indeed!

LYDIA. How mortifying to remember the dear delicious shifts I used to be put to, to gain half a minute's conversation with this fellow! How often have I stole forth in the coldest night in January, and found him in the garden, stuck like a dripping statue! There would he kneel to me in the snow, and sneeze and cough so pathetically! he shivering with cold, and I with apprehension! and while the freezing blast numbed our joints, how warmly would he press me to pity his flame, and glow with mutual ardour! Ah, Julia, that was something like being in love!

JULIA. If I were in spirits, Lydia, I should chide you only by laughing heartily at you: but it suits more the situation of my mind, at present, earnestly to entreat you not to let a man, who loves you with sincerity, suffer that unhappiness from your caprice, which I know too well caprice can inflict.

LYDIA. O lud! what has brought my aunt here?

[*Enter* MRS. MALAPROP, FAG, *and* DAVID.]

MRS. MALAPROP. So! so! here's fine work!—here's fine suicide, parricide, and simulation[3] going on in the fields! and Sir Anthony not to be found to prevent the antistrophe![4]

---

1. Article of commercial trade. Smithfield was a district of London known for its markets, particularly its meat market.
2. English couples frequently eloped to Scotland.
3. Homicide and dissimulation.
4. Catastrophe.

JULIA.   For heaven's sake, Madam, what's the meaning of this?

MRS. MALAPROP.   That gentleman can tell you—'twas he enveloped[5] the affair to me.

LYDIA [*to* FAG].   Do, Sir, will you inform us.

FAG.   Ma'am, I should hold myself very deficient in every requisite that forms the man of breeding if I delayed a moment to give all the information in my power to a lady so deeply interested in the affair as you are.

LYDIA.   But quick! quick, Sir!

FAG.   True, Ma'am, as you say, one should be quick in divulging matters of this nature; for should we be tedious, perhaps while we are flourishing on the subject, two or three lives may be lost!

LYDIA.   O patience! Do, Ma'am, for heaven's sake! tell us what is the matter!

MRS. MALAPROP.   Why, murder's the matter! slaughter's the matter! killing's the matter! But he can tell you the perpendiculars.[6]

LYDIA.   Then, prithee, Sir, be brief.

FAG.   Why then, Ma'am—as to murder, I cannot take upon me to say—and as to slaughter, or manslaughter, that will be as the jury finds it.

LYDIA.   But who, Sir—who are engaged in this?

FAG.   Faith, Ma'am, one is a young gentleman whom I should be very sorry anything was to happen to—a very pretty behaved gentleman! We have lived much together, and always on terms.

LYDIA.   But who is this? who! who! who!

FAG.   My master, Ma'am, my master—I speak of my master.

LYDIA.   Heavens! What, Captain Absolute!

MRS. MALAPROP.   Oh, to be sure, you are frightened now!

JULIA.   But who are with him, Sir?

FAG.   As to the rest, Ma'am, this gentleman can inform you better than I.

JULIA [*to* DAVID].   Do speak, friend.

DAVID.   Look'ee, my lady—by the Mass! there's mischief going on. Folks don't use to meet for amusement with fire-arms, fire-locks, fire-engines, fire-screens, fire-office, and the devil knows what other crackers[7] beside! This, my lady, I say, has an angry favour.

JULIA.   But who is there beside Captain Absolute, friend?

DAVID.   My poor master—under favour, for mentioning him first. You know me, my lady—I am David, and my master, of course, is, or *was*, Squire Acres. Then comes Squire Faulkland.

JULIA.   Do, Ma'am, let us instantly endeavour to prevent mischief.

MRS. MALAPROP.   Oh fie—it would be very inelegant in us: we should only participate[8] things.

DAVID.   Ah! do, Mrs. Aunt, save a few lives. They are desperately given, believe me. Above all, there is that bloodthirsty Philistine, Sir Lucius O'Trigger.

MRS. MALAPROP.   Sir Lucius O'Trigger! O mercy! have they drawn poor

---

5. Unfolded.
6. Particulars.
7. Explosives.
8. Precipitate.

little dear Sir Lucius into the scrape? Why, how you stand, girl! you have no more feeling than one of the Derbyshire putrefactions![9]

LYDIA.   What are we to do, Madam?

MRS. MALAPROP.   Why, fly with the utmost felicity,[10] to be sure, to prevent mischief. Here, friend—you can show us the place?

FAG.   If you please, Ma'am, I will conduct you.——David, do you look for Sir Anthony.   [*Exit* DAVID.]

MRS. MALAPROP.   Come, girls!—this gentleman will exhort us,[11]—— Come, Sir, you're our envoy—lead the way, and we'll precede.[12]

FAG.   Not a step before the ladies for the world!

MRS. MALAPROP.   You're sure you know the spot?

FAG.   I think I can find it, Ma'am; and one good thing is we shall hear the report of the pistols as we draw near, so we can't well miss them; never fear, Ma'am, never fear.   [*Exeunt, he talking.*]

Scene II.   [*South parade*]

[*Enter* ABSOLUTE, *putting his sword under his greatcoat.*]

ABSOLUTE.   A sword seen in the streets of Bath would raise as great an alarm as a mad dog. How provoking this is in Faulkland! never punctual! I shall be obliged to go without him at last. Oh, the devil! here's Sir Anthony! How shall I escape him? [*Muffles up his face, and takes a circle to go off. Enter* SIR ANTHONY.]

SIR ANTHONY.   How one may be deceived at a little distance! Only that I see he don't know me, I could have sworn that was Jack!——Hey! 'Gad's life! it is. Why, Jack!—what are you afraid of, hey!—Sure I'm right.—Why, Jack! —Jack Absolute! [*Goes up to him.*]

ABSOLUTE.   Really, Sir, you have the advantage of me: I don't remember ever to have had the honour. My name is Saunderson, at your service.

SIR ANTHONY.   Sir, I beg your pardon—I took you—hey!—why, zounds! it is—stay—[*Looks up to his face.*] So, so—your humble servant, Mr. Saunderson! Why, you scoundrel, what tricks are you after now?

ABSOLUTE.   Oh! a joke, Sir, a joke! I came here on purpose to look for you, Sir.

SIR ANTHONY.   You did! Well, I am glad you were so lucky. But what are you muffled up so for? What's this for?—hey?

ABSOLUTE.   'Tis cool, Sir; isn't it?—rather chilly, somehow. But I shall be late—I have a particular engagement.

SIR ANTHONY.   Stay. Why, I thought you were looking for me? Pray, Jack, where is't you are going?

ABSOLUTE.   Going, Sir!

SIR ANTHONY.   Aye—where are you going?

ABSOLUTE.   Where am I going?

SIR ANTHONY.   You unmannerly puppy!

---

9. Petrifications—rock formations in Derbyshire.
10. Facility.
11. Escort.
12. Proceed.

ABSOLUTE. I was going, Sir, to—to—to—to Lydia—Sir, to Lydia, to make matters up if I could; and I was looking for you, Sir, to—to——

SIR ANTHONY. To go with you, I suppose. Well, come along.

ABSOLUTE. Oh! zounds! no, Sir, not for the world! I wished to meet with you, Sir—to—to—to——You find it cool, I'm sure, Sir—you'd better not stay out.

SIR ANTHONY. Cool!—not at all. Well Jack—and what will you say to Lydia?

ABSOLUTE. O, Sir, beg her pardon, humour her, promise and vow. But I detain you, Sir—consider the cold air on your gout.

SIR ANTHONY. Oh, not at all!—not at all! I'm in no hurry. Ah! Jack, you youngsters, when once you are wounded here—[*putting his hand to* ABSOLUTE's *breast*] Hey! what the deuce have you got here?

ABSOLUTE. Nothing, Sir—nothing.

SIR ANTHONY. What's this? here's something damned hard!

ABSOLUTE. Oh, trinkets, Sir! trinkets—a bauble for Lydia!

SIR ANTHONY. Nay, let me see your taste. [*Pulls his coat open, the sword falls.*] Trinkets!—a bauble for Lydia! Zounds! Sirrah, you are not going to cut her throat, are you?

ABSOLUTE. Ha! ha! ha! I thought it would divert you, Sir; though I didn't mean to tell you till afterwards.

SIR ANTHONY. You didn't? Yes, this is a very diverting trinket, truly!

ABSOLUTE. Sir, I'll explain to you. You know, Sir, Lydia is romantic, dev'lish romantic, and very absurd of course. Now, Sir, I intend, if she refuses to forgive me, to unsheathe this sword and swear I'll fall upon its point, and expire at her feet!

SIR ANTHONY. Fall upon a fiddle-stick's end! Why, I suppose it is the very thing that would please her. Get along, you fool.

ABSOLUTE. Well, Sir, you shall hear of my success—you shall hear. "O Lydia!—forgive me, or this pointed steel"—says I.

SIR ANTHONY. "O, booby! stab away and welcome"—says she. Get along!—and damn your trinkets! [*Exit* ABSOLUTE.]

[*Enter* DAVID, *running.*]

DAVID. Stop him! Stop him! Murder! Thief! Fire! Stop fire! Stop fire! O! Sir Anthony—call! call! bid 'em stop! Murder! Fire!

SIR ANTHONY. Fire! Murder! Where?

DAVID. Oons! he's out of sight! and I'm out of breath, for my part! O, Sir Anthony, why didn't you stop him? why didn't you stop him?

SIR ANTHONY. Zounds! the fellow's mad. Stop whom? Stop Jack?

DAVID. Aye, the Captain, Sir! there's murder and slaughter——

SIR ANTHONY. Murder!

DAVID. Aye, please you, Sir Anthony, there's all kinds of murder, all sorts of slaughter to be seen in the fields: there's fighting going on, Sir—bloody sword-and-gun fighting!

SIR ANTHONY. Who are going to fight, dunce?

DAVID. Everybody that I know of, Sir Anthony—everybody is going to fight; my poor master, Sir Lucius O'Trigger, your son, the Captain——

SIR ANTHONY. Oh, the dog! I see his tricks.——Do you know the place?

DAVID. King's-Mead-Fields.

SIR ANTHONY. You know the way?

DAVID. Not an inch; but I'll call the mayor—aldermen—constables—church-wardens—and beadles—we can't be too many to part them.

SIR ANTHONY. Come along—give me your shoulder! we'll get assistance as we go. The lying villain! Well, I shall be in such a frenzy! So—this was the history of his trinkets! I'll bauble him! [*Exeunt.*]

Scene III. [*King's-Mead-Fields*]

[SIR LUCIUS *and* ACRES, *with pistols.*]

ACRES. By my valour! then, Sir Lucius, forty yards is a good distance. Odds levels and aims! I say it is a good distance.

SIR LUCIUS. Is it for muskets or small-field-pieces? Upon my conscience, Mr. Acres, you must leave those things to me. Stay now—I'll show you. [*Measures paces along the stage.*] There now, that is a very pretty distance—a pretty gentleman's distance.

ACRES. Zounds! we might as well fight in a sentry-box! I tell you, Sir Lucius, the farther he is off, the cooler I shall take my aim.

SIR LUCIUS. Faith! then I suppose you would aim at him best of all if he was out of sight!

ACRES. No, Sir Lucius, but I should think forty, or eight and thirty yards——

SIR LUCIUS. Pho! pho! nonsense! Three or four feet between the mouths of your pistols is as good as a mile.

ACRES. Odds bullets, no! By my valour! there is no merit in killing him so near: do, my dear Sir Lucius, let me bring him down at a long shot—a long shot, Sir Lucius, if you love me!

SIR LUCIUS. Well—the gentleman's friend and I must settle that. But tell me now, Mr. Acres, in case of an accident, is there any little will or commission I could execute for you?

ACRES. I am much obliged to you, Sir Lucius, but I don't understand——

SIR LUCIUS. Why, you may think, there's no being shot at without a little risk, and if an unlucky bullet should carry a *quietus*[1] with it—I say it will be no time then to be bothering you about family matters.

ACRES. A *quietus*!

SIR LUCIUS. For instance, now—if that should be the case—would you choose to be pickled and sent home? or would it be the same to you to lie here in the Abbey? I'm told there is very snug lying in the Abbey.

ACRES. Pickled! Snug lying in the Abbey! Odds tremors! Sir Lucius, don't talk so!

SIR LUCIUS. I suppose, Mr. Acres, you never were engaged in an affair of this kind before?

ACRES. No, Sir Lucius, never before.

SIR LUCIUS. Ah! that's a pity! there's nothing like being used to a thing. Pray now, how would you receive the gentleman's shot?

ACRES. Odds files! I've practised that. There, Sir Lucius—there [*Puts

---

1. Release from life.

himself in an attitude.]—a side-front, hey? Odd! I'll make myself small enough: I'll stand edge-ways.

SIR LUCIUS.   Now—you're quite out, for if you stand so when I take my aim——[*levelling at him.*]

ACRES.   Zounds! Sir Lucius—are you sure it is not cocked?

SIR LUCIUS.   Never fear.

ACRES.   But—but—you don't know—it may go off of its own head!

SIR LUCIUS.   Pho! be easy. Well, now if I hit you in the body, my bullet has a double chance, for if it misses a vital part on your right side, 'twill be very hard if it don't succeed on the left!

ACRES.   A vital part!

SIR LUCIUS.   But, there—fix yourself so. [*Placing him.*] Let him see the broad side of your full front—there—now a ball or two may pass clean through your body, and never do any harm at all.

ACRES.   Clean through me! a ball or two clean through me!

SIR LUCIUS.   Aye, may they; and it is much the genteelest attitude into the bargain.

ACRES.   Look'ee! Sir Lucius—I'd just as lieve be shot in an awkward posture as a genteel one—so, by my valour! I will stand edge-ways.

SIR LUCIUS [*looking at his watch*].   Sure they don't mean to disappoint us. Hah? No, faith—I think I see them coming.

ACRES.   Hey! what!—coming!——

SIR LUCIUS.   Aye. Who are those yonder getting over the stile?

ACRES.   There are two of them indeed! Well—let them come—hey, Sir Lucius? We—we—we—we—won't run.

SIR LUCIUS.   Run!

ACRES.   No—I say—we *won't* run, by my valour!

SIR LUCIUS.   What the devil's the matter with you?

ACRES.   Nothing—nothing—my dear friend—my dear Sir Lucius—but —I—I—I don't feel quite so bold, somehow—as I did.

SIR LUCIUS.   Oh fie! consider your honour.

ACRES.   Aye—true—my honour. Do, Sir Lucius, edge in a word or two every now and then about my honour.

SIR LUCIUS [*looking*].   Well, here they're coming.

ACRES.   Sir Lucius—if I wa'n't with you, I should almost think I was afraid. If my valour should leave me! Valour will come and go.

SIR LUCIUS.   Then, pray, keep it fast while you have it.

ACRES.   Sir Lucius—I doubt[2] it is going—yes—my valour is certainly going! it is sneaking off! I feel it oozing out as it were at the palms of my hands!

SIR LUCIUS.   Your honour—your honour. Here they are.

ACRES.   Oh mercy! now that I were safe at Clod-Hall! or could be shot before I was aware!

[*Enter* FAULKLAND *and* ABSOLUTE.]

SIR LUCIUS.   Gentlemen, your most obedient—hah!—what—Captain Absolute! So, I suppose, Sir, you are come here, just like myself—to do a kind

---

2. Fear.

office, first for your friend—then to proceed to business on your own account.

ACRES. What, Jack! my dear Jack! my dear friend!

ABSOLUTE. Hark'ee, Bob, Beverley's at hand.

SIR LUCIUS. Well, Mr. Acres, I don't blame your saluting the gentleman civilly. So, Mr. Beverley [*to* FAULKLAND], if you'll choose your weapons, the Captain and I will measure the ground.

FAULKLAND. *My* weapons, Sir!

ACRES. Odd's life! Sir Lucius, I'm not going to fight Mr. Faulkland; these are my particular friends.

SIR LUCIUS. What, Sir, did not you come here to fight Mr. Acres?

FAULKLAND. Not I, upon my word, Sir.

SIR LUCIUS. Well, now, that's mighty provoking! But I hope, Mr. Faulkland, as there are three of us come on purpose for the game, you won't be so cantankerous as to spoil the party by sitting out.

ABSOLUTE. Oh pray, Faulkland, fight to oblige Sir Lucius.

FAULKLAND. Nay, if Mr. Acres is so bent on the matter—

ACRES. No, no, Mr. Faulkland—I'll bear my disappointment like a Christian. Look'ee, Sir Lucius, there's no occasion at all for me to fight; and if it is the same to you, I'd as lieve let it alone.

SIR LUCIUS. Observe me, Mr. Acres—I must not be trifled with. You have certainly challenged somebody, and you came here to fight him. Now, if that gentleman is willing to represent him, I can't see, for my soul, why it isn't just the same thing.

ACRES. Why no, Sir Lucius—I tell you, 'tis one Beverley I've challenged—a fellow you see, that dare not show his face! If *he* were here, I'd make him give up his pretensions directly!

ABSOLUTE. Hold, Bob—let me set you right. There is no such man as Beverley in the case. The person who assumed that name is before you; and as his pretensions are the same in both characters, he is ready to support them in whatever way you please.

SIR LUCIUS. Well, this is lucky! Now you have an opportunity——

ACRES. What, quarrel with my dear friend Jack Absolute? Not if he were fifty Beverleys! Zounds! Sir Lucius, you would not have me be so unnatural.

SIR LUCIUS. Upon my conscience, Mr. Acres, your valour has *oozed* away with a vengeance!

ACRES. Not in the least! Odds backs and abettors! I'll be your second with all my heart, and if you should get a *quietus*, you may command me entirely. I'll get you *snug lying* in the *Abbey here;* or *pickle* you, and send you over to Blunderbuss-Hall, or anything of the kind, with the greatest pleasure.

SIR LUCIUS. Pho! pho! you are little better than a coward.

ACRES. Mind, gentlemen, he calls me a *coward;* coward was the word, by my valour!

SIR LUCIUS. Well, Sir?

ACRES. Look'ee, Sir Lucius, 'tisn't that I mind the word coward—*coward* may be said in joke. But if you had called me a *poltroon,*[3] odds daggers and balls!——

---

3. Coward.

SIR LUCIUS.   Well, Sir?

ACRES.   ——I should have thought you a very ill-bred man.

SIR LUCIUS.   Pho! you are beneath my notice.

ABSOLUTE.   Nay, Sir Lucius, you can't have a better second than my friend Acres. He is a most *determined dog,* called in the country, *Fighting Bob.* He generally *kills a man a week;* don't you, Bob?

ACRES.   Aye—at home!

SIR LUCIUS.   Well then, Captain, 'tis we must begin. So come out, my little counsellor [*draws his sword*], and ask the gentleman whether he will resign the lady without forcing you to proceed against him.

ABSOLUTE.   Come on then, Sir [*draws*]; since you won't let it be an amicable suit, here's my reply.

[*Enter* SIR ANTHONY, DAVID, *and the Women.*]

DAVID.   Knock 'em all down, sweet Sir Anthony; knock down my master in particular, and bind his hands over to their good behaviour!

SIR ANTHONY.   Put up, Jack, put up, or I shall be in a frenzy. How came you in a duel, Sir?

ABSOLUTE.   Faith, Sir, that gentleman can tell you better than I; 'twas he called on me, and you know, Sir, I serve his Majesty.

SIR ANTHONY.   Here's a pretty fellow! I catch him going to cut a man's throat, and he tells me he serves his Majesty! Zounds! Sirrah, then how durst you draw the King's sword against one of his subjects?

ABSOLUTE.   Sir, I tell you! That gentleman called me out, without explaining his reasons.

SIR ANTHONY.   Gad! Sir, how came you to call my son out, without explaining your reasons?

SIR LUCIUS.   Your son, Sir, insulted me in a manner which my honour could not brook.

SIR ANTHONY.   Zounds! Jack, how durst you insult the gentleman in a manner which his honour could not brook?

MRS. MALAPROP.   Come, come, let's have no honour before ladies. Captain Absolute, come here. How could you intimidate us so? Here's Lydia has been terrified to death for you.

ABSOLUTE.   For fear I should be killed, or escape, Ma'am?

MRS. MALAPROP.   Nay, no delusions[4] to the past. Lydia is convinced; speak, child.

SIR LUCIUS.   With your leave, Ma'am, I must put in a word here. I believe I could interpret the young lady's silence. Now mark——

LYDIA.   What is it you mean, Sir?

SIR LUCIUS.   Come, come, Delia, we must be serious now—this is no time for trifling.

LYDIA.   'Tis true, Sir; and your reproof bids me offer this gentleman my hand, and solicit the return of his affections.

ABSOLUTE.   O! my little angel, say you so? Sir Lucius, I perceive there must be some mistake here. With regard to the affront which you affirm I have

---

4. Allusions.

given you, I can only say that it could not have been intentional. And as you must be convinced that I should not fear to support a real injury, you shall now see that I am not ashamed to atone for an inadvertency. I ask your pardon. But for this lady, while honoured with her approbation, I will support my claim against any man whatever.

SIR ANTHONY.   Well said, Jack! and I'll stand by you, my boy.

ACRES.   Mind, I give up all my claim—I make no pretensions to anything in the world—and if I can't get a wife without fighting for her, by my valour! I'll live a bachelor.

SIR LUCIUS.   Captain, give me your hand—an affront handsomely acknowledged becomes an obligation—and as for the lady, if she chooses to deny her own handwriting here——[*Takes out letters.*]

MRS. MALAPROP.   Oh, he will dissolve[5] my mystery! Sir Lucius, perhaps there's some mistake—perhaps, I can illuminate[6]——

SIR LUCIUS.   Pray, old gentlewoman, don't interfere where you have no business. Miss Languish, are you my Delia, or not?

LYDIA.   Indeed, Sir Lucius, I am not. [LYDIA *and* ABSOLUTE *walk aside.*]

MRS. MALAPROP.   Sir Lucius O'Trigger, ungrateful as you are, I own the soft impeachment—pardon my blushes, I am Delia.

SIR LUCIUS.   You Delia!—pho! pho! be easy.

MRS. MALAPROP.   Why, thou barbarous Vandyke![7]—those letters are mine. When you are more sensible of my benignity, perhaps I may be brought to encourage your addresses.

SIR LUCIUS.   Mrs. Malaprop, I am extremely sensible of your condescension; and whether you or Lucy have put this trick upon me, I am equally beholden to you. And to show you I'm not ungrateful——Captain Absolute! since you have taken that lady from me, I'll give you my Delia into the bargain.

ABSOLUTE.   I am much obliged to you, Sir Lucius; but here's our friend, Fighting Bob, unprovided for.

SIR LUCIUS.   Hah! little Valour—here, will you make your fortune?

ACRES.   Odds wrinkles! No. But give me your hand, Sir Lucius; forget and forgive; but if ever I give you a chance of *pickling* me again, say Bob Acres is a dunce, that's all.

SIR ANTHONY.   Come, Mrs. Malaprop, don't be cast down—you are in your bloom yet.

MRS. MALAPROP.   O Sir Anthony!—men are all barbarians——

[*All retire but* JULIA *and* FAULKLAND.]

JULIA [*aside*].   He seems dejected and unhappy—not sullen. There was some foundation, however, for the tale he told me. O woman! how true should be your judgment, when your resolution is so weak!

FAULKLAND.   Julia! how can I sue for what I so little deserve? I dare not presume—yet Hope is the child of Penitence.

JULIA.   Oh! Faulkland, you have not been more faulty in your unkind

---

5. Resolve.
6. Elucidate.
7. Vandal.

treatment of me than I am now in wanting inclination to resent it. As my heart honestly bids me place my weakness to the account of love, I should be ungenerous not to admit the same plea for yours.

FAULKLAND.   Now I shall be blest indeed!

[SIR ANTHONY *comes forward.*]

SIR ANTHONY.   What's going on here? So you have been quarrelling too, I warrant. Come, Julia, I never interfered before; but let me have a hand in the matter at last. All the faults I have ever seen in my friend Faulkland seemed to proceed from what he calls the *delicacy* and *warmth* of his affection for you. There, marry him directly, Julia; you'll find he'll mend surprisingly!

[*The rest come forward.*]

SIR LUCIUS.   Come now, I hope there is no dissatisfied person but what is content; for as I have been disappointed myself, it will be very hard if I have not the satisfaction of seeing other people succeed better——

ACRES.   You are right, Sir Lucius. So, Jack, I wish you joy—Mr. Faulkland the same.——Ladies,—come now, to show you I'm neither vexed nor angry, odds tabours and pipes! I'll order the fiddles in half an hour to the New Rooms, and I insist on your all meeting me there.

SIR ANTHONY.   Gad! Sir, I like your spirit; and at night we single lads will drink a health to the young couples, and a husband to Mrs. Malaprop.

FAULKLAND.   Our partners are stolen from us, Jack—I hope to be congratulated by each other—*yours* for having checked in time the errors of an ill-directed imagination, which might have betrayed an innocent heart; and *mine,* for having, by her gentleness and candour, reformed the unhappy temper of one who by it made wretched whom he loved most, and tortured the heart he ought to have adored.

ABSOLUTE.   Well, Faulkland, we have both tasted the bitters, as well as the sweets, of love—with this difference only, that *you* always prepared the bitter cup for yourself, while *I*——

LYDIA.   Was always obliged to *me* for it, hey! Mr. Modesty?——But come, no more of that: our happiness is now as unalloyed as general.

JULIA.   Then let us study to preserve it so; and while Hope pictures to us a flattering scene of future Bliss, let us deny its pencil those colours which are too bright to be lasting. When Hearts deserving Happiness would unite their fortunes, Virtue would crown them with an unfading garland of modest, hurtless flowers; but ill-judging Passion will force the gaudier Rose into the wreath, whose thorn offends them, when its leaves are dropt!   [*Exeunt.*]

Questions for Study

1. The plot of *The Rivals* develops a series of humorous deceptions. Describe the essential ones, pointing out which characters are deceiving whom. Why does Sheridan let the audience in on the secret of what is happening at the beginning of the play?

2. The ending of this comedy works out a happy conclusion for two couples. What type of ending does the play indicate for Bob Acres, Sir Lucius O'Trigger, and Mrs. Malaprop? In what sense may we say that each gets what he or she deserves? Explain.

3. Intrigues, unexpected turns of events, surprise appearances, disguises, and letters are used in developing the plot of *The Rivals*. Point out at least two instances in which each of these devices is employed.

4. Contrasts between characters are used to work out the actions of the play. How do the contrasts between Captain Absolute and Faulkand, between Lydia and Julia, show the character of each?

5. What function do Fag, David, and Lucy have in the play? Are they developed as characters who are interesting in themselves? How does Sheridan characterize each of them?

6. What essential character flaws would you attribute to Captain Absolute and Faulk-land? Is the "punishment" of each given according to the cause? What character flaws would you attribute to Lydia and Julia? Has Sheridan devised a pattern of flaws-punishments-rewards in the play? Explain.

7. Compare the attitudes of Lydia and Julia, and then those of Captain Absolute and Faulkland, on harmony and quarreling, health and sickness, togetherness and separation. Why won't Captain Absolute elope with Lydia when she thinks he is Ensign Beverley? Why won't she elope when she discovers that the man her aunt wants her to marry is the man she loves?

8. Why does Sir Lucius provoke Bob Acres into dueling? Is Sir Lucius an evil man?

9. What various assumptions about courtship are suggested in the play? Which ones are acted upon? Which ones, in your opinion, does the play seem to recommend?

10. What are the arguments against female education proposed by *The Rivals?* How does the play itself refute them?

11. Describe the argument in Act IV, scene I, between David and Bob Acres. In what ways does it remind you of the discussion of reputation between Iago and Cassio in *Othello* (Act II, scene III)? How does this argument relate to the theme of *The Rivals?*

12. Identify specific subjects and fashions Sheridan satirizes in *The Rivals*.

Chapter 2
Realism

When a piece of literature is described as realistic, what is usually meant is that the author has avoided romantic or idealistic conventions and has carefully reported the object or the situation depicted. In literature, **realism** is the attempt to create an accurate impression of reality as it appears to an objective consciousness. Here, however, realism will be used in an even more specific sense—to refer to a style, or a manner of writing, which arose during the nineteenth century in Europe and America and which stressed direct experience, a faithful reporting of facts and details, and a view of the world within a general humanistic framework.[1] It first appeared in the novels of such writers as Honoré de Balzac (1799–1850), Gustave Flaubert (1821–1880), and Leo Tolstoy (1828–1910).

During the last quarter of the nineteenth century, realism gradually became the predominant style in drama. Its purpose was **representation,** the attempt to approximate real life on the stage. The realists rebelled against the stilted and artificial conventions of the stage by drawing their material from real life as they experienced it. Influenced by the advance of modern science, they wanted to dramatize the problems of everyday life as directly and as objectively as possible. Their only written sources were to be historical, social, and political documents. Careful observation and research were to be their only inspiration.

Because realism has dominated the stage for the last one hundred years, we have come to take many of its innovations for granted. To recognize how radical these innovations were, we need to consider briefly the kind of theater realism replaced. The drama against which the

---

1. In contrast, **literary naturalism** was an adaptation to the arts of a deterministic philosophy developed during roughly the same period. It is characterized by an intensification of realistic methods of composition, usually through an emphasis on scientific materials, techniques, and theories.

realists reacted was highly conventional and unoriginal because playwrights wished to please a conservative, middle-class audience. As a result, the plays of the time were artificial and divorced from everyday life. The most popular forms were **sentimental comedy,** or comedy designed to elicit tears before the inevitable happy ending, and **melodrama,** or plays in which the completely virtuous battled the completely wicked until justice prevailed. When dramatists attempted to treat social problems, the result was usually an artificial concoction in which Victorian platitudes were exchanged over the tea table. In general, plot overpowered characterization and theme. The most influential kind of drama during the nineteenth century was the **well-made play,** in which the suspense generated by an intricate plot overcame all other theatrical considerations. The well-made play was structured according to a formula: exposition in Act I, complication in Act II, resolution in Act III.

The appearance of the prerealistic stage reflected the artificiality of the play itself. Sets were constructed entirely of painted canvas—even the doorknobs were painted on. Doors would shake with each entrance and exit. Since objects depicted on the painted canvas at the back were diminished in size to suggest distance, an actor venturing too far to the rear might find himself eye to eye with a second-story window. Consequently, the action took place at the front of the stage, the players declaiming their lines, often in verse. Asides and soliloquies were common. The performers were constantly aware of the spectators and, in effect, spoke to them. Dramatist, designers, and actors regarded the theater as a spectacle, as a conscious presentation made to an audience.

In order to suit the emerging realistic drama, new methods of production and acting had to be established. A new kind of theater set, the box set, was developed. The **box set** represents a room, three walls and a ceiling, which gives the audience the illusion that it is witnessing a real-life episode. **Properties** ("props") such as furniture, paintings, books, and utensils were intended to be used by the actors. Because they portrayed characters who were more true to life and therefore psychologically more complex, the performers were required to be more subtle and natural in their delivery. Instead of declaiming grand speeches to the audience, they spoke their lines to one another as if the fourth wall of the room were actually in place. If previous theater had been presentation, the new realistic plays became a representation of life.

The plays of Henrik Ibsen (1828–1906), often called the father of modern dramatic realism, are generally thought to be the first to require this kind of theatrical presentation. In place of the intricate plot, he focused the action upon climactic events and reduced all prior events to exposition. In place of purely virtuous or villainous stereotypes, he created recognizable, human characters, shaped by their heredities and social environments. In place of poetic speeches, soliloquies, and asides, he wrote dialog which approximated real-life conversation.

The plays of Ibsen which broke new ground involve discussion, both dispassionate and heated, of a central social problem. Like many later realistic dramas, most of his works are **problem plays,** or plays which hardheadedly expose and investigate actual problems facing society. In *The Pillars of Society* (1877), the whole social structure is indicted as Ibsen exposes the hypocrisy with which its most respected members mask their real nature. *The Doll's House* (1879) treats the place of women in the modern social order; and *An Enemy of the People* (1882) treats the struggle of a naive idealist to overcome the greed and complacency of a small town that refuses to act to clean up its polluted waters. By constantly questioning the complacent assumptions of society, Ibsen's drama was as unconventional in content as it was in form. In attempting to create drama out of contemporary materials, Ibsen found the pathos and the tragedy in everyday life.

Considered as objective social inquiries, Ibsen's plays come close to the conception of theater advocated by his French contemporary Émile Zola (1840–1903). In Zola's work, realism, a style of writing, and naturalism, a deterministic philosophy, momentarily merge. **Naturalism** is a late-nineteenth-century philosophy fostered by several popular scientific theories of the time. It was particularly influenced by Darwin's theory of evolution, or the human descent from the animal kingdom, and by Social Darwinism, or the application of theories such as "the survival of the fittest" to human society. Naturalism usually is deterministic— that is, it holds that human fate is determined solely by heredity and environment. It tends to be pessimistic in its assumption that human morality and idealism are inevitably overcome by biological and social conditions.

In a series of essays, Zola advocated a theater which analyzed human behavior clinically, taking into primary consideration environment and biological motivation. He described his own play *Therese Raquin* (1873), which concerns the murder of a man by his wife and her lover, as the analytic study of a "strong man and a dissatisfied woman." He had attempted "to see in them the beast, to see nothing but the beast, to throw them in violent drama and note scrupulously the sensations and acts of these creatures." Zola's goal was to bring the theater "into closer relation with the great movement toward truth and experimental science."

Zola's emphasis on heredity and environment and his insistence on an objective, scientific attitude influenced many realist playwrights. Ibsen's treatment of heredity and venereal disease in *Ghosts* (1881), for example, certainly owes something to Zola. But perhaps the most important effect of Zola's writing was to further the attack on theatrical conventionality. He called for a pure re-creation of life without the selection and the rearrangement of detail and event. With all artifice eliminated, drama would become a **slice-of-life,** a literal representation of everyday existence. Since it is in fact impossible for an artist to re-create life without transforming it to some degree, slice-of-life has never been completely realized on the stage. But the mere conception discredited the more sentimental or artificial forms such as melodrama or the well-made play.

The well-made play and the slice-of-life are two opposing extremes. When we speak of a dramatist as a realist, we can assume his work occupies a position somewhere between these extremes. The realist, to varying degrees and in varying ways, attempts to represent life as he knows it and to limit and conceal the artifice in doing so. The two examples of dramatic realism in this chapter differ considerably from one another. August Strindberg's *Miss Julie* (1888) shows the influence of both Ibsen and Zola. Lillian Hellman's *The Little Foxes* (1939) is conventional in its structure and less clinical in its objectivity. But it too is a realistic play.

The plays of Strindberg, like those of his predecessor Ibsen, represent several phases in the author's development. On several counts, *Miss Julie* can be regarded as typical of the realistic phase. Its subject, for instance, is social change—the demise of the old aristocracy and the rise of the lower classes. Strindberg's attitude is clinical and objective. In his detailed preface to the play, he wrote: "There is no such thing as absolute evil; the downfall of one family is the good fortune of another, which thereby gets a chance to rise, and, fortune being only comparative, the alternation of rising and falling is one of life's principal charms." In a statement which suggests his affinity for naturalism, he adds that in society, as in the animal kingdom, the stronger will devour the weaker.

The characters whose interaction exemplifies this social evolution are drawn in typically realistic fashion. Neither good nor evil, they are driven by complex motivation. Miss Julie, the aristocrat who gives herself to her father's valet, is motivated by her peculiar heredity, upbringing, and environment. In his preface, Strindberg lists several immediate causes for her action: "the festive mood of Midsummer Eve, her father's absence, her monthly indisposition, her pre-occupation with animals, the excitement of dancing, the magic of dusk, the strongly aphrodisiac influence of flowers, and finally the chance that drives the couple into a room alone." She is a "victim" of her mother's upbringing and also partially a victim of her own biology which demands sexual love. Heredity and environment have created an internal conflict which renders Miss Julie an unstable young woman.

Jean, the valet, is characterized with almost as much care. He is a laborer's son who has educated himself toward becoming a gentleman.

Although ambitious and willing to use other people to gain his own ends, he is not a single-minded automaton. He wavers between awe and respect for the upper classes and hatred of those born to the position he desires. Unlike the typical social climber who is equally ambitious and crude, he has learned the ways of the upper class. Yet his polish disguises a true vulgarity and an indifference to aristocratic values.

The dialog has all the irregularity of a prolonged, fatiguing debate. The participants continually touch upon a subject, move on to another, and then return to an earlier subject and develop it further. The attraction and repulsion which Miss Julie feels for Jean, and the reverence and disdain which he feels for her find alternating expression. The dialog is designed not to impress with its beauty or its elegance, but to reveal the psychological process going on within each character.

The plot of the play is simple. All the action includes only the events immediately preceding Miss Julie's demise. The actions of her mother, her complex relationship with her fiance, her own mixed attitudes—all of which an earlier playwright might have dramatized—are relegated to exposition. The action of the play is really a struggle for dominance between man and woman, servant and woman of the house, until Jean, unhampered by the aristocratic sense of honor, prevails. To increase the illusion of reality, Strindberg dispenses with the traditional act division and writes a single unified action with merely a brief interlude in which the peasants take the stage to sing and dance.

In fact, Strindberg has expended much concealed art in creating the illusion of reality. A considerable portion of his preface is given over to instructions for the set, which is to be a box set without "painted pots and pans," and directions for the actors, who are to play their roles without "greeting" the audience. In terms of content, characterization, dialog, plot, and stage production, then, *Miss Julie* confirms the pattern of realistic drama.

In contrast with Strindberg, Lillian Hellman, an American dramatist writing fifty years later, is considerably less innovative in her technique. *The Little Foxes* is, for example, an intricately plotted play. Regina's conflict with her brothers for control of the cotton mill about to be built passes through exposition, complication, crisis, and finally resolution in the last act. The unfolding of the action suggests the well-made play. Hellman's concern with the social implications of this action, however, places her among the realists. Like that of Strindberg, her subject is social change—the rise of an inhumane industrial order in place of the romanticized agricultural society wiped out by the Civil War. Hellman never loses sight of the social and the economic conditions which allow the Hubbards to rise through cunning, graft, and exploitation. Nor does she lose sight of their destructiveness: they "pound the bones of the town," as Horace points out, "to make dividends."

Her characters are shaped by their social and historical environment. Birdie, for example, is the child of the old "high-toned" aristocracy unable to adapt to the new order of things. She lives in a dream of the past and in an alcoholic daze. In contrast, Regina, the third generation of a merchant family on the rise, is unscrupulously determined to achieve her goal. Her aggressive strength is bolstered by her dream of living the "high-toned" life in Chicago. With some of the clinical objectivity of the realist, Hellman does not idealize any of her major characters. Even Horace, who alone seems to see the evil connected with the rise of the Hubbards, is depicted as sick and ineffectual, having waited too long to oppose what he knows is wrong.

Similarly, the attempt at representation is evident throughout the play. The dialog is colloquial, even regional, and it is used to individualize each of the characters. The instructions for the set are specific and detailed. "The room is good-looking," Hellman sums up at the end of her first stage direction, "but it reflects no particular taste. Everything is the best, and that is all." Even the set is intended to contribute to the realistic picture of an ambitious, vulgar family on the rise.

What finally distinguishes Hellman's realism from that of Strindberg, however, is the touch of American idealism which appears at the play's conclusion. The action suggests that the strongest will prevail regardless of moral questions. The Old South represented by Birdie is dispossessed because it could not adapt to new conditions. With the rising industrial class—whose members could adapt—Regina seems to emerge triumphant because she is the strongest, and her strength is evident in her capacity to commit a crime far worse than the mere theft committed by her brothers. But in her last speech, Alexandra, who has been shaped throughout the play by the more positive figures in her environment, makes a statement which seems to reflect Hellman's attitude:

> Addie said there were people who ate the earth and other people who stood around and watched them do it. And just now Uncle Ben said the same thing. . . . Well, tell him for me, Mama, I am not going to stand around and watch you do it. Tell him I'll be fighting as hard as he'll be fighting someplace where people don't just stand around and watch.

This final statement before the end of the play suggests that social change involves moral questions and that evil, no matter what forms it takes, must be combatted.

Among those dramatists who can be called realists, then, we find varying social philosophies. Realism has dominated the stage for over a hundred years in societies as different as Czarist Russia, Sweden, France, and the United States. It has been influenced by naturalism, Marxism, and even American idealism. The constant factor is not simply a particular philosophy but an awareness of vital, human questions. And it is this sensitivity to historical, social, and psychological conditions, as well as imaginative attempts to represent life by a faithful reporting of these conditions, that must constitute our final definition of realism.

August Strindberg   (1849–1912)
Miss Julie

Characters

MISS JULIE, *aged 25*
JEAN, *aged 30*
KRISTIN, *the cook, aged 35*

SCENE: *The large kitchen of a Swedish manor house in a country district in
the 1880s. Midsummer Eve.*[1]

> *The kitchen has three doors, two small ones into* JEAN's *and* KRISTIN's
> *bedrooms, and a large, glass-fronted double one, opening on to a court-
> yard. This is the only way to the rest of the house.*
> *Through these glass doors can be seen part of a fountain with a cupid, lilac
> bushes in flower and the tops of some Lombardy poplars. On one wall are
> shelves edged with scalloped paper on which are kitchen utensils of cop-
> per, iron and tin.*
> *To the left is the corner of a large tiled range and part of its chimney-hood,
> to the right the end of the servants' dinner table with chairs beside it.*
> *The stove is decorated with birch boughs, the floor strewn with twigs of
> juniper. On the end of the table is a large Japanese spice jar full of lilac.*
> *There are also an ice-box, a scullery table and a sink.*
> *Above the double door hangs a big old-fashioned bell; near it is a
> speaking-tube.*
> *A fiddle can be heard from the dance in the barn near-by.*
> KRISTIN *is standing at the stove, frying something in a pan. She wears a
> light-colored cotton dress and a big apron.*
> JEAN *enters, wearing livery and carrying a pair of large riding-boots with
> spurs, which he puts in a conspicuous place.*

JEAN.   Miss Julie's crazy again to-night, absolutely crazy.
KRISTIN.   Oh, so you're back, are you?
JEAN.   When I'd taken the Count to the station, I came back and dropped
in at the Barn for a dance. And who did I see there but our young lady leading off
with the gamekeeper. But the moment she sets eyes on me, up she rushes and

---

1. The night of June 23, during which all-night festivals are held in Sweden to celebrate the return
of summer; among young people especially it is a time of renewed hopes for romance.

invites me to waltz with her. And how she waltzed—I've never seen anything like it! She's crazy.

KRISTIN. Always has been, but never so bad as this last fortnight since the engagement was broken off.

JEAN. Yes, that was a pretty business, to be sure. He's a decent enough chap, too, even if he isn't rich. Oh, but they're choosy! [*Sits down at the end of the table*] In any case, it's a bit odd that our young—er—lady would rather stay at home with yokels than go with her father to visit her relations.

KRISTIN. Perhaps she feels a bit awkward, after that bust-up with her fiancé.

JEAN. Maybe. That chap had some guts, though. Do you know the sort of thing that was going on, Kristin? I saw it with my own eyes, though I didn't let on I had.

KRISTIN. You saw them . . . ?

JEAN. Didn't I just! Came across the pair of them one evening in the stable-yard. Miss Julie was doing what she called "training" him. Know what that was? Making him jump over her riding whip—the way you teach a dog. He did it twice and got a cut each time for his pains, but when it came to the third go, he snatched the whip out of her hand and broke it into smithereens. And then he cleared off.

KRISTIN. What goings on! I never did!

JEAN. Well, that's how it was with that little affair . . . Now, what have you got for me, Kristin? Something tasty?

KRISTIN [*Serving from the pan to his plate*]. Well, it's just a little bit of kidney I cut off their joint.

JEAN [*Smelling it*]. Fine! That's my special delice.[2] [*Feels the plate*] But you might have warmed the plate.

KRISTIN. When you choose to be finicky you're worse than the Count himself. [*Pulls his hair affectionately*]

JEAN [*Crossly*]. Stop pulling my hair. You know how sensitive I am.

KRISTIN. There, there! It's only love, you know.

[JEAN *eats.* KRISTIN *brings a bottle of beer*]

JEAN. Beer on Midsummer Eve? No thanks! I've got something better than that. [*From a drawer in the table brings out a bottle of red wine with a yellow seal*] Yellow seal, see! Now get me a glass. You use a glass with a stem of course when you're drinking it straight.

KRISTIN [*Giving him a wine-glass*]. Lord help the woman who gets you for a husband, you old fusser! [*She puts the beer in the ice-box and sets a small saucepan on the stove*]

JEAN. Nonsense! You'll be glad enough to get a fellow as smart as me. And I don't think it's done you any harm, people calling me your fiancé. [*Tastes the wine*] Good. Very good indeed. But not quite warmed enough. [*Warms the glass in his hand*] We bought this in Dijon. Four francs the liter without the bottle, and duty on top of that. What are you cooking now? It stinks.

KRISTIN. Some bloody muck Miss Julie wants for Diana.

---

2. Delicacy.

JEAN. You should be more refined in your speech, Kristin. But why should you spend a holiday cooking for that bitch? Is she sick or what?

KRISTIN. Yes, she's sick. She sneaked out with the pug at the lodge and got in the usual mess. And that, you know, Miss Julie won't have.

JEAN. Miss Julie's too high-and-mighty in some respects, and not enough in others, just like her mother before her. The Countess was more at home in the kitchen and cowsheds than anywhere else, but would she ever go driving with only one horse? She went round with her cuffs filthy, but she had to have the coronet on the cuff-links. Our young lady—to come back to her—hasn't any proper respect for herself or her position. I mean she isn't refined. In the Barn just now she dragged the gamekeeper away from Anna and made him dance with her—no waiting to be asked. We wouldn't do a thing like that. But that's what happens when the gentry try to behave like the common people—they become common . . . Still she's a fine girl. Smashing! What shoulders! And what—er—etcetera!

KRISTIN. Oh come off it! I know what Clara says, and she dresses her.

JEAN. Clara? Pooh, you're all jealous! But I've been out riding with her . . . and as for her dancing!

KRISTIN. Listen, Jean. You will dance with me, won't you, as soon as I'm through.

JEAN. Of course I will.

KRISTIN. Promise?

JEAN. Promise? When I say I'll do a thing I do it. Well, thanks for the supper. It was a real treat. [*Corks the bottle*]

[JULIE *appears in the doorway, speaking to someone outside*]

JULIE. I'll be back in a moment. Don't wait.

[JEAN *slips the bottle into the drawer and rises respectfully.* JULIE *enters and joins* KRISTIN *at the stove*]

Well, have you made it? [KRISTIN *signs that* JEAN *is near them*]

JEAN [*Gallantly*]. Have you ladies got some secret?

JULIE [*Flipping his face with her handkerchief*]. You're very inquisitive.

JEAN. What a delicious smell! Violets.

JULIE [*Coquettishly*]. Impertinence! Are you an expert of scent too? I must say you know how to dance. Now don't look. Go away. [*The music of a schottische³ begins*]

JEAN [*With impudent politeness*]. Is it some witches' brew you're cooking on Midsummer Eve? Something to tell your stars by, so you can see your future?

JULIE [*Sharply*]. If you could see that you'd have good eyes. [*To* KRISTIN] Put it in a bottle and cork it tight. Come and dance this schottische with me, Jean.

JEAN [*Hesitating*]. I don't want to be rude, but I've promised to dance this one with Kristin.

---

3. Lively dance characterized by gliding and hopping steps.

JULIE.   Well, she can have another, can't you, Kristin? You'll lend me Jean, won't you?

KRISTIN [*Bottling*].   It's nothing to do with me. When you're so condescending, Miss, it's not his place to say no. Go on, Jean, and thank Miss Julie for the honor.

JEAN.   Frankly speaking, Miss, and no offense meant, I wonder if it's wise for you to dance twice running with the same partner, specially as those people are so ready to jump to conclusions.

JULIE [*Flaring up*].   What did you say? What sort of conclusions? What do you mean?

JEAN [*Meekly*].   As you choose not to understand, Miss Julie, I'll have to speak more plainly. It looks bad to show a preference for one of your retainers when they're all hoping for the same unusual favor.

JULIE.   Show a preference! The very idea! I'm surprised at you. I'm doing the people an honor by attending their ball when I'm mistress of the house, but if I'm really going to dance, I mean to have a partner who can lead and doesn't make me look ridiculous.

JEAN.   If those are your orders, Miss, I'm at your service.

JULIE [*Gently*].   Don't take it as an order. Tonight we're all just people enjoying a party. There's no question of class. So now give me your arm. Don't worry, Kristin. I shan't steal your sweetheart.

[JEAN *gives* JULIE *his arm and leads her out*]
[*Left alone,* KRISTIN *plays her scene in an unhurried, natural way, humming to the tune of the schottische, played on a distant violin. She clears* JEAN's *place, washes up and puts things away, then takes off her apron, brings out a small mirror from a drawer, props it against the jar of lilac, lights a candle, warms a small pair of tongs and curls her fringe. She goes to the door and listens, then turning back to the table finds* MISS JULIE's *handkerchief. She smells it, then meditatively smooths it out and folds it*]
[*Enter* JEAN]

JEAN.   She really *is* crazy. What a way to dance! With people standing grinning at her too from behind the doors. What's got into her, Kristin?

KRISTIN.   Oh, it's just her time coming on. She's always queer then. Are you going to dance with me now?

JEAN.   Then you're not wild with me for cutting that one.

KRISTIN.   You know I'm not—for a little thing like that. Besides, I know my place.

JEAN [*Putting his arm round her waist*].   You're a sensible girl, Kristin, and you'll make a very good wife . . .

[*Enter* JULIE, *unpleasantly surprised*]

JULIE [*With forced gaiety*].   You're a fine beau—running away from your partner.

JEAN.   Not away, Miss Julie, but as you see back to the one I deserted.

JULIE [*Changing her tone*].   You really can dance, you know. But why are you wearing your livery on a holiday. Take it off at once.

JEAN.   Then I must ask you to go away for a moment, Miss. My black coat's here. [*Indicates it hanging on the door to his room*]

JULIE.   Are you so shy of me—just over changing a coat? Go into your room then—or stay here and I'll turn my back.

JEAN.   Excuse me then, Miss. [*He goes to his room and is partly visible as he changes his coat*]

JULIE.   Tell me, Kristin, is Jean your fiancé? You seem very intimate.

KRISTIN.   My fiancé? Yes, if you like. We call it that.

JULIE.   Call it?

KRISTIN.   Well, you've had a fiancé yourself, Miss, and . . .

JULIE.   But we really were engaged.

KRISTIN.   All the same it didn't come to anything.

[JEAN *returns in his black coat*]

JULIE.   *Très gentil, Monsieur Jean. Très gentil.*[4]

JEAN.   *Vous voulez plaisanter, Madame.*

JULIE.   *Et vous voulez parler français.* Where did you learn it?

JEAN.   In Switzerland, when I was steward at one of the biggest hotels in Lucerne.

JULIE.   You look quite the gentleman in that get-up. Charming. [*Sits at the table*]

JEAN.   Oh, you're just flattering me!

JULIE [*Annoyed*].   Flattering you?

JEAN.   I'm too modest to believe you would pay real compliments to a man like me, so I must take it you are exaggerating—that this is what's known as flattery.

JULIE.   Where on earth did you learn to make speeches like that? Perhaps you've been to the theater a lot.

JEAN.   That's right. And traveled a lot too.

JULIE.   But you come from this neighborhood, don't you?

JEAN.   Yes, my father was a laborer on the next estate—the District Attorney's place. I often used to see you, Miss Julie, when you were little, though you never noticed me.

JULIE.   Did you really?

JEAN.   Yes. One time specially I remember . . . but I can't tell you about that.

JULIE.   Oh do! Why not? This is just the time.

JEAN.   No, I really can't now. Another time perhaps.

JULIE.   Another time means never. What harm in now?

JEAN.   No harm, but I'd rather not. [*Points to* KRISTIN, *now fast asleep*] Look at her.

JULIE.   She'll make a charming wife, won't she? I wonder if she snores.

JEAN.   No, she doesn't, but she talks in her sleep.

JULIE [*Cynically*].   How do you know she talks in her sleep?

---

4. JULIE.   Very nice, Monsieur Jean, very nice.
    JEAN.   You are joking, Madam.
    JULIE.   And you are speaking French.

JEAN [*Brazenly*]. I've heard her. [*Pause. They look at one another*]
JULIE. Why don't you sit down?
JEAN. I can't take such a liberty in your presence.
JULIE. Supposing I order you to.
JEAN. I'll obey.
JULIE. Then sit down. No, wait a minute. Will you get me a drink first?
JEAN. I don't know what's in the ice-box. Only beer, I expect.
JULIE. There's no only about it. My taste is so simple I prefer it to wine.

[JEAN *takes a bottle from the ice-box, fetches a glass and plate and serves the beer*]

JEAN. At your service.
JULIE. Thank you. Won't you have some yourself?
JEAN. I'm not really a beer-drinker, but if it's an order . . .
JULIE. Order? I should have thought it was ordinary manners to keep your partner company.
JEAN. That's a good way of putting it. [*He opens another bottle and fetches a glass*]
JULIE. Now drink my health. [*He hesitates*] I believe the man really is shy.

[JEAN *kneels and raises his glass with mock ceremony*]

JEAN. To the health of my lady!
JULIE. Bravo! Now kiss my shoe and everything will be perfect. [*He hesitates, then boldly takes hold of her foot and lightly kisses it*] Splendid. You ought to have been an actor.
JEAN [*Rising*]. We can't go on like this, Miss Julie. Someone might come in and see us.
JULIE. Why would that matter?
JEAN. For the simple reason that they'd talk. And if you knew the way their tongues were wagging out there just now, you . . .
JULIE. What were they saying? Tell me. Sit down.
JEAN [*Sitting*]. No offense meant, Miss, but . . . well, their language wasn't nice, and they were hinting . . . oh, you know quite well what. You're not a child, and if a lady's seen drinking alone at night with a man—and a servant at that—then . . .
JULIE. Then what? Besides, we're not alone. Kristin's here.
JEAN. Yes, asleep.
JULIE. I'll wake her up. [*Rises*] Kristin, are you asleep? [KRISTIN *mumbles in her sleep*] Kristin! Goodness, how she sleeps!
KRISTIN [*In her sleep*]. The Count's boots are cleaned—put the coffee on—yes, yes, at once . . . [*Mumbles incoherently*]
JULIE [*Tweaking her nose*]. Wake up, can't you!
JEAN [*Sharply*]. Let her sleep.
JULIE. What?
JEAN. When you've been standing at the stove all day you're likely to be tired at night. And sleep should be respected.

JULIE [*Changing her tone*]. What a nice idea. It does you credit. Thank you for it. [*Holds out her hand to him*] Now come out and pick some lilac for me.

[*During the following* KRISTIN *goes sleepily in to her bedroom*]

JEAN. Out with you, Miss Julie?

JULIE. Yes.

JEAN. It wouldn't do. It really wouldn't.

JULIE. I don't know what you mean. You can't possibly imagine that . . .

JEAN. I don't, but others do.

JULIE. What? That I'm in love with the valet?

JEAN. I'm not a conceited man, but such a thing's been known to happen, and to these rustics nothing's sacred.

JULIE. You, I take it, are an aristocrat.

JEAN. Yes, I am.

JULIE. And I am coming down in the world.

JEAN. Don't come down, Miss Julie. Take my advice. No one will believe you came down of your own accord. They'll all say you fell.

JULIE. I have a higher opinion of our people than you. Come and put it to the test. Come on. [*Gazes into his eyes*]

JEAN. You're very strange, you know.

JULIE. Perhaps I am, but so are you. For that matter everything is strange. Life, human beings, everything, just scum drifting about on the water until it sinks—down and down. That reminds me of a dream I sometimes have, in which I'm on top of a pillar and can't see any way of getting down. When I look down I'm dizzy; I have to get down but I haven't the courage to jump. I can't stay there and I long to fall, but I don't fall. There's no respite. There can't be any peace at all for me until I'm down, right down on the ground. And if I did get to the ground I'd want to be under the ground . . . Have you ever felt like that?

JEAN. No. In my dream I'm lying under a great tree in a dark wood. I want to get up, up to the top of it, and look out over the bright landscape where the sun is shining and rob that high nest of its golden eggs. And I climb and climb, but the trunk is so thick and smooth and it's so far to the first branch. But I know if I can once reach that first branch I'll go to the top just as if I'm on a ladder. I haven't reached it yet, but I shall get there, even if only in my dreams.

JULIE. Here I am chattering about dreams with you. Come on. Only into the park. [*She takes his arm and they go toward the door*]

JEAN. We must sleep on nine midsummer flowers tonight; then our dreams will come true,[5] Miss Julie.

[*They turn at the door. He has a hand to his eye*]

JULIE. Have you got something in your eye? Let me see.

JEAN. Oh, it's nothing. Just a speck of dust. It'll be gone in a minute.

JULIE. My sleeve must have rubbed against you. Sit down and let me see

---

5. It was said that young girls who slept with nine different kinds of flowers under their pillows on Midsummer Eve would dream of their future loves.

to it. [*Takes him by the arm and makes him sit down, bends his head back and tries to get the speck out with the corner of her handkerchief*] Keep still now, quite still. [*Slaps his hand*] Do as I tell you. Why, I believe you're trembling, big, strong man though you are! [*Feels his biceps*] What muscles!

JEAN [*Warning*].   Miss Julie!

JULIE.   Yes, Monsieur Jean?

JEAN.   *Attention. Je ne suis qu'un homme.*[6]

JULIE.   Will you stay still! There now. It's out. Kiss my hand and say thank you.

JEAN [*Rising*].   Miss Julie, listen. Kristin's gone to bed now. Will you listen?

JULIE.   Kiss my hand first.

JEAN.   Very well, but you'll have only yourself to blame.

JULIE.   For what?

JEAN.   For what! Are you still a child at twenty-five? Don't you know it's dangerous to play with fire?

JULIE.   Not for me. I'm insured.

JEAN [*Bluntly*].   No, you're not. And even if you are, there's still stuff here to kindle a flame.

JULIE.   Meaning yourself?

JEAN.   Yes. Not because I'm me, but because I'm a man and young and . . .

JULIE.   And good-looking? What incredible conceit! A Don Juan perhaps? Or a Joseph?[7] Good Lord, I do believe you are a Joseph!

JEAN.   Do you?

JULIE.   I'm rather afraid so.

[JEAN *goes boldly up and tries to put his arms round her and kiss her. She boxes his ears*]

How dare you!

JEAN.   Was that in earnest or a joke?

JULIE.   In earnest.

JEAN.   Then what went before was in earnest too. You take your games too seriously and that's dangerous. Anyhow I'm tired of playing now and beg leave to return to my work. The Count will want his boots first thing and it's past midnight now.

JULIE.   Put those boots down.

JEAN.   No. This is my work, which it's my duty to do. But I never undertook to be your playfellow and I never will be. I consider myself too good for that.

JULIE.   You're proud.

JEAN.   In some ways—not all.

JULIE.   Have you ever been in love?

JEAN.   We don't put it that way, but I've been gone on quite a few girls.

---

6. "Careful, I am only a man."

7. In the Bible, Joseph, son of Jacob, resisted the advances of his Egyptian master's wife, who then had him imprisoned on false charges. Because he correctly forecast for Egypt seven abundant years followed by seven years of famine, he was made prime minister by the Pharaoh.

And once I went sick because I couldn't have the one I wanted. Sick, I mean, like those princes in the Arabian Nights who couldn't eat or drink for love.

JULIE. Who was she? [*No answer*] Who was she?

JEAN. You can't force me to tell you that.

JULIE. If I ask as an equal, ask as a—friend? Who was she?

JEAN. You.

JULIE [*Sitting*]. How absurd!

JEAN. Yes, ludicrous if you like. That's the story I wouldn't tell you before, see, but now I will . . . Do you know what the world looks like from below? No, you don't. No more than the hawks and falcons do whose backs one hardly ever sees because they're always soaring up aloft. I lived in a laborer's hovel with seven other children and a pig, out in the gray fields where there isn't a single tree. But from the window I could see the wall round the Count's park with apple-trees above it. That was the Garden of Eden, guarded by many terrible angels with flaming swords. All the same I and the other boys managed to get to the tree of life. Does all this make you despise me?

JULIE. Goodness, all boys steal apples!

JEAN. You say that now, but all the same you do despise me. However, one time I went into the Garden of Eden with my mother to weed the onion beds. Close to the kitchen garden there was a Turkish pavilion hung all over with jasmine and honeysuckle. I hadn't any idea what it was used for, but I'd never seen such a beautiful building. People used to go in and then come out again, and one day the door was left open. I crept up and saw the walls covered with pictures of kings and emperors, and the windows had red curtains with fringes—you know now what the place was, don't you? I . . . [*Breaks off a piece of lilac and holds it for* JULIE *to smell. As he talks, she takes it from him*] I had never been inside the manor, never seen anything but the church, and this was more beautiful. No matter where my thoughts went, they always came back—to that place. The longing went on growing in me to enjoy it fully, just once. *Enfin,*[8] I sneaked in, gazed and admired. Then I heard someone coming. There was only one way out for the gentry, but for me there was another and I had no choice but to take it. [JULIE *drops the lilac on the table*] Then I took to my heels, plunged through the raspberry canes, dashed across the strawberry beds and found myself on the rose terrace. There I saw a pink dress and a pair of white stockings—it was you. I crawled into a weed pile and lay there right under it among prickly thistles and damp rank earth. I watched you walking among the roses and said to myself: "If it's true that a thief can get to heaven and be with the angels, it's pretty strange that a laborer's child here on God's earth mayn't come in the park and play with the Count's daughter."

JULIE [*Sentimentally*]. Do you think all poor children feel the way you did?

JEAN [*Taken aback, then rallying*]. All poor children? . . . Yes, of course they do. Of course.

JULIE. It must be terrible to be poor.

JEAN [*With exaggerated distress*]. Oh yes, Miss Julie, yes. A dog may lie on the Countess's sofa, a horse may have his nose stroked by a young lady, but a servant . . . [*Change of tone*] well, yes, now and then you meet one with guts

---

8. "Finally."

enough to rise in the world, but how often? Anyhow, do you know what I did? Jumped in the millstream with my clothes on, was pulled out and got a hiding. But the next Sunday, when Father and all the rest went to Granny's, I managed to get left behind. Then I washed with soap and hot water, put my best clothes on and went to church so as to see you. I did see you and went home determined to die. But I wanted to die beautifully and peacefully, without any pain. Then I remembered it was dangerous to sleep under an elder bush. We had a big one in full bloom, so I stripped it and climbed into the oats-bin with the flowers. Have you ever noticed how smooth oats are? Soft to touch as human skin . . . Well, I closed the lid and shut my eyes, fell asleep, and when they woke me I was very ill. But I didn't die, as you see. What I meant by all that I don't know. There was no hope of winning you—you were simply a symbol of the hopelessness of ever getting out of the class I was born in.

JULIE.   You put things very well, you know. Did you go to school?

JEAN.   For a while. But I've read a lot of novels and been to the theater. Besides, I've heard educated folk talking—that's what's taught me most.

JULIE.   Do you stand round listening to what we're saying?

JEAN.   Yes, of course. And I've heard quite a bit too! On the carriage box or rowing the boat. Once I heard you, Miss Julie, and one of your young lady friends . . .

JULIE.   Oh! Whatever did you hear?

JEAN.   Well, it wouldn't be nice to repeat it. And I must say I was pretty startled. I couldn't think where you had learnt such words. Perhaps, at bottom, there isn't as much difference between people as one's led to believe.

JULIE.   How dare you! We don't behave as you do when we're engaged.

JEAN [*Looking hard at her*].   Are you sure? It's no use making out so innocent to me.

JULIE.   The man I gave my love to was a scoundrel.

JEAN.   That's what you always say—afterward.

JULIE.   Always?

JEAN.   I think it must be always. I've heard the expression several times in similar circumstances.

JULIE.   What circumstances?

JEAN.   Like those in question. The last time . . .

JULIE [*Rising*].   Stop. I don't want to hear any more.

JEAN.   Nor did *she*—curiously enough. May I go to bed now please?

JULIE [*Gently*].   Go to bed on Midsummer Eve?

JEAN.   Yes. Dancing with that crowd doesn't really amuse me.

JULIE.   Get the key of the boathouse and row me out on the lake. I want to see the sun rise.

JEAN.   Would that be wise?

JULIE.   You sound as though you're frightened for your reputation.

JEAN.   Why not? I don't want to be made a fool of, nor to be sent packing without references when I'm trying to better myself. Besides, I have Kristin to consider.

JULIE.   So now it's Kristin.

JEAN.   Yes, but it's you I'm thinking about too. Take my advice and go to bed.

JULIE.   Am I to take orders from you?

JEAN. Just this once, for your own sake. Please. It's very late and sleepiness goes to one's head and makes one rash. Go to bed. What's more, if my ears don't deceive me, I hear people coming this way. They'll be looking for me, and if they find us here, you're done for.

[*The* CHORUS *approaches, singing. During the following dialogue the song is heard in snatches, and in full when the peasants enter*]

Out of the wood two women came,
Tridiri-ralla, tridiri-ra.
The feet of one were bare and cold,
Tridiri-ralla-la.

The other talked of bags of gold,
Tridiri-ralla, tridiri-ra.
But neither had a sou to her name,
Tridiri-ralla-la.

The bridal wreath I give to you,
Tridiri-ralla, tridiri-ra.
But to another I'll be true,
Tridiri-ralla-la.

JULIE. I know our people and I love them, just as they do me. Let them come. You'll see.

JEAN. No, Miss Julie, they don't love you. They take your food, then spit at it. You must believe me. Listen to them, just listen to what they're singing . . . No, don't listen.

JULIE [*Listening*]. What are they singing?

JEAN. They're mocking—you and me.

JULIE. Oh no! How horrible! What cowards!

JEAN. A pack like that's always cowardly. But against such odds there's nothing we can do but run away.

JULIE. Run away? Where to? We can't get out and we can't go into Kristin's room.

JEAN. Into mine then. Necessity knows no rules. And you can trust me. I really am your true and devoted friend.

JULIE. But supposing . . . supposing they were to look for you in there?

JEAN. I'll bolt the door, and if they try to break in I'll shoot. Come on. [*Pleading*] Please come.

JULIE [*Tensely*]. Do you promise . . . ?

JEAN. I swear!

[JULIE *goes quickly into his room and he excitedly follows her.
Led by the fiddler, the peasants enter in festive attire with flowers in their hats. They put a barrel of beer and a keg of spirits, garlanded with leaves, on the table, fetch glasses and begin to carouse. The scene becomes a ballet. They form a ring and dance and sing and mime:* "Out of the wood two women came." *Finally they go out, still singing.*]

JULIE *comes in alone. She looks at the havoc in the kitchen, wrings her hands, then takes out her powder puff and powders her face.*
JEAN *enters in high spirits*]

JEAN.   Now you see! And you heard, didn't you? Do you still think it's possible for us to stay here?
JULIE.   No, I don't. But what can we do?
JEAN.   Run away. Far away. Take a journey.
JULIE.   Journey? But where to?
JEAN.   Switzerland. The Italian lakes. Ever been there?
JULIE.   No. Is it nice?
JEAN.   Ah! Eternal summer, oranges, evergreens . . . ah!
JULIE.   But what would we do there?
JEAN.   I'll start a hotel. First-class accommodation and first-class customers.
JULIE.   Hotel?
JEAN.   There's life for you. New faces all the time, new languages—no time for nerves or worries, no need to look for something to do—work rolling up of its own accord. Bells ringing night and day, trains whistling, buses coming and going, and all the time gold pieces rolling on to the counter. There's life for you!
JULIE.   For *you*. And I?
JEAN.   Mistress of the house, ornament of the firm. With your looks, and your style . . . oh, it's bound to be a success! Terrific! You'll sit like a queen in the office and set your slaves in motion by pressing an electric button. The guests will file past your throne and nervously lay their treasure on your table. You've no idea the way people tremble when they get their bills. I'll salt the bills[9] and you'll sugar them with your sweetest smiles. Ah, let's get away from here! [*Produces a time-table*] At once, by the next train. We shall be at Malmö at six-thirty, Hamburg eight-forty next morning, Frankfurt-Basle the following day, and Como by the St. Gotthard Pass in—let's see—three days. Three days!
JULIE.   That's all very well. But Jean, you must give me courage. Tell me you love me. Come and take me in your arms.
JEAN [*Reluctantly*].   I'd like to, but I daren't. Not again in this house. I love you—that goes without saying. You can't doubt that, Miss Julie, can you?
JULIE [*Shyly, very feminine*].   Miss? Call me Julie. There aren't any barriers between us now. Call me Julie.
JEAN [*Uneasily*].   I can't. As long as we're in this house, there *are* barriers between us. There's the past and there's the Count. I've never been so servile to anyone as I am to him. I've only got to see his gloves on a chair to feel small. I've only to hear his bell and I shy like a horse. Even now, when I look at his boots, standing there so proud and stiff, I feel my back beginning to bend. [*Kicks the boots*] It's those old, narrow-minded notions drummed into us as children . . . but they can soon be forgotten. You've only got to get to another country, a republic, and people will bend themselves double before my porter's livery. Yes, double they'll bend themselves, but I shan't. I wasn't born to bend. I've got guts, I've got character, and once I reach that first branch, you'll watch

---

9. I.e., make them hard to swallow.

me climb. Today I'm valet, next year I'll be proprietor, in ten years I'll have made a fortune, and then I'll go to Rumania, get myself decorated and I may, I only say *may,* mind you, end up as a Count.

JULIE [*Sadly*]. That would be very nice.

JEAN. You see in Rumania one can buy a title, and then you'll be a Countess after all. My Countess.

JULIE. What do I care about all that? I'm putting those things behind me. Tell me you love me, because if you don't . . . if you don't, what am I?

JEAN. I'll tell you a thousand times over—later. But not here. No sentimentality now or everything will be lost. We must consider this thing calmly like reasonable people. [*Takes a cigar, cuts and lights it*] You sit down there and I'll sit here and we'll talk as if nothing has happened.

JULIE. My God, have you no feelings at all?

JEAN. Nobody has more. But I know how to control them.

JULIE. A short time ago you were kissing my shoe. And now . . .

JEAN [*Harshly*]. Yes, that was then. Now we have something else to think about.

JULIE. Don't speak to me so brutally.

JEAN. I'm not. Just sensibly. One folly's been committed, don't let's have more. The Count will be back at any moment and we've got to settle our future before that. Now, what do you think of my plans? Do you approve?

JULIE. It seems a very good idea—but just one thing. Such a big undertaking would need a lot of capital. Have you got any?

JEAN [*Chewing his cigar*]. I certainly have. I've got my professional skill, my wide experience and my knowledge of foreign languages. That's capital worth having, it seems to me.

JULIE. But it won't buy even one railway ticket.

JEAN. Quite true. That's why I need a backer to advance some ready cash.

JULIE. How could you get that at a moment's notice?

JEAN. You must get it, if you want to be my partner.

JULIE. I can't. I haven't any money of my own. [*Pause*]

JEAN. Then the whole thing's off.

JULIE. And . . . ?

JEAN. We go on as we are.

JULIE. Do you think I'm going to stay under this roof as your mistress? With everyone pointing at me. Do you think I can face my father after this? No. Take me away from here, away from this shame, this humiliation. Oh my God, what have I done? My God, my God! [*Weeps*]

JEAN. So that's the tune now, is it? What have you done? Same as many before you.

JULIE [*Hysterically*]. And now you despise me. I'm falling, I'm falling.

JEAN. Fall as far as me and I'll lift you up again.

JULIE. Why was I so terribly attracted to you? The weak to the strong, the falling to the rising? Or was it love? Is that love? Do you know what love is?

JEAN. Do I? You bet I do. Do you think I never had a girl before?

JULIE. The things you say, the things you think!

JEAN. That's what life's taught me, and that's what I am. It's no good getting hysterical or giving yourself airs. We're both in the same boat now. Here, my dear girl, let me give you a glass of something special. [*Opens the drawer, takes out the bottle of wine and fills two used glasses*]

JULIE.   Where did you get that wine?

JEAN.   From the cellar.

JULIE.   My father's burgundy.

JEAN.   Why not, for his son-in-law?

JULIE.   And I drink beer.

JEAN.   That only shows your taste's not so good as mine.

JULIE.   Thief!

JEAN.   Are you going to tell on me?

JULIE.   Oh God! The accomplice of a petty thief! Was I blind drunk? Have I dreamt this whole night? Midsummer Eve, the night for innocent merrymaking.

JEAN.   Innocent, eh?

JULIE.   Is anyone on earth as wretched as I am now?

JEAN.   Why should *you* be? After such a conquest. What about Kristin in there? Don't you think she has any feelings?

JULIE.   I did think so, but I don't any longer. No. A menial is a menial . . .

JEAN.   And a whore is a whore.

JULIE [*Falling to her knees, her hands clasped*].   O God in heaven, put an end to my miserable life! Lift me out of this filth in which I'm sinking. Save me! Save me!

JEAN.   I must admit I'm sorry for you. When I was in the onion bed and saw you up there among the roses, I . . . yes, I'll tell you now . . . I had the same dirty thoughts as all boys.

JULIE.   You, who wanted to die because of me?

JEAN.   In the oats-bin? That was just talk.

JULIE.   Lies, you mean.

JEAN [*Getting sleepy*].   More or less. I think I read a story in some paper about a chimney-sweep who shut himself up in a chest full of lilac because he'd been summonsed for not supporting some brat . . .

JULIE.   So this is what you're like.

JEAN.   I had to think up something. It's always the fancy stuff that catches the women.

JULIE.   Beast!

JEAN.   *Merde!*[10]

JULIE.   Now you have seen the falcon's back.

JEAN.   Not exactly its *back*.

JULIE.   I was to be the first branch.

JEAN.   But the branch was rotten.

JULIE.   I was to be a hotel sign.

JEAN.   And I the hotel.

JULIE.   Sit at your counter, attract your clients and cook their accounts.

JEAN.   I'd have done that myself.

JULIE.   That any human being can be so steeped in filth!

JEAN.   Clean it up then.

---

10. Vulgar French term for excrement.

JULIE. Menial! Lackey! Stand up when I speak to you.

JEAN. Menial's whore, lackey's harlot, shut your mouth and get out of here! Are you the one to lecture me for being coarse? Nobody of my kind would ever be as coarse as you were tonight. Do you think any servant girl would throw herself at a man that way? Have you ever seen a girl of my class asking for it like that? I haven't. Only animals and prostitutes.

JULIE [*Broken*]. Go on. Hit me, trample on me—it's all I deserve. I'm rotten. But help me! If there's any way out at all, help me.

JEAN [*More gently*]. I'm not denying myself a share in the honor of seducing you, but do you think anybody in my place would have dared look in your direction if you yourself hadn't asked for it? I'm still amazed . . .

JULIE. And proud.

JEAN. Why not? Though I must admit the victory was too easy to make me lose my head.

JULIE. Go on hitting me.

JEAN [*Rising*]. No. On the contrary I apologize for what I've said. I don't hit a person who's down—least of all a woman. I can't deny there's a certain satisfaction in finding that what dazzled one below was just moonshine, that that falcon's back is gray after all, that there's powder on the lovely cheek, that polished nails can have black tips, that the handkerchief is dirty although it smells of scent. On the other hand it hurts to find that what I was struggling to reach wasn't high and isn't real. It hurts to see you fallen so low you're far lower than your own cook. Hurts like when you see the last flowers of summer lashed to pieces by rain and turned to mud.

JULIE. You're talking as if you're already my superior.

JEAN. I am. I might make you a Countess, but you could never make me a Count, you know.

JULIE. But I am the child of a Count, and you could never be that.

JEAN. True, but I might be the father of Counts if . . .

JULIE. You're a thief. I'm not.

JEAN. There are worse things than being a thief—much lower. Besides, when I'm in a place I regard myself as a member of the family to some extent, as one of the children. You don't call it stealing when children pinch a berry from overladen bushes. [*His passion is roused again*] Miss Julie, you're a glorious woman, far too good for a man like me. You were carried away by some kind of madness, and now you're trying to cover up your mistake by persuading yourself you're in love with me. You're not, although you may find me physically attractive, which means your love's no better than mine. But I wouldn't be satisfied with being nothing but an animal for you, and I could never make you love me.

JULIE. Are you sure?

JEAN. You think there's a chance? Of my loving you, yes, of course. You're beautiful, refined, [*Takes her hand*] educated, and you can be nice when you want to be. The fire you kindle in a man isn't likely to go out. [*Puts his arm round her*] You're like mulled wine, full of spices, and your kisses . . . [*He tries to pull her to him, but she breaks away*]

JULIE. Let go of me! You won't win me that way.

JEAN. Not that way, how then? Not by kisses and fine speeches, not by planning the future and saving you from shame? How then?

JULIE.   How? How? I don't know. There isn't any way. I loathe you—
loathe you as I loathe rats, but I can't escape from you.

JEAN.   Escape with me.

JULIE [*Pulling herself together*].   Escape? Yes, we must escape. But I'm
so tired. Give me a glass of wine. [*He pours it out. She looks at her watch*] First
we must talk. We still have a little time. [*Empties the glass and holds it out for
more*]

JEAN.   Don't drink like that. You'll get tipsy.

JULIE.   What's that matter?

JEAN.   What's it matter? It's vulgar to get drunk. Well, what have you got
to say?

JULIE.   We've got to run away, but we must talk first—or rather, I must,
for so far you've done all the talking. You've told me about your life, now I want
to tell you about mine, so that we really know each other before we begin this
journey together.

JEAN.   Wait. Excuse my saying so, but don't you think you may be sorry
afterward if you give away your secrets to me?

JULIE.   Aren't you my friend?

JEAN.   On the whole. But don't rely on me.

JULIE.   You can't mean that. But anyway everyone knows my secrets.
Listen. My mother wasn't well-born; she came of quite humble people, and was
brought up with all those new ideas of sex-equality and women's rights and so
on. She thought marriage was quite wrong. So when my father proposed to her,
she said she would never become his *wife* . . .   but in the end she did. I came into the world, as far as I can make out, against my mother's will, and I was left to
run wild, but I had to do all the things a boy does—to prove women are as good
as men. I had to wear boys' clothes; I was taught to handle horses—and I wasn't
allowed in the dairy. She made me groom and harness and go out hunting; I even
had to try to plough. All the men on the estate were given the women's jobs, and
the women the men's, until the whole place went to rack and ruin and we were
the laughing-stock of the neighborhood. At last my father seemed to have come
to his senses and rebelled. He changed everything and ran the place his own way.
My mother got ill—I don't know what was the matter with her, but she used to
have strange attacks and hide herself in the attic or the garden. Sometimes she
stayed out all night. Then came the great fire which you have heard people
talking about. The house and the stables and the barns—the whole place burnt to
the ground. In very suspicious circumstances. Because the accident happened
the very day the insurance had to be renewed, and my father had sent the new
premium, but through some carelessness of the messenger it arrived too late.
[*Refills her glass and drinks*]

JEAN.   Don't drink any more.

JULIE.   Oh, what does it matter? We were destitute and had to sleep in the
carriages. My father didn't know how to get money to rebuild, and then my
mother suggested he should borrow from an old friend of hers, a local brick
manufacturer. My father got the loan and, to his surprise, without having to pay
interest. So the place was rebuilt. [*Drinks*] Do you know who set fire to it?

JEAN.   Your lady mother.

JULIE.   Do you know who the brick manufacturer was?

JEAN.   Your mother's lover?

JULIE. Do you know whose the money was?

JEAN. Wait . . . no, I don't know that.

JULIE. It was my mother's.

JEAN. In other words the Count's, unless there was a settlement.

JULIE. There wasn't any settlement. My mother had a little money of her own which she didn't want my father to control, so she invested it with her—friend.

JEAN. Who grabbed it.

JULIE. Exactly. He appropriated it. My father came to know all this. He couldn't bring an action, couldn't pay his wife's lover, nor prove it was his wife's money. That was my mother's revenge because he made himself master in his own house. He nearly shot himself then—at least there's a rumor he tried and didn't bring it off. So he went on living, and my mother had to pay dearly for what she'd done. Imagine what those five years were like for me. My natural sympathies were with my father, yet I took my mother's side, because I didn't know the facts. I'd learnt from her to hate and distrust men—you know how she loathed the whole male sex. And I swore to her I'd never become the slave of any man.

JEAN. And so you got engaged to that attorney.

JULIE. So that he should be my slave.

JEAN. But he wouldn't be.

JULIE. Oh yes, he wanted to be, but he didn't have the chance. I got bored with him.

JEAN. Is that what I saw—in the stable-yard?

JULIE. What did you see?

JEAN. What I saw was him breaking off the engagement.

JULIE. That's a lie. It was I who broke it off. Did he say it was him? The cad.

JEAN. He's not a cad. Do you hate men, Miss Julie?

JULIE. Yes . . . most of the time. But when that weakness comes, oh . . . the shame!

JEAN. Then do you hate me?

JULIE. Beyond words. I'd gladly have you killed like an animal.

JEAN. Quick as you'd shoot a mad dog, eh?

JULIE. Yes.

JEAN. But there's nothing here to shoot with—and there isn't a dog. So what do we do now?

JULIE. Go abroad.

JEAN. To make each other miserable for the rest of our lives?

JULIE. No, to enjoy ourselves for a day or two, for a week, for as long as enjoyment lasts, and then—to die . . .

JEAN. Die? How silly! I think it would be far better to start a hotel.

JULIE [*Without listening*]. . . . die on the shores of Lake Como, where the sun always shines and at Christmas time there are green trees and glowing oranges.

JEAN. Lake Como's a rainy hole and I didn't see any oranges outside the shops. But it's a good place for tourists. Plenty of villas to be rented by—er—honeymoon couples. Profitable business that. Know why? Because they all sign a lease for six months and all leave after three weeks.

JULIE [*Naively*].   After three weeks? Why?

JEAN.   They quarrel, of course. But the rent has to be paid just the same. And then it's let again. So it goes on and on, for there's plenty of love although it doesn't last long.

JULIE.   You don't want to die with me?

JEAN.   I don't want to die at all. For one thing I like living and for another I consider suicide's a sin against the Creator who gave us life.

JULIE.   You believe in God—*you?*

JEAN.   Yes, of course. And I go to church every Sunday. Look here, I'm tired of all this. I'm going to bed.

JULIE.   Indeed! And do you think I'm going to leave things like this? Don't you know what you owe the woman you've ruined?

JEAN [*Taking out his purse and throwing a silver coin on the table*]. There you are. I don't want to be in anybody's debt.

JULIE [*Pretending not to notice the insult*].   Don't you know what the law is?

JEAN.   There's no law unfortunately that punishes a woman for seducing a man.

JULIE.   But can you see anything for it but to go abroad, get married and then divorce?

JEAN.   What if I refuse this misalliance?

JULIE.   Misalliance?

JEAN.   Yes, for me. I'm better bred than you, see! Nobody in my family committed arson.

JULIE.   How do you know?

JEAN.   Well, you can't prove otherwise, because we haven't any family records outside the Registrar's office. But I've seen your family tree in that book on the drawing-room table. Do you know who the founder of your family was? A miller who let his wife sleep with the King one night during the Danish war. I haven't any ancestors like that. I haven't any ancestors at all, but I might become one.

JULIE.   This is what I get for confiding in someone so low, for sacrificing my family honor . . .

JEAN.   Dishonor! Well, I told you so. One shouldn't drink, because then one talks. And one shouldn't talk.

JULIE.   Oh, how ashamed I am, how bitterly ashamed! If at least you loved me!

JEAN.   Look here—for the last time—what do you want? Am I to burst into tears? Am I to jump over your riding whip? Shall I kiss you and carry you off to Lake Como for three weeks, after which . . . What am I to do? What do you want? This is getting unbearable, but that's what comes of playing around with women. Miss Julie, I can see how miserable you are; I know you're going through hell, but I don't understand you. We don't have scenes like this; we don't go in for hating each other. We make love for fun in our spare time, but we haven't all day and all night for it like you. I think you must be ill. I'm sure you're ill.

JULIE.   Then you must be kind to me. You sound almost human now.

JEAN.   Well, be human yourself. You spit at me, then won't let me wipe it off—on you.

JULIE. Help me, help me! Tell me what to do, where to go.

JEAN. Jesus, as if I knew!

JULIE. I've been mad, raving mad, but there must be a way out.

JEAN. Stay here and keep quiet. Nobody knows anything.

JULIE. I can't. People do know. Kristin knows.

JEAN. They don't know and they wouldn't believe such a thing.

JULIE [*Hesitating*]. But—it might happen again.

JEAN. That's true.

JULIE. And there might be—consequences.

JEAN [*In panic*]. Consequences! Fool that I am I never thought of that. Yes, there's nothing for it but to go. At once. I can't come with you. That would be a complete give-away. You must go alone—abroad—anywhere.

JULIE. Alone? Where to? I can't.

JEAN. You must. And before the Count gets back. If you stay, we know what will happen. Once you've sinned you feel you might as well go on, as the harm's done. Then you get more and more reckless and in the end you're found out. No. You must go abroad. Then write to the Count and tell him everything, except that it was me. He'll never guess that—and I don't think he'll want to.

JULIE. I'll go if you come with me.

JEAN. Are you crazy, woman? "Miss Julie elopes with valet." Next day it would be in the headlines, and the Count would never live it down.

JULIE. I can't go. I can't stay. I'm so tired, so completely worn out. Give me orders. Set me going. I can't think any more, can't act . . .

JEAN. You see what weaklings you are. Why do you give yourselves airs and turn up your noses as if you're the lords of creation? Very well, I'll give you your orders. Go upstairs and dress. Get money for the journey and come down here again.

JULIE [*Softly*]. Come up with me.

JEAN. To your room? Now you've gone crazy again. [*Hesitates a moment*] No! Go along at once. [*Takes her hand and pulls her to the door*]

JULIE [*As she goes*]. Speak kindly to me, Jean.

JEAN. Orders always sound unkind. Now you know. Now you know.

[*Left alone,* JEAN *sighs with relief, sits down at the table, takes out a note-book and pencil and adds up figures, now and then aloud. Dawn begins to break.* KRISTIN *enters dressed for church, carrying his white dickey and tie*]

KRISTIN. Lord Jesus, look at the state the place is in! What have you been up to? [*Turns out the lamp*]

JEAN. Oh, Miss Julie invited the crowd in. Did you sleep through it? Didn't you hear anything?

KRISTIN. I slept like a log.

JEAN. And dressed for church already.

KRISTIN. Yes, you promised to come to Communion with me today.

JEAN. Why, so I did. And you've got my bib and tucker, I see. Come on then. [*Sits.* KRISTIN *begins to put his things on. Pause. Sleepily*] What's the lesson today?

KRISTIN. It's about the beheading of John the Baptist, I think.

JEAN.   That's sure to be horribly long. Hi, you're choking me! Oh Lord, I'm so sleepy, so sleepy!

KRISTIN.   Yes, what have you been doing up all night? You look absolutely green.

JEAN.   Just sitting here talking with Miss Julie.

KRISTIN.   She doesn't know what's proper, that one. [*Pause*]

JEAN.   I say, Kristin.

KRISTIN.   What?

JEAN.   It's queer really, isn't it, when you come to think of it? Her.

KRISTIN.   What's queer?

JEAN.   The whole thing. [*Pause*]

KRISTIN [*Looking at the half-filled glasses on the table*].   Have you been drinking together too?

JEAN.   Yes.

KRISTIN.   More shame you. Look me straight in the face.

JEAN.   Yes.

KRISTIN.   Is it possible? Is it possible?

JEAN [*After a moment*]. Yes, it is.

KRISTIN.   Oh! This I would never have believed. How low!

JEAN.   You're not jealous of her, surely?

KRISTIN.   No, I'm not. If it had been Clara or Sophie I'd have scratched your eyes out. But not of her. I don't know why; that's how it is though. But it's disgusting.

JEAN.   You're angry with her then.

KRISTIN.   No. With you. It was wicked of you, very very wicked. Poor girl. And, mark my words, I won't stay here any longer now—in a place where one can't respect one's employers.

JEAN.   Why should one respect them?

KRISTIN.   You should know since you're so smart. But you don't want to stay in the service of people who aren't respectable, do you? I wouldn't demean myself.

JEAN.   But it's rather a comfort to find out they're no better than us.

KRISTIN.   I don't think so. If they're no better there's nothing for us to live up to. Oh and think of the Count! Think of him. He's been through so much already. No, I won't stay in the place any longer. A fellow like you too! If it had been that attorney now or somebody of her own class . . .

JEAN.   Why, what's wrong with . . .

KRISTIN.   Oh, you're all right in your own way, but when all's said and done there is a difference between one class and another. No, this is something I'll never be able to stomach. That our young lady who was so proud and so down on men you'd never believe she'd let one come near her should go and give herself to one like you. She who wanted to have poor Diana shot for running after the lodge-keeper's pug. No. I must say . . . ! Well, I won't stay here any longer. On the twenty-fourth of October I quit.

JEAN.   And then?

KRISTIN.   Well, since you mention it, it's about time you began to look around, if we're ever going to get married.

JEAN.   But what am I to look for? I shan't get a place like this when I'm married.

KRISTIN. I know you won't. But you might get a job as porter or caretaker in some public institution. Government rations are small but sure, and there's a pension for the widow and children.

JEAN. That's all very fine, but it's not in my line to start thinking at once about dying for my wife and children. I must say I had rather bigger ideas.

KRISTIN. You and your ideas! You've got obligations too, and you'd better start thinking about them.

JEAN. Don't *you* start pestering me about obligations. I've had enough of that. [*Listens to a sound upstairs*] Anyway we've plenty of time to work things out. Go and get ready now and we'll be off to church.

KRISTIN. Who's that walking about upstairs?

JEAN. Don't know—unless it's Clara.

KRISTIN [*Going*]. You don't think the Count could have come back without our hearing him?

JEAN [*Scared*]. The Count? No, he can't have. He'd have rung for me.

KRISTIN. God help us! I've never known such goings on. [*Exit*]

[*The sun has now risen and is shining on the tree-tops. The light gradually changes until it slants in through the windows.* JEAN *goes to the door and beckons.* JULIE *enters in traveling clothes, carrying a small bird-cage covered with a cloth which she puts on a chair*]

JULIE. I'm ready.

JEAN. Hush! Kristin's up.

JULIE [*In a very nervous state*]. Does she suspect anything?

JEAN. Not a thing. But, my God, what a sight you are!

JULIE. Sight? What do you mean?

JEAN. You're white as a corpse and—pardon me—your face is dirty.

JULIE. Let me wash then. [*Goes to the sink and washes her face and hands*] There. Give me a towel. Oh! The sun is rising!

JEAN. And that breaks the spell.

JULIE. Yes. The spell of Midsummer Eve . . . But listen, Jean. Come with me. I've got the money.

JEAN [*Skeptically*]. Enough?

JULIE. Enough to start with. Come with me. I can't travel alone today. It's Midsummer Day, remember. I'd be packed into a suffocating train among crowds of people who'd all stare at me. And it would stop at every station while I yearned for wings. No, I can't do that, I simply can't. There will be memories too; memories of Midsummer Days when I was little. The leafy church—birch and lilac—the gaily spread dinner table, relatives, friends—evening in the park—dancing and music and flowers and fun. Oh, however far you run away—there'll always be memories in the baggage car—and remorse and guilt.

JEAN. I will come with you, but quickly now then, before it's too late. At once.

JULIE. Put on your things. [*Picks up the cage*]

JEAN. No luggage, mind. That would give us away.

JULIE. No, only what we can take with us in the carriage.

JEAN [*Fetching his hat*]. What on earth have you got there? What is it?

JULIE. Only my greenfinch. I don't want to leave it behind.

JEAN. Well, I'll be damned! We're to take a bird-cage along, are we? You're crazy. Put that cage down.

JULIE. It's the only thing I'm taking from my home. The only living creature who cares for me since Diana went off like that. Don't be cruel. Let me take it.

JEAN. Put that cage down, I tell you—and don't talk so loud. Kristin will hear.

JULIE. No, I won't leave it in strange hands. I'd rather you killed it.

JEAN. Give the little beast here then and I'll wring its neck.

JULIE. But don't hurt it, don't . . . no, I can't.

JEAN. Give it here. I *can*.

JULIE [*Taking the bird out of the cage and kissing it*]. Dear little Serena, must you die and leave your mistress?

JEAN. Please don't make a scene. It's *your* life and future we're worrying about. Come on, quick now!

[*He snatches the bird from her, puts it on a board and picks up a chopper.* JULIE *turns away*]

You should have learnt how to kill chickens instead of target-shooting. Then you wouldn't faint at a drop of blood.

JULIE [*Screaming*]. Kill me too! Kill me! You who can butcher an innocent creature without a quiver. Oh, how I hate you, how I loathe you! There is blood between us now. I curse the hour I first saw you. I curse the hour I was conceived in my mother's womb.

JEAN. What's the use of cursing. Let's go.

JULIE [*Going to the chopping-block as if drawn against her will*]. No, I won't go yet. I can't . . . I must look. Listen! There's a carriage. [*Listens without taking her eyes off the board and chopper*] You don't think I can bear the sight of blood. You think I'm so weak. Oh, how I should like to see your blood and your brains on a chopping-block! I'd like to see the whole of your sex swimming like that in a sea of blood. I think I could drink out of your skull, bathe my feet in your broken breast and eat your heart roasted whole. You think I'm weak. You think I love you, that my womb yearned for your seed and I want to carry your offspring under my heart and nourish it with my blood. You think I want to bear your child and take your name. By the way, what is your name? I've never heard your surname. I don't suppose you've got one. I should be "Mrs. Hovel" or "Madam Dunghill." You dog wearing my collar, you lackey with my crest on your buttons! I share you with my cook; I'm my own servant's rival! Oh! Oh! Oh! . . . You think I'm a coward and will run away. No, now I'm going to stay—and let the storm break. My father will come back . . . find his desk broken open . . . his money gone. Then he'll ring that bell—twice for the valet—and then he'll send for the police . . . and I shall tell everything. Everything. Oh how wonderful to make an end of it all—a real end! He has a stroke and dies and that's the end of all of us. Just peace and quietness . . . eternal rest. The coat of arms broken on the coffin and the Count's line extinct . . . But the valet's line goes on in an orphanage, wins laurels in the gutter and ends in jail.

JEAN. There speaks the noble blood! Bravo, Miss Julie. But now, don't let the cat out of the bag.

[KRISTIN *enters dressed for church, carrying a prayer-book.* JULIE *rushes to her and flings herself into her arms for protection*]

JULIE. Help me, Kristin! Protect me from this man!

KRISTIN [*Unmoved and cold*]. What goings-on for a feast day morning! [*Sees the board*] And what a filthy mess. What's it all about? Why are you screaming and carrying on so?

JULIE. Kristin, you're a woman and my friend. Beware of that scoundrel!

JEAN [*Embarrassed*]. While you ladies are talking things over, I'll go and shave. [*Slips into his room*]

JULIE. You must understand. You must listen to me.

KRISTIN. I certainly don't understand such loose ways. Where are you off to in those traveling clothes? And he had his hat on, didn't he, eh?

JULIE. Listen, Kristin. Listen, I'll tell you everything.

KRISTIN. I don't want to know anything.

JULIE. You must listen.

KRISTIN. What to? Your nonsense with Jean? I don't care a rap about that; it's nothing to do with me. But if you're thinking of getting him to run off with you, we'll soon put a stop to that.

JULIE [*Very nervously*]. Please try to be calm, Kristin, and listen. I can't stay here, nor can Jean—so we must go abroad.

KRISTIN. Hm, hm!

JULIE [*Brightening*]. But you see, I've had an idea. Supposing we all three go—abroad—to Switzerland and start a hotel together . . . I've got some money, you see . . . and Jean and I could run the whole thing—and I thought you would take charge of the kitchen. Wouldn't that be splendid? Say yes, do. If you come with us everything will be fine. Oh do say yes! [*Puts her arms round* KRISTIN]

KRISTIN [*Coolly thinking*]. Hm, hm.

JULIE [*Presto tempo*]. You've never traveled, Kristin. You should go abroad and see the world. You've no idea how nice it is traveling by train—new faces all the time and new countries. On our way through Hamburg we'll go to the zoo—you'll love that—and we'll go to the theater and the opera too . . . and when we get to Munich there'll be the museums, dear, and pictures by Rubens and Raphael—the great painters, you know . . . You've heard of Munich, haven't you? Where King Ludwig lived—you know, the king who went mad. . . . We'll see his castles—some of his castles are still just like in fairy-tales . . . and from there it's not far to Switzerland—and the Alps. Think of the Alps, Kristin dear, covered with snow in the middle of summer . . . and there are oranges there and trees that are green the whole year round . . .

[JEAN *is seen in the door of his room, sharpening his razor on a strop which he holds with his teeth and his left hand. He listens to the talk with satisfaction and now and then nods approval.* JULIE *continues, tempo prestissimo*[11]]

And then we'll get a hotel . . . and I'll sit at the desk, while Jean receives the guests and goes out marketing and writes letters . . . There's life for you! Trains

---

11. Very quickly.

whistling, buses driving up, bells ringing upstairs and downstairs . . . and I shall make out the bills—and I shall cook them too . . . you've no idea how nervous travelers are when it comes to paying their bills. And you—you'll sit like a queen in the kitchen . . . of course there won't be any standing at the stove for you. You'll always have to be nicely dressed and ready to be seen, and with your looks—no, I'm not flattering you—one fine day you'll catch yourself a husband . . . some rich Englishman, I shouldn't wonder—they're the ones who are easy [*Slowing down*] to catch . . . and then we'll get rich and build ourselves a villa on Lake Como . . . of course it rains there a little now and then—but [*Dully*] the sun must shine there too sometimes—even though it seems gloomy—and if not—then we can come home again—come back— [*Pause*]—here—or somewhere else . . .

KRISTIN. Look here, Miss Julie, do you believe all that yourself?

JULIE [*Exhausted*]. Do I believe it?

KRISTIN. Yes.

JULIE [*Wearily*]. I don't know. I don't believe anything any more. [*Sinks down on the bench; her head in her arms on the table*] Nothing. Nothing at all.

KRISTIN [*Turning to* JEAN]. So you meant to beat it, did you?

JEAN [*Disconcerted, putting the razor on the table*]. Beat it? What are you talking about? You've heard Miss Julie's plan, and though she's tired now with being up all night, it's a perfectly sound plan.

KRISTIN. Oh, is it? If you thought I'd work for that . . .

JEAN [*Interrupting*]. Kindly use decent language in front of your mistress. Do you hear?

KRISTIN. Mistress?

JEAN. Yes.

KRISTIN. Well, well, just listen to that!

JEAN. Yes, it would be a good thing if you did listen and talked less. Miss Julie is your mistress and what's made you lose your respect for her now ought to make you feel the same about yourself.

KRISTIN. I've always had enough self-respect——

JEAN. To despise other people.

KRISTIN. —not to go below my own station. Has the Count's cook ever gone with the groom or the swineherd? Tell me that.

JEAN. No, you were lucky enough to have a high-class chap for your beau.

KRISTIN. High-class all right—selling the oats out of the Count's stable.

JEAN. You're a fine one to talk—taking a commission on the groceries and bribes from the butcher.

KRISTIN. What the devil . . . ?

JEAN. And now you can't feel any respect for your employers. You, you!

KRISTIN. Are you coming to church with me? I should think you need a good sermon after your fine deeds.

JEAN. No, I'm not going to church today. You can go alone and confess your own sins.

KRISTIN. Yes, I'll do that and bring back enough forgiveness to cover yours too. The Savior suffered and died on the cross for all our sins, and if we go to Him with faith and a penitent heart, He takes all our sins upon Himself.

JEAN. Even grocery thefts?

JULIE. Do you believe that, Kristin?

KRISTIN. That is my living faith, as sure as I stand here. The faith I learnt as a child and have kept ever since, Miss Julie. "But where sin abounded, grace did much more abound."

JULIE. Oh, if I had your faith! Oh, if . . .

KRISTIN. But you see you can't have it without God's special grace, and it's not given to all to have that.

JULIE. Who is it given to then?

KRISTIN. That's the great secret of the workings of grace, Miss Julie. God is no respecter of persons, and with Him the last shall be first . . .

JULIE. Then I suppose He does respect the last.

KRISTIN [*Continuing*]. . . . and it is easier for a camel to go through the eye of a needle than for a rich man to enter into the kingdom of God. That's how it is, Miss Julie. Now I'm going—alone, and on my way I shall tell the groom not to let any of the horses out, in case anyone should want to leave before the Count gets back. Good-by.

[*Exit*]

JEAN. What a devil! And all on account of a greenfinch.

JULIE [*Wearily*]. Never mind the greenfinch. Do you see any way out of this, any end to it?

JEAN [*Pondering*]. No.

JULIE. If you were in my place, what would you do?

JEAN. In your place? Wait a bit. If I was a woman—a lady of rank who had—fallen. I don't know. Yes, I do know now.

JULIE [*Picking up the razor and making a gesture*]. This?

JEAN. Yes. But *I* wouldn't do it, you know. There's a difference between us.

JULIE. Because you're a man and I'm a woman? What is the difference?

JEAN. The usual difference—between man and woman.

JULIE [*Holding the razor*]. I'd like to. But I can't. My father couldn't either, that time he wanted to.

JEAN. No, he didn't want to. He had to be revenged first.

JULIE. And now my mother is revenged again, through me.

JEAN. Didn't you ever love your father, Miss Julie?

JULIE. Deeply, but I must have hated him too—unconsciously. And he let me be brought up to despise my own sex, to be half woman, half man. Whose fault is what's happened? My father's, my mother's, or my own? My own? I haven't anything that's my own. I haven't one single thought that I didn't get from my father, one emotion that didn't come from my mother, and as for this last idea—about all people being equal—I got that from him, my fiancé—that's why I call him a cad. How can it be my fault? Push the responsibility on to Jesus, like Kristin does? No, I'm too proud and—thanks to my father's teaching—too intelligent. As for all that about a rich person not being able to get into heaven, it's just a lie, but Kristin, who has money in the savings-bank, will certainly not get in. Whose fault is it? What does it matter whose fault it is? In any case I must take the blame and bear the consequences.

JEAN. Yes, but . . . [*There are two sharp rings on the bell.* JULIE *jumps to her feet.* JEAN *changes into his livery*] The Count is back. Supposing Kristin . . . [*Goes to the speaking-tube, presses it and listens*]

JULIE. Has he been to his desk yet?

JEAN. This is Jean, sir. [*Listens*] Yes, sir. [*Listens*] Yes, sir, very good, sir. [*Listens*] At once, sir? [*Listens*] Very good, sir. In half an hour.

JULIE [*In panic*]. What did he say? My God, what did he say?

JEAN. He ordered his boots and his coffee in half an hour.

JULIE. Then there's half an hour . . . Oh, I'm so tired! I can't do anything. Can't be sorry, can't run away, can't stay, can't live—can't die. Help me. Order me, and I'll obey like a dog. Do me this last service—save my honor, save his name. You know what I ought to do, but haven't the strength to do. Use your strength and order me to do it.

JEAN. I don't know why—I can't now—I don't understand . . . It's just as if this coat made me—I can't give you orders—and now that the Count has spoken to me—I can't quite explain, but . . . well, that devil of a lackey is bending my back again. I believe if the Count came down now and ordered me to cut my throat, I'd do it on the spot.

JULIE. Then pretend you're him and I'm you. You did some fine acting before, when you knelt to me and played the aristocrat. Or . . . Have you ever seen a hypnotist at the theater? [*He nods*] He says to the person "Take the broom," and he takes it. He says "Sweep," and he sweeps . . .

JEAN. But the person has to be asleep.

JULIE [*As if in a trance*]. I am asleep already . . . the whole room has turned to smoke—and you look like a stove—a stove like a man in black with a tall hat—your eyes are glowing like coals when the fire is low—and your face is a white patch like ashes. [*The sunlight has now reached the floor and lights up* JEAN] How nice and warm it is! [*She holds out her hands as though warming them at a fire*] And so light—and so peaceful.

JEAN [*Putting the razor in her hand*]. Here is the broom. Go now while it's light—out to the barn—and . . . [*Whispers in her ear*]

JULIE [*Waking*]. Thank you. I am going now—to rest. But just tell me that even the first can receive the gift of grace.

JEAN. The first? No, I can't tell you that. But wait . . . Miss Julie, I've got it! You aren't one of the first any longer. You're one of the last.

JULIE. That's true. I'm one of the very last. I *am* the last. Oh! . . . But now I can't go. Tell me again to go.

JEAN. No, I can't now either, I can't.

JULIE. And the first shall be last.

JEAN. Don't think, don't think. You're taking my strength away too and making me a coward. What's that? I thought I saw the bell move . . . To be so frightened of a bell! Yes, but it's not just a bell. There's somebody behind it—a hand moving it—and something else moving the hand—and if you stop your ears—if you stop your ears—yes, then it rings louder than ever. Rings and rings until you answer—and then it's too late. Then the police come and . . . and . . . [*The bell rings twice loudly.* JEAN *flinches, then straightens himself up*] It's horrible. But there's no other way to end it . . . Go!

[JULIE *walks firmly out through the door*]

Questions for Study

1. *Miss Julie* takes place during one long night. What is the implication of its being Midsummer Eve? What role do the peasants outside the kitchen setting play in the drama? What influence do flowers and dancing have upon the outcome of this long night?

2. Define the two distinct social classes represented in the play. How is Miss Julie a social snob? How is Jean a social climber? Why are Miss Julie and Jean afraid of trying to cross social barriers?

3. Miss Julie's parents clearly brought her up with ideas that were unusual. What is the father's influence upon Miss Julie's character and attitudes? What is the mother's? How is Miss Julie a young woman who is divided against herself?

4. Explain the relationship between Jean and Miss Julie's father. Is Jean afraid of him? Describe Jean's attitude toward the bell which the Count rings as a summons. What finally does Jean's dream of running off to Switzerland tell us about him?

5. Describe Kristin and her function in the play. What does her attitude toward the Swedish nobility tell us about her character? If she cares for Jean, why does she not try to keep him from Miss Julie? Is she afraid of Miss Julie or merely indifferent to her?

6. Interpret Miss Julie's suicide. Be sure to point out why, in your view, she takes Jean's razor and kills herself. Has she turned to suicide because of her loss of honor or because of other circumstances portrayed in the play? Does the play present Miss Julie's situation as truly tragic or as one that ends with merely a mad action?

7. Is Miss Julie only half a woman? Does she hate men? Describe her relationship with her fiancé and comment on how it reveals important features of her character.

8. What role does Miss Julie try to play in life? How do you interpret her frantic search for affection and happiness?

9. Is Miss Julie attracted to Jean merely because of his masculinity or because she has fallen in love with him? What are the ingredients of her attraction to him? Why is he attracted to her?

10. Comment on the way Strindberg has structured the interior scene of the play against a background of exterior festivities. What does this staging of events suggest?

11. How many examples of dominance/submission do you find in the play? Do you find a balanced awareness of what men can do to women and of what women can do to men? Or does Strindberg seem to you to be biased against the "new woman"? Explain.

Lillian Hellman (b. 1905)
The Little Foxes

Take us the foxes, the little foxes,
that spoil the vines; for our vines have tender grapes.

—SONG OF SOLOMON 2:15

Characters, *in order of their appearance*

ADDIE
CAL
BIRDIE HUBBARD
OSCAR HUBBARD
LEO HUBBARD
REGINA GIDDENS
WILLIAM MARSHALL
BENJAMIN HUBBARD
ALEXANDRA GIDDENS
HORACE GIDDENS

The scene of the play is the living room of the Giddens house, in a small town in the South.

ACT I: *The Spring of 1900, evening.*
ACT II: *A week later, early morning.*
ACT III: *Two weeks later, late afternoon.*

There has been no attempt to write Southern dialect. It is to be understood that the accents are Southern.

ACT I.

SCENE: *The living room of the Giddens home, in a small town in the deep South, the spring of 1900. Upstage is a staircase leading to the second story. Upstage, right, are double doors to the dining room. When these doors are open we see a section of the dining room and the furniture. Upstage, left, is an entrance hall with a coatrack and umbrella stand. There are large lace-curtained windows on the left wall. The room is lit by a center gas chandelier and painted china oil lamps on the tables. Against the wall is a large piano. Downstage, right, are a high couch, a large table, several chairs. Against the left back wall are a table and several chairs. Near the window there are a smaller couch and tables. The room is good-looking, the furniture expensive; but it reflects no particular taste. Everything is of the best and that is all.*

AT RISE: ADDIE, *a tall, nice-looking Negro woman of about fifty-five, is closing the windows. From behind the closed dining-room doors there is the sound of voices. After a second,* CAL, *a middle-aged Negro, comes in from the entrance hall carrying a tray with glasses and a bottle of port.* ADDIE *crosses, takes the tray from him, puts it on table, begins to arrange it.*

ADDIE [*pointing to the bottle*].   You gone stark out of your head?

CAL.   No, smart lady, I ain't. Miss Regina told me to get out that bottle. [*Points to bottle*] That very bottle for the mighty honored guest. When Miss Regina changes orders like that you can bet your dime she got her reason.

ADDIE [*points to dining room*].   Go on. You'll be needed.

CAL.   Miss Zan she had two helpings frozen fruit cream and she tell that honored guest, she tell him that you make the best frozen fruit cream in all the South.

ADDIE.   Did she? Well, see that Belle saves a little for her. She like it right before she go to bed. Save a few little cakes, too, she like—

[*The dining-room doors are opened and closed again by* BIRDIE HUB-BARD. BIRDIE *is a woman of about forty, with a pretty, well-bred, faded face. Her movements are usually nervous and timid, but now, as she comes running into the room, she is gay and excited.* CAL *turns to* BIRDIE.]

BIRDIE.   Oh, Cal. I want you to get one of the kitchen boys to run home for me. He's to look in my desk drawer and—[*To* ADDIE] My, Addie. What a good supper! Just as good as good can be.

ADDIE.   You look pretty this evening, Miss Birdie, and young.

BIRDIE [*laughing*].   Me, young? [*Turns back to* CAL] Maybe you better find Simon and tell him to do it himself. He's to look in my desk, the left drawer, and bring my music album right away. Mr. Marshall is very anxious to see it because of his father and the opera in Chicago. [*To* ADDIE] Mr. Marshall is such a polite man with his manners and very educated and cultured and I've told him all about how my mama and papa used to go to Europe for the music—[*Laughs*] Imagine going all the way to Europe just to listen to music. Wouldn't that be nice, Addie? Just to sit there and listen and—[*Turns*] Left drawer, Cal. Tell him that twice because he forgets. And tell him not to let any of the things drop out of the album and to bring it right in here when he comes back.

[*The dining-room doors are opened and quickly closed by* OSCAR HUB-BARD. *He is a man in his late forties.*]

CAL.   Simon he won't get it right. But I'll tell him.

BIRDIE.   Left drawer, Cal, and tell him to bring the blue book and—

OSCAR [*sharply*].   Birdie.

BIRDIE [*turning nervously*].   Oh, Oscar. I was just sending Simon for my music album.

OSCAR [*to* CAL].   Never mind about the album. Miss Birdie has changed her mind.

BIRDIE.   But, really, Oscar. Really I promised Mr. Marshall. I—

[CAL *exits*.]

OSCAR.   Why do you leave the dinner table and go running about like a child?

BIRDIE.   But, Oscar, Mr. Marshall said most specially he *wanted* to see my album. I told him about the time Mama met Wagner,[1] and Mrs. Wagner gave her the signed program and the big picture. Mr. Marshall wants to see that. Very, very much. We had such a nice talk and—

OSCAR.   You have been chattering to him like a magpie. You haven't let him be for a second. I can't think he came South to be bored with you.

BIRDIE [*quickly, hurt*].   He wasn't bored. I don't believe he was bored. He's a very educated, cultured gentleman. [*Her voice rises*] I just don't believe it. You always talk like that when I'm having a nice time.

OSCAR [*turning to her, sharply*].   You have had too much wine. Get yourself in hand now.

BIRDIE [*drawing back, about to cry, shrilly*].   What am I doing? I am not doing anything. What am I doing?

OSCAR [*taking a step to her*].   I said get yourself in hand. Stop acting like a fool.

BIRDIE.   I don't believe he was bored. I just don't believe it. Some people like music and like to talk about it. That's all I was doing.

[LEO HUBBARD *comes hurrying through the dining-room door. He is a young man of twenty, with a weak kind of good looks.*]

LEO.   Mama! Papa! They are coming in now.

OSCAR [*softly*].   Sit down, Birdie. Sit down now. [BIRDIE *sits down, bows her head as if to hide her face.*]

[*The dining-room doors are opened by* CAL. *We see people beginning to rise from the table.* REGINA GIDDENS *comes in with* WILLIAM MARSHALL. REGINA *is a handsome woman of forty.* MARSHALL *is forty-five, pleasant-looking, self-possessed. Behind them comes* ALEXANDRA GIDDENS, *a pretty, rather delicate-looking girl of seventeen. She is followed by* BEN-JAMIN HUBBARD, *fifty-five, with a large jovial face and the light graceful movements that one often finds in large men.*]

REGINA.   Mr. Marshall, I think you're trying to console me. Chicago may be the noisiest, dirtiest city in the world but I should still prefer it to the sound of

---

1. Richard Wagner (1813–83), celebrated and distinguished German composer.

our horses and the smell of our azaleas. I should like crowds of people, and theaters, and lovely women—*Very* lovely women, Mr. Marshall?

MARSHALL.   In Chicago? Oh, I suppose so. But I can tell you this: I've never dined there with *three* such lovely ladies.

[ADDIE *begins to pass the port.*]

BEN.   Our Southern women are well favored.

LEO [*laughs*].   But one must go to Mobile for the ladies, sir. Very elegant worldly ladies, too.

BEN [*looks at him*].   Worldly, eh? *Worldly,* did you say?

OSCAR [*hastily, to* LEO].   Your Uncle Ben means that worldliness is not a mark of beauty in any woman.

LEO [*quickly*].   Of course, Uncle Ben. I didn't mean—

MARSHALL.   Your port is excellent, Mrs. Giddens.

REGINA.   Thank you, Mr. Marshall. We had been saving that bottle, hoping we could open it just for you.

ALEXANDRA [*as* ADDIE *comes to her with the tray*].   Oh. May I *really*, Addie?

ADDIE.   Better ask Mama.

ALEXANDRA.   May I, Mama?

REGINA [*nods, smiles*].   In Mr. Marshall's honor.

ALEXANDRA.   Mr. Marshall, this will be the first taste of port I've ever had.

MARSHALL.   No one ever had their first taste of a better port. [*He lifts his glass in a toast; she lifts hers; they both drink*] Well, I suppose it is all true, Mrs. Giddens.

REGINA.   What is true?

MARSHALL.   That you Southerners occupy a unique position in America. You live better than the rest of us, you eat better, you drink better. I wonder you find time, or want to find time, to do business.

BEN.   A great many Southerners don't.

MARSHALL.   Do all of you live here together?

REGINA.   Here with me? [*Laughs*] Oh, no. My brother Ben lives next door. My brother Oscar and his family live in the next square.

BEN.   But we are a very close family. We've always wanted it that way.

MARSHALL.   That is very pleasant. Keeping your family together to share each other's lives. My family moves around too much. My children seem never to come home. Away at school in the winter; in the summer, Europe with their mother—

REGINA [*eagerly*].   Oh, yes. Even down here we read about Mrs. Marshall in the society pages.

MARSHALL.   I dare say. She moves about a great deal. And all of you are part of the same business? Hubbard Sons?

BEN [*motions to* OSCAR].   Oscar and me. [*Motions to* REGINA] My sister's good husband is a banker.

MARSHALL [*looks at* REGINA, *surprised*].   Oh.

REGINA.   I am so sorry that my husband isn't here to meet you. He's been very ill. He is at Johns Hopkins.[2] But he will be home soon. We think he is getting better now.

LEO.   I work for Uncle Horace. [REGINA *looks at him*] I mean I work for Uncle Horace at his bank. I keep an eye on things while he's away.

REGINA [*smiles*].   Really, Leo?

BEN [*looks at* LEO, *then to* MARSHALL].   Modesty in the young is as excellent as it is rare.

OSCAR [*to* LEO].   Your uncle means that a young man should speak more modestly.

LEO [*hastily, taking a step to* BEN].   Oh, I didn't mean, sir—

MARSHALL.   Oh, Mrs. Hubbard. Where's that Wagner autograph you promised to let me see? My train will be leaving soon and—

BIRDIE.   The autograph? Oh. Well. Really, Mr. Marshall, I didn't mean to chatter so about it. Really I—[*Nervously, looking at* OSCAR] You must excuse me. I didn't get it because, well, because I had—I—I had a little headache and—

OSCAR.   My wife is a miserable victim of headaches.

REGINA [*quickly*].   Mr. Marshall said at supper that he would like you to play for him, Alexandra.

ALEXANDRA [*who has been looking at* BIRDIE].   It's not I who play well, sir. It's my aunt. She plays just wonderfully. She's my teacher. [*Rises. Eagerly*] May we play a duet? May we, Mama?

BIRDIE.   Thank you, dear. But I have my headache now. I—

OSCAR [*sharply*].   Don't be stubborn, Birdie. Mr. Marshall wants you to play.

MARSHALL.   Indeed I do. If your headache isn't—

BIRDIE [*hesitates, then gets up, pleased*].   But I'd like to, sir. Very much. [*She and* ALEXANDRA *go to the piano.*]

MARSHALL.   It's very remarkable how you Southern aristocrats have kept together. Kept together and kept what belonged to you.

BEN.   You misunderstand, sir. Southern aristocrats have *not* kept together and have *not* kept what belonged to them.

MARSHALL [*laughs, indicates room*].   You don't call this keeping what belongs to you?

BEN.   But we are not aristocrats. [*Points to* BIRDIE *at the piano*] Our brother's wife is the only one of us who belongs to the Southern aristocracy.

[BIRDIE *looks toward* BEN.]

MARSHALL [*smiles*].   My information is that you people have been here, and solidly here, for a long time.

OSCAR.   And so we have. Since our great-grandfather.

BEN.   Who was *not* an aristocrat, like Birdie's.

MARSHALL.   You make great distinctions.

BEN.   Oh, they have been made for us. And maybe they are important

---

2. Johns Hopkins Hospital, Baltimore; a prestigious teaching and research center which provided the finest treatment available in the country at the time.

distinctions. Now you take Birdie's family. When my great-grandfather came here they were the highest-tone plantation owners in this state.

LEO [*steps to* MARSHALL. *Proudly*]. My mother's grandfather was *governor* of the state before the war.

OSCAR. They owned the plantation Lionnet. You may have heard of it, sir?

MARSHALL [*laughs*]. No, I've never heard of anything but brick houses on a lake, and cotton mills.

BEN. Lionnet in its day was the best cotton land in the South. It still brings us in a fair crop. Ah, they were great days for those people—even when I can remember. They had the best of everything. [BIRDIE *turns to them*] Cloth from Paris, trips to Europe, horses you can't raise anymore, niggers to lift their fingers—

BIRDIE. We were good to our people. Everybody knew that. We were better to them than—

REGINA [*quickly*]. Why, Birdie. You aren't playing.

BEN. But when the war comes these fine gentlemen ride off and leave the cotton, *and* the women, to rot.

BIRDIE. My father was killed in the war. He was a fine soldier, Mr. Marshall. A fine man.

REGINA. Oh, certainly, Birdie. A famous soldier.

BEN [*to* BIRDIE]. But that isn't the tale I am telling Mr. Marshall. [*To* MARSHALL] Well, sir, the war ends. Lionnet is almost ruined, and the sons finish ruining it. And there were thousands like them. Why? Because the Southern aristocrat can adapt himself to nothing. Too high-tone to try.

MARSHALL. Sometimes it is difficult to learn new ways. [BIRDIE *and* ALEXANDRA *begin to play.* MARSHALL *leans forward, listening.*]

BEN. Perhaps, perhaps. [*He sees that* MARSHALL *is listening to the music. Irritated, he turns to* BIRDIE *and* ALEXANDRA *at the piano, then back to* MARSHALL] You're right, Mr. Marshall. It is difficult to learn new ways. But maybe that's why it's profitable. *Our* grandfather and *our* father learned the new ways and learned how to make them pay. [*Smiles*] *They* were in trade. Hubbard Sons, Merchandise. Others, Birdie's family, for example, looked down on them. [*Settles back in chair*] To make a long story short, Lionnet now belongs to us. [BIRDIE *stops playing*] Twenty years ago we took over their land, their cotton, and their daughter. [BIRDIE *rises and stands stiffly by the piano.* MARSHALL, *who has been watching her, rises.*]

MARSHALL. May I bring you a glass of port, Mrs. Hubbard?

BIRDIE [*softly*]. No, thank you, sir. You are most polite.

REGINA [*sharply, to* BEN]. You are boring Mr. Marshall with these ancient family tales.

BEN. I hope not. I hope not. I am trying to make an important point— [*Bows to* MARSHALL] for our future business partner.

OSCAR [*to* MARSHALL]. My brother always says that it's folks like us who have struggled and fought to bring to our land some of the prosperity of your land.

BEN. Some people call that patriotism.

REGINA [*laughs gaily*]. I hope you don't find my brothers too obvious,

Mr. Marshall. I'm afraid they mean that this is the time for the ladies to leave the gentlemen to talk business.

MARSHALL [*hastily*]. Not at all. We settled everything this afternoon. [*He looks at his watch*] I have only a few minutes before I must leave for the train. [*Smiles at her*] And I insist they be spent with you.

REGINA. *And* with another glass of port.

MARSHALL. Thank you.

BEN. My sister is right. [*To* MARSHALL] I am a plain man and I am trying to say a plain thing. A man ain't only in business for what he can get out of it. It's got to give him something here. [*Puts hand to his breast*] That's every bit as true for the nigger picking cotton for a silver quarter, as it is for you and me. [REGINA *gives* MARSHALL *a glass of port*] If it don't give him something here, then he don't pick the cotton right. Money isn't all. Not by three shots.

MARSHALL. Really? Well, I always thought it was a great deal.

REGINA. And so did I, Mr. Marshall.

MARSHALL [*pleasantly, but with meaning*]. Now you don't have to convince me that you are the right people for the deal. I wouldn't be here if you hadn't convinced me six months ago. You want the mill here, and I want it here. It isn't my business to find out why you want it.

BEN. To bring the machine to the cotton, and not the cotton to the machine.

MARSHALL [*amused*]. You have a turn for neat phrases, Hubbard. Well, however grand your reasons are, mine are simple: I want to make money and I believe I'll make it on you. [*As* BEN *starts to speak, he smiles*] Mind you, I have no objections to more high-minded reasons. They are mighty valuable in business. It's fine to have partners who so closely follow the teachings of Christ. [*Gets up*] And now I must leave for my train.

REGINA. I'm sorry you won't stay over with us, Mr. Marshall, but you'll come again. Anytime you like.

BEN [*motions to* LEO, *indicating the bottle*]. Fill them up, boy, fill them up. [LEO *moves around filling the glasses as* BEN *speaks*] Down here, sir, we have a strange custom. We drink the *last* drink for a toast. That's to prove that the Southerner is always still on his feet for the last drink. [*Picks up his glass*] It was Henry Frick,[3] your Mr. Henry Frick, who said, "Railroads are the Rembrandts of investments." Well, *I* say, "Southern cotton mills *will be* the Rembrandts of investment." So I give you the firm of Hubbard Sons and Marshall, Cotton Mills, and to it a long and prosperous life. [*They all pick up their glasses.* MARSHALL *looks at them, amused. Then he, too, lifts his glass, smiles.*]

OSCAR. The children will drive you to the depot. Leo! Alexandra! You will drive Mr. Marshall down.

LEO [*eagerly, looks at* BEN *who nods*]. Yes, sir. [*To* MARSHALL] Not often Uncle Ben lets *me* drive the horses. And a beautiful pair they are. [*Starts for hall*] Come on, Zan.

ALEXANDRA. May I drive tonight, Uncle Ben, please? I'd like to and—

BEN [*shakes his head, laughs*]. In your evening clothes? Oh, no, my dear.

---

3. Henry Clay Frick (1849–1919), wealthy American steel executive, railroad baron, and art collector.

ALEXANDRA.   But Leo always —[*Stops, exits quickly.*]
REGINA.   I don't like to say good-bye to you, Mr. Marshall.
MARSHALL.   Then we won't say good-bye. You have promised that you would come and let me show you Chicago. Do I have to make you promise again?
REGINA [*looks at him as he presses her hand*].   I promise again.
MARSHALL [*moves to* BIRDIE].   Good-bye, Mrs. Hubbard.
BIRDIE.   Good-bye, sir.
MARSHALL [*as he passes* REGINA].   Remember.
REGINA.   I will.

[MARSHALL *exits, followed by* BEN *and* OSCAR. *For a second* REGINA *and* BIRDIE *stand looking after them. Then* REGINA *throws up her arms, laughs happily.*]

REGINA.   And there, Birdie, goes the man who has opened the door to our future.
BIRDIE [*surprised at the unaccustomed friendliness*].   What?
REGINA.   *Our future.* Yours and mine, Ben's and Oscar's, the children —[*Looks at* BIRDIE's *puzzled face, laughs*] Our future! [*Gaily*] You were charming at supper, Birdie. Mr. Marshall certainly thought so.
BIRDIE [*pleased*].   Why, Regina! Do you think he did?
REGINA.   Can't you tell when you're being admired?
BIRDIE.   Oscar said I bored Mr. Marshall. But he admired *you*. He told me so.
REGINA.   What did he say?
BIRDIE.   He said to me, "I hope your sister-in-law will come to Chicago. Chicago will be at her feet." He said the ladies would bow to your manners and the gentlemen to your looks.
REGINA.   Did he? He seems a lonely man. Imagine being lonely with all that money. I don't think he likes his wife.
BIRDIE.   Not like his wife? What a thing to say.
REGINA.   She's away a great deal. He said that several times. And once he made fun of her being so social and high-tone. But that fits in all right. [*Sits back, stretches*] Her being social, I mean. She can introduce me. It won't take long with an introduction from her.
BIRDIE [*bewildered*].   Introduce you? In Chicago? You mean you really might go? Oh, Regina, you can't leave here. What about Horace?
REGINA.   Don't look so scared about everything, Birdie. I'm going to live in Chicago. I've always wanted to. And now there'll be plenty of money to go with.
BIRDIE.   But Horace won't be able to move around. You know what the doctor wrote.
REGINA.   There'll be millions, Birdie, millions. You know what I've always said when people told me we were rich? I said I think you should either be a nigger or a millionaire. In between, like us, what for? [*Laughs*] But I'm not going away tomorrow, Birdie. There's plenty of time to worry about Horace when he comes home. If he ever decides to come home.
BIRDIE.   Will we be going to Chicago? I mean, Oscar and Leo and me?

REGINA. You? I shouldn't think so. [*Laughs*] Well, we must remember tonight. It's a very important night and we mustn't forget it. We shall plan all the things we'd like to have and then we'll really have them. Make a wish, Birdie, any wish. It's bound to come true now. [BEN *and* OSCAR *enter.*]

BIRDIE [*laughs*]. Well. Well, I don't know. Maybe. [REGINA *turns to look at* BEN] Well, I guess I'd know right off what I wanted. [OSCAR *stands by the upper window, waves to the departing carriage.*]

REGINA [*looks up at* BEN, *smiles. He smiles back at her*]. Well, you did it.

BEN. Looks like it might be we did.

REGINA [*springs up*]. Looks like it! Don't pretend. You're like a cat who's been licking the cream. [*Crosses to wine bottle*] Now we must all have a drink to celebrate.

OSCAR. The children, Alexandra and Leo, make a very handsome couple, Regina. Marshall remarked himself what fine young folks they were. How well they looked together!

REGINA [*sharply*]. Yes. You said that before, Oscar.

BEN. Yes, sir. It's beginning to look as if the deal's all set. I may not be a subtle man—but—[*Turns to them. After a second*] Now somebody ask me how I know the deal is set.

OSCAR. What do you mean, Ben?

BEN. You remember I told him that down here we drink the *last* drink for a toast?

OSCAR [*thoughtfully*]. Yes. I never heard that before.

BEN. Nobody's ever heard it before. God forgives those who invent what they need. I already had his signature. But we've all done business with men whose word over a glass is better than a bond. Anyway it don't hurt to have both.

OSCAR [*turns to* REGINA]. You understand what Ben means?

REGINA. Yes, Oscar. I understand. I understood immediately.

BEN [*looks at her admiringly*]. Did you, Regina? Well, when he lifted his glass to drink, I closed my eyes and saw the bricks going into place.

REGINA. And *I* saw a lot more than that.

BEN. Slowly, slowly. As yet we have only our hopes.

REGINA. Birdie and I have just been planning what we want. I know what I want. What will you want, Ben?

BEN. Caution. Don't count the chickens. [*Leans back, laughs*] Well, God would allow us a little daydreaming. Good for the soul when you've worked hard enough to deserve it. [*Pauses*] I think I'll have a stable. For a long time I've had my good eyes on Carter's in Savannah. A rich man's pleasure, the sport of kings, why not the sport of Hubbards? Why not?

REGINA [*smiles*]. Why not? What will you have, Oscar?

OSCAR. I don't know. [*Thoughtfully*] The pleasure of seeing the bricks grow will be enough for me.

BEN. Oh, of course. Our greatest pleasure will be to see the bricks grow. But we are all entitled to a little side indulgence.

OSCAR. Yes, I suppose so. Well, then, I think we might take a few trips here and there, eh, Birdie?

BIRDIE [*surprised at being consulted*]. Yes, Oscar. I'd like that.

OSCAR. We might even make a regular trip to Jekyll Island.[4] I've heard the Cornelly place is for sale. We might think about buying it. Make a nice change. Do you good, Birdie, a change of climate. Fine shooting on Jekyll, the best.

BIRDIE. I'd like—

OSCAR [*indulgently*]. What would you like?

BIRDIE. Two things. Two things I'd like most.

REGINA. Two! I should like a thousand. You are modest, Birdie.

BIRDIE [*warmly, delighted with the unexpected interest*]. I should like to have Lionnet back. I know you own it now, but I'd like to see it fixed up again, the way Mama and Papa had it. Every year it used to get a nice coat of paint—Papa was very particular about the paint—and the lawn was so smooth all the way down to the river, with the trims of zinnias and red-feather plush. And the figs and blue little plums and the scuppernongs—[*Smiles. Turns to* REGINA] The organ is still there and it wouldn't cost much to fix. We could have parties for Zan, the way Mama used to have for me.

BEN. That's a pretty picture, Birdie. Might be a most pleasant way to live. [*Dismissing* BIRDIE] What do you want, Regina?

BIRDIE [*very happily, not noticing that they are no longer listening to her*]. I could have a cutting garden. Just where Mama's used to be. Oh, I do think we could be happier there. Papa used to say that *nobody* had ever lost their temper at Lionnet, and *nobody* ever would. Papa would never let anybody be nasty-spoken or mean. No, sir. He just didn't like it.

BEN. What do you want, Regina?

REGINA. I'm going to Chicago. And when I'm settled there and know the right people and the right things to buy—because I certainly don't now—I shall go to Paris and buy them. [*Laughs*] I'm going to leave you and Oscar to count the bricks.

BIRDIE. Oscar. Please let me have Lionnet back.

OSCAR [*to* REGINA]. You are serious about moving to Chicago?

BEN. She is going to see the great world and leave us in the little one. Well, we'll come and visit you and meet all the great and be proud you are our sister.

REGINA [*gaily*]. Certainly. And you won't even have to learn to be subtle, Ben. Stay as you are. You will be rich and the rich don't have to be subtle.

OSCAR. But what about Alexandra? She's seventeen. Old enough to be thinking about marrying.

BIRDIE. And, Oscar, I have one more wish. Just one more wish.

OSCAR [*turns*]. What is it, Birdie? What are you saying?

BIRDIE. I want you to stop shooting. I mean, so much. I don't like to see animals and birds killed just for the killing. You only throw them away—

BEN [*to* REGINA]. It'll take a great deal of money to live as you're planning, Regina.

REGINA. Certainly. But there'll be plenty of money. You have estimated the profits very high.

---

4. Exclusive resort island situated just off the coast of Georgia; at the time it was privately owned.

BEN. I have—

BIRDIE [OSCAR *is looking at her furiously*].   And you never let anybody else shoot, and the niggers need it so much to keep from starving. It's wicked to shoot food just because you like to shoot, when poor people need it so—

BEN [*laughs*].   I have estimated the profits very high—for myself.

REGINA.   What did you say?

BIRDIE.   I've always wanted to speak about it, Oscar.

OSCAR [*slowly, carefully*].   What are you chattering about?

BIRDIE [*nervously*].   I was talking about Lionnet and—and about your shooting—

OSCAR.   You are exciting yourself.

REGINA [*to* BEN].   I didn't hear you. There was so much talking.

OSCAR [*to* BIRDIE].   You have been acting very childish, very excited, all evening.

BIRDIE.   Regina asked me what I'd like.

REGINA.   What did you say, Ben?

BIRDIE.   Now that we'll be so rich everybody was saying what they would like, so *I* said what *I* would like, too.

BEN.   I said—[*He is interrupted by* OSCAR.]

OSCAR [*to* BIRDIE].   Very well. We've all heard you. That's enough now.

BEN.   I am waiting. [*They stop*] I am waiting for you to finish. You and Birdie. Four conversations are three too many. [BIRDIE *slowly sits down.* BEN *smiles, to* REGINA] I said that I had, and I do, estimate the profits very high—for myself, and Oscar, of course.

REGINA.   And what does that mean? [BEN *shrugs, looks toward* OSCAR.]

OSCAR [*looks at* BEN, *clears throat*].   Well, Regina, it's like this. For forty-nine percent Marshall will put up four hundred thousand dollars. For fifty-one percent—[*Smiles archly*] a controlling interest, mind you—we will put up two hundred and twenty-five thousand dollars besides offering him certain benefits that our [*looks at* BEN] local position allows us to manage. Ben means that two hundred and twenty-five thousand dollars is a lot of money.

REGINA.   I know the terms and I know it's a lot of money.

BEN [*nodding*].   It is.

OSCAR.   Ben means that we are ready with our two-thirds of the money. Your third, Horace's I mean, doesn't seem to be ready. [*Raises his hand as* REGINA *starts to speak*] Ben has written to Horace, I have written, and you have written. He answers. But he never mentions this business. Yet we have explained to him in great detail, and told him the urgency. Still he never mentions it. Ben has been very patient, Regina. Naturally, you are our sister and we want you to benefit from anything we do.

REGINA.   And in addition to your concern for me, you do not want control to go out of the family. [*To* BEN] That right, Ben?

BEN.   That's cynical. [*Smiles*] Cynicism is an unpleasant way of saying the truth.

OSCAR.   No need to be cynical. We'd have no trouble raising the third share, the share that you want to take.

REGINA.   I am sure you could get the third share, the share you were saving for me. But that would give you a strange partner. And strange partners sometimes want a great deal. [*Smiles unpleasantly*] But perhaps it would be wise for you to find him.

OSCAR. Now, now. Nobody says we *want* to do that. We would like to have you in and you would like to come in.

REGINA. Yes. I certainly would.

BEN [*laughs, puts up his hand*]. But we haven't heard from Horace.

REGINA. I've given my word that Horace will put up the money. That should be enough.

BEN. Oh, it was enough. I took your word. But I've got to have more than your word now. The contracts will be signed this week, and Marshall will want to see our money soon after. Regina, Horace has been in Baltimore for five months. I know that you've written him to come home, and that he hasn't come.

OSCAR. It's beginning to look as if he doesn't want to come home.

REGINA. Of course he wants to come home. You can't move around with heart trouble at any moment you choose. You know what doctors are like once they get their hands on a case like this—

OSCAR. They can't very well keep him from answering letters, can they? [REGINA *turns to* BEN] They couldn't keep him from arranging for the money if he wanted to—

REGINA. Has it occurred to you that Horace is also a good businessman?

BEN. Certainly. He is a shrewd trader. Always has been. The bank is proof of that.

REGINA. Then, possibly, he may be keeping silent because he doesn't think he is getting enough for his money. Seventy-five thousand he has to put up. That's a lot of money, too.

OSCAR. Nonsense. He knows a good thing when he hears it. He knows that we can make *twice* the profit on cotton goods manufactured here than can be made in the North.

BEN. That isn't what Regina means. May I interpret you, Regina? [*To* OSCAR] Regina is saying that Horace wants *more* than a third of our share.

OSCAR. But he's only putting up a third of the money. You put up a third and you get a third. What else could he expect?

REGINA. Well, *I* don't know. I don't know about these things. It would seem that if you put up a third you should only get a third. But then again, there's no law about it, is there? I should think that if you knew your money was very badly needed, well, you just might say, I want more, I want a bigger share. You boys have done that. I've heard you say so.

BEN [*after a pause, laughs*]. So you believe he has deliberately held out? For a larger share? Well, I don't believe it. But I do believe that's what *you* want. Am I right, Regina?

REGINA. Oh, I shouldn't like to be too definite. But I could say that I wouldn't like to persuade Horace unless he did get a larger share. I must look after his interests. It seems only natural—

OSCAR. And where would the larger share come from?

REGINA. I don't know. That's not my business. [*Giggles*] But perhaps it could come off your share, Oscar. [REGINA *and* BEN *laugh.*]

OSCAR [*rises and wheels on both of them as they laugh*]. What kind of talk is this?

BEN. I haven't said a thing.

OSCAR [*to* REGINA]. *You* are talking very big tonight.

REGINA [*stops laughing*]. Am I? Well, you should know me well enough to know that I wouldn't be asking for things I didn't think I could get.

OSCAR. Listen. I don't believe you can even get Horace to come home, much less get money from him or talk quite so big about what you want.

REGINA. Oh, I can get him home.

OSCAR. Then why haven't you?

REGINA. I thought I should fight his battles for him, before he came home. Horace is a very sick man. And even if *you* don't care how sick he is, I do.

BEN. Stop this foolish squabbling. How can you get him home?

REGINA. I will send Alexandra to Baltimore. She will ask him to come home. She will say that she wants him to come home, and that *I* want him to come home.

BIRDIE [*rises*]. Well, of course she wants him here, but he's sick and maybe he's happy where he is.

REGINA [*ignores* BIRDIE, *to* BEN] You agree that he will come home if she asks him to, if she says that I miss him and want him—

BEN [*looks at her, smiles*]. I admire you, Regina. And I agree. That's settled now and—[*Starts to rise.*]

REGINA [*quickly*]. But before she brings him home, I want to know what he's going to get.

BEN. What do you want?

REGINA. Twice what you offered.

BEN. Well, you won't get it.

OSCAR [*to* REGINA]. I think you've gone crazy.

REGINA. I don't want to fight, Ben—

BEN. I don't either. You won't get it. There isn't any chance of that. [*Roguishly*] You're holding us up, and that's not pretty, Regina, not pretty. [*Holds up his hand as he sees she is about to speak*] But we need you, and I don't want to fight. Here's what I'll do: I'll give Horace forty percent, instead of the thirty-three and a third he really should get. I'll do that, provided he is home and his money is up within two weeks. How's that?

REGINA. All right.

OSCAR. I've asked before: where is this extra share coming from?

BEN [*pleasantly*]. From you. From your share.

OSCAR [*furiously*]. From me, is it? That's just fine and dandy. That's my reward. For thirty-five years I've worked my hands to the bone for you. For thirty-five years I've done all the things you didn't want to do. And this is what I—

BEN [*turns to look at* OSCAR. OSCAR *breaks off*]. My, my. I am being attacked tonight on all sides. First by my sister, then by my brother. And I ain't a man who likes being attacked. I can't believe that God wants the strong to parade their strength, but I don't mind doing it if it's got to be done. You ought to take these things better, Oscar. I've made you money in the past. I'm going to make you more money now. You'll be a very rich man. What's the difference to any of us if a little more goes here, a little less goes there—it's all in the family. And it will stay in the family. I'll never marry. [ADDIE *enters, begins to gather the glasses from the table*] So my money will go to Alexandra and Leo. They may even marry someday and—[ADDIE *looks at* BEN.]

BIRDIE [*rising*]. Marry—Zan and Leo—

OSCAR [*carefully*]. That would make a great difference in my feelings. If they married.

BEN. Yes, that's what I mean. Of course it would make a difference.

OSCAR [*carefully*]. Is that what *you* mean, Regina?

REGINA. Oh, it's too far away. We'll talk about it in a few years.

OSCAR. I want to talk about it now.

BEN [*nods*]. Naturally.

REGINA. There's a lot of things to consider. They are first cousins, and—

OSCAR. That isn't unusual. Our grandmother and grandfather were first cousins.

REGINA [*giggles*]. And look at us. [BEN *giggles.*]

OSCAR [*angrily*]. You're both being very gay with my money.

BEN [*sighs*]. These quarrels. I dislike them so. [*To* REGINA] A marriage might be a very wise arrangement, for several reasons. And then, Oscar has given up something for you. You should try to manage something for him.

REGINA. I haven't said I was opposed to it. But Leo is a wild boy. There were those times when he took a little money from the bank and—

OSCAR. That's all past history—

REGINA. Oh, I know. And I know all young men are wild. I'm only mentioning it to show you that there are considerations—

BEN [*irritated because she does not understand that he is trying to keep* OSCAR *quiet*]. All right, so there are. But please assure Oscar that you will think about it very seriously.

REGINA [*smiles, nods*]. Very well. I assure Oscar that I will think about it seriously.

OSCAR [*sharply*]. That is not an answer.

REGINA [*rises*]. My, you're in a bad humor and you shall put me in one. I have said all that I am willing to say now. After all, Horace has to give his consent, too.

OSCAR. Horace will do what you tell him to.

REGINA. Yes, I think he will.

OSCAR. And I have your word that you will try to—

REGINA [*patiently*]. Yes, Oscar. You have my word that I will think about it. Now do leave me alone. [*There is the sound of the front door being closed.*]

BIRDIE. I—Alexandra is only seventeen. She—

LEO [*comes into the room*]. Mr. Marshall got off safe and sound. Weren't those fine clothes he had? You can always spot clothes made in a good place. Looks like maybe they were done in England. Lots of men in the North send all the way to England for their stuff.

BEN [*to* LEO]. Were you careful driving the horses?

LEO. Oh, yes, sir. I was. [ALEXANDRA *has come in on* BEN'S *question, hears the answer, looks angrily at* LEO.]

ALEXANDRA. It's a lovely night. You should have come, Aunt Birdie.

REGINA. Were you gracious to Mr. Marshall?

ALEXANDRA. I think so, Mama. I liked him.

REGINA.   Good. And now I have great news for you. You are going to Baltimore in the morning to bring your father home.

ALEXANDRA [*gasps, then delighted*].   Me? Papa said I should come? That must mean—[*Turns to* ADDIE] Addie, he must be well. Think of it, he'll be back home again. We'll bring him home.

REGINA.   You are going alone, Alexandra.

ADDIE [ALEXANDRA *has turned in surprise*].   Going alone? Going by herself? A child that age! Mr. Horace ain't going to like Zan traipsing up there by herself.

REGINA [*sharply*].   Go upstairs and lay out Alexandra's things.

ADDIE.   He'd expect me to be along—

REGINA.   I'll be up in a few minutes to tell you what to pack. [ADDIE *slowly begins to climb the steps. To* ALEXANDRA] I should think you'd like going alone. At your age it certainly would have delighted me. You're a strange girl, Alexandra. Addie has babied you so much.

ALEXANDRA.   I only thought it would be more fun if Addie and I went together.

BIRDIE [*timidly*].   Maybe I could go with her, Regina. I'd really like to.

REGINA.   She is going alone. She is getting old enough to take some responsibilities.

OSCAR.   She'd better learn now. She's almost old enough to get married. [*Jovially, to* LEO, *slapping him on shoulder*] Eh, son?

LEO.   Huh?

OSCAR [*annoyed with* LEO *for not understanding*].   Old enough to get married, you're thinking, eh?

LEO.   Oh, yes, sir. [*Feebly*] Lots of girls get married at Zan's age. Look at Mary Prester and Johanna and—

REGINA.   Well, she's not getting married tomorrow. But she is going to Baltimore tomorrow, so let's talk about that. [*To* ALEXANDRA] You'll be glad to have Papa home again.

ALEXANDRA.   I wanted to go before, Mama. You remember that. But you said *you* couldn't go, and that *I* couldn't go alone.

REGINA.   I've changed my mind. [*Too casually*] You're to tell Papa how much you missed him, and that he must come home now—for your sake. Tell him that you *need* him home.

ALEXANDRA.   Need him home? I don't understand.

REGINA.   There is nothing for you to understand. You are simply to say what I have told you.

BIRDIE [*rises*].   He may be too sick. She couldn't do that—

ALEXANDRA.   Yes. He may be too sick to travel. I couldn't make him think he had to come home for me, if he is too sick to—

REGINA [*looks at her, sharply, challengingly*].   You *couldn't* do what I tell you to do, Alexandra?

ALEXANDRA [*quietly*].   No. I couldn't. If I thought it would hurt him.

REGINA [*after a second's silence, smiles pleasantly*].   But you are doing this for Papa's own good. [*Takes* ALEXANDRA'S *hand*] You must let me be the judge of his condition. It's the best possible cure for him to come home and be taken care of here. He mustn't stay there any longer and listen to those alarmist doctors. You are doing this entirely for his sake. Tell your papa that I want him to come home, that I miss him very much.

ALEXANDRA [*slowly*]. Yes, Mama.

REGINA [*to the others*]. I must go and start getting Alexandra ready now. Why don't you all go home?

BEN [*rises*]. I'll attend to the railroad ticket. One of the boys will bring it over. Good night, everybody. Have a nice trip, Alexandra. The food on the train is very good. The celery is so crisp. Have a good time and act like a little lady.

[*Exits*]

REGINA. Good night, Ben. Good night, Oscar—[*Playfully*] Don't be so glum, Oscar. It makes you look as if you had chronic indigestion.

BIRDIE. Good night, Regina.

REGINA. Good night, Birdie. [*Exits upstairs.*]

OSCAR [*starts for hall*]. Come along.

LEO [*to* ALEXANDRA]. Imagine your not wanting to go! What a little fool you are. Wish it were me. What I could do in a place like Baltimore!

ALEXANDRA. Mind your business. I can guess the kind of things *you* could do.

LEO [*laughs*]. Oh, no, you couldn't. [*He exits.*]

REGINA [*calling from the top of the stairs*]. Come on, Alexandra.

BIRDIE [*quickly, softly*]. Zan.

ALEXANDRA. I don't understand about my going, Aunt Birdie. [*Shrugs*] But anyway, Papa will be home again. [*Pats* BIRDIE'*s arm*] Don't worry about me. I can take care of myself. Really I can.

BIRDIE [*shakes her head, softly*]. That's not what I'm worried about. Zan—

ALEXANDRA [*comes close to her*]. What's the matter?

BIRDIE. It's about Leo—

ALEXANDRA [*whispering*]. He beat the horses. That's why we were late getting back. We had to wait until they cooled off. He always beats the horses as if—

BIRDIE [*whispering frantically, holding* ALEXANDRA'*s hands*]. He's my son. My own son. But you are more to me—more to me than my own child. I love you more than anybody else—

ALEXANDRA. Don't worry about the horses. I'm sorry I told you.

BIRDIE [*her voice rising*]. *I am not worrying about the horses.* I am worrying about *you*. You are *not* going to marry Leo. I am not going to let them do that to you—

ALEXANDRA. Marry? To Leo? [*Laughs*] I wouldn't marry, Aunt Birdie. I've never even thought about it—

BIRDIE. But they have thought about it. [*Wildly*] Zan, I couldn't stand to think about such a thing. You and—[OSCAR *has come into the doorway on* ALEXANDRA'S *speech. He is standing quietly, listening.*]

ALEXANDRA [*laughs*]. But I'm not going to marry. And I'm certainly not going to marry Leo.

BIRDIE. Don't you understand? They'll make you. They'll make you—

ALEXANDRA [*takes* BIRDIE'S *hands, quietly, firmly*]. That's foolish, Aunt Birdie. I'm grown now. Nobody can make me do anything.

BIRDIE. I just couldn't stand—

OSCAR [*sharply*]. Birdie. [BIRDIE *looks up, draws quickly away from* ALEXANDRA. *She stands rigid, frightened.*] Birdie, get your hat and coat.

ADDIE [*calls from upstairs*]. Come on, baby. Your mama's waiting for you, and she ain't nobody to keep waiting.

ALEXANDRA. All right. [*Then softly, embracing* BIRDIE] Good night, Aunt Birdie. [*As she passes* OSCAR] Good night, Uncle Oscar. [BIRDIE *begins to move slowly toward the door as* ALEXANDRA *climbs the stairs.* ALEXANDRA *is almost out of view when* BIRDIE *reaches* OSCAR *in the doorway. As* BIRDIE *attempts to pass him, he slaps her hard, across the face.* BIRDIE *cries out, puts her hand to her face. On the cry,* ALEXANDRA *turns, begins to run down the stairs*] Aunt Birdie! What happened? What happened? I—

BIRDIE [*softly, without turning*]. Nothing, darling. Nothing happened. [*Anxious to keep* ALEXANDRA *from coming close*] Now go to bed. [OSCAR *exits*] Nothing happened. I only—I only twisted my ankle. [*She goes out.* ALEXANDRA *stands on the stairs looking after her.*]

ACT II.

SCENE: *Same as Act One. A week later, morning.*

AT RISE: *The light comes from the open shutter of the right window; the other shutters are tightly closed.* ADDIE *is standing at the window, looking out. Near the dining-room doors are brooms, mops, rags, etc. After a second,* OSCAR *comes into the entrance hall, looks in the room, shivers, decides not to take his hat and coat off, comes into the room. At the sound of the door,* ADDIE *turns.*

ADDIE [*without interest*]. Oh, it's you, Mr. Oscar.

OSCAR. What is this? It's not night. What's the matter here? [*Shivers*] Fine thing at this time of the morning. Blinds all closed. [ADDIE *begins to open shutters*] Where's Miss Regina? It's cold in here.

ADDIE. Miss Regina ain't down yet.

OSCAR. She had any word?

ADDIE. No, sir.

OSCAR. Wouldn't you think a girl that age could get on a train at one place and have sense enough to get off at another?

ADDIE. Something must have happened. If Zan say she was coming last night, she's coming last night. Unless something happened. Sure fire disgrace to let a baby like that go all that way alone to bring home a sick man without—

OSCAR. You do a lot of judging around here, Addie, eh? Judging of your white folks, I mean.

REGINA [*speaking from the upstairs hall*]. Who's downstairs, Addie? [*She appears in a dressing gown, peers down from the landing.* ADDIE *picks up broom, dustpan and brush and exits*] Oh, it's you, Oscar. What are you doing here so early? I haven't been down yet. I'm not finished dressing.

OSCAR [*speaking up to her*]. You had any word from them?

REGINA. No.

OSCAR. Then something certainly has happened. People don't just say they are arriving on Thursday night, and they haven't come by Friday morning.

REGINA. Oh, nothing has happened. Alexandra just hasn't got sense enough to send a message.

OSCAR. If nothing's happened, then why aren't they here?

REGINA. You asked me that ten times last night. My, you do fret so, Oscar. Anything might have happened. They may have missed connections in Atlanta, the train may have been delayed—oh, a hundred things could have kept them.

OSCAR. Where's Ben?

REGINA [*as she disappears upstairs*]. Where should he be? At home, probably. Really, Oscar, I don't tuck him in his bed and I don't take him out of it. Have some coffee and don't worry so much.

OSCAR. Have some coffee? There isn't any coffee. [*Looks at his watch, shakes his head. After a second* CAL *enters with a large silver tray, coffee urn, small cups, newspaper*] Oh, there you are. Is everything in this fancy house always late?

CAL [*looks at him, surprised*]. You ain't out shooting this morning, Mr. Oscar?

OSCAR. First day I missed since I had my head cold. First day I missed in eight years.

CAL. Yes, sir. I bet you. Simon he say you had a mighty good day yesterday morning. That's what Simon say. [*Brings* OSCAR *coffee and newspaper.*]

OSCAR. Pretty good, pretty good.

CAL [*laughs, slyly*]. Bet you got enough bobwhite[1] and squirrel to give every nigger in town a Jesus-party.[2] Most of 'em ain't had no meat since the cotton picking was over. Bet they'd give anything for a little piece of that meat—

OSCAR [*turns his head to look at* CAL]. Cal, if I catch a nigger in this town going shooting, you know what's going to happen. [LEO *enters.*]

CAL [*hastily*]. Yes, sir, Mr. Oscar. It was Simon who told me and—Morning, Mr. Leo. You gentlemen having your breakfast with us here?

LEO. The boys in the bank don't know a thing. They haven't had any message. [CAL *waits for an answer, gets none, shrugs, exits.*]

OSCAR [*peers at* LEO]. What you doing here, son?

LEO. You told me to find out if the boys at the bank had any message from Uncle Horace or Zan—

OSCAR. I told you if they had a message to bring it here. I told you that if they didn't have a message to stay at the bank and do your work.

LEO. Oh, I guess I misunderstood.

OSCAR. You didn't misunderstand. You just were looking for any excuse to take an hour off. [LEO *pours a cup of coffee*] You got to stop that kind of thing. You got to start settling down. You going to be a married man one of these days.

LEO. Yes, sir.

OSCAR. You also got to stop with that woman in Mobile. [*As* LEO *is about*

---

1. Quail.
2. Celebration held to give thanks to the Lord for an increase in good fortune.

to speak] You're young and I haven't got no objections to outside women. That is, I haven't got no objections so long as they don't interfere with serious things. Outside women are all right in their place, but *now* isn't their place. You got to realize that.

LEO [*nods*]. Yes, sir. I'll tell her. She'll act all right about it.

OSCAR. Also, you got to start working harder at the bank. You got to convince your Uncle Horace you going to make a fit husband for Alexandra.

LEO. What do you think has happened to them? Supposed to be here last night—[*Laughs*] Bet you Uncle Ben's mighty worried. Seventy-five thousand dollars worried.

OSCAR [*smiles happily*]. Ought to be worried. Damn well ought to be. First he don't answer the letters, then he don't come home—[*Giggles.*]

LEO. What will happen if Uncle Horace don't come home or don't—

OSCAR. Or don't put up the money? Oh, we'll get it from outside. Easy enough.

LEO [*surprised*]. But *you* don't want outsiders.

OSCAR. What do I care who gets my share? I been shaved already. Serve Ben right if he had to give away some of his.

LEO. Damn shame what they did to you.

OSCAR [*looking up the stairs*]. Don't talk so loud. Don't you worry. When I die, you'll have as much as the rest. You might have yours *and* Alexandra's. I'm not so easily licked.

LEO. I wasn't thinking of myself, Papa—

OSCAR. Well, you should be, you should be. It's every man's duty to think of himself.

LEO. You think Uncle Horace don't want to go in on this?

OSCAR [*giggles*]. That's my hunch. He hasn't showed any signs of loving it yet.

LEO [*laughs*]. But he hasn't listened to Aunt Regina yet, either. Oh, he'll go along. It's too good a thing. Why wouldn't he want to? He's got plenty and plenty to invest with. He don't even have to sell anything. Eighty-eight thousand worth of Union Pacific bonds sitting right in his safe deposit box. All he's got to do is open the box.

OSCAR [*after a pause. Looks at his watch*]. Mighty late breakfast in this fancy house. Yes, he's had those bonds for fifteen years. Bought them when they were low and just locked them up.

LEO. Yeah. Just has to open the box and take them out. That's all. Easy as easy can be. [*Laughs*] The things in that box! There's all those bonds, looking mighty fine. [OSCAR *slowly puts down his newspaper and turns to* LEO] Then right next to them is a baby shoe of Zan's and a cheap old cameo on a string, and, *and*—nobody'd believe this—a piece of an old violin. Not even a whole violin. Just a piece of an old thing, a piece of a violin.

OSCAR [*very softly, as if he were trying to control his voice*]. A piece of a violin! What do you think of that!

LEO. Yes, sirree. A lot of other crazy things, too. A poem, I guess it is, signed with his mother's name, and two old schoolbooks with notes and—[LEO *catches* OSCAR's *look. His voice trails off. He turns his head away.*]

OSCAR [*very softly*]. How do you know what's in the box, son?

LEO [*draws back, frightened, realizing what he has said*]. Oh, well. Well, er. Well, one of the boys, sir. It was one of the boys at the bank. He took old Manders' keys. It was Joe Horns. He just up and took Manders' keys and, and—well, took the box out. [*Quickly*] Then they all asked me if I wanted to see, too. So I looked a little, I guess, but then I made them close up the box quick and I told them never—

OSCAR [*looks at him*]. Joe Horns, you say? He opened it?

LEO. Yes, sir, yes, he did. My word of honor. [*Very nervous now*] I suppose that don't excuse *me* for looking—[*Looking at* OSCAR] but I did make him close it up and put the keys back in Manders' drawer—

OSCAR [*leans forward, very softly*]. Tell me the truth, Leo. I am not going to be angry with you. Did you open the box yourself?

LEO. *No, sir, I didn't.* I told you I didn't. No, I—

OSCAR [*irritated, patient*]. I am *not* going to be angry with you. [*Watching* LEO *carefully*] Sometimes a young fellow deserves credit for looking round him to see what's going on. Sometimes that's a good sign in a fellow your age. Many great men have made their fortune with their eyes. Did you open the box?

LEO [*very puzzled*]. No. I—

OSCAR [*moves to* LEO]. Did you open the box? It may have been—well, it may have been a good thing if you had.

LEO [*after a long pause*]. I opened it.

OSCAR [*quickly*]. Is that the truth? [LEO *nods*] Does anybody else know that you opened it? Come, Leo, don't be afraid of speaking the truth to me.

LEO. No. Nobody knew. Nobody was in the bank when I did it. But—

OSCAR. Did your Uncle Horace ever know you opened it?

LEO [*shakes his head*]. He only looks in it once every six months when he cuts the coupons, and sometimes Manders even does that for him. Uncle Horace don't even have the keys. Manders keeps them for him. Imagine not looking at all that. You can bet if I had the bonds, I'd watch 'em like—

OSCAR. If you had them. *If* you had them. Then you could have a share in the mill, you and me. A fine, big share, too. [*Pauses, shrugs*] Well, a man can't be shot for wanting to see his son get on in the world, can he, boy?

LEO [*looks up, begins to understand*]. No, he can't. Natural enough. [*Laughs*] But I haven't got the bonds and Uncle Horace has. And now he can just sit back and wait to be a millionaire.

OSCAR [*innocently*]. You think your Uncle Horace likes you well enough to lend you the bonds if he decides not to use them himself?

LEO. Papa, it must be that you haven't had your breakfast! [*Laughs loudly*] Lend me the bonds! My God—

OSCAR [*disappointed*]. No, I suppose not. Just a fancy of mine. A loan for three months, maybe four, easy enough for us to pay it back then. Anyway, this is only April—[*Slowly counting the months on his fingers*] and if he doesn't look at them until Autumn he wouldn't even miss them out of the box.

LEO. That's it. He wouldn't even miss them. Ah, well—

OSCAR. No, sir. Wouldn't even miss them. How could he miss them if he never looks at them? [*Sighs as* LEO *stares at him*] Well, here we are sitting around waiting for him to come home and invest his money in something he hasn't lifted his hand to get. But I can't help thinking he's acting strange. You laugh when I say he could lend you the bonds if he's not going to use them himself. But would it hurt him?

LEO [*slowly looking at* OSCAR].   No. No, it wouldn't.

OSCAR.   People ought to help other people. But that's not always the way it happens. [BEN *enters, hangs his coat and hat in hall. Very carefully*] And so sometimes you got to think of yourself. [*As* LEO *stares at him,* BEN *appears in the doorway*] Morning, Ben.

BEN [*coming in, carrying his newspaper*].   Fine sunny morning. Any news from the runaways?

REGINA [*on the staircase*].   There's no news or you would have heard it. Quite a convention so early in the morning, aren't you all? [*Goes to coffee urn.*]

OSCAR.   You rising mighty late these days. Is that the way they do things in Chicago society?

BEN [*looking at his paper*].   Old Carter died up in Senateville. Eighty-one is a good time for us all, eh? What do you think has really happened to Horace, Regina?

REGINA.   Nothing.

BEN.   You don't think maybe he never started from Baltimore and never intends to start?

REGINA [*irritated*].   Of course they've started. Didn't I have a letter from Alexandra? What is so strange about people arriving late? He has that cousin in Savannah he's so fond of. He may have stopped to see him. They'll be along today sometime, very flattered that you and Oscar are so worried about them.

BEN.   I'm a natural worrier. Especially when I am getting ready to close a business deal and one of my partners remains silent *and* invisible.

REGINA [*laughs*].   Oh, is that it? I thought you were worried about Horace's health.

OSCAR.   Oh, that too. Who could help but worry? I'm worried. This is the first day I haven't been shooting since my head cold.

REGINA [*starts toward dining room*].   Then you haven't had your breakfast. Come along. [OSCAR *and* LEO *follow her.*]

BEN.   Regina. [*She turns at dining-room door*] That cousin of Horace's has been dead for years and, in any case, the train does not go through Savannah.

REGINA [*laughs, continues into dining room, seats herself*].   Did he die? You're always remembering about people dying. [BEN *rises*] Now I intend to eat my breakfast in peace, and read my newspaper.

BEN [*goes toward dining room as he talks*].   This is second breakfast for me. My first was bad. Celia ain't the cook she used to be. Too old to have taste anymore. If she hadn't belonged to Mama, I'd send her off to the country.

[OSCAR *and* LEO *start to eat.* BEN *seats himself.*]

LEO.   Uncle Horace will have some tales to tell, I bet. Baltimore is a lively town.

REGINA [*to* CAL].   The grits isn't hot enough. Take it back.

CAL.   Oh, yes'm. [*Calling into the kitchen as he exits*] Grits didn't hold the heat. Grits didn't hold the heat.

LEO.   When I was at school three of the boys and myself took a train once and went over to Baltimore. It was so big we thought we were in Europe. I was just a kid then—

REGINA.   I find it very pleasant [ADDIE *enters*] to have breakfast alone. I hate chattering before I've had something hot. [CAL *closes the dining-room doors*] Do be still, Leo.

[ADDIE *comes into the room, begins gathering up the cups, carries them to the large tray. Outside there are the sounds of voices. Quickly* ADDIE *runs into the hall. A few seconds later she appears again in the doorway, her arm around the shoulders of* HORACE GIDDENS, *supporting him.* HORACE *is a tall man of about forty-five. He has been good looking, but now his face is tired and ill. He walks stiffly, as if it were an enormous effort, and carefully, as if he were unsure of his balance.* ADDIE *takes off his overcoat and hangs it on the hall tree. She then helps him to a chair.*]

HORACE.   How are you, Addie? How have you been?
ADDIE.   I'm all right, Mr. Horace. I've just been worried about you.

[ALEXANDRA *enters. She is flushed and excited, her hat awry, her face dirty. Her arms are full of packages, but she comes quickly to* ADDIE.]

ALEXANDRA.   Don't tell me how worried you were. We couldn't help it and there was no way to send a message.
ADDIE [*begins to take packages from* ALEXANDRA].   Yes, sir, I was mighty worried.
ALEXANDRA.   We had to stop in Mobile overnight. Papa didn't feel well. The trip was too much for him, and I made him stop and rest—[*As* ADDIE *takes the last package*] No, don't take that. That's Father's medicine. I'll hold it. It mustn't break. Now, about the stuff outside. Papa must have his wheelchair. I'll get that and the valises—
ADDIE [*very happy, holding* ALEXANDRA'S *arms*]. Since when you got to carry your own valises? Since when I ain't old enough to hold a bottle of medicine? [HORACE *coughs*] You feel all right, Mr. Horace?
HORACE [*nods*].   Glad to be sitting down.
ALEXANDRA [*opening package of medicine*].   He doesn't feel all right. He just says that. The trip was very hard on him, and now he must go right to bed.
ADDIE [*looking at him carefully*].   Them fancy doctors, they give you help?
HORACE.   They did their best.
ALEXANDRA [*has become conscious of the voices in the dining room*].   I bet Mama was worried. I better tell her we're here now. [*She starts for door.*]
HORACE.   Zan. [*She stops*] Not for a minute, dear.
ALEXANDRA.   Oh, Papa, you feel bad again. I knew you did. Do you want your medicine?
HORACE.   No, I don't feel that way. I'm just tired, darling. Let me rest a little.
ADDIE.   They're all in there eating breakfast.
ALEXANDRA.   Oh, are they all here? Why do they *always* have to be here? I was hoping Papa wouldn't have to see anybody, that it would be nice for him and quiet.
ADDIE.   Then let your papa rest for a minute.
HORACE.   Addie, I bet your coffee's as good as ever. They don't have

such good coffee up North. Is it as good, Addie? [ADDIE *starts for coffee urn.*]

ALEXANDRA.   No. Dr. Reeves said not much coffee. Just now and then. I'm the nurse now, Addie.

ADDIE.   You'd be a better one if you didn't look so dirty. Now go take a bath. Change your linens, get out a fresh dress, give your hair a good brushing—go on—

ALEXANDRA.   Will you be all right, Papa?

ADDIE.   Go on.

ALEXANDRA [*on stairs, talks as she goes up*].   The pills Papa must take once every four hours. And the bottle only when—only if he feels very bad. Now don't move until I come back and don't talk much and remember about his medicine, Addie—[*As she disappers*] How's Aunt Birdie? Is she here?

ADDIE.   It ain't right for you to have coffee? It will hurt you?

HORACE [*slowly*].   Nothing can make much difference now. Get me a cup, Addie. [*She crosses to urn, pours a cup*] Funny. They can't make coffee up North. [ADDIE *brings him a cup*] They don't like red pepper, either. [*He takes the cup and gulps it greedily*] God, that's good. You remember how I used to drink it? Ten, twelve cups a day. So strong it had to stain the cup. [*Then slowly*] Addie, before I see anybody else, I want to know why Zan came to fetch me home. She's tried to tell me, but she doesn't seem to know herself.

ADDIE.   I don't know. All I know is big things are going on. Everybody going to be high-tone rich. Big rich. You too. All because smoke's going to start out of a building that ain't even up yet.

HORACE.   I've heard about it.

ADDIE.   And, er—[*Hesitates, steps to him*] and—well, Zan, maybe she going to marry Mr. Leo in a little while.

HORACE [*looks at her, then very slowly*].   What are you talking about?

ADDIE.   That's right. That's the talk, God help us.

HORACE [*angrily*].   What's the talk?

ADDIE.   I'm telling you. There's going to be a wedding—

HORACE [*after a second, quietly*].   Go and tell them I'm home.

ADDIE [*hesitates*].   Now you ain't to get excited. You're to be in your bed—

HORACE.   Go on, Addie. Go and say I'm back. [ADDIE *opens dining-room doors. He rises with difficulty, stands stiff, as if he were in pain, facing the dining room.*]

ADDIE.   Miss Regina. They're home. They got here—

REGINA.   Horace! [REGINA *quickly, rises, runs into the room. Warmly*] Horace! You've finally arrived. [*As she kisses him, the others come forward, all talking together.*]

BEN [*in doorway, carrying a napkin*].   Well, sir, you had us all mighty worried. [*He steps forward. They shake hands.* ADDIE *exits.*]

OSCAR.   You're a sight for sore eyes.

HORACE.   Hello, Ben.

[LEO *enters, eating a biscuit.*]

OSCAR.   And how you feel? Tip-top, I bet, because that's the way you're looking.

HORACE [*irritated with* OSCAR'S *lie*].   Hello, Oscar. Hello, Leo, how are you?

LEO [*shaking hands*].   I'm fine, sir. But a lot better now that you're back.

REGINA.   Now sit down. What did happen to you and where's Alexandra? I am so excited about seeing you that I almost forgot about her.

HORACE.   I didn't feel good, a little weak, I guess, and we stopped overnight to rest. Zan's upstairs washing off the train dirt.

REGINA.   Oh, I am so sorry the trip was hard on you. I didn't think that—

HORACE.   Well, it's just as if I had never been away. All of you here—

BEN.   Waiting to welcome you home.

[BIRDIE *bursts in. She is wearing a flannel kimono and her face is flushed and excited.*]

BIRDIE [*runs to him, kisses him*].   Horace!

HORACE [*warmly pressing her arm*].   I was just wondering where you were, Birdie.

BIRDIE [*excited*].   Oh, I would have been here. I didn't know you were back until Simon said he saw the buggy. [*She draws back to look at him. Her face sobers*] Oh, you don't look well, Horace. No, you don't.

REGINA [*laughs*].   Birdie, what a thing to say—

HORACE.   Oscar thinks I look very well.

OSCAR [*annoyed. Turns on* LEO].   Don't stand there holding that biscuit in your hand.

LEO.   Oh, well. I'll just finish my breakfast, Uncle Horace, and then I'll give you all the news about the bank—[*He exits into the dining room.*]

OSCAR.   And what is that costume you have on?

BIRDIE [*looking at* HORACE].   Now that you're home, you'll feel better. Plenty of good rest and we'll take such fine care of you. [*Stops*] But where is Zan? I missed her so much.

OSCAR.   I asked you what is that strange costume you're parading around in?

BIRDIE [*nervously, backing toward stairs*].   Me? Oh! It's my wrapper. I was so excited about Horace I just rushed out of the house—

OSCAR.   Did you come across the square dressed that way? My dear Birdie, I—

HORACE [*to* REGINA, *wearily*].   Yes, it's just like old times.

REGINA [*quickly to* OSCAR].   Now, no fights. This is a holiday.

BIRDIE [*runs quickly up the stairs*].   Zan! Zannie!

OSCAR.   Birdie! [*She stops.*]

BIRDIE.   Oh. Tell Zan I'll be back in a little while. [*Whispers*] Sorry, Oscar. [*Exits.*]

REGINA [*to* OSCAR *and* BEN].   Why don't you go finish your breakfast and let Horace rest for a minute?

BEN [*crossing to dining room with* OSCAR].   Never leave a meal unfinished. There are too many poor people who need the food. Mighty glad to see you home, Horace. Fine to have you back. Fine to have you back.

OSCAR [*to* LEO *as* BEN *closes dining-room doors*].   Your mother has gone crazy. Running around the streets like a woman—

[*The moment* REGINA *and* HORACE *are alone, they become awkward and self-conscious.*]

REGINA [*laughs awkwardly*]. Well. Here we are. It's been a long time. [HORACE *smiles*] Five months. You know, Horace, I wanted to come and be with you in the hospital, but I didn't know where my duty was. Here, or with you. But you know how much I *wanted* to come.

HORACE. That's kind of you, Regina. There was no need to come.

REGINA. Oh, but there was. Five months lying there all by yourself, no kinfolks, no friends. Don't try to tell me you didn't have a bad time of it.

HORACE. I didn't have a bad time. [*As she shakes her head, he becomes insistent*] No, I didn't, Regina. Oh, at first when I—when I heard the news about myself—but after I got used to that, I liked it there.

REGINA. You *liked* it? Isn't that strange. You liked it so well you didn't want to come home?

HORACE. That's not the way to put it. [*Then, kindly, as he sees her turn her head away*] But there I was and I got kind of used to it, kind of to like lying there and thinking. I never had much time to think before. And time's become valuable to me.

REGINA. It sounds almost like a holiday.

HORACE [*laughs*]. It was, sort of. The first holiday I've had since I was a little kid.

REGINA. And here I was thinking you were in pain and—

HORACE [*quietly*]. I was in pain.

REGINA. And instead you were having a holiday! A holiday of thinking. Couldn't you have done that here?

HORACE. I wanted to do it before I came here. I was thinking about us.

REGINA. About us? About you and me? Thinking about you and me after all these years. You shall tell me everything you thought—someday.

HORACE [*there is silence for a minute*]. Regina. [*She turns to him*] Why did you send Zan to Baltimore?

REGINA. Why? Because I wanted you home. You can't make anything suspicious out of that, can you?

HORACE. I didn't mean to make anything suspicious about it. [*Hesitantly, taking her hand*] Zan said you wanted me to come home. I was so pleased at that and touched. It made me feel good.

REGINA [*taking away her hand*]. Touched that I should want you home?

HORACE. I'm saying all the wrong things as usual. Let's try to get along better. There isn't so much more time. Regina, what's all this crazy talk I've been hearing about Zan and Leo? Zan and Leo marrying?

REGINA [*turning to him, sharply*]. Who gossips so much around here?

HORACE [*shocked*]. Regina!

REGINA [*anxious to quiet him*]. It's some foolishness that Oscar thought up. I'll explain later. I have no intention of allowing any such arrangement. It was simply a way of keeping Oscar quiet in all this business I've been writing you about—

HORACE [*carefully*]. What has Zan to do with any business of Oscar's? Whatever it is, you had better put it out of Oscar's head immediately. You know what I think of Leo.

REGINA. But there's no need to talk about it now.

HORACE. There is no need to talk about it ever. Not as long as I live. [HORACE *stops, slowly turns to look at her*] As long as I live. I've been in a hospital for five months. Yet since I've been here you have not once asked me about—about my health. [*Then gently*] Well, I suppose they've written you. I can't live very long.

REGINA. I've never understood why people have to talk about this kind of thing.

HORACE [*there is a silence. Then he looks up at her, his face cold*]. You misunderstand. I don't intend to gossip about my sickness. I thought it was only fair to tell you. I was not asking for your sympathy.

REGINA [*sharply, turns to him*]. What do the doctors think caused your bad heart?

HORACE. What do you mean?

REGINA. They didn't think it possible, did they, that your fancy women may have—

HORACE [*smiles unpleasantly*]. Caused my heart to be bad? I don't think that's the best scientific theory. You don't catch heart trouble in bed.

REGINA [*angrily*]. I thought you might catch a bad conscience—in bed, as you say.

HORACE. I didn't tell them about my bad conscience. Or about my fancy women. Nor did I tell them that my wife has not wanted me in bed with her for—[*Sharply*] How long is it, Regina? Ten years? Did you bring me home for this, to make me feel guilty again? That means you want something. But you'll not make me feel guilty anymore. My "thinking" has made a difference.

REGINA. I see that it has. [*She looks toward dining-room door. Then comes to him, her manner warm and friendly*] It's foolish for us to fight this way. I didn't mean to be unpleasant. I was stupid.

HORACE [*wearily*]. God knows I didn't either. I came home wanting so much not to fight, and then all of a sudden there we were.

REGINA [*hastily*]. It's all my fault. I didn't ask about—about your illness because I didn't want to remind you of it. Anyway, I never believe doctors when they talk about—[*Brightly*] when they talk like that.

HORACE. I understand. Well, we'll try our best with each other. [*He rises.*]

REGINA [*quickly*]. I'll try. Honestly, I will. Horace, Horace, I know you're tired but, but—couldn't you stay down here a few minutes longer? I want Ben to tell you something.

HORACE. Tomorrow.

REGINA. I'd like to now. It's very important to me. It's very important to all of us. [*Gaily, as she moves toward dining room*] Important to your beloved daughter. She'll be a very great heiress—

HORACE. Will she? That's nice.

REGINA [*opens doors*]. Ben, are you finished breakfast?

HORACE. Is this the mill business I've had so many letters about?

REGINA [*to* BEN]. Horace would like to talk to you now.

HORACE. Horace would not like to talk to you now. I am very tired, Regina—

REGINA [*comes to him*]. Please. You've said we'll try our best with each other. I'll try. Really, I will. Please do this for me now. You will see what I've done while you've been away. How I watched your interests. [*Laughs gaily*] And I've done very well too. But things can't be delayed any longer. Everything must be settled this week—[HORACE *sits down.* BEN *enters.* OSCAR *has stayed in the dining room, his head turned to watch them.* LEO *is pretending to read the newspaper*] Now you must tell Horace all about it. Only be quick because he is very tired and must go to bed. [HORACE *is looking at her. His face hardens as she speaks*] But I think your news will be better for him than all the medicine in the world.

BEN [*looking at* HORACE].   It could wait. Horace may not feel like talking today.

REGINA.   What an old faker you are! You know it can't wait. You know it must be finished this week. You've been just as anxious for Horace to get here as I've been.

BEN [*very jovial*].   I suppose I have been. And why not? Horace has done Hubbard Sons many a good turn. Why shouldn't I be anxious to help him now?

REGINA [*laughs*].   Help him! Help him when you need him, that's what you mean.

BEN.   What a woman you married, Horace. [*Laughs awkwardly when* HORACE *does not answer*] Well, then I'll make it quick. You know what I've been telling you for years. How I've always said that every one of us little Southern businessmen had great things—[*Extends his arm*]—right beyond our fingertips. It's been my dream: my dream to make those fingers grow longer. I'm a lucky man, Horace, a lucky man. To dream and to live to get what you've dreamed of. That's *my* idea of a lucky man. For thirty years I've cried bring the cotton mills to the cotton. [HORACE *opens the medicine bottle*] Well finally I got up nerve to go to Marshall Company in Chicago.

HORACE.   I know all this. [*He takes the medicine.* REGINA *rises, steps to him.*]

BEN.   Can I get you something?

HORACE.   Some water, please.

REGINA [*turns quickly*].   Oh, I'm sorry. [*Brings him a glass of water. He drinks as they wait in silence*] You feel all right now?

HORACE.   Yes. You wrote me. I know all that.

[OSCAR *enters from dining room.*]

REGINA [*triumphantly*].   But you don't know that in the last few days Ben has agreed to give us—you, I mean—a much larger share.

HORACE.   Really? That's very generous of him.

BEN [*laughs*].   It wasn't so generous of me. It was smart of Regina.

REGINA [*as if she were signaling* HORACE].   I explained to Ben that perhaps you hadn't answered his letters because you didn't think he was offering you enough, and that the time was getting short and you could guess how much he needed you—

HORACE [*smiles at her, nods*].   And I could guess that he wants to keep control in the family.

REGINA [*triumphantly*].   Exactly. So I did a little bargaining for you and convinced my brothers they weren't the only Hubbards who had a business sense.

HORACE.   Did you have to convince them of that? How little people know about each other! [*laughs*] But you'll know better about Regina next time, eh, Ben? [BEN, REGINA, HORACE *laugh together*. OSCAR's *face is angry*] Now let's see. We're getting a bigger share. [*Looking at* OSCAR] Who's getting less?

BEN.   Oscar.

HORACE.   Well, Oscar, you've grown very unselfish. What's happened to you?

[LEO *enters from dining room*.]

BEN [*quickly*].   Oscar doesn't mind. Not worth fighting about now, eh, Oscar?

OSCAR [*angrily*].   I'll get mine in the end. You can be sure of that. I've got my son's future to think about.

HORACE [*sharply*].   Leo? Oh, I see. [*Puts his head back, laughs.* REGINA *looks at him nervously*] I am beginning to see. Everybody will get theirs.

BEN.   I knew you'd see it. Seventy-five thousand, and that seventy-five thousand will make you a million.

REGINA.   It will, Horace, it will.

HORACE.   I believe you. [*After a second*] Now I can understand Oscar's self-sacrifice, but what did you have to promise Marshall Company besides the money you're putting up?

BEN.   They wouldn't take promises. They wanted guarantees.

HORACE.   Of what?

BEN.   Water power. Free and plenty of it.

HORACE.   You got them that, of course.

BEN.   Cheap. You'd think the Governor of a great state would make his price a little higher. From pride, you know. [HORACE *smiles*. BEN *smiles*] Cheap wages. "What do you mean by cheap wages?" I say to Marshall. "Less than Massachusetts," he says to me, "and that averages eight a week." "Eight a week! By God," I tell him, "*I'd* work for eight a week myself." Why, there ain't a mountain white or a town nigger but wouldn't give his right arm for three silver dollars every week, eh, Horace?

HORACE.   Sure. And they'll take less than that when you get around to playing them off against each other. You can save a little money that way, Ben. And make them hate each other just a little more than they do now.

REGINA.   What's all this about?

BEN [*laughs*].   There'll be no trouble from anybody, white or black. Marshall said that to me. "What about strikes? That's all we've had in Massachusetts for the last three years." I say to him, "What's a strike? I never heard of one. Come South, Marshall. We got good folks and we don't stand for any fancy fooling."

HORACE.   You're right. [*Slowly*] Well, it looks like you made a good deal for yourselves, and for Marshall, too. Your father used to say he made the thousands and you boys would make the millions. I think he was right. [*Rises.*]

REGINA [*as they look at* HORACE. *She laughs nervously*].   Millions for *us,* too.

HORACE.   Us? You and me? I don't think so. We've got enough money, Regina. We'll just sit by and watch the boys grow rich. [*They watch* HORACE *as he begins to move toward the staircase. He passes* LEO, *looks at him for a second*] How's everything at the bank, Leo?

LEO.   Fine, sir. Everything is fine.

HORACE.   How are all the ladies in Mobile? [HORACE *turns to* REGINA, *sharply*] Whatever made you think I'd let Zan marry—

REGINA.   Do you mean that you are turning this down? Is it possible that's what you mean?

BEN.   No, that's not what he means. Turning down a fortune. Horace is tired. He'd rather talk about it tomorrow—

REGINA.   We can't keep putting it off this way. Oscar must be in Chicago by the end of the week with the money and contracts.

OSCAR [*giggles, pleased*]. Yes, sir. Got to be there end of the week. No sense going without the money.

REGINA [*tensely*]. I've waited long enough for your answer. I'm not going to wait any longer.

HORACE [*very deliberately*].   I'm very tired now, Regina.

BEN [*quickly*].   Now, Horace probably has his reasons. Things he'd like explained. Tomorrow will do. I can—

REGINA [*turns to* BEN, *sharply*].   I want to know his reasons now!

HORACE [*as he climbs the steps*].   I don't know them all myself. Let's leave it at that.

REGINA.   We shall not leave it at that! We have waited for you here like children. Waited for you to come home.

HORACE.   So that you could invest my money. So that is why you wanted me home? Well, I had hoped—[*Quietly*] If you are disappointed, Regina, I'm sorry. But I must do what I think best. We'll talk about it another day.

REGINA.   We'll talk about it now. Just you and me.

HORACE [*looks down at her. His voice is tense*].   Please, Regina, it's been a hard trip. I don't feel well. Please leave me alone now.

REGINA [*quietly*].   I want to talk to you, Horace. [*He looks at her for a minute, then moves on, out of sight. She begins to climb the stairs.*]

BEN [*softly.* REGINA *turns to him as he speaks*].   Sometimes it is better to wait for the sun to rise again. [*She does not answer*] And sometimes, as our mother used to tell you, [REGINA *continues up stairs*] it's unwise for a good-looking woman to frown. [BEN *rises, moves toward stairs*] Softness and a smile do more to the heart of men—[*She disappears.* BEN *stands looking up the stairs. There is a long silence. Then* OSCAR *giggles.*]

OSCAR.   Let us hope she'll change his mind. Let us hope. [*After a second* BEN *crosses to table, picks up his newspaper.* OSCAR *looks at* BEN. *The silence makes Leo uncomfortable.*]

LEO.   The paper says twenty-seven cases of yellow fever in New Orleans. Guess the floodwaters caused it. [*Nobody pays attention*] Thought they were building the levees high enough. Like the niggers always say: a man born of woman can't build nothing high enough for the Mississippi. [*Gets no answer. Gives an embarrassed laugh.*]

[*Upstairs there is the sound of voices. The voices are not loud, but* BEN, OSCAR, LEO *become conscious of them.* LEO *crosses to landing, looks up, listens.*]

OSCAR [*pointing up*]. Now just suppose she don't change his mind? Just suppose he keeps on refusing?

BEN [*without conviction*]. He's tired. It was a mistake to talk to him today. He's a sick man, but he isn't a crazy one.

OSCAR. But just suppose he is crazy. What then?

BEN [*puts down his paper, peers at* OSCAR]. Then we'll go outside for the money. There's plenty who would give it.

OSCAR. And plenty who will want a lot for what they give. The ones who are rich enough to give will be smart enough to want. That means we'd be working for them, don't it, Ben?

BEN. You don't have to tell me the things I told you six months ago.

OSCAR. Oh, you're right not to worry. She'll change his mind. She always has. [*There is a silence. Suddenly* REGINA'S *voice becomes louder and sharper. All of them begin to listen now. Slowly* BEN *rises, goes to listen by the staircase.* OSCAR, *watching him, smiles. As they listen* REGINA'S *voice becomes very loud.* HORACE'S *voice is no longer heard*] Maybe. But I don't believe it. I never did believe he was going in with us.

BEN [*turning on him*]. What the hell do you expect me to do?

OSCAR [*mildly*]. Nothing. You done your almighty best. Nobody could blame you if the whole thing just dripped away right through our fingers. You can't do a thing. But there may be something I could do for us. [OSCAR *rises*] Or, I might better say, Leo could do for us. [BEN *turns, looks at* OSCAR. LEO *is staring at* OSCAR] Ain't that true, son? Ain't it true you might be able to help your own kinfolks?

LEO [*nervously taking a step to him*]. Papa, I—

BEN [*slowly*]. How would he help us, Oscar?

OSCAR. Leo's got a friend. Leo's friend owns eighty-eight thousand dollars in Union Pacific bonds. [BEN *turns to look at* LEO] Leo's friend don't look at the bonds much—not for five or six months at a time.

BEN [*after a pause*]. Union Pacific. Uh, huh. Let me understand. Leo's friend would—would lend him these bonds and he—

OSCAR [*nods*]. Would be kind enough to lend them to us.

BEN. Leo.

LEO [*excited, comes to him*]. Yes, sir?

BEN. When would your friend be wanting the bonds back?

LEO [*very nervous*]. I don't know. I—well, I—

OSCAR [*sharply. Steps to him*]. You told me he won't look at them until Autumn—

LEO. Oh, that's right. But I—not till Autumn. Uncle Horace never—

BEN [*sharply*]. Be still.

OSCAR [*smiles at* LEO].   Your uncle doesn't wish to know your friend's name.

LEO [*starts to laugh*].   That's a good one. Not know his name—

OSCAR.   Shut up, Leo! [LEO *turns away*] He won't look at them again until September. That gives us five months. Leo will return the bonds in three months. And we'll have no trouble raising the money once the mills are going up. Will Marshall accept bonds?

[BEN *stops to listen to the voices from above. The voices are now very angry and very loud.*]

BEN [*smiling*].   Why not? Why not? [*Laughs*] Good. We are lucky. We'll take the loan from Leo's friend—I think he will make a safer partner than our sister. [*Nods toward stairs. Turns to* LEO] How soon can you get them?

LEO.   Today. Right now. They're in the safe-deposit box and—

BEN [*sharply*].   I don't want to know where they are.

OSCAR [*laughs*].   We will keep it secret from you. [*Pats* BEN's *arm.*]

BEN.   Good. Draw a check for our part. You can take the night train for Chicago. Well, Oscar [*Holds out his hand*], good luck to us.

OSCAR.   Leo will be taken care of?

LEO.   I'm entitled to Uncle Horace's share. I'd enjoy being a partner—

BEN [*wheels on him*].   You would? You can go to hell, you little— [*Starts toward* LEO.]

OSCAR [*nervously*].   Now, now. He didn't mean that. I only want to be sure he'll get something out of all this.

BEN.   Of course. We'll take care of him. We won't have any trouble about that. I'll see you at the store.

OSCAR [*nods*].   That's settled then. Come on, son. [*Starts for door.*]

LEO [*puts out his hand*].   I was only going to say what a great day this was for me and—

BEN.   Go on.

[LEO *turns, follows* OSCAR *out. Again the voices upstairs can be heard.* REGINA's *voice is high and furious.* BEN *looks up, smiles, winces at the noise.*]

ALEXANDRA [*upstairs*].   Mama—Mama—don't . . . [*The noise of running footsteps is heard and* ALEXANDRA *comes running down the steps, speaking as she comes*] Uncle Ben! Uncle Ben! Please go up. Please make Mama stop. Uncle Ben, he's sick, he's so sick. How can Mama talk to him like that—please, make her stop. She'll—

BEN.   Alexandra, you have a tender heart.

ALEXANDRA [*crying*].   Go on up, Uncle Ben, please—

[*Suddenly the voices stop. A second later there is the sound of a door being slammed.*]

BEN.   Now you see. Everything is over. Don't worry. [*He starts for the door*] Alexandra, I want you to tell your mother how sorry I am that I had to leave. And don't worry so, my dear. Married folk frequently raise their voices, unfortunately. [*He starts to put on his hat and coat as* REGINA *appears on the stairs.*]

ALEXANDRA [*furiously*].   How can you treat Papa like this? He's sick. He's very sick. Don't you know that? I won't let you.

REGINA.   Mind your business, Alexandra. [*To* BEN. *Her voice is cold and calm*] How much longer can you wait for the money?

BEN [*putting on his coat*].   He has refused? My, that's too bad.

REGINA.   He will change his mind. I'll find a way to make him. What's the longest you can wait now?

BEN.   I could wait until next week. But I can't wait until next week. [*He giggles, pleased*] I could but I can't. Could and can't. Well, I must go now. I'm very late—

REGINA [*coming downstairs toward him*].   You're not going. I want to talk to you.

BEN.   I was about to give Alexandra a message for you. I wanted to tell you that Oscar is going to Chicago tonight, so we can't be here for our usual Friday supper.

REGINA [*tensely*].   Oscar is going to Chi— [*Softly*] What do you mean?

BEN.   Just that. Everything is settled. He's going on to deliver to Marshall—

REGINA [*taking a step to him*].   I demand to know what—You are lying. You are trying to scare me. *You haven't got the money.* How could you have it? You can't have—[BEN *laughs*] You will wait until I—

[HORACE *comes into view on the landing.*]

BEN.   You are getting out of hand. Since when do I take orders from you?

REGINA.   Wait, you— [BEN *stops*] How *can* he go to Chicago? Did a ghost arrive with the money? [BEN *starts for the hall*] I don't believe you. Come back here. [REGINA *starts after him*] Come back here, you— [*The door slams. She stops in the doorway, staring, her fists clenched. After a pause she turns slowly.*]

HORACE [*very quietly*].   It's a great day when you and Ben cross swords. I've been waiting for it for years.

ALEXANDRA.   Papa, Papa, please go back! You will—

HORACE.   And so they don't need you, and so you will not have your millions, after all.

REGINA [*turns slowly*].   You hate to see anybody live now, don't you? You hate to think that I'm going to be alive and have what I want.

HORACE.   I should have known you'd think that was the reason.

REGINA.   Because you're going to die and you know you're going to die.

ALEXANDRA [*shrilly*].   Mama! Don't—Don't listen, Papa. Just don't listen. Go away—

HORACE.   Not to keep you from getting what you want. Not even partly that. I'm sick of you, sick of this house, sick of my life here. I'm sick of your brothers and their dirty tricks to make a dime. Why should I give you the money? [*Very angrily*] To pound the bones of this town to make dividends for you to spend? You wreck the town, you and your brothers, *you* wreck the town and live on it. Not me. Maybe it's easy for the dying to be honest. But it's not my fault I'm dying. I'll do no more harm now. I've done enough. I'll die my own way. And I'll do it without making the world any worse. I leave that to you.

REGINA [*looks up at him*].   I hope you die. I hope you die soon. [*Smiles*] I'll be waiting for you to die.

ALEXANDRA [*shrieking*].   Papa! Don't—Don't listen—Don't—

[HORACE *turns slowly and starts upstairs.*]

ACT III.

SCENE: *Same as Act One. Two weeks later. It is late afternoon and it is raining.*

AT RISE: HORACE *is sitting near the window in a wheelchair. On the table next to him is a safe-deposit box, and a small bottle of medicine. *BIRDIE *and *ALEXANDRA *are playing the piano. On a chair is a large sewing basket.*

BIRDIE [*counting for* ALEXANDRA].   One and two and three and four. One and two and three and four. [*Nods—turns to* HORACE] We once played together, Horace. Remember?

HORACE [*has been looking out of the window*].   What, Birdie?

BIRDIE.   We played together. You and me.

ALEXANDRA.   *Papa* used to play?

BIRDIE.   Indeed he did. [ADDIE *appears at the door in a large kitchen apron*] He played the fiddle and very well, too.

ALEXANDRA [*turns to smile at* HORACE].   I never knew—

ADDIE.   Where's your mama?

ALEXANDRA.   Gone to Miss Safronia's to fit her dresses.

[ADDIE *nods, starts to exit.*]

HORACE.   Addie. Tell Cal to get on his things. I want him to go on an errand.

[ADDIE *nods, exits.* HORACE *moves nervously in his chair, looks out of the window.*]

ALEXANDRA [*who has been watching him*].   It's too bad it's been raining all day, Papa. But you can go out in the yard tomorrow. Don't be restless.

HORACE.   I'm not restless, darling.

BIRDIE.   I remember so well the time we played together, your papa and me. It was the first time Oscar brought me here to supper. I had never seen all the Hubbards together before, and you know what a ninny I am and how shy. [*Turns to look at* HORACE] You said you could play the fiddle and you'd be much obliged if I'd play with you. *I* was obliged to *you*, all right, all right. [*Laughs when he does not answer her*] Horace, you haven't heard a word I've said.

HORACE. Birdie, when did Oscar get back from Chicago?

BIRDIE. Yesterday. Hasn't he been here yet?

ALEXANDRA [*stops playing*]. No. Neither has Uncle Ben since—since that day.

BIRDIE. Oh, I didn't know it was *that* bad. Oscar never tells me anything—

HORACE. The Hubbards have had their great quarrel. I knew it would come someday. [*Laughs*] It came.

ALEXANDRA. It came. It certainly came all right.

BIRDIE [*amazed*]. But Oscar was in such a good humor when he got home, I didn't—

HORACE. Yes, I can understand that.

[ADDIE *enters carrying a large tray with glasses, a carafe of elderberry wine and a plate of cookies, which she puts on the table.*]

ALEXANDRA. Addie! A party! What for?

ADDIE. Nothing for. I had the fresh butter, so I made the cakes, and a little elderberry does the stomach good in the rain.

BIRDIE. Isn't this nice! A party just for us. Let's play party music, Zan.

[ALEXANDRA *begins to play a gay piece.*]

ADDIE [*to* HORACE, *wheeling his chair to center*]. Come over here, Mr. Horace, and don't be thinking so much. A glass of elderberry will do more good.

[ALEXANDRA *reaches for a cake.* BIRDIE *pours herself a glass of wine.*]

ALEXANDRA. Good cakes, Addie. It's nice here. Just us. Be nice if it could always be this way.

BIRDIE [*nods happily*]. Quiet and restful.

ADDIE. Well, it won't be that way long. Little while now, even sitting here, you'll hear the red bricks going into place. The next day the smoke'll be pushing out the chimneys and by church time that Sunday every human born of woman will be living on chicken. That's how Mr. Ben's been telling the story.

HORACE. They believe it that way?

ADDIE. Believe it? They use to believing what Mr. Ben orders. There ain't been so much talk around here since Sherman's army didn't come near.

HORACE [*softly*]. They are fools.

ADDIE [*nods, sits down with the sewing basket*]. You ain't born in the South unless you're a fool.

BIRDIE [*has drunk another glass of wine*]. But we didn't play together after that night. Oscar said he didn't like me to play on the piano. [*Turns to* ALEXANDRA] You know what he said that night?

ALEXANDRA. Who?

BIRDIE. Oscar. He said that music made him nervous. He said he just sat and waited for the next note. [ALEXANDRA *laughs*] He wasn't poking fun. He meant it. Ah, well—[*She finishes her glass, shakes her head.* HORACE *looks at her, smiles*] Your papa don't like to admit it, but he's been mighty kind to me all these years. [*Running her hand along his sleeve*] Often he'd step in when somebody said something and once—[*She stops, turns away, her face still*] Once he stopped Oscar from—[*She stops, turns. Quickly*] I'm sorry I said that. Why, here I am so happy and yet I think about bad things. [*Laughs nervously*] That's not right, now, is it? [*She pours a drink.* CAL *appears in the door. He has on an old coat and is carrying a torn umbrella.*]

ALEXANDRA.   Have a cake, Cal.

CAL [*comes in, takes a cake*].   You want me, Mr. Horace?

HORACE.   What time is it, Cal?

CAL.   'Bout ten minutes before it's five.

HORACE.   All right. Now you walk yourself down to the bank.

CAL.   It'll be closed. Nobody'll be there but Mr. Manders, Mr. Joe Horns, Mr. Leo—

HORACE.   Go in the back way. They'll be at the table, going over the day's business. [*Points to the deposit box*] See that box?

CAL [*nods*].   Yes, sir.

HORACE.   You tell Mr. Manders that Mr. Horace says he's much obliged to him for bringing the box, it arrived all right.

CAL [*bewildered*].   He know you got the box. He bring it himself Wednesday. I opened the door to him and he say, "Hello, Cal, coming on to summer weather."

HORACE.   You say just what I tell you. Understand?

[BIRDIE *pours another drink, stands at table.*]

CAL.   No, sir. I ain't going to say I understand. I'm going down and tell a man he give you something he already know he give you, and you say "understand."

HORACE.   Now, Cal.

CAL.   Yes, sir. I just going to say you obliged for the box coming all right. I ain't going to understand it, but I'm going to say it.

HORACE.   And tell him I want him to come over here after supper, and to bring Mr. Sol Fowler with him.

CAL [*nods*].   He's to come after supper and bring Mr. Sol Fowler, your attorney-at-law, with him.

HORACE.   That's right. Just walk right in the back room and say your piece. [*Slowly*] In front of everybody.

CAL.   Yes, sir. [*Mumbles to himself as he exits.*]

ALEXANDRA [*who has been watching* HORACE].   Is anything the matter, Papa?

HORACE.   Oh, no. Nothing.

ADDIE.   Miss Birdie, that elderberry going to give you a headache spell.

BIRDIE [*beginning to be drunk. Gaily*].   Oh, I don't think so. I don't think it will.

ALEXANDRA [*as* HORACE *puts his hand to his throat*].   Do you want your medicine, Papa?

HORACE.   No, no. I'm all right, darling.

BIRDIE.   Mama used to give me elderberry wine when I was a little girl. For hiccoughs. [*Laughs*] You know, I don't think people get hiccoughs anymore. Isn't that funny? [BIRDIE *laughs*. HORACE *and* ALEXANDRA *smile*] I used to get hiccoughs just when I shouldn't have.

ADDIE [*nods*].   And nobody gets growing pains no more. That is funny. Just as if there was some style in what you get. One year an ailment's stylish and the next year it ain't.

BIRDIE.   I remember. It was my first big party, at Lionnet I mean, and I was so excited, and there I was with hiccoughs and Mama laughing. [*Softly. Looking at carafe*] Mama always laughed. [*Picks up carafe*] A big party, a lovely dress from Mr. Worth in Paris, France, and hiccoughs. [*Pours drink*] My brother pounding me on the back and Mama with the elderberry bottle, laughing at me. Everybody was on their way to come, and I was such a ninny, hiccoughing away. [*Drinks*] You know, that was the first day I ever saw Oscar Hubbard. The Ballongs were selling their horses and he was going there to buy. He passed and lifted his hat—we could see him from the window—and my brother, to tease Mama, said maybe we should have invited the Hubbards to the party. He said Mama didn't like them because they kept a store, and he said that was old-fashioned of her. [*Her face lights up*] And then, and *then,* I saw Mama angry for the first time in my life. She said that wasn't the reason. She said she was old-fashioned, but not that way. She said she was old-fashioned enough not to like people who killed animals they couldn't use, and who made their money charging awful interest to ignorant niggers and cheating them on what they bought. She was very angry, Mama was. I had never seen her face like that. And then suddenly she laughed and said, "Look, I've frightened Birdie out of the hiccoughs." [*Her head drops. Then softly*] And so she had. They were all gone. [*Moves to sofa, sits.*]

ADDIE.   Yeah, they got mighty well-off cheating niggers. Well, there are people who eat the earth and eat all the people on it like in the Bible with the locusts. And other people who stand around and watch them eat it. [*Softly*] Sometimes I think it ain't right to stand and watch them do it.

BIRDIE [*thoughtfully*].   Like I say, if we could only go back to Lionnet. Everybody'd be better there. They'd be good and kind. I like people to be kind. [*Pours drink*] Don't you, Horace; don't you like people to be kind?

HORACE.   Yes, Birdie.

BIRDIE [*very drunk now*].   Yes, that was the first day I ever saw Oscar. Who would have thought—You all want to know something? Well, I don't like Leo. My very own son, and I don't like him. [*Laughs, gaily*] My, I guess I even like Oscar more.

ALEXANDRA.   Why did you marry Uncle Oscar?

ADDIE.   That's no question for you to be asking.

HORACE [*sharply*].   Why not? She's heard enough around here to ask anything.

BIRDIE.   I don't know. I thought I liked him. He was kind to me and I thought it was because he liked me too. But that wasn't the reason—[*Wheels on* ALEXANDRA] Ask why *he* married *me*. I can tell you that: he's told it to me often enough.

ADDIE.   Miss Birdie, don't—

BIRDIE [*speaking very rapidly*].   My family was good and the cotton on Lionnet's fields was better. Ben Hubbard wanted the cotton and Oscar Hubbard married it for him. He was kind to me, then. He used to smile at me. He hasn't smiled at me since. Everybody knew that's what he married me for. [ADDIE *rises*] Everybody but me. Stupid, stupid me.

ALEXANDRA [*to* HORACE, *softly*]. I see. [*Hesitates*] Papa, I mean— when you feel better couldn't we go away? I mean, by ourselves. Couldn't we find a way to go?

HORACE. Yes, I know what you mean. We'll try to find a way. I promise you, darling.

ADDIE [*moves to* BIRDIE]. Rest a bit, Miss Birdie. You get talking like this you'll get a headache and—

BIRDIE [*sharply*]. I've never had a headache in my life. [*Begins to cry*] You know it as well as I do. [*Turns to* ALEXANDRA] I never had a headache, Zan. That's a lie they tell for me. I drink. All by myself, in my own room, by myself, I drink. Then, when they want to hide it, they say, "Birdie's got a headache again"—

ALEXANDRA [*comes to her*]. Aunt Birdie.

BIRDIE. Even you won't like me now. You won't like me any more.

ALEXANDRA. I love you. I'll always love you.

BIRDIE [*angrily*]. Well, don't. Don't love me. Because in twenty years you'll just be like me. They'll do all the same things to you. [*Begins to laugh*] You know what? In twenty-two years I haven't had a whole day of happiness. Oh, a little, like today with you all. But never a single, whole day. I say to myself, if only I had one more *whole* day, then—[*The laugh stops*] And that's the way you'll be. And you'll trail after them, just like me, hoping they won't be so mean that day or say something to make you feel so bad—only you'll be worse off because you haven't got my Mama to remember—[*Turns away, her head drops. She stands quietly, swaying a little, holding to the sofa*].

ALEXANDRA [*to* BIRDIE]. I guess we were all trying to make a happy day. You know, we sit around and try to pretend nothing's happened. We try to pretend we are not here. We make believe we are just by ourselves, someplace else, and it doesn't seem to work. [*Kisses* BIRDIE'S *hand*] Come now, Aunt Birdie, I'll walk you home. You and me. [*She takes* BIRDIE'S *arm. They move slowly out.*]

BIRDIE [*softly as they exit*]. You and me.

ADDIE [*after a minute*]. Well, First time I ever heard Miss Birdie say a word. Maybe it's good for her. I'm just sorry Zan had to hear it. [HORACE *moves his head as if he were uncomfortable*] You feel bad, don't you? [*He shrugs.*]

HORACE. So you didn't want Zan to hear? It would be nice to let her stay innocent, like Birdie at her age. Let her listen now. Let her see everything. How else is she going to know that she's got to get away? I'm trying to show her that. I'm trying, but I've only got a little time left. She can even hate me when I'm dead, if she'll only learn to hate and fear this.

ADDIE. Mr. Horace—

HORACE. Pretty soon there'll be nobody to help her but you.

ADDIE. What can I do?

HORACE. Take her away.

ADDIE. How can I do that? Do you think they'd let me just go away with her?

HORACE. I'll fix it so they can't stop you when you're ready to go. You'll go, Addie?

ADDIE [*after a second, softly*].   Yes, sir. I promise. [*He touches her arm, nods.*]

HORACE [*quietly*].   I'm going to have Sol Fowler make me a new will. They'll make trouble, but you make Zan stand firm and Fowler'll do the rest. Addie, I'd like to leave you something for yourself. I always wanted to.

ADDIE [*laughs*].   Don't you do that, Mr. Horace. A nigger woman in a white man's will! I'd never get it nohow.

HORACE.   I know. But upstairs in the armoire drawer there's thirty-seven hundred-dollar bills. It's money left from my trip. It's in an envelope with your name. It's for you.

ADDIE.   It's mighty kind and good of you. I don't know what to say for thanks—

CAL [*appears in doorway*].   I'm back. [*No answer*] I'm back.

ADDIE.   So we see.

HORACE.   Well?

CAL.   Nothing. I just went down and spoke my piece. Just like you told me. I say, "Mr. Horace he thank you mightily for the safe box arriving in good shape and he say you come right after supper to his house and bring Mr. Attorney-at-law Sol Fowler with you." Then I wipe my hands on my coat. Every time I ever told a lie in my whole life, I wipe my hands right after. Well, while I'm wiping my hands, Mr. Leo jump up and say to me, "What box? What you talking about?"

HORACE [*smiles*].   Did he?

CAL.   And Mr. Leo say he got to leave a little early cause he got something to do. And then Mr. Manders say Mr. Leo should sit right down and finish up his work and stop acting like somebody made him Mr. President. So he sit down. Now, just like I told you, Mr. Manders was mighty surprised with the message because he knows right well he brought the box—[*Points to box, sighs*] But he took it all right. Some men take everything easy and some do not.

HORACE [*laughs*].   Mr. Leo was telling the truth; he *has* got something to do. I hope Manders don't keep him too long. [*Outside there is the sound of voices.* CAL *exits.* ADDIE *crosses quickly to* HORACE, *begins to wheel his chair toward the stairs*] No. Leave me where I am.

ADDIE.   But that's Miss Regina coming back.

HORACE [*nods, looking at door*].   Go away, Addie.

ADDIE [*hesitates*].   Mr. Horace. Don't talk no more today. You don't feel well and it won't do no good—

HORACE [*as he hears footsteps in the hall*].   Go on. [*She looks at him for a second, then picks up her sewing from table and exits as* REGINA *comes in from hall.* HORACE's *chair is now so placed that he is in front of the table with the medicine.* REGINA *stands in the hall, shakes umbrella, stands it in the corner, takes off her cloak and throws it over the banister. She stares at* HORACE.]

REGINA [*as she takes off her gloves*].   We had agreed that you were to stay in your part of this house and I in mine. This room is *my* part of the house. Please don't come down here again.

HORACE.   I won't.

REGINA [*crosses toward bell cord*].   I'll get Cal to take you upstairs.

HORACE.   Before you do I want to tell you that after all, we have invested our money in Hubbard Sons and Marshall, Cotton Manufacturers.

REGINA [*stops, turns, stares at him*]. What are you talking about? You haven't seen Ben—When did you change your mind?

HORACE. I didn't change my mind. *I* didn't invest the money. [*Smiles*] It was invested for me.

REGINA [*angrily*]. What—?

HORACE. I had eighty-eight thousand dollars' worth of Union Pacific bonds in that safe-deposit box. They are not there now. Go and look. [*As she stares at him, he points to the box*] Go and look, Regina. [*She crosses quickly to the box, opens it*] Those bonds are as negotiable as money.

REGINA [*turns back to him*]. What kind of joke are you playing now? Is this for my benefit?

HORACE. I don't look in that box very often, but three days ago, on Wednesday it was, because I had made a decision—

REGINA. I want to know what you are talking about.

HORACE. Don't interrupt me again. Because I had made a decision, I sent for the box. The bonds were gone. Eighty-eight thousand dollars gone. [*He smiles at her.*]

REGINA [*after a moment's silence, quietly*]. Do you think I'm crazy enough to believe what you're saying?

HORACE. Believe anything you like.

REGINA [*slowly*]. Where did they go to?

HORACE. They are in Chicago. With Mr. Marshall, I should guess.

REGINA. What did they do? Walk to Chicago? Have you really gone crazy?

HORACE. Leo took the bonds.

REGINA [*turns sharply, then speaks softly, without conviction*]. I don't believe it.

HORACE. I wasn't there but I can guess what happened. This fine gentle-man, with whom you were bargaining your daughter, took the keys and opened the box. You remember that the day of the fight Oscar went to Chicago? Well, he went with my bonds that his son Leo had stolen for him. [*Pleasantly*] And for Ben.

REGINA [*slowly, nods*]. When did you find out the bonds were gone?

HORACE. Wednesday night.

REGINA. I thought that's what you said. Why have you waited three days to do anything? [*Suddenly laughs*] This *will* make a fine story.

HORACE [*nods*]. Couldn't it?

REGINA. A fine story to hold over their heads. How could they be such fools?

HORACE. But I'm not going to hold it over their heads.

REGINA [*the laugh stops*]. What?

HORACE [*turns his chair to face her*]. I'm going to let them keep the bonds—as a loan from you. An eighty-eight-thousand-dollar loan; they should be grateful to you. They will be, I think.

REGINA [*slowly, smiles*]. I see. You are punishing me. But I won't let you punish me. If you won't do anything, I will. Now. [*She starts for door.*]

HORACE. You won't do anything. Because you can't. [REGINA *stops*] It won't do you any good to make trouble because I shall simply say that I lent them the bonds.

REGINA [*slowly*]. You would do that?

HORACE. Yes. For once in your life I am tying your hands. There is nothing for you to do. [*There is silence. Then she sits down.*]

REGINA. I see. You are going to lend them the bonds and let them keep all the profit they make on them and there is nothing I can do about it. Is that right?

HORACE. Yes.

REGINA [*softly*]. Why did you say that I was making this gift?

HORACE. I was coming to that. I am going to make a new will, Regina, leaving you eighty-eight thousand dollars in Union Pacific bonds. The rest will go to Zan. It's true that your brothers have borrowed your share for a little while. After my death I advise you to talk to Ben and Oscar. They won't admit anything and Ben, I think, will be smart enough to see that he's safe. Because I knew about the theft and said nothing. Nor will I say anything as long as I live. Is that clear to you?

REGINA [*nods, softly, without looking at him*]. You will not say anything as long as you live.

HORACE. That's right. And by that time they will probably have replaced your bonds, and then they'll belong to you and nobody but us will ever know what happened. They'll be around any minute to see what I am going to do. I took good care to see that word reached Leo. They'll be mighty relieved to know I'm going to do nothing and Ben will think it all a capital joke on you. And that will be the end of that. There's nothing you can do to them, nothing you can do to me.

REGINA. You hate me very much.

HORACE. No.

REGINA. Oh, I think you do. [*Puts her head back, sighs*] Well, we haven't been very good together. Anyway, I don't hate you either. I have only contempt for you. I've always had.

HORACE. From the very first?

REGINA. I think so.

HORACE. I was in love with *you*. But why did *you* marry *me?*

REGINA. I was lonely when I was young.

HORACE. *You* were lonely?

REGINA. Not the way people usually mean. Lonely for all the things I wasn't going to get. Everybody in this house was so busy and there was so little place for what I wanted. I wanted the world. Then, and then—[*Smiles*] Papa died and left the money to Ben and Oscar.

HORACE. And you married me?

REGINA. Yes, I thought—But I was wrong. You were a small-town clerk then. You haven't changed.

HORACE [*nods*]. And that wasn't what you wanted.

REGINA. No. No, it wasn't what I wanted. [*Pleasantly*] It took me a little while to find out I had made a mistake. As for you—I don't know. It was almost as if I couldn't stand the kind of man you were—[*Smiles, softly*] I used to lie there at night, praying you wouldn't come near—

HORACE. Really? It was as bad as that?

REGINA. Remember when I went to Doctor Sloan and I told you he said there was something the matter with me and that you shouldn't touch me anymore?

HORACE. I remember.

REGINA. But you believed it. I couldn't understand that. I couldn't understand that anybody could be such a soft fool. That was when I began to despise you.

HORACE [*puts his hand to his throat, looks at the bottle of medicine on table*]. Why didn't you leave me?

REGINA. I told you I married you for something. It turned out it was only for this. [*Carefully*] This wasn't what I wanted, but it was something. I never thought about it much, but if I had I'd have known that you would die before I would. But I couldn't have known that you would get heart trouble so early and so bad. I'm lucky, Horace. I've always been lucky. [HORACE *turns slowly to the medicine*] I'll be lucky again. [HORACE *looks at her. Then he puts his hand to his throat. Because he cannot reach the bottle he moves the chair closer. He reaches for the medicine, takes out the cork, picks up the spoon. The bottle slips and smashes on the table. He draws in his breath, gasps.*]

HORACE. Please. Tell Addie—The other bottle is upstairs. [REGINA *has not moved. She does not move now. He stares at her. Then, suddenly as if he understood, he raises his voice. It is a panic-stricken whisper, too small to be heard outside the room*] Addie! Addie! Come—[*Stops as he hears the softness of his voice. He makes a sudden, furious spring from the chair to the stairs, taking the first few steps as if he were a desperate runner. Then he slips, gasps, grasps the rail, makes a great effort to reach the landing. When he reaches the landing, he is on his knees. His knees give way, he falls on the landing, out of view. REGINA *has not turned during his climb up the stairs. Now she waits a second. Then she goes below the landing, speaks up.*]

REGINA. Horace. Horace. [*When there is no answer, she turns, calls*] Addie! Cal! Come in here. [*She starts up the steps.* ADDIE *and* CAL *appear. Both run toward the stairs*] He's had an attack. Come up here. [*They run up the steps quickly.*]

CAL. My God. Mr. Horace—

[*They cannot be seen now.*]

REGINA [*her voice comes from the head of the stairs*]. Be still, Cal. Bring him in here.

[*Before the footsteps and the voices have completely died away,* ALEXANDRA *appears in the hall door, in her raincloak and hood. She comes into the room, begins to unfasten the cloak, suddenly looks around, sees the empty wheelchair, stares, begins to move swiftly as if to look in the dining room. At the same moment* ADDIE *runs down the stairs.* ALEXANDRA *turns and stares up at* ADDIE.]

ALEXANDRA. Addie! What?

ADDIE [*takes* ALEXANDRA *by the shoulders*]. I'm going for the doctor. Go upstairs. [ALEXANDRA *looks at her, then quickly breaks away and runs up the steps.* ADDIE *exits. The stage is empty for a minute. Then the front doorbell begins to ring. When there is no answer, it rings again. A second later* LEO *appears in the hall, talking as he comes in.*]

LEO [*very nervous*].   Hello. [*Irritably*] Never saw any use ringing a bell when a door was open. If you are going to ring a bell, then somebody should answer it. [*Gets in the room, looks around, puzzled, listens, hears no sound*] Aunt Regina. [*He moves around restlessly*] Addie. [*Waits*] Where the hell— [*Crosses to the bell cord, rings it impatiently, waits, gets no answer, calls*] Cal! Cal! [CAL *appears on the stair landing.*]

CAL [*his voice is soft, shaken*].   Mr. Leo. Miss Regina says you stop that screaming noise.

LEO [*angrily*].   Where is everybody?

CAL.   Mr. Horace he got an attack. He's bad. Miss Regina says you stop that noise.

LEO.   Uncle Horace—What—What happened? [CAL *starts down the stairs, shakes his head, begins to move swiftly off.* LEO *looks around wildly*] But when—You seen Mr. Oscar or Mr. Ben? [CAL *shakes his head. Moves on.* LEO *grabs him by the arm*] Answer me, will you?

CAL.   No, I ain't seen 'em. I ain't got time to answer you. I got to get things. [CAL *runs off.*]

LEO.   But what's the matter with him? When did this happen—[*Calling after* CAL] You'd think Papa'd be someplace where you could find him. I been chasing him all afternoon.

[OSCAR *and* BEN *come quickly into the room.*]

LEO.   Papa, I've been looking all over town for you and Uncle Ben—

BEN.   Where is he?

OSCAR.   Addie just told us it was a sudden attack, and—

BEN [*to* LEO].   Where is he? When did it happen?

LEO.   Upstairs. Will you listen to me, please? I been looking for you for—

OSCAR [*to* BEN].   You think we should go up? [BEN, *looking up the steps, shakes his head.*]

BEN.   I don't know. I don't know.

OSCAR.   But he was all right—

LEO [*yelling*].   *Will you listen to me?*

OSCAR.   What is the matter with you?

LEO.   I been trying to tell you. I been trying to find you for an hour—

OSCAR.   Tell me what?

LEO.   Uncle Horace knows about the bonds. He knows about them. He's had the box since Wednesday—

BEN [*sharply*].   Stop shouting! What the hell are you talking about?

LEO [*furiously*].   I'm telling you he knows about the bonds. Ain't that clear enough—

BEN [*grabbing* LEO's *arm*].   You God-damn fool! Stop screaming! Now what happened? Talk quietly.

LEO.   You heard me. Uncle Horace knows about the bonds. He's known since Wednesday.

BEN [*after a second*].   How do you know that?

LEO.   Because Cal comes down to Manders and says the box came okay and—

OSCAR [*trembling*].   That might not mean a thing—

LEO [*angrily*]. No? It might not, huh? Then he says Manders should come here tonight and bring Sol Fowler with him. I guess that don't mean a thing either.

OSCAR [*to* BEN]. Ben—What—Do you think he's seen the—

BEN [*motions to the box*]. There's the box. [*Both* OSCAR *and* LEO *turn sharply.* LEO *makes a leap to the box*] You ass. Put it down. What are you going to do with it, eat it?

LEO. I'm going to—

BEN [*furiously*]. Put it down. Don't touch it again. Now sit down and shut up for a minute.

OSCAR. Since Wednesday. [*To* LEO] You said he had it since Wednesday. Why didn't he say something—[*To* BEN] I don't understand—

LEO [*taking a step*]. I can put it back. I can put it back before anybody knows.

BEN [*who is standing at the table, softly*]. He's had it since Wednesday. Yet he hasn't said a word to us.

OSCAR. Why? Why?

LEO. What's the difference why? He was getting ready to say plenty. He was going to say it to Fowler tonight—

OSCAR [*angrily*]. Be still. [*Turns to* BEN, *looks at him, waits.*]

BEN [*after a minute*]. I don't believe that.

LEO [*wildly*]. *You* don't believe it? What do I care what *you* believe? I do the dirty work and then—

BEN [*turning his head to* LEO]. I'm remembering that. I'm remembering that, Leo.

OSCAR. What do you mean?

LEO. You—

BEN [*to* OSCAR]. If you don't shut that little fool up, I'll show you what I mean. For some reason he knows, but he don't say a word.

OSCAR. Maybe he didn't know that *we*—

BEN [*quickly*]. That *Leo*—He's no fool. Does Manders know the bonds are missing?

LEO. How could I tell? I was half crazy. I don't think so. Because Manders seemed kind of puzzled and—

OSCAR. But we got to find out—[*He breaks off as* CAL *comes into the room carrying a kettle of hot water.*]

BEN. How is he, Cal?

CAL. I don't know, Mr. Ben. He was bad. [*Going toward stairs.*]

OSCAR. But when did it happen?

CAL [*shrugs*]. He wasn't feeling bad early. [ADDIE *comes in quickly from the hall*] Then there he is next thing on the landing, fallen over, his eyes tight—

ADDIE [*to* CAL]. Dr. Sloan's over at the Ballongs. Hitch the buggy and go get him. [*She takes the kettle and cloths from him, pushes him, runs up the stairs*] Go on. [*She disappears.* CAL *exits.*]

BEN. Never seen Sloan anywhere when you need him.

OSCAR [*softly*]. Sounds bad.

LEO. He would have told *her* about it. Aunt Regina. He would have told his own wife—

BEN [*turning to* LEO]. Yes, he might have told her. But they weren't on such pretty terms and maybe he didn't. Maybe he didn't. [*Goes quickly to* LEO] Now listen to me. If she doesn't know, it may work out all right. If she does know, you're to say he lent you the bonds.

LEO. Lent them to me! Who's going to believe that?

BEN. Nobody.

OSCAR [*to* LEO]. Don't you understand? It can't do no harm to say it—

LEO. Why should I say he lent them to me? Why not to you? [*Carefully*] Why not to Uncle Ben?

BEN [*smiles*]. Just because he didn't lend them to me. Remember that.

LEO. But all he has to do is say he didn't lend them to me—

BEN [*furiously*]. But for some reason, he doesn't seem to be talking, does he?

[*There are footsteps above. They all stand looking at the stairs.* REGINA *begins to come slowly down.*]

BEN. What happened?

REGINA. He's had a bad attack.

OSCAR. Too bad. I'm sorry we weren't here when—when Horace needed us.

BEN. When *you* needed us.

REGINA [*looks at him*]. Yes.

BEN. How is he? Can we—can we go up?

REGINA [*shakes her head*]. He's not conscious.

OSCAR [*pacing around*]. It's that—it's that bad? Wouldn't you think Sloan could be found quickly, just once, just once?

REGINA. I don't think there is much for him to do.

BEN. Oh, don't talk like that. He's come through attacks before. He will now.

[REGINA *sits down. After a second she speaks softly.*]

REGINA. Well. We haven't seen each other since the day of our fight.

BEN [*tenderly*]. That was nothing. Why, you and Oscar and I used to fight when we were kids.

OSCAR [*hurriedly*]. Don't you think we should grow up? Is there anything we can do for Horace—

BEN. You don't feel well. Ah—

REGINA [*without looking at them*]. No, I don't. [*Slight pause*] Horace told me about the bonds this afternoon. [*There is an immediate shocked silence.*]

LEO. The bonds. What do you mean? What bonds? What—

BEN [*looks at him furiously. Then to* REGINA]. The Union Pacific bonds? *Horace's* Union Pacific bonds?

REGINA. Yes.

OSCAR [*steps to her, very nervously*]. Well. Well what—what about them? What—what could he say?

REGINA. He said that Leo had stolen the bonds and given them to you.

OSCAR [*aghast, very loudly*]. That's ridiculous, Regina, absolutely—

LEO. I don't know what you're talking about. What would I—Why—

REGINA [*wearily to* BEN]. Isn't it enough that he stole them? Do I have to listen to this in the bargain?

OSCAR. You are talking—

LEO. I didn't steal anything. I don't know why—

REGINA [*to* BEN]. Would you ask them to stop that, please? [*There is silence.* BEN *glowers at* OSCAR *and* LEO.]

BEN. Aren't we starting at the wrong end, Regina? What did Horace tell you?

REGINA [*smiles at him*]. He told me that Leo had stolen the bonds.

LEO. I didn't steal—

REGINA. Please. Let me finish. Then he told me that he was going to pretend that he had lent them to you [LEO *turns sharply to* REGINA, *then looks at* OSCAR, *then looks back at* REGINA] as a present from me—to my brothers. He said there was nothing I could do about it. He said the rest of his money would go to Alexandra. That is all. [*There is a silence,* OSCAR *coughs,* LEO *smiles slyly.*]

LEO [*taking a step to her*]. I told you he had lent them—I could have told you—

REGINA [*ignores him, smiles sadly at* BEN]. So I'm very badly off, you see. Horace said there was nothing I could do about it as long as he was alive to say he had lent you the bonds.

BEN. You shouldn't feel that way. It can all be explained, all be adjusted. It isn't as bad—

REGINA. So you, at least, are willing to admit the bonds were stolen?

BEN [OSCAR *laughs nervously*]. I admit no such thing. It's possible that Horace made up that part of the story to tease you—[*Looks at her*] Or perhaps to punish you. Punish you.

REGINA [*sadly*]. It's not a pleasant story. I feel bad, Ben, naturally. I hadn't thought—

BEN. Now you shall have the bonds safely back. That was the understanding, wasn't it, Oscar?

OSCAR. Yes.

REGINA. I'm glad to know that. [*Smiles*] Ah, I had greater hopes—

BEN. Don't talk that way. That's foolish. [*Looks at his watch*] I think we ought to drive out for Sloan ourselves. If we can't find him we'll go over to Senateville for Doctor Morris. And don't think I'm dismissing this other business. I'm not. We'll have it all out on a more appropriate day.

REGINA. I don't think you had better go yet. I think you had better stay and sit down.

BEN. We'll be back with Sloan.

REGINA. Cal has gone for him. I don't want you to go.

BEN. Now don't worry and—

REGINA. You will come back in this room and sit down. I have something more to say.

BEN [*turns, comes toward her*]. Since when do I take orders from you?

REGINA [*smiles*]. You don't—yet. [*Sharply*] Come back, Oscar. You too, Leo.

OSCAR [*sure of himself, laughs*]. My dear Regina—

BEN [*softly, pats her hand*]. Horace has already clipped your wings and very wittily. Do I have to clip them, too? [*Smiles at her*] You'd get farther with a smile, Regina. I'm a soft man for a woman's smile.

REGINA. I'm smiling, Ben. I'm smiling because you are quite safe while Horace lives. But I don't think Horace will live. And if he doesn't live I shall want seventy-five percent in exchange for the bonds.

BEN [*steps back, whistles, laughs*]. Greedy! What a greedy girl you are! You want so much of everything.

REGINA. Yes. And if I don't get what I want I am going to put all three of you in jail.

OSCAR [*furiously*]. You're mighty crazy. Having just admitted—

BEN. And on what evidence would you put Oscar and Leo in jail?

REGINA [*laughs, gaily*]. Oscar, listen to him. He's getting ready to swear that it was you and Leo! What do you say to that? [OSCAR *turns furiously toward* BEN] Oh, don't be angry, Oscar. I'm going to see that he goes in with you.

BEN. Try anything you like, Regina. [*Sharply*] And now we can stop all this and say good-bye to you. [ALEXANDRA *comes slowly down the steps*] It's his money and he's obviously willing to let us borrow it. [*More pleasantly*] Learn to make threats when you can carry them through. For how many years have I told you a good-looking woman gets more by being soft and appealing? Mama used to tell you that. [*Looks at his watch*] Where the hell is Sloan? [*To* OSCAR] Take the buggy and—[*As* BEN *turns to* OSCAR, *he sees* ALEXANDRA. *She walks stiffly. She goes slowly to the lower window, her head bent. They all turn to look at her.*]

OSCAR [*after a second, moving toward her*]. What? Alexandra—[*She does not answer. After a second,* ADDIE *comes slowly down the stairs, moving as if she were very tired. At foot of steps, she looks at* ALEXANDRA, *then turns and slowly crosses to door and exits.* REGINA *rises.* BEN *looks nervously at* ALEXANDRA, *at* REGINA.]

OSCAR [*as* ADDIE *passes him, irritably to* ALEXANDRA]. Well, what is—[*Turns into room—sees* ADDIE *at foot of steps*]—what's? [BEN *puts up a hand, shakes his head*] My God, I didn't know—who *could* have known—I didn't know he was that sick. Well, well—I—[REGINA *stands quietly, her back to them.*]

BEN [*softly, sincerely*]. Seems like yesterday when he first came here.

OSCAR. Yes, that's true. [*Turns to* BEN] The whole town loved him and respected him.

ALEXANDRA [*turns*]. Did you love him, Uncle Oscar?

OSCAR. Certainly, I—What a strange thing to ask! I—

ALEXANDRA. Did you love him, Uncle Ben?

BEN [*simply*]. Alexandra, I—

ALEXANDRA [*starts to laugh very loudly*]. And you, Mama, did you love him, too?

REGINA. I know what you feel, Alexandra, but please try to control yourself.

ALEXANDRA. I'm trying, Mama. I'm trying very hard.

BEN. Grief makes some people laugh and some people cry. It's better to cry, Alexandra.

ALEXANDRA [*the laugh has stopped. She moves toward* REGINA]. What was Papa doing on the staircase?

[BEN *turns to look at* ALEXANDRA.]

REGINA. Please go and lie down, my dear. We all need time to get over shocks like this. [ALEXANDRA *does not move.* REGINA'S *voice becomes softer, more insistent*] Please go, Alexandra.

ALEXANDRA. No, Mama. I'll wait. I've got to talk to you.

REGINA. Later. Go and rest now.

ALEXANDRA [*quietly*]. I'll wait, Mama. I've plenty of time.

REGINA [*hesitates, stares, makes a half shrug, turns back to* BEN]. As I was saying. Tomorrow morning I am going up to Judge Simmes. I shall tell him about Leo.

BEN [*motioning toward* ALEXANDRA]. Not in front of the child, Regina. I—

REGINA [*turns to him. Sharply*]. I didn't ask her to stay. Tomorrow morning I go to Judge Simmes—

OSCAR. And what proof? What proof of all this—

REGINA [*turns sharply*]. None. I won't need any. The bonds are missing and they are with Marshall. That will be enough. If it isn't, I'll add what's necessary.

BEN. I'm sure of that.

REGINA [*turns to* BEN]. You can be quite sure.

OSCAR. We'll deny—

REGINA. Deny your heads off. You couldn't find a jury that wouldn't weep for a woman whose brothers steal from her. And you couldn't find twelve men in this state you haven't cheated and who hate you for it.

OSCAR. What kind of talk is this? You couldn't do anything like that! We're your own brothers. [*Points upstairs*] How can you talk that way when upstairs not five minutes ago—

REGINA. Where was I? [*Smiles at* BEN] Well, they'll convict you. But I won't care much if they don't. Because by that time you'll be ruined. I shall also tell my story to Mr. Marshall, who likes me, I think, and who will not want to be involved in your scandal. A respectable firm like Marshall and Company. The deal would be off in an hour. [*Turns to them angrily*] And you know it. Now I don't want to hear any more from any of you. *You'll do no more bargaining in this house.* I'll take my seventy-five percent and we'll forget the story forever. That's one way of doing it, and the way I prefer. You know me well enough to know that I don't mind taking the other way.

BEN [*after a second, slowly*]. None of us has ever known you well enough, Regina.

REGINA. You're getting old, Ben. Your tricks aren't as smart as they used to be. [*There is no answer. She waits, then smiles*] All right. I take it that's settled and I get what I asked for.

OSCAR [*furiously to* BEN]. Are you going to let her do this—

BEN [*turns to look at him, slowly*]. You have a suggestion?

REGINA [*puts her arms above her head, stretches, laughs*]. No, he hasn't. All right. Now, Leo, I have forgotten that you ever saw the bonds. [*Archly, to* BEN *and* OSCAR] And as long as you boys both behave yourselves, I've forgotten that we ever even talked about them. You can draw up the necessary papers tomorrow. [BEN *laughs.* LEO *stares at him, starts for door.*

Exits. OSCAR *moves toward door angrily.* REGINA *looks at* BEN, *nods, laughs with him. For a second,* OSCAR *stands in the door, looking back at them. Then he exits.*]

REGINA.   You're a good loser, Ben. I like that.

BEN [*picks up his coat, turns to her*].   Well, I say to myself, what's the good? You and I aren't like Oscar. We're not sour people. I think that comes from a good digestion. Then, too, one loses today and wins tomorrow. I say to myself, years of planning and I get what I want. Then I don't get it. But I'm not discouraged. The century's turning, the world is open. Open for people like you and me. Ready for us, waiting for us. After all this is just the beginning. There are hundreds of Hubbards sitting in rooms like this throughout the country. All their names aren't Hubbard, but they are all Hubbards and they will own this country someday. We'll get along.

REGINA [*smiles*].   I think so.

BEN.   Then, too, I say to myself, things may change. [*Looks at* ALEXANDRA] I agree with Alexandra. What is a man in a wheelchair doing on a staircase? I ask myself that.

REGINA [*looks up at him*].   And what do you answer?

BEN.   I have no answer. But maybe someday I will. Maybe never, but maybe someday. [*Smiles. Pats her arm*] When I do, I'll let you know. [*Goes toward hall.*]

REGINA.   When you do, write me. I will be in Chicago. [*Gaily*] Ah, Ben, if Papa had only left me his money.

BEN.   I'll see you tomorrow.

REGINA.   Oh, yes. Certainly. You'll be sort of working for me now.

BEN [*as he passes* ALEXANDRA].   Alexandra, you're turning out to be a right interesting girl. Well, good night all. [*He exits.*]

REGINA [*sits quietly for a second, stretches*].   What do you want to talk to me about, Alexandra?

ALEXANDRA [*slowly*].   I've changed my mind. I don't want to talk.

REGINA.   You're acting very strange. Not like yourself. You've had a bad shock today. I know that. And you loved Papa, but you must have expected this to come someday. You knew how sick he was.

ALEXANDRA.   I knew. We all knew.

REGINA.   It will be good for you to get away from here. Good for me, too. Time heals most wounds, Alexandra. You're young, you shall have all the things I wanted. I'll make the world for you the way I wanted it to be for me. [*Uncomfortably*] Don't sit there staring. You've been around Birdie so much you're getting just like her.

ALEXANDRA [*nods*].   Funny. That's what Aunt Birdie said today.

REGINA.   Be good for you to get away from all this.

[ADDIE *enters.*]

ADDIE.   Cal is back, Miss Regina. He says Dr. Sloan will be coming in a few minutes.

REGINA.   We'll leave in a few weeks. A few weeks! That means two or three Saturdays, two or three Sundays. [*Sighs*] Well, I'm very tired. I shall go to bed. I don't want any supper. Put the lights out and lock up. [ADDIE *moves to the piano lamp, turns it out*] You go to your room, Alexandra. Addie will bring you something hot. You look very tired. [*Rises. To* ADDIE] Call me when Dr. Sloan gets here. I don't want to see anybody else. I don't want any condolence calls tonight. The whole town will be over.

ALEXANDRA.   Mama, I'm not coming with you. I'm not going to Chicago.

REGINA [*turns to her*].   You're very upset, Alexandra.

ALEXANDRA.   I mean what I say. With all my heart.

REGINA.   We'll talk about it tomorrow. The morning will make a difference.

ALEXANDRA.   It won't make any difference. And there isn't anything to talk about. I am going away from you. Because I want to. Because I know Papa would want me to.

REGINA [*careful, polite*].   You *know* your papa wanted you to go away from me?

ALEXANDRA.   Yes.

REGINA [*softly*].   And if I say no?

ALEXANDRA.   Say it Mama, say it. And see what happens.

REGINA [*softly, after a pause*].   And if I make you stay?

ALEXANDRA.   That would be foolish. It wouldn't work in the end.

REGINA.   You're very serious about it, aren't you? [*Crosses to stairs*] Well, you'll change your mind in a few days.

ALEXANDRA.   No.

REGINA [*going up the steps*].   Alexandra, I've come to the end of my rope. Somewhere there has to be what I want, too. Life goes too fast. Do what you want; think what you want; go where you want. I'd like to keep you with me, but I won't make you stay. Too many people used to make me do too many things. No, I won't make you stay.

ALEXANDRA.   You couldn't, Mama, because I want to leave here. As I've never wanted anything in my life before. Because now I understand what Papa was trying to tell me. All in one day: Addie said there were people who ate the earth and other people who stood around and watched them do it. And just now Uncle Ben said the same thing. Really, he said the same thing. [*Tensely*] Well, tell him for me, Mama, I'm not going to stand around and watch you do it. I'll be fighting as hard as he'll be fighting [*Rises*] someplace else.

REGINA.   Well, you have spirit, after all. I used to think you were all sugar water. We don't have to be bad friends. I don't want us to be bad friends, Alexandra. [*Starts, stops, turns to* ALEXANDRA] Would you like to come and talk to me, Alexandra? Would you—would you like to sleep in my room tonight?

ALEXANDRA [*takes a step toward the stairs*].   Are you afraid, Mama? [REGINA *does not answer. She moves up the stairs and out of sight.* ADDIE, *smiling, begins to put out the lamps.*]

Questions for Study

1. What significance can you attribute to the setting of the play—the South at the turn of the century? Specifically, how important as background are the qualities of small-town life and the family relationships that Hellman depicts? From Marshall's descriptions of life in the North, how would you contrast the differences between life in the North and in the South?

2. In Act I, Regina, Ben, Oscar, and Birdie imagine what they will do with the money from the cotton mill. How do their wishes differ? What do their wishes reveal about each of them?

3. What are the contents of Horace Giddens' vault box? Why does he keep the broken violin?

4. Oscar Hubbard likes to hunt. What does he do with the game he kills? What does this reveal about his character?

5. Describe the relationship between Horace and Regina Giddens. Why are they estranged?

6. Why do Horace and Oscar accept Regina's terms in Act I? What do they hope to achieve by marrying Alexandra to Leo?

7. Describe the relationship between Oscar and Birdie Hubbard. Why did they marry?

8. Why does Horace oppose the building of the cotton mill? Do you believe the reasons he gives or do you see more in them than he himself declares?

9. Why does Horace want his daughter Alexandra to leave after his death? How would you describe the differences between the two generations, that of the parents and the children, in the play?

10. Why does Horace decide not to prosecute the Hubbards and Leo when he discovers the theft of his bonds? How does his death affect what happens to them and to Regina?

11. In the final act of the play, what two kinds of people does Regina say that there are? Point out which kind each of the following is: the Hubbard brothers, Leo, Birdie, Regina, and Horace.

12. Why does Alexandra decide to leave home? Why does Regina allow her to leave?

13. *The Little Foxes* is a drama about degenerating family relationships. Are there also larger implications to the actions and characters it dramatizes? Explain.

14. Which character or characters most appealed to you? Which one(s) had the least appeal? Justify your responses.

15. Many critics have pointed out that *The Little Foxes* is a tightly organized, well-crafted play. If you agree, identify several dramatic devices that Hellman uses in structuring her actions and scenes. Also identify the scene which, in your opinion, is the most effective. Explain the reasons for your choice.

16. How does Hellman build suspense in the play? How is such suspense intensified in the last act? Does the intrigue about the bonds seem to you to be too contrived for "realistic" drama? Does Alexandra's final speech seem thematically appropriate? Explain.

Chapter 3
Symbolism
and Expressionism

Between 1875 and 1900, realism became the dominant form of theatrical productions. Committed to a representation of the surfaces of everyday life and preoccupied with contemporary social problems, realism was bound to provoke the opposition of those concerned with the life of the mind and with individual psychological processes. The realists assumed that reality lies in the external world. Opponents of realism pointed out that the external world is transformed in the very act of perceiving it. Perceptions of reality therefore are influenced by personal emotions and reshaped by relating them to previous experiences. Because of its attempt at scientific objectivity, realism, its opponents argued, actually involves an artificial way of looking at things.

The opponents of realism favored stylization in the theater. **Stylized representation** does not merely imitate nature but transforms and even distorts it to emphasize its subjective, human significance. A realistic stage set for Shakespeare's *Macbeth*, for example, might include the stone walls, winding stairs, and arched windows of a typical medieval castle. In a stylized set created for the play by the designer Robert Edmund Jones in 1922, the medieval castle was transformed into bizarre, slanted arches which suggested Macbeth's disturbance of the prevailing feudal order. The effects of such stylization were evident in nearly every other aspect of the theatrical presentation as well.

Symbolism and expressionism are two particularly influential forms of stylized theater which developed in opposition to realism. **Symbolism** presented the earliest challenge to realism. Its chief characteristic is its use of **symbols,** concrete elements which express a range of meanings and associations in rich, suggestive, and often complex ways. Modern symbols tend to be open-ended, suggesting a variety of emotions and thoughts that often do not have an easily identifiable meaning. As concrete manifestations of subtle emotions and thoughts, symbols became ideal tools for dramatists who wished to explore the psychological implications of reality.

Another means of externalizing reality is through **myths**—tales of gods and superhuman figures. Since myths are anonymous, they can be said to arise from and to be reshaped by the collective consciousness of a race, tribe, or people. The Swiss psychoanalyst Carl Jung (1875–1961) argued, during the early years of symbolist theater, that certain symbols and myths are **archetypes**, or inborn, unconscious patterns which express a collective memory of the human race. As such, they reveal fundamental and even universal psychological responses to human experiences. It is not surprising therefore that many symbolist playwrights carefully studied myths and folktales and introduced them (or elements of them) directly or indirectly into their dramas.

The symbolist movement in France, which grew up around lyric poets such as Paul Verlaine (1844–1896) and Stéphane Mallarmé (1842–1898), developed literary techniques which would be used in the symbolist theater. Verlaine and Mallarmé avoided in their poetry discursiveness, or logical, sequential statements, and attempted to communicate by means of symbols that make multiple suggestions to the imagination. They attempted to create a strong, unified mood or emotional atmosphere in each poem. The relationship among symbols, the intense mood, and the heavy verbal music of the words moved readers toward their own formulation of a poem's theme. Frequently, that theme related in some way to the connection between the material world and a spiritual or a psychological sphere.

Maurice Maeterlinck (1862–1949), who was Mallarme's disciple, applied the master's techniques to the theater. His powerful one-act play *The Intruder* (1890) is often cited as one of the principal examples of symbolist drama. In the play, a family sits at a table and talks intermittently of the mother who is recuperating from a difficult childbirth in an adjoining room. With little or no action, the play's characters merely report what they perceive: the swans that are disturbed on the pond outside the window; the sound of mowing that rises from the shadows near the house; the cold draft that penetrates the room; and the lamp that flickers out. Through the increasingly agitated commentary of the grandfather, the audience gradually recognizes that all these tangible sensations indicate (or symbolize) the intrusion of death into the house. The mother eventually dies, still unseen, in the next room.

A symbolist drama like *The Intruder* cannot be judged by the same standards applied to realistic drama. Action and conflict have disappeared, replaced by a sense of growing expectation and, finally, by the terrifying realization of expectation. Beyond minimal distinctions like age and sex, characters are not individualized at all. Their lines are delivered in an increasingly intense and musical manner until the audience is almost hypnotized. No attempt is made to imitate real conversation.

It was precisely this kind of theater which the Irish poet William Butler Yeats encouraged during his years as manager of the Abbey Theatre in Dublin, Ireland. He viewed realism as the product of rationalism and materialism, and he was opposed to both. Seeking alternatives to realistic drama, Yeats turned to Maeterlinck and other symbolists and also to Japanese **Noh,** a highly stylized form of drama in which ghosts or deities reenact the most significant moments of their existence for travelers who encounter them.

Although *Purgatory* (1938) was written by Yeats after the vogue of symbolism had subsided, it retains many of the characteristics of the symbolist dramas Yeats admired. Based on an Irish folk legend which had fascinated him for years, the play concerns the relationship between life and life-after-death. In accordance with folklore, the spirits of the dead are compelled to reenact the transgressions which they committed during life. Similarly, their ritual reenactments powerfully affect the attitudes and the actions of their living descendants. Yeats blends Irish folklore, Noh theater, and symbolist technique in treating this theme of the interaction between matter and spirit.

The action of the play is simple. A peddler and his bastard son stand before the window of a ruined house in which the ghost of the peddler's mother appears. Her foolhardy marriage to a drunken stableman years before had resulted in her early death in childbirth, the dissipation of her family fortune, and the degeneration of her family, the only survivors of which are the peddler and his drunken and vicious son. Obsessed even after death by her transgression, the ghost seems to reenact, on each anniversary of her wedding night, her fateful actions. Moved by this reenactment, the peddler murders his son in an attempt to end the tainted line and to relieve his mother's guilt. But the bizarre murder is in vain. Although it removes the external consequences of the ghost's crime, it cannot eradicate her remorse at her own degeneration.

In contrasting *Purgatory* with Strindberg's *Miss Julie* (Chapter 2), which also concerns misalliance and the end of a great family, we can see how deliberately Yeats has set aside realistic techniques. His characters are types—a peddler and a bastard—or ghosts. His dialog is highly rhetorical poetry, spoken mostly by the peddler and ignored or misunderstood by his son. The action largely concerns ritual reenactment by spirits. The one act committed by a living character—the murder of a son—has that illogicality and lack of apparent motive which force the audience to work out its meaning. In other words, it is a symbolic act.

Also typical of symbolist theater is Yeats' description of the set: "a ruined house and a bare tree in the background." As the action proceeds, the house actually becomes a visual symbol for the family that now has fallen into decay. Similarly, the tree is present not to suggest the reality of the scene but to symbolize the decadent state of the family. When the ghost was a living girl, the tree had "green leaves, ripe leaves, leaves thick as butter"; now it is stripped bare. When the murder is committed in an attempted expiation of the old crime, the tree lights up with an eerie white glow.

One could describe *Purgatory,* with its supernatural and violent action, as the acting out of the peddler's inner conflicts. The child of a sensual, illiterate drunkard and a refined, highly educated aristocrat, he has a dual nature—half sensuous body, half spiritual soul. His action suggests the attempt to sacrifice the bestial side of his nature to the spiritual, but the gesture fails. Quite typically, Yeats hints that as the ghost relives her wedding night "pleasure and remorse must both be there." That is, the soul desires the body. In light of this interpretation of the action, the play becomes a projection of the protagonist's inner consciousness in a process that is similar to expressionism.

Expressionism is a style of art and literature which imitates the world as perceived by an individual consciousness. It differs radically from realism, which attempts to imitate the objective world. And it differs subtly from symbolism, which attempts to work with universal or archetypal patterns of perception and meaning. A few expressionistic dramas, like Strindberg's later plays, *The Dream Play* (1902) and *The Ghost Sonata* (1907), are projections onto the stage of the dramatist's response to his material. In many later expressionistic plays, the focus is on the individual psychological responses of the protagonists.

This feat is often accomplished by deliberate, even violent distortions of reality. Characters whose responses seem mechanical actually become machines and act with mechanical stiffness. Fantasies come to life and are acted out in brief, highly stylized scenes. Sets are grossly exaggerated, often dwarfing characters or closing in and threatening to smother them. Scenery and props may shake to suggest the agitation of a protagonist. When, for example, the meek protagonist of Elmer Rice's *The Adding Machine* (1923) attacks his boss, the whole set spins around, suggesting the motion of an adding machine.

Expressionism also has its own unique form of characterization, dialog, and action. Characters tend to be depersonalized, with names like Mr. Zero, the Nameless, or even Man and Woman. Individuals are not as much human beings as they are representations of particular attitudes. The dialog, often known as **telegraphic dialog,** is terse and disjointed. In a few instances, some of the unessential parts of speech, articles, adjectives, and adverbs, for example, are eliminated. And so verbal communication is minimized. Characters often make oblique speeches, long and seemingly unnecessary statements of their attitudes, to which no one listens. The action is similarly abrupt and disjointed.

Unlike symbolist playwrights who attempt to build a mood slowly through a long, single act, expressionists favor a series of brief, intense scenes. Each tends to be another crisis in a series leading to a final resolution.

Expressionism developed in Germany before and after World War I. Among its chief proponents were Georg Kaiser, whose trilogy *The Choral, Gas I,* and *Gas II* (1918–1920) is a strong indictment of industrialism; and Fritz Von Unruh, whose *Officers* (1911) and *Family* (1917) condemn militarism. In America after World War I, Eugene O'Neill began experimenting with expressionistic techniques. The results were *The Emperor Jones* (1920) and *The Hairy Ape* (1922), the latter of which, as O'Neill explained, treats the dilemma of Yank, "a symbol of man, who has lost his old harmony with nature, the harmony which he used to have as an animal and has not yet acquired in a spiritual way."

Elements of expressionism pervade *The Hairy Ape.* In the opening stage direction, O'Neill writes: "The treatment of this scene, or of any other scene in the play, should by no means be naturalistic." He goes on to speak of cramped space and the sense of imprisonment the set should convey. The low ceilings force the characters to stoop, giving them the appearance of Neanderthal men. The images suggest imprisonment (jails, cages, steel girders) and beasts (monkey fur, apes, and apemen). Such images are present in almost every scene and suggest Yank's dilemma as an animal trapped in a world of mechanization. Even the gestures of the actors suggest the dehumanization of people by an industrial society. At the end of Scene I, for instance, the stokers file out "through the door silently, close upon each others' heels in what is very like a prisoners' lockstep."

In the manner of other expressionists, O'Neill develops the action through brief scenes—eight in *The Hairy Ape.* After two scenes which introduce Yank and Mildred Douglas, the society woman whose horrified gaze destroys Yank's complacency, each scene depicts another crisis in his quest for a sense of "belonging." The dialog is disjointed, often "telegraphic." The longer speeches are often "oblique." (Long, the socialist, and Paddy, the romantic, both express their attitudes in lengthy monologs which are misunderstood or simply rejected.) Perhaps none of the scenes is so purely expressionistic as Scene V, which depicts Yank's response to the opulence of New York City's Fifth Avenue. The set is comprised of shopwindows displaying gigantic ropes of jewelry from which are hung enormous price tags. The upper-class crowds who move past him like "a procession of gaudy marionettes," are totally unaware of the existence of Yank or of laborers like him. In their "detached, mechanical unawareness," they fail to respond even to his worst taunts and insults. The whole scene has the air of a nightmare and yet makes a cogent social comment.

Today, some of the effects in *The Hairy Ape* (and even in *Purgatory*) may seem somewhat obvious. Since the establishment of realism as the standard method in the theater, various forms of stylized drama have regularly challenged its dominance. For an audience accustomed to realism, highly stylized drama has an initial shock value which, unfortunately, disappears with familiarity. Certainly, modified forms of symbolism and expressionism will endure, and often very moving drama has been created from the synthesis of realistic and various stylized techniques. From its inception, realism has gravitated toward symbolism. In Anton Chekhov's *The Cherry Orchard* (in "Plays for Further Study"), a realistic treatment of social change written in 1904, the orchard emerges as a symbol of the humanistic but impractical luxuries which the aristocracy has maintained to its own detriment. Yet, in Arthur Miller's *Death of a Salesman* (1949), expressionistic flashbacks are blended with a realistic treatment of the American dream and disillusionment. The kind of synthesis found in these plays may well indicate the future development of drama. But until such a time as this synthesis is worked out, audiences will have to value the considerable variety of styles and techniques modern theater offers.

William Butler Yeats (1865–1939)
Purgatory[1]

Persons in the Play

A BOY
AN OLD MAN

SCENE: *A ruined house and a bare tree in the background.*

     BOY. Half-door, hall door,
Hither and thither day and night,
Hill or hollow, shouldering this pack,
Hearing you talk.
     OLD MAN. Study that house.
I think about its jokes and stories;
I try to remember what the butler
Said to a drunken gamekeeper
In mid-October, but I cannot.
If I cannot, none living can.
Where are the jokes and stories of a house,   10
Its threshold gone to patch a pig-sty?
     BOY. So you have come this path before?
     OLD MAN. The moonlight falls upon the path,
The shadow of a cloud upon the house,
And that's symbolical; study that tree,
What is it like?
     BOY.   A silly old man.
     OLD MAN. It's like—no matter what it's like.
I saw it a year ago stripped bare as now,
So I chose a better trade.
I saw it fifty years ago   20
Before the thunderbolt had riven it,
Green leaves, ripe leaves, leaves thick as butter,
Fat, greasy life. Stand there and look,
Because there is somebody in that house.
               [*The* BOY *puts down pack and stands in the doorway.*]
     BOY. There's nobody here.

---

1. In the Roman Catholic Church, purgatory is the state or place in which souls who have died in God's grace and are thus destined for heaven undergo a temporary period of expiation for their sins.

OLD MAN.   There's somebody there.
BOY.   The floor is gone, the windows gone,
And where there should be roof there's sky,
And here's a bit of an egg-shell thrown
Out of a jackdaw's nest.
OLD MAN.   But there are some
That do not care what's gone, what's left: 30
The souls in Purgatory that come back
To habitations and familiar spots.
BOY.   Your wits are out again.
OLD MAN.   Re-live
Their transgressions, and that not once
But many times; they know at last
The consequence of those transgressions
Whether upon others or upon themselves;
Upon others, others may bring help,
For when the consequence is at an end
The dream must end; if upon themselves,   40
There is no help but in themselves
And in the mercy of God.
BOY.   I have had enough!
Talk to the jackdaws, if talk you must.
OLD MAN.   Stop! Sit there upon that stone.
That is the house where I was born.
BOY.   The big old house that was burnt down?
OLD MAN.   My mother that was your grand-dam owned it,
This scenery and this countryside,
Kennel and stable, horse and hound—
She had a horse at the Curragh,[2] and there met   50
My father, a groom in a training stable,
Looked at him and married him.
Her mother never spoke to her again,
And she did right.
BOY.   What's right and wrong?
My grand-dad got the girl and the money.
OLD MAN.   Looked at him and married him,
And he squandered everything she had.
She never knew the worst, because
She died in giving birth to me,
But now she knows it all, being dead.   60
Great people lived and died in this house;
Magistrates, colonels, members of Parliament,
Captains and Governors, and long ago
Men that had fought at Aughrim and the Boyne.[3]
Some that had gone on Government work

---

2. Scene of Ireland's most important horse races.
3. In 1690 at the Boyne River, the Protestant forces of William III of England defeated Catholic troops led by James II, former king who was attempting to regain the throne. The following year the Catholics were dealt an even more decisive blow at Aughrim.

To London or to India came home to die,
Or came from London every spring
To look at the may-blossom in the park.
They had loved the trees that he cut down
To pay what he had lost at cards   70
Or spent on horses, drink and women;
Had loved the house, had loved all
The intricate passages of the house,
But he killed the house; to kill a house
Where great men grew up, married, died,
I here declare a capital offence.
     BOY.   My God, but you had luck! Grand clothes,
And maybe a grand horse to ride.
     OLD MAN.   That he might keep me upon his level
He never sent me to school, but some   80
Half-loved me for my half of her:
A gamekeeper's wife taught me to read,
A Catholic curate taught me Latin.
There were old books and books made fine
By eighteenth-century French binding, books
Modern and ancient, books by the ton.
     BOY.   What education have you given me?
     OLD MAN.   I gave the education that befits
A bastard that a pedlar got
Upon a tinker's[4] daughter in a ditch.   90
When I had come to sixteen years old
My father burned down the house when drunk.
     BOY.   But that is my age, sixteen years old,
At the Puck Fair.[5]
     OLD MAN.   And everything was burnt;
Books, library, all were burnt.
     BOY.   Is what I have heard upon the road the truth,
That you killed him in the burning house?
     OLD MAN.   There's nobody here but our two selves?
     BOY.   Nobody, Father.
     OLD MAN.   I stuck him with a knife,
That knife that cuts my dinner now,   100
And after that I left him in the fire.
They dragged him out, somebody saw
The knife-wound but could not be certain
Because the body was all black and charred.
Then some that were his drunken friends
Swore they would put me upon trial,
Spoke of quarrels, a threat I had made.
The gamekeeper gave me some old clothes,

---

4. Itinerant repairman; gypsy.
5. Festival held on Midsummer Day (June 24) celebrating the mischievous spirit of English and Irish legend.

I ran away, worked here and there
Till I became a pedlar on the roads,   110
No good trade, but good enough
Because I am my father's son,
Because of what I did or may do.
Listen to the hoof-beats! Listen, listen!
   BOY. I cannot hear a sound.
   OLD MAN.   Beat! Beat!
This night is the anniversary
Of my mother's wedding night,
Or of the night wherein I was begotten.
My father is riding from the public-house,
A whiskey-bottle under his arm.   120
     [*A window is lit showing a young girl.*]
Look at the window; she stands there
Listening, the servants are all in bed,
She is alone, he has stayed late
Bragging and drinking in the public-house.
   BOY. There's nothing but an empty gap in the wall.
You have made it up. No, you are mad!
You are getting madder every day.
   OLD MAN. It's louder now because he rides
Upon a gravelled avenue
All grass to-day. The hoof-beat stops,   130
He has gone to the other side of the house,
Gone to the stable, put the horse up.
She has gone down to open the door.
This night she is no better than her man
And does not mind that he is half drunk,
She is mad about him. They mount the stairs,
She brings him into her own chamber.
And that is the marriage-chamber now.
The window is dimly lit again.

Do not let him touch you! It is not true   140
That drunken men cannot beget,
And if he touch he must beget
And you must bear his murderer.
Deaf! Both deaf! If I should throw
A stick or a stone they would not hear;
And that's a proof my wits are out.
But there's a problem: she must live
Through everything in exact detail,
Driven to it by remorse, and yet
Can she renew the sexual act   150
And find no pleasure in it, and if not,
If pleasure and remorse must both be there,
Which is the greater?
     I lack schooling.

Go fetch Tertullian;[6] he and I
Will ravel all that problem out
Whilst those two lie upon the mattress
Begetting me.
        Come back! Come back!
And so you thought to slip away,
My bag of money between your fingers,
And that I could not talk and see!   160
You have been rummaging in the pack.
        [*The light in the window has faded out.*]
    BOY.   You never gave me my right share.
    OLD MAN.   And had I given it, young as you are,
You would have spent it upon drink.
    BOY.   What if I did? I had a right
To get it and spend it as I chose.
    OLD MAN.   Give me that bag and no more words.
    BOY.   I will not.
    OLD MAN.   I will break your fingers.

[*They struggle for the bag. In the struggle it drops, scattering the money.
The* OLD MAN *staggers but does not fall. They stand looking at each other.
The window is lit up. A man is seen pouring whiskey into a glass.*]

    BOY.   What if I killed you? You killed my grand-dad,
Because you were young and he was old.   170
Now I am young and you are old.
    OLD MAN [*staring at window*].   Better-looking, those sixteen years—
    BOY.   What are you muttering?
    OLD MAN.   Younger—and yet
She should have known he was not her kind.
    BOY.   What are you saying? Out with it! [OLD MAN *points to window.*]
My God! The window is lit up
And somebody stands there, although
The floorboards are all burnt away.
    OLD MAN.   The window is lit up because my father
Has come to find a glass for his whiskey.   180
He leans there like some tired beast.
    BOY.   A dead, living, murdered man!
    OLD MAN.   'Then the bride-sleep fell upon Adam':
Where did I read those words?
           And yet
There's nothing leaning in the window
But the impression upon my mother's mind;
Being dead she is alone in her remorse.
    BOY.   A body that was a bundle of old bones
Before I was born. Horrible! Horrible!   [*He covers his eyes.*]
    OLD MAN.   That beast there would know nothing, being nothing, 190

---

6. Early Christian author, polemicist, and moralist (A.D. 155?–220?).

If I should kill a man under the window
He would not even turn his head.   [*He stabs the* BOY.]
My father and my son on the same jack-knife!
That finishes—there—there—there—
                    [*He stabs again and again. The window grows dark.*]
'Hush-a-bye baby, thy father's a knight,
Thy mother a lady, lovely and bright.'
No, that is something that I read in a book,
And if I sing it must be to my mother,
And I lack rhyme.
        [*The stage has grown dark except where the tree stands in white light.*]
                    Study that tree.
It stands there like a purified soul,   200
All cold, sweet, glistening light.
Dear mother, the window is dark again,
But you are in the light because
I finished all that consequence.
I killed that lad because had he grown up
He would have struck a woman's fancy,
Begot, and passed pollution on.
I am a wretched foul old man
And therefore harmless. When I have stuck
This old jack-knife into a sod   210
And pulled it out all bright again,
And picked up all the money that he dropped,
I'll to a distant place, and there
Tell my old jokes among new men.
                    [*He cleans the knife and begins to pick up money.*]
Hoof-beats! Dear God,
How quickly it returns—beat—beat—!

Her mind cannot hold up that dream.
Twice a murderer and all for nothing,
And she must animate that dead night
Not once but many times!
                    O God,   220
Release my mother's soul from its dream!
Mankind can do no more. Appease
The misery of the living and the remorse of the dead.

Questions for Study

1. How does the setting function in this play?
2. Describe what actually happens in *Purgatory*. Are these actions believable? Explain why or why not.
3. Interpret the character of the Old Man.
4. What does the Old Man think of as his father's "crime"? What differences do you see between the groom's real offenses and the Old Man's theories about them? When the Old Man says that his father "killed the house," what does the house symbolize? What other examples can you find of the Old Man's habit of dealing in symbols?
5. What does the Old Man think of as his mother's "crime"? Did he know his mother? Why does he want to sing to her?
6. What role does the Boy play in the dramatized events? In what ways does he contrast with the Old Man?
7. Why does the Boy at first not see the light and the figure in the house? Why do you think he suddenly can see them? Why does he cover his eyes? Why can the audience see these mysterious sights?
8. What are the Old Man's crimes? What ironic differences do you see between what the Old Man intended to do and what he actually did?
9. Interpret the final speech of the Old Man. Relate your comments to what, in your view, this speech means to the play.
10. How is light used symbolically in the play? What other staging techniques do you find employed in establishing the meaning of the play?
11. What implications in the title suggest the theme of the play? Does the Old Man understand the concept of purgatory? What does the play imply about human guilt and divine grace?

Eugene O'Neill (1888–1953)
The Hairy Ape

A Comedy of Ancient and Modern Life in Eight Scenes

Characters

ROBERT SMITH, "YANK"
PADDY
LONG
MILDRED DOUGLAS
HER AUNT
SECOND ENGINEER
A GUARD
A SECRETARY OF AN ORGANIZATION
STOKERS, LADIES, GENTLEMEN, *etc.*

SCENE I: *The firemen's forecastle of an ocean liner—an hour after sailing from New York.*
SCENE II: *Section of promenade deck, two days out—morning.*
SCENE III: *The stokehole. A few minutes later.*
SCENE IV: *Same as Scene I. Half an hour later.*
SCENE V: *Fifth Avenue, New York. Three weeks later.*
SCENE VI: *An island near the city. The next night.*
SCENE VII: *In the city. About a month later.*
SCENE VIII: *In the city. Twilight of the next day.*

Scene I.

The firemen's forecastle of a transatlantic liner an hour after sailing from New York for the voyage across. Tiers of narrow, steel bunks, three deep, on all sides. An entrance in rear. Benches on the floor before the bunks. The room is crowded with men, shouting, cursing, laughing, singing—a confused, inchoate uproar swelling into a sort of unity, a meaning—the bewildered, furious, baffled defiance of a beast in a cage. Nearly all the men are drunk. Many bottles are passed from hand to hand. All are dressed in dungaree pants, heavy ugly shoes. Some wear singlets, but the majority are stripped to the waist.

The treatment of this scene, or of any other scene in the play, should by no means be naturalistic. The effect sought after is a cramped space in the bowels of a ship, imprisoned by white steel. The lines of bunks, the uprights supporting them, cross each other like the steel framework of a cage. The ceiling crushes down upon the men's heads. They cannot stand upright. This accentuates the natural stooping posture which shoveling coal and the resultant over-development of back and shoulder muscles have given them. The men themselves should resemble those pictures in which the appearance of Neanderthal Man is guessed at. All are hairy-chested, with long arms of tremendous power, and low, receding brows above their small, fierce, resentful eyes. All the civilized white races are represented, but except for the slight differentiation in color of hair, skin, eyes, all these men are alike.

The curtain rises on a tumult of sound. YANK *is seated in the foreground. He seems broader, fiercer, more truculent, more powerful, more sure of himself than the rest. They respect his superior strength—the grudging respect of fear. Then, too, he represents to them a self-expression, the very last word in what they are, their most highly developed individual.*

VOICES. Gif me trink dere, you!
'Ave a wet!
Salute!
Gesundheit!
Skoal![1]
Drunk as a lord, God stiffen you!
Here's how!
Luck!
Pass back that bottle, damn you!
Pourin' it down his neck!
Ho, Froggy! Where the devil have you been?
La Touraine.
I hit him smash in yaw, py Gott!
Jenkins—the First[2]—he's a rotten swine—
And the coppers nabbed him—and I run—
I like peer better. It don't pig head gif you.
A slut, I'm sayin'! She robbed me aslape—
To hell with 'em all!
You're a bloody liar!
Say dot again! [*Commotion. Two men about to fight are pulled apart*]
No scrappin' now!
Tonight—
See who's the best man!
Bloody Dutchman!
Tonight on the for'ard square.[3]
I'll bet on Dutchy.
He packa da wallop, I tella you!

---

1. *Salute, Gesundheit,* and *Skoal* are Italian, German, and Danish drinking toasts meaning "Health" or "To your health."
2. The ship's First Engineer.
3. Forward deck.

Shut up, Wop!
No fightin', maties. We're all chums, ain't we?
[*A voice starts bawling a song*]

"Beer, beer, glorious beer!
Fill yourselves right up to here."

YANK [*for the first time seeming to take notice of the uproar about him, turns around threateningly—in a tone of contemptuous authority*]. Choke off dat noise! Where d'yuh get dat beer stuff? Beer, hell! Beer's for goils—and Dutchmen. Me for somep'n wit a kick to it! Gimme a drink, one of youse guys. [*Several bottles are eagerly offered. He takes a tremendous gulp at one of them; then, keeping the bottle in his hand, glares belligerently at the owner, who hastens to acquiesce in this robbery by saying*] All righto, Yank. Keep it and have another. [YANK *contemptuously turns his back on the crowd again. For a second there is an embarrassed silence. Then—*]

VOICES. We must be passing the Hook.[4]
She's beginning to roll to it.
Six days in hell—and then Southampton.[5]
Py Yesus, I vish somepody take my first vatch for me!
Gittin' seasick, Square-head?
Drink up and forget it!
What's in your bottle?
Gin.
Dot's nigger trink.
Absinthe?[6] It's doped. You'll go off your chump, Froggy!
Cochon![7]
Whisky, that's the ticket!
Where's Paddy?
Going asleep.
Sing us that whisky song, Paddy. [*They all turn to an old, wizened Irishman who is dozing, very drunk, on the benches forward. His face is extremely monkey-like with all the sad, patient pathos of that animal in his small eyes*]
Singa da song, Caruso Pat!
He's gettin' old. The drink is too much for him.
He's too drunk.

PADDY [*blinking about him, starts to his feet resentfully, swaying, holding on to the edge of a bunk*]. I'm never too drunk to sing. 'Tis only when I'm dead to the world I'd be wishful to sing at all. [*With a sort of sad contempt*] "Whisky Johnny," ye want? A chanty, ye want? Now that's a queer wish from the ugly like of you, God help you. But no matther. [*He starts to sing in a thin, nasal, doleful tone*]

---

4. Sandy Hook, peninsula on the New Jersey coast jutting into the Atlantic toward New York City.
5. Chief English port for transatlantic voyages.
6. Very strong, licorice-flavored liqueur prohibited today by law from being manufactured or sold in Europe or the United States.
7. "Pig!" (French).

Oh, whisky is the life of man!
  Whisky! O Johnny! [*They all join in on this*]
Oh, whisky is the life of man!
  Whisky for my Johnny! [*Again chorus*]

Oh, whisky drove my old man mad!
  Whisky! O Johnny!
Oh, whisky drove my old man mad!
  Whisky for my Johnny!

YANK [*again turning around scornfully*].   Aw hell! Nix on dat old sailing ship stuff! All dat bull's dead, see? And you're dead, too, yuh damned old Harp,[8] on'y yuh don't know it. Take it easy, see. Give us a rest. Nix on de loud noise. [*With a cynical grin*] Can't youse see I'm tryin' to t'ink?

ALL [*repeating the word after him as one with the same cynical amused mockery*]. Think! [*The chorused word has a brazen metallic quality as if their throats were phonograph horns. It is followed by a general uproar of hard, barking laughter*]

VOICES. Don't be cracking your head wit ut, Yank.
  You gat headache, py yingo!
  One thing about it—it rhymes with drink!
  Ha, ha, ha!
  Drink, don't think!
  Drink, don't think!
  Drink, don't think! [*A whole chorus of voices has taken up this refrain, stamping on the floor, pounding on the benches with fists*]

YANK [*taking a gulp from his bottle—good-naturedly*].   Aw right. Can de noise. I got yuh de foist time. [*The uproar subsides. A very drunken sentimental tenor begins to sing*]

"Far away in Canada,
  Far across the sea,
There's a lass who fondly waits
  Making a home for me—"

YANK [*fiercely contemptuous*].   Shut up, yuh lousy boob! Where d'yuh get dat tripe? Home? Home, hell! I'll make a home for yuh! I'll knock yuh dead. Home! T'hell wit home! Where d'yuh get dat tripe? Dis is home, see? What d'yuh want wit home? [*Proudly*] I runned away from mine when I was a kid. On'y too glad to beat it, dat was me. Home was lickings for me, dat's all. But yuh can bet your shoit no one ain't never licked me since! Wanter try it, any of youse? Huh! I guess not. [*In a more placated but still contemptuous tone*] Goils waitin' for yuh, huh? Aw, hell! Dat's all tripe. Dey don't wait for no one. Dey'd double-cross yuh for a nickel. Dey're all tarts, get me? Treat 'em rough, dat's me. To hell wit 'em. Tarts, dat's what, de whole bunch of 'em.

LONG [*very drunk, jumps on a bench excitedly, gesticulating with a bottle*

---

8. Slang term for a person of Irish descent; later in the play, the more derogatory term *Mick* is used.

in his hand]. Listen 'ere, Comrades! Yank 'ere is right. 'E says this 'ere stinkin' ship is our 'ome. And 'e says as 'ome is 'ell. And 'e's right! This is 'ell. We lives in 'ell, Comrades—and right enough we'll die in it. [*Raging*] And who's ter blame, I arsks yer. We ain't. We wasn't born this rotten way. All men is born free and ekal. That's in the bleedin' Bible, maties. But what d'they care for the Bible—them lazy, bloated swine what travels first cabin? Them's the ones. They dragged us down 'til we're on'y wage slaves in the bowels of a bloody ship, sweatin', burnin' up, eatin' coal dust! Hit's them's ter blame—the damned Capitalist clarss! [*There had been a gradual murmur of contemptuous resentment rising among the men until now he is interrupted by a storm of catcalls, hisses, boos, hard laughter*]

    VOICES. Turn it off!

             Shut up!

             Sit down!

             Closa da face!

             Tamn fool! [*Etc.*]

    YANK [*standing up and glaring at* LONG]. Sit down before I knock yuh down! [LONG *makes haste to efface himself.* YANK *goes on contemptuously*] De Bible, huh? De Cap'tlist class, huh? Aw nix on dat Salvation Army-Socialist bull. Git a soapbox! Hire a hall! Come and be saved, huh? Jerk us to Jesus, huh? Aw g'wan! I've listened to lots of guys like you, see. Yuh're all wrong. Wanter know what I t'ink? Yuh ain't no good for no one. Yuh're de bunk. Yuh ain't got no noive, get me? Yuh're yellow, dat's what. Yellow, dat's you. Say! What's dem slobs in de foist cabin got to do wit us? We're better men dan dey are, ain't we? Sure! One of us guys could clean up de whole mob wit one mit. Put one of 'em down here for one watch in de stokehole, what'd happen? Dey'd carry him off on a stretcher. Dem boids don't amount to nothin'. Dey're just baggage. Who makes dis old tub run? Ain't it us guys? Well den, we belong, don't we? We belong and dey don't. Dat's all. [*A loud chorus of approval.* YANK *goes on*] As for dis bein' hell—aw, nuts! Yuh lost your noive, dat's what. Dis is a man's job, get me? It belongs. It runs dis tub. No stiffs need apply. But yuh're a stiff, see? Yuh're yellow, dat's you.

    VOICES [*with a great hard pride in them*].

             Righto!

             A man's job!

             Talk is cheap, Long.

             He never could hold up his end.

             Divil take him!

             Yank's right. We make it go.

             Py Gott, Yank say right ting!

             We don't need no one cryin' over us.

             Makin' speeches.

             Throw him out!

             Yellow!

             Chuck him overboard!

             I'll break his jaw for him!

             [*They crowd around* LONG *threateningly*]

    YANK [*half good-natured again–contemptuously*]. Aw, take it easy.

Leave him alone. He ain't woith a punch. Drink up. Here's how, whoever owns dis. [*He takes a long swallow from his bottle. All drink with him. In a flash all is hilarious amiability again, backslapping, loud talk, etc.*]

PADDY [*who has been sitting in a blinking, melancholy daze—suddenly cries out in a voice full of old sorrow*].   We belong to this, you're saying? We make the ship to go, you're saying? Yerra then, that Almighty God have pity on us! [*His voice runs into the wail of a keen,*[9] *he rocks back and forth on his bench. The men stare at him, startled and impressed in spite of themselves*] Oh, to be back in the fine days of my youth, ochone![10] Oh, there was fine beautiful ships them days—clippers wid tall masts touching the sky—fine strong men in them—men that was sons of the sea as if 'twas the mother that bore them. Oh, the clean skins of them, and the clear eyes, the straight backs and full chests of them! Brave men they was, and bold men surely! We'd be sailing out, bound down round the Horn[11] maybe. We'd be making sail in the dawn, with a fair breeze, singing a chanty song wid no care to it. And astern the land would be sinking low and dying out, but we'd give it no heed but a laugh, and never a look behind. For the day that was, was enough, for we was free men—and I'm thinking 'tis only slaves do be giving heed to the day that's gone or the day to come—until they're old like me. [*With a sort of religious exaltation*] Oh, to be scudding south again wid the power of the Trade Wind driving her on steady through the nights and the days! Full sail on her! Nights and days! Nights when the foam of the wake would be flaming wid fire, when the sky'd be blazing and winking wid stars. Or the full of the moon maybe. Then you'd see her driving through the gray night, her sails stretching aloft all silver and white, not a sound on the deck, the lot of us dreaming dreams, till you'd believe 'twas no real ship at all you was on but a ghost ship like the *Flying Dutchman* they say does be roaming the seas forevermore widout touching a port. And there was the days, too. A warm sun on the clean decks. Sun warming the blood of you, and wind over the miles of shiny green ocean like strong drink to your lungs. Work—aye, hard work—but who'd mind that at all? Sure, you worked under the sky and 'twas work wid skill and daring to it. And wid the day done, in the dog watch,[12] smoking me pipe at ease, the lookout would be raising land maybe, and we'd see the mountains of South Americy wid the red fire of the setting sun painting their white tops and the clouds floating by them! [*His tone of exaltation ceases. He goes on mournfully*] Yerra, what's the use of talking? 'Tis a dead man's whisper. [*To* YANK *resentfully*] 'Twas them days men belonged to ships, not now. 'Twas them days a ship was part of the sea, and a man was part of a ship, and the sea joined all together and made it one. [*Scornfully*] Is it one wid this you'd be, Yank—black smoke from the funnels smudging the sea, smudging the decks—the bloody engines pounding and throbbing and shaking—wid divil a sight of sun or a breath of clean air—choking our lungs wid coal dust—breaking our backs and hearts in the hell of the stokehole—feeding the bloody furnace—feeding our lives along wid the coal, I'm thinking—caged in by steel from a sight of the sky like bloody apes in

---

9. Ritualized Irish cry of sorrow.
10. Irish exclamation of regret.
11. Cape Horn, the southern tip of South America. In the days of sailing ships, "rounding the Horn" was a noteworthy event in the life of a sailor.
12. Either of two duty watches, one from 4 to 6 p.m., the other from 6 to 8 p.m.

the Zoo! [*With a harsh laugh*] Ho-ho, divil mend you! Is it to belong to that you're wishing? Is it a flesh and blood wheel of the engines you'd be?

YANK [*who has been listening with a contemptuous sneer, barks out the answer*].   Sure ting! Dat's me. What about it?

PADDY [*as if to himself—with great sorrow*].   Me time is past due. That a great wave wid sun in the heart of it may sweep me over the side sometime I'd be dreaming of the days that's gone!

YANK.   Aw, yuh crazy Mick! [*He springs to his feet and advances on* PADDY *threateningly—then stops, fighting some queer struggle within himself—lets his hands fall to his sides—contemptuously*] Aw, take it easy. Yuh're aw right, at dat. Yuh're bugs, dat's all—nutty as a cuckoo. All dat tripe yuh been pullin'—Aw, dat's all right. On'y it's dead, get me? Yuh don't belong no more, see. Yuh don't get de stuff. Yuh're too old. [*Disgustedly*] But aw say, come up for air onct in a while, can't yuh? See what's happened since yuh croaked. [*He suddenly bursts forth vehemently, growing more and more excited*] Say! Sure! Sure I meant it! What de hell—Say, lemme talk! Hey! Hey, you old Harp! Hey, youse guys! Say, listen to me—wait a moment—I gotter talk, see. I belong and he don't. He's dead but I'm livin'. Listen to me! Sure I'm part of de engines! Why de hell not! Dey move, don't dey? Dey're speed, ain't dey? Dey smash trou, don't dey? Twenty-five knots a hour! Dat's goin' some! Dat's new stuff! Dat belongs! But him, he's too old. He gets dizzy. Say, listen. All dat crazy tripe about nights and days; all dat crazy tripe about stars and moons; all dat crazy tripe about suns and winds, fresh air and de rest of it—Aw hell, dat's all a dope dream! Hittin' de pipe of de past, dat's what he's doin'. He's old and don't belong no more. But me, I'm young! I'm in de pink! I move wit it! It, get me! I mean de ting dat's de guts of all dis. It ploughs trou all de tripe he's been sayin'. It blows dat up! It knocks dat dead! It slams dat offen de face of de oith! It, get me! De engines and de coal and de smoke and all de rest of it! He can't breathe and swallow coal dust, but I kin, see? Dat's fresh air for me! Dat's food for me! I'm new, get me? Hell in de stokehole? Sure! It takes a man to work in hell. Hell, sure, dat's my fav'rite climate. I eat it up! I git fat on it! It's me makes it hot! It's me makes it roar! It's me makes it move! Sure, on'y for me everyting stops. It all goes dead, get me? De noise and smoke and all de engines movin' de woild, dey stop. Dere ain't nothin' no more! Dat's what I'm sayin'. Everyting else dat makes de woild move, somep'n makes it move. It can't move without somep'n else, see? Den yuh get down to me. I'm at de bottom, get me! Dere ain't nothin' foither. I'm de end! I'm de start! I start somep'n and de woild moves! It—dat's me!—de new dat's moiderin' de old! I'm de ting in coal dat makes it boin; I'm steam and oil for de engines; I'm de ting in noise dat makes yuh hear it; I'm smoke and express trains and steamers and factory whistles; I'm de ting in gold dat makes it money! And I'm what makes iron into steel! Steel, dat stands for de whole ting! And I'm steel—steel—steel! I'm de muscles in steel, de punch behind it! [*As he says this he pounds with his fist against the steel bunks. All the men, roused to a pitch of frenzied self-glorification by his speech, do likewise. There is a deafening metallic roar, through which* YANK's *voice can be heard bellowing*] Slaves, hell! We run de whole woiks. All de rich guys dat tink dey're somep'n, dey ain't nothin'! Dey don't belong. But us guys, we're in de move, we're at de bottom, de whole ting is us! [PADDY *from the start of* YANK's *speech has been taking one gulp after another from his bottle, at first frightened-*

ly, as if he were afraid to listen, then desperately, as if to drown his senses, but finally has achieved complete indifferent, even amused, drunkenness. YANK *sees his lips moving. He quells the uproar with a shout*] Hey, youse guys, take it easy! Wait a moment! De nutty Harp is sayin' somep'n.

PADDY [*is heard now—throws his head back with a mocking burst of laughter*].   Ho-ho-ho-ho-ho—

YANK [*drawing back his fist, with a snarl*].   Aw! Look out who yuh're givin' the bark!

PADDY [*begins to sing the "Miller of Dee" with enormous good nature*].

"I care for nobody, no, not I,
And nobody cares for me."

YANK [*good-natured himself in a flash, interrupts* PADDY *with a slap on the bare back like a report*].   Dat's de stuff! Now yuh're gettin' wise to somep'n. Care for nobody, dat's de dope! To hell wit'em all! And nix on nobody else carin'. I kin care for myself, get me! [*Eight bells sound, muffled, vibrating through the steel walls as if some enormous brazen gong were imbedded in the heart of the ship. All the men jump up mechanically, file through the door silently close upon each other's heels in what is very like a prisoners' lockstep.* YANK *slaps* PADDY *on the back*] Our watch, yuh old Harp! [*Mockingly*] Come on down in hell. Eat up de coal dust. Drink in de heat. It's it, see! Act like yuh liked it, yuh better—or croak yuhself.

PADDY [*with jovial defiance*].   To the divil wid it! I'll not report this watch. Let thim log me and be damned. I'm no slave the like of you. I'll be sittin' here at me ease, and drinking, and thinking, and dreaming dreams.

YANK [*contemptuously*].   Tinkin' and dreamin', what'll that get yuh? What's tinkin' got to do wit it? We move, don't we? Speed, ain't it? Fog, dat's all you stand for. But we drive trou dat, don't we? We split dat up and smash trou—twenty-five knots a hour! [*Turns his back on* PADDY *scornfully*] Aw, yuh make me sick! Yuh don't belong! [*He strides out the door in rear.* PADDY *hums to himself, blinking drowsily*]

Scene II.

Two *days out. A section of the promenade deck.* MILDRED DOUGLAS *and her aunt are discovered reclining in deck chairs. The former is a girl of twenty, slender, delicate, with a pale, pretty face marred by a self-conscious expression of disdainful superiority. She looks fretful, nervous and discontented, bored by her own anemia.*[1] *Her aunt is a pompous and proud—and fat—old lady. She is a type even to the point of a double chin and lorgnettes.*[2] *She is dressed pretentiously, as if afraid her face alone would never indicate her position in life.* MILDRED *is dressed all in white.*

The impression to be conveyed by this scene is one of the beautiful, vivid life of the sea all about—sunshine on the deck in a great flood, the fresh sea wind blowing across it. In the midst of this, these two incongruous,

---

1. General lack of vitality and color.
2. Eyeglasses with a handle.

*artificial figures, inert and disharmonious, the elder like a gray lump of
dough touched up with rouge, the younger looking as if the vitality of her
stock had been sapped before she was conceived, so that she is the
expression not of its life energy but merely of the artificialities that energy
had won for itself in the spending.*

MILDRED [*looking up with affected dreaminess*].   How the black smoke
swirls back against the sky! Is it not beautiful?
AUNT [*without looking up*].   I dislike smoke of any kind.
MILDRED.   My great-grandmother smoked a pipe—a clay pipe.
AUNT [*ruffling*].   Vulgar!
MILDRED.   She was too distant a relative to be vulgar. Time mellows
pipes.
AUNT [*pretending boredom but irritated*].   Did the sociology you took up
at college teach you that—to play the ghoul on every possible occasion, excavat-
ing old bones? Why not let your great-grandmother rest in her grave?
MILDRED [*dreamily*].   With her pipe beside her—puffing in Paradise.
AUNT [*with spite*].   Yes, you are a natural born ghoul. You are even
getting to look like one, my dear.
MILDRED [*in a passionless tone*].   I detest you, Aunt. [*Looking at her
critically*] Do you know what you remind me of? Of a cold pork pudding against a
background of linoleum tablecloth in the kitchen of a—but the possibilities are
wearisome. [*She closes her eyes*]
AUNT [*with a bitter laugh*].   Merci for your candor. But since I am and
must be your chaperon—in appearance, at least—let us patch up some sort of
armed truce. For my part you are quite free to indulge any pose of eccentricity
that beguiles you—as long as you observe the amenities—
MILDRED [*drawling*].   The inanities?
AUNT [*going on as if she hadn't heard*].   After exhausting the morbid
thrills of social service work on New York's East Side—how they must have
hated you, by the way, the poor that you made so much poorer in their own
eyes!—you are now bent on making your slumming international. Well, I hope
Whitechapel[3] will provide the needed nerve tonic. Do not ask me to chaperon
you there, however. I told your father I would not. I loathe deformity. We will
hire an army of detectives and you may investigate everything—they allow you
to see.
MILDRED [*protesting with a trace of genuine earnestness*].   Please do not
mock at my attempts to discover how the other half lives. Give me credit for
some sort of groping sincerity in that at least. I would like to help them. I would
like to be some use in the world. Is it my fault I don't know how? I would like to
be sincere, to touch life somewhere. [*With weary bitterness*] But I'm afraid I
have neither the vitality nor integrity. All that was burnt out in our stock before I
was born. Grandfather's blast furnaces, flaming to the sky, melting steel, making
millions—then father keeping those home fires burning, making more
millions—and little me at the tail-end of it all. I'm a waste product in the
Bessemer process[4]—like the millions. Or rather, I inherit the acquired trait of
the by-product, wealth, but none of the energy, none of the strength of the steel

---

3. At the time, a poverty-stricken district of London.
4. The modern process of refining pig iron into steel.

that made it. I am sired by gold and damned by it, as they say at the race track—damned in more ways than one. [*She laughs mirthlessly*]

AUNT [*unimpressed—superciliously*]. You seem to be going in for sincerity today. It isn't becoming to you, really—except as an obvious pose. Be as artificial as you are, I advise. There's a sort of sincerity in that, you know. And, after all, you must confess you like that better.

MILDRED [*again affected and bored*]. Yes, I suppose I do. Pardon me for my outburst. When a leopard complains of its spots, it must sound rather grotesque. [*In a mocking tone*] Purr, little leopard. Purr, scratch, tear, kill, gorge yourself and be happy—only stay in the jungle where your spots are camouflage. In a cage they make you conspicuous.

AUNT. I don't know what you are talking about.

MILDRED. It would be rude to talk about anything to you. Let's just talk. [*She looks at her wrist watch*] Well, thank goodness, it's about time for them to come for me. That ought to give me a new thrill, Aunt.

AUNT [*affectedly troubled*]. You don't mean to say you're really going? The dirt—the heat must be frightful—

MILDRED. Grandfather started as a puddler.[5] I should have inherited an immunity to heat that would make a salamander shiver. It will be fun to put it to the test.

AUNT. But don't you have to have the captain's—or someone's—permission to visit the stokehole?

MILDRED [*with a triumphant smile*]. I have it—both his and the chief engineer's. Oh, they didn't want to at first, in spite of my social service credentials. They didn't seem a bit anxious that I should investigate how the other half lives and works on a ship. So I had to tell them that my father, the president of Nazareth Steel, chairman of the board of directors of this line, had told me it would be all right.

AUNT. He didn't.

MILDRED. How naïve age makes one! But I said he did, Aunt. I even said he had given me a letter to them—which I had lost. And they were afraid to take the chance that I might be lying. [*Excitedly*] So it's ho! for the stokehole. The second engineer is to escort me. [*Looking at her watch again*] It's time. And here he comes, I think. [*The* SECOND ENGINEER *enters. He is a husky, fine-looking man of thirty-five or so. He stops before the two and tips his cap, visibly embarrassed and ill-at-ease*]

SECOND ENGINEER. Miss Douglas?

MILDRED. Yes. [*Throwing off her rugs and getting to her feet*] Are we all ready to start?

SECOND ENGINEER. In just a second, ma'am. I'm waiting for the Fourth. He's coming along.

MILDRED [*with a scornful smile*]. You don't care to shoulder this responsibility alone, is that it?

SECOND ENGINEER [*forcing a smile*]. Two are better than one. [*Disturbed by her eyes, glances out to sea—blurts out*] A fine day we're having.

MILDRED. Is it?

SECOND ENGINEER. A nice warm breeze—

---

5. Worker who tends the blast furnace in a steel mill.

MILDRED.   It feels cold to me.

SECOND ENGINEER.   But it's hot enough in the sun—

MILDRED.   Not hot enough for me. I don't like Nature. I was never athletic.

SECOND ENGINEER [*forcing a smile*].   Well, you'll find it hot enough where you're going.

MILDRED.   Do you mean hell?

SECOND ENGINEER [*flabbergasted, decides to laugh*].   Ho-ho! No, I mean the stokehole.

MILDRED.   My grandfather was a puddler. He played with boiling steel.

SECOND ENGINEER [*all at sea—uneasily*].   Is that so? Hum, you'll excuse me, ma'am, but are you intending to wear that dress?

MILDRED.   Why not?

SECOND ENGINEER.   You'll likely rub against oil and dirt. It can't be helped.

MILDRED.   It doesn't matter. I have lots of white dresses.

SECOND ENGINEER.   I have an old coat you might throw over—

MILDRED.   I have fifty dresses like this. I will throw this one into the sea when I come back. That ought to wash it clean, don't you think?

SECOND ENGINEER [*doggedly*].   There's ladders to climb down that are none too clean—and dark alleyways—

MILDRED.   I will wear this very dress and none other.

SECOND ENGINEER.   No offense meant. It's none of my business. I was only warning you—

MILDRED.   Warning? That sounds thrilling.

SECOND ENGINEER [*looking down the deck—with a sigh of relief*]. There's the Fourth now. He's waiting for us. If you'll come—

MILDRED.   Go on. I'll follow you. [*He goes.* MILDRED *turns a mocking smile on her aunt*] An oaf—but a handsome, virile oaf.

AUNT [*scornfully*].   Poser!

MILDRED.   Take care. He said there were dark alleyways—

AUNT [*in the same tone*].   Poser!

MILDRED [*biting her lips angrily*].   You are right. But would that my millions were not so anemically chaste!

AUNT.   Yes, for a fresh pose I have no doubt you would drag the name of Douglas in the gutter!

MILDRED.   From which it sprang. Good-by, Aunt. Don't pray too hard that I may fall into the fiery furnace.

AUNT.   Poser!

MILDRED [*viciously*].   Old hag! [*She slaps her aunt insultingly across the face and walks off, laughing gaily*]

AUNT [*screams after her*].   I said poser!

Scene III.

The stokehole. In the rear, the dimly-outlined bulks of the furnaces and boilers. High overhead one hanging electric bulb sheds just enough light through the murky air laden with coal dust to pile up masses of shadows everywhere. A line of men, stripped to the waist, is before the furnace doors. They bend over, looking neither to right nor left, handling their shovels as if they were part of their bodies, with a strange, awkward, swinging rhythm. They use the shovels to throw open the furnace doors. Then from these fiery round holes in the black a flood of terrific light and heat pours full upon the men who are outlined in silhouette in the crouching, inhuman attitudes of chained gorillas. The men shovel with a rhythmic motion, swinging as on a pivot from the coal which lies in heaps on the floor behind to hurl it into the flaming mouths before them. There is a tumult of noise—the brazen clang of the furnace doors as they are flung open or slammed shut, the grating, teeth-gritting grind of steel against steel, of crunching coal. This clash of sounds stuns one's ears with its rending dissonance. But there is order in it, rhythm, a mechanical regulated recurrence, a tempo. And rising above all, making the air hum with the quiver of liberated energy, the roar of leaping flames in the furnaces, the monotonous throbbing beat of the engines.

As the curtain rises, the furnace doors are shut. The men are taking a breathing spell. One or two are arranging the coal behind them, pulling it into more accessible heaps. The others can be dimly made out leaning on their shovels in relaxed attitudes of exhaustion.

PADDY [*from somewhere in the line—plaintively*].   Yerra, will this divil's own watch nivir end? Me back is broke. I'm destroyed entirely.

YANK [*from the center of the line—with exuberant scorn*].   Aw, yuh make me sick! Lie down and croak, why don't yuh? Always beefin', dat's you! Say, dis is a cinch! Dis was made for me! It's my meat, get me! [*A whistle is blown—a thin, shrill note from somewhere overhead in the darkness.* YANK *curses without resentment*] Dere's de damn engineer crackin' de whip. He tinks we're loafin'.

PADDY [*vindictively*].   God stiffen him!

YANK [*in an exultant tone of command*].   Come on, youse guys! Git into de game! She's gittin' hungry! Pile some grub in her. Trow it into her belly! Come on now, all of youse! Open her up! [*At this last all the men, who have followed his movements of getting into position, throw open their furnace doors with a deafening clang. The fiery light floods over their shoulders as they bend round for the coal. Rivulets of sooty sweat have traced maps on their backs. The enlarged muscles form bunches of high light and shadow*]

YANK [*chanting a count as he shovels without seeming effort*].   One—two—tree—[*His voice rising exultantly in the joy of battle*] Dat's de stuff! Let her have it! All togedder now! Sling it into her! Let her ride! Shoot de piece now! Call de toin on her! Drive her into it! Feel her move! Watch her smoke! Speed, dat's her middle name! Give her coal, youse guys! Coal, dat's her booze! Drink it up, baby! Let's see yuh sprint! Dig in and gain a lap! Dere she go-o-es. [*This last in the chanting formula of the gallery gods at the six-day bike race. He slams his furnace door shut. The others do likewise with as much unison as their wearied bodies will permit. The effect is of one fiery eye after another being blotted out with a series of accompanying bangs*]

PADDY [*groaning*].   Me back is broke. I'm bate out—bate—[*There is a pause. Then the inexorable whistle sounds again from the dim regions above the electric light. There is a growl of cursing rage from all sides*]

YANK [*shaking his fist upward—contemptuously*].   Take it easy dere, you! Who d'yuh tink's runnin' dis game, me or you? When I git ready, we move. Not before! When I git ready, get me!

VOICES [*approvingly*]. That's the stuff!

Yank tal him, py golly!

Yank ain't affeerd.

Goot poy, Yank!

Give him hell!

Tell 'im 'e's a bloody swine!

Bloody slave-driver!

YANK [*contemptuously*]. He ain't got no noive. He's yellow, get me? All de engineers is yellow. Dey got streaks a mile wide. Aw, to hell wit him! Let's move, youse guys. We had a rest. Come on, she needs it! Give her pep! It ain't for him. Him and his whistle, dey don't belong. But we belong, see! We gotter feed de baby! Come on! [*He turns and flings his furnace door open. They all follow his lead. At this instant the* SECOND *and* FOURTH ENGINEERS *enter from the darkness on the left with* MILDRED *between them. She starts, turns paler, her pose is crumbling, she shivers with fright in spite of the blazing heat, but forces herself to leave the* ENGINEERS *and take a few steps nearer the men. She is right behind* YANK. *All this happens quickly while the men have their backs turned*]

YANK. Come on, youse guys! [*He is turning to get coal when the whistle sounds again in a peremptory, irritating note. This drives* YANK *into a sudden fury. While the other men have turned full around and stopped dumfounded by the spectacle of* MILDRED *standing there in her white dress,* YANK *does not turn far enough to see her. Besides, his head is thrown back, he blinks upward through the murk trying to find the owner of the whistle, he brandishes his shovel murderously over his head in one hand, pounding on his chest, gorilla-like, with the other, shouting*] Toin off dat whistle! Come down outa dere, yuh yellow, brass-buttoned, Belfast bum, yuh! Come down and I'll knock yer brains out! Yuh lousy, stinkin', yellow mut of a Catholic-moiderin' bastard! Come down and I'll moider yuh! Pullin' dat whistle on me, huh! I'll show yuh! I'll crash yer skull in! I'll drive yer teet' down yer troat! I'll slam yer nose trou de back of yer head! I'll cut yer guts out for a nickel, yuh lousy boob, yuh dirty, crummy, muck-eatin' son of a—[*Suddenly he becomes conscious of all the other men staring at something directly behind his back. He whirls defensively with a snarling, murderous growl, crouching to spring, his lips drawn back over his teeth, his small eyes gleaming ferociously. He sees* MILDRED, *like a white apparition in the full light from the open furnace doors. He glares into her eyes, turned to stone. As for her, during his speech she has listened, paralyzed with horror, terror, her whole personality crushed, beaten in, collapsed, by the terrific impact of this unknown, abysmal brutality, naked and shameless. As she looks at his gorilla face, as his eyes bore into hers, she utters a low, choking cry and shrinks away from him, putting both hands up before her eyes to shut out the sight of his face, to protect her own. This startles* YANK *to a reaction. His mouth falls open, his eyes grow bewildered*]

MILDRED [*about to faint—to the* ENGINEERS, *who now have her one by each arm—whimperingly*]. Take me away! Oh, the filthy beast! [*She faints. They carry her quickly back, disappearing in the darkness at the left, rear. An iron door clangs shut. Rage and bewildered fury rush back on* YANK. *He feels himself insulted in some unknown fashion in the very heart of his pride. He roars*]

God damn yuh! [*And hurls his shovel after them at the door which has just closed. It hits the steel bulkhead with a clang and falls clattering on the steel floor. From overhead the whistle sounds again in a long, angry, insistent command*]

Scene IV.

 The firemen's forecastle. YANK'S *watch has just come off duty and had dinner. Their faces and bodies shine from a soap and water scrubbing but around their eyes, where a hasty dousing does not touch, the coal dust sticks like black make-up, giving them a queer, sinister expression.* YANK *has not washed either face or body. He stands out in contrast to them, a blackened, brooding figure. He is seated forward on a bench in the exact attitude of Rodin's* The Thinker.[1] *The others, most of them smoking pipes, are staring at* YANK *half-apprehensively, as if fearing an outburst; half-amusedly, as if they saw a joke somewhere that tickled them.*

  VOICES. He ain't ate nothin'.
    Py golly, a fallar gat to gat grub in him.
    Divil a lie.
    Yank feeda da fire, no feeda da face.
    Ha-ha.
    He ain't even washed hisself.
    He's forgot.
    Hey, Yank, you forgot to wash.
  YANK [*sullenly*]. Forgot nothin'! To hell wit washin'.
  VOICES. It'll stick to you.
    It'll get under your skin.
    Give yer the bleedin' itch, that's wot.
    It makes spots on you—like a leopard.
    Like a piebald nigger, you mean.
    Better wash up, Yank.
    You sleep better.
    Wash up, Yank.
    Wash up! Wash up!
  YANK [*resentfully*]. Aw say, youse guys. Lemme alone. Can't youse see I'm tryin' to tink?
  ALL [*repeating the word after him as one with cynical mockery*]. Think! [*The word has a brazen, metallic quality as if their throats were phonograph horns. It is followed by a chorus of hard, barking laughter*]
  YANK [*springing to his feet and glaring at them belligerently*]. Yes, tink! Tink, dat's what I said! What about it? [*They are silent, puzzled by his sudden resentment at what used to be one of his jokes.* YANK *sits down again in the same attitude of* The Thinker].
  VOICES. Leave him alone.
    He's got a grouch on.
    Why wouldn't he?

---

 1. Auguste Rodin (1840–1917), French sculptor. *The Thinker* is the figure of a muscular man seated in a pose of deep contemplation.

PADDY [*with a wink at the others*].   Sure I know what's the matter. 'Tis aisy to see. He's fallen in love, I'm telling you.

ALL [*repeating the word after him as one with cynical mockery*].   Love! [*The word has a brazen, metallic quality as if their throats were phonograph horns. It is followed by a chorus of hard, barking laughter*]

YANK [*with a contemptuous snort*].   Love, hell! Hate, dat's what. I've fallen in hate, get me?

PADDY [*philosophically*].   'Twould take a wise man to tell one from the other. [*With a bitter, ironical scorn, increasing as he goes on*] But I'm telling you it's love that's in it. Sure what else but love for us poor bastes in the stokehole would be bringing a fine lady, dressed like a white quane, down a mile of ladders and steps to be havin' a look at us? [*A growl of anger goes up from all sides*]

LONG [*jumping on a bench—hecticly*].   Hinsultin' us! Hinsultin' us, the bloody cow! And them bloody engineers! What right 'as they got to be exhibitin' us 's if we was bleedin' monkeys in a menagerie! Did we sign for hinsults to our dignity as 'onset workers? Is that in the ship's articles? You kin bloody well bet it ain't! But I knows why they done it. I arsked a deck steward 'o she was and 'e told me. 'Er old man's a bleedin' millionaire, a bloody Capitalist! 'E's got enuf bloody gold to sink this bleedin' ship! 'E makes arf the bloody steel in the world! 'E owns this bloody boat! And you and me, Comrades, we're 'is slaves! And the skipper and mates and engineers, they're 'is slaves! And she's 'is bloody daughter and we're all 'er slaves, too! And she gives 'er orders as 'ow she wants to see the bloody animals below decks and down they takes 'er! [*There is a roar of rage from all sides*]

YANK [*blinking at him bewilderedly*].   Say! Wait a moment! Is all dat straight goods?

LONG.   Straight as string! The bleedin' steward as waits on 'em, 'e told me about 'er. And what're we goin' ter do, I arsks yer? 'Ave we got ter swaller 'er hinsults like dogs? It ain't in the ship's articles. I tell yer we got a case. We kin go to law—

YANK [*with abysmal contempt*].   Hell! Law!

ALL [*repeating the word after him as one with cynical mockery*].   Law! [*The word has a brazen metallic quality as if their throats were phonograph horns. It is followed by a chorus of hard, barking laughter*]

LONG [*feeling the ground slipping from under his feet—desperately*]. As voters and citizens we kin force the bloody governments—

YANK [*with abysmal contempt*].   Hell! Governments!

ALL [*repeating the word after him as one with cynical mockery*]. Governments!   [*The word has a brazen metallic quality as if their throats were phonograph horns. It is followed by a chorus of hard, barking laughter*]

LONG [*hysterically*].   We're free and equal in the sight of God.

YANK [*with abysmal contempt*].   Hell! God!

ALL [*repeating the word after him as one with cynical mockery*].   God! [*The word has a brazen metallic quality as if their throats were phonograph horns. It is followed by a chorus of hard, barking laughter*]

YANK [*witheringly*].   Aw, join de Salvation Army!

ALL.   Sit down! Shut up! Damn fool! Sea-lawyer! [LONG *slinks back out of sight*]

PADDY [*continuing the trend of his thoughts as if he had never been interrupted—bitterly*].   And there she was standing behind us, and the Second pointing at us like a man you'd hear in a circus would be saying: In this cage is a queerer kind of baboon than ever you'd find in darkest Africy. We roast them in their own sweat—and be damned if you won't heart some of thim saying they like it! [*He glances scornfully at* YANK]

YANK [*with a bewildered uncertain growl*].   Aw!

PADDY.   And there was Yank roarin' curses and turning round wid his shovel to brain her—and she looked at him, and him at her—

YANK [*slowly*].   She was all white. I tought she was a ghost. Sure.

PADDY [*with heavy, biting sarcasm*].   'Twas love at first sight, divil a doubt of it! If you'd seen the endearin' look on her pale mug when she shriveled away with her hands over her eyes to shut out the sight of him! Sure, 'twas as if she'd seen a great hairy ape escaped from the Zoo!

YANK [*stung—with a growl of rage*].   Aw!

PADDY.   And the loving way Yank heaved his shovel at the skull of her, only she was out the door! [*A grin breaking over his face*] 'Twas touching, I'm telling you! It put the touch of home, swate home in the stokehole. [*There is a roar of laughter from all*]

YANK [*glaring at* PADDY *menacingly*].   Aw, choke dat off, see!

PADDY [*not heeding him—to the others*].   And her grabbin' at the Second's arm for protection. [*With a grotesque imitation of a woman's voice*] Kiss me, Engineer dear, for it's dark down here and me old man's in Wall Street making money! Hug me tight, darlin', for I'm afeerd in the dark and me mother's on deck makin' eyes at the skipper! [*Another roar of laughter*]

YANK [*threateningly*].   Say! What yuh tryin' to do, kid me, yuh old Harp?

PADDY.   Divil a bit! Ain't I wishin' myself you'd brained her?

YANK [*fiercely*].   I'll brain her! I'll brain her yet, wait 'n' see! [*Coming over to* PADDY—*slowly*] Say, is dat what she called me—a hairy ape?

PADDY.   She looked it at you if she didn't say the word itself.

YANK [*grinning horribly*].   Hairy ape, huh? Sure! Dat's de way she looked at me, aw right. Hairy ape! So dat's me, huh? [*Bursting into rage—as if she were still in front of him*] Yuh skinny tart! Yuh white-faced bum, yuh! I'll show yuh who's a ape! [*Turning to the others, bewilderment seizing him again*] Say, youse guys. I was bawlin' him out for pullin' de whistle on us. You heard me. And den I seen youse lookin' at somep'n and I tought he'd sneaked down to come up in back of me, and I hopped round to knock him dead wit de shovel. And dere she was wit de light on her! Christ, yuh coulda pushed me over with a finger! I was scared, get me? Sure! I tought she was a ghost, see? She was all in white like dey wrap around stiffs. You seen her. Kin yuh blame me? She didn't belong, dat's what. And den when I come to and seen it was a real skoit and seen de way she was lookin' at me—like Paddy said—Christ, I was sore, get me? I don't stand for dat stuff from nobody. And I flung de shovel—on'y she'd beat it. [*Furiously*] I wished it'd banged her! I wished it'd knocked her block off!

LONG.   And be 'anged for murder or 'lectrocuted? She ain't bleedin' well worth it.

YANK.   I don't give a damn what! I'd be square wit her, wouldn't I? Tink I wanter let her put somep'n over on me? Tink I'm goin' to let her git away wit dat stuff? Yuh don't know me! No one ain't never put nothin' over on me and got away wit it, see!—not dat kind of stuff—no guy and no skoit neither! I'll fix her! Maybe she'll come down again—

VOICE. No chance, Yank. You scared her out of a year's growth.

YANK. I scared her? Why de hell should I scare her? Who de hell is she? Ain't she de same as me? Hairy ape, huh? [*With his old confident bravado*] I'll show her I'm better'n her, if she on'y knew it. I belong and she don't, see! I move and she's dead! Twenty-five knots a hour, dat's me! Dat carries her but I make dat. She's on'y baggage. Sure! [*Again bewilderedly*] But, Christ, she was funny lookin'! Did yuh pipe her hands? White and skinny. Yuh could see de bones through 'em. And her mush,[2] dat was dead white, too. And her eyes, dey was like dey'd seen a ghost. Me, dat was! Sure! Hairy ape! Ghost, huh? Look at dat arm! [*He extends his right arm, swelling out the great muscles*] I coulda took her wit dat, wit just my little finger even, and broke her in two. [*Again bewilderedly*] Say, who is dat skoit, huh? What is she? What's she come from? Who made her? Who give her de noive to look at me like dat? Dis ting's got my goat right. I don't get her. She's new to me. What does a skoit like her mean, huh? She don't belong, get me! I can't see her. [*With growing anger*] But one ting I'm wise to, aw right, aw right! Youse all kin bet your shoits I'll git even wit her. I'll show her if she tinks she— She grinds de organ and I'm on de string, huh? I'll fix her! Let her come down again and I'll fling her in de furnace! She'll move den! She won't shiver at nothin', den! Speed, dat'll be her! She'll belong den! [*He grins horribly*]

PADDY. She'll never come. She's had her belly-full, I'm telling you. She'll be in bed now, I'm thinking, wid ten doctors and nurses feedin' her salts to clean the fear out of her.

YANK [*enraged*]. Yuh tink I made her sick, too, do yuh? Just lookin' at me, huh? Hairy ape, huh? [*In a frenzy of rage*] I'll fix her! I'll tell her where to git off! She'll git down on her knees and take it back or I'll bust de face offen her! [*Shaking one fist upward and beating on his chest with the other*] I'll find yuh! I'm comin', d'yuh hear? I'll fix yuh, God damn yuh! [*He makes a rush for the door*]

VOICES. Stop him!
He'll get shot!
He'll murder her!
Trip him up!
Hold him!
He's gone crazy!
Gott, he's strong!
Hold him down!
Look out for a kick!
Pin his arms!

[*They have all piled on him and, after a fierce struggle, by sheer weight of numbers have borne him to the floor just inside the door*]

PADDY [*who has remained detached*]. Kape him down till he's cooled off. [*Scornfully*] Yerra, Yank, you're a great fool. Is it payin' attention at all you are to the like of that skinny sow widout one drop of rale blood in her?

YANK [*frenziedly, from the bottom of the heap*]. She done me doit! She done me doit, didn't she? I'll git square wit her! I'll get her some way! Git offen me, youse guys! Lemme up! I'll show her who's a ape!

---

2. Face.

Scene V.

> *Three weeks later. A corner of Fifth Avenue in the Fifties on a fine Sunday morning. A general atmosphere of clean, well-tidied, wide street; a flood of mellow, tempered sunshine; gentle, genteel breezes. In the rear, the show windows of two shops, a jewelry establishment on the corner, a furrier's next to it. Here the adornments of extreme wealth are tantalizingly displayed. The jeweler's window is gaudy with glittering diamonds, emeralds, rubies, pearls, etc., fashioned in ornate tiaras, crowns, necklaces, collars, etc. From each piece hangs an enormous tag from which a dollar sign and numerals in intermittent electric lights wink out the incredible prices. The same in the furrier's. Rich furs of all varieties hang there bathed in a downpour of artificial light. The general effect is of a background of magnificence cheapened and made grotesque by commercialism, a background in tawdry disharmony with the clear light and sunshine on the street itself.*
>
> *Up the side street* YANK *and* LONG *come swaggering.* LONG *is dressed in shore clothes, wears a black Windsor tie, cloth cap.* YANK *is in his dirty dungarees. A fireman's cap with black peak is cocked defiantly on the side of his head. He has not shaved for days and around his fierce, resentful eyes — as around those of* LONG *to a lesser degree — the black smudge of coal dust still sticks like make-up. They hesitate and stand together at the corner, swaggering, looking about them with a forced, defiant contempt.*

LONG [*indicating it all with an oratorical gesture*].   Well, 'ere we are. Fif' Avenoo. This 'ere's their bleedin' private lane, as yer might say. [*Bitterly*] We're trespassers 'ere. Proletarians keep orf the grass!

YANK [*dully*].   I don't see no grass, yuh boob. [*Staring at the sidewalk*] Clean, ain't it? Yuh could eat a fried egg offen it. The white wings[1] got some job sweepin' dis up. [*Looking up and down the avenue — surlily*] Where's all de white-collar stiffs yuh said was here — and de skoits — *her* kind?

LONG.   In church, blarst 'em! Arskin' Jesus to give 'em more money.

YANK.   Choich, huh? I useter go to choich onct — sure — when I was a kid. Me old man and woman, dey made me. Dey never went demselves, dough. Always got too big a head on Sunday mornin', dat was dem. [*With a grin*] Dey was scrappers for fair, bot' of dem. On Satiday nights when dey bot' got a skinful dey could put up a bout oughter been staged at de Garden.[2] When dey got trough dere wasn't a chair or table wit a leg under it. Or else dey bot' jumped on me for somep'n. Dat was where I loined to take punishment. [*With a grin and a swagger*] I'm a chip offen de old block, get me?

LONG.   Did yer old man follow the sea?

YANK.   Naw. Worked along shore. I runned away· when me ole lady croaked wit de tremens. I helped at truckin' and in de market. Den I shipped in de stokehole. Sure. Dat belongs. De rest was nothin'. [*Looking around him*] I ain't never seen dis before. De Brooklyn waterfront, dat was where I was dragged up. [*Taking a deep breath*] Dis ain't so bad at dat, huh?

---

1. Once-common term for white-coated street sweepers.
2. Madison Square Garden, New York.

LONG.   Not bad? Well, we pays for it wiv our bloody sweat, if yer wants to know!

YANK [*with sudden angry disgust*].   Aw, hell! I don't see no one, see—like her. All dis gives me a pain. It don't belong. Say, ain't dere a back room around dis dump? Let's go shoot a ball. All dis is too clean and quiet and dolled-up, get me! It gives me a pain.

LONG.   Wait and yer'll bloody well see—

YANK.   I don't wait for no one. I keep on de move. Say, what yuh drag me up here for, anyway? Tryin' to kid me, yuh simp, yuh?

LONG.   Yer wants to get back at 'er, don't yer? That's what yer been sayin' every bloomin' hour since she hinsulted yer.

YANK [*vehemently*].   Sure ting I do! Didn't I try to get even wit her in Southampton? Didn't I sneak on de dock and wait for her by de gangplank? I was goin' to spit in her pale mug, see! Sure, right in her pop-eyes! Dat woulda made me even, see? But no chanct. Dere was a whole army of plainclothes bulls around. Dey spotted me and gimme de bum's rush. I never seen her. But I'll git square wit her yet, you watch! [*Furiously*] De lousy tart! She tinks she kin get away wit moider—but not wit me! I'll fix her! I'll tink of a way!

LONG [*as disgusted as he dares to be*].   Ain't that why I brought yer up 'ere—to show yer? Yer been lookin' at this 'ere 'ole affair wrong. Yer been actin' an' talkin' 's if it was all a bleedin' personal matter between yer and that bloody cow. I wants to convince yer she was on'y a representative of 'er clarss. I wants to awaken yer bloody clarss consciousness. Then yer'll see it's 'er clarss yer've got to fight, not 'er alone. There's a 'ole mob of 'em like 'er, Gawd blind 'em!

YANK [*spitting on his hands—belligerently*].   De more de merrier when I gits started. Bring on de gang!

LONG.   Yer'll see 'em in arf a mo', when that church lets out. [*He turns and sees the window display in the two stores for the first time*] Blimey! Look at that, will yer? [*They both walk back and stand looking in the jeweler's*. LONG *flies into a fury*] Just look at this 'ere bloomin' mess! Just look at it! Look at the bleedin' prices on 'em—more'n our 'ole bloody stokehole makes in ten voyages sweatin' in 'ell! And they—'er and 'er bloody clarss—buys 'em for toys to dangle on 'em! One of these 'ere would buy scoff[3] for a starvin' family for a year!

YANK.   Aw, cut de sob stuff! T' hell wit de starvin' family! Yuh'll be passin' de hat to me next. [*With naïve admiration*] Say, dem tings is pretty, huh? Bet yuh dey'd hock for a piece of change aw right. [*Then turning away, bored*] But, aw hell, what good are dey? Let her have 'em. Dey don't belong no more'n she does. [*With a gesture of sweeping the jewelers into oblivion*] All dat don't count, get me?

LONG [*who has moved to the furrier's—indignantly*].   And I s'pose his 'ere don't count neither—skins of poor, 'armless animals slaughered so as 'er and 'ers can keep their bleedin' noses warm!

YANK [*who has been staring at something inside—with queer excitement*].   Take a slant at dat! Give it de once-over! Monkey fur—two t'ousand bucks! [*Bewilderedly*] Is dat straight goods—monkey fur? What de hell—?

LONG [*bitterly*].   It's straight enuf. [*With grim humor*] They wouldn't

---

3. Food.

bloody well pay that for a 'airy ape's skin—no, nor for the 'ole livin' ape with all 'is 'ead, and body, and soul thrown in!

YANK [*clenching his fists, his face growing pale with rage as if the skin in the window were a personal insult*]. Trowin' it up in my face! Christ! I'll fix her!

LONG [*excitedly*]. Church is out. 'Ere they come, the bleedin' swine. [*After a glance at* YANK's *lowering face—uneasily*]. Easy goes, Comrade. Keep yer bloomin' temper. Remember force defeats itself. It ain't our weapon. We must impress our demands through peaceful means—the votes of the on-marching proletarians of the bloody world!

YANK [*with abysmal contempt*]. Votes, hell! Votes is a joke, see. Votes for women! Let dem do it!

LONG [*still more uneasily*]. Calm, now. Treat 'em wiv the proper contempt. Observe the bleedin' parasites but 'old yer 'orses.

YANK [*angrily*]. Git away from me! Yuh're yellow, dat's what. Force, dat's me! De punch, dat's me every time, see! [*The crowd from church enter from the right, sauntering slowly and affectedly, their heads held stiffly up, looking neither to right nor left, talking in toneless, simpering voices. The women are rouged, calcimined, dyed, overdressed to the nth degree. The men are in Prince Alberts,[4] high hats, spats, canes, etc. A procession of gaudy marionettes, yet with something of the relentless horror of Frankensteins in their detached, mechanical unawareness*]

VOICES. Dear Doctor Caiaphas! He is so sincere!

What was the sermon? I dozed off.

About the radicals, my dear—and the false doctrines that are being preached.

We must organize a hundred per cent American bazaar.

And let everyone contribute one one-hundredth per cent of their income tax.

What an original idea!

We can devote the proceeds to rehabilitating the veil of the temple.

But that has been done so many times.

YANK [*glaring from one to the other of them—with an insulting snort of scorn*]. Huh! Huh! [*Without seeming to see him, they make wide detours to avoid the spot where he stands in the middle of the sidewalk*]

LONG [*frightenedly*]. Keep yer bloomin' mouth shut, I tells yer.

YANK [*viciously*]. G'wan! Tell it to Sweeney![5] [*He swaggers away and deliberately lurches into a top-hatted gentleman, then glares at him pugnaciously*] Say, who d'yuh tink yuh're bumpin'? Tink yuh own de oith?

GENTLEMAN [*coldly and affectedly*]. I beg your pardon. [*He has not looked at* YANK *and passes on without a glance, leaving him bewildered*]

LONG [*rushing up and grabbing* YANK's *arm*]. 'Ere! Come away! This wasn't what I meant. Yer'll 'ave the bloody coppers down on us.

YANK [*savagely—giving him a push that sends him sprawling*]. G'wan!

LONG [*picks himself up—hysterically*]. I'll pop orf then. This ain't what I meant. And whatever 'appens, yer can't blame me. [*He slinks off left*]

---

4. Long double-breasted outercoats named for England's Prince Albert (1841–1910).
5. Once-common expression of contemptuous disbelief.

YANK.   T' hell wit youse! [*He approaches a lady—with a vicious grin and a smirking wink*] Hello, Kiddo. How's every little ting? Got anyting on for tonight? I know an old boiler down to de docks we kin crawl into. [*The lady stalks by without a look, without a change of pace.* YANK *turns to others—insultingly*] Holy smokes, what a mug! Go hide yuhself before de horses shy at yuh. Gee, pipe de heine[6] on dat one! Say, youse, yuh look like de stoin of a ferryboat. Paint and powder! All dolled up to kill! Yuh look like stiffs laid out for de boneyard! Aw, g'wan, de lot of youse! Yuh give me de eye-ache. Yuh don't belong, get me! Look at me, why don't youse dare? I belong, dat's me! [*Pointing to a skyscraper across the street which is in process of construction—with bravado*] See dat building goin' up dere? See de steel work? Steel, dat's me! Youse guys live on it and tink yuh're somep'n. But I'm *in* it, see! I'm de hoistin' engine dat makes it go up! I'm it—de inside and bottom of it! Sure! I'm steel and steam and smoke and de rest of it! It moves—speed—twenty-five stories up—and me at de top and bottom—movin'! Youse simps don't move. Yuh're on'y dolls I winds up to see 'm spin. Yuh're de garbage, get me—de leavins—de ashes we dump over de side! Now, what 'a' yuh gotta say? [*But as they seem neither to see nor hear him, he flies into a fury*] Bums! Pigs! Tarts! Bitches! [*He turns in a rage on the men, bumping viciously into them but not jarring them the least bit. Rather it is he who recoils after each collision. He keeps growling*] Git off de oith! G'wan, yuh bum! Look where yuh're goin', can't yuh? Git outa here! Fight, why don't yuh? Put up yer mits! Don't be a dog! Fight or I'll knock yuh dead! [*But, without seeming to see him, they all answer with mechanical affected politeness*] I beg your pardon. [*Then at a cry from one of the women, they all scurry to the furrier's window*]

THE WOMAN [*estatically, with a gasp of delight*].   Monkey fur! [*The whole crowd of men and women chorus after her in the same tone of affected delight*] Monkey fur!

YANK [*with a jerk of his head back on his shoulders, as if he had received a punch full in the face—raging*].   I see yuh, all in white! I see yuh, yuh white-faced tart, yuh! Hairy ape, huh? I'll hairy ape yuh! [*He bends down and grips at the street curbing as if to pluck it out and hurl it. Foiled in this, snarling with passion, he leaps to the lamp-post on the corner and tries to pull it up for a club. Just at that moment a bus is heard rumbling up. A fat, high-hatted, spatted gentleman runs out from the side street. He calls out plaintively*] Bus! Bus! Stop there! [*and runs full tilt into the bending, straining* YANK, *who is bowled off his balance*]

YANK [*seeing a fight—with a roar of joy as he springs to his feet*] At last! Bus, huh? I'll bust yuh! [*He lets drive a terrific swing, his fist landing full on the fat gentleman's face. But the gentleman stands unmoved as if nothing had happened*]

GENTLEMAN.   I beg your pardon. [*Then irritably*] You have made me lose my bus. [*He claps his hands and begins to scream*] Officer! Officer! [*Many police whistles shrill out on the instant and a whole platoon of policemen rush in on* YANK *from all sides. He tries to fight but is clubbed to the pavement and fallen upon. The crowd at the window have not moved or noticed this disturbance. The clanging gong of the patrol wagon approaches with a clamoring din*]

---

6. I.e., "look at the rump."

Scene VI.

> *Night of the following day. A row of cells in the prison on Blackwells Island.*[1] *The cells extend back diagonally from right front to left rear. They do not stop, but disappear in the dark background as if they ran on, numberless, into infinity. One electric bulb from the low ceiling of the narrow corridor sheds its light through the heavy steel bars of the cell at the extreme front and reveals part of the interior.* YANK *can be seen within, crouched on the edge of his cot in the attitude of Rodin's* The Thinker. *His face is spotted with black and blue bruises. A blood-stained bandage is wrapped around his head.*

YANK [*suddenly starting as if awakening from a dream, reaches out and shakes the bars—aloud to himself, wonderingly*]. Steel. Dis is de Zoo, huh? [*A burst of hard, barking laughter comes from the unseen occupants of the cells, runs back down the tier, and abruptly ceases*]

VOICES [*mockingly*]. The Zoo? That's a new name for this coop—a damn good name!

Steel, eh? You said a mouthful. This is the old iron house.

Who is that boob talkin'?

He's the bloke they brung in out of his head. The bulls had beat him up fierce.

YANK [*dully*]. I musta been dreamin'. I tought I was in a cage at de Zoo—but de apes don't talk, do dey?

VOICES [*with mocking laughter*]. You're in a cage aw right.

A coop!

A pen!

A sty!

A kennel! [*Hard laughter—a pause*]

Say, guy! Who are you? No, never mind lying. What are you?

Yes, tell us your sad story. What's your game?

What did they jug yuh for?

YANK [*dully*]. I was a fireman—stokin' on de liners. [*Then with sudden rage, rattling his cell bars*] I'm a hairy ape, get me? And I'll bust youse all in de jaw if yuh don't lay off kiddin' me.

VOICES. Huh! You're a hard boiled duck, ain't you!

When you spit, it bounces! [*Laughter*]

Aw, can it. He's a regular guy. Ain't you?

What did he say he was—a ape?

YANK [*defiantly*]. Sure ting! Ain't dat what youse all are—apes? [*A silence. Then a furious rattling of bars from down the corridor*]

A VOICE [*thick with rage*]. I'll show yuh who's a ape, yuh bum!

VOICES. Sshh! Nix!

Can de noise!

Piano!

You'll have the guard down on us!

---

1. Known since 1921 as Welfare Island. Located in the East River between Manhattan and Queens in New York City, its once notorious prison has since been demolished.

YANK [*scornfully*]. De guard? Yuh mean de keeper, don't yuh? [*Angry exclamations from all the cells*]

VOICE [*placatingly*]. Aw, don't pay no attention to him. He's off his nut from the beatin'-up he got. Say, you guy! We're waitin' to hear what they landed you for—or ain't yuh tellin'?

YANK. Sure, I'll tell youse. Sure! Why de hell not? On'y—youse won't get me. Nobody gets me but me, see? I started to tell de Judge and all he says was: "Toity days to tink it over." Tink it over! Christ, dat's all I been doin' for weeks! [*After a pause*] I was tryin' to git even wit someone, see?—someone dat done me doit.

VOICES [*cynically*]. De old stuff, I bet. Your goil, huh?
　　　　Give yuh the double-cross, huh?
　　　　That's them every time!
　　　　Did yuh beat up de odder guy?

YANK [*disgustedly*]. Aw, yuh're all wrong! Sure dere was a skoit in it—but not what youse mean, not dat old tripe. Dis was a new kind of skoit. She was dolled up all in white—in de stokehole. I tought she was a ghost. Sure. [*A pause*]

VOICES [*whispering*]. Gee, he's still nutty.
　　　　Let him rave. It's fun listenin'.

YANK [*unheeding—groping in his thoughts*]. Her hands—dey was skinny and white like dey wasn't real but painted on somep'n. Dere was a million miles from me to her—twenty-five knots a hour. She was like some dead ting de cat brung in. Sure, dat's what. She didn't belong. She belonged in de window of a toy store, or on de top of a garbage can, see! Sure! [*He breaks out angrily*] But would yuh believe it, she had de noive to do me doit. She lamped[2] me like she was seein' somep'n broke loose from de menagerie. Christ, yuh'd oughter seen her eyes! [*He rattles the bars of his cell furiously*] But I'll get back at her yet, you watch! And if I can't find her I'll take it out on de gang she runs wit. I'm wise to where dey hangs out now. I'll show her who belongs! I'll show her who's in de move and who ain't. You watch my smoke!

VOICES [*serious and joking*]. Dat's de talkin'!
　　　　Take her for all she's got!
　　　　What was this dame, anyway? Who was she, eh?

YANK. I dunno. First cabin stiff. Her old man's a millionaire, dey says—name of Douglas.

VOICES. Douglas? That's the president of the Steel Trust, I bet.
　　　　Sure. I seen his mug in de papers.
　　　　He's filthy with dough.

VOICE. Hey, feller, take a tip from me. If you want to get back at that dame, you better join the Wobblies.[3] You'll get some action then.

YANK. Wobblies? What de hell's dat?

VOICE. Ain't you ever heard of the I.W.W.?

YANK. Naw. What is it?

VOICE. A gang of blokes—a tough gang. I been readin' about 'em today

---

2. Looked at.

3. Term for members of the Industrial Workers of the World (I.W.W.), labor organization founded in 1905 on socialistic principles. Its reputation for advocating sabotage and general strikes to overthrow capitalism and to achieve economic equality for the working classes led to its disintegration in the 1920s.

in the paper. The guard give me the *Sunday Times*. There's a long spiel about 'em. It's from a speech made in the Senate by a guy named Senator Queen. [*He is in the cell next to* YANK's. *There is a rustling of paper*] Wait'll I see if I got light enough and I'll read you. Listen. [*He reads*] "There is a menace existing in this country today which threatens the vitals of our fair Republic—as foul a menace against the very life-blood of the American Eagle as was the foul conspiracy of Catiline against the eagles of ancient Rome!"[4]

VOICE [*disgustedly*]. Aw, hell! Tell him to salt de tail of dat eagle!

VOICE [*reading*]. "I refer to that devil's brew of rascals, jailbirds, murderers and cutthroats who libel all honest working men by calling themselves the Industrial Workers of the World; but in the light of their nefarious plots, I call them the Industrious *Wreckers* of the World!"

YANK [*with vengeful satisfaction*]. Wreckers, dat's de right dope! Dat belongs! Me for dem!

VOICE. Ssshh! [*reading*] "This fiendish organization is a foul ulcer on the fair body of our Democracy—"

VOICE. Democracy, hell! Give him the boid, fellers—the raspberry! [*They do*]

VOICE. Ssshh! [*reading*] "Like Cato[5] I say to this Senate, the I.W.W. must be destroyed! For they represent an ever-present dagger pointed at the heart of the greatest nation the world has ever known, where all men are born free and equal, with equal opportunities to all, where the Founding Fathers have guaranteed to each one happiness, where Truth, Honor, Liberty, Justice, and the Brotherhood of Man are a religion absorbed with one's mother's milk, taught at our father's knee, sealed, signed, and stamped upon in the glorious Constitution of these United States!" [*A perfect storm of hisses, catcalls, boos, and hard laughter*]

VOICES [*scornfully*]. Hurrah for de Fort' of July!
　　　　　Pass de hat!
　　　　　Liberty!
　　　　　Justice!
　　　　　Honor!
　　　　　Opportunity!
　　　　　Brotherhood!

ALL [*with abysmal scorn*]. Aw, hell!

VOICE. Give that Queen Senator guy the bark! All togedder now—one—two—tree—[*A terrific chorus of barking and yapping*]

GUARD [*from a distance*]. Quiet there, youse—or I'll git the hose. [*The noise subsides*]

YANK [*with growling rage*]. I'd like to catch dat senator guy alone for a second. I'd loin him some trute!

VOICE. Ssshh! Here's where he gits down to cases on the Wobblies. [*Reads*] "They plot with fire in one hand and dynamite in the other. They stop not before murder to gain their ends, nor at the outraging of defenseless woman-

---

4. Lucius Sergius Catalina (108?–62 B.C.), Roman statesman whose thwarted political ambitions led him to conspire unsuccessfully against the conservative ruling party in Rome.

5. Marcus Porcius Cato, the Elder (234–149 B.C.), Roman statesman and general. In his efforts to initiate a war against Rome's old enemy Carthage, he closed every speech in the Senate with the words, "Furthermore, I am of the opinion that Carthage must be destroyed."

hood. They would tear down society, put the lowest scum in the seats of the mighty, turn Almighty God's revealed plan for the world topsy-turvy, and make of our sweet and lovely civilization a shambles, a desolation where man, God's masterpiece, would soon degenerate back to the ape!''

VOICE [*to* YANK]. Hey, you guy. There's your ape stuff again.

YANK [*with a growl of fury*]. I got him. So dey blow up tings, do dey? Dey turn tings round, do dey? Hey, lend me dat paper, will yuh?

VOICE. Sure. Give it to him. On'y keep it to yourself, see. We don't wanter listen to no more of that slop.

VOICE. Here you are. Hide it under your mattress.

YANK [*reaching out*]. Tanks I can't read much but I kin manage. [*He sits, the paper in the hand at his side, in the attitude of Rodin's* The Thinker. *A pause. Several snores from down the corridor. Suddenly* YANK *jumps to his feet with a furious groan as if some appalling thought had crashed on him—bewilderedly*] Sure—her old man—president of de Steel Trust—makes half de steel in de world—steel—where I tought I belonged—drivin' trou—movin'—in dat—to make *her*—and cage me in for her to spit on! Christ! [*He shakes the bars of his cell door till the whole tier trembles. Irritated, protesting exclamations from those awakened or trying to get to sleep*] He made dis—dis cage! Steel! *It* don't belong, dat's what! Cages, cells, locks, bolts, bars—dat's what it means!— holdin' me down wit him at de top! But I'll drive trou! Fire, dat melts it! I'll be fire—under de heap—fire dat never goes out—hot as hell—breakin' out in de night—[*While he has been saying this last he has shaken his cell door to a clanging accompaniment. As he comes to the "breakin' out" he seizes one bar with both hands and, putting his two feet up against the others so that his position is parallel to the floor like a monkey's, he gives a great wrench backwards. The bar bends like a licorice stick under his tremendous strength. Just at this moment the* PRISON GUARD *rushes in, dragging a hose behind him*]

GUARD [*angrily*]. I'll loin youse bums to wake me up! [*Sees* YANK] Hello, it's you, huh? Got the D. Ts.,[6] hey? Well, I'll cure 'em. I'll drown your snakes for yuh! [*Noticing the bar*] Hell, look at dat bar bended! On'y a bug is strong enough for dat!

YANK [*glaring at him*]. Or a hairy ape, yuh big yellow bum! Look out! Here I come! [*He grabs another bar*]

GUARD [*scared now—yelling off left*]. Toin de hose on, Ben!—full pressure! And call de others—and a straitjacket! [*The curtain is falling. As it hides* YANK *from view, there is a splattering smash as the stream of water hits the steel of* YANK'S *cell*]

Scene VII.

Nearly a month later. An I.W.W. local near the waterfront, showing the interior of a front room on the ground floor, and the street outside. Moonlight on the narrow street, buildings massed in black shadow. The interior of the room, which is general assembly room, office, and reading room, resembles some dingy settlement boys' club. A desk and high stool are in

---

6. Delirium tremens, acute delirium caused by excessive and prolonged use of alcohol.

one corner. A table with papers, stacks of pamphlets, chairs about it, is at center. The whole is decidedly cheap, banal, commonplace and unmys- terious as a room could well be. The secretary is perched on the stool making entries in a large ledger. An eye shade casts his face into shadows. Eight or ten men, longshoremen, iron workers, and the like, are grouped about the table. Two are playing checkers. One is writing a letter. Most of them are smoking pipes. A big sign-board is on the wall at the rear, "Industrial Workers of the World—Local No. 57."

YANK [*comes down the street outside. He is dressed as in Scene Five. He moves cautiously, mysteriously. He comes to a point opposite the door; tiptoes softly up to it, listens, is impressed by the silence within, knocks carefully, as if he were guessing at the password to some secret rite. Listens. No answer. Knocks again a bit louder. No answer. Knocks impatiently, much louder*]
    SECRETARY [*turning around on his stool*].   What the hell is that— someone knocking? [*Shouts*] Come in, why don't you? [*All the men in the room look up. YANK opens the door slowly, gingerly, as if afraid of an ambush. He looks around for secret doors, mystery, is taken aback by the commonplaceness of the room and the men in it, thinks he may have gotten in the wrong place, then sees the signboard on the wall and is reassured*]
    YANK [*blurts out*].   Hello.
    MEN [*reservedly*].   Hello.
    YANK [*more easily*].   I tought I'd bumped into de wrong dump.
    SECRETARY [*scrutinizing him carefully*].   Maybe you have. Are you a member?
    YANK.   Naw, not yet. Dat's what I come for—to join.
    SECRETARY.   That's easy. What's your job—longshore?
    YANK.   Naw. Fireman—stoker on de liners.
    SECRETARY [*with satisfaction*].   Welcome to our city. Glad to know you people are waking up at last. We haven't got many members in your line.
    YANK.   Naw. Dey're all dead to de woild.
    SECRETARY.   Well, you can help to wake 'em. What's your name? I'll make out your card.
    YANK [*confused*].   Name? Lemme tink.
    SECRETARY [*sharply*].   Don't you know your own name?
    YANK.   Sure; but I been just Yank for so long—Bob, dat's it—Bob Smith.
    SECRETARY [*writing*].   Robert Smith. [*Fills out the rest of card*] Here you are. Cost you half a dollar.
    YANK.   Is dat all—four bits? Dat's easy. [*Gives the SECRETARY the money*]
    SECRETARY [*throwing it in drawer*].   Thanks. Well, make yourself at home. No introductions needed. There's literature on the table. Take some of those pamphlets with you to distribute aboard ship. They may bring results. Sow the seed, only go about it right. Don't get caught and fired. We got plenty out of work. What we need is men who can hold their jobs—and work for us at the same time.
    YANK.   Sure. [*But he still stands, embarrassed and uneasy*]
    SECRETARY [*looking at him—curiously*].   What did you knock for? Think we had a coon in uniform to open doors?

YANK. Naw. I tought it was locked—and dat yuh'd wanter give me the once-over trou a peep-hole or somep'n to see if I was right.

SECRETARY [*alert and suspicious but with an easy laugh*]. Think we were running a crap game? That door is never locked. What put that in your nut?

YANK [*with a knowing grin, convinced that this is all camouflage, a part of the secrecy*]. Dis burg is full of bulls, ain't it?

SECRETARY [*sharply*]. What have the cops got to do with us? We're breaking no laws.

YANK [*with a knowing wink*]. Sure. Youse wouldn't for woilds. Sure. I'm wise to dat.

SECRETARY. You seem to be wise to a lot of stuff none of us knows about.

YANK [*with another wink*]. Aw, dat's aw right, see. [*Then made a bit resentful by the suspicious glances from all sides*] Aw, can it! Youse needn't put me trou de toid degree. Can't youse see I belong? Sure! I'm reg'lar. I'll stick, get me? I'll shoot de woiks for youse. Dat's why I wanted to join in.

SECRETARY [*breezily, feeling him out*]. That's the right spirit. Only are you sure you understand what you've joined? It's all plain and above board; still, some guys get a wrong slant on us. [*Sharply*] What's your notion of the purpose of the I.W.W.?

YANK. Aw, I know all about it.

SECRETARY [*sarcastically*]. Well, give us some of your valuable information.

YANK [*cunningly*]. I know enough not to speak outa my toin. [*Then resentfully again*] Aw, say! I'm reg'lar. I'm wise to de game. I know yuh got to watch your step wit a stranger. For all youse know, I might be a plain-clothes dick, or somep'n, dat's what yuh're tinkin', huh? Aw, forget it! I belong, see? Ask any guy down to de docks if I don't.

SECRETARY. Who said you didn't?

YANK. After I'm 'nitiated, I'll show yuh.

SECRETARY [*astounded*]. Initiated? There's no initiation.

YANK [*disappointed*]. Ain't there no password—no grip nor nothin'?

SECRETARY. What'd you think this is—the Elks—or the Black Hand?[1]

YANK. De Elks, hell! De Black Hand, dey're a lot of yellow back-stickin' Ginees. Naw. Dis is a man's gang, ain't it?

SECRETARY. You said it! That's why we stand on our two feet in the open. We got no secrets.

YANK [*surprised but admiringly*]. Yuh mean to say yuh always run wide open—like dis?

SECRETARY. Exactly.

YANK. Den yuh sure got your noive wit youse!

SECRETARY [*sharply*]. Just what was it made you want to join us? Come out with that straight.

YANK. Yuh call me? Well, I got noive, too! Here's my hand. Yuh wanter blow tings up, don't yuh? Well, dat's me! I belong!

SECRETARY [*with pretended carelessness*]. You mean change the unequal conditions of society by legitimate direct action—or with dynamite?

---

1. The Elks is a fraternal service organization. The Black Hand was a secret Sicilian organization involved in crime and terrorism in the United States at the time. *Ginees* below is a derogatory name for persons of Italian descent.

YANK. Dynamite! Blow it offen de oith—steel—all de cages—all de factories, steamers, buildings, jails—de Steel Trust and all dat makes it go.

SECRETARY. So—that's your idea, eh? And did you have any special job in that line you wanted to propose to us? [*He makes a sign to the men, who get up cautiously one by one and group behind* YANK].

YANK [*boldly*]. Sure, I'll come out wit it. I'll show youse I'm one of de gang. Dere's dat millionaire guy, Douglas—

SECRETARY. President of the Steel Trust, you mean? Do you want to assassinate him?

YANK. Naw, dat don't get yuh nothin'. I mean blow up de factory, de woiks, where he makes de steel. Dat's what I'm after—to blow up de steel, knock all de steel in de woild up to de moon. Dat'll fix tings! [*Eagerly, with a touch of bravado*] I'll do it by me lonesome! I'll show yuh! Tell me where his woiks is, how to git there, all de dope. Gimme de stuff, de old butter—and watch me do de rest! Watch de smoke and see it move! I don't give a damn if dey nab me—long as it's done! I'll soive life for it—and give 'em de laugh! [*Half to himself*] And I'll write her a letter and tell her de hairy ape done it. Dat'll square tings.

SECRETARY [*stepping away from* YANK]. Very interesting. [*He gives a signal. The men, huskies all, throw themselves on* YANK *and before he knows it they have his legs and arms pinioned. But he is too flabbergasted to make a struggle, anyway. They feel him over for weapons*].

MAN. No gat, no knife. Shall we give him what's what and put the boots to him?

SECRETARY. No. He isn't worth the trouble we'd get into. He's too stupid. [*He comes closer and laughs mockingly in* YANK's *face*] Ho-ho! By God, this is the biggest joke they've put up on us yet. Hey, you Joke! Who sent you—Burns or Pinkerton?[2] No, by God, you're such a bonehead I'll bet you're in the Secret Service! Well, you dirty spy, you rotten agent provocateur, you can go back and tell whatever skunk is paying you blood-money for betraying your brothers that he's wasting his coin. You couldn't catch a cold. And tell him that all he'll ever get on us, or ever has got, is just his own sneaking plots that he's framed up to put us in jail. We are what our manifesto says we are, neither more nor less—and we'll give him a copy of that any time he calls. And as for you—[*He glares scornfully at* YANK, *who is sunk in an oblivious stupor*] Oh, hell, what's the use of talking? You're a brainless ape.

YANK [*aroused by the word to fierce but futile struggles*]. What's dat, yuh Sheeny bum, yuh!

SECRETARY. Throw him out, boys. [*In spite of his struggles, this is done with gusto and éclat. Propelled by several parting kicks,* YANK *lands sprawling in the middle of the narrow cobbled street. With a growl he starts to get up and storm the closed door, but stops bewildered by the confusion in his brain, pathetically impotent. He sits there, brooding, in as near to the attitude of Rodin's* Thinker *as he can get in his position*]

YANK [*bitterly*]. So dem boids don't tink I belong, neider. Aw, to hell wit 'em! Dey're in de wrong pew—de same old bull—soapboxes and Salvation

---

2. Two private detective agencies which at the time were engaged in infiltrating radical labor organizations.

Army—no guts! Cut out an hour offen de job a day and make me happy! Gimme a dollar more a day and make me happy! Tree square a day, and cauliflowers in de front yard—ekal rights—a woman and kids—a lousy vote—and I'm all fixed for Jesus, huh? Aw, hell! What does dat get yuh? Dis ting's in your inside, but it ain't your belly. Feedin' your face—sinkers[3] and coffee—dat don't touch it. It's way down—at de bottom. Yuh can't grab it, and yuh can't stop it. It moves, and everything moves. It stops and de whole woild stops. Dat's me now—I don't tick, see?—I'm a busted Ingersoll,[4] dat's what. Steel was me, and I owned de woild. Now I ain't steel, and de woild owns me. Aw, hell! I can't see—it's all dark, get me? It's all wrong! [*He turns a bitter mocking face up like an ape gibbering at the moon*] Say, youse up dere, Man in de Moon, yuh look so wise, gimme de answer, huh? Slip me de inside dope, de information right from de stable—where do I get off at, huh?

A POLICEMAN [*who has come up the street in time to hear this last—with grim humor*]. You'll get off at the station, you boob, if you don't get up out of that and keep movin'.

YANK [*looking up at him—with a hard, bitter laugh*]. Sure! Lock me up! Put me in a cage! Dat's de on'y answer yuh know. G'wan, lock me up!

POLICEMAN. What you been doin'?

YANK. Enuf to gimme life for! I was born, see? Sure, dat's de charge. Write it in de blotter. I was born, get me!

POLICEMAN [*jocosely*]. God pity your old woman! [*Then matter-of-fact*] But I've no time for kidding. You're soused. I'd run you in but it's too long a walk to the station. Come on now, get up, or I'll fan your ears with this club. Beat it now! [*He hauls* YANK *to his feet*]

YANK [*in a vague mocking tone*]. Say, where do I go from here?

POLICEMAN [*giving him a push—with a grin, indifferently*] Go to hell.

Scene VIII.

> *Twilight of the next day. The monkey house at the Zoo. One spot of clear gray light falls on the front of one cage so that the interior can be seen. The other cages are vague, shrouded in shadow from which chatterings pitched in a conversational tone can be heard. On the one cage a sign from which the word "gorilla" stands out. The gigantic animal himself is seen squatting on his haunches on a bench in much the same attitude as Rodin's Thinker.* YANK *enters from the left. Immediately a chorus of angry chattering and screeching breaks out. The gorilla turns his eyes but makes no sound or move.*

YANK [*with a hard, bitter laugh*]. Welcome to your city, huh? Hail, hail, de gang's all here! [*At the sound of his voice the chattering dies away into an attentive silence.* YANK *walks up to the gorilla's cage and, leaning over the railing, stares in at its occupant, who stares back at him, silent and motionless. There is a pause of dead stillness. Then* YANK *begins to talk in a friendly confidential tone, half-mockingly, but with a deep undercurrent of sympathy*]

---

3. Doughnuts.
4. Brand name of a mass-produced and low-priced pocket watch of the time.

Say, yuh're some hard-lookin' guy, ain't yuh? I seen lots of tough nuts dat de
gang called gorillas, but yuh're de foist real one I ever seen. Some chest yuh got,
and shoulders, and dem arms and mits! I bet yuh got a punch in eider fist dat'd
knock 'em all silly! [*This with genuine admiration. The gorilla, as if he understood, stands upright, swelling out his chest and pounding on it with his fist.*
YANK *grins sympathetically*] Sure, I get yuh. Yuh challenge de whole woild,
huh? Yuh got what I was sayin' even if yuh muffed de woids. [*Then bitterness
creeping in*] And why wouldn't yuh get me? Ain't we both members of de same
club—de Hairy Apes? [*They stare at each other—a pause—then* YANK *goes
on slowly and bitterly*] So yuh're what she seen when she looked at me, de
white-faced tart! I was you to her, get me? On'y outa de cage—broke out—free
to moider her, see? Sure! Dat's what she tought. She wasn't wise dat I was in a
cage, too—worser'n yours—sure—a damn sight—'cause you got some chanct
to bust loose—but me—[*He grows confused*] Aw, hell! It's all wrong, ain't it?
[*A pause*] I s'pose yuh wanter know what I'm doin' here, huh? I been warmin' a
bench down to de Battery[1]—ever since last night. Sure. I seen de sun come up.
Dat was pretty, too—all red and pink and green. I was lookin' at de
skyscrapers—steel—and all de ships comin' in, sailin' out, all over de oith—
and dey was steel, too. De sun was warm, dey wasn't no clouds, and dere was a
breeze blowin'. Sure, it was great stuff. I got it aw right—what Paddy said about
dat bein' de right dope—on'y I couldn't get *in* it, see? I couldn't belong in dat. It
was over my head. And I kept tinkin'—and den I beat it up here to see what
youse was like. And I waited till dey was all gone to git yuh alone. Say, how
d'yuh feel sittin' in dat pen all de time, havin' to stand for 'em comin' and starin'
at yuh—de white-faced, skinny tarts and de boobs what marry 'em—makin' fun
of yuh, laughin' at yuh, gittin' scared of yuh—damn 'em! [*He pounds on the rail
with his fist. The gorilla rattles the bars of his cage and snarls. All the other
monkeys set up an angry chattering in the darkness.* YANK *goes on excitedly*]
Sure! Dat's de way it hits me, too. On'y yuh're lucky, see? Yuh don't belong wit
'em and yuh know it. But me, I belong wit 'em—but I don't, see? Dey don't
belong wit me, dat's what. Get me? Tinkin' is hard—[*He passes one hand
across his forehead with a painful gesture. The gorilla growls impatiently.* YANK
goes on gropingly] It's dis way, what I'm drivin' at. Youse can sit and dope
dream in de past, green woods, de jungle and de rest of it. Den yuh belong and
dey don't. Den yuh kin laugh at 'em, see? Yuh're de champ of de woild. But
me—I ain't got no past to tink in, nor nothin' dat's comin', on'y what's now—
and dat don't belong. Sure, you're de best off! Yuh can't tink, can yuh? Yuh
can't talk neider. But I kin make a bluff at talkin' and tinkin'—a'most git away
wit it—a'most!—and dat's where de joker comes in. [*He laughs*] I ain't on oith
and I ain't in heaven, get me? I'm in de middle tryin' to separate 'em, takin' all de
woist punches from bot' of 'em. Maybe dat's what dey call hell, huh? But you,
yuh're at de bottom. You belong! Sure! Yuh're de on'y one in de woild dat does,
yuh lucky stiff! [*The gorilla growls proudly*] And dat's why dey gotter put yuh in
a cage, see? [*The gorilla roars angrily*] Sure! Yuh get me. It beats it when you try
to tink it or talk it—it's way down—deep—behind—you 'n' me we feel it. Sure!
Bot' members of dis club! [*He laughs—then in a savage tone*] What de hell! T'
hell wit it! A little action, dat's our meat! Dat belongs! Knock 'em down and keep

---

1. Battery Park, at the southern tip of Manhattan.

bustin' 'em till dey croaks yuh wit a gat—wit steel! Sure! Are yuh game? Dey've looked at youse, ain't dey—in a cage? Wanter git even? Wanter wind up like a sport 'stead of croakin' slow in dere? [*The gorilla roars an emphatic affirmative.* YANK *goes on with a sort of furious exaltation*] Sure! Yuh're reg'lar! Yuh'll stick to de finish! Me 'n' you, huh?—bot' members of this club! We'll put up one last star bout dat'll knock 'em offen deir seats! Dey'll have to make de cages stronger after we're trou! [*The gorilla is straining at his bars, growling, hopping from one foot to the other.* YANK *takes a jimmy from under his coat and forces the lock on the cage door. He throws this open*] Pardon from de governor! Step out and shake hands. I'll take yuh for a walk down Fif' Avenoo. We'll knock 'em offen de oith and croak wit de band playin'. Come on, Brother. [*The gorilla scrambles gingerly out of his cage. Goes to* YANK *and stands looking at him.* YANK *keeps his mocking tone—holds out his hand*] Shake—de secret grip of our order. [*Something, the tone of mockery, perhaps, suddenly enrages the animal. With a spring he wraps his huge arms around* YANK *in a murderous hug. There is a crackling snap of crushed ribs—a gasping cry, still mocking, from* YANK] Hey, I didn't say kiss me! [*The gorilla lets the crushed body slip to the floor; stands over it uncertainly, considering; then picks it up, throws it in the cage, shuts the door, and shuffles off menacingly into the darkness at left. A great uproar of frightened chattering and whimpering comes from the other cages. Then* YANK *moves, groaning, opening his eyes, and there is silence. He mutters painfully*] Say—dey oughter match him—wit Zybszko.[2] He got me, aw right. I'm trou. Even him didn't tink I belonged. [*Then, with sudden passionate despair*] Christ, where do I get off at? Where do I fit in? [*Checking himself as suddenly*] Aw, what de hell! No squawkin', see! No quittin', get me! Croak wit your boots on! [*He grabs hold of the bars of the cage and hauls himself painfully to his feet—looks around him bewilderedly—forces a mocking laugh*] In de cage, huh? [*In the strident tones of a circus barker*] Ladies and gents, step forward and take a slant at de one and only—[*His voice weakening*]—one and original—Hairy Ape from de wilds of—[*He slips in a heap on the floor and dies. The monkeys set up a chattering, whimpering wail. And, perhaps, the Hairy Ape at last belongs*]

---

2. Misspelling for Stanislaus Zbyszko (1879–1967), once-popular professional wrestler.

Questions for Study

1. Several of the scenes in *The Hairy Ape* have settings which actually contain or strongly suggest cages. Identify these scenes and comment on their function in the play. How do other scenes contrast with these cage scenes? In your discussion, point out O'Neill's use of furniture and of miscellaneous items which surround Yank.

2. O'Neill dramatizes certain aspects of reality through exaggerated, symbolic scenes. In what ways then does he achieve realism and credibility in the play? Study in particular Scene V in determining how he accomplishes these effects.

3. How does Yank get along with his fellow crew members? What specific views does he advocate, and how do the crew members respond to these views?

4. Describe Paddy's thoughts about ships, sailing, and sailors. Why are he and Yank contrasted?

5. Describe Mildred Douglas. What are her motives for being a social worker, and why is she going to England? How does Mildred's aunt view her?

6. Interpret the confrontation between Mildred and the men in the stokehole. Why is Yank so enraged at her, and what reaction does he have to her?

7. Describe Yank's motives for attempting to join the I.W.W. Why is he misunderstood?

8. Is *The Hairy Ape*, as was *Miss Julie,* concerned, at least in part, with social classes? What social barriers do you see dramatized, and how does Yank respond to them?

9. First in Scene IV and later on in several other instances, Yank is described as assuming the pose of Rodin's *The Thinker,* a pose the gorilla takes up in Scene VIII. What implications do these parallels suggest? How do they figure in the final transposition of man and ape?

10. What does Yank mean by "belonging"? Name as many ways as you can by which he is deluded into thinking that he belongs. Where, or to what, does he belong? What does O'Neill mean by his final comment in the last stage direction?

Plays for
Further Study

Sophocles (496?–406 B.C.)
Antigone

Characters

ANTIGONE
ISMENE
EURYDICE
CREON
HAIMON
TEIRESIAS
A SENTRY
A MESSENGER
CHORUS

SCENE: *Before the palace of* CREON, *King of Thebes. A central double door and two lateral doors. A platform extends the length of the façade, and from this platform three steps lead down into the "orchestra," or chorus-ground.*

TIME: *Dawn of the day after the repulse of the Argive army from the assault on Thebes.*

PROLOGUE[1]

Antigone and Ismene enter from the central door of the Palace.

Antigone. Ismene, dear sister,
You would think that we had already suffered enough
For the curse on Oedipus:
I cannot imagine any grief
That you and I have not gone through. And now—
Have they told you of the new decree of our King Creon?
    Ismene. I have heard nothing: I know
That two sisters lost two brothers, a double death
In a single hour; and I know that the Argive army
Fled in the night; but beyond this nothing.   10
    Antigone. I thought so. And that is why I wanted you
To come out here with me. There is something we must do.
    Ismene. Why do you speak so strangely?
    Antigone. Listen, Ismene:
Creon buried our brother Eteocles
With military honors, gave him a soldier's funeral,
And it was right that he should; but Polyneices,
Who fought as bravely and died as miserably,—
They say that Creon has sworn
No one shall bury him, no one mourn for him,   20
But his body must lie in the fields, a sweet treasure
For carrion birds to find as they search for food.
That is what they say, and our good Creon is coming here
To announce it publicly; and the penalty—
Stoning to death in the public square!
                            There it is,
And now you can prove what you are:
A true sister, or a traitor to your family.
    Ismene. Antigone, you are mad! What could I possibly do?
    Antigone. You must decide whether you will help me or not.
    Ismene. I do not understand you. Help you in what?   30
    Antigone. Ismene, I am going to bury him. Will you come?
    Ismene. Bury him! You have just said the new law forbids it.
    Antigone. He is my brother. And he is your brother, too.
    Ismene. But think of the danger! Think what Creon will do!
    Antigone. Creon is not strong enough to stand in my way.
    Ismene. Ah sister!

---

1. Greek audiences were familiar with the events preceding those in the play. Although Oedipus, King of Thebes, tried to defy the prophecy that he would kill his father Laïos and marry his mother Iocaste, he unknowingly fulfilled these dire predictions. Discovering his horrible acts, he gouged out his eyes and banished himself from Thebes, leaving two daughters, Antigone and Ismene, and two sons, Polyneices and Eteocles. (This story is recounted by Sophocles in his *Oedipus Rex.*) The sons were to rule Thebes in alternate years, but Eteocles refused to yield the throne. Polyneices led the Argive army in an unsuccessful attack on the city, and the two brothers killed each other. Creon, their uncle (Iocaste's brother), became king, and his son Haimon became betrothed to Antigone.

Oedipus died, everyone hating him
For what his own search brought to light, his eyes
Ripped out by his own hand; and Iocaste died,
His mother and wife at once: she twisted the cords   40
That strangled her life; and our two brothers died,
Each killed by the other's sword. And we are left:
But oh, Antigone,
Think how much more terrible than these
Our own death would be if we should go against Creon
And do what he has forbidden! We are only women,
We cannot fight with men, Antigone!
The law is strong, we must give in to the law
In this thing, and in worse. I beg the Dead
To forgive me, but I am helpless: I must yield   50
To those in authority. And I think it is dangerous business
To be always meddling.

    ANTIGONE.   If that is what you think,
I should not want you, even if you asked to come.
You have made your choice, you can be what you want to be.
But I will bury him; and if I must die,
I say that this crime is holy: I shall lie down
With him in death, and I shall be as dear
To him as he to me.

                It is the dead,
Not the living, who make the longest demands:
We die for ever . . .

                You may do as you like,   60
Since apparently the laws of the gods mean nothing to you.

    ISMENE.   They mean a great deal to me; but I have no strength
To break laws that were made for the public good.

    ANTIGONE.   That must be your excuse, I suppose. But as for me,
I will bury the brother I love.

    ISMENE.   Antigone,
I am so afraid for you!

    ANTIGONE.   You need not be:
You have yourself to consider, after all.

    ISMENE.   But no one must hear of this, you must tell no one!
I will keep it a secret, I promise!

    ANTIGONE.   Oh, tell it! Tell everyone!
Think how they'll hate you when it all comes out   70
If they learn that you knew about it all the time!

    ISMENE.   So fiery! You should be cold with fear.

    ANTIGONE.   Perhaps. But I am doing only what I must.

    ISMENE.   But can you do it? I say that you cannot.

    ANTIGONE.   Very well: when my strength gives out, I shall do no more.

    ISMENE.   Impossible things should not be tried at all.

    ANTIGONE.   Go away, Ismene:
I shall be hating you soon, and the dead will too,

For your words are hateful. Leave me my foolish plan:
I am not afraid of the danger; if it means death, 80
It will not be the worst of deaths—death without honor.
    ISMENE. Go then, if you feel that you must.
You are unwise,
But a loyal friend indeed to those who love you.

       [*Exit into the Palace.* ANTIGONE *goes off, L. Enter the* CHORUS.]

PARADOS[2]

Strophe 1

    CHORUS. Now the long blade of the sun, lying
Level east to west, touches with glory
Thebes of the Seven Gates. Open, unlidded
Eye of golden day! O marching light
Across the eddy and rush of Dirce's stream,[3]
Striking the white shields of the enemy
Thrown headlong backward from the blaze of morning!
    CHORAGOS. Polyneices their commander
Roused them with windy phrases,
He the wild eagle screaming 10
Insults above our land,
His wings their shields of snow,
His crest their marshalled helms.

Antistrophe 2

    CHORUS. Against our seven gates in a yawning ring
The famished spears came onward in the night;
But before his jaws were sated with our blood,
Or pinefire took the garland of our towers,
He was thrown back; and as he turned, great Thebes—
No tender victim for his noisy power—
Rose like a dragon behind him, shouting war. 20
    CHORAGOS. For God hates utterly
The bray of bragging tongues;
And when he beheld their smiling,
Their swagger of golden helms,
The frown of his thunder blasted
Their first man from our walls.

---

    2. The song or ode sung by the chorus (here representing the elders of Thebes) on its entry to the stage area. Led by the *choragos,* the chorus sang the strophe and the antistrophe as it moved back and forth across the stage.
    3. A stream near Thebes.

Strophe 2

CHORUS.   We heard his shout of triumph high in the air
Turn to a scream; far out in a flaming arc
He fell with his windy torch, and the earth struck him.
And others storming in fury no less than his   30
Found stock of death in the dusty joy of battle.
CHORAGOS.   Seven captains at seven gates
Yielded their clanging arms to the god
That bends the battle-line and breaks it.
These two only, brothers in blood,
Face to face in matchless rage,
Mirroring each the other's death,
Clashed in long combat.

Antistrophe 2

CHORUS.   But now in the beautiful morning of victory
Let Thebes of the many chariots sing for joy!   40
With hearts for dancing we'll take leave of war:
Our temples shall be sweet with hymns of praise,
And the long night shall echo with our chorus.

SCENE I

CHORAGOS.   But now at last our new King is coming:
Creon of Thebes, Menoikeus' son.
In this auspicious dawn of his reign
What are the new complexities
That shifting Fate has woven for him?
What is his counsel? Why has he summoned
The old men to hear him?

[*Enter* CREON *from the Palace, C. He addresses the* CHORUS *from the top step.*]

CREON.   Gentlemen: I have the honor to inform you that our Ship of
State, which recent storms have threatened to destroy, has come safely to harbor at last, guided by the merciful wisdom of Heaven. I have summoned you
here this morning because I know that I can depend upon you: your devotion
to King Laıos was absolute; you never hesitated in your duty to our late ruler
Oedipus; and when Oedipus died, your loyalty was transferred to his children.
Unfortunately, as you know, his two sons, the princes Eteocles and Polyneices,
have killed each other in battle; and I, as the next in blood, have succeeded to
the full power of the throne.   16
I am aware, of course, that no Ruler can expect complete loyalty from his
subjects until he has been tested in office. Nevertheless, I say to you at the very
outset that I have nothing but contempt for the kind of Governor who is afraid,

for whatever reason, to follow the course that he knows is best for the State; and as for the man who sets private friendship above the public welfare—I have no use for him, either. I call God to witness that if I saw my country headed for ruin, I should not be afraid to speak out plainly; and I need hardly remind you that I would never have any dealings with an enemy of the people. No one values friendship more highly than I; but we must remember that friends made at the risk of wrecking our Ship are not real friends at all. 26

These are my principles, at any rate, and that is why I have made the following decision concerning the sons of Oedipus: Eteocles, who died as a man should die, fighting for his country, is to be buried with full military honors, with all the ceremony that is usual when the greatest heroes die; but his brother Polyneices, who broke his exile to come back with fire and sword against his native city and the shrines of his father's gods, whose one idea was to spill the blood of his blood and sell his own people into slavery—Polyneices, I say, is to have no burial: no man is to touch him or say the least prayer for him; he shall lie on the plain, unburied; and the birds and the scavenging dogs can do with him whatever they like. 36

This is my command, and you can see the wisdom behind it. As long as I am King, no traitor is going to be honored with the loyal man. But whoever shows by word and deed that he is on the side of the State—he shall have my respect while he is living, and my reverence when he is dead. 40

CHORAGOS. If that is your will, Creon son of Menoikeus,
You have the right to enforce it: we are yours.
CREON. That is my will. Take care that you do your part.
CHORAGOS. We are old men: let the younger ones carry it out.
CREON. I do not mean that: the sentries have been appointed.
CHORAGOS. Then what is it that you would have us do?
CREON. You will give no support to whoever breaks this law.
CHORAGOS. Only a crazy man is in love with death!
CREON. And death it is; yet money talks, and the wisest
Have sometimes been known to count a few coins too many. 50

[Enter SENTRY *from L.]*

SENTRY. I'll not say that I'm out of breath from running, King, because every time I stopped to think about what I have to tell you, I felt like going back. And all the time a voice kept saying, "You fool, don't you know you're walking straight into trouble?"; and then another voice: "Yes, but if you let somebody else get the news to Creon first, it will be even worse than that for you!" But good sense won out, at least I hope it was good sense, and here I am with a story that makes no sense at all; but I'll tell it anyhow, because, as they say, what's going to happen's going to happen, and—
CREON. Come to the point. What have you to say?
SENTRY. I did not do it. I did not see who did it. You must not punish me for what someone else has done. 61
CREON. A comprehensive defense! More effective, perhaps,
If I knew its purpose. Come: what is it?
SENTRY. A dreadful thing . . . I don't know how to put it—
CREON. Out with it!

SENTRY.   Well, then;
The dead man—
         Polyneices—

[*Pause. The* SENTRY *is overcome, fumbles for words.* CREON *waits impassively.*]

                out there—
                    someone—
New dust on the slimy flesh!

[*Pause. No sign from* CREON.]

Someone has given it burial that way, and
Gone . . .

[*Long pause.* CREON *finally speaks with deadly control.*]

CREON.   And the man who dared do this?
SENTRY.   I swear I   70
Do not know! You must believe me!
                  Listen:
The ground was dry, not a sign of digging, no,
Not a wheeltrack in the dust, no trace of anyone.
It was when they relieved us this morning: and one of them,
The corporal, pointed to it.
                There it was,
The strangest—
        Look:
The body, just mounded over with light dust: you see?
Not buried really, but as if they'd covered it
Just enough for the ghost's peace. And no sign
Of dogs or any wild animal that had been there.   80

And then what a scene there was! Every man of us
Accusing the other: we all proved the other man did it,
We all had proof that we could not have done it.
We were ready to take hot iron in our hands,
Walk through fire, swear by all the gods,
It was not I!
I do not know who it was, but it was not I!

[CREON's *rage has been mounting steadily, but the* SENTRY *is too intent upon his story to notice it.*]

And then, when this came to nothing, someone said
A thing that silenced us and made us stare
Down at the ground: you had to be told the news,   90
And one of us had to do it! We threw the dice,
And the bad luck fell to me. So here I am,

No happier to be here than you are to have me:
Nobody likes the man who brings bad news.
    CHORAGOS.   I have been wondering, King: can it be that the gods have
done this?
    CREON [*furiously*]. Stop!
Must you doddering wrecks
Go out of your heads entirely? "The gods!"
Intolerable!
The gods favor this corpse? Why? How had he served them?   100
Tried to loot their temples, burn their images,
Yes, and the whole State, and its laws with it!
Is it your senile opinion that the gods love to honor bad men?
A pious thought!—

                No, from the very beginning
There have been those who have whispered together,
Stiff-necked anarchists, putting their heads together,
Scheming against me in alleys. These are the men,
And they have bribed my own guard to do this thing.
[*Sententiously.*] Money!
There's nothing in the world so demoralizing as money.   110
Down go your cities,
Homes gone, men gone, honest hearts corrupted,
Crookedness of all kinds, and all for money!
[*To* SENTRY]   But you—!
I swear by God and by the throne of God,
The man who has done this thing shall pay for it!
Find that man, bring him here to me, or your death
Will be the least of your problems: I'll string you up
Alive, and there will be certain ways to make you
Discover your employer before you die;
And the process may teach you a lesson you seem to have missed: 120
The dearest profit is sometimes all too dear:
That depends on the source. Do you understand me?
A fortune won is often misfortune.
    SENTRY.   King, may I speak?
    CREON.   Your very voice distresses me.
    SENTRY.   Are you sure that it is my voice, and not your conscience?
    CREON.   By God, he wants to analyze me now!
    SENTRY.   It is not what I say, but what has been done, that hurts you.
    CREON.   You talk too much.
    SENTRY.   Maybe; but I've done nothing.
    CREON.   Sold your soul for some silver: that's all you've done.
    SENTRY.   How dreadful it is when the right judge judges wrong! 130
    CREON.   Your figures of speech
May entertain you now; but unless you bring me the man,
You will get little profit from them in the end.

                           [*Exit* CREON *into the Palace.*]
    SENTRY.   "Bring me the man"—!
I'd like nothing better than bringing him the man!

But bring him or not, you have seen the last of me here.
At any rate, I am safe!

[Exit SENTRY.]

ODE I

Strophe 1

    CHORUS. Numberless are the world's wonders, but none
More wonderful than man; the stormgray sea
Yields to his prows, the huge crests bear him high;
Earth, holy and inexhaustible, is graven
With shining furrows where his plows have gone
Year after year, the timeless labor of stallions.

Antistrophe 1

The lightboned birds and beasts that cling to cover,
The lithe fish lighting their reaches of dim water,
All are taken, tamed in the net of his mind;
The lion on the hill, the wild horse windy-maned,   10
Resign to him; and his blunt yoke has broken
The sultry shoulders of the mountain bull.

Strophe 2

Words also, and thought as rapid as air,
He fashions to his good use; statecraft is his,
And his the skill that deflects the arrows of snow,
The spears of winter rain: from every wind
He has made himself secure—from all but one:
In the late wind of death he cannot stand.

Antistrophe 2

A clear intelligence, force beyond all measure!
O fate of man, working both good and evil!   20
When the laws are kept, how proudly his city stands!
When the laws are broken, what of his city then?
Never may the anarchic man find rest at my hearth,
Never be it said that my thoughts are his thoughts.

SCENE II

    [*Re-enter* SENTRY, *leading* ANTIGONE.]

CHORAGOS.   What does this mean? Surely this captive woman
Is the Princess, Antigone. Why should she be taken?
   SENTRY.   Here is the one who did it! We caught her
In the very act of burying him.—Where is Creon?
   CHORAGOS.   Just coming from the house.

[*Enter* CREON, *C.*]

CREON.   What has happened?
Why have you come back so soon?
   SENTRY [*expansively*].   O King,
A man should never be too sure of anything: I would have sworn
That you'd not see me here again: your anger
Frightened me so, and the things you threatened me with;
But how could I tell then   10
That I'd be able to solve the case so soon?

No dice-throwing this time: I was only too glad to come!

Here is this woman. She is the guilty one:
We found her trying to bury him.
Take her, then; question her; judge her as you will.
I am through with the whole thing now, and glád óf it.
   CREON.   But this is Antigone! Why have you brought her here?
   SENTRY.   She was burying him, I tell you!
   CREON [*severely*].   Is this the truth?
   SENTRY.   I saw her with my own eyes. Can I say more?
   CREON.   The details: come, tell me quickly!
   SENTRY.   It was like this: 20
After those terrible threats of yours, King,
We went back and brushed the dust away from the body.
The flesh was soft by now, and stinking,
So we sat on a hill to windward and kept guard.
No napping this time! We kept each other awake.
But nothing happened until the white round sun
Whirled in the center of the round sky over us:
Then, suddenly,
A storm of dust roared up from the earth, and the sky
Went out, the plain vanished with all its trees   30
In the stinging dark. We closed our eyes and endured it.
The whirlwind lasted a long time, but it passed;
And then we looked, and there was Antigone!
I have seen
A mother bird come back to a stripped nest, heard
Her crying bitterly a broken note or two
For the young ones stolen. Just so, when this girl
Found the bare corpse, and all her love's work wasted,
She wept, and cried on heaven to damn the hands
That had done this thing.

And then she brought more dust   40
And sprinkled wine three times for her brother's ghost.

We ran and took her at once. She was not afraid,
Not even when we charged her with what she had done.
She denied nothing.
     And this was a comfort to me,
And some uneasiness: for it is a good thing
To escape from death, but it is no great pleasure
To bring death to a friend.
     Yet I always say
There is nothing so comfortable as your own safe skin!
  CREON [*slowly, dangerously*].   And you, Antigone,
You with your head hanging—do you confess this thing?   50
  ANTIGONE.   I do. I deny nothing.
  CREON [*to* SENTRY].   You may go.   [*Exit* SENTRY.]
[*To* ANTIGONE] Tell me, tell me briefly:
Had you heard my proclamation touching this matter?
  ANTIGONE.   It was public. Could I help hearing it?
  CREON.   And yet you dared defy the law.
  ANTIGONE.   I dared.
It was not God's proclamation. That final Justice
That rules the world below makes no such laws.
Your edict, King, was strong,
But all your strength is weakness itself against
The immortal unrecorded laws of God.   60
They are not merely now: they were, and shall be,
Operative for ever, beyond man utterly.

I knew I must die, even without your decree:
I am only mortal. And if I must die
Now, before it is my time to die,
Surely this is no hardship: can anyone
Living, as I live, with evil all about me,
Think Death less than a friend? This death of mine
Is of no importance; but if I had left my brother
Lying in death unburied, I should have suffered.   70
Now I do not.
    You smile at me. Ah Creon,
Think me a fool, if you like; but it may well be
That a fool convicts me of folly.
  CHORAGOS.   Like father, like daughter: both headstrong, deaf to reason!
She has never learned to yield.
  CREON.   She has much to learn.
The inflexible heart breaks first, the toughest iron
Cracks first, and the wildest horses bend their necks
At the pull of the smallest curb.
     Pride? In a slave?
The girl is guilty of a double insolence,

Breaking the given laws and boasting of it.   80
Who is the man here,
She or I, if this crime goes unpunished?
Sister's child, or more than sister's child,
Or closer yet in blood—she and her sister
Win bitter death for this!
[*To* SERVANTS]   Go, some of you,
Arrest Ismene. I accuse her equally.
Bring her: you will find her sniffling in the house there.

Her mind's a traitor: crimes kept in the dark
Cry for light, and the guardian brain shudders;
But how much worse than this   90
Is brazen boasting of barefaced anarchy!
   ANTIGONE.   Creon, what more do you want than my death?
   CREON.   Nothing.
That gives me everything.
   ANTIGONE.   Then I beg you: kill me.
This talking is a great weariness: your words
Are distasteful to me, and I am sure that mine
Seem so to you. And yet they should not seem so:
I should have praise and honor for what I have done.
All these men here would praise me
Were their lips not frozen shut with fear of you.
[*Bitterly*.] Ah the good fortune of kings,   100
Licensed to say and do whatever they please!
   CREON.   You are alone here in that opinion.
   ANTIGONE.   No, they are with me. But they keep their tongues in leash.
   CREON.   Maybe. But you are guilty, and they are not.
   ANTIGONE.   There is no guilt in reverence for the dead.
   CREON.   But Eteocles—was he not your brother too?
   ANTIGONE.   My brother too.
   CREON.   And you insult his memory?
   ANTIGONE [*softly*].   The dead man would not say that I insult it.
   CREON.   He would: for you honor a traitor as much as him.
   ANTIGONE.   His own brother, traitor or not, and equal in blood.   110
   CREON.   He made war on his country. Eteocles defended it.
   ANTIGONE.   Nevertheless, there are honors due all the dead.
   CREON.   But not the same for the wicked as for the just.
   ANTIGONE.   Ah Creon, Creon,
Which of us can say what the gods hold wicked?
   CREON.   An enemy is an enemy, even dead.
   ANTIGONE.   It is my nature to join in love, not hate.
   CREON [*finally losing patience*].   Go join them, then; if you must have your love,
Find it in hell!
   CHORAGOS.   But see, Ismene comes: 120

[*Enter* ISMENE, *guarded*.]

Those tears are sisterly, the cloud
That shadows her eyes rains down gentle sorrow.
    CREON. You too, Ismene,
Snake in my ordered house, sucking my blood
Stealthily—and all the time I never knew
That these two sisters were aiming at my throne!

                               Ismene,
Do you confess your share in this crime, or deny it?
Answer me.
    ISMENE. Yes, if she will let me say so. I am guilty.
    ANTIGONE [*coldly*]. No, Ismene. You have no right to say so.   130
You would not help me, and I will not have you help me.
    ISMENE. But now I know what you meant; and I am here
To join you, to take my share of punishment.
    ANTIGONE. The dead man and the gods who rule the dead
Know whose act this was. Words are not friends.
    ISMENE. Do you refuse me, Antigone? I want to die with you:
I too have a duty that I must discharge to the dead.
    ANTIGONE. You shall not lessen my death by sharing it.
    ISMENE. What do I care for life when you are dead?
    ANTIGONE. Ask Creon. You're always hanging on his opinions.   140
    ISMENE. You are laughing at me. Why, Antigone?
    ANTIGONE. It's a joyless laughter, Ismene.
    ISMENE.   But can I do nothing?
    ANTIGONE. Yes. Save yourself. I shall not envy you.
There are those who will praise you; I shall have honor, too.
    ISMENE. But we are equally guilty!
    ANTIGONE.   No more, Ismene.
You are alive, but I belong to Death.
    CREON [*to the* CHORUS]. Gentlemen, I beg you to observe these girls:
One has just now lost her mind; the other,
It seems, has never had a mind at all.
    ISMENE. Grief teaches the steadiest minds to waver, King.   150
    CREON. Yours certainly did, when you assumed guilt with the guilty!
    ISMENE. But how could I go on living without her?
    CREON.   You are.
She is already dead.
    ISMENE.   But your own son's bride!
    CREON. There are places enough for him to push his plow.
I want no wicked women for my sons!
    ISMENE. O dearest Haimon, how your father wrongs you!
    CREON. I've had enough of your childish talk of marriage!
    CHORAGOS. Do you really intend to steal this girl from your son?
    CREON. No; Death will do that for me.
    CHORAGOS.   Then she must die?
    CREON [*ironically*]. You dazzle me.
                      —But enough of this talk!   160
[*To* GUARDS.] You, there, take them away and guard them well:
For they are but women, and even brave men run

When they see Death Coming.

[*Exeunt* ISMENE, ANTIGONE, *and* GUARDS.]

ODE II

Strophe 1

CHORUS.   Fortunate is the man who has never tasted God's vengeance!
Where once the anger of heaven has struck, that house is shaken
For ever: damnation rises behind each child
Like a wave cresting out of the black northeast,
When the long darkness under sea roars up
And bursts drumming death upon the windwhipped sand.

Antistrophe 1

I have seen this gathering sorrow from time long past
Loom upon Oedipus' children: generation from generation
Takes the compulsive rage of the enemy god.
So lately this last flower of Oedipus' line   10
Drank the sunlight! but now a passionate word
And a handful of dust have closed up all its beauty.

Strophe 2

What mortal arrogance
Transcends the wrath of Zeus?
Sleep cannot lull him, nor the effortless long months
Of the timeless gods: but he is young for ever,
And his house is the shining day of high Olympos.
All that is and shall be,
And all the past, is his.
No pride on earth is free of the curse of heaven.   20

Antistrophe 2

The straying dreams of men
May bring them ghosts of joy:
But as they drowse, the waking embers burn them;
Or they walk with fixed éyes, as blind men walk.
But the ancient wisdom speaks for our own time:
Fate works most for woe
With Folly's fairest show.
Man's little pleasure is the spring of sorrow.

SCENE III

CHORAGOS.   But here is Haimon, King, the last of all your sons.
Is it grief for Antigone that brings him here,
And bitterness at being robbed of his bride?

[*Enter* HAIMON.]

CREON.   We shall soon see, and no need of diviners.
                                                        —Son,
You have heard my final judgment on that girl:
Have you come here hating me, or have you come
With deference and with love, whatever I do?
   HAIMON.   I am your son, father. You are my guide.
You make things clear for me, and I obey you.
No marriage means more to me than your continuing wisdom.   10
   CREON.   Good. That is the way to behave: subordinate
Everything else, my son, to your father's will.
That is what a man prays for, that he may get
Sons attentive and dutiful in his house,
Each one hating his father's enemies,
Honoring his father's friends. But if his sons
Fail him, if they turn out unprofitably,
What has he fathered but trouble for himself
And amusement for the malicious?
                                      So you are right
Not to lose your head over this woman.   20
Your pleasure with her would soon grow cold, Haimon,
And then you'd have a hellcat in bed and elsewhere.
Let her find her husband in Hell!
Of all the people in this city, only she
Has had contempt for my law and broken it.
Do you want me to show myself weak before the people?
Or to break my sworn word? No, and I will not.
The woman dies.
I suppose she'll plead "family ties." Well, let her.
If I permit my own family to rebel,   30
How shall I earn the world's obedience?
Show me the man who keeps his house in hand,
He's fit for public authority.
                            I'll have no dealings
With law-breakers, critics of the government:
Whoever is chosen to govern should be obeyed—
Must be obeyed, in all things, great and small,
Just and unjust! O Haimon,
The man who knows how to obey, and that man only,
Knows how to give commands when the time comes.
You can depend on him, no matter how fast   40

The spears come: he's a good soldier, he'll stick it out.

Anarchy, anarchy! Show me a greater evil!
This is why cities tumble and the great houses rain down,
This is what scatters armies!

No, no: good lives are made so by discipline.
We keep the laws then, and the lawmakers,
And no woman shall seduce us. If we must lose,
Let's lose to a man, at least! Is a woman stronger than we?
    CHORAGOS.   Unless time has rusted my wits,
What you say, King, is said with point and dignity.   50
    HAIMON [*boyishly earnest*].   Father:
Reason is God's crowning gift to man, and you are right
To warn me against losing mine. I cannot say—
I hope that I shall never want to say!—that you
Have reasoned badly. Yet there are other men
Who can reason, too; and their opinions might be helpful.
You are not in a position to know everything
That people say or do, or what they feel:
Your temper terrifies them—everyone
Will tell you only what you like to hear.   60
But I, at any rate, can listen; and I have heard them
Muttering and whispering in the dark about this girl.
They say no woman has ever, so unreasonably,
Died so shameful a death for a generous act:
"She covered her brother's body. Is this indecent?
She kept him from dogs and vultures. Is this a crime?
Death?—She should have all the honor that we can give her!"

This is the way they talk out there in the city.

You must believe me:
Nothing is closer to me than your happiness.
What could be closer? Must not any son   70
Value his father's fortune as his father does his?
I beg you, do not be unchangeable:
Do not believe that you alone can be right.
The man who thinks that,
The man who maintains that only he has the power
To reason correctly, the gift to speak, the soul—
A man like that, when you know him, turns out empty.

It is not reason never to yield to reason!

In flood time you can see how some trees bend,   80
And because they bend, even their twigs are safe,
While stubborn trees are torn up, roots and all.
And the same thing happens in sailing:
Make your sheet fast, never slacken—and over you go,

Head over heels and under: and there's your voyage.
Forget you are angry! Let yourself be moved!
I know I am young; but please let me say this:
The ideal condition
Would be, I admit, that men should be right by instinct;
But since we are all too likely to go astray,   90
The reasonable thing is to learn from those who can teach.
    CHORAGOS.   You will do well to listen to him, King,
If what he says is sensible. And you, Haimon,
Must listen to your father.—Both speak well.
    CREON.   You consider it right for a man of my years and experience
To go to school to a boy?
    HAIMON.   It is not right
If I am wrong. But if I am young, and right,
What does my age matter?
    CREON.   You think it right to stand up for an anarchist?
    HAIMON.   Not at all. I pay no respect to criminals.   100
    CREON.   Then she is not a criminal?
    HAIMON.   The City would deny it, to a man.
    CREON.   And the City proposes to teach me how to rule?
    HAIMON.   Ah. Who is it that's talking like a boy now?
    CREON.   My voice is the one voice giving orders in this City!
    HAIMON.   It is no City if it takes orders from one voice.
    CREON.   The State is the King!
    HAIMON.   Yes, if the State is a desert.

    [*Pause.*]

    CREON.   This boy, it seems, has sold out to a woman.
    HAIMON.   If you are a woman: my concern is only for you.
    CREON.   So? Your "concern"! In a public brawl with your
father!   110
    HAIMON.   How about you, in a public brawl with justice?
    CREON.   With justice, when all that I do is within my rights?
    HAIMON.   You have no right to trample on God's right.
    CREON [*completely out of control*].   Fool, adolescent fool! Taken in by a
woman!
    HAIMON.   You'll never see me taken in by anything vile.
    CREON.   Every word you say is for her!
    HAIMON [*quickly, darkly*].   And for you.
And for me. And for the gods under the earth.
    CREON.   You'll never marry her while she lives.
    HAIMON.   Then she must die.—But her death will cause another.
    CREON.   Another?   120
Have you lost your senses? Is this an open threat?
    HAIMON.   There is no threat in speaking to emptiness.
    CREON.   I swear you'll regret this superior tone of yours!
You are the empty one!
    HAIMON.   If you were not my father,

I'd say you were perverse.

      CREON.   You girlstruck fool, don't play at words with me!

      HAIMON.   I am sorry. You prefer silence.

      CREON.   Now, by God—!

I swear, by all the gods in heaven above us,

You'll watch it, I swear you shall!

[*To the* SERVANTS]   Bring her out!

Bring the woman out! Let her die before his eyes!   130

Here, this instant, with her bridegroom beside her!

      HAIMON.   Not here, no; she will not die here, King.

And you will never see my face again.

Go on raving as long as you've a friend to endure you.

[Exit HAIMON.*]*

      CHORAGOS.   Gone, gone.

Creon, a young man in a rage is dangerous!

      CREON.   Let him do, or dream to do, more than a man can.

He shall not save these girls from death.

      CHORAGOS.   These girls?

You have sentenced them both?

      CREON.   No, you are right.

I will not kill the one whose hands are clean.   140

      CHORAGOS.   But Antigone?

      CREON [*somberly*].   I will carry her far away

Out there in the wilderness, and lock her

Living in a vault of stone. She shall have food,

As the custom is, to absolve the State of her death.

And there let her pray to the gods of hell:

They are her only gods:

Perhaps they will show her an escape from death,

Or she may learn,

          though late,

That piety shown the dead is pity in vain.   150

[Exit CREON.*]*

ODE III

Strophe

      CHORUS.   Love, unconquerable

Waster of rich men, keeper

Of warm lights and all-night vigil

In the soft face of a girl:

Sea-wanderer, forest-visitor!

Even the pure Immortals cannot escape you,

Any mortal man, in his one day's dusk,
Trembles before your glory.

Antistrophe

Surely you swerve upon ruin
The just man's consenting heart,
As here you have made bright anger
Strike between father and son—
And none has conquered but Love!
A girl's glánce wórking the will of heaven:
Pleasure to her alone who mocks us,
Merciless Aphrodite.[4]

10

SCENE IV

[*As* ANTIGONE *enters guarded.*]

CHORAGOS.   But I can no longer stand in awe of this,
Nor, seeing what I see, keep back my tears.
Here is Antigone, passing to that chamber
Where all find sleep at last.

Strophe 1

ANTIGONE.   Look upon me, friends, and pity me
Turning back at the night's edge to say
Good-by to the sun that shines for me no longer;
Now sleepy Death
Summons me down to Acheron,[5] that cold shore:
There is no bridesong there, nor any music.

10

CHORUS.   Yet not unpraised, not without a kind of honor,
You walk at last into the underworld;
Untouched by sickness, broken by no sword.
What woman has ever found your way to death?

Antistrophe 1

ANTIGONE.   How often I have heard the story of Niobe,[6]
Tantalos' wretched daughter, how the stone
Clung fast about her, ivy-close: and they say
The rain falls endlessly
And sifting soft snow; her tears are never done.
I feel the loneliness of her death in mine

20

---

4. Goddess of love.
5. A river of Hades, the underworld of Greek mythology.
6. Because Niobe, an early queen of Thebes, boasted of her twelve children, the angry gods killed them. Zeus eventually transformed her into a statue which wept perpetually.

CHORUS. But she was born of heaven, and you
Are woman, woman-born. If her death is yours,
A mortal woman's, is this not for you
Glory in our world and in the world beyond?

Strophe 2

ANTIGONE. You laugh at me. Ah, friends, friends,
Can you not wait until I am dead? O Thebes,
O men many-charioted, in love with Fortune,
Dear springs of Dirce, sacred Theban grove,
Be witnesses for me, denied all pity,
Unjustly judged! and think a word of love   30
For her whose path turns
Under dark earth, where there are no more tears.
CHORUS. You have passed beyond human daring and come at last
Into a place of stone where Justice sits.
I cannot tell
What shape of your father's guilt appears in this.

Antistrophe 2

ANTIGONE. You have touched it at last: that bridal bed
Unspeakable, horror of son and mother mingling:
Their crime, infection of all our family!
O Oedipus, father and brother!   40
Your marriage strikes from the grave to murder mine.
I have been a stranger here in my own land:
All my life
The blasphemy of my birth has followed me.
CHORUS. Reverence is a virtue, but strength
Lives in established law: that must prevail.
You have made your choice,
Your death is the doing of your conscious hand.

Epode[7]

ANTIGONE. Then let me go, since all your words are bitter,
And the very light of the sun is cold to me.   50
Lead me to my vigil, where I must have
Neither love nor lamentation; no song, but silence.

[CREON *interrupts impatiently.*]

CREON. If dirges and planned lamentations could put off death,
Men would be singing for ever.
[*To the* SERVANTS]   Take her, go!
You know your orders: take her to the vault

---

7. The third part of the three-part ode, following the strophe and the antistrophe.

And leave her alone there. And if she lives or dies;
That's her affair, not ours; our hands are clean.
      ANTIGONE. O tomb, vaulted bride-bed in eternal rock,
Soon I shall be with my own again
Where Persephone[8] welcomes the thin ghosts underground: 60
And I shall see my father again, and you, mother,
And dearest Polyneices—
                      dearest indeed
To me, since it was my hand
That washed him clean and poured the ritual wine:
And my reward is death before my time!

And yet, as men's hearts know, I have done no wrong,
I have not sinned before God. Or if I have,
I shall know the truth in death. But if the guilt
Lies upon Creon who judged me, then, I pray,
May his punishment equal my own.
      CHORAGOS.   O passionate heart,   70
Unyielding, tormented still by the same winds!
      CREON. Her guards shall have good cause to regret their delaying.
      ANTIGONE. Ah! That voice is like the voice of death!
      CREON. I can give you no reason to think you are mistaken.
      ANTIGONE. Thebes, and you my father's gods,
And rulers of Thebes, you see me now, the last
Unhappy daughter of a line of kings,
Your kings, led away to death. You will remember
Because I would not transgress the laws of heaven.
What things I suffer, and at what men's hands,   80
      [*To the* GUARDS, *simply*] Come: let us wait no longer.

                              [*Exit* ANTIGONE, *L., guarded.*]

ODE IV

Strophe 1

      CHORUS. All Danae's[9] beauty was locked away
In a brazen cell where the sunlight could not come:
A small room, still as any grave, enclosed her.
Yet she was a princess too,
And Zeus in a rain of gold poured love upon her.
O child, child,
No power in wealth or war

---

    8. Queen of the underworld.
    9. An oracle told Danae's father that she would bear a child who would kill him, so he imprisoned
her in a bronze tower. Zeus, however, visited her in a shower of gold, and she gave birth to Perseus, who
fulfilled the prophecy by killing his grandfather.

Or tough sea-blackened ships
Can prevail against untiring Destiny!

Antistrophe 1

And Dryas' son[10] also, that furious king,   10
Bore the god's prisoning anger for his pride:
Sealed up by Dionysos in deaf stone,
His madness died among echoes.
So at the last he learned what dreadful power
His tongue had mocked:
For he had profaned the revels,
And fired the wrath of the nine
Implacable Sisters[11] that love the sound of the flute.

Strophe 2

And old men tell a half-remembered tale[12]
Of horror done where a dark ledge splits the sea   20
And a double surf beats on the gráy shóres:
How a king's new woman, sick
With hatred for the queen he had imprisoned,
Ripped out his two sons' eyes with her bloody hands
While grinning Ares[13] watched the shuttle plunge
Four times: four blind wounds crying for revenge,

Antistrophe 2

Crying, tears and blood mingled.—Piteously born,
Those sons whose mother was of heavenly birth!
Her father was the god of the North Wind
And she was cradled by gales,   30
She raced with young colts on the glittering hills
And walked untrammeled in the open light:
But in her marriage deathless Fate found means
To build a tomb like yours for all her joy.

SCENE V

[*Enter blind* TEIRESIAS,[14] *led by a boy. The opening speeches of* TEIRESIAS *should be in singsong contrast to the realistic lines of* CREON.]

---

10. Lycurgus, King of Thrace, who insulted Dionysos, god of revelry and wine, and who attempted to dissuade the god's followers from worshiping him. Lycurgus was driven insane by the god and was eventually killed.
11. The nine Muses.
12. The second wife of King Phineus of Thrace blinded the king's two sons out of jealousy over his first wife Cleopatra. Daughter of Boreas, god of the North Wind, Cleopatra had been shut up in a cave by Phineus.
13. God of war.
14. Aged prophet who foretold the future by interpreting various signs in nature.

TEIRESIAS. This is the way the blind man comes, Princes, Princes,
Lock-step, two heads lit by the eyes of one.
    CREON. What new thing have you to tell us, old Teiresias?
    TEIRESIAS. I have much to tell you: listen to the prophet, Creon.
    CREON. I am not aware that I have ever failed to listen.
    TEIRESIAS. Then you have done wisely, King, and ruled well.
    CREON. I admit my debt to you. But what have you to say?
    TEIRESIAS. This, Creon: you stand once more on the edge of fate.
    CREON. What do you mean? Your words are a kind of dread.
    TEIRESIAS. Listen, Creon: 10
I was sitting in my chair of augury, at the place
Where the birds gather about me. They were all a-chatter,
As is their habit, when suddenly I heard
A strange note in their jangling, a scream, a
Whirring fury; I knew that they were fighting,
Tearing each other, dying
In a whirlwind of wings clashing. And I was afraid.
I began the rites of burnt-offering at the altar,
But Hephaistos[15] failed me: instead of bright flame,
There was only the sputtering slime of the fat thigh-flesh 20
Melting: the entrails dissolved in gray smoke,
The bare bone burst from the welter. And no blaze!

This was a sign from heaven. My boy described it,
Seeing for me as I see for others.

I tell you, Creon, you yourself have brought
This new calamity upon us. Our hearths and altars
Are stained with the corruption of dogs and carrion birds
That glut themselves on the corpse of Oedipus' son.
The gods are deaf when we pray to them, their fire
Recoils from our offering, their birds of omen 30
Have no cry of comfort, for they are gorged
With the thick blood of the dead.
                O my son,
These are no trifles! Think: all men make mistakes,
But a good man yields when he knows his course is wrong,
And repairs the evil. The only crime is pride.

Give in to the dead man, then: do not fight with a corpse—
What glory is it to kill a man who is dead?
Think, I beg you:
It is for your own good that I speak as I do.
You should be able to yield for your own good. 40

    CREON. It seems that prophets have made me their especial province.
All my life long
I have been a kind of butt for the dull arrows

---

15. God of fire.

Of doddering fortune-tellers!
                          No, Teiresias:
If your birds—if the great eagles of God himself
Should carry him stinking bit by bit to heaven,
I would not yield. I am not afraid of pollution:
No man can defile the gods.
                          Do what you will,
Go into business, make money, speculate
In India gold or that synthetic gold from Sardis,   50
Get rich otherwise than by my consent to bury him.
Teiresias, it is a sorry thing when a wise man
Sells his wisdom, lets out his words for hire!

TEIRESIAS.   Ah Creon! Is there no man left in the world—
CREON.   To do what?—Come, let's have the aphorism!
TEIRESIAS.   No man who knows that wisdom outweighs any wealth?
CREON.   As surely as bribes are baser than any baseness.
TEIRESIAS.   You are sick, Creon! You are deathly sick!
CREON.   As you say: it is not my place to challenge a prophet.
TEIRESIAS.   Yet you have said my prophecy is for sale.   60
CREON.   The generation of prophets has always loved gold.
TEIRESIAS.   The generation of kings has always loved brass.
CREON.   You forget yourself! You are speaking to your King.
TEIRESIAS.   I know it. You are a king because of me.
CREON.   You have a certain skill; but you have sold out.
TEIRESIAS.   King, you will drive me to words that—
CREON.   Say them, say them!
Only remember: I will not pay you for them.
TEIRESIAS.   No, you will find them too costly.
CREON.   No doubt. Speak:
Whatever you say, you will not change my will.
  TEIRESIAS.   Then take this, and take it to heart!   70
The time is not far off when you shall pay back
Corpse for corpse, flesh of your own flesh.
You have thrust the child of this world into living night,
You have kept from the gods below the child that is theirs:
The one in a grave before her death, the other,
Dead, denied the grave. This is your crime:
And the Furies[16] and the dark gods of Hell
Are swift with terrible punishment for you.

Do you want to buy me now, Creon?

                          Not many days,
And your house will be full of men and women weeping,   80
And curses will be hurled at you from far
Cities grieving for sons unburied, left to rot
Before the walls of Thebes.

---

16. Goddesses of vengeance who punished certain crimes, especially those involving blood relations.

These are my arrows, Creon: they are all for you.

[*To* BOY] But come, child: lead me home.
Let him waste his fine anger upon younger men.
Maybe he will learn at last
To control a wiser tongue in a better head.

[*Exit* TEIRESIAS.]

CHORAGOS.   The old man has gone, King, but his words
Remain to plague us. I am old, too,   90
But I cannot remember that he was ever false.
    CREON.   That is true. . . . It troubles me.
Oh it is hard to give in! but it is worse
To risk everything for stubborn pride.
    CHORAGOS.   Creon: take my advice.
    CREON.   What shall I do?
    CHORAGOS.   Go quickly: free Antigone from her vault
And build a tomb for the body of Polyneices.
    CREON.   You would have me do this?
    CHORAGOS.   Creon, yes!
And it must be done at once: God moves
Swiftly to cancel the folly of stubborn men.   100
    CREON.   It is hard to deny the heart! But I
Will do it: I will not fight with destiny.
    CHORAGOS.   You must go yourself, you cannot leave it to others.
    CREON.   I will go.
                    —Bring axes, servants:
Come with me to the tomb. I buried her, I
Will set her free.
                Oh, quickly!
My mind misgives—
The laws of the gods are mighty, and a man must serve them
To the last day of his life!

[*Exit* CREON.]

PAEAN[17]

Strophe 1

CHORAGOS.   God of many names
CHORUS.   O Iacchos[18]
                                        son

—————
17. A hymn sung to the gods.
18. Also known as Dionysos, son of Zeus ("the Thunderer") and of Sémele, daughter of Kadmos,
founder and first king of Thebes. Dionysos was honored at rituals held on the plain of Eleusis, near
Athens. The Maenads were his female worshipers, who shouted "'Evohé" and "Io" during their wild
celebrations.

of Kadmeian Sémele
O born of the Thunder!
Guardian of the West
Regent
of Eleusis' plain
O Prince of maenad Thebes
and the Dragon Field by rippling Ismenos:[19]

Antistrophe 1

CHORAGOS. God of many names
CHORUS. the flame of torches
flares on our hills
the nymphs of Iacchos
dance at the spring of Castalia:[20]
from the vine-close mountain
come ah come in ivy:
Evohé evohé! sings through the streets of Thebes   10

Strophe 2

CHORAGOS. God of many names
CHORUS. Iacchos of Thebes
heavenly Child
of Sémele bride of the Thunderer!
The shadow of plague is upon us:
come
with clement feet
oh come from Parnasos
down the long slopes
across the lamenting water

Antistrophe 2

CHORAGOS. Io Fire! Chorister of the throbbing stars!
O purest among the voices of the night!
Thou son of God, blaze for us!
CHORUS. Come with choric rapture of circling Maenads
Who cry *Io Iacche!*
God of many names!   20

EXODOS[21]

[*Enter* MESSENGER, *L.*]

---

19. A river near Thebes. In a nearby field Kadmos had slain a sacred dragon and sown its teeth, from which sprang the ancestors of the nobility of Thebes.
20. Spring on Mount Parnasos, the abode of Apollo and the Muses.
21. The last scene following the final ode.

MESSENGER.   Men of the line of Kadmos, you who live
Near Amphion's citadel[22]
                              I cannot say
Of any condition of human life "This is fixed,
This is clearly good, or bad." Fate raises up,
And Fate casts down the happy and unhappy alike:
No man can foretell his fate.
                              Take the case of Creon:
Creon was happy once, as I count happiness:
Victorious in battle, sole governor of the land,
Fortunate father of children nobly born.
And now it has all gone from him! Who can say   10
That a man is still alive when his life's joy fails?
He is a walking dead man. Grant him rich,
Let him live like a king in his great house:
If his pleasure is gone, I would not give
So much as the shadow of smoke for all he owns.
   ·CHORAGOS.   Your words hint at sorrow: what is your news for us?
   MESSENGER.   They are dead. The living are guilty of their death.
   CHORAGOS.   Who is guilty? Who is dead? Speak!
   MESSENGER.   Haimon.
Haimon is dead; and the hand that killed him
Is his own hand.
   CHORAGOS.   His father's? or his own?   20
   MESSENGER.   His own, driven mad by the murder his father had done.
   CHORAGOS.   Teiresias, Teiresias, how clearly you saw it all!
   MESSENGER.   This is my news: you must draw what conclusions you can
from it.
   CHORAGOS.   But look: Eurydice, our Queen:
Has she overheard us?

[*Enter* EURYDICE *from the Palace, C.*]

   EURYDICE.   I have heard something, friends:
As I was unlocking the gate of Pallas'[23] shrine,
For I needed her help today, I heard a voice
Telling of some new sorrow. And I fainted
There at the temple with all my maidens about me.   30
But speak again: whatever it is, I can bear it:
Grief and I are no strangers.
   MESSENGER.   Dearest Lady,
I will tell you plainly all that I have seen.
I shall not try to comfort you: what is the use,
Since comfort could lie only in what is not true?
The truth is always best.
                          I went with Creon

---

22. Amphion's lute-playing was so melodious that it moved huge stones into forming the fortified
lower part of Thebes.
23. Pallas Athene, goddess of wisdom.

To the outer plain where Polyneices was lying,
No friend to pity him, his body shredded by dogs.
We made our prayers in that place to Hecate
And Pluto,[24] that they would be merciful. And we bathed   40
The corpse with holy water, and we brought
Fresh-broken branches to burn what was left of it,
And upon the urn we heaped up a towering barrow
Of the earth of his own land.
                         When we were done, we ran
To the vault where Antigone lay on her couch of stone.
One of the servants had gone ahead,
And while he was yet far off he heard a voice
Grieving within the chamber, and he came back
And told Creon. And as the King went closer,
The air was full of wailing, the words lost,   50
And he begged us to make all haste. "Am I a prophet?"
He said, weeping, "And must I walk this road,
The saddest of all that I have gone before?
My son's voice calls me on. Oh quickly, quickly!
Look through the crevice there, and tell me
If it is Haimon, or some deception of the gods!"
We obeyed; and in the cavern's farthest corner
We saw her lying:
She had made a noose of her fine linen veil
And hanged herself. Haimon lay beside her,   60
His arms about her waist, lamenting her,
His love lost under ground, crying out
That his father had stolen her away from him.
When Creon saw him the tears rushed to his eyes
And he called to him: "What have you done, child? Speak to me.
What are you thinking that makes your eyes so strange?
O my son, my son, I come to you on my knees!"
But Haimon spat in his face. He said not a word,
Staring—
            And suddenly drew his sword
And lunged. Creon shrank back, the blade missed; and the boy,   70
Desperate against himself, drove it half its length
Into his own side, and fell. And as he died
He gathered Antigone close in his arms again,
Choking, his blood bright red on her white cheek.
And now he lies dead with the dead, and she is his
At last, his bride in the houses of the dead.

                        [*Exit* Eurydice *into the Palace.*]

CHORAGOS.   She has left us without a word. What can this mean?
MESSENGER.   It troubles me, too; yet she knows what is best,

---

24. Hecate was one of the goddesses of the underworld; Pluto was its supreme god.

Her grief is too great for public lamentation,
And doubtless she has gone to her chamber to weep   80
For her dead son, leading her maidens in his dirge.
    CHORAGOS.   It may be so: but I fear this deep silence.

[*Pause.*]

    MESSENGER.   I will see what she is doing. I will go in.

[*Exit* MESSENGER *into the Palace.*]

[*Enter* CREON *with attendants, bearing* HAIMON'S *body.*]

    CHORAGOS.   But here is the King himself: oh look at him,
Bearing his own damnation in his arms.
    CREON.   Nothing you say can touch me any more.
My own blind heart has brought me
From darkness to final darkness. Here you see
The father murdering, the murdered son—
And all my civic wisdom!   90

Haimon my son, so young, so young to die,
I was the fool, not you; and you died for me.
    CHORAGOS.   That is the truth; but you were late in learning it.
    CREON.   This truth is hard to bear. Surely a god
Has crushed me beneath the hugest weight of heaven.
And driven me headlong a barbaric way
To trample out the thing I held most dear.

The pains that men will take to come to pain!

[*Enter* MESSENGER *from the Palace.*]

    MESSENGER.   The burden you carry in your hands is heavy,
But it is not all: you will find more in your house.   100
    CREON.   What burden worse than this shall I find there?
    MESSENGER.   The Queen is dead.
    CREON.   O port of death, deaf world,
Is there no pity for me? And you, Angel of evil,
I was dead, and your words are death again.
Is it true, boy? Can it be true?
Is my wife dead? Has death bred death?
    MESSENGER.   You can see for yourself.

[*The doors are opened, and the body of* EURYDICE *is disclosed within.*]

    CREON.   Oh pity!
All true, all true, and more than I can bear!   110
O my wife, my son!

MESSENGER. She stood before the altar, and her heart
Welcomed the knife her own hand guided,
And a great cry burst from her lips for Megareus[25] dead,
And for Haimon dead, her sons; and her last breath
Was a curse for their father, the murderer of her sons.
And she fell, and the dark flowed in through her closing eyes.
    CREON. O God, I am sick with fear.
Are there no swords here? Has no one a blow for me?
    MESSENGER. Her curse is upon you for the deaths of both.   120
    CREON. It is right that it should be. I alone am guilty.
I know it, and I say it. Lead me in,
Quickly, friends.
I have neither life nor substance. Lead me in.
    CHORAGOS. You are right, if there can be right in so much wrong.
The briefest way is best in a world of sorrow.
    CREON. Let it come,
Let death come quickly, and be kind to me.
I would not ever see the sun again.
    CHORAGOS. All that will come when it will; but we, meanwhile,   130
Have much to do. Leave the future to itself.
    CREON. All my heart was in that prayer!
    CHORAGOS. Then do not pray any more: the sky is deaf.
    CREON. Lead me away. I have been rash and foolish.
I have killed my son and my wife.
I look for comfort; my comfort lies here dead.
Whatever my hands have touched has come to nothing.
Fate has brought all my pride to a thought of dust.

[*As* CREON *is being led into the house, the* CHORAGOS *advances and speaks directly to the audience.*]

    CHORAGOS. There is no happiness where there is no wisdom;
No wisdom but in submission to the gods.   140
Big words are always punished,
And proud men in old age learn to be wise.

---

25. One of Creon's sons; he sacrificed himself to Ares in order to spare Thebes from Polyneices' attack.

Anton Chekhov (1860–1904)
The Cherry Orchard
A Comedy in Four Acts

Characters[1]

LYUBOV ANDREYEVNA RANEVSKY, *a landowner*
ANYA, *her daughter, aged 17*
VARYA, *her adopted daughter, aged 27*
LEONID ANDREYEVICH GAYEV, *brother of* Lyubov Andreyevna
YERMOLAY ALEXEICH LOPAKHIN, *a merchant*
PETR SERGEICH TROFIMOV, *a student*
BORIS BORISOVICH SEMEONOV-PISHCHIK, *a landowner*
CHARLOTTA IVANOVNA, *a governess*
SEMEN PANTALEYEVICH EPIKHODOV, *a clerk*
DUNYASHA, *a maid*
FIRS, *the butler, an old man of 87*
YASHA, *a young footman*
A WAYFARER
THE STATION MASTER
A POST-OFFICE OFFICIAL
GUESTS *and* SERVANTS

SCENE: *The country estate of* LYUBOV ANDREYEVNA RANEVSKY

ACT I

A room that is still called the nursery. One of the doors leads into ANYA'S room. Day is breaking. The sun will soon rise. It is May, and the cherry tress are in bloom, but it is cold in the orchard, and a light frost lies on the ground. The windows in the room are closed. DUNYASHA enters with a candle, and LOPAKHIN with a book in his hand.

LOPAKHIN. The train has come, thank Heaven! What time is it?

---

1. At the time of the play, Russians used various forms and combinations of their names in different circumstances: for formal occasions and relationships, the title and surname (Madame Ranevsky); for less formal circumstances, the given mame (Lyubov) and the patronymic, a name derived from a father or from a paternal ancestor (Andreyevna); for affectionate relationships, the given name only; and for intimate or for contemptuously familiar circumstances, a diminutive of the given name (Lyuba).

DUNYASHA. Almost two o'clock. [*Blows out the candle.*] It's beginning to get light already.

LOPAKHIN. How late was the train, anyway? At least a couple of hours. [*Yawns and stretches.*] I'm a fine one! I surely made a fool of myself. Here I came over on purpose to meet them at the station, and then all at once I fell asleep . . . sitting up! What a nuisance! . . . You might have waked me.

DUNYASHA. I thought you had gone. [*Listens.*] I think they're coming now.

LOPAKHIN [*listens*]. No, they have to collect their baggage and so forth. [*Pause.*] Lyubov Andreyevna has been living abroad now for five years, and I don't know how she may have changed. She's a good soul, a simple, easy-going woman. I remember when I was a young sprout, fifteen years old, my father— he's dead now, but he used to have a little shop in the village then—struck me in the face with his fist one day, and my nose began to bleed. We'd gone out of doors together for some reason or other and he was drunk. I remember just as though it were now, how Lyubov Andreyevna—she was still a slim young thing—led me over to the washbasin here in this very room, the nursery. "Come, come, don't cry your eyes away; you'll live to dance on your wedding day, little peasant," says she. [*Pause.*] Little peasant! . . . True, my father was a peasant, and here I am wearing a white waistcoat and yellow shoes. From the sow's ear to the silk purse. . . . I've grown rich, made a lot of money, but when you come to think of it, to figure it out, I'm still a peasant. . . . [*Fingers the pages of the book.*] Here I've been reading this book, and haven't understood a word of it. I fell asleep reading. [*Pause.*]

DUNYASHA. Even the dogs haven't slept all night long. They seem to feel their masters are returning.

LOPAKHIN. What's the matter with you, Dunyasha? You're so . . .

DUNYASHA. My hands are trembling. I'm going to faint.

LOPAKHIN. You're a tender, spoiled little thing, Dunyasha. Why, you even dress like a lady, and comb your hair to match. It's not right. You ought to remember your place.

[EPIKHODOV *enters, carrying a bouquet. He wears a short coat, and highly polished boots, which squeak loudly. As he enters, he drops the bouquet.*]

EPIKHODOV [*picking up the bouquet*]. The gardener sent these, and said to put them in the dining-room. [*Hands the bouquet to* DUNYASHA.]

LOPAKHIN. And bring me some kvass.[2]

DUNYASHA. Yes, sir. [*Goes out.*]

EPIKHODOV. There's a frost this morning. Six degrees below freezing, and the cherry trees all in bloom. I can't praise our climate. [*Sighs.*] No, that I can't. It won't favor us even this once. Just listen to this, Yermolay Alexeich—I bought myself some boots day before yesterday, and I tell you, they squeak so loudly you wouldn't believe it. What shall I grease them with?

LOPAKHIN. Leave me alone. I'm sick of you.

EPIKHODOV. Every day some bad luck or other overtakes me, but I don't grumble. I'm used to it. I just smile.

---

2. Mild Russian beer.

[DUNYASHA *enters and hands* LOPAKHIN *the kvass.*]

EPIKHODOV. I'm going. [*Stumbles against a chair, knocking it over.*] There! . . . [*With apparent triumph.*] There, if you'll pardon the expression, you see the kind of circumstance that pursues me. This is positively remarkable. [*Goes out.*]

DUNYASHA. Did you know, Yermolay Alexeich, Epikhodov's made me a proposal?

LOPAKHIN. Aha!

DUNYASHA. I don't know how to . . . He's a quiet sort of fellow, only sometimes when he begins talking, you can't make out a word. It's first-rate and full of feeling, only you can't understand it. I half like him, too. He's madly in love with me. An unlucky man. Something goes wrong with him every day. We tease him, and call him two-and-twenty troubles.

LOPAKHIN [*listening*]. I think they're coming now.

DUNYASHA. Coming! What's the matter with me! . . . I'm all goose-flesh!

LOPAKHIN. They're really coming. Let's go out and meet them. Will she recognize me? It's five years since we've seen each other.

DUNYASHA [*in agitation*]. I'm going to faint. . . . Oh, I'm going to faint!

[*Two carriages are heard drawing up to the house.* LOPAKHIN *and* DUNYASHA *go out quickly. The stage remains empty. There is noise and stir in the adjoining room. Across the stage, leaning on his stick, hastens* FIRS, *who has met* LYUBOV ANDREYEVNA *at the station. He wears an old-fashioned livery and a tall hat. He is muttering to himself, but not a word is distinguishable. The noise behind the scenes continually increases. A voice is heard, saying, "Come in this way. . . ."* LYUBOV ANDREYEVNA, ANYA, *and* CHARLOTTA IVANOVNA, *all wearing traveling clothes, cross the room, accompanied by* VARYA, *clad in a heavy coat and kerchief,* GAYEV, SEMEONOV-PISHCHIK, LOPAKHIN, DUNYASHA, *with a bundle and an umbrella, and a servant carrying the bags.* CHARLOTTA IVANOVNA *is leading a little dog by a chain.*]

ANYA. Let's come in here. Do you remember this room, mama?

LYUBOV ANDREYEVNA [*joyfully, through her tears*]. The nursery!

VARYA. It's so cold my hands are numb. [*To* LYUBOV ANDREYEVNA.] Mama, your rooms, the white one and the lavender, have been left just as they were.

LYUBOV ANDREYEVNA. The nursery, my dear, beautiful room! . . . It was here I slept when I was little. . . . [*Weeps.*] And now I feel as though I were a little child again. . . . [*Kisses her brother, then* VARYA, *and then her brother once more.*] And Varya hasn't changed a bit—she's just like a little nun. And if here isn't Dunyasha. [*She kisses* DUNYASHA.]

GAYEV. The train was two hours late. How did it happen? Do you call that punctuality?

CHARLOTTA [*to* PISHCHIK]. My dog even eats nuts.

PISHCHIK [*surprised*]. Just think of that!

[*They all go out, with the exception of* ANYA *and* DUNYASHA.]

DUNYASHA. Here you are at last. . . . [*She takes off* ANYA'S *hat and coat.*]

ANYA. I didn't sleep the four nights we were on the road. . . . Now I'm chilled through.

DUNYASHA. You went away during Lent. There was snow on the ground then, there was frost—and now? My darling! [*Laughs and kisses* ANYA.] I've waited for you so long, my joy, my dear one. . . . I must tell you right now; I can't keep it a minute longer. . . .

ANYA [*listlessly*]. What now? . . .

DUNYASHA. Epikhodov, the clerk, made me a proposal right after Easter.

ANYA. Always harping on the same thing. . . . [*Arranges her hair.*] I've lost all my hairpins. . . . [*She is very tired, can hardly stand.*]

DUNYASHA. I'm all of a flutter. He loves me—he loves me so!

ANYA [*glancing tenderly through the door into her own room*]. My room, my windows—just as though I had never gone away. I'm at home! To-morrow morning I shall get up and run out into the orchard. . . . Oh, if I could only sleep! During the whole journey I couldn't sleep a wink. I was restless.

DUNYASHA. Petr Sergeich arrived day before yesterday.

ANYA [*joyfully*]. Petya!

DUNYASHA. He's sleeping in the bath house, and living there too. He says he's afraid he'll inconvenience us. [*Looks at her watch.*] I'd wake him up, but Varvara Mikhailovna told me not to. "Don't waken him," said she.

[VARYA *comes in with a bunch of keys at her belt.*]

VARYA. Dunyasha, bring us some coffee right away. . . . Mama's asking for it.

DUNYASHA. Right away. [*Goes out.*]

VARYA. Well, thank Heaven, you're here! Once more you are at home. [*Caressing* ANYA.] My darling is here! My pretty one has come home!

ANYA. I was impatient, too.

VARYA. I can just imagine!

ANYA. I left home during Holy Week. It was cold then. Charlotta talked all the way, and did tricks. Why, why did you tie me to Charlotta's apron strings?

VARYA. You couldn't have traveled alone, my dear. Seventeen years old!

ANYA. When we arrived in Paris, it was cold. There was snow on the ground. I speak French horribly. Mama was living on the fifth floor. I went to find her. There were a few Frenchmen there, and some ladies, and an old priest with a prayer book, and it was full of tobacco smoke and uncomfortable. Suddenly I became sorry for mama, so sorry. I hugged her head, squeezed it tight, and could not let her go. And after that mama kept caressing me and weeping. . . .

VARYA [*through her tears*]. Don't tell me any more, don't! . . .

ANYA. She'd already sold her country house near Mentone.[3] She had nothing left, nothing. And I didn't have a kopek[4] left—we just managed to get

---

3. Small town on the French Riviera.
4. Roughly equivalent to one cent; 100 kopecks equal one ruble.

there. But mama doesn't realize! We had dinner at the station, and she ordered the most expensive things, and tipped the servants a ruble apiece. Charlotta did too. And Yasha demands his share also: it's just awful! You know mama has a footman—Yasha. We brought him back with us.

VARYA. I saw the good-for-nothing.

ANYA. Well, how are things? Is the interest paid up?

VARYA. Not much!

ANYA. Good heavens, how awful!

VARYA. The estate will be sold in August.

ANYA. God help us!

LOPAKHIN [*looks through the door and moos*]. Moo-oo-oo! [*Withdraws.*]

VARYA [*through her tears*]. I'd like to give him that! . . . [*Shakes her fist.*]

ANYA [*softly, embracing* VARYA]. Varya, has he proposed to you? [*Varya shakes her head.*] But he does love you. . . . Why don't you both speak out plainly? What are you waiting for?

VARYA. I don't believe anything will come of it. His business takes up so much of his interest—he hasn't time for me. . . . And he doesn't pay any attention to me. Deuce take him anyhow, I'm tired of seeing him. . . . Every one's talking about our marriage, wishing us well—but there's really nothing at all in it. It's like a dream. . . . [*In another tone.*] You have a little brooch shaped like a bee.

ANYA [*sadly*]. Mama bought it for me. [*Goes into her own room and calls back in a happy, childlike voice.*] While I was in Paris I went up in a balloon!

VARYA. My darling has come home! My pretty one is here!

[DUNYASHA *has already returned with the coffeepot, and is making coffee.*]

VARYA [*standing near the door*]. All day long, my darling, I go to and fro, looking after the housekeeping and daydreaming. We must marry you to a rich man, and then I'd be easier in my mind. I'd go to some hermitage, then to Kiev, then to Moscow. I'd go from one holy shrine to another. . . . I'd wander and wander. . . . How lovely! . . .

ANYA. The birds are singing in the orchard. What time is it now?

VARYA. It must be three. It's time for you to sleep, my darling. [*Going into* ANYA'S *room.*] How lovely!

[YASHA *comes in with a steamer rug and a traveling bag.*]

YASHA [*tiptoeing across the stage*]. May I come through this way?

DUNYASHA. Why, I wouldn't have recognized you, Yasha. You've changed so while you were abroad.

YASHA. Hm. . . . And who are you?

DUNYASHA. When you went away, I was just so high. . . . [*Holds out her hand.*] I'm Dunyasha, Fedor Kozoyedov's daughter. Don't you remember?

YASHA. Hm. . . . Little cucumber! [*Glances hastily around and embraces her. She screams and drops a saucer.* YASHA *goes out hurriedly.*]

VARYA [*in the doorway, annoyed*]. What's the matter here?

DUNYASHA [*through her tears*]. I broke a saucer.

VARYA. That's good luck.

ANYA [*emerging from her room*]. We must warn mama. Petya is here. . . .

VARYA. I told them not to wake him.

ANYA [*musingly*]. Six years ago father died, and a month later brother Grisha was drowned in the river—such a darling little seven-year-old boy. Mama couldn't stand the shock; she went away, went away without looking behind her. . . . [*Shudders.*] How I understand her, if she only knew it! [*Pause.*] And Petya Trofimov was Grisha's tutor—he may remind her. . . .

[FIRS *comes in. He wears a waiter's jacket and a white waistcoat.*]

FIRS [*going over to the coffeepot with a preoccupied air*]. The Mistress is going to eat in here. [*Puts on his white gloves.*] Is the coffee ready? [*To* DUNYASHA *sternly.*] You there! Where's the cream?

DUNYASHA. Oh, good Lord! [*She goes out hurriedly.*]

FIRS [*bustling around the coffee pot*]. Eh, you're a lummox. . . . [*Mutters to himself.*] So they're back from Paris. . . . The Master visited Paris once too . . . in a coach and four. . . . [*Laughs.*]

VARYA. What are you saying, Firs?

FIRS. Beg pardon? [*Joyfully.*] My Lady's come home! I've lived to see it. I might as well die now. [*Weeps with joy.*]

[LYUBOV ANDREYEVNA, GAYEV, *and* SEMEONOV-PISHCHIK *come in.* SEMEONOV-PISHCHIK *wears a sleeveless coat of light-weight material, and loose trousers.* GAYEV, *as he enters, goes through the motions of a pool player.*]

LYUBOV ANDREYEVNA. How does it go? Let me see if I can remember! Yellow into the corner! Cross the table to the center![5]

GAYEV. Graze it into the corner! You and I, sister, slept here in this very room once, and now I'm fifty-one, strange though it may seem. . . .

LOPAKHIN. Yes, time flies.

GAYEV. What's that?

LOPAKHIN. I say, time flies.

GAYEV. It smells of patchouli[6] in here.

ANYA. I'm going to bed. Good night, mama. [*Kisses her mother.*]

LYUBOV ANDREYEVNA. My darling girlie! [*Kisses her hands.*] Are you glad to be home? Somehow I can't calm myself.

ANYA. Good night, uncle.

GAYEV [*kissing her face and hands*]. God bless you! How you resemble your mother! [*To his sister.*] Lyuba, at her age, you were just like her.

[ANYA *gives her hand to* LOPAKHIN *and* PISHCHIK, *and goes out of the room, closing the door behind her.*]

LYUBOV ANDREYEVNA. She is very tired.

---

5. Descriptions of billiard shots. Throughout the play, Gayev alludes to many others.
6. Heavily scented perfume sometimes used by men as shaving lotion.

PISHCHIK.   It must have been a long journey.

VARYA [*to* LOPAKHIN *and* PISHCHIK].   Well, gentlemen? It's past two o'clock. Time to be decent.

LYUBOV ANDREYEVNA [*laughing*].   You are still the same Varya. [*Draws* VARYA *close and kisses her.*] See, I'll drink my coffee and then we'll all disperse. [FIRS *places a cushion under her feet.*] Thank you, my friend. I've become addicted to coffee. I drink it day and night. Thank you, dear old man. [*Kisses him.*]

VARYA.   I'll go and see whether they've brought in all your things. [*Goes out.*]

LYUBOV ANDREYEVNA.   Is it really I sitting here? [*Laughs.*] I want to wave my arms and jump for joy. [*Covers her face with her hands.*] And all of a sudden I drop off dozing! God knows, I love my country, I love it dearly. I couldn't look through the train window—I cried all the time. [*Through her tears.*] However, I must drink the coffee. Thank you, Firs. Thank you, dear old man. I am so glad you are still alive.

FIRS.   Day before yesterday.

GAYEV.   He is hard of hearing.

LOPAKHIN.   I must leave shortly, between four and five, for Harkov. What a nuisance! I wanted to have a look at you, and to chat a little. . . . You are just as handsome as ever.

PISHCHIK [*breathing heavily*].   She's even more beautiful. She's dressed Paris style. "This is more than we could hope for, most astonishingly fine."

LOPAKHIN.   Your brother there, Leonid Andreich, says I'm a low sort of fellow, a skinflint, but that doesn't bother me. Let him talk. I only want you to have faith in me as before, to see your marvelous, touching eyes look upon me as they used to. God is merciful! My father was the serf of your grandfather and your father, but you, you yourself, once did so much for me that I have forgotten all old wrongs, and love you as though you were my own kin—no, even more.

LYUBOV ANDREYEVNA.   I can't sit still—I simply can't. . . . [*She springs up and walks about excitedly.*] I cannot survive this joy. . . . Laugh at me—I'm a silly woman. . . . My darling bookcase! . . . [*Kisses the bookcase.*] My desk! . . .

GAYEV.   Nurse died during your absence.

LYUBOV ANDREYEVNA [*sits down and drinks her coffee.*].   Yes, God rest her soul! They wrote me about it.

GAYEV.   And Anastasy died. Petrushka Kosoy has left me, and is living in the city now at the Police Inspector's house. [*Takes a little box of lozenges out of his pocket and sucks one.*]

PISHCHIK.   My daughter Dashenka . . . sends you her regards.

LOPAKHIN.   I have something very pleasant and heartening to tell you. [*Looks at his watch.*] I must go at once—there's no time to explain it. . . . Oh, well, here it is in a nutshell. You know already that your cherry orchard is to be sold for debts, and that the auction has been set for the twenty-second of August. But don't you worry, dear lady, put your mind at rest—there's a way out. . . . Here's my proposition: let me have your attention. Your estate is situated only thirteen miles from the city, the railroad runs past it, and if the cherry orchard and the land along the river were divided into plots for cottages and then leased, you would get an annual return of at least twenty-five thousand rubles.

GAYEV. Pardon me, what utter nonsense!

LYUBOV ANDREYEVNA. I don't understand you at all, Yermolay Alexeich.

LOPAKHIN. You'll receive from the cottagers annually at least twenty-five rubles per desyatina,[7] and if you advertise it now, I'll wager anything you please that you won't have a vacant plot left by autumn. They'll all be taken. In short—I congratulate you—you're saved! The site is marvelous, the river deep. Only, of course, you'll have to fix it up a bit, clear it off. . . . Tear down all the old buildings—for instance, this house, which is no use to any one now, cut down the old cherry orchard—

LYUBOV ANDREYEVNA. Cut it down? My dear friend, forgive me, but you don't understand at all. If there is anything interesting—I might say remarkable—in our province it is our cherry orchard.

LOPAKHIN. The orchard is remarkable only for its size. The cherries ripen only every other year, and even then there's no way to dispose of them. Nobody buys them.

GAYEV. Even the encyclopedia mentions this cherry orchard.

LOPAKHIN [*looking at his watch*]. Unless we devise some plan and arrive at a definite decision, the cherry orchard and the entire estate will be sold at auction on the twenty-second of August. Make up your minds then! I assure you there's no other alternative. There is absolutely none!

FIRS. In times past, forty or fifty years ago, they used to dry the cherries, preserve them, and spice them; they made jam of them, and sometimes—

GAYEV. Be quiet, Firs.

FIRS. And sometimes they sent the dried cherries by cartloads to Moscow and Harkov. Ah, they brought in the money! And the dried cherries were soft, moist, sweet, fragrant. . . . They knew a way then. . . .

LYUBOV ANDREYEVNA. But who has the recipe now?

FIRS. They've forgotten how. No one remembers it.

PISHCHIK [*to* LYUBOV ANDREYEVNA]. What did you do in Paris? Tell us! Did you eat frogs?

LYUBOV ANDREYEVNA. I ate crocodiles.

PISHCHIK. Just think of that! . . .

LOPAKHIN. Only gentry and peasants have lived in the country prior to our time, but now the cottager makes his appearance. Every city—even the smallest—is now surrounded by cottages. And one may safely foretell that within twenty years the number of cottagers will have increased remarkably. Now he only drinks tea on the balcony, but the time may come when he will busy himself with farming on his one desyatina, and then your cherry orchard will become joyous, rich, and luxuriant. . . .

GAYEV [*becoming indignant*]. What nonsense!

[VARYA *and* YASHA *come in.*]

VARYA. There are two telegrams for you here, mama. [*She takes out a key and opens the squeaking lock of the old bookcase.*] Here they are.

---

7. Area of land roughly equivalent to 2.5 acres.

LYUBOV ANDREYEVNA.   They're from Paris. [*Tears them across without reading them.*] I am through with Paris. . . .

GAYEV.   Do you know, Lyuba, how old this bookcase is? A week ago I pulled out the bottom drawer, and there I saw figures burned into the wood. This bookcase was made just a hundred years ago. What do you think of that, eh? We ought to celebrate its jubilee. It's an inanimate object, but just the same, say what you will, it's a fine old bookcase.

PISHCHIK [*surprised*].   A hundred years! . . . Just think of that!

GAYEV.   Yes. . . . This object. . . . [*Laying his hand on the bookcase.*] Dear, venerated bookcase! I greet thine existence, which for more than a hundred years now has been consecrated to the bright ideals of goodness and justice; thy mute summons to fruitful labor has grown no weaker during the course of these hundred years, as thou hast upheld through generations of our stock [*Tearfully.*] courage, faith in a better future, and hast developed within us ideals of goodness and social conscience. [*Pause.*]

LOPAKHIN.   Yes. . . .

LYUBOV ANDREYEVNA.   You haven't changed a bit, Lenya.

GAYEV [*somewhat confused*].   Right ball to the corner pocket! Close shot to the center!

LOPAKHIN [*looking at his watch*].   Well, it's time for me to go.

YASHA [*handing LYUBOV ANDREYEVNA a vial*].   You must take your pills now. . . .

PISHCHIK.   You shouldn't take medicine, my dear. It does you neither harm nor good. . . . Give it to me, most honored lady. [*Takes the pills, pours them out on his palm, blows on them, puts them in his mouth and drinks some kvass.*] There now!

LYUBOV ANDREYEVNA [*frightened*].   Why, you're crazy!

PISHCHIK.   I swallowed every pill.

LOPAKHIN.   What a glutton! [*They all laugh.*]

FIRS.   He was at our house on Easter, and ate half a gallon of cucumbers. . . . [*Mutters.*]

LYUBOV ANDREYEVNA.   What is he talking about?

VARYA.   He's been mumbling that way for ten years now. We've grown used to it.

YASHA.   In his dotage.

[CHARLOTTA IVANOVNA, *a very thin, tightly-laced woman, dressed in white, and with a lorgnette*[8] *at her waist, crosses the stage.*]

LOPAKHIN.   Excuse me, Charlotta Ivanovna, I haven't had a chance yet to greet you. [*Tries to kiss her hand.*]

CHARLOTTA [*drawing away her hand*].   If I let you kiss my hand, you'll want to kiss my elbow next, then my shoulder. . . .

LOPAKHIN.   I'm out of luck to-day. [*All laugh.*] Charlotta Ivanovna, show us a trick!

LYUBOV ANDREYEVNA.   Charlotta, show us a trick!

---

8. A pair of eyeglasses with a handle.

CHARLOTTA. Not I. I'm too sleepy. [*Goes out.*]

LOPAKHIN. I'll see you again in three weeks. [*Kisses the hand of* LYUBOV ANDREYEVNA.] In the meantime, good-by. [*To* GAYEV] Time to go. Good-by. [*Exchanges kisses with* PISHCHIK.] Goodby. [*Gives his hand to* VARYA, *then to* FIRS *and* YASHA.] I don't want to leave. [*To* LYUBOV ANDREYEVNA.] If you can come to a decision regarding the subdivision, and make up your mind, let me know. I'll get you a loan of fifty thousand. Think it over seriously.

VARYA [*angrily*]. Do go and be done with it!

LOPAKHIN. I'm going, I'm going. [*He goes out.*]

GAYEV. A low fellow, that. But no—your pardon! . . . Varya's going to marry him. That's Varya's suitor.

VARYA. Don't talk nonsense, uncle.

LYUBOV ANDREYEVNA. Why, Varya, I should be very glad. He's a good man.

PISHCHIK. A most worthy man, one must admit. . . . Even my Dashenka . . . says also that . . . she says a lot . . . [*Snores, but rouses himself immediately.*] But still, dear lady, loan me two hundred and forty rubles . . . to pay the interest on our mortgage.

VARYA [*frightened*]. We haven't any, we haven't!

LYUBOV ANDREYEVNA. Really, I haven't any money.

PISHCHIK. You'll find some. [*Laughs.*] I never lose hope. Here I used to think that everything was lost, ruined, and then—the railroad was built across my land, and . . . they paid me. And so, just watch and see—something else will turn up, if not to-day, then to-morrow. . . . Dashenka is going to win two hundred thousand. . . . She has a lottery ticket.

LYUBOV ANDREYEVNA. The coffee's all gone. We can go to bed.

FIRS [*in a lecturing tone, as he brushes off* GAYEV]. You've put on the wrong trousers again. What shall I do with you?

VARYA [*softly*]. Anya's asleep. [*Opens the window gently.*] The sun has risen already. It's not cold any more. Look, mama, what wonderful trees! How glorious the air is! The starlings are singing!

GAYEV [*opening another window*]. The whole orchard is white. Do you remember, Lyuba? There is that long vista; straight, straight as an arrow it shines on moonlight nights. Do you remember? You haven't forgotten?

LYUBOV ANDREYEVNA [*looks out of the window into the orchard*]. Oh, my childhood, those pure and happy years! Here in this nursery I used to sleep; from here I looked out upon the orchard. Gladness awakened with me every morning, and it was just the same then—as now—not a bit changed. [*Laughs joyously*] White, all white! Oh, my orchard! After the dark, rainy autumns and the cold winters, you are young again, full of gladness. The heavenly angels have not abandoned you. . . . If only I might cast from my shoulders and breast the heavy stone, if only I could forget my past!

GAYEV. Yes, and they'll sell the orchard to pay our debts. How strange it seems! . . .

LYUBOV ANDREYEVNA. Look, the spirit of our mother is walking in the orchard . . . in a white dress! [*Laughs joyously.*] It is she.

GAYEV. Where?

VARYA. Lord help you, mama!

LYUBOV ANDREYEVNA. There's no one there. I only thought it looked so. On the right, at the turn to the summerhouse, a white tree was bent so that it resembled a woman. . . .

[TROFIMOV *comes in. He is dressed in a shabby student's uniform, and wears glasses.*]

LYUBOV ANDREYEVNA. What a wonderful orchard! White masses of flowers, the blue sky! . . .

TROFIMOV. Lyubov Andreyevna! [*She looks at him.*] I shall only pay you my respects, and then go immediately. [*Kissing her hand warmly.*] They told me to wait until morning, but I didn't have the patience. . . .

[LYUBOV ANDREYEVNA *looks at him in bewilderment.*]

VARYA [*through her tears*]. It is Petya Trofimov.

TROFIMOV. Petya Trofimov, who used to be tutor to your Grisha. . . . Can I really have changed so?

[LYUBOV ANDREYEVNA *embraces him and weeps quietly.*]

GAYEV [*embarrassed*]. That's enough, Lyuba, that's enough.

VARYA [*weeping*]. But I told you, Petya, to wait till to-morrow.

LYUBOV ANDREYEVNA. My Grisha . . . my boy . . . Grisha . . . my son! . . .

VARYA. What's the use, mama? It's God's will.

TROFIMOV [*softly, through his tears*]. There . . . there. . . .

LYUBOV ANDREYEVNA [*weeping quietly*]. My little boy is dead, he was drowned . . . Why did it happen? Why, my dear? [*More softly.*] Anya is asleep in there and I am talking in a loud voice . . . disturbing her. . . . What's the matter, Petya? Why have you lost your good looks? Why have you grown old?

TROFIMOV. On the train a village woman called me "a gentleman gone to seed."

LYUBOV ANDREYEVNA. You were just a boy then, a dear, young student, but now your hair is thin, and you're wearing spectacles. Is it possible you're still a student? [*Going toward the door.*]

TROFIMOV. I suppose I shall be a student forever.

LYUBOV ANDREYEVNA [*kisses her brother, then* VARYA]. Well, let's go to bed. Even you have grown older, Leonid.

PISHCHIK [*following her*]. So then, we must go to bed. . . . Oh, my gout! I'll stay the night. . . . Lyubov Andreyevna, my dear friend, if you could just get me two hundred and forty rubles by to-morrow morning!

GAYEV. That's all he can think of!

PISHCHIK. Two hundred and forty rubles . . . to pay the interest on the mortgage.

LYUBOV ANDREYEVNA. I haven't any money, my dear man.

PISHCHIK. I'll give it back, my dear, it's a trifling sum. . . .

LYUBOV ANDREYEVNA. Well, all right then. Leonid will give it to you. . . . Give it to him, Leonid.

GAYEV. I'll give it to him—you just watch me!

LYUBOV ANDREYEVNA.   What's the use? Give it to him. . . . He needs it. . . . He'll return it.

[TROFIMOV. LYUBOV ANDREYEVNA, PISHCHIK, *and* FIRS *go out.* GAYEV, VARYA, *and* YASHA *remain.*]

GAYEV.   My sister has not yet broken herself of the habit of squandering money. [*To* YASHA.] Get away, my dear fellow. You smell like a chicken.

YASHA [*with a grin*].   And you haven't changed a bit, Leonid Andreyevich.

GAYEV.   What's he talking about? [*To* VARYA.] What did he say?

VARYA [*to* YASHA].   Your mother has come in from the village. She's been sitting in the servants' room since yesterday. She wants to see you.

YASHA.   Devil a bit I care!

VARYA.   Ah, you're a shameless fellow!

YASHA.   Much use her being here. She might have come to-morrow. [*He goes out.*]

VARYA.   Mama is just the same as always. She hasn't changed a bit. If you'd let her, she'd give away everything she had.

GAYEV.   Yes. . . . [*Pause.*] When a great many remedies are suggested for some ailment, it means that the ailment is incurable. I think, rack my brains, I find many solutions, very many, which means that in reality there isn't one. It would be splendid if some one would make us a bequest, splendid if we could marry our Anya to a very wealthy man, splendid to go to Yaroslavl and try our luck with our aunt, the Countess. Auntie is very, very rich.

VARYA [*weeping*].   If only God would help us!

GAYEV.   Don't cry. Auntie is very rich, but she doesn't like us. My sister, in the first place, married an attorney, a man below her class.

[ANYA *appears in the doorway.*]

GAYEV.   She not only married below her class, but conducted herself, I must admit, in a manner far from virtuous. She is a kind, admirable, fine woman, I love her very much. But however diligently you may think up extenuating circumstances, you must still admit that she is immoral. One feels it in her slightest movement.

VARYA [*in a whisper*].   Anya is in the doorway.

GAYEV.   Who? [*Pause.*] That's strange—I've got something in my right eye—I can't see out of it. And on Thursday, when I was in the district court—

[ANYA *comes in.*]

VARYA.   Why aren't you asleep, Anya?

ANYA.   I'm not sleepy. I can't go to sleep.

GAYEV.   My darling! [*Kisses* ANYA's *face and hands.*] My child! . . . [*Through his tears.*] You're not only my niece—you're my angel—everything in the world to me. Believe in me, believe. . . .

ANYA.   I believe in you, uncle. Every one loves you, respects you . . . but, dear uncle, you must keep still—only keep still. What were you just saying about my mother, your sister? Why did you say that?

GAYEV.   Yes, yes. . . . [*Covers his face with her hand.*] This is indeed terrible! My God! Save me, God! And just a little while ago I delivered an oration over the bookcase . . . so silly! And it was only when I had finished that I realized it was silly.

VARYA.   Yes, uncle dear, you truly must keep still. Just keep still, that's all.

ANYA.   You'll be happier yourself if you just keep still.

GAYEV.   I'll keep still. [*Kisses their hands.*] I'll keep still. Only here's some news about money matters. I was at the district court on Thursday. Well, people came in, the talk turned from one thing to another, from this to that, and I gathered that we might arrange a loan on a note, to pay the interest at the bank.

VARYA.   If only God would help us.

GAYEV.   I'll go over on Tuesday and talk it over with them again. [*To* VARYA.] Don't sob so. [*To* ANYA.] Your mama will have a talk with Lopakhin—of course he'll not refuse her. . . . And when you've rested up a bit, you will go to Yaroslavl to see your great-aunt, the Countess. So you see, we'll be working from three points, and the trick is turned already. I'm sure we shall pay off the interest. . . . [*Puts a piece of candy in his mouth.*] On my honor, I swear by whatever pledge you please, the estate shall not be sold! [*Excitedly.*] By my happiness I swear! Here's my hand on it. You may call me a wretched, dishonorable man if I let it be put up at auction. By my whole being I swear it!

ANYA [*cheerfully, her composure restored*].   How good and clever you are, uncle! [*Embraces him.*] I am quite calm now, quite calm and happy.

[FIRS *comes in.*]

FIRS [*reproachfully*].   Leonid Andreich, you're conscienceless! When are you going to bed?

GAYEV.   Right away, right away. You may go, Firs. I'll take off my things without your help. Well, children, bye-bye. . . . I'll give you the details to-morrow, but now, go and sleep. [*Kisses* ANYA *and* VARYA.] I'm a man of the eighties. . . . People don't praise those times much, but just the same, I may say that I've suffered a lot for my convictions. The peasant loves me with good reason. One must understand the peasant, one must understand what—

ANYA.   There you go again, uncle!

VARYA.   You must keep still, uncle dear!

FIRS [*angrily*].   Leonid Andreich!

GAYEV.   I'm coming, I'm coming. . . . Go to bed now. Off two cushions into the center! I'll turn over a new leaf. [*He goes out,* FIRS *shuffling behind him.*]

ANYA.   My mind is at peace now. I don't want to go to Yaroslavl, I don't like auntie; but just the same, I feel calmer, thanks to uncle. [*She sits down.*]

VARYA.   We must sleep. I'm going to bed. Things went all to pieces while you were gone. You know, only the old servants live in the servants' quarters:

Efimyushka, Polya, Evstigney, and Karp, too. They began to let in tramps to spend the night. I didn't say a word. But then the rumor got around to me that they were saying I didn't let them have anything but peas to eat. Out of stinginess—you see? And Evstigney was to blame all the time. Very well, I thought. If that's so, I thought, you just wait! So I called Evstigney in. [*Yawns.*] He came. . . . "What's the matter with you, Evstigney? You're making a fool of yourself." . . . [*Looks at* ANYA.] Anya darling! [*Pause.*] She's fallen asleep. [*Takes* ANYA *by the arm.*] Let's go to bed! Come! [*Leading her.*] My darling has fallen asleep! Come on! [*They start to go.*]

> [*In the far distance beyond the orchard a shepherd plays on his pipe.* TROFIMOV *walks across the stage, and seeing* VARYA *and* ANYA, *stops still.*]

VARYA.   Sh . . . sh. She's sleeping . . . sleeping. Come, dear.
ANYA [*softly, and half asleep*].   I am so tired. . . . All the little bells . . . dear uncle . . . mama and uncle. . . .
VARYA.   Come, dear, come on. . . . [*They go into* ANYA'S *room.*]
TROFIMOV [*tenderly*].   My sun! My springtime!

ACT II

> An old, ruined, long-since-abandoned shrine. Near it a well; and a few big stones, evidently at one time tombstones. An old bench. The road leading to GAYEV'S *farmhouse can be seen. At one side poplar trees tower up, dark and tall; beyond them, the cherry orchard begins. In the distance a row of telegraph poles, and far off along the horizon are dimly visible the outlines of a great city, which can be seen only during fine, clear weather. It is nearly sunset.* CHARLOTTA, YASHA, *and* DUNYASHA *are sitting on the bench:* EPIKHODOV *is standing nearby and playing the guitar. They are all thoughtful.* CHARLOTTA *is wearing a man's old cap; she has lowered a rifle from her shoulder, and is adjusting a buckle on the strap.*

CHARLOTTA [*thoughtfully*].   I haven't a real passport. I don't know how old I am, and I always feel I am young. When I was a little girl my father and mother used to travel from fair to fair and give performances—very good ones. And I used to do the salto-mortale,[1] and other tricks. Then, when papa and mama died, a German woman took me to live with her and began to teach me. Well and good. I grew up, and later I became a governess. But who I am or where I come from—that I don't know. Who my parents were, I don't know. Perhaps they weren't married. [*Takes a cucumber out of her pocket and begins to eat it.*] I don't know anything. [*Pause.*] I long so to talk, but there's no one to talk to. . . . I haven't anybody at all.
EPIKHODOV [*playing on the guitar and singing*].

---

1. Literally, "leap of death"—a standing somersault.

What care I for friends and foes?
What care I for the noisy world?

How jolly it is to play on the mandolin!

DUNYASHA.   That's a guitar, not a mandolin! [*Glances into a little mirror and powders her nose.*]

EPIKHODOV.   To the poor idiot who's in love, it's a mandolin. [*Hums.*]

With the flame of a mutual love
Would that your heart were burning!

[YASHA *joins in.*]

CHARLOTTA.   These men sing horribly. . . . Foh! Like jackals.

DUNYASHA [*to* YAHSA].   Just the same, it must be fine to live abroad.

YASHA.   Yes, to be sure. I can't contradict you. [*Yawns and lights a cigar.*]

EPIKHODOV.   That's easy to understand. Things have been properly established abroad for a long time.

YASHA.   Of course.

EPIKHODOV.   I'm an educated fellow, I read many remarkable books; but I simply can't understand my own state of mind—what I really want—whether to live, or to shoot myself, so to speak. But just the same, I always carry a revolver around with me. Here it is. . . . [*Produces a revolver.*]

CHARLOTTA.   Now I'm through. I'm going. [*Slings the rifle over her shoulder.*] Epikhodov, you are a very clever and very terrifying man. Women must fall madly in love with you. Br-r-r! [*Walks away.*] Those smart boys are all so stupid that I haven't a soul to talk to. I'm always alone, alone, no one belongs to me, and . . . and I don't know who I am nor why I was born. [*She goes slowly out.*]

EPIKHODOV.   Without mentioning other matters, I should, properly speaking, say of myself among other things that fate has treated me as mercilessly as a storm does a little ship. Supposing you say I am wrong—then tell me why it was that this morning, for instance, I waked up and saw on my chest a spider of terrific size? It was so big. . . . [*Illustrates with both hands.*] And then, when I took up some kvass to have a drink, why there I saw something in the highest degree indecent, in the nature of a cockroach. [*Pause.*] Have you ever read Buckle?[2] [*Pause.*] May I speak a couple of words to you, Avdotya Fedorovna?

DUNYASHA.   Speak up.

EPIKHODOV.   I should prefer to speak with you alone. [*Sighs.*]

DUNYASHA [*disconcerted*].   Very well. . . . Only bring me my cloak first. . . . It's near the bookcase. . . . It's a little damp here.

EPIKHODOV.   Very well. I'll bring it to you. . . . Now I know what to do with my revolver. . . . [*Picks up the guitar and goes out, playing.*]

YASHA.   Two-and-twenty troubles! Between you and me, he's a stupid fellow. [*Yawns.*]

---

2. Henry Thomas Buckle (1821–62), English historian.

DUNYASHA.   God grant he doesn't shoot himself! [*Pause.*] I'm afraid. I'm all upset. They took me to live with gentlefolk when I was still a little girl, and now I'm not used to humble living. Why, my hands here are snowy white like a lady's. I've grown tender and delicate, and turned into a lady—I'm afraid of everything. It's terrible to be that way. And if you should deceive me, Yasha, then I don't know what would become of my nerves.

YASHA [*kisses her*].   Little cucumber! Of course, every girl should respect herself, and I should be the first to despise one whose conduct was not above reproach.

DUNYASHA.   I'm head over heels in love with you; you're well educated, you can discourse on every subject. [*Pause.*]

YASHA [*yawning*].   Oh, yes. . . . To my mind it's this way: if a girl loves some one, that means she's immoral. [*Pause.*] It's nice to smoke a cigar in the open air. . . . [*Listening.*] Some one's coming this way. . . . It's the gentry. . . .

[DUNYASHA *embraces him impulsively.*]

YASHA.   Go on home as if you'd been down to the river to bathe. Take that little path, or else they'll meet you and think I've had a rendezvous with you. I couldn't stand that.

DUNYASHA [*coughing softly*].   My head aches a little from the cigar smoke. [*She goes out.*]

[YASHA *remains sitting near the shrine.* LYUBOV ANDREYEVNA, GAYEV, *and* LOPAKHIN *come in.*]

LOPAKHIN.   You absolutely must make up your mind—time will not wait. The question is perfectly simple. Are you willing to lease the land for cottages, or not? Answer me in a word: yes or no? One word only!

LYUBOV ANDREYEVNA.   Who has been smoking disgusting cigars out here? [*Seats herself.*]

GAYEV.   It's convenient since they built the railroad. [*Sits down.*] We rode into town and had lunch. . . . Yellow to the center! I'd like to go into the house first and play just one game. . . .

LYUBOV ANDREYEVNA.   You'll have time.

LOPAKHIN.   Only one word! [*Beseechingly.*] Please give me an answer!

GAYEV [*yawning*].   What's that?

LYUBOV ANDREYEVNA [*looking into her purse*].   Yesterday I had a lot of money, but to-day there's very little. My poor Varya is scrimping along, feeding every one on milk soup; they're giving the old people in the kitchen nothing but peas to eat, and here I'm squandering money senselessly. . . . [*Drops her purse, scattering gold coins. In vexation.*] Look, they're all scattered. . . .

YASHA.   By your leave, I'll pick them up right away. [*Picks up the coins.*]

LYUBOV ANDREYEVNA.   Yes, please, Yasha. Why did I go out to lunch anyway! . . . Your vile restaurant with its music, the tablecloths smelling of soap! . . . Why do people drink so much, Lenya? Why do they eat so much? Why do they talk so much? To-day in the restaurant you rambled on and on, and all about nothing. About the seventies, about the decadents.[3] And to whom? Talking to the waiters about the decadents!

LOPAKHIN. Yes.

GAYEV [*waving his hand*]. I'm incorrigible, that's obvious. . . . [*Exasperatedly to* YASHA.] What's the matter? Why are you always under our noses?

YASHA [*laughing*]. I can't listen to your voice without laughing.

GAYEV [*to his sister*]. Either he or I . . .

LYUBOV ANDREYEVNA. Go away, Yasha, get along with you.

YASHA [*handing* LYUBOV ANDREYEVNA *her purse*]. I'm going right away. [*With difficulty restraining his laughter.*] This very minute. [*He goes out.*]

LOPAKHIN. Deriganov, the rich man, is planning to buy your estate. They say he's coming to the auction himself.

LYUBOV ANDREYEVNA. Where did you hear that?

LOPAKHIN. That's the rumor in town.

GAYEV. Our aunt in Yaroslavl has promised to send some money, but how much she will send, and when, we don't know. . . .

LOPAKHIN. How much will she send? A hundred thousand? Two hundred?

LYUBOV ANDREYEVNA. Well! . . . ten or fifteen thousand, and we'll be grateful for that.

LOPAKHIN. Pardon me for saying so, but I have never yet met such frivolous, unbusinesslike, queer people as you, my friends. People tell you in plain Russian that your estate is to be sold, but you don't take it in.

LYUBOV ANDREYEVNA. What can we do about it? Tell us, what?

LOPAKHIN. Every day I tell you. Every day I repeat the same thing. The cherry orchard, and the land as well, simply must be leased for cottages, and this must be done now, now, without delay! The date of the auction is almost here! You must realize this! Just make up your mind definitely once for all to accept the leasing plan, and people will loan you as much money as you wish. Then you'll be saved.

LYUBOV ANDREYEVNA. Cottages and cottagers—forgive me, that's so vulgar.

GAYEV. I agree with you perfectly.

LOPAKHIN. I shall either sob, or scream, or fall in a faint. I can't stand it! You've worn me out. [*To* GAYEV.] You old woman!

GAYEV. What's that?

LOPAKHIN. Old woman! [*He turns to go.*]

LYUBOV ANDREYEVNA [*frightened*]. No, don't go away. Stay here, my dear friend, I beg you. Perhaps we shall find a way.

LOPAKHIN. What's there to think about?

LYUBOV ANDREYEVNA. Don't go away, I beg of you. It's more cheerful with you here anyway. . . . [*Pause.*] All the time I feel as though I were waiting for something—as though the house were going to fall in ruins above us.

GAYEV [*musing deeply*]. Double into the corner . . . back shot to the center. . . .

---

3. A group of late nineteenth-century artists and writers, predominantly in France and England, whose unconventional ideas about art and morals shocked many of their contemporaries.

LYUBOV ANDREYEVNA. We have committed many sins.

LOPAKHIN. What sins have you committed? . . .

GAYEV [*putting a piece of candy into his mouth*]. They say I've gobbled up all my substance in sugar candy. . . . [*Laughs.*]

LYUBOV ANDREYEVNA. Oh, my sins! . . . I've always squandered my money like a mad woman, and I married a man who only created more debts. My husband died from too much champagne—he drank horribly—and I, to my own misfortune, fell in love with another man, and at the very same time—this was my first punishment, a mortal blow—my little boy was drowned here in the river. I went abroad, broke all ties, planning never to return, never to see that river again. I covered my eyes and fled in desperation, and *he* followed me, with brutal, merciless persistence. I bought a villa near Mentone, for *he* became ill there, and for three years I knew no rest day or night. The sick man exhausted me, my soul shriveled up. And then, last year, when they sold the villa for debts, I went to Paris, and there he plundered me, abandoned me, and took up with another woman. I tried to poison myself. . . . It was so stupid and shameful. . . . And suddenly I was drawn back to Russia, to my native land, to my little girl. . . . [*Wipes away her tears.*] Lord, Lord, be merciful, forgive my sins! Do not punish me any more! [*Takes a telegram out of her pocket.*] I received this to-day from Paris. He asks forgiveness, entreats me to come back. . . . [*Tears up the telegram.*] Don't I hear music somewhere? [*Listens.*]

GAYEV. That's our famous Jewish orchestra. Do you remember? Four violins, a flute, and a double-bass.

LYUBOV ANDREYEVNA. So it's still in existence? We ought to ask them over sometime and have an evening party.

LOPAKHIN [*listening*]. I can't hear. . . . [*Humming softly.*] "Germans, if paid well enough, can make Russians Frenchmen."[4] [*Laughs.*] What a funny thing I saw in the theatre yesterday! It was very amusing.

LYUBOV ANDREYEVNA. I'm sure it wasn't a bit funny. You shouldn't go to plays, but observe yourself more closely. What a drab life you live, how many unnecessary things you say!

LOPAKHIN. That's true enough. One must frankly admit that we lead a fool's life. . . . [*Pause.*] My dad was a peasant and a stupid one, he understood nothing, taught me nothing, but only beat me when he was drunk, and always with a stick. And in reality, I am just the same sort of blockhead and idiot that he was. I never studied anything, my handwriting is wretched. I write like a pig—I feel ashamed of it.

LYUBOV ANDREYEVNA. You ought to get married, my dear man.

LOPAKHIN. Yes, that's true.

LYUBOV ANDREYEVNA. And to our Varya? She's a good girl.

LOPAKHIN. True.

LYUBOV ANDREYEVNA. She's a simple-hearted child, she works the whole day long, and most important of all, she loves you. And you—you've liked her for a long time.

LOPAKHIN. Well? I've no objection. . . . She's a good girl. [*Pause.*]

---

4. I.e., "If given enough money, German tutors can transform uncivilized Russians into refined people like the French."

GAYEV. They've offered me a place in the bank. Six thousand a year. . . . Did you hear about it?

LYUBOV ANDREYEVNA. To a man like you! . . . Just sit still. . . .

[FIRS *comes in, carrying an overcoat.*]

FIRS [*to* GAYEV]. Please put this on, sir, or you'll feel the dampness.

GAYEV [*putting on the coat*]. You're a bother, old man.

FIRS. Never mind. . . . You went off this morning without saying a word to anybody. [*Surveys him.*]

LYUBOV ANDREYEVNA. How old you've grown, Firs!

FIRS. Beg pardon?

LOPAKHIN. She says that you've grown very old.

FIRS. I've lived a long time. They were getting ready to marry me off before your daddy was born. . . . [*Laughs.*] And when the Emancipation[5] came, I was already head valet. I didn't approve of the Emancipation then, I stayed with my masters. . . . [*Pause.*] And I remember, every one was happy, but *why* they were happy they didn't know themselves.

LOPAKHIN. It was fine before the Emancipation, all right. At least, there used to be flogging.

FIRS [*who has not understood him*]. Yes, indeed. The peasants for the masters, the masters for the peasants, but now they're all split up. You can't make head or tail of it.

GAYEV. Be quiet, Firs. I've got to go to town to-morrow. They promised to introduce me to some general who may loan us some money on a note.

LOPAKHIN. Nothing will come of it. And you'll not pay your interest— you can depend on that.

LYUBOV ANDREYEVNA. He's talking nonsense. There aren't any generals.

[TROFIMOV, ANYA, *and* VARYA *come in.*]

GAYEV. Here come our people.

ANYA. Mama's sitting out here.

LYUBOV ANDREYEVNA [*tenderly*]. Come here, come here, Anya. . . . My dear ones! . . . [*Embracing* ANYA *and* VARYA.] If you only both knew how I love you. Sit down beside me, so. [*They all sit down.*]

LOPAKHIN. Our eternal student is always with the young ladies.

TROFIMOV. That's none of your business.

LOPAKHIN. He'll be fifty pretty soon, but he's still a student.

TROFIMOV. Quit your idiotic jokes.

LOPAKHIN. What are you getting huffy about, you freak?

TROFIMOV. Let me alone.

LOPAKHIN [*laughs*]. Well, what do you think of *me,* anyhow, pray tell?

TROFIMOV. Here's what I think of you, Yermolay Alexeich: You are a

---

5. The emancipation of the Russian serfs in 1861.

wealthy man, you'll be a millionaire soon. And just as a ravenous beast that devours everything crossing his path, is necessary to the transmutation of the elements, even so you are necessary. [*All laugh.*]

VARYA. You'd better talk about the planets, Petya.

LYUBOV ANDREYEVNA. No, please, let's continue our discussion of yesterday.

TROFIMOV. What were we discussing?

GAYEV. The proud man.

TROFIMOV. We talked at length yesterday, but we didn't come to any conclusion. There is, in your opinion, something mystical in a proud man. Possibly from your own point of view you are right, but if you reason it out simply, without evasion, what pride can there be, what grounds for pride can exist if a man's physiological structure is of a poor sort, if in the great majority of cases he is crude, stupid, profoundly unhappy? He must moderate his self-admiration. He must apply himself to work alone.

GAYEV. You'll die just the same.

TROFIMOV. Who knows? And what does it mean—to die? Perhaps a man has a hundred senses, and only the five we know are annihilated by death, while the remaining ninety-five continue to live.

LYUBOV ANDREYEVNA. How clever you are, Petya!

LOPAKHIN [*ironically*]. Awfully!

TROFIMOV. Humanity advances, perfecting its forces. Everything that is unattainable for it now, will sometime become near and comprehensible; only we must work and help to our fullest ability those who are seeking the truth. Only a few are thus far working among us here in Russia. The vast majority of those intellectuals whom I know, are seeking nothing, do nothing, and are as yet incapable of labor. They call themselves intellectuals, but they speak condescendingly to their servants, and treat the peasants like animals. They are wretched students, they don't read anything seriously, they are utterly idle, they only talk about the sciences, and they understand little about art. They are all solemn, they pull long faces and discuss only portentous matters, they philosophize—but in the meantime the enormous majority of us—ninety-nine out of a hundred—are living like wild beasts, wrangling and fighting at the least pretext. We have vile table manners, we sleep in filth, in stifling rooms, there are bedbugs everywhere, stench, dampness, moral impurity. . . . And evidently all our nice conversations have only the purpose of fooling ourselves and others. Show me the day nurseries of which people speak so frequently and at such length, and the reading rooms! Where are they? People only write about them in stories—they really don't exist at all. There's only dirt, vulgarity, Asiatic backwardness. I dislike and fear deeply serious faces, I dread serious conversations. Best to keep silence.

LOPAKHIN. You know, I get up before five o'clock, I work from morning till night. Well, I'm always handling money, my own and other people's, and I observe those around me. You need only start some project of your own to discover how few honorable, decent people there are. Sometimes when I lie in bed awake I think, "Lord, thou hast given us vast forests, boundless fields, remote horizons, and we, living in their midst, should really be giants."

LYUBOV ANDREYEVNA. You want giants? . . . They're only good in fairy tales—they'd frighten you.

[EPIKHODOV *crosses back stage, playing on his guitar.*]

LYUBOV ANDREYEVNA [*thoughtfully*].   Epikhodov is coming.
ANYA [*thoughtfully*].   Epikhodov is coming.
GAYEV.   The sun has set, friends.
TROFIMOV.   Yes.
GAYEV [*softly, as though declaiming to himself*].   O marvelous Nature, serene and beautiful, thou gleamest with an eternal radiance; thou whom we call our mother unitest within thyself life and death, thou livest and destroyest—
VARYA [*entreatingly*].   Uncle dear!
ANYA.   Uncle! At it again!
TROFIMOV.   You'd better make it, "Yellow across the table to the center."
GAYEV.   I'll keep still, I'll keep still.

[*They all sit pondering. Silence. Only the soft muttering of* FIRS *is audible. Suddenly a distant sound, seemingly from the skies, is heard; a melancholy sound, which dies away like the snapping of a violin string.*]

LYUBOV ANDREYEVNA.   What's that?
LOPAKHIN.   I don't know. Maybe a cable snapped in a shaft somewhere far off. But it was very far away.
GAYEV.   Maybe it's a bird—a heron, perhaps.
TROFIMOV.   Or an owl.
LYUBOV ANDREYEVNA [*shudders*].   It depresses me, somehow.

[*Pause.*]

FIRS.   It was the same way before the great misfortune. An owl hooted, and the samovar[6] hissed and hissed.
GAYEV.   Before what misfortune?
FIRS.   Before the Emancipation.

[*Pause.*]

LYUBOV ANDREYEVNA.   Come, my friends. It's growing dark already. [*To* ANYA.] There are tears in your eyes. What's troubling you, little girl? [*Embraces her.*]
ANYA.   Never mind, mama. Nothing's the matter.
TROFIMOV.   Some one is coming.

[*A* WAYFARER *makes his appearance. He has on a long coat and a worn, white cap. He is a little tipsy.*]

WAYFARER.   Pray tell me, does this road lead directly to the station?
GAYEV.   Yes. Follow the road.
WAYFARER.   I'm deeply grateful to you. [*Coughing.*] It's fine

---

6. Urn used to boil water for making tea.

weather. . . . [*Dramatically.*] "My brother, my suffering brother!" . . . "Go
to the Volga, whose groan—?" [*To* VARYA.] Mademoiselle, please give a
hungry Russian thirty kopeks. . . .

[VARYA *is frightened, and screams.*]

LOPAKHIN [*angrily*]. There's a limit to every sort of impudence!
LYUBOV ANDREYEVNA [*panic-stricken*]. Take this. . . . Here it
is. . . . [*Searches in her purse.*] There's no silver. . . . Oh well, here's a gold
piece for you. . . .
WAYFARER. I'm deeply grateful to you! [*Goes out.*]

[*They all laugh.*]

VARYA [*frightened*]. I'm going, I'm going home. Oh, mama dear, there's
nothing at home for the servants to eat, and there you gave him a gold piece!
LYUBOV ANDREYEVNA. What's to be done with poor, foolish me? When
we get home I'll give you everything I have. Yermolay Alexeich, make me
another loan!
LOPAKHIN. Very well.
LYUBOV ANDREYEVNA. Come, friends, it's time to go home. And see
here, Varya, we've found a husband for you. I congratulate you!
VARYA [*through her tears*]. Please don't joke about it, mama.
LOPAKHIN. Go to a nunnery, Okhmelia![7]
GAYEV. My hands are trembling. I haven't played pool for a long time.
LOPAKHIN. Okhmelia, nymph, remember me in your prayers!
LYUBOV ANDREYEVNA. Come, every one, we'll have supper soon.
VARYA. He frightened me. My heart's fairly pounding.
LOPAKHIN. Let me remind you, my friends: the cherry orchard will be
sold on the twenty-second of August. Think that over! Think that over!

[*They all go out, with the exception of* ANYA *and* TROFIMOV.]

ANYA [*laughing*]. We're alone, now, thanks to the wayfarer who
frightened Varya.
TROFIMOV. Varya's afraid that we'll suddenly fall in love with each
other; and for days on end she hasn't budged from our side. Her trifling little
mind cannot comprehend that we are superior to love. To avoid the petty and
deluding things that prevent one from being free and happy—this is the aim and
significance of our life. Forward! We shall press on irresistibly toward the
bright star that shines beyond in the distance! Forward! Do not fall behind,
friends!
ANYA [*clapping her hands*]. How splendidly you say it! [*Pause.*] It's
marvelous here to-day.
TROFIMOV. Yes, the weather is wonderful.
ANYA. What have you done to me, Petya, that I no longer love the cherry

---

7. Here and below Lopakhin paraphrases lines from Shakespeare's *Hamlet* in which Hamlet gives
contemptuous advice to Ophelia.

orchard as I did before? I used to love it so tenderly. It seemed to me that there was no place on earth more beautiful than our orchard.

TROFIMOV.   All Russia is our orchard. The land is vast and glorious, there are many marvelous places in it. [*Pause.*] Think of it, Anya! Your grandfather, your great-grandfather, and all your ancestors were serf-owners, ruling over living souls. Don't you hear voices and see human beings looking at you from every cherry in the orchard, from every little leaf, from every tree trunk? . . . Oh, it is terrible, your orchard is a fearful place, and when one walks through it in the evening or at night, the ancient bark is lit then with a dull gleam, and the cherry trees seem to be dreaming of things that happened a hundred, two hundred years ago, and grievous visions harass them. What's the use of talking! We are at least two hundred years behind the times, we have nothing of our own, no definite relationship with the past; we do nothing but philosophize, complain of our own unhappiness, or drink vodka. But it's all so clear: in order to begin living in the present, we must first redeem our past, make an end of it. But we may redeem it only through suffering, only through strenuous, constant labor. You must realize this, Anya.

ANYA.   The house in which we are living has for a long time ceased to belong to us, and I will go away, I give you my word.

TROFIMOV.   If you have the housekeeper's keys, throw them into the well and go away. Be as free as the wind.

ANYA [*in ecstasy*].   How well you said that!

TROFIMOV.   Have faith in me, Anya, have faith in me. I am not yet thirty, I am young, I am still a student, but how much I have endured already! I'm as famished as the winter, sick, distraught, poor as a beggar, and wherever fate has driven me, I have gone. But always my soul has been my own; at every moment, day and night it has been filled with inexplicable premonitions. I feel that happiness is on its way, Anya; I already see it. . . .

ANYA [*thoughtfully*].   The moon is rising.

[EPIKHODOV *is heard strumming over and over on the guitar the same melancholy song. The moon rises slowly.* VARYA *is searching for* ANYA *somewhere near the poplars, and calling* "Anya, where are you?"]

TROFIMOV.   Yes, the moon is rising. [*Pause.*] Ah yes, happiness is coming, drawing ever nearer and nearer. Already I hear its footsteps. And if we do not see it, do not recognize it, what matter? Others will see it!

VARYA'S *voice*.   Anya! Where are you?

TROFIMOV.   It's that Varya again! [*Angrily.*] Exasperating!

ANYA.   Never mind. Let's go down to the river. It's nice there.

TROFIMOV.   All right. [*They go out.*]

VARYA'S *voice*.   Anya! Anya!

ACT III

A drawing-room, separated by an arch from the ballroom. A lighted chandelier. The Jewish orchestra—the same orchestra mentioned in the second act—is heard playing in the hall. It is evening. They are dancing the grand rond[1] *in the ballroom. The voice of* SEMEONOV-PISHCHIK *is heard, calling,* "Promenade à une paire!" PISHCHIK *and* CHARLOTTA IVANOVNA *are the first couple to enter the drawing-room;* TROFIMOV *and* LYUBOV ANDREYEVNA *follow; then* ANYA *and the* POST OFFICE OFFI-CIAL, *then* VARYA *and the* STATION MASTER, *and so on.* VARYA *is weeping softly, wiping away her tears as she dances.* DUNYASHA *and her partner form the last couple. They circle around the drawing-room.* PISHCHIK *cries out,* "Grand rond, balancez!" *and then,* "Les cavaliers à genoux, et remerciez vos dames!"

FIRS, *wearing a dress coat, is carrying about a tray with seltzer water.* PISHCHIK *and* TROFIMOV *reenter the drawing-room.*

PISHCHIK.   I'm full-blooded, I've had two strokes already, it's hard for me to dance, but, as the saying goes, "If you join the pack and cannot bay, wag your tail, anyway!" I have the constitution of a horse. My dear father—may he rest in peace—was a great joker, and he used to say in speaking of our ancestry, that the ancient stock of the Semeonov-Pishchiks was descended from the identical horse appointed senator by Caligula.[2] . . . [*Sits down.*] But here's the pity of it; I've no money! A hungry dog believes only in meat. . . . [*Snores, and suddenly rouses himself.*] And so I, too . . . can think of nothing but money. . . .

TROFIMOV.   True, there really is something about you that reminds one of a horse.

PISHCHIK.   Well . . . a horse is a good beast. . . . You can sell a horse. . . .

[*The click of billiard balls is heard in the next room.* VARYA *appears in the hall under the archway.*]

TROFIMOV [*tesasingly*].   Madam Lopakhin! Madam Lopakhin!

VARYA [*angrily*].   Gentleman-gone-to-seed!

TROFIMOV.   Yes, I'm a gentleman gone to seed, and I'm proud of it!

VARYA [*musing bitterly*].   We've hired musicians, but who's going to pay them? [*Goes out.*]

TROFIMOV [*to* PISHCHIK].   If the energy you've wasted all your life dig-ging up money to pay interest, had been directed to something else, I believe that eventually you could have turned the world upside down.

PISHCHIK.   Nietzsche,[3] the philosopher . . . most noted . . . most fa-mous . . . a man of vast intellect, says in his books that one can make counter-feit money.

TROFIMOV.   Have you read Nietzsche then?

PISHCHIK.   Bah! Dashenka told me about him. But things have come to

1. Literally, the "great circle," a dance similar in pattern to the American square dance. Below Pishchik calls out: "Each couple promenade"; "Great circle, swing!"; and "Gentlemen, on your knees and thank your ladies."

2. Nickname of Gaius Caesar (A.D. 12–41), Roman emperor noted for his tyrannical misrule and erratic behavior.

3. Friedrich Nietzsche (1844–1900), influential German philosopher.

such a pass with me now, that I'd even make counterfeit money. . . . Day after to-morrow I must pay out three hundred and ten rubles. . . . I've scraped together a hundred and thirty already. . . . [*Feels through his pockets excitedly.*] It's gone! I've lost my money! [*In tears.*] Where's my money? . . . [*Joyfully.*] Here it is, under the lining. . . . Why, that raised a sweat on me! . . .

[LYUBOV ANDREYEVNA *and* CHARLOTTA IVANOVNA *come in.*]

LYUBOV ANDREYEVNA [*humming a Caucasian air*]. Why is Leonid so long in coming? What is he doing in town? [*To* DUNYASHA.] Dunyasha, give the musicians some tea.

TROFIMOV. Most likely the auction wasn't held.

LYUBOV ANDREYEVNA. And so we needn't have asked the musicians to come, and there was no reason for planning a ball. . . . Well, no matter. . . . [*She sits down and hums softly.*]

CHARLOTTA [*handing* PISHCHIK *a pack of cards*]. Here's a pack of cards. Think of a card.

PISHCHIK. I've thought of one.

CHARLOTTA. Now, shuffle the pack. Very good. Give it to me, my dear Mr. Pishchik. *Ein, zwei, drei!*[4] Take a look now—it's in your hip pocket. . . .

PISHCHIK [*takes a card out of his hip pocket*]. The eight of spades. Quite right! [*In astonishment.*] Just think of that!

CHARLOTTA [*holding the pack of cards in her hands and speaking to* TROFIMOV]. Tell me quick! What's the top card?

TROFIMOV. Eh? Why, the queen of spades.

CHARLOTTA. Right! [*To* PISHCHIK.] Well, what's the top card?

PISHCHIK. The ace of hearts.

CHARLOTTA. Right! [*Claps her hands, and the pack of cards disappears.*] But what fine weather we've had to-day! [*A mysterious voice—a woman's—coming as though from beneath the floor, answers her:* "Oh yes, the weather is splendid, madam."] You are charming—my ideal type of person. . . . [*Voice:* "And I likes you fery much too, Madam."]

STATION MASTER [*applauding*]. Bravo, Madam Ventriloquist, bravo!

PISHCHICK [*in amazement*]. Just think of that! Most enchanting Charlotta Ivanovna! . . . I'm fairly in love with you! . . .

CHARLOTTA. In love? [*Shrugging her shoulders.*] Can you really love? *Guter Mensch, aber schlechter Musikant.*[5]

TROFIMOV [*clapping* PISHCHIK *on the shoulder*]. What a horse you are!

CHARLOTTA. Attention, please! Here's another trick. [*Takes a steamer rug from a chair.*] Here's a very good rug, I want to sell it. . . . [*Shakes it.*] Doesn't some one want to buy it?

PISHCHIK [*in amazement*]. Just think of that!

CHARLOTTA. *Ein, zwei, drei!* [*She raises the rug quickly, behind it stands* ANYA. *She makes a low curtsey, runs over to her mother, embraces her, and flies back to the drawing-room amid general delight.*]

LYUBOV ANDREYEVNA [*applauding*]. Bravo, bravo!

---

4. "One, two, three!"
5. "A good man, but a bad musician."

CHARLOTTA.   Once more now. *Ein, zwei, drei!* [*Raises the rug; behind it stands* VARYA, *bowing.*]

PISHCHIK [*marveling*].   Just think of that!

CHARLOTTA.   That's all! [*She throws the rug over* PISHCHIK, *makes a low curtsey, and runs into the ballroom.*]

PISHCHIK [*hurrying after her*].   Rascal! . . . You would then? You would? [*Goes out.*]

LYUBOV ANDREYEVNA.   And Leonid's not come yet. What's he doing in the city to keep him so long? I don't understand it. Why, everything must be finished there by now; the estate is sold, or else the sale didn't take place. Why must we be kept so long in ignorance?

VARYA [*trying to console her*].   Uncle has bought it, I'm sure.

TROFIMOV [*mockingly*].   Oh, yes!

VARYA.   Auntie gave him authority to buy it in her name and transfer the debt. She did it for Anya. And I'm convinced that with God's help uncle will buy it.

LYUBOV ANDREYEVNA.   Our aunt in Yaroslavl sent fifteen thousand rubles with which to purchase the estate in her name—she doesn't trust us—but that sum wouldn't be enough even to pay the interest. [*Covers her face with her hands.*] To-day my fate is decided . . . my fate . . .

TROFIMOV [*teasing* VARYA].   Madam Lopakhin!

VARYA [*angrily*].   Eternal student! He's been expelled from the University twice already.

LYUBOV ANDREYEVNA.   Why do you lose your temper, Varya? He's teasing you about Lopakhin—well, what of it? Marry Lopakhin if you want to, he's a nice, good man. If you don't want to, don't marry him. No one is forcing you, dear.

VARYA.   To be frank, mother dear, I do regard this matter seriously. He's a good man, I like him.

LYUBOV ANDREYEVNA.   Well then, marry him. I don't understand what you're waiting for.

VARYA.   I surely can't propose to him myself, mama. Every one has been talking to me about him for two years, but he either says nothing or jokes. I understand. He's making money, taken up with business. He hasn't time for me. If I had some money, even a little, even a hundred rubles, I'd give up everything and go far away. I'd enter a convent.

TROFIMOV.   Magnificent!

VARYA [*to* TROFIMOV].   A student ought to have some sense! [*Softly, and weeping.*] How old and ugly you've grown, Petya! [*To* LYUBOV ANDREYEVNA, *drying her tears.*] Only I can't stand it to be idle, mama. I must have something to do every minute.

[YASHA *comes in.*]

YASHA [*with difficulty restraining his laughter*].   Epikhodov has broken a billiard cue! . . . [*Goes out.*]

VARYA.   And why is Epikhodov in here? Who gave him permission to play pool? I don't understand these people. . . . [*Goes out.*]

LYUBOV ANDREYEVNA.   Don't tease her, Petya. You can see she's unhappy enough without it.

TROFIMOV. She takes a lot of pains minding other people's business. All summer she's given Anya and me no peace. She was afraid a romance might spring up between us. What business is it of hers? And moreover, I gave her no occasion—I am beyond such vulgarity. We are superior to love.

LYUBOV ANDREYEVNA. Then I must be inferior to love. [*Deeply agitated.*] Why isn't Leonid here? If only I knew whether the estate had been sold or not! The catastrophe seems so incredible to me that I don't even know what to think. I'm losing my mind. . . . I may cry out or do some idiotic thing. Help me, Petya; say something, do ! . . .

TROFIMOV. Isn't it all the same whether or no the estate is sold today? The matter's been settled for a long time; there is no turning back, the path is overgrown. Be calm, my dear friend, no need to deceive yourself. For once in your life at least, you must look truth straight in the eyes.

LYUBOV ANDREYEVNA. What truth? You can see where truth and falsehood lie, but I have quite lost that vision, I see nothing. You settle all important questions boldly, but tell me, my dear boy, is this not because you are young, because you haven't had time to put to painful test a single one of your questions? You look bravely forward—but isn't it because you do not see nor expect any terrible thing, inasmuch as life is still concealed from your young eyes? You are more fearless, more honest, more profound than we, but take thought for a moment, be a tiny bit magnanimous, and have pity on me. You see, I was born here, my father and mother lived here, and my grandfather too. I love this house; without the cherry orchard life is meaningless to me, and if it must be sold now, why then, you must sell me along with the orchard. . . . [*Embraces* TROFIMOV *and kisses him on the forehead.*] You see, my son was drowned here. . . . [*Weeps.*] Pity me, my good, kind friend.

TROFIMOV. You know that I sympathize with all my heart.

LYUBOV ANDREYEVNA. But you must say it differently, differently. [*Takes out her handkerchief and a telegram falls to the floor.*] You cannot imagine how heavy my heart is to-day. Things are so noisy and confusing, my very being shudders at every sound, I quiver all over, but I can't go off by myself—when I'm alone the silence terrifies me. Do not condemn me, Petya. I love you as though you belonged to my own family. I would gladly let Anya marry you, I swear it. Only, my dear boy, you must study, you must finish your course. You aren't doing anything but let fate bear you from place to place, strange as that may seem. . . . Isn't it so? And you simply must do something with your beard to make it grow decently. [*Laughs.*] You're so funny!

TROFIMOV [*picks up the telegram*]. I don't want to be a dandy.

LYUBOV ANDREYEVNA. That's a telegram from Paris. Every day I receive one. That wild man is sick again and in trouble. He asks forgiveness, begs me to come to him; and really, I ought to go to Paris to be near him. Your face is stern, Petya, but what can I do, my dear? What can I do? He is sick, he is alone, unhappy, and who is there to look after him, who will keep him from making mistakes, and give him his medicine at the right time? And why should I keep silence or conceal anything? I love him, that is clear to me. I love him, I love him. . . . This is the stone around my neck, I shall sink with it into the depths, but I love this stone and I cannot live without it. [*Presses* TROFIMOV's *hand.*] Don't think ill of me, Petya; don't say anything to me, don't say . . .

TROFIMOV [*through his tears*]. Forgive my bluntness, for God's sake— but he robbed you!

LYUBOV ANDREYEVNA.   No, no, no, you mustn't say that. . . . [*Covers her ears.*]

TROFIMOV.   Why, he's a rascal—you're the only one who doesn't realize it. He's a petty thief, a good-for-nothing . . .

LYUBOV ANDREYEVNA [*restrained, but angry*].   You're twenty-six or seven now, but you're still a high school sophomore!

TROFIMOV.   Well?

LYUBOV ANDREYEVNA.   You should be a man, at your age you should understand those who love. And you should be in love yourself . . . you must fall in love! [*Angrily.*] Yes, yes! And you're not virtuous, you're only a prude, a sort of freak and monstrosity. . . .

TROFIMOV [*horrified*].   What is she saying?

LYUBOV ANDREYEVNA.   "I am superior to love!" You're not superior to love, you're only what our Firs always calls a "lummox." To think of not having a mistress at your age!

TROFIMOV [*horrified*].   This is horrible! What is she saying! [*He walks quickly into the ballroom, clutching his head.*] This is horrible! I can't listen, I'll go away. . . . [*He goes out but returns immediately.*] Everything is over between us! [*Goes out into the hall.*]

LYUBOV ANDREYEVNA [*calling after him*].   Petya, wait! Foolish man, I was joking! Petya!

[*Some one is heard quickly ascending the stairway in the hall, then all of a sudden loudly falling downstairs. ANYA and VARYA scream, but immediately laughter is heard.*]

LYUBOV ANDREYEVNA.   What's the matter out there?

[*ANYA runs in.*]

ANYA [*laughing*].   Petya fell downstairs! [*She runs out.*]

LYUBOV ANDREYEVNA.   That Petya's a funny boy.

[*The STATION MASTER stops in the middle of the ballroom and begins to recite Alexey Tolstoy's "The Magdalen."*[6] *The others listen to him, but after a few stanzas the strains of a waltz are borne in from the hallway, and the recitation breaks off. They all dance. TROFIMOV, ANYA, VARYA, and LYUBOV ANDREYEVNA come back from the hallway.*]

LYUBOV ANDREYEVNA.   Well, Petya . . . well, pure soul. . . . I beg your forgiveness. . . . Come, let's dance. . . . [*She and PETYA dance.*]

[*ANYA and VARYA dance together. FIRS comes in and leans his stick up near the side door. YASHA has also entered from the dining-room and is watching the dancing.*]

YASHA.   What's the matter, grandfather?

---

6. Alexey Tolstoy (1817–75), popular Russian poet; the poem describes Christ's sudden appearance at a sumptuous banquet.

FIRS. I'm not well. In the old days generals, admirals and barons used to dance at our balls, and now we send for the postal official and the station master, and even they don't come very graciously. I'm not as strong as I used to be. My dead master, their grandfather, used to cure everybody of every disease with sealing wax. I've been taking sealing wax every day for twenty years now, and maybe more; maybe that's what's kept me alive.

YASHA. You make me tired, grandfather. [*Yawns.*] It's time you croaked.

FIRS. Eh, you lummox! . . . [*Mutters.*]

[TROFIMOV *and* LYUBOV ANDREYEVNA *are dancing in the ballroom; then they pass into the drawing-room.*]

LYUBOV ANDREYEVNA. *Merci!* I think I'll sit down . . . [*Seats herself.*] I'm tired.

[ANYA *comes in.*]

ANYA [*excitedly*]. Some man just told them in the kitchen that the cherry orchard was sold to-day.

LYUBOV ANDREYEVNA. Sold to whom?

ANYA. He didn't say to whom. He went away. [*She dances off with* TROFIMOV *into the ballroom.*]

YASHA. Some old fellow was gossiping about it a while ago. A stranger.

FIRS. And Leonid Andreich hasn't come yet. He was wearing a light-weight overcoat. He'd better look out or he'll catch cold. Eh, these green young things!

LYUBOV ANDREYEVNA. I shall die this very minute! Go, Yasha, and find out who's bought it.

YASHA. The old man's been gone a long time. [*Laughs.*]

LYUBOV ANDREYEVNA [*somewhat annoyed*]. Well, what are you laughing at? What are you so happy about?

YASHA. Epikhodov's very amusing. A stupid fellow. Two-and-twenty troubles.

LYUBOV ANDREYEVNA. Firs, if they sell the estate, where will you go?

FIRS. I will go wherever you command.

LYUBOV ANDREYEVNA. Why do you look so strange? Are you sick? You ought to go to bed.

FIRS. Yes. . . . [*With a grimace.*] I'd go to bed, but when I'm gone, who'll hand things around and manage everything? The whole house depends on me.

YASHA [*to* LYUBOV ANDREYEVNA]. Lyubov Andreyevna, permit me to make a request. Be so good! If you go back to Paris, kindly take me with you! It's absolutely impossible for me to remain here. [*In a low voice and looking around him.*] What's the use of talking? You can see for yourself, it's an uncivilized country, the people are immoral, and besides that, it's dull, they give you wretched food in the kitchen, and that Firs is always walking around muttering all kinds of stupidities. Please do take me with you!

[PISHCHIK *comes in.*]

PISHCHIK. May I ask you . . . most lovely lady . . . for a little waltz? . . . [LYUBOV ANDREYEVNA *dances off with him.*] Bewitching one, I'm going to borrow a hundred and eighty little rubles from you, I'm going to borrow . . . [*Dancing.*] a hundred and eighty little rubles. . . . [*They pass out into the ballroom.*]

YASHA [*humming softly*]. "Oh, canst thou comprehend the tumult of my soul?"

[*Out in the ballroom a figure in a gray top hat and checkered pantaloons waves its arms and jumps about; cries of "Bravo, Charlotta Ivanovna!"*]

DUNYASHA [*stopping to powder her nose*]. My young mistress told me to come in and dance. There are many gentlemen, and only a few ladies, but my head whirls when I dance, my heart beats, Firs Nikolayevich, and the post office clerk just said something to me that quite took my breath away.

[*The music stops.*]

FIRS. What did he say to you?
DUNYASHA. "You're like a flower," says he.
YASHA [*yawns*]. The bumpkin! . . . [*Goes out.*]
DUNYASHA. Like a little flower. . . . I'm such a delicate girl, I just love tender words.
FIRS. You'll lose your head.

[EPIKHODOV *comes in.*]

EPIKHODOV. You refuse to look at me, Avdotya Fedorovna . . . as if I were a sort of insect. . . . [*Sighing.*] Ah, well, that's life!
DUNYASHA. What do you want?
EPIKHODOV. Of course, you're probably right. [*Sighs.*] But then, if you want to regard it from this point of view, it's you, if you'll pardon my bluntness, who have brought me to such a pass. I know my fate. Every day some misfortune befalls me, and I've long since grown so accustomed to it that I smile at my fate. You gave me your promise, and though I—
DUNYASHA. Please let's talk later and leave me in peace now. I'm musing. [*Plays with her fan.*]
EPIKHODOV. Every day a mishap befalls me, and I—if I may say so—only smile, I even laugh.

[VARYA *comes in from the hall.*]

VARYA. Haven't you gone yet, Semen? What a presuming fellow you are, anyway. [*To* DUNYASHA.] Leave the room, Dunyasha. [*To* EPIKHODOV.] First you play billiards and break a cue, and then you swagger around in the drawing-room as though you were a guest.
EPIKHODOV. You can't expect much of me, if I may say so.
VARYA. I'm not expecting much of you, I'm just telling you the truth. All you know how to do is to walk from place to place, but you don't tend to your business. We keep a clerk, but goodness knows what for!

EPIKHODOV [*offended*]. Only my elders and people who know what they're talking about can pass judgment as to whether I work, or walk, or eat, or play pool.

VARYA. You dare speak to me so? [*Flying into a passion.*] You dare? You mean to imply that I don't know what I'm talking about? Get out of here! This instant!

EPIKHODOV [*cringing*]. Speak more politely, I beg you.

VARYA [*beside herself*]. Get out of here this instant! Out! [*He goes towards the door, she following him.*] Two-and-twenty troubles! Don't let me set eyes on you again! Go away and stay! [EPIKHODOV *goes out. His voice comes back from outside the door:* "I'll call you to account for this."] What, coming back? [*She snatches up the stick* FIRS *has left earlier near the door.*] Come on, then, come on, come on, I'll show you! Well, are you coming? Are you coming? Then take that! . . . [*She deals a blow with the stick just as* LOPAKHIN *enters.*]

LOPAKHIN. I thank you humbly.

VARYA [*angrily and mockingly*]. I beg your pardon.

LOPAKHIN. Don't mention it. I thank you humbly for a pleasant welcome.

VARYA. It deserves no appreciation. [*She moves away, then looks back and asks softly.*] I didn't hurt you, did I?

LOPAKHIN. Oh no, that's all right. All the same, there'll be a big bump.

VOICE [*in the hall*]. Lopakhin's come! Yermolay Alexeyevich!

PISHCHIK. We'll see with our eyes and hear with our ears! [*Exchanges kisses with* LOPAKHIN.] You smell of cognac, my dear fellow. Well, we've been having a jolly time here too.

[LYUBOV ANDREYEVNA *comes in.*]

LYUBOV ANDREYEVNA. So it's you, Yermolay Alexeich? Why were you so long? Where's Leonid?

LOPAKHIN. Leonid Andreich returned with me, he'll be in directly. . . .

LYUBOV ANDREYEVNA [*excitedly*]. Well, what happened? Did the sale take place? Do tell us!

LOPAKHIN [*in confusion and fearing to show his joy*]. The sale was over at four o'clock. . . . We missed the train and had to wait until half past nine. [*Sighing deeply.*] Uh! I'm a little bit dizzy. . . .

[GAYEV *comes in. His right arm is full of bundles; with his left hand he wipes away his tears.*]

LYUBOV ANDREYEVNA. Lenya, what's happened? Come, Lenya? [*Impatiently, through her tears.*] Quickly, for God's sake! . . .

GAYEV [*he does not answer her but only gestures; then to* FIRS, *weeping*]. Come, take these things. . . . Here are anchovies, Crimean herring. . . . I haven't eaten a thing to-day. . . . What I've been through! [*The door into the billiard room is open; one can hear the click of balls and* YASHA'S *voice saying,* "Seven and eighteen!" GAYEV'S *expression changes, he stops weeping.*] I'm terribly tired. Help me change my clothes, Firs. [*Goes into his own room across the hall,* FIRS *following him.*]

PISHCHIK. What happened? Please tell us.
LYUBOV ANDREYEVNA. Was the cherry orchard sold?
LOPAKHIN. Yes.
LYUBOV ANDREYEVNA. Who bought it?
LOPAKHIN. *I* bought it.

[*Pause.* LYUBOV ANDREYEVNA *is stunned. She would fall were she not leaning against the table and the armchair.* VARYA *takes the bunch of keys from her belt, throws them into the middle of the drawing-room floor, and goes out.*]

LOPAKHIN. *I* bought it! Wait a little, ladies and gentlemen, have patience, my head's swimming, I can't talk. . . . [*Laughs.*] When we arrived at the auction, Deriganov was already there. Leonid Andreich had on hand only fifteen thousand, while Deriganov immediately bid thirty thousand above the amount of the mortgage. I saw I was going to have a tussle with him, and bid forty. He raised to forty-five. I bid fifty-five. So he kept raising me five and I raised him ten. . . . Well, it was over at last. I offered ninety thousand over the mortgage, and it went to me. The cherry orchard's mine now! Mine! [*Roars with laughter.*] O Lord my God, the cherry orchard's mine! Tell me I'm drunk, out of my head, or dreaming. . . . [*Stamps his feet.*] Don't laugh at me! If only my father and grandfather could rise from their graves and see all these things that have come to pass—how their Yermolay, beaten, illiterate little Yermolay, who used to go barefoot in the winter, has bought an estate—the most beautiful one in the world! I have bought the estate where my father and grandfather were slaves, where they weren't allowed even to set foot in the kitchen. I'm asleep, this is only a dream, an hallucination. . . . This is the fruit of my imagination, veiled with the mist of uncertainty. . . . [*Picks up the keys with a caressing smile.*] She threw away the keys, she wants to show that she's no longer housekeeper here. . . . [*Jingles the keys.*] Well, no matter! . . . [*The orchestra is heard tuning up.*] Come, musicians, play, I want to hear you! Come, every one, and watch Yermolay Lopakhin swing his ax through the cherry orchard, see the trees fall to the ground! We'll build cottages here, and our grandsons and great-grandsons will see a new life arising here. . . . Let the music play!

[*Music.* LYUBOV ANDREYEVNA *falls into a chair and weeps bitterly.*]

LOPAKHIN [*reproachfully*]. Why, oh, why didn't you listen to me? My poor, dear friend, you cannot return to your home now. [*Weeping.*] Ah, if only this might swiftly pass by, if only we might swiftly change this unhappy, incoherent life of ours!

PISHCHIK [*in a low voice, taking him by the arm*]. She is weeping. Let us go into the ballroom and leave her alone. . . . Come on! . . . [*Takes him by the arm and leads him into the ballroom.*]

LOPAKHIN. What's the matter? Mind your notes, musicians! Let my wishes be obeyed. [*With irony.*] The new proprietor is coming, the lord of the cherry orchard! [*He unexpectedly bumps against a table, almost upsetting the candelabra.*] I can pay for everything! [*He goes out with* PISHCHIK.]

[*The ballroom and the drawing-room are empty save for* LYUBOV AN-
DREYEVNA, *who is huddled in her chair, weeping bitterly. The music plays
softly.* ANYA *and* TROFIMOV *come in quickly.* ANYA *goes over to her
mother and kneels before her.* TROFIMOV *remains near the ballroom door.*]

ANYA. Mama! . . . Mama, are you crying? My dear, good, kind mama,
my beautiful mama, I love you. . . . I bless you. The cherry orchard is sold, it is
gone, that is true, true, but don't cry, mama. Your life to come is left you, your
good, pure soul is left you. . . . Come with me, come away with me, darling,
come away! . . . We'll plant a new orchard, a more beautiful one; you shall
see it, shall understand it; and joy, deep and quiet, shall descend upon your
soul like the evening sunlight, and you will smile again, mama. Come, darling,
come!

ACT IV

The same as in Act I. There are no curtains at the windows, no pictures;
a little furniture remains, which has been piled in one corner, apparently to
be sold. There is a feeling of emptiness. Trunks, strapped bundles, etc.,
are piled near the outside door and back stage. The door to the left is open,
and through it may be heard the voices of ANYA and VARYA. LOPAKHIN is
standing in the room, waiting. YASHA is holding a tray with glasses filled
with champagne. EPIKHODOV is roping a box in the entry-way. There
is a droning behind scenes—the voices of the peasants who have come
to say good-by. GAYEV'S voice is heard, saying, "Thank you, my lads,
thank you."

YASHA. The peasants have come to say good-by. It's my opinion, Yermolay Alexeich, that the peasants are a good lot, but unintelligent.

[*The voices die away.* LYUBOV ANDREYEVNA *and* GAYEV *come in through
the hall. She is not weeping, but her face is pale and quivering. She
cannot speak.*]

GAYEV. You gave them your purse, Lyuba. You mustn't do such things,
you must not.
LYUBOV ANDREYEVNA. I couldn't help myself! I couldn't help it! [*They
both go out.*]
LOPAKHIN [*calling after them from the doorway*]. Please, I beg of you!
Come and have a farewell glass. I forgot to bring any from town, and I could only
find one bottle at the station. Please do! [*Pause.*] Don't you really want any?
[*Moves away from the door.*] If I'd only known, I wouldn't have bought it. Well,
then, I shan't drink any either. [YASHA *places the tray carefully on a chair.*]
Yasha, you have a drink anyway!
YASHA. To the departing! Good luck to them! [*Drinks.*] This isn't real
champagne, I can tell you that.
LOPAKHIN. It's eight rubles a bottle. [*Pause.*] It's cold as the devil here.

YASHA. We didn't build any fires to-day—it's all the same, we're going away. [*Laughs.*]

LOPAKHIN. Why are you laughing?

YASHA. Because I'm happy.

LOPAKHIN. Here it is October, but it's as quiet and sunny as though it were summer. Good building weather. [*Glances at his watch and calls through the door.*] Well, ladies and gentlemen, remember, it's just forty-seven minutes before train time. That means you must leave for the station in twenty minutes. Hurry up!

[TROFIMOV, *wearing an overcoat, comes in from outside.*]

TROFIMOV. I think it's time to go now. The horses have been brought around. Where the devil are my galoshes? They're lost. . . . [*Calls through the doorway.*] Anya, I can't find my galoshes. They're gone!

LOPAKHIN. I've got to go to Harkov. I'll take the same train you do. I shall spend the whole winter in Harkov. I've been frittering away my time with you people, I'm miserable without work. I can't live without something to do. I don't know what to do with my hands. They fidget around as though they belonged to some one else.

TROFIMOV. We'll be gone soon, and you can turn to your useful labors again.

LOPAKHIN. Have a glass, do.

TROFIMOV. No, thank you.

LOPAKHIN. So you're going on to Moscow now?

TROFIMOV. Yes, I'll accompany them as far as town, and then tomorrow I'll go on to Moscow.

LOPAKHIN. Yes. . . . I suppose the professors are holding up their lectures, every one will wait until you get there!

TROFIMOV. That's none of your business.

LOPAKHIN. How many years have you been studying at the University?

TROFIMOV. Think up a new question. That one's old and worn. [*Looking for his galoshes.*] You know, we probably shan't see each other again, so permit me to give you one parting bit of advice: Don't flourish your hands so! Break yourself of that habit of flourishing. And then too—all this building of cottages and figuring that in time their tenants will become land-owners—that's just another way of flourishing your hands. But for all that, I like you just the same. You have slender, delicate fingers like those of an artist; you have a slender, delicate soul. . . .

LOPAKHIN [*embracing him*]. Good-by, my dear fellow. Thank you for everything. If you need money for your trip, let me lend you some.

TROFIMOV. I don't need any.

LOPAKHIN. But you have none!

TROFIMOV. Oh yes, thank you. I received some for a translation. Here it is, in my pocket. [*Anxiously.*] But I can't find my galoshes!

VARYA [*from the other room*]. Here, take your rubbish! [*Throws a pair of rubber galoshes out on the stage.*]

TROFIMOV. Why are you so angry, Varya? Hm. . . . Those aren't my galoshes.

LOPAKHIN.   Last spring I sowed three thousand acres to poppies, and now I've cleared forty thousand on them. And when my poppies were in bloom, what a picture it was! As I was saying, I made forty thousand clear, and I'm offering you a loan because I'm able to. Why turn up your nose at me? I'm a peasant—a plain, blunt fellow.

TROFIMOV.   Your father was a peasant, mine an apothecary, and that fact is of no consequence whatever. [LOPAKHIN *takes out his wallet.*] Hold on there, hold on—if you gave me two hundred thousand I wouldn't take it. I am a free man; and everything which you all, rich and poor alike, value so highly and dearly, has not the slightest power over me, even as thistledown borne upon the breeze. I can get along without you, I can pass you by. I am strong and proud. Humanity is moving towards the highest truth, towards the highest happiness attainable on earth; and I am in the front ranks.

LOPAKHIN.   Shall you get there?

TROFIMOV.   I shall. [*Pause.*] I shall get there, or else I will show others the road whereby they may arrive.

[*The sound of an ax striking against wood is heard in the distance.*]

LOPAKHIN.   Well, good-by, my dear fellow. It's time to go. Here we stand chaffing each other, but life goes on just the same. When I work without stopping for a long time, then my thoughts grow clearer somehow, and it seems as though I too knew the reason for my existence. But how many people there are in Russia, brother, who do not know why they are alive! Oh, well—the world wags on just the same. They say Leonid Andreich has taken a position in a bank, six thousand a year. . . . Only you know he won't stay there, he's very lazy.

ANYA [*in the doorway*].   Mama asks you please not to let them cut down the orchard before she goes.

TROFIMOV.   Really, haven't you the consideration to . . . [*He goes out through the hall.*]

LOPAKHIN.   Right away . . . right away. . . . What people! . . . [*Follows him out.*]

ANYA.   Has Firs been taken to the hospital?

YASHA.   I told them to this morning. They must have taken him.

ANYA [*to* EPIKHODOV, *who is passing through the hall*].   Semen Panteleich, please find out if Firs has been taken to the hospital.

YASHA [*offended*].   I told Yegor this morning. Why do you have to ask about it a dozen times!

EPIKHODOV.   It's my firm opinion that that superannuated Firs isn't worth repairs. It's time he joined his forefathers. I can only envy him. [*Puts a trunk down on top of a hat box and crushes it.*] Well, of course, that had to happen—I knew it! [*Goes out.*]

YASHA [*mockingly*].   Two-and-twenty troubles. . . .

VARYA [*outside the door*].   Have they taken Firs to the hospital?

ANYA.   Yes.

VARYA.   Why didn't they take the letter to the doctor?

ANYA.   We'll have to send it after him. [*Goes out.*]

VARYA [*from the next room*].   Where's Yasha? Tell him that his mother has come and wants to say good-by to him.

YASHA [*waves his hand*].   She bothers me to death!

[*All this time* DUNYASHA *has been bustling about the baggage. Now that* YASHA *is alone on the stage, she approaches him.*]

DUNYASHA.   You might look at me just once more, Yasha. You're going away . . . leaving me. . . . [*She bursts into tears and falls on his neck.*]

YASHA.   What's the use of crying? [*Drinks champagne.*] In six days I'll be back in Paris again. To-morrow we'll take the express and roll along so fast they can hardly see us flying by. I can scarcely believe it. Veev la France! . . . I don't like it here, I can't live here. . . . There's nothing to do. I have looked my fill at ignorance—that's enough for me. [*Drinks champagne.*] What's the use of crying? Act like a lady, then you won't cry.

DUNYASHA [*glancing in the mirror and powdering her nose*].   Write me a letter from Paris. You know I've loved you, Yasha—oh, how I've loved you! I'm a tender little creature, Yasha.

YASHA.   They're coming. [*Bustles around the trunks, humming softly.*]

[LYUBOV ANDREYEVNA, GAYEV, ANYA, *and* CHARLOTTA IVANOVNA *come in.*]

GAYEV.   We ought to be on our way. Time's short. [*Glancing at* YASHA.] Who is it smells of herring around here?

LYUBOV ANDREYEVNA.   In ten minutes we shall be sitting in the carriage. . . . [*Surveys the room.*] Good-by, dear house, old grandfather! The winter will pass, spring will return, and then you'll be here no longer, they will tear you down. How many things these walls have seen! [*Kisses her daughter warmly.*] My treasure, you are radiant, your eyes are dancing like two diamonds. Are you happy? Very?

ANYA.   Very. A new life is beginning, mama!

GAYEV [*cheerfully*].   Indeed, everything is all right now. Before the cherry orchard was sold, we were all restless, unhappy; but now that the question has been definitely and irrevocably settled, we have all become calm and even cheerful. I'm a bank official now, I'm a financier. . . . Yellow into the middle! While you, Lyuba, somehow look better, no doubt of it.

LYUBOV ANDREYEVNA.   Yes, my nerves are quieter, that's true. [*Some one hands her her hat and coat.*] I'm sleeping well. Carry my bags out, Yasha. It's time to go. [*To* ANYA.] My little girl, we shall see each other soon. . . . I am going to Paris, I shall live there on the money your great-aunt from Yaroslavl sent to buy the estate—long life to auntie!—but that money won't last long.

ANYA.   You'll come back very, very soon, won't you, mama? I'll study to pass the high school examinations, and then I'll work and help you. We'll read so many books together, mama . . . won't we? [*Kisses her mother's hands.*] We'll read on the autumn evenings, lots of books, and a wonderful new world will open up before us. . . . [*Dreamily.*] Be sure to come, mama.

LYUBOV ANDREYEVNA.   I will come back, my treasure. [*Embraces* ANYA.]

[LOPAKHIN *comes in.* CHARLOTTA *is singing softly.*]

GAYEV.   Happy Charlotta! She is singing!

CHARLOTTA [*picking up a bundle shaped like a swaddled baby*].   Bye-o-bye, my baby. . . . [*A child's cry is heard:* "Wah! wah!"] Keep quiet, my darling, my nice boy! ["Wah! wah!"] Oh, too bad, too bad! [*Tosses the bundle back to its place.*] Please find a situation for me, I can't manage otherwise.

LOPAKHIN.   We'll find one for you, Charlotta Ivanovna, don't you worry.

GAYEV.   They're all leaving us. Varya's going away. . . . All of a sudden, nobody needs us.

CHARLOTTA.   I've no place to live in town. I'll have to leave you. . . . [*Hums.*] Oh, well! . . .

[PISHCHIK *comes in.*]

LOPAKHIN.   Nature's miracle!

PISHCHIK [*panting*].   Oh, let me get my breath! I'm all worn out! Most dear and honored friends—give me some water. . . .

GAYEV.   You've come after money, I suppose? Your humble servant! . . . But just the same I'm going to flee temptation. [*Goes out.*]

PISHCHIK.   I haven't been to see you for a long time, most lovely lady. . . . [*To* LOPAKHIN.] So you're here. . . . I'm glad to see you . . . man of vast intellect. . . . Here, take this. . . . [*Hands* LOPAKHIN *some money.*] Four hundred rubles. . . . Eight hundred and forty left on my account. . . .

LOPAKHIN [*shrugging his shoulders in bewilderment*].   I'm dreaming. . . . Where did you get it?

PISHCHIK.   Wait a minute. . . . I'm too warm. . . . A most unusual circumstance. Some Englishmen came to see me and found some white clay on my land. . . . [*To* LYUBOV ANDREYEVNA.] And four hundred for you . . . most beautiful and marvelous lady. . . . [*Hands her the money.*] I'll have the rest for you later. [*Drinks some water.*] A young man told me on the train just a little while ago how some great philosopher or other told a man how to jump off roofs. . . . "Just jump!" says he, and that's all there is to it. [*In wonderment.*] Just think of that! Water!

LOPAKHIN.   But who are these Englishmen?

PISHCHIK.   I've leased them the piece of land with the clay for twenty-four years. . . . But excuse me, I haven't time to tell you about it now. . . . I've got to hurry on. . . . I'm going to see Znoykov . . . and Kardamonov. . . . I'm in debt to every one. . . . [*Drinks.*] Your health! . . . I'll call in on Thursday. . . .

LYUBOV ANDREYEVNA.   We're just leaving for the city, and to-morrow I'm going abroad.

PISHCHIK.   What? [*In alarm.*] Why are you going to town? Ah, now I see the furniture . . . the trunks. . . . Well, no matter. . . . [*Through his tears.*] No matter. . . . People of great intelligence . . . these Englishmen. . . . No matter. Good luck. . . . God will take care of you. . . . No matter. . . . There's an end to everything on earth. . . . [*Kisses the hand of* LYUBOV ANDREYEVNA.] And should you ever happen to hear that my end has come, remember this old . . . horse, and say, "There used to live upon this earth a certain . . . Semeonov-Pishchik. . . . The heavenly kingdom to him!" . . . It's wonderful weather. . . . Yes. . . . [*He goes out deeply moved, but returns immediately and says from the doorway.*] Dashenka sent her regards! [*Goes out.*]

LYUBOV ANDREYEVNA. Well, we can go now. I'm leaving with two cares on my mind. The first one is poor, sick, old Firs. [*Looks at her watch.*] I have still five minutes to spare. . . .

ANYA. They've sent Firs to the hospital already, mama. Yasha saw to it this morning.

LYUBOV ANDREYEVNA. My second worry is Varya. She is accustomed to early rising and work; and now, with nothing to do, she's like a fish out of water. She's grown thin and pale, and she weeps, poor girl. . . . [*Pause.*] You know very well, Yermolay Alexeich, I have dreamed . . . of giving her to you, for it's quite obvious that you'll marry some one. [*She whispers to* ANYA, *who nods to* CHARLOTTA, *and they both go out.*] She loves you, she's congenial to you, and I really don't know why you avoid each other so. I don't understand it at all!

LOPAKHIN. To tell the truth, I don't understand it myself. It's all strange somehow. . . . If there's still time, why I'm ready now. . . . We'll make an end of it right away and have done with it. But without your help, I feel I shan't propose.

LYUBOV ANDREYEVNA. That's fine now. It'll take only a moment, you know. I'll call her right away.

LOPAKHIN. By the way, there's some champagne. . . . [*Looking at the glasses.*] They're empty. Some one's drained them dry already. [YASHA *coughs.*] That's real guzzling, that is!

LYUBOV ANDREYEVNA [*with animation*]. Splendid! We'll go out. . . . Yasha, *allez!*[1] I'll call her. . . . [*In the doorway.*] Varya, leave everything and come here. Come! [*Goes out with* YASHA.]

LOPAKHIN [*looking at his watch*]. Yes. . . . [*Pause.*]

[*There is a restrained laugh behind the door, and whispering. At last* VARYA *comes in.*]

VARYA [*looking over the baggage carefully*]. That's strange, I can't find it anywhere. . . .

LOPAKHIN. What are you looking for?

VARYA. I packed it myself, and now I've forgotten where. [*Pause.*]

LOPAKHIN. Where are you going now, Varvara Mikhaylovna?

VARYA. I? To the Ragulins. . . . I've agreed to take over the housekeeping—something like that. . . .

LOPAKHIN. Don't they live in Yashnevo? That's fifty miles from here. [*Pause.*] So life in this old house is finished. . . .

VARYA [*surveying the bundles*]. Where can it be? . . . Or perhaps I packed it in the trunk. . . . Yes, life in this house is over—it will never return.

LOPAKHIN. And I'm off to Harkov now . . . on this same train. I've a lot to attend to. And I'm going to leave Epikhodov here. . . . I've hired him.

VARYA. You don't say!

LOPAKHIN. Last year at this time, if you remember, snow was already

---

1. "Go!"

falling, but now it's quiet and sunny. Only it's cold . . . six degrees below freezing.

VARYA.   I haven't looked to see. [*Pause.*] But then, our thermometer is broken anyway. . . . [*Pause.*]

VOICE [*at the door*].   Yermolay Alexeich!

LOPAKHIN [*as though he had long been waiting that call*].   Right away. [*He goes out quickly.*]

[VARYA, *sitting on the floor, lays her head on a bundle of wraps and sobs softly. The door opens and* LYUBOV ANDREYEVNA *tiptoes in.*]

LYUBOV ANDREYEVNA.   Well? [*Pause.*] We must be going.

VARYA [*stops crying and wipes her eyes*].   Yes, it's time to go, mama. I'll arrive at the Ragulins' to-day, if only I don't miss the train.

LYUBOV ANDREYEVNA [*standing in the doorway*].   Anya, put on your things.

[ANYA *comes in;* GAYEV *and* CHARLOTTA IVANOVNA *follow her.* GAYEV *is wearing a warm overcoat with a cape. The* SERVANTS *and* COACHMEN *assemble.* EPIKHODOV *bustles around the baggage.*]

LYUBOV ANDREYEVNA.   Now we can start on our way.

ANYA [*joyously*].   On our way!

GAYEV.   My friends, my dear, good friends! In leaving this house forever, can I possibly remain silent, restrain myself, and not express at parting the emotions that now fill my whole being? . . .

ANYA [*beseechingly*].   Uncle!

VARYA.   Uncle dear, you mustn't!

GAYEV [*mournfully*].   Yellow across the table into the middle. . . . I'll keep still. . . .

[TROFIMOV *comes in, after him* LOPAKHIN.]

TROFIMOV.   Well, ladies and gentlemen, it's time to go!

LOPAKHIN.   Epikhodov, my coat!

LYUBOV ANDREYEVNA.   I'll sit here just one moment longer. It's as though I'd never really seen these walls, these ceilings before, and now I look at them eagerly, with such tender love. . . .

GAYEV.   I remember when I was six years old sitting in this window on Trinity Sunday, and watching father go to church.

LYUBOV ANDREYEVNA.   Has everything been taken out?

LOPAKHIN.   I think so. [*To* EPIKHODOV, *who is helping him on with his overcoat.*] Epikhodov, look and see if everything is all ready.

EPIKHODOV [*in a hoarse voice*].   Put your mind at rest, Yermolay Alexeich.

LOPAKHIN.   What's the matter with your voice?

EPIKHODOV.   I just drank some water and swallowed it wrong.

YASHA [*contemptuously*].   Bumpkin!

LYUBOV ANDREYEVNA.   If we go, there won't be a soul left behind. . . .

LOPAKHIN.   Not until spring.

VARYA [*pulls an umbrella out of a bundle and seems about to swing it.* LOPAKHIN *pretends to be frightened*].   What's the matter? What's the matter? . . . I never dreamed of it.

TROFIMOV.   Let's climb into the carriages, ladies and gentlemen. It's time to go. It's nearly train time.

VARYA.   Petya, there are your galoshes, near that trunk . . . [*Tearfully.*] And how dirty and old they are! . . .

TROFIMOV [*putting on his galoshes*].   Well, let's be on our way!

GAYEV [*deeply moved, on the verge of unwilling tears*].   The train . . . the station. . . . Back shot to the middle, white across the table to the corner. . . .

LYUBOV ANDREYEVNA.   We must go!

LOPAKHIN.   Is every one here? No one left? [*He locks the door on the left.*] There are some things stored here, we'll have to lock them up. Come on!

ANYA.   Good-by, old house! Good-by, old life!

TROFIMOV.   Welcome, new life! [*He goes out with* ANYA.]

[VARYA *casts a glance around the room and goes slowly out.* YASHA, *and* CHARLOTTA, *her lap dog in her arms, follow.*]

LOPAKHIN.   Until spring then! Come on, my friends! Till we meet again! [*Goes out.*]

[LYUBOV ANDREYEVNA *and* GAYEV *are left together. They seem to have been waiting for this moment. They fall into each other's arms and sob softly, restrainedly, as though fearing lest some one hear them.*]

GAYEV [*in despair*].   My sister, my sister! . . .

LYUBOV ANDREYEVNA.   Oh, my dear orchard, my tender, beautiful orchard! My life, my youth, my happiness, farewell! Farewell!

ANYA's *voice* [*joyously, appealingly*].   Mama! . . .

TROFIMOV's *voice* [*joyously and with ardor*].   Yoo-hoo!

LYUBOV ANDREYEVNA.   To look at the walls, at the windows, for the last time! . . . Our dead mother loved to walk to and fro in this room. . . .

GAYEV.   My sister, my sister!

ANYA's *voice*.   Mama!

TROFIMOV's *voice*.   Yoo-hoo!

LYUBOV ANDREYEVNA.   We're coming! . . . [*They go out.*]

[*The stage is empty. One can hear keys turning in the locks of all the doors, the carriages roll away. Then the sound of an ax striking against wood, a sad and lonely sound, rings out amid the stillness. Footsteps are heard.* FIRS *emerges from the door on the right. He is dressed as usual in a waiter's jacket and white waistcoat, with slippers on his feet. He is ill.*]

FIRS [*going over to the door and pulling at the knob*].   Locked! They've gone away. . . . [*Sits down on the sofa.*] They've forgotten me. . . . No matter. . . . I'll sit here a little while. . . . And I suppose Leonid Andreich didn't put on his fur coat and went off in a light one. . . . [*Sighs anxiously.*] I never looked to see. . . . Young and green! [*Mutters something unintelligible.*] So life has gone by—just as though I'd never lived at all. . . . [*Lies down.*] I'll lie here a little while. . . . You've no strength in you, nothing's left, nothing. . . . Eh, you're a . . . lummox! [*Lies motionless.*]

[*A distant sound is heard, like the melancholy twang of a string, breaking in the heavens. It dies away. Silence, save for the dull sound of an ax chopping, far off in the orchard.*]

Eugène Ionesco   (b. 1912)
The Gap

Cast of Characters

THE FRIEND
THE ACADEMICIAN
THE ACADEMICIAN'S WIFE
THE MAID

SET: *A rich bourgeois living room with artistic pretensions. One or two sofas, a number of armchairs, among which, a green, Régence style[1] one, right in the middle of the room. The walls are covered with framed diplomas. One can make out, written in heavy script at the top of a particularly large one, "Doctor Honoris causa." This is followed by an almost illegible Latin inscription. Another equally impressive diploma states: "Doctorat honoris causa,"[2] again followed by a long, illegible text. There is an abundance of smaller diplomas, each of which bears a clearly written "doctorate."*
   A door to the right of the audience.
   As the curtain rises, one can see THE ACADEMICIAN'S WIFE *dressed in a rather crumpled robe. She has obviously just gotten out of bed, and has not had time to dress.* THE FRIEND *faces her. He is well dressed: hat, umbrella in hand, stiff collar, black jacket and striped trousers, shiny black shoes.*

THE WIFE.   Dear friend, tell me all.
THE FRIEND.   I don't know what to say.
THE WIFE.   I know.
THE FRIEND.   I heard the news last night. I did not want to call you. At the same time I couldn't wait any longer. Please forgive me for coming so early with such terrible news.
THE WIFE.   He didn't make it! How terrible! We were still hoping. . . .
THE FRIEND.   It's hard, I know. He still had a chance. Not much of one. We had to expect it.
THE WIFE.   I didn't expect it. He was always so successful. He could always manage somehow, at the last moment.
THE FRIEND.   In that state of exhaustion. You shouldn't have let him!

---

   1. Furniture style originating in France in the early 1700s; it is characterized by gentle curves, subdued brass and tortoise-shell ornamentation, and woods such as walnut and rosewood.
   2. These are honorary doctorate degrees, ones granted in recognition of a distinctive accomplishment not achieved in a regular course of study.

THE WIFE. What can we do, what can we do! . . . How awful!

THE FRIEND. Come on, dear friend, be brave. That's life.

THE WIFE. I feel faint: I'm going to faint. [*She falls in one of the armchairs.*]

THE FRIEND [*holding her, gently slapping her cheeks and hands*]. I shouldn't have blurted it out like that. I'm sorry.

THE WIFE. No, you were right to do so. I had to find out somehow or other.

THE FRIEND. I should have prepared you, carefully.

THE WIFE. I've got to be strong. I can't help thinking of him, the wretched man. I hope they won't put it in the papers. Can we count on the journalists' discretion?

THE FRIEND. Close your door. Don't answer the telephone. It will still get around. You could go to the country. In a couple of months, when you are better, you'll come back, you'll go on with your life. People forget such things.

THE WIFE. People won't forget so fast. That's all they were waiting for. Some friends will feel sorry, but the others, the others. . . . [THE ACADEMICIAN *comes in, fully dressed: uniform, chest covered with decorations, his sword on his side.*]

THE ACADEMICIAN. Up so early, my dear? [*To* THE FRIEND.] You've come early too. What's happening? Do you have the final results?

THE WIFE. What a disgrace!

THE FRIEND. You mustn't crush him like this, dear friend. [*To* THE ACADEMICIAN.] You have failed.

THE ACADEMICIAN. Are you quite sure?

THE FRIEND. You should never have tried to pass the baccalaureate examination.

THE ACADEMICIAN. They failed me. The rats! How dare they do this to me!

THE FRIEND. The marks were posted late in the evening.

THE ACADEMICIAN. Perhaps it was difficult to make them out in the dark. How could you read them?

THE FRIEND. They had set up spotlights.

THE ACADEMICIAN. They're doing everything to ruin me.

THE FRIEND. I passed by in the morning; the marks were still up.

THE ACADEMICIAN. You could have bribed the concierge[3] into pulling them down.

THE FRIEND. That's exactly what I did. Unfortunately the police were there. Your name heads the list of those who failed. Everyone's standing in line to get a look. There's an awful crush.

THE ACADEMICIAN. Who's there? The parents of the candidates?

THE FRIEND. Not only they.

THE WIFE. All your rivals, all your colleagues must be there. All those you attacked in the press for ignorance: your undergraduates, your graduate students, all those you failed when you were chairman of the board of examiners.

THE ACADEMICIAN. I am discredited! But I won't let them. There must be some mistake.

---

3. Building attendant.

THE FRIEND. I saw the examiners. I spoke with them. They gave me your marks. Zero in mathematics.

THE ACADEMICIAN. I had no scientific training.

THE FRIEND. Zero in Greek, zero in Latin.

THE WIFE [*to her husband*]. You, a humanist, the spokesman for humanism, the author of that famous treatise "The Defense of Poesy and Humanism."

THE ACADEMICIAN. I beg your pardon, but my book concerns itself with twentieth century humanism. [*To* THE FRIEND.] What about composition? What grade did I get in composition?

THE FRIEND. Nine hundred. You have nine hundred points.

THE ACADEMICIAN. That's perfect. My average must be all the way up.

THE FRIEND. Unfortunately not. They're marking on the basis of two thousand. The passing grade is one thousand.

THE ACADEMICIAN. They must have changed the regulations.

THE WIFE. They didn't change them just for you. You have a frightful persecution complex.

THE ACADEMICIAN. I tell you they changed them.

THE FRIEND. They went back to the old ones, back to the time of Napoleon.

THE ACADEMICIAN. Utterly outmoded. Besides, when did they make those changes? It isn't legal. I'm chairman of the Baccalaureate Commission of the Ministry of Public Education. They didn't consult me, and they cannot make any changes without my approval. I'm going to expose them. I'm going to bring government charges against them.

THE WIFE. Darling, you don't know what you're doing. You're in your dotage. Don't you recall handing in your resignation just before taking the examination so that no one could doubt the complete objectivity of the board of examiners?

THE ACADEMICIAN. I'll take it back.

THE WIFE. You should never have taken that test. I warned you. After all, it's not as if you needed it. But you have to collect all the honors, don't you? You're never satisfied. What did you need this diploma for? Now all is lost. You have your Doctorate, your Master's, your high school diploma, your elementary school certificate, and even the first part of the baccalaureate.

THE ACADEMICIAN. There was a gap.

THE WIFE. No one suspected it.

THE ACADEMICIAN. But *I* knew it. Others might have found out. I went to the office of the Registrar and asked for a transcript of my record. They said to me: "Certainly Professor, Mr. President, Your Excellency. . . ." Then they looked up my file, and the Chief Registrar came back looking embarrassed, most embarrassed indeed. He said: "There's something peculiar, very peculiar. You have your Master's, certainly, but it's no longer valid." I asked him why, of course. He answered: "There's a gap behind your Master's. I don't know how it happened. You must have registered and been accepted at the University without having passed the second part of the baccalaureate examination."

THE FRIEND. And then?

THE WIFE. Your Master's degree is no longer valid?

THE ACADEMICIAN. No, not quite. It's suspended. "The duplicate you are asking for will be delivered to you upon completion of the baccalaureate. Of course you will pass the examination with no trouble.'' That's what I was told, so you see now that I had to take it.

THE FRIEND. Your husband, dear friend, wanted to fill the gap. He's a conscientious person.

THE WIFE. It's clear you don't know him as I do. That's not it at all. He wants fame, honors. He never has enough. What does one diploma more or less matter? No one notices them anyway, but he sneaks in at night, on tiptoe, into the living room, just to look at them, and count them.

THE ACADEMICIAN. What else can I do when I have insomnia?

THE FRIEND. The questions asked at the baccalaureate are usually known in advance. You were admirably situated to get this particular information. You could also have sent in a replacement to take the test for you. One of your students, perhaps. Or if you wanted to take the test without people realizing that you already knew the questions, you could have sent your maid to the black market, where one can buy them.

THE ACADEMICIAN. I don't understand how I could have failed in my composition. I filled three sheets of paper. I treated the subject fully, taking into account the historical background. I interpreted the situation accurately . . . at least plausibly. I didn't deserve a bad grade.

THE FRIEND. Do you recall the subject?

THE ACADEMICIAN. Hum . . . let's see. . . .

THE FRIEND. He doesn't even remember what he discussed.

THE ACADEMICIAN. I do . . . wait . . . hum.

THE FRIEND. The subject to be treated was the following: ''Discuss the influence of Renaissance painters on novelists of the Third Republic.''[4] I have here a photostatic copy of your examination paper. Here is what you wrote.

THE ACADEMICIAN [*grabbing the photostat and reading*]. ''The trial of Benjamin: After Benjamin was tried and acquitted, the assessors holding a different opinion from that of the President murdered him, and condemned Benjamin to the suspension of his civic rights, imposing on him a fine of nine hundred francs. . . .''

THE FRIEND. That's where the nine hundred points come from.

THE ACADEMICIAN. ''Benjamin appealed his case . . . Benjamin appealed his case. . . .'' I can't make out the rest. I've always had bad handwriting. I ought to have taken a typewriter along with me.

THE WIFE. Horrible handwriting, scribbling and crossing out; ink spots didn't help you much.

THE ACADEMICIAN [*goes on with his reading after having retrieved the text his wife had pulled out of his hand*]. ''Benjamin appealed his case. Flanked by policemen dressed in zouave uniforms[5] . . . in zouave uniforms. . . .'' It's getting dark. I can't see the rest. . . . I don't have my glasses.

THE WIFE. What you've written has nothing to do with the subject.

THE FRIEND. Your wife's quite right, friend. It has nothing to do with the subject.

---

4. Period of rule in France from 1871 to 1940; it was marked by relative stability, increased democratization, and greater social equality.

5. Characterized by baggy trousers, short colorful jackets, and tasseled caps.

THE ACADEMICIAN. Yes, it has. Indirectly.

THE FRIEND. Not even indirectly.

THE ACADEMICIAN. Perhaps I chose the second question.

THE FRIEND. There was only one.

THE ACADEMICIAN. Even if there was only that one, I treated another quite adequately. I went to the end of the story. I stressed the important points, explaining the motivations of the characters, highlighting their behavior. I explained the mystery, making it plain and clear. There was even a conclusion at the end. I can't make out the rest. [*To* THE FRIEND.] Can you read it?

THE FRIEND. It's illegible. I don't have my glasses either.

THE WIFE [*taking the text*]. It's illegible and I have excellent eyes. You pretended to write. Mere scribbling.

THE ACADEMICIAN. That's not true. I've even provided a conclusion. It's clearly marked here in heavy print: "Conclusion or sanction . . . Conclusion or sanction. . . ." They can't get away with it. I'll have this examination rendered null and void.

THE WIFE. Since you treated the wrong subject, and treated it badly, setting down only titles, and writing nothing in between, the mark you received is justified. You'd lose your case.

THE FRIEND. You'd most certainly lose. Drop it. Take a vacation.

THE ACADEMICIAN. You're always on the side of the Others.

THE WIFE. After all, these professors know what they're doing. They haven't been granted their rank for nothing. They passed examinations, received serious training. They know the rules of composition.

THE ACADEMICIAN. Who was on the board of examiners?

THE FRIEND. For Mathematics, a movie star. For Greek, one of the Beatles. For Latin, the champion of the automobile race, and many others.

THE ACADEMICIAN. But these people aren't any more qualified than I am. And for composition?

THE FRIEND. A woman, a secretary in the editorial division of the review *Yesterday, the Day Before Yesterday, and Today.*

THE ACADEMICIAN. Now I know. This wretch gave me a poor grade out of spite because I never joined her political party. It's an act of vengeance. But I have ways and means of rendering the examination null and void. I'm going to call the President.

THE WIFE. Don't! You'll make yourself look even more ridiculous. [*To* THE FRIEND.] Please try to restrain him. He listens to you more than to me. [THE FRIEND *shrugs his shoulders, unable to cope with the situation.* THE WIFE *turns to her husband, who has just lifted the receiver off the hook.*] Don't call!

THE ACADEMICIAN [*on the telephone*]. Hello, John? It is I . . . What? . . . What did you say? . . . But, listen, my dear friend . . . but, listen to me . . . Hello! Hello! [*Puts down the receiver.*]

THE FRIEND. What did he say?

THE ACADEMICIAN. He said . . . He said. . . . "I don't want to talk to you. My mummy won't let me make friends with boys at the bottom of the class." Then he hung up on me.

THE WIFE. You should have expected it. All is lost. How could you do this to me? How could you do this to me?

THE ACADEMICIAN. Think of it! I lectured at the Sorbonne, at Oxford, at

American universities. Ten thousand theses have been written on my work; hundreds of critics have analyzed it. I hold an *honoris causa* doctorate from Amsterdam as well as a secret university Chair with the Duchy of Luxembourg. I received the Nobel Prize three times. The King of Sweden himself was amazed by my erudition. A doctorate *honoris causa, honoris causa . . .* and I failed the baccalaureate examination!

THE WIFE.   Everyone will laugh at us!

[THE ACADEMICIAN *takes off his sword and breaks it on his knee.*]

THE FRIEND [*picking up the two pieces*].   I wish to preserve these in memory of our ancient glory.

[THE ACADEMICIAN *meanwhile in a fit of rage is tearing down his decorations, throwing them on the floor, and stepping on them.*]

THE WIFE [*trying to salvage the remains*].   Don't do this! Don't! That's all we've got left.

Writing Themes about Literature

When your instructor makes the announcement, "The first paper will be due Friday," there is no need to let this news upset you. Writing an interpretive paper about a short story, poem, or play does not have to be an unpleasant experience. Students who find themselves gazing at a blank piece of paper the night before the assignment is due usually have only themselves to blame. They have already made two errors in judgment which threaten to turn an interesting experience into an agonizing all-nighter.

First, they should not have let the assignment go until the last night. Few inexperienced writers (and many experienced ones) can produce an honest and intelligent paper in one evening. If professional writers agree on any single idea, it is that a good piece of prose involves prolonged concentration and some unconscious activity as well. The English philosopher and mathematician, Bertrand Russell, once wrote:

> I have found that if I have to write upon some rather difficult topic, the best plan is to think about it with very great intensity—the greatest intensity of which I am capable—for a few hours or days, and at the end of that time give orders, so to speak, that the work is to proceed underground. After some time I return consciously to the topic and find that the work has been done.

Russell is not suggesting that you can count on your unconscious to write your paper for you. He means merely that you must involve your whole mind in the problem you are writing about. And the human mind creates at its own slow pace, so set it to work early.

Even if they have thought seriously about their papers after the assignment was made, students who find themselves with nothing to say are probably making a second, more serious mistake. Pressed by time, they are trying to write their papers without going through the essential preliminary steps. The creation of any long, written statement involves a process which will take a few hours for several successive days. The actual writing of your paper is a late stage in this process. It follows the choice of a topic, the defining of a thesis, the collecting of evidence, and the outlining of the argument. With a statement of thesis, a pile of index cards covered with notes and a rough outline spread out on your desk, the actual writing of your paper should go smoothly.

Interpreting Literature

There is, however, one very important activity which must precede all others in this process—the interpretation of the text. An effective interpretive paper invariably treats one aspect of a piece of literature— theme, style, imagery, or characterization, just to name a few. But before you begin concentrating on your particular topic, it is essential that you consider the story, poem or play as an object of delight and instruction in its own right. No matter how narrow the topic you have been assigned or have chosen, an intelligent treatment will require a thorough study of the work as a unified piece of literature.

Interpreting a story, poem, or play is very much like interpreting your daily experiences. Imagine that you and a friend meet a classmate for the first time who seems anxious to impress you. He talks rapidly and tells several amusing stories. In later weeks, you run into him again, and he recounts further anecdotes. After the third or fourth meeting, you might comment to your friend, "Did you notice how all his stories have to do with fraternities?" "Yes," your friend responds, "and none of them too complimentary." Then you remember how frequently words like *solitude, individualism,* and *independence* occurred in his conversation. You are beginning to note a central preoccupation in your acquaintance; you are beginning to analyze character. If you persist, you may eventually come to understand the dynamics of this individual's personality. Analyzing literature is a very similar activity. And it could be argued that it is a less difficult activity since living experience tends to be diffuse and difficult to grasp, but literature is an imitation of life concentrated to make a strong and lasting impact.

The terms which are discussed in each of the chapters of this text and which are listed again in the Glossary can help you a great deal in interpreting literature. Yet it is not advisable to use these terms merely to add a sophisticated tone to your paper. In fact, a paper in which they are used loosely will sound pretentious rather than sophisticated. Critical terminology is a tool designed to help us isolate and discuss the various aspects of a writer's technique. Analysis begins with the examination of such components of a work as *plot, characterization, setting, imagery, point of view,* and *tone.* About each of these aspects of the work you should ask the all-important question "why?" Why did the author adopt this point of view? Why this kind of imagery? Why this particular setting?

Ideally, the answers to these and similar questions will relate to each other. A piece of literature is distinguished by its unity: all its parts are subordinated to the creation of a unified effect. Thus, your study of its various aspects should lead you to a general understanding of the literary work as a whole. It is crucial that you understand your selection as an integral statement before you begin to write. You will not be able to write about any one aspect until you have understood its relation to the whole.

Analyzing the Assignment

When you feel you understand the text that you will be writing about, you are ready to begin the first part of your work—the important preliminary steps. Examine your assignment first. Who is to read your paper? What is the assigned length? What is the topic you are to treat?

This first question may at first seem unnecessary. Class assignments are almost always read by the instructor or by a grader who has received directions from the instructor. Yet in preparing all forms of communication, including writing, the nature of your audience will be one of your primary considerations. What you will say or write, for instance, is determined by the amount of knowledge possessed by your listeners or readers. Plot summary is a waste of space if you are writing for an instructor, who is familiar with the work. Similarly, a general biographical sketch of the author is unnecessary and will seem like padding to someone who has taught that author's works.

There is, however, a more subtle problem involved in considering the nature of your audience. Because any piece of writing that you do should be an honest statement which represents your own thoughts on a subject, you should not write solely to please your audience. It is equally unwise to alienate your reader by explicitly or implicitly contradicting all of his or her assumptions in your first paragraph. This problem is aggravated when the reader is your instructor. From class discussion, you know something about his or her attitudes toward literature and perhaps toward the work you are treating. A simple rehashing of a class lecture or discussion may indicate that you have been listening closely but thinking carelessly. A paper which is totally unrelated to what was said in class may suggest inattentiveness or arrogance. You will often disagree with the attitudes and assumptions of your instructor and classmates, but you cannot ignore them any more than you can ignore another person's argument in a debate. Whenever it is relevant, acknowledge what has been said or implied during class and then go on to refine or supplement it with your own well-reasoned ideas.

Like the nature of your reading audience, the assigned length of your paper is a consideration too often ignored. The length of your paper will determine both the amount of subject matter you cover and the approach you use. If you are asked to write a 1200-word paper, for instance, you have only five typewritten pages in which to cover your material and complete your argument. Students who choose to write on characterization in *Othello* and decide to demonstrate their point by analyzing the three major characters will soon discover, however, that they have only two or three paragraphs in which to treat each of these complex figures. As a result, their papers will be thin indeed. In such a situation, you would do better to devote your paper to a study of Desdemona, a subject which might conceivably be handled in five pages. And so you must limit the scope of your paper with regard to the assigned length.

The last and most important consideration in analyzing your assignment is the topic. Your instructor will probably choose a topic which directs your attention to one particular aspect of a work. Let us say you are asked to write on point of view in John Updike's "A & P." After analyzing the story as a whole, you should direct your attention to the critical conception of "point of view." Check the chapter in this text which discusses the subject and also refer to the Glossary. Review your class notes and look for comments on point of view in other stories. You are not being asked to write simply about a work but about a particular aspect of that work. Before you begin to write, you should have thought as much about point of view as you have about Updike's story.

Your instructor may, however, merely ask you to write a paper on any one of the selections which the class has been reading. The choice of topic is yours and will therefore require careful deliberation. Select a work which moves you in some way, and then analyze it. The selection of a particular work, however, is not the choice of a topic. If you try to write simply *about* a work, you will probably produce a sophisticated version of the grammar-school book report. Go on to consider which aspect of the selection seems most significant. Is it plot structure, setting, theme, tone, diction? Often it is that aspect of a work which at first strikes you as strange that eventually yields the most profitable topic. Let us say you have been analyzing T. S. Eliot's "The Love Song of J. Alfred Prufrock" and you are intrigued by the imagery and allusions. Consider your audience. The instructor has just spent a considerable amount of class time discussing imagery and allusions. What about the length? You only have five pages, and there is the sea imagery, the fog, the tea-party images and all those allusions. You might well decide to limit your topic to allusions in Eliot's "Prufrock" and then refer to related patterns of imagery if you have the space. After careful consideration, you have decided on what will probably be a workable topic.

Defining Your Thesis

The isolation of a topic is by no means the signal to start writing. You have only begun the preliminary work. The next step will take you from consideration of your topic to definition of a thesis. A topic is an area to be studied; a thesis is a proposition to be demonstrated and defended. For example, the topic is point of view in Updike's "A & P." The student who starts to write with merely this topic in mind will probably produce one or two paragraphs. He will identify and describe first-person point of view. He may quote a passage or two which show Sammy telling his own story. But after beginning in this way, he will probably come to a dead end.

Many questions must be asked before this topic yields a fruitful thesis. Why does Updike use the first-person point of view? What is gained through Sammy's describing the incident in his own words? Does this narrative technique contribute to the theme of social convention which seems central to the story? Eventually, you may conclude that Sammy's deceptively naive narration and the words in which he describes the incident and the people involved actually establish the conflict between freedom and conventionality. You are now approaching a thesis for your paper.

When you have arrived at this thesis, it should be written on a piece of paper or on an index card, because you will want to keep it in mind as you think, take notes, and finally write. The thesis for an effective paper on point of view in "A & P" might be stated in this way:

> By using first-person point of view, Updike leads his reader to see the significance of a seemingly trivial event. Sammy's account of this incident and his description of the three girls as opposed to his description of Lengel and the other customers establish the story's central conflict—freedom versus conventionality.

The success of your paper depends upon carefully choosing and clearly defining an intelligent thesis. Your thesis is actually a statement of your paper's purpose. It establishes the point you will demonstrate and, to some extent, the line of argument you will follow. During the remaining preliminary steps, you will be finding and arranging support for your thesis. And when you begin to write, you will probably include it in the first paragraph. You must, therefore, give careful consideration to both choosing and defining a thesis.

Gathering Your Evidence

Once your thesis has been defined, it is time to reread the work. You should now read with a specific purpose in mind: to collect the evidence with which you will construct your argument. Your primary evidence is always found within the work itself—in the language with which the author or his characters describe motivation, actions, responses, and situations. This internal evidence from the work will make up the core of your argument. Do not try to keep it all in your head. The relevant phrase or quotation, the number of the page on which it appears, and your observation about it should be written down. It is helpful to take these notes on index cards, which can be later reshuffled and arranged in the order indicated by your argument.

Some of your evidence may of course be external. That is, you may read a biography of the author or a critical study of the selection. (Find out if your instructor wants you to go beyond the primary text. Some instructors place a higher value on original thinking than on research.) The relevant facts or opinions found in such books should also be noted on index cards. On the top of your card, write the name of the biographer or critic, the title of his book, the name of the publisher, and the date and place of publication. Copy the relevant statement and the page number underneath. Then check again to be certain that you have quoted correctly.

To illustrate the process of gathering evidence, let us return to the hypothetical paper on the characterization of Desdemona in *Othello*. You have defined the following thesis:

> Although Desdemona may at first seem to be an implausible character who simply accepts the brutal treatment by her husband, her characterization is in fact convincingly consistent and creates one of the great ironies in the play: a totally loyal wife is accused of adultery and proves her loyalty by submitting to the vengeance of her jealous husband.

There are two points here that you will have to demonstrate—the consistency of characterization and the willing submission to Othello's vengeance. In rereading the drama, examine Desdemona's actions, her statements and the statements of other characters about her. Examine the words she uses and the metaphors she employs. What is her attitude toward her role as wife as opposed to the attitude of other characters in the drama? (Do not overlook the playful but significant discussion of this subject in Act II, scene i.) In regard to your second point, carefully study Act IV, scene iii, in which Desdemona prepares for bed on the night of her murder. Write down each relevant speech and your comment. Be sure to include act, scene and line numbers.

As you collect your evidence, consider opposing arguments. Whenever possible, anticipate the other side of the argument and take it into account. In this case, it might be pointed out that Desdemona is very eloquent in her own defense in Act I, but seems defenseless in later scenes. Do not simply overlook her speech in Act I, scene iii, lines 180–189. Copy it onto a card labeled "negative evidence," and then think about it. You may conclude that this speech, though an elegant defense and quite defiant, actually concerns the loyalty owed to one's husband. Thus, you might argue, Desdemona remains a very consistent character. Note your observation under the quotation so that you will not forget it at a later stage of your work.

In addition to this kind of internal evidence, there are some external facts which are relevant to this thesis. In 1603, when *Othello* was written, the conception of a woman's role in society was considerably different from our own. You might read about the status of seventeenth-century women in a book of literary history which discusses social conditions, or perhaps in a sociology book which deals with the role of women through history. Search for a relevant quotation or two on the subject. Similarly, a history of the theater will indicate that boys played female parts in Shakespeare's day. This fact, too, may prove relevant when you shape your argument. You can also look at some of the many critical books that have been written about Shakespearean tragedy. In one of them you may find an opinion sufficiently close or opposed to your own to be of use. You may or may not include this material in your paper, but it is helpful to have it on hand. The more evidence you have to choose from, the stronger your argument will be.

Organizing Your Argument

When you have finished gathering your evidence, you will have a statement of thesis and a pile of note cards lying on your desk. You are now ready to organize this material into a logical argument. The best way to shape your argument is to write an outline. Whether it consists merely of phrases or of complete sentences, an outline will help you order your argument effectively, separate the useful evidence from the extraneous, and, finally, see what further evidence you need to bolster a particular phase of your argument.

There are two generally recognized kinds of arguments. Inductive argument moves from the specific evidence to the general conclusion. Deductive argument moves from the general assertion to the supporting evidence. In working inductively, you actually imitate the process of thought by which you reached your conclusion. You lay out the evidence, evaluate it, and finally show how it leads to a particular conclusion. While inductive arguments can be very convincing, they are difficult to write. You have to lead your reader through all the pieces of evidence toward the conclusion without explaining it prematurely. Unless you are a very experienced writer, you may lose your reader before making your point.

Your first few papers, therefore, should be organized deductively, moving from a general assertion through the supporting evidence and back to a final reiteration of the assertion. The outline of a deductive argument follows a fairly obvious pattern. You place your statement of thesis under the heading "Introduction," categorize your supporting evidence and divide it among successive headings, and then restate your thesis more broadly under the final heading "Conclusion."

Your actual outline, however, will be slightly more complex than this pattern would indicate. In the outline, your generalizations (your thesis statements, or adaptations of them) appear in the introduction and conclusion; your concrete evidence and specific examples, in the body of the outline. Obviously, you have to guide your reader through all this evidence to be certain he or she draws the appropriate conclusions from it. Each of your headings (and, later, each of your paragraphs) will include both generalizations which *tell* and specific evidence which *shows*. The constant alternation between telling and showing creates the rhythm of your paper. In the introduction and conclusion, there will be more generalizations than evidence. In the body of the paper, the proportion will be reversed. Both the generalizations and the evidence should be indicated in your outline. (Incidentally, the kind of outline we are discussing here is the rough plan which you will use in organizing your material. Unless your instructor specifies otherwise, the outline should not be submitted with the finished paper.)

If you are writing on allusions in Eliot's "Prufrock," for example, you place your thesis under the Roman numeral I and then write the following:

II. Constant allusion to secular and religious heroes
   A. Examples (index card 12)
      1. St. John the Baptist, 1. 83
      2. Either one or both of the Lazaruses, 1. 94
      3. Hamlet, 1. 111
      4. Ulysses, 1. 124
   B. In each case, allusion is contrasted with Prufrock
      1. Lazarus—rhetorical question—answer is no
      2. Ulysses' mermaids will not sing to Prufrock
   C. Prufrock dwells on heroes who diminish his own stature

Notice the interplay of generalizations and specific examples here. The major heading generalizes about the types of allusions. Under subheading A, there is a list of examples which illustrate the generalization. Subheading B generalizes further about these specific examples and then refers specifically to the two allusions, Lazarus and Ulysses, which might seem to some readers to contradict this second generalization. (Potential objections should be dealt with before they can be raised.) Finally, subheading C introduces a generalization which concludes this phase of the argument.

Most of the headings in the body of your outline should include a considerable amount of evidence. Generalizations help readers see your point; concrete examples convince then of the validity of your point. But occasionally, a heading will be followed by only one piece of evidence, usually a quotation from the work or a critical book. Here you need only indicate the index card on which you have copied the quotation. The rest of your subheadings will suggest what relevance this quotation has to your argument. Do not assume that the relevance will be apparent. Point it out before you go on to your next heading.

For example, in a paper on allusions in "Prufrock," you have decided to treat the refrain, "In the room the women come and go / Talking of Michelangelo." And so, you might include the following in your outline:

III. Refrain alludes indirectly to heroes and heroic endeavor
   A. Quotation, (index card 15)
   B. Michelangelo—heroic artist who created great works of sculpture
      1. *David*
      2. *Moses*
      3. *Night* and *Day*
   C. Sculpted powerful physiques of great men which contrast with Prufrock's self-image
   D. Prufrock—uncomfortable in room where women talk of Michelangelo and his art

Subheadings B and C generalize about Michelangelo, although even here some supporting evidence—the names of specific statues—is introduced. The last subheading, D, relates all this material back to the general argument about the poem.

In writing your outline, give serious thought to the sequence of your headings. Is there a logical connection between two subsequent headings? (Both headings in the outline above refer to heroes; the transition between the two phases of argument will be easy to make.) Does each heading and its subheadings move the argument towards the conclusion? (Again, in both of the examples from the "Prufrock' outline, the last subheading refers to the general argument and adds more support to it.) Is any heading digressive, or any subheading extraneous? By eliminating digressions and excess material at this point, you will greatly simplify the actual writing of your paper.

Finally, some attention should be given to the last heading, "Conclusion." If your outline has progressed deductively from an introduction containing your thesis statement through the evidence which supports that thesis statement, you may feel that you have nothing more to say. Often, you can strengthen your conclusion by adapting something from the introduction. For example, the thesis statement for the paper on Desdemona contained two points: first, her characterization is consistent and, second, this consistent characterization creates one of the great ironies of the play. This second point could conceivably be saved for the conclusion. Or it might be given heavier emphasis in the conclusion. In general, a good conclusion restates the thesis more broadly than the introduction. It should ring with conviction because it is your last chance to present the nub of your argument.

When your outline is completed, you will probably have material which you have not included. Look through your remaining cards for any particular argument which you think is essential, but do not add digressive material to your outline merely to show the breadth of your knowledge or to pad your paper. If your outline shows a lack of evidence in some particular phase of your argument, include material now. When you begin to write you should have all the material you need recorded on your index cards and indicated in your outline.

Writing Your Paper

When it is time to write the first draft of your paper, the most difficult part of your work has been done. All you have to do now is expand the notations found in your outline, provide the transitions and add those sentences which will make your paragraphs read smoothly. Do not begin looking for three-syllable, Latinate words which you would never use under ordinary circumstances. Express yourself in the sort of language which you would use in making an oral report in class. That is, avoid both the erudite terminology which would make your classmates laugh at your pretentiousness and the hip expressions which would either befuddle or exasperate your instructor. Neither formal nor informal, the correct English for an interpretive paper is the middle range of the language.

The section of the outline on page 1120 is easily transformed into a full, well-developed paragraph.

> During his monolog, Prufrock constantly alludes to secular and religious heroes. The prophet to whom he refers in line 84 is John the Baptist, whose head was in fact "brought in" on a platter or shield to Salome. Lazarus, either the one raised from the dead by Christ or the beggar who was prevented from warning the rich man's brothers of the torments of hell (or perhaps both), is mentioned immediately afterwards (1. 94). Towards the end of his "song," Prufrock constrasts himself to Hamlet and then speaks of the mermaids who sang to Ulysses (1. 124). Significantly, each allusion suggests a contrast with himself. He quite explicitly states that he is "no prophet" and "not Prince Hamlet." When he asks if it would be worthwhile to say, "I am Lazarus," the implicit answer is no. Furthermore, the mermaids who sang to Ulysses will not sing to him. And so, Prufrock continually imagines heroes against whom he cannot measure up.

A new sentence not indicated in the outline and several phrases have been added to make the paragraph flow. But the essential sequence of generalizations and evidence established in the outline is followed closely here.

Although many instructors will be more concerned with the quality of your argument than in technical matters, there is no excuse for mistakes in spelling or grammar in your paper. Keep a dictionary by your side and use it. If you have the slightest doubt concerning the definition or spelling of a word, check it out. Similarly, you should use a handbook of grammar, usage, and mechanics so that you can look up matters of language which you are unsure of.

In the presentation of your evidence, you need to keep a few practical points in mind. Any prose quotation which is more than three lines in length should be centered on the page and, if you are typing, single-spaced. More than two lines of poetry should also be centered and single-spaced. More significantly, you must cite a source for any words or thoughts which are not your own. Failure to mention your source amounts to plagiarism. The usual method of citation is a footnote in which author, title of book, place of publication, publisher, date of publication and page number are included. The precise form of the footnote varies. Ask your instructor what form he prefers and then use it consistently throughout your paper.

When you have finished your first draft, you should read it aloud to yourself several times. During each reading, concentrate on a different problem. For example, read it once for errors in diction. Have you chosen the right word and spelled it correctly? Read the draft once again for errors in sentence structure. Are your sentences grammatically correct and varied in kind? Have you included any excess verbiage? Read the draft yet again for errors in paragraphing. Is each paragraph a well-developed, integral unit of thought linked explicitly or implicitly to the preceding paragraph? Then read the draft one last time to check the overall organization. Is your argument clearly defined? Does the succession of paragraphs flow smoothly without a break from introduction to conclusion? Errors in spelling, word choice and sentence structure can be corrected by marking over in ink. More extensive revisions can be written on separate pieces of paper and then pasted or clipped into place.

Set aside the corrected draft at least for a few hours, preferably overnight. In the cold light of a new day, many of the errors you missed in your previous readings should be clearly visible. It should also be apparent whether you can type or transcribe from your corrected draft or whether you need to write a second draft before putting your paper in its final form. The number of drafts required to produce a well-written paper will vary from student to student and from paper to paper.

Proofreading Your Final Version

It is certainly preferable to type the final copy of your paper. Readers are conditioned to regard a printed text with great deference, a typed text with some respect, and a handwritten text with an eye for errors. If you can type your paper or can have it typed for you, do so. If not, write it out in longhand as neatly and clearly as possible.

When the final version is completed, you are ready for the last step—proofreading. You must catch and correct all mechanical errors—typos, omitted spaces, omitted words—which may have cropped up as the final draft was prepared. Go through it word by word, even letter by letter. You may even want to try reading your final version backwards. When you read backwards, content ceases to occupy your mind and all your attention can be directed toward catching mechanical errors. Leave sufficient time for proofreading. Typos detract from the quality of your paper, and even a few can result in a lower grade.

Conclusion

Following the procedure here should help you write successful papers with effectiveness and ease. To review briefly, there are eight steps in the process:

1. Interpret the text as a unified work of art.
2. Analyze your assignment in regard to audience, length and topic.
3. Define your thesis and write a brief thesis statement.
4. Collect your evidence on index cards.
5. Organize your argument by writing an outline.
6. Write and revise your first draft or drafts.
7. Prepare your final draft.
8. Proofread.

Writing an interpretive paper is, like other activities ranging from crocheting to painting a portrait, a creative endeavor. There is no recipe for creativity. You might follow this procedure while preparing your first few papers, and then, if you wish, revise it to suit yourself. If you find, however, that doing things your own way increases the effort involved in actually writing your paper, you should continue to follow the conventional procedure. In time, you will find the system that works best for you. Continual but careful experimentation will teach you what steps you can most profitably add, omit, or combine.

Glossary of Literary
and Critical Terms

The number (or numbers) following each of the entries below indicates the page (or pages) in the text on which the term is more fully discussed and exemplified.

allegory A narrative or a descriptive technique in which objects, names, and qualities are employed in a more or less interrelated pattern that points beyond the surface level of a work to other, usually abstract, meanings. (282–284, 531–535)

alliteration The repetition of identical or nearly identical consonant sounds in two or more words in close or immediate succession. Depending on where the consonant sounds appear in a word, alliteration can be classified as either *initial* or *internal* (or *hidden*). (582) See *consonance*.

allusion A reference (technically an indirect reference) to something real or fictitious outside of the work in which it appears. The reference is often taken from history, the Bible, mythology, or other literary works. (281–282, 535–537)

ambiguity The deliberate use of a word or a statement to suggest more than one, usually opposed, meaning. (246, 547–548)

amphibrach See *meter*.

anagnorisis A Greek term which denotes the recognition by the protagonist in a tragedy of the real situation and its implications. It usually comes near the end of the action. (758)

anapest See *meter*.

animation The attribution of lifelike, but not necessarily human, traits to nonhuman objects, events, and the like; it is usually generalized under the term *personification*. (513)

antagonist The force that opposes the *protagonist*. Most often another character, it may also be an aspect of society or the environment, some facet of the protagonist himself, or a complex of many forces that work against him internally and externally. (46, 758)

anti-hero A main character who is less sophisticated, savory, or admirable than a traditional hero. (46)

apostrophe In poetry, a figure of speech in which someone or something absent is addressed as if present, dead as if living, or inanimate as if animate. (513–514)

archetype A term introduced by Carl G. Jung (1875–1961) to indicate inborn, unconscious patterns which express the collective memory of the human race and which are represented as "images of the archetypes" by such figures as the savior-redeemer, the hero, the mother, the father, the old wise man, and the miraculous child. (303–304, 539–540, 991)

aside   A brief statement by a character in a play which is overheard by the audience but supposedly unheard by other characters on stage (756)

assonance   The repetition of identical or related vowel sounds which occur either initially or internally within a word. (582)

ballad   A narrative in verse written about popular subjects and intended for oral presentation, normally for singing. (457)

  literary ballad   A ballad consciously written for a literary purpose; as such, it differs from folk or popular ballads, which are usually anonymous. (653–654)

  popular (or **folk**) **ballad**   A narrative poem which, in its origin, was intended for oral presentation, usually for singing, and which is usually anonymous. (457)

ballad stanza   A four-line stanza which often employs lines of alternating iambic tetrameter and iambic trimeter, riming *abcb*. (626–627)

beginning rime   See *rime*.

blank verse   A frequently employed verse form consisting of lines of unrimed iambic pentameter. (622–624)

box set   A stage set which represents realistically the three walls and the ceiling of a room, giving audiences the illusion of witnessing a real-life episode. (907)

cacophony   Sound patterns which are harsh and displeasing to the ear. (581)

cadence   Various rhythmic effects used in *free verse* as a substitute for regular meter. Such effects are so irregular that they are noticeable only within larger units of a poem, such as a stanza or a verse paragraph. (630)

caesura   A pause within a verse line frequently marked by punctuation and indicated in scanning a line of poetry by two perpendicular lines (‖). (600)

catharsis   A term used by Aristotle to refer to an audience's individual emotional purgation, which results from its vicarious participation in a protagonist's ordeal and suffering in a dramatic tragedy. (760)

character   A person in a story, poem, or play; occasionally, it is an animal or object given human attributes. (45–50)

  dynamic character   A character whose attitudes and values are affected by the events in a work. (47)

  flat character   A term used by E. M. Forster to denote a character having only a single trait or quality. (49–50)

  round character   A term used by E. M. Forster to refer to a multidimensional or a complex character. (49)

  static character   A character whose personality, attitudes, and beliefs remain fixed no matter what kinds of situations he encounters. (47)

  stock character   A recognizable, ready-made figure such as a hard-boiled detective or a dumb blonde. (50)

characterization   The way in which an author presents and defines his characters in a literary work. (48–49, 756)

direct presentation Characterization through a narrator's statements or explanations. (48–49)

indirect presentation Characterization through the action and speech of the characters themselves. (48–49)

characternym A suggestive or a symbolic name that identifies the character's major trait or basic nature. (49)

clerihew A humorous variation of the quatrain, named for its originator, Edmund Clerihew Bentley (1875–1956). It consists of two rimed couplets; the line lengths usually increase, with the fourth line the longest. Its subject must be a famous person whose name must appear in the first line. (628)

climax The point toward which the plot and the conflict rise and at which the fate of the major character (or characters) is determined. (757)

closed couplet See *couplet*.

closet drama A play intended solely for reading. (755)

comedy Originating in the ritual celebrating the resurrection of Dionysus and the simultaneous renewal of nature in the spring, ancient comedy invariably ended with a feast or a wedding-dance. Until the modern period, the standard plot has remained essentially very simple: an attractive young man desires an attractive young woman but is prevented from winning her by an older man, usually her father, uncle, or guardian; yet near the end of the play, a discovery is made which allows the young man to overcome all obstacles and to win his bride. (760–764)

romantic comedy A type of comedy often set in a never-never land and focused closely on two lovers in their struggles to achieve happiness. The ending usually unites all the characters in a celebration which concludes the action. Romantic comedy exposes human folly and often leads to character reform. (763)

satiric comedy A type of comedy in which human foibles and actions are exposed and exaggerated, often in cruel fashion. (763)

sentimental comedy A type of comedy designed to elicit the sentimental emotions of the audience through its depiction of such stock characters as the totally virtuous lovers who triumph over the obstacles set in their path by completely evil villains. (907)

complication In a plot, the development and intensification of the *conflict*. (20)

conceit A figure of speech which is especially ingenious and farfetched in its comparison of two dissimilar things. An even more ingenious variety of the conceit is the **metaphysical conceit,** named for the English metaphysical poets of the seventeenth century who used this elaborate device often in their poetry. (512)

confidant In comedy, a character (often a faithful friend or a companion) in whom one of the lovers can confide without resorting to soliloquy. (761)

conflict In a plot, the opposition between forces that is intensified and then resolved during the narrative. Conflict usually takes three basic forms: individual against individual, an individual against nature or the environment, or an individual against himself. (19–20 and 211–213, 758)

connotation A word's suggested or implied meanings which, through time and usage, have become associated with it. (176, 483)

consonance The use of words having identical or related consonant sounds but different vowels. (582) Compare *alliteration*.

consonantal rime See *rime*.

conventional symbol See *symbol*.

couplet A unit of poetry consisting of two successive lines of verse usually of the same metrical length and with the same end rime. (624–625)

> **heroic** (or **closed**) **couplet** A couplet in iambic pentameter which usually presents a complete thought within its two lines. (624–625)

> **open couplet** A couplet in which the thought and the grammatical structure of the second line are continued into the next couplet. (625)

crisis In a plot, the moment of the conflict's greatest intensity, usually that point at which opposing forces interlock or reach a standstill. (20)

curtal sonnet See *sonnet*.

dactyl See *meter*.

denotation The literal or dictionary meaning of a word. (176, 482–483)

dénouement Literally, the "untying," it occurs in a plot after the crisis. At this point, the conflict between opposing forces is settled, the narrative loose ends are tied up, and the action is brought to a close. (20, 757)

detective story A type of fiction in which a crime, usually a murder, is solved by a detective through careful analysis and logical interpretation of clues. (21)

dialog Speech exchanged between two or more characters in a literary work. (756)

diction An author's choice of words. Diction may be characterized as formal or informal; words may be complex or simple, old or new, long or short; and their origins and accumulated associations may give them particular or highly suggestive meanings. (175–177, 475)

dimeter See *meter*.

direct presentation See *characterization*.

dramatic irony See *irony*.

dramatic monolog In poetry, a dramatic method of presentation in which a speaker gradually reveals something highly significant about himself or about his circumstances to a listener (who may also speak but who often remains silent). (657)

dramatic poetry A broadly used term that denotes poetry rendered in some dramatic form or, at least, in a form that utilizes elements of dramatic technique. The term may also refer to poems whose method of presentation is partly or largely dramatic. (656–657)

dramatic point of view See *point of view*.

dynamic character See *character*.

elegiac quatrain A variation of the standard quatrain in its use of a five-foot, rather than the regular four-foot, line; so named following Thomas Gray's employment of it in his "Elegy Written in a Country Churchyard." (627–628)

elegy A poem occasioned by the death of a specific person which expresses the pensive thoughts of a poet as he reflects on death and on other solemn subjects. (628)

ellipsis   The omission of one or more words or of an entire phrase or statement. (476)

end rime   See *rime*.

end-stopped line   A line of verse that ends with a full pause, either punctuated or dictated by the rhythm of the poetic line. (601)

English sonnet   See *sonnet*.

enjambement   In poetry, the continuation of the thought from one line to the next. (601)

epic   A narrative poem of considerable length written in a serious tone and concerned with heroic characters and situations that illustrate the origins, history, and destiny of a race, culture, or nation. (654)

epigram   A type of very short poem that strives to capture in summary fashion a personal judgment, sentiment, or thought, often in a humorous or a satiric manner. (640)

epiphany   A term used by James Joyce (1884–1941) to describe a moment of profound insight, illumination, or revelation that a fictional protagonist experiences. (47–48)

epitaph   A short commemorative poem used to mark burial places or at least written as if this were the intention. (641)

euphony   A sound pattern that is pleasing to the ear. (580–581)

exposition   In a narrative or a dramatic work, the introductory or the background information—such as time, place, details about characters—which serves as preparation for subsequent actions and conflicts. (19, 757)

expressionism   A style of art, later adapted to drama and other forms of literature, which imitates the world as perceived by an individual consciousness. It differs radically from realism, which attempts to imitate the objective world; and it differs subtly from symbolism, which attempts to work with universal or archetypal patterns of perception and meaning. (993–995)

extended figure (or **extended metaphor** or **extended simile**)   The continuation of a figure of speech throughout several lines, occasionally throughout a stanza or an entire poem. (511–512)

eye rime   See *rime*.

fable   A short tale, in verse or in prose, that contains a moral and whose characters are often animals given various human qualities. (538)

fairy tale   A type of narrative that relates the lives and adventures of supernatural spirits, or at least of mysterious and strangely endowed creatures, whose behavior and actions are often playful and benevolent but also sometimes sinister and wicked. (538)

falling action   That part of a plot following the climax and in which the major character of a tragedy gradually loses control, or in a comedy gradually gains control, of the situation. (757)

falling meter   See *meter*.

fantasy   A personal and a highly imaginative creation which usually defies the limits of any known reality, often doing so by placing apparently realistic characters in an unrealistic setting, or unrealistic characters in a realistic setting. (300–302)

feminine rime   See *rime*.

figurative language (also called **figures of speech** or **tropes**) An imaginative departure from literal, straightforward statements in which two essentially dissimilar things are compared in a particular way. (510–521)

first-person point of view See *point of view*.

fixed forms Specific types of poems that use traditionally accepted structures and conventions of composition; some examples are the sonnet, the limerick, the villanelle, and the sestina. (632)

flashback In fiction, the presentation of scenes which took place prior to the time of a particular narrative. (20)

flat character See *character*.

foil A character whose main purpose is to set off through contrast the qualities of one of the major characters. (761)

folk ballad See *ballad*.

folklore Defined by Jan Harold Brunvand as "those materials in culture that circulate traditionally among members of any group in different versions, whether in oral form or by means of customary example." Folklore may include orally transmitted information about such things as folk arts and crafts, cooking and architecture, even furniture and clothing. It may also include references to such partly verbal lore as beliefs, games, dances, and customs. (313, 538)

folktale A narrative highly saturated with the superstitions, anecdotes, proverbs, legends, and customs of a particular group, race, geographical region, or culture. Usually anonymous and passed orally from generation to generation, a folktale may contain semihistorical materials or express largely mythic imaginings. (538)

foot See *meter*.

foreshadowing In fiction, the use of subtle hints that suggest what is to come later in the story. (21)

form In fiction, the organization of a story in relation to the ways various elements shape and determine its total effect. Many elements of a narrative may contribute to its form—for example, the point and counterpoint of its plot actions, the pattern(s) of images and symbols, the arrangement of scenes and details, the development and the resolution of its conflict, and the point of view of the narrative. (210–213)

In poetry, *form* may designate commonly used types of verses and stanzas, but it may also indicate a particular kind of poem such as epic, ballad, ode, or sonnet. (621–641)

frame In fiction, a device which presents a story from the past within a context of more recent events. (21)

free verse (sometimes called **vers libre**) A verse form lacking a regular metrical pattern or a definite rime scheme. For regular meter, it substitutes various rhythmic effects that are usually so irregular that they are noticeable only within larger units such as a stanza or a verse paragraph. (630–632)

haiku A traditional form of Japanese poetry that usually consists of seventeen syllables, normally arranged in three lines of five, seven, and five syllables respectively. Haiku strives, through one striking image, to paint a vivid picture that suggests an insight into nature or human existence. (506–508)

hamartia Often translated as "tragic flaw," hamartia, as used by Aristotle, is that weakness of character or error in judgment which causes the downfall of the protagonist in a tragedy. (758)

heptameter See *meter.*

heroic couplet See *couplet.*

hexameter See *meter.*

hubris In tragedy, the "excessive pride" of a protagonist which eventually leads to his downfall. (758)

humor Derives from an incongruity between what seems logical, possible, or expected and what actually happens. Humor often reveals how appropriate the seemingly inappropriate really is. (248)

humour character A type of character in Renaissance drama who was completely overpowered by a single obsessive emotion, such as greed, jealousy, melancholia, anger, and so forth. In terms of Renaissance physiology, one of his *humours,* or bodily fluids—blood, phlegm, cholor, or bile—was overly predominant, thus upsetting the balance of his personality. (761)

hyperbole See *overstatement.*

iamb See *meter.*

image A word or a phrase that conveys a sensory impression, appealing to one or more of the senses—seeing, hearing, smelling, tasting, or touching. (177, 492–500)

imagery All of the images in a section of a literary work or in an entire work. (492–500)

indirect presentation See *characterization.*

internal rime See *rime.*

irony Expresses a discrepancy between what is said and what is meant, between what is presented and what actually is revealed—and thus between appearance and reality. (244–248, 548–556, 762–763)

    dramatic irony Expresses a discrepancy between what a character says or does and what the reader understands to be true; called "dramatic" because in the theater an audience often has access to knowledge that a character (or characters) on stage lack. (246–247, 554, 762)

    situational irony Expresses a discrepancy between what happens and what is really the situation, thus between expectation and fulfillment. (247, 550–554)

    verbal irony Expresses one thing through speech when another thing, usually its opposite, is meant. (245–246, 548–550, 762–763)

Italian sonnet See *sonnet.*

legend A tale that normally is semihistorical in origin and tied closely to an actual time and place (e.g., tales about western gunfighters). A legend is usually less cosmic and sweeping in intention or implications than a myth. (538)

limerick A fixed form of English poetry which usually consists of five short lines of anapests, riming *aabba,* and which is often humorous and frequently satiric. (639–640)

limited subjective point of view See *point of view.*

literary ballad See *ballad.*

literary naturalism See *naturalism.*

literary symbol See *symbol.*

loose sentence A prose sentence that follows the normal subject-verb-object pattern. (178)

lyric poetry A poem that expresses the feelings, attitudes, and thoughts of a poet or a persona within the work. (659)

masculine rime See *rime.*

mask (or **persona**) The voice in a work through which an author speaks. In some cases, however, the thoughts, feelings, and actions of the mask or the persona are in opposition to the meaning of the work. (108–109, 554)

melodrama A type of play in which completely virtuous individuals battle completely wicked ones until justice prevails. (907)

metaphor An implied comparison between two dissimilar things which relates and fuses one to the other by expressing an identity between them. (177, 511)

metaphysical conceit See *conceit.*

meter The more or less regular pattern of stressed and unstressed syllables in a line, a stanza, or an entire poem. (603–615) The process of determining the kinds and the number of such syllables in these units of poetry is called **scansion**; it also consists of determining the *rimes* or the *rime scheme,* when applicable. (599–615)

A **foot** (pl., **feet**) is the basic unit of English verse and normally consists of one stressed and one or more unstressed syllables. In scanning verse, a short, slanted mark (´) indicates a stressed syllable, and a curved line (⌣) shows an unstressed one. (599–600) The principal feet employed in English verse are the following. (604–605)

> **iamb** (adj., **iambic**) Consists of one unstressed syllable followed by a stressed one: |⌣ ´|
>
> **trochee** (adj., **trochaic**) Consists of one stressed syllable followed by an unstressed one: |´ ⌣|
>
> **anapest** (adj., **anapestic**) Consists of two unstressed syllables followed by a stressed one: |⌣ ⌣ ´|
>
> **dactyl** (adj., **dactylic**) Consists of one stressed syllable followed by two unstressed ones: |´ ⌣ ⌣|

Iambic and anapestic feet are sometimes called *rising meters* because the movement is from unstressed to stressed units. Trochaic and dactylic feet are sometimes called *falling meters* because the movement is from stressed to unstressed units.

The basic variant feet, used normally for substitutions and variety, are the following. (605)

> **monosyllable** (adj., **monosyllabic**) Consists of one stressed syllable: |´ |
>
> **spondee** (adj., **spondaic**) Consists of two stressed syllables: |´ ´|

pyrrhic Consists of two unstressed syllables: $\smile\smile$

amphibrach (adj., **amphibrachic**) Consists of an unstressed, a stressed, and another unstressed syllable: $\smile\,\prime\,\smile$

The principal line lengths of English verse are the following. (606)

monometer	one foot	**pentameter**	five feet
dimeter	two feet	**hexameter**	six feet
trimeter	three feet	**heptameter**	seven feet
tetrameter	four feet	**octameter**	eight feet

metonymy A figure of speech which is marked by the substitution of a thing or of a quality attributed to or closely associated with it for the thing itself—*crown* for *king, smoke* for *cigarette*. (518–520)

metrical romance A narrative poem of considerable length which treats love, intrigue, and chivalric adventures and romances. (654)

monolog A long, uninterrupted speech addressed to one or more characters in a play. (756)

monometer See *meter*.

monosyllable See *meter*.

myth A story or a group of interrelated stories that people accept, for various reasons, as making important statements about the universe and human life that could not be made in any other way. Stories of pre-Hellenic Greek gods and goddesses are examples of myths. (302–305, 538–540, 991)

mythology A fully developed pattern of interrelated myths, such as those of ancient Greece and Rome. (303, 548)

narrative poem Verses that tell a story, with characters, a setting, and various elements of plot, such as a rising action, a falling action, a conflict, and a resolution. (653–654)

naturalism A late nineteenth-century philosophy fostered by several scientific theories of that time. It was particularly influenced by Charles Darwin's theory of evolution, or the descent of human beings from the animal kingdom, and by Social Darwinism, or the application of theories such as "the survival of the fittest" to human society. Naturalism holds that human fate is determined solely by heredity and environment. It tends toward pessimism in its assumption that human morality and idealism are inevitably overcome by biological and social conditioning. (908)

    literary naturalism An adaptation to literature of the principles of naturalistic philosophy and characterized by an intensification of realistic methods of composition, usually through an emphasis on scientific materials, techniques, and theories. (906)

natural symbol See *symbol*.

Noh play A type of highly stylized drama developed in Japan in which ghosts or deities reenact the most significant moments of their existence for travelers who encounter them. The Noh play influenced modern western dramatists who were seeking alternatives to realistic drama. (992)

novel An extended prose narrative that portrays fictional characters engaging in actions and conflicts held together by a plot or by a pattern of themes or ideas. In contrast to the short story, the novel generally contains a more complicated plot, a greater number of fully developed characters, and a wider range of settings, events, and themes. (376–378)

objective point of view See *point of view*.

octameter See *meter*.

octave See *sonnet*.

ode A poetic form which originated in ancient Greece as verse spoken aloud by a chorus and accompanied by music. Traditionally, the ode, one of the *fixed forms* of poetry, has treated dignified, serious themes within a complex metrical framework. (663)

off rime See *rime*.

omniscient point of view See *point of view*.

onomatopoeia The suggestion of a word's meaning by its actual sound. Words such as *buzz, crash, hiss, sneeze,* and *squeak* approximate in sound their literal meanings. (581–582)

open couplet See *couplet*.

overstatement (or **hyperbole**) A form of verbal irony which exaggerates something and thus represents it as more significant than it really is. (245–246, 556–557)

paradox Attempts to show that things which seem contradictory are the same or at least that they are ultimately related. Paradox reveals that opposites may be joined and resolved in ways that often defy explanation. Thus paradox is an apparent contradiction that actually proves true, though at another level or in a certain way. (248–249, 557–559)

paraphrase A restatement which retains the meaning, essential facts, and details of an original source, although the exact wording of that original source is changed. (22)

pentameter See *meter*.

periodic sentence A sentence in which a word or phrase essential to the meaning is withheld until the end or near the end of the sentence. (178)

peripeteia (or **peripity**) As used by Aristotle, it is the reversal or change of fortune which the protagonist in a dramatic tragedy experiences. (758)

persona See *mask*.

personification The attribution of human characteristics to objects, animals, events, or abstract ideas. (513)

Petrarchan sonnet See *sonnet*.

plot In a narrative or a dramatic work, not only the sum total and the sequence of events but also the selecting, ordering, and arranging of incidents to suggest their relationships and their actual interdependence on one another. (18–22)

point of view The vantage point or angle from which an author tells a story and reveals the characters, setting, and events. (101–109)

  first-person point of view One of the characters in the story narrates the events. (105–108)

limited subjective point of view (often called the *limited omniscient*) An author tells the story from the perspective of a single character only, using the third person to describe action and dialog but freely telling the reader what the central character feels and thinks. (104–105)

objective point of view An author records in the third person only the actions and dialog of his characters, making no attempt to reveal or interpret their inner thoughts and feelings. Another name for this perspective is the **dramatic point of view,** a term which suggests that the reader is overhearing and observing things happen, as if seeing them acted out on a stage. (103–104)

omniscient point of view The most common and conventional of the third-person perspectives in which an author is literally "all-knowing," placing himself at some distance from events and freely interpreting and commenting on the thoughts, feelings, and behavior of the characters. (102–103)

popular ballad See *ballad*.

problem play A type of play which exposes and investigates actual problems that face a particular group or society. (908)

propaganda Fiction intended to achieve immediate, short-term, or limited purposes, such as getting people to believe a certain idea or to join a particular organization. (151–152)

properties (or **props**) On the stage, such things as furniture, paintings, books, rugs, lamps, and household utensils intended to be used by the actors in a play. (907)

protagonist The chief figure in a narrative or dramatic work who struggles against opposing forces, which are often personified by an *antagonist*. (46, 758)

pun A deliberate confusion of words that are alike in sound and/or spelling but are different in meaning, e.g., "The king, sir, is no *subject* for a pun." (558)

pyrrhic See *meter*.

quatrain A four-line stanza, usually appearing with two- or three-foot line lengths. Many nursery rimes, proverbs, hymns, and popular songs are composed in this popular and enduring form. (626)

realism In literature, the attempt to create an accurate impression of reality as it appears to the senses or to an objective consciousness. In a more technical sense, *realism* refers to a style, or to a manner of writing, which arose during the second half of the nineteenth century in Europe and America and which stressed direct experience, a faithful reporting of facts and details, and a view of the world within a general humanistic framework. (906–912)

refrain A word or a group of words or verse lines repeated at regular intervals throughout a poem, often at the end of each stanza. (580)

representation The attempt by nineteenth-century realistic dramatists to approximate real life and everyday events on the stage. (906)

rhythm   The repetition at measured intervals of stressed and unstressed syllables in order to establish a definite pattern of rising and falling inflections.
(599–603)

rime (also **rhyme**)   In poetry, the repetition of identical or similar sounds; more
specifically, the repetition of similar or identical vowel sounds in stressed
syllables which are preceded by unlike consonants. When a consonant
follows the stressed vowel sound, it must be the same consonant if true rime
is to occur—*day/pay*. (586–593)

> **beginning rime**   Rime which occurs in the first word of two or more lines.
> (586)

> **consonantal rime**   A correspondence of sounds between consonants
> (sometimes merely a resemblance of sound), as in *matter/mutter,
> simple/supple, floor/flair*. (587)

> **end rime**   Rime at the end of two or more lines of poetry. (586)

> **feminine rime**   Rime which occurs in the final two syllables (a stressed
> followed by an unstressed one) at the end of two or more lines—
> *miser/wiser*. (586)

> **internal rime**   Rime occurring within a line of poetry. (586)

> **masculine rime**   Rime which occurs in the final stressed syllables at the end
> of two or more lines, when the stressed syllables are preceded by
> different consonants—*bed/head, St. Ives/wives*. (586)

> **sight** (or **eye**) **rime**   A variant of rime occurring not in the sound but simply
> in the spelling—*dew/sew*. (587–588)

> **slant** (or **off**) **rime**   Rime in which final consonants sounds that are alike are
> preceded by vowel sounds that are different—*bard/heard*. (587)

> **triple rime**   A correspondence of sound in three syllables, one stressed
> followed by two unstressed ones, as in *vainglorious* and *meritorious*.
> This rime is so pronounced and melodious that it is usually reserved
> for light or humorous verse. (586)

rime scheme   The pattern or order in which rimes occur in a poem, or in a part of
a poem. In marking the rime scheme of a poem, a letter of the alphabet is
given to each corresponding end rime, e.g., *abab, cdcd*. (588)

rising action   The sequence of events which complicate the original situation in
a plot; called "rising" because the momentum of events is directed toward
an eventual high point or climax of the action. (757)

rising meter   See *meter*.

romantic comedy   See *comedy*.

round character   See *character*.

run-on line   A line of poetry that moves directly into the next line without any
end punctuation and without a noticeable pause in the thought. (601)

sarcasm   An ironic statement that is deeply cutting or mocking and intended to
injure or ridicule. (245, 548)

satire   A way of ridiculing human follies and vices that finds the discrepancy
between what is and what ought to be neither appropriate nor desirable.
Satire supposes an ideal of human behavior and exposes departures from
that ideal, doing so in the hope of correcting the situation. (248, 548)

satiric comedy   See *comedy.*

scansion   See *meter.*

science fiction   A form of imaginative story based on scientific facts, assumptions, and hypotheses which are logically projected beyond present-day actualities and known realities. (301–302)

sentimental comedy   See *comedy.*

sentimentality   An attempt to draw from the reader a greater emotional response than is warranted by the subject or by its treatment. Sentimentality results not so much from the subject itself as from an author's failure to treat the subject properly. (570)

sestet   See *sonnet.*

setting   The physical location and the specific time or historical period in which an action occurs; it can also be the psychological and the social environment of a narrative. (82–84)

Shakespearean sonnet   See *sonnet.*

sight rime   See *rime.*

simile   An expressed direct comparison, almost always introduced by the word *like* or *as,* that shows a similarity between two dissimilar things by relating them in specific ways. (177, 510–511)

situational irony   See *irony.*

slant rime   See *rime.*

slice-of-life   The attempt, in a narrative or dramatic work, to re-create as closely as possible the random and disjointed qualities of real life. As a major concept of literary naturalism, *slice-of-life* discredited the more sentimental and artificial literary techniques popular during the nineteenth century. (909)

soliloquy   A speech in a dramatic poem or in a poetic drama uttered by a character while alone. (672, 756)

song   Verses adapted to musical expression. (455)

sonnet   One of the notable *fixed forms* of English poetry, the sonnet is a lyric poem traditionally consisting of fourteen lines with several alternate rime schemes and normally employing iambic pentameter but occasionally iambic tetrameter. (632–635)

>   **curtal sonnet**   A variation of the traditional sonnet form devised by Gerard Manley Hopkins (1844–1889). Literally, a "curtailed" sonnet, it consists of ten lines plus—in most cases—a fraction of an additional line. (635)

>   **English** (or **Shakespearean**) **sonnet**   Derived from the Italian sonnet, this form contains three quatrains and a couplet, a rime scheme *abab, cdcd, efef, gg,* and an organization which provides great flexibility and which allows the treatment of different aspects of a situation, problem, or experience. The resolution in the couplet tends to be pointed and succinct. (633–634)

>   **Italian** (or **Petrarchan**) **sonnet**   A sonnet consisting of two parts: the **octave,** eight lines riming *abbaabba,* which presents a situation, sets a problem, or gives an observation; and the **sestet,** six lines of variable rime scheme (for instance, *cdecde* or *cdccdc*), which usually offers a response, resolution, or closing appropriate to the subject. (632–633)

>   **Spenserian sonnet**   A variation of the English sonnet, the only difference

being its use of five interrelated rimes, *abab, bcbc, cdcd, ee,* which link various elements of the poem closely together. (634)

sonnet sequence Consists of a number of sonnets joined by a common purpose or a unified subject. Notable sonnet sequences in English poetry are Edmund Spenser's *Amoretti* (1595), Sir Philip Sidney's *Astrophel and Stella* (1580–1581), and Elizabeth Barrett Browning's *Sonnets from the Portuguese* (1850). (634–635)

Spenserian sonnet See *sonnet.*

spondee See *meter.*

sprung rhythm Devised by Gerard Manley Hopkins (1844–1889), it is essentially a way of organizing sounds in poetry by stressed syllables regardless of the number of unstressed syllables in a poetic foot or in a line. (614)

stage directions Instructions by a dramatist about the setting and the physical features of a play, as well as about the actions and the emotional responses of the actors. Printed in italics and sometimes set off in brackets, stage directions range from a mere indication of entrances and exits to detailed descriptions of characters and scenes. (756)

stanza A group of two or more lines of poetry that have a demonstrated metrical integrity or a similar kind of organizational unity. Divisions into stanzas are normally indicated in print by an extra line or two of space and in oral reading by a heavy pause, or occasionally (as in a song) by a chorus or a refrain. In the technical sense, the term *stanza* is correctly employed only when the pattern of the lines is repeated in a poem. (621)

static character See *character.*

stock character See *character.*

stream of consciousness A narrative technique in which an author represents a character's perceptions, thoughts, and feelings, often conveying the actual flow of and the interplay between a character's conscious, semiconscious, or even unconscious operations. (108)

structure The overall design of a poem which is shaped, for example, by a central image or an idea, by a controlling allusion or an extended analogy, or even by the tone or the point of view. In addition, structure may also result from the scene a poem develops or from the situation it describes. (648–653)

style An author's use and arrangement of language, his selection of words, and the pacing and the patterning with which he puts words together. (175–180)

stylized representation A type of drama which does not merely imitate nature but transforms and even distorts it to emphasize its subjective, human significance. (990)

subplot A secondary sequence of actions which normally mirror or contrast with the main plot. (758)

suspense In narrative and dramatic works, the creation of an intense desire in the reader or spectator to know the outcome of a particular sequence of events. (21, 757)

symbol An example of figurative language in which one thing is used to suggest another. A symbol remains itself and yet stands for or suggests something else. (280–284, 525–531, 990–991)

>   **conventional symbol** A symbol that, through time and usage, has taken on a customary significance or conventional meaning recognized by a particular culture. (281, 530)

literary symbol A symbol whose meaning is located in or defined by the work in which it appears; literary symbols sometimes represent an author's complex system of ideas. (281, 530)

natural symbol A symbol that suggests meanings, associations, and implications that are not limited to a particular literary work or culture. (281, 530–531)

symbolism A literary movement which developed in the last part of the nineteenth century and which presented a direct challenge to realism. In drama, its chief characteristic is its use of symbols, which, as concrete manifestations of subtle emotions and thoughts, are ideal tools for playwrights in exploring the psychological dimensions and implications of character and action. (990–993)

synecdoche A figure of speech in which the part is substituted for the whole, or the container for the contained. (518–520)

syntax The ordering and the relationships between words within a phrase or a sentence. (177–179, 476)

telegraphic dialog A terse and disjointed form of dialog employed by expressionistic dramatists in which some of the parts of speech—articles, adjectives, and adverbs—are eliminated so that verbal communication is minimized. Characters often make long, apparently oblique and irrelevant speeches to which no one seems to listen. (993)

tercet (or **triplet**) A group of three successive lines in poetry, usually of the same metrical length and frequently with the same end rime. (625–626)

terza rima A three-line stanza whose first and third lines rime and whose second line rimes with the first and third lines of the next stanza; thus the rime scheme is *aba, bcb, cdc,* and so on. (626)

tetrameter See *meter.*

theme The central idea or the understanding around which a story is constructed. (149–153)

tone The attitude of an implied author, as expressed in a literary work, toward the subject, theme, and audience. (180–181, 564–570)

tragedy In his *Poetics,* Aristotle (384–322 B.C.) examined the nature of classical tragedy, a discussion which is vital to an understanding of this dramatic form. Aristotle emphasized the "high importance" of the action, the nobility of the protagonist, the "tragic flaw," and the reversal or change of fortune that leads to the downfall of the protagonist and to his final recognition of the situation and its implications. (758–760)

tragic flaw See *hamartia.*

tragicomedy A dramatic work which combines many of the elements of tragedy and comedy. The tone and the plot are similar to those of tragedy, but the ending is a happy one. (764)

trimeter See *meter.*

triple rime See *rime.*

triplet See *tercet.*

trochee See *meter.*

tropes See *figurative language.*

typography The literal arrangement of characters, words, and lines on a printed page. (479)

understatement A form of verbal irony which represents something as less important than it really is in order to emphasize rather than to diminish the significance of a point or a situation. (245, 556–557)

verbal irony See *irony*.

verisimilitude In fiction, the creation of the appearance or likeness of what is true and actual in real life. (8)

verse One line or more of poetry. A verse line is usually defined according to the kind and the number of stressed and unstressed syllables it contains— iambic pentameter or anapestic tetrameter, for example. (621)

verse paragraph In general, any marked division or section of poetry not ordered by a regular scheme of lines or rimes; the term refers more specifically to units of *free verse*. (630)

vers libre See *free verse*.

well-made play A conventional and artificial kind of drama popular during the nineteenth century in which the suspense generated by an intricate plot overcomes all other theatrical considerations. It was structured according to a formula: exposition in Act I, complication in Act II, resolution in Act III. (907)

Anthony Hecht. "The Dover Bitch" from *The Hard Hours* by Anthony Hecht. Copyright © 1960 by Anthony Hecht. Reprinted by permission of Atheneum Publishers. Appeared originally in *Transatlantic Review*.

Lillian Hellman. *The Little Foxes* by Lillian Hellman. Copyright 1939 and renewed 1967 by Lillian Hellman. Reprinted by permission of Random House, Inc. *Caution:* professionals and amateurs are hereby warned that *The Little Foxes*, being fully protected under the copyright laws of the United States of America, the British Empire, including the Dominion of Canada, and all other countries of the Copyright Union, is subject to a royalty. All rights, including professional, amateur, motion picture, recitation, public reading, radio broadcasting, and the rights of translation into foreign languages, are strictly reserved. In its present form this play is dedicated to the reading public only. All inquiries regarding this play should be addressed to the author, care of Random House, Inc., 201 East 50th Street, New York City.

Ernest Hemingway. "The Capital of the World" (copyright 1936 Ernest Hemingway) is reprinted by permission of Charles Scribner's Sons from *The Short Stories of Ernest Hemingway* by Ernest Hemingway.

William Heven. "Driving at Dawn" and "In Memoriam: Theodore Roethke" from *Depth of Field* by William Heyen. Copyright 1970 by William Heyen. Reprinted by permission of Louisiana State University Press.

Gerard Manley Hopkins. "Pied Beauty," "Felix Randal," "Spring and Fall," and "No Worst, There Is None" reprinted from *The Poems of Gerard Manley Hopkins,* Oxford University Press, 1967.

A. E. Housman. "They Say My Verse Is Sad: No Wonder" from *The Collected Poems of A. E. Housman.* Copyright 1936 by Barclays Bank Ltd. Copyright © 1964 by Robert E. Symons, "Loveliest of Trees," "Terence, This Is Stupid Stuff," "When I Was One–and–Twenty," and "Is My Team Ploughing" from "A Shropshire Lad"—Authorized Edition—from *The Collected Poems of A. E. Housman.* Copyright 1939, 1940, © 1965 by Holt, Rinehart and Winston, Inc. Copyright 1967, 1968 by Robert E. Symons. All poems reprinted by permission of Holt, Rinehart and Winston, Inc., The Society of Authors as the literary representative of the Estate of A. E. Housman; and Jonathan Cape Ltd., publishers of A. E. Housman's *Collected Poems.*

Langston Hughes. "On the Road" from *Laughing to Keep from Crying.* Copyright 1935 by Langston Hughes. Renewed 1952. Reprinted by permission of Harold Ober Associates Incorporated. "Dream Deferred" copyright 1951 by Langston Hughes. Reprinted from *The Panther and the Lash* by Langston Hughes. "Dreams" from *The Dream Keeper and Other Poems* by Langston Hughes. Copyright 1932 by Alfred A. Knopf, Inc. and renewed 1960 by Langston Hughes. "I, Too, Sing America" from *Selected Poems* by Langston Hughes. Copyright 1926 by Alfred A. Knopf, Inc. and renewed 1954 by Langston Hughes. All poems reprinted by permission of Alfred A. Knopf, Inc.

Ted Hughes. "Secretary" from *The Hawk in the Rain* by Ted Hughes. Copyright © 1957 by Ted Hughes. By permission of Harper & Row, Publishers.

Eugène Ionesco. *The Gap* by Eugène Ionesco, translated by Rosette Lamont. Reprinted from *The Massachusetts Review*, Vol. X, No. 1, Winter 1969. © 1969 The Massachusetts Review, Inc.

Hakyō Ishida. "The Captive Eagle" from *Anthology of Modern Japanese Poetry*, translated and edited by Edith Marcombe Shiffert and Yuki Sawa. Reprinted by permission of Charles E. Tuttle Co., Inc.

Kobayashi Issa. "The Place Where I Was Born" and "Contentment in Poverty" from *An Introduction to Haiku* by Harold G. Henderson. Copyright © 1958 by Harold G. Henderson. Reprinted by permission of Doubleday & Company, Inc.

Dan Jacobson. "Beggar My Neighbor" reprinted with permission of Macmillan Publishing Co., Inc., Dan Jacobson and Weidenfeld & Nicolson Ltd. from *Through the Wilderness and Other Stories* by Dan Jacobson. © Dan Jacobson 1962. Originally published in *The New Yorker* as "A Gift Too Late."

Randall Jarrell. "The Death of the Ball Turret Gunner" and "Eighth Air Force" reprinted with the permission of Farrar, Straus & Giroux, Inc. from *The Complete Poems* by Randall Jarrell. Copyright 1945, 1947 by Randall Jarrell, copyright renewed 1973, 1975 by Mary von Schrader Jarrell.

Robinson Jeffers. "November Surf" copyright 1932 and renewed 1960 by Robinson Jeffers. Reprinted from *The Selected Poetry of Robinson Jeffers* by Robinson Jeffers, by permission of Random House, Inc.

Joan Johnson. "Continental Drift" copyright © 1977 by Joan Johnson. Reprinted by permission.

James Joyce. "Araby" from *Dubliners* by James Joyce. Copyright © 1967 by the Estate of James Joyce. All rights reserved. Reprinted by permission of The Viking Press, Inc.

Franz Kafka. "Jackals and Arabs" reprinted by permission of Schocken Books Inc. from *The Penal Colony* by Franz Kafka. Copyright 1948 by Schocken Books Inc.

X. J. Kennedy. "Epitaph for a Postal Clerk," copyright © 1956 by X. J. Kennedy, originally appeared in *The New Yorker*. "Nude Descending a Staircase," copyright © 1960 by X. J. Kennedy. Both poems reprinted from the book *Nude Descending a Staircase* by X. J. Kennedy, by permission of Doubleday & Company, Inc.

Rudyard Kipling. "Danny Deever" from *Rudyard Kipling's Verse:* Definitive Edition (British source: *Barrack Room Ballads*). Reprinted by permission of Mrs. George Bambridge, Doubleday & Company, Inc., and Eyre Methuen Ltd.

Maxine Kumin. "A Family Man" from *The Nightmare Factory* by Maxine Kumin. Copyright © 1970 by Maxine Kumin. By permission of Harper & Row, Publishers.

Peter LaFarge. "Vision of a Past Warrior" from *As Long as the Grass Shall Grow* by Peter LaFarge. © 1963 United International Copyright Representatives Ltd. Used by permission. All rights reserved.

Pär Lagerkvist. "The Children's Campaign" reprinted with the permission of Farrar, Straus & Giroux, Inc., the Author's Literary Estate, and Chatto & Windus Ltd. From *The Marriage Feast* by Pär Lagerkvist, translated by Alan Blair and Carl Eric Lindin. Copyright 1954 by Albert Bonniers Forlag.

Philip Larkin. "Wedding–Wind" reprinted from *The Less Deceived* by permission of The Marvell Press, England.

D. H. Lawrence. "The White Stocking" from *The Complete Short Stories of D. H. Lawrence*, Volume I. All rights reserved. Reprinted by permission of The Viking Press, Inc. "Bavarian Gentians" and "Piano" from *The Complete Poems of D. H. Lawrence*, edited by Vivian de Sola Pinto and F. Warren Roberts. Copyright © 1964, 1971 by Angelo Ravagli and C. M. Weekley, Executors of the Estate of Frieda Lawrence Ravagli. All rights reserved. Reprinted by permission of The Viking Press, Inc.

John Lennon and Paul McCartney. "A Day in the Life," © 1967 Northern Songs Limited. All rights for the United States, Canada, Mexico, and the Philippines controlled by Maclen Music, Inc. Used by permission. All Rights Reserved.

Doris Lessing. "The Old Chief Mshlanga" from *African Stories* by Doris Lessing. Copyright © 1951, 1953, 1954, 1957, 1958, 1962, 1963, 1964, 1965 by Doris Lessing. Reprinted by permission of Simon & Schuster, Inc. and John Cushman Associates, Inc.

Denise Levertov. "The Ache of Marriage" from *O Taste and See* by Denise Levertov. Copyright © 1964 by Denise Levertov Goodman. Reprinted by permission of New Directions Publishing Corporation.

Gordon Lightfoot. "Early Morning Rain," © 1967 Warner Bros. Inc. All rights reserved. Used by permission.

Robert Lowell. "The Mouth of the Hudson" reprinted with the permission of Farrar, Straus & Giroux, Inc. from *For the Union Dead* by Robert Lowell. Copyright © 1964 by Robert Lowell. "Christmas Eve under Hooker's Statue" and "France" from *Lord Weary's Castle,* copyright 1946, 1974 by Robert Lowell. Reprinted by permission of Harcourt Brace Jovanovich, Inc.

Archibald MacLeish. "Ars Poetica," "Dr. Sigmund Freud Discovers the Sea Shell," and "The Snowflake Which Is Now and Hence Forever" from *The Collected Poems of Archibald MacLeish.* Copyright 1952 by Archibald MacLeish. Reprinted by permission of Houghton Mifflin Company.

Louis MacNeice. "Museums" from *The Collected Poems of Louis MacNeice,* edited by E. R. Dodds. Copyright © The Estate of Louis MacNeice 1966. Reprinted by permission of Oxford University Press, Inc., and Faber and Faber Ltd.

Bernard Malamud. "Take Pity" reprinted with the permission of Farrar, Straus & Giroux, Inc. From *The Magic Barrel* by Bernard Malamud. Copyright ©1956, 1958 by Bernard Malamud.

(copyright © 1959, 1968 by Gary Snyder) from *The Back Country* by Gary Snyder. Reprinted by permission of New Directions Publishing Corporation.

Sophocles. *The Antigone of Sophocles:* An English Version, by Dudley Fitts and Robert Fitzgerald, copyright 1939 by Harcourt Brace Jovanovich, Inc.; renewed 1967 by Dudley Fitts and Robert Fitzgerald. Reprinted by permission of Harcourt Brace Jovanovich, Inc. *Caution:* all rights, including professional, amateur, motion picture, recitation, lecturing, performance, public reading, radio broadcasting and television are strictly reserved. Inquiries on all rights should be addressed to Harcourt Brace Jovanovich, Inc., 757 Third Avenue, New York, New York 10017.

Stephen Spender. "An Elementary School Classroom in a Slum," copyright 1942 and renewed 1970 by Stephen Spender. Reprinted from *Selected Poems* by Stephen Spender (British title: *Collected Poems*), by permission of Random House, Inc. and Faber and Faber Ltd.

Jean Stafford. "The Maiden" reprinted with the permission of Farrar, Straus & Giroux, Inc. from *The Collected Stories of Jean Stafford*. Copyright © 1950, 1969 by Jean Stafford. "The Maiden" originally appeared in *The New Yorker*.

Wallace Stevens. "A High–Toned Old Christian Woman" and "The Snow Man," copyright 1923 and renewed 1951 by Wallace Stevens. "Of Modern Poetry" and "The Candle a Saint," copyright 1942 and renewed 1970 by Holly Stevens. All poems reprinted from *The Collected Poems of Wallace Stevens* by Wallace Stevens, by permission of Alfred A. Knopf, Inc.

August Strindberg. *Miss Julie,* translated by Elizabeth Sprigge, from *Six Plays of Strindberg.* Copyright © 1955 by Elizabeth Sprigge. Reprinted by permission of Collins–Knowlton–Wing, Inc.

Allen Tate. "Sonnets at Christmas" reprinted from *Poems* by Allen Tate with the permission of The Swallow Press.

Dylan Thomas. "A Refusal to Mourn the Death, by Fire, of a Child in London," "Fern Hill," and "In My Craft or Sullen Art" from *The Poems of Dylan Thomas*. Copyright 1946 by New Directions Publishing Corporation. Reprinted by permission of New Directions Publishing Corporation, J. M. Dent & Sons Ltd., and the Trustees for the Copyrights of the late Dylan Thomas.

Kyoshi Tkkahama. "A Butterfly's Noises" from *Anthology of Modern Japanese Poetry,* translated and edited by Edith Marcombe Shiffert and Yuki Sawa. Reprinted by permission of Charles E. Tuttle Co., Inc.

Leo Tolstoy. "The Death of Ivan Ilych" from *The Death of Ivan Ilych and Other Stories* by Leo Tolstoy. Translated by Louise and Aylmer Maude and published by Oxford University Press.

John Updike. "A & P," copyright © 1962 by John Updike. Reprinted from *Pigeon Feathers and Other Stories* by John Updike, by permission of Alfred A. Knopf, Inc. Originally appeared in *The New Yorker*. "Player Piano" in *The Carpentered Hen and Other Tame Creatures* by John Updike. Copyright 1954 by John Updike. Originally appeared in *The New Yorker*. By permission of Harper & Row, Publishers, Inc.

Eudora Welty. "Keela, the Outcast Indian Maiden" from *A Curtain of Green and Other Stories,* copyright © 1941, renewed 1969 by Eudora Welty. Reprinted by permission of Harcourt Brace Jovanovich, Inc.

Richard Wilbur. "A Dubious Night" from *The Beautiful Changes,* copyright 1947 by Richard Wilbur. "A Simile for Her Smile" from *Ceremony and Other Poems,* copyright 1948, 1949, 1950 by Richard Wilbur. Both reprinted by permission of Harcourt Brace Jovanovich, Inc.

William Carlos Williams. "The Red Wheelbarrow" and "This Is Just to Say" from *Collected Earlier Poems* by William Carlos Williams. Copyright 1938 by New Directions Publishing Corporation. "The Pause" from *Collected Later Poems* by William Carlos Williams. Copyright 1950 by William Carlos Williams. All reprinted by permission of New Directions Publishing Corporation.

James Wright. "The Jewel," copyright © 1962, 1968 by James Wright. Reprinted from *Collected Poems* by James Wright, by permission of Wesleyan University Press.

William Butler Yeats. "The Second Coming" (copyright 1924 by Macmillan Publishing Co., Inc., renewed 1952 by Bertha Georgie Yeats), "The Choice" (copyright 1933 by Macmillan Publishing Co., Inc., renewed 1961 by Bertha Georgie Yeats), "Leda and the Swan" and "Sailing to Byzantium" (copyright 1928 by Macmillan Publishing Co., Inc., renewed 1956 by Georgie Yeats), "Long–Legged Fly" (copyright 1940 by Georgie Yeats, renewed 1968 by Bertha Georgie Yeats), "The Wild Swans at Coole" (copyright 1919 by Macmillan Publishing Co., Inc., renewed 1947 by Bertha Georgie Yeats), "That the Night Come" (copyright 1912 by Macmillan Publishing Co., Inc., renewed 1940 by Bertha Georgie Yeats), "The Old Men Admiring Themselves in the Water" all reprinted with permission of Macmillan Publishing Co., Inc., M. B. Yeats, Miss Anne Yeats, and Macmillan of London & Basingstoke, from *Collected Poems* by William Butler Yeats. *Purgatory* reprinted with permission of Macmillan Publishing Co., Inc., M. B. Yeats, Miss Anne Yeats, and Macmillan of London & Basingstoke, from *Collected Plays* by William Butler Yeats. Copyright 1934, 1952 by Macmillan Publishing Co., Inc.

Al Young. "Birthday Poem" from *Dancing* by Al Young. Copyright © 1969 by Al Young. Reprinted by permission of Corinth Books.

Index of Authors, Titles, and First Lines

Authors' names are in capitals, titles of selections in italics, and first lines of poems in roman type.